Birnbaum's 9

Canada

A BIRNBAUM TRAVEL GUIDE

Alex
EDITOR

Lois
Editori

Laur
Manag

Mary
Beth
Senior

Jill K
Editor

Patri
Gene
Susa
Assoc

Marc
Map C

Susa
Editor

H
A

For Stephen, who merely made all this possible.

FIRST EDITION

ISSN 0749-2561 (Birnbaum Travel Guides)
ISSN 0884-1039 (Canada)
ISBN 0-06-278220-7 (pbk.)

96 97 98 ❖/RRD 5 4 3 2

BIRNBAUM TRAVEL GUIDES

Bahamas, and Turks & Caicos
Bermuda
Canada
Cancun, Cozumel & Isla Mujeres
Caribbean
Country Inns and Back Roads
Disneyland
Hawaii
Mexico
Miami & Ft. Lauderdale
United States
Walt Disney World
Walt Disney World for Kids, By Kids
Walt Disney World Without Kids

Contributing Editors

Andrew Allentuck
Diana Barkley
Cristine Bye
Susan Campbell
Elizabeth Carroll
Elizabeth Chambers
Colette Copeland
Sarah Downey
Louise Gagnon
Margot Gibb-Clark
Geoff Johnson
Mark Kalish
David Katz
Susan Kelly
Hazel Lowe
Patricia Lowe
Gordon Morash
Brigit Paradis
Len Russo
Jonathan Siskin
Joan Sullivan
Anne Marie Tedesco
Colleen Thompson
Ian Thompson
Glenn Wanamaker
Loralee Wenger
Leslie Westbrook

Maps

B. Andrew Mudryk
Mark Stein Studios

Contents

Getting Ready to Go

Practical information for planning your trip.

The Cities

Thorough, qualitative guides to each of the nine cities most often visited by vacationers and businesspeople. Each section offers a comprehensive report on the city's most compelling attractions and amenities—highlighting our top choices in every category.

Diversions

A selective guide to active and/or cerebral vacation themes, pinpointing the best places to pursue them.

Exceptional Pleasures and Treasures

For the Experience

For the Body

Directions

Canada's most spectacular routes and roads, most arresting natural wonders, most magnificent parks and forests, all organized into 33 specific driving tours.

Glossary

Foreword

Part of the problem of comprehending all that Canada has to offer is the sheer size of the undertaking. Few countries offer as vast a panorama or as diverse a spectrum of landscapes—to say nothing of the variety of ethnic and cultural influences. To even the most cursory observer, Canada seems at least three countries: the marvelously austere Maritimes of the east, the fiercely French Québécois nearer the center of the continent, and the vast sweep of the pioneer west that stretches from the province of Ontario (just above the Great Lakes) to the Pacific Ocean. And that doesn't even begin to consider the trackless wilderness of the Yukon and the Northwest Territories.

Canada is one of my own favorite travel destinations. For visitors from the US, the foreign quality of Canada can take on quite a different cast from place to place. The dour demeanor of the Atlantic provinces is an extension (and occasionally an exaggeration) of the inscrutable mien that is regularly encountered in Maine. In contrast, the Canadian west—from the flat prairies of Saskatchewan and Manitoba to the islands of Vancouver Harbour—is almost unfailingly and heartily friendly; this is the segment of Canada where it is most difficult to realize that you have crossed a national border.

French Canada is a somewhat different matter, and Montreal's advertisement of itself as "the second-largest French-speaking city in the world" has its own meaning. (We won't tell them that they've dropped to third place, behind Paris and Kinshasa.) As a vacation alternative to Paris, Montreal has substantial appeal both in its ambience and in the fact that the US dollar continues to fare far better in Canada than in Europe. And the continuing separatist spirit shows its face in myriad ways, including the frequent reluctance of Montreal cab drivers to speak English to US visitors. For the visitor, however, this slight inconvenience may prove welcome; it means that setting foot in a Montreal taxi now more closely approximates a foreign visitor's introduction to France.

This guide tries as much as possible to offer some insights into a country that we consider vastly underrated as a tourist destination. But I should, I think, apologize for at least one indulgence in this text that is baldly chauvinistic, and that is our constant reference to citizens of the US as "Americans." Strictly speaking, Canadian citizens are just as much residents of the North American continent as US citizens, and we apologize for any slight our Canadian readers may feel about our having appropriated this terminology. It was done strictly in an effort to simplify the narrative, rather than an attempt to appropriate a common continental distinction.

A large part of Canada's appeal is its extremely wide variety of terrain and cultural influence. And although Canada is often referred to as a single destination, it is actually a dazzling blend of ethnic and historic diversity. While this diversity often spawns internal political confrontations, a visitor is more likely to notice environments and atmospheres that are almost always intriguing and often unique.

The increasing and broadening sophistication of US travelers—no matter where they are headed—has made it essential that any Canadian guidebook reflect and keep pace with the real needs of its prospective readers. That's why we have created a guide to Canada that's specifically organized, written, and edited for today's demanding traveler, one for whom qualitative information is infinitely more desirable than mere quantities of unappraised data. We realize that it's impossible for any single travel writer to visit hundreds of restaurants (and nearly that many hotels) in any given year and provide accurate appraisals of each. And even if it were physically possible for one human being to survive such an itinerary, it would of necessity have to be done at a dead sprint, and the perceptions derived therefrom would probably be less valid than those of any other intelligent individual visiting the same establishments. It is, therefore, both impractical and undesirable (especially in an annually revised and updated guidebook series such as we offer) to have only one person provide all the data on the entire world. Instead, we have chosen what we like to describe as the "thee and me" approach to restaurant and hotel appraisal and, to a somewhat more limited degree, to the sites and sights we have included in the other sections of our text. What this really reflects is personal sampling tempered by intelligent counsel from informed local sources.

This guidebook is directed to the "visitor," and such elements as restaurants have been specifically picked to provide the visitor with a representative, enlightening, and above all pleasant experience. Since so many extraneous considerations can affect the reception and service accorded a regular restaurant patron, our choices can in no way be construed as an exhaustive guide to resident dining. We think we've listed all the best places in various price ranges, but they were chosen with a visitor's enjoyment in mind.

Other evidence of how we've tried to tailor our text to reflect modern travel habits is apparent in the section we call DIVERSIONS. Where once it was common for travelers to spend a foreign visit seeing only the obvious sights, today's traveler is more likely to want to pursue a special interest or to venture off the beaten path. In response to this trend, we have collected a series of special experiences so that it is no longer necessary to wade through a pound or two of superfluous prose just to find exceptional pleasures and treasures.

Finally, I should point out that every good travel guide is a living enterprise; that is, no part of this text is carved in stone. In our annual revisions, we refine, expand, and further hone all our material to serve your travel needs better. To this end, no contribution is of greater value to us than your personal reaction to what we have written, as well as information reflecting your own experiences while using the book. Please write to us at 10 E. 53rd St., New York, NY 10022.

We sincerely hope to hear from you.

Alexandra Mayes Birnbaum

ALEXANDRA MAYES BIRNBAUM, editorial consultant to the *Birnbaum Travel Guides*, worked with her late husband, Stephen Birnbaum, as co-editor of the series. She has been a world traveler since childhood and is known for her travel reports on radio on what's hot and what's not.

Canada

ARCTIC OCEAN
Beaufort Sea
Parry Islands
Melville
Banks I.
Bathurst I.
Victoria I.
Brooks Range
ALASKA
Yukon R.
Arctic Circle
Aklavik
Ft. McPherson
Inuvik
KLONDIKE REGION
Dawson
ROCKY MOUNTAINS
McKenzie Mts
Great Bear Lake
McKenzie R.
Beaver Creek
YUKON
Carmacks
Faro
Pelly Mts
Whitehorse
Carcross
Skagway
NORTH WEST TERRITORIES
Arctic Circle
Ft. Simpson
McKenzie R.
Yellowknife
COAST MOUNTAINS
Stikine Mts
Hay River
Great Slave Lake
Ft. Smith
Ft. Nelson
Peace R.
Lake Athabasca
Queen Charlotte Islands
Hazelton
Prince Rupert
Ft. St. John
Peace River
Dawson Creek
Lesser Slave Lake
Slave Lake
Grande Prairie
Vanderhoof
Prince George
Athabasca R.
Athabasca
Reindeer Lake
Churchill
Churchill R.
Nelson
Churchill R.
La Ronge
BRITISH COLUMBIA
Edmonton
ALBERTA
Jasper
SASKATCHEWAN
Flin Flon
MANITOBA
Red Deer
Lloydminster
The Pas
Selkirk Mts
Fraser R.
Banff
N. Battleford
Prince Albert
Saskatoon
L. Winnipeg
Winnipegosis
Vancouver Island
Kamloops
Columbia R.
Revelstoke
Calgary
Drumheller
Vancouver
Victoria
Penticton
Swift Current
Yorkton
Regina
L. Manitoba
Dauphin
PACIFIC OCEAN
WASHINTON
Lethbridge
Medicine Hat
Moose Jaw
Seattle
MONTANA
Estevan
Brandon
Winnipeg
IDAHO
Missouri R.
Columbia R.
Portland
NORTH DAKOTA
Red R.
MINNE
Missouri R.
CANADA
0 Miles 500
0 km 800

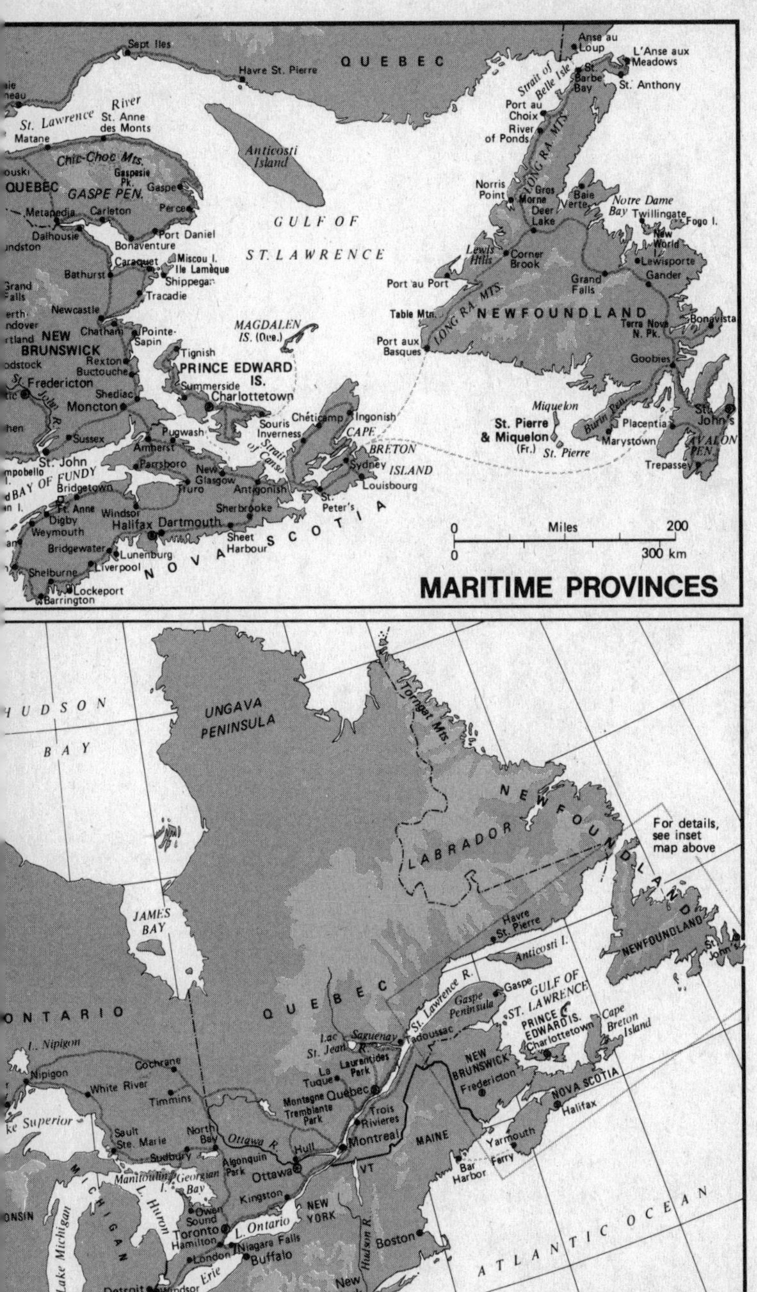
MARITIME PROVINCES
QUEBEC
GULF OF ST. LAWRENCE
NEWFOUNDLAND
NEW BRUNSWICK
PRINCE EDWARD IS.
NOVA SCOTIA
CAPE BRETON ISLAND
Anticosti Island
St. Pierre & Miquelon (Fr.)
Miles 0 200
0 300 km
For details, see inset map above
HUDSON BAY
UNGAVA PENINSULA
LABRADOR
JAMES BAY
ONTARIO
MAINE
NEW YORK
ATLANTIC OCEAN

How to Use This Guide

A great deal of care has gone into the special organization of this guidebook, and we believe it represents a real breakthrough in the presentation of travel material.

Our text is divided into five basic sections in order to present information in the best way on every possible aspect of a vacation to Canada. Our aim is to highlight what's where and to provide basic information—how, when, where, how much, and what's best—to assist you in making the most intelligent choices possible.

Here is a brief summary of what you can expect to find in each section. We believe that you will find both your travel planning and en route enjoyment enhanced by having this book at your side.

GETTING READY TO GO

A mini-encyclopedia of practical travel facts with all the precise data necessary to create a successful trip to Canada. Here you will find how to get where you're going, plus selected resources—including useful publications and companies and organizations specializing in discount and special-interest travel—providing a wealth of information and assistance useful both before and during your trip.

THE CITIES

Our individual reports on the nine Canadian cities most visited by travelers and businesspeople offer a short-stay guide, including an essay introducing the city as a historic entity and as a contemporary place to visit; an *At-a-Glance* section that's a site-by-site survey of the most important, interesting, and unique sights to see and things to do; *Sources and Resources,* a concise listing of pertinent tourism information, such as the address of the local tourist office, which sightseeing tours to take, where to find the best nightspot, which are the shops that have the finest merchandise and/or the most irresistible bargains, and where the best museums and theater are to be found; and *Best in Town,* which lists our collection of cost-and-quality choices of the best places to eat and sleep on a variety of budgets.

DIVERSIONS

This section is designed to help travelers find the best places to engage in a variety of exceptional experiences, without having to wade through endless pages of unrelated text. In every case, our particular suggestions are intended to guide you to that special place where the quality of experience is likely to be highest.

DIRECTIONS

Here are 33 Canadian driving itineraries, from Prince Edward Island to British Columbia, that follow Canada's most beautiful routes, taking you past its most spectacular natural wonders and through its most magnificent parks and forests. DIRECTIONS is the only section of this book that is organized geographically; its itineraries cover Canada in short, independent segments that each describe a journey of several days' duration. Itineraries can be "connected" for longer sojourns or used individually for short, intensive explorations.

GLOSSARY

This section provides helpful information that you may need on your trip. A climate chart includes seasonal temperatures throughout the country. A weights and measures table will help you translate metric measurements and temperatures in Celsius to their US equivalents.

To use this book to full advantage, take a few minutes to read the table of contents and random entries in each section to get a firsthand feel for how it all fits together. You will find that the sections of this book are building blocks designed to help you put together the best possible trip. Use them selectively as a tool, a source of ideas, a reference work for accurate facts, and a guidebook to the best buys, the most exciting sights, the most pleasant accommodations, the tastiest food—*the best travel experience* that you can possibly have.

Getting Ready to Go

Getting Ready to Go

When to Go

It is difficult to generalize about Canadian weather—climatic differences between one part of the country and another can be dramatic. Although summer generally is the peak travel period for touring and sightseeing, excellent skiing and other cold-weather sports make many areas popular winter destinations as well. And Canada's major cities are wonderful long-weekend destinations in any season. In short, timing a visit to Canada depends more on your own interests than on weather or the tourist facilities available.

Travel during the off-seasons (which vary throughout the country) and shoulder seasons (the months immediately before and after the peak months) can offer relatively fair weather and smaller crowds. During these periods, travel often is less expensive—although high-season rates may prevail because of an important local event.

If you have a touch-tone phone, you can call *The Weather Channel Connection* (phone: 900-WEATHER) for current worldwide weather forecasts. This service, available from *The Weather Channel* (2600 Cumberland Pkwy., Atlanta, GA 30339), costs 95¢ per minute; the charge will appear on your phone bill.

Traveling by Plane

SCHEDULED FLIGHTS

Airlines offering flights between the US and Canada include *Air Canada* (and some of its subsidiaries, such as *Air Nova* and *Air Ontario*), *Alaska Airlines, American, Canadian Airlines International, Delta, Horizon Air, Northwest, NW Airlink, United, USAir,* and *USAir Express.*

FARES The great variety of airfares can be reduced to the following basic categories: first class, business class, coach (also called economy or tourist class), excursion or discount, and standby, as well as various promotional fares. For information on applicable fares and restrictions, contact the airlines listed above or ask your travel agent. Most airfares are offered for a limited time. Once you've found the lowest fare for which you can qualify, purchase your ticket as soon as possible.

RESERVATIONS Reconfirmation is strongly recommended for all international flights. It is essential that you confirm your round-trip reservations—*especially the return leg*—as well as any flights within Canada.

SEATING Airline seats usually are assigned on a first-come, first-served basis at check-in, although you may be able to reserve a seat when purchasing your ticket. Seating charts may be available from airlines and are included in the *Desktop Flight Guide* (Official Airline Guides, 2000 Clearwater Dr., Oak Brook, IL 60521; phone: 800-342-5624 or 708-574-6000; fax: 708-574-6565).

SMOKING US law prohibits smoking on flights scheduled for six hours or less within the US and its territories on both US and foreign carriers. Although these restrictions do not apply to nonstop flights between the US and international destinations, none of the major US carriers permit smoking on flights to Canada, and *Air Canada* and *Canadian Airlines International* both prohibit smoking on all their domestic and international flights. A free wallet-size guide that describes the rights of nonsmokers under current regulations is available from *ASH* (*Action on Smoking and Health;* DOT Card, 2013 H St. NW, Washington, DC 20006; phone: 202-659-4310).

SPECIAL MEALS When making your reservation, you can request one of the airline's alternate menu choices for no additional charge. Though it is not always required, it's a good idea to reconfirm your request the day before departure.

BAGGAGE On major international airlines, passengers usually are allowed to carry on board one bag that will fit under a seat or in an overhead bin and to check two bags in the cargo hold. Specific regulations regarding dimensions and weight restrictions vary among airlines, but a checked bag usually cannot exceed 62 inches in combined dimensions (length, width, and depth) or weigh more than 70 pounds. There may be charges for additional, oversize, or overweight luggage, and for special equipment or sporting gear. Note that baggage allowances may be more limited on some domestic routes in Canada. Check that the tags the airline attaches are correctly coded for your destination.

CHARTER FLIGHTS

By booking a block of seats on a specially arranged flight, charter operators frequently can offer travelers bargain airfares. If you do fly on a charter, however, read the contract's fine print carefully. Federal regulations permit charter operators to cancel a flight or assess surcharges of as much as 10% of the airfare up to 10 days before departure. You usually must book in advance, and once booked, no changes are permitted, so buy trip cancellation insurance. Also, make your check out to the company's escrow account, which provides some protection for your investment in the event that the charter operator fails. For further information, consult the publication *Jax Fax* (397 Post Rd., Darien, CT 06820; phone: 203-655-8746; fax: 203-655-6257).

DISCOUNTS ON SCHEDULED FLIGHTS

CONSOLIDATORS AND BUCKET SHOPS These companies buy blocks of tickets from airlines and sell them at a discount to travel agents or directly to consumers.

Since many bucket shops operate on a thin margin, be sure to check a company's record with the *Better Business Bureau*—before parting with any money.

Cheap Tickets (8320 Lincoln Blvd., Suite 101, Los Angeles, CA 90045; phone: 800-377-1000; fax: 800-454-2500).

Council Charter (205 E. 42nd St., New York, NY 10017; phone: 800-800-8222 or 212-661-0311; fax: 212-972-0194).

Fare Deals Travel (9350 E. Arapahoe Rd., Suite 330, Englewood, CO 80112; phone: 800-878-2929 or 303-792-2929; fax: 303-792-2954).

Omniglobe Travel (690 Market St., Suite 510, San Francisco, CA 94104; phone: 800-894-9942 or 415-433-9312; fax: 415-433-9315).

Southwest Travel Systems (1001 N. Central Ave., Suite 575, Phoenix, AZ 85004; phone: 800-STS-TRAVEL or 602-255-0234; fax: 602-255-0220).

STT Worldwide Travel (9880 SW Beaverton Hillsdale Hwy., Beaverton, OR 97005; phone: 800-348-0886 or 503-641-8866; fax: 503-641-2171).

Travac Tours and Charters (989 Ave. of the Americas, New York, NY 10018; phone: 800-872-8800 or 212-563-3303; fax: 212-563-3631).

Unitravel (1177 N. Warson Rd., St. Louis, MO 63132; phone: 800-325-2222 or 314-569-0900; fax: 314-569-2503).

LAST-MINUTE TRAVEL CLUBS Members of such clubs receive information on imminent trips and other bargain travel opportunities. Some clubs charge an annual fee; others offer free membership. Despite the names of some of the clubs listed below, you don't have to wait until literally the last minute to make travel plans.

Discount Travel International (169 W. 81st St., New York, NY 10024; phone: 212-362-3636; fax: 212-362-3236).

FLY ASAP (PO Box 9808, Scottsdale, AZ 85252-3808; phone: 800-FLY-ASAP or 602-956-1987; fax: 602-956-6414).

Last Minute Travel (1249 Boylston St., Boston, MA 02215; phone: 800-LAST-MIN or 617-267-9800; fax: 617-424-1943).

Moment's Notice (425 Madison Ave., New York, NY 10017; phone: 212-486-0500/1/2/3; fax: 212-486-0783).

Spur of the Moment Cruises (411 N. Harbor Blvd., Suite 302, San Pedro, CA 90731; phone: 800-4-CRUISES or 310-521-1070 in California; 800-343-1991 elsewhere in the US; 24-hour hotline: 310-521-1060; fax: 310-521-1061).

Traveler's Advantage (3033 S. Parker Rd., Suite 900, Aurora, CO 80014; phone: 800-548-1116 for membership services; 800-835-8747 for reservations; fax: 303-368-3985).

Vacations to Go (1502 Augusta Dr., Suite 415, Houston, TX 77057; phone: 713-974-2121 in Texas; 800-338-4962 elsewhere in the US; fax: 713-974-0445).

Worldwide Discount Travel Club (1674 Meridian Ave., Miami Beach, FL 33139; phone: 305-534-2082).

GENERIC AIR TRAVEL These organizations operate much like an ordinary airline standby service, except that they offer seats on not one but several scheduled and charter airlines. One pioneer of generic flights is *Airhitch* (2472 Broadway, Suite 200, New York, NY 10025; phone: 212-864-2000; fax: 212-864-5489).

BARTERED TRAVEL SOURCES Barter—the exchange of commodities or services in lieu of cash payment—is a common practice among travel suppliers. Companies that have obtained travel services through barter may sell these services at substantial discounts to travel clubs, who pass along the savings to members. One organization offering bartered travel opportunities is *Travel World Leisure Club* (225 W. 34th St., Suite 909, New York, NY 10122; phone: 800-444-TWLC or 212-239-4855; fax: 212-564-5158).

CONSUMER PROTECTION

Passengers whose complaints have not been satisfactorily addressed by the airline can contact the *US Department of Transportation* (*DOT;* Consumer Affairs Division, 400 Seventh St. SW, Room 10405, Washington, DC 20590; phone: 202-366-2220). Also see *Fly Rights* (*Consumer Information Center,* Dept. 133B, Pueblo, CO 81009; phone: 718-948-3334; fax: 718-948-9724). If you have safety-related questions or concerns, write to the *Federal Aviation Administration* (*FAA;* 800 Independence Ave. SW, Washington, DC 20591) or call the *FAA Consumer Hotline* (phone: 800-322-7873). If you have a complaint against a Canadian travel service, contact the provincial tourist authorities.

Traveling by Ship

Your cruise fare usually includes all meals, recreational activities, and entertainment. Shore excursions are available at extra cost, and can be booked in advance or once you're on board. An important factor in the price of a cruise is the location (and sometimes the size) of your cabin. Charts issued by the *Cruise Lines International Association* (*CLIA;* 500 Fifth Ave., Suite 1407, New York, NY 10110; phone: 212-921-0066; fax: 212-921-0549) provide information on ship layouts and facilities, and are available at some *CLIA*-affiliated travel agencies.

The *US Public Health Service (PHS)* inspects all passenger vessels calling at US ports. For the most recent summary or a particular inspection report, write to the *National Center for Environmental Health* (Attention: Chief, Vessel Sanitation Program, 1015 N. America Way, Room 107, Miami, FL 33132; phone: 305-536-4307). Most cruise ships have a doctor on board, plus medical facilities.

For further information on cruises and cruise lines, consult *Ocean and Cruise News* (PO Box 92, Stamford, CT 06904; phone/fax: 203-329-2787). And for a free list of travel agencies specializing in cruises, contact the *National Association of Cruise Only Agencies* (*NACOA;* 3191 Coral Way, Suite 630, Miami, FL 33145; phone: 305-446-7732; fax: 305-446-9732).

A number of international lines offer cruises that call at Canadian coastal ports, and some companies offer excursions along the St. Lawrence River and other inland waterways. In addition, ferry services link Canada and the US, often carrying both passengers and vehicles. Note, however, that not all routes are in service year-round.

International Cruise Lines

Alaska Sightseeing/Cruise West (Fourth and Battery Building, Suite 700, Seattle, WA 98121; phone: 800-426-7702 or 206-441-8687; fax: 206-441-4757).

American Canadian Caribbean Line (PO Box 368, Warren, RI 02885; phone: 401-247-0955 in Rhode Island; 800-556-7450 elsewhere in the US; fax: 401-245-8303).

Clipper Cruises (7711 Bonhomme Ave., St. Louis, MO 63105-1956; phone: 800-325-0010 or 314-727-2929; fax: 314-727-6576).

Holland America Line/West Tours (300 Elliot Ave. W., Seattle, WA 98119; phone: 800-426-0327 or 206-281-3535; fax: 800-628-4855 or 206-281-7110).

INTRAV (7711 Bonhomme Ave., St. Louis, MO 63105-1961; phone: 800-456-8100 or 314-747-0500; fax: 314-727-0908).

Prince of Fundy Cruises (468 Commercial St., Portland, ME 04101-0416; phone: 800-341-7540; fax: 207-773-7403).

Princess Cruises (10100 Santa Monica Blvd., Los Angeles, CA 90067; phone: 800-421-0522 or 310-553-1770; fax: 310-284-2844).

Regency Cruises (260 Madison Ave., New York, NY 10016; phone: 212-972-4774 in New York State; 800-388-5500 elsewhere in the US; fax: 800-388-8833).

Royal Cruise Line (1 Maritime Plaza, Suite 1400, San Francisco, CA 94111; phone: 800-792-2992 in California; 800-227-4534 elsewhere in the US; fax: 415-956-1656).

Seabourn Cruise Line (55 Francisco St., Suite 710, San Francisco, CA 94133; phone: 800-929-9595 or 415-391-7444; fax: 415-391-8518).

Special Expeditions (720 Fifth Ave., New York, NY 10019; phone: 800-762-0003 or 212-765-7740; fax: 212-265-3770).

Inland Waterway Cruise Companies

American Canadian Caribbean Line (address above).

OdessAmerica Cruise Company (170 Old Country Rd., Mineola, NY 11501; phone: 800-221-3254 or 516-747-8880; fax: 516-747-8367).

St. Lawrence Cruise Lines (253 Ontario St., Kingston, Ontario K7L 2Z4, Canada; phone: 800-267-7868 or 613-549-8091; fax: 613-549-8410).

Ferry Companies

Clipper Navigation (2701 Alaskan Way, Pier 69, Seattle, WA 98121; phone: 800-888-2535 or 206-443-2560; fax: 206-443-2583).

Marine Atlantic (121 Eden St., Bar Harbor, ME 04609; phone: 800-341-7981 or 207-288-3395; fax: 207-288-9521).

Nordic Cruise (21 Rue du Marché Champlain, Quebec City, Quebec G1K 8Z8, Canada; phone: 800-692-8002 or 418-692-8002; fax: 418-692-6044).

Victoria Line (main office: 185 Dallas Rd., Victoria, British Columbia V8V 1A1, Canada; phone: 604-480-5555; fax: 604-480-5222; US office: 101 Alaskan Way S., Seattle, WA 98104; phone: 800-668-1167 or 206-625-1880; fax: 206-625-1881).

Washington State Ferry (801 Alaskan Way, Pier 52, Seattle, WA 98104-1487; phone: 206-464-6400).

Traveling by Train

For those interested in traveling *to* Canada by rail, *Amtrak* (phone: 800-USA-RAIL) offers limited service to Toronto from Chicago and New York City. (At the time of this writing, *Amtrak*'s overnight Montrealer service between Washington, DC and Montreal had been cancelled.)

VIA Rail Canada (PO Box 8116, Station C, Montreal, Quebec H3C 3N3, Canada; phone: 514-871-1331) is the country's national railroad company. Although cutbacks in recent years have reduced the number of trains, transcontinental service—such as the first class *Silver and Blue* line, connecting Toronto and Vancouver—still exists. *VIA Rail* also runs shorter lines—between the major eastern cities, as well as between Winnipeg and Churchill (both in Manitoba), and between Jasper (Alberta) and Prince Rupert (British Columbia) on the Pacific Coast. Schedules and other publications providing information on Canadian rail service can be obtained at *VIA Rail* stations and by phone or mail from *VIA Rail* at the address above.

Several classes of tickets are sold. On most trains, coach seats are unreserved and are allocated on a first-come, first-served basis; first class seats (in the more comfortable "club cars") can be reserved. Sleeping berths, called "section accommodations," with shared washroom facilities, as well as "roomettes" (small rooms with single beds) and double occupancy bedrooms with private washrooms, also may be available. (These accommodations are in demand on both transcontinental and longer regional routes—especially in summer—and should be booked well in advance.) Meal service ranges from snacks to full meals in dining cars.

Long-distance trains usually have baggage cars, and bags can be checked through to your destination. Baggage allowances are 100 pounds for adults and 75 pounds for children ages 2 through 11 (who travel at half fare). There are porters or self-service carts at major train stations, and many stations also have storage lockers.

Canadian rail tickets are good for one year. Only one-way tickets are sold; discounted round-trip excursion tickets are not offered. However, senior citizens', youth/student, and children's discount fares are available. Passengers usually can stop anywhere en route as long as they reach their final destination before the ticket expires. Tickets can be purchased in person, by phone, or by mail from *VIA Rail* ticket offices (located in train stations), as well as through travel agents.

VIA Rail's Canrailpass allows unlimited travel in selected areas for specified periods. It can be purchased in person at *VIA Rail* ticket offices or at travel agencies (phone or mail orders are not accepted).

Packaged rail tours in Canada are offered by *Accent on Travel* (112 N. Fifth St., Klamath Falls, OR 97601; phone: 503-885-7330), which also sells the Canrailpass and individual *VIA Rail* tickets. *Rocky Mountaineer Railtours* (340 Brooksbank Ave., Suite 104, N. Vancouver, British Columbia V7J 2C1, Canada; phone: 800-665-7245 or 604-984-3315; fax: 604-984-2883) also arranges packages of this type in the Canadian Rockies. Rail tours in the Niagara Falls and Toronto areas are offered by *Key Tours* (main office: 525 Windsor Ave., Windsor, Ontario N9A 6X2, Canada; phone: 800-265-5888 in Wisconsin and throughout Canada; 519-258-7477 elsewhere in the US; fax: 519-258-2268; US office: PO Box 517, Detroit, MI 48231; phone: 313-963-8787).

Traveling by Bus

For those interested in traveling to Canada by bus, *Greyhound* (phone: 800-231-2222) offers direct service to Montreal (Quebec) from Boston (Massachusetts), Detroit (Michigan), and Buffalo and New York City (New York). Direct service to Toronto (Ontario) is available from Detroit, Buffalo, and New York City. US travelers also can make connections to Canadian bus lines in Buffalo and Niagara Falls (New York), Detroit, Fargo (North Dakota), Great Falls (Montana), and Seattle (Washington). In addition, *Greyhound*'s Ameripass covers travel to Montreal and Vancouver (British Columbia), although passengers traveling to Vancouver must transfer to a *Greyhound Canada* bus in Seattle.

Bus service constitutes the most comprehensive transportation network in Canada. Buses reach most populated areas (except in the far north), including many towns without airports or railway stations. *Greyhound Lines of Canada* (phone: 416-367-8747), the country's major bus company, offers service between the Pacific coast and Ottawa (Ontario). In addition, *Voyageur* (phone: 416-393-7911) serves eastern Ontario and southern Quebec; *SMT Eastern, Ltd.* (phone: 506-859-5100) covers New Brunswick, Nova Scotia, and parts of Quebec; and *Acadian* (phone: 902-454-9321) serves Nova Scotia only. A number of smaller regional bus lines operate within other areas, provinces, and territories.

Reservations are not necessary on most bus routes. Tickets usually can be obtained at bus stations or from a central office; on some routes, tickets can be purchased from the bus driver. Companies often allow passengers to make free stopovers along a given route, although these stopovers may be limited to cities where passengers must make connections. Most long-distance buses have air conditioning, heating, toilets, reading lamps, and other amenities.

Grayline (phone: 212-397-2600 in the US; 514-934-1222 in Montreal; 418-622-7420 in Quebec City) offers one-day bus tours of Montreal and Quebec City. For information, contact a *Grayline* office or a travel agent. Local bus lines and other organizations also frequently offer guided day tours in their respective areas. For information, contact the provincial tourist offices.

Traveling by Car

Driving is the most flexible way to explore Canada. To drive in Canada, a US citizen must have a valid US driver's license. If driving your own car into Canada, you also must bring proof of liability insurance.

Canadians drive on the right and observe traffic rules similar to those in the US. However, distances are expressed in kilometers (km) rather than miles (1 kilometer equals approximately .62 mile; 1 mile = approximately 1.6 kilometers), and speed limits are posted in kilometers per hour (kmh). Common speed limits are 100 kmh (62 mph) on freeways, 80 kmh (50 mph) on highways, and 50 kmh (31 mph) on city streets.

Road signs and traffic symbols are standardized under the International Roadsign System and their meanings are indicated by their shapes—triangular signs indicate danger, circular signs give instructions, and rectangular signs provide information. So even in Quebec, where road signs are in French, you should be able to understand the rules of the road.

Seat belts are compulsory for the driver and both front- and back-seat passengers—except in the Yukon Territory, where seat belts are required only for children under six years of age or weighing 48 pounds (approximately 22 kilograms) or less. Throughout Canada, children weighing 20 pounds (about 9 kilograms) or less must ride in rear-facing safety seats in the front seat of the car; children weighing between 21 and 40 pounds (9.5 to 18 kilograms) must ride in forward-facing safety seats in the back seat of the car. Note that forward-facing safety seats must be tethered to the car, in addition to being strapped into place with seat belts. (Tethers can be purchased from most US safety seat manufacturers.)

MAPS

Free maps can be obtained by contacting provincial tourist offices. Canadian road maps can be purchased at service stations on both sides of the border. Automobile clubs may provide maps and route instructions to members, and sometimes these maps also can be purchased by non-members.

MapArt (72 Bloor St. E., Oshawa, Ontario L1H 3M2, Canada; phone: 905-436-2525; fax: 905-723-6677) publishes atlases and a wide range of national, provincial, regional, and municipal maps of Canada. *Hildebrand* (Schönberger Weg 15-17, Frankfurt 60488, Germany; phone: 49-69-762031; no fax) issues *Canada: The East* and *Canada: The West* road atlases and *Canada East* and *Canada West* maps. Other useful resources include Michelin's *Green Guide to Canada* (Michelin Travel Publications, PO Box 19008, Greenville, SC 29602-9008; phone: 803-458-5000 in South Carolina; 800-423-0485 elsewhere in the US; fax: 803-458-5665 in South Carolina; 800-378-7471 elsewhere in the US); the *Hammond Road Atlas of America* (Hammond, 515 Valley St., Maplewood, NJ 07040; phone: 800-526-4953 or 201-763-6000; fax: 201-763-7658); and the *Rand McNally Road Atlas: US, Canada and Mexico* (Rand McNally, 8255 N. Central Park Ave., Skokie, IL 60076; phone: 800-333-0136 or 708-673-9100; fax: 708-673-0813). These maps and atlases can be obtained at travel and general book stores and from mail order suppliers such as *Map Link* (25 E. Mason St., Suite 201, Santa Barbara, CA 93101; phone: 805-965-4402; fax: 800-MAP-SPOT or 805-962-0884).

AUTOMOBILE CLUBS AND BREAKDOWNS

To protect yourself in case of breakdowns while driving to and through Canada, and for travel information and other benefits, consider joining a reputable automobile club. The largest of these is the *American Automobile Association* (*AAA;* 1000 AAA Dr., Heathrow, FL 32746-5063; phone: 407-444-7000; fax: 407-444-7380). Before joining this or any other automobile club, check whether it has reciprocity with the *Canadian Automobile Association* (*CAA;* 60 Commerce Valley Dr. E., Thornhill, Ontario L3T 7P9, Canada; phone: 905-771-3035; fax: 905-771-3101), a federation of provincial Canadian auto clubs.

GASOLINE

Gasoline is sold in liters (approximately 3.8 liters = 1 US gallon). Leaded, unleaded, and diesel fuel are available.

RENTING A CAR

You can rent a car through a travel agent or international rental firm before leaving home, or from a regional or local company once in Canada. Reserve in advance.

Most car rental companies require a credit card, although some will accept a substantial cash deposit. The minimum age to rent a car is set by the company; some also may impose special conditions on drivers above a certain age. Electing to pay for collision or loss damage waiver (CDW or LDW) protection will add to the cost of renting a car, but releases you from financial liability for the vehicle. Additional costs include drop-off charges or one-way service fees.

National Car Rental Companies

Avis (phone: 800-331-1084).
Budget (phone: 800-472-3325).
Dollar Rent A Car (phone: 800-800-4000).
Hertz (phone: 800-654-3001).
Kemwel Group (phone: 800-678-0678).
National (phone: 800-CAR-RENT; affiliated with *Tilden Rent-A-Car* in Canada).
Sears (phone: 800-527-0770).
Thrifty (phone: 800-367-2277).

NOTE

Rent-A-Wreck **rents cars that are well worn but (presumably) mechanically sound, and has franchises throughout the US and Canada (phone: 800-421-7253 for locations).**

Package Tours

A package is a collection of travel services that can be purchased in a single transaction. Its principal advantages are convenience and economy—the cost usually is lower than that of the same services purchased separately. Tour programs generally can be divided into two categories: escorted or locally hosted (with a set itinerary) and independent (which usually are more flexible).

When considering a package tour, read the brochure *carefully* to determine exactly what is included and any conditions that may apply, and check the company's record with the *Better Business Bureau.* The *United States Tour Operators Association* (*USTOA;* 211 E. 51st St., Suite 12B, New York, NY 10022; phone: 212-750-7371; fax: 212-421-1285) also can be helpful in determining a package tour operator's reliability. As with charter flights, to safeguard your funds, always make your check out to the company's escrow account.

Many tour operators offer packages focused on special interests such as the arts, nature study, or sports. *All Adventure Travel* (5589 Arapahoe, Suite 208, Boulder, CO 80303; phone: 800-537-4025 or 303-440-7924; fax: 303-440-4160) represents such specialized packagers. Many also are listed in the *Specialty Travel Index* (305 San Anselmo Ave., Suite 313, San Anselmo, CA 94960; phone: 415-459-4900 in California; 800-442-4922 elsewhere in the US; fax: 415-459-4974).

Below is a list of companies offering package tours to Canada. Note that companies described as wholesalers accept bookings only through travel agents.

Package Tour Operators

Adventure Center (1311 63rd St., Suite 200, Emeryville, CA 94608; phone: 510-654-1879 in northern California; 800-227-8747 elsewhere in the US; fax: 510-654-4200).

Adventure Tours (10612 Beaver Dam Rd., Hunt Valley, MD 21030-2205; phone: 410-785-3500 in the Baltimore area; 800-638-9040 elsewhere in the US; fax: 410-584-2771). Wholesaler.

Adventures in Golf (29 Valencia Dr., Nashua, NH 03062; phone: 603-882-8367; fax: 603-595-6514).

Alaska Sightseeing/Cruise West (Fourth and Battery Building, Suite 700, Seattle, WA 98121; phone: 800-426-7702 or 206-441-8687; fax: 206-441-4757).

American Airlines FlyAAway Vacations (offices throughout the US; phone: 800-321-2121).

American Wilderness Experience (PO Box 1486, Boulder, CO 80306; phone: 800-444-0099 or 303-444-2622; fax: 303-444-3999).

Anglers Travel (1280 Terminal Way, Suite 30, Reno, NV 89502; phone: 800-624-8429 or 702-324-0580; fax: 702-324-0583).

Angling Travel and Tours (c/o *John Eustice & Associates,* 1445 SW 84th Ave., Portland, OR 97225; phone: 800-288-0886 or 503-297-2468; fax: 503-297-3048).

Backcountry (PO Box 4029, Bozeman, MT 59772; phone: 406-586-3556; fax: 406-586-4288).

Backroads (1516 Fifth St., Berkeley, CA 94710; phone: 800-462-2848 or 510-527-1555; fax: 510-527-1444).

Biological Journeys (1696 Ocean Dr., McKinleyville, CA 95521; phone: 800-548-7555 or 707-839-0178; fax: 707-839-4656).

Biss Tours (62-85 Woodhaven Blvd., Rego Park, NY 11374; phone: 718-426-4000).

Black Feather Wilderness Adventures (1960 Scott St., Ottawa, Ontario K1Z 8L8, Canada; phone: 613-722-9717; fax: 613-722-0245).

Brendan Tours (15137 Califa St., Van Nuys, CA 91411; phone: 800-421-8446 or 818-785-9696; fax: 818-902-9876). Wholesaler.

Brian Moore International Tours (116 Main St., Medway, MA 02053; phone: 800-982-2299 or 508-533-6683; fax: 508-533-3812). Wholesaler.

Butterfield & Robinson (70 Bond St., Suite 300, Toronto, Ontario M5B 1X3, Canada; phone: 800-387-1147 or 416-864-1354; fax: 416-864-0541).

California Academy of Sciences (Attention: Travel Division; Golden Gate Park, San Francisco, CA, 94118; phone: 415-750-7222; fax: 415-750-7346).

Canoe Country Escapes (194 S. Franklin St., Denver, CO 80209; phone: 303-722-6482).

Capitol Tours (PO Box 4241, Springfield, IL 62708; phone: 800-252-8924 for reservations; 217-529-8166 for information; fax: 217-529-5831).

Cartan Tours (2809 Butterfield Rd., Suite 350, Oak Brook, IL 60521; phone: 800-422-7826 or 708-571-1400; fax: 708-574-8074). Wholesaler.

Central Holidays** and **Steve Lohr's Holidays (206 Central Ave., Jersey City, NJ 07307; phone: 800-935-5000, 800-929-5647, or 201-798-5777; fax: 201-963-0966).

Certified Vacations (110 E. Broward Blvd., Ft. Lauderdale, FL 33302; phone: 800-233-7260 or 305-522-1440; fax: 305-468-4781).

City Tours (PO Box 333, Rutherford, NJ 07070; phone: 800-248-9868 or 201-939-4154; fax: 201-939-6230).

Classic Adventures (PO Box 153, Hamlin, NY 14464-0153; phone: 800-777-8090 or 716-964-8488; fax: 716-964-7297).

Collette Tours (162 Middle St., Pawtucket, RI 02860; phone: 800-752-2655 in New England; 800-832-4656 elsewhere in the US; fax: 401-727-4745).

Contiki Holidays (300 Plaza Alicante, Suite 900, Garden Grove, CA 92640; phone: 800-266-8454 or 714-740-0808; fax: 714-740-0818). Wholesaler.

Corliss Tours (436 W. Foothill Blvd., Monrovia, CA 91016; phone: 800-456-5717 or 818-359-5358; fax: 818-359-0724).

Creative World Rallies and Caravans (4005 Toulouse St., New Orleans, LA 70119; phone: 800-732-8337 or 504-486-7259; fax: 504-483-8830).

Cross Country International Equestrian Vacations (PO Box 1170, Millbrook, NY 12545; phone: 800-828-8768 or 914-677-6000; fax: 914-677-6077).

Delta's Dream Vacations (PO Box 1525, Ft. Lauderdale, FL 33302; phone: 800-872-7786).

Earthwatch (680 Mt. Auburn St., PO Box 403BG, Watertown, MA 02272; phone: 800-776-0188 or 617-926-8200; fax: 617-926-8532).

Easy Rider Tours (PO Box 228, Newburyport, MA 01950; phone: 800-488-8332 or 508-463-6955; fax: 508-463-6988).

Ecosummer Expeditions (main office: 1516 Duranleau St., Vancouver, British Columbia V6H 3S4, Canada; phone: 800-688-8605 in the US; 800-465-8884 or 604-669-7741 in Canada; fax: 604-669-3244; US mailing address: 936 Peace Portal Dr., PO Box 8014-240, Blaine, WA 98231).

Equitour (PO Box 807, Dubois, WY 82513; phone: 307-455-3363 in Wyoming; 800-545-0019 elsewhere in the US; fax: 307-455-2354).

Federation of Ontario Naturalists (355 Lesmill Rd., Don Mills, Ontario M3B 2W8, Canada; phone: 416-444-8419; fax: 416-444-9866).

Fishing International (PO Box 2132, Santa Rosa, CA 95405; phone: 800-950-4242 or 707-539-3366; fax: 707-539-1320).

FITS Equestrian (685 Lateen Rd., Solvang, CA 93463; phone: 800-666-3487 or 805-688-9494; fax: 805-688-2943).

Forum Travel International (91 Gregory La., Suite 21, Pleasant Hill, CA 94523; phone: 510-671-2900; fax: 510-671-2993 or 510-946-1500).

Frontiers International (PO Box 959, Wexford, PA 15090-0959; phone: 412-935-1577 in Pennsylvania; 800-245-1950 elsewhere in the US; fax: 412-935-5388).

Gadabout Tours (700 E. Tahquitz Canyon Way, Palm Springs, CA 92262; phone: 800-952-5068 or 619-325-5556; fax: 619-325-5127).

Globus and Cosmos (5301 S. Federal Circle, Littleton, CO 80123; phone: 800-221-0090, 800-851-0728, or 303-797-2800; fax: 303-347-2080). Wholesaler.

Golfing Holidays (231 E. Millbrae Ave., Millbrae, CA 94030; phone: 800-652-7847 or 415-697-0230; fax: 415-697-8687).

Hiking Holidays (PO Box 750, Bristol, VT 05443-0750; phone: 802-453-4816; fax: 802-453-4806).

Horizon Air Holidays (PO Box 48309, Seattle, WA 98148; phone: 800-547-9308; fax: 206-248-6336).

InterGolf (PO Box 500608, Atlanta, GA 31150; phone: 800-468-0051 or 404-518-1250; fax: 404-518-1272).

ITC Golf Tours (4134 Atlantic Ave., Suite 205, Long Beach, CA 90807; phone: 800-257-4981 or 310-595-6905; fax: 310-424-6683).

Jefferson Tours (1206 Currie Ave., Minneapolis, MN 55403; phone: 800-767-7433 or 612-338-4174; fax: 612-332-5532).

Joseph Van Os Photo Safaris (PO Box 655, Vashon Island, WA 98070; phone: 206-463-5383; fax: 206-463-5484).

Kaufmann's Fly Fishing Expeditions (PO Box 23032, Portland, OR 97281-3032; phone: 800-442-4359 or 503-684-7025; fax: 503-639-6400).

Kerrville Tours (PO Box 79, Shreveport, LA 71161-0079; phone: 800-442-8705 or 318-227-2882; fax: 318-227-2486).

Le Ob's Tours (4635 Touro St., New Orleans, LA 70122-3933; phone: 800-827-0932 or 504-288-3478; fax: 504-288-8517).

Liberty Travel (for the nearest location, contact the central office: 69 Spring St., Ramsey, NJ 07446; phone: 201-934-3500; fax: 201-934-3888).

M.A.D. World Adventure Club (PO Box 400, Ingersoll, Ontario N5C 3V3, Canada; phone: 519-485-1306).

Maupintour (PO Box 807, Lawrence, KS 66044; phone: 800-255-4266 or 913-843-1211; fax: 913-843-8351). Wholesaler.

Mayflower (1225 Warren Ave., PO Box 490, Downers Grove, IL 60515; phone: 800-323-7604 or 708-960-3430; fax: 708-960-3575).

Mountain Travel-Sobek (6420 Fairmount Ave., El Cerrito, CA 94530; phone: 510-527-8100 in California; 800-227-2384 elsewhere in the US; fax: 510-525-7710).

National Outdoor Leadership School (288 Main St., Lander, WY 82520; phone: 307-332-6973; fax: 307-332-1220).

New England Hiking Holidays (PO Box 1648, N. Conway, NH 03860; phone: 800-869-0949 or 603-356-9696).

New England Vacation Tours (PO Box 560, West Dover, VT 05356; phone: 800-742-7669 or 802-464-2076; fax: 802-464-2629).

Oceanic Society Expeditions (Ft. Mason Center, Building E, San Francisco, CA 94123; phone: 800-326-7491 or 415-441-1106; fax: 415-474-3395).

Outland Adventures (PO Box 16343, Seattle, WA 98116; phone/fax: 206-932-7012).

Overseas Adventure Travel (349 Broadway, Cambridge, MA 02139; phone: 800-221-0814 or 617-876-0533; fax: 617-876-0455).

Pacific Rim Paddling Company (621 Discovery St., PO Box 1840, Victoria, British Columbia V8W 2Y3, Canada; phone: 604-384-6103; fax: 604-361-2686).

PanAngling Travel Service (180 N. Michigan Ave., Room 303, Chicago, IL 60601; phone: 800-533-4353 or 312-263-0328; fax: 312-263-5246).

Panorama Tours (600 N. Sprigg St., Cape Girardeau, MO 63701; phone: 800-962-8687 in Missouri and adjacent states; 314-335-9098 elsewhere in the US; fax: 314-335-7824).

Questers Tours & Travel (257 Park Ave. S., New York, NY 10010; phone: 800-468-8668 or 212-673-3120; fax: 212-473-0178).

Ramblers Holidays (13 Longcroft House, Fretherne Rd., Welwyn Garden City, Hertfordshire AL8 6PQ, England; phone: 44-170-733-1133; fax: 44-170-733-3276).

Regina Tours (401 South St., Room 4B, Chardon, OH 44024; phone: 800-228-4654 or 216-286-9166; fax: 216-286-4231).

REI Adventures (PO Box 1938, Sumner, WA 98390-0800; phone: 800-622-2236 or 206-891-2631; fax: 206-891-2523).

Rocky Mountain Worldwide Cycle Tours (PO Box 1978, Canmore, Alberta T0L 0M0, Canada; phone: 800-661-2453 or 403-678-6770; fax: 403-678-4451).

Sierra Club Outings (730 Polk St., San Francisco, CA 94109; phone: 415-923-5630).

Smithsonian Associates Study Tours and Seminars (1100 Jefferson Dr. SW, Room 3045, Washington, DC 20560; phone: 202-357-4700; fax: 202-786-2315).

Sportsworld International (3350 Cumberland Circle, Suite 1940, Atlanta, GA 30339; phone: 404-850-3260; fax: 404-850-3261).

Tauck Tours (PO Box 5027, Westport, CT 06881; phone: 800-468-2825 or 203-226-6911; fax: 203-221-6828).

Thomas Cook Vacations (headquarters: 45 Berkeley St., Piccadilly, London W1A 1EB, England; phone: 44-171-499-4000; fax: 44-171-408-4299; main US office: 100 Cambridge Park Dr., Cambridge, MA 02140; phone: 800-846-6272 or 617-868-2666; fax: 617-349-1094).

Tours and Travel Odyssey (230 E. McClellan Ave., Livingston, NJ 07039; phone: 800-527-2989 or 201-992-5459; fax: 201-994-1618).

TravelTours International (250 W. 49th St., Suite 600, New York, NY 10019; phone: 800-767-8777 or 212-262-0700; fax: 212-944-5854). Wholesaler.

TravelWild International (PO Box 1637, Vashon Island, WA 98070; phone: 800-368-0077 or 206-463-5362; fax: 206-463-5484).

Trek America (PO Box 470, Blairstown, NJ 07825; phone: 800-221-0596 or 908-362-9198; fax: 908-362-9313).

Uniworld (16000 Ventura Blvd., Suite 210, Encino, CA 91436; phone: 800-733-7820 or 818-382-7820; fax: 818-382-7829). Wholesaler.

Vermont Bicycle Touring (PO Box 711, Bristol, VT 05443-0711; phone: 802-453-4811; fax: 802-453-4806).

Victor Emanuel Nature Tours (PO Box 33008, Austin, TX 78764; phone: 800-328-VENT or 512-328-5221; fax: 512-328-2919).

Waymark Holidays (44 Windsor Rd., Slough SL1 2EJ, England; phone: 44-175-351-6477; fax: 44-175-351-7016).

Wide World of Golf (PO Box 5217, Carmel, CA 93921; phone: 800-214-4653 or 408-624-6667; fax: 408-625-9671).

Wildland Adventures (3516 NE 155th St., Seattle, WA 98155; phone: 800-345-4453 or 206-365-0686; fax: 206-363-6615).

Willard's Adventure Club (PO Box 10, Barrie, Ontario L4M 4S9, Canada; phone: 705-737-1881; fax: 705-737-5123).

Yamnuska (PO Box 1920, Canmore, Alberta T0L 0M0, Canada; phone: 403-678-4164; fax: 403-678-4450).

Yankee Holidays (435 Newbury St., Suite 210, Danvers, MA 01923-1065; phone: 800-225-2550 or 508-750-9688; fax: 508-750-9692). Wholesaler.

Insurance

The first person with whom you should discuss travel insurance is your own insurance broker. You may discover that the insurance you already carry protects you adequately while traveling and that you need little additional coverage. If you charge travel services, the credit card company also may provide some insurance coverage (and other safeguards). Below is a list of the basic types of travel insurance and companies specializing in such policies.

Types of Travel Insurance

Automobile insurance: Provides collision, theft, property damage, and personal liability protection while driving.

Baggage and personal effects insurance: Protects your bags and their contents in case of damage or theft at any point during your travels.

Default and/or bankruptcy insurance: Provides coverage in the event of default and/or bankruptcy on the part of the tour operator, airline, or other travel supplier.

Flight insurance: Covers accidental injury or death while flying.

Personal accident and sickness insurance: Covers cases of illness, injury, or death in an accident while traveling.

Trip cancellation and interruption insurance: Guarantees a refund if you must cancel a trip; may reimburse you for additional travel costs incurred in catching up with a tour or traveling home early.

Combination policies: Include any or all of the above.

Travel Insurance Providers

Access America International (PO Box 90315, Richmond, VA 23230; phone: 800-284-8300 or 804-285-3300; fax: 804-673-1491).

Carefree (c/o *Berkely Care,* Arm Coverage, PO Box 310, Mineola, NY 11501; phone: 800-645-2424 or 516-294-0220; fax: 516-294-0258).

NEAR Services (PO Box 1339, Calumet City, IL 60409; phone: 708-868-6700 in the Chicago area; 800-654-6700 elsewhere in the US; fax: 708-868-6706).

Tele-Trip (3201 Farnam St., Omaha, NE 68131; phone: 800-228-9792 or 402-345-2400; fax: 402-978-2456).

Travel Assistance International (c/o *Worldwide Assistance Services,* 1133 15th St. NW, Suite 400, Washington, DC 20005; phone: 800-821-2828 or 202-331-1609; fax: 202-331-1530).

Travel Guard International (1145 Clark St., Stevens Point, WI 54481; phone: 800-826-1300 or 715-345-0505; fax: 800-955-8785).

Travel Insurance PAK Worldwide Coverage (c/o *Travel Insured International,* PO Box 280568, East Hartford, CT 06128-0568; phone: 800-243-3174 or 203-528-7663; fax: 203-528-8005).

Disabled Travelers

Make travel arrangements well in advance. Specify to all services involved the nature of your disability to determine if there are accommodations and facilities that meet your needs. Accommodations guides available from the Canadian provincial tourist boards use the standard symbol of access (person in a wheelchair) to indicate establishments that are accessible to the disabled.

International Organizations

ACCENT on Living (PO Box 700, Bloomington, IL 61702; phone: 800-787-8444 or 309-378-2961; fax: 309-378-4420).

Access: The Foundation for Accessibility by the Disabled (PO Box 356, Malverne, NY 11565; phone/fax: 516-568-2715).

American Foundation for the Blind (15 W. 16th St., New York, NY 10011; phone: 800-232-5463 or 212-620-2147; fax: 212-727-7418).

Canadian March of Dimes (branches throughout Canada; for information, contact the Toronto office: 10 Overlook Blvd., Toronto, Ontario M4H 1A4, Canada; phone: 416-425-3463; fax: 416-425-1920).

Canadian Paraplegic Association (1101 Prince of Wales Dr., Suite 320, Ottawa, Ontario K2C 3W7, Canada; phone: 613-723-1033; fax: 613-723-1060).

Canadian Rehabilitation Council for the Disabled (45 Sheppard Ave. E., Suite 801, Toronto, Ontario M2N 5W9, Canada; phone/TDD: 416-250-7490; fax: 416-229-1371).

Holiday Care Service (2 Old Bank Chambers, Station Rd., Horley, Surrey RH6 9HW, England; phone: 44-1293-774535; fax: 44-1293-784647).

Information Center for Individuals with Disabilities (Ft. Point Pl., 27-43 Wormwood St., Boston, MA 02210; phone: 800-462-5015 in Massachusetts; 617-727-5540 elsewhere in the US; TDD: 617-345-9743; fax: 617-345-5318).

Keroul (4545 Pierre du Coubertin, CP1000, Box M, Montreal, Quebec H1V 3R2, Canada; phone/TDD: 514-252-3104; fax: 514-254-0766).

Mobility International (main office: 25 Rue de Manchester, Brussels B-1070, Belgium; phone: 32-2-410-6297; fax: 32-2-410-6874; US office: *MIUSA,* PO Box 10767, Eugene, OR 97440; phone/TDD: 503-343-1284; fax: 503-343-6812).

Moss Rehabilitation Hospital Travel Information Service (telephone referrals only; phone: 215-456-9600; TDD: 215-456-9602).

National Rehabilitation Information Center (8455 Colesville Rd., Suite 935, Silver Spring, MD 20910-3319; phone: 301-588-9284; fax: 301-587-1967).

Paralyzed Veterans of America (*PVA;* PVA/Access to the Skies Program, 801 18th St. NW, Washington, DC 20006-3585; phone: 202-872-1300 in Washington, DC; 800-424-8200 elsewhere in the US; fax: 202-785-4452).

Royal Association for Disability and Rehabilitation (*RADAR;* 12 City Forum, 250 City Rd., London EC1V 8AF, England; phone: 44-171-250-3222; fax: 44-171-250-0212).

Society for the Advancement of Travel for the Handicapped (*SATH;* 347 Fifth Ave., Suite 610, New York, NY 10016; phone: 212-447-7284; fax: 212-725-8253).

Travel Industry and Disabled Exchange (*TIDE;* Attention: Yvonne Nau, 5435 Donna Ave., Tarzana, CA 91356; phone: 818-344-3640; fax: 818-344-0078).

Tripscope (The Courtyard, Evelyn Rd., London W4 5JL, England; phone: 44-181-994-9294; fax: 44-181-994-3618).

Publications

Access Travel: A Guide to the Accessibility of Airport Terminals (Consumer Information Center, Dept. 575A, Pueblo, CO 81009; phone: 719-948-3334; fax: 719-948-9724).

Accessibility of Tourism-Related Services (*Keroul,* address above).

Air Transportation of Handicapped Persons (Publication #AC-120-32; *US Department of Transportation,* Distribution Unit, Utilization and Storage Section, M-45.3, 400 Seventh St. SW, Washington, DC 20590; phone: 202-366-0039; fax: 202-366-2795).

The Diabetic Traveler (PO Box 8223 RW, Stamford, CT 06905; phone: 203-327-5832; fax: 203-975-1748).

Directory of Travel Agencies for the Disabled *and* ***Travel for the Disabled,*** both by Helen Hecker (Twin Peaks Press, PO Box 129, Vancouver, WA 98666; phone: 800-637-CALM for orders; 206-694-2462 for information; fax: 206-696-3210).

The Disabled Driver's Mobility Guide (*American Automobile Association,* Traffic Safety Dept., 1000 AAA Dr., Heathrow, FL 32746-5063; phone: 407-444-7961; fax: 407-444-7956).

Guide to Traveling with Arthritis (*Upjohn Company,* 7000 Portage Rd., Kalamazoo, MI 49001; phone: 800-253-9860).

Handicapped Travel Newsletter (PO Box 269, Athens, TX 75751; phone/fax: 903-677-1260).

Handi-Travel: A Resource Book for Disabled and Elderly Travellers, by Cinnie Noble (*Canadian Rehabilitation Council for the Disabled,* address above).

Holidays and Travel Abroad, edited by John Stanford (*Royal Association for Disability and Rehabilitation,* address above).

On the Go, Go Safely, Plan Ahead (*American Diabetes Association,* 1660 Duke St., Alexandria, VA 22314; phone: 800-232-3472 or 703-549-1500; fax: 703-863-7439).

Travel for the Patient with Chronic Obstructive Pulmonary Disease (Dr. Harold Silver, 1601 18th St. NW, Washington, DC 20009; phone: 202-667-0134; fax: 202-667-0148).

Travel Tips for Hearing-Impaired People (*American Academy of Otolaryngology,* 1 Prince St., Alexandria, VA 22314; phone: 703-836-4444; fax: 703-683-5100).

Travel Tips for People with Arthritis (*Arthritis Foundation,* 1314 Spring St. NW, Atlanta, GA 30309; phone: 800-283-7800 or 404-872-7100; fax: 404-872-0457).

Traveling Like Everybody Else: A Practical Guide for Disabled Travelers, by Jacqueline Freedman and Susan Gersten (Modan Publishing, PO Box 1202, Bellmore, NY 11710; phone: 516-679-1380; fax: 516-679-1448).

The Wheelchair Traveler, by Douglass R. Annand (123 Ball Hill Rd., Milford, NH 03055; phone: 603-673-4539).

Package Tour Operators

Accessible Journeys (35 W. Sellers Ave., Ridley Park, PA 19078; phone: 800-846-4537 or 610-521-0339; fax: 610-521-6959).

Accessible Tours/Directions Unlimited (Attention: Lois Bonanni, 720 N. Bedford Rd., Bedford Hills, NY 10507; phone: 800-533-5343 or 914-241-1700; fax: 914-241-0243).

Classic Travel Service (8 W. 40th St., New York, NY 10018; phone: 212-869-2560 in New York State; 800-247-0909 elsewhere in the US; fax: 212-944-4493).

CTM Beehive Travel (77 W. 200 S., Suite 500, Salt Lake City, UT 84101; phone: 800-777-5727 or 801-578-9000; fax: 801-297-2828).

Dahl's Good Neighbor Travel Service (124 S. Main St., Viroqua, WI 54665; phone: 800-338-3245 or 608-637-2128; fax: 608-637-3030).

Dialysis at Sea Cruises (PO Box 218, Indian Rocks Beach, FL 34635; phone: 800-544-7604 or 813-596-4614; fax: 813-596-0203).

Flying Wheels Travel (PO Box 382, Owatonna, MN 55060; phone: 800-535-6790 or 507-451-1966; fax: 507-451-1685).

The Guided Tour (7900 Old York Rd., Suite 114B, Elkins Park, PA 19027-2339; phone: 800-783-5841 or 215-782-1370; fax: 215-635-2637).

Hinsdale Travel (201 E. Ogden Ave., Hinsdale, IL 60521; phone: 708-325-1335 or 708-469-7349; fax: 708-325-1342).

MedEscort International (*Lehigh Valley International Airport,* PO Box 8766, Allentown, PA 18105-8766; phone: 800-255-7182 or 215-791-3111; fax: 215-791-9189).

Prestige World Travel (5710-X High Point Rd., Greensboro, NC 27407; phone: 800-476-7737 or 910-292-6690; fax: 910-632-9404).

Sprout (893 Amsterdam Ave., New York, NY 10025; phone: 212-222-9575; fax: 212-222-9768).

Weston Travel Agency (134 N. Cass Ave., Westmont, IL 60559; phone: 708-968-2513 in Illinois; 800-633-3725 elsewhere in the US; fax: 708-968-2539).

Single Travelers

The travel industry is not very fair to people who vacation by themselves—they often end up paying more than those traveling in pairs. There are services catering to single travelers, however, that match travel companions, offer travel arrangements with shared accommodations, and provide information and discounts. Useful publications include *Going Solo* (Doerfer Communications, PO Box 123, Apalachicola, FL 32329; phone/fax: 904-653-8848) and *Traveling on Your Own,* by Eleanor Berman (Random House, Order Dept., 400 Hahn Rd., Westminster, MD 21157; phone: 800-733-3000; fax: 800-659-2436).

Organizations and Companies

Contiki Holidays (300 Plaza Alicante, Suite 900, Garden Grove, CA 92640; phone: 800-266-8454 or 714-740-0808; fax: 714-740-0818).

Gallivanting (515 E. 79th St., Suite 20F, New York, NY 10021; phone: 800-933-9699 or 212-988-0617; fax: 212-988-0144).

Globus and Cosmos (5301 S. Federal Circle, Littleton, CO 80123; phone: 800-221-0090, 800-851-0728, or 303-797-2800; fax: 303-347-2080).

Jane's International Travel and Sophisticated Women Travelers (2603 Bath Ave., Brooklyn, NY 11214; phone: 800-613-9226 or 718-266-2045; fax: 718-266-4062).

Marion Smith Singles (611 Prescott Pl., N. Woodmere, NY 11581; phone: 800-698-TRIP, 516-791-4852, 516-791-4865, or 212-944-2112; fax: 516-791-4879).

Partners-in-Travel (11660 Chenault St., Suite 119, Los Angeles, CA 90049; phone: 310-476-4869).

Solo Flights (612 Penfield Rd., Fairfield, CT 06430; phone: 800-266-1566 or 203-256-1235).

Suddenly Singles Tours (161 Dreiser Loop, Bronx, NY 10475; phone: 718-379-8800 in New York City; 800-859-8396 elsewhere in the US; fax: 718-379-8858).

Travel Companion Exchange (PO Box 833, Amityville, NY 11701; phone: 516-454-0880; fax: 516-454-0170).

Travel Companions (Atrium Financial Center, 1515 N. Federal Hwy., Suite 300, Boca Raton, FL 33432; phone: 800-383-7211 or 407-393-6448; fax: 407-451-8560 or 407-393-6448).

Travel in Two's (239 N. Broadway, Suite 3, N. Tarrytown, NY 10591; phone: 914-631-8301 in New York State; 800-692-5252 elsewhere in the US).

Umbrella Singles (PO Box 157, Woodbourne, NY 12788; phone: 800-537-2797 or 914-434-6871; fax: 914-434-3532).

Older Travelers

Special discounts and more free time are just two factors that have given older travelers a chance to see the world at affordable prices. Many travel suppliers offer senior discounts—sometimes only to members of certain senior citizens organizations (which provide benefits of their own). When considering a particular package, make sure the facilities—and the pace of the tour—match your needs and physical condition.

Publications

Going Abroad: 101 Tips for Mature Travelers (*Grand Circle Travel,* 347 Congress St., Boston, MA 02210; phone: 800-221-2610 or 617-350-7500; fax: 617-423-0445).

The Mature Traveler (PO Box 50820, Reno, NV 89513-0820; phone: 702-786-7419).

The Senior Citizen's Guide to Budget Travel in the US and Canada, by Paige Palmer (Pilot Books, 103 Cooper St., Babylon, NY 11702; phone: 516-422-2225; fax: 516-422-2227).

Take a Camel to Lunch and Other Adventures for Mature Travelers, by Nancy O'Connell (Bristol Publishing Enterprises, PO Box 1737, San Leandro, CA 94577; phone: 510-895-4461 in California; 800-346-4889 elsewhere in the US; fax: 510-895-4459).

Unbelievably Good Deals & Great Adventures That You Absolutely Can't Get Unless You're Over 50, by Joan Rattner Heilman (Contemporary Books, 180 N. Stetson Ave., Suite 1200, Chicago, IL 60601; phone: 312-782-9181; fax: 312-540-4687).

Organizations

American Association of Retired Persons (*AARP;* 601 E St. NW, Washington, DC 20049; phone: 202-434-2277).

Golden Companions (PO Box 754, Pullman, WA 99163-0754; phone: 208-858-2183).

Mature Outlook (Customer Service Center, 6001 N. Clark St., Chicago, IL 60660; phone: 800-336-6330; fax: 312-764-5036).

National Council of Senior Citizens (1331 F St. NW, Washington, DC 20004; phone: 202-347-8800; fax: 202-624-9595).

Package Tour Operators

Elderhostel (75 Federal St., Boston, MA 02110-1941; phone: 617-426-7788; fax: 617-426-8351).

Gadabout Tours (700 E. Tahquitz Canyon Way, Palm Springs, CA 92262; phone: 800-952-5068 or 619-325-5556; fax: 619-325-5127).

Grand Circle Travel (347 Congress St., Boston, MA 02210; phone: 800-221-2610 or 617-350-7500; fax: 617-542-2887).

Grandtravel (6900 Wisconsin Ave., Suite 706, Chevy Chase, MD 20815; phone: 800-247-7651 or 301-986-0790; fax: 301-913-0166).

Interhostel (*University of New Hampshire,* Division of Continuing Education, 6 Garrison Ave., Durham, NH 03824; phone: 800-733-9753 or 603-862-1147; fax: 603-862-1113).

Mature Tours (c/o *Solo Flights,* 612 Penfield Rd., Fairfield, CT 06430; phone: 800-266-1566 or 203-256-1235).

OmniTours (104 Wilmot Rd., Deerfield, IL 60015; phone: 800-962-0060 or 708-374-0088; fax: 708-374-9515).

Saga International Holidays (222 Berkeley St., Boston, MA 02116; phone: 800-343-0273 or 617-262-2262; fax: 617-375-5950).

Traveling with Children

Sharing the excitement and discovery of travel with your family can bring special meaning to any trip. Although traveling with your children requires some additional preparation and planning, it does not have to be a burden or an excessive expense. An increasing number of hotels and other travel services cater to families and offer family packages and discounts for children. In addition, there are numerous publications that provide valuable information on family travel.

Publications

Doing Children's Museums: A Guide to 265 Hands-On Museums, by Joanne Cleaver (Williamson Publishing, PO Box 185, Charlotte, VT 05445; phone: 800-234-8791; fax: 802-425-2199).

Family Travel Times newsletter (*Travel with Your Children; TWYCH;* 80 Eighth Ave., New York, NY 10011; phone: 212-206-0688). Subscription includes copy of "Airline Guide" issue (also available separately).

Farm, Ranch & Country Vacations, by Pat Dickerman (Adventure Guides, 7550 E. McDonald Dr., Scottsdale, AZ 85250; phone: 800-252-7899 or 602-596-0226; fax: 602-596-1722).

Recommended Family Resorts in the United States, Canada, and the Caribbean: 100 Quality Resorts with Leisure Activities for Children and Adults, by Jane Wilson with Janet Tice (Globe Pequot Press, PO Box 833, Old Saybrook, CT 06475; phone: 800-243-0495 or 203-395-0440; fax: 203-395-0312).

Super Family Vacations, by Martha Shirk and Nancy Klepper (HarperCollins Publishers, 10 E. 53rd St., New York, NY 10022; phone: 800-242-7737 for orders; 212-207-7000 for information; fax: 800-822-4090).

Travel with Children, by Maureen Wheeler (Lonely Planet Publications, Embarcadero West, 112 Linden St., Oakland, CA 94607; phone: 510-893-8555; fax: 510-893-8563).

Traveling with Children and Enjoying It, by A. B. Butler (Globe Pequot Press, address above).

Trouble-Free Travel with Children: Helpful Hints for Parents on the Go, by Vicki Lansky (The Book Peddlers, 18326 Minnetonka Blvd., Deephaven, MN 55391; phone: 800-255-3379 or 612-475-3527; fax: 612-475-1505).

When Kids Fly (*Massport,* Public Affairs Dept., 10 Park Plaza, Boston, MA 02116-3971; phone: 617-973-5600; fax: 617-973-5611).

Money Matters

Travelers from the US should have little difficulty using Canadian currency. Like the US, Canada's monetary system is based on dollars and cents, although the US and Canadian dollars are not equal in value. (At the time of this writing, the exchange rate for the Canadian dollar was CN$1.38 to $1 US.) Canadian currency is distributed in coin denominations of $1, 25¢,

10¢, 5¢, and 1¢, and in bills of $1,000, $500, $100, $50, $20, $10, $5, and $2. Although 50¢ coins and $1 bills no longer are issued, some still are in circulation and are legal tender.

Exchange rates are listed in international newspapers such as the *International Herald Tribune.* Foreign currency information and related services are provided by banks and companies such as *Thomas Cook Foreign Exchange* (for the nearest location, call 800-621-0666 or 312-236-0042; fax: 312-807-4895); *Harold Reuter and Company* (200 Park Ave., Suite 332E, New York, NY 10166; phone: 800-258-0456 or 212-661-0826; fax: 212-557-6622); and *Ruesch International* (for the nearest location, call 800-424-2923 or 202-408-1200; fax: 202-408-1211). In Canada, you will find the official rate of exchange posted in banks, airports, money exchange houses, hotels, and some shops. Since you will get more Canadian currency for your US dollar at banks and money exchanges, don't change more than $10 at other commercial establishments. Ask how much commission you're being charged and the exchange rate, and don't buy money on the black market (it may be counterfeit). Estimate your needs carefully; if you overbuy, you lose twice—buying and selling back.

CREDIT CARDS AND TRAVELER'S CHECKS

Most major credit cards enjoy wide domestic and international acceptance; however, not every hotel, restaurant, or shop in Canada accepts all (or in some cases any) credit cards. When making purchases with a credit card, note that the rate of exchange depends on when the charge is processed. Most credit card companies charge a 1% fee for converting foreign currency charges.

It's also wise to carry traveler's checks while on the road, since they are widely accepted and replaceable if stolen or lost. You can buy traveler's checks at banks and some are available by mail or phone. Keep a separate list of all traveler's checks (noting those that you have cashed) and the names and numbers of your credit cards. Both traveler's check and credit card companies have international numbers to call for information or in the event of loss or theft.

CASH MACHINES

Automated teller machines (ATMs) are increasingly common worldwide, and most banks participate in international ATM networks such as *MasterCard/Cirrus* (phone: 800-4-CIRRUS) and *Visa/PLUS* (phone: 800-THE-PLUS). Using a card—with an assigned Personal Identification Number (PIN)—from an affiliated bank or credit card company, you can withdraw cash from any machine in the same network. The *MasterCard/Cirrus ATM Travel Directory* and the *Visa/PLUS International ATM Locator Guide 1996* provide the locations of network ATMs worldwide and are available from banks and other financial institutions.

SENDING MONEY ABROAD

Should the need arise, you can have money sent to you throughout most of Canada via the services provided by *American Express MoneyGram* (phone: 800-926-9400 for information; 800-866-8800 for money transfers) or *Western Union Financial Services* (phone: 800-325-6000 or 800-325-4176). You also can have money wired to you in Canada via a direct bank-to-bank transfer from the US; arrangements can be made with the participating institutions. If you are down to your last cent and have no other way to obtain cash, the nearest *US Consulate* (see *Consular Services* for addresses) will let you call home to set matters in motion.

Accommodations

For specific information on hotels, resorts, and other selected accommodations, see *Checking In* in THE CITIES, sections throughout DIVERSIONS, and *Best en Route* in DIRECTIONS. The provincial tourist boards all publish booklets that provide information on licensed establishments in their respective areas, and the Alberta, Manitoba, New Brunswick, Newfoundland, Nova Scotia, Ontario, Prince Edward Island, and Quebec booklets also include ratings for some of the establishments listed. In addition, the provincial tourist boards of Alberta, British Columbia, Ontario, and Nova Scotia offer free accommodations reservations services.

RELAIS & CHÂTEAUX

Founded in France, the *Relais & Châteaux* association has grown to include establishments in numerous countries. At press time there were eight members in Canada. All maintain very high standards in order to retain their memberships, as they are reviewed annually. An illustrated catalogue of properties is available from *Relais & Châteaux* (11 E. 44th St., Suite 707, New York, NY 10017; phone: 212-856-0115; fax: 212-856-0193).

BED AND BREAKFAST ESTABLISHMENTS

Commonly known as B&Bs, bed and breakfast establishments provide exactly what the name implies. A private bath isn't always offered, so check before you reserve. Although some hosts may be contacted directly, most prefer that arrangements be made through reservations services. Provincial tourist offices are the best sources of information on bed and breakfast establishments and reservations services in Canada.

For lists of B&B reservations services in Canada, contact *Bed & Breakfast: The National Network* (PO Box 4616, Springfield, MA 01101; no phone), and *Bed & Breakfast Reservations Services World-Wide* (*A Trade Association;* PO Box 14841, Baton Rouge, LA 70898-4841; phone: 504-336-4035; fax: 504-343-0672). The latter organization also will fax information on reservations services and specific establishments; for this service, call the *B&B/Innfo-Fax Line* (phone: 800-364-7242).

Publications

America's Wonderful Little Hotels and Inns, by Sandra W. Soule (St. Martin's Press, 175 Fifth Ave., New York, NY 10010; phone: 800-288-2131 for orders; 212-674-5151, ext. 311 for information; fax: 212-254-8175).

Bed & Breakfasts and Country Inns (*Association of American Historic Inns,* PO Box 336, Dana Point, CA 92629; phone: 800-397-4667 or 714-496-6953; fax: 714-499-4022).

Birnbaum's Country Inns and Back Roads (HarperCollins Publishers, PO Box 588, Dunmore, PA 18512; phone: 800-331-3761; fax: 800-822-4090).

The Complete Guide to Bed & Breakfasts, Inns, & Guesthouses in the United States and Canada, by Pamela Lanier (Lanier Publishing International, PO Box 20467, Oakland, CA 94620-0467; phone: 510-644-8018; fax: 510-644-2651).

Gracious Stays & Special Places (*Person to Person Travel Productions,* 2856 Hundred Oaks St., Baton Rouge, LA 70808; phone/fax: 504-343-0672).

Waterside Escapes, by Nancy Webster and Richard Woodworth (Wood Pond Press, 365 Ridgewood Rd., West Hartford, CT 06107; phone: 203-521-0389).

RENTAL OPTIONS

An attractive accommodations alternative for the visitor content to stay in one spot is a vacation rental. For a family or group, the per-person cost can be reasonable. To have your pick of the properties available throughout Canada, make inquiries at least six months in advance. The *Worldwide Home Rental Guide* (3501 Indian School Rd. NE, Suite 303, Albuquerque, NM 87106; phone/fax: 505-255-4271) lists rental properties and managing agencies.

Rental Property Agents

Barclay International Group (150 E. 52nd St., New York, NY 10022; phone: 212-832-3777 in New York City; 800-U4-LONDON elsewhere in the US; fax: 212-753-1139).

Hideaways International (767 Islington St., Portsmouth, NH 03801; phone: 800-843-4433 or 603-430-4433; fax: 603-430-4444).

Keith Prowse & Co. (USA) Ltd. (234 W. 44th St., Suite 1000, New York, NY 10036; phone: 800-669-8687 or 212-398-1430; fax: 212-302-4251).

Property Rentals International (1 Park W. Circle, Suite 108, Midlothian, VA 23113; phone: 800-220-3332 or 804-378-6054; fax: 804-379-2073).

Rent a Home International (7200 34th Ave. NW, Seattle, WA 98117; phone: 206-789-9377; fax: 206-789-9379).

HOME EXCHANGES

For comfortable, reasonable living quarters with amenities that no hotel could possibly offer, consider trading homes with someone abroad. The following companies provide information on exchanges:

Home Base Holidays (7 Park Ave., London N13 5PG, England; phone/fax: 44-181-886-8752).

Intervac US/International Home Exchange (PO Box 590504, San Francisco, CA 94159; phone: 800-756-HOME or 415-435-3497; fax: 415-435-7440).

Loan-A-Home (2 Park La., Apt. 6E, Mt. Vernon, NY 10552-3443; phone: 914-664-7640).

Vacation Exchange Club (PO Box 650, Key West, FL 33041; phone: 800-638-3841; phone/fax: 305-294-1448).

Worldwide Home Exchange Club (main office: 50 Hans Crescent, London SW1X 0NA, England; phone: 44-171-589-6055; US office: 806 Brantford Ave., Silver Spring, MD 20904; phone: 301-680-8950).

HOME STAYS

United States Servas (11 John St., Room 407, New York, NY 10038; phone: 212-267-0252; fax: 212-267-0292) maintains a list of hosts worldwide willing to accommodate visitors free of charge. The aim of this nonprofit cultural program is to promote international understanding and peace, and *Servas* emphasizes that member travelers should be interested mainly in their hosts, not in sightseeing, during their stays.

ACCOMMODATIONS DISCOUNTS

The following organizations offer discounts of up to 50% on accommodations throughout Canada:

Carte Royale (131 N. State St., Suite J, Lake Oswego, OR 97034; phone: 800-847-7002 or 503-635-6300; fax: 503-635-4937).

Encore Marketing International (4501 Forbes Blvd., Lanham, MD 20706; phone: 800-638-0930 or 301-459-8020; fax: 301-731-0525).

Entertainment Publications (2125 Butterfield Rd., Troy, MI 48084; phone: 800-477-3234 or 810-637-8400; fax: 810-637-9779).

Great American Traveler (Access Development Corp., PO Box 27965, Salt Lake City, UT 84127; phone: 800-331-8867 or 801-262-2233; fax: 801-262-2311).

Hotel Express International (International Concepts Group, 707 E. Arapaho Rd., Richardson, TX 75081-2260; phone: 800-866-2015, 800-770-2015, or 214-497-9792; fax: 214-994-2298).

Impulse (6143 S. Willow Dr., Suite 410, Englewood, CO 80111; phone: 303-741-2457; fax: 303-721-6011).

International Travel Card (6001 N. Clark St., Chicago, IL 60660; phone: 800-342-0558 or 312-465-8891; fax: 312-764-8066).

Privilege Card (3391 Peachtree Rd. NE, Suite 110, Atlanta, GA 30326; phone: 800-236-9732 or 404-262-0255; fax: 404-262-0235).

Quest International (402 E. Yakima Ave., Suite 1200, Yakima, WA 98901; phone: 800-325-2400 or 509-248-7512; fax: 509-457-8399).

Time Zones

Canada is divided into six time zones, but because the two most easterly zones are only a half hour apart, there is only a 4½-hour difference between the country's east and west coasts. Canada's eastern, central, mountain, and pacific standard time zones are the same as the corresponding time zones in the US; the time is later in the two time zones covering provinces east of the US. Note, however, that the government of each province or territory has the authority to determine the time observed within its boundaries, so there may be some exceptions.

Canadian Time Zones

Newfoundland standard time (Labrador; Newfoundland): 1½ hours later than eastern standard time.

Atlantic standard time (Maritime Provinces): 1 hour later than eastern standard time.

Eastern standard time (Gaspé Peninsula; Quebec; all of Ontario east of 90° longitude): the same as eastern standard time in the US.

Central standard time (Ontario west of 90° longitude; Manitoba; Saskatchewan): 1 hour earlier than eastern standard time.

Mountain standard time (Alberta; sections of the Northwest Territories directly north of Alberta and Saskatchewan; some parts of northeastern British Columbia): 2 hours earlier than eastern standard time.

Pacific standard time (the remainder of British Columbia; the Yukon Territory): 3 hours earlier than eastern standard time.

Saskatchewan is the only Canadian province that does not observe daylight saving time. In the rest of the country, daylight saving time is observed from the first Sunday in April until the last Sunday in October, as in the US. Canadian timetables use a 24-hour clock to denote arrival and departure times, which means that hours are expressed sequentially from 1 AM—for example, 1:30 PM would be "1330 hours" ("13h30" in Quebec).

Business and Shopping Hours

Business hours throughout Canada are fairly standard and similar to those in the US: 9 AM to 5 PM, Mondays through Fridays. Retail stores usually are open weekdays and Saturdays from 9 or 9:30 AM to between 5 and 6 PM, although in major cities, stores may stay open later (until around 8 or 9 PM) Wednesdays through Fridays (and sometimes Saturdays). Department stores and malls may be open weekdays and Saturdays from 10 AM to 9 or 10 PM; some malls also are open Sundays from around noon to 5 PM.

Banking hours are weekdays from 10 AM to 3 PM, except on Fridays, when most banks stay open until 6 PM. The trend is toward longer hours, however, and some stay open every weekday until 6 PM. Most banks are closed on weekends, although an increasing number are offering Saturday morning hours (typically from 10 AM to 2 PM). Currency exchange houses usually are open weekdays (and often Saturdays as well) from 9 or 10 AM to 5 or 6 PM. Money exchanges at major airports may be open 24 hours daily, seven days a week.

Holidays

Below is a list of Canadian national and provincial holidays and the dates they will be observed this year. (Note that the dates of some holidays vary from year to year; others occur on the same day every year.)

National Holidays

New Year's Day (January 1)
Good Friday (April 5)
Easter Monday (April 8)
Victoria Day (May 20)
Canada Day (July 1)
Labour Day (September 2)
Thanksgiving Day (October 14)
Remembrance Day (November 11)
Christmas Day (December 25)
Boxing Day (December 26)

Provincial Holidays

Alberta

Heritage Day (August 5)

British Columbia

British Columbia Day (August 5)

Newfoundland

St. Patrick's Day (March 18)
St. George's Day (April 22)
Discovery Day (June 24)
Memorial Day (July 1)
Orangeman's Day (July 12)

Quebec

Saint-Jean Baptiste Day (also known as *Quebec Day;* June 24)

Manitoba, Northwest Territories, and Ontario

Civic holiday (August 5)

New Brunswick

New Brunswick Day (August 5)

Yukon

Discovery Day (August 19)

Mail

Main post offices and branches (called "postal stations") in Canada are open weekdays from 8:30 AM to around 5:30 PM; some offices may be open on Saturdays as well. Stamps also are sold at most hotels and some stores and newsstands, as well as from public vending machines.

When sending mail between Canada and the US, allow at least seven days for delivery. Note that the inclusion of postal codes in Canadian addresses is essential; delivery of your letter or parcel may depend on it. If your correspondence is especially important, you may want to send it via an international courier service, such as *FedEx* (*Federal Express;* phone: 800-238-5355 in the US; 800-463-3339 in Canada) or *DHL Worldwide Express* (phone: 800-225-5345 in the US; in Canada, contact the nearest local office).

You can have mail sent to you care of your hotel (marked "Guest Mail, Hold for Arrival") or to a post office (the address should include "c/o General Delivery" or, in French-speaking areas, "c/o *Poste Restante*"). *American Express* offices in Canada also will hold mail for customers ("c/o Client Letter Service"); information is provided in their pamphlet *Travelers' Companion.* Note that *US Embassies* and *Consulates* abroad will hold mail for US citizens *only* in emergency situations.

Telephone

The procedure for making calls between the US and Canada, as well as long-distance calls within Canada, is the same as in the US: Dial 1 + the area code + the local number. To call a number within the same area code, dial the local number. The nationwide number for information is 555-1212; in most areas, you also can dial 411 for local information. If you need a number in another area code, dial 1 + the area code + 555-1212. (If you don't know an area code in Canada, call 555-1212 or 411 for directory assistance.)

In metropolitan areas throughout the country, the number to dial in emergencies is 911. In smaller towns and rural areas, you may need to dial 0 for an operator, who will connect you to the police or other emergency services.

Although most public telephones in Canada still take coins, pay phones that accept special phone debit cards are increasingly common. Marketed under the name "HELLO Phone Pass" (*"La télécarte ALLÔ"* in Quebec), these cards are available from most of the regional telephone companies in Canada. They can be purchased at "PhoneCenters" in malls and other shopping areas, and also may be sold in pharmacies and convenience stores.

You can use a telephone company calling card number on any phone, and some pay phones take major credit cards (*American Express, MasterCard, Visa,* and so on). Also available are combined telephone calling/bank credit cards, such as the *AT&T Universal Card* (PO Box 44167, Jacksonville, FL 32231-4167; phone: 800-423-4343). Similarly, *Sprint* (8140 Ward Pkwy., Kansas City, MO 64114; phone: 800-669-8585) offers *VisaPhone,* through which you can add phone card privileges to your existing *Visa* card. Companies offering long-distance phone cards without additional credit card privileges include *AT&T* (phone: 800-CALL-ATT), *Executive Telecard International* (4260 E. Evans Ave., Suite 6, Denver, CO 80222; phone: 800-950-3800), *LDDS/Metromedia Communications* (1 International Center, 100 NE Loop 410, San Antonio, TX 78216; phone: 800-275-0200), *MCI* (323 Third St. SE, Cedar Rapids, IA 52401; phone: 800-444-4444; and 12790 Merit Dr., Dallas, TX 75251; phone: 800-444-3333), and *Sprint* (address above; phone: 800-THE-MOST).

Hotels routinely add surcharges to the cost of phone calls made from their rooms. Long-distance telephone services that may help you avoid this added expense are provided by a number of companies, including *AT&T* (International Information Service, 635 Grant St., Pittsburgh, PA 15219; phone: 800-874-4000), *LDDS/Metromedia Communications, MCI,* and *Sprint* (addresses above). Note that some of these services can be accessed only with the companies' long-distance calling cards (see above). In addition, even when you use such long-distance services, some hotels still may charge a fee for line usage.

Useful telephone directories for travelers include the *AT&T Toll-Free 800 National Shopper's Guide* and the *AT&T Toll-Free 800 National Business Guide* (phone: 800-426-8686 for orders), the *Toll-Free Travel & Vacation Information Directory* (Pilot Books, 103 Cooper St., Babylon, NY 11702; phone: 516-422-2225; fax: 516-422-2227), and *The Phone Booklet* (Scott American Corporation, PO Box 88, W. Redding, CT 06896; no phone).

Electricity

Like the US, Canada uses 110-volt, 60-cycle, alternating current (AC). Travelers from the US can use appliances they have brought from home without converters or plug adapters.

Staying Healthy

For up-to-date information on current health conditions, call the Centers for Disease Control's *International Travelers' Hotline:* 404-332-4559. The Centers for Disease Control also publishes *Health Information for International Travel, 1996,* which provides worldwide information on health risks and vaccination requirements. It can be ordered from the Superintendent of Documents (*US Government Printing Office,* PO Box 371954, Pittsburgh, PA 15250-7954; phone: 202-512-1800; fax: 202-512-2250).

Travelers to Canada face few serious health risks. Tap water generally is clean and potable throughout the country—if you are at all uncertain, ask. Milk is pasteurized and dairy products are safe to eat, as are fresh fruit, vegetables, meat, poultry, and fish.

When swimming in the ocean, be careful of the undertow (the water running back down the beach after a wave has washed ashore), which can knock you off your feet, and riptides (currents running against the tide), which can pull you out to sea. Sharks are found in coastal waters, but rarely come close to shore. Jellyfish and sea urchins also are fairly common in some areas. Though rare, bites from spiders, snakes, or any wild animal can be serious and should be treated immediately.

Although Canada has a government-run medical system, and health care is free (or inexpensive) for Canadian citizens, this does not apply to travelers from the US. US health insurance policies *may* cover medical care in Canada. Check with your insurance company before your trip.

Most major cities in Canada have at least one drugstore that is open 24 hours a day. In some areas, pharmacies may take turns staying open. Stores that have closed may display the name and phone number of the nearest all-night pharmacy. Information about 24-hour or on-call pharmacists also can be obtained from a local hospital or medical clinic, and may be provided in local newspapers.

Should you need non-emergency medical attention, ask at your hotel for the house physician or for help in reaching a doctor. Lists of local doctors and dentists also may be available from the *US Embassy* or a *US Consulate.* **In an emergency: Dial 911 for emergency services or 0 for an operator, or go directly to the emergency room of the nearest hospital.**

Additional Resources

Global Emergency Services (2720 Enterprise Pkwy., Suite 106, Richmond, VA 23294; phone: 804-527-1094; fax: 804-527-1941).

Health Care Abroad/Global (c/o *Wallach and Co.,* PO Box 480, Middleburg, VA 22117-0480; phone: 800-237-6615 or 703-687-3166; fax: 703-687-3172).

International Association for Medical Assistance to Travelers (*IAMAT;* 417 Center St., Lewiston, NY 14092; phone: 716-754-4883; and 40 Regal Rd., Guelph, Ontario N1K 1B5, Canada; phone: 519-836-0102; fax: 519-836-3412).

International Health Care Service (440 E. 69th St., New York, NY 10021; phone: 212-746-1601).

International SOS Assistance (PO Box 11568, Philadelphia, PA 19116; phone: 800-523-8930 or 215-244-1500; fax: 215-244-2227).

Medic Alert Foundation (2323 Colorado Ave., Turlock, CA 95382; phone: 800-ID-ALERT or 209-668-3333; fax: 209-669-2495).

Travel Care International (*Eagle River Airport,* PO Box 846, Eagle River, WI 54521; phone: 800-5-AIR-MED or 715-479-8881; fax: 715-479-8178).

Traveler's Emergency Network (*TEN;* PO Box 238, Hyattsville, MD 20797-8108; phone: 800-ASK-4-TEN; fax: 301-559-5167).

TravMed (PO Box 10623, Baltimore, MD 21285-0623; phone: 800-732-5309 or 410-296-5225; fax: 410-825-7523).

Consular Services

The American Services section of the *US Consulate* is a vital source of assistance and advice for US citizens abroad. If you are injured or become seriously ill, the consulate can direct you to sources of medical attention and notify your relatives. If you become involved in a dispute that could lead to legal action, the consulate can provide a list of local attorneys. In cases of natural disasters or civil unrest, consulates handle the evacuation of US citizens if necessary.

The *US State Department* operates an automated 24-hour *Citizens' Emergency Center* travel advisory hotline (phone: 202-647-5225). You also can reach a duty officer at this number from 5:15 PM to 10 PM, eastern standard time, seven days a week; at other times, call 202-647-4000. For faxed travel advisories and other consular information, call 202-647-3000 using the handset on your fax machine; instructions will be provided. Using a personal computer with a modem, you can access the consular affairs electronic bulletin board (phone: 202-647-9225).

The US Embassy and Consulates in Canada

Embassy

Ottawa: 100 Wellington St., Ottawa, Ontario K1P 5T1, Canada (phone: 613-238-5335; fax: 613-238-5720).

Consulates

Calgary: *Consulate General,* 615 Macleod Trail SE, Room 1000, Calgary, Alberta T2G 4T8, Canada (phone: 403-266-8962; fax: 403-264-6630).

Halifax: *Consulate General,* Cogswell Tower, Suite 910, Scotia Square, Halifax, Nova Scotia B3J 3K1, Canada (phone: 902-429-2480; fax: 902-423-6861).

Montreal: *Consulate General,* PO Box 65, Station Desjardins, Montreal, Quebec H5B 1G1, Canada (phone: 514-398-9695; fax: 514-398-0973).

Quebec City: *Consulate General,* 1 Ste-Geneviève Ave., Quebec City, Quebec G1R 4C9, Canada (phone: 418-692-2095; fax: 418-692-4640).

Toronto: *Consulate General,* 360 University Ave., Toronto, Ontario M5G 1S4, Canada (phone: 416-595-1700; fax: 416-595-0051).

Vancouver: *Consulate General,* 1095 W. Pender St., Vancouver, British Columbia V6E 2M6, Canada (phone: 604-685-4311; fax: 604-685-5285).

Entry Requirements and Customs Regulations

ENTERING CANADA

To cross the Canadian border, US citizens need a valid passport or another official form of identification (such as a driver's license, original or certified birth certificate, baptismal certificate, or voter registration card). If the identification does not include a photograph, it must be accompanied by some form of official photo ID. Proof of current residency also may be requested. Naturalized US citizens should carry their naturalization certificate or other evidence of citizenship. Permanent residents of the US who are not American citizens should have Alien Registration Receipt cards (US Form I-151 or Form I-551). Visitors under 18 years of age not accompanied by an adult must carry a letter from a parent or guardian giving them permission to travel to Canada.

Travelers from the US can stay in Canada for up to six months as tourists. Vehicles and trailers are allowed into the country for this period duty-free. Sporting equipment also can be brought into Canada duty-free. (In rare cases, a refundable deposit may be required to ensure that this equipment is not being imported to be sold.) Although a permit is not required to bring tackle for sport fishing into the country, provincial governments require travelers to obtain fishing licenses.

The standard duty-free allowances for travelers entering Canada are as follows: 50 cigars, 200 cigarettes (one carton), 400 grams (approximately one pound) of processed tobacco, and a "reasonable" amount of food for your stay. If you are over the legal drinking age (which varies among provinces and territories), you also can bring up to 40 ounces (1.1 liters) of liquor or wine, or 288 ounces of beer or ale (equal to 24 12-ounce cans or bottles) duty-free. All plants and plant material must be declared at the border; house plants from the continental US may be permitted, but bonsai, all outdoor plants (including bulbs), and all seeds, require permits.

DUTY-FREE SHOPS

Located in international airports, duty-free shops provide bargains on the purchase of goods imported to Canada from other countries. But beware: Not all foreign goods are automatically less expensive. You *can* get a good deal on some items, but know what they cost elsewhere. Also note that although these goods are free of the duty that *Canadian Customs* normally would assess, they will be subject to US import duty upon your return to the US (see below).

GOODS AND SERVICES TAX (GST)

Similar to the Value Added Tax imposed in many European countries, this Canadian sales tax is applicable to most goods and services. Although everyone must pay the tax, foreign visitors with total purchases of at least CN$100 during their stay are eligible for a refund. The procedure is as follows: Request a rebate application at the store at the time of purchase. Send this application, along with the original receipts, to *Revenue Canada* (Customs and Excise Visitors' Rebate Program, Ottawa, Ontario K1A 1J5, Canada; phone: 800-66-VISIT in Canada; 613-991-3346 in the US). A refund check (in US dollars) will be mailed to you in the US.

Note that some provinces and territories also impose their own sales taxes, and, in some cases, these are refundable as well. For information, contact the provincial tourist authorities.

RETURNING TO THE US

You must declare to the *US Customs* official at the point of entry everything you have acquired in Canada. The standard duty-free allowance for US citizens returning to the US is $400. If your trip is shorter than 48 continuous hours, or if you have been outside the US within 30 days of your current trip, the duty-free allowance is reduced to $25. Families traveling together may make a joint customs declaration. To avoid paying duty unnecessarily on expensive items (such as computer equipment) that you plan to take with you on your trip, register these items with *US Customs* before you depart.

A flat 10% duty is assessed on the next $1,000 worth of merchandise; additional items are taxed at a variety of rates (see *Tariff Schedules of the United States* in a library or any *US Customs Service* office). Some articles are duty-free only up to certain limits. The $400 allowance includes 200 cigarettes (one carton), 100 cigars (not Cuban), and one liter of liquor or wine (for those over 21); the $25 allowance includes 10 cigars, 50 cigarettes, and four ounces of perfume. Antiques (at least 100 years old) and paintings or drawings done entirely by hand are duty-free. Each day you are abroad, you also can ship up to $200 in gifts (excluding alcohol, perfume, and tobacco) to the US duty-free.

FORBIDDEN IMPORTS

Note that US regulations prohibit the import of some goods sold abroad, such as fresh fruits and vegetables, and most meat products (except certain canned goods). Also prohibited are articles made from plants or animals on the endangered species list.

FOR ADDITIONAL INFORMATION Consult one of the following publications, available from the *US Customs Service* (PO Box 7407, Washington, DC 20044):

Currency Reporting; Importing a Car; International Mail Imports; Know Before You Go; Pets, Wildlife, US Customs; and *Pocket Hints. Travelers' Tips on Bringing Food, Plant, and Animal Products into the United States* is available from the *United States Department of Agriculture, Animal and Plant Health Inspection Service* (*USDA-APHIS;* 6505 Belcrest Rd., Room 613-FB, Hyattsville, MD 20782; phone: 301-436-7799; fax: 301-436-5221). For tape-recorded information on customs-related topics, call 202-927-2095 from any touch-tone phone.

For Further Information

The provincial government tourist offices in Canada are the best sources of travel information. Offices generally are open on weekdays, during normal business hours, and—except for the Yukon office—all can be called toll-free from the US. For information on entry requirements and customs regulations, contact the *Canadian Embassy* or a *Canadian Consulate.*

Provincial Tourist Offices

Alberta: *Alberta Tourism,* 10155 102nd St., Commerce Place Building, Third Floor, Edmonton, Alberta T5J 4L6, Canada (phone: 800-661-8888 or 403-427-4321; fax: 403-427-0867).

British Columbia: *Ministry of Small Business, Tourism, and Culture,* Parliament Buildings, Victoria, British Columbia V8V 1X4, Canada (phone: 800-663-6000 or 604-685-0032; fax: 604-660-3383).

Labrador and Newfoundland: *Newfoundland and Labrador Tourism & Culture,* PO Box 8700, St. John's, Newfoundland A1B 4J6, Canada (phone: 800-563-6353 or 709-729-2830; fax: 709-729-1965).

Manitoba: *Travel Manitoba,* 155 Carlton St., Seventh Floor, Winnipeg, Manitoba R3C 3H8, Canada (phone: 800-665-0040 or 204-945-3777; fax: 204-948-2517).

New Brunswick: *New Brunswick Economic Development & Tourism,* PO Box 6000, Fredericton, New Brunswick E3B 5H1, Canada (phone: 800-561-0123 or 506-453-2496).

Northwest Territories: *Department of Economic Development & Tourism, Government of Northwest Territories,* PO Box 1320, Yellowknife, Northwest Territories X1A 2L9, Canada (phone: 800-661-0788 or 403-873-7200; fax: 403-873-0294).

Nova Scotia: *Nova Scotia Economic Renewal Agency,* PO Box 519, Halifax, Nova Scotia B3J 2R7, Canada (phone: 800-341-6096 in the US; 800-565-0000 or 902-424-8920 in Canada; fax: 902-420-1286).

Ontario: *Ontario Travel, Eaton Centre,* 77 Bloor St. W., Ninth Floor, Toronto, Ontario M7A 2R9, Canada (phone: 800-668-2746 or 416-314-0944; fax: 416-314-7372).

Prince Edward Island: *Department of Economic Development and Tourism,* PO Box 940, Charlottetown, Prince Edward Island C1A

7M5, Canada (phone: 800-463-4734 or 902-368-4444; fax: 902-368-4438).

Quebec: *Tourisme Québec,* PO Box 979, Montreal, Quebec H3B 1G2, Canada (phone: 800-363-7777 or 514-873-2015; fax: 514-864-3838).

Saskatchewan: *Tourism Saskatchewan,* 1919 Saskatchewan Dr., Regina, Saskatchewan S4P 3V7, Canada (phone: 800-667-7191 or 306-787-2300; fax: 306-787-5744).

Yukon Territory: *Tourism Yukon,* PO Box 2703, Whitehorse, Yukon Y1A 2C6, Canada (phone: 403-667-5340; fax: 403-667-2634).

The Canadian Embassy and Consulates in the US

Embassy

Washington, DC: 501 Pennsylvania Ave. NW, Washington, DC 20001 (phone: 202-682-1740; fax: 202-682-7726).

Consulates

California: *Consulate General,* 300 S. Grand Ave., 10th Floor, Los Angeles, CA 90071 (phone: 213-346-2700; fax: 213-620-8827).

Georgia: *Consulate General,* 1 CNN Center, Suite 400, Atlanta, GA 30303-2705 (phone: 404-577-6810; fax: 404-524-5046).

Illinois: *Consulate General,* 2 Prudential Plaza, 180 N. Stetson Ave., Suite 2400, Chicago, IL 60601 (phone: 312-616-1860; fax: 312-616-1877).

Massachusetts: *Consulate General,* 3 Copley Place, Suite 400, Boston, MA 02116 (phone: 617-262-3760; fax: 617-262-3415).

Michigan: *Consulate General,* 600 Renaissance Center, Suite 1100, Detroit, MI 42843-1798 (phone: 313-567-2340; fax: 313-567-2164).

Minnesota: *Consulate General,* 701 Fourth Ave. S., Suite 900, Minneapolis, MN 55415-1899 (phone: 612-333-4641; fax: 612-332-4601).

New York: *Consulate General,* 3000 Marine Midland Center, Buffalo, NY 14203-2884 (phone: 716-858-9500; fax: 716-852-4340); *Consulate General,* 1251 Ave. of the Americas, New York, NY 10020-1175 (phone: 212-596-1600; fax: 212-596-1790).

Texas: *Consulate General,* 750 N. St. Paul St., Suite 1700, Dallas, TX 75201 (phone: 214-922-9806; fax: 214-922-9815).

Washington State: *Consulate General,* 412 Plaza 600 Building, Sixth Ave. and Stewart St., Seattle, WA 98101-1286 (phone: 206-443-1777; fax: 206-443-1782).

The Cities

Calgary

For a long time Calgary was Canada's best kept secret. Folks in the cattle business knew it as a railhead, and oil drillers came into town to change clothes on their way to or from the big drilling fields, but to the rest of the world Calgary was known mostly as a town out near the Rockies where they had a hell of a rodeo once a year.

That all changed in 1988, when Calgary hosted the *Winter Olympics.* Suddenly, people from all over the world wanted to see Calgary for themselves, and what they found was a warm, welcoming metropolis on the vast Canadian prairie, with the jagged, snow-capped peaks of the Rockies jutting up to the west and fields of golden grain extending to the east.

Situated at the western end of the Great Plains that sweep across Manitoba, Saskatchewan, and Alberta to wash against the eastern face of the Rockies, Calgary sits in the foothills of the mountains at an altitude of 3,440 feet. The city is built around the confluence of the Bow and Elbow Rivers, which meet near downtown. Its altitude assures that Calgary gets lots of sun, and on clear days—that is, almost every day—the mountains are visible some 50 miles to the west.

Calgary was founded in 1875 by a contingent of the North West Mounted Police (now the Royal Canadian Mounted Police), who set up camp near the joining of the Bow and Elbow Rivers. They had come west to control the whiskey traders, who were creating havoc among the Native American tribes, and to prepare the way for the thousands of eastern Canadians and immigrants who wanted to homestead here. They subsequently built a fort, which their leader, Colonel James Macleod, named after Calgary Bay in Scotland.

In 1877 the five nomadic tribes inhabiting southern Alberta—the Blackfoot, Stoney, Sarcee, Blood, and Peigan—signed a treaty ceding all rights to the land except for areas designated for them by the government. In return the government agreed to provide the tribes with education, medical care, hunting rights, ammunition money, farm implements, and suits of clothing for the chiefs. Controversy over the terms, and whether the government ever fulfilled its end of the bargain, still rages. Nevertheless, the agreement was reached without bloodshed, and the government gained complete access to the lands of southern Alberta for agriculture and for the railroad, which rolled into Calgary in 1883. By the end of that year, the settlement's population had reached 600; by 1889 it had risen to 2,000. In the coming years thousands of people making their way west stopped in Calgary, and many stayed.

The abundance of grassy plains in southern and central Alberta spawned the development of a huge ranching industry, of which Calgary was the center. As the lush grazing lands encouraged US cattle owners to move their

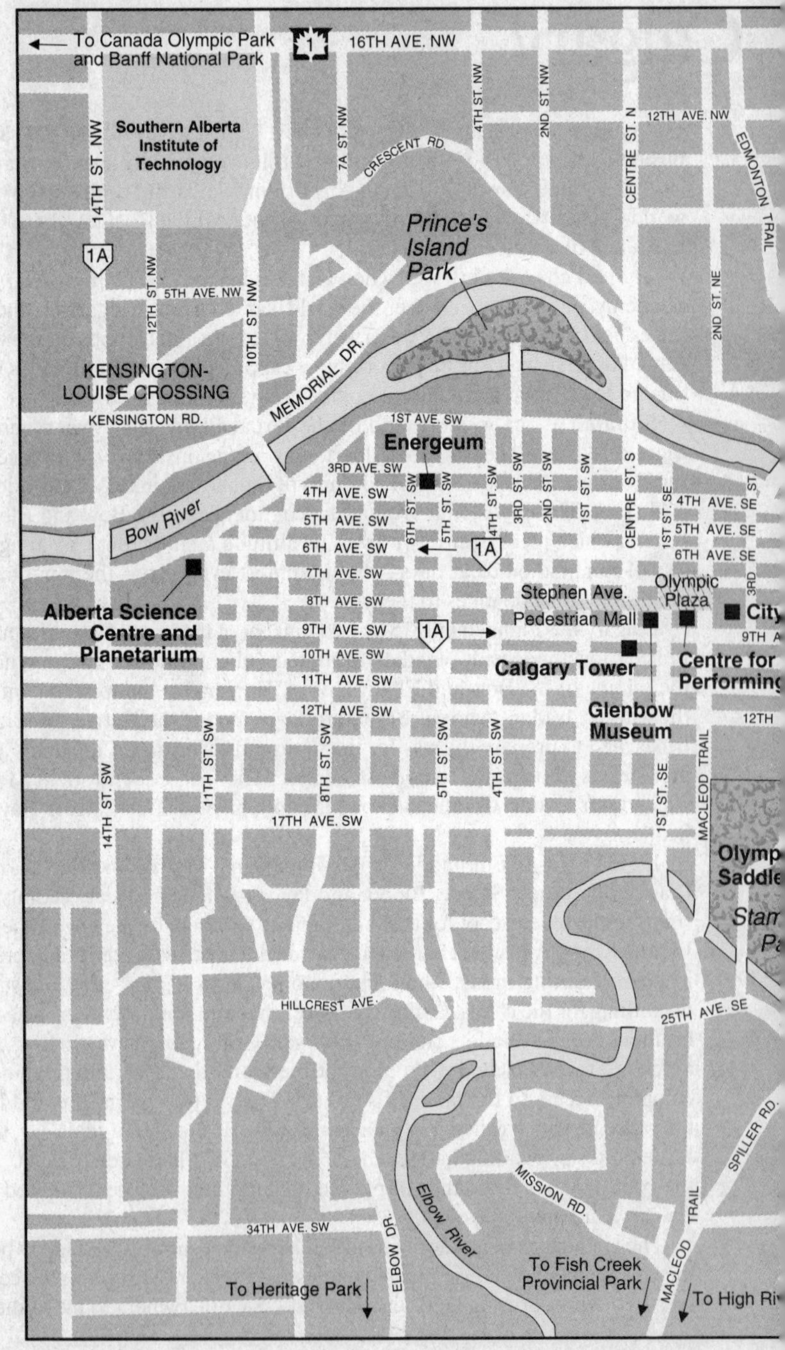

To Canada Olympic Park and Banff National Park
1
16TH AVE. NW
Southern Alberta Institute of Technology
14TH ST. NW
1A
12TH ST. NW
5TH AVE. NW
10TH ST. NW
7A ST. NW
CRESCENT RD.
4TH ST. NW
2ND ST. NW
CENTRE ST. N
12TH AVE. NW
EDMONTON TRAIL
2ND ST. NE
Prince's Island Park
KENSINGTON-LOUISE CROSSING
KENSINGTON RD.
MEMORIAL DR.
1ST AVE. SW
Energeum
3RD AVE. SW
4TH AVE. SW
5TH AVE. SW
6TH AVE. SW
7TH AVE. SW
8TH AVE. SW
9TH AVE. SW
10TH AVE. SW
11TH AVE. SW
12TH AVE. SW
Bow River
6TH ST. SW
5TH ST. SW
4TH ST. SW
3RD ST. SW
2ND ST. SW
1ST ST. SW
CENTRE ST. S
1ST ST. SE
4TH AVE. SE
5TH AVE. SE
6TH AVE. SE
Olympic Plaza
Stephen Ave. Pedestrian Mall
Alberta Science Centre and Planetarium
Calgary Tower
Glenbow Museum
Centre for Performing
City
9TH A
12TH
11TH ST. SW
8TH ST. SW
5TH ST. SW
4TH ST. SW
14TH ST. SW
1ST ST. SE
MACLEOD TRAIL
17TH AVE. SW
Olymp Saddle
Stam
HILLCREST AVE.
25TH AVE. SE
SPILLER RD.
MISSION RD.
Elbow River
ELBOW DR.
34TH AVE. SW
To Heritage Park
To Fish Creek Provincial Park
MACLEOD TRAIL
To High Ri

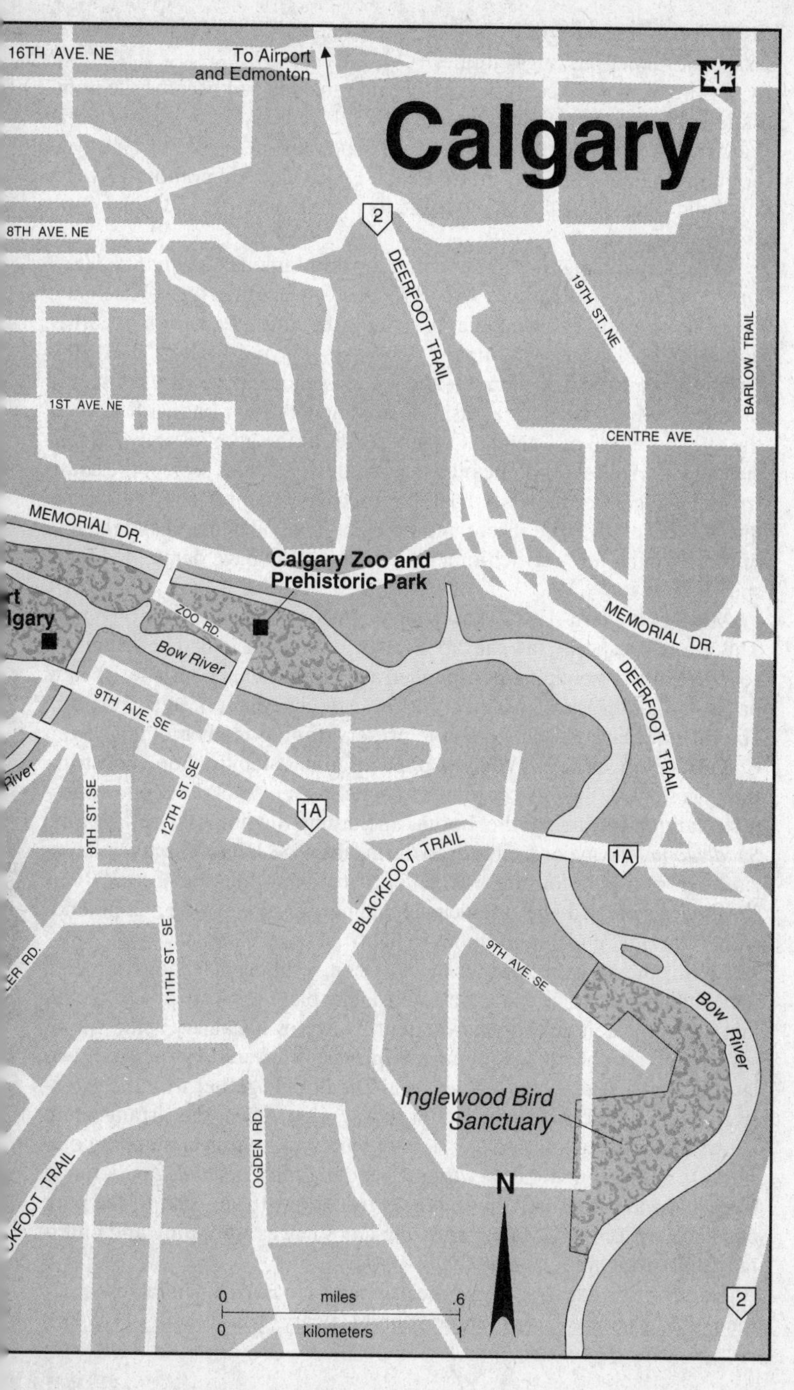

Calgary
16TH AVE. NE
To Airport
and Edmonton
1
2
8TH AVE. NE
DEERFOOT TRAIL
19TH ST. NE
BARLOW TRAIL
1ST AVE. NE
CENTRE AVE.
MEMORIAL DR.
Calgary Zoo and
Prehistoric Park
ZOO RD.
Bow River
MEMORIAL DR.
DEERFOOT TRAIL
9TH AVE. SE
12TH ST. SE
8TH ST. SE
1A
BLACKFOOT TRAIL
1A
9TH AVE. SE
11TH ST. SE
Bow River
Inglewood Bird
Sanctuary
OGDEN RD.
N
0
miles
.6
0
kilometers
1
2

tremendous herds north from overgrazed ranges, Calgary also developed as a major meat-packing center.

By the turn of the century farming and ranching had become the foundation of Calgary's thriving economy. In 1914, when oil was discovered at Turner Valley, just south of town, an era of new prosperity began. However, not until the big discovery in the Leduc Fields near Edmonton, 33 years later, did Calgary really start to make its mark as a center of Canada's oil and gas industry.

Once a year Calgary still puts on the world-famous *Calgary Exhibition and Stampede*—that Rolls-Royce of rodeos—in an effort to fool itself and everyone else into believing that it remains the simple cow town of earlier days. Don't believe it for a minute. Nowadays this prairie city of 738,000 is heavily into oil—and oil money—and the ten-gallon hat, cowboy boots, and saddle have been shed for a business suit and a cellular phone. Known as the energy capital of Canada, Calgary serves as the administrative, financial, and service center of the oil and gas industry. About 83% of the country's oil and gas producers and 60% of its coal companies have their headquarters here. Even the recent unpredictability of oil demand and the loss of more than a few get-rich-quick fortunes hardly have dampened local spirits.

Much of modern-day Calgary's appearance is the result of the oil boom. This era of prosperity saw the city swell by more than 20,000 newcomers a year, as Calgary's boundaries expanded at a phenomenal rate. Those heady days left their legacy in an almost entirely new city center of steel and glass. Happily, public concern led to the preservation of many buildings from Calgary's pioneer days. While its population has stabilized and construction has slowed, the city continues to benefit from several ambitious projects launched during the boom, including the impressive *Olympic Saddledome,* the major facility used during the 1988 *Winter Olympics;* a spacious downtown performing arts center that incorporates the historic *Burns Building;* a mirrored-glass municipal building, next door to the quaint sandstone *City Hall;* and an ultramodern light-rail transit system.

During the most recent surge of expansion, resulting in millions of square feet of high-rise office space downtown, city planners were able to maintain a comfortable urban environment. Downtown Calgary is the site of several interconnected shopping complexes, bracketed by the city's two largest department stores, *Eaton's* and *The Bay.* Together with the extensive system of enclosed overhead walkways downtown, this arrangement allows residents to shop in a variety of stores without ever stepping outside. On balmy summer days workers head to *Prince's Island,* a park full of trees and waterways only three blocks from downtown. Next to the park entrance, on Barclay Mall, stands the city's newest shopping and entertainment attraction, the *Eau Claire Market.*

Hardly surprising for a city whose prosperity is based on natural resources, the hand of nature is writ large around Calgary. Just 80 miles (128 km) away is *Banff National Park* in the Canadian Rockies, gateway to some of the best skiing in the world. To the east are the endless plains, and over the western ridge of the Rockies, the Pacific Ocean. While Canadian prairie winters can mean plunging temperatures, there are also the chinooks—the amazingly warm winds that sweep in from the Pacific on even the most bitterly cold days, raising the temperature 30 or 40 degrees in a matter of hours. The chinooks create a dramatic phenomenon known as the "chinook arch," a curve of brilliant blue sky rimmed by dove-gray clouds. At sunset the chinooks produce even more astonishing contrasts of light and dark in this brash, bustling prairie city's skies.

Calgary At-a-Glance

SEEING THE CITY

The best view of the city is from the top of the 626-foot *Calgary Tower* (Ninth Ave. and Centre St. S.; phone: 266-7171). On a clear day the Rocky Mountains are visible to the west. Have a meal or drinks in the revolving dining room and cocktail lounge, or just admire the scenery from the observation deck (where there's a snack bar). Hours vary with the time of year, so call ahead to confirm. The tower is open daily; admission charge.

SPECIAL PLACES

It's easy to get around downtown Calgary, because there is no traffic on the downtown mall, and overhead walkways allow pedestrians to cross streets above traffic. The streets are numbered and laid out in a north-south, east-west grid.

OLYMPIC PLAZA In summer, musicians and other entertainers often perform in this downtown park, which in winter is turned into an outdoor skating rink. Across from *City Hall* on Macleod Trail, between Seventh and Eighth Aves.

GLENBOW MUSEUM Operated by the *Glenbow-Alberta Institute,* this museum houses a large collection of art and artifacts of the Inuit and other native peoples of North America, including one of the most outstanding Plains tribe collections in the world. The second-floor contemporary and historical art galleries focus primarily on western Canadian artists. Located between the *Calgary Tower* and *Olympic Plaza,* this is a fascinating stop for both sightseers and scholars. Closed Mondays. Admission charge. 130 Ninth Ave. SE (phone: 268-4100).

ALBERTA SCIENCE CENTRE AND PLANETARIUM In the "star chamber" the wonders of the universe are revealed by 100 special-effects projectors and a sophisticated sound system. *Discovery Hall* has hands-on exhibits on everything from holograms to frozen shadows, as well as special theme displays that change every few months. Open daily in summer; closed Mondays the rest of the year. Admission charge. Seventh Ave. SW and 11th St. (phone: 221-3700).

FORT CALGARY HISTORIC PARK On the site of the original *North West Mounted Police Fort* built in 1875, this 40-acre park at the confluence of the Bow and Elbow Rivers contains an interpretive center with exhibits and audiovisual presentations recounting Calgary's early days. Guides dressed in the red-coated uniforms of the old-time Mounties give tours of the park; part of the tour encourages visitors to help rebuild the original fort using 1875 building techniques. The nearby *Deane House* (phone: 269-7747), built in 1906 by NWMP Captain Richard Deane, offers lunch and afternoon tea and charming views of the Elbow River; reservations are advised. The interpretive center is open daily May through the first week of October; closed the rest of the year. The park is open daily year-round. Admission charge for the interpretive center. 750 Ninth Ave. SE (phone: 290-1875).

CALGARY ZOO, BOTANICAL GARDEN, AND PREHISTORIC PARK An exotic experience in winter or summer, this complex features a *Botanical Garden* with displays that include an indoor tropical rain forest and an enclosed butterfly garden. The *Prehistoric Park,* with its fern-filled swamp, life-size dinosaur and reptile replicas, and realistic re-creations of rock formations (including a volcano and examples of the rock columns known as hoodoos) presents a glimpse of western Canada as it was millions of years ago. The zoo is engaged in developing the innovative *Canadian Wilds* project, consisting of five distinct ecosystems. Look for bighorn sheep, grizzly bears, cougars, and eagles in the *Rocky Mountain* section, and elk, great horned owls, porcupines, and deer in the *Aspen Woodlands.* All animals live in their natural habitats here; there are no barred cages. Open daily. Admission charge. Access to the zoo is from Memorial Drive (parking lot is on the north side). There is also a *C-Train* stop on Memorial Drive at the zoo. 1300 Zoo Rd. NE (phone: 232-9372).

INGLEWOOD BIRD SANCTUARY Just 1½ miles downstream from the zoo, this patch of nature offers visitors a chance to observe some 265 varieties of birds year-round. In summer wildlife experts give guided tours. Open daily. No admission charge. Ninth Ave. and Sanctuary Rd. SE (phone: 269-6688).

STEPHEN AVENUE PEDESTRIAN MALL A six-block, pedestrians-only zone by day, it features local artwork, old-fashioned street lamps, and wrought-iron benches. In the summer, especially around noon, it is full of workers taking breaks, shoppers, street vendors with old-style pushcarts, musicians, and other performers. Many of the city's original sandstone buildings stand on the block between Second Street SE (Macleod Trail) and Fourth Street SW. The second floor of the *Lancaster Building* (304 Eighth Ave. SW) has many food kiosks serving international fare. Stephen Ave. between First St. E. and Third St. W. along Eighth Ave. Vehicular traffic allowed after 6 PM.

DOWNTOWN SHOPPING AREA Overlooking the *Stephen Avenue Pedestrian Mall*, this huge indoor shopping complex comprises four large malls (*Toronto-Dominion Square, Scotia Fashion Centre, Bankers Hall*, and *Calgary Eaton Centre*), *The Bay* department store, *Eaton's* department store, and hundreds of smaller shops, all connected by skywalks. *Bankers Hall* is a striking office tower with four levels of shops found nowhere else in Calgary and excellent restaurants in a variety of price ranges. The *Devonian Gardens*, a two-and-a-half-acre tropical park inside *Toronto-Dominion Square*, is a popular gathering place. Three blocks between First and Fifth Sts. SW, and Seventh and Eighth Aves.

KENSINGTON This revitalized older neighborhood is thick with trendy restaurants, pubs, boutiques, bookstores, crafts shops, and tiny places that serve first-rate ice cream. The area stretches west along Kensington Road for several blocks from 10th Street NW. A lovely Bow River pathway follows Memorial Drive, one block south of Kensington Road.

EAU CLAIRE MARKET With 240,000 square feet of one-of-a-kind shops, popular restaurants and cafés, a farmer's market in a park-like setting, and an *IMAX* theater with a five-and-a-half-story movie screen, this is downtown Calgary's newest entertainment center. Third St. SW (Barclay Mall) at *Prince's Island Park* entrance, along the Bow River.

SUBURBS

HERITAGE PARK Buildings were transplanted here from small Alberta towns to re-create a pre-1915 pioneer village, the largest of its kind in Canada. Structures include a working blacksmith's shop, a bakery that sells fresh bread, a small log church still used for services and weddings, and an office distributing the park's own newspaper. The houses are furnished with period pieces, and costumed interpreters tell the stories of the buildings' original occupants. Also on the site are an old steam train, an electric streetcar, a carousel, a horse-drawn wagon, and the SS *Moyie*, a paddle wheeler that plies the waters of the Glenmore Reservoir. Refreshments range from ice cream and snack-bar fare to great Alberta beef and homemade apple pie served in the dining room of the elegant *Wainwright Hotel*. During months when the park is closed, the hotel still opens for breakfast on Sundays. The park is open daily from the third weekend in May through the first week in September; then closed weekdays through mid-October; closed the rest of the year. Admission charge. West of 14th St. and Heritage Dr. SW (phone: 259-1900).

FISH CREEK PROVINCIAL PARK These 2,800 acres on the city's southern edge—stretching more than 12 miles, from the Bow River in the east to 37th Street in the west—shelter a mixture of grassland, poplar and spruce groves, and native shrubs. Also here are 54 miles of walking and bicycling trails, 12 picnic areas, a horseback-riding operation, a new 18-hole golf course (opening this year), a wildlife refuge, and Sikome Lake, a small artificial lake where people swim in the summer. Open daily. No admission charge. To reach the golf course, exit off Route 22 at the Lake McKenzie area (watch for signs). To reach the visitors' center and Sikome Lake, follow Bow Bottom Trail off Canyon Meadows Dr. SE (phone: 297-5293).

Sources and Resources

TOURIST INFORMATION

The *Calgary Convention and Visitors Bureau* operates two locations for walk-in visitors: one at the airport at the arrivals level and the other at the base of the *Calgary Tower* (Ninth Ave. and Centre St. S). Both are open daily. To receive information by phone or mail, contact the bureau on weekdays at 237 Eighth Ave. SE, Calgary, AB T2G OK8 (phone: 263-8510; 800-661-1678; fax: 262-3809). The bureau supplies maps, accommodation assistance, and an extensive annual visitor's guide. The non-profit *Child Friendly Calgary* organization (720 *Lancaster Bldg.*, 304 Eighth Ave. SW, Calgary, AB T2P 1C2; phone: 266-5300) offers a list of accredited attractions, restaurants, and hotels that cater especially to children and families. It also puts together entertainment and education packages for children whose parents are in town on business.

LOCAL COVERAGE The *Calgary Sun* and *Calgary Herald* are morning dailies; *Cityscope* and *Where/Calgary* are free monthly magazines.

TELEPHONE The area code for Calgary is 403.

SALES TAX Alberta imposes no provincial sales tax, but a 7% federal Goods and Services Tax (GST) is levied on most purchases. For information on obtaining rebates on the federal tax, see GETTING READY TO GO or contact *Revenue Canada* (phone: 292-6990 in Calgary).

CLIMATE Calgary is sunny and dry most of the year. Temperatures range from an average of 10F (-12C) in January to an average of 75F (24C) in July. From May to the middle of September expect warm days and cool nights. During the winter the city gets about 50 inches of snow and unpredictable chinooks—warm westerly winds that can boost the temperature 30 to 40 degrees in a few hours. Anyone who ventures to Calgary in the winter should bring along boots, a heavy coat, gloves, and a hat.

GETTING AROUND

AIRPORT The *Airporter Bus* (phone: 531-3909) provides transportation between *Calgary International Airport* and several spots in downtown Calgary.

BUS *Calgary Transit* (phone: 262-1000, between 6 AM and 11 PM) serves all parts of the city. Bus fare (CN$1.50/$1.10 US at press time) must be paid in exact change.

CAR RENTAL All major firms are represented at the airport and downtown.

TAXI Cabs generally cannot be hailed on the streets, but they are available at hotels and by telephone. Major companies are *Associated Cab* (phone: 299-1111); *Checker Cab* (phone: 299-9999); and *Red Top Cabs* (phone: 974-4444).

TOURS *Brewster Transportation and Tours* (808 Centre St. SE; phone: 221-8242; 800-661-1152) and *White Stetson Tours* (6312 Travois Crescent NW; phone: 274-2281) offer bus tours of the city.

TRAINS The *Light Rail Transit* line (a modern, high-speed version of the old cable-car system, locally referred to as the *LRT,* or the *C-Train*) links downtown with the southern, northeast, and northwest reaches of the city. The *C-Train* is free along Seventh Avenue between *City Hall* and 10th Street SW; otherwise, the fare (at press time) is CN$1.50 ($1.10 US). For detailed route information, call *Calgary Transit* (see *Bus,* above).

SPECIAL EVENTS

Calgary shifts into high gear each year in early July, when the *Stampede* rolls into town.

BEST FESTIVAL

Calgary Exhibition and Stampede During Canada's 10-day self-styled "Greatest Outdoor Show on Earth" each July, thousands come to see Calgary celebrate its heritage with rodeos, world championship chuck wagon races, and other carryings-on. The *Half Million Dollar Rodeo,* which takes place daily during the celebration, ranks among the top events on the circuit. Cowboys compete for prize money in bareback-bronc riding, saddle-bronc riding, bull riding, steer wrestling, calf roping, barrel racing, wild-horse racing, wild-cow milking, and buffalo riding. But there also are native dance competitions, rock concerts, agricultural exhibits, a casino, a midway, a big parade, and a vast array of free entertainment. *Stampede* dates vary slightly every year; check before coming and reserve tickets for grandstand events well in advance (PO Box 2890, Station M, Calgary, AB T2P 3C3; phone: 269-9822; 800-661-1767; fax: 233-9736). Most of the action takes place within walking distance of downtown, at *Stampede Park,* but the malls, suburban shopping centers, and other parks are also filled with cowboys in wagons, members of native tribes in traditional dress, and western bands. The *Calgary Convention and Visitors Bureau* (see *Tourist Information*) can handle accommodations. If you can't make the *Stampede, Rodeo Royale* is held inside the *Stampede Corral* (in *Stampede Park*) in March. For information on all events at *Stampede Park,* call 261-0101.

MUSEUMS

In addition to those described in *Special Places,* Calgary museums worth a visit include the following:

ENERGEUM Oil field memorabilia and interactive video displays tell the tale of the energy industry in Alberta. Closed Saturdays June through August; closed weekends the rest of the year. No admission charge. 640 Fifth Ave. SW (phone: 297-4293).

MUSEUM OF THE REGIMENTS Displays at this large military museum cover the history of Calgary's four regiments dating back to the Boer War of 1900. Displays simulate life at the front line in World Wars I and II: Visitors can view a trench scene, listen to conversations between soldiers, and hear the sounds of battle. Closed Wednesdays. No admission charge. Crowchild Trail and Flanders Ave. (phone: 240-7057).

OLYMPIC HALL OF FAME Located on the site of the 1988 *Winter Olympics,* this is the world's largest Olympic museum, offering interactive video displays, bobsled and ski-jump simulators, and a panoramic view of *Canada Olympic Park.* Guided tours of the park are available; call ahead to check times. Open daily. Admission charge. Take Rte. 1A north to Route 1 (the Trans-Canada Hwy.) and turn left at Canada Olympic Drive at the city's western limits (phone: 247-5452).

SHOPPING

The *Downtown Shopping Area* is the site of four large shopping malls, and the *Eau Claire Market* is a cosmopolitan mixture of unique shops, cinemas, restaurants, and fresh produce (see *Special Places* for details on both). The *Uptown 17* shopping area (17th Avenue between Second St. and 14th St. SW), features trendy clothing shops, antiques stores, art galleries, restaurants, pubs, and bookstores. The 38 local merchants in *Mount Royal Village* (16th Ave. SW and Eighth St.), the area's upscale centerpiece, sell everything from women's fashions, jewelry, childrenswear, and luggage, to china and stationery. Similar shopping opportunities may be found in the Kensington district (Kensington Rd. and 10th St. NW). Special goods in Calgary include westernwear, furs, and Native American crafts. Most stores are open Mondays through Saturdays from 9 or 10 AM to 5:30 PM, with later hours on Thursdays or Fridays. Many stores, especially those in shopping malls and trendy shopping districts, are open Sundays (call ahead on Sundays to check).

Alberta Boot Co. The province's only cowboy boot manufacturer stocks authentic western footwear in every imaginable leather, from cowhide to kangaroo. 614 Tenth Ave. SW (phone: 263-4623).

Benzing-Charlebois Furs Calgary's oldest furrier, offering distinctive designs and impeccable service. 1506 Fourth St. SW (phone: 229-1431).

Chocolaterie Bernard Callebaut The factory where renowned, Belgium-born chocolate maker Bernard Callebaut turns out his premium chocolates. Take a self-guided tour through the factory and Callebaut's museum of antique chocolate molds and finish off with a stop at his flagship retail store. Closed weekends. 1313 First St. SE (phone: 265-5777; 800-661-8367).

Cottage Craft Gifts and Fine Arts World renowned for its authentic native art and Canadiana—everything from Inuit sculptures to moccasins—in all price categories. 6503 Elbow Dr. SW (phone: 252-3797).

Galleria The largest arts and crafts store in Canada, representing more than 550 Canadian artisans. 1141 Kensington Rd. NW (phone: 270-3612).

Glenbow Museum Shop Native-made crafts from western and northern Canada, including soapstone carvings and beadwork, are found here. Also look for unique jewelry, children's toys, and books on local history, art, and nature. Open daily. On the museum's main floor, at 130 Ninth Ave. SE (phone: 268-4119).

Grand Saddlery and Western Wear Everything a cowboy or cowgirl needs. 108 Eighth Ave. SE (phone: 265-3400).

Heartland Country Store A combination gift and coffee shop located in an old building just outside the hurly-burly of Kensington. Shop for rustic gifts or lovely linen goods. 940 Second Ave. NW (phone: 270-4541).

Holt Renfrew This elegant department store is known for clothing, furs, cosmetics, shoes, and accessories. *Eaton Centre,* Eighth Ave. SW and Fourth St. (phone: 269-7341).

Pages on Kensington Peter Oliva, a local author, and Maria Caffaro are the personable owners of this cozy bookstore focusing on works by Canadians. 1135 Kensington Rd. (phone: 283-6655).

Riley and McCormick Great westernwear and riding gear. 209 Eighth Ave. SW (phone: 262-1556).

Western Outfitters In the Pomerance family for four decades, this shop sells cowboy hats, jeans, boots, and western shirts for the entire family. On the *Stephen Avenue Pedestrian Mall,* 128 Eighth Ave. SE (phone: 266-3656).

SPORTS

Though Calgary is 80 miles (128 km) from the Rocky Mountain skiing centers, it has its own fair share of diversions. Contact the *Calgary Area Outdoor Council* (1111 Memorial Dr. NW, Calgary, AB T2N 3E4; phone: 270-2262) to obtain a copy of the inexpensive *Guide to Outdoor Recreation In and Around Calgary,* which lists outdoor opportunities such as bicycling, rafting, canoeing, hiking, ballooning, and climbing, as well as recreational organizations, retailers, and classes.

AUTO RACING The 160-acre *Race City Speedway* (114th Ave. and 68th St. SE; phone: 264-6515) hosts major national and international stock car, motorcycle, hot rod, and formula Grand Prix–style competitions throughout the summer.

BASEBALL The Calgary *Cannons,* a farm team for the Pittsburgh *Pirates* and part of the *Pacific Coast League,* play at *Foothills Baseball Stadium* (24th Ave. and Crowchild Trail; phone: 284-1111) April through mid-September.

BOATING There's sailing on the Glenmore Reservoir in the southwest section of the city. The *City of Calgary Parks and Recreation Department* (90th Ave. and 24th St. SW; phone: 221-3858) rents sailboats weekends in July and August; call well in advance, and be ready to show proof of sailing proficiency. During the spring and summer many people canoe, raft, and kayak on the Bow and Elbow Rivers; *University of Calgary Campus Recreation Rentals* (2500 University Dr. NW; phone: 220-5038) can supply equipment. Canoes and rafts also are available from *Sports Rent* (4424 16th Ave. NW; phone: 292-0077).

FISHING AND HUNTING The Calgary area supports upland birds, big game, waterfowl, and freshwater fish. For information, contact *Alberta Fish and Wildlife* (5920 1A St. SW, Rm. 200, Calgary, AB T2H OG3; phone: 297-6423). The Bow River downstream from Calgary is reputed to be one of the finest fishing grounds in the world for brown and rainbow trout. For a list of tour operators in the area, consult the "Float Fishing" section at the back of the *Accommodation Guide* published by *Alberta Economic Development and Tourism* (PO Box 2500, Edmonton, AB T5J 2ZA; phone: 427-4321; 800-661-8888).

FOOTBALL The professional *Stampeders* of the *Canadian Football League* play from June through November at *McMahon Stadium* in northwest Calgary (1817 Crowchild Trail NW; phone: 289-0258).

GOLF Six municipal courses and numerous private courses will accept visiting players. For information on municipal courses, call 268-3888. *Shaganappi Point* (Bow Trail and 26th St. SW; phone: 974-1810) is the closest 18-hole municipal course to downtown.

HOCKEY The Calgary *Flames,* members of the *NHL,* play from October through May at the *Olympic Saddledome* (555 Saddledome Rise, *Stampede Park;* phone: 777-4630).

HORSE RACING Harness and thoroughbred racing can be enjoyed year-round at *Stampede Park* (2300 Stampede Trail; phone: 261-0214).

HORSEBACK RIDING Lessons, group trail rides, and hayrides are available at *Fish Creek Provincial Park* (phone: 251-3344). *Spruce Meadows* (phone: 974-4200), just southwest of the city, is the site of several annual international equestrian competitions.

SKATING The *Olympic Oval* on the *University of Calgary* campus (288 Collegiate Blvd.; phone: 220-7890) is the first covered 400-meter speed-skating track in North America, and the first ever used in *Olympic* competition. Visitors can bring their own blades or rent them here. *Olympic Plaza* (see *Special Places*) becomes an outdoor skating rink in winter.

SKIING One of the newest ski destinations in the Canadian Rockies is *Nakiska* at Mount Allen, about 60 miles (96 km) west of Calgary, where an *Olympic* alpine competition was held in 1988 (*Kananaskis Village;* phone: 591-7777). Three big areas near Banff, 80 miles (128 km) west, are *Sunshine Village* (phone: 762-6500), *Skiing Louise* (phone: 522-3555), and *Mystic Ridge and Norquay* (phone: 762-4421); for information, see *Downhill Skiing* in DIVERSIONS. For the novice or the experienced downhill skier who just wants a little practice near town, *Canada Olympic Park* (Rte. 1 W. at Bowfort Rd., at the edge of Calgary; phone: 286-2632) has trails, rents equipment, and offers lessons.

SWIMMING The city-owned *Lindsay Park Sports Centre* (2225 Macleod Trail S.; phone: 233-8393) has three indoor pools, in addition to such facilities as squash courts, a running track, a sauna, and a weight room.

TENNIS There are private and public courts throughout the city. For information on public courts, call 268-3888.

THEATER

Tickets for most events in Calgary can be purchased in advance through *Ticketmaster,* either by telephone (phone: 299-8888) or in person at *Ticketmaster* outlets in *Eaton's* department stores and other locations throughout the city. There is a small service charge based on the price of the ticket. Three of the city's professional companies—*Alberta Theatre Projects, One Yellow Rabbit Performance Theatre,* and *Theatre Calgary*—stage works at the *Calgary Centre for the Performing Arts* (205 Eighth Ave. SE; phone: 294-7455 for information; 264-8131 for *One Yellow Rabbit* tickets; call *Ticketmaster* for *Alberta Theatre Projects* and *Theatre Calgary* tickets). The *Garry Theater* in Inglewood (1229 Ninth Ave. SE; phone: 233-9100) presents mainstream Canadian and international theater in a historic movie house. Short noontime productions are staged at the *Lunchbox Theatre* (Bow Valley Sq., downtown; phone: 265-4292) Mondays through Saturdays. The *Stage West* dinner theater (727 42nd Ave. SE; phone: 243-6642) presents popular Broadway shows starring celebrity actors. (For complete listings of theatrical events, consult the publications cited in *Local Coverage,* above.)

MUSIC AND DANCE

The *Calgary Philharmonic Orchestra* presents concerts from September through May at the *Jack Singer Concert Hall* in the *Calgary Centre for the Performing Arts* (205 Eighth Ave. SE; phone: 294-7420 for information; call

Ticketmaster at 299-8888 for tickets). The *Calgary Opera*'s season runs from October through May. The *Alberta Ballet,* a 20-member professional company, performs repertoire from traditional classical ballet to world premieres from September through the spring. Both perform at the *Jubilee Auditorium* (1415 14th Ave. NW; phone: 297-8000 for information; call *Ticketmaster* for tickets).

NIGHTCLUBS AND NIGHTLIFE

"Electric Avenue" is the name Calgarians have given to a neon-lit strip of bistros and dance clubs along 11th Avenue Southwest between Fourth and Eighth Streets. It's heaven for barhoppers, and revelers can even engage a muscular young rickshaw puller to transport them from one watering hole to the next. *Buzzards Café* (phone: 264-6959) has an excellent wine bar and offers casual bistro dining, while the adjacent *Bottlescrew Bill's Old English Pub* (phone: 263-7900) features more than 100 types of beer—including "Buzzard Breath Ale." Both are at the corner of First St. and 10th Ave. SW. The *King Edward* hotel (438 Ninth Ave. SE; phone: 262-1680), at the east edge of downtown, is known for bringing in the best names in blues. A few blocks away is the *Hose and Hydrant* (1030 Ninth Ave. SE; phone: 263-7900), a converted firehouse offering 13 beers on tap, darts, pool, and two fireplaces. A wide variety of wine bars, nightclubs, pubs, and coffee bars also can be found along 17th Avenue Southwest between First Street Southeast and 10th Street Southwest. If you want to listen or dance to western music in the company of real cowboys and cowgirls, head to *Ranchman's* in southern Calgary (9615 Macleod Trail; phone: 253-1100), one of a number of country-and-western dance hall/bars in the area. Calgary drinking establishments tend to operate until midnight Sundays through Wednesdays, and until 2 AM Thursdays, Fridays, and Saturdays. Many are closed Sundays.

Best in Town

CHECKING IN

Calgary has several first class hotels downtown and a spate of motels on the two primary approaches to the city—along the southern end of Macleod Trail from the south and, north of downtown, along 16th Avenue from the Trans-Canada Highway. Accommodations are often booked solid during the *Stampede;* the city also hosts many conventions, so reserve rooms in advance. For one night, expect to pay $110 or more for a double room in the places listed as expensive and $50 to $110 for those in the moderate category. All hotels feature air conditioning, private baths, TV sets, and telephones unless otherwise indicated. We recommend no inexpensive hotels in Calgary, though bed and breakfast establishments are a low-cost option. Contact the *Bed and Breakfast Association of Calgary* (6016 Thornburn Dr. NW, Calgary, AB T2K 3P7; phone: 531-0065; fax: 531-0069).

The *University of Calgary* (phone: 220-3210 or 220-3203), *Mount Royal College* (phone: 240-6275), and the *Southern Alberta Institute of Technology* (phone: 284-8013) all rent out student housing over the summer. For further assistance, check with the *Calgary Convention and Visitors Bureau* (see *Tourist Information,* above). All telephone numbers are in the 403 area code unless otherwise indicated.

EXPENSIVE

Delta Bow Valley Inn This 398-room establishment has two dining rooms, a lobby lounge, meeting and banquet facilities, nonsmoking floors, plus exercise facilities, a pool, a sauna, and a Jacuzzi. Special services for people with children, and "business zone" bedrooms equipped with computers, printers, and other office supplies are available. 209 Fourth Ave. SE (phone: 266-1980; 800-268-1133 in Canada; 800-877-1133 in the US; fax: 298-5060).

Palliser A gracious old hotel constructed in 1914 by the *Canadian Pacific Railway Company,* it's still a link in the company chain. The 11-story sandstone structure has 406 restored rooms. Solid brass doors, original marble pillars and staircases, and a large chandelier decorate the elegant lobby. The *Rimrock* dining room has an Old West flavor in its decor and menu. There are also two coffee shops, plus banquet and meeting facilities. Covered walkways lead to the *Calgary Tower* complex of shops, movie theaters, and offices. 133 Ninth Ave. SW (phone: 262-1234; 800-441-1414; fax: 260-1260).

Radisson Plaza Located in the *Convention Centre* complex, it has 365 rooms and features a lobby lounge, a pool, an exercise room, a sun deck, two restaurants, and business services. Floors are available for nonsmokers. Ninth Ave. and Centre St. SE (phone: 266-7331; 800-333-3333; fax: 262-8442).

Westin Calgary This 525-room establishment is one of Calgary's best known. Its *Owl's Nest* restaurant is among the city's finest (see *Eating Out*), and there's also an informal dining room and cocktail lounge. Other facilities include a pool, lobby shops, and underground parking. Rooms for nonsmokers, business services, and special programs for children are available. Fourth Ave. and Third St. SW (phone: 266-1611; 800-228-3000; fax: 233-7471).

MODERATE

Prince Royal Inn Great for families, each of the 301 suites in this property has a fully equipped kitchen. There's also a dining room, a lounge, an outdoor garden patio, two meeting rooms, and a health club. Note that rooms are not air conditioned. Continental breakfast is complimentary. 618 Fifth Ave. SW (phone: 263-0520; 800-661-1592; fax: 298-4888).

Quality Inn Built around an inner courtyard with a swimming pool, this 101-room hotel in the *Choice Hotel* chain has a poolside dining room, a lounge, and business services. Rooms for nonsmokers are available. 2359 Banff Trail

NW (phone: 289-1973; 800-661-4667 in Canada; 800-221-2222 in the US; fax: 282-1241).

Stampeder Inn In south Calgary, this modern hostelry has 140 guestrooms, a dining room, a cocktail lounge, an indoor pool, a hot tub, and business services. Children under 12 may stay in their parents' room at no additional charge; rooms for nonsmokers are available. 3828 Macleod Trail S. (phone: 243-5531; 800-361-3422; fax: 243-6962).

Travelodge–Calgary Airport This 203-room hostelry has an indoor pool, a hot tub, a restaurant, a lounge, three nonsmoking floors, business services, and a free shuttle service to and from the airport. 2750 Sunridge Blvd. NE (phone: 291-1260; 800-578-7878; fax: 291-9170).

Travelodge–Macleod Trail A hotel with 260 rooms, it offers some of the most reasonably priced accommodations in the city. A floor for nonsmokers and an indoor pool and hot tub are on the premises. There's no restaurant. 9206 Macleod Trail S. (phone: 253-7070; 800-578-7878; fax: 255-6740).

EATING OUT

At the crossroads of the prairies, Calgary should—and does—have some of the best beef in North America. But it's also known for serving up excellent Alberta-grown lamb, bison, game, and a broad range of international dishes. Expect to pay $50 or more for dinner for two in the places we've listed as expensive; $30 to $50 in the moderate range; and $25 or less in the inexpensive category. Prices do not include drinks, wine, or tip. Unless otherwise noted, all telephone numbers are in the 403 area code, and all restaurants are open for lunch and dinner.

EXPENSIVE

La Chaumière French food and fine service are this restaurant's hallmarks. Specialties include breast of duck with peppercorns, flambéed in brandy, and fresh Alberta rack of lamb. The extensive wine list, with more than 300 rare vintages, attracts connoisseurs from all over North America. Closed Saturday lunch and Sundays. Reservations advised. Major credit cards accepted. 121 17th Ave. SE (phone: 228-5690; fax: 228-4448).

Owl's Nest Renowned for its beef entrées, British Columbia salmon, medallions of venison, and quail, this plush place in the *Westin Calgary* hotel is a local institution. Closed weekend lunch. Reservations necessary. Major credit cards accepted. 320 Fourth Ave. SW (phone: 267-2823/4; fax: 233-7471).

Da Paola Ristorante Paola De Minico and Claudio Carnali have used their considerable culinary experience to create a popular, elegant-yet-friendly Italian restaurant serving excellent veal, seafood, and pasta. Closed Saturday lunch and Sundays. Reservations necessary. Major credit cards accepted. 510 17th Ave. SW (phone: 228-5556).

MODERATE

Cilantro Dine in the relaxing lounge decorated with Mexican rugs, the dining room featuring a beautiful stained glass window, or the pleasant summer garden. The pheasant, quail, and rack of lamb, or, for a more casual mood, the pizza topped with fresh pears, gorgonzola cheese, and roasted pine nuts are all exquisite. Open daily. Reservations advised. Major credit cards accepted. 338 17th Ave. SW (phone: 229-1177; fax: 245-5239).

Jennifer's Jamaican Cuisine This cozy, Caribbean-style spot offers up curried goat, shrimp creole, and oxtail and broad-bean stew—just a few of owner Jennifer Clarke's specialties. Closed Sunday lunch. Reservations advised. Major credit cards accepted. 2015 Fourth St. SW, No. 5 (phone: 228-6966).

The King & I Thai Cuisine Enjoy contemporary decor, jazz music, and authentic Thai dishes featuring fresh herbs, coconut, and exotic spices. The *pad kai long song* (chicken sautéed in spicy peanut sauce), sticky rice, and mango dessert are popular. Closed weekend lunch. Reservations advised. Major credit cards accepted. 820 11th Ave. SW (phone: 264-7241; fax: 264-8490).

INEXPENSIVE

Decadent Desserts This café is the perfect spot for a chocolate fix. Sample exquisite Seymours (caramel and pecans on shortbread dipped in chocolate) or, for true chocoholics, the popular Chocolate Overdose Cake. Specialty coffees, teas, Italian ice creams, and birthday cakes also are available. Open daily. No reservations. Major credit cards accepted. 924 17th Ave. SW (phone: 245-5535).

4 St. Rose Centrally located, this eatery serves a multiethnic menu of dishes from 17 different countries, including soups, salads, sandwiches, pizza, frittatas, stir fries, *fajitas,* and tempting desserts. The atmosphere is cozy, and the offbeat clientele is great for people watching. Open daily. Reservations necessary for six or more people; no reservations for smaller parties. Major credit cards accepted. 2116 Fourth St. SW (phone: 228-5377; fax: 244-0408).

Good Earth Two locations in the downtown area, offering a coffeehouse atmosphere and salads, soups, breads, lasagna, and stews made with chicken, seafood, or vegetables (no red meat). No liquor license. Open daily. No reservations. Visa accepted. 1502 11th St. SW (phone: 228-9543), or *Eau Claire Market,* Third St. SW at *Prince's Island Park* entrance (phone: 237-8684).

Joey Tomato's This busy, upbeat place specializes in sandwiches, pasta, and traditional thin-crust pizza baked in a birchwood-burning oven imported from Italy. All ingredients are fresh, and the pasta is made from scratch. Kitchen tours available. No reservations. Major credit cards accepted. *Eau Claire Market,* Third St. SW at *Prince's Island Park* entrance (phone: 263-6336).

Edmonton

From Charlie Chaplin's epic film of Alaskan misadventure, *The Gold Rush,* to Robert Altman's classic *McCabe and Mrs. Miller,* the boomtown is embedded in our culture as an arena where both the brave and the foolish try to strike it rich—and where they most often fail. And when they fail and the mine or well runs dry, the boomtown suddenly finds itself a ghost town.

But consider Edmonton, the capital of the province of Alberta, the most northerly large city in the Americas (with a metropolitan area population of 840,000) and the wiliest boomtown in the Northern Hemisphere. It has experienced the frenetic explosion of a boom three times: in the days of the Hudson's Bay Company and "King Fur," during the Gold Rush of 1898, and in the late 1970s and early 1980s, with extensive oil and gas development. Unlike most boomtowns, however, Edmonton emerged from each period of bounty stronger and more beautiful than before.

Fort Edmonton was established as a fur trading post in 1795 on the mighty North Saskatchewan River. Chief Factor John Rowand, the first commander of the fort in the early 19th century, was regent of a realm known as Rupert's Land, which comprised the southern half of Alberta and part of Saskatchewan. From the very beginning Edmonton was north-central Canada's seat of commerce and power.

While Hudson's Bay fur traders roamed the north in search of beaver, muskrat, and mink pelts, a number of missionaries traveled around southern Alberta, attempting to convert the local Wood, Cree, and Blackfoot tribes. They built schools and churches, but their efforts were subverted when Rupert's Land became part of Canada in 1869, and whiskey traders and other unscrupulous characters moved up from the Montana Territory, founding *Fort Whoop-Up* (situated in modern-day Lethbridge) and bedeviling the population. Most God-fearing citizens in the new province had to wait five years before the North West Mounted Police (now the Royal Canadian Mounted Police) arrived to restore order.

It was in 1871, in the midst of this lawless era, that Edmonton was incorporated as a town, with a population of about 600. Soon after, when Canada's first transcontinental railway was laid, Edmonton became an important crossroads. In many ways the true source of Edmonton's wealth, the railroad is the reason the settlement became known as Canada's "gateway to the north."

After gold was discovered in the Klondike in 1898, the tiny town mushroomed to a respectably sized population of 4,000. A disaster for most of the unfortunate prospectors, the Gold Rush is remembered fondly by Edmonton folks, whose warm nostalgia takes yearly expression in a colorful bacchanalia known as *Klondike Days,* held during the last two weeks of July (see *Special Events*). The oil boom, too, was particularly kind to

Edmonton, and, while wallowing in its profitable wake, Edmontonians further benefited from the discovery of natural gas reserves at Viking and the development of tar sands at *Fort McMurray*. (As a result of this natural bounty, there is no provincial sales tax in Alberta.)

Far from being the amorphous hodgepodge of slums and mansions one might expect in a boomtown, Edmonton is an extremely well designed, modern city that has made a valiant effort to retain and even reconstruct valuable artifacts of its past. For example, a replica of *Fort Edmonton* now stands on a 158-acre park in the southwestern suburbs, and reconstructions of Edmonton in its various stages of development are being erected in the same place. Also contributing to the city's pleasant ambience is *Capital City Recreation Park.* Set along the banks of the North Saskatchewan River, this 2,100-acre retreat separates the city's downtown from its suburbs. In summer, when it's often light until 10 or 11 PM, these green acres are filled with people cycling, riding horses, playing baseball, picnicking, and simply enjoying the outdoors. In the winter Edmontonians venture outdoors to use these same parks for skating and cross-country skiing. And rather than struggle through unplowed streets and icy sidewalks, they can take advantage of extensive underground and overhead walkways that crisscross the downtown area.

Today visitors to Edmonton will be struck by the dynamic high-rise skyline, starkly silhouetted against the deep blue western sky; they also may marvel at the sleek lines of the massive *Commonwealth Stadium* or at the ultramodern technological grace of the *Muttart Conservatory,* four huge glass pyramids near the downtown area. Currently, the recession that has infected Canada as a whole is affecting Edmonton as well, slowing its economic growth and development. But Edmonton still has an abundance of sunlight and space, which it has saved for its most important natural resource—its people. As a result this is a town that will probably find a way to boom again.

Edmonton At-a-Glance

SEEING THE CITY

The only vantage point affording a view from on high—and it's only a partial one—is *La Ronde,* the revolving restaurant on the 24th floor of the *Holiday Inn Crowne Plaza* hotel (10111 Bellamy Hill; phone: 428-6611). Open nightly to about 11 PM, it has a bar and lounge.

SPECIAL PLACES

It's easy to walk around the streets of downtown Edmonton, but in the winter, the under- and aboveground "pedways" make more sense. The streets are laid out in a geometric grid and, except for the major routes, are numbered.

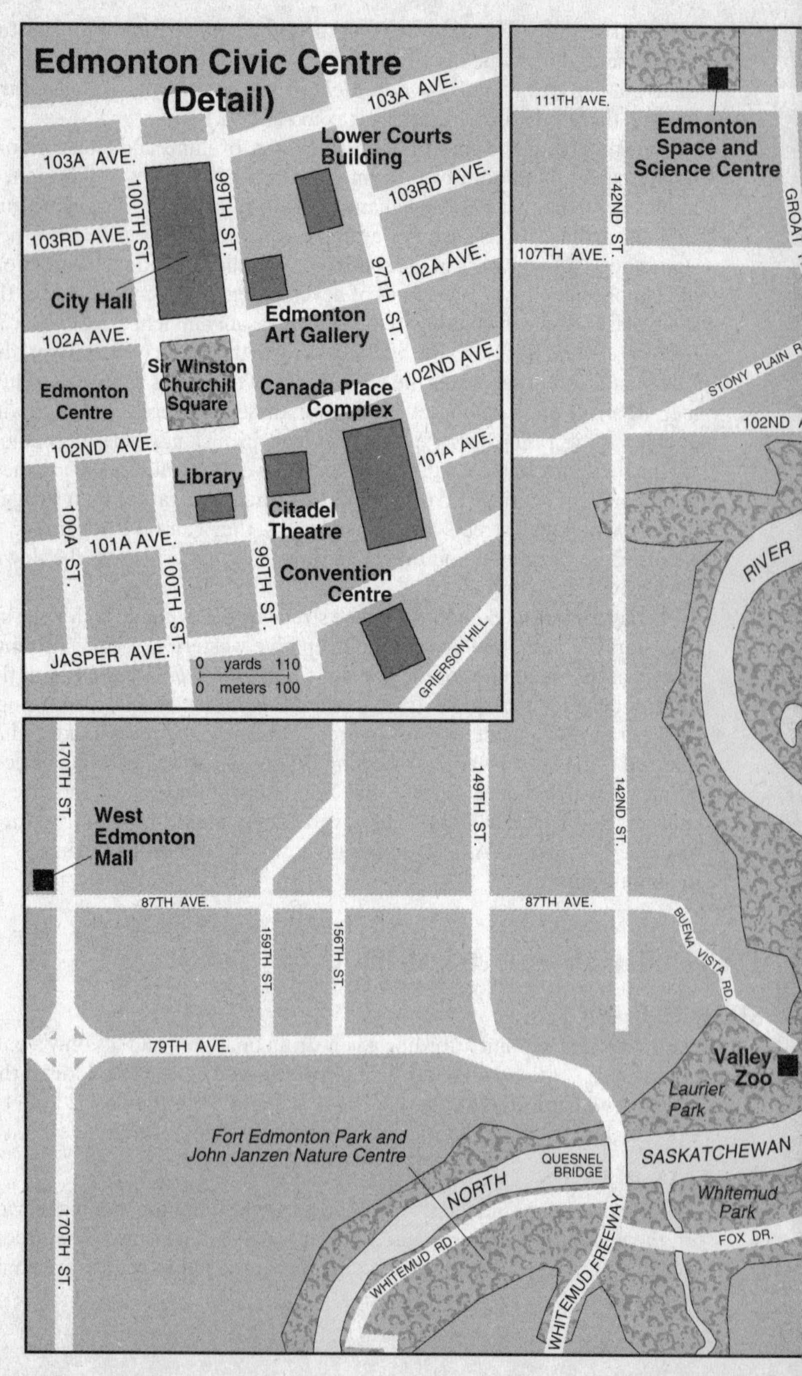

Edmonton Civic Centre (Detail)
103A AVE.
Lower Courts Building
103A AVE.
103RD AVE.
99TH ST.
100TH ST.
103RD AVE.
97TH ST.
102A AVE.
City Hall
Edmonton Art Gallery
102A AVE.
Sir Winston Churchill Square
Edmonton Centre
Canada Place Complex
102ND AVE.
102ND AVE.
101A AVE.
Library
Citadel Theatre
100A ST.
101A AVE.
100TH ST.
99TH ST.
Convention Centre
GRIERSON HILL
JASPER AVE.
0 yards 110
0 meters 100
111TH AVE.
Edmonton Space and Science Centre
142ND ST.
107TH AVE.
STONY PLAIN R
102ND
RIVER
170TH ST.
West Edmonton Mall
149TH ST.
142ND ST.
87TH AVE.
87TH AVE.
BUENA VISTA RD.
159TH ST.
156TH ST.
79TH AVE.
Valley Zoo
Laurier Park
Fort Edmonton Park and John Janzen Nature Centre
QUESNEL BRIDGE
SASKATCHEWAN
NORTH
Whitemud Park
FOX DR.
WHITEMUD RD.
WHITEMUD FREEWAY
170TH ST.

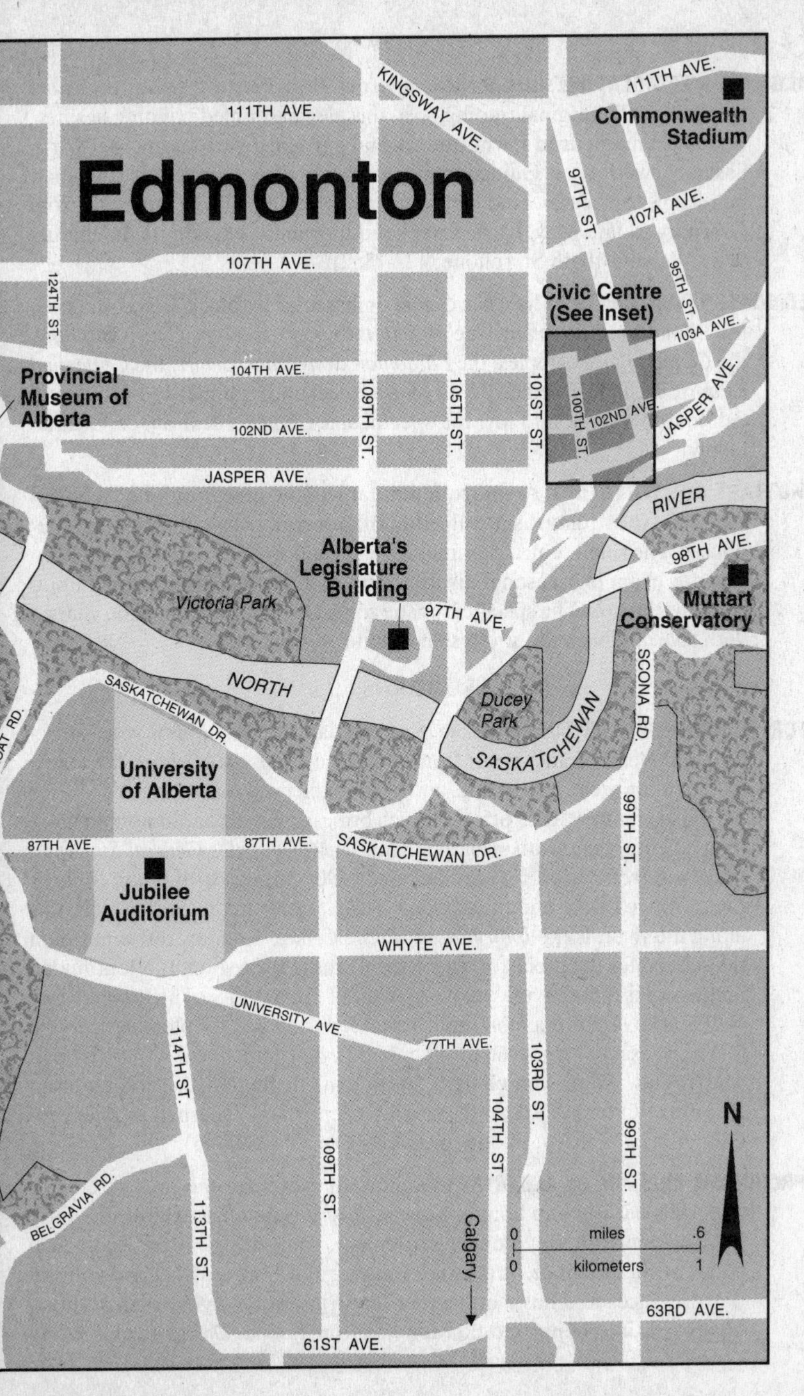

Edmonton
111TH AVE.
KINGSWAY AVE.
111TH AVE.
Commonwealth Stadium
97TH ST.
107A AVE.
107TH AVE.
95TH ST.
124TH ST.
Civic Centre (See Inset)
103A AVE.
Provincial Museum of Alberta
104TH AVE.
109TH ST.
105TH ST.
101ST ST.
100TH ST.
102ND AVE.
JASPER AVE.
102ND AVE.
JASPER AVE.
RIVER
98TH AVE.
Alberta's Legislature Building
Muttart Conservatory
Victoria Park
97TH AVE.
NORTH
SASKATCHEWAN DR.
Ducey Park
SASKATCHEWAN
SCONA RD.
University of Alberta
99TH ST.
87TH AVE.
87TH AVE.
SASKATCHEWAN DR.
Jubilee Auditorium
WHYTE AVE.
UNIVERSITY AVE.
77TH AVE.
114TH ST.
103RD ST.
104TH ST.
109TH ST.
99TH ST.
N
BELGRAVIA RD.
113TH ST.
Calgary
0 miles .6
0 kilometers 1
63RD AVE.
61ST AVE.

DOWNTOWN

ALBERTA'S LEGISLATURE BUILDING Constructed in 1912 on the site of *Fort Edmonton,* the original trading post, this elegant domed building lies nestled amid manicured lawns and formal gardens overlooking the North Saskatchewan River. Guided tours are offered daily year-round; Canadian politicians can be observed lobbying and legislating in November and from February to late May. Closed weekend mornings. No admission charge. 97th Ave. and 109th St. (phone: 427-7362).

EDMONTON CIVIC CENTRE The *Civic Centre* embraces a six-block area containing the *Edmonton Art Gallery* (see *Museums,* below); the *Law Courts Building;* the *Canada Place* complex; the *Edmonton Convention Centre;* the *Centennial Library;* the light-filled *City Hall* (closed weekends; phone: 496-8200); and Edmonton's pride and joy, the spectacular *Citadel Theatre* (see *Theater,* below).

MUTTART CONSERVATORY A controlled botanical incubator unique to North America, the *Muttart* is a collection of graceful, pyramid-shaped greenhouses. The small central pyramid is the reception foyer; another is a showcase for changing seasonal displays; and each of the remaining pyramids contains the flora of a specific climatic zone. Open daily. Admission charge. 96th Ave. and 96A St., south side (phone: 496-8755).

SUBURBS

FORT EDMONTON PARK The centerpiece of this park is an authentic reconstruction of the early trading post from which the city grew. Visitors can take a look at a fur press, a stockade, and a clay oven used for baking bread. The park also features "1885 Street," which brings to life urban Edmonton more than a century ago with such highlights as *McDougall's General Store* and the *North West Mounted Police Jail;* and "1905 Street," with *Ernest Brown's Photography Studio* and the *Masonic Temple.* Also in the park, which runs along the river, is the *John Janzen Nature Centre,* an interpretive museum that illustrates the prehistoric geological eras in the region. It offers guided nature walks that provide a close-up view of the North Saskatchewan River Valley. The *Fort Edmonton* replica is closed from early September through late May, except for special programs and events; the *Janzen Centre* is open year-round. Admission charge. South bank of the North Saskatchewan River off Whitemud Rd., at the southwest end of the Quesnell Bridge (general phone: 496-8787; phone for *Janzen Centre:* 434-7446).

PROVINCIAL MUSEUM OF ALBERTA An important center for the preservation of Alberta's natural and human history, this museum has exhibits on early Native American life, pioneer settlement, and geological and ecological zones of the province. It also presents regular film festivals and cultural performances and has a bookstore featuring works by Alberta authors. Open daily in summer; closed Mondays from *Labour Day* through *Victoria*

Day (the third Monday in May). No admission charge. 12845 102nd Ave. (phone: 427-1786 or 453-9100).

VALLEY ZOO Featuring fairy-tale dioramas, farm animals, and a miniature train, the zoo also has buildings for reptiles and nocturnal animals as well as winter quarters for tropical birds and animals. Open daily. Admission charge. 13315 Buena Vista Rd. at 87th Ave. and 134th St. (phone: 496-6911).

EDMONTON SPACE AND SCIENCE CENTRE One of Edmonton's major attractions, the center houses a planetarium, an *IMAX* theater with a 60-by-40-foot screen, both interactive and conventional exhibits, a public observatory, a shop, and a café. Open daily; shows Tuesdays through Sundays. Admission charge. 112th Ave. and 142nd St. (phone: 493-9000).

WEST EDMONTON MALL This five-million-plus-square-foot mall/entertainment complex is listed in the *Guinness Book of World Records* as the planet's largest, with more than 800 stores and service outlets. It features a five-acre water park with slides and submarine rides, a 20-ride indoor amusement park, and 19 cinemas. Scattered throughout the complex are animal displays, aviaries, and aquariums, and there also are a tremendous, multi-theme hotel (*Fantasyland;* see *Best in Town*); reasonable facsimiles of Bourbon Street and a fashionable Parisian boulevard; the *Ice Palace,* an *NHL*-size ice rink; and a miniature version of California's *Pebble Beach* golf course. Open daily. Shuttle bus and limousine services operate from many downtown hotels for a small charge (20,000 parking spaces are available!). Admission charge for most attractions. 8770 170th St. (phone: 444-5200).

Sources and Resources

TOURIST INFORMATION

For general information, brochures, and maps, contact the *Edmonton Tourism Visitor Information Centre* (9797 Jasper Ave., No. 104; phone: 496-8400; 800-463-4667 in Canada; fax: 463-4667). It's open daily, May 20 through *Labour Day;* closed weekends the rest of the year.

LOCAL COVERAGE The *Edmonton Sun* and the *Edmonton Journal* are dailies; *Alberta Report* is a weekly news magazine; *Western Living* is a monthly lifestyle magazine. Free publications that are distributed at area hotels, restaurants, and shops are *See* magazine, a weekly arts and entertainment publication, and the monthlies *Edmontonions* and *Culture Shock.*

TELEPHONE The area code for Edmonton is 403.

SALES TAX Alberta has no provincial sales tax, but a 7% federal Goods and Services Tax (GST) is levied on most purchases. See GETTING READY TO GO for information on obtaining rebates on the federal tax.

CLIMATE At an altitude of 2,182 feet, the city averages 6.25 hours of sunshine a day. This is the result of Edmonton's extreme northerly position, which, in summer, gives it daylight past 11 PM and average temperatures of 68F (20C). The city's location also makes for very cold winters, with the mean January temperature a mere 5F (-15C).

GETTING AROUND

AIRPORT Edmonton has two airports: *Edmonton International Airport* (about 40 minutes south of downtown on Hwy. 2; phone: 890-8382) and *Edmonton Municipal Airport* (121st St. and Kingsway Ave.; phone: 496-2842). *Yellow Cab* (phone: 462-3456) operates inexpensive buses to and from the international airport and major hotels; they run daily about every 45 minutes from 6 AM to 2:45 AM. The best way to get to the municipal airport is by taxi (see below).

BUS *Edmonton Transit* (phone: 496-1611) provides service around the city and its environs. The fare was CN$1.60 (about $1.20 US) at press time.

CAR RENTAL Most major North American firms are represented, many with offices at both airports and downtown.

TAXI Hail cabs on street corners and at taxi stands in front of major hotels and at the airports. In the middle of winter, however, telephoning is often preferable to venturing outside. Try *Co-Op Taxi* (phone: 425-8310) or *Yellow Cab* (phone: 462-3456).

TOURS *Royal Tours* (phone: 488-9040; fax: 488-9110) offers guided excursions to various attractions from mid-June through late September. Most hotels can make reservations.

TRAMWAY *Light Rail Transit (LRT),* operated by *Edmonton Transit* (see *Bus,* above), offers tram service in the downtown area, to the *University of Alberta,* and in the northeastern section of the city. At press time the fare was CN$1.60 (about $1.20 US).

SPECIAL EVENTS

The days of the gold panner are re-created in Edmonton each July in a brawling festival that sends the city back 100 years into its history. Meanwhile, plays from the world of fringe theater have their day here in August.

BEST FESTIVALS

Fringe Theatre Festival What started as a daring experiment more than 10 years ago is now regarded as the largest, most exciting festival of alternative theater in North America. *Fringe*-goers can choose from among nearly 200 new plays staged in 15 theaters, plus dance, music, mime, and street entertainment by performers from around the world. The 650 performances of the festival are held in the Old Strathcona district. Theater buffs have been known to spend the third week of August racing feverishly from one play to the next. For information, contact the *Fringe Theatre Festival, Chinook Theatre,* 10329 83rd Ave. (phone: 448-9000; fax: 431-1893), or the *Edmonton Tourism Visitor Information Centre* (see *Tourist Information,* above).

Klondike Days The fact that Edmonton is even on the map today is almost exclusively the result of the turn-of-the-century gold rush to the Yukon, when the community became a supply depot and departure point for northbound fortune seekers. So, when the town fathers were casting around for a theme for a community celebration, this colorful bit of local heritage was a natural choice. Everyone dresses in Gay Nineties garb, and buildings all over town disappear behind colorful 19th-century storefronts. What makes the festival so much fun—for residents as well as tourists—is the lively program of activities, featuring everything from marching bands and flapjack breakfasts to river raft and bathtub races, street entertainment, community dances, and Canada's biggest midway. *Klondike Days* takes place annually during the last half of July, just after the *Calgary Stampede.* The festivities also include the *World Championship Sourdough Raft Race* on the North Saskatchewan River, parades, garden parties, sporting events, and more. For information, contact the *Edmonton Klondike Days Association, Phipps McKinnon Bldg.*, Suite 1660, 10020 101A Ave. (phone: 426-4055; fax: 424-0418).

In June, Edmonton hosts *Jazz City* (phone: 432-0428), a week-long, world class jazz festival. August brings the *Edmonton Folk Music Festival* (phone: 429-1899), four days on a sunny hillside with some of the world's best folk artists. Then there's the *Heritage Festival* (phone: 488-3378), a two-day event in early August that celebrates Edmonton's multicultural heritage. Thousands flock to *William Hawrelak Park* (south of the river, off Groat Rd.) for this event, which features the food, music, dance, art, and crafts of more than 40 nations.

MUSEUMS

In addition to those described in *Special Places,* other Edmonton museums of note include the following:

EDMONTON ART GALLERY Traditional and contemporary Canadian art. Open daily. Admission charge. 2 Sir Winston Churchill Sq., in the *Edmonton Civic Centre* (phone: 422-6223).

FATHER LACOMBE CHAPEL This is the original log chapel built in 1861 by Father Albert Lacombe, the prairie priest who translated the New Testament into the language of the Cree. Closed *Labour Day* through May 15. No admission charge. St. Albert, 12 miles (19 km) north of Edmonton off Hwy. 2 (phone: 459-7663, 458-9199, or 427-3995).

OLD STRATHCONA MODEL AND TOY MUSEUM Here are more than 450 models and toys made exclusively from paper, all assembled by the husband-and-wife team of Bob and Gerry Bell. Open daily June through August; closed Mondays and Tuesdays the rest of the year. Donation suggested. 8603 104th St. (phone: 433-4512).

RUTHERFORD HOUSE Alberta's first restored historical home. Open daily. Admission charge. 11153 Saskatchewan Dr. (phone: 427-3995).

UKRAINIAN CULTURAL HERITAGE VILLAGE Exhibits here on the history of Ukrainian pioneers include full-scale replicas of a railway town, farmstead area, and rural community. Open daily; closed early October to May 15. No admission charge Tuesdays. Yellowhead Hwy. 16, 30 miles (48 km) east of Edmonton (phone: 662-3640).

SHOPPING

The greater Edmonton area boasts some 25 shopping malls. Among them are *Edmonton Centre* (102nd Ave. and 100th St.) and *Eaton Centre* (102nd Ave. and 101st St.), both in the heart of downtown; *Londonderry Shopping Mall* (137th Ave. and 66th St.) and *Heritage Mall* (23rd Ave. and 111th St.), in the southwest section of the city; and *West Edmonton Mall* (see *Special Places,* above). Edmonton is a good place to look for native arts and crafts, particularly Inuit work. For standard shopping hours see GETTING READY TO GO.

Bearclaw Gallery Contemporary crafts and paintings of the Inuit and other native tribes from across the continent. 9724 111th Ave. (phone: 479-8502).

Birks Jewelers A wide selection of sterling silver goods. *West Edmonton Mall* (phone: 444-1656), *Edmonton Centre* (phone: 426-7290), and *Southgate Shopping Centre* (111th St. and 51st Ave.; phone: 435-4602).

Chocolaterie Bernard Callebaut Some of the best chocolate in Canada. At several locations: 12325 102nd Ave. (phone: 488-0690); *ManuLife Place,* 10180 101st St. (phone: 423-3083); and 11004 51st Ave. (phone: 436-0908).

Dennis Miller Beverage Company A wide variety of wines, liqueurs, and hard-to-find beers from Canadian microbreweries. Several locations, including 5708 111th St. (phone: 436-9463), 10185 Jasper Ave. (phone: 421-9463), and 10421 82nd Ave. (phone: 433-2337).

Greenwoods' Bookshoppe New and out-of-print books, including books for children. 10355 Whyte Ave. (phone: 439-2005).

Holt Renfrew An elegant selection of clothing, perfume, furs, and more. *ManuLife Place,* 10180 101st St. (phone: 425-5300).

Lister Furs Fur coats and other fashions. 10200 102nd Ave., Suite 1211 (phone: 428-1774).

Pat Henning Custom Tailor & Shirt Maker Clothes and furnishings for men. In the *Edmonton Hilton International,* 10235 101st St. (phone: 424-5679 or 425-8558).

Sam Abouhassan Designer for Men One of the best men's designers in Edmonton. 10180 101st St. (phone: 429-7998).

Silversmith Jewelry Designs Co. Imported and Canadian silver goods, in both classic and contemporary designs. 201 *Edmonton Centre* (phone: 424-8539).

Village Books for Children Children's books plus general literature at its parent shop, *Volume II,* both at the same address. 12433 102nd Ave. (phone: 488-2665 and 488-4597).

Wine Cellar A wide selection of vintages plus a tasting bar. 12421 102nd Ave. (phone: 488-9463).

Zenari's Fancy foodstuffs, cookware, and coffee paraphernalia, plus some of the best espresso in town, and a surprisingly eclectic selection of pizzas, soups, and salads to eat in or take out. *ManuLife Place,* 10180 101st St. (phone: 423-5409).

SPORTS

BASEBALL The Edmonton *Trappers* of the *Pacific Coast League* play in *John Ducey Park* (10233 96th Ave.), minutes from downtown. Call 429-2934 for schedule information.

FOOTBALL Edmonton's *Canadian Football League* franchise, the *Eskimos,* play from July through November at *Commonwealth Stadium* (Stadium Rd.; phone for box office: 448-3757).

GOLF Good municipal courses include *Riverside* (Rowland Rd. and 86th St.; phone: 428-5330) and the *Victoria Golf Course and Driving Range* (12130 River Rd.; phone: 428-8095).

HOCKEY The Edmonton's *NHL* team, the *Oilers,* who have brought home the *Stanley Cup* many times, play their regular season from October through April (longer if they make the playoffs); home games are held at *The Coliseum* (7424 118th Ave.; phone: 474-8561, for information; 471-2191, for tickets). The *University of Alberta* has one of the country's leading college teams, the *Golden Bears;* their home ice is the university's *Clare Drake Arena* (*Faculty of Physical Education and Recreation;* phone: 492-2327).

HORSEBACK RIDING The *Whitemud Equine Centre* (12505 Keillor Rd.; phone: 435-3597) offers guided trail rides (summer only) through the North Saskatchewan River Valley and hayrides year-round.

SKIING The *Snow Valley Ski Club* (45th Ave. and 132nd St.; phone: 434-3991) has a ski hill (130-foot vertical drop) with artificial snow. Operating from mid-November to mid-March, facilities include a lodge with food and drink concessions, as well as snowboard and ski rentals.

SWIMMING There are several indoor and outdoor municipal pools. For information, call the *Parks and Recreation Department*'s *Swim Line* at 496-7946.

TENNIS Edmonton has a number of municipal courts. For information call the *Parks and Recreation Department* (phone: 496-4898 or 496-4999).

THEATER

Edmonton caters to theatergoers, with more theaters and theater companies per capita than any other Canadian city. The modern *Citadel Theatre* (9828 101A Ave.; phone: 425-1820) is the city's largest, with five stages. One of the country's major performing arts centers, it might on any given night present productions of Shaw, Pinter, Shakespeare, and a revival of *Man of La Mancha.* The *Phoenix Theatre* (phone: 429-4015) is a highly respected group that stages productions—often of recent major Broadway hits—at the *Kaasa Theatre* (lower level of the *Jubilee Auditorium,* 11455 87th Ave.; phone: 432-0925). Other places to take in a show are the *Mayfield Inn* dinner-theater (see *Checking In*); the *University of Alberta*'s *Studio Theatre* (*Timms Centre for the Arts,* 87th Ave. and 112th St.; phone: 492-2495); the prominent *Northern Light Theatre* (phone: 471-1586), a troupe that performs at the *Jubilee Auditorium* (11455 87th Ave.) and other locations; and the *Walterdale Playhouse* (10322 83rd Ave.; phone: 439-2845), Edmonton's oldest community theater. *Workshop West Playwright's Theatre* (phone: 477-5955) specializes in and also commissions new work by Canadian playwrights, with performances at the *Kaasa Theatre* in the *Jubilee Auditorium* (see above) and other locations from September through May. Also see *Special Events* for information on the *Fringe Theatre Festival.*

MUSIC

The *Edmonton Symphony Orchestra* (phone: 428-1414) presents concerts (except in summer) at the *Jubilee Auditorium* (11455 87th Ave.). The *Jubilee Auditorium* also is home to the *Edmonton Opera.*

NIGHTCLUBS AND NIGHTLIFE

The *Yardbird Suite* (86th Ave. and 102nd St.; phone: 432-0428) occasionally features live jazz. For a singles bar with dancing, try *Barry T's Grand Central Station* (6111 104th St.; phone: 438-2582) or the lively, country-and-western–style *Cook County Saloon* (8010 103rd St.; phone: 432-2665), where the 18-to-25 set goes to see and be seen. The *Rose and Crown Pub* (in the *Edmonton Hilton International;* see *Checking In*) has a piano bar that attracts a more sophisticated, professional crowd. Most bars are open daily and close at 2 AM.

Gambling is a favorite pastime of Edmontonians, and as a result there's usually a casino with a temporary government permit operating somewhere in the city. For the time and place, consult the local papers.

Best in Town

CHECKING IN

Edmonton has several first class hotels as well as dozens of more moderately priced establishments. Per night, expect to pay $65 or more for a double room in the hotels listed as expensive, between $40 and $65 in those categorized as moderate, and under $40 in the one labeled inexpensive. (The 5% hotel tax and 7% GST are not included in quoted rates.) All hotels feature air conditioning, private baths, TV sets, and telephones unless otherwise indicated. All telephone numbers are in the 403 area code unless otherwise noted.

EXPENSIVE

Edmonton Hilton International Connected by a pedestrian walkway to the *Edmonton Centre* shopping mall, it has 314 rooms (27 of which are suites), nonsmoking floors, a concierge, a fitness center, an indoor pool, a sauna, and a whirlpool bath. There are also two lounges, a café, an Old English–style pub, and a dining room. Weekend rates are available. 10235 101st St. (phone: 428-7111; 800-HILTONS; fax: 441-3098).

Fantasyland Part of the *West Edmonton Mall* complex, this place features imaginative motifs (Polynesian, Arabian, Victorian, and western—where the bed is in the flatbed of a pickup truck) in a third of its 355 rooms—most with Jacuzzis. Amenities include a cocktail lounge, the *Fantasy Grill* dining room, and the more casual *Café Europa.* Rooms for nonsmokers are available; children under 12 can stay in their parents' room at no additional charge. 87th Ave. and 170th St. (phone: 444-3000; 800-661-6454; fax: 444-3294).

Macdonald This establishment maintains its original 1915 grandeur. The exterior façade, lobby, *Confederation Lounge, Wedgwood Room,* and *Empire Ballroom* are designated Municipal Historic Resources. There are 172 rooms, six two-bedroom suites, two mini-suites, and a deluxe presidential suite. Facilities include a good restaurant, indoor tennis and squash courts, an indoor pool, a sauna, steamrooms, and exercise and gamerooms. Overlooking the North Saskatchewan River Valley at Jasper Ave. and 100th St. (phone: 424-5181; fax: 424-8017).

Mayfield Inn Located in the west end of the city, this 330-room property has a recreation center with a pool, squash and racquetball courts, a gym, a dinner-theater, four restaurants, and a lounge. 109th Ave. and 166th St. (phone: 484-0821; 800-661-9804; fax: 486-1634).

Westin This handsome establishment is where both royalty and rock stars stay. In it are 413 rooms and suites, a pool, a sauna, a whirlpool bath, and one of the finest dining rooms in the city, the *Carvery of Edmonton* (see *Eating Out*). A family plan and weekend rates are available year-round. 10135 100th St. at 101A Ave. (phone: 426-3636; 800-228-3000; fax: 428-1454).

MODERATE

Kingsway Inn Five minutes from downtown and just blocks from the midtown municipal airport, this place has 70 rooms, banquet and meeting facilities, free parking, a restaurant, and pubs. 10812 Kingsway Ave. (phone: 479-4266; fax: 471-4868).

Mayfair This 123-room property has suites for business travelers who require an office on the road. There are three restaurants. Seven blocks from the city center, at 10815 Jasper Ave. (phone: 423-1650; 800-463-7666; fax: 425-6834).

Renford Inn at Fifth Between downtown Edmonton and the legislature grounds, this hotel has 107 rooms, an indoor pool, a dining room, a cocktail lounge, and a British-style pub. Children under 12 can stay in their parents' room at no additional charge. 100th Ave. and 104th St. (phone: 423-5611; 800-661-6498; fax: 425-9791).

Travelodge Edmonton South/Travelodge Edmonton West Two very reasonably priced motels on the southern and western edges of the city, one just off the highway to Calgary and the international airport (South), the other on the highway to Jasper (West). Each has an indoor pool and whirlpool; there are a total of 447 rooms. *Travelodge Edmonton South,* 10320 45th Ave. (phone: 436-9770; 800-578-7878; fax: 436-3529); *Travelodge Edmonton West,* 18320 Stony Plain Rd. (phone: 483-6031; 800-578-7878; fax: 484-2358).

INEXPENSIVE

Klondike Valley Tent and Trailer Park This comfortable campground has 148 camping sites, 84 with electricity and water and 64 with sewage hookups. There are also flush toilets, showers, a playground, laundry facilities, a barbecue, and a small grocery store. 1660 Calgary Trail Southbound (phone: 988-5067).

EATING OUT

Besides making the city rich, all those booms brought a wide range of people into Edmonton. As a result, regular prairie fare—which centers on Alberta beef, some of the best in the country—has been augmented with a potpourri of truly delightful ethnic foods. Expect to pay about $40 or more for a meal for two at restaurants listed as expensive, between $20 and $40 in the moderate range, and under $20 in the inexpensive category. Prices do not include drinks, wine, or tip. Unless otherwise noted, all restaurants are open for lunch and dinner, and all telephone numbers are in the 403 area code.

EXPENSIVE

Carvery of Edmonton Known for its mammoth servings, this fine establishment with a woodsy, hunting-hall atmosphere serves some of the best beef that Alberta produces, along with wild game such as buffalo. The chicken dishes are also good. Closed Saturday lunch. Reservations advised. Major credit cards accepted. At the *Westin Hotel,* 10135 100th St. at 101A Ave. (phone: 426-3636; fax: 428-1454).

Chef's Table One of Edmonton's most creative restaurants is incongruously located in an industrial area. Hong Kong–born, Edmonton-trained chef Peter Lai prepares delicious California-style dishes. The menu features a wide variety of seafood, fowl, pasta, and veal—all prepared with unexpected touches: The fried oysters appetizer comes stuffed with fresh ginger and chives; the lobster and pasta entrée has perfectly cooked seafood and crisp asparagus; and the honeydew melon balls are topped with a Tahitian vanilla-Riesling sauce. Open daily. Reservations necessary. Major credit cards accepted. 11121 156th St. (phone: 453-3532; fax: 453-3534).

Hy's Steak Loft Edmonton's premier steakhouse features a well-appointed dining room and tuxedoed waiters. Though seafood, fowl, and lamb fill out the menu, steaks are what this place does best; considering that Alberta beef is among the best in the world, it would be a shame to order anything else. Closed Sundays. Reservations necessary. Major credit cards accepted. 10013 101A Ave. (phone: 424-4444; fax: 425-9566).

Jack's Grill Schooled in California's wine valleys, chef-owner Peter Jackson prepares intriguing California-influenced dishes. The menu changes monthly, using fresh produce from the local markets. There is an excellent wine list. Open for dinner only; closed Mondays and Tuesdays. Reservations necessary. Major credit cards accepted. 290 Saddleback Rd. (phone: 434-1113).

Sushi Tomi Raw fish in a landlocked town can be iffy, but Edmonton's top sushi bar (downstairs at the *Japanese Village* restaurant) has garnered the praise of connoisseurs from both coasts. Traditionally prepared Japanese dishes also are available. Open daily. Reservations advised. Major credit cards accepted. 10126 100th St. (phone: 422-6083; fax: 425-0099).

Unheardof The intercom at the entrance gives this small restaurant a speakeasy feel, but the standards are much higher. The six-course prix fixe menu runs from a light pâté that changes with the best ingredients available, through a main course of lamb, beef, or game hen in a maple glaze, to light, delicious desserts. Open for dinner only; closed Sundays and Mondays. Reservations necessary as far in advance as possible. Major credit cards accepted. 9602 82nd Ave. (phone: 432-0480; fax: 432-1863).

MODERATE

Da-De-O This inviting Cajun joint offers a bit of high and low culture. There are working tableside jukeboxes, but the waiters will also flambé your bananas Foster with a flourish at your table. The oyster po' boys are surprisingly good, considering this is a landlocked city; the seven-green gumbo (which, as its name implies, contains a variety of greens) is also worth a try. Open daily. No reservations (except for parties of six or more). Major credit cards accepted. 10548A 82nd Ave. (phone: 433-0930).

New Asian Village For the best Indian food in Edmonton, visit this pleasant restaurant with a lounge serving Indian beers (and rarely seen Indian scotches) and a view of the North Saskatchewan River Valley. The chicken *tikka,* marinated in herbs and spices and cooked in a tandoor oven, is excellent. Or try a *biryani* dish—lamb or chicken cooked with rice, cashews, and currants, and served with grated *ponir* cheese. Vegetarian offerings are plentiful and tasty. Open daily. Reservations advised. Major credit cards accepted. 1030 Saskatchewan Dr. (phone: 433-3804).

INEXPENSIVE

Bul-Go-Gi House One of several Korean restaurants in town, it started as a small café but has undergone steady expansion. Tops on the menu are the *bul-go-gi,* a mélange of vegetables and marinated beef grilled at your table; the side dish of hot pickled *kim chee;* and *bee-bim-bab,* a bowl of vegetables capped by a fried egg. No liquor license. Closed Sundays. Reservations advised. Major credit cards accepted. 8813 92nd St. (phone: 466-2330).

Halifax

The largest city on Canada's eastern seaboard (pop. 114,500), Halifax has a long, rich military and naval heritage, thanks to its strategic location overlooking the mouth of one of the world's great natural harbors. Since its earliest days, Halifax has been a center of maritime activity: It was first a tiny summer fishing settlement for the local native tribes, and was known as Chebucto, or "at the biggest harbor."

Today, Halifax is the capital of Nova Scotia and the commercial, administrative, and military center of Atlantic Canada. In 1995 the city even played host to the annual summit meeting of the world's top seven industrialized nations. Still, it retains the charm of a small city. Ask a cross section of Haligonians (residents of Halifax) why they like their town, and most will reply that they enjoy all the cultural amenities of a bigger metropolis without the disadvantages of size and impersonality. The streets are lined with trees; there are beautiful, relaxing parks and fine old buildings; and the downtown area is a nicely balanced mixture of modern office towers and older restored shops. In addition, Halifax is home to Canada's oldest Protestant church, *St. Paul's Anglican Church,* and one of Canada's better art schools, the *Nova Scotia College of Art and Design.*

Halifax was founded in 1749, when, in the wake of the Treaty of Aix-la-Chapelle that returned *Fortress Louisbourg* to France, the British recognized the need to establish an English fortress on mainland Nova Scotia. When British control over all of Canada was established in 1763, Halifax became the chief station of His Majesty's Army and Navy on the Atlantic seaboard.

The American Revolution and the War of 1812 affected Halifax in a number of ways. The city enjoyed all the benefits of war—military spending and employment—and none of the horror. It thrived, and its population grew. After the Revolutionary War, 25,000 Loyalists fled to Nova Scotia from the United States, and, after the War of 1812, thousands of blacks escaped from slavery in the US and settled in the Halifax-Dartmouth region (a mile-wide strip of water separates the two cities).

When peace finally came, the Haligonians experienced a severe and sudden depression. However, the gradual development of a civilian shipbuilding industry, alongside the traditional military economy, led to increased affluence. Then, with the outbreak of World War I, Halifax again became a military base—a vital link in the North American lifeline to Europe's embattled countries.

Halifax suffered one of the world's most serious maritime disasters late in the war. In fact, it was the worst recorded manmade explosion before the atomic bombing of Hiroshima in 1945. In 1917, the munitions ship *Mont Blanc,* laden with 2,500 tons of explosives, collided with the Belgian relief

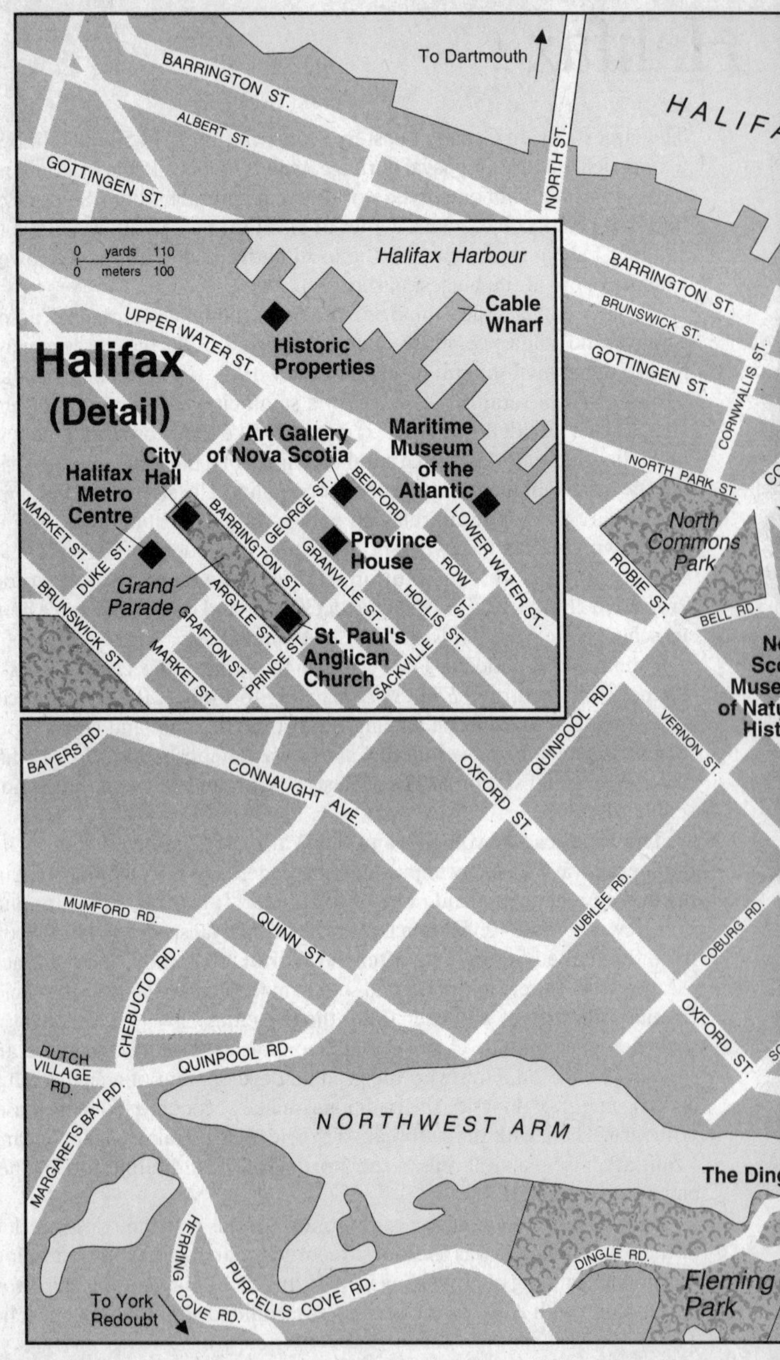

To Dartmouth
BARRINGTON ST.
ALBERT ST.
GOTTINGEN ST.
NORTH ST.
HALIFA
0 yards 110
0 meters 100
Halifax Harbour
Cable Wharf
UPPER WATER ST.
Historic Properties
Halifax
(Detail)
Art Gallery of Nova Scotia
Maritime Museum of the Atlantic
City Hall
Halifax Metro Centre
MARKET ST.
DUKE ST.
BARRINGTON ST.
GEORGE ST.
BEDFORD
Province House
GRANVILLE ST.
ROW
LOWER WATER ST.
Grand Parade
ARGYLE ST.
HOLLIS ST.
ST.
BRUNSWICK ST.
GRAFTON ST.
PRINCE ST.
St. Paul's Anglican Church
SACKVILLE
MARKET ST.
BARRINGTON ST.
BRUNSWICK ST.
GOTTINGEN ST.
CORNWALLIS ST.
NORTH PARK ST.
North Commons Park
ROBIE ST.
BELL RD.
BAYERS RD.
CONNAUGHT AVE.
OXFORD ST.
QUINPOOL RD.
VERNON ST.
MUMFORD RD.
QUINN ST.
JUBILEE RD.
COBURG RD.
CHEBUCTO RD.
OXFORD ST.
DUTCH VILLAGE RD.
QUINPOOL RD.
MARGARETS BAY RD.
NORTHWEST ARM
The Ding
HERRING COVE RD.
PURCELLS COVE RD.
DINGLE RD.
Fleming Park
To York Redoubt

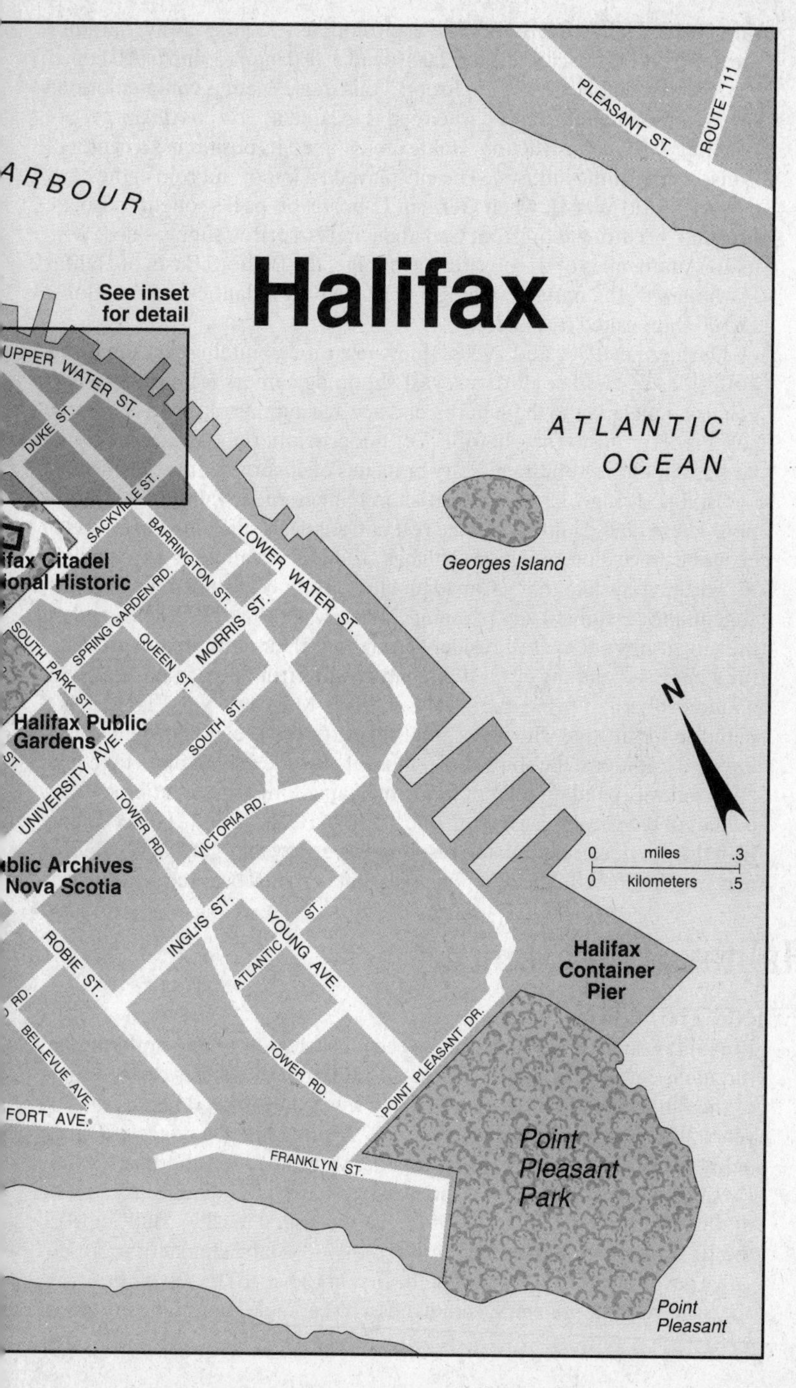

Halifax
ARBOUR
PLEASANT ST.
ROUTE 111
See inset for detail
UPPER WATER ST.
DUKE ST.
SACKVILLE ST.
BARRINGTON ST.
LOWER WATER ST.
ATLANTIC OCEAN
Georges Island
ifax Citadel
ional Historic
SPRING GARDEN RD.
QUEEN ST.
MORRIS ST.
SOUTH PARK ST.
Halifax Public Gardens
SOUTH ST.
UNIVERSITY AVE.
TOWER RD.
VICTORIA RD.
blic Archives
Nova Scotia
INGLIS ST.
YOUNG AVE.
ATLANTIC ST.
ROBIE ST.
BELLEVUE AVE.
TOWER RD.
POINT PLEASANT DR.
FORT AVE.
FRANKLYN ST.
N
0 miles .3
0 kilometers .5
Halifax Container Pier
Point Pleasant Park
Point Pleasant

ship *Imo* in Halifax Harbour. The explosion, felt 52 miles away, flattened the north end of the city, leaving 2,000 dead, 9,000 injured, and 6,000 homeless. Known simply as "the Explosion," this tragic event is commemorated yearly; a monument to those who died is located at *Fort Needham.*

After swift reconstruction, Halifax reassumed its position as a center of Canada's maritime industry. The city played an important role in the early days of World War II, when German U-boat wolf packs sought to isolate England by cutting it off from Canadian and American supply ships. With its 10 square miles of deep-water anchorage, the Bedford Basin of Halifax Harbour was the natural staging area for North Atlantic convoys. Some 17,500 ships sailed from here.

During the 1970s and 1980s, shiny new office buildings sprang up on both sides of Halifax Harbour, vast shopping centers followed the burgeoning population to the suburbs, and new restaurants reflected a far more cosmopolitan taste than before. Yet underneath, the city has remained largely dependent on the military branches of government for its income, and still is strongly English and Irish in temperament, culture, and tradition. These days, Halifax, like the rest of Canada, is suffering the effects of economic recession, and its growth has ground to an almost complete halt.

Fortunately, like many Canadian cities, Halifax has been blessed with cogent and restrained city planning. When wealth has been bestowed on the city, it has not caused residents to ignore their cultural and architectural heritage, and the city's 19th-century waterfront area is suffused with an atmosphere of brine, barnacles, and Her Majesty's Navy. Halifax is a paradise for anyone who loves great seaports, the accompanying nautical lore and traditions, the ships, and—most of all—the sea. At press time final approval was pending on a plan to amalgamate the surrounding municipalities of the City of Dartmouth, the Town of Bedford, and Halifax County with the provincial capital; the resulting super-city may get a new name, as may certain streets in the different areas that currently bear the same names.

Halifax At-a-Glance

SEEING THE CITY

In Halifax, an ordinance prohibits the construction of any building that threatens certain "view planes." As a result, today's visitors can see some of the same views that the Loyalists did when they arrived here some 200 years ago. The *Halifax Citadel National Historic Site* (see *Special Places,* below) affords a fine vista. For a broader view, head to suburban *Fleming Park,* on the western shore of the northwest arm of Halifax Harbour, site of the *Memorial Tower* (or the *Dingle,* as it is called locally). Built in 1912, the 10-story structure commemorates the 1758 establishment of representative government in Nova Scotia, the first in Canada. The top of the tower, accessible via interior steps, commands a remarkable view of the northwest arm, its yacht clubs and beautiful homes, *Dalhousie University,* and other sections of the city, as well as the harbor's mouth. The park is open daily; no admission charge.

SPECIAL PLACES

Downtown Halifax easily can be seen on foot, although there is a steep grade from the harbor to the *Halifax Citadel National Historic Site.* Motorists are cautioned about the large number of one-way streets.

DOWNTOWN

HALIFAX CITADEL NATIONAL HISTORIC SITE Once the key to the defense of Halifax, the *Citadel* is a fort built of granite and ironstone quarried at nearby Purcell's Cove. Conceived as a bastion of British power in North America and shaped, like the other fortresses of the period, in the form of a star, the structure—begun in 1749—took 79 years to complete. The on-site *Army Museum* (on the second floor of the *Cavalier Building*) is devoted to military artifacts. A 50-minute sound-and-light show, called "Tides of History," reviews 300 years of life in the harbor; see it before exploring the ramparts. At noon every day a cannon is fired from Citadel Hill, as it has been for 150 years. Summertime events here include concerts, candlelight tours, and dinners featuring hosts in historic costumes. The *Old Town Clock,* which stands on the eastern slope of the hill and has faces on all four sides, was commissioned by the Duke of Kent, father of Queen Victoria and head of the garrison at Halifax from 1794 to 1800. Grounds are open daily year-round, but there are reduced activities and opening hours for the museum in winter. Guided tours are available. Admission charge from June 15 to *Labour Day.* Accessible from Cogswell or Sackville St. (phone: 426-5080).

HISTORIC PROPERTIES On the waterfront, below the *Halifax Citadel National Historic Site,* is a retail development that has brought life back to the 18th-century buildings that once were the city's center of activity. Known as the *Historic Properties,* this hodgepodge of specialty shops and restaurants, many housed in renovated historic buildings, is a powerful magnet for tourists and Haligonians alike. The three-acre site is open daily (phone: 429-0530).

PROVINCE HOUSE Built between 1811 and 1818, this structure was described as a "gem of Georgian architecture" by none other than Charles Dickens. Indeed, it is one of the finest examples of that style on the continent. When the Nova Scotia legislature is in session, visitors can hear debates from the *Public Gallery.* The handsome *Legislative Library* features tall windows, two curving staircases leading to a mezzanine balcony, and alcoves adorned with fine woodcarvings and metal tracery. The building is generally open to visitors daily in July and August; closed weekends the rest of the year. The staff usually provides tours on request. No admission charge. 1690 Hollis St. (phone: 424-5980 or 434-5982).

ST. PAUL'S ANGLICAN CHURCH Built in 1750, this is the oldest existing building in Halifax and the oldest Protestant church in Canada. Its oak frame and pine timbers were brought by sea from Boston and Portsmouth, New Hampshire. *St. Paul's Cemetery,* three blocks south, also known as the *Old Burying Ground,* has a unique memorial to two Nova Scotians killed in the Crimean War. General Robert Ross, who burned Washington, DC during the War of 1812, also is buried here. Barrington St., across from *City Hall* on the Grand Parade (phone: 429-2240).

HALIFAX PUBLIC GARDENS Covering close to 18 acres, these are reputed to be the oldest and finest surviving Victorian gardens in North America, and among the finest public gardens in the country. Created in 1867, they were enlarged in 1874 to their present size. Tree-shaded gravel walks wind among the many flower beds (arranged in French formal and English Romantic fashion) and around fountains and a large pond. A bandstand commemorating Queen Victoria's *Golden Jubilee* in 1887 stands near the center of the gardens and, during summer, serves as a stage for Sunday concerts. Closed November through mid-May. Bordered by Spring Garden Rd. and Summer, Sackville, and S. Park Sts.

POINT PLEASANT PARK This 186-acre wooded park at the extreme southerly end of peninsular Halifax, off limits to private cars, offers countless trails, picnic areas, a supervised beach on the harbor side, and several fortresses that are national historic sites, including, most notably, a Martello tower, a circular stone fortification that was the first of its kind in North America. Accessible from the end of Tower Rd. or Point Pleasant Dr. (phone: 421-6519).

HALIFAX CONTAINER PIER *Halterm,* one of the busiest container piers in Canada, can be seen close up from the breakwater off the *Point Pleasant Park* parking lot. From here, onlookers are literally within a stone's throw of huge ocean vessels unloading cargoes day and night. Off Hollis St. just before *Point Pleasant Park.*

NOVA SCOTIA MUSEUM OF NATURAL HISTORY Located near the *Halifax Citadel National Historic Site* and *Halifax Public Gardens,* this museum contains countless displays and exhibits on all aspects of Nova Scotia's history—from its geological formation to the arrival of the first inhabitants 11,000 years ago, through European settlement up to the present day. The spacious foyer is dominated by a 10-foot lens from the 18th-century *Sambro Lighthouse* and a stagecoach that operated between Yarmouth and Tusket in the late 19th century. Open daily. Admission charge from June to October 15. 1747 Summer St. (phone: 424-7353 or 424-6099).

HMCS SACKVILLE: CANADA'S NAVAL MEMORIAL One of the heroic corvettes used to escort convoys during World War II, this ship has been restored as a memorial to all who served in Canada's Navy. Open daily from early June to late September; by appointment only the rest of the year. No admission charge to the wharf's interpretive center; admission charge to board the ship. At the wharf of the *Maritime Museum of the Atlantic* (see *Museums,* below).

SUBURBS

YORK REDOUBT About 10 miles (16 km) outside Halifax on Herring Cove Road, *York Redoubt* is a more-than-200-year-old fort overlooking the harbor. A national historic site, the park features an exhibit of old muzzle-loaders, a photographic display, a viewing tower, and picnic facilities. It also offers a good view of *Mauger's* (pronounced Major's) *Beach Lighthouse,* on a sand spit projecting into the harbor from McNab's Island. Farther along Herring Cove Road are small fishing communities typical of those around the province—Herring Cove, Portuguese Cove, Ketch Harbour, and Sambro. The shops in Sambro usually have lobsters for sale. Sandy Cove Road affords a good view of 82-foot *Sambro Lighthouse* on Sambro Island. Built in 1759, it was originally operated by three men, with seal oil for fuel. The round trip from Halifax to Sambro is about 50 miles (80 km).

EXTRA SPECIAL

Peggy's Cove is a photographers' and artists' colony that is well-nigh legendary in Canada, thanks to its status as one of the best-preserved fishing villages in North America. Named for one of its original inhabitants, it has a number of quaint gift shops as well as two spectacular murals in *St. John's Anglican Church.* About 27 miles (43 km) southwest of Halifax on Rte. 333 (also see *Quintessential Canada* in DIVERSIONS).

Sources and Resources

TOURIST INFORMATION

For general information, brochures, and maps, contact the *Nova Scotia Tourist Bureau* (*Old Red Store, Historic Properties;* phone: 424-4247), which is open daily from late May to mid-October; closed weekends the rest of the year. *Tourism Halifax,* in *City Hall* (Duke St.; phone: 421-8736), is closed weekends.

LOCAL COVERAGE The *Chronicle-Herald* is a morning daily; the *Mail-Star* is an afternoon daily (same entertainment listings in both papers); and the *Daily News* is a morning daily tabloid.

Where Magazine: Halifax-Dartmouth is one of the best guides to the city. Published monthly by Metro Guide Publishing Ltd. (1496 Lower Water St.; phone: 420-9943), it is distributed free in hotels, restaurants, some stores, area tourist offices (see above), and *Air Canada* ticket offices. The magazine describes a walking route of historic downtown Halifax and

Dartmouth and outlines a driving tour of Halifax known as the *Kingfisher Motor Tour* and marked by street signs. The *Halifax Visitor's Guide,* also published by Metro Guide, is a good source of up-to-date information on tours of all types, as well as museums, libraries, parks and recreation, dining out, and shopping. It can be found at *Tourism Halifax* or the *Nova Scotia Tourist Bureau* (see above). A city and district map produced by the Royal Bank of Canada also is widely available.

TELEPHONE The area code for Halifax is 902. A recent change in the telephone system means that now, to call from one community in Nova Scotia to another, you must dial the area code first; previously, it was unnecessary to use the area code for calls within the province.

SALES TAX Nova Scotia has an 11% provincial sales tax in addition to the 7% federal Goods and Services Tax (GST). The provincial tax is nonrefundable; for information on obtaining rebates on the federal tax, see GETTING READY TO GO.

CLIMATE Compared with the rest of Canada, Nova Scotia has relatively moderate temperatures, and thanks to the Gulf Stream, Halifax is even a bit more temperate than that. In February, the coldest month of the year, the average low is 16F (-9C), and the average high is 31F (-1C); in July and August, the average daytime high is 74F (23C), and the average nighttime low is 57F (14C). Water temperature is rarely above 70F (22C). The climate is not particularly humid; in summer months the rainfall is usually less than four inches, although in the rainiest month, December, precipitation can be as much as seven inches. For weather information, call 426-9090.

GETTING AROUND

AIRPORT *Zinck Bus Company Ltd.* (phone: 468-4342) provides transport to and from *Halifax International Airport.* The buses operate daily, stopping at major hotels in Halifax and Dartmouth. Call the company or ask your hotel concierge for a timetable of departures. Taxis to and from the airport tend to be expensive.

BUS The *Metropolitan Transit Authority* (commonly known as *Metro Transit*) operates regular service. Exact fare (CN$1.20/about 90¢ US at press time) in coins is required. For schedule and route information, call 421-6600.

CAR RENTAL All major international firms are represented; many have offices both at the airport and downtown.

FERRIES They link downtown Halifax with its sister city (at press time slated to become part of Halifax itself), Dartmouth, across the harbor. Schedule information is available from *Metro Transit* (see *Bus,* above).

TAXI Cabs may be hailed in the streets or found at taxi stands at the airport, major hotels, shopping areas, and elsewhere around the city. To call a cab, try *Y*

Taxi (phone: 422-4433) or *Yellow Taxi* (phone: 422-1551). Meters are used on all trips except for some outside the city (to the airport, for example), for which flat rates apply.

TOURS The *Mar II* (phone: 420-1015; fax: 423-7942), a 75-foot Danish ketch, offers one- and two-hour sailing tours of the harbor from *Cable Wharf* (next to *Historic Properties*) from May 15 through October. (Charters are available.) *Gray Line of Halifax* (phone: 454-9321) and *Metro Transit* (see *Bus,* above) offer city bus tours.

SPECIAL EVENTS

The Nova Scotia International Tattoo, which takes place in late June, is a military pageant featuring marching bands, dancing, singing, and traditional athletic competitions (such as the British Navy "gun run"). Rated among the top three tattoos in the world, it is staged indoors at the *Metro Centre* (5284 Duke St., across from *Scotia Square;* phone: 451-1221), Halifax's 10,000-seat entertainment-sports arena. *Halifax Natal Day,* which commemorates the founding of the city in 1749 and rivals *Canada Day* (July 1) for its display of civic pride, is celebrated the first weekend in August. The festivities include a parade, concerts, picnics, and fireworks. The *Nova Scotia Festival of the Arts,* held in mid-August, features a large display of local arts and crafts.

MUSEUMS

In addition to those described in *Special Places,* other notable Halifax museums include the following:

ART GALLERY OF NOVA SCOTIA Here are paintings and sculptures from the area, in addition to some traveling exhibitions; check the lecture schedule, too. Tours are given daily at 2 PM in July and August. Closed Mondays. No admission charge Tuesdays. 1741 Hollis St., across from *Province House* (phone: 424-7542).

MARITIME MUSEUM OF THE ATLANTIC Exhibits here chronicle the history of sailing and steam vessels and the Canadian Navy. There's also a gallery devoted to shipwrecks and an exhibit about the 1917 harbor explosion. Closed Mondays. Admission charge from June to October 15. 1675 Lower Water St. (phone: 424-7490).

PUBLIC ARCHIVES OF NOVA SCOTIA This is a popular spot for genealogical research. Open daily. No admission charge. 6016 University Ave. at Robie St. (phone: 424-6060).

SHOPPING

Halifax's many native craftspeople produce a wide range of goods, including pottery, jewelry, ceramics, rugs, quilts, woodwork, and all manner of dolls. You can visit them at their shops, which more often than not double as their homes. While some artisans keep shop hours, others are open by appointment only; call in advance. A list of local weavers is available from the *Atlantic Spinners and Handweavers Association,* through the *Nova Scotia Museum of Natural History* (see *Special Places*). For more extensive information, contact the *Nova Scotia Department of Education, Nova Scotia Centre for Arts, Crafts and Design* (1683 Barrington St.; phone: 424-4062) and ask for a copy of its *Buyer's Guide to Arts and Crafts in Nova Scotia,* a free publication that also is available at tourist bureaus and crafts outlets. The *Nova Scotia Designer Crafts Council* (5516 Spring Garden Rd.; phone: 423-3837) also can supply information on local artisans and crafts fairs around the province.

Spring Garden Road, which runs perpendicular to Barrington Street, is the most heavily traveled downtown street for shopping. Major malls outside the downtown area include the *West End Mall* on Mumford Road, and the *Halifax Shopping Centre* and the *Bayers Road Shopping Centre,* both on Bayers Road. Most retail stores are open Mondays, Tuesdays, and Saturdays from 10 AM to 5:30 PM; Wednesdays through Fridays to 9 PM; closed Sundays. Below is a list of Halifax's best shopping locations:

Binnacle Sweaters, slickers, yachting supplies (including navigational instruments and charts), and books on nautical themes make for good browsing and buying. 15 Purcell's Cove Rd. (phone: 423-6464).

Fireworks Gallery Somewhat high-priced jewelry, crafts in silver, and "wearable art" are the stock items here. 1569 Barrington St. (phone: 420-1735).

Jennifer's of Nova Scotia Arts and crafts by local talent are the specialty, at slightly better prices than elsewhere. 5636 Spring Garden Rd. (phone: 425-3119).

Pewter House This shop carries a large stock of pewter items, ranging from jewelry to tableware, many of them made by Nova Scotia's own Seagull Pewter, one of Canada's leading manufacturers and exporters. 1875 Granville St. (phone: 423-8843).

Plaid Place A bit of Scotland in Halifax, this is the place for custom-made kilts, family tartans, even bagpipes. 1903 Barrington Pl. (phone: 423-0112).

Stornoway Gift Shop Next door to the *Pewter House,* it offers a diverse (but somewhat pricey) selection of arts and crafts by local artisans—everything from quilts to lampshades. 1873 Granville St. (phone: 422-9507).

Suttles and Seawinds Featured here are distinctive hand-crafted sportswear and quilts, often blending cotton prints in clever designs, made by artisans in Mahone Bay, Nova Scotia. 1869 Upper Water St. (phone: 423-9077).

SPORTS

BICYCLING The *Velo Halifax Club* (phone: 453-5091) is a noncompetitive touring and recreational club. Visitors to the city with access to a bicycle are welcome to join club members on weekend rides. Weather permitting, members travel 30 to 50 miles (48 to 80 km). For those not up to tackling such an excursion, the club publishes a pamphlet suggesting shorter routes, which is available at the *Nova Scotia Tourist Bureau* (see *Tourist Information*). Also useful is *Bicycle Tours in Nova Scotia,* a 50-page book published by *Bicycle Nova Scotia's Touring Committee* (PO Box 3010 South, Halifax, NS B3J 3G6; no phone). *Down East Tours* (PO Box 632, Milton, NS B0T 1P0; phone: 354-4667) organizes weekend and six-day guided tours that originate in Halifax, as well as self-guided bicycle tours and nature hikes. Guides and van support are provided, and accommodations are in bed and breakfast establishments along the way. Bike rentals are also available.

FISHING Trout fishing in stocked lakes is possible within Dartmouth's city limits; however, anglers seeking real trout and salmon fishing will want to check out the lakes and streams along Marine Drive on the road between Halifax and Sherbrooke, about 125 miles (200 km) to the east.

GOLF Golfers have their choice of five 18-hole layouts, all 10 miles (16 km) or less from downtown hotels. Among them is one of our favorite Canadian courses.

TOP TEE-OFF SPOT

Brightwood Golf and Country Club Located right in the center of Dartmouth across the bay, this 18-hole course is perched high on a hill on what must surely be the area's choicest site. The views are as beautiful as the golf holes are difficult. A non-member can play by showing a membership card from another club. 227 School St., Dartmouth (phone: 469-7879).

There also are two *Ashburn* golf courses, the newer one in Fall River just north of town (Fall River Rd. at Windsor Junction; phone: 861-4013) and the older inside Halifax (Dutch Village Rd., between Mumford and Bayers Rds.; phone: 443-9415). Both allow non-members to play on weekdays. The *Hartlen Point Forces* golf course (Eastern Passage; phone: 465-6353) and *Oakfield Country Club* (Grand Lake; phone: 861-2658) are open to the public. Along with the *Ashburn* courses, *Oakfield* is one of Halifax's prime layouts. It's as wide open as the *Ashburn* courses are wooded, but no less difficult. The constant breeze that blows over the lakeside setting makes each hole a bit trickier than it initially appears.

JOGGING Haligonians love to jog, and those looking for companionship should have no trouble finding some. The *YMCA* (1565 S. Park St.; phone: 422-6437) is a good spot to meet joggers, particularly at noon and shortly after 5 PM, when businesspeople leave the *Y* to jog around the city. *Halifax Common* (in the city center, just beside The Citadel) and *Point Pleasant Park* (see *Special Places*) are frequented by joggers during the day.

SAILING For information on area sailing and cruising schools, contact the *Nova Scotia Sailing Association,* c/o *Sport Nova Scotia* (5516 Spring Garden Rd., Suite 401; phone: 425-5450).

TENNIS There are public courts on *Halifax Common,* near the *Holiday Inn* and *Château Halifax* hotels (see *Checking In*). The *Nova Scotia Open Tennis Tournament* is held in late August at the *Waegwoltic Club* (6549 Coburg Rd.; phone: 429-2822).

THEATER

The *Neptune Theatre* (5216 Sackville St.; phone: 429-7070) presents a varied repertoire of plays—drama and comedy, classic and contemporary—in an intimate setting. Lunchtime shows are sometimes offered; check newspapers for performance schedules. Summer dinner-theater is featured around town; again, check newspaper listings.

MUSIC

Dalhousie University's *Rebecca Cohn Auditorium* schedules frequent performances by visiting artists of all stripes. It is located in the *Dalhousie Arts Centre* (University Ave., off Coburg Rd.; phone: 494-2646). Other concerts are held regularly at *Metro Centre* (5284 Duke St., across from *Scotia Square;* phone: 451-1221).

NIGHTCLUBS AND NIGHTLIFE

Visitors to Halifax, particularly during the summer, are often surprised to discover how much of a party town it is. The festive atmosphere is particularly noticeable on Friday and Saturday nights along Argyle Street downtown, where pubs—and their patrons—seem to be everywhere. In recent years, more bars and lounges have been opening their doors in the area—some only to close down shortly afterward. (To keep up to date, check the *Halifax Visitor's Guide*—see *Local Coverage,* above.) Pub crawlers will find plenty of nightspots within walking distance of one another. The *Thirsty Duck* (upstairs at 5472 Spring Garden Rd.; phone: 422-1548) features live entertainment on Fridays and Saturdays, ranging from traditional Celtic music to top 40. The good pub fare served from 11 AM to 10 PM is an added enticement, and the shuffleboard or darts enthusiast won't be disappointed, either. Or dance to live rock music at *My Apartment* (1740 Argyle St.; phone: 422-5453), which is usually loud and packed; it's open daily. At the *Lower Deck* (phone: 425-1501), the entertainment often features traditional Irish and Nova Scotia folk music; upstairs, the *Middle Deck* (phone: 425-1500) schedules a variety of live bands. Both are in the *Privateer's Warehouse* (see *Eating Out,* below). *O'Carroll's Oyster Bar* (1860 Upper Water St.; phone: 423-4405) has a piano bar. For cabaret entertainment, check out the *Palace* (1721 Brunswick St.; phone: 420-0015 or 420-5959). Other popular nightspots are *Thackeray's Pub* (5407 Spring Garden Rd.; phone: 423-5995) and *Maxwell's Plum* (1600 Grafton St.; phone: 423-8465).

Best in Town

CHECKING IN

For one night, expect to pay $75 or more for a double room at those places classified as expensive, and between $40 and $75 at the inn described as moderate. Prices quoted do not include taxes. All hotels feature air conditioning, private baths, TV sets, and telephones unless otherwise indicated.

A toll-free number (phone: 800-341-6096 in the US) is available for reservations throughout the province. All hotels below are in the 902 area code unless otherwise indicated.

EXPENSIVE

Château Halifax Operated by Canadian Pacific Hotels and ideally situated in the downtown *Scotia Square* complex, the hotel has 305 rooms; an enclosed patio garden and a tower with views of the harbor, Citadel Hill, and Bedford Basin; a restaurant, *The Crown Bistrot,* specializing in grilled meat and lobster; a lounge, *Sam Slick's;* a heated indoor-outdoor pool; and a sauna, whirlpool, and fitness center. Ask about special weekend rates. 1990 Barrington St. (phone: 425-6700; 800-441-1414; fax: 425-6214).

Citadel Halifax Not quite as posh as the *Château Halifax,* it's also slightly less expensive. Some of the 278 rooms have harbor views. There are nonsmoking floors, a pool, a sun deck, and a fitness center. There's also a restaurant, *Arthur's,* which features a lunch buffet, and a lounge. Near *Scotia Square* and *Metro Centre,* at 1960 Brunswick St. (phone: 422-1391; 800-565-7162; fax: 429-6672).

Delta Barrington Inn This 200-room hostelry belongs to the respected Delta chain. Housed in four converted mid-19th-century warehouses, it is about three blocks from the waterfront, between the *Scotia Square* complex and *Historic Properties.* Facilities include a seafood restaurant, *McNab's;* the *Trader's Lounge,* with a daily luncheon buffet; a heated indoor pool, sauna, and whirlpool; a nonsmoking floor; and business services. 1875 Barrington St., at the corner of Duke (phone: 429-7410; 800-268-1133 in Canada; 800-887-1133 in the US; fax: 420-6524).

Halifax Sheraton A classy, low-rise, 352-room hostelry, it blends well with the *Historic Properties* development next door along the waterfront. A great location, lovely surroundings, and tasteful decor are its hallmarks. *The Library* restaurant offers fine dining, and there's a new casino and Scottish-style pub. 1919 Upper Water St. (phone: 421-1700; 800-325-3535; fax: 422-5805).

Holiday Inn This member of the worldwide chain overlooks *Halifax Common,* where hundreds of amateur athletes play such games as cricket year-round.

There are 203 rooms; amenities include a heated indoor pool and a restaurant and lounge, *Willow's Bistro and Wine Bar.* Quinpool and Robie Sts. (phone: 423-1161; 800-HOLIDAY; fax: 423-9069).

Prince George With 205 rooms and six suites, this place enjoys a convenient, central location, just a block from the Grand Parade at *City Hall.* Handy indoor parking connects with an underground walkway to the *World Trade and Convention Centre* and the adjacent *Metro Centre.* Guests can enjoy a pool, a whirlpool bath, a sauna, and an exercise room; there are two restaurants—*The Terrace,* for breakfast, and *Giorgio's,* for lunch and dinner. 1725 Market St. (phone: 425-1986; 800-565-1567; fax: 429-6048).

MODERATE

Chebucto Inn Although removed from downtown, this 32-room modern hostelry is situated near the main roads in and out of the city. A dining room, *The Lady Hammond Grill,* offers a standard continental menu. 6151 Lady Hammond Rd. (phone: 453-4330; fax: 454-7043).

EATING OUT

Halifax's restaurants have improved dramatically over the last two decades, although some critics still complain that, given the city's proximity to some of the world's best fishing grounds, there is not enough high-quality seafood available. Expect to pay more than $45 for dinner for two in those restaurants we've categorized as expensive; between $35 to $45 in the moderate range; and $35 or less at an inexpensive place. Prices do not include wine, drinks, or tip. Unless otherwise noted, all restaurants are open for lunch and dinner, and all are in the 902 area code.

EXPENSIVE

La Perla This unpretentious restaurant has wonderful food plus Old World charm. The quickest and most entertaining way to get there is via a ferry across the harbor to Dartmouth. The restaurant has recently moved to new quarters just next door to its former location; outside the terminal, look across the street for a distinctive pink door. The quiet and intimate dining room is now housed on the second and third floors of the building. Primarily northern Italian, the menu is not limited to mounds of pasta: Salads are especially good here, and the main courses are a delight. Closed weekends for lunch. Reservations necessary. Major credit cards accepted. 73 Alderney Dr., Dartmouth (phone: 469-3241; fax: 466-6043).

Scanway Tucked away in a two-story boutique complex, this eatery features great Scandinavian fare. Seafood is a specialty. Closed Sundays. Reservations advised. Major credit cards accepted. 1569 Dresden Row, off Spring Garden Rd. (phone: 422-3733; fax: 422-5743).

MODERATE

Lawrence of Oregano Across the street from the Grand Parade at *City Hall,* it caters to a youthful clientele of office workers and university students, and is a good spot to grab a pizza and a beer in lively, pleasant surroundings. Closed Sundays. Reservations unnecessary. Major credit cards accepted. 726 Argyle St. (phone: 422-6907).

McKelvie's The decor is nautical, dress is informal, and the specialty is fish. The restaurant is housed in a grand old converted firehouse; there's also a terrace for summer dining. Open daily. Reservations advised. Major credit cards accepted. Conveniently located opposite the *Maritime Museum of the Atlantic* on the waterfront, next to *Historic Properties,* at 1680 Lower Water St. (phone: 421-6161; fax: 425-8949).

Mother Tucker's Close to *Historic Properties* and the business district, this is a popular spot for seafood and prime ribs, with a huge salad bar. Open daily. Reservations advised. 1668 Lower Water St. (phone: 422-4436; fax: 425-2024).

Old Man Morias This eatery serves authentic Greek food in a converted townhouse. Closed Sundays. Reservations advised. Major credit cards accepted. 1150 Barrington St. (phone: 422-7960).

Privateer's Warehouse There are three entities here: The *Lower Deck* and *Middle Deck* are lounges with entertainment (see *Nightclubs and Nightlife*), and the *Upper Deck* is one of the best places to eat in town. Seafood and steaks are served by a friendly, efficient staff; the dining room's stone walls and wooden beams are decorated with things nautical, as befits the building's history. Closed Sundays. Reservations advised. Major credit cards accepted. At *Historic Properties* (phone: 422-1289; fax: 423-1575).

Silver Spoon The quaint coffeehouse/tearoom here has satisfied many a sweet tooth, while the restaurant has delighted patrons with its more substantial fare. Closed Sundays. Reservations necessary for the dining room. Major credit cards accepted. 1813 Granville St. (phone: 422-1519).

Thackeray's This pleasant and sophisticated dining spot, located on one of Halifax's busiest streets, specializes in meat and poultry dishes and also produces very good desserts. Open daily. Reservations advised. Major credit cards accepted. 5435 Spring Garden Rd. (phone: 423-5995; fax: 425-5675).

INEXPENSIVE

Midtown Tavern A student hangout, this is a place for draft-beer drinkers not concerned about surroundings—or smoke. The food is surprisingly good, particularly the fish and chips and the corned beef and cabbage. Closed Sundays. No reservations. No credit cards accepted. 1684 Grafton St. at Prince St. (phone: 422-5213).

FISH AND CHIPS—OR JUST CHIPS

Haligonians have a penchant for deep-fried fish and potatoes (clams and scallops usually are available too). Wrapped in brown paper, this fast food is great for a picnic in one of the city parks or along the waterfront. Local favorites are *Camille's* (2654 Barrington St.; phone: 423-8869) and *Fries and Company* (Chebucto Rd. and Connolly St.; phone: 455-5250). *Camille's* is open daily; *Fries and Company* is closed Sundays. Neither accepts credit cards.

For some of the best French fries in town, try *Bud the Spud*'s popular chip wagon. It's usually parked at noon outside the *Halifax Regional Public Library* at Spring Garden Road and Grafton Street.

Montreal

Since 1535—when Jacques Cartier first laid eyes on the St. Lawrence River village of Hochelaga, climbed with its native residents to the top of its 764-foot mountain, took a look at the 50-mile view, and exclaimed, "What a royal mount!"—the place has emerged as Canada's second-largest city. Yet some of the most dramatic changes in Montreal have occurred in the past 30 years, with the construction of luxury hotels; the addition of a vast underground network of shops and services linked by a clean, efficient *Métro* (subway) system; an accretion of fashionable boutiques and excellent restaurants; and careful restorations in the historic quarter. Montreal's current look was sparked in the 1960s by a midtown face-lift which gained momentum during *EXPO '67,* a world's fair that brought the city international attention. A concomitant increase in tourism reached its peak in 1976, when Montreal hosted the *Summer Olympic Games.*

A second building boom in the 1980s transformed the downtown area, with the completion of a dozen major projects that included the conversion of two former hotels on Rue Peel into chic commercial complexes, along with the construction of several showy office towers. Indeed, the transformation was so complete that some residents claim they can't remember what Montreal used to look like. However, a key priority when construction began was the preservation of Vieux Montréal (Old Montreal). The protection of special buildings extended to modern Montreal as well: The city's *Stade Olympique* (Olympic Stadium) has become a spectacular public sports facility, and the *EXPO '67* grounds on Ile Notre-Dame are now the site of the *Casino de Montréal,* Quebec's province-operated gambling casino, which opened in 1993.

Compelling and cosmopolitan, Montreal sits on a flat (except for Mont-Royal), anvil-shape island 32 miles long and 10 miles wide in the middle of the St. Lawrence River, some 170 miles (272 km) northeast of Lake Ontario. The river, which borders the city on the south and east, provides a crucial navigable link between the inland Great Lakes and the Atlantic Ocean. A narrow branch of the St. Lawrence, known as Rivière des Prairies, borders Montreal on the west and the north.

The most appealing thing about Montreal, especially for Americans, is its Frenchness. Without jet lag and with a minimum of cost and bother, Americans have easy access to a North American city that still provides the best of the traditional French experience. Two thirds of greater Montreal's more than three million inhabitants are of French origin, and the French Canadian patois is heard all around town. Though nearly everyone in the urban center is bilingual, there is no question of the primary tongue.

Montreal's cosmopolitan ambience is due in part to the city's diverse population, which includes more than a hundred ethnic groups. While the

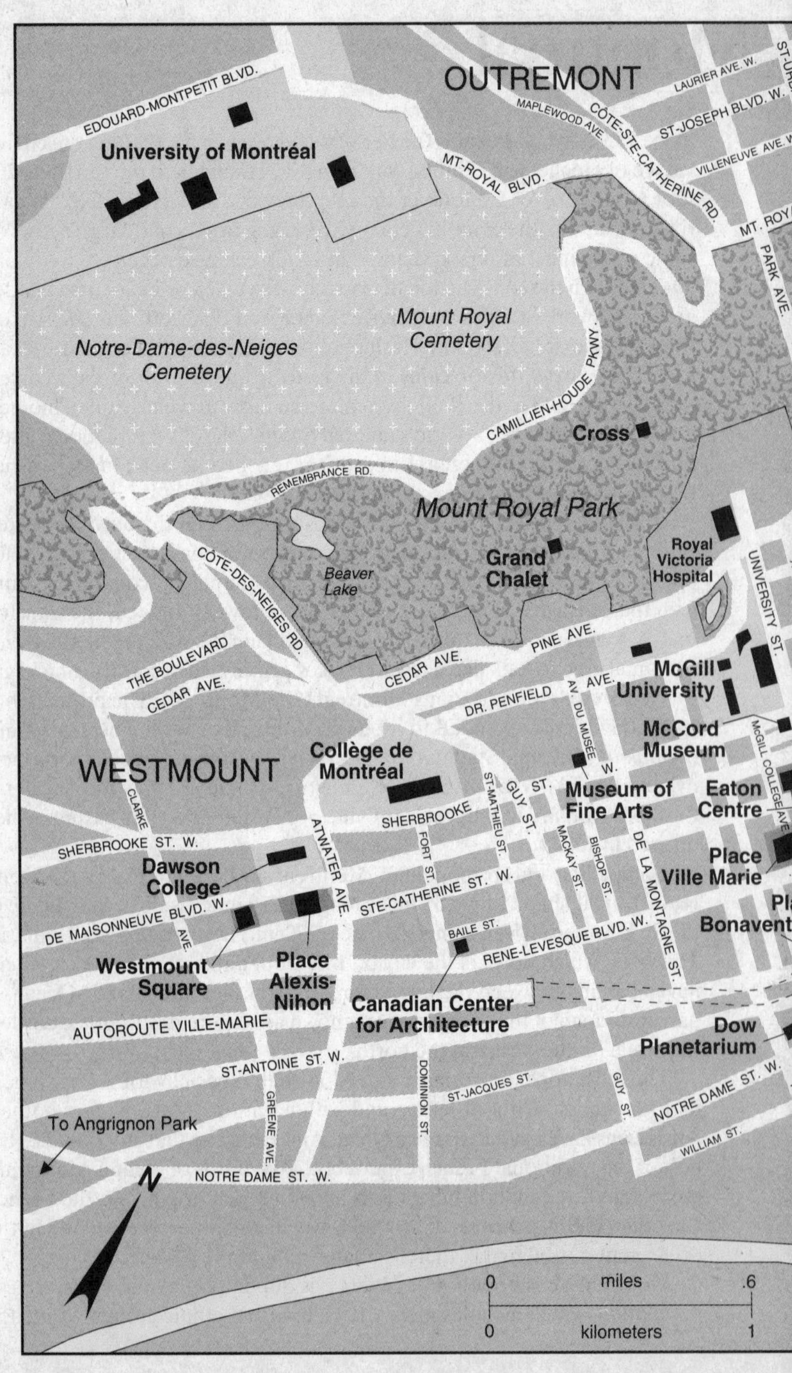
OUTREMONT
EDOUARD-MONTPETIT BLVD.
University of Montréal
LAURIER AVE. W.
MAPLEWOOD AVE.
CÔTE-STE-CATHERINE RD.
ST-JOSEPH BLVD. W.
VILLENEUVE AVE. W.
MT-ROYAL BLVD.
PARK AVE.
Mount Royal Cemetery
Notre-Dame-des-Neiges Cemetery
CAMILLIEN-HOUDE PKWY.
Cross
REMEMBRANCE RD.
Mount Royal Park
Beaver Lake
CÔTE-DES-NEIGES RD.
Grand Chalet
Royal Victoria Hospital
UNIVERSITY ST.
THE BOULEVARD
CEDAR AVE.
PINE AVE.
McGill University
DR. PENFIELD AVE.
AV. DU MUSÉE
McCord Museum
WESTMOUNT
Collège de Montréal
CLARKE AVE.
ST-MATHIEU ST.
GUY ST.
SHERBROOKE ST. W.
Museum of Fine Arts
Eaton Centre
McGILL COLLEGE AVE.
ATWATER AVE.
FORT ST.
MACKAY ST.
BISHOP ST.
DE LA MONTAGNE ST.
Dawson College
Place Ville Marie
STE-CATHERINE ST. W.
DE MAISONNEUVE BLVD. W.
BAILE ST.
RENE-LEVESQUE BLVD. W.
Westmount Square
Place Alexis-Nihon
Canadian Center for Architecture
AUTOROUTE VILLE-MARIE
Dow Planetarium
ST-ANTOINE ST. W.
DOMINION ST.
ST-JACQUES ST.
GUY ST.
NOTRE DAME ST. W.
GREENE AVE.
To Angrignon Park
WILLIAM ST.
N
0 miles .6
0 kilometers 1

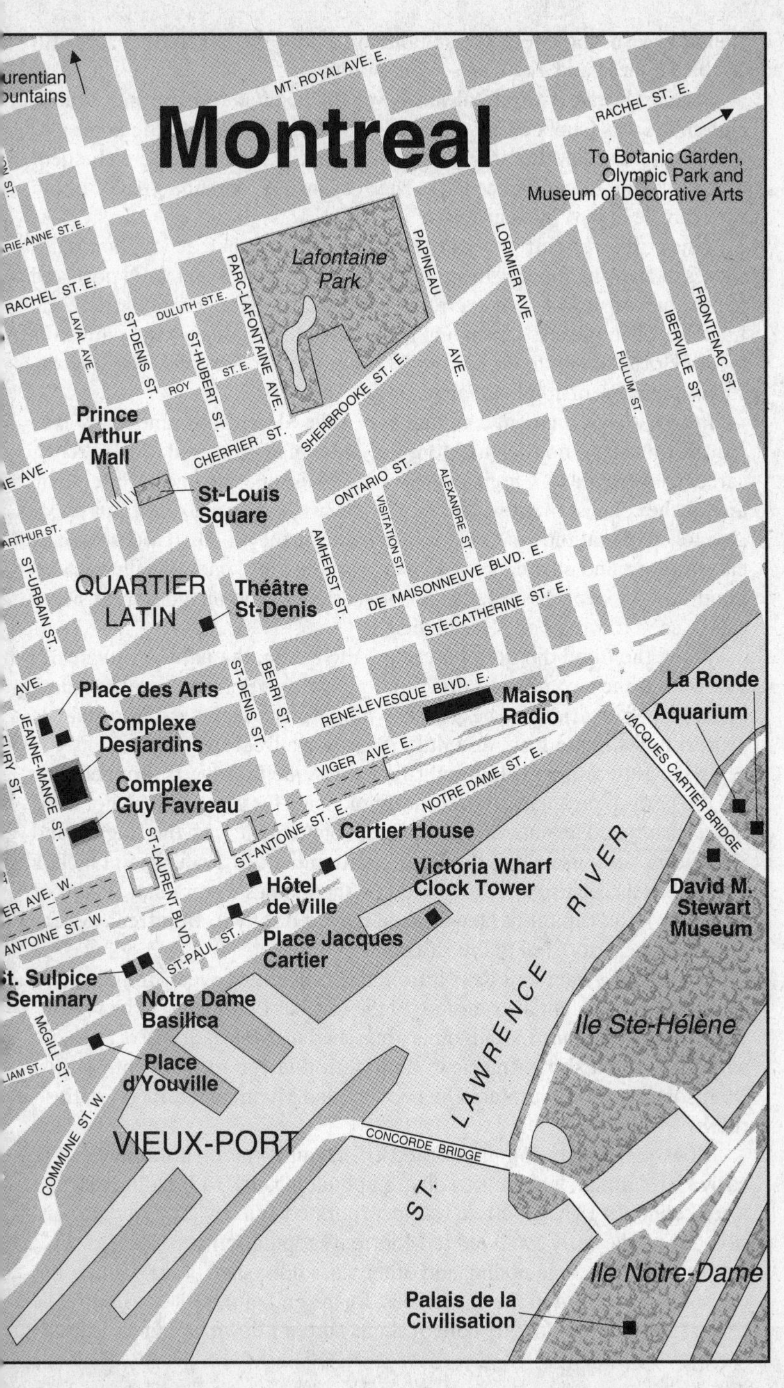

Montreal
urentian
ountains
MT. ROYAL AVE. E.
RACHEL ST. E.
To Botanic Garden,
Olympic Park and
Museum of Decorative Arts
Lafontaine
Park
PAPINEAU
AVE.
LORIMIER AVE.
FRONTENAC ST.
IBERVILLE ST.
FULLUM ST.
RIE-ANNE ST. E.
RACHEL ST. E.
LAVAL AVE.
ST-DENIS ST.
DULUTH ST.E.
ST-HUBERT ST.
PARC-LAFONTAINE AVE.
ROY ST. E.
SHERBROOKE ST. E.
CHERRIER ST.
Prince
Arthur
Mall
St-Louis
Square
ONTARIO ST.
VISITATION ST.
ALEXANDRE ST.
ARTHUR ST.
ST-URBAIN ST.
QUARTIER
LATIN
Théâtre
St-Denis
AMHERST ST.
DE MAISONNEUVE BLVD. E.
STE-CATHERINE ST. E.
ST-DENIS ST.
BERRI ST.
RENE-LEVESQUE BLVD. E.
Maison
Radio
La Ronde
Aquarium
Place des Arts
Complexe
Desjardins
JEANNE-MANCE ST.
VIGER AVE. E.
NOTRE DAME ST. E.
JACQUES CARTIER BRIDGE
Complexe
Guy Favreau
ST-ANTOINE ST. E.
Cartier House
ST-LAURENT BLVD.
Victoria Wharf
Clock Tower
RIVER
Hôtel
de Ville
David M.
Stewart
Museum
Place Jacques
Cartier
ANTOINE ST. W.
ST-PAUL ST.
St. Sulpice
Seminary
Notre Dame
Basilica
McGILL ST.
Ile Ste-Hélène
Place
d'Youville
LAWRENCE
COMMUNE ST. W.
VIEUX-PORT
CONCORDE BRIDGE
ST.
Ile Notre-Dame
Palais de la
Civilisation

Italian, Jewish, and Greek populations are among the largest, there are also sizable Chinese and Portuguese communities.

Perhaps because Montreal was never the headquarters of the Catholic church (as was Quebec City, its cousin 153 miles/245 km to the north), or because it passed part of this century as a "sin city," it seems more ebullient and easygoing than Quebec City. The reasons for this subtle flavor of life certainly lie in part in its history.

When explorer-entrepreneur Samuel de Champlain reached Montreal's shores in 1603, he foresaw the great value of the area as an inland port, and he returned in 1611 to erect a trading post near the foot of the Rapides de Lachine. (The ravages of warring tribes had left no trace of the native village of Hochelaga visited by Cartier.) The spot, later christened Place Royale, still is a nucleus of commercial activity.

In 1642 the permanent community of Ville Marie was founded at Place Royale (in what is now Vieux Montréal) by a small group led by the French career soldier Paul de Chomedey, Sieur de Maisonneuve. Shortly after their arrival, the colonists narrowly escaped being swept away in a disastrous flood. As a token of gratitude to God for their survival, they climbed Mont-Royal's eastern slope and planted a wooden cross at the top. Today, the illuminated hundred-foot steel cross that stands in its stead—and on a different site—can be seen for miles on clear nights.

While the flood did not obliterate Ville Marie, the natives very nearly did. During the next 60 years, the rapidly growing colony of traders, explorers, and missionaries was besieged by numerous attacks; an open state of war existed with the Iroquois until 1701, when a treaty was signed.

In the 18th century, Montreal (the name Ville Marie was dropped during this period) prospered through its burgeoning fur trade, though not without difficulties. The natives were quieted, but trouble with the English and Americans took its toll on the French settlement. In 1759, when Quebec City fell to the British after the battle on the Plaines d'Abraham (Plains of Abraham), the capital of New France moved briefly to Montreal. A year later Montreal, too, fell to the British.

During the American Revolution, the Americans eyed Montreal and Quebec City as potential extensions of the original 13 colonies. In November 1775, General Richard Montgomery marched on Montreal and occupied it without firing a shot. American domination lasted only seven months; Montgomery failed to capture Quebec City, and Montreal returned to British rule.

Montreal's expansion under the British gained momentum during the early 19th century, when fur trading, shipbuilding, and railroading reached a crescendo. In 1832 Montreal was incorporated as a city. The city's expansion during the early 1900s led to Montreal's reputation as a "wicked city"; prostitution, illegal gambling, and other vices flourished, mostly under the well-paid protection of the authorities. By the end of the 1940s, Montreal's central section was a dreary core of slums and run-down buildings. But this blot on the face of the city has since completely vanished, thanks to a war on corruption mounted during the 1950s by city official Jean Drapeau and more recent efforts.

The first renovation was the construction of *Place Ville-Marie,* an underground complex of shops, restaurants, and services in the heart of downtown, built to hide the ugly pit yards of the *Canadian National Railways. Place Ville-Marie* was the first of several such complexes to be built in the heart of Montreal; today these complexes are found in various parts of the city and provide weatherproof access to hotels, office buildings, banks, stores, and two railway stations.

In the 1960s and 1970s, Montreal put up a stunning cultural and performing arts center, *Place des Arts,* and became one of the two Canadian cities with a major league baseball team, the Montreal *Expos* (Toronto has the *Blue Jays*). The city followed up *EXPO '67* by hosting the *1976 Summer Olympics.* As Montreal was acquiring its new look, municipal and provincial ordinances wisely assured the preservation of Vieux Montréal, designating the 95-acre waterfront sector a historical site.

The city spreads out in all directions from Mont-Royal, and probably the best way to appreciate the mountain and its surrounding *Parc du Mont-Royal* is to hire a calèche (horse-drawn carriage). Meandering through the park, it's possible to assimilate a little local sociology along with an appreciation of the scenic beauty. A certain tension has always existed between the descendants of the original French founders and those of the British conquerors. They enjoy a fairly cordial coexistence today, although former antipathies are still evident in Montreal's neighborhood patterns. To the west is Westmount, the "bedroom" for Montreal's prosperous English community. On the other side of the mountain is Outremont, the turf of the wealthy French inhabitants. Each community is equally affluent but entirely separate, and it is easy to distinguish the lines of demarcation. As you ride along, just note the names of the passing apartment buildings: as *The Trafalgar*'s give way to *Le Trianon*'s, you'll know that you have "crossed the Channel."

Whichever course the province of Quebec chooses to follow in the near future—continued confederation or possible separation from the rest of Canada—it's safe to say that the city of Montreal always will offer a wide spectrum of sights and sounds for visitors.

Montreal At-a-Glance

SEEING THE CITY

There are several vantage points from which to capture the sweep of Montreal. Two lookout points on 764-foot Mont-Royal offer spectacular views. To reach the *Belvédère Mont-Royal* at the *Grand Chalet,* follow the path up from the *Parc du Mont-Royal* parking lot or walk up Rue Peel from downtown. Those traveling by car have access to an impressive view of the north and east at the *Observatoire de l'Est* lookout on the eastern slope of Voie Camillien-Houde, the only road over the mountain on which automobiles are permitted. Also on Mont-Royal, the *Oratoire St-Joseph* (see *Special Places*) offers an excellent view of the northern part of the city.

The *Belvédère Westmount* (on Chemin Belvédère in Westmount), accessible by car, affords an excellent view of the southwestern section of the city and surroundings. Arrows on the lookout's ledge indicate 22 points of interest, extending to the Green Mountains of Vermont and New York's Adirondacks. Iles Ste-Hélène and Notre-Dame offer magnificent views of downtown with a mountain backdrop.

From the *Stade Olympique*'s 575-foot-high tower (4141 Av. Pierre-de-Coubertin; phone: 252-TOUR), the view extends more than 50 miles on a clear day. A cable car with bay windows takes visitors to the top in two minutes. It's open daily; closed mid-January to mid-February. There's an admission charge.

The old *Tour de l'Horloge* (Clock Tower) on Quai de l'Horloge (phone: 496-PORT), now an interpretive center tracing the Vieux (Old) Port's past, commands a vista of the harbor from its top story. It's open daily; closed *Labour Day* through May. There's no admission charge. Other panoramas of Montreal can be seen from the *Château Champlain*'s *l'Escapade* restaurant and *Le Tour de Ville* dining room at the *Radisson-Gouverneurs* (see *Checking In* for both).

SPECIAL PLACES

To get a feel for Montreal, walk through its streets and parks; the city's layout makes it easy to navigate on foot. Montreal's street plan is laid out on a roughly north-south, east-west axis. Each block covers approximately a hundred numbers. East-west numbering starts at Boulevard St-Laurent, so the street number 900 Ouest, for example, is nine blocks west of St-Laurent. (The directionals E and O—designating *est,* or east, and *ouest,* or west—follow the addresses.) North-south numbers start at the river and run north, following the same formula. Most interesting to the visitor is the area wedged between the river on the south and east and Mont-Royal on the north and west.

An easy way to visit places farther afield is to head for the nearest *Métro* station and hop aboard a train on one of the city's four subway lines; most put visitors near the important attractions.

DOWNTOWN

MUSÉE DES BEAUX-ARTS DE MONTRÉAL (MUSEUM OF FINE ARTS OF MONTREAL)

The main neoclassical structure of Canada's oldest fine arts museum (1860) boasts an airy, glass-walled atrium and space for more than 3,000 works. The permanent collection of this first-rate institution includes Western European art from the medieval period to the present, as well as relics of ancient civilizations in Europe, Egypt, China, Japan, and pre-Columbian

America. Works by Canadian, Inuit, and Native American artists are noteworthy, as is the collection of period furnishings. The building also hosts major exhibitions, such as the recent *Lost Paradise: Symbolist Europe,* which featured works by Munch, Rodin, Moreau, and others. Closed Mondays. Admission charge. 1379 and 1380 Rue Sherbrooke O. (phone: 285-1600).

RUES MACKAY TO DE LA MONTAGNE A concentration of restaurants, pubs, discos, trendy fashion boutiques, and art galleries ensconced in brownstone and gray-stone Victorian houses is centered in this nine-square-block downtown area. Whether for browsing, shopping, or barhopping, there is plenty of action here, and in good weather much of it takes place out on the street. Rues Mackay, Bishop, Crescent, and de la Montagne, between Rue Sherbrooke and Blvd. René-Lévesque.

UNIVERSITÉ MCGILL (MCGILL UNIVERSITY) Chartered in 1821, this prestigious school was built with funds from the estate of Scottish immigrant James McGill, who amassed a fortune as a fur trader and served in Lower Canada's Parliament. The campus is on the site of the 16th-century native village of Hochelaga, stumbled on by Cartier in 1535. A stroll around the campus and down fashionable Rue Sherbrooke reveals a number of interesting façades, including some fine old mansions that now belong to the university. Guided tours of the grounds are available; visitors also can arrange to be students for a day and sit in on classes during October, November, February, and March. Rue Sherbrooke, between Rue University and Rue McTavish (phone: 398-6555).

CATHÉDRALE MARIE-REINE-DU-MONDE (CATHEDRAL OF MARY, QUEEN OF THE WORLD) A scaled-down replica of Rome's *St. Peter's Basilica,* complete with a row of statues depicting the patron saints of the Archdiocese of Montreal on the roof and a reproduction of Bernini's altar columns, this cathedral was under construction from 1870 to 1894. Its vast, dark interior space (architects of the time believed that the darker the church, the brighter the candles would glow and, thus, the brighter the stained glass would appear) is a symbol of the era when the Catholic church was a powerful influence on the city and the province. The domed mass is now dwarfed by the towers of modern Montreal, but it remains a monument to Quebec's Catholic heritage. 1085 Rue Cathédrale at the corner of Blvd. René-Lévesque O. (phone: 866-1661).

VOIE PIÉTONNIÈRE PRINCE-ARTHUR (PRINCE ARTHUR PEDESTRIAN MALL) Once a quiet residential street and then part of *McGill*'s low-cost student ghetto from the 1950s to the early 1970s, today the stretch of Rue Prince-Arthur from Boulevard St-Laurent to Carré (Square) St-Louis is an attractive outdoor mall. Enhanced by a fountain, overflowing tubs of flowers, and streetlamps, it is home to an array of moderately priced restaurants running the gamut of ethnicities from Greek and Italian to Vietnamese, Polish, and Québécois. In summer, people watchers take advantage of the many outdoor cafés lining this lovely street. Most of the restaurants are BYOW (bring your own wine).

Summer is also the season for outdoor performances by local musicians, magicians, and acrobats.

RUE ST-DENIS Known as Montreal's Latin Quarter, this area is the site of the *Université du Québec à Montréal (UQAM)* campus. The façade of historic *Eglise St-Jacques* has been integrated into the institution's main building. Rue St-Denis also is lined with popular restaurants, clothing stores, and cafés. Across Rue Sherbrooke away from the river, the street is a fashion hub, where many Quebec designers have showrooms and boutiques.

VILLE SOUTERRAINE (UNDERGROUND MONTREAL)

This subterranean network of downtown commercial-business-residential complexes is for many as vital a part of Montreal as the city above ground. *Place Ville-Marie,* Montreal's first underground complex, opened in 1962; its successful reception prompted a gradual expansion, and today the network extends some 18 miles. All the centers are linked by the *Métro* system. Plans are in the works for further subterranean development in coming years.

It's possible to spend days in Montreal without ever going outside. Many Montrealers do just that—especially when winter dumps a hundred inches of snow on the city. The complex networks offer access to the city's main exhibition halls and performing arts center, about 1,700 shops, 200 restaurants, eight major hotels, the two main rail stations and two bus terminals, numerous banks and apartment buildings, more than 30 cinemas and theaters, some 10,000 indoor parking spaces, and even a municipal library branch at the *McGill Métro* station. Guided tours of the Ville Souterraine can be arranged through *Gray Line* (phone: 934-1222); *Guidatour* (phone: 844-4021); *Hertz Tourist Guide* (phone: 739-7454); *Les Tours Diamant* (phone: 744-3009); and *Visites de Montréal* (phone: 933-6674).

PLACE VILLE-MARIE Conceived by architect I. M. Pei and developer William Zeckendorf during the 1950s, the city's first underground complex now houses over 110 boutiques as well as an elegant marble-and-brass food court offering a wide range of menus from pizza to Vietnamese cuisine. Promenades link *Place Ville-Marie* with the *Centre Eaton, Place Bonaventure,* three hotels, and *l'Amphithéatre Bell,* an indoor ice skating rink. Indoor parking is available. Enter *Place Ville-Marie* through the *Bonaventure* or *McGill* Métro stations. Street level entrances on Blvd. René-Lévesque O., Rue Cathcart at the foot of Av. McGill College, and Rues Mansfield and University.

PLACE BONAVENTURE Linked to *Place Ville-Marie* by walkways leading through the *Gare Centrale* (Central Station), this six-acre arcade houses about a hundred shops and restaurants. Above the shopping concourse are the *Bonaventure Hilton Montreal* hotel (see *Checking In*) and an exhibition hall that hosts numerous shows, such as Canada's largest antiques show. Enter *Place Bonaventure* through the *Bonaventure Hilton Montreal* (Rues de la

Gauchetière and Mansfield) or through the *Château Champlain* (1050 Rue de la Gauchetière O.; see *Checking In*).

PLACE MONTREAL TRUST This five-level underground atrium houses 120 specialty stores, boutiques, and restaurants in a sunny, California-style setting of cool pastels, waterfalls, reflecting pools, and greenery. Sunlight filters through a rooftop skylight into the second basement level. The *place* has underground links with its neighbors above and below Rue Ste-Catherine. Following the *Métro* corridors, shoppers can walk from here to the *Centre Eaton, Les Promenades de la Cathédrale,* and *La Baie* (The Bay). Enter via the *McGill Métro* station or 1500 Av. McGill College.

CENTRE EATON Downtown's largest shopping center has five tiers of boutique-lined galleries under its glass roof. Linked to *Eaton's* department store, the center houses more than 200 stores and includes a food court on the lower level. There's a cinema complex with six movie theaters on the top floor. Enter via the *McGill Métro* station or 705 Rue Ste-Catherine O.

LES PROMENADES DE LA CATHÉDRALE Two levels of underground shopping are hidden away beneath *Cathédrale Christ Church,* with more than a hundred shops linked to *La Baie, Centre Eaton,* and the *Métro.* Enter via the *McGill Métro* station or 625 Rue Ste-Catherine O.

LES COURS MONT-ROYAL Formerly a hotel, this complex now houses luxury condominiums, offices, and four levels of elegant commercial space including 60 boutiques, three restaurants, a fast-food court, and a movie theater. Enter via the *Peel Métro* station; street-level entrances at 1455 Rue Peel and 1550 Rue Metcalfe.

PLACE VICTORIA Facing Square Victoria, this massive office tower is home to the *Bourse de Montréal* (Montreal Stock Exchange) and a small underground shopping mall. The complex is connected to the *Radisson-Gouverneurs* hotel and the *Place Victoria Métro* station. The *Bourse* trading floor is open to visitors. Guided tours can be arranged; no admission charge (phone: 871-2424).

PLACE ALEXIS-NIHON A short subway ride from the city center, this plaza offers more weatherproof shopping. Some 80,000 people pass through the complex daily en route to the office building, apartment tower, three-floor shopping mall, and covered parking levels. Take the *Métro* to *Atwater;* 1500 Av. Atwater.

COMPLEXE WESTMOUNT SQUARE High-fashion shops share this posh underground plaza with *Le Marché Westmount Square,* an extensive food mart featuring everything from imported delicacies to fast-food snacks. Linked by underground passage to *Place Alexis-Nihon,* the upscale marketplace is situated directly beneath three gleaming office towers designed by Mies van der Rohe. Take the *Métro* to *Atwater.* West of Av. Atwater on Rue Ste-Catherine O.

PLACE DES ARTS The heart of Montreal's cultural life is its lavish performing arts center, which contains a stunning and acoustically superb concert hall and theater accommodating over 3,000 people. Home of the *Orchestre Symphonique de Montréal, Les Grands Ballets Canadiens,* and the *Opéra de Montréal,* it is also the setting for chamber music concerts, ballet recitals, jazz performances, and plays. Approximately every other Sunday morning, the lobby of the center hosts "Sons et Brioches," informal concerts served up with a continental breakfast. (Very reasonably priced tickets are available at *Place des Arts* in advance or on the day of the performance.) 175 Rue Ste-Catherine O.; take the *Métro* to the *Place des Arts* stop (phone: 842-2112).

COMPLEXE DESJARDINS This impressive complex contains meeting halls, offices, and an enclosed shopping center with some one hundred boutiques and specialty stores, a cinema complex with four movie theaters, a miniature golf course, a hotel, and 20 restaurants. Sculptures, fountains, plants, and a regular series of entertainment events and special exhibits make it a popular gathering place. It's linked by underground walkways to *Place des Arts,* the *Palais des Congrès* (Convention Center), and the *Musée d'Art Contemporain de Montréal* (Montreal Museum of Contemporary Art).

VIEUX MONTRÉAL (OLD MONTREAL)

Private enterprise and government funds are contributing to the restoration of important buildings in Vieux Montréal, the city's historic waterfront section. The area can be toured by car or calèche, but the best way to get a feel for it is by strolling through the narrow streets. Get a free copy of *A Walking Tour of Vieux Montréal* from *INFOTOURISTE* (see *Tourist Information,* below).

BASILIQUE NOTRE-DAME Completed in 1829, this twin-towered Gothic Revival church was designed by New York architect James O'Donnell, whose grave lies in the crypt. It is notable for its lavishly decorated interior, which includes a monumental altar, exquisite woodcarvings and paintings, exceptional stained glass windows, and an organ with nearly 7,000 pipes. There is also a museum in the sacristy. Adjacent to the main church is the restored *Chapelle du Sacré-Coeur* (Sacred Heart Chapel), a place of calm in the crush of Vieux Montréal. After leaving the basilica, step into the Place d'Armes and glance up at the twin spires for a true perspective of the church's scale. Museum closed weekdays. Admission charge to the museum. Take the *Métro* to *Place-d'Armes*. 116 Rue Notre-Dame O. (phone: 849-1070).

VIEUX SÉMINAIRE ST-SULPICE (OLD ST. SULPICE SEMINARY) Sightseers aren't welcome inside the oldest building in Montreal (1683) because it's still a private home for Sulpician priests, but they can admire its weathered graystone façade through the wrought-iron gateway to the front courtyard. Photographers and students of historic architecture admire the symmetrical windows and dormers and the campanile over the main entrance, which, according to local historians, is the oldest outdoor clock in North America (1701). 130 Rue Notre-Dame O.

PLACE JACQUES-CARTIER This cobblestone square, the largest in Vieux Montréal, was once the main marketplace. Dominating the square is a statue of Horatio Nelson atop a 35-foot column (erected in 1809). In warm weather, the base of the column is the venue for a flower market that offers blossoms of every conceivable variety; in autumn, apples and pumpkins are sold. Lining both sides of the square are alfresco cafés, perfect for relaxing and drinking in the early-19th-century flavor. Between Rues St-Paul and Notre-Dame.

VIEUX-PORT (OLD PORT) The award-winning redevelopment of the Vieux-Port transformed it into a summertime entertainment center. Whether they are strolling, biking, or in-line skating, people of all ages enjoy this riverfront park. The Vieux-Port's rich history is highlighted along the promenade, with historical facts and points of interest marked along the way. Pleasure craft dock at the marina *Bassin Jacques Cartier.* The port's restored piers are also departure points for harbor cruises and Rapides de Lachine jet-boat excursions (see *Getting Around*). There are interactive exhibitions in summertime at *Expotec* (phone: 496-4629) and *Image du Futur* (phone: 849-1612), both on Quai King-Edward (Rue de la Commune and Blvd. St-Laurent); both are open daily mid-May to mid-September. The *Cinéma IMAX* has a giant seven-story-high screen (phone: 496-IMAX); it's open daily. Admission to the *Cinéma IMAX* includes *Expotec.* Separate admission to *Image du Futur.* An immense flea market full of secondhand bargains also takes place on Quai King-Edward Wednesdays through Sundays from May to early September, except in July and August, when it's also open on Tuesdays. A favorite summer stop is the garden terrace at *Gibby's* (see *Eating Out*). The Vieux-Port also offers an abundance of wintertime activities, including sleigh rides and ice skating (skate rentals are available). Parking is available. Take the *Métro* to *Place-d'Armes* or *Champ-de-Mars.* For information and schedules of events, call 496-PORT.

CHÂTEAU RAMEZAY The manor, built in 1705, was the official residence of Claude de Ramezay, 11th Governor of Montreal, who occupied this modest version of a Norman château during his 20 years in office. It later housed the offices of the West India Company and, still later, was the residence of English governors. During the American occupation (1775–76), the Continental Army, under Generals Richard Montgomery and Benedict Arnold, established its headquarters here. A museum since 1895, the château houses a collection of artifacts representing the history of Montreal during the 18th and 19th centuries. The big cellar kitchen, with its cavernous fireplace and the latest innovations in 18th-century appliances, is particularly noteworthy. Open daily May through August; closed Mondays September through April. Admission charge. 280 Rue Notre-Dame E. (phone: 861-3708).

CHAPELLE NOTRE-DAME-DE-BON-SECOURS One of the city's oldest churches, it is also called the *Eglise des Matelots* (Sailors' Church) because of the large number of sailors who worshiped here. Built originally in 1657, it was destroyed by fire and twice rebuilt and modified. The on-site museum pays homage to Marguerite Bourgeoys, the first Catholic saint to live and die in Canada. Museum closed Mondays. Admission charge to the museum. 400 Rue St-Paul E. (phone: 845-9991).

CENTRE D'HISTOIRE (HISTORY CENTER) Place d'Youville—one of Montreal's first civic centers—is now surrounded by monuments and historic sites. One interesting landmark is the restored *Caserne de Pompiers* (Fire Station 1), which houses the *Centre d'Histoire.* The center re-creates daily life in Montreal from 1642 to the present through audiovisual presentations and display rooms that portray scenes from the city's past—for example, a replica of a 19th-century shoe factory. Periodic expositions showcase different aspects of Montreal's history. Open daily May 11 through late September; closed Mondays late September through May 10. Admission charge. 335 Place d'Youville, corner of Rue St. Pierre (phone: 872-3207).

ELSEWHERE IN MONTREAL

PARC ANGRIGNON A 262-acre recreational oasis, this park is at its busiest from mid-December to late March, when it is the city's winter wonderland, a place for all kinds of outdoor fun, from cross-country skiing, snowshoeing, and skating on the decorated rink to thrilling slides down the icy toboggan run. Get off at the *Angrignon Métro* station. 3400 Blvd. des Trinitaires.

PARC OLYMPIQUE (OLYMPIC PARK) Having hosted the *1976 Summer Olympic Games,* Montreal is now using these spectacular facilities for all types of events and exhibits. Both the *Expos* and rock musicians play at the *Stade Olympique* (Olympic Stadium), known locally as the "Big O." Atop the unique inclined tower overlooking the *Stade,* a restaurant and observation deck offer panoramic views of the city (see *Seeing the City,* above). Meets, classes, and public swimming periods are held regularly in the 50-meter pool and 50-foot diving pool. Half-hour guided tours are conducted in English daily, except holidays. Admission charge. Take the *Métro* to *Viau.* 4141 Av. Pierre-de-Coubertin (phone: 252-TOUR).

BIODÔME Housed in the *Parc Olympique*'s former *Vélodrome* are four natural ecosystems, representing South, Central, and North America. More than 5,000 animals (not counting the invertebrates) inhabit such settings as a tropical rain forest, a beaver lake, a salt marsh, and an Arctic snowbank. In the St. Lawrence Marine Ecosystem, fish and other ocean dwellers patrol a salty artificial sea, while scores of starfish, anemones, crabs, and sea urchins make their home in a tidal pool near the salt marsh habitat of black ducks and shorebirds. The Polar Ecosystem represents the two icy worlds of the Arctic and Antarctic, which can be viewed from a glass-enclosed observation site. Open daily. Admission charge. Take the *Métro* to *Viau.* 4777 Av. Pierre-de-Coubertin (phone: 868-3000).

JARDIN BOTANIQUE (BOTANICAL GARDEN) Across from the *Parc Olympique* and the *Biodôme,* this noted horticultural showplace was founded by naturalist Brother Marie Victorin. Actually a complex of some 30 specialized gardens and 10 greenhouses, the garden displays more than 26,000 different species of plants, grouped according to use and habitat. The garden is said to have North America's most complete collection of bonsai trees. With the highly acclaimed *Jardin Japonais* (Japanese Garden), the *Insectarium*—a giant house with thousands of live insects on display—and the addition of the traditional *Jardin de Chine* (Chinese Garden), Montreal's botanical garden is now considered one of the most important in the world. The visitors' reception center offers video presentations and bilingual guides. Open daily. Admission charge. Take the *Métro* to *Viau* or *Pie-IX.* 4101 Rue Sherbrooke E. (phone: 872-1400).

MONT-ROYAL Because it dominates the city scene, visitors can't avoid seeing Mont-Royal from one angle or another (the mountain has two peaks: Mont-Royal and Westmount). Not only is it a fine vantage point from which to view the St. Lawrence River, Montreal, and the mountains beyond; it's also a good place to observe Montrealers at their leisure. The park is bounded by Av. du Parc on the east and, continuing counterclockwise, Blvd. Mont-Royal, Voie Camillien-Houde, Chemin Remembrance, Chemin de la Côte-des-Neiges, and Av. des Pins.

ORATOIRE ST-JOSEPH (ST. JOSEPH'S ORATORY) Founded as a tiny chapel in 1904 by Brother André, a member of the Holy Cross Order of Roman Catholic brothers, this oratory had grown into a 3,000-seat basilica by 1922. Barely literate and in poor health, Brother André purportedly had healing powers, and he had a vast following among the faithful of Quebec (he is entombed here). André is said to have cured hundreds of people, invoking the aid of St. Joseph. The church commands the hillside on the northwest slopes of Mont-Royal, with 99 steps cut into the steep slope below the main entrance. At one time the most humble of suppliants made the ascent on their knees; today, some two million people visit the site annually. At 856 feet above sea level, the oratory observatory is the highest point on the Montreal skyline, with a view that stretches as far west as Lake St-Louis and over the northwest section of the city. Its carillon of bells, which was designed for the *Eiffel Tower,* was judged unsuitable for the famous Parisian landmark and came to the oratory on loan in 1955; it was later anonymously purchased and donated as a permanent fixture. Carillon concerts are held Wednesdays through Fridays at noon and 3 PM; Saturdays and Sundays at noon and 2:30 PM. Organ recitals are given Wednesday evenings in the summer, and *Les Petits Chanteurs du Mont-Royal* children's choir performs during Sunday morning mass. The on-site museum houses religious art and a few relics of the founder, including one of his cassocks; during the *Christmas* season, exhibitions feature 250 crèches from more than 90 countries. The museum is open daily; donations accepted. 3800 Chemin Queen-Mary (phone: 733-8211).

WESTMOUNT The heights of this mountainside "city within a city" were traditionally the enclave of Montreal's well-heeled English-speaking population. Today, the residents of Upper Westmount must still be wealthy to maintain their stately homes, but the "English-only" requisite has eased somewhat as the city's cultures have blended. This is the section of town for mansion staring. *West Mount,* the palatial stone house that gave the area its name and was owned by *Beaver Steamship Line*'s William Murray, has been torn down, but a number of other impressive 19th- and early-20th-century homes (and a few even earlier landmarks) fill the gap. The sturdy of limb can take the *Métro* to *Atwater* station, which is linked to the elegant *Complexe Westmount Square* (see above), and start a walking tour of the area from there. But because of Westmount's hills, the less hearty may prefer to see it by car. The most interesting sights fall between Rues Sherbrooke and Edgehill, from Avenues Greene to Victoria.

OUTREMONT The traditional French-speaking counterpart to English-speaking Westmount is the *"ville"* of Outremont, hidden on the northeast slope of Mont-Royal. Incorporated in 1875, the village principally comprised large tracts of farmland owned and cultivated by "gentleman farmers" from Scotland and England. While the farms have long since been divided into smaller building lots, some of the original farmhouses still exist. Parts of Outremont's terrain are easily as demanding as Westmount's, so it is best explored by car. The section's main thoroughfare, Chemin de la Côte Ste-Catherine, and the parallel Avenue Maplewood display the best of Outremont's landmark mansions, and Avenue Laurier is lined with smart boutiques and cafés. Try *Café Laurier* (394 Av. Laurier O.; phone: 273-2484) for a relaxing coffee break. Bounded north and south by Av. Glendale and Blvd. Mont-Royal; east and west by Avs. Hutchison and Canterbury.

UNIVERSITÉ DE MONTRÉAL Opened in 1878 as a branch of Quebec City's *Université Laval,* the *U of M* has developed into the largest French-language university outside of Paris, with over 50,000 students and more than 200 undergraduate programs. The Mont-Royal campus, which opened in 1943, now accommodates 13 faculties, more than 100 research units, and affiliated schools of engineering and commerce, as well as a huge sports complex. 2900 Blvd. Edouard-Montpetit (phone: 343-6111).

PLANÉTARIUM DOW This giant theater of the stars, one of Canada's first planetariums, was a gift to the city from the Dow Brewery in the mid-1960s. Its programs change throughout the year and are narrated in French and English on alternate hours (call for times). Closed Mondays. Admission charge. 1000 Rue St-Jacques O. (phone: 872-4530).

MAISON DE RADIO-CANADA Headquarters of French radio and television Canadian Broadcasting Company (CBC) programming, this center sprawls over 25 acres in downtown Montreal. The 23-story hexagonal building that houses the studios also has galleries and an extensive collection of paintings, sculptures, and graphics done mostly by artists of Quebec and the Atlantic provinces. Visitors are allowed at only a limited number of shows; call ahead for information. Guided tours of the center, including the television studio and *CBC Museum,* are also available. No admission charge. 1400 Blvd. René-Lévesque E. (phone: 597-7787).

ST. LAWRENCE SEAWAY Montreal is the starting point of this modern engineering miracle, which makes it possible for ocean-bound ships to travel all the way through from the Great Lakes. Often missed by the average visitor, the observatory at the *Ecluse de St-Lambert* (St. Lambert Lock) offers a close look at the intricate locking procedures as well as a fine view of Montreal's skyline across the river. A scenic bicycle path runs along the lock. Open daily; closed from mid-November to mid-April. No admission charge. Take the Pont Victoria (Victoria Bridge) from downtown across to *Ecluse de St-Lambert* on Route 132, on the south shore of the river (phone: 672-4110).

ST. LAWRENCE RIVER ISLANDS/PARC DES ILES

The largest of Montreal's St. Lawrence River satellite islands is Ile Ste-Hélène, which Samuel de Champlain named after his wife, Hélène Boulé. It was once the site of a military installation and, somewhat more recently, part of the extensive grounds of *EXPO '67,* which also included its neighboring island, Ile Notre-Dame. These islands now make up an oasis of greenery called *Parc des Iles.* Access is via the Autoroute Bonaventure or Pont Jacques-Cartier by car or the *Métro* system (*Ile Ste-Hélène* stop).

ILE NOTRE-DAME Home of Montreal's only downtown beach, this popular park offers something for everyone. In summer beautiful gardens can be explored on foot, while pedal boats are an ideal way to navigate the island's lagoon. In winter the *Bassin Olympique* (Olympic Rowing Basin) becomes a skating rink, and snowshoeing, cross-country skiing, and horse-drawn sleigh rides can be enjoyed. Other sites here include the *Grand Prix Molson* racetrack, *Circuit Gilles Villeneuve,* and the *Casino de Montréal* (see *Nightclubs and Nightlife*).

ILE STE-HÉLÈNE *La Ronde,* a rollicking amusement park, covers 135 acres of this island. In addition to rides, the park has spirited restaurants and pubs that Montrealers frequent on warm summer evenings—especially from the end of May to the end of July, when *La Ronde* is the launching pad for an international fireworks competition. *La Ronde* is open daily until 9 PM; closed September through May. There's an admission charge (phone: 872-6222).

The *Biosphère,* built as the American pavilion for *EXPO '67,* is now a unique museum and research center with multimedia displays on the subject of water and water conservation. Created by architect Buckminster

Fuller, the *Biosphère* is easily recognizable by its impressive geodesic dome. The largest spherical structure in the world, the dome is a landmark in contemporary architecture. In 1976 a fire destroyed the structure's skin-like outer layer, leaving only the tubular frame intact. Abandoned for more than 15 years, the *Biosphère* was recently resurrected as part of an agreement between the federal and municipal governments to develop the *Parc des Iles.* The museum is open daily; admission charge (phone: 283-5000).

The *Musée David M. Stewart* in Ile Ste-Hélène's *Fort* (built in the early 1820s by order of the Duke of Wellington) houses artifacts that outline Canada's history, such as antique firearms, old maps, period kitchen utensils, and navigational and scientific instruments. In the summer, two colorfully uniformed resident companies of colonial troops—the Compagnie Franche de la Marine (French) and the 78th Fraser Highlanders (Scottish)—perform authentic 18th-century drills and marches. The museum is closed Tuesdays; admission charge (phone: 861-6701).

The *Fort*'s *Festin du Gouverneur* restaurant (phone: 879-1141; reservations necessary) invites diners to enjoy a 17th-century banquet served by costumed performers who sing, dance, and draw patrons into the act. *Hélène-de-Champlain* (phone: 395-2424) is a restaurant in an attractive Norman-style building overlooking the river and rose gardens.

Sources and Resources

TOURIST INFORMATION

INFOTOURISTE (1001 Sq. Dorchester at Rue Peel; phone: 873-2015; 800-363-7777) offers a full range of travel services, including hotel reservations, currency exchange, and car rentals. Information, maps, and brochures about Montreal also are available at the tourist bureau kiosk in Vieux Montréal (Place Jacques-Cartier at Rue Notre-Dame; no phone). Both offices are open daily.

LOCAL COVERAGE There is one daily English-language newspaper, the *Montreal Gazette.* Two free weekly English newspapers, *Mirror* and *Hour,* which are available in restaurants, cafés, and bars, give a complete listing of entertainment and cultural activities. The monthly *Scope* magazine, available at newsstands, also has entertainment and restaurant listings.

TELEPHONE The area code for Montreal is 514.

SALES TAX Quebec has a provincial sales tax (QST) of 6.5%, in addition to the 7% federal Goods and Services Tax (GST). In many cases, visitors can receive refunds of both the provincial and federal taxes. For details on Quebec tax rebates, call *Revenue Quebec* (phone: 873-4692); for more information on obtaining rebates on the federal tax, see GETTING READY TO GO.

CLIMATE Montreal winters are long, cold, and snowy, but the rest of the year the city enjoys a fairly temperate climate. Summer temperatures average a pleasant 55 to 80F—although hotter weather is not unknown. Spring also is mild, with temperatures between 50 and 70F; fall temperatures average between 40 and 55F. Early spring and fall are the rainiest times of year.

GETTING AROUND

AIRPORT *Dorval International Airport* is about 12 miles (19 km) west of the city, and *Mirabel International Airport* is about 34 miles (54 km) to the northwest. The most convenient way to travel between the airports and downtown is to take the inexpensive shuttle bus *Autocar Connoisseur* (phone: 934-1222); cabs are more expensive.

CAR RENTAL All major international firms are represented. Most have offices downtown and at both airports.

HARBOR CRUISES A scenic and restful way to see the entire island is from the St. Lawrence. *Croisières du Port de Montréal* (phone: 842-3871) offers a variety of voyages up and down the river, lasting from two to four hours, from May to mid-October. At least five excursions depart daily from the foot of Rue Berri. Tickets are available at major hotels and kiosks on the Quai de l'Horloge; phone ahead for reservations in peak season. In addition, *Amphi Tour* (phone: 386-1298) travels on the streets of the port, then takes to the water; the intriguing "amphi-bus" departs daily from Rue de la Commune at the corner of Boulevard St-Laurent. Tours run from noon to 10 PM; until midnight in summertime. *Les Tours St-Louis* (300 Chemin du Canal, Lachine; phone: 365-4440) schedules several two-hour cruises daily around Lac St-Louis on the *St-Louis IV,* which boards 180 passengers per voyage. Tours run from May 15 to October 15; advance reservations are advised.

HORSE-DRAWN CARRIAGE A romantic way to see the town is by calèches, which are stationed on Rues Notre-Dame and de la Commune in Vieux Montréal, at Place Jacques-Cartier, at Square Dorchester, and atop Mont-Royal. *Calèches A. Boisvert* (phone: 653-0751) operates carriages and, in winter, one-horse sleighs on Mont-Royal.

JET-BOAT TOURS Organized expeditions over the Rapides de Lachine, in large aluminum jet boats, leave from the Quai de l'Horloge at the foot of Rue Berri in Vieux Montréal. From May to late September they depart daily every other hour from 10 AM to 6 PM. Contact *Expéditions sur les Rapides de Lachine* (105 Rue de la Commune O.; phone: 284-9607).

MÉTRO AND BUS *STCUM* (phone: 288-6287), Montreal's efficient transit system, links various areas of the city via four underground lines and 176 bus lines. The same tickets—which cost CN$1.75 (about $1.28 US at press time)—are used on the *Métro* and the buses. *Métro* trains are clean and quiet, whizzing underground on rubber-tired wheels. The price of the ride admits visitors to a veritable underground art gallery of murals, sculptures, stained glass windows, enameled steel frescoes, and ceramics built into the 65 stations of the system. The *Carte Touristique,* one- and three-day passes offering unlimited access to the *Métro* and buses, can be purchased at various hotels and *INFOTOURISTE* (see *Tourist Information,* above). *STCUM* issues a helpful route map, available free at hotel desks, at the *STCUM* service desk at *Berri/UQAM Métro* station, and at *STCUM*'s head office (*Place Bonaventure,* 800 Rue de la Gauchetière O.).

TAXI Cabs may be hailed on the street; taxi stands are located on the corners of main intersections, near the railway stations, at the airports, and at hotels.

TOURS Some taxicab drivers are licensed tour guides; *Taxi LaSalle* (phone: 277-2552) is one outfit that offers tours. Sightseeing tours leaving from *INFOTOURISTE* at Square Dorchester are provided by *Autocar Connoisseur Gray Line* (Rue du Sq.-Dorchester; phone: 934-1222) and *Murray Hill* (Rue du Sq.-Dorchester; phone: 871-4733). Other private tour companies include *Guidatour* (phone: 844-4021); *Hertz Tourist Guides* (phone: 739-7454); *Step-on-Guides* (phone: 935-5131); and *Visites de Montréal* (phone: 933-6674). For more information on guided tours, call *INFOTOURISTE* (see *Tourist Information,* above). *A Walking Tour of Vieux Montréal,* available free from *INFOTOURISTE,* is a boon for those who choose to go it alone.

SPECIAL EVENTS

Ile Ste-Hélène and Ile Notre-Dame host the *Fêtes des Neiges,* a 10-day pre-Lenten snow carnival that features costume balls on ice, skating races, sledding, and other outdoor activities, plus plentiful refreshments. Imaginative ice sculptures are part of the fun.

With over 40,000 cyclists competing, early June's *Tour de l'Ile de Montreal* (phone: 521-8356) is fast becoming one of the most popular bicycle races in North America. The route encircles the island of Montreal via city streets. The *Grand Prix Molson du Canada* (phone: 392-0000) is a Formula One automobile racing event held in mid-June at the 4.41-km *Gilles Villeneuve* track on Ile Notre-Dame. Also in mid-June, the *Festival International du Nouveau Cinéma et de la Vidéo de Montréal* (Montreal Festival of New Cinema and Video; phone: 834-4725) holds indoor and outdoor screenings of avant-garde films, while *Le Mondial de la Bière* (phone: 722-9640), a lively beer-tasting festival, serves up more than 250 brands of beer from over 25 countries at the Vieux-Port.

The 10-day *Festival International de Jazz de Montréal* (phone 871-1881) draws music greats—and more than one million of their fans—every year in late June. With the streets surrounding *Place des Arts* (see *Special Places*) blocked to traffic, music lovers can roam day and night from one outdoor stage to another. Major indoor concerts are held at *Place des Arts* and the *Spectrum* (318 Rue Ste-Catherine O.). The *Festival Juste pour Rire* (Just for Laughs Festival; phone: 845-3155) is a 10-day event held in late July that attracts comedians from all over the world who match wits in French and English. Outdoor events take place at the Vieux-Port. Indoor venues include *Place des Arts* (see *Special Places*) and *Club Soda* (5240 Av. du Parc).

At *Les Fêtes Gourmandes* (Gourmet Festival; phone: 861-8241), which takes place in mid-August, food lovers converge on Ile Notre-Dame to sample gastronomic delights from around the world. The *Festival des Films du Monde* (World Film Festival; phone: 848-3883) brings an array of the latest international movies and their stars to Montreal at the end of August. Renowned choreographers dazzle audiences with their latest works at the *Festival International de Nouvelle Danse* (phone: 287-1423), held at the beginning of October.

MUSEUMS

In addition to those mentioned in *Special Places,* other notable Montreal museums include the following:

CENTRE CANADIEN D'ARCHITECTURE (CANADIAN CENTRE FOR ARCHITECTURE) The world's first nonprofit institution devoted solely to the study of architecture is the brainchild of Canadian-born architect Phyllis Lambert. Available here are study and research facilities, a lecture hall, and the founder's exhaustive collection of manuscripts, folios, artwork, and archives that include 47,000 prints and drawings, 45,000 photographs, and 35,000 books spanning the history of architecture from the Renaissance to the 20th century. The center's bookstore offers a good selection of architectural books. The sculpture garden across Boulevard René-Lévesque Ouest from the museum is an enchanting spot to rest during a visit here. Closed Mondays June through September; closed Mondays and Tuesdays October through May. Admission charge except on Thursdays from 6 PM to 8 PM. 1920 Rue Baile (phone: 939-7026).

CENTRE SAIDYE BRONFMAN Contemporary works by national and international artists. Closed Saturdays. No admission charge. 5170 Chemin de la Côte Ste-Catherine (phone: 739-2301).

MAISON DE SIR GEORGE-ETIENNE-CARTIER Some of the rooms in this building—the Montreal home of one of Canada's founding fathers—have been restored to their former Victorian glory; others are reserved for various exhibitions. Open daily mid-May to *Labour Day;* closed Mondays and Tuesdays the rest of the year. Admission charge. *Métro* stop *Champ-de-Mars.* 458 Rue Notre-Dame E. (phone: 283-2282).

MUSÉE D'ART CONTEMPORAIN DE MONTRÉAL (MONTREAL CONTEMPORARY ART MUSEUM) The museum features art since 1939 by Québécois and other Canadian and international artists. Included are pieces by Quebec-based artists Jean-Paul Riopelle, Paul-Emile Borduas, David Moore, and Alfred Pellan as well as national artists Barbara Steinman, Jack Bush, and Michael Snow. Guided tours for groups are available. Closed Mondays. Admission charge except on Wednesdays from 6 PM to 9 PM. 185 Rue Ste-Catherine O. (phone: 847-6226).

MUSÉE D'ART DE ST-LAURENT This arts and crafts center is housed in the old chapel that once served the *Collège St-Laurent.* Closed mornings and Mondays. No admission charge; contributions are welcome. *Métro* stop *Du Collège.* 615 Blvd. Ste-Croix, St-Laurent (phone: 747-7367).

MUSÉE DES ARTS DÉCORATIFS DE MONTRÉAL (MONTREAL MUSEUM OF DECORATIVE ARTS)–CHÂTEAU DUFRESNE Built between 1915 and 1918 by the Dufresne family, this restored early-20th-century mansion is the site of the *Liliane and David M. Stewart Collection of International Design;* temporary exhibitions of furniture, textiles, ceramics, and graphic arts also are mounted. Closed Mondays through Thursdays. Admission charge. 2929 Rue Jeanne-d'Arc (phone: 259-2575).

MUSÉE DE LA BANQUE DE MONTRÉAL (BANK OF MONTREAL MUSEUM) Early currency and bank memorabilia. Closed weekends and holidays. No admission charge. 129 Rue St-Jacques at Pl. d'Armes (phone: 877-6892).

MUSÉE DU COMMERCE DE LA FOURRURE À LACHINE (LACHINE FUR TRADE MUSEUM) A warehouse within a national historic site displays memorabilia from the area's rich fur-trading past. Open daily April through October 15; closed Mondays and Tuesdays October 16 through December 8; closed December 9 through March. Admission charge. 1255 Blvd. St-Joseph at Av. 12e, Lachine (phone: 637-7433).

MUSÉE MARC-AURÈLE-FORTIN Works and memorabilia of the Canadian landscape artist. Closed Mondays and December 24 through February 5. Admission charge. 118 Rue St-Pierre (phone: 845-6108).

MUSÉE MARGUERITE D'YOUVILLE This is the motherhouse of the Grey Nuns (Sisters of Charity of Montreal), a religious order founded by Marguerite d'Youville. Guided tours are given of the chapel and crypt where she is buried. Closed Mondays, Tuesdays, and mornings. No admission charge. 1185 Rue St-Matthew (phone: 937-9501).

MUSÉE MCCORD D'HISTOIRE CANADIENNE (MCCORD MUSEUM OF CANADIAN HISTORY) Here is one of Canada's largest collections of aboriginal art and artifacts, plus a good selection of the works of such masters as Cornelius Kreighoff and Théophile Hamel. Built in 1906 by Perry E. Nobbs, the museum is a hybrid of Baroque, Gothic, and classical architecture. Its galleries contain a treasure trove of period costumes, furniture, religious art, toys, and photographs from the *Notman Archives,* a collection which comprises some 700,000 historical images, including both original glass plate negatives and prints. Closed Mondays and holidays. Admission charge. 690 Rue Sherbrooke O. (phone: 398-7100).

MUSÉE REDPATH Located on *McGill*'s campus, this ethnology and natural history museum houses an impressive collection, including Egyptian mummies and rare fossils. Closed Saturdays and holidays; also closed Fridays during the summer. No admission charge. Take the *Métro* to *Peel* or *McGill.* 859 Rue Sherbrooke O. (phone: 398-4086).

POINTE-À-CALLIÈRE, MUSÉE D'ARCHÉOLOGIE ET D'HISTOIRE (MUSEUM OF ARCHAEOLOGY AND HISTORY) A landmark in the heart of Vieux Montréal's historic sector, it sits on the spot where the city was founded in 1642. Featured are relics collected from the archaeological exploration at Place Royale and Pointe-à-Callière, where the first settlers landed. The complex includes three historic sites: the *Edifice de l'Eperon* (Eperon Building), the *Crypte Archéologique* (Archaeological Crypt), and the *Ancienne Douane* (Old Customs House). Its restaurant, *L'Arrivage,* overlooks the Vieux-Port. Guided tours available. Closed Mondays. Admission charge. 350 Pl. Royale (phone: 872-9150).

SHOPPING

Since the US dollar is strong north of the border, there are excellent bargains to be found on a shopping spree in Montreal. Canadian import tariffs may be less heavy in some cases than those in the US, occasionally making for even better buys (as well as a usually wider selection of imported products).

The underground shopping areas (see *Special Places*) provide an enormous variety of shops—including branches of many Paris fashion houses—that satisfy most shopping needs. Montreal's department stores also have fine selections of clothing, china, crystal, and furniture. In general, shopping hours are from 9:30 or 10 AM to 6 PM Mondays through Wednesdays; until 9 PM Thursdays and Fridays; and until 5 PM Saturdays. Many stores are also open all day on Sundays.

ANTIQUES

Antiquités Phyllis Friedman Those looking for precious pine pieces usually make their first stop here, where the blanket boxes, spinning wheels, chests, and armoires are all at least 150 years old. 5012 Rue Sherbrooke O. (phone: 483-6185).

Blue Pillow Antiques A tiny shop in the *Queen Elizabeth* hotel's underground shopping mall, it might offer such treasures as a Royal Crown Derby tea set or a diamond-encrusted platinum brooch (its specialty is estate jewelry). 900 Blvd. René-Lévesque O. (phone: 871-0225).

Coach House Antiques This gallery is the place to look for a sterling silver tea service or a mahogany-framed hunting print among the fine antiques, art, and estate jewelry. 1325 Av. Greene, Westmount (phone: 937-6191).

Daniel J. Malynowsky Antiques Sterling silver and fine bone china stand out here, along with marble-topped Victorian tables, étagères, and high-backed chairs. Closed Mondays. 1642 Rue Notre-Dame O. (phone: 937-3727).

Deuxièmement A grab bag of secondhand furniture, household items, china, and toys. 1880 Rue Notre-Dame O. (phone: 933-8560).

Henrietta Antony This Westmount establishment houses four floors of fine antiques, with an accent on chandeliers. 4192 Rue Ste-Catherine O. (phone: 935-9116).

Petit Musée Probably one of the most intriguing and expensive of Montreal's antiques shops, it is really more of a fine arts gallery, with an eclectic collection of furniture, china, and objets d'art from Europe, the Middle East, and the Far East. 1494 Rue Sherbrooke O. (phone: 937-6161).

Retro-Ville On Rue Notre-Dame Ouest's "attic row," a 10-block stretch of antiques and secondhand shops, this store deals mainly in nostalgia—old signs, toys, magazines, sports collectibles, and the like. Closed Mondays. 2652 Rue Notre-Dame O. (phone: 939-3589).

ART

Dominion Gallery Easily recognizable by Rodin's *Bourgeois de Calais* and Henry Moore's *Upright Motif* on the plaza in front of its limestone townhouse, it is a leader in Canada's art world, displaying and selling paintings and sculptures by international and Canadian artists. Closed Mondays. 1438 Rue Sherbrooke O. (phone: 845-7471).

Galerie d'Art Vente et Location (Art Sales and Rental Gallery) A part of the *Musée des Beaux Arts,* this unique gallery rents and sells works by Canadian contemporary artists. 1390 Rue Sherbrooke O. (phone: 285-1611).

Galerie Claude Lafitte A showcase for the best of Canadian art, including the work of Jean-Paul Riopelle. 1480 Rue Sherbrooke O. (phone: 939-9898).

Galerie Jean-Pierre Valentin Canadian and European paintings. Closed Mondays. 1434 Rue Sherbrooke O. (phone: 849-3637).

Galerie Lippel One of the few sources of pre-Columbian artwork in Montreal. Closed Mondays through Wednesdays and mornings. 2157 Rue Mackay (phone: 842-6369).

Galerie Tansu Japanese and Chinese antiques, bronzes, embroidered silks, lacquer works, kimonos, obis, and ancient dolls. 1460 Rue Sherbrooke O. (phone: 845-8604).

Galerie Walter Klinkhoff This family-owned gallery is among the most respected in the city. The Klinkhoffs show primarily Canadian artists, although they have international works as well. 1200 Rue Sherbrooke O. (phone: 288-7306).

BOOKS

Bibliomania A haven for browsers, its shelves are well stocked with titles old and new, in French and English, including some rare collectors' items. Closed mornings. 4872 Av. du Parc (phone: 278-6401).

Coles There are outlets of this bookstore all over the city, selling a variety of French and English publications. The flagship store is at 1171 Rue Ste-Catherine O. (phone: 849-8825).

Double Hook A quaint Victorian house is the site of this bookshop with a cozy atmosphere and a specialty in Canadian authors. 1235 Av. Greene, Westmount (phone: 932-5093).

Paragraph A bookstore-cum-coffee shop, it attracts serious bibliophiles and students from nearby *Université McGill.* The store occasionaly hosts lectures and readings by well-known Canadian authors. 2065 Rue Mansfield (phone: 845-5811).

Russell Though it's somewhat shabby, its shelves are well stocked with out-of-print and secondhand books. A must stop for collectors. 275 Rue St-Antoine O. (phone: 866-0564).

Ulysses Travel publications on Montreal, Canada, and the world, plus globes and travel cases. Three locations: in the basement at *Ogilvy,* 1307 Rue Ste-Catherine O. (phone: 842-7711, ext. 362); 560 Av. du Président-Kennedy (phone: 843-7222); and 4176 Rue St-Denis (phone: 843-9447).

W. H. Smith Best sellers, paperbacks, and magazines are its stock-in-trade. Two downtown branches: *Place Ville-Marie* (phone: 861-1736) and *Promenades de la Cathédrale* (phone: 289-8737).

CHILDREN'S CLOTHING

Gamineries This neat little boutique on the street level of a 19th-century townhouse specializes in expensive but unusual European- and US-made fashions for chic children. 1458 Rue Sherbrooke O. (phone: 843-4614).

Jacadi Sweaters and pleated skirts, knitted suits, and smart chapeaus from France are in the affordable range in this *Centre Eaton* boutique for fashion-conscious kids. 705 Rue Ste-Catherine O. (phone: 282-1933).

Oink-Oink This Westmount store for preteens also stocks a nice selection of toys. 1361 Av. Greene (phone: 939-2634).

DEPARTMENT STORES

La Baie (The Bay) Founded in 1845 as Henry Morgan and Company, it was purchased by the Hudson's Bay Company in 1969. While it's strong on new trends, French boutique styles, and campus fashions, the store no longer sells furs. Dining spots within include a cafeteria, a dining room, and *La*

Soupière, which serves soup and sandwiches. 585 Rue Ste-Catherine O., at Sq. Phillips (phone: 281-4422).

Eaton This branch of the Canadian department store chain dates back to 1925. Its merchandise runs the gamut from appliances to works of art, and a personalized shopping service will do all the work for reluctant shoppers. The ninth-floor Art Deco restaurant is modeled after the dining room of the steamship *Ile de France.* 677 Rue Ste-Catherine O. (phone: 284-8411).

Holt Renfrew This firm traces its heritage to the 1837 furriers Henderson, Holt, and Renfrew. It is still known for its truly chic fur fashions as well as haute couture lines, a *Gucci* boutique, and stylish men's clothing. 1300 Rue Sherbrooke O. (phone: 842-5111).

Ogilvy This once tartan-trimmed testament to days gone by is now a glossy complex of boutiques and elegant counters. However, the columns and grand main-floor chandeliers have been retained, and traditional goods still can be found. The store's Scottish heritage manifests itself at noon, when shoppers hear bagpipes played by a kilted piper. Every *Christmas* since 1947, Montrealers have looked forward to *Ogilvy*'s main window display of animated Steiff toys. *Ogilvy pour Enfants,* on the fourth floor, offers a good selection of children's clothing. 1307 Rue Ste-Catherine O. (phone: 842-7711).

FASHION

Aquascutum Two branches of the British fashion house offer the best in raincoats, blazers, and other classic clothing. *Ogilvy,* 1307 Rue Ste-Catherine O.: second floor for women (phone: 843-7836), main floor for men (phone: 843-8428); and 1 *Place Ville-Marie* for men and women (phone: 875-7010).

Brisson & Brisson Catering to the well-dressed Montreal male, it carries elegant European-style suits, vests, and designer silk ties. 1472 Rue Sherbrooke O. (phone: 937-7456).

Chakok Youthful styles incorporating riots of color distinguish the designs in this French import outlet in the *Cacharel* boutique. *Ogilvy,* 1307 Rue Ste-Catherine O. (phone: 842-7711, ext. 386).

Jaeger The *Ogilvy* branch of one of Britain's top-of-the-line fashion houses carries fine English woolens, tweeds, classic suits, coats, and dresses. 1307 Rue Ste-Catherine O. (phone: 845-5834).

Marks & Spencer The Montreal outpost of Britain's venerable fashion and food chain carries a wide selection of men's, women's, and children's clothing that's both affordable and serviceable. *Place Montreal Trust,* 1500 Av. McGill College (phone: 499-8558).

Polo Ralph Lauren A townhouse has been transformed into a showcase for fashions by the internationally popular designer. 1290 Rue Sherbrooke O. (phone: 288-3988).

Rodier Paris Knits and ensembles from the exclusive French house. At *Ogilvy,* 1307 Rue Ste-Catherine O. (phone: 284-0234).

l'Uomo Boutique Trendsetting menswear. 1452 Rue Peel (phone: 844-1008).

FURS

Alexandor's One of the finer salons dealing in Canadian-made furs. 2055 Rue Peel (phone: 288-1119).

Birger Christensen The Danish fur fashion house has its Quebec salon in *Holt Renfrew,* 1300 Rue Sherbrooke O. (phone: 842-5111).

Desjardins Fourrures This large, two-story house has served generations of customers. 325 Blvd. René-Lévesque E. (phone: 288-4151).

McComber Canadian-made fur coats for women. 440 Blvd. de Maisonneuve O. (phone: 845-1167).

Shuchat High-fashion designs in furs. 418 Blvd. de Maisonneuve O. (phone: 843-8883).

FURNITURE

Décors et Confort de France Elegant French furniture and decorative fixtures are featured here, all of them expensive. 1434 Rue Sherbrooke O. (phone: 281-9281).

Roche-Bobois For those seeking the latest in leather sectionals, chrome-frame furniture, and glass-topped tables on arty pedestals. 1425 Blvd. René-Lévesque O. (phone: 871-9070).

HANDICRAFTS

Les Artisans du Meuble Québécois Located in Vieux Montréal, this boutique offers furniture and arts and crafts by more than 300 Quebec artists. 88 Rue St-Paul (phone: 866-1836).

Canadian Guild of Crafts, Quebec Devoted to authentic Inuit carvings, prints, and other crafts, the collection is open to viewing, while the boutique is regarded as the best place in Montreal to learn about the artists of Canada's Far North. 2025 Rue Peel (phone: 849-6091).

Centre de Céramique Bon Secours Original ceramics and sculpture by Quebec artists are displayed and sold here. Call for information on current exhibits. 444 Rue St-Gabriel, Vieux Montréal (phone: 866-6581).

Galerie le Chariot In the heart of the historic quarter, this place stocks a wide selection of signed Inuit carvings from Cape Dorset and other parts of the Canadian North. 446 Pl. Jacques-Cartier (phone: 875-4994).

Galerie Elena Lee-Verre d'Art The one-of-a-kind pieces on display in this gallery/boutique are true works of art: plates, vases, and other *objets* the artist infuses with glowing color. Closed Mondays. 1428 Rue Sherbrooke O. (phone: 844-6009).

Le Rouet Métiers d'Art Three downtown branches of this boutique feature tasteful, reasonably priced ceramics, weaving, copper and enamel jewelry, wooden toys, and carvings. 1300 Rue St-Patrick, Vieux Montréal (phone: 935-8266); 1 *Place Ville-Marie* (phone: 866-4774); and *Place Montreal Trust,* 1500 Av. McGill College (phone: 843-5253).

JEWELRY

Birks Canada's most prestigious jewelry store also has been the source of sterling silver, china, and crystal for generations. Crystal chandeliers and marble pillars set the tone. 1240 Sq. Phillips (phone: 397-2511).

Cartier This treasure chest of a boutique carries a representative selection from the famous Paris *joaillier.* 1498 Rue Sherbrooke O. (phone: 939-0000).

Kaufmann A long-established midtown company where Rolex and Piaget watches share display cases with diamond bijoux. 2195 Rue Crescent (phone: 848-0595).

Oz Bijoux Young fashionables on a budget patronize this boutique known for its original designs in chunky silver and copper. 3955 Rue St-Denis (phone: 845-9568).

LINEN

Bleu Nuit Specializing in imported bed and table linen, this boutique also carries luxurious white goose-down duvets and a selection of fine French toiletries. 3913 Rue St-Denis (phone: 843-5702).

Linen Chest The largest branch of this Canadian enterprise stocks a bountiful supply of bed and bath linen, china, crystal, gift items, and home accessories. *Les Promenades de la Cathédrale,* 625 Rue Ste-Catherine O. (phone: 282-9525).

SHOES

Bally Affordable yet stylish men's shoes and boots by *Bally of Canada. Place Montreal Trust,* 1500 Av. McGill College (phone: 499-9766).

Brown's A popular chain for high-fashion women's shoes, boots, and bags. 1 *Place Ville-Marie* (phone: 334-5512).

Pegabo For the latest in youthful footwear for women, particularly boots, this chain is a good bet. Main store at 4065 Rue St-Denis (phone: 848-0272).

Roots Canada's own health-shoe company is a big hit in this walkers' city, where both men and women like to combine style with comfort. 716 Rue Ste-Catherine O. (phone: 875-4374).

SWEETS

Lenôtre Paris For chocolates and pastries with a European flair, the Montreal branches of this French pâtisserie are worth the trip. 1050 Av. Laurier O. (phone: 270-2702); 1277 Av. Greene, Westmount (phone: 939-6000); and *Place Montreal Trust,* 1500 Av. McGill College (phone: 844-2244).

Pâtisserie Belge Fine pastries, baguettes, and extraordinary cheeses are sold here. The adjoining restaurant serves breakfast and light lunch. 3487 Av du Parc (phone: 845-1245) and 1075 Av. Laurier O. (phone: 279-5274).

Pâtisserie La Brioche Lyonnaise This distinctly Québécois pastry shop is also a restaurant where you can sip coffee and savor a cream-filled cake or two. An outdoor terrace is open in spring and summer. 1593 Rue St-Denis (phone: 842-7017).

TOBACCO

Davidoff An upmarket establishment, it stocks imported tobacco products (including Cuban cigars—it's legal to sell them here), pipes, lighters, and other smoker's accessories. 1452 Rue Sherbrooke O. (phone: 289-9118).

SPORTS

BASEBALL The *National League*'s *Expos* play at the spectacular *Stade Olympique* (Olympic Stadium) in *Parc Olympique* (see *Special Places;* phone: 253-3434).

BICYCLING Among the most popular bicycle trails in the city are the 7.8-mile (12-km) path along the Canal de Lachine (Lachine Canal), once the only way to bypass the Rapides de Lachine; the St. Lawrence Seaway path, which is 10 miles (16 km) long and begins at the *Ecluse de St-Lambert* (St-Lambert Lock) on its south side and ends in the community of Côte Ste-Catherine, at the foot of the Rapides de Lachine; the 1½-mile (2.4-km) scenic path in Vieux Montréal's ever-growing waterfront park; the well-maintained bicycle track in *Parc Maisonneuve,* near the *Parc Olympique;* and *Parc Angrignon*'s 4-mile (6.5-km) cycling path. In addition, both Ile Ste-Hélène and Ile Notre-Dame are captivating places to explore on two wheels, although neither maintains trails exclusively for cyclists. Altogether, the city of Montreal has a network of bike paths spanning more than 87 miles (140 km). For transportation to trails, *Métro* trains open the doors of their first cars to cyclists and their wheels (except during city-wide special events) weekdays between 10 AM and 3 PM and again after 7 PM, as well as weekends at all hours. For biking maps and information on commercial rentals, call *Vélo-Québec* (1251 Rue Rachel E.; phone: 521-8356). Rentals also are available at *La Cordée* (2159 Rue Ste-Catherine E.; phone: 524-1515); *Vélo Aventure,* near the

Cinéma IMAX in the Vieux-Port, open April through October (phone: 847-0666); and *Cyclo-Touriste* in the *INFOTOURISTE* center on Square Dorchester (see *Tourist Information,* above).

GOLF The nine-hole *Golf Municipal de Montréal* (phone: 872-1143) is located at Rues Sherbrooke and Viau. All told, there are more than 50 courses on the island of Montreal and in the surrounding area.

HOCKEY From October through May, the ice is hotly contested by *Les Canadiens* and their *NHL* challengers at a new *Forum,* scheduled to open later this year (*Métro* stop *Bonaventure;* 1200 Rue de la Gauchetière; phone at press time: 932-2582). Hockey dominates the skating scene, and aspiring professionals begin early. Drop into any community center/arena to see the small fry in action. Montreal boasts 170 outdoor rinks and more than 20 indoor arenas for hockey and public skating (see *Skating,* below).

HORSE RACING Harness racing takes place nightly, except Tuesdays and Thursdays, at the *Hippodrome Blue Bonnets* (7440 Blvd. Décarie; phone: 739-2741). Races begin at 7:30 PM; 1:30 PM on Sundays.

JOGGING *Parcs du Mont-Royal* and *Angrignon* have paved trails for taking a pleasant run. There is another good trail from Vieux Montréal along the Canal de Lachine.

ROLLER BLADING While in-line skaters can be seen virtually everywhere in warm weather, the Vieux-Port is a favorite spot. Rentals are available at *Vélo Aventure,* on the Vieux-Port's promenade (see *Bicycling,* above).

SKATING Throughout the week, day and night, locals throng to open-air rinks (there are close to 200) that the city government maintains—at *Parc du Mont-Royal* and *Parc Lafontaine* (both lighted at night and near downtown); at *Parc Angrignon;* at the Vieux-Port; and on Ile Notre-Dame, where there's skating on *Bassin Olympique.* Indoor skating takes place at *l'Amphithéatre Bell,* a huge public rink inside Montreal's tallest building (1000 Rue de la Gauchetière; *Métro* stop *Bonaventure;* phone: 395-0555).

SWIMMING The Olympic-size pool at the *Parc Olympique* (see *Special Places;* phone: 252-4622) is open to the public year-round; admission charge. The city operates some 50 additional indoor and outdoor pools, including the large ones on Ile Ste-Hélène (phone: 872-6093); admission charge. Two of the best indoor pools are the *Cégep du Vieux Montréal* (255 Rue Ontario E.; phone: 982-3457) and the *Centre Claude-Robillard* (1000 Rue Emile-Journault; phone: 872-6911); neither charges admission. Montreal's only downtown beach is on Ile Notre-Dame (*Métro* stop *Ile Ste-Hélène*).

TENNIS The *Omnium DuMaurier* (DuMaurier Limited Open) championships are held each summer at the *Stade de Tennis Jarry* (*Parc Jarry;* phone: 273-1515). Men's tournaments are held in odd-numbered years; women's, in even-numbered years. Montreal's more than 200 municipal courts are open to the public, for a reasonable fee. For information contact the *Service des Sports et Loisirs de la Ville de Montréal* (Montreal Department of Sports and Recreation; phone: 872-6211).

WINTER SPORTS In addition to skating and hockey, the city counts among its facilities 11 cross-country ski areas, each with several trails; eight large snowshoeing areas; seven alpine slopes; and 12 toboggan runs. For information, call the *Service des Sports et Loisirs de la Ville de Montréal* (see *Tennis,* above). The Laurentides (Laurentian Mountains), which extend from 20 to 80 miles (32 to 128 km) north of Montreal, boast some of the best ski resorts in eastern North America. For more information see *Downhill Skiing* and *Cross-Country Skiing* in DIVERSIONS.

THEATER

French-language productions are presented at more than a dozen theaters around town, including such well-known stages as the *Théâtre de Quat' Sous* (100 Av. des Pins E.; phone: 845-7277); the *Théâtre du Nouveau Monde* (84 Rue Ste-Catherine O.; phone: 866-8667); and the *Théâtre du Rideau Vert* (4664 Rue St-Denis; phone: 844-1793). The *Théâtre Centaur* (453 Rue St-François-Xavier; phone: 288-3161) schedules a regular season of mainly English-language drama and musicals. Local newspapers and in-hotel magazine guides list current attractions. The *Théâtre Biscuit* (221 Rue St-Paul O.; phone: 845-7306) is a puppet theater featuring shows on weekends. When it is not on tour (usually in summer), Montreal's unique and now world-famous *Cirque du Soleil* (phone: 522-2324) performs its delightful circus antics at the Vieux-Port.

CINEMA

Visitors to Montreal can see the latest film releases from Hollywood in English and from Paris, Algiers, and other French-language cities in French. Most movies are screened in multiple complexes like the six-theater hub on the top floor of the *Centre Eaton* (see *Special Places;* phone: 985-5730), where films are shown in both languages. Other centrally located cinema complexes are the *Cineplex Odéon Centre-Ville* (2001 Rue University; phone: 849-3456); *Loews* (954 Rue Ste-Catherine O.; phone: 861-7437); *Palace 6* (698 Rue Ste-Catherine O.; phone: 866-6991); and *Egyptian* (1455 Rue Peel; phone: 843-3112). Repertory theaters include the *Cinéma de Paris* (896 Rue Ste-Catherine O.; phone: 875-7284) and the *Cinéma Parallèle* (362 Blvd. St-Laurent; phone: 843-6001).

The *National Film Board* (*NFB;* 1564 Rue St-Denis; phone: 496-6895), Canada's main government-supported film organization, presents a regular program of made-in-Canada films, some of which have won international acclaim. Devoted chiefly to Québécois cinema, the *Cinémathèque Québécoise* (335 Blvd. de Maisonneuve E.; phone: 842-9763) presents two different films a day. Screenings are scheduled Tuesdays through Saturdays at 6:35 and 8:35 PM; Sundays at 3, 6:35, and 8:35 PM.

MUSIC

The *Orchestre Symphonique de Montréal* (phone: 842-3402) performs at the *Salle Wilfrid-Pelletier* in the *Place des Arts* (see *Special Places*), as do *Les Grand Ballets Canadiens, L'Opéra de Montréal,* and various guest companies and soloists. Programs of chamber music are held at the *Théâtre Maisonneuve* and *Théâtre Port-Royale,* also located in the *Place des Arts. McGill's Pollack Concert Hall* (555 Rue Sherbrooke O.; phone: 398-4547) regularly schedules varied musical programs. Throughout the year, rock stars perform at the *Forum* (see *Hockey*) and *Stade Olympique* (in the *Parc Olympique;* phone: 252-4670). Special productions, such as a summer *Mozart Festival* and *Christmastime* performances of Handel's *Messiah,* are presented at the *Basilique Notre-Dame* (see *Special Places*) and at other churches; call the *Orchestre Symphonique de Montréal* office (see above) for information. Up-to-date schedules of musical events are printed in the guides listed in *Local Coverage* (see above).

NIGHTCLUBS AND NIGHTLIFE

The supper-club crowd can choose from among the many hotel and restaurant dining-entertainment spots in Montreal. On weekends, the *Château Champlain*'s 36th-floor *l'Escapade* restaurant (see *Checking In*) affords a good view along with music. The *Queen Elizabeth's Beaver Club* restaurant (see *Eating Out*) features a duo that plays music for dancing on Saturday nights, and there's nightly dancing at the *Radisson-Gouverneurs*'s revolving *Tour de Ville* restaurant (see *Checking In*). The *Ritz-Carlton Kempinski*'s *Café de Paris* (see *Eating Out*) has piano music. *Solmar* (111 Rue St-Paul E.; phone: 861-4562) has Portuguese cuisine and fado music. *Vieux Munich* (1170 Rue St-Denis; phone: 288-8011) features dining and dancing to a Bavarian orchestra nightly after 6 PM, while *Sabayon* (666 Rue Sherbrooke O.; phone: 288-0373) offers a dance band and Greek music and food.

Disco- and barhopping abound around Rues Crescent, de la Montagne, Bishop, Mackay, St-Denis, and St-Laurent, and a number of side streets between Boulevard René-Lévesque and Rue Sherbrooke. Currently popular are the *Grand Prix Bar,* the *Ritz-Carlton Kempinski*'s rendezvous for mature singles on expense accounts (see *Checking In*); *Angel's* (3604 Blvd. St-Laurent; phone: 282-9944), offering two floors of late-night pub-club action; and *Club DiSalvio* (3519 Blvd. St-Laurent; phone: 845-4337), which attracts a fashion-conscious crowd. More nightlife can be found at *Thursday's* (1449 Rue Crescent; phone: 281-5320), the city's original singles bar; *Biddles,* for great jazz and ribs (2060 Rue Aylmer; phone: 842-8656); *Cheers* (1260 Rue Mackay; phone: 932-3138); *Metropolis* (59 Rue Ste-Catherine E.; phone: 288-2020), a turn-of-the-century theater with five bars and dancing on three floors; *Salsathèque* (1220 Rue Peel; phone: 875-0016), for Latin music and dancing; the *Sir Winston Churchill Pub* (1459 Rue Crescent; phone: 288-0616); and *Winnie's* (1455 Rue Crescent; phone: 288-0623). For live music, check out *Club Soda* (5240 Av. du Parc; phone: 270-7848), which hosts local and international acts.

Favorite places in Vieux Montréal include the vintage jazz joint *l'Air du Temps* (191 Rue St-Paul O.; phone: 842-2003); *Chez Brandy* (21 Rue St-Paul E.; phone: 871-9178); and *La Cage aux Sports* (395 Le Moyne; phone: 288-1115), popular with sports personalities. For gamblers, Ile Notre-Dame is home to the *Casino de Montréal* (phone: 392-2746; 800-665-2274), an international class venue that moved into the former French pavilion on the *EXPO '67* grounds in 1993. The casino has over 85 gaming tables and 1,500 slot machines; players can try their luck at blackjack, baccarat, roulette, and keno. The complex also includes five levels of dining, shopping, and entertainment. Minimum age is 18. It's open daily from 11 AM to 3 AM. (Most bars are open daily and close at 3 AM.)

Best in Town

CHECKING IN

With more than 16,000 hotel rooms in downtown Montreal, there is no difficulty finding suitable accommodations. Hotels in all categories dot the downtown area, close to shopping centers, restaurants, and the city's other attractions. Double room rates per night will run more than $200 in the very expensive category; from $140 to $200 in the expensive category; and from $75 to $140 in the moderate category, excluding taxes. Some luxury hotels offer weekend packages that are real bargains, including the small extras that make a stay more pleasant. Prices can vary significantly depending on the season; generally, as the temperature rises, so does the cost of accommodations. Unless otherwise noted, all hotels feature air conditioning, private baths, TV sets, and telephones. Among the firms that handle bed and breakfast lodgings are *Bed & Breakfast de Chez Nous* (3717 Rue Ste-Famille; phone: 845-7711); *Bed & Breakfast Downtown Network* (3458 Av. Laval; phone: 289-9749); *Bed & Breakfast Montreal* (PO Box 575, Snowdon Station, Montreal, QUE H3X 3T8; phone: 738-9410); *Relais Montréal Hospitalité* (3977 Av. Laval; phone: 287-9635); and *Welcome Bed & Breakfast* (3950 Av. Laval; phone: 844-5897).

The downtown *YMCA* (1450 Rue Stanley; phone: 849-8393) and *YWCA* (1355 Blvd. René-Lévesque O.; phone: 866-9941), as well as the youth hostel (1030 Rue Mackay; phone: 843-3317), offer inexpensive accommodations. In the summer, *Université McGill* (see *Special Places;* phone: 398-6367) and the *Université de Montréal* (see *Special Places*), *Collège MacDonald* (2111 Rue Lakeshore, Ste-Anne de Bellevue; phone: 398-7716), and the *Collège Français* (Rue Fairmont O.; phone: 495-2581) also have inexpensive rooms to let. Reservations are advised. All telephone numbers are in the 514 area code unless otherwise indicated.

We begin with our favorite haven, which falls in the "very expensive" category, followed by recommended hotels listed by price category.

GRAND HOTEL

Ritz-Carlton Kempinski The details matter at this 230-room, European-style hotel in the heart of Montreal. The secret is making luxury seem natural. Even the ducks in the hotel's flower-fringed pond are forever young—when they reach a certain age, they are retired to the country and replaced by more youthful birds. Opened more than 80 years ago by the legendary hotelier César Ritz, the Montreal establishment became an instant institution, catering to Canada's high and mighty, and a loyal international clientele. The *Café de Paris* restaurant here (see *Eating Out*) is consummately elegant. The hotel (now managed by the German Kempinski Group, which has not compromised an iota of comfort) sets the standard for amenities—not just the now-ubiquitous toiletries, but an umbrella in each room. Since the days of transatlantic cruises (the *Ritz* opened in 1912, the year the *Titanic* sailed and sank), the custom of unpacking and packing guests' steamer trunks (or suitcases) persists. Just ask, and your garment bag will be looked after, wrinkled suits pressed, and shoes shined. This is, after all, the *Ritz.* 1228 Rue Sherbrooke O. (phone: 842-4212; 800-363-0366 in Canada; 800-426-3135 in the US; fax: 842-3383).

VERY EXPENSIVE

Inter-Continental Montreal A stunning blend of the old and new, this property is a favorite in Vieux Montréal. The reception area and guestrooms are located in a turret-topped, 26-story tower. The Victorian-style *Nordheimer* building, where such stars as Sarah Bernhardt and P. T. Barnum's celebrated Tom Thumb once entertained, now houses the hotel's public rooms and three vaulted event rooms, including *La Cave,* which boasts an impressive fresco. Historians believe these vaults, which predate the building itself, were part of Montreal's early fortification system. Both the foyer, with its natural wood wainscoting and stenciled frieze, and the ballroom's vast plaster ceiling are equally grand. In *Chez Plume,* a casual bistro bar, the upper walls are painted with friezes of stylized peacocks in full plumage. All 22 suites and 335 rooms are decorated in gentle pastel shades, with spacious marble bathrooms. Guests can work out in the 10th-floor health club or do laps in the 50-foot indoor pool and then relax in the sauna, steam, and massage rooms. The hotel's fine dining room, *Les Continents,* features eclectic Southwestern, Asian, and Cajun cuisine. Concierge services and 24-hour room service are available to guests; other amenities include complimentary newspapers and twice-daily maid service. One of the best business centers in town offers secretarial, translation, fax, and courier services, to name a few. 360 Rue St-Antoine O. (phone: 987-9900; 800-361-3600; fax: 987-9904).

Westin–Mont Royal A leader among the prime properties on Rue Sherbrooke, this is a favorite for those who choose contemporary luxury with traditional comforts. The 31-story, 300-room tower appeals to business travelers, young fashionables, and show-biz bigwigs; its two split-level suites are especially popular among Hollywood types. Those here on business can plug in a computer, have business calls routed to one of two phones, and work at a larger-than-average, well-lit desk. Fitness fanatics can stay in shape at the health club, where they'll find Kaiser and Nautilus equipment, a sauna, a whirlpool bath, a steamroom, and an outdoor pool for all seasons (in winter, it's heated to a steamy 85F). There's a minimal charge for shiatsu massage and the services of a personal trainer. Joggers will find a map in their rooms with directions to the best trails in nearby *Parc du Mont-Royal,* just a sprint away up Rue Peel. The hotel's main restaurant, *Le Cercle,* offers a menu of French, Californian, and Italian cuisine. At *Zen,* one of the best Chinese restaurants in town, dinner is served Szechuan-style (see *Eating Out*). 1050 Rue Sherbrooke O. (phone: 284-1110; 800-228-3000; fax: 845-3025).

EXPENSIVE

Bonaventure Hilton Montreal Located at the top of the *Place Bonaventure* in the heart of the city's business district is an oasis of comfort. Guests enter the elevator on the ground level in the most commercial part of Montreal and are whisked up 17 stories to the lobby to check in. In winter the heated, rooftop outdoor pool is surrounded by evergreens covered in snow (swimmers enter the pool through a narrow covered passageway). Guests with a garden-view room often wake up to the sight of a pheasant strutting across the Japanese garden, complete with babbling brooks, cascades, and tree-shaded ponds. Yet only an elevator ride away are the mall and exhibition hall, the *Métro, Place Ville-Marie,* and the *Gare Centrale,* all major gateways to the Ville Souterraine. There are 400 contemporary rooms in this penthouse location, including six executive and 12 junior suites. Convention and business facilities are located on the floor below the hotel's lobby, where the main ballroom can accommodate 2,000, and meeting rooms and secretarial services are available on request. The cozy wood-and-stone main dining room, *Le Castillon,* features floor-to-ceiling windows overlooking the garden and a terrace for warm-weather dining. 1 *Place Bonaventure* (phone: 878-2332; 800-HILTONS; fax: 878-3881).

Château Champlain The huge, arched picture windows covering the 36-story façade of this Canadian Pacific property make it a distinctive landmark on Montreal's skyline (it's known to locals as the "Cheese Grater"). The 617 rooms and suites are spacious and elegantly furnished, and there also is a health club and a pool. The top-floor *L'Escapade* restaurant (open weekends only) offers a good view. 1 Pl. du Canada (phone: 878-9000; 800-441-1414; fax: 878-6761).

Delta Here is a luxury high-rise with 453 rooms (most with balconies), a dining room, a health club, an indoor pool, and an innovative Creativity Center designed to keep young travelers occupied while their parents are sight-seeing. Conveniently located downtown, on the corner of Rues Sherbrooke and City Councillors (phone: 286-1986; 800-268-1133 in Canada; 800-877-1133 in the US; fax: 284-4342).

Le Méridien Montréal This 600-room property is the focal point of the *Complexe Desjardins,* adjacent to the *Place des Arts,* Montreal's performing arts center. There is an indoor pool with a whirlpool, and three restaurants. 4 *Complexe Desjardins;* enter at Rue Jeanne-Mance (phone: 285-1450; 800-361-8234 in Canada; 800-543-4300 in the US; fax: 285-1243).

Queen Elizabeth With 1,020 rooms, this is the city's largest hotel. Offering direct access to underground *Place Ville-Marie*'s shops and services and the *Gare Centrale,* it is one of the most conveniently located, too. In addition to the restaurants in the hotel, including the well-known *Beaver Club* (see *Eating Out*), the building features an elegant shopping arcade in the lower lobby, separate from the shops of *Place Ville-Marie.* 900 Blvd. René-Lévesque O. (phone: 861-3511; 800-268-9420 in Canada; 800-828-7447 in the US; fax: 954-2256).

Radisson-Gouverneurs Linked to *Place Victoria,* this 568-room hotel has a 40-foot-high atrium lobby with glass-enclosed elevators, an indoor pool, and a sauna. Its main dining room, *Le Tour de Ville,* is the city's only revolving rooftop restaurant. 777 Rue University (phone: 879-1370; 800-333-3333; fax: 879-1761).

Vogue Representing a new approach to upmarket innkeeping, this midtown establishment opposite the *Ogilvy* department store has transformed an ordinary office building into a classy little hostelry reminiscent of those traditionally favored by affluent European travelers. The comforting Old World touches—goosedown duvets and pillows and, in some cases, canopy beds—in its 126 rooms and 16 suites are complemented by modern amenities such as fax machines; the luxurious bathrooms feature whirlpool baths. There's a restaurant, and corporate pluses include three meeting rooms equipped with audio-visual and computer projection systems, as well as secretarial, translation, and courier services. 1425 Rue de la Montagne (phone: 285-5555; 800-465-6654; fax: 849-8903).

MODERATE

Best Western Ville-Marie This high-rise has 162 well-appointed rooms, an agreeable ambience, and the glass-enclosed sidewalk *Café Park Express.* 3407 Rue Peel (phone: 288-4141; 800-361-7791; fax: 288-3021).

Château Versailles This European-style hotel with 70 deluxe rooms attracts many repeat visitors. It serves only breakfast (included in the rate), but it's located in an area abounding in good, moderately priced restaurants. 1659 Rue Sherbrooke O. (phone: 933-3611; 800-361-7199 in Canada; 800-361-3664 in the US; fax: 933-6867).

Holiday Inn Centre Ville Holiday Inn's newest Montreal property has added an exotic new dimension to the small Chinese quarter with its illuminated rooftop pagodas and a reflection pool and cascade in the dining area. Across the street from the *Palais des Congrès* (Convention Center), it has 235 well-appointed rooms, six suites, and an executive floor. There's also a 40-shop mini-mall and a fitness center with an indoor pool and exercise room. 99 Av. Viger O. (phone: 878-9888; 800-HOLIDAY; fax: 878-6341).

Holiday Inn Crowne Plaza The largest and most convenient of the several *Holiday Inn*s in the area, this 486-room link in the chain has an indoor pool and a restaurant. 420 Rue Sherbrooke O. (phone: 842-6111; 800-HOLIDAY; fax: 842-9381).

Manoir LeMoyne The hotel's 265 suites all come with fully equipped kitchens, dining alcoves, and spacious balconies. *Le Bistro de l'Hôtel,* a fairly good restaurant and bar, is on the premises. There's a whirlpool and sauna, as well as a business center. 2100 Blvd. de Maisonneuve (phone: 931-8861; 800-361-7191; fax: 931-7726).

De la Montagne This 136-room hostelry is within a stone's throw of the chic boutiques and restaurants in the Rue Crescent–Rue de la Montagne area. Its rooftop pool and terrace are popular for summer rendezvous, and its dining room, *Le Lutetia,* is highly regarded. 1430 Rue de la Montagne (phone: 288-5656; 800-361-6262; fax: 288-9658).

Du Parc The hub of a major office-apartment-shopping complex at the base of Mont-Royal, this 445-room hostelry has an attractive lounge and a restaurant. Included in the rate is access to extensive health club facilities in the adjacent complex, including indoor and outdoor pools, a sauna, and indoor tennis. 3625 Av. du Parc (phone: 288-6666; 800-363-0735; fax: 288-2469).

Tour Versailles This 107-room hotel is located in a converted high-rise apartment building across the street from its cousin, the *Château Versailles* (see above). Rooms have Shaker-style furniture, and the bathrooms are decorated with Italian marble. The more expensive rooms have a Jacuzzi, microwave oven, and refrigerator. Next door is the elegant little French restaurant *Champs-Elysées* (phone: 939-1212), under the same management as the two hotels.

1808 Rue Sherbrooke O. (phone: 933-3611; 800-361-7199 in Canada; 800-361-3664 in the US; fax: 933-7102).

EATING OUT

For the Francophile gastronome, Montreal provides a cornucopia of delights comparable to anything available on the other side of the Atlantic. Even homegrown French Canadian cuisine takes a back seat to the French variety, although local influences show up in the form of *ragoût de pattes* (pig's feet in a garlic stew) or *ragoût de boulettes* (a stew of pork meatballs). Many of the city's ethnic restaurants, as well as its seafood spots and steakhouses, are excellent. Montrealers put a high value on ambience, too, and our choices reflect this native concern. Expect to pay more than $100 for a dinner for two in a restaurant rated very expensive; from $80 to $100 in a place in the expensive range; from $40 to $80 in a moderate restaurant; and $40 or less in an inexpensive one. Prices do not include drinks, wine, tip, or tax. By law, all menus must be posted outside the establishment. Unless otherwise noted, all restaurants are open for lunch and dinner, and all are in the 514 area code.

VERY EXPENSIVE

Café de Paris This is Montreal's most beautiful restaurant, the *Ritz-Carlton Kempinski*'s main dining room. It is best described as an elegant salon, an island of blue-and-gold civility off the mainstream of Rue Sherbrooke shopping. Its walls are covered in watered silk, and gilt-framed mirrors reflect intimate groupings of velvet banquettes and French doors that open onto the *Ritz Garden,* a lovely warm-weather dining terrace. The cuisine is every bit as fine as the ambience, but be prepared: The golden accents in the decor are reflected in the menu's prices. (Gourmet Impérial, a selection of beluga, ossetra, and sevruga caviar, adds up to more than $300!) Chicken 21 with wild rice is a longtime favorite, as are Dover sole, Gaspé salmon, venison, and other game dishes. The traditional baron of beef is a carnivore's delight. Open daily. Reservations advised. Major credit cards accepted. 1228 Rue Sherbrooke O. (phone: 842-4212).

EXPENSIVE

Auberge le Vieux St-Gabriel Long favored for its good French Canadian food and old-time ambience, this restaurant rambles through a Vieux Montréal building that dates from fur-trading days, complete with a tunnel leading to a room (now a cozy bar) once used to store pelts. For a taste of Old Quebec, this is the place. Open daily. Reservations advised. Major credit cards accepted. 426 Rue St-Gabriel (phone: 878-3561; fax: 878-4492).

Bagel-Etc. Perfect for the insomniac, this jazzy, late-night rendezvous spot prepares everything from caviar dishes to hamburgers. Sunday brunch features the widest variety of egg dishes in town. Open Sundays to 1 AM; Mondays through

Wednesdays to 2 AM; Thursdays to 3 AM; Fridays and Saturdays to 5 AM. Reservations advised for Sunday brunch. Major credit cards accepted. 4320 Blvd. St-Laurent (phone: 845-9462; fax: 845-7537).

Beaver Club Founded in 1785 by the 19 fur-trading partners of the North West Company, the original *Beaver Club* was a private enclave for those hardy souls who had spent a winter in the Northwest. The club disbanded in the early 1800s, and, despite attempts by the Hudson's Bay Company to revive it, the group re-emerged only in the 1950s as a restaurant in the *Queen Elizabeth* hotel. Far more advanced than the banquet fare of the old Nor' Westers, the à la carte menu is as varied as it is sophisticated. Specialties include cutlet of venison in blueberry-wine sauce; loin of lamb with a marjoram, apricot, and shallot crust; and grilled salmon in sorrel herb sauce. Regulars favor the roast beef, either sliced thin, English-style, or in juicy, steak-thick slabs. Open daily. Reservations advised. Major credit cards accepted. 900 Blvd. René-Lévesque O. (phone: 861-3511; fax: 954-2256).

Les Chenêts At this small, intimate French place, decorated with copper pots, try the oysters from France (called *portuguese*), mussels *marinière* (prepared in white wine with herbs), fresh Pacific salmon, pheasant with mushrooms, or anything else—it's all very good. The excellent wine list also includes 60 varieties of cognac. Open daily. Reservations advised. Major credit cards accepted. 2075 Rue Bishop (phone: 844-1842; fax: 844-0552).

Chez Delmo Well-prepared seafood draws locals to this restaurant in the financial district of Vieux Montréal. At lunchtime seafood also is served up at the Victorian-style mahogany bar. Closed Sundays, Monday dinner, and some holidays. Reservations advised. Major credit cards accepted. 211 Rue Notre-Dame O. (phone: 849-4061).

Chez Desjardins A favorite since 1892, it features a nautically inspired menu, yet the elegant setting is far from the typical nets-hanging-from-the-ceiling, buoys-bobbing-in-your-face kind of place. Open daily. Reservations advised. Major credit cards accepted. 1175 Rue Mackay (phone: 866-9741; fax: 866-0145).

Chez la Mère Michel In this fine old stone house converted to an attractive, dark-beamed, candlelit dining spot, French fare achieves authentic excellence. The lobster soufflé is a special treat, and don't miss having a drink in the snug downstairs bar. Closed Sundays. Reservations necessary. Major credit cards accepted. 1209 Rue Guy (phone: 934-0473; fax: 939-0709).

Claude Postel One of the city's finest French restaurants is located in Vieux Montréal in the old *Richelieu* hotel. Specialties include veal liver with raspberry sauce; salmon in a sherry, shallot, and cream sauce; smoked seafood; and home-made pastries. Open daily. Reservations advised. Major credit cards accepted. 443 Rue St-Vincent (phone: 875-5067; fax: 875-7294).

Le Fadeau Seventeenth-century ambience and excellent food and service are offered at this classic Gallic restaurant in a Vieux Montréal house. Selections from an excellent wine cellar complement the cuisine. Closed Sundays. Reservations necessary. Major credit cards accepted. 423 Rue St-Claude (phone: 878-3959; fax: 871-1134).

Gibby's If you are after good steaks and atmosphere, try this spot in Vieux Montréal's restored, early-18th-century *Ecuries d'Youville* (Youville Stables). While tucking into the large portions, take your time to enjoy the attractive stone-walled, beamed interior. Though most diners order a beef dish, there are other entrées as well, all accompanied by fresh, hot bread and a generous salad. Open daily for dinner only. Reservations necessary. Major credit cards accepted. 298 Pl. d'Youville (phone: 282-1837; fax: 282-9771).

Les Halles The great charm of this townhouse is attributable to proprietor Jacques Landurie, whose hearty welcome sets the tone for a delightful dining experience. A nostalgic version of the bistros that once surrounded the eponymous Paris marketplace, it's decorated with murals of the erstwhile market scene, café signs salvaged from the old *quartier,* and other memorabilia of a sadly missed Parisian landmark. Chef Dominique Crevoisier's robust pot-au-feu (tender boiled beef and fresh garden vegetables) draws the lunchtime crowd; for dinner try the warm appetizer of grapefruit, lobster, and scallops dressed with mayonnaise and French mustard, or the king-size ravioli with four varieties of imported mushrooms. Marinated venison, a favorite wintertime entrée, gives way to rack of Quebec lamb in summer. Among the wicked temptations from the dessert trolley are strawberries *feuillantine* (strawberry mousse sandwiched between two thin slices of chocolate topped with marinated strawberries and *sauce anglaise*). The *carte des vins* is an encyclopedia of fine if pricey wines. Closed Sundays and holidays. Reservations necessary. Major credit cards accepted. 1450 Rue Crescent (phone: 844-2328; fax: 849-1294).

Le Latini A different pasta dish is featured every day, and the veal specialties are tasty and tender. In summer, guests may dine alfresco on the terrace. Closed Sundays. Reservations necessary. Major credit cards accepted. 1130 Rue Jeanne-Mance, near *Complexe Desjardins* (phone: 861-3166; 861-8294).

La Marée Once a private residence, this restored property is home to one of the best seafood restaurants in town. Though meals are served by formally dressed waiters in a velvet-draped dining room, the menu is shaped more by the quality and freshness of the food than by culinary flourishes. Much of the fish and seafood is imported daily from France, and the kitchen turns out such satisfying yet simply prepared specialties as bouillabaisse, sole meunière, halibut in creamy lobster sauce, and poached or grilled salmon. The chef is not averse to adding hearty old-fashioned favorites such as onion soup gratinée. Open daily. Reservations advised. Major credit cards accepted. 404 Pl. Jacques-Cartier (phone: 861-8126; fax: 861-3944).

Le Mas des Oliviers If you're gearing up for a night in one of Montreal's best disco areas (in the neighborhood of Rues Stanley, de la Montagne, and Bishop), start off the way Montrealers do—by having dinner here. The lamb dishes are chef Pierre Domonikea's specialty. Open daily. Reservations necessary. Major credit cards accepted. 1216 Rue Bishop (phone: 861-6733; fax: 861-7838).

Le Pavillon de l'Atlantique This seafood establishment, with its classic nautical decor, dominates the atrium of the *Maison Alcan* office building. Among the best dishes are grilled scampi and lobster thermidor. The Arctic char, when available, is also quite good. *Moby Dick's* is the lively bar section, a popular lunchtime and cocktail-hour destination, where the menu offers the same seafood specials as the restaurant. Open daily; *Moby Dick's* is closed Sundays. Reservations advised. Major credit cards accepted. 1188 Rue Sherbrooke O.; *Moby Dick's* also has an entrance at 2121 Rue Drummond (phone: 285-1636; fax: 285-1675).

MODERATE

Le Caveau French food is served in this cozy little house in the heart of town. Checkered tablecloths and candlelight add to the intimate atmosphere. The less expensive of the two menus offers good value and has almost the same selection as the other. The tournedos, house wine, and *crème caramel* are all of high quality. Open daily. Reservations advised. Major credit cards accepted. 2063 Rue Victoria (phone: 844-1624; fax: 844-0854).

LUX This futuristic-style bistro serves French-influenced American fare. In a converted textile mill, it has a spacious, circular main room with a steel floor and a glass-enclosed second level, reached by two spiral staircases. Open daily, 24 hours a day. Reservations advised for parties of six or more on weekends. Major credit cards accepted. 5220 Blvd. St-Laurent (phone: 271-9272; fax: 274-2622).

Le Paris Yet another fine French eatery with a truly Parisian atmosphere. Closed Sundays and holidays. Reservations advised. Major credit cards accepted. 1812 Rue Ste-Catherine O. (phone: 937-4898).

Le Père St-Vincent Nestled in the oldest house in Vieux Montréal (1658), this eatery specializes in French dishes served beside a cozy hearth. The decor is rough-hewn, early Montreal, but the ambience is warm and inviting. Open daily. Reservations advised. Major credit cards accepted. 431 Rue St-Vincent (phone: 397-9610; fax: 878-3627).

La Transition Traditional Italian dishes on the main menu are complemented by a more adventurous *table d'hôte* at this Westmount eatery. Open daily. Reservations advised. Major credit cards accepted. 4785 Rue Sherbrooke O. (phone: 486-2742).

La Tulipe Noire This Parisian-style café and pastry shop in the *Maison Alcan* office building is one of the few midtown restaurants where you can get a moderately priced bite after the theater. Also a busy spot for breakfast, lunch, and Sunday brunch, it overlooks a garden court and its own summer café terrace. Open daily. No reservations. Major credit cards accepted. 2100 Rue Stanley (phone: 285-1225).

Zen The only North American branch of the London-based restaurant, this is one of the best places in town for haute cuisine Szechuan-style. Aromatic crispy duck is a favorite, among such specialties as lobster prepared five different ways, sesame shrimp, and whole abalone. Open daily. Reservations advised. Major credit cards accepted. In the *Westin–Mont Royal Hotel,* 1050 Rue Sherbrooke O. (phone: 499-0801; fax: 499-2037).

INEXPENSIVE

Beautys Locals seem to have a soft spot for this long-standing establishment, which has been serving breakfast and lunch since 1942. Famous for its "Mish-Mash" omelette (a unique blend of hot dog, salami, green pepper, and fried onions), it also packs in the crowds for its blueberry pancakes and fresh-squeezed orange juice. There's usually a line for Sunday brunch, but it's worth the wait. Open daily from 7 AM to 5 PM. No reservations. Major credit cards accepted. 93 Av. du Mont-Royal O. at the corner of Rue St-Urbain (phone: 849-8883).

Brûlerie St-Denis Coffee lovers will appreciate this Rue St-Denis spot, where more than 70 types of beans are roasted on the premises. The menu offers sandwiches, salads, and a variety of tempting desserts. The outdoor terrace fills up quickly as soon as it's warm enough to sit outside. Open daily. No reservations. Visa and MasterCard accepted. 3967 Rue St-Denis (phone: 286-9158).

Chez Vito Near thc *Université de Montréal,* this popular place has fine Italian fare. Open daily. No reservations. Major credit cards accepted. 5408-12 Chemin de la Côte-des-Neiges (phone: 735-3623).

La Maison Grecque A reasonable, no-frills place featuring moussaka and fish en brochette. Diners can bring their own wine. Open daily. Reservations advised. Visa and MasterCard accepted. 450 Rue Duluth E. (phone: 842-0969; fax: 987-1146).

Charcuterie Hébraïque de Montréal Known locally as *Schwartz's,* this deli is famous for its smoked meat, grilled steaks, and possibly the best French fries on the continent. Closed *Yom Kippur.* No reservations. No credit cards accepted. 3895 Blvd. St-Laurent (phone: 842-4813).

Rôtisserie Laurier Chicken here is roasted Quebec-style and served with a side of barbecue sauce. Open daily. No reservations. Major credit cards accepted. 381 Av. Laurier O. (phone: 273-3671).

Stash's Café Bazaar This Vieux Montréal establishment specializes in Polish food. The decor is simple; the atmosphere, friendly. Open daily. No reservations. Visa and MasterCard accepted. 200 Rue St-Paul O. (phone: 845-6611).

Sucrerie de la Montagne Anyone with a sweet tooth should make the trip to this spot 20 miles (32 km) southwest of the city. The traditional feast includes *tourtière* (meat pie) and baked beans, finished off with delectable maple syrup pie, more commonly served in Quebec City. Open from 11 AM to 8 PM. Reservations necessary for groups. Major credit cards accepted. 300 Rang St-Georges, Rigaud, off Rte. 40 (phone: 451-5204 or 451-0831; fax: 451-0340).

Ottawa

Ottawa, Ontario, is Canada's national capital. The city is situated on the southern bank of the Ottawa River at its junction with the Rideau River. Canada's *Parliament* is perched on top of a hill on the riverbank, dominating its surroundings with a Gothic grandeur that may seem overblown for a city of only 600,000. But on the river's opposite bank, in the province of Quebec, the predominantly French-speaking city of Hull and adjoining municipalities bring the population of what is known as the National Capital Region to just under one million.

Ottawa is predominantly English-speaking, but about 35 percent of the people consider French their mother tongue, providing a mix that lends this city much of its multicultural flair. One of the oldest ethnic groups in Ottawa is Italian; the city's Little Italy is concentrated in the Preston Street area.

A place of human proportions, Ottawa is much admired for its clean streets, open spaces, restaurants, recreations, and cultural activities. It also is a city of contrasts. In it are Rockcliffe Village, home of the "old-money crowd," and most of Canada's diplomatic and political elite; Lower Town, a once-seedy area whose brick frontages have been sandblasted into chic respectability; and vast stretches of new suburban housing. Linking them all together is one of North America's most ambitious mass transit systems.

Because of its national significance, Ottawa has amenities other cities of its size could not support, such as an array of excellent museums crowned by the architecturally stunning *National Gallery of Canada* and the equally spectacular *National Museum of Civilization* on the Hull side of the river. The heart of the performing arts world here is the *National Arts Centre,* with an opera house, theater, and *The Studio,* an all-purpose performance and conference space.

Ottawa's current eminence stands in stark contrast to its humble beginnings. French explorer Samuel de Champlain paused here briefly in 1613 to admire the Chaudière Falls near what is now Parliament Hill, pronounced himself impressed, and then hurried on in search of more rewarding discoveries.

In 1796 a hardy, puritanical New Englander named Philemon Wright carved out a small settlement on the Quebec side of the river, near what is now Hull. Thirteen years later, more settlers tackled the forests and beaver swamps in what was to become Ottawa. In 1826 they were joined by the Royal Engineers, a ragtag band of Irish laborers and British veterans of the Napoleonic and American wars, who had been assigned to build a canal from Ottawa to Kingston to serve as a supply route in the event of an American invasion. The threat never materialized, and the canal—today called the Rideau Canal—became a commercial venture almost as soon as it was completed in 1832.

Even today, the canal, a 123-mile system of locks, dams, and artificial lakes, is seen as an engineering marvel. But the engineer who pulled it off, Lieutenant Colonel John By (from whom Ottawa got its original name, Bytown, now a historic market area), overspent his budget by several thousand pounds and was ordered home in disgrace by his government. Today Americans regularly invade Canada via the Rideau Canal aboard pleasure craft.

The city's location at the midpoint of the then-main water route between Montreal and the growing cities on the Great Lakes briefly gave Ottawa a sense of commercial purpose. That, in turn, attracted a group of American lumber barons, who for a time set up mills, hired workers, and jammed up the Ottawa River with gigantic log booms.

In 1858, Queen Victoria declared the Bytown area the capital of the merged colonies of Upper and Lower Canada (Ontario and Quebec, respectively), and named it Ottawa after the Outaouac tribe, who had used the town as a stopover. Some said the queen may have been influenced by watercolors that painted a rather romantic picture of the region. In any event, the business and political elite reacted with disbelief to the choice, snidely referring to Ottawa as the "wilderness Westminster." Today all that has changed. Even diplomats bid for a posting to the city that as recently as 30 years ago was perceived by some foreign governments as a "hardship posting" because of its weather extremes and "cultural limitations."

Lacking the European sophistication of Montreal or the bustling cultural diversity of Toronto, Ottawa has staked out its own claim as a living, breathing model of what people-oriented urban planning is all about. From the real-life theater of the daily House of Commons Question Period, which allows opposition politicians to grill the government of the day, to the beauty of *Gatineau Park* just 15 minutes away by car, Canada's capital today no longer lacks allure.

Ottawa At-a-Glance

SEEING THE CITY

The best overview of the capital is from the lookout of the *Peace Tower,* one of the *Parliament Buildings* (see *Special Places*), on Wellington Street in the center of the city. Just a touch over 300 feet high, the tower opens up a panoramic view extending 40 miles in all directions.

SPECIAL PLACES

Many of Ottawa's most interesting sights, including the must-see *National Gallery,* lie within easy walking distance of the *Parliament Buildings.* Some are in Hull, the Quebec half of the National Capital Region. The not-to-

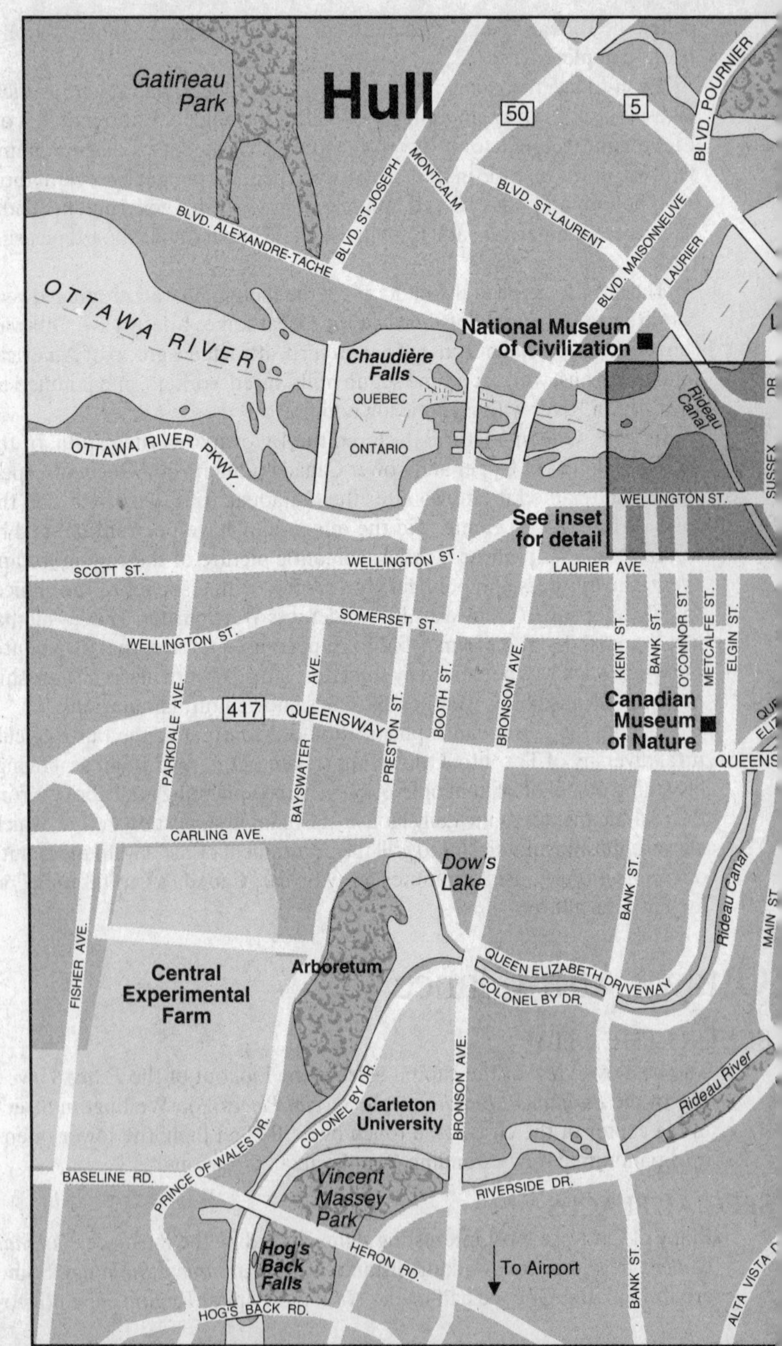
Hull
Gatineau Park
50
5
BLVD. POURNIER
BLVD. ST-JOSEPH
MONTCALM
BLVD. ST-LAURENT
BLVD. MAISONNEUVE
LAURIER
BLVD. ALEXANDRE-TACHE
OTTAWA RIVER
National Museum of Civilization
Chaudière Falls
QUEBEC
ONTARIO
Rideau Canal
SUSSEX DR
OTTAWA RIVER PKWY.
WELLINGTON ST.
See inset for detail
SCOTT ST.
WELLINGTON ST.
LAURIER AVE.
SOMERSET ST.
WELLINGTON ST.
KENT ST.
BANK ST.
O'CONNOR ST.
METCALFE ST.
ELGIN ST.
BRONSON AVE.
BOOTH ST.
PRESTON ST.
BAYSWATER AVE.
PARKDALE AVE.
417
QUEENSWAY
Canadian Museum of Nature
QUEENS
CARLING AVE.
Dow's Lake
BANK ST.
Rideau Canal
MAIN ST
FISHER AVE.
Central Experimental Farm
Arboretum
QUEEN ELIZABETH DRIVEWAY
COLONEL BY DR.
Rideau River
COLONEL BY DR.
Carleton University
BRONSON AVE.
PRINCE OF WALES DR.
BASELINE RD.
Vincent Massey Park
RIVERSIDE DR.
Hog's Back Falls
HERON RD.
To Airport
BANK ST.
ALTA VISTA
HOG'S BACK RD.

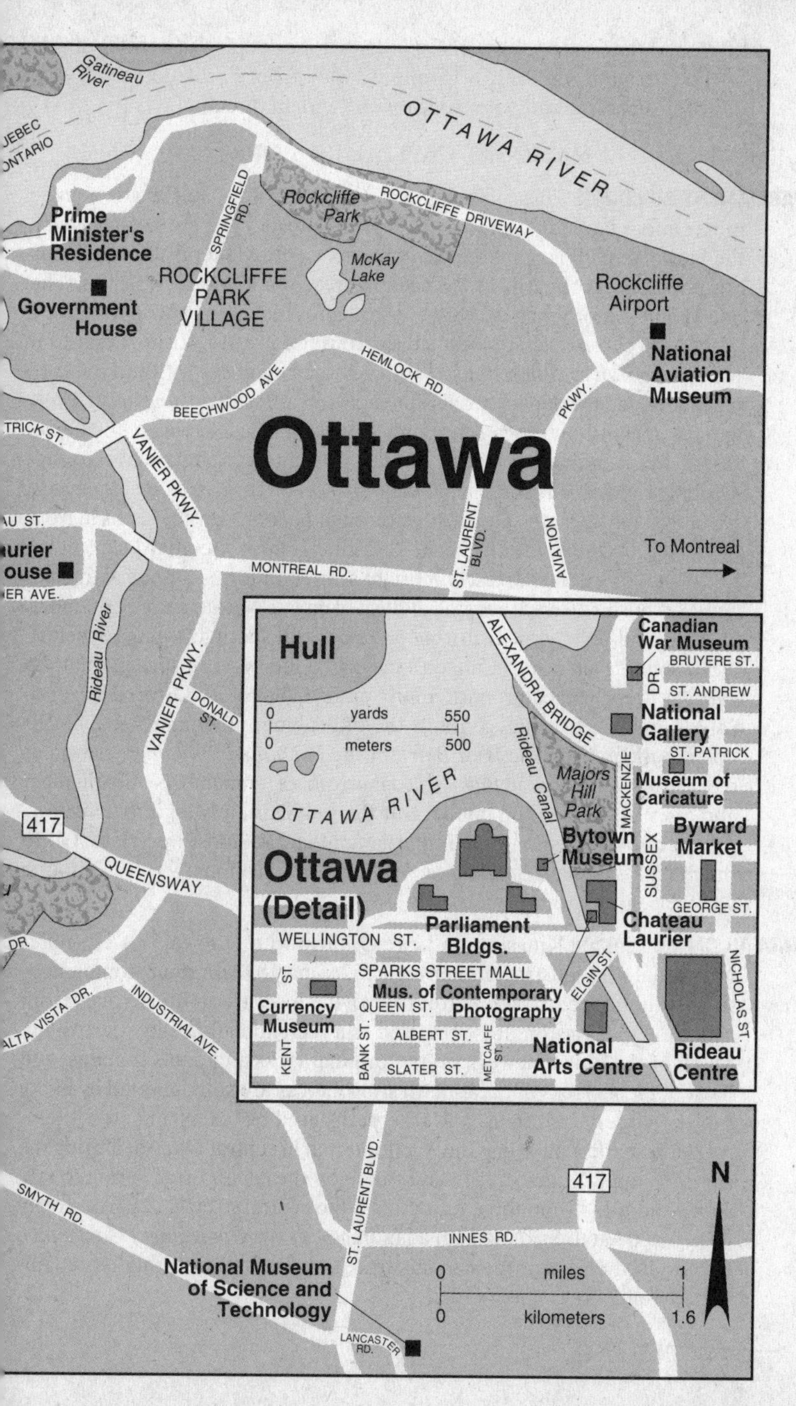

Gatineau River
QUEBEC
ONTARIO
OTTAWA RIVER
Rockcliffe Park
ROCKCLIFFE DRIVEWAY
SPRINGFIELD RD.
Prime Minister's Residence
McKay Lake
ROCKCLIFFE PARK VILLAGE
Government House
Rockcliffe Airport
National Aviation Museum
HEMLOCK RD.
BEECHWOOD AVE.
PKWY.
Ottawa
VANIER PKWY.
ST. LAURENT BLVD.
AVIATION
To Montreal
MONTREAL RD.
Rideau River
DONALD ST.
417
QUEENSWAY
ALTA VISTA DR.
INDUSTRIAL AVE.
Hull
ALEXANDRA BRIDGE
Canadian War Museum
BRUYERE ST.
ST. ANDREW
DR.
National Gallery
yards 0 550
meters 0 500
Rideau Canal
ST. PATRICK
Majors Hill Park
MACKENZIE
Museum of Caricature
OTTAWA RIVER
Byward Market
Bytown Museum
SUSSEX
Ottawa (Detail)
GEORGE ST.
Chateau Laurier
Parliament Bldgs.
WELLINGTON ST.
ELGIN ST.
NICHOLAS ST.
SPARKS STREET MALL
Mus. of Contemporary Photography
Currency Museum
QUEEN ST.
ALBERT ST.
National Arts Centre
Rideau Centre
KENT ST.
BANK ST.
SLATER ST.
METCALFE ST.
ST. LAURENT BLVD.
417
N
SMYTH RD.
INNES RD.
National Museum of Science and Technology
miles 0 1
kilometers 0 1.6
LANCASTER RD.

be-missed *National Museum of Civilization*, for example, is on the Hull side of the Ottawa River, only a 15-minute walk from Parliament Hill. Any downtown habitué can point a visitor in the right direction.

NATIONAL CAPITAL REGION

PARLIAMENT BUILDINGS These impressive Gothic structures are Canada's single most famous landmark. Erected on a promontory above the Ottawa River, the Parliament Hill complex once housed the entire federal administration but now serves primarily as the meeting place of federal politicians. The only original, more-than-century-old structures remaining are on the *Centre Block;* others were rebuilt after a disastrous fire in 1916. Visitors may tour the *Centre Block,* which houses not only the chambers for the House of Commons and the Senate but also the opulent, domed *Parliamentary Library* and the magnificent *Peace Tower.* Free English-language tours of the *Centre Block,* which include a trip to the top of the tower, start daily (except *Christmas* and *New Year's Day*) at the *Info-Tent* on the east side of the block. At 10 AM daily from the end of June through *Labour Day,* the lawns in front of the *Centre Block* are the scene of a changing-of-the-guard ceremony, involving 125 soldiers dressed in bright scarlet uniforms topped with giant bearskin busbies. Every evening at dusk from late May to early September, a sound-and-light show featuring 600 powerful spotlights and a synchronized soundtrack brings Canada's history to life here. In spring, the tulip gardens are spectacular, particularly along Colonel By Drive. The renovated *East Block,* which contains the old cabinet meeting rooms, also is open to the public. The *West Block* of the *Parliament Buildings,* as well as the nearby *Confederation Building,* contain offices for members of Parliament and are not open to the public. But the public is allowed into a visitors' gallery during question time in Parliament at 2 PM most weekdays. Go to the main *Parliament Building* on Wellington St. (phone: 992-4793, tours; 996-0896, group tours).

RIDEAU CANAL Linking Kingston on Lake Ontario with Ottawa, this 125-mile-long canal was constructed between 1826 and 1832 on the recommendation of the Duke of Wellington to provide a secure military route from Montreal to Kingston. It is now used as a recreational facility year-round. Much of the old stonework on the original locks and dams remains, and most of the 45 locks of hand-hewn stone blocks are still operated by hand. Flower gardens, tall trees, and bike paths used by hikers and cross-country skiers in the winter line the 5-mile stretch in central Ottawa. During the summer, many Ottawans sail and canoe on the canal. From spring to fall, a one-and-a-half-hour boat tour cruises the central stretch, departing daily from 11:30 AM to 8:30 PM from a landing near the *Government Conference Centre.* In the winter, the canal is transformed into an excellently maintained 5-mile-long skating rink.

RIDEAU CENTRE Costing $250 million, this multilevel complex boasts a luxury hotel (the *Westin;* see *Checking In*) as well as over 200 stores, 18 restaurants, and three movie houses. On top of it is a five-acre park with winding paths, benches, and trees. The center has had an impressive impact on the heart of Ottawa, reversing the trend begun in the 1960s when the city retreated into the suburbs every evening at 5 o'clock. 50 Rideau St. (phone: 236-6565).

SPARKS STREET MALL Here are five outdoor city blocks filled with boutiques, department stores, historic buildings, rock gardens, sculptures, live entertainment, and the best people watching in the capital: Canada's first permanent pedestrians-only street. In summer, the mall comes alive with flower and fruit stalls, musicians, street-corner orators, and armies of lunch-hour civil servants trying to catch a little sun. The building known as *240 Sparks* is a giant glass enclosure housing federal government offices, a variety of lunch-on-a-bun spots, and stores selling elegant apparel. Open daily. Sparks St., between Elgin and Lyon.

BYWARD MARKET This market has been an Ottawa institution since the mid-1800s, when farmers from the area first set up their stalls and peddled fresh produce. In recent years, the farmers have been joined by local artists and craftspeople who display their wares in the renovated market building. The market also houses an impressive array of ethnic grocery stores, fish markets, cheese shops, and cozy restaurants. On summer nights, its cobblestone courtyards and side streets become impromptu stages for sidewalk entertainers. The market itself is open daily, May through October. Between Clarence and George Sts.

ROYAL CANADIAN MINT Commemorative coins, medals, and bullion investment coins for countries all over the world are minted in this turn-of-the-century castle-like building next to the *Canadian War Museum.* It's also one of the largest gold, silver, and platinum refineries in the West. One-hour tours are available by reservation only. Visitors can watch the process from a walkway above the production floor. The mint is open weekdays, except public holidays, early May through August. No admission charge for children six and under or for large groups. 320 Sussex Dr. (phone: 993-8990).

NATIONAL GALLERY OF CANADA A veritable glass mountain illuminated by natural light, this is a breathtaking work of architecture. A major attraction for its design alone, the gallery houses the country's largest collection of fine art: more than 25,000 paintings, sculptures and drawings, plus an international collection of over 17,000 photographs. European masters from the Middle Ages through the 20th century are represented, with important pieces by Rembrandt, van Gogh, and Picasso. Its prized Canadian holdings include works by the 20th-century landscape artists known as the Group of Seven, including Paul Kane's paintings of native people and caricaturist Cornelius Kreigoff's vignettes of pioneer life. The museum also contains a restored 19th-century chapel with a neo-Gothic fan-vaulted ceiling and a large selection of silver pieces and 19th-century wooden church sculptures. Open daily May through early October; closed Mondays and Tuesdays the rest of the year. Admission charge, though the gallery finds an excuse to open its doors for free sometimes. 380 Sussex Dr. (phone: 990-1985).

LAURIER HOUSE Purchased by Canada's seventh prime minister, Sir Wilfrid Laurier, after his election in 1896, this 18-room brick house was also the home of Canada's 10th prime minister—Laurier's fellow Liberal, William Lyon Mackenzie King. A popular leader, King held power longer than any other prime minister (1921–30 and 1935–48); he died in 1950. He bequeathed the house—now a showcase of the furniture and personal effects of the two men (right down to King's shaving mug in the bathroom)—to the people of Canada. Closed Mondays. No admission charge. 335 Laurier Ave. (phone: 992-8142).

CANADIAN MUSEUM OF NATURE With two million zoological specimens, from the Daspletosaurus (a four-ton, 28-foot-long Tyrannosaurus) skeleton on up the evolutionary ladder, this museum is particularly fascinating for children. The building housing the exhibits is a castle-like structure where the House of Commons met after the *Parliament Buildings* were destroyed by a fire in 1916. Open daily; Thursdays to 8 PM. Admission charge. Metcalfe at McLeod (phone: 996-3102).

NATIONAL MUSEUM OF CIVILIZATION The main hall of this $225 million museum bears little resemblance to the traditional (and decrepit) *Victoria Memorial Museum* in Ottawa that it replaced. Half of the vast structure is a stack of curving tiers that resemble a space-age version of a pueblo; the other half is a series of copper domes. Designed by Métis architect Douglas Cardinal, it is the length of a football field and five stories high, with one entire wall of glass providing a panoramic view of the Ottawa River and Parliament Hill. It contains a re-creation of a rain forest and six full-size reconstructions of Pacific Coast Native American homes, in which actors depict how members of the tribes lived. A domed theater presents *IMAX* and *OMNIMAX* movies featuring huge, crystal-clear images, with *OMNIMAX* shows projected on a giant, wrap-around screen. There also is a children's museum. Open Thursdays to 8 PM year-round; open daily May through October; closed Mondays the rest of the year. No admission charge for children under 15. 100 Laurier St., across the river in Hull (phone: 819-776-7000).

CANADIAN WAR MUSEUM Exhibits here are related to Canada's military history. Displays include skulls taken by Native Americans as spoils of war, a mock-up of a German bunker overlooking Normandy's beaches on *D-Day,* and Goering's staff car. Open daily. Admission charge. 330 Sussex Dr. (phone: 992-2774).

ENVIRONS

GOVERNMENT HOUSE Diagonally across the street from the *Prime Minister's Residence* at 24 Sussex Drive (not open to the public) is the 88-acre estate of the governor-general, the queen's official Canadian representative. In addition to the governor-general's rambling mansion and a guesthouse for the queen and other foreign dignitaries, the tree-lined grounds also have gardens, a skating rink, and even a cricket pitch to add a British touch. Concerts are held on the grounds in summer. Free hourly guided tours of the grounds are available daily in summer; state occasions permitting, free tours of the house are available weekends in July and August and by appointment in winter. 1 Sussex Dr. (phone: 998-7113).

CENTRAL EXPERIMENTAL FARM Established in 1886 as the headquarters of the research branch of the federal *Department of Agriculture,* the farm sprawls over 1,200 acres within the city limits. Its spectacular ornamental gardens are a favorite spot for local wedding photographs, and the arboretum is a showplace of rare trees. In the farm's *Neatby Building* are displays of more than 10 million insect samples, and farm animals inhabit the dairy barn and piggery. Ninety-minute tours, by appointment, include horse-drawn wagon rides in summer and horse-drawn sleigh rides in winter. Open daily. Admission charge. Prince of Wales Dr., between The Driveway and Baseline Rd. (phone: 995-5222).

HOG'S BACK FALLS Near *Carleton University,* at the south end of Colonel By Drive, the foaming Rideau River plunges through a picturesque 40-foot gorge. In winter, it's an ice palace; in summer, youngsters often jump off rocky ledges into the water (we don't recommend it, though, since it's not only dangerous but illegal). The nearby locks and canal that enable boats to travel around the falls were built by British military engineer Lieutenant Colonel John By in the 1830s. (The job was difficult, since the locks collapsed three times during their construction.) There is a bicycle path along Colonel By Drive, and parking is available nearby. Five miles (8 km) south of the downtown area. For information, contact the *Ottawa Tourism and Convention Authority* (see *Tourist Information,* below) or the nearby canal lock station (phone: 223-5033).

ROCKCLIFFE PARK VILLAGE A community of 22,000 set among stately mansions and narrow, tree-lined streets, it is the city's most elegant residential area. The village's first home was *Rideau Hall* (Sussex Dr.), built in 1838, which has been the residence of all Canada's governor-generals since confederation. Many of the area's other residents are also government officials (close to 600 diplomats live here). Most ambassadors' residences are identifiable by their country's emblems decorating the entranceways, in a section of Ottawa that is a little over a mile northeast of the *Parliament Buildings.*

NATIONAL MUSEUM OF SCIENCE AND TECHNOLOGY This popular museum encourages involvement; visitors can clamber aboard a train or ring the bell of a ship's wheelhouse. Displays range from early motorcars to a non-radioactive, charred chunk of a Soviet satellite that crashed in northern Canada back in 1978. "Canada in Space," which focuses on space science and exploration, includes video programs, satellites and spacecraft, and hands-on exhibits on weightlessness, spacesuits, and other aspects of life in outer space. Open Thursdays to 9 PM year-round; open daily May through October; closed Mondays the rest of the year. Admission charge. 1867 St. Laurent Blvd. (phone: 991-3044).

NATIONAL AVIATION MUSEUM Housed in dilapidated World War II hangars until 1988, this fine collection of more than 50 aircraft dating back to the turn of the century is now displayed in an $18-million showplace at *Rockcliffe Airport.* Exhibits include the *Silver Dart,* the first plane ever flown in the British Empire—at Baddeck, Nova Scotia, in 1909. There's a small art gallery on the second floor. Open Thursdays to 8 PM year-round; open daily May through October; closed Mondays the rest of the year. Admission charge. *Rockcliffe Airport*, off St. Laurent Blvd. (phone: 993-2010).

VINCENT MASSEY PARK This spot was named after the first native-born Governor-General of Canada. A pleasant break from sightseeing, these 52 acres of country within the city limits offer cycling paths, barbecue pits, picnic tables, ample parking, and plenty of grass and trees in which to frolic. The park also offers a great view of Hog's Back Falls (see above). There's cross-country skiing and tobogganing in winter. Open daily. Parking charge. Base Line Rd. west of Riverside Dr.

GATINEAU PARK Just 15 minutes from the *Parliament Buildings* on the Quebec side of the Ottawa River is an 88,000-acre wilderness and recreation area with more than 60 miles of hiking and cross-country trails (see also *Hiking and Backpacking* in DIVERSIONS); 40 lakes for fishing, swimming, and boating; plenty of camping and picnic facilities; and a lion's share of the area's beautiful scenery. In western Hull, the park is open year-round and has a visitors' center (phone: 819-827-2020). On the drive, which wanders through the rolling hills of the park, is *Moorside*, the summer home of former Canadian Prime Minister William Lyon Mackenzie King. The grounds are decorated with the ruins of old British and Ottawa buildings, and delightful lunches, afternoon tea, and dinners are served. *Moorside* is closed mornings and mid-October to mid-May; no admission charge (phone: 819-827-3405).

Sources and Resources

TOURIST INFORMATION

The *Ottawa Tourism and Convention Authority* (in the *National Arts Centre*, at 65 Elgin St.; phone: 237-5158) provides all manner of maps, brochures, and helpful hints. It's open daily. The *National Capital Commission (NCC)* visitors' center, opposite the *Parliament Buildings* (14 Metcalfe St.; phone: 239-5000; 800-465-1867 in Canada), offers maps of the various *NCC*-operated cycling, hiking, and nature trails in the region; it's open daily. From mid-May to *Labour Day,* the *NCC* staffs an *Info-Tent* on Parliament Hill. For information, you also can write to the *NCC* (151 Laurier Ave. W., Ottawa, ONT K1P 6J6).

LOCAL COVERAGE The *Ottawa Citizen* is the city's largest daily; the much smaller tabloid *Ottawa Sun* does not publish on Sunday. *Le Droit* is the city's French-language daily. The national English-language paper, *The Toronto Globe and Mail,* also is published daily. *Where* magazine, available free at hotels and many restaurants, provides tourist information. Numerous magazines offer arts and entertainment news. For the inside story on Ottawa, ask for *Frank* magazine. Not all newsstands stock it (its controversial subject matter makes some of them nervous).

TELEPHONE The area code for Ottawa is 613; the area code for Hull is 819. All phone numbers in this chapter are in the 613 area code unless otherwise indicated. No area code is necessary to call between Ottawa and Hull.

SALES TAX Ontario has a provincial sales tax of 8% in addition to the 7% federal Goods and Services Tax (GST). The provincial tax is nonrefundable, but visitors can receive refunds of the federal tax.

CLIMATE Ottawa's weather is variable: The temperature has been known to top 98F (37C) at the height of summer and to plummet to -25F (-31C) in the depths of winter. The warmest month is July and the coldest is January; rain falls about a hundred days a year, snow during another 45. June is notorious for its humidity.

GETTING AROUND

Daytime downtown parking is expensive, so look for less expensive lots just outside the core area. Parking is banned on main traffic arteries downtown during morning and afternoon rush hours; pay special attention to the black and white signs showing tow trucks in action—they mean it.

BUS Although many places of interest are within walking distance, especially in summer, try the bus system anyway. The modern, $500-million, high-speed *Transitway* system (a route—mostly set below ground—on which only buses run) is a novelty as well as a way of beating traffic jams. Regular service is from 6 AM to midnight, and a computer tracking facility lets passengers know exactly when a bus will arrive. Maps that show the best way to see the city by bus are widely available; for information, call 741-4390. *Winterlude* has excellent shuttle bus service between the main sites. The *Nightstop* program, designed with safety, the disabled, and the elderly in mind, allows passengers to get off between regularly scheduled stops after 9 PM. Bus fares vary depending on the time of day.

CAR RENTAL All major international firms are represented.

TAXI You can hail a cab in Ottawa, but the quickest way to get one is to call one of the major companies, such as *A-1* (phone: 746-1616), *Blue Line* (phone: 238-1111), or *Capital* (phone: 746-2233). All cabs are metered. Cabstands are located at major hotels and at the train station.

TOURS It's possible to view this lovely city by land, water, or air, or on foot. *Capital Trolley Tours* (phone: 241-0658) offers a bargain-priced sightseeing tour with stops at 19 major tourist attractions along a 22-mile route which crosses the river to the *Museum of Civilization* in Hull. You can ride the green-and-gold trolley buses all day on one ticket and stay as long as you like at any of the stops (another trolley comes along every 30 minutes). *Piccadilly Bus Tours* (phone: 235-7674) conducts tours of the city on double-decker buses from Confederation Square (near Parliament Hill) from May to late October. Or hail a *Velvet Wheels* rickshaw on the street; the fit young students who pull them provide a running commentary. *Paul's Boat Lines* (phone: 225-6781) cruises the Ottawa River and Rideau Canal all summer; the *Ottawa Riverboat Company* (phone: 562-4888) schedules party and brunch cruises aboard the *Sea Prince II.* Head toward Confederation Square, and ticket sellers for both companies will find you. The *Bytown Pumper* steamship offers two-hour cruises on the calm waters of the Rideau River starting near Hog's Back Falls (phone: 736-9893). Beautifully restored, the wood-burning *Pumper* was the first steel-hulled vessel on the Great Lakes; it celebrated its 100th birthday in 1995.

Riding in hot-air balloons is a popular way to see the city, and five companies offer such excursions: *Blue Sky* (phone: 739-9035); *Bytown Ballooning* (phone: 749-7502); *Great Canadian* (phone: 741-5627); *Skyview* (phone: 724-7784); and *Windborne* (phone: 739-7388). For those who prefer to keep their feet on the ground, daily walking tours are organized during the summer by the *NCC* (phone: 239-5000). For a nominal charge, these expeditions explore areas of the Lower Town that are off limits to traffic. Highly recommended is the five-hour round trip from Hull to the picturesque ski village of Wakefield aboard a 1907 steam engine with 1940s wooden rolling stock (phone: 819-77-TRAIN; fax: 819-778-5007). Great photo ops abound as the train winds its way up the Gatineau Valley. Group rates are available, and reservations are necessary. The train operates May through October; it runs daily in July and August, weekends only in May, June, September, and October.

SPECIAL EVENTS

Winter and spring are the liveliest times of year in the Canadian federal capital thanks to two lively festivals celebrating these seasons.

BEST FESTIVALS

Winterlude What began in the 1970s as a minor party on skates, a gesture of defiance against the long, hard winter, has developed into North America's biggest party on ice. On three consecutive weekends in February, the Rideau Canal becomes the world's longest skating rink, bedecked with flags, huts, exotic food stands, and elaborate snow and ice sculptures created by amateurs and professionals from as far away as China and Australia. Events range from figure-skating shows and zany hospital-bed races (on ice) to the dramatic *Winterman Triathalon*—a 16-mile course covered on foot, skates, and skis. Events spill over into *Jacques Cartier Park,* on the opposite bank of the Ottawa River; the children's ice playground is sheer magic. Try one of the festival's most popular snack foods: a "beavertail" (a crispy pancake served with a variety of toppings). Skates can be rented and sharpened at many sites along the canal, and there are numerous heated changing huts and restrooms. If you need first aid or other assistance, radio-equipped patrollers on skates are never far away (look for the red crosses on their jackets). *Winterlude* is capped off on the final day by an international 55-mile (88-km) cross-country ski race in *Gatineau Park.* For information, contact the *NCC* or the *Ottawa Tourism and Convention Authority* (see *Tourist Information*).

Canadian Tulip Festival To commemorate Ottawa's having given haven to the exiled Dutch royal family during World War II, the Netherlands presented the capital city with 100,000 tulip bulbs in 1945. An additional 20,000 bulbs have been sent every year since, making this display the largest of its kind in North America. The spectacular blossoming of these Dutch flowers serves as the impetus for a five-day, mid-May program of outdoor entertainment for all ages, including a procession of decorated boats on the Rideau Canal, street dancing, a huge crafts market, hot-air balloon and helicopter rides, fireworks displays, and more. A focal point of the festival is *Major's Hill Park,* behind the *Château Laurier* hotel, where many key events take place. For information, contact the *Canadian Tulip Festival* (360 Albert St., Ste. 1720, Ottawa, ONT K1R 7X7; phone: 567-5757).

Canada Day (July 1) celebrates the nation's birthday, and naturally the capital sets the pace. The downtown core—closed to traffic all day—is turned over to free concerts and special events, culminating at night in a stage show and fireworks display on Parliament Hill. The 10-day *Ottawa International Jazz Festival* in mid-July has become one of the city's best summer attractions. Jazz bands and soloists from Canada and the US perform on street corners and in parks and concert halls throughout the downtown area. Street performances and most outdoor lunchtime shows are free; a bargain-priced passport gets you into everything else (phone: 594-3580).

The *International Cycling Festival* in Hull is held the first two weeks of August. In Ottawa, the *SuperEx* at *Landsdowne Park* during the last two weeks of August mixes the noise and lights of a giant midway with agricultural displays, food fairs, and outdoor concerts. The first week of September is marked by the spectacular *Hot Air Balloon Festival* at *La Baie Park* in Gatineau, on the Quebec side of the river (phone: 819-243-2330; 800-668-8383). It features approximately 150 manned balloons from Europe and America, many in novel shapes. The *Ottawa Wine and Food Show* at the *Congress Centre* (next to the *Westin* hotel; phone: 236-9931) in the third week of October is the capital's culinary event of the year, with more than 200 exhibits of food, fine wine, beer, and spirits from around the world and cooking demonstrations by celebrity chefs. Minimum age for entry is 19, and the admission charge includes tastings.

MUSEUMS

In addition to those described in *Special Places,* Ottawa is the home of several other interesting museums:

BYTOWN MUSEUM The city's oldest building houses a museum saluting the builders of the canal and the rough, tough lumber town Ottawa once was. It's closed Sunday mornings April through mid-October; open by appointment only the rest of the year. Admission charge. Next to the *Canadian Museum of Contemporary Photography* (see below), near the canal locks' entrance (phone: 234-4570).

CANADIAN MUSEUM OF CARICATURE A collection of works dating back to the 18th century, it includes some of the merciless caricatures at which modern Canadian political cartoonists excel. From the queen to hockey great Wayne Gretsky, no one is spared. Open daily. No admission charge. 136 St. Patrick St., near the *National Gallery* (phone: 995-3145).

CANADIAN MUSEUM OF CONTEMPORARY PHOTOGRAPHY This museum has a permanent collection of 150,000 photographs; it also features special exhibitions, an audiovisual theater, and a boutique selling items of interest to photographers. Open Wednesdays from 4 to 8 PM and Thursdays from 11 AM to 8 PM year-round; open daily May through October; closed Mondays and Tuesdays the rest of the year. Admission charge. In a reconstructed railway tunnel near the *Château Laurier* hotel (phone: 990-8257).

CURRENCY MUSEUM The Bank of Canada's collection includes international currencies along with such ancient monies as Chinese bronze "knife money" and a three-ton Yap stone from the South Pacific. Closed Sunday mornings May through September; closed Sunday morning and Mondays October through April. Admission charge. 245 Sparks St. (phone: 782-8914).

SHOPPING

The region's large shopping centers include *Rideau Centre* (see *Special Places*) and the *Place d'Orléans* (110 Place d'Orléans; phone: 824-9468), which has 200 stores and an indoor playground. Also in the east end, *St. Laurent* (1200 St. Laurent St.) and *Gloucester Centre* (1980 Ogilvie Rd.) both have restaurants, movie theaters, and shops big and small. On the west end, *Bayshore* (100 Bayshore Dr.) and *Carlingwood* (2121 Carling St.) are the major shopping centers; in the south, it's *Billings Bridge* (2323 Riverside Dr.). The *Byward Market* (see *Special Places*) is for sidewalk browsers interested in bric-a-brac and the work of local artisans. The *Sparks Street Mall,* an outdoor, pedestrians-only street, is a popular shopping and socializing venue (see *Special Places*). In addition, Bank Street has a number of antiques shops and used bookstores worth browsing through. Outside Ottawa's city limits, shopping centers stay open evenings Mondays through Saturdays; within the city, they close at 6 PM, with later hours on Fridays and Saturdays. All malls are open Sundays, and many stores open at noon on Sundays.

Some shops to explore:

Architectural Antique Company As the name implies, antique architectural elements are featured here. 1240 Bank St. (phone: 738-9243).

Baldwin House Antique furniture, historic military medals, and vintage European toys are sold. 1115 Bank St. (phone: 232-7296).

Bloomsbury and Company The focus here is on antique furniture. 1090 Bank St. (phone: 730-1926).

Burkholder Furs A good selection of fine furs. 119 Bank St. (phone: 232-2626).

Davis Agency Canadiana Shop A must for Canadian crafts—everything from handwoven British Columbia blankets to Inuit carvings. *Sparks Street Mall* (phone: 236-7446).

Domus A combined bookstore, restaurant, and kitchenware shop. On the corner of Dalhousie and Murray Sts. (phone: 241-6410).

Dworkin Furs Another fine furrier. 256 Rideau St. (phone: 241-4213).

Four Corners Inuit and other Native American arts and crafts. *Sparks Street Mall* (phone: 233-2322).

Penelope Specializes in one-of-a-kind mohair sweaters for women. 703 Bank St. (phone: 233-0223).

Snow Goose A good selection of Inuit and other Native American arts and crafts. *Sparks Street Mall* (phone: 232-2213).

Suttles and Seawinds Distinctively Canadian clothing—most of it made in Nova Scotia. 535 Sussex Dr. (phone: 241-8101).

Valley Goods Company This shop in a 19th-century limestone building whisks you back to the era of the general store, offering Ottawa Valley art and crafts, clothing, furnishings, and food. *Byward Market* at 41 York St. (phone: 241-3000).

A Very Special Place Tapestries, hand-crafted ceramics, and Raku pottery. 463 Sussex Dr. (phone: 241-6100).

Yardley's One of the largest collections of antique lamps in Canada. 1124 Bank St. (phone: 238-6695) and nearby at 1095 Bank St. (phone: 730-9111).

SPORTS

BASEBALL Triple A baseball arrived in Ottawa in 1993 in the form of the Ottawa *Lynx,* a farm team of the Montreal *Expos.* The club's home is the 10,000-seat *Ottawa Stadium* (Coventry Rd.; phone: 747-5969). Take the Queensway east and exit at Vanier Parkway; parking is plentiful. There's bus service, too (phone: 741-4390). The regular season runs from late April to mid-September.

BICYCLING The *NCC* maintains more than 65 miles of trails. Rent wheels from *Rent-A-Bike* (*Château Laurier* hotel; phone: 241-4140). The best places to ride are on Colonel By Drive and the Ottawa River parkways, which wind around the city. The *Ottawa Bicycle Club* (*OBC*; PO Box 4298, Station E, Ottawa, ONT KIS 5B3; phone: 230-1064) welcomes kindred spirits seeking guidance on the many cycle routes and upcoming events; it also makes its newsletter and path maps free on request to non-residents.

FOOTBALL The Ottawa *Rough Riders,* a professional team in the *Canadian Football League,* play regular-season home games from July through November in *Lansdowne Park* (phone: 563-4551). The city provides additional bus service on game days.

GOLF There are more than 30 public and private golf courses within easy reach of Ottawa. The season is short (April through November), but greens and fairways are usually excellent despite the hard winters. The best public courses on the Ontario side include *Emerald Links* (6357 Emerald Lakes Dr., Greeley, ONT K4P 1M4; phone: 822-4653); *Loch Marsh* (1755 Old Carp Rd., Kanata, ONT K2K 1X7; phone: 839-5885); *Manderlay* (RR 3, North Gower, ONT K0A 2T0; phone: 489-2066); and *Metcalfe* (PO Box 279, Metcalfe, ONT K0A 2P0; phone: 821-2701).

HIKING Information on area trails is available from the *NCC* (see *Tourist Information*) or the *Ontario Ministry of Natural Resources* (phone: 836-1237). The Rideau Trail stretches for 125 miles (200 km) from the outskirts of Ottawa to Kingston, Ontario; for information contact the *Rideau Trail Association* (phone: 730-2229). *Ottawa Valley Field Trips* (phone: 591-1722) offers scenic hiking or driving day trips in the Ottawa Valley. A contact for bird watchers and insect, mushroom, and botany lovers is the *Ottawa Field*

Naturalists' Club (PO Box 3264, Postal Station C, Ottawa, ONT K1Y 4K5; phone: 722-3050). The club arranges day trips (free for individual travelers) and publishes a naturalist's history of the area, *Nature and Natural Areas in Canada's Capital*.

HOCKEY One of the newer franchises in the *National Hockey League,* the Ottawa *Senators* play at the *Civic Centre* (*Lansdowne Park;* phone: 564-1490) while they wait for their own stadium, the *Palladium,* to be built in Kanata, a western suburb. The *Civic Centre* is also home to the Ottawa *67s,* members of the *Ontario Hockey League* (phone: 232-6767). Their Quebec counterparts, the *Olympiques,* play at the *Guertin Arena* in Hull (phone: 819-771-6111). The regular season runs from September through April.

HORSE RACING Two tracks offer harness racing: the *Rideau-Carleton Raceway* (July through November), on the southern edge of Ottawa (phone: 822-2211); and the *Connaught Park Raceway* (closed Tuesdays year-round), near Aylmer, in Quebec (phone: 819-771-6111).

JOGGING Ottawa has many wonderful jogging paths. Two of them, each about 5 miles (8 km) long, run along either side of the Rideau Canal. Another runs parallel to the Ottawa River Parkway.

SAILING Canoes and paddleboats can be rented at many locations, including the Rideau Canal on Fifth Avenue and Dows Lake at the southern end of the main stretch of the canal (phone: 232-5278; also see *Canoeing and Rafting* in DIVERSIONS). For information about nearby sailing and cruising opportunities, contact the *Canadian Yachting Association* (*CYA*; 1600 James Naismith Dr., Ste. 504; phone: 748-5687). Those interested in cruising the entire Rideau Canal, about a three-day journey, can rent a boat or seek a cruise organizer (for details, see *Sailing Canada's Many Waters* in DIVERSIONS).

SKATING During the winter, the Rideau Canal is transformed into a 5-mile-long outdoor skating rink, stretching south from the Ottawa River between Colonel By Drive and Queen Elizabeth Driveway. During the day and at night, when the rink is lighted, thousands of people skate on the world's longest outdoor rink; in the morning, some people even skate to work. There are heated changing rooms on the canal January through February. For canal conditions, call 232-1234, or tune into *The Weather Channel* on TV at 27 minutes past the hour.

SKIING Four ski centers are within a 30-minute drive of downtown Ottawa. Although they're not world class in terms of vertical drops, among them they offer something for everyone, including some advanced-level slopes not for the timid or inexperienced. All have night skiing (except Sundays) and good facilities, including ski schools, equipment rentals, and cafeterias. Some centers offer two-for-one ticket days during the week and skiing by the hour. Note that all of these centers are just over the border, in Quebec.

SUPERB SLOPES

Edelweiss Younger, more aggressive skiers tend to favor this ski area, 16 miles (26 km) from Ottawa on Rte. 366 (phone: 819-459-2328).

Mont Cascades It also has a range of runs for skiers of all levels of expertise. By-the-hour lift passes are offered, a popular recent innovation. Rte. 307, 8 miles (13 km) from Cantley and 12 miles (19 km) from Ottawa (phone: 819-827-0301).

Ski Fortune Resort After deteriorating badly in recent years, the once-great *Camp Fortune Ski Club* in *Gatineau Park* has a new lease on life with new owners, a new name, and greatly improved facilities—including a 325-seat bar and restaurant in the lodge. The slopes are ideal for intermediate and family skiing, and there are also two expert-level runs. This area is being groomed to become a year-round resort, with mountain biking trails and outdoor entertainment in summer. Take the McDonald-Cartier bridge to Quebec and follow the signs (phone: 819-827-1717).

Vorlage Ideal for beginners and families with toddlers. Burnside Ave., Wakefield, 15 miles (24 km) from Ottawa (phone: 819-459-2301).

The *Mont-Ste-Marie* ski area near Kazabazua, about an hour's drive from the city, has far more extensive facilities. (For details, see *Downhill Skiing* in DIVERSIONS.) There also are more than 60 miles of groomed and patrolled cross-country ski trails in the Gatineau Hills. Passes are available on-site for a nominal charge.

SOCCER Now the leading sport in the region, soccer is played throughout the city from May through early October. The region hosts several major international youth tournaments every summer. While they are predominantly for boys, the biggest tournament, held in early August, is for female players ages 14 and older. For information, call 722-7774.

SWIMMING Among the region's 20 or so outdoor facilities are several wave pools. Mooney's Bay Beach on the Rideau River near Hog's Back Falls (see *Special Places*) is a good family swimming and picnic spot, with lifeguards on duty. For information on Ottawa pools and beaches, call 564-1414.

TENNIS Free courts—many of them floodlit for night play—are located throughout the city. Call the city recreation department (phone: 564-1180) for information.

THEATER

Touring companies often appear at the three theaters located in the *National Arts Centre* (53 Elgin St.; phone: 996-5051). The *Ottawa Little Theatre* (400 King Edward Ave.; phone: 233-8948) presents amateur productions with a professional flair in a modern, 510-seat hall. The *Great Canadian Theatre Company* (910 Gladstone; phone: 236-5192) has a reputation for strong theme plays. The *Arts Court* (2 Daly Ave., around the corner from the *Rideau Centre;* phone: 233-3449), an imposing building that once housed the criminal courts, now is a major center for the visual and performing arts. The *Théâtre de l'Ile* (1 Rue Wellington, Hull; phone: 819-595-7455) stages popular works in French; additionally, a French-language repertory company makes its home in the *National Arts Centre* (see above).

MUSIC

Canada's *National Arts Centre Orchestra,* the local *Ottawa Symphony Orchestra,* and many guest artists perform at the *National Arts Centre* (see *Theater,* above). The *Orpheus Operatic Society* stages musicals at the *High School of Commerce Auditorium* (Rochester St. at the Queensway; phone: 729-4318). For information on instrumental and choral concerts taking place around the city, consult the "City Lights" supplement published every Thursday in the *Ottawa Citizen* (see *Local Coverage*).

NIGHTCLUBS AND NIGHTLIFE

There are no more jokes about Ottawa rolling up the sidewalks at 6 PM. After dark, the city offers everything from the big band sound to hot jazz, from male strippers to *Second City*–style comedy. Once dreary, Elgin and Somerset Streets downtown now are stretches of chic sidewalk restaurants and boutiques. *Byward Market* (see *Special Places*) is even livelier, with street entertainers on warm summer nights adding to the appeal of dozens of good restaurants and clubs. The top rock spot for live dance music nightly (except Sundays) is *Grand Central* (141 George St.; phone: 233-1216).

Good downtown spots for live blues are the *Penguin* (292 Elgin St.; phone: 233-0057); *Rainbow Bistro* (76 Murray St.; phone: 594-5123); *Tucson Road House* (2440 Bank St.; phone: 738-7596); and *Zaphod Beeblebrox* (27 York St.; phone: 562-1010). Upstairs from *Mexicali Rosa's* restaurant (see *Eating Out*) is *Mexi's Creeque Alley,* which presents live bands Sunday afternoons and nightly except Mondays; the bar downstairs now caters to a darts-and-gossip crowd. For both blues and folk music, *Rasputin's* (696 Bronson Ave.; phone: 230-5102) is the current favorite, which makes getting in tough (it's a small place). Other popular clubs are the *Cajun Attic* (594 Rideau St.; phone: 789-1185) and *Ozzie's* (85 Holland Ave.; phone: 722-8500).

Jazz is popular in Ottawa; to find out what's happening and where, call the *Jazzline* (phone: 730-7755). Mainstream groups play at the *Glue Pot Inn* (340 Queen St.; phone: 594-8222) Monday evenings. Other jazz venues include *Vineyard's Wine Bar* (54 York St.; phone: 563-4270) and the *Applause* restaurant (246 Slater St.; phone: 594-4524).

If your ears demand something a little more soothing, there are also lots of piano bars: Try *Lautrec's,* in the *Radisson* hotel; *Zoe's,* in the *Château Laurier* (see *Checking In* for both hotels); *Friday's Roast Beef House* (see

Eating Out); or the *Full House* restaurant (Somerset St. W.; phone: 238-6734). The *Courtyard* restaurant (see *Eating Out*) offers classical music performances with its Sunday brunch.

English-style pubs are very popular here. Good places to try include the loud and lively *Alfie's* (14 Waller St.; phone: 235-5050); *Brigadier's Pump* (23 York St.; phone: 230-6368), which has a courtyard with tables plus a patio for summer evenings; *Mayflower II* (201 Queen St.; phone: 238-1138), which has an upstairs bar as well as a downstairs restaurant; *Earl of Sussex* (431 Sussex Dr.; phone: 233-5544); and the *Newfoundland Pub* (940 Montreal Rd.; phone: 745-0962).

For stand-up comedy, there's *Yuk Yuk's* at the *Capital Hill* hotel (see *Checking In*); reservations are necessary Friday and Saturday nights. Around midnight it's common for Ottawans to head over to "The Strip"—an area of Hull jammed with clubs and pubs that stay open late. Taxi drivers know the way from Ottawa, but be warned that it can get pretty wild and woolly.

Most bars in Ottawa are open daily and close at midnight or 1 AM. On Saturday nights at around 1 AM, serious night owls travel across the river to Hull, where bars remain open until 3 AM.

Best in Town

CHECKING IN

Finding accommodations in Canada's capital is not a problem, thanks to the hotel construction boom of the late 1980s. However, vacancies in the downtown core can be scarce during February's *Winterlude,* spring's *Canadian Tulip Festival,* and summer's conventions and conferences. For a double room, expect to pay $120 or more per night in an establishment listed as very expensive; from $80 to $115 in expensive places; from $55 to $80 in those classed as moderate; and $50 or less in the ones described as inexpensive. All hotels feature such amenities as air conditioning, private baths, TV sets, and telephones unless otherwise indicated.

In addition, more and more private homes are offering bed and breakfast accommodations to travelers. The *Ottawa Bed and Breakfast Association* (phone: 563-0106) represents those that submit to regular inspections and meet certain standards, and it acts as a referral service. *Carleton University* (phone: 788-5611) and the *University of Ottawa* (phone: 564-3463) make student residences available for short stays in the summer, but the latter does not provide breakfast. All telephone numbers are in the 613 area code unless otherwise indicated.

For an unforgettable experience, we begin with our favorite Ottawa hostelry, followed by our cost and quality choices of hotels, listed by price category.

A GRAND HOTEL

Château Laurier The *Grand Trunk Railway* built the *Laurier* as a palace to honor Canada's capital, naming it after Prime Minister Wilfred Laurier, who retired in 1911, a year before the hotel opened. Since its beginnings, it has been an ornate, conservative landmark of the city. The 450 guestrooms are bright and airy, and the atmosphere is light, but it remains the traditional den for the country's leading political figures. On any given day, you might see the current prime minister's entourage lunching at elegant *Wilfrid's* or run into members of Parliament sipping tea or cocktails in *Zoe's* lounge. The hotel is located on the picturesque Rideau Canal, where guests can sled or skate in the winter; there's also an indoor pool and exercise room. *Parliament* is right next door, and the impressive *National Arts Centre* is just across the street. Several underground walkways connect the 17 meeting rooms to the *Conference Centre.* 1 Rideau St., Confederation Sq. (phone: 232-6411; 800-828-7447; fax: 786-8030).

VERY EXPENSIVE

Westin Part of a vast shopping and convention complex, this 24-story establishment has 475 rooms, a pool, a gym, a hot tub, and squash courts. *Daly's* restaurant serves good food (see *Eating Out*). At lobby level, the hotel connects with *Rideau Centre.* 11 Colonel By Dr. (phone: 560-7000; 800-228-3000; fax: 234-5396).

EXPENSIVE

Cartier Place One of an increasing number of apartment hotels springing up in Ottawa, it offers good facilities at rates below those of the major hotels. There are 132 apartments (studios and one- and two-bedroom units) available for any length of stay; maid service is included. There's a dining room. Downtown, at 180 Cooper St. (phone: 236-5000; fax: 238-3842).

Chimo Inn Across from the huge *St. Laurent Shopping Centre,* a 10-minute drive from downtown Ottawa, this rapidly expanding and well-equipped inn is popular with families. The 261 rooms include 18 executive suites. It has an indoor pool, a sauna, a whirlpool bath, exercise facilities, and a gameroom. *Quincy's* and *Clancy's* restaurants offer a vast menu range, and there's a lively lobby bar. Parking is free. St. Laurent exit north from Queensway, 1199 Joseph Cyr St. (phone: 744-1060; 800-387-9779; fax: 744-7845).

Delta Ottawa Sparkling from a $5-million makeover, this hotel boasts one of the most impressive lobbies in the capital, done in gleaming white marble, with a fireplace and a skylight. The 329 bright, well-equipped rooms include 63 suites; *Perrier's* and the more formal *Capital Club* offer good dining. The *Business Centre and Lounge,* with boardroom and clerical help, is a favorite breakfast spot for judges from Canada's *Supreme Court*, a block away. Next to the pool are a 115-foot, two-story water slide and a Jacuzzi. Ask about the free "Delta Privilege" service, which offers, in addition to some remarkable service guarantees, a free coffee maker in your room. Close to downtown, at 361 Queen St. (phone: 238-6000; 800-268-1133 in Canada; 800-877-1133 in the US; fax: 238-2290).

Lord Elgin The "dean" of Ottawa accommodations, this imposing granite landmark just below Parliament Hill has 312 large, bright, and well-equipped rooms. There also is a restaurant, a bar, and conference facilities. 100 Elgin St. (phone: 235-3333; 800-267-4298; fax: 235-3223).

Minto Place Six blocks from Parliament Hill, this impressive apartment hotel offers daily, weekly, and monthly rates, with longer-stay discounts. The 418 attractive suites with one, two, or three rooms have everything from fully equipped kitchens to computer-compatible phone lines; most also have two bathrooms. There are two restaurants, an indoor pool, and a fitness center. 433 Laurier Ave. W. (phone: 232-2200; 800-267-3377; fax: 232-6962).

Radisson An upscale, modern high-rise, it has 504 spacious rooms featuring such high-tech novelties as TV sets that display your bill at the touch of a button and mini-bars that can be locked by a computer at the front desk (for when the kids are by themselves). Other pluses are a pool and a fitness club; *La Ronde,* the revolving rooftop restaurant; and an underground shopping concourse. *Café Toulouse* is a popular lunch spot, with outdoor tables in summer. 100 Kent St. (phone: 238-1122; 800-333-3333; fax: 783-4229).

Victoria Park Bathroom mirrors that automatically defog are typical of the extras provided by this all-suite hotel, a 10-minute stroll from Parliament Hill. The 62 warm and elegant studio units and the 38 bedroom/living room suites have mahogany furniture and kitchenettes with microwave ovens. There's no restaurant, but a commissary downstairs offers "microwaveable" snacks. Continental breakfast is included in the rate. 377 O'Connor St. at Gladstone St. (phone: 567-7275; 800-465-7275; fax: 567-1161).

MODERATE

Capital Hill Considering the location of this 158-room landmark—only a few blocks from Parliament Hill—the rates are a bargain. There's a restaurant. 88 Albert St. (phone: 235-1413; 800-463-7705 in Canada; fax: 235-6047).

Quality Inn Downtown, this 211-room member of the popular chain offers a dining room, a laundry, and meeting facilities. 290 Rideau St., next to the *Ottawa Little Theatre* (phone: 789-7511; 800-668-4200).

INEXPENSIVE

Comfort Inns On the main freeway at the east and west ends of the city, these no-frills motels offer clean, pleasant accommodations. The one at the east end has 69 rooms and housekeeping units; continental breakfast is offered, but there is no restaurant. In the west end property are 104 guestrooms and a restaurant. East end (St. Laurent Blvd. exit; phone: 744-2900; 800-668-4200); west end (Eagleson Rd. exit; phone: 592-2200; 800-668-4200).

Nicholas Street International Hostel The walls of many of the tiny cells in this 19th-century jail have been removed to convert them into dormitories and rooms, but the bars have been left to preserve the heritage atmosphere (privacy is a bit limited). The gallows and trapdoor from the last hanging are still here, yet it's a surprisingly cheerful and comfy place, and the 160 beds are in great demand in the separate male and female dorms; a few family rooms are available by reservation. There are lockers, a laundry room, showers, and access to kitchen facilities, but no private baths, phones, or TV sets in the rooms. Open to everyone, though members of the international hostel organization are entitled to discounts. There are buses that take you right to the door: from the airport, No. 96; from the train station, No. 95; from the intercity bus depot, No. 4. 75 Nicholas St. (phone: 235-2595).

EATING OUT

Because of the city's role as a host for foreign government missions, Ottawa is a great place for almost any kind of food. French and French Canadian fare are specialties in this bilingual city, but there's also a strong showing of other ethnic foods, ranging from Russian to Chinese. For a meal for two, expect to pay $50 or more in restaurants classed as expensive; from $30 to $50 at those places listed as moderate; and $30 or less in the establishments categorized as inexpensive. Prices do not include drinks, wine, taxes, or tip. All restaurants are open for lunch and dinner unless otherwise noted. All telephone numbers are in the 613 area code unless otherwise indicated.

EXPENSIVE

Chez Jean Pierre Former *US Embassy* chef Jean Pierre Muller works culinary wonders in his French dining spot. The fine dishes, often featuring Atlantic salmon, veal, and venison, are reasonably priced, but be warned: Due to taxes, the accompanying bottle of wine may double the cost of the meal. Closed Sundays, Mondays, and Saturdays for lunch. Reservations necessary. Major credit cards accepted. 210 Somerset St. (phone: 235-9711).

Friday's Roast Beef House A five-minute stroll from the *National Arts Centre* and *Parliament Buildings,* this Victorian-era landmark serves excellent roast beef, aged steaks, rack of lamb, poultry, and seafood in a candlelight atmosphere. Try the Wexfordshire beef soup, and leave room for the Victorian chocolate truffle cake. Fireside tables are available in winter. Closed weekends for lunch. Reservations advised. Major credit cards accepted. 150 Elgin St. (phone: 237-5353).

Le Jardin Widely acknowledged for its excellent food and consistent quality (no canned or frozen products are used), this place specializes in French fare. The decor is pleasing: The restaurant is in an 1875 stone house that has won a Heritage Canada award for its renovation. Closed for lunch. Reservations advised. Major credit cards accepted. 127 York St. (phone: 241-1828).

L'Orée du Bois A 15-minute drive across the river from Ottawa and up in the Gatineau Hills near the *Ski Fortune* resort, this restaurant enjoys a beautiful wooded setting and a reputation for excellent French fare. Specialties include seafood stew, salmon in pastry, and duck in cider. Closed January, Sundays, and Mondays. Reservations necessary Saturday nights and for groups of more than four at lunch. Major credit cards accepted. Kingsmere Rd., Old Chelsea (phone: 819-827-0332).

MODERATE

Bay Street Bistro A popular eatery near Parliament Hill, the bistro has an ecletic menu (ask about the escargots in champagne for adults, or the grilled chicken breasts for children) and good-value "early bird" pasta dinner specials. Open daily. Reservations advised. Major credit cards accepted. 160 Bay St. (phone: 234-1111).

Bistro 115 Well known for its mussels with saffron-and–white wine sauce, this eatery is located in a lovely old home on the fringe of *Byward Market,* complete with a courtyard patio in the summer. The soups and desserts are homemade, and the wine bar offers vintages by the glass. Open daily. Reservations advised. Major credit cards accepted. 110 Murray St. (phone: 562-7244).

Courtyard In a delightful setting near the *Byward Market* and tucked away in a cobblestone courtyard, this restaurant has a summer patio. Specialties include beef tenderloin Wellington, rack of lamb, sautéed shrimp and scallops, and raspberry cottage cake. Special dietary needs are accommodated. Open daily, with a Sunday brunch. Reservations advised on weekends. Major credit cards accepted. 21 George St. (phone: 238-4623).

Daly's Long and narrow so everyone can share the view of the canal and the *National Arts Centre,* this pleasant eatery in the *Westin* hotel is classy without being pretentious or overpriced. Lunch offerings include poached salmon in Indian tea and prime ribs; at dinner, rib-eye steaks and tiger prawns are among the selections. On request, youngsters are supplied with crayons and drawing paper. The staff is efficient and friendly. Open daily.

Reservations advised for dinner. Major credit cards accepted. 11 Colonel By Dr. (phone: 560-7333).

Domus Café Part of this fresh, bright establishment is devoted to kitchenware, the rest to a very good restaurant that offers a unique feature: a daily menu item adapted from a cookbook available in the store. Most of the produce comes from the nearby farmers' market. Everything about this place is welcoming and professional, and the open kitchen invites inspection. Open daily; brunch and dinner on Sundays. Reservations recommended. Major credit cards accepted. 85 Murray St. (phone: 241-6007).

Haveli This East Indian restaurant has grown in size and popularity; its much-talked-about specialties include marinated leg of lamb and a complete vegetarian dinner made of yogurt, rice, cauliflower, and other healthful ingredients. The decor glows with opulent dark wood and burnished brass. Closed Saturdays for lunch and Sundays for dinner. Reservations advised. Major credit cards accepted. 87 George St., upstairs in the *Byward Market* (phone: 241-1700).

Mamma Teresa Veal is the specialty at this firmly ensconced Italian restaurant, known for its fine food and comfortable atmosphere. Dishes come with homemade pasta, plenty of fresh bread, and deep-fried zucchini. There's a good selection of Italian wines. Open daily. Reservations advised. Major credit cards accepted. 300 Somerset St. W. (phone: 236-3023).

Silk Roads Local food critics rave about this Afghan restaurant, which serves lamb, quail, duck, and vegetarian dishes. Try the sweet cheese balls and at least one of the magnificent desserts. The decor is attractive; the service, pleasant. Open daily. Reservations advised. Major credit cards accepted. A short stroll from Parliament Hill, at 300 Sparks St. (phone: 236-4352).

INEXPENSIVE

Mexicali Rosa's The branch of this restaurant in the new boathouse on Dow's Lake (phone: 234-8156) has a picturesque setting; the other two, at 895 Bank St. (phone: 236-9499) and at 207 Rideau Street (phone: 234-7044), make up in liveliness what they lack in decor. All three serve very good guacamole, burritos, tostadas, tacos, enchiladas, and chili; be sure to indicate how hot you like them. Open daily. Reservations advised for groups of eight or more. Major credit cards accepted.

Trattoria Italia Preston Street is so Italian that red and green street signs designate it "Corso Italia." Good restaurants abound on this strip (a five-minute taxi ride from downtown, walkable on a summer evening), but the Carrozza family runs one of the best. It's unpretentious, and the warm, relaxed atmosphere makes the food seem even better. The pasta is daughter Connie's specialty; the *tiramisù* is not to be missed. Open daily. Reservations advised. Major credit cards accepted. 228 Preston St. (phone: 236-1081).

Zak's Highlighted by vinyl banquettes, metal paper-napkin dispensers, and "Wake Up, Little Susie" playing on the jukebox, the food at this 1950s-era diner is exactly what you'd expect, with such specialties as great burgers and deep-fried clams. Open daily to at least midnight. Reservations necessary for groups of 15 or more. Major credit cards accepted. 14 *Byward Market* (phone: 241-2401).

Quebec City

The key battle that determined the fate of French Canada lasted only about 20 minutes. It occurred on the morning of September 13, 1759, on the Plaines d'Abraham (Plains of Abraham) in Quebec City, the capital of New France. Under siege by the British General James Wolfe since July, the city had stood firm against the attacks. On the evening of September 12, however, Wolfe led a group of soldiers up the steep hill from Anse au Foulon and assembled the force on the Plaines d'Abraham. That is where the astonished and horrified French found them the following morning when the Marquis de Montcalm, commander of the city's defenses, rushed his troops into battle. In the ensuing struggle, both Wolfe and Montcalm were killed (Wolfe died on the battlefield, Montcalm shortly after in the city), and the French were decisively defeated. But according to legend, as smoke obscured the battlefield and the dream of New France died with its last defenders, a voice was heard across the plains crying, *"Je me souviens"*—"I remember."

Those words have become the motto of the province of Quebec, and nowhere do they resound with more conviction than in Quebec City, itself the most tangible remnant of New France in Canada. Rising on the massive cliff of Cap Diamant (Cape Diamond) some 350 feet above the St. Lawrence River, Quebec City is the rock upon which the nation's federalism often has nearly foundered. Though the English won control of Canada, Quebec City retained its French language, culture, and heritage. And through subsequent invasions by the British and Americans in the course of its history and the contemporary French-English controversy concerning the independence of Quebec, the city survives as a stronghold of Canada's French culture on an English-speaking continent.

In no other city in Canada can you see so clearly the places where the two worlds of the French and English collide. The *Monument Wolfe-Montcalm* in Lower Town, for example, commemorates both the victors and the vanquished. At the *Musée du Fort,* the guide explaining the diorama of the fateful battle in 1759 refers to the British as "the enemy." Even in the sports world, French and English clashes of Canadian culture reveal themselves: Quebec City nationalists charged that top hockey prospect Eric Lindros was anti-French when he turned down an offer to play for the hometown *Nordiques.*

Quebec City was the first permanent French settlement in North America, and, despite two centuries of English rule, it remains fiercely French. Most everyone here speaks French; newspapers, plays, and conversations generally are in French, though many people can and do speak English, particularly those who work in businesses catering to tourists.

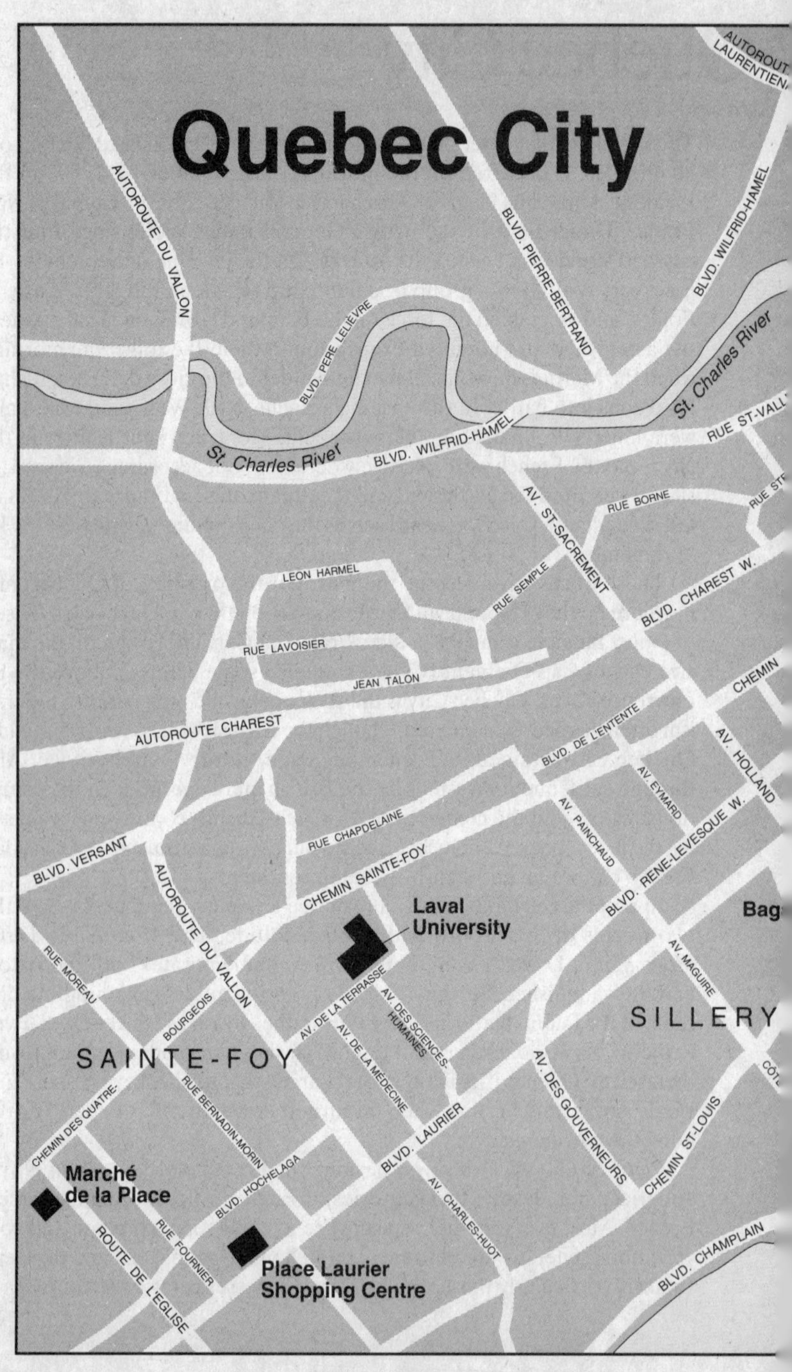
Quebec City
AUTOROUTE LAURENTIENNE
AUTOROUTE DU VALLON
BLVD. PIERRE-BERTRAND
BLVD. WILFRID-HAMEL
BLVD. PERE LELIÈVRE
St. Charles River
St. Charles River
BLVD. WILFRID-HAMEL
RUE ST-VALL
AV. ST-SACREMENT
RUE BORNE
LEON HARMEL
RUE SEMPLE
BLVD. CHAREST W.
RUE LAVOISIER
JEAN TALON
CHEMIN
AUTOROUTE CHAREST
BLVD. DE L'ENTENTE
AV. HOLLAND
AV. EYMARD
AV. PAINCHAUD
RUE CHAPDELAINE
BLVD. VERSANT
BLVD. RENE-LEVESQUE W.
CHEMIN SAINTE-FOY
AUTOROUTE DU VALLON
Laval University
AV. MAGUIRE
RUE MOREAU
BOURGEOIS
AV. DE LA TERRASSE
AV. DES SCIENCES-HUMAINES
SILLERY
SAINTE-FOY
AV. DE LA MÉDECINE
AV. DES GOUVERNEURS
CHEMIN DES QUATRE-
RUE BERNADIN-MORIN
BLVD. LAURIER
CHEMIN ST-LOUIS
Marché de la Place
BLVD. HOCHELAGA
AV. CHARLES-HUOT
RUE FOURNIER
ROUTE DE L'EGLISE
BLVD. CHAMPLAIN
Place Laurier Shopping Centre

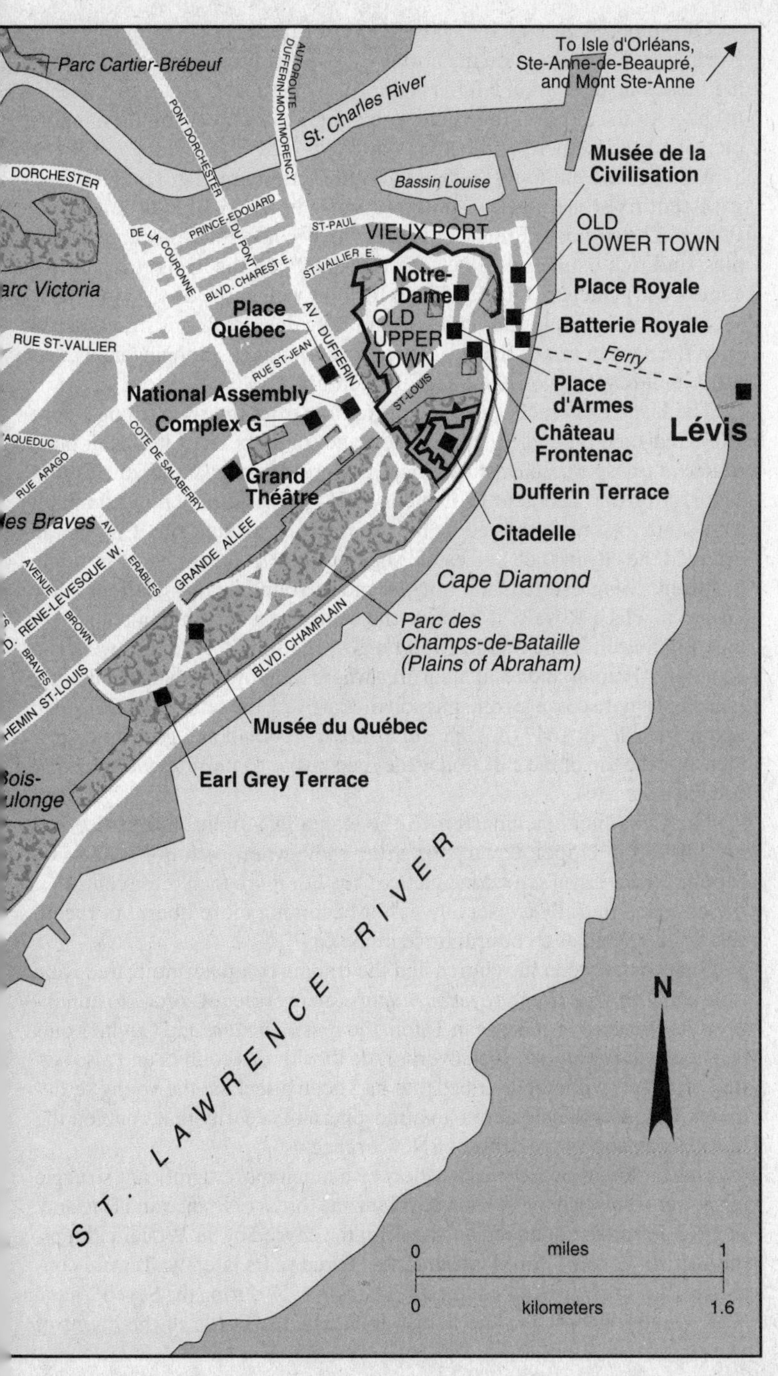

Parc Cartier-Brébeuf
AUTOROUTE DUFFERIN-MONTMORENCY
PONT DORCHESTER
St. Charles River
To Isle d'Orléans, Ste-Anne-de-Beaupré, and Mont Ste-Anne
DORCHESTER
Bassin Louise
Musée de la Civilisation
PRINCE-EDOUARD
DU PONT
DE LA COURONNE
BLVD. CHAREST E.
ST-PAUL
ST-VALLIER E.
VIEUX PORT
OLD LOWER TOWN
Notre-Dame
Place Royale
arc Victoria
Place Québec
AV. DUFFERIN
OLD UPPER TOWN
Batterie Royale
RUE ST-VALLIER
RUE ST-JEAN
Ferry
National Assembly
ST-LOUIS
Place d'Armes
Complex G
Château Frontenac
Lévis
AQUEDUC
COTE DE SALABERRY
RUE ARAGO
Grand Théâtre
Dufferin Terrace
des Braves
AV.
Citadelle
AVENUE
RENE-LEVESQUE W.
ERABLES
GRANDE ALLEE
Cape Diamond
BROWN
D.
BRAVES
BLVD. CHAMPLAIN
Parc des Champs-de-Bataille (Plains of Abraham)
HEMIN ST-LOUIS
Musée du Québec
Bois-
ulonge
Earl Grey Terrace
ST. LAWRENCE RIVER
N
0
miles
1
0
kilometers
1.6

Of the population of 165,000, 95% is of French stock, primarily from Normandy and Brittany on the northwest coast of France. True Québécois are those who have never left the province—some actually trace their ancestry back to the 17th century. They are a family-oriented, traditional people, an attitude which is reflected in their city.

Many of the buildings in the city's old section are restored 17th- and 18th-century stone houses, similar to those in the villages of provincial France. The cuisine is French or hearty Québécois—thick pea soups, meat pies, and rich maple syrup pies for dessert. Even the walls surrounding Vieux (Old) Québec (Quebec City is the only walled city on the continent) seem to protect its insular culture, and they demarcate historic Quebec from the newer parts of the city, where modern hotels, shopping malls, and office buildings acknowledge the 20th century.

The history of Quebec City seems to flow from the river, along whose banks indigenous peoples lived for thousands of years, using it as their main source of transportation. And although explorer Jacques Cartier, the Breton sailor, gave Cap Diamant its name in 1535, it was Samuel de Champlain who came to stay. Attracted by the strategically located site, Champlain founded the city in 1608 and established his first *habitation* here, a trading post comprising a store, a few houses, and surrounding fortifications. Now known as Place Royale, it became the center of a fur-trading colony—a meeting place for the merchants who governed the territory as well as a commercial center and residential area where wealthy merchants built their homes. As more colonists and missionaries arrived, the settlement expanded up the hillside. In 1647 the *Château St-Louis* was built as a governor's residence at the top of the cliff (today the spectacular *Château Frontenac* hotel occupies the site).

The Canadian headquarters of the Roman Catholic church also was established in Upper Town soon after 1659, when Bishop François de Montmorency Laval settled in Quebec City. For more than three centuries, the church—initially conservative, but becoming more liberal in recent years—has acted as a cultural force in the city.

Quarrels between the church and the trading company motivated King Louis XIV to send over a royal *intendant*—an overseer of sorts—to administer the province in 1663. Jean Talon, the first *intendant,* and Comte Louis de Buade de Frontenac, the governor, dealt with this conflict and also settled problems with native tribes that had been attacking the young settlement. Together they fostered an atmosphere of security that enabled the town to develop as the center of New France.

This period of peace was cut short by a much more significant struggle for power—between the two major colonizing forces of France and England. In 1690, Frontenac subdued an attack on the city led by Sir William Phipps, the British Governor of Massachusetts. Three years later, walls were constructed to fortify the city's defenses. Then, in 1759 during the Seven Years' War, Quebec City fell to the British following the Battle of the Plains of

Abraham. The settlement, known as the Act of Quebec (1774), guaranteed French Canadians "as much as British laws would allow" in terms of cultural and religious rights. But the battle had a profound effect on the Québécois psyche. Many members of the aristocratic class returned to France, and those who stayed taught their children what had been lost on the Plaines d'Abraham: *"Je me souviens."*

The British weren't the only outsiders with an interest in Quebec. In 1775, the Québécois resisted an invasion by American troops led by Generals Richard Montgomery and Benedict Arnold. This siege lasted a little more than a month, ending with the arrival of the British fleet and the retreat of the exhausted American troops. Concerned over further attacks, the English completed the wall surrounding the city.

Throughout the 19th century Quebec City remained an important political center, becoming the province's capital in 1867. Peace brought economic change. Timber and shipbuilding became the major industries, and the city maintained its position as a significant commercial center until the mid-19th century, when Montreal and Toronto surpassed it.

But Quebec City remains the most important historical center of Canada. The restored city walls, now a historic site, surround the most interesting section of the city, Vieux Québec. More than 90% of the 17th- and 18th-century houses and buildings in the area around Place Royale have been restored and now house museums, art galleries, and restaurants. Upper Town is a well-preserved area of narrow cobblestone streets lined with historic buildings.

Beyond the city walls, farther up the hill, lies 20th-century Quebec. Here are all the amenities found in any other modern provincial capital—a convention center; several luxurious high-rise hotels; and the stately buildings of the *Hôtel du Parlement* (National Assembly, as the legislature is called). Beyond this sprawls the suburb of Ste-Foy, rapidly developed in the past three decades to accommodate a growing population. Many Québécois work in Ste-Foy at the suburb's two major shopping malls or at *Université Laval.* The largest employer of all is the provincial government, with more than 53,000 civil servants.

Around Colline Parlementaire (Parliament Hill) stands further evidence that Quebec City's present is inextricably bound up with its past. Sculptures of historically prominent Canadians are carved into niches in the *Hôtel du Parlement.* These figures and the nearby Plaines d'Abraham and *Citadelle*—the star-shaped fortress that won the city the sobriquet "Gibraltar of America"—record Quebec City's struggle to become what it is today.

The French-English controversy in Canada still simmers. It's often said if you scratch the surface, you will find some level of nationalism in every Québécois. The province's current generation aspires to economic stability over political turmoil. In fact, even the fiercely separatist Parti Québécois wants to continue using the Canadian dollar and Canadian passports and to maintain trade relations with the rest of Canada. With the onset of a severe nationwide recession and high unemployment, however, the Quebec business community is suffering, and some enthusiasm for independence has cooled.

Quebec's current political crisis began when it refused to sign the Constitution. In 1987 Prime Minister Brian Mulroney proposed the Meech Lake Accord to give the provinces more power. Under the accord Quebec would have been recognized as a "distinct society" and, along with the other provinces, would have been given veto power over future constitutional changes. When Manitoba and Newfoundland refused to ratify the agreement in 1990, the accord failed—giving rise to a new movement toward Quebec's secession from Canada. The Meech Lake debacle was followed in 1992 by a nationwide referendum on a new agreement, the Charlottetown Accord. Quebec and five other provinces turned down the revised constitutional package. Quebeckers insisted the new deal failed to meet their demands, while most Canadians, weary of constitutional wrangling, felt it did not address the concerns of the country as a whole in its efforts to accommodate Quebec.

With the constitutional issue still in limbo, the question of sovereignty was a key issue in the 1993 federal election, when, for the first time in Canada's history, a separatist party, the Bloc Québécois, won enough votes to become parliament's official opposition. Sovereignty was also a major issue in the 1994 provincial election, which resulted in the return to power of the Parti Québécois (PQ) after 10 years in opposition (although according to pundits the election result says little about voters' support for the party's separatist platform—Quebeckers have shown a marked tendency to vote simply for a change of ruling party, regardless of its agenda). As promised by PQ leader Jacques Parizeau throughout the election campaign, the wheels were immediately set in motion toward another referendum on Quebec's future, despite public opinion polls which have shown support for independence running consistently at less than 50% since the last referendum.

Regardless of the outcome of a provincial referendum, Quebec City will continue to be proud of its very particular history and character. Whatever the future holds, Quebec City will certainly remain—as it has through almost four centuries and six invasions—authentically French. The strength of its collective memory continues to hold fast.

Quebec City At-a-Glance

SEEING THE CITY

Set on a hill, Quebec City affords a spectacular panoramic view. To the northeast is the Gaspé Peninsula, with its poor but picturesque villages; to the south, Montreal, 153 miles (245 km) away; straight up to the north are the fabulous Laurentian slopes, which the Québécois call the Laurentides.

L'Astral, the *Loews Le Concorde* hotel's revolving rooftop restaurant-bar (see *Eating Out*), is situated on the highest point of Cap Diamant, and it commands a great panorama of Quebec City and surrounding areas, day or night. On a clear day you can see as far as Ile d'Orléans, in summer a verdant island of apple orchards, strawberry farms, and country homes; some 25 miles away, the surrounding peaks of the Laurentians are dominated by Mont Ste-Anne, site of the region's best ski resort. Also check out the view from the city's highest observation point, the 31st floor of *Edifice Marie-Guyart* (*Complexe G,* 1037 Rue de la Chevrotière, off the Grande Allée; phone: 643-9841). While enjoying the view, tour exhibitions of works by some of Quebec's best artists in the sky-high *Galerie Anima G.* The observation gallery is closed weekend mornings and December 15 to January 15; no admission charge.

Two of the best views of the river are from the *Terrasse Dufferin,* a terrace flanking the *Château Frontenac* hotel, and the *Terrasse Earl-Grey,* an observatory adjoining the Plaines d'Abraham, between Rues Wolfe and Montcalm, in *Parc des Champs-de-Bataille.*

SPECIAL PLACES

The best way to see the city is by strolling down its streets and alleys. Quebec City is a people-size place where the scale of sites is that of an easy day's perambulation—quaint cobbled streets, historic houses, and the sort of secure claustrophobia conferred by a city that you can almost drape around your shoulders. But before setting out, get a good map. The streets are laid out haphazardly, particularly in the older sections. Lower Town revolves around Place Royale at river level. To the north and west, there's a cluster of cafés, pubs, art galleries, boutiques, and antiques stores in what was once the city's financial district. Just a few blocks north is the spruced-up port area, with old warehouses reincarnated as fashionable boutiques. Place d'Armes, at the top of the funicular next to the *Château Frontenac,* stands at the center of Upper Town. (The funicular, which links Lower and Upper Towns, operates daily from 7:30 AM to 11 PM; there's an admission charge.) Colline Parlementaire, farther up, is the site of government buildings abutting sleek high-rise hotels. Beyond them all are the suburbs. The Plaines d'Abraham have been made into a lovely park *(Parc des Champs-de-Bataille),* with miles of walking and jogging paths, picnic tables, bird-feeding stations, gardens, and great river views.

LOWER TOWN

PLACE ROYALE This small, cobblestone square—a historic zone—was the site of Champlain's first *habitation* (1608), which included buildings for lodging, a store, a stockade, and gardens. During the French regime, the square was used as a marketplace, and successful merchants built their homes here. In the center of the square is a bronze bust of Louis XIV. Despite the destruction of some of the houses, the *place* and the streets leading off it are lined with the greatest concentration of 17th- and 18th-century buildings in North America. As the centuries slipped by, the area went downhill, and the townsfolk simply forgot its history. Then, in 1960, a fire bared some mysterious brick walls that eventually were discovered to be genuine historic treasures. Most of the buildings clustered around the *Eglise Notre-Dame-des-Victoires* are architectural gems that began life as the houses of wealthy merchants. The main floors of a number of these homes are open to the public as museums, art galleries, and restaurants, while the upper floors are home to modern-day Quebeckers, many of whom own businesses in the area. Off Notre-Dame at the foot of Cap Diamant near the river.

EGLISE NOTRE-DAME-DES-VICTOIRES (OUR LADY OF VICTORIES CHURCH) Built over the foundations of the settlement that Samuel de Champlain founded in the early 1600s, this small, gray stone church has been clinging to its original site for more than three centuries. Despite its meek appearance, *Notre-Dame* owes its name to two French victories over British aggression, one in 1690, just two years after the church celebrated its first mass, and another in 1711. Destroyed in the bombardment that preceded the Battle of the Plains of Abraham and the conquest of 1759, the church has been restored twice. Today it looks much as it did when it was the heart and soul of community life in the French colony's burgeoning port district. The pretty, pastel-tinted interior is dominated by an unusual castle-shaped high altar. A scale model of a ship, suspended above the nave, recalls *Le Brezé,* the vessel that transported troops to New France in 1664. Mass is said Saturdays at 7 PM and Sundays (call for hours). Open daily May to October 15; closed Mondays the rest of the year. Pl. Royale (phone: 692-1650).

MAISONS BRUNEAU, DRAPEAU, AND RAGEOT The multimedia production "Place Royale: Centre of Trade in New France," which describes the business activities of the area during colonial times, is presented here daily from June 7 through September. No admission charge. 3A Pl. Royale (phone: 643-6631).

MAISON DES VINS (HOUSE OF WINES) In this restored home is an excellent wine store with an extensive selection of imported bottles. The establishment is worth a visit for its exposed brick walls, vaulted and candlelit cellars, and a wide array of wines, ranging from a Mouton Rothschild 1879 (valued between $13,000 and $21,000) to the local favorite, *caribou,* a potent mixture of wine and alcohol. Closed Sundays and Mondays. Reservations necessary for guided tours. No admission charge. Beside *Maisons Bruneau, Drapeau,* and *Rageot* (above), at 1 Pl. Royale (phone: 643-1214).

PLACE DE PARIS In 1984 France paid tribute to Quebec by christening the Place du Québec in Paris. To reciprocate, Quebec City erected a monument on the exact spot where the French first set foot here—at the corner of today's Rues de la Place and de l'Union—and dubbed it Place de Paris.

BATTERIE ROYALE (ROYAL BATTERY) Built in 1691, this artillery emplacement, one of the oldest in Quebec City, has been entirely restored. Corner of Rues Sous-le-Fort and St-Pierre.

MAISON FORNEL With foundations dating back to 1658 and vaulted cellars constructed in 1735, this house was reconstructed in 1964, initiating the Place Royale restoration project. It now houses the exhibition "Place Royale: 400 Years of History," which provides a good perspective on the area's past and ongoing restoration; a brochure in English is available. Open daily June 7 through September; closed the rest of the year. No admission charge. 25 Rue St-Pierre, just south of Ruelle de la Place (phone: 643-6631).

MAISON CHEVALIER Constructed in the 17th and 18th centuries for several merchants, including Jean-Baptiste Chevalier, these three buildings together form an interesting ethnographic museum. The changing exhibits include old toys, costumes, furniture, and folk art. Open daily mid-May to mid-October; closed the rest of the year. No admission charge. Corner of Cul-de-Sac and Notre-Dame (phone: 643-9689).

MAISON JOLLIET This restored house was the home of explorer Louis Jolliet, who, accompanied by Jacques Marquette, discovered the Mississippi River in 1672. His house now contains the entrance to the funicular that transports passengers to Upper Town. Opposite Sous-le-Fort at the foot of Escalier Casse-Cou.

VIEUX PORT (OLD PORT) Quebec's old port area today features a 6,000-seat open-air amphitheater and a number of boutiques, all connected by enclosed aerial walkways. At the confluence of the St. Lawrence and St. Charles Rivers lies a lock-controlled marina big enough to accommodate several hundred pleasure craft; oceangoing merchant vessels and cruise ships moor along the wharf. The area also houses restaurants, pubs, and cafés and is easily accessible by pedestrians and cyclists from the waterfront promenade. 84 Rue Dalhousie.

CENTRE D'INTERPRETATION DU VIEUX-PORT-DE-QUÉBEC (OLD PORT OF QUEBEC INTERPRETATION CENTER) Four exhibition floors in a refurbished cement factory trace the salty history of Vieux Québec when it was the center of Canada's lumber and shipbuilding trade. Run by *Parks Canada,* it displays a ship's prow, rum kegs, and a working capstan set up for visitors to try their hand. The top floor affords views of the city skyline and marina. Open daily early May to *Labour Day;* closed mornings *Labour Day* to late October; open by reservation only the rest of the year. No admission charge. 100 Rue St-André (phone: 648-3300).

MUSÉE DE LA CIVILISATION All aspects of Quebec society are explored in this stunning complex in the restored Vieux Port near Place Royale. Architect Moshe Safdie brought old and new together in 1988, creating a structure that covers a city block between Rues Dalhousie and St-Pierre, with a contemporary core joining three historic properties and a space-age steeple of glass and steel. Summer visitors can stroll from one street to the other via a series of connecting stairways and terraces, taking in the port panorama as they go. The centerpiece in the massive entrance hall is a reflecting pool where Astri Reusch's *La Débacle* sculpture symbolizes the drama of the spring thaw on the ice-choked St. Lawrence. The museum takes a hands-on approach, involving children and adults in many of the exhibits through computers and video screens. Its four permanent exhibits trace the history of Quebec by way of an impressive collection of artifacts, including a 250-foot boat that was found on the building's site. Open daily June 24 to *Labour Day;* closed Mondays the rest of the year. No admission charge Tuesdays and for children under 16. 85 Rue Dalhousie (phone: 643-2158).

UPPER TOWN

PLACE D'ARMES A small square, it served as a meeting place and parade ground during the French regime. In its center stands a Gothic fountain surmounted by the granite and bronze *Monument de la Foi* (Monument of Faith), constructed in 1916 in memory of the Récollets (Franciscan) missionaries who arrived in 1615. Today the square is a good orientation point in Upper Town, the section of Vieux Québec built above the cliff, where military, religious, and residential buildings from the 17th, 18th, and 19th centuries have been restored. One of the loveliest, *Maison Vallée* (which dates from 1732), is the home of the *Musée de Cire* (see *Museums,* below). For traditional French Canadian fare and decor, check out *Aux Anciens Canadiens* (see *Eating Out*), in a house built in 1677 and named after the classic Canadian volume whose author, Philippe Aubert de Gaspé, once lived on the premises.

CHÂTEAU FRONTENAC What the *Eiffel Tower* is to Paris and the *Leaning Tower* is to Pisa, this grand hotel is to Quebec City. Everything about the present structure, built in 1893, is grand, from its broad, slanting copper roof, its turrets and towers, and its imposing red brick walls to its magnificent setting high above the St. Lawrence River. The site on which it is built has undergone numerous transitions. First a fort built by Champlain in 1620, it eventually became the *Château St-Louis,* a regal residence of the governors of New France. It was razed by fire in 1834. During World War II, Allied officers accompanying Roosevelt and Churchill stayed here and planned the invasion of France. In the main lobby is an interesting display tracing the château's past. Stroll around the lobby or the inner courtyard, or enjoy the majestic river view from the circular cocktail lounge. The *Terrasse Dufferin,* built in 1838, with its spectacular view of Lower Town and the Ile d'Orléans, is a favorite spot for relaxing on summer nights. At the north end of the terrace stands a statue of Samuel de Champlain, watching over the city he founded in 1608. 1 Av. des Carrières (phone: 692-3861).

JARDIN DES GOUVERNEURS (GARDEN OF THE GOVERNORS) Originally the private garden of the *Château St-Louis,* it was opened to the public in 1838. Here stands the *Monument Wolfe-Montcalm,* erected in 1828. It is one of the few monuments in the world commemorating both the triumphant and the defeated: As its inscription reads in translation, "Their courage gave them the same lot; history, the same fame; posterity, the same monument." Open daily. No admission charge. Next to the *Château Frontenac* at Av. des Carrières and Rue Mont-Carmel.

CAVALIER DU MOULIN (WINDMILL OUTPOST) This restful little park once was an important link in the Old City's defense works. Named for the windmill that once occupied the site, the military outpost was first activated in 1693; its men had orders to destroy the Cap Diamant redoubt and the *St-Louis* bastion if they were to fall to the enemy. Open daily; closed December through April. No admission charge. At the western end of Rue Mont-Carmel.

MUSÉE DU FORT Visitors can get their historical bearings in this museum. A 30-minute sound-and-light show presented on a model of the 18th-century city re-creates the most important battles and sieges of Quebec, including the Battle of the Plains of Abraham and the attack by Arnold and Montgomery during the American Revolution. Also available here are a wide variety of guides and history books in English. Shows alternate in English and French. Open daily; closed December 1 through *Christmas.* Admission charge. 10 Rue Ste-Anne (phone: 692-2175).

BASILIQUE NOTRE-DAME-DE-QUÉBEC Probably the finest example of Baroque architecture in Quebec, the basilica stands on the site of *Notre-Dame-de-Recouvrance,* built in 1633 by Samuel de Champlain, who probably was buried there (the gravesite has never been found). Destroyed by fire seven years later, it was rebuilt as *Notre-Dame-de-la-Paix,* the place where Monseigneur François-Xavier de Montmorency-Laval, first Bishop of Quebec, established the first Roman Catholic diocese in North America (outside of Mexico) in 1674. The cathedral was renovated and its façade remodeled in the early 1700s, but like the *Eglise Notre-Dame-des-Victoires,* it was destroyed during the British bombardment of 1759. Repairs and additions over the next century resulted in a building that recalls the 18th-century structure. Its ornate interior (largely reconstructed after a 1922 fire) is decorated with works of art and illuminated by stained glass windows. The basilica's treasures include an episcopal throne and a chancel lamp presented by French King Louis XIV. Three governors of New France and most of the Bishops of Quebec are buried in the crypt. Guided tours of the basilica and crypt are available May through October. Rue Buade and Côte de la Fabrique (phone: 692-2533).

SÉMINAIRE DE QUÉBEC (QUEBEC SEMINARY) Beyond the iron gates lies a group of 17th-century buildings that were part of a training school for Catholic priests founded in 1663 by Monseigneur François-Xavier de Montmorency-Laval, the first Bishop of Quebec. The main chapel is worth a visit for a look at its marble altars, valuable relics, and sarcophagus of Bishop Laval; the sundial over the door dates to 1773. The *Musée de l'Amérique française* (Museum of Francophone America) here is devoted to the French presence in North America. Displays of both religious and secular objects create a revealing portrait of the Québécois. The museum (9 Rue de l'Université; phone: 692-2843) is open daily June through September; closed Mondays the rest of the year. There's an admission charge. Visits to other parts of the seminary, which must be arranged in advance, are possible June through August; admission charge (phone: 692-3981).

CATHÉDRALE ANGLICANE (HOLY TRINITY ANGLICAN CATHEDRAL) *Holy Trinity* is a relic of the British colonial era in Quebec. The first Church of England cathedral ever built beyond the British Isles, it has served the capital's Anglican community since 1804. Erected by royal decree of King George III—who donated the silver communion set now used on royal occasions—it was inspired by London's *St. Martin in the Fields,* with pews of stalwart English oak. The cathedral still honors the monarchy with a sacrosanct royal pew reserved for the use of a visiting British sovereign or designated representative. Memorial plaques under the stained glass windows trace the history of Quebec City's English-speaking establishment in war and peace. Open daily May through mid-October; closed weekends the rest of the year. 31 Rue des Jardins (phone: 692-2193).

COUVENT DES URSULINES (URSULINE CONVENT) Founded in 1639, it runs the oldest school for women in North America. The convent itself was twice damaged by fire, but some original walls still stand. A few of the present buildings date from the 17th century. It is not open to the public, but the chapel, which contains a number of relics and valuable paintings, welcomes visitors. Its votive lamp, first lit in 1717, has never been extinguished, and the defeated Montcalm is buried in a tomb in the chapel. His skull is preserved under glass in the *Musée des Ursulines,* adjoining the chapel (see below). The chapel is closed Sundays and Mondays May through October; closed the rest of the year. No admission charge. 12 Rue Donnacona (phone: 694-0694).

MUSÉE DES URSULINES Fascinating and oddly touching, this repository of early Quebec memorabilia includes trappings of convent life—furniture, kitchenware, and richly embroidered altar clothes—all exhibited on three silent, dimly lighted floors. Some items date from 1639, when three intrepid members of this French teaching order arrived in the port of "Kebec." Replicas of the sisters' enclosed "cabin beds"—for warmth (they didn't install stoves in the convent until 1668)—share exhibition space with the elegant furniture of the order's wealthy cofounder, Madame de la Peltrie, and the skull (under glass) of Marquis Louis-Joseph de Montcalm, defeated commander of the French Army in the Battle of the Plains of Abraham. The general is buried in the convent chapel next door, and many of his personal effects are on display in the museum. One of the more endearing exhibits is the shirt that Murdoch Stewart, a British soldier and paymaster, wore to his wedding to Angélique Cartier, making him the first of the "enemy" to marry a Canadian girl after the conquest of 1759. Hand-stitched in sheer linen, with a frilled jabot, the Fraser Highlander's dress shirt is as fresh as the day it was made more than two centuries ago. Closed Mondays and December. Admission charge. 12 Rue Donnacona (phone: 694-0694).

CENTRE MARIE-DE-L'INCARNATION Next door to the convent, the *Centre Marie-de-l'Incarnation* displays a collection of objects belonging to the order's cofounder, Mother Marie-de-l'Incarnation. It also operates a bookstore and shows a film tracing the Ursulines' history under French rule. The center is closed Mondays and December. Admission charge (10 Rue Donnacona; phone: 692-1569).

PARC MONTMORENCY Named in honor of François de Montmorency-Laval, this park, straddling the hill between Upper and Lower Town, affords good views of Lower Town, the harbor, and the surrounding area. A monument to Sir Georges-Etienne-Cartier, a French Canadian political leader, and another to Louis Hébert, the first farmer to settle in Quebec City, stand in the center of the park. On the hill off Côte de la Montagne.

MONUMENT DE LAVAL (LAVAL MONUMENT) This impressive statue honors Laval, Canada's first bishop, who arrived in 1659 and was one of the most prominent citizens of New France. He founded the *Séminaire de Québec,* the predecessor of *Université Laval.* Sculpted by Philippe Hébert, the work was unveiled in 1908. At Côte de la Montagne across from *Parc Montmorency.*

COLLINE PARLEMENTAIRE (PARLIAMENT HILL) AND THE PLAINES D'ABRAHAM (PLAINS OF ABRAHAM)

PROMENADE DES GOUVERNEURS (GOVERNORS' PROMENADE) This 2,200-foot-long walkway leads from the *Terrasse Dufferin* up Cap Diamant, beside the *Citadelle,* all the way to the Plaines d'Abraham. The walk offers excellent views of the river upstream to the Pont de Québec (Quebec Bridge) and downstream to the Ile d'Orléans. Open daily late May through September; closed the rest of the year. No admission charge.

CITADELLE This massive star-shaped fortress commands a strategic position at the highest point on Quebec's promontory, 350 feet above the St. Lawrence. The French built previous fortifications on this site, but the present citadel was constructed between 1820 and 1832 by the British government as a defense against American attack following the War of 1812. The fortress was never subjected to enemy fire. It was first occupied by British troops, then by the Royal Canadian Artillery, and since 1920 by the Royal 22nd Regiment. A 1750 structure within the fort houses the *Regimental Museum,* with displays of ancient weapons, uniforms, and rare documents—some dating back to the time of the French regime. From mid-June to the first Monday in September, the changing of the guard occurs daily at 10 AM, and a ceremonial retreat is enacted at 7 PM on Tuesdays, Thursdays, and weekends. Closed December through February, except to groups with reservations (write to *Musée de la Citadelle,* CP 6020, Haute-Ville, Quebec City, QC G1R 4V7) and during *Carnaval de Québec* in early February (see *Special Events*). Admission charge. Reached by Côte de la Citadelle off Rue St-Louis (phone: 648-3563).

FORTIFICATIONS DE QUÉBEC The walls encircling the Old City and its four gates, now the domain of *Parks Canada,* offer a 3-mile (5-km) walk along the western section, which overlooks Vieux Québec and the surrounding area. The federal government has been actively restoring the walls since 1971. At *Porte St-Louis,* the *Poudrière de l'Esplanade* (Esplanade Powder Magazine; 100 Rue St-Louis; phone: 648-7016) is an 1810 defense site reincarnated as a reception and interpretation center, as well as the departure point for guided tours of the fortifications. The *Poudrière* is open daily mid-May through *Labour Day;* by reservation only the rest of the year, except during *Carnaval,* when it is closed mornings. There's no admission charge.

Parc de l'Artillerie, also part of the fortifications system, preserves defense works raised during the French regime, including the *Redoute Dauphine* (Dauphine Redoubt, built from 1712 to 1748) and military structures installed by the British in the early 18th century. Visit the reception center (an old iron foundry) and the officers' quarters, which have been converted to an interpretive center for children. The reception and interpretive centers are closed Monday mornings April through September; closed weekends the rest of the year. No admission charge. 2 Rue d'Auteuil (phone: 648-4205).

PLAINES D'ABRAHAM (PLAINS OF ABRAHAM) Named for Abraham Martin, the first St. Lawrence River pilot, this is where Canada's French-English struggle was decided in 1759. Now part of the 250-acre *Parc des Champs-de-Bataille* (phone: 648-4071), the Plaines d'Abraham were the site of the battle between the British forces led by General James Wolfe and the French under the Marquis de Montcalm that sealed the fate of New France. On the grounds are various monuments and statues plus the *Musée du Québec* (see below). The *National Battlefields Park Interpretation Centre,* located in a wing of the *Musée du Quebec,* offers a high-tech history of the Plaines. The center is open daily from *Victoria Day* (late May) to *Labour Day;* closed Mondays the rest of the year. There's an admission charge (phone: 648-5641). The observation post affords excellent river views. Beyond the *Citadelle* to the west, off Grande Allée.

MUSÉE DU QUÉBEC Not many fine arts museums boast a criminal connection, but Quebec City is proud to claim a city jail as part of its landmark complex on the Plaines d'Abraham. Linked to the *Musée*'s original neoclassical gallery in the *Parc des Champs-de-Bataille,* the jail's former cellblocks have been transformed into airy exhibition spaces, along with a library, a documentation center, administrative offices, and the *National Battlefields Park Interpretation Centre* (above). The *Grand Salle* (Grand Hall), the hub of the museum complex, links the old and new pavilions; with glass walls and a lofty cruciform skylight, it's a work of art in itself. The *Grand Salle* was built partially underground, and its connecting corridors are roofed in a landscaped lawn to blend harmoniously with the natural park setting. The dramatic entry houses the museum's auditorium, a gift shop, and a restaurant with a terrace overlooking the plains and the St. Lawrence River. A sculpture garden occupies an inner court between the *Grand Salle* and the original *Pavillon Gérard-Morisset,* where six galleries are devoted to a permanent collection that traces Quebec's fine arts history from the late 1700s to the present. More than 18,000 works by artists from Quebec and other parts of the world make up the collection. Open daily *Victoria Day* (late May) to *Labour Day* (to 9:45 PM Wednesdays); closed Mondays the rest of the year. No admission charge Wednesdays. 1 Av. Wolfe-Montcalm (phone: 643-2150).

HÔTEL DU PARLEMENT (NATIONAL ASSEMBLY BUILDINGS) These imposing French Renaissance structures were built between 1877 and 1886. The 12 bronze statues in niches on the façade, commemorating people prominent in Quebec's and Canada's history, were executed by the Quebec sculptor Philippe Hébert. The buildings are open for guided tours, in French and English, weekdays from *Labour Day* through May; daily, June 24 to *Labour Day;* no tours June 1 through June 23. If you want to see Quebec's legislators in action, keep in mind that the Assembly is not in session from June 24 through October or from December 22 to mid-March. No admission charge. Bounded by Rue Dufferin, Blvd. René-Lévesque E., Rue St-Augustin, and Grande Allée (phone: 643-7239).

CHAPELLE HISTORIQUE BON-PASTEUR (HISTORIC CHAPEL OF THE GOOD SHEPHERD) A designated historic monument, the chapel of the motherhouse of the sisters of Bon-Pasteur de Québec was completed in 1868. The high altar of delicately carved wood and gold leaf dates from 1730. Many paintings displayed in the chapel were done by members of the order more than a century ago. Concerts are held here regularly, and a special Sunday mass for artists is celebrated at 11 AM, following a 15-minute musical prelude. Closed mornings and Mondays in July and August; closed mornings, Sundays, and Mondays the rest of the year; open other times by request. 1080 Rue de la Chevrotière (phone: 648-9710).

GRAND THÉÂTRE DE QUÉBEC This sleek structure built in 1970 comprises a music conservatory and two entertainment halls. 269 Blvd. René-Lévesque, at the corner of Rue Claire-Fontaine (phone: 643-8131).

STE-FOY This town has grown quickly since the 1960s to become Quebec City's bedroom community of choice, a sprawling, American-style suburb of modern condominiums and apartments. In addition to its Route 175 motel strip, the town supports two large shopping malls, *Place Laurier* and *Place Ste-Foy,* and a growing number of restaurants, bars, and discos. Follow Grande Allée about 2 miles (3 km) west from the *Hôtel du Parlement,* or take bus No. 11 or 25 or Metrobus No. 800 or 801 from downtown.

SILLERY This was estate country in the early 19th century, when wealthy lumber and shipping magnates built their mansions here close to the St. Lawrence River and the shipyards at the base of the cliffs. Once inhabited by mostly English speakers, today this charming residential neighborhood is decidedly more French. It's a tranquil retreat of quiet, tree-shaded streets and expensive homes, surrounded by manicured lawns and well-tended gardens. Avenue Magurie is Sillery's chic commercial zone, with several stylish restaurants. An interpretive center devoted to Sillery's past, the *Villa Bagatelle* (1563 Chemin St-Louis; phone: 688-8074), recalls the Belle Epoque of Quebec's English and Scots lumber barons and shipbuilders. In summer, the villa is the departure point for walking tours of what remains of the old baronial domain. Its popular English gardens bloom with more than 350 varieties of plants, and the adjoining studio exhibits works of promising young artists. The villa and its grounds are closed Mondays; admission charge. Nearby *Bois-de-Coulonge* is one of the prettiest parks in the area. Sillery is a 10-minute drive from the city center en route to Ste-Foy, or take buses Nos. 11 or 25 from downtown.

UNIVERSITÉ LAVAL An outgrowth of the *Séminaire de Québec* founded by Bishop Laval, it is the oldest French-language university on the continent. The construction of a sprawling 465-acre campus was begun in 1946 to accommodate the growing numbers of students. One of the school's 25 modern buildings is the physical education and sports complex. Its excellent facilities, including an Olympic-size pool, are open to the public at certain hours, mainly on weekends. Off Blvd. Laurier (Rte. 175) and bounded by the Autoroute du Vallon, Av. Myrand, and Chemin Ste-Foy (phone: 656-3333).

ILE D'ORLÉANS This island in the St. Lawrence River below Quebec was relatively isolated until 1935, when a suspension bridge was built to connect it with the mainland. The island retains a great deal of its 18th-century French Canadian influence. Most of the islanders are of Norman or Breton stock, and, like their ancestors, most are farmers. (Island apples, raspberries, and strawberries are especially good.) The island is only 21 miles long and about 5 miles wide. Visitors can easily make a complete driving tour in a grand circle, stopping in village after village of 17th- and 18th-century houses and churches. (Route 368 forms a 42-mile/67-km ring around the island.) Ste-Famille has the most interesting church on the island—a triple-spired structure built in 1742. On the east side of the island are some summer cottages and Ste-Pétronille, a resort village which hosts a summer-long festival of chamber music featuring international performers.

If you visit during March or April, keep an eye out for smoke coming from buildings off the main road. These are "sugar shacks," stark, wooden structures where Quebec's famous maple syrup is made. In a scene more reminiscent of a Breton landscape than of a North American village, ruddy-faced men stand around steaming metal bins, watching for just the right moment when the liquid is ready. Follow the mist: The grounds—with maple trees bearing metal spigots and buckets—lead to the shack where, more often than not, the proprietor will invite you in and even give you a sample of his oh-so-sweet product. Two of the best on Ile d'Orléans are the *Sucrerie Jean-Pierre Verret* (Chemin Royal, St-Jean; phone: 522-8217 or 829-3189) and the *Cabane à Sucre l'En-Tailleur* (1447 Chemin Royal, St-Pierre; phone: 828-2344 or 828-1269). Even when the sap is not running, these shacks are open for business, selling maple sugar products; both are closed November through February.

To get to Ile d'Orléans, take Autoroute Dufferin down the hill near the *Hôtel du Parlement,* then follow Route 138. *Beautemps Mauvaistemps* (phone: 828-2275) organizes personalized tours of the island.

EXTRA SPECIAL

Ste-Anne-de-Beaupré is a small village near the ski center of *Mont Ste-Anne* (see *Cross-Country Skiing,* below), dominated by a massive cathedral which is an internationally renowned Catholic shrine. Millions of people have made pilgrimages here; the piles of crutches, canes, and folding wheelchairs in the cathedral attest to healings that the faithful believe have taken place. The present building dates from 1923. The fountain of Ste-Anne in front is said to have healing powers. The sanctuary has a marble statue of Ste-Anne as well as other venerable religious items. There's an information bureau, and guides are available to lead tours (phone: 827-3781). To get to Ste-Anne-de-Beaupré, about 25 miles (40 km) northeast of Quebec City, follow Route 138. A more picturesque route leaves 138 at Beaupré and continues along Route 360.

Just east of *Mont Ste-Anne* is the *Réserve Nationale de la Faune du Cap Tourmente,* developed by naturalists to protect the greater snow goose, along with 250 other bird species, which stop here during their seasonal migrations. The noisy October gatherings can easily attract 100,000 screeching birds. In May, ducks, herons, swallows, and red-winged blackbirds build their nests in the many ponds of the region. The reserve also has a nature-interpretation center. To visit, head east on Route 138 from Ste-Anne-de-Beaupré and watch for signs for *Cap Tourmente* (phone: 827-4591, April through October; 827-3776, the rest of the year).

En route to Ste-Anne-de-Beaupré or on the return to Quebec City, stop off at the 274-foot-high Chute Montmorency (Montmorency Falls). Take in the view from a cable car that climbs to the top, where the English General Wolfe established his headquarters in 1759. Wolfe's headquarters were eventually converted into a beautiful hotel that was destroyed in a tragic fire in 1993. The new *Manoir Montmorency* (2490 Av. Royale, Beauport; phone: 663-2877) reopened in 1994, and its dining room still offers a fantastic view of Ile d'Orléans.

Sources and Resources

TOURIST INFORMATION

For maps, brochures, and the like, contact the *Office du Tourisme et des Congrès de la Communauté Urbaine de Québec* (Greater Quebec Area Tourism and Convention Bureau; 60 Rue d'Auteuil; phone: 692-2471) or the reception office of the *Maison du Tourisme* (12 Rue Ste-Anne; phone: 800-363-7777 in Canada and the US, except Alaska), both open daily. The Place Royale restoration has its own information center in *Entrepôt Thibodeau* (Thibodeau Warehouse; Pl. Marché-Finlay; phone: 643-6631), which is open daily June 7 through September only. Another government tourist information center is in Ste-Foy, off the Pont Pierre-Laporte (3005 Blvd. Laurier; phone: 651-2882); it's open daily.

LOCAL COVERAGE *Le Soleil* and *Le Journal de Québec* are French morning dailies; *Québec Chronicle-Telegraph* is an English weekly that hits the newsstands on Wednesdays. *Voilà Québec* is a bilingual quarterly entertainment, sightseeing, and dining guide distributed free in hotels and at the various tourist information centers. For English-language television programs, tune to CKMI, Channel 5 (Cable 3); the English radio station is CBVE at 104.7 FM.

English-language city guidebooks are hard to find. The *Librairie Garneau* (a bookstore at 24 Côte de la Fabrique; phone: 692-4262) and the *Musée du Fort* (10 Rue Ste-Anne; phone: 692-2175) have a fair selection. One useful (and free) publication is the *Quebec City Area* tourist guide, published by the provincial government and available at the *Office du Tourisme et des Congrès de la Communauté Urbaine de Québec* (see above).

TELEPHONE The area code for Quebec City is 418.

SALES TAX Quebec has a provincial sales tax of 6.5%, depending on what is being purchased. In addition, a 7% federal tax, called the Goods and Services Tax (GST), is levied on most purchases. In many cases, visitors can receive refunds of both the provincial and federal taxes. For details on Quebec tax rebates, call *Revenue Québec* (phone: 659-4692; 800-567-4692 in Canada);

for more information on obtaining rebates on the federal tax, see GETTING READY TO GO.

CLIMATE Winters in Quebec can be bitterly cold and snowy, but spring and summer are pleasantly temperate. In summer, temperatures average 55 to 80F, while in spring they're normally between 50 and 70F. Fall temperatures average between 40 and 55F. Early spring and fall are the rainiest times of year.

GETTING AROUND

AIRPORT *Jean-Lesage International Airport* is about 11 miles (18 km) west of the city. *Maple Leaf Sightseeing Tours* (phone: 649-9226) operates an inexpensive bus that shuttles between the airport and most major hotels (from mid-May to early October only). Taxis are more expensive.

BUS Buses serve the metropolitan area from approximately 5:30 AM to 1 AM. Exact change, CN$1.80 (about $1.30 US at press time), is required; tickets also can be purchased at tobacconists and convenience stores for CN$1.45 ($1.05 US). For CN$3.50 ($2.55 US) you can buy a pass good for one day's unlimited travel. The Metrobus (No. 800 or 801) offers express service from downtown to the outlying suburbs. For route information, call the *Société de Transports de la Communauté Urbaine de Québec* (*STCUQ;* phone: 627-2511).

CAR RENTALS All major international firms are represented. Most have offices both at the airport and downtown.

CRUISES St. Lawrence cruises are available aboard the M/V *Louis Jolliet* from Quai Chouinard (10 Rue Dalhousie; phone: 692-1159), in the Place Royale section of the city, daily from May to early October; children under five ride for free. Sailing aficionados should look into the variety of trips organized by *Vieux Port Yachting* (Quai Renaud, 80 Rue St-André; phone: 692-0017), with cruises of up to 14 days and as far as the Saguenay River, 200 miles north of Quebec City and one of the greatest fjords in the world.

FERRY Year-round service links Quebec and its suburb of Lévis, operating every hour from 6 AM to 2 AM. The ride affords panoramic views of both cities (10 Rue des Traversiers, across from Place Royale; phone: 644-3704).

HORSE-DRAWN CARRIAGES Calèches tour Vieux Québec, the Parliament area, and the Plaines d'Abraham year-round. A tip for the driver is customary. Calèches line up at four locations: near the main office of the *Office du Tourisme et des Congrès de la Communauté Urbaine de Québec* (see *Tourist Information*); at the *Porte St-Louis;* at *Parc de l'Esplanade* (west side of Rue St-Louis inside the walls); and at Place d'Armes near the *Château Frontenac.* For information, call 683-9222. For information on horse-drawn trolley tours, call 624-3062.

TAXI Most cabs cannot be hailed in the streets. Some cabbies speak French only, so have your phrasebook ready. There are cabstands at the airport, at major hotels, and in Vieux Québec at Place d'Armes and at Place d'Youville. The principal cab companies are *Taxi Co-op* (phone: 525-5191; 653-7777 in Ste-Foy) and *Taxi Québec* (phone: 525-8123).

WALKING TOURS Quebec City is best seen on foot. Pick up a free copy of *Quebec City Region*—which includes walking tours—at the tourist office (see *Tourist Information,* above). The *Quebec Ministry of Cultural Affairs* publishes a folder about Place Royale, which can be obtained at the Place Royale information center in *Entrepôt Thibodeau* (see *Tourist Information*). *Baillairgé Cultural Tours* (phone: 692-5737) offers two-and-a-quarter-hour walking tours of the Old City in English, with emphasis on history and architecture, departing from the *Musée du Fort* (see *Special Places*) across the street from the *Château Frontenac,* at 9:30 AM and 2 PM daily. The tour guides are especially interesting and knowledgeable. Tours are available from late June to mid-October. For those interested in the city's impressive religious history, the booklet "Living Stones of Old Quebec" outlines three walking tours. The free publication can be obtained through any tourist office or through the *Religious Tourism Corporation* (20 Rue Buade; phone: 694-0665). The latter organization also offers guided tours emphasizing the city's religious background. Two tours with different itineraries depart daily from the entrance of the *Basilique Notre-Dame* (see *Special Places*).

SPECIAL EVENTS

After New Orleans's *Mardi Gras,* the *Carnaval de Québec,* a 10-day affair starting on the first Thursday in February every year, is one of the biggest blowouts in North America.

BEST FESTIVAL

Carnaval Over half a million people from all over Canada and the US flood the city for this winter celebration. Festivities include two parades, snow sculpture contests, fireworks, a queen's coronation and ball, a variety of theme parties, and lots of winter sports and events—hockey, skiing, and a canoe race on the frozen St. Lawrence River. Hotels are generally booked solid during *Carnaval,* so make arrangements several months in advance. The best bet for last-minute reservations is through the *Carnaval*'s lodging committee, which can sometimes book rooms in motels or guesthouses, from December 15 to *Carnaval* time. For general information, contact the *Carnaval de Québec* (290 Rue Joly, Quebec City, QC G1L 1N8; phone: 626-3716). Also see *Quintessential Canada* in DIVERSIONS.

For two weeks in July, between 600 and 800 musicians from all parts of the world and all musical backgrounds gather in the city for the *Festival d'Eté International de Québec* (Quebec International Summer Festival; PO Box 24, Station B, Quebec City, QC G1K 7A1; phone: 692-4540; 800-361-5405 in Canada), one of the largest cultural events in the French-speaking world. Rock, jazz, and classical music all can be heard in public squares and on stages around the city. Most presentations are free of charge.

In early August of odd-numbered years, Quebec becomes the backdrop for a stunning five-day festival celebrating the Middle Ages and the Renaissance. During *Les Médiévales de Québec* (Quebec Medievals) the streets of the Old City teem with costumed participants who re-create the daily life of the period—from a functioning blacksmith's forge to the excitement of a jousting tournament. Because this festival draws an enormous number of visitors to the city, it's wise to book rooms well in advance. For information contact *Les Médiévales de Québec* (126 Rue St-Pierre, Bureau 600, Quebec, QC G1K 4A8; phone: 692-1993; 800-648-1997; fax: 692-2017).

MUSEUMS

In addition to those mentioned in *Special Places,* other noteworthy museums include the following:

CENTRE D'INTERPRÉTATION DE LA VIE URBAINE (URBAN LIFE INTERPRETATION CENTER) This small museum in the basement of the *Hôtel de Ville* (City Hall) concentrates on contemporary life in the provincial capital. Closed Mondays and *Labour Day* to June 23. No admission charge. 43 Côte de la Fabrique (phone: 691-4606).

MUSÉE DES AUGUSTINES DE L'HÔTEL-DIEU DE QUÉBEC (MUSEUM OF THE AUGUSTINES OF THE HÔTEL-DIEU OF QUEBEC) Dedicated to the founders of Canada's first hospital, the small museum displays antique surgical instruments, furniture, and 17th-century memorabilia related to the order of nursing sisters. Guided tours of cellar vaults where the nuns took refuge during the 1759 siege are available. Closed Mondays. No admission charge. 32 Rue Charlevoix (phone: 692-2492).

MUSÉE DE CIRE A wax museum featuring figures who have played a role in Quebec's history. Open daily. Admission charge. 22 Rue Ste-Anne (phone: 692-2289).

PARC CARTIER-BRÉBEUF A replica of Jacques Cartier's ship is moored on the St. Charles River. Open daily. No admission charge. 175 Rue de l'Espinay (phone: 648-4038).

PARKS CANADA EXHIBITION ROOM Housed on the ground floor of the *Edifice Louis-St-Laurent,* with a post office that dates from 1871, the *Parks Canada* salon presents changing exhibitions relating to Canada's national heritage. Open daily. No admission charge. 3 Rue Buade (phone: 648-4177).

SHOPPING

Venues in Quebec City and the surrounding area include 63 shopping centers, elegant boutiques, and flea markets, but the best buys are in the city's many galleries and crafts studios, where the works of local and national artists are featured. The main concentration of shopping malls is in Ste-Foy, about 2 miles (3 km) west of the *Château Frontenac.* Travelers with children should make a beeline to *Les Galeries de la Capitale,* a vast shopping center and amusement park with rides, a giant carousel, a year-round indoor skating rink, and a mini-golf course, located northwest of the city. For shopping in town, the best streets are Rue St-Jean, Côte de la Fabrique, Rue Ste-Anne, and Rue Buade within the walls of the Upper Town, and the Avenue Cartier neighborhood between Grande Allée Ouest (West) and Boulevard René-Lévesque Ouest.

Most stores are open from 9:30 AM to 5:30 PM Mondays and Tuesdays; to 9 PM Wednesdays through Fridays; to 5 PM Saturdays; and from noon to 5 PM Sundays.

ANTIQUES

Antique Chez Ti-Père Good reproductions of country pine as well as traditional pieces. Follow Route 20 from the Pont Pierre-Laporte (Pierre Laporte Bridge) toward Montreal and take Exit 278 (about 33 miles/53 km). 128 Rue Olivier, Laurier-Station (phone: 728-4031).

Antiquité Brocante A treasure trove for collectors of old silver and china, heirloom lace, antique furniture, clocks, and estate jewelry. 65 Rue St-Jean (phone: 522-2500).

Antiquités Zaor A serious collectors' rendezvous for over 30 years, it specializes in objets d'art, fine porcelain pieces, silver, and bronze. 112 Rue St-Paul (phone: 692-0581).

Gérard Bourguet Antiquaire Specialists in 18th-century Quebec furniture and vintage ceramics. 97 Rue St-Paul (phone: 694-0896).

Heritage Antiquité A favorite of clock collectors, it also carries a selection of furniture, oil lamps, ceramics, and pottery. 109 Rue St-Paul (phone: 692-1681).

Rendez-Vous du Collectionneur Check out a uniquely Canadian obsession: hockey-card collecting. Antique dolls and old games share the premises. 123 Rue St-Paul (phone: 692-3099).

ART

Brousseau & Brousseau An exclusive showcase of Inuit artists. Signed prints and carvings are shipped to most destinations around the world. 1 Rue des Carrières (phone: 694-1828).

Galerie d'Art Le Portal This impressive architectural space is devoted to works by Quebec artists. 139 Rue St-Pierre (phone: 692-0354).

Galerie Le Chien d'Or The "Golden Dog Gallery" is devoted exclusively to the works of Quebec artists. François Faucher has regular exhibitions here. 8 Rue du Fort (phone: 694-9949).

Galerie Christin One of a dozen or more galleries along Rue St-Paul, it features works by such well-known national artists as Lemieux, Suzor-Côté, Riopelle, Cosgrove, Roberts, and Picher. 113 Rue St-Paul (phone: 692-4471).

Galerie Eliette Dufour This salon specializes in the works of such Canadian sculptors as Jordi Bonet, Donald Liardi, and Claude Dufour. 169 Rue St-Paul (phone: 692-2041).

Galerie Estampe Plus Monthly exhibitions are mounted here. Contemporary artists include Danielle April, Guy Langevin, and Paul Béliveau. 49 Rue St-Pierre (phone: 694-1303).

Galerie Georgette Pihay An award-winning Belgian sculptor, Pihay exhibits works in aluminum and bronze in her studio-salesroom in the *quartier.* 53 Rue du Petit-Champlain (phone: 692-0297).

Galerie Linda Verge Avant-garde painters Michel Rivest, Guy Labbé, and Joseph Veilleux are featured here. 1049 Av. des Erables (phone: 525-8393).

Aux Multiples Collections The Brousseau family stocks the city's best collection of Inuit carvings, drawings, and prints, each piece signed by the artist. 69 Rue Ste-Anne (phone: 692-1230) and 43 Rue Buade (phone: 692-4298).

Tirage Limité Works by Calder, Miró, and Riopelle, as well as tapestry art and original prints. 334 Blvd. René-Lévesque E. (phone: 522-1234).

Verrerie la Mailloche The master glass blower Jean Vallières invites visitors to watch him at work, using a technique that has changed little since it was developed in ancient Egypt. Finished pieces are on sale in a boutique upstairs. 58 Rue Sous-le-Fort (phone: 694-0445).

CRAFTS

Boutique La Corriveau Two Upper Town outlets specialize in Québécois arts and crafts—from homemade jams to hand-carved waterfowl decoys to sheepskin slippers—all from the looms, studios, and kitchens of local artisans. 49 Rue St-Louis (phone: 692-3781) and 42 Rue Garneau (phone: 692-3781).

Boutique Sachem Sells authentic (and reasonably priced) native Canadian arts and crafts, from moccasins and jewelry to Inuit sculpture. 17 Rue des Jardins (phone: 692-3056).

Créaly Decorative leather masks, costume jewelry in leather, and works in semiprecious stones by local artisans. 26 Rue du Petit-Champlain (phone: 692-4753).

Galerie Le Fil du Temps Handmade dolls are the stock-in-trade at this Vieux Québec boutique. Strictly collectibles, these one-of-a-kind creations aren't for kids. 88 Rue du Petit-Champlain (phone: 692-5867).

L'Iroquois A Native American souvenir outlet whose best buys are moccasins, toys, baskets, jewelry, and woodcarvings. 39 Rue Sous-le-Fort (phone: 692-3366).

Le Jardin de l'Argile Canada's exclusive outlet for the popular "Lorteau" figurines, the sleepy-faced little people cast in clay by the Quebec ceramist of the same name and glazed in pastel shades of pink and turquoise. Here also are exclusive woodcarvings and ornamental duck decoys, as well as hand-crafted toys, games, and marionettes. 51 Rue du Petit-Champlain (phone: 692-4870).

Petit Galerie de Pauline Pelletier Exotica from India, China, Thailand, and Bali complement works of this Quebec ceramist and other Quebec craftspeople. 30 Rue du Petit-Champlain (phone: 692-4871).

Pot-en-Ciel The work of more than a dozen top potters, ceramists, and wood sculptors from all over Quebec. 27 Rue du Petit-Champlain (phone: 692-1743).

Les Trois Colombes Crafts from Quebec, Atlantic Canada, Ontario, and the Canadian North in a three-story building. Fashion items include designer sweaters in handwoven mohair, decorated with leather, silk, and lace, and custom-designed coats, each an original by Quebec designer Lise Dupuis. 46 Rue St-Louis (phone: 694-1114).

NATIVE ARTISTRY

For those looking for the best in Native American crafts, there are outlets in Wendake, the Huron Village near suburban Loretteville, about 20 minutes west of the walled city via Route 73, followed by Route 369. These include *A & Artisanat OKI* (152 Blvd. Bastien; phone: 847-0574), which specializes in snowshoes, moccasins, baskets, dolls, jewelry, fringed jackets, and other hand-crafted items; *Artisanat Gros-Louis* (125 Blvd. Bastien; phone: 843-2503); Le Huron (25 Huron Village; phone: 842-4308); and *Artisanats Indiens du Québec* (540 Rue Max Gros-Louis; phone: 845-2150).

FASHION

Atelier Ibiza This small Lower Town salon specializes in high-fashion leatherwear, handbags, and other accessories. 47 Rue du Petit-Champlain (phone: 692-2103).

Atelier La Pomme House designers work with the finest Argentine leather, suede, and pigskin to produce a prêt-à-porter collection of clothing and accessories for men and women. 47 Rue Sous-le-Fort (phone: 692-2875).

Le Capitain d'à Bord Everything for the well-dressed sailor. 63 Rue du Petit-Champlain (phone: 694-0624).

Frederik et Cie. This well-established boutique in the heart of Upper Town's old business core features imported woolens from Britain. 49 Rue Buade (phone: 692-5244).

La Maison Darlington A senior member of Rue Buade's little fashion enclave, it is known for its British tweeds, Scottish cashmeres, and fine mohair shawls. There's also a good selection of Austrian sportswear and a beguiling collection of hand-smocked dresses for infants and little girls, including small sizes in Liberty-print fabrics with matching panties. 7 Rue Buade (phone: 692-2268).

La Maison Simons Established in 1840, the doyenne of Vieux Québec department stores stocks its fashion floor with designs by Anne Klein, Ralph Lauren, and Marithé and François Girbaud, plus an affordable private-label collection. 20 Côte de la Fabrique (phone: 692-3630).

Peau sur Peau This high-fashion house of leather features clothing, shoes, and accessories for men and women. Fine luggage is a specialty. Two locations: 85 Rue du Petit-Champlain (phone: 694-1921) and 70 Blvd. Champlain (phone: 692-5132).

Promenades du Vieux Québec The latest arrival on Upper Town's fashion scene has converted *Holt Renfrew*'s stately old store into a stylish complex of boutiques for young fashionables of both sexes. 43 Rue Buade (phone: 692-6000).

Les Vêteries Distinctive made-in-Quebec fashions in silk, wool, and cotton. Best buys are from an exclusive collection of high-fashion and après-ski sweaters. 31½ Rue du Petit-Champlain (phone: 694-1215).

FURS

J. B. Laliberté A leading retailer in high-fashion furs. 595 Rue St-Joseph E. (phone: 525-4841).

Joseph Robitaille For a hundred years this place has been the acknowledged leader of the city's huge fur-trade community. Top-quality fur designs at realistic prices. 2450 Blvd. Laurier (phone: 650-6185).

LACE

La Dentellière Lace curtains to fit all shapes and sizes of windows are a specialty. It also carries the best in handmade tablecloths and lace accessories for boudoir and bathroom, clothing, and lace trimmings. 56 Blvd. Champlain (phone: 692-2807).

MARKETS

Marché de la Place Fruit and vegetable farmers and flower sellers converge here daily from May through November. One of the best flea markets in the area, *Marché aux Puces de Ste-Foy,* is nearby. From downtown, take Metrobus No. 800 or 801. 939 Pl. de Ville, Ste-Foy (phone: 654-4394 or 654-4070).

Marché du Vieux Port This farmers' market in the restored Vieux Port area is renowned for its flowers. Closed November through February. From downtown, take bus No. 1. 160 Rue St-André (phone: 692-2517).

SWEETS

Chocolaterie Erico Hand-dipped confections in an Upper Town candy boutique. 634 Rue St-Jean (phone: 524-2122).

Confiserie d'Epoque Madame Gigi Offering homemade chocolate of every conceivable variety, it's a crowd-pleaser. In Lower Town, at 84 Rue du Petit-Champlain (phone: 694-2269).

Delicatesse Nourcy Creamy chocolate creations are featured at its two chic outlets. 1622 Chemin St-Louis, Sillery (phone: 527-2739), and 1035 Av. Cartier (phone: 523-4772).

Au Palet d'Or Hand-dipped chocolates and other custom-made bonbons share the celebrated pastry salon of Roger Geslin in the restaurant complex of chef Serge Bruyère. 60 Rue Garneau (phone: 692-2488).

TOYS

L'Echelle Hand-crafted playthings and other diversions. 1039 Rue St-Jean (phone: 694-9133).

Le Fou du Roi Wee royals will test their minds (and bodies) in this boutique of educational toys, both domestic and imported. 57 Rue du Petit-Champlain (phone: 692-4439).

SPORTS

BICYCLING Some of the most rewarding bike paths in eastern Canada can be found outside the historic *quartier.* Favorite city cycling spots include a trail that's less than 1 mile (1.6 km) long in *Parc des Champs-de-Bataille;* the 3-mile (5-km) St. Charles River Bikeway; Montmorency Bikeway, a challenging path of just over 6 miles (10 km) that leads all the way out to Chute Montmorency; and *Parc du Mont-Ste-Anne,* a top spot for mountain biking, with 157 trails. Explorers can rent wheels in the latter park at *Bicycles Marius* (phone: 827-2420 or 827-4561). For rentals in Quebec City, try *Location Petit-Champlain* (94 Rue du Petit-Champlain; phone: 692-2817).

CROSS-COUNTRY SKIING Lovers of the sport will find some of the province's best cross-country skiing within an hour's drive of the city at and around *Mont*

Ste-Anne; there are also good trails at the *Station Forestière Duchesnay* and *Camp Mercier* (see *Cross-Country Skiing* in DIVERSIONS). Urbanites also take to the Plaines d'Abraham right within the city limits—like New Yorkers to *Central Park*—to keep in shape; though the skiing isn't the best, the views are fine.

DOWNHILL SKIING There are a number of ski resorts an hour or less from Quebec City, and the attractions of the city are such that many skiers headquarter in town and travel to the slopes every day, rather than the other way around. Many of Quebec City's major hotels offer ski packages, and a shuttle service to the slopes, the *Skibus* (phone: 653-9722), is available from several. For information on the four major ski areas nearby, see *Downhill Skiing* in DIVERSIONS.

GOLF Though no courses exist within the city limits, about a dozen nine-hole and 18-hole courses are within a 20-mile (32-km) radius. For more information, see *Golf in Canada: A Land of Links* in DIVERSIONS.

HARNESS RACING They're off and running at the *Hippodrome de Québec* in the *Parc de l'Exposition* (Exhibition Grounds; phone: 524-5283). To get there, follow Boulevard Dorchester until you see the signs. Call ahead for the schedule.

HOCKEY Sadly for Quebeckers, the city's *National Hockey League* team, the *Nordiques,* was sold to Denver last year. But, as always, from December to May Quebec's ponds, lakes, rivers, and streams turn into natural rinks that are ideal for playing hockey (see *Skating,* below).

SKATING Join the locals in *Parc de l'Esplanade,* off Rue d'Auteuil (no admission charge). Other popular spots are the 2-mile (3-km) circuit on the St. Charles River (between the Ponts, or Bridges, Samson and Marie-de-l'Incarnation; phone: 691-7188) and Place d'Youville (just outside the *Porte St-Jean* in Vieux Québec; phone: 691-4685); no admission charge to either. *L'Anneau de Glace Gaétan Boucher* (930 Rue Place-de-Ville, Ste-Foy; phone: 654-4462) is an outdoor Olympic-size skating track, while *Village des Sports* in St-Gabriel-de-Valcartier, 25 miles (40 km) north of the city (take Autoroute de la Capitale, then Rte. 371; phone: 844-3725), offers skating paths through the woods; there's an admission charge to both. Skating begins in mid-October and usually lasts through March.

SWIMMING Some hotels have pools (see *Checking In*). The *Physical Education and Sports Pavilion* at *Université Laval* in Ste-Foy (off Blvd. Laurier; phone: 656-2807) has an Olympic-size pool that is open to the public for a fee; the *YMCA* (835 Blvd. René-Lévesque O.; phone: 527-2518) and the *YWCA* (855 Rue Holland; phone: 683-2155) also have pools the public can use for a fee at certain hours; call ahead.

TENNIS Indoor and outdoor tennis courts (as well as squash courts) are available at the *Club de Tennis Montcalm* (901 Blvd. Champlain; phone: 687-1250).

Courts are also available for rent at *Nautilus Plus* (4230 Blvd. Hamel; phone: 872-0111) and at the *Club de Tennis Avantage* (1080 Rue Bouvier, Charlesbourg O.; phone: 627-3343), a 15-minute drive from town via Route 73.

TOBOGGANING There are toboggan runs at the *Village des Sports* in St-Gabriel-de-Valcartier (see *Skating,* above).

THEATER

Plays rarely are performed in English, but for those who are fluent in this city's language, there is a great selection.

CENTER STAGE

Grand Théâtre de Québec Quebec's preeminent stage since it opened in 1971, this is the home of the *Orchestre Symphonique de Québec,* Canada's oldest symphony orchestra; *Opéra de Québec;* the *Théâtre du Trident* repertory company; and the *Danse-Partout* dance troupe. The symphony schedules a full concert season in the *Salle Louis-Fréchette,* one of *Le Grand's* two splendid auditoriums. From September through May, the theater company mounts productions that range from the classics to new works by Canadian, European, and American playwrights, and the opera takes over the big stage for a series of spring and fall productions. Designed by Victor Prus, the huge building is a stunning example of contemporary architecture. The interior is decorated with three massive murals in concrete by Spanish artist Jordi Bonet titled *Death, Space,* and *Liberty.* Both the building and the murals are controversial—not everyone likes Prus's bold design or Bonet's aggressive style—but they're worth seeing even if you're not staying for the concert. 269 Blvd. René-Lévesque E. (phone: 643-8131).

Other theaters include *Palais Montcalm* (995 Pl. d'Youville; phone: 670-9011); *Bibliothèque Gabrielle-Roy* (350 Rue St-Joseph E.; phone: 529-0924); and *Salle Albert-Rousseau* (Cégep Ste-Foy; phone: 659-6710). Student productions are presented at the *Conservatoire d'Art Dramatique* (13 Rue St-Stanislas; phone: 643-9833) and at the *Théâtre de la Cité Universitaire* (on the *Laval* campus, Ste-Foy—see *Special Places;* phone: 656-2765). Summer theaters are the *Théâtre de la Fenière* (1500 Rue de la Fenière, L'Ancienne-Lorette; phone: 872-1424); *Théâtre Beaumont–St-Michel* (Rte. 132 between St-Etienne-de-Beaumont and St-Michel on the south bank of the river, about a 40-minute drive from town; phone: 884-3344); and *Théâtre du Bois de Coulonge* (Blvd. Laurier; phone: 681-0088). Among the small theaters are the *Théâtre Petit-Champlain* (*Maison de la Chanson,* 78 Rue du Petit-Champlain; phone: 692-2631), which often hosts folk singers; *Théâtre*

Périscope (2 Rue Crémazie E.; phone: 529-2183); and *Théâtre d'Eté Saint-Pierre* (342 Rue du Galendor, St-Pierre, Ile d'Orléans; phone: 828-9411).

CINEMA

With one exception Quebec City theaters screen all films in French. English-language versions of current movies are shown at the *Cinéma Ste-Foy* (Pl. Ste-Foy, 2450 Blvd. Laurier, Ste-Foy; phone: 656-0592).

MUSIC

The *Orchestre Symphonique de Québec* (phone: 643-8486) performs at the *Salle Louis-Fréchette* in the *Grand Théâtre de Québec.* Touring musical groups usually play at the *Palais Montcalm* or at the *Salle Albert-Rousseau* (see *Theater,* above, for all three halls). The small pubs located along Rue St-Jean between Rue d'Auteuil and Côte de la Fabrique; on Grande Allée; and in the Vieux Port area (see *Nightclubs and Nightlife,* below) have live music, ranging from Québécois folk to rock and blues.

NIGHTCLUBS AND NIGHTLIFE

The city's brightest lights shine along the Grande Allée, beyond the Old City's walls. In summer, locals and visitors alike gather here from about 5 PM to plan their evening strategy over a pre-dinner aperitif or two. The liveliest corner on this sophisticated strip is at the intersection of the Rue d'Artigny and Grande Allée. Here, *Vogue* (1170 Rue d'Artigny; phone: 529-9973), with a café-bar on the main floor and a disco upstairs, is hopping until 3 AM, the hour most boîtes (clubs) in town call it a night. *Sherlock Holmes* (phone: 529-9973), a decidedly British pub, shares the premises. Around the corner and up the street, there's the *Cosmos Café* (575 Grande Allée E.; phone: 640-0606), an upscale watering hole that attracts a similarly toney, if boisterous crowd. Across the street is *Chez Dagobert* (600 Grande Allée E.; phone: 522-0393), where the capital's young congregate. There's live music for dancing downstairs and a disco for the under-30 crowd upstairs.

Disco fans—especially the younger set—favor *Le Quartier de Lune* (799 Av. Cartier; phone: 532-4011). *Le Dancing* at *Loews Le Concorde* (see *Checking In*) attracts customers with its upmarket glitter. Often referred to as the "executive's disco," it's closed Mondays and Tuesdays. Confirmed discomaniacs looking for action on a grand scale converge on *Le Palladium Bar* (2327 Blvd. Versant N., Ste-Foy; phone: 682-8783), near the *Université Laval* campus. *Beaugarte* (2600 Blvd. Laurier, Ste-Foy; phone: 659-2442) is an expense-account singles bar and disco for those 35 or so.

There's plenty of action in the part of the walled city known as the Latin Quarter, which was a center of academic life when the *Université Laval* was located here, and still attracts students today. However, caution is advised when casing some of the raunchier places in the Old City's busiest entertainment zone. On the whole it's safe and low-key, but not as geared to the tourist trade as Grande Allée. Try *Bistro Plus* (1063 Rue St-Jean; phone:

694-9252), a singles bar, or *Danse-Bar l'Arlequin* (1070 Rue St-Jean; phone: 694-1422), for hard rock fans. At the *Bar Chez Son Père* (24 Rue St-Stanislas; phone: 692-5308) a house minstrel serenades night owls with sweet Québécois ballads. Another Latin Quarter boîte, *Le Petit Paris* (48 Côte de la Fabrique; phone: 694-0383), also features chansonnier entertainment. Quebec City's only source of authentic contemporary jazz is *l'Emprise,* the Art Nouveau café-bar in the *Clarendon* hotel (see *Checking In*). Four-hour sessions start at 11 PM nightly.

The *Bar du Grand Hall,* the piano bar in the lobby of the *Château Frontenac* (see *Checking In*), always attracts an interesting mix of hotel guests and after-dark explorers. Many revelers choose to top off the evening romantically at the *l'Astral* (see *Eating Out*) bar in *Loews Le Concorde*'s revolving rooftop restaurant (see *Checking In*).

Best in Town

CHECKING IN

Quebec City has a wide range of hostelries, from the magnificent *Château Frontenac* and modern high-rise hotels to small, family-run guesthouses. To avoid having to drive in the Old City, motoring visitors should consider checking into a motel in Ste-Foy. Those planning to visit Quebec City during *Carnaval* in early February or during the summer should make reservations as far in advance as possible. During the winter, rooms generally are available, and most places even offer discount rates. Expect to pay more than $200 per night for a double room in hotels listed as very expensive; from $100 to $200 in an expensive hotel; and from $70 to $100 in those designated moderate. Unless otherwise noted all hotels feature air conditioning, private baths, TV sets, and telephones. All are in the 418 area code unless otherwise indicated.

We begin with our favorite haven, which falls in the "very expensive" category, followed by recommended hotels listed by price category.

A GRAND HOTEL

Château Frontenac Towering above the walled city and visible for miles, this hotel built by the Canadian Pacific Railway is Quebec City's most recognizable landmark (see also *Special Places*). Constantly renovated, the grande dame still reigns supreme. With its imposing brick walls, turrets, towers, and copper roof, green with age, it was designed to resemble a 16th-century French château. Within, modern comforts have been added without compromising the hotel's Old World appeal. Many of the 620 rooms have river views. In the central tower attic are split-level "spa" units where turn-of-the-century travelers lodged their maids and valets. Today the former servants' quarters are mini-suites with individual hot tubs. The newly-constructed Pratt Wing offers a gym and an elegantly designed indoor pool area. The fare at *Le Champlain,* where waiters wear 16th-century costume, is superb (see *Eating Out*). There's also an attractive circular cocktail lounge overlooking the St. Lawrence, an inviting inner courtyard, the casual *Café de la Terrasse* (see *Eating Out*), and a small gallery of shops. The *Terrasse Dufferin,* built in 1838, has a spectacular view of the historic Lower Town and the Ile d'Orléans, and is a lovely place to relax on a summer night. 1 Rue des Carrières (phone: 692-3861; 800-268-9411 in Canada; 800-282-7447 in the US; fax: 692-1751).

VERY EXPENSIVE

Château Bonne Entente When retired army colonel Charles Hugh Le Pailleur Jones invested his savings in a spacious frame manor house set on 120 acres around Ste-Foy more than 70 years ago, the last thing on his mind was a resort hotel. But 30 years later, the colonel's son, Mowbray, launched the *Bonne Entente.* At first a small, eight-bedroom inn, before long it was sprouting additional wings and services. Today a 170-room mini-resort, this château retains the *bonne entente* (loosely translated as "good vibes") of the colonel's original country retreat. Its many features make it ideal for family vacationers; in fact, kids are VIP guests at a complimentary child-care center with an outdoor playground. Guests have the run of what remains of the original estate—11 landscaped acres with tennis courts, a jogging trail, a pool, and a trout pond. Enjoy some excellent wild game at *Le Pailleur,* the *Château*'s fine restaurant, or at any one of the three other less formal dining rooms. Complimentary afternoon tea is a daily ritual at *Le Salon de Thé.* A business center provides a complete range of services. Fifteen minutes by car or No. 11 bus from the walls of Vieux Québec, at 3400 Chemin Ste-Foy (phone: 653-5221; 800-463-4390; fax: 653-3098).

Loews Le Concorde The preferred choice of business travelers, it has a stunning lobby—a golden-beige blend of marble, brass, and glass, with a hint of the exotic Orient in its delicate cherry-wood paneling and tropical greenery. Set on the edge of the Grande Allée's after-dark playground and just a 10-minute walk from *Porte St-Louis* and Vieux Québec, the geometric pyramid on the Plaines d'Abraham has a backyard as big as all outdoors in the *Parc des Champs-de-Bataille.* Not surprisingly, the views are the best in town: Each of the 422 rooms looks out on the St. Lawrence River and the Plaines d'Abraham. *Club 1225* on the private-access 12th floor has its own exclusive lounge, and a full American breakfast is included. The two top-floor presidential suites feature wood-burning fireplaces in their duplex apartments, as well as saunas and whirlpool baths. Non-presidential guests have to make do with the hotel's health club, saunas, and whirlpool bath, located next to the heated outdoor pool. Executive amenities include a business center with secretarial, photocopy, fax, and telex services. The hotel's crowning glory, *l'Astral,* a revolving rooftop restaurant-bar, offers a 360-degree view of the Old City, picturesque Ile d'Orléans, and the Laurentian Mountains (see *Eating Out*); there's also a popular nightclub, *Le Dancing.* 1225 Pl. Montcalm (phone: 647-2222; 800-463-5256 in Canada; 800-223-LOEWS in the US and Mexico; fax: 647-4710).

Quebec Hilton International A five-minute walk from the walled city, the 565-room terraced tower near Colline Parlementaire is conveniently close to the capital's legislative and corporate office blocks and all the shopping and nightlife temptations of Grande Allée. And no other spot is as close to the chic boutiques and fine restaurants of *Place Québec,* the only underground shopping mall of its type in the downtown area. Business travelers like the hotel's underground link to the *Centre Municipal des Congrès* (Convention Center), its two floors of executive-class accommodations, and its extensive meeting facilities. In addition to a restaurant and bar, there's an outdoor pool (closed in winter) and a health club equipped with a sauna, a whirlpool bath, massage facilities, and a big Jacuzzi. Health-conscious guests will appreciate that seven floors are reserved for nonsmokers. 3 *Place Québec* (phone: 647-2411; 800-268-9275 in Canada; 800-HILTONS in the US; fax: 647-6488).

EXPENSIVE

Clarendon Within the Old City walls, this 96-room hotel, built in 1870, is constantly undergoing renovations. Situated just opposite the *Hôtel de Ville,* it's very convenient for sightseeing. The *Charles Baillargé* restaurant serves dinner accompanied by performances of classical music on weekends; *l'Emprise* bar, also on the premises, has the best jazz in town. 57 Rue Ste-Anne, near Rue des Jardins (phone: 692-2480; 800-361-6162 in Canada; fax: 692-4652).

Holiday Inn Ste-Foy This property has 233 spacious rooms, including VIP suites with Jacuzzis. There also is an indoor pool, a health club with a sauna, an elaborate dining room, and a cocktail lounge. Free limousine service to and from the airport is available. 3125 Blvd. Hochelaga, Ste-Foy (phone: 653-4901; 800-463-5241 in Canada; 800-HOLIDAY in the US; fax: 653-1836).

Hôtel des Gouverneurs Ste-Foy This suburban hostelry has 318 attractive rooms, a sophisticated restaurant, a piano bar, and a heated outdoor pool (open in summer). 3030 Blvd. Laurier (phone: 651-3030; 800-463-2820 in the eastern US and Canada; fax: 658-6638).

Hôtel du Théâtre The nearly century-old former *Théâtre Capitole* has been restored to its 1920s splendor, this time around as an intimate, Parisian-style hotel with eight double rooms, 23 standard suites, and nine split-level suites. The complex also is home to a bistro, a dinner-theater, and boutiques. 972 Rue St-Jean (phone: 694-4040; fax: 694-9924).

Manoir Victoria The most striking aspect of this establishment in a lovely historical setting is its vast and richly decorated entry hall. It has 145 rooms, boutiques, an indoor pool, a fitness center, and valet parking. The hotel's dining room, *La Table du Manoir,* serves continental fare, while the more casual *Pub St-James* specializes in pasta. Ski packages are offered. 44 Côte-du-Palais (phone: 692-1030; 800-463-6283; fax: 692-3822).

Plaza Québec The straightforward, massive exterior of this building contrasts with the refinement of its interior, which is all marble, dark paneling, and cozy, stylish furniture. The large indoor pool and the dining room are both glass-enclosed. There are 220 rooms and 11 suites. 3031 Blvd. Laurier, Ste-Foy (phone: 658-2727; 800-361-4495 in Canada; fax: 658-6587).

Radisson Gouverneurs Quebec Adjacent to the *Quebec Hilton International,* this modern high-rise has 377 nicely appointed rooms, an elaborate dining room, a health club, and a heated outdoor pool (open June through September). 690 Blvd. René-Lévesque E. (phone: 647-1717; 800-463-2820 in Canada; 800-333-3333 in the US; fax: 647-2146).

MODERATE

Auberge du Trésor This 300-year-old building has 21 rooms, many overlooking Place d'Armes. Conveniently situated for those whose main objective is sightseeing, the hotel also has a cocktail lounge, a fine dining room with a multiethnic menu, and a café in summer. 20 Rue Ste-Anne at Rue du Trésor (phone: 694-1876; fax: 694-0563).

Le Germain-des-Prés Decorated in European Art Deco style, this 127-room hostelry offers personalized service. Rooms include such amenities as bathrobes and fresh fruit. The hotel has a continental breakfast room. Transportation to and from the airport is complimentary. Near shopping centers, at 1200 Rue Germain-des-Prés, Ste-Foy (phone: 658-1224; 800-463-5253 in Canada; fax: 658-8846).

Manoir Ste-Geneviève Built in the early 1800s, this house was one of the first in the *Jardin des Gouverneurs.* All nine rooms are individually decorated with old family pieces; three have kitchenettes (none have telephones). There's no restaurant. 13 Av. Ste-Geneviève at Rue Laporte (phone/fax: 694-1666).

EATING OUT

Even visitors who don't know the difference between flambé and soufflé will become well acquainted with Gallic fare, thanks to the myriad French restaurants in Vieux Québec. Although French nouvelle cuisine is on most menus, a few restaurants still serve typical Québécois meals of *soupe aux pois* (pea soup), *tourtière* (meat pie), and maple sugar–based desserts. The best Québécois chefs combine the wild game and succulent lamb of the countryside and farm with the sauces of their French ancestry to create an exciting cuisine. The city's gastronomic landscape includes a variety of ethnic establishments, including Chinese and Indian. The city also boasts *salons de thé* (tearooms) where one can enjoy the traditional ritual of tea or wonderful chocolate desserts. Expect to pay $85 or more for a very expensive dinner for two; between $70 and $85 in the expensive range; $40 to $70 in the moderate range; and $40 or less in the inexpensive range. Prices do not include drinks, wine, or tip. Unless otherwise noted all restaurants are open for lunch and dinner, and all are in the 418 area code.

VERY EXPENSIVE

L'Atre This 1680 farmhouse-turned-fashionable-restaurant is the pride of Ile d'Orléans. The menu is Québécois. Open daily; closed early September to mid-June. Reservations necessary. Major credit cards accepted. 4403 Rue Royal (Rte. 368) near Ste-Famille, east of the island bridge (phone: 829-2474; fax: 829-1146).

Le Champlain Crossing the threshold here is like entering a time warp. Attentive waiters in formal colonial dress glide around the richly paneled room; majestic oak pillars and exposed beams support the lofty, stenciled ceiling; high-backed tapestry chairs surround damask-covered tables; a massive, hooded fireplace burns; and a harpist plucks out delicate airs. Chef Jean Soulard's cuisine reflects a respect for the traditional coupled with a keen sense of innovation: Witness his braised leg of duck with olives, or the shellfish mousse. Soulard also makes a point of highlighting Quebec delicacies, such as Gaspésie seafood bisque. The *carte des vins* is long, lavish, and priced accordingly, but wine may be ordered by the glass. This restaurant, the best (and most expensive) in the *Château Frontenac,* is open daily for dinner, for lunch Sundays only. Reservations advised. Major credit cards accepted. 1 Rue des Carrières (phone: 692-3861; fax: 692-1751).

La Closerie One of several restaurants in the region that offer refined French fare. The menu changes every season. Chef-owner Jacques Le Pluart has been known to go so far as to import expensive ($400 per pound!) black truffles from the Périgord region of France for a special dish on the *menu dégustation.* A moderately priced menu is available at lunchtime. Closed Sundays and Mondays. Reservations advised. Major credit cards accepted. 966 Blvd. René-Lévesque O. (phone: 687-9975).

L'Elysée Mandarin The best place in town for authentic Szechuan and other regional Chinese food. The dining room is spacious in a minimalist style; the service courteous and discreet. Open daily. Reservations advised. Major credit cards accepted. 65 Rue d'Auteuil (phone: 692-0909).

Le Marie Clarisse A very good seafood spot near the bottom of the *funiculaire*. Closed Sundays. Reservations necessary on weekends. Major credit cards accepted. 12 Rue du Petit-Champlain (phone: 692-0857).

El Michelangelo For over 20 years patrons have enjoyed this restaurant's homemade pasta and seafood, as well as its other Italian specialties. It's a favorite of the area's businesspeople. Open daily. Reservations advised. Major credit cards accepted. 3111 Chemin St-Louis, Ste-Foy (phone: 651-6262; fax: 651-6771).

Le Paris-Brest Art Nouveau decor combined with stained glass windows and brass fittings creates an engaging environment in which to enjoy the restaurant's French specialties. Open daily. Reservations necessary on weekends. Major credit cards accepted. 590 Grande Allée E. (phone: 529-2243).

A la Table de Serge Bruyère There's only one sitting per evening in the two small rooms of this second-floor dining room, located in a historic building. Happily, things haven't changed much since Bruyère, a Lyons-born disciple of Paul Bocuse, opened this establishment in the 1980s. Exposed brick and stone walls, log fires crackling on the hearths, burnished antique copper reflecting the candlelight, and tables set with pastel linen, fresh flowers, and fine china create an Old World ambience. Try the tender young Quebec lamb, thin slices of rare pheasant in blueberry sauce, or roast duckling with raspberry vinegar. Diners who can't choose between fresh scallops from the Iles de la Madeleine and filet of pork spiced with green peppercorns solve their dilemma with the nightly seven-course *table d'hôte menu découverte* (tasting menu). Bruyère also boasts the best-stocked wine cellar in town. Closed Sundays and Mondays. Reservations necessary. In the same mid-19th-century house, Serge Bruyère Entreprises operates a small tearoom (inexpensive); *Le Bistro la Petite Table* for light lunches (inexpensive); and an upmarket delicatessen and caterer, *Le Traiteur.* All three are open daily, and reservations are advised. Major credit cards accepted. In the heart of the Old City, at 1200 Rue St-Jean (phone: 694-0618; fax: 694-2120).

EXPENSIVE

Aux Anciens Canadiens For travelers looking for a complete French Canadian experience, this dining spot has no equal. It's housed in the charming, white-walled *Maison Jacquet,* built about 1675 and the only example of original 17th-century architecture in Vieux Québec. Its thick white plaster walls are crowded with corner cupboards and bolstered with hand-hewn joists. Furnished in the charming, authentic style of a colonial homestead, it serves customers in four rooms, each with its own thematic decor. The *table d'hôte* selections go beyond the salt pork and *soupe aux pois* that nourished generations of Québécois families to include braised goose leg with sour cream and herbs, duckling with maple syrup, and breast of pheasant in puff pastry. Such traditional dishes as *fèves au lard* (pork and beans), *cretons maison* (pork pâté), *tourtière,* and *ragoût de pattes de cochon et de boulettes* (pigs' knuckles and meatball stew) are always available. Open daily. Reservations advised. Major credit cards accepted. 34 Rue St-Louis (phone: 692-1627; fax: 692-5419).

Apsara A good place for adventurous dining, it serves Thai, Cambodian, and Vietnamese fare. The plate of assorted appetizers is a wise selection for the uninitiated. Open daily. Reservations advised. Major credit cards accepted. 71 Rue d'Auteuil (phone: 694-0232).

L'Astral The only revolving rooftop restaurant in Quebec City is popular for its Saturday-night dinner buffet, and both locals and visitors flock to its Sunday brunch. The eatery also offers an à la carte menu at lunch and dinner. Open daily. Reservations advised. Major credit cards accepted. *Loews Le Concorde,* 1225 Pl. Montcalm (phone: 647-2222; fax: 647-4710).

Auberge Louis Hébert This restaurant offers friendly service and an attractive setting, with calico lampshades dangling above the tables. Specialties include fresh Quebec lamb and *confit d'oie,* a goose pâté. The outdoor terrace is open for summer dining. Open daily. Reservations advised. Major credit cards accepted. 668 Grande Allée E. (phone: 525-7812; fax: 525-6294).

Café de la Paix This landmark started life quietly back in the 1960s, when lawyers from the old courthouse across the street discovered a new lunchtime spot that offered fine food at fair prices. Good news traveled fast: Before long, food critics from New York to Los Angeles were singing the praises of chef Jean-Marc Bass. Although genial host Benito Terzini's convivial establishment is now a Vieux Québec tourist tradition, old patrons still turn up regularly. From the outside, the café is a photographer's dream. The French *auberge* of white-plastered stone sits flush with the hillside street; an old-fashioned lantern lights a narrow doorway; and window boxes brim with flowers. Inside, it's pure back-street Paris, with lamp-lit tables, sideboards, hutches, wine racks and bar, and Desrosiers landscapes on the paneled walls—the kind of *mère-et-père* operation where locals come for lunch and linger through a lazy afternoon. Reliable classics include *boeuf bourguignon,* Dover sole, frogs' legs, rack of lamb, and, in season, pheasant, partridge, venison, wild boar, and moose. The dessert trolley is loaded with sherry-laced trifle, chocolate cake, custard-filled pastry, and bowls of whipped cream. Open daily. Reservations advised. Major credit cards accepted. 44 Rue des Jardins (phone: 692-1430; fax: 692-3949).

Café de Paris Robust French cuisine complements this place's romantic atmosphere. Entrées include chateaubriand, leg of lamb, and seafood dishes. A chansonnier serenades diners six nights a week. Open daily. Reservations advised. Major credit cards accepted. 66 Rue St-Louis (phone: 694-9626; fax: 694-2260).

Café de la Terrasse Window-table diners at the *Château Frontenac*'s bistro restaurant linger here to watch the nonstop promenade on the *Terrasse Dufferin.* This informal spot features a bountiful prix fixe buffet and à la carte specials from the grill. Open daily for breakfast, lunch, and dinner. Reservations advised. Major credit cards accepted. 1 Rue des Carrières (phone: 692-3861; fax: 692-1751).

La Caravelle Traditional French and Spanish dishes—including a first-rate paella—are featured in this well-respected dining establishment. A chansonnier enhances the 18th-century atmosphere in two rustic rooms with wood-burning fireplaces. Open daily. Reservations advised. Major credit cards accepted. 68½ Rue St-Louis (phone: 694-9022; fax: 694-0352).

Le Continental The cuisine could hardly be a surprise—an extensive menu of European specialties ranging from sweetbreads *madère* to steaks *flambés au poivre.* For starters, try the *gaspé en crêpe* (seafood crêpe). The oak-paneled dining room is attractive and spacious, and the service is usually very good. Open daily. Reservations advised. Major credit cards accepted. 26 Rue St-Louis (phone: 694-9995; fax: 694-2109).

L'Echaudé In Lower Town, this spot's Art Deco interior is cool and relaxing, its nouvelle cuisine menu intriguing, and its desserts sumptuous. Try the *bavaroise aux framboises,* a raspberry custard with a tangy sauce. Open daily. Reservations advised. Major credit cards accepted. 73 Rue Sault-au-Matelot (phone: 692-1299; fax: 694-0448).

Gambrinus *Quel scandale!* Imagine a modern-looking restaurant in Upper Town—under the *Musée du Fort,* no less—serving nouvelle cuisine in a nouvelle setting. No exposed stone walls or colonial fireplaces here. Despite its ancient surroundings, this place has the contemporary atmosphere of a classy private club, with ceiling beams and wall panels aglow with a satiny mahogany finish; polished brass fixtures; and sheer café curtains. The chefs are best described as food designers, innovators who combine Italian and French classics with Québécois flair. Try the seafood and veal dishes, usually coupled with pasta, or rack of lamb, duckling in madeira sauce, and several variations of beef filet. The chocolate mousse *gâteau* is one of Vieux Québec's best. The menu changes daily for lunch and weekly for dinner. Open daily. Reservations advised. Major credit cards accepted. 15 Rue du Fort (phone: 692-5144; fax: 694-9557).

Le Graffiti Connoisseurs relish the creative *cuisine légère* menu that features such artistically presented dishes as a mille-feuille of three fish with fresh cucumbers and tomatoes, salmon tartare, and rabbit in a light mustard sauce. A reasonably priced menu geared toward businesspeople *(menu d'affaires)* is served at lunch. Open daily. Reservations advised. Major credit cards accepted. 1191 Av. Cartier (phone: 529-4949; fax: 523-1956).

Kyoto The place to go if you've got a yen for Japanese food, it's decorated in bamboo, with Japanese prints on the wall, and has long tables that seat eight. On a gas burner right on your table, the chef—who loves to show off and make people laugh—prepares chicken, steaks, shrimp, or lobster dishes, with all the traditional accompaniments. Open daily; closed weekends for lunch. Reservations advised. Major credit cards accepted. 560 Grande Allée E. (phone: 529-6141).

Le Melrose At first glance it looks like grandmother's cottage, a prim Victorian villa of rose-trimmed gray brick, rose-colored awnings, and roses growing in rose-colored window boxes. It's as cozy inside as out: The small rooms are curtained in old-fashioned lace, with the original dark wood trim framing plain, pastel-painted walls. Only 60 guests can be seated at the intimate, candlelit tables, arranged around the fireplace in the front parlor, in the dining room, and on the second floor, in what once were the bedrooms. Behind the country-cottage ambience, chef Mario Martel invents such specialties as filet of caribou in a sauce of gingery peaches; pink, juicy tenderloin of lamb, seasoned with mustard and green peppercorns; and a mousse of duckling foie gras in chestnut cream. Closed Sundays. Reservations advised. Major credit cards accepted. A 10-minute cab ride from the Old City, at 1648 Chemin St-Louis, Sillery (phone: 681-7752; fax: 681-6867).

Au Parmesan For those with a taste for Italy, this is the place. Irrepressible host Luigi Leoni presides over traditional Italian meals in a room decorated with his collection of wine bottles. There's live Italian accordion music, too. Open daily. Reservations advised. Major credit cards accepted. 38 Rue St-Louis (phone: 692-0341; fax: 692-4256).

Le St-Amour Young gourmets-about-town swear by this romantic hideaway in a refurbished Victorian house within the walls of Vieux Québec. Normandy-born chef Jean-Luc Boulay and his partner Jacques Fortier have ensured that the main dining room lives up to its romantic name: It's a roseate blush of candlelight, pink table linen, and reproductions of Renoir's rose-lipped maidens. From May through October, ask for a table in the glass-enclosed terrace of greenery with a retractable roof. Specialties include tiny quail stuffed with roasted scampi, sliced into succulent rounds and served with fresh asparagus; cornets of escargots in a creamy herb sauce; and sautéed scallops with snow peas in lobster sauce. Calorie counters can take comfort in the chef's light sauces, which he concocts without butter or flour—but the desserts are bound to undo you. Open daily. Reservations advised. Major credit cards accepted. 48 Rue Ste-Ursule (phone: 694-0667).

MODERATE

Balico Off the usual tourist trail, this intimate little place specializes in Provençal fare. The fish soups are delicious, and the aiole (garlic mayonnaise) unforgettable. Closed Mondays and for lunch on weekends. Reservations advised. Major credit cards accepted. 935 Rue Bourlamaque (phone: 648-1880).

Le Biarritz It's an intimate spot for cozy dining on Basque specialties. The escargots are a good choice for starters, and any of the many veal dishes will make a satisfying entrée. Open daily. Reservations advised. Major credit cards accepted. 136 Rue Ste-Anne (phone: 692-2433).

Café du Monde Next to the *Musée de la Civilisation,* this funky diner-style eatery offers everything from an emperor-size Caesar salad to a traditional five-course dinner. The fare is first-rate, the setting whimsical—featuring crystal chandeliers and hot-pink neon. Open daily. Reservations advised for groups of eight or more. Major credit cards accepted. 57 Rue Dalhousie (phone: 692-4455; fax: 692-4448).

Au Café Suisse For a change of pace, try the fondues at this festive, multi-story place. Some suggestions: the Chinese fondue, thinly sliced beef served in a heated beef bouillon; raclette, a grilled cheese dish; or a traditional Swiss cheese fondue. Since it's one of the few restaurants in town open past 11 PM, its regulars include provincial politicians when the *National Assembly* is in session. Open daily. Reservations advised. Major credit cards accepted. 32 Rue Ste-Anne (phone: 694-1320; fax: 694-1315).

Fleur de Lotus Near the *Hôtel de Ville,* this Cambodian restaurant also serves Vietnamese and Thai food. Bring your own wine. Open daily. Reservations advised. MasterCard and Visa accepted. 38 Côte de la Fabrique (phone: 692-4286).

Nupur This Indian spot is well worth the 15-minute drive from town. Although the decor is modest, the atmosphere is warm and the service exceptional. Try any of the tandoori or curry dishes. Open daily. Reservations advised. Major credit cards accepted. 850 Av. Myrand, Ste-Foy (phone: 683-4770).

Optimum A luxurious, two-story Victorian house with a Mediterranean deli on the first floor and a café on the second, where nouvelle cuisine is served and the desserts are delectable. Closed weekends. Reservations advised. Major credit cards accepted. 64 Blvd. René-Lévesque O. (phone: 648-0768).

Le d'Orsay This restaurant-pub boasts a good location and an excellent selection of European beers. The menu offers both hearty pub food—burgers, nachos, and the like—and, for more refined tastes, a good selection of seafood, poultry, and meat entrées. Open daily. Reservations advised. Major credit cards accepted. 65 Rue Buade, across from the *Hôtel de Ville* (phone: 694-1582; fax: 694-1587).

INEXPENSIVE

Chez Victor Hamburgers with flair (topped with goat cheese, for example) are the specialty in this intimate little place. And the house *frites* (French fries), which are served *à l'européen*—with a dollop of mayonnaise and poppy seeds—are a must. Closed Mondays. No reservations; expect a wait on weekends. Major credit cards accepted. 145 Rue St-Jean (phone: 529-7702).

Mille-Feuille This was the first establishment in the region to specialize in vegetarian fare. No clichés about health food hold here, however—the menu features such innovative dishes as fresh pasta with artichoke sauce, and tofu Stroganoff. Open daily. Reservations advised for lunch and weekend brunch. MasterCard and Visa accepted. 1405 Chemin Ste-Foy (phone: 681-4520; fax: 681-9920).

Au Petit Coin Breton The Grande Allée branch of this small *crêperie* chain is best in summer, when the terrace café looks out on the passing parade. Crêpes, salads, onion soup, and other light fare are reasonably priced à la carte specials. Open daily. Reservations unnecessary. Major credit cards accepted. 655 Grande Allée E. (phone: 525-6904).

Le Petit Coin Latin A lovely place to dawdle over an espresso, sandwich, quiche, or salad to the accompaniment of taped classical music. It also has the best maple sugar pie in town. Dine outdoors on the terrace in summer. Open daily. Reservations unnecessary. Major credit cards accepted. 8½ Rue Ste-Ursule (phone: 692-2022).

QUEBEC QUAFFS

Pubs, particularly those inspired by the traditional London variety, are increasingly popular in Quebec City. But unlike their British counterparts, most keep late-night hours to compete with the bar trade. *Le d'Orsay* (65 Rue Buade; phone: 694-1582), opposite the *Hôtel de Ville,* is a soigné version of the real thing, with rich cashew-wood paneling and all the requisite polished brass appointments (there's a good restaurant upstairs for those tired of pub grub). Across from the *Gare du Palais* railway station, *Thomas Dunn* (369 Rue St-Paul; phone: 692-4693) serves imported beer to match its imported atmosphere. *L'Inox,* in the restored Vieux Port district (37 Rue St-André; phone: 692-2877), cold-shoulders the trendy import image in favor of the home-brewed product. It's the only independent brewery in Quebec City, and pub customers can watch three exclusive brands of suds in the making before deciding on their preference. It's as notable for its king-size hot dogs as for its house potables.

Toronto

There was a time when Toronto was provincial, strait-laced, and somewhat lacking in soul; one of its nicknames was Toronto the Good. In the days before its population outstripped Montreal's (Toronto surged ahead in the 1970s to its current population of more than three million), the city still slept under the influence of its old British traditions or, where these had waned, too readily picked up on the cultural influences of the US.

But the dreams of farm kids and an influx of immigrants, plus a surprising combination of economic and political factors, transformed Toronto from a minor North American city into the cultural, commercial, and communications powerhouse it is today. Dominating the skyline are two buildings, the *CN Tower*—the tallest freestanding structure in the world—and *Royal Bank Plaza,* whose two triangular towers appear to be made of solid gold. The construction and eminence of both structures symbolize the city's ascendancy, a rise that occurred during the past two decades.

Toronto may have the greatest ethnic diversity of any major city in the world, with some 70 nationalities speaking a hundred languages. The city has the largest Italian population outside of Italy, as well as large numbers of French speakers of Canadian and other origins, plus East Indians, Portuguese, Greeks, Ukrainians, Germans, Asians, West Indians, and other substantial minority communities, all with their own newspapers and traditions. Present-day Toronto is also home to a sizable Native American community, largely made up of Ojibwa and members of the Iroquois Six Nations Confederacy. Roberta Jamieson, Canada's first female Native American lawyer, hails from Toronto.

Mass-scale immigration was largely responsible for Toronto's evolution. Refugees from the war-ravaged countries of Western and Central Europe came here in a great wave during the early 1950s in search of jobs; jobs brought people, and people brought more jobs. Thousands of industrial plants in and around the city account for about one-fifth of all Canadian manufacturing. Most of the nation's companies are headquartered here, and many international firms maintain offices. The defection of many head offices from Montreal to Toronto, because of Quebec's separatist stance, also played a role in the city's growth.

Rising on the north bank of Lake Ontario, Toronto covers 244 square miles, embracing six municipalities stretching from the flat, central downtown section to numerous hills in the sprawling suburbs. It is laid out on a rectangular grid, but the neat order of the plan is interrupted by a green belt of wooded ravines created by two small rivers—the Humber in the west and the Don in the east—that cut through the city. The miles of wooded parkland along the rivers are among Toronto's prime recreational areas;

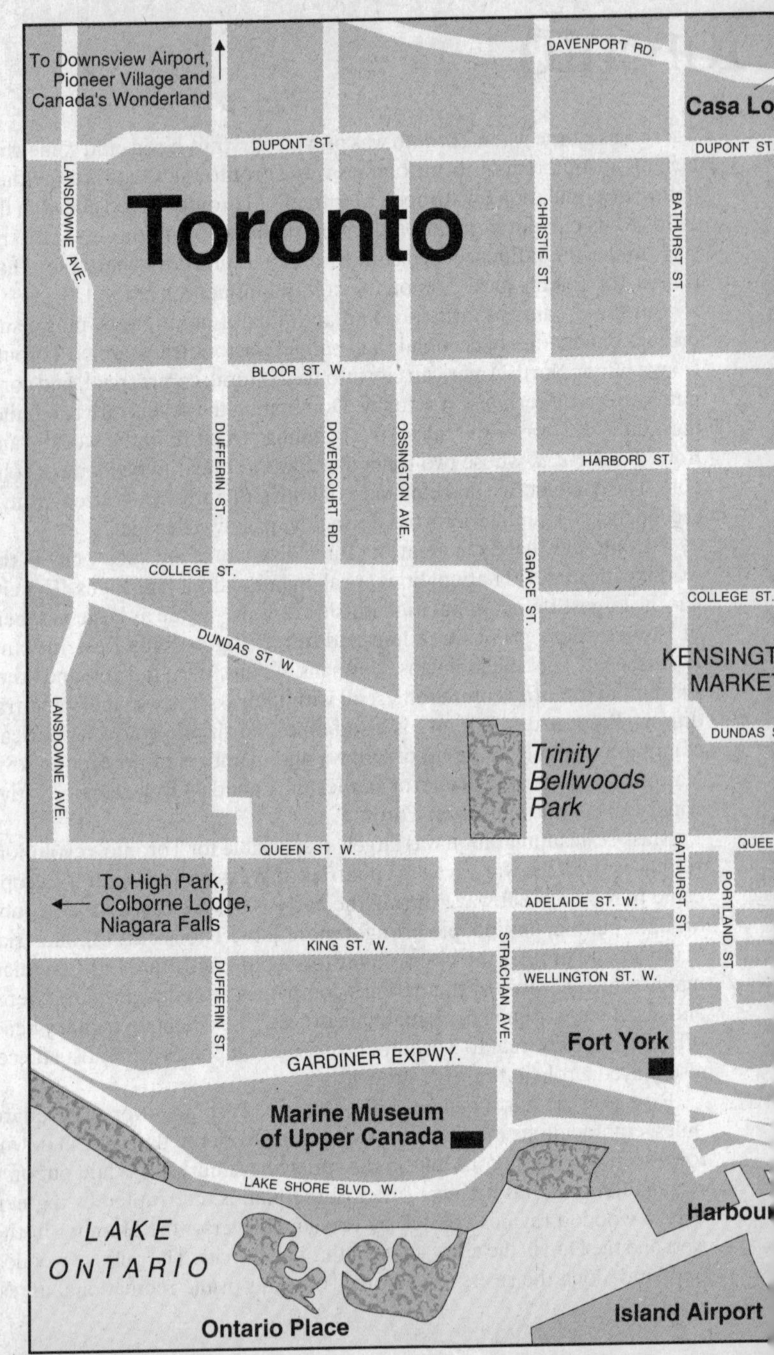

Toronto
To Downsview Airport,
Pioneer Village and
Canada's Wonderland
DAVENPORT RD.
Casa Lo
DUPONT ST.
DUPONT ST.
LANSDOWNE AVE.
CHRISTIE ST.
BATHURST ST.
BLOOR ST. W.
DUFFERIN ST.
DOVERCOURT RD.
OSSINGTON AVE.
HARBORD ST.
COLLEGE ST.
GRACE ST.
COLLEGE ST.
DUNDAS ST. W.
KENSINGT
MARKE
LANSDOWNE AVE.
DUNDAS
Trinity
Bellwoods
Park
QUEEN ST. W.
QUEE
BATHURST ST.
PORTLAND ST.
To High Park,
Colborne Lodge,
Niagara Falls
ADELAIDE ST. W.
KING ST. W.
STRACHAN AVE.
WELLINGTON ST. W.
DUFFERIN ST.
Fort York
GARDINER EXPWY.
Marine Museum
of Upper Canada
LAKE SHORE BLVD. W.
Harbou
LAKE
ONTARIO
Ontario Place
Island Airport

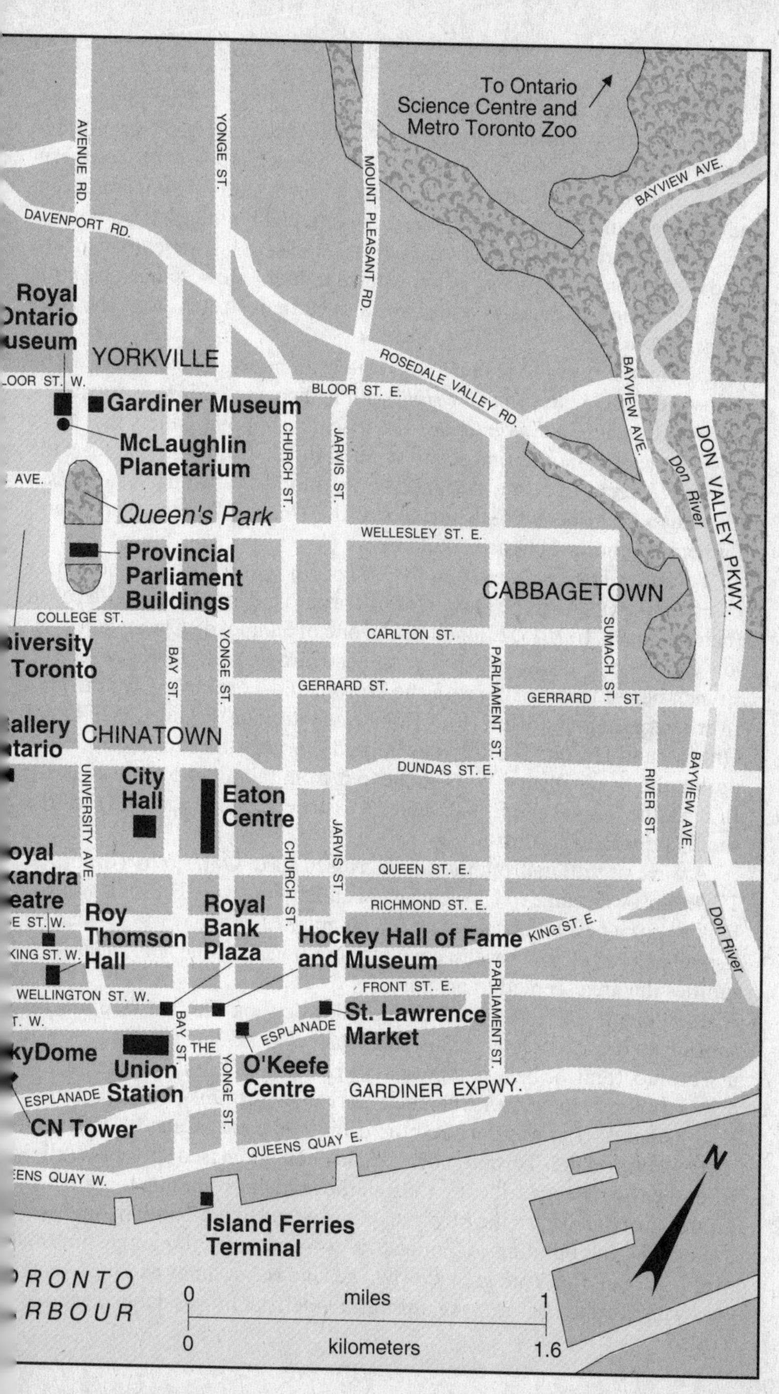

To Ontario
Science Centre and
Metro Toronto Zoo
AVENUE RD.
YONGE ST.
MOUNT PLEASANT RD.
BAYVIEW AVE.
DAVENPORT RD.
Royal
Ontario
Museum
YORKVILLE
ROSEDALE VALLEY RD.
BLOOR ST. W.
BLOOR ST. E.
Gardiner Museum
McLaughlin
Planetarium
CHURCH ST.
JARVIS ST.
DON VALLEY PKWY.
Don River
Queen's Park
WELLESLEY ST. E.
Provincial
Parliament
Buildings
CABBAGETOWN
COLLEGE ST.
CARLTON ST.
University
Toronto
BAY ST.
SUMACH ST.
GERRARD ST.
GERRARD ST.
PARLIAMENT ST.
Gallery
Ontario
CHINATOWN
DUNDAS ST. E.
RIVER ST.
UNIVERSITY AVE.
City
Hall
Eaton
Centre
Royal
Alexandra
Theatre
QUEEN ST. E.
Roy
Thomson
Hall
Royal
Bank
Plaza
RICHMOND ST. E.
Hockey Hall of Fame
and Museum
KING ST. E.
KING ST. W.
WELLINGTON ST. W.
FRONT ST. E.
St. Lawrence
Market
ESPLANADE
THE
SkyDome
Union
Station
O'Keefe
Centre
GARDINER EXPWY.
ESPLANADE
CN Tower
QUEENS QUAY E.
QUEENS QUAY W.
Island Ferries
Terminal
N
TORONTO
HARBOUR
0
miles
1
0
kilometers
1.6

summer and winter, residents use the space to hike, jog, and cross-country ski.

Lake Ontario's wide, deep harbor accommodates oceangoing vessels, making Toronto a major port on the St. Lawrence Seaway. The renovated waterfront area close to downtown is the site of *Harbourfront,* a government-funded complex that includes recreational, cultural, and crafts centers, restaurants, and residential and commercial buildings. Also bordering the lake are *Harbour Square,* exclusive, modern high-rise apartments, and the *Westin Harbour Castle,* a spectacular double-towered, luxury hotel (see *Checking In*). Beaches, walkways, and marinas stretch along the lakefront.

Downtown rises to the north. Innovative architecture characterizes the city—the banking towers; *City Hall,* with its two curved towers surrounding a lower rotunda; *Eaton Centre,* the spacious shopping gallery that looks like a huge greenhouse (inside are some of the best shops in Canada); the *Central Reference Library,* designed by Raymond Moriyama, a Japanese-Canadian architect who also designed the *Ontario Science Centre;* and numerous other avant-garde buildings.

Toronto's history dates from the early 17th century, when it became a camp for members of the Huron tribe; Toronto means "Meeting Place" in their language. In 1615, Etienne Brulé, one of Samuel de Champlain's fellow explorers, was one of the first known Europeans to arrive here. The French began trading furs with the Huron, and Toronto evolved from a river camp to a military fort (Fort Rouillé), controlling the junction of Lakes Ontario and Huron. The fort was burned down by the French in 1759—during the Seven Years' War—to keep it from falling into British hands. In 1763, the French and British signed a treaty ending the war, and the area came under British control.

A wave of settlers from the south crossed Lake Ontario to Toronto in 1784. Most who came to Upper Canada at that time were British Loyalists, looking for a new homeland after US independence. They were joined by a small number of non-Loyalist compatriots attracted by the land and opportunities the area seemed to promise.

Lieutenant-Governor John Graves Simcoe took the first step toward shoring up the tiny colony against US invaders in 1793 by founding a town at Toronto. (Simcoe believed it would be easier to secure than Niagara, the area's capital at the time.) Renamed York after the Duke of York, son of King George III, it was declared the capital of Upper Canada. The land where metropolitan Toronto now sits had been purchased six years earlier from the Mississauga tribe; by 1805 all the lands surrounding the site had been appropriated from the Mississauga and added to the Toronto Purchase.

In 1794, the building of Yonge Street—said to be the longest in the world—began. But York grew slowly. The land was swampy and the streets nearly impassable; before long, this future metropolis was dubbed Muddy York.

During the War of 1812, the town was attacked by US troops, who destroyed the Parliament buildings and archives and stole the mace, the symbol of British sovereignty and authority. The invaders withdrew after four days, on May 1, 1813, and then reoccupied the town for two more days that summer before leaving for good. The British retaliated by marching on Washington, DC, burning all of its public buildings. In 1934, President Franklin D. Roosevelt returned the mace to the government of Ontario as a goodwill gesture.

The city was incorporated in 1834, and its name reverted from York to the original Toronto. By 1901 its population had soared to 200,000, and its business connections extended throughout Canada. The Toronto of that era was essentially built by Scottish bankers, its character heavily indebted to classic British traits. Its business world was run like a select British club, with the reins of financial and corporate power held tightly in a few hands. The view of what constituted a good and satisfying life was vividly perceived and rigidly maintained. Until World War II, Toronto was a predominantly WASP town, so immersed in the work ethic that anything that even resembled fun was assumed to be harmful, sinful, prideful, or all three. Life in the city was governed by stringent blue laws. In the words of the late Gordon Sinclair, Toronto's outspoken radio and TV broadcaster, "Everyday life was dreary enough, but Sundays were murder. Everything but the churches shut down tight. *Eaton's,* the major department store, even drew its curtains to prevent the small enjoyment of window shopping on the Sabbath."

What turned Toronto the Good into Toronto the Human was the infusion of diverse cultures, which transformed it into a city of greatly varied neighborhoods. Toronto celebrates its ethnicity every year at the end of June in a 10-day blowout known as *Caravan.* A year-round legacy of its newer residents has been a proliferation of theaters, clubs, ethnic restaurants, and, even more important, the effect that such social and cultural offerings has had on the city's living habits. With so much to choose from, Toronto has opened up at night. Instead of becoming a ghost town after working hours, as it did just a few decades ago, downtown Toronto now remains vibrant.

While the immigrants tended to settle in the city center, older inhabitants fled to the suburbs each evening. The newcomers opened up perceptions of downtown Toronto as a place to live, and neighborhoods that were formerly thought of as strictly commercial became popular places for the young middle class to live. But what really sparked the revival of the decaying neighborhoods was the election in 1972 of a reform-minded city council, which reversed developers' plans for massive demolition to make way for inner-city high-rises. Instead, the council promoted city-run nonprofit housing, rent control, and tenants' rights, and the restoration of old neighborhoods began in earnest.

Toronto residents continue to work to create and maintain a lively and livable city, one still relatively safe for an urban area its size. As a result, it holds many attractions for visitors. Whether you intend to visit the spectacular *Ontario Science Centre* or the *Metro Toronto Zoo* (one of the largest and best in the world)—see *Special Places* for both—or attend an event at *SkyDome* stadium, you won't see the self-critical city of old but a vibrant, new Toronto.

Toronto At-a-Glance

SEEING THE CITY

The best way to grasp the lay of the land is from the *CN Tower* (301 Front St. W.; phone: 360-8500), Toronto's most visible and famous landmark. The property of *Canadian National,* the publicly owned railway, this communications tower is the world's tallest freestanding structure—from the base of the reflecting pool, it stretches to just over 1,815 feet. (There are taller TV antennas in the world, but they're supported by guy wires and thus are not freestanding.) Four exterior glass elevators whisk visitors 1,122 feet up to the *Sky Pod,* which has an outdoor observation deck, an indoor deck with zoom-lens peritelescopes, the world's highest revolving restaurant, *Top of Toronto,* and a nightclub called *Sparkles.* On a clear day, Buffalo, Niagara Falls, and everything in between is visible. Another elevator leads to the 1,500-foot level, where you can look up at the transmission mast and down on nearly everything else. The tower is open daily; admission charge.

SPECIAL PLACES

Toronto is designed on a grid, which makes it easy to walk around downtown; nearly all streets have names rather than numbers, however, so finding a specific address can be difficult for a newcomer. The north end of the city is bounded by Route 401; the south end, by Lake Ontario. The main north-south arterial, Yonge Street, defines the heart of the city; anything west of Spadina Avenue (pronounced Spa-*dye*-na) is considered the West End; anything east of Jarvis, the East End. Most north-south streets are designated by blue street signs. Bloor Street (which becomes Danforth Avenue east of the viaduct) is the main east-west thoroughfare, and other east-west streets have yellow signs. Downtown extends from Bloor south to Lake Ontario, between Spadina Avenue and Jarvis Street. Midtown covers the area north of Bloor to Eglinton Avenue.

Unless you need to take your car into the central city, don't. Toronto streets can get very congested, and on-street parking is severely restricted during peak hours. Overtime parking at meters can end in an expensive ticket, and if you park in a restricted zone, your car may be towed. Parking lots are expensive as well; it's best to use the modern, efficient, clean, and safe public transit system (see *Getting Around*).

DOWNTOWN

SKYDOME Occupying eight acres, this 31-story amphitheater is one of the world's largest, accommodating 60,000 spectators. Home of the *Blue Jays* baseball team and the *Canadian Football League*'s *Argonauts,* it also hosts other major-league sporting events, concerts, exhibitions, and more. The retractable dome roof covers the stadium during inclement weather and opens when the weather is good. The amphitheater also boasts the world's largest scoreboard/replay machine (35 by 115 feet); *Windows on the SkyDome,* a restaurant overlooking one of the football end zones (see *Eating Out*); several bars; a health club; the 346-suite *SkyDome* hotel, with 70 rooms overlooking the stadium (see *Checking In*); a *Hard Rock Café* (see *Eating Out*); and a *McDonald's* seating 500 people. Parking is limited, so most fans reach the stadium via public transportation. 277 Front St. W. (phone: 341-3663, general information; 393-4636, information on public transport).

ART GALLERY OF ONTARIO This white concrete structure houses the *Henry Moore Sculpture Centre,* with the world's largest public collection of Moore's work (300 pieces, including five large bronzes and 40 major original plasters, as well as drawings, woodcuts, and etchings). Natural light pours in through the ceiling of the *Moore Gallery,* designed by the sculptor to exhibit 15 of his larger works. Other highlights displayed in the museum's 50 galleries are works by Tintoretto, Augustus John, Renoir, Rubens, and other Old Masters, Impressionists, and early-20th-century artists. More than half of the permanent collection is devoted to works of Canadian artists, including the Group of Seven landscape painters and contemporary artists (including Inuit). One of the most important collections in the country, it is the heart of English Canada's art world. Connected to the museum through the *Sculpture Atrium* is the *Grange,* Toronto's oldest remaining brick house (ca. 1817). Some say it's haunted, but its atmosphere is warm and cheery. The gallery and the *Grange* are closed Mondays and Tuesdays, although both are open many holiday Mondays; on Wednesdays, both have evening hours. The admission charge covers entrance to both. 317 Dundas St. W., between McCaul and Beverley Sts. (phone: 977-0414).

ROYAL ONTARIO MUSEUM Affectionately known as the *ROM,* this is Canada's largest public museum. Twenty departments cover art, archaeology, and science. One highlight is the internationally acclaimed 800-piece Chinese collection, displayed in period-room settings, which includes the only Chinese tomb in the Western world. Textiles, weapons, and Egyptian mummies are the focus of some of the other permanent collections. Among the popular science exhibits are a gallery of dinosaur skeletons; the *Life Sciences Gallery,* with living insects; and the *Bat Cave,* with live specimens. Other areas include the *European Gallery,* the *Gallery of Birds,* and the *Ethnology Gallery of the Native Peoples of North America.* The adjacent *McLaughlin Planetarium* has interactive displays, computer games, and laser and other shows (*Laserium* shows are presented Wednesdays through Sundays; call 586-5750 for times and admission prices; children under six not admitted). Two other *ROM* buildings are a short walk from the main museum: the *Sigmund Samuel Building,* devoted to Canadian decorative arts, and the *George R. Gardiner Museum* (111 Queen's Park; phone: 586-8080), North America's only specialized ceramics museum. The *ROM* gift shop sells items from around the world. And the museum's new restaurant, *J. K. ROM,* run by the highly respected Toronto chef Jamie Kennedy, serves excellent lunches and Sunday brunch (phone: 586-5578).

The main museum, the *Sigmund Samuel Building,* and *J. K. ROM* are closed Mondays from *Labour Day* to *Victoria Day* (May 20 this year); the *Gardiner Museum* and planetarium are closed Mondays; the entire complex is closed *New Year's Day* and *Christmas.* Admission charge. 100 *Queen's Park* (phone: 586-5549).

PROVINCIAL PARLIAMENT BUILDINGS In *Queen's Park,* synonymous with the provincial legislature, that pile of pink Romanesque rock is the back of the *Provincial Parliament Buildings;* from the front they are striking brownstones. Enthroned beside the buildings is a resplendent statue of Queen Victoria. Her equally regal son, Edward VII, astride his sturdy steed, has become a shrine for local pigeons. Sir John A. Macdonald, Canada's first prime minister and the chief architect of the Canadian Confederation, and George Brown, his adversary, who first proposed a federal system of government, also are represented here. Here's a bit of Canadiana to put these two characters in proper perspective: Once, during a legislative debate, Brown charged Macdonald with being drunk (a fairly safe accusation). Macdonald's reply was immortalized in the annals of Canadian history: "Better Sir John A. drunk," he said, "than George Brown sober." The legislature convenes Mondays through Wednesdays from 1:30 to 6 PM and on Thursdays from 10 AM to noon. Sessions are open to the public; register at the information desk at entry. With its sweeping lawns and old trees, *Queen's Park* is a favorite picnic ground, with outdoor musical events held regularly during the summer. Also in summer, guided tours are conducted daily, every hour; the rest of the year, tours are arranged based on demand. Call ahead to book off-season tours. No admission charge. Queen's Park Crescent at University Ave. (phone: 325-7500).

UNIVERSITY OF TORONTO Dating from 1827, this is one of North America's better universities. The campus sprawls over several city blocks; the best route for a short tour is around King's College Circle. Take a look inside *Hart House,* the Gothic student center built with Massey money (the family of the late Hollywood actor Raymond and his brother, Vincent, former Governor-General of Canada). Among the other buildings are the *Old Observatory, University College, Knox College,* and the *Medical Sciences Building.* Many scientific firsts have occurred in this last building: It was here that Dr. Frederick Banting and Dr. Charles Best isolated insulin, in

1922; it was also here that the first electric heart pacemaker was developed, as well as the formula for Pablum, the first precooked, vitamin-enriched cereal. Student guides lead free walking tours weekdays at 10:30 AM and 1 and 2:30 PM June through August. Groups should book ahead; no admission charge. *Hart House* (*Alumni and Community Relations, University of Toronto,* 21 King's College Cir.; phone: 978-5000).

TOUR OF THE UNIVERSE For those who've always wondered what it's like to be an astronaut, this attraction is a must-see. The year is 2019; "astronauts" are checked in by security, insert their 3-D passes into a computer terminal, and pass through customs. Then it's blast-off time for a simulated ride to Jupiter. Open daily. Admission charge. At the base of *CN Tower* (phone: 364-3134).

CHINATOWN Several blocks downtown (north of *City Hall* and west of *Eaton Centre*) is the focal point of Toronto's Chinese community. Here are many interesting grocery stores and restaurants. One of the many excellent restaurants is *Young Lok* (see *Eating Out*). The spillover from Chinatown at Gerrard Street and Broadview Avenue has become "Vietnam Town." There's another Chinatown in the suburb of Scarborough.

EATON CENTRE A modern, four-level shopping complex, the center has a high glass roof and lots of space and light. *Eaton's,* an institution in Canadian merchandising (whose founder, Timothy Eaton, first set up shop in Toronto in 1869), has its plush flagship store here. The center houses another 300 shops, boutiques, and restaurants. Constructed in accordance with Toronto's policy for architectural preservation, it was built around two of the city's oldest buildings, *Trinity Church* and *Scadding House,* the former home of an early Toronto historian. Shops and some restaurants are open daily. 220 Yonge St. (phone: 598-2322).

HOCKEY HALL OF FAME AND MUSEUM For the serious hockey fan, a visit to this shrine is a must. The *Stanley Cup,* the oldest of North America's professional sports trophies, is officially housed here, although it is occasionally displayed elsewhere. Here also are most of the sport's other famous trophies—the *Challenge Cup,* the *Canada Cup,* and all of the *National Hockey League*'s major prizes. Sections are devoted to famous goalies, hockey skates and sticks used by legendary players, and other paraphernalia of the sport; audiovisual presentations and regular programs also are scheduled. Open daily. Admission charge. 30 Yonge St., on the lower concourse of *BCE Place* (phone: 360-7765).

YORKVILLE Once a hangout for Toronto hippies before they headed west, this area is now the city's most chic. Renovated townhouses, boutiques with designer fashions and expensive jewelry, quiet courtyards, wrought-iron lampposts, and art galleries flank the narrow streets. There are several cafés where patrons sit by window boxes, sipping an aperitif and watching the world go by. Yorkville Village was incorporated in 1853, and eagle-eyed explorers will find the original coat of arms—indicating a brewer, smith, brick maker, carpenter, or farmer—outside many of the specialty stores. *Hazelton Lanes* is a classy commercial-residential complex with some 70 boutiques and an outdoor courtyard that becomes a skating rink in winter. Bounded by Bloor St., Avenue Rd., Bay St., and Scollard St.

QUEEN STREET WEST This once-moribund stretch west of *City Hall* now hums with colorful street life, sidewalk jewelry vendors, funky restaurants and nightclubs, and shops selling everything from new and used furniture and books to state-of-the-art computers. Nearby is the *Ontario College of Art,* whose proximity played a big role in the development of this area: When graduates from the acclaimed art school needed places to show their work, they opened shops along this street. From John St. to Spadina Ave.

KENSINGTON MARKET A colorful, folksy area jammed with cafés, street musicians, and shops where everything from salted fish and fresh produce to clothing and stereos is sold, this outdoor market has lots of character and a heavy ethnic flavor. Jewish, Portuguese, Caribbean, and Italian influences are apparent. The market is at its best Saturday mornings. Closed Sundays. College and Dundas Sts., west of Spadina Ave.

ST. LAWRENCE MARKET Erected in 1844 to serve as Toronto's first *City Hall,* this bustling marketplace now is a clearinghouse for farmers, butchers, and fishmongers. It's crammed with ethnic foods, coffees, fresh pies, flowers, fantastic breads, and crafts, as well as delis and juice bars. The big day here is Saturday, when the area farmers truck their produce to the *Farmers' Market* across the street. Closed Sundays and Mondays. 95 Front St. E.

CASA LOMA This magnificent, rambling, eccentric, turreted mansion was built between 1911 and 1914 by financier Sir Henry Pellatt—a pioneer of the use of hydroelectric power in Canada—to house the collection of antique furniture and grandiose art he had collected from Europe. He imported European craftsmen to build this 98-room mock-medieval castle, which features a secret staircase; vast, carpeted horse stables, lined in mahogany and marble; *Peacock Alley,* a corridor running the length of the house, copied and named after the *Peacock Alley* in the royal residence of *Windsor Castle;* the *Great Hall,* with suits of armor and a 60-foot ceiling; the *Oak Room,* where three artisans worked for three years to chisel the French oak paneling; 15 bathrooms; 25 fireplaces; and a wine cellar accommodating 1,700 bottles. In the 1920s, when Toronto's electric utilities went public and the city took over his company, Pellatt gave up *Casa Loma* to the city because of unpaid back taxes. In 1937, the *Kiwanis Club of West Toronto* restored the castle and still runs it today as a tourist attraction, with proceeds going to community projects. The *Garden Club of Toronto* renovated *Casa Loma*'s 10 acres of gardens. Climb the two towers; the *Norman Tower* is open, and the *Scottish Tower* is enclosed. On Saturday nights in summer, you can enjoy ballroom dancing under the stars that shine through the dome of the old *Conservatory.* Open daily. Admission charge includes self-guided audio tours, or arrange guided tours in advance. 1 Austin Ter. (phone: 923-1171).

SPADINA The Native American name of this house means "Hill"; it is located just east of *Casa Loma.* Built in 1866 as a home for James Austin, a major shareholder in Consumer Gas and founder of the Dominion Bank (now the Toronto Dominion), it has 50 rooms and halls, which were restored by the *Toronto Historic Board.* Most of the Victorian and Edwardian furnishings belonged to the family, and many pieces were made by the Jakes & Haye Company in Toronto. The *Garden Club of Toronto* planted more than 300 varieties of flowers and plants. Open daily. Admission charge. 285 Spadina Rd. (phone: 392-6910).

FORT YORK This site marks Toronto's founding in 1793, when a small garrison was constructed to protect the entrance to Toronto Bay. Today the defensive walls of old *Fort York* surround gunpowder magazines, soldiers' barracks, and officers' quarters. Other restored structures are on site, and guards in period costume conduct tours. Open daily. Admission charge. Garrison Rd. off Fleet St., between Bathurst St. and Strachan Ave., near *Exhibition Pl.* Take the No. 511 *Bathurst* streetcar to the stop after Front St. (phone: 392-6907).

MACKENZIE HOUSE This row house near *Eaton Centre* honors one of the most colorful early political leaders of English Canada. William Lyon Mackenzie's populist views—reflected in his newspaper, the *Colonial Advocate*—earned him a dedicated following among laborers and farmers. Mackenzie became the first Mayor of Toronto for nine months from 1834 to 1835—even though he suspected that the incorporation of the town of York into a city called Toronto was "a Tory plot to raise. . . taxes." But his views veered to the extreme, and in 1837 he fomented an uprising of 750 rural supporters that took the form of two skirmishes in and near Toronto. The Upper Canada Rebellion of 1837 (as it became known), the only one of its kind in Ontario, was quickly put down, and Mackenzie fled to the US. Still popular with Canadian elitists, he returned under amnesty 12 years later, but many of his supporters were hanged or sent to prison camps in Australia. On his return, Mackenzie served as a member of the legislative assembly for eight years. This house, which a committee of his friends bought for him, has changed little since he lived here: Costumed guides show pieces from 1857, including clothing and kitchen utensils as well as heavy period furniture and linen tablecloths. A reconstructed print shop tells the story of this political visionary. Open daily. Admission charge. 82 Bond St. (phone: 392-6915).

HIGH PARK Covering 400 acres in the west end of the city, this is the largest recreation area in Toronto. In an area known as the West End, its open and wooded spaces and ravines are the restful setting for two playgrounds, a small zoo and bird sanctuary, and facilities for swimming, tennis, baseball, soccer, and lawn bowling. Grenadier Pond is a great spot to fish, row, and feed the ducks; *Hillside Gardens*—three beautiful and elaborate gardens on the west side—are popular for wedding photographs. On the grounds is *Colborne Lodge*, an 1837 Regency country cottage that was once the home of John G. Howard, city engineer and architect. He donated much of the present *High Park* to the city of Toronto. A living museum with costumed staff re-creating Victorian times, it is furnished with period pieces and fine examples of early Canadian art. Open daily. Admission charge. Colborne Lodge Dr. (phone: 392-6916).

CABBAGETOWN In the east end of the city, bordered by Sherbourne, Don Valley Parkway, and Bloor Street East, this is Toronto's best-preserved Victorian neighborhood. Once called "the largest Anglo-Saxon slum in North America" and named after the inhabitants' staple food, it is now among the city's trendiest places to live. For a bit of country in the city, visit *Riverdale Farm* (201 Winchester St.; phone: 392-6794), a tiny working farm with a Victorian-style farmhouse, an 1858 barn, and a menagerie of cows, sheep, pigs, ducks, geese, turkeys, chickens, goats, and horses. The farm is open daily; no admission charge. Subway exit *College;* then take the *Carlton* streetcar east to Parliament St.

HARBOURFRONT The federal government restored this 92-acre waterfront area and built a recreation/culture complex. The *Metropolitan Toronto Convention and Visitors Association* has its offices (with a contemporary art exhibit) in the *Queen's Quay Terminal.* Outdoor music is featured mainly in July and August, but visitors can shop, dine, listen to jazz, make crafts, participate in sports, examine old steam engines, feed the ducks, or just watch the yachts sail around the refurbished terminal and surrounding park. The area is divided into several sections: *York Quay* has an art gallery, theater, and café featuring jazz and poetry readings; *Spadina Quay* features a marina and picnic facilities; and *Bathurst Quay* includes a park and cooperative housing projects among its attractions. An antiques market takes place here Tuesdays through Sundays year-round, and a flea market is held here Sundays in summer. Open daily. No admission charge, though sometimes there's a charge for a specific event. 235 Queen's Quay W. (phone: 973-3000).

BEYOND DOWNTOWN

ONTARIO SCIENCE CENTRE Designed by architect Raymond Moriyama, this spectacular facility is handsomely set on the Don River ravine; its glass-enclosed escalators offer views of the surrounding wooded valley. The museum focuses on modern science. Each exhibit—including the *Hall of Food and Earth, Exploring Space,* the *Hall of Communication,* the *Hall of Life,* the *Hall of Transportation,* the *Science Arcade,* and the *Hall of the Atom*—offers a degree of interaction. You can generate electricity with a bicycle, play Hangman with a computer, make a machine talk, and test your fitness and perception; the *Space Hall* features a hands-on shuttle mission.

Demonstrations, films, and theater performances are presented regularly. There are no guided tours, although knowledgeable "hosts" are on hand to offer assistance if needed. Open daily. Admission charge. 770 Don Mills Rd. (phone: 696-3127).

ONTARIO PLACE A 96-acre theme park on the edge of Lake Ontario, it is part playground, part exposition and cultural center, and mostly lush green park. The *Cinesphere,* a giant structure shaped like a dimpled basketball and spiked with luminous eyeballs, houses a curved six-story movie screen, where films are shown in the winter. At the *Forum* (capacity 10,000), music lovers can listen to the *Toronto Symphony,* to jazz, or to popular performers. *Children's Village* is an imaginative area for kids under 12 (there's a height restriction of 58 inches). The *Pavilion,* a series of interconnected pods built right in Lake Ontario, houses good restaurants and exhibits. The west island features a wilderness flume ride and water stage facility showcasing Ontario talent. Closed *Labour Day* to mid-May; admission charge. 955 Lakeshore Blvd. W. (phone: 965-7711). Subway exit *Union;* then take the *Harbourfront Rapid Transit Line* west to the last stop and walk a quarter of a mile along the lakeshore.

TORONTO ISLANDS Known locally as "the Island," this archipelago off the Toronto shore of Lake Ontario encompasses Hanlan's Point, Ward's Island, Centre Island, Algonquin Island, and four small islands. The 15-minute ferry ride is the least expensive and quickest escape from the intensity of city life. (The islands are populated by 650 people, at least one sly red fox, and thousands of Canada geese and mallards.) Cars aren't allowed on the ferry; bicycles (you may bring your own on weekdays only) and foot power are the standard modes of transportation. The most popular spot, Centre Island, has 612 acres of park, picnic grounds, restaurants, boating, a barnyard zoo, and *Centreville,* a child-size replica of a 19th-century Ontario village with lots of rides (closed *Labour Day* to May 23). Ward's Island and Hanlan's Point feature fewer facilities and attract fewer people, but swimming is good at Ward's Island, and public tennis courts are available at Hanlan's Point. There also are boat rentals.

METRO TORONTO ZOO This impressive zoo is one of the largest in the world. Stretched between two arms of the Rouge River, these 710 acres of river valley and eight pavilions simulate the natural habitats of the zoo's nearly 4,000 residents. The geographic regions represented include Africa, Australia, Eurasia, Indo-Malaysia, North America, and South America. The largest area, the *African Pavilion,* contains ponds and a jungle atmosphere to keep the gorillas, hippos, and monkeys feeling at home. Orangutans and gibbons swing through trees in the rain forest environment of Indo-Malaysia. Other settings accommodate polar bears, alligators, zebras, Japanese macaques, and South African fur seals. A slow, rubber-wheeled train negotiates the 3½-mile path though the *Canadian Domain,* where deer,

Arctic wolves, caribou, moose, and antelope play. Seeing the zoo can easily occupy a full day. In addition to the train, there are various walking tours. Closed *Christmas.* Admission charge. Just north of Rte. 401 on Meadowvale Rd., 10 miles (16 km) east of the Don Valley Pkwy. (phone: 392-5900; 392-5901, recorded information).

BLACK CREEK PIONEER VILLAGE The buildings at this restored 19th-century town include a homestead and farm, a general store, a blacksmith's shop, a town hall, and a flour mill. Costumed folk in last century's fashions perform such tasks as shoeing horses, churning butter, and weaving rugs. The buildings are closed January through February, but a sports program features skating and horse-drawn sleigh rides. Admission charge. There is no easy way to get here, but, if you have the time, take the scenic route west along the Gardiner Exprwy. to Jane St. and then north 12 miles (19 km) to Steeles Ave. Jane St. at Steeles Ave. W. (phone: 736-1733).

MCMICHAEL CANADIAN ART COLLECTION Built of hand-hewn logs and fieldstone and set amid a hundred acres of breathtaking conserved land overlooking the Humber River Valley, these attractive galleries shelter many works of the Group of Seven, an informal school of artists who broke away from traditional British painting early in the 20th century and immortalized the Canadian landscape. There also are exhibits of Northwest Coast, Inuit, and contemporary Native American art. Lively weekend programs include tours, talks, films, and Sunday-afternoon jazz concerts. A full-service restaurant and book and gift shop with exclusive hand-crafted Canadian goods are on the premises. Open daily May through October; closed Mondays the rest of the year. Admission charge. In Kleinburg, about 25 miles (40 km) north of Toronto. Take Rte. 401 W. and exit at Rte. 400 N., then take Major Mackenzie Dr. west to Kleinburg and follow the signs (phone: 893-1121).

CANADA'S WONDERLAND Canada's major theme park is 20 miles (32 km) northwest of downtown Toronto. The park features five live stage shows and some 30 thrilling rides, including the only stand-up looping roller coaster in Canada. Shops and restaurants line International Street, which leads to six theme areas. Top entertainers perform in the *Kingswood Music Theatre* (capacity 15,000). Children's and adults' pay-one-price passports allow unlimited use of the park (except *Kingswood*) for the day. Open daily June through *Labour Day;* closed weekdays May and October; closed the rest of the year. Rte. 400 between Rutherford Rd. and Major Mackenzie Dr. (phone: 832-7000 or 832-2205).

Sources and Resources

TOURIST INFORMATION

For brochures, maps, a copy of an annually updated guide to Toronto's hotels, restaurants, and attractions, and other information, contact the

Metropolitan Toronto Convention and Visitors Association (*Queen's Quay Terminal;* Ste. 509; phone: 203-2600; fax: 867-3995), which is closed weekends. The association maintains several outdoor kiosks that provide quick information and a *Visitor Information Centre* outside *Eaton Centre* (Yonge and Dundas Sts.; no phone). Its city map has plenty of helpful information and an insert on the subway routes. The *Toronto Visitor Information Line* (phone: 203-2500; 800-363-1990) is a good source for activities taking place in and around town.

LOCAL COVERAGE *The Globe and Mail,* a national paper, appears every morning except Sundays; the local tabloid-size *Sun* comes out daily; another local paper, the Toronto *Star,* is the country's largest daily; and the *Financial Post,* owned by the *Sun,* is a morning daily.

The monthly magazine *Toronto Life* highlights the latest restaurants, theater, music, and fashion. *About Town,* a quarterly booklet with lists of what's going on in town, is available from the *Metropolitan Toronto Convention and Visitors Association* (see *Tourist Information*). *Where Toronto* is a monthly magazine distributed free to hotel guests by the *Hotel Association of Metropolitan Toronto;* it's also available from the *Metropolitan Toronto Convention and Visitors Association. NOW* and *EYE* are two weekly tabloids available free at most newsstands, bars, and cafés. Both print information about music, film, theater, dining, and shopping.

The best street maps of Toronto are in *Perly's* city street guide, used by all taxi drivers. If you're browsing in a city bookstore, look for works by William Kilbourn—especially his *Toronto Book,* an anthology of Toronto literature—or anything written by Mike Filey. Both local historians have chronicled features of the city, from the history of its streetcars to the interesting experience of strolling through its cemeteries.

TELEPHONE The area code for metropolitan Toronto is 416; outside the metropolitan area, the area code is 905. Unless otherwise indicated, all phone numbers in this chapter begin with 416.

SALES TAX Ontario has a provincial sales tax of 8%, in addition to the federal 7% Goods and Services Tax (GST). The provincial tax is nonrefundable, but visitors can receive refunds of the federal tax (see GETTING READY TO GO).

CLIMATE Toronto gets a lot of sunshine all year. Summers are warm and often humid, with average daytime temperatures around 83F (25C). Winters are cold, with average temperatures around 23F (-5C) and a fair amount of snowfall. For weather information, call 676-3066, 24 hours a day.

GETTING AROUND

AIRPORT *P. W. Transportation* (phone: 905-672-0293) runs relatively inexpensive airport coaches to and from *Lester B. Pearson Airport* (phone: 247-7678) and major hotels; call for schedule. Taxis are more expensive.

CAR RENTAL All major North American firms are represented.

PUBLIC TRANSIT The *Toronto Transit Commission (TTC)* operates an efficient, clean, safe, and modern system covering over 700 miles of routes. It publishes a handy pocket-size *Ride Guide,* which is available free from station collectors; from the *TTC* center at the *Bloor-Yonge* subway station; by calling 393-INFO; or writing to the *TTC* (1900 Yonge St., Toronto, ONT M4S 1Z2). Buses, trolleys, streetcars, and subways make up this interconnecting system. Exact change, a ticket, or a token is required for the first fare, but transfers along the same route are free (including subway-bus-trolley transfers); round-trip tickets cost less. The fare is CN$2 (about $1.45 US at press time); there are discounts for buying more than one ticket or token at a time, and family passes are available for use on Sundays and holidays.

TAXI Cabs are easy to hail on any downtown street, and there are taxi stands at every hotel. Major cab companies are *Beck's Taxi* (phone: 449-6911); *Co-op Taxi* (phone: 364-8161); *Diamond Cab* (phone: 366-6868); *Metro* (phone: 363-5611); and *Yellow Cab* (phone: 363-4141).

TOURS *Gray Coach* (610 Bay St.; phone: 351-3311) has excellent bus tours of the city during the summer, with passenger pickups at all major hotels and the main bus terminal. The *TTC* (see above) also offers a tour of the city on a restored antique trolley.

SPECIAL EVENTS

Toronto's calendar of celebrations is full throughout the year, but the standout event is August's *Canadian National Exhibition (CNE),* which turns the waterfront into a sprawling fairground.

BEST FESTIVAL

Canadian National Exhibition The world's largest annual exposition, this enormous Canadian version of a state fair keeps over two million visitors entertained with everything from a mile-and-a-half-long midway with games of chance and concession stands to agricultural displays and competitions. Artisans compete for prizes with quilts and other handiwork. There are nightly grandstand shows with name performers such as Whitney Houston, Bonnie Raitt, and Paul Simon; daily water shows; roller coasters; bungee jumping; and the *Canadian International Air Show* during the last four days of the fair. The *Food Building* offers taste treats from every corner of the world. Founded in 1878 as a promotional showcase for Canada's agricultural produce and industrial products, the *CNE* runs from mid-August to *Labour Day.* For information, call 393-6349.

For 10 days in January, the *Toronto International Boat Show* brings yachting enthusiasts to *Exhibition Place,* at the *Canadian National Exhibition (CNE)* grounds; later that month, motorcycle buffs converge for the three-day *Toronto Motorcycle Show* (phone: 695-0311). In February, the 10-day *International Auto Show* (phone: 585-8000) fills the downtown *Metro Toronto Convention Centre* with state-of-the-art and possible future automobile designs. Held in March, the *Toronto Sportsmen's Show* (phone: 695-0311) draws hundreds of thousands of visitors during its annual 10-day run at the *CNE* grounds. It features displays of state-of-the-art sporting equipment and technology and provides information about hunting and fishing lodges throughout North America.

In May, the *International Children's Festival* (phone: 973-3000) at *Harbourfront* features over a hundred performances by international companies and free shows by jugglers, mimes, and more. Two music festivals held in June bring huge crowds to Toronto from as far away as Chicago. The *du Maurier Ltd. Downtown Jazz Festival* (phone: 363-8717) features concerts (many free) in city squares, concert halls, theaters, and clubs and on street corners. The *Harbourfront Jazz Festival* (phone: 973-3000) offers free music in the outdoor concert spaces, indoor cafés, and grassy parks that make up the 3-mile-long waterfront area.

The *Caravan* festival is held at the end of June, when about 50 of Toronto's ethnic communities set up national pavilions in church basements, school gyms, public halls, and tents to show off their food, music, dance, costumes, and traditions. Patrons purchase a ticket in the form of a passport, which gets "stamped" at each pavilion visited during their international tour. For information, contact the *Metro Caravan* (263 Adelaide St. W.; phone: 977-0466). The *Benson & Hedges International Fireworks Festival,* which lasts for two weeks in June and July, brings together the most talented pyrotechnicians from around the world, who compete for the most spectacular presentation. The best place from which to view these celestial sights is the grounds of *Ontario Place.* For more information, call 965-6332.

The *Canada Day* holiday weekend in July always brings the *International Picnic,* a free bash sponsored by the multilingual radio station CHIN (637 College St.; phone: 531-9991). It features everything from pie-eating contests and games to music and a parade.

In mid-July, Toronto hosts the *Molson Indy* auto race (phone: 595-5445), during which cars roar through the streets near the lakeshore and barrel past bleachers specially built along the harborfront. Held about the same time is the annual *Outdoor Art Exhibition,* in which dozens of artists display their work in and around Nathan Phillips Square.

Caribana is a 10-day West Indies carnival that takes place the last two weeks in July. Its highlight is a colorful parade that winds through town, complete with floats and Caribbean displays, reggae music, and street-corner stands selling grilled jerk pork. For information, call 925-5435 or consult *About Town* or *Where Toronto.*

The *Player's Limited International Championships,* a tennis contest held in Toronto each summer, alternate between men's and women's events (men's tournaments are held in even-numbered years; women's in odd-numbered years). For information, call 667-9777.

The first two weeks of September are a cineast's dream, as the annual *Festival of Festivals* (phone: 967-7371) introduces more than 300 films from around the globe. International filmmakers, movie stars, and journalists crowd into the city for this prestigious public festival. Also held in the beginning of September is the four-day-long *Canadian Open Golf Championship,* which takes place at the *Glen Abbey* golf course, about 40 minutes from Toronto (1333 Dorval Dr., Oakville; phone: 905-844-1800).

The *International Festival of Authors* (phone: 973-4000) at *Harbourfront* features some of the finest writers from around the world for nine days in September. Events include readings, lectures, onstage interviews, and the popular *Lives & Times* presentations (prominent biographers and critics speaking on their subjects), plus the *Book-Keepers Café,* with free appraisals of up to 10 of your favorite old books. *Artsweek* (phone: 597-8223), for nine days in September and October, offers free special events throughout the city in all arts disciplines: behind-the-scenes tours, rehearsals, workshops, and performances.

The *Royal Agricultural Winter Fair* at *Exhibition Place* (phone: 393-6400) on Lakeshore Boulevard is the largest agricultural fair under one roof (27½ acres). Running for 10 days in mid-October, it traditionally marks the beginning of winter. Its *Royal Horse Show* attracts international competition in every field.

MUSEUMS

The *Art Gallery of Ontario* distributes an excellent guidebook with information about more than 30 galleries around the city. In addition to those described in *Special Places,* other interesting museums include the following:

BATA SHOE MUSEUM One of the only museums in the Western Hemisphere exclusively devoted to footwear, this collection contains almost 10,000 pairs of shoes spanning 4,500 years of history. Among the articles displayed in this striking building (designed by Raymond Moriyama) are shoes worn by Queen Victoria, Elvis Presley, Elton John, writer Margaret Atwood, and Pierre Trudeau. Closed Mondays, except for holidays. No admission charge the first Tuesday of the month and for children under five. 327 Bloor St. W. (phone: 979-7799).

GIBSON HOUSE A restored 19th-century home. Closed Mondays, except holidays. Admission charge. 5172 Yonge St. (phone: 395-7432).

MARINE MUSEUM OF UPPER CANADA The last surviving structure of seven buildings built in 1841 to replace the original *Fort York,* it now features exhibits on the history of shipping and waterways. There is a fine display of model ships and marine artwork, as well as an audiovisual presentation on the economic history of the Great Lakes. Closed *New Year's Day, Christmas,* and *Boxing Day* (December 26). Admission charge. Lakeshore Blvd., *Stanley Barracks, Exhibition Pl.* (phone: 392-1765).

MARKET GALLERY On the second level of the *St. Lawrence Market,* this display chronicles the history of Toronto through old photographs. Until 1899, this was the site of Toronto's second *City Hall,* and the city's extensive archival and artistic collections are housed here. Closed Mondays and Tuesdays. No admission charge. 95 Front St. E. (phone: 392-7604).

MUSEUM FOR TEXTILES Tucked away in a condominium building a few blocks east of the *Art Gallery of Ontario* is the only museum in Canada devoted to handmade textiles and carpets. Exhibits range from complex loom-woven tapestries to pounded and painted bark cloth. A special gallery is devoted to contemporary artists. Closed Mondays. Admission charge. 55 Centre Ave. (phone: 599-5515).

R. C. HARRIS WATER FILTRATION PLANT In spite of its less than intriguing name, this building—still in operation—offers fine examples of Art Deco design and marble work. The plant is open to the public for guided tours on weekends only. East end of the Beach area, at Queen St. E. at *Victoria Park* (phone: 392-9652, weekdays only). Subway exit *Queen St.;* then take the *Neville Park* streetcar east to the end of the line.

SHOPPING

Toronto's stores carry imported goods, native crafts—and everything in between. There's a broad selection of shopping areas as well, ranging from the exclusive *Hazelton Lanes* (55 Avenue Rd.), which houses the biggest names in fashion and design, to *Kensington Market* (see *Special Places*). There's more to shopping here than initially meets the eye—some 1,400 shops are underground, many of them in *Eaton Centre* (see *Special Places*). Here are many goods not readily found elsewhere in town, such as Scottish woolens and Eskimo carvings and prints, as well as the ubiquitous *Blue Jays* merchandise.

Shoppers looking for clothing head to the Spadina Avenue area, the established garment district, where they can find merchandise for a third of the prices charged at shops in the Bloor-Yonge area or at chic Yorkville boutiques. Specialty items—like an authentic Chinese wok—can be tracked down along the Dundas West strip of Chinatown; funky fashions can be found in the quirky little shops lining Queen Street West; and more expensive items—from a designer suit to a new yacht—can be purchased in the smart shops of *Queen's Quay Terminal.*

Most shops in Toronto are open on Sundays.

ANTIQUES

The ideal spot for browsing in myriad antiques-cum-kitsch shops is Queen Street West between University Avenue and Bathurst Street or the ever-popular *Harbourfront Antique Market* (390 Queen's Quay W.; phone: 340-8377), which houses hundreds of dealers purveying everything from furniture to tiny toy soldiers under one huge roof. Scattered throughout the city are more specialized shops:

Hickl-Szabo Antiques and Fine Art A good selection of artwork. 66 Avenue Rd. (phone: 962-4140).

Jalan Eclectic, unusual antiques from Southeast Asia. 699 Queen St. W. (phone: 366-3473).

Lorenz Antiques Specialists in antique silver and china. 701 Mt. Pleasant Ave. (phone: 487-2066).

Map Room Historical maps and globes. 18 Birch Ave. (phone: 922-5153).

ART

Toronto's numerous galleries feature everything from historic Canadian art (by the Group of Seven) to popular contemporary pieces (Robert Bateman) to photojournalism (Barbara Cole). Many galleries occupy the Yorkville section; one could easily spend an entire day browsing in a dozen galleries in only a few short blocks. There also are a number of good galleries under one roof at 80 Spadina Avenue. Some shops to explore:

Art Med Artifacts, decorative items, and fine art in various media, all from Mediterranean countries. *Hazelton Lanes* (phone: 929-1026).

Eskimo Art Gallery Hundreds of native sculptures from the northern reaches of Canada. 10 Queen's Quay W. (phone: 366-3000).

Isaacs/Inuit Gallery Primitive carvings, sculptures, prints, and wall hangings. 9 Prince Arthur Ave. (phone: 921-9985).

Jane Corkin Gallery Historical and modern photography. 179 John St. (phone: 979-1980).

Libby's of Toronto Contemporary Canadian art. 463 King St. E. (phone: 364-3730).

Marci Lipman Graphics Specializing in "art to wear," this shop offers T-shirts and sweats creatively designed by Lipman. Some prints and posters are available as well. 231 Avenue Rd. (phone: 922-7061).

Marianne Friedland Gallery One of the city's most distinguished galleries. 122 Scollard St. (phone: 961-4900).

Mira Godard Gallery Considered preeminent in the city, it concentrates on contemporary Canadian oil painters. Closed Mondays. 22 Hazelton Ave. (phone: 964-8197).

Nancy Poole's Studio Another fine gallery, it focuses on contemporary Canadian painting, sculpture, folk art, and American ceramics. Closed Mondays. 16 Hazelton Ave. (phone: 964-9050).

BOOKS, MAGAZINES, AND NEWSPAPERS

Britnell's Hard-to-find titles. 765 Yonge St. (phone: 924-3321).

Coles, The World's Biggest Bookstore It lives up to its name: You can find just about any book on its rows of shelves. 20 Edward St. (phone: 977-7009).

Gulliver's Travel Bookshop This place should satisfy those touched by armchair wanderlust. 609 Bloor St. W. (phone: 537-7700).

Lichtman's News and Books The stores in this chain are the best spots for international newspapers and magazines. Main store at Yonge and Richmond Sts. (phone: 368-7390).

Longhouse Bookstore Canadian subjects and authors. 497 Bloor St. W. (phone: 921-9995).

Open Air Books and Maps A treasure trove of nature, travel, and outdoor books. 25 Toronto St. (phone: 363-0719).

CHINA, CRYSTAL, AND SILVER

Ashley China Finest and most distinctive English bone china dinnerware, as well as a huge selection of the best silver and crystal, all at great discounts. At the *Manulife Centre,* Bloor St. W. (phone: 964-2900).

Irish Import House Waterford crystal plus Belleek china, books, sweatshirts, and other Irish goods at lower-than-usual prices. 444 Yonge St. (phone: 595-0500).

CLOTHING

For elegance at any price, go to *Hazelton Lanes* (55 Avenue Rd.), a classy commercial-residential complex in Yorkville with some 70 boutiques, or Bloor Street West, the city's equivalent of New York City's Fifth Avenue. For gritty chic, check out the shops on Queen Street West; for suburban trendiness, head for Yonge Street North. Favorite shops:

Chez Catherine Distinctive apparel. 20A *Hazelton Lanes* (phone: 967-5666).

Cobblestones Fine men's and women's sportswear in a store with a Shaker decor. 87 Avenue Rd. (phone: 925-1680).

David's Pricey purses, women's shoes, and luggage. Bloor and Bay Sts. (phone: 920-1000).

Holt Renfrew & Co. High fashion and furs. 50 Bloor St. W. (phone: 922-2333).

Irish Shop A delectable (if expensive) selection of knitwear and other clothing from Irish designers. 110 Bloor St. W. (phone: 922-9400).

Norma Pure wool sweaters, jackets, and suits by Canadian designer Norma Lepofsky. 116 Cumberland St. (phone: 923-5514).

Richardson's Tartan Shop Scottish woolens and knits. 546 Yonge St. (phone: 922-3141).

CRAFTS

Arts on King Vibrant, imaginative Canadian crafts and fine and folk arts. 169 King St. E., corner of Jarvis (phone: 777-9617).

Guild Shop A nonprofit retail outlet for Canadian craftspeople. Returning US residents do not have to pay duty on original works of Inuit art. 140 Cumberland St. (phone: 921-1721).

Matmata Unusual pottery and artifacts, as well as high-quality leather goods from Morocco, Tunisia, and Algeria. 465 Queen St. W. (phone: 504-1317).

FOOD

For the freshest fruits, vegetables, fish, meats, and baked goods, visit the *St. Lawrence* and *Kensington Markets* (see *Special Places* for both).

Teuscher Switzerland Delicious but pricey Swiss chocolates are air-expressed here weekly from Zurich. *Hazelton Lanes* (phone: 961-1303).

FURS

The Spadina Avenue garment district—where most of the city's retail furriers are located—is the best place for comparison shopping. In the *Balfour Building* alone (119 Spadina Ave.) are dozens of showrooms and specialty shops. Other worthwhile emporia are spread throughout the city, but the garment district has the best prices.

Alan Cherry An upscale shop outside the garment district, at 33 Avenue Rd. (phone: 967-1115).

Alaska Furs In the garment district, at 116 Spadina Ave. (phone: 362-0097).

Aristotelis Creation Specializes in fur hats. *Balfour Bldg.,* 119 Spadina Ave. (phone: 504-6965).

Class Furs Company 89 In the garment district, at 383 Adelaide St. W. (phone: 360-6568).

Eaton's Fur Salon In *Eaton Centre* (phone: 343-2111).

Green Brothers Fur Manufacturing In the garment district, at 332 Richmond St. W. (phone: 593-8860).

JEWELRY

Richard Booth Custom-designed jewelry by this master craftsman. 138 Cumberland St. (phone: 960-3207).

Royal de Versailles Jewellers Elegant and distinctive pieces. 101 Bloor St. W. (phone: 967-7201).

LEATHER GOODS

Danier Leather and Suede A good range of quality and styles. Several locations throughout the city including *Eaton Centre* (phone: 598-1159) and a factory outlet shop at 365 Weston Rd. (phone: 762-6631).

Zanelle's Funky leather and suede fashions. 288 Queen St. W. (phone: 593-0776).

SPORTS

The *Metro Parks Department* maintains good facilities around the city for participatory sports.

BASEBALL The *SkyDome* (see *Special Places*) is home base for the 1992 and 1993 *World Series* champion *Blue Jays.*

BASKETBALL The city has finally realized its hoop dreams. The Toronto *Raptors* (phone: 214-2255), Canada's first *NBA* expansion franchise, currently play at various locations, including the *SkyDome* (see *Special Places*). Plans are in the works to build a new arena next year that will be the *Raptors'* home court.

BICYCLING Those keen on biking can cycle on some excellent paths around Toronto's parks. Many of them are described in *The Great Toronto Bicycling Guide,* by Elliot Katz (Great North Books; $3.95). *Boardwalk Cycle* (748 Markham Rd.; phone: 431-1961) rents the wheels.

FOOTBALL The *Argonauts,* members of the *Canadian Football League,* play from June through November at the *SkyDome* (see *Special Places*).

GOLF Of the many pay-as-you-play courses in and around Toronto, one is truly topnotch.

TOP TEE-OFF SPOT

Glen Abbey The critic's choice, designed by Jack Nicklaus, this par 73 course hosts the annual *Canadian Open.* The high greens fees include the cart; it's about a 40-minute drive west of Toronto. 1333 Dorval Dr., Oakville (phone: 905-844-1800).

In addition, the par 71, 18-hole *Don Valley* (6½ miles/10½ km from the center of downtown, at 4200 Yonge St., south of Rte. 401; phone: 392-2465) has the Don River as its main hazard. *Lakeview* (1190 Dixie Rd., ¾ mile/1 km south of Queen Elizabeth Way; phone: 905-278-4411) is a good, narrow 18-hole course with a pro shop, lockers, showers, and a snack bar.

HOCKEY Large crowds convene whenever the *Maple Leafs* defend their home ice at *Maple Leaf Gardens* (60 Carlton St.; phone: 977-1641). Since 1927, when the team was established, the *Leafs* have won the *Stanley Cup,* the symbol of hockey supremacy, 11 times—a record second only to that of the Montreal *Canadiens.* However, these days tickets are easier to come by than they used to be. Toronto is also home to two of the top collegiate hockey teams in the country. For ticket information, contact the *University of Toronto* (phone: 978-2011) and *York University* (phone: 736-2100).

HORSE RACING *Woodbine Race Track* (Rexdale Blvd. at Rte. 27; phone: 675-6110) is the place for thoroughbred and standardbred racing. Every July, it hosts the *Queen's Plate*—the oldest continuously run stake event in North America and the highlight of the Canadian racing season for Canadian-bred three-year-olds. A member of Britain's royal family usually officiates during the ceremonies.

JOGGING *City Hall* has a jogging track. In central Toronto, jog at the *University of Toronto* or *Queens Park.* The Martin Goodman Trail along the harborfront also is pleasant, as are the stretches of wooded green cutting through the city along the Humber and Don Rivers.

SKIING Cross-country skiing is a way of life around Toronto, and you can do it around the Toronto islands or along the green-belted ravines running through the city from downtown to the *Ontario Science Centre.* Rental equipment is available at *Rudy's Sport Centre Ltd.* (1055 Eglinton Ave. W.; phone: 781-9196). The Collingwood area, 90 miles (144 km) north of town, has the closest downhill skiing resorts, including *Blue Mountain* (6½ miles/10½ km west of Collingwood on Blue Mountain Rd.; phone: 705-445-0231), with 15 lifts and 29 trails.

TENNIS Hanlan's Point, one of the Toronto islands, has good public courts, as does *Ramsden Park* on Yonge Street. The *Player's Limited International Championships* are held in Toronto each summer (see *Special Events*).

THEATER

For complete listings of current performances, check the publications listed above (see *Local Coverage*), or contact the *Toronto Theatre Alliance* (phone: 536-6468). Toronto has a large variety of theatrical offerings, ranging from its own repertory groups to stagings of London shows by English performers. *5 Star Tickets* (outside *Eaton Centre* at Yonge and Dundas Sts., and in *Eaton Centre* itself; phone: 596-8211) sells half-price tickets to events staged by professional companies on the day of performance. It's open daily; cash only.

Of the city's more than 40 theatrical venues, four stars really shine.

CENTER STAGE

O'Keefe Centre This is the home of the *National Ballet of Canada,* where classical and experimental contemporary works meet. The company (157 King St. E.; phone: 362-1041) is under the command of its first Canadian-born artistic director, Reid Anderson. Homegrown talent has included such dancers as Karen Kain, Veronica Tennant, and Peter Ottman. The center also hosts visiting Broadway shows. It's located at the edge of the Esplanade, a street of many restaurants and pubs, so it's easy to find a place to have dinner before or after the show. 1 Front St. E. (phone: 872-2262).

Old Fire Hall An offbeat comedy troupe à la "Saturday Night Live," *Second City* presents satirical sketches here nightly in a nightclub–supper club setting. The building, which once was a fire station (it dates from 1867), is now a 200-seat theater and restaurant. An offshoot of the original Chicago-based comedy company, *Second City* has been presenting its particular brand of biting and topical humor in Toronto since 1974. Well-known comedians Dan Aykroyd, Martin Short, and the late John Candy, among others, got started here. 110 Lombard St. (phone: 863-1111).

Princess of Wales Theatre With a 2,000-seat capacity, this stage opened in 1993 for the Canadian premiere of the musical *Miss Saigon;* the blockbuster has been here ever since (and will remain for the indefinite future). Glass and earth tones are its main visual themes, and the many-windowed structure also houses a series of large murals by Frank Stella. 300 King St. (phone: 872-1212).

Royal Alexandra Theatre Acquired and restored to Edwardian splendor by Toronto entrepreneur Ed Mirvish in 1963, this theater stages shows from New York and London, as well as local productions. Don't expect anything experimental, but it's Broadway-quality theater; locals refer to it as the *Royal Alex.* 260 King St. W. (phone: 593-4211).

Opportunities to see shows in Toronto abound. *Phantom of the Opera* has been playing at the *Pantages Theatre* (263 Yonge St.; phone: 362-3216) since 1988. Other notable venues are the *Elgin and Winter Garden* (189 Yonge St.; phone: 968-0455), a fully restored historic theater, and the *St. Lawrence Centre for the Performing Arts* (27 Front St. E.; phone: 366-7723), for Toronto repertory groups. *Laugh Resort* (26 Lombard St.; phone: 364-5233) presents stand-up comedy at its best. The *Tarragon Theatre* (30 Bridgman Ave.; phone: 531-1827) stages new Canadian plays.

Dinner-theater is popular at such places as *Stage West,* in nearby Mississauga (5400 Dixie Rd.; phone: 905-238-0042); *Zasu* (26 Lombard St.; phone: 362-1088); and *His Majesty's Feast* (1926 Lakeshore Blvd. W.; phone: 769-1165), which features a musical comedy set in King Henry VIII's time, accompanied by a lavish, period-style banquet.

From early July to mid-August, every night except Mondays, the *Canadian Stage Company* (phone: 367-8243) presents *The Dream in High Park,* a free series of Shakespearean plays performed under the stars in *High Park.*

MUSIC

Concerts are presented in a variety of halls throughout the city, including one extra-special spot.

HIGH NOTE

Roy Thomson Hall Home of the *Toronto Symphony Orchestra,* this unique round structure is clad in diamond-shaped glass panels that glisten in the sunlight and allow the lights of evening performances to shine through at night. Designed by Canadian architect Arthur Erickson, the building is considered daring by some, inspiring by others. Controlled by state-of-the-art technology, the acoustics are excellent. 60 Simcoe St. (phone: 593-4828).

Musical performances by the *University of Tornoto* music faculty are held in the *Edward Johnson Building* (phone: 978-3744) and at *Convocation Hall* (phone: 978-2100), both on campus; in the *Ontario Place Forum* (955 Lakeshore Blvd. W.; phone: 314-9900); and downtown, in Nathan Phillips Square (phone: 392-7341). The *Canadian Opera Company* mounts a number of interesting works at its home stage (227 Front St. E.; phone: 363-6671), as well as at the *O'Keefe Centre* (see *Theater*), which also hosts concerts by a wide range of popular artists. In addition, classical concerts are performed in the city's churches and schools.

NIGHTCLUBS AND NIGHTLIFE

Toronto's nightspots cater to every taste. *BamBoo* (see *Eating Out*) features live reggae, salsa, and Latin music for dancing. *Berlin* (2335 Yonge St.; phone: 489-7777) combines dining and dancing, with music ranging from salsa to Top 40 hits. The largest and liveliest discos include *RPM* (132 Queen's Quay E.; phone: 869-1462); the *Big Bop* (651 Queen St. W.; phone: 366-6699); and *Spectrum* (2714 Danforth Ave.; phone: 699-9913). The city's most impressive supper club is the *Imperial Room* in the *Royal York* hotel, where you dine and dance to a live band (reservations necessary; see *Checking In*). *Barrister's Bar* in the *Hilton International* (see *Checking In*) is a quiet, elegant library lounge. The trendiest nightclub in which to see and be seen remains *Stilife* (217 Richmond St. W.; phone: 593-6116).

Queen Street West, where such groups as *Blue Rodeo* and the *Cowboy Junkies* got their start, is the place to hear many different styles of contemporary music. Raucous performances take place at the *Black Bull* (298 Queen St. W.; phone: 593-2766) and the classic *Horseshoe Tavern* (368 Queen St. W.; phone: 598-4753). Jazz aficionados should check out the *Montreal Jazz Club* (65 Sherbourne St.; phone: 363-0179); *Judy Jazz,* at the *Holiday Inn on King* (370 King St. W.; phone: 593-7788); *Pilot Tavern* (22 Cumberland St.; phone: 923-5716); and *Top o' the Senator* (253 Victoria St.; phone: 364-7517).

Mingle with hockey players after a game at *George's,* the piano bar at *George Bigliardi's* restaurant (463 Church St.; phone: 922-9594). *Sparkles* (301 Front St. W.; phone: 362-5411) is a nightclub located two-thirds of the way up the *CN Tower. El Mocambo* (464 Spadina Ave.; phone: 961-2558) is *the* place for alternative and mainstream rock in Canada. The *Lounge* at the *King Edward* hotel (see *Checking In*) is a popular meeting spot.

Bars are open daily; last call is at 1 AM.

Best in Town

CHECKING IN

Toronto's proliferation of hotels accommodates its large numbers of visitors; even so, reservations are recommended. The *Hotel Association of Metropolitan Toronto* (phone: 629-7770) offers information about room availability and makes reservations free of charge.

For travelers who prefer alternatives to standard lodgings, *Executive Travel Apartments* (40 St. Mary St., Toronto, ONT M4Y 2S8; phone: 923-1000) provides fully equipped apartments—ranging from simple studios to three-bedroom setups—throughout the city. Some units are in modern high-rises; others can be found in Victorian houses in residential neighborhoods. All apartments are completely furnished, with full baths and kitchens. A less expensive option is a bed and breakfast establishment. Contact the *Metropolitan Toronto Convention and Visitors Association* (see *Tourist Information*) for a complete list, or call the *Hotel Association of Metropolitan Toronto* (see above), which handles more than 20 host houses, many of which are refurbished Victorian homes. Most feature clean, large bedrooms and hearty, homemade breakfasts, and your hosts will keep you apprised of what's happening around town better than most hotel concierges. Other agencies providing B&B accommodations are *Toronto Bed and Breakfast* (phone: 588-8800 or 596-1118) and *Bed and Breakfast Accommodators* (phone: 461-7095).

For a double room for one night, expect to pay $175 or more in the places listed as very expensive; from $125 to $175 in the expensive range; from $70 to $125 in the moderate range; and $70 or less in the inexpensive category. All hotels feature private baths, air conditioning, TV sets, and telephones unless otherwise indicated. All telephone numbers are in the 416 area code unless otherwise noted.

VERY EXPENSIVE

Four Seasons Inn on the Park Within 30 minutes of downtown, this resort on 600 acres of parkland has 568 luxurious rooms (half of them reserved for nonsmokers), a 24-hour concierge and room service, five restaurants, two lounges, and meeting facilities for over 2,000. For those bent on fitness, there are indoor and outdoor pools, a health club, tennis, toboggans, cross-country skis, and bicycles. There also are supervised children's programs. 1100 Eglinton Ave. E. (phone: 444-2561; 800-332-3442; fax: 446-3308).

Four Seasons Toronto Nicely positioned right in the heart of Yorkville, a colorful area of boutiques, galleries, sidewalk cafés, and clubs, it has 381 beautifully appointed rooms and suites. Special touches include a 24-hour concierge and room service, a health club, an indoor-outdoor pool, and a multilingual staff. French cuisine is served at *Truffles* (see *Eating Out*), and *La Serre,* the hotel's bar, is a nice choice for lunch. 21 Avenue Rd. (phone: 964-0411; 800-332-3442; fax: 964-2301).

King Edward Warmly referred to by locals as the "King Eddie," this place is everything a first class hotel should be. Built in 1903, the 315-room Edwardian establishment has long been a favorite with visiting VIPs: Elizabeth Taylor and Richard Burton spent their second honeymoon here; the *Lounge* bar has greeted Rockefellers and royalty; and former British Prime Minister Margaret Thatcher even made her own tea in the Royal Suite. On the Crown Club floor, members enjoy special rates and services. *Chiaro's,* the Baroque-ceilinged dining room, is known for its tea-smoked salmon and corn chowder. The *Café Victoria* serves breakfast, lunch, and pre- and post-theater suppers. 37 King St. E. (phone: 863-9700; 800-225-5843; fax: 367-5515).

Park Plaza At the crossroads of Toronto chic—Avenue Road and Bloor Street—this landmark 261-room property was built in the 1930s. The lounge has soft piano music, an intimate atmosphere, and good food. The *Prince Arthur* dining room serves continental fare, as does the *Roof* restaurant, which affords a spectacular view of Toronto and the islands. Banquets and professional conferences are held in the *Ballroom.* 4 Avenue Rd. (phone: 924-5471; 800-268-4927; fax: 924-4933).

Radisson Plaza Hotel Admiral This lovely 157-unit place is right on the harbor; each of its 17 suites overlooks the water (as does almost every guestroom). The fourth-floor outdoor pool offers a panoramic vista of the Toronto Islands and a relaxing Jacuzzi. The romantic *Commodore* dining room provides lovely views of yachts sailing by, but the fare is unremarkable. 249 Queen's Quay W. (phone: 203-3333; 800-333-3333; fax: 364-2975).

Renaissance on Bloor In this property are 256 rooms and 18 suites. There's 24-hour room service and complimentary use of the squash, gym, and pool facilities of the exclusive *Bloor Park Club,* located in the same building. The glass-enclosed dining room serves good continental fare, and the lobby-level cocktail lounge offers afternoon tea. 90 Bloor St. E. (phone: 961-8000; 800-228-9898; fax: 961-9581).

Sutton Place Grand Hotel Le Méridien Toronto A member of the Leading Hotels of the World group, this 280-unit property with the long-winded name has attracted such celebrities as Al Pacino, Faye Dunaway, and Paul Newman. Guests seeking extra-special service stay in Regency Floor suites, which provide 24-hour butler service. All guests have access to the exercise, business, and banquet facilities. Visit *Alexandra's Piano Bar,* the hotel's chic lunch spot, filled with photos of stars who have eaten here. 955 Bay St. (phone: 924-9221; 800-268-3790; fax: 924-1778).

EXPENSIVE

Bradgate Arms Ensconced in a residential downtown neighborhood, this stately hideaway has 109 rooms—all characterized by idiosyncrasies in design and decor, owing to the establishment's former incarnation as two apartment buildings. Each guestroom has a mini-refrigerator and a wet bar. The style is Old World elegance. The restaurant, *Avenues,* boasts a formidable wine list (see *Eating Out*). 54 Foxbar Ave. (phone: 968-1331; 800-268-7171; fax: 968-3743).

Bristol Place A top-of-the-line hotel on the airport strip and surprisingly quiet for its location, it has 287 attractive rooms and suites furnished in mahogany, right down to the mini-bar. There are two pools, indoor and outdoor; a health club; and a children's activity center. The main dining room serves high-caliber continental fare; there's also a café. In summer, barbecues are served on the patio by the outdoor pool. The hotel operates an airport shuttle; parking is free, and there is public transportation (subway and bus) to downtown. 950 Dixon Rd. (phone: 675-9444; fax: 675-4426).

Metropolitan Just behind *City Hall* on the fringes of Chinatown and next to the *Museum of Textiles,* this 491-room hotel, formerly a member of the Best Western chain, has undergone extensive renovations under new management. Amenities include a pool, a sauna, a health club, 24-hour room service, and eight nonsmoking floors. There are also three restaurants, including a new Chinese eatery, *Lai Wah Heen.* 108 Chestnut St. (phone: 977-5000; 800-223-5652; fax: 599-3317).

Crowne Plaza Toronto Centre A first class business property connected to the *Metro Toronto Convention Centre* at the base of the *CN Tower,* it has 600 rooms and suites in a variety of styles, all with complimentary in-room coffee service. The *Crowne Club* on the eighth and ninth floors offers separate check-in and checkout facilities, concierge and limousine services, and complimentary local phone calls and newspapers. The two restaurants include *Chanterelles* (see *Eating Out*). Other facilities include two lounges, a heated pool, a whirlpool, saunas, squash courts, and an exercise room. 225 Front St. W. (phone: 597-1400; 800-828-7447; fax: 597-8128).

Delta Chelsea Inn An ideal place for families, Canada's largest hotel has 1,586 rooms, some with kitchen facilities. The property is conveniently located two blocks north of *Eaton Centre.* In it are two good restaurants (with children's menus, and children under six eat free), a lounge, a health club, a sauna, free day-care in a children's creative center, and an indoor pool. 33 Gerrard St. W. (phone: 595-1975; 800-877-1133; fax: 585-4362).

Hilton International This striking showpiece has 601 large, lovely rooms and features a good selection of restaurants. There also are a sauna and indoor and outdoor pools. Located downtown near theaters, shopping, and major office buildings, at 145 Richmond St. W. (phone: 869-3456; 800-HILTONS; fax: 869-3187).

Inter-Continental One of the most luxurious of Toronto's lodging establishments, it offers 201 elegantly appointed rooms and 12 suites. The rooms feature rich fabric wall coverings, shiny brass fixtures, and marble baths. The cherrywood atrium lobby provides a respite from the hustle and bustle of Bloor Street. *Signatures,* the hotel's main restaurant, serves sweet-corn and lobster chowder, shrimp tempura, and Muscovit duck breast with sun-dried cherries and black-olive chutney. In the fitness center are a pool and a sauna. 220 Bloor St. W. (phone: 960-5200; 800-327-0200; fax: 960-8269).

Novotel Toronto Centre Perfect for a weekend at the theater, this 266-room hotel is close to the *O'Keefe Centre* and several other Front Street venues. Don't be put off by its grim, gray exterior: The accommodations are bright and cheerful. The property includes a pool, a sauna, a whirlpool, and a health club plus the European-style *Café Nicole.* Children under 16—who stay for free when accompanied by a parent—receive a complimentary full buffet breakfast (a maximum of two children per family). 45 The Esplanade (phone: 367-8900; 800-221-4542; fax: 360-8285).

Prince In the northern section of town, this 406-unit hotel provides easy access to such attractions as the *Ontario Science Centre, Canada's Wonderland,* and the *Metro Toronto Zoo.* It has a resort ambience, with a pool, a health club, a sauna, 24-hour room service, and three outdoor clay-surface tennis courts. There are three restaurants as well, including *Katsura,* which boasts a good sushi bar. The lounge features live entertainment nightly. 900 York Mills Rd., North York (phone: 444-2511; 800-542-8686; fax: 444-9597).

Royal York This grande dame has been a landmark since 1929, when it was built. While its 1,438 rooms (including a hundred suites) may be a trifle cramped, it has a dozen restaurants and lounges, and it's located in the core of the city. Two floors are available for conventions. The *Imperial Room* offers dinner and dancing, and the *Royal Tea Room* provides an elegant setting for light lunches and English-style afternoon tea. An underground gallery features stores, airline offices (airport buses are at the west door of the hotel), and restaurants. 100 Front St. W. (phone: 368-2511; 800-828-7447; fax: 368-2884).

Sheraton Centre A city within a city, this landmark has 1,400 rooms, a waterfall cascading three stories into the lobby, gardens and paths on the grounds, over 60 stores and boutiques, two theaters, and 18 restaurants and lounges, including the *Winter Palace* (see *Eating Out*). This is also home to *Good Queen Bess,* an intimate English pub literally shipped from Great Britain. The hotel's square shape contrasts nicely with the curved structure of *City Hall,* to which it is linked by a footbridge. There is a sauna and an indoor-outdoor pool. 123 Queen St. W. (phone: 361-1000; 800-325-3535; fax: 947-4854).

SkyDome Seventy of the hotel's 346 large rooms look out on the *SkyDome*'s field, where baseball's *Blue Jays* and football's *Argonauts* play, making this the lodging of choice for sports aficionados. Other pluses include a state-of-the-art fitness center and a private billiards room. Its chief draw, however, is the novelty of its location. On the premises are several restaurants that overlook the playing field, including *Windows on the SkyDome* and the trendy *Hard Rock Café* (see *Eating Out* for both). 45 Peter St. S. (phone: 360-7100; 800-828-7447; fax: 341-5090).

Swissôtel Toronto Located in *Trillium Terminal 3* at the international airport, this $57-million establishment has 494 rooms decorated in neoclassical style. There is a café, a lounge, and a Mediterranean-style restaurant. The sports and fitness center features a workout room, steamrooms and saunas, a pool, and a whirlpool. At *Pearson International Airport* (phone: 672-7000; 800-63-SWISS; fax: 672-0889).

Toronto Airport Marriott This 423-room property is five minutes from the airport and 20 minutes from downtown Toronto. In it are two restaurants, a lounge, an indoor pool, a hydrotherapy pool, a weight room, and saunas. 901 Dixon Rd. (phone: 674-9400; 800-228-9290; fax: 674-8292).

Toronto Marriott/Eaton Centre Next to *Eaton Centre* in the heart of downtown, this 459-room property overlooks 17th-century *Holy Trinity Church,* one of the city's oldest buildings. On the premises are an indoor pool, a health club, and two restaurants. Twenty-four-hour room service is available. 525 Bay St. (phone: 597-9200; 800-228-9290; fax: 597-9211).

Westin Harbour Castle This sleek, twin-towered structure dominates the waterfront. Its architecture is well integrated with its surroundings, creating a luxurious and comfortable atmosphere. Its revolving *Lighthouse* restaurant affords panoramic views of the area, and all 978 rooms offer vistas of either Lake Ontario and the islands or the city skyline. The health club has an indoor pool, a whirlpool, a sauna, a steamroom, a gym, squash courts, and an outdoor track equipped to melt snow so it can be used year-round. The *Poseidon* restaurant serves seafood, and there are three lounges in the lobby. A free shuttle bus connects the hotel and *Eaton Centre, City Hall,* and other downtown locations. 1 Harbour Sq. (phone: 869-1600; 800-228-3000; fax: 869-0573).

MODERATE

Bond Place One block from *Eaton Centre* and near the *Pantages* and *Elgin and Winter Garden* theaters, this hotel has 286 small but functional rooms. Fifty-one of the units feature a queen-size bed plus a pull-out couch, ideal for families. The service is prompt and friendly. There is a good restaurant and a cheery lounge, as well as a health club, a pool, and a sauna. 65 Dundas St. E. (phone: 362-6061; 800-268-9390; fax: 360-6406).

Holiday Inn on King This unusually shaped white-and-aqua building is within walking distance of the *SkyDome,* the *CN Tower,* and the *Convention Centre.* The hotel occupies the top 12 floors of a 20-story office building. Overlooking the downtown skyline and the lake are 426 rooms and executive suites. There also is a small outdoor pool, a good fitness center, and a restaurant; a Japanese restaurant and a deli are located elsewhere in the building. Baseball and theater packages are available. 370 King St. W. (phone: 599-4000; 800-HOLIDAY; fax: 599-8889).

Journey's End Typical of the properties in this hotel chain, the guestrooms here are very reasonably priced. Amenities at most locations include fax and photocopy facilities, in-room movies, on-site parking, and a no-frills coffee shop. Children 16 years of age and under stay for free when accompanied by a parent; pets are allowed in most locations. Several locations in Toronto include downtown (111 Lombard St.; phone: 367-5555; fax: 367-3470); North York (66 Norfinch Dr.; phone: 736-4700; fax: 736-4842); Bloor Street (280 Bloor St. W.; phone: 968-0010; fax: 968-7765); the airport vicinity (262 Carlingview Dr.; phone: 674-8442; fax: 674-3088); and east of the airport (2180 Islington Ave.; phone: 240-9090; fax: 240-9944). There's a toll-free number for all locations (phone: 800-668-4200).

Primrose The 320 guestrooms in this Best Western member are surprisingly well appointed for their price range. The dining room offers good, solid fare; also on the premises are an outdoor pool and a sauna. There are six non-smoking floors. 111 Carlton St. (phone: 977-8000; 800-268-8082; fax: 977-6323).

Toronto Colony Formerly the *Downtown Holiday Inn,* this property features 717 guestrooms. It boasts an attractive lounge and a good eatery, and is also steps away from some of the best restaurants in Chinatown. There are indoor and outdoor pools, a sauna, and a small health club. 89 Chestnut St. (phone: 977-0707; 800-777-1700; fax: 977-1136).

Victoria This 48-room property is across the street from the famed *Shopsy's* deli (see *Eating Out*) and around the corner from the *O'Keefe Centre.* Commonly referred to as "the Old Vic," it offers few amenities save good, clean rooms and a popular restaurant called *56 Yonge* (see *Eating Out*). 56 Yonge St. (phone: 363-1666; fax: 363-7327).

INEXPENSIVE

Carlton Inn Most of the 536 modern rooms here have small refrigerators, and there's also a dining room, two pubs, a pool, and a sauna. Next door to *Maple Leaf Gardens,* at 30 Carlton St. (phone: 977-6655; 800-268-9076; fax: 977-0502).

EATING OUT

Today, Toronto is home to about 5,000 restaurants, many of which offer ethnic fare. The choice of food, which once ran the gamut from roast beef to Yorkshire pudding, represents a veritable United Nations of culinary options: Chinese, French, Italian, Moroccan, Vietnamese, Indian, Greek, Japanese, Malaysian, Thai, and Caribbean, to name just a few. Because of the fierce competition, the quality generally is high. For a dinner for two, expect to pay $90 to $125 at a restaurant in the expensive category; from $40 to $80 at a place rated moderate; and $40 or less for a restaurant in the inexpensive range. Prices do not include drinks, wine, tip, or taxes. All restaurants are open for lunch and dinner unless otherwise noted. All telephone numbers are in the 416 area code unless otherwise indicated.

EXPENSIVE

Avenues Intimate and pastel-hued, this hotel dining room is known for its attention to detail and the kitchen's imaginative entrées, such as succulent breast of goose with sautéed scallions and morel-truffle butter. The service is solicitous, and the wine cellar houses a selection broad enough to appeal to every palate. Open daily. Reservations advised. Major credit cards accepted. In the *Bradgate Arms Hotel,* 54 Foxbar Rd. (phone: 968-1331).

Barberian's Just off Yonge Street, this small restaurant prides itself on its old-fashioned dinner-club ambience, and it serves food to match. Baskets of toasted bread and plates of dill pickles, olives, and vegetables magically appear on the table; follow those up with a huge bacon-wrapped sirloin steak and an even larger baked potato, accompanied by a seemingly endless supply of sour cream. Also of note are the late-night fondues and après-theater baked Alaska. The decor is warm and muted; the wine list, extensive. Closed for lunch on weekends. Reservations advised. Major credit cards accepted. 7 Elm St. (phone: 597-0225).

Barolo This Cabbagetown spot serves generous portions of such Italian specialties as sun-dried-tomato fettuccine and scallops Barolo (the shellfish is marinated in jalapeño peppers, garlic, and other spices, then grilled and served in a white wine sauce). The dining area is pleasantly quirky, in keeping with the colorful neighborhood. The wine selection is excellent, and the *tiramisù* and gelati are worth saving room for. Closed Sundays. Reservations advised. Major credit cards accepted. 193 Carlton St. (phone: 961-4747).

Bistro 990 It looks like an old wine cellar with its heavy pillars, vaulted ceiling, and line drawings on stucco walls, but this dining room is softly lit, and the kitchen prepares French country-style dishes like duck *confit,* steak in roquefort sauce, garlicky roast chicken, and tiger prawns. Closed Saturday lunch and Sundays. Reservations advised. Major credit cards accepted. 990 Bay St. (phone: 921-9990).

La Bodega Despite its Spanish name, this eatery in a Victorian mansion serves distinctly French fare, such as breast of duck with raspberry sauce and veal filets with a cranberry *coulis.* The daily blackboard menu features specials designed around the fresh foodstuffs that owner Philip Wharton chooses every morning at the city's markets. The impressive wine list invariably includes the best lot of the season's beaujolais. The rooms adjoining the main one are elegant, and there is an outdoor patio as well. Closed Sundays. Reservations advised. Major credit cards accepted. 30 Baldwin St. (phone: 977-8600).

Carman's While trendier spots may come and go, this steakhouse has been a tried-and-true favorite for many years. The style is English Tudor, and the dining area features four wood-burning fireplaces. Sirloin is trimmed of all fat, lamb is garlic-charged, and the Dover sole and lobster are excellent. Closed for lunch. Reservations advised. Major credit cards accepted. 26 Alexander St. (phone: 924-6306).

Centro Grill & Wine Bar Franco Prevedello, the restaurateur with the Midas touch, opened this top dining spot in the mid-1980s. Modern Italian decor—including leather armchairs and Art Deco lighting—sets the tone for this chic, crowded, and sometimes noisy place. Appetizers include pepper beef carpaccio with shaved fennel and arugula parmigiana, and lobster and bay scallops with tarragon. Typical of the inventive main courses are mesquite-grilled veal chops with sage and black-olive paste, served with wild-rice pancakes. For dessert, try the vanilla bean *crème brûlée* with lemon-blossom gelato. Arrive early for a glass of wine and a complimentary hot snack in the relaxing piano bar. Closed Sundays. Reservations necessary. Major credit cards accepted. 2472 Yonge St. (phone: 483-2211).

Chanterelles Superb food, solicitous service, and a handsome setting off the lobby of the *Crowne Plaza Toronto Centre* make this a fine dining choice. The menu includes everything from oysters and caviar to saddle of rabbit. There's a pre-theater dinner, but you may want to go after the performance just to try the sinful but heavenly signature cake. Closed Sundays. Reservations advised. Major credit cards accepted. 225 Front St. W. (phone: 597-8142).

George Bigliardi's Popular with the hockey crowd and high-powered business types, this elegant dining lounge serves steaks, seafood, pasta, and sausages—all with that special Italian touch. Enjoy the house cocktail, the Midnight George, at the brass-railed bar or the piano bar. Closed Sundays and for lunch. Reservations advised. Major credit cards accepted. 463 Church St., two blocks north of *Maple Leaf Gardens* (phone: 922-9594).

Grappa This eatery is popular for its tasty northern Italian cuisine with a California touch. Surrounded by prints of Venice and a mural depicting a vineyard, patrons treat themselves to hearty pasta like linguine Capri with shrimp, scallops, and squid napped in baby clam tomato sauce and garnished with mussels. There also are warm salads, lamb, and daily specials like grilled tuna with mango salsa. Desserts include a warm raspberry *clafouti* (a country-style French dessert made of fruit with a baked batter topping), dark chocolate mousse meringue, and ices, all made on the premises. Closed for lunch. Reservations advised. Major credit cards accepted. In Little Italy, at 797 College St. (phone: 535-3337).

Joso's The theme of this place—the female form—is all-pervasive, from the numerous paintings and statuary to the Rubenesque busts literally protruding from the walls. Located in a two-story mansion just off Avenue Road, this establishment specializes in seafood, usually prepared imaginatively (try the crispy calamari with spicy saffron risotto). Although the wine list is not extensive, the house wine is a good bet. Closed Sundays. Reservations advised. Major credit cards accepted. 202 Davenport Rd. (phone: 925-1903).

Lotus Local foodies flock here to taste the blend of the best of French and Chinese cooking. Chef Susur Lee has created a serene space (with courteous service) for 30 diners and a menu that changes daily. His offerings might include charred tuna, shrimp in crawfish bisque, marinated barbecued pork, or such unusual organic vegetables as purple potatoes and wild leeks. The wine list is good, too. Expect to wait for your meal: Everything is made to order. Closed Sundays. Reservations necessary. Major credit cards accepted. 96 Tecumseh St. (phone: 368-7620).

Nami The indoor Japanese-style grill will be the first thing to catch your eye as you enter this elegant restaurant. Sushi lovers gather here to sample delicate raw shrimp or lobster; others prefer the seafood lightly grilled. Also outstanding is anything tempura, with a thin, exquisitely crispy batter. The wine list is limited; most patrons stick with hot sake or cold Kirin beer. Open daily. Reservations advised. Major credit cards accepted. 55 Adelaide St. E. (phone: 362-7373).

North 44° The name refers to Toronto's geographical latitude. This ultra-chic spot boasts the considerable skills of chef/owner Mark McEwan, which are manifested in such culinary tours de force as corn-fried oysters with sweet pepper and jalapeño sauce; capon with rosemary and ratatouille; pasta; sweet potato fries; and Caribbean-spiced, charred seafood stew. Upstairs in the piano bar, sit on comfortable sofas and enjoy pasta dishes. Desserts include homemade ice cream and sorbets; the wine list is excellent. Closed Sundays. Reservations necessary. Major credit cards accepted. 2537 Yonge St. (phone: 487-4897).

Orso Created by New York restaurateur Joe Allen and managed by the redoubtable John Maxwell, this converted two-story, sandblasted-brick structure is decorated with pastel pinks and marbled walls. While the decor is somewhat formal, the ambience and staff are congenial. The wafer-thin pizza, topped with mussels or mushrooms, makes a perfect starter; notable entrées include grilled swordfish with cream and mango relish and sautéed sweetbreads in a thick cream sauce with onions and mustard. The wine and beer lists are exemplary, and regulars often drop in for a cappuccino (or a shot of grappa) at the tiny stand-up bar. Closed for lunch on weekends. Reservations advised. Major credit cards accepted. 106 John St. (phone: 596-1989).

Roppongi Named for a Tokyo district where the Chinese owner once lived, this restaurant has clean lines and a restful feeling. The Szechuan, Cantonese, and Chiu-Chow food emphasizes freshness. Try the *kung-po* chicken; steamed, marinated duck with ginger sauce; or pork served with a sauce of green onion, garlic, chili oil, and wine. No MSG is used. The service is attentive, and there's a good selection of wines, mostly nonvintage French. Closed for lunch on weekends. Reservations advised. Major credit cards accepted. 230 Richmond St. W. (phone: 977-6622).

Scaramouche Some of the best dishes here are the smoked salmon and trout, veal served with sweet morels and Jerusalem artichokes, sautéed calamari with sweet peppers, and lamb. All are served in an elegant, candlelit dining room in the upscale neighborhood of Forest Hills, with views of the bright lights of downtown. There's also a pasta bar. The wine list features French and Italian vintages plus wines from Oregon and California. A must for dessert is the bittersweet-chocolate and praline truffle. Closed Sundays and for lunch. Reservations necessary. Major credit cards accepted. On a small side street off Avenue Rd.; ask for directions. 1 Benvenuto Pl. (phone: 961-8011).

Splendido Chef Arpi Magyar's trattoria and his garlic mashed potatoes are major reasons to venture into this residential area. The two-story front windows allow for a sunny atmosphere that complements the bright color combinations of the meals served here, which might include seared rack of lamb, accompanied by green mint, orange yams, and white beets; quail with fresh pasta; lamb sausage with velvety polenta and rosemary sauce; and rabbit served with kale and *porcini* mushrooms. Particularly noteworthy are the restaurant's pesto creations—try the pesto pizza, cooked in an old-fashioned brick oven. The homemade desserts are some of the best in town. Italian fixtures and the long bar at the entrance give it a Mediterranean-via-New York feel. The wines are Italian and good (available by the glass). Closed Mondays. Reservations necessary. Major credit cards accepted. 88 Harbord St. (phone: 929-7788).

Truffles This dining room at the *Four Seasons Toronto* only enhances the hotel's already sterling reputation. Designed to offer fine fare as well as soup-and-salad meals, the menu includes a three-fish (salmon, black bass, and sautéed skate) main course with a tomato-lemon-thyme sauce, as well as lobster, rabbit, and grilled squid. Try the sumptuous seared Quebec duck liver for an appetizer and one of the elaborate pastries or pies for dessert. The service is white-glove perfect; the wine list, with more than 200 vintages from around the world, is pricey. Works by local artists adorn the restaurant's soaring spaces. Closed Sundays and for lunch. Reservations necessary. Major credit cards accepted. 21 Avenue Rd. (phone: 964-0411).

Waves Behind this little storefront is some of Toronto's best bouillabaisse and paella. The creative fare here runs the gamut from "Med bread"—which comes with various toppings—to swordfish. The hand-painted tables add to the sunny ambience, and the light, pastel-colored walls are the perfect backdrop for the restaurant's rotating art exhibit. Closed for lunch. Reservations advised. Major credit cards accepted. 347 Danforth Ave. (phone: 466-4644).

Windows on the SkyDome This 650-seat restaurant offers a spectacular view of the *SkyDome*'s playing fields. Excellent prime ribs, steaks, and seafood are served. The international buffet is very popular. Open only during major sports events. Reservations advised. Major credit cards accepted. 300 Bremner Rd. (phone: 341-2300 or 341-2324).

Winter Palace Atop the *Sheraton Centre* complex, this place commands an excellent view of *City Hall* and Nathan Phillips Square. Dining is enhanced in the summer by the multicolored lights shimmering from the reflecting pool 43 stories below and, in winter, by the soft glow bathing the skaters in front of *City Hall.* The interior is elegant, and the menu features French dishes with a Russian flair. Sample the *zakuska*—a dish of seven hors d'oeuvres, including caviar, partridge pâté, and smoked salmon—then follow up with the veal tenderloin or scampi Fabergé. There's an extensive wine list. Closed Sundays. Reservations necessary. Major credit cards accepted. 123 Queen St. W. (phone: 361-1000).

MODERATE

Babur This Indian restaurant is small and softly lit. The appetizers are tasty and fragrant, as is the snack platter with such items as chicken *tikka,* vegetable fritters, and ground beef kebab. Vegetarian dishes include cheese in saffron cream, and *dahl* (lentils). *Jardaloo sali boti,* a tender lamb dish with nuts and dried fruit, and the tandoori chicken are good, as is the service. Open daily. Reservations advised. Major credit cards accepted. 279 Dundas St. W. (phone: 599-7720).

BamBoo Long regarded as the heart of the funky Queen Street West strip, this spot serves some of the city's finest Caribbean, Thai, and other Asian concoctions. The *pad thai*—a mound of thin noodles, chicken, shrimp, and blended spices—is a meal in itself, and the Key lime pie is appropriately light and tart. Although the wine list is decent, beer seems to be the drink of choice here. There's also a great rooftop patio in the summer. This is one of Toronto's hottest nightspots; arrive early to avoid paying a cover charge for the live reggae, salsa, and Latin music played here in the evenings. Closed Sundays. Reservations necessary. Major credit cards accepted. 312 Queen St. W. (phone: 593-5771).

Bellair Café Serving pasta, salads, seafood, and frozen yogurt and sorbet in a contemporary dining room, this is a popular spot for business lunches and shopping breaks. Celebrities can sometimes be seen dining here. Open daily. Reservations advised. Major credit cards accepted. 100 Cumberland St. at Bellair (phone: 964-2222).

C'est What? Just east of Yonge Street, this underground café attracts an eclectic after-work and late-night clientele. The fare is standard pub grub—chicken fingers, wings, and burgers—and the owners pride themselves on their microbrewery beer selection and local wine list. Entertainment includes board games and live music, from blues to classical. Open to 4 AM weekends and 2:30 AM weekdays. No reservations. Major credit cards accepted. 67 Front St. E. (phone: 867-9791).

Coyote Grill Located in the upper shopping floors of the *Queen's Quay Terminal,* this Tex-Mex diner overlooks the harbor. The chicken *fajitas* are especially good; order them with thick corn bread, black-bean soup, and spicy guacamole. Sit either by the (very) open kitchen, where you can watch food cooking on the grill, or, better yet, by the window, where you can see sailboats gliding on the water. Open daily. Reservations advised for lunch. Major credit cards accepted. 207 *Queen's Quay Terminal* (phone: 203-0504).

Ed's Warehouse When Ed Mirvish bought and restored the *Royal Alexandra Theatre,* he also launched a restaurant empire, seating 1,300 guests, next door. Garish, with Tiffany-style lamps and plush old-time autos, this restaurant is great for beef and atmosphere. Closed for lunch on weekends. Reservations necessary for parties of 20 or more. Major credit cards accepted. 270 King St. W. (phone: 593-6676).

Filet of Sole Fishing scenes of Peggy's Cove in Nova Scotia line the walls of this informal seafood spot. The menu revolves around the day's best fresh fish selections. Try the shellfish platters. The place caters to theater lovers who like to linger at their tables. Closed for lunch on weekends. Reservations necessary. Major credit cards accepted. 11 Duncan St. (phone: 598-3256).

Grano Sunny colors, Byzantine-style mosaics, and Renaissance sculptures combine to create an Italian ambience in this pretty café run by a popular young Italian couple. The soups and antipasti are wonderful, as are the pizza and pasta. Their assortment of breads (*grano* in Italian means grain), as well as the desserts and the pizza dough, are made daily on the premises. There is a patio, and the boutique sells ceramics, art, books, and other items in a southern Italian vein. Closed Sundays. Reservations advised. Major credit cards accepted. 2035 Yonge St. (phone: 440-1086).

Jacques Bistro du Parc This Yorkville eatery overlooking an unusual little park has a French à la carte menu, a *table d'hôte,* and a reputation for superb omelettes. The omelette niçoise and grilled salmon with basil butter sauce are highly recommended. Closed Sunday lunch. Reservations advised. Major credit cards accepted. 126 Cumberland Ave. (phone: 961-1893).

Lakes Regulars fight their way through the crowd at the tiny front bar here because they know that the superb dishes created in the open kitchen are well worth the trouble. This friendly place combines the feel of a neighborhood watering hole with that of a chic dinner spot. Try the *bruschetta* (toasted bread topped with tomatoes, garlic, and cheese) or the mouth-watering chilled gazpacho (summer only) for starters; the beef filet in port sauce is a highly recommended entrée. The wine list is good, too. Closed Sundays. Reservations necessary. Major credit cards accepted. 1112 Yonge St. (phone: 966-0185).

Marché This stylish eating complex is a unique link among Toronto's locations of the popular Swiss *Mövenpick* restaurant chain. It is modeled after a French village square, complete with a marketplace. Diners move from one cooking station to another armed with a blank card, running up a tab to be paid on leaving; the food may be eaten here or taken out. The cooking is done before you—pasta, seafood, pizza, steaks, and quail—and there also are salad, oyster, and wine bars. The breads and desserts are made on the premises. Everything is fresh, from the salmon down to the bacon bits. The staff is cheery, and you can read the provided newspapers, have a shoeshine, or buy fresh flowers while you dine. Open daily until 2 AM. No reservations. Major credit cards accepted. *BCE Place,* 42 Yonge St. (phone: 366-8986).

Masa The focus here is on authentic Japanese fare. Customers can sit in a standard booth or dine in traditional Japanese style on tatami mats in partitioned lounges. Closed for lunch on weekends. Reservations advised on weekends. Major credit cards accepted. 205 Richmond St. W. (phone: 977-9519).

Metropolis Cheeky murals depict the city in this popular spot, which serves up contemporary interpretations of traditional Canadian fare. Specialties include cornmeal fritters, potato-leek pancakes, Mennonite sausage, East Coast shrimp and mussels steeped in wine made from Niagara grapes, and heavy-duty maple cheesecake. Closed Sundays. Reservations advised. Major credit cards accepted. 838 Yonge St. (phone: 924-4100).

Ouzeri This funky, noisy Greek dining spot, the throbbing heart of Danforth Avenue, has been a hit since the day it opened. The superb fare includes a flaky, tender rabbit-and-onion phyllo pie, and grilled lamb with garlic, lemon, and oregano. The extensive beer list complements the food, and retsina and ouzo are always on hand. The decor is reminiscent of a sunny Greek island; at weekday lunches, the Greek equivalent of dim sum is offered. In summer, the dining area extends onto the sidewalk, and the street scene swells until 4 AM with festive customers. Open daily. Reservations advised, though you may still have to wait for a table. Major credit cards accepted. 500A Danforth Ave. (phone: 778-0500).

Pink Pearl Specializing in Cantonese and Szechuan food, this eatery features distinguished surroundings and service; dining here is a leisurely affair. Highlights of the extensive menu include Rainbow Chopped in Crystal Fold (chopped meat and vegetables sautéed together and served with crispy noodles); Peking Supreme Beef Filet (sliced beef tenderloin sautéed with oyster sauce and served sizzling hot); and braised lobster in black bean-and-garlic sauce. Open daily. Reservations advised for dinner. Major credit cards accepted. Two locations: 120 Avenue Rd. (phone: 966-3631) and at the *Queen's Quay Terminal* (phone: 366-9162).

Rodney's Oyster House Ensconced in the basement of an old office building, this tiny establishment will satisfy even the most demanding seafood connoisseur. Oysters, mussels, and clams arrive fresh daily; order clam or oyster chowder. The beer list is robust. Though the place gets crowded at night and at lunch during the week, it is relaxing on Saturday afternoons. Closed Sundays. Reservations advised. Major credit cards accepted. 209 Adelaide St. E. (phone: 363-8105).

Round Window One of Toronto's veteran fish and seafood restaurants, this no-frills establishment was a pioneer in the Danforth area. Its reputation has withstood the test of time, as the filet of sole and salmon steaks attest. The atmosphere is homey, with brisk, friendly service in the two small, cozy rooms. The clientele ranges from lingering couples to families to executives. Closed Mondays. Reservations advised. Major credit cards accepted. 729 Danforth Ave. (phone: 465-3892).

Select Bistro This spot on trendy Queen Street West has a genuine zinc bar, taped jazz and classical music, a first-rate wine list, and baskets of homemade bread suspended on pulleys above diners' heads. The food is a bit inconsistent (the fresh green and Caesar salads and garlic cheese bread are safe bets), but the lively atmosphere is the main reason for its continuing popularity. Be prepared to wait in line. Open daily. Reservations advised for groups of five or more. Major credit cards accepted. 328 Queen St. W. (phone: 596-6405).

Senator Located behind the *Pantages Theatre* and *Eaton Centre,* the establishment comprises a renovated 1940s-era diner, an upscale restaurant, and *Top o' the Senator,* one of the finest jazz clubs in town. The diner is renowned for its great deli sandwiches, baked goods, thick shakes, and fizzy sodas, while the elegant dining room features rib steaks and top-quality grilled veal chops. The after-work crowd heads for the patio in the summer to enjoy the ever-changing jazz program. Open daily. Reservations advised. Major credit cards accepted. 249 Victoria St. (phone: 364-7517).

Southern Accent This small, easygoing restaurant with a friendly bar serves up some of the best Cajun and creole food in the city. Chef Elena Embrioni prepares authentic Louisiana dishes like jambalaya, as well as less familiar—but very popular—creations such as blackened chicken livers and blackened grilled rack of lamb. Try to save room for the excellent bread pudding with bourbon sauce. The wine selection is good, and the service attentive. On Tuesdays and Thursdays you can have your palm or tarot cards read, and there's a stand-up comedy night twice a month (call for details). Open daily; closed for lunch except in summer. Reservations advised. Major credit cards accepted. 595 Markham St. (phone: 536-3211).

Spiaggia Trattoria Located in the Beaches (*spiaggia* is Italian for "beach"), this tiny, usually crowded place is a neighborhood institution. The blackboard menu changes daily, depending on what chef-owner Stephen Young has purchased at the market that morning. His pasta is inventive and delicious; the vegetables are served al dente; and the all-important pesto has the proper tangy taste. Try not to miss the mushroom risotto with grilled lamb sausage. The wine list is limited but exemplary. Closed Mondays. Reservations necessary. Major credit cards accepted. 2318 Queen St. E. (phone: 699-4656).

Sultan's Tent For an intriguing change, try some authentic Moroccan food in the Yorkville shopping district. The decor features rich tapestries, low, round tables, and comfortable divans and brass vases. Specialties include lamb with honey and almonds, chicken with lemon and olives, and couscous with various meat and vegetables. For dessert try the dense combinations of honey, nuts, and layers of phyllo pastry with some strong Moorish coffee or mint tea. At night, Arabic music and belly dancers add to the ambience. Closed Sundays. Reservations advised. Major credit cards accepted. 1280 Bay St. (phone: 961-0601).

Thai Magic This place has a devoted following among area residents, who come for its curry dishes, *satay* and stir-fry specialties, and sumptuous appetizers, such as fish cakes and spring rolls. Closed Saturday lunch and Sundays.

Reservations advised. Major credit cards accepted. 1118 Yonge St. (phone: 968-7366).

INEXPENSIVE

Arax Popular for its fine dining, this spotless eatery in the Beaches serves fresh Armenian and Middle Eastern food, prepared with a light hand. The Special Combo is a platter of six appetizers, and the snapper and salmon are particularly good. Closed Sunday lunch. Reservations advised. Major credit cards accepted. 1966 Queen St. E. (phone: 693-5707).

Boulevard Café A Peruvian accent pervades this place, from the eclectic decor to the food. Appetizers include *tamales verdes* and salad with garlic cream. Most of the main dishes are deliciously tangy, from the spicy marinade of chicken or jumbo shrimp to the sea bass kebabs. If it's on the list of specials, the grilled chicken with yogurt marinade is a must. The Key lime pie will cool you off. Open daily. No reservations, but come early for a patio seat. Major credit cards accepted. 161 Harbord St. (phone: 961-7676).

56 Yonge Located in the *Victoria* hotel, this restaurant is much like its host establishment: good, dependable, and inexpensive. The service is casual; most regulars are on a first-name basis with the staff. The continental fare ranges from an appetizer of steamed mussels in lemon-saffron tea to a generous entrée of calf's liver, accompanied by fresh vegetables purchased at the nearby *St. Lawrence Market.* Also featured is a prix fixe pre-theater dinner. The somewhat limited wine list has many Canadian labels. Closed weekends, and Mondays through Wednesdays for dinner. Reservations unnecessary. Major credit cards accepted. 56 Yonge St. (phone: 363-1666).

Friendly Greek Friendly it is, starting with Sula, who greets guests effusively as they enter her domain. The lamb souvlaki is more than generous; the village salad boasts crisp greens and pure olive oil; and the calamari is some of the best in town. Stick with the Greek wines; for dessert, have a glass of ouzo along with thick black coffee and honey-soaked baklava. Open daily. No reservations. Major credit cards accepted. 551 Danforth Ave. (phone: 469-8422).

Hard Rock Café A member of the popular chain, this is a rock 'n' roll museum, restaurant, and tourist attraction rolled into one. The menu is basic burgers-and-fries fare, but the food's not the main draw: People flock here to see the memorabilia (guitars used by Elvis, Jimi Hendrix, and Stevie Ray Vaughan; some of Elton John's outrageous Captain Fantastic outfits; and one of John Lennon's early *Beatles* suits are displayed here); listen to the loud background music; and soak up the atmosphere. The place overlooks the playing field of the *SkyDome,* and it sells tickets to watch baseball and football games from this vantage point (the price of the seat includes dinner). Open daily. Reservations necessary for groups of 10 or more. Major credit cards accepted. In the *SkyDome Hotel,* 45 Peter St. S. (phone: 341-2388).

Just Desserts Virtually all manner of baked goods, from oversize butter tarts—an adaptation of the English treacle tart made with raisins, butter, brown sugar, eggs, and corn syrup—to hefty pieces of cheesecake, as well as salads and quiche, are on the menu here. The desserts are the cream of the crop of the best bakeries across town. Also sample one of the many coffees, teas, or juices. Open until 3 AM during the week; 24 hours Fridays and Saturdays. No reservations or credit cards accepted. 306 Davenport Rd. (phone: 922-6824).

Real Jerk Reggae music is in the air, the corrugated tin walls are painted in bright colors, and patrons chow down on Jamaican jerk pork and chicken entrées. Service is gracious but slow. Open daily, but only from 1:30 PM on Saturdays and 3 PM on Sundays. Reservations accepted for large groups only. Major credit cards accepted. 709 Queen St. E. (phone: 463-6906).

Shopsy's Sam Shopsowitz first opened this deli generations ago, in the middle of the predominantly Jewish garment district on Spadina Avenue. Although it now occupies a different site—across from the *O'Keefe Centre*—it still remains Toronto's quintessential delicatessen. The outdoor patio and late hours accommodate the après-theater crowd; the corned beef on rye, Montreal smoked meat, homemade hot dogs, creamy potato salad, thick fries, and chicken noodle soup all make for a good nosh. Open daily for all three meals. Reservations necessary at peak dining hours. Major credit cards accepted. 33 Yonge St. (phone: 365-3333).

Vines Across the street from the *St. Lawrence Centre* and the *O'Keefe Centre,* this wine bar is an ideal place to spend an hour or two dissecting the latest play or opera. Bistro-style hot dishes and light fare—cold roast beef, pâtés, and cheese plates—complement a wide variety of international wines. A special vintage is featured daily. Closed Sundays. No reservations. Major credit cards accepted. 38 Wellington St. E. (phone: 869-0744).

Young Lok Szechuan and Hunan regional food featuring lobster and other seafood, dim sum lunches, and a tasty Mongolian grill are served here. The wooden booths are reminiscent of the soda-pop stands of the 1950s. Open daily. Reservations necessary for six or more. Major credit cards accepted. 122 St. Patrick St. (phone: 593-9819).

PEPPERONI TO GO

If you're assailed by an intense craving for pizza at night, relax—you're in a city full of pizza parlors that take orders for delivery to downtown hotels. *Pizza Gigi* (phone: 535-4444) offers a wide choice of toppings from pepperoni and olives to banana peppers and pineapple; it's open to 4 am.

Joel's Gourmet Pizza (phone: 787-7263) has unusual, vegetarian, and standard toppings; it's open to 11 pm (to midnight on weekends). *Panzerotto and Pizza* (phone: 222-2221) is open until 1 am, and *Pizza Pizza* (phone: 967-1111), with more than 200 locations, is open to 2 am. All but *Pizza Gigi* accept major credit cards.

Vancouver

In Vancouver, life is dominated by the elements—the ocean, the mountains, and the weather that the two brew up between them. Pale buildings gleam in the marine air like opals set against varied hues of green—the translucent emerald ocean, the lush greenery of the city's many gardens, and the verdant fir-covered slopes to the east. The skyline is high-rise steel and glass, with snow-capped mountains for a backdrop. Around almost any corner is a glimpse of water, usually streaked by the white wake of an oceangoing freighter or dotted by white triangles of sailboats boasting colorful spinnakers.

Tucked into the southwestern corner of British Columbia, downtown Vancouver sits on a peninsula bounded by English Bay to the west, the Fraser River to the south, and Burrard Inlet to the north. Across Burrard Inlet is residential North Vancouver, flanked by the tall peaks of the Coastal Range—Grouse Mountain, Mt. Seymour, and Hollyburn. These 3,000- to 4,000-foot peaks provide a magnificent backdrop to the city, and, by capturing the storms that sweep in from the ocean and down from the Alaskan panhandle, they create Vancouver's foggy, wet climate, the gardener's delight and the sun worshiper's despair.

Vancouver's geography is also largely responsible for the city's distinctively West Coast atmosphere. Business does get done here, but in a more relaxed manner than in Canada's two largest cities, Toronto and Montreal. (Vancouver, with just over 1.6 million residents in its metropolitan area, is Canada's third-largest city and home to half of British Columbia's population.) Vancouver's sense of remoteness from its eastern sisters is reinforced by the great natural barrier of the Rocky Mountains, 400 miles (640 km) east of the city. The US border, however, is only 30 miles (48 km) south (San Francisco is two hours away by air).

Vancouver's excellent natural harbor fosters the city's healthy flow of commerce. Wheat, timber, lumber, oil, and manufactured goods move through the port in a steady stream, providing a crucial economic link with the rest of the world, especially Japan. Ships transport grain and lumber from Vancouver and return with cars, appliances, and other Japanese-made consumer goods.

The many rivers that flow from the Coastal Range into the ocean along the Vancouver coast make the area prime salmon country. (Salmon—smoked, fresh, or frozen and packed to travel—is offered everywhere.) All the water in and around Vancouver means most residents have to cross one of the city's 20 bridges at least twice a day.

While the pulse of money, youth, and drive around the aggressively new high-rise office buildings is discernible, most locals seem to favor a balance between work and leisure. Below the high-rises, people stroll along the waterfront development at the foot of Granville Street and linger over lunch

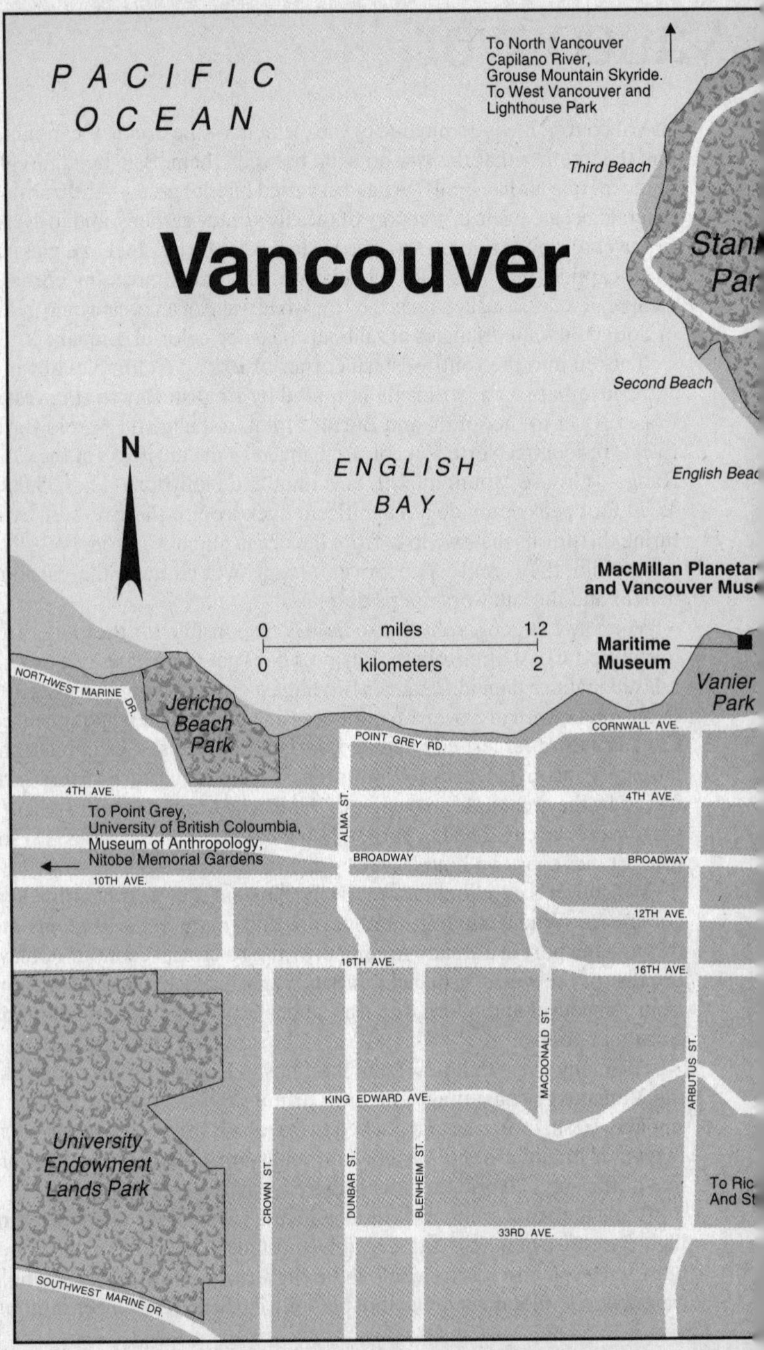

Vancouver

PACIFIC OCEAN

To North Vancouver
Capilano River,
Grouse Mountain Skyride.
To West Vancouver and
Lighthouse Park

Third Beach

Stanl
Par

Second Beach

N

ENGLISH BAY

English Beac

MacMillan Planetar
and Vancouver Muse

0 miles 1.2
0 kilometers 2

Maritime
Museum

Vanier
Park

NORTHWEST MARINE DR.

Jericho
Beach
Park

POINT GREY RD.

CORNWALL AVE.

4TH AVE.

4TH AVE.

ALMA ST.

To Point Grey,
University of British Coloumbia,
Museum of Anthropology,
Nitobe Memorial Gardens

BROADWAY

BROADWAY

10TH AVE.

12TH AVE.

16TH AVE.

16TH AVE.

MACDONALD ST.

ARBUTUS ST.

KING EDWARD AVE.

University
Endowment
Lands Park

CROWN ST.

DUNBAR ST.

BLENHEIM ST.

To Ric
And St

33RD AVE.

SOUTHWEST MARINE DR.

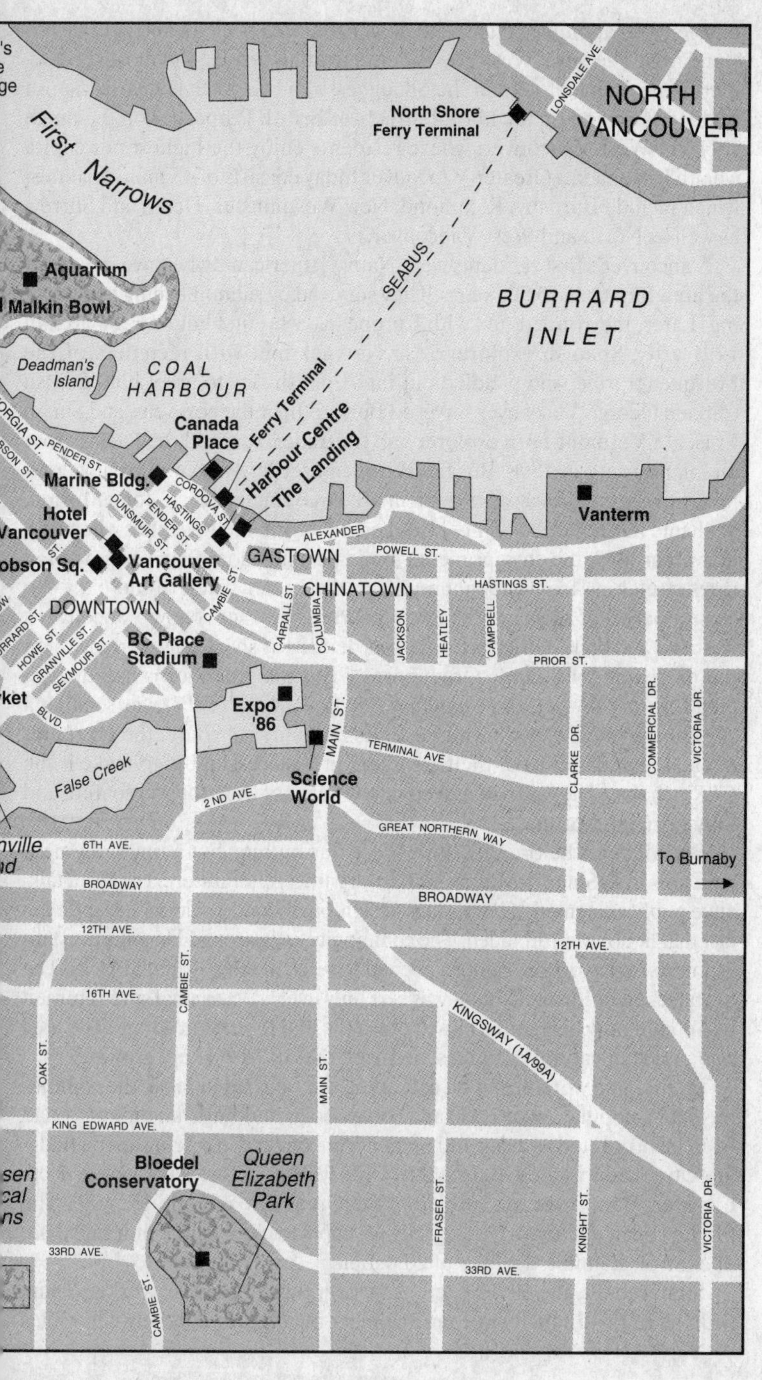

NORTH VANCOUVER
LONSDALE AVE.
North Shore Ferry Terminal
First Narrows
SEABUS
BURRARD INLET
Aquarium
Malkin Bowl
Deadman's Island
COAL HARBOUR
Canada Place
Ferry Terminal
Harbour Centre
The Landing
Marine Bldg.
PENDER ST.
CORDOVA ST.
HASTINGS
DUNSMUIR ST.
Hotel Vancouver
Vancouver Art Gallery
CAMBIE ST.
DOWNTOWN
HOWE ST.
GRANVILLE ST.
SEYMOUR ST.
BC Place Stadium
Vanterm
ALEXANDER
POWELL ST.
GASTOWN
CHINATOWN
HASTINGS ST.
CARRALL ST.
COLUMBIA
JACKSON
HEATLEY
CAMPBELL
PRIOR ST.
Expo '86
MAIN ST.
TERMINAL AVE
Science World
CLARKE DR.
COMMERCIAL DR.
VICTORIA DR.
False Creek
2 ND AVE.
GREAT NORTHERN WAY
6TH AVE.
BROADWAY
To Burnaby
12TH AVE.
16TH AVE.
KINGSWAY (1A/99A)
OAK ST.
KING EDWARD AVE.
Bloedel Conservatory
Queen Elizabeth Park
FRASER ST.
KNIGHT ST.
33RD AVE.

on the grass at *Stanley Park.* The downtown area is clean and safe by US standards. The city's West End is dense with high-rises; the most spectacular homes can be found in the Shaugnessy and Kerrisdale districts south of downtown and on the hillside streets of British Properties on the north shore in West Vancouver, where residents enjoy the highest per capita wealth in Canada. (Greater Vancouver today consists of 18 municipalities, which include Burnaby, Richmond, New Westminster, Delta, and Surrey, as well as North and West Vancouver.)

Vancouver's first residents were Native Americans, who have inhabited the area for at least 3,000 years. They survived by salmon fishing and whaling. Later, they traded furs with Europeans, who first entered the area in 1791 after Spanish explorer José Narváez met with members of the Musqueam tribe who paddled out into English Bay to greet him. British Captain George Vancouver surveyed Burrard Inlet the next year, and Simon Fraser, a Vermont-born explorer and fur trader, reached the Pacific from an inland route in 1808. But the European settlers who are usually credited with the city's early development are three Englishmen—John Morton, William Hailstone, and Samuel Brighouse. Only in their twenties when they arrived in 1862, the entrepreneurs found nothing more than a stand of tall trees stretching from the mountains to the ocean. Their grand plan—to clear a parcel of the vast 150-acre wilderness in what is now Vancouver's west end and build a brick factory—was derided as sheer folly, earning them the nickname "the Three Greenhorns." But the greenhorns had the last laugh. In 1884, when the *Canadian Pacific Railway (CPR)* was seeking a site for the West Coast terminus of its national rail route, the entrepreneurs donated a third of their own land in a successful bid to make it the *CPR*'s choice. The railroad moved in, the value of the property soared, and folly turned to fortune.

But for years before that time, there was nothing but a tiny settlement here known as Stamp's Mill, a shack town with a general store. In 1867 a talkative publican named "Gassy" Jack Deighton opened a saloon—despite the fact that liquor was forbidden. The community grew around Deighton's establishment, and two more saloons opened to serve the thirsty lumberjacks. The town lacked refinement, but it was certainly lively. Occasional sprees turned into community binges that closed down the mill for days at a time. The area was so rich in natural resources, however, that the town kept growing.

By the time work began on extending the railroad in 1886, the community had a population of 2,500 and 350 wooden buildings, and it finally had been incorporated as a city and named Vancouver. To celebrate, the fledgling city's leaders ordered a brand-new fire wagon. Before the wagon arrived, however, Vancouver was leveled in the Great Fire of June 13, 1886. The fire had been deliberately set by city planners to clear land, but it raged out of control, claiming the lives of 20 people.

Soon rebuilt, the city thrived. A large influx of Chinese workers came with the railroad, and thus began a number of ugly incidents between whites and Chinese. When the Chinese were forcibly deported to Victoria on Vancouver Island, the provincial government stepped in with constables to restore order, even revoking the city's charter for a period of time. As a result of these racial conflicts, Vancouver's Chinese community segregated itself in Chinatown and established something of a parallel community.

The *CPR* finally arrived in 1887, and Vancouver began to flourish. That same year the city's first hotel, the *Hotel Vancouver,* opened its doors, and the Hudson's Bay Company launched the city's first department store. (Now known as *The Bay,* it still is open for business.)

In the 20th century Vancouver has grown by leaps and bounds. The opening of the Panama Canal in 1914 strengthened the city by providing access to Europe for grain shipments from the western prairies. During US Prohibition, rumrunners plied the coast for intrepid entrepreneurs who smuggled spirits southward.

Although the modern city's roots were predominantly British, Vancouver now teems with newcomers from all over the world. Today nearly half the metropolitan area's residents are of non-British descent. Vancouver's East Indian population is one of Canada's largest and most vibrant, but the fastest growth has been in the number of immigrants from Pacific Rim countries, especially Hong Kong. (Canada has a favorable immigration policy for well-to-do Hong Kong Chinese, and Vancouver has been their destination of choice with the approach of their homeland's reversion to the People's Republic of China in 1997.) One of the most tangible benefits brought by this varied population has been to the city's food: The ethnic restaurants are among the best on the continent; the dim sum served in Vancouver's Chinatown rivals the savories served on restaurant row in Kowloon; and exotic goods and groceries abound.

Besides good food, Vancouver now has all the accoutrements of a major city: a symphony orchestra, an opera company, several dance companies, and good shopping. West Vancouver's luxurious *Park Royal Shopping Centre* was the first strip shopping mall in Canada. There is ongoing restoration of original downtown buildings, which now house boutiques, restaurants, art and filmmaking studios in Yaletown; antiques stores and galleries on South Granville Street; Asian crafts stores and vegetable markets in Chinatown; and restaurants, boutiques, and specialty stores in historic Gastown, where Vancouver began. But when visitors have had their fill of shopping, they should head for the place where Vancouverites spend most of their free time—the great outdoors.

Vancouver At-a-Glance

SEEING THE CITY

Grouse Mountain, rising 4,100 feet above sea level in North Vancouver, commands a spectacular view of the city and the surrounding coastal area.

Take the *Grouse Mountain Skyride* (at the top of Capilano Rd. on Nancy Greene Way in North Vancouver; phone: 984-0661), an aerial tramway that runs from the parking lot to the 3,700-foot level, and enjoy panoramic views along the way. The *Skyride* runs daily, weather permitting; there is an admission charge.

More than 550 feet above the harbor, *The Lookout!* at *Harbour Centre* (see *Special Places*) is a viewing deck and orientation center where visitors can watch cruise ships, freighters, sailboats, and seaplanes go by. Staff members will point out special sights. After enjoying the breathtaking city scene, stop at the video theater for a changing program of films on the region, then have a snack at the cappuccino bar. The facilities are open daily; there's an admission charge.

Perched atop Little Mountain, the highest natural elevation within the city limits, *Queen Elizabeth Park* (Cambie and 33rd Sts.) affords spectacular views of the city; if you want to look even farther, telescopes bring the mountains into clear sight.

SPECIAL PLACES

Walking is the best way to get a feel for certain sections of Vancouver, including Gastown, Chinatown, the Granville Island complex, *Canada Place,* and *Stanley Park.* The fastest way to get from one neighborhood to another is to use the city's efficient *Skytrain,* which serves some of the areas listed below (see *Getting Around*). It is more convenient to drive to some of the area's attractions that lie in the suburbs and outlying districts.

DOWNTOWN

CHINATOWN North America's second-largest Chinese quarter (only San Francisco's is bigger) encompasses a fair-size piece of downtown. Centered on Pender Street between Gore and Carrall Streets, this area has been the nucleus of the Chinese community for over a century, first as a self-imposed ghetto where the immigrants clung to their culture in the face of animosity from whites, today as a vibrant commercial community. Restaurants offer Cantonese, Mandarin, and Shanghai cooking as well as Chinese-Canadian fare, similar to Chinese-American. The stores range from large import emporiums to holes-in-the-wall, with mah-jongg sets, jade and ivory carvings, dried litchi nuts, and dozens of other intriguing items. The groceries feature smoked duck, bok choy, ginger root, and squid. One experience not to miss here is the *Dr. Sun Yat-Sen Classical Chinese Garden* (578 Carrall St., behind the *Chinese Community Centre;* phone: 662-3207). A sublime mix of pavilions, ponds, plantings, and rocks, the garden—completed for *EXPO '86*—is unique in North America. Only traditional methods and tools were used to construct this peaceful haven, created mainly by traditional artisans from China's Jiangsu province. The garden is open daily; admission charge. Other interesting Chinatown landmarks are the *Kuomintang Building* (529 Gore St.); the *Chinese Cultural Centre* (50 E. Pender St.); and

Wong's Benevolent Society (121-125 E. Pender St.), which is a good example of the balcony style of architecture prevalent in the area.

STANLEY PARK Surrounded by the ocean on three sides, this 1,000-acre park is one of the most beautiful in the world. Located at the foot of West Georgia Street, it's bespeckled with tall evergreens, gardens, lakes, lagoons, 50 miles of trails, tennis courts, a miniature golf course, bowling greens, restaurants (see the *Teahouse* in *Eating Out*), coffee shops, snack bars, a zoo, and the *Vancouver Aquarium* (see below). Residents use the park for hiking, jogging, biking, concerts, picnicking, and simple relaxing. The seawall that flanks the water for 5 miles makes a lovely walk. Open daily. Admission charge for some attractions.

VANCOUVER AQUARIUM With over 9,000 aquatic inhabitants, this is Canada's largest and most famous aquarium. Attractions include the *H. R. MacMillan Gallery of Whales,* the *Marine Mammal Center,* and the *Arctic Sea* display. Popular exhibitions are the *Amazon Gallery* and the *British Columbia Hall of Fish,* displaying local sea life. There are public feedings of sharks, sea otters, and harbor seals. The gift shop features local craftwork. Open daily. Admission charge. In *Stanley Park* (phone: 682-1118).

GASTOWN Named for "Gassy" Jack Deighton, first citizen and saloon keeper, this is where Vancouver began as a rowdy mill town. Later it was the city's skid row and, still later, home of its drug culture. Today it is a living example of successful urban renewal: Extensive renovation has transformed many of the warehouses into upscale condos, antiques stores, boutiques, galleries, and restaurants with lovely brick façades and gaslight fixtures. *The Landing* (at the Cordova St. entrance to Gastown) is an upscale shopping center. Loosely bounded by Water, Columbia, Cordova, and Richards Sts.

GASTOWN STEAM CLOCK The world's first steam-powered timepiece is fueled by the vapor rising beneath the city streets. It whistles and puffs on the quarter hour and serenades with Westminster chimes each hour. The landmark is a favorite with TV and film production crews. Its creator, Ray Saunders, will fill you in on the details from his eponymous clock shop around the corner (123 Cambie St.; phone: 669-3525). Cambie and Water Sts.

GRANVILLE ISLAND MARKET Under the south end of the Granville Bridge, this large indoor market has become the prime gathering spot for those in search of the freshest seafood and produce. You can get salmon vacuum-packed to go. A number of the stalls sell food that visitors can eat outdoors while watching the two independent ferry services, *Granville Island Ferries* and the *Aquabus,* that run daily between Vancouver's West End and Granville Island. The complex is also home to three theaters, arts and crafts galleries, assorted shops, and a number of restaurants.

ROBSON STREET By day it has been compared to Beverly Hills' Rodeo Drive, with its chic and pricey designer boutiques like *Ferragamo.* But on balmy evenings it's like a European village square, with strollers stopping for ice cream at *Cows Vancouver* (see *Shopping*) or coffee at ubiquitous coffee bars like *Starbucks,* browsing at the *Book Warehouse* (see *Shopping*), or just window shopping en route to any of the various restaurants. The atmosphere is convivial; the people watching, superb.

ROBSON SQUARE This innovative complex designed by Arthur Erickson (who also designed the *Canadian Embassy* in Washington, DC, and much of *Simon Fraser University;* see below) houses the provincial government offices, the courthouse, and shopping facilities in a multilevel galleria. Among the attractions are a theater and a small skating rink that's open from early November to late February. Robson and Hornby Sts.

CANADA PLACE Built for *EXPO '86,* this building is known for its ship-like appearance, with a roof designed to resemble five billowing sails. It houses the *Trade and Convention Centre,* the *Pan Pacific* hotel (see *Checking In*), and the *CN IMAX (Canadian National Image Maximum) Theatre.* Designed and developed in Canada, the IMAX process increases the size of the screen image tenfold, making you feel as if you're in the picture. Open daily. Admission charge. 999 Canada Pl., at the north end of Howe St. (phone: 682-4629).

VANCOUVER ART GALLERY Francis Rattenbury, the designer of the regal *Empress* hotel and the *Parliament Buildings* in Victoria on Vancouver Island, built the *Old Court House* at Georgia and Hornby Streets in 1906; since 1980 it has been home to the city's major art gallery. At the front of the sandstone-and-granite structure, the *BC Centennial Fountain* celebrates the mainland's union with Vancouver Island in 1866. Of the four exhibition halls, one is devoted to the works of Victoria artist Emily Carr, whose early 1900s paintings of forests and totems are renowned. Open daily May through September; closed Mondays and Tuesdays the rest of the year. No admission charge Thursday evenings. 750 Hornby St. (phone: 682-4668).

SCIENCE WORLD With hands-on, interactive exhibits highlighting everything from bugs to beaver lodges and lightning bolts to laser beams, this museum is for children of all ages. Housed in a 17-story geodesic dome, another legacy of *EXPO '86,* it contains the *Omnimax Theatre,* which features "sense-surround" films projected on the world's largest domed screen. Open daily. Admission charge. 1455 Quebec St. (phone: 268-6363).

CHRIST CHURCH CATHEDRAL Construction of the oldest surviving church in Vancouver began in 1889; since 1929 it has served as the cathedral of the Anglican diocese of New Westminster. A granite basement was the first segment completed, earning the church the moniker *Root House.* With its stained glass windows and Douglas fir beams and roof, the church proper took six years to complete. After heated public controversy halted a 1974 attempt to replace the cathedral with a modern tower, it was designated a historic landmark. 690 Burrard St. at Georgia St. (phone: 682-3848).

CATHEDRAL OF OUR LADY OF THE HOLY ROSARY In 1900, when this Gothic Revival Roman Catholic parish church was completed, its spire dominated the city skyline. Despite the coming of loftier buildings, it still is impressive. The church was the first in the city (1916) to be designated a cathedral, 13 years before the Anglican *Christ Church Cathedral* achieved that status. Dunsmuir and Richards Sts. (phone: 682-6774).

BC PLACE STADIUM From rock concerts to BC *Lions* football games to trade shows and tractor pulls, this stadium, beneath its pillowy, air-supported dome (the world's largest), is the permanent site of the *BC Sports Hall of Fame* (entrance at Gate A; phone: 687-5520). On the main floor, it celebrates over a century of sporting achievement by the province's athletes, with medals and memorabilia from local competitions to the *Olympic Games.* The *Hall of Fame* also features a high-tech "participation gallery," where visitors can sprint, row, climb a wall, or throw a ball using special, computerized equipment. In front of the stadium stands a monument to local hero Terry Fox, the gallant one-legged runner who was struck down by cancer. The permanent exhibit on Fox's life is one of the museum's most popular. The *Hall of Fame* is closed Mondays. Admission charge. The rest of the stadium is open to the public only during scheduled events. 777 Pacific Blvd. S. (phone: 669-2300).

ENGLISH BAY BEACH With the exception of Sydney, Australia, no major city has so many fine beaches (11). Since the turn of the century, English Bay Beach has attracted swimmers, sun worshipers, and, in more recent years, windsurfers. The summer venue for the *Vancouver Sea Festival,* it was here, too, that the annual *Polar Bear Swim* got its start on *New Year's Day* 1919. Today hardy souls, often numbering in the hundreds, begin the year with a plunge into the frigid waters. Those on foot downtown can get here by heading west on Robson St. to Denman St. Turn left on Denman and continue to Beach Ave.

HARBOUR CENTRE For years this was *Eaton's* department store, one of the city's largest. The current structure, in part a reconstruction of that emporium, now also includes 21 floors of offices, a shopping mall, and the downtown branch of *Simon Fraser University.* Two outdoor glass elevators offer a view of the city as they whiz visitors to *The Lookout!*, an observation deck topped by a revolving restaurant. The flying saucer–shape top is one of the most recognized features of downtown Vancouver. 555 W. Hastings St. (phone: 689-0421).

MARINE BUILDING Perhaps the city's most beloved building, this Art Deco "wedding cake" structure with its precise stone carvings and small but lavishly ornate lobby was erected in 1929, just in time to be hit hard by the Depression. Vancouver's first skyscraper survived bad times and threats of the wrecking ball; today, thanks to its city-sanctioned landmark status, it is untouchable. It now houses the *Imperial* (see *Eating Out*), one of the city's best Chinese restaurants, and two other small eateries, as well as the eclectic gift shop *Tangram Designs* (phone: 669-6789). Stand across the street for a good look at the terra cotta trim. 355 Burrard St., corner of Hastings St.

PORTAL PARK Downtown Vancouver's breathing space of choice features a relief map beneath a glass dome that illustrates the city's geographical relationship to its Pacific Rim neighbors. The tiny park has four freestanding arches with stained glass inserts on stone pillars, as well as curved stone benches that overlook the harbor. W. Hastings St. at the foot of Thurlow St.

ST. JAMES ANGLICAN CHURCH This Gothic-style structure, with its vaguely Byzantine interior, was designed in the late 1930s by Adrian Gilbert Scott; he had recently built a church in Cairo, and the edifice reflects his interest in things Egyptian. Constructed of reinforced concrete, it replaced a church built in 1881 and destroyed in a fire five years later. A two-foot space between the inner and outer walls adds depth to the windows and arches. Cordova and Gore Sts. (phone: 685-7503).

BEYOND DOWNTOWN AND ENVIRONS

VAN DUSEN BOTANICAL GARDENS Gardening is such a passion in Vancouver that it has been called the city's religion. If that's the case, *Van Dusen* must be its cathedral. These 55 acres of formal gardens and lakes are given over to displays of native and exotic plants. The fountain at the entrance, a gift from the *Swedish Society,* depicts the contribution of Swedish Canadians to the economic and cultural life of British Columbia. Open daily. Admission charge. 37th Ave. and Oak St. (phone: 878-9274).

SIMON FRASER UNIVERSITY Sitting atop Burnaby Mountain, the campus commands beautiful views of the city and the surrounding coastal areas. Most of its striking modern buildings were designed by Vancouver architect Arthur Erickson (who also designed *Robson Square*—see above—and the *Museum of Anthropology*—see below). Hourly tours of the campus are conducted daily in July and August; weekends the rest of the year. Open daily. No admission charge. Burnaby (phone: 291-3111).

BLOEDEL CONSERVATORY Some 350 exotic plants and flowers thrive in this three-sectioned dome, which houses a desert, a rain forest, and a tropical environment. There are also 50 varieties of birds from throughout the world. In *Queen Elizabeth Park,* a spectacularly lush park that was once a rock quarry. Open daily. Admission charge. Cambie and 33rd Sts. (phone: 872-5513).

NITOBE MEMORIAL GARDENS This traditional Japanese garden on the *University of BC* campus is a serene, tranquil setting for contemplation. Though the gardens are small, they encourage lingering. There's a tea house for ceremonial occasions. Open daily from April to early October; closed weekends the rest of the year. NW Marine Dr. (phone: 822-6038).

LIGHTHOUSE PARK Eight miles of trails lead through a pristine forest, one of the most beautiful in the region. A half-mile hiking trail leads to the park's namesake, the 60-foot *Point Atkinson Lighthouse,* and ends at a rocky bluff overlooking the Strait of Georgia. Five miles (8 km) west of Lions Gate Bridge on Marine Dr., West Vancouver.

GROUSE MOUNTAIN In addition to the *Skyride* and stunning views of the city from the summit (see *Seeing the City,* above), this 4,100-foot mountain—only 20 minutes from downtown—also offers good skiing (see *Sports,* below), and in summertime, its many paths are great for hiking. Another attraction here is the *Theatre in the Sky,* which shows a multi-image presentation about the history of Vancouver on three large screens and several television monitors. The *Grouse Nest* dining room has excellent views. Open daily. Admission charge for the *Skyride* and theater. At the top of Capilano Rd. in North Vancouver (phone: 984-0661).

CAPILANO SUSPENSION BRIDGE The world's longest—and highest—suspension footbridge hangs 230 feet above the Capilano River and stretches 450 feet across the canyon. The original bridge was erected in 1889; the bridge that stands now was built in 1956. Those who walk across the span will feel it move under their feet. Also here are the *Rock of Ages* center, which explores the region's geology; a *Story Centre,* with historical exhibits; walking trails through coastal rain forest; the *Trading Post* gift shop, with a cantilevered deck jutting over the canyon; Native American craftspeople carving totem poles; and a totem-pole park. Open in July and August until 10:30 PM; until dark the rest of the year. Admission charge. 3735 Capilano Rd., North Vancouver (phone: 985-7474).

CYPRESS PROVINCIAL PARK This mountain park overlooking the city has meadows, lakes, and forests spanning 7,037 acres of the North Shore mountains. Hiking, snowshoeing, and cross-country and downhill skiing are favorite activities here. North of downtown (phone: 929-1291).

BURNABY VILLAGE MUSEUM Life in the Vancouver area from 1890 to 1925—complete with a village smithy, a bandstand, a chapel, a school, log cabins, and a restored carousel—is re-created at this living museum with costumed interpreters. Some of the structures were moved from other locations; others, like the chapel, were erected for the museum (although its pews date from 1905). There's also a bakery, a general store, a drugstore with its identifying red-and-green globes in the window, a theater showing silent movies, and a Chinese herbalist. An ice-cream parlor and an occasional vaudeville show at the bandstand add to the charm. At *Christmas,* the scene is festively lighted. Open daily April through September, *Thanksgiving* weekend (the second weekend in October), and part of December; closed the rest of the year. Admission charge. 6501 Deer Lake Ave., Burnaby (phone: 293-6501).

MUSEUM OF ANTHROPOLOGY An award-winning glass-and-concrete structure on a cliff, the *University of British Columbia*'s seaside museum houses a major collection of Native American art and artifacts, focusing on the northwest and coastal tribes. There are also displays on other indigenous peoples of the Americas, the Pacific Islands, Asia, and Africa. Architect Arthur Erickson's most arresting innovation is the 45-foot-high glass enclosure in the *Great Hall,* which contains a magnificent collection of Haida and Kwakiutl totem poles. The cedar entry doors were carved by 'Ksan craftsmen (Native Americans from the Hazelton area). A major repository of cultural riches lost to European settlement, the museum gives visitors access to additional information about each item via a computerized catalogue. Closed Mondays; open Tuesdays to 9 PM. Admission charge. 6393 NW Marine Dr. (phone: 822-3825).

H. R. MACMILLAN PLANETARIUM Part of the *Pacific Space Centre,* this planetarium offers astronomy and laser shows on a 60-foot dome with high-tech projection and sound equipment. There also are family matinees and laser light shows set to music. Programs change frequently; make reservations in advance. Closed Mondays, except holidays. Admission charge. 1100 Chestnut St., *Vanier Park* (phone: 738-7827).

GORDON SOUTHAM OBSERVATORY The other major component of the *Pacific Space Centre,* this was the first public observatory in western Canada. It houses a number of telescopes, some of which are from time to time removed for public use outside the facility. Visitors are invited to "Shoot the Moon" when the moon is full; for a small fee per camera, shutterbugs can attach their 35mm SLRs to the telescopes and indulge in lunar photography. In the same complex as the *Pacific Space Centre,* the observatory is usually closed weekends and holidays, depending on the weather and availability of volunteers; call ahead to check. No admission charge. 1100 Chestnut St., *Vanier Park* (phone: 738-7827 or 738-2855).

VANCOUVER MUSEUM Canada's largest civic museum and one of Vancouver's oldest cultural organizations features a charming permanent display of reconstructed rooms and settings from the first days of the settlement through the Edwardian era. There's ample free parking on site. Open daily May through September; closed Mondays the rest of the year. No admission charge the first Thursday of each month from 5 to 9 PM. In the *Pacific Space Centre* complex, 1100 Chestnut St., *Vanier Park* (phone: 736-4431).

MARITIME MUSEUM Not far from the three attractions above, this is the place for those with a fascination for the sea. It's home to numerous artifacts that tell the story of the Port of Vancouver, such as pieces from the SS *Beaver,* which went aground off Prospect Point in 1888. Here, too, is the *St. Roch,* the RCMP Arctic patrol vessel that in the 1940s was the first ship to cross the North American continent in both directions by way of the treacherous Northwest Passage. Down at the museum's *Heritage Harbour* is a revolving display of local and international historic vessels. Open daily. Admission charge. 1905 Ogden Ave., *Vanier Park,* one block from the *Pacific Space Centre* (phone: 257-8300).

LYNN CANYON ECOLOGY CENTRE A not-to-be-missed experience for nature lovers, this popular place has areas devoted to plant, human, and animal life; kids love the well-equipped play area. Few nature centers are so aptly located: Forested *Lynn Canyon Park* has extensive hiking trails, a picnic site, and a swaying suspension bridge that spans the roaring white water of Lynn Canyon Creek; there's also a concession stand. Open daily February through November; closed weekends December and January. In summer, guided walks through the park are available. From downtown take Hastings St. east to Cassiar St., cross the Second Narrows Bridge, then take the fifth exit, Lynn Valley Rd. Turn right onto Peters Rd. and then right again into the park. Pedestrians should take the *SeaBus* to North Vancouver, then *BC Transit* (see *Bus,* below, for information). In *Lynn Canyon Park,* North Vancouver, at 3633 Park Rd. (phone: 987-5922).

OUTSIDE THE CITY

REIFEL BIRD SANCTUARY Home and nesting ground of about 245 species of swans, geese, and ducks, this wild bird sanctuary has footpaths and observation towers. The 850-acre site is open daily. Admission charge. Take Rte. 99 south to the Ladner exit, then River Rd. west; cross the Westham Island Bridge and continue to the end of the road (phone: 946-6980).

GREATER VANCOUVER ZOOLOGICAL CENTRE Lions and tigers and bears, as well as monkeys, zebras, and giraffes, are among the 126 species from all over the world that inhabit these 120 acres of farmland. Visitors can amble around the grounds or take the farm train. There also are picnic facilities and a gift shop and restaurant. Open daily. Admission charge. 5048 264th St., Aldergrove, 45 miles (60 km) southeast of the city; take Hwy. 1, then exit south at Rte. 13/264th St. (phone: 856-6825).

FORT LANGLEY NATIONAL HISTORIC SITE Built in 1827 as a Hudson's Bay Company fort, this park includes the original company store and restored gates, palisades, living quarters, and shops. The fort is historically interesting because it predates Vancouver by a number of years. In fact, it was the site of the founding of British Columbia. Each November 19, Langley sponsors a banquet and historical program in tribute to the day in 1858 when Governor James Douglas signed the decree making BC a British colony. A visit here recalls the fort's boom period in 1859, when gold seekers spent as much as $1,500 daily outfitting themselves. The camp was dominated by the Hudson's Bay Company, which even organized dances for the prospectors. Open daily. Admission charge (except in winter). In Fort Langley, 30 miles (48 km) southeast of the city via Hwy. 1; exit at 232nd St. (phone: 888-4424).

ROYAL HUDSON STEAM TRAIN, ENGINE 2860 A must for train buffs, this is a journey into the past aboard a genuine steam engine. Day trips leave from North Vancouver, follow Howe Sound, with its magnificent ocean and mountain views, and proceed up the coast to the logging community of Squamish. The train features a bar car and several refurbished passenger cars. The round trip takes a good six hours, including a lunch stop in Squamish (see below for a diverting attraction while you're there). Another—perhaps better—way to make the excursion is to take a combination boat-train day trip that transports travelers one way on the train and then returns them via the MV *Britannia,* Canada's largest sightseeing vessel. Trips are made Wednesdays through Sundays from early June to mid-September. Reservations necessary. Tickets and details from *Harbour Ferries,* at the north end of Denman St. (phone: 688-7246).

WEST COAST RAILWAY HERITAGE PARK Located across the road from the *Royal Hudson Steam Train*'s Squamish station, this 12-acre site is itself worth the trip for railroad buffs. The park displays Western Canada's largest collection of historic railway rolling stock, including a restored 1890 business car (a special car outfitted as an office for district superintendents touring their territory), conventional rail cars, vintage cabooses, and locomotives. There's also a 1914 Pacific Great Eastern repair shop, which was transported here from the Squamish station. Added attractions include picnic facilities, nature trails, and magnificent mountain scenery. Open daily; closed November through April. Admission charge. Just north of Squamish, a mile (2 km) west of Rte. 99, at 39645 Government Rd. (phone: 524-1011; 800-722-1233).

EXTRA SPECIAL

Just a 90-minute ferry ride through the spectacular Gulf Islands is Vancouver Island, 24 miles across the Strait of Georgia from the mainland. Some 285 miles (456 km) in length, Canada's largest Pacific island is quite spectacular. Actually the top of a partially submerged mountain system, much of the island is heavily forested and mountainous. From the ferry terminal at Swartz Bay, it's a 45-minute drive to Victoria, the provincial capital and the most English community on the continent. For detailed information about Vancouver Island and its capital, see *British Columbia* in DIRECTIONS.

Sources and Resources

TOURIST INFORMATION

For general information, brochures, and maps, contact the *Vancouver Travel InfoCentre* located next to the *Waterfront Centre* hotel (*Waterfront Centre,* Plaza Level, 200 Burrard St.; phone: 683-2000). It's open daily mid-May through *Labour Day;* closed Sundays the rest of the year. City street maps are available at most newsstands and department stores.

LOCAL COVERAGE The *Province* is a morning daily and the only Sunday paper; the *Sun* comes out mornings daily except Sundays. *Vancouver* and *Western Living* are monthly magazines that focus on West Coast lifestyles. The free monthly *Where Vancouver* includes maps and information on shopping and entertainment and is distributed widely. Another free publication, the weekly *Georgia Straight,* covers entertainment and dining and often includes discount coupons; it can be found in many restaurants and shops. The *BC Transit* bus system publishes a booklet, *Discover Vancouver on Transit,* that shows routes to attractions in the area (see *Bus,* below).

TELEPHONE The area code for Vancouver is 604.

SALES TAX British Columbia has a provincial sales tax of 6% in addition to a 7% federal Goods and Services Tax (GST). In many cases, visitors can receive refunds of both the provincial and federal taxes. Some stores that deal with tourists generally carry British Columbia and federal tax rebate forms. For more information on obtaining rebates on the federal tax, see GETTING READY TO GO.

CLIMATE Rain is a fact of life in Vancouver, so an umbrella and a raincoat are de rigueur year-round. Some snow usually falls during the winter months, although it rarely stays on the ground very long. Winter mornings can be nippy; the average winter temperature is around 39F (4C). Summers are warm and pleasant, with temperatures averaging in the 60s and 70s F (15–23C).

GETTING AROUND

AIRPORT *Vancouver Airporter* (phone: 244-9888) runs a minibus service to *Vancouver International Airport* (phone: 276-6101), leaving downtown from 5:25 AM to 10 PM and stopping at major downtown hotels.

BUS The *BC Transit* bus system (phone: 521-0400) covers most of Greater Vancouver, with extensive downtown service. The fare depends on the time of day and distance traveled, but at press time it ranged between $1.50CN ($1.10 US at press time) and $3CN ($2.20 US). A single fare entitles the traveler to use any combination of conveyances to reach the desired destination (bus, *Skytrain,* and *SeaBus*—see below for latter two). During off-peak hours (weekdays from 9:30 AM to 3 PM and after 6 PM, and all day on weekends) you can travel throughout the system's three zones for the basic one-zone fare. Service is greatly reduced after midnight. The booklet *Discover Vancouver on Transit,* available at transit system information outlets for a small fee, gives easy-to-follow routes to attractions throughout the Greater Vancouver area.

CAR RENTAL All major international firms are represented; most have offices both at the airport and downtown.

FERRY *SeaBus* is a ferry system that links the North Shore with downtown Vancouver. The *Burrard Otter* and the *Burrard Beaver* shuttle passengers between the North Shore's *Lonsdale Quay Market* and *Skytrain*'s *Waterfront* station, at the foot of Granville Street downtown. Ferries depart every 15 minutes from the downtown terminal, which is within the *CP Rail* station, and from the North Vancouver terminal. Each can carry as many as 400 people at a time. The fare at press time was CN$1.50 ($1.10 US), making this an inexpensive way to view the busy harbor. For schedule and fare information call *BC Transit* (see *Bus,* above). For information on service to Vancouver Island, contact *BC Ferries* (phone: 277-0277), which sail to Victoria and Nanaimo, farther north on the island.

SKYTRAIN The *Automated Light Rapid Transit (ALRT)* system makes 10 convenient stops in the city and serves the suburbs of Burnaby, New Westminster, and Surrey. The fare varies depending on the time of day and distance traveled; at press time fares were between CN$1.50 ($1.10 US) and CN$3 ($2.20 US). For information call *BC Transit* (see above).

TAXI Major companies are *Advance* (phone: 876-5555); *Black Top Cabs* (phone: 681-2181); *Maclure's* (phone: 731-9211); and *Yellow Cab* (phone: 681-3311). Cabs cannot be hailed in the streets, but there are taxi stands at the airport, throughout the city, and at most hotels.

TOURS *Gray Line* (phone: 879-3363) operates bus tours from most downtown hotels. From mid-April to mid-October, colorful British double-deckers join the fleet. *Vancouver Trolley Tours* (phone: 451-5581) has old-style trolleys that stop at 16 attractions on a narrated 90-minute circuit. You can get out and look around as frequently as you wish along the route, then pick up the next trolley, until you've made the complete circuit. *West Coast City/Nature Tours* (phone: 451-5581) offers year-round narrated bus tours with an emphasis on parks and gardens.

SPECIAL EVENTS

Outdoor life is an essential part of Vancouver, and year-round outdoor events proliferate, rain notwithstanding. At the *Polar Bear Swim,* held every *New Year's Day* since 1919, hardy souls of all ages dip into the Pacific at English Bay. The *Chinese New Year* is celebrated (on February 18 this year) with a parade, lion dances (the traditional Chinese dance featuring a giant-size, dragon-like puppet manned by several revelers), and firecrackers in Chinatown as well as celebrations in city and suburban malls and parks.

In May, the annual *Children's Festival*—considered one of the best of its kind in North America—features a lively program of puppet shows, mime, dancers, singers, and plays, all performed under colorful tents in *Vanier Park.* During the *Canadian International Dragon Boat Festival* in June, ornately decorated boats propelled by up to four dozen rowers race down False Creek for the honor of representing Canada at the world championships in Hong Kong.

In late June, the annual *Vancouver International Jazz Festival* attracts legendary artists, along with thousands of jazz buffs, to indoor and outdoor venues throughout the city and to a three-day open-air spectacular at the Plaza of Nations, on the *EXPO '86* site.

The city celebrates *Canada Day* (July 1) with picnics, fireworks, and a star-studded musical show at *Canada Place* (see *Special Places*). For three days in mid-July, during the *Vancouver Sea Festival,* the city becomes a feast of salmon barbecues and seafood, accompanied by parades, concerts, and sports events. The concurrent *Symphony of Fire* is an international fireworks competition synchronized to music. Best views are from the water; several boat charters are available. Also held in conjunction with the *Sea Festival* is the *World Champion Bathtub Race,* perhaps Canada's wackiest event. During this madcap race, "sailors" in wild getups pilot modified bathtubs from Nanaimo (Vancouver Island) to Vancouver, a distance of 35 miles. For details on the *Sea Festival* and related events, check with the *Vancouver Travel InfoCentre* (see *Tourist Information,* above). Also taking place in mid-July is the *Vancouver Folk Music Festival,* a long weekend filled with performances by musicians from all over North America.

Held on a weekend in early August, the *Abbotsford International Air Show* (phone: 857-1142) features aerobatics and aircraft displays of everything from Piper Cubs to 747s. It takes place at the *Abbotsford Airport,* 45 miles (72 km) east of Vancouver. Every year in late August, a grand parade through downtown Vancouver kicks off the *Pacific National Exhibition* (phone: 253-2311), with concerts by renowned artists, logging sports exhibitions, livestock and agricultural displays, horse races, food fairs, and a good midway.

Local restaurants and ethnic groups provide samplings of their specialties in August at the annual *Taste of Nations Food Fair* at the Plaza of Nations, on the *EXPO '86* site. The same month, Granville Island is the home of the yearly *International Comedy Festival,* during which the area's three theaters and several outdoor stages—along with off-island venues—showcase the best in humor from around the world. In late summer the roads around *BC Place Stadium* (see *Special Places*) are converted to a 2-km circuit for the *Molson Indy 500,* which attracts the biggest names in non–Formula One racing.

During the *International Film Festival,* held in September, filmmakers from Europe, the Far East, and the US screen their best. There's a special segment featuring Canadian films. Also in September, the Mt. Pleasant area, east of downtown, hosts the annual *Fringe Festival.* Offbeat plays are the norm, although there usually are a few traditional productions as well. Hundreds of productions and dozens of plays are mounted during this marathon day-and-night theaterfest.

In December, the *Christmas Carol Ship,* with a troupe of carolers on board, leads a flotilla all lit up for *Christmas* around Vancouver Harbour evenings during a 10-day period before the 25th. More than a dozen charter companies offer holiday harbor cruises that accompany the flotilla, but book well in advance, as this local favorite is usually sold out early. For information on participating companies, call the *Vancouver Travel InfoCentre* (see *Tourist Information,* above).

MUSEUMS

In addition to those described in *Special Places,* other museums of interest include the following:

CANADIAN CRAFT MUSEUM Set in the soaring *Cathedral Place* complex, this captivating museum displays international, historical, and Canadian contemporary artwork, with an emphasis on crafts. Open daily May through August; closed Tuesdays the rest of the year. Admission charge. 639 Hornby St. (phone: 687-8266).

CANADIAN LACROSSE HALL OF FAME AND MUSEUM The only facility in Canada devoted to the country's national summer sport, artifacts here date back to 1867, the year Canada was founded. Open by prior arrangement only. No admission charge. 65 East 6th St., New Westminster (phone: 521-7656).

CANADIAN MUSEUM OF FLIGHT AND TRANSPORTATION Newly relocated to a hangar at *Langley Airport,* this place displays biplanes, gliders, and other historic aircraft, along with support vehicles. There's also a gift shop selling aviation-related items and a children's play area. Taped guided tours are available. Open daily. Admission charge. 5333 216th St., Langley, southeast of town off Rte. 1A (phone: 535-1115).

IRVING HOUSE HISTORIC CENTRE Built in 1865 for a pioneer riverboat captain, this stately Victorian home contains 14 rooms furnished with antiques that reflect an 1890s lifestyle. Located 12 miles (19 km) southeast of downtown Vancouver, the site is a three-block uphill walk from the *Columbia* station on the *Skytrain.* Closed Mondays (except holidays) May through September 15; open weekend afternoons only the rest of the year. Donations accepted. 302 Royal Ave., New Westminster (phone: 521-7656).

SS SAMSON V This steam-powered paddle wheeler plied the Fraser River from 1937 to 1980. Its history, and that of other ships dating back to early settler days, is told by way of pictures and memorabilia. The craft is moored on the Fraser, one block from the *New Westminster Skytrain* station, alongside the *Westminster Quay Public Market.* Closed weekdays and weekend mornings September through April; closed Mondays (except holidays) the rest of the year. Donations accepted. 810 Front St., New Westminster (phone: 521-7656).

VANCOUVER POLICE CENTENNIAL MUSEUM Located in the old coroner's building and the former morgue, this museum, with its "storage" drawers, well-equipped autopsy room, and minutely detailed crime exhibit about a woman murdered in a rooming house, is no ordinary house of constabulary collectibles. The story of the force's first century is told through displays of police badges, weapons, and a variety of artifacts, including marked cards, counterfeit currency, and opium paraphernalia. Closed weekends. Admission charge. Close to Gastown and Chinatown, at 240 E. Cordova St. (phone: 665-3346).

SHOPPING

The best upscale shopping and browsing are found in the designer boutiques along Robson Street and on South Granville Street, site of expensive antiques stores and fine arts galleries. Both areas have good restaurants and coffee bars. Gastown, with its restored buildings and old town ambience, has a mix of chic designer boutiques as well as stores that sell antiques and arts and crafts. The city has 17 major shopping centers, including three in the downtown area. The largest is the 400-store *Metrotown,* in Burnaby, a 20-minute trip by *Skytrain.* Minutes from the *Main Street Skytrain* station is the *Vancouver Flea Market* (703 Terminal Ave.; phone: 685-0666); with over 350 stalls and huge crowds to match, it is the fair-weather choice of weekend and holiday shoppers. Just look for the red barn.

Most shops are open from 9 or 10 AM to 6 PM Saturdays through Tuesdays; to 9 PM Wednesdays through Fridays. Most malls are open Sunday afternoons, and shops in tourist-frequented areas such as Gastown and Robson St. are open all day Sundays. The following are some of the city's favorite shopping haunts.

Angel's This is a favorite stop for visiting actors and musicians, who buy from the rack or custom-order hand-painted, one-of-a-kind shirts, jackets, and other wearable art, including infantswear. Check out the full line of fabric paints for do-it-yourselfers. 1293 Robson St. (phone: 681-0947).

Atkinson's Exclusive lines of linen, crystal, china, silver, French perfume, evening bags, even upscale teddy bears. 3057 Granville St. (phone: 736-3378).

Bakers Dozen Two and Bakers Dozen The first has artifacts and furniture of western Canada and hand-crafted pond boats from Nova Scotia; the second, across the street, has toy collectibles. *Bakers Dozen Two,* 3520 Main St. (phone: 879-3348); *Bakers Dozen,* 3467 Main St. (phone: 873-9611).

Birk's Canada's most prestigious jeweler for over a century, it likens itself to *Tiffany's,* right down to the blue boxes. At *Birk's Centre,* Granville and Hastings Sts. (phone: 669-3333).

Bollum's Books With over 85,000 titles for sale in its 21,500 square feet of floor space, this two-story addition to downtown is Vancouver's largest bookstore. Browse the selections amid a pleasant atmosphere of piped-in classical music, overstuffed sofas, cherry wood shelves, and marble walls. The store also sells a wide selection of out-of-town newspapers, and there's a café in which to peruse them. Open daily to 10 PM, and to midnight on

Fridays and Saturdays. Corner of Granville and Georgia Sts. (phone: 689-1802).

Book Warehouse Here is a profusion of discounted books, with some great bargains. Several locations, including 1150 Robson St. (phone: 685-5711).

Cheena BC Ltd. For those who want to take home a taste of Vancouver, this specialty shop features BC smoked salmon packed for travel. 667 Howe St. (phone: 684-5374).

Cows Vancouver A unique collection of things bovine—T-shirts, caps, mugs, and more—it began life as an ice-cream shop, and all-natural ice cream and waffle cones also are made and sold here. 1301 Robson St. (phone: 682-2622).

Crafthouse This non-profit place linked to the *Crafts Association of BC* offers the best from BC's artists and craftspeople. 1386 Cartwright St. (phone: 687-7270).

Crystal Ark Behind *Kids Only Market* (see below) is this storehouse of New Age energy, carrying natural crystals and gemstones from around the world, including crystal balls, geodes, and rock clusters. Jewelry is made on the premises. 1496 Cartwright St., Granville Island (phone: 681-8900).

Deeler's Antiques One of the largest importers of antique furniture in town, it offers good browsing. *North Mall* at the *Park Royal Shopping Centre,* West Vancouver (phone: 922-0213).

Derek Simpkins Gallery of Tribal Art Collectors of Northwest Coast art seek out this gallery, which specializes in the works of Robert Davidson, Joe David, and Richard Hunt. 2329 Granville St. (phone: 732-4555).

Duthie Books Every title you can imagine is housed in spacious downtown quarters. Out of print searches are a specialty. Six locations, including the main store at 919 Robson St. (phone: 684-4496).

Edinburgh Tartan Shop This specialty shop offers an array of clan tartans, along with woolens, cashmeres, kilts, and other fine Scotland-related goods. 375 Water St. (phone: 681-8889).

Edward Chapman For over a century, this has been *the* place for men's classic British woolens. 833 W. Pender (phone: 685-6207) and *Westin Bayshore Inn* (see *Checking In;* phone: 685-6734).

Frances Hill This clothing store emphasizes sweaters, parkas, and coats that put fashion into cold-weather wear. 151 Water St. (phone: 685-1828).

Gallery of BC Ceramics Over 60 potters, each with a distinctive style, are represented at this Granville Island gallery. 1359 Cartwright St. (phone: 669-5645).

Garden Antiques The specialty here is antique garden tools, old jardinieres, garden ornaments, and other things botanical, plus additional antiques and collectibles. 3518 Main St. (phone: 876-2311).

Heritage Canada Authentic native arts, including carvings, large totem poles, moccasins, and mukluks, are featured. 356 Water St. (phone: 669-6375).

Hill's Indian Crafts Masks, rattles, bentwood boxes, baskets, beadwork, jewelry, Haida argillite (lava-like stone) sculptures, Cowichan sweaters, and totem poles make this shop as interesting as any museum. 165 Water St. (phone: 685-4249).

Holt Renfrew The Canadian fur company is also a trendsetter in men's and women's fashions. Opposite the entrance to the *Four Seasons Hotel* in *Pacific Centre,* 633 Granville St. (phone: 681-3121).

Images for a Canadian Heritage This charming shop specializes in Inuit sculptures, Northwest Coast woodcarvings, limited-edition prints, and other original art. 164 Water St. (phone: 685-7046).

Inuit Gallery One of Canada's most highly regarded emporiums of Inuit works and Northwest Coast Native American art. 345 Water St. (phone: 688-7323).

Jade World For a fascinating behind-the-scenes look at the making of jade sculpture and jewelry from rough stone, check out the factory and carving studio (on the premises) before entering here. 1696 W. First Ave. (phone: 733-7212).

Kids Only Market Play areas and live entertainment add fun to shopping in a unique, kids-are-welcome setting. Twenty-five shops are clustered in this sprawling, colorful area that caters to the younger set with clothing, toys, and games. 1496 Cartwright St., Granville Island (phone: 689-8447).

Leona Lattimer Gallery Traditionally carved silver jewelry, Inuit soapstone sculptures, cedar bentwood boxes, bowls, blankets adorned with button designs, and masks are displayed in a gallery-like setting in a simulated cedar longhouse. 1590 W. Second Ave. (phone: 732-4556).

Leone's Socialites and celebrities shop here for European fashions by such designers as Gianni Versace and Giorgio Armani as well as stylish accessories. At *Sinclair Centre,* 757 W. Hastings St. (phone: 683-1133).

Mammoth Enterprises Designer Richard Marcus creates unusual and pleasing jewelry and sculptures from mastodon tusks, whose segments are colored with natural mineralization. The firm has US and Canadian export permits. (Pieces also are available at *Birk's* and at some hotel gift shops or, by appointment, from the artist's studio.) 320-80 W. First Ave. (phone: 988-1299).

Murchie's This ultimate among coffee and tea outlets began blending imported coffees in 1894. Today, it dispenses over 90 varieties and carries all the accessories to make and serve its brews. 970 Robson St. (phone: 662-3776).

Pappas Furs Creations of leading designers have made this furrier one of Canada's best known for three generations. Call for limo service. 449 Hamilton St. (phone: 681-6391).

Railway World Here is everything for the train buff, from models to engineers' caps to books. 150 Water St. (phone: 681-4811).

The Source A great mix of antiques and collectibles, including old British pub items. 929 Main St. (phone: 684-9914).

Tony Cavelti This European craftsman creates distinctive jewelry in gold and platinum. 565 W. Georgia St. (phone: 681-3481).

Uno Langmann Antiques & Art A superb selection that includes 18th- and 19th-century furniture and paintings and some Northwest Coast Native American works. 2117 Granville St. (phone: 736-8825).

Vancouver Antique Centre Housed in a historic building, about 15 shops offer an eclectic selection of antiques and other collectibles. 422 Richards St. (phone: 682-3573).

Vancouver Pen Shop With the largest pen selection in the Canadian West, it has supplies for calligraphers of all levels. 512 W. Hastings St. (phone: 681-1612).

Zonda Nellis The designer, whose handwoven garments are found in elite stores in major US cities, lives in Vancouver. Check out her chic line of men's sweaters. 2203 Granville St. (phone: 736-5668).

SPORTS

BASEBALL The *Canadians,* the triple-A farm team of the California *Angels,* fill the stands at *Nat Bailey Stadium* (4601 Ontario St.; phone: 872-5232).

BASKETBALL A new entry in the *NBA,* the *Vancouver Grizzlies* (phone: 688-5867) take on opponents at the *GM Arena,* Griffith's Way, across from *BC Place Stadium.*

BICYCLING The line-divided *Stanley Park* seawall is a favorite among cyclists of all levels. The more energetic continue on past the *EXPO '86* lands and around False Creek. Rent one- to five-speed bikes, mountain bikes, or tandems from *Spokes* (phone: 688-5141) or *Stanley Park Bike Rentals* (phone: 681-5581). Both are at 1798 W. Georgia Street.

FISHING Vancouver offers easy access to both freshwater and deep-sea fishing. Steelhead and Dolly Varden trout are caught in the Capilano River and in any of the bays surrounding the city, but the main catch is salmon. Fishing charter companies include *Westin Bayshore Yacht Charter* at the *Westin Bayshore Inn* (see *Checking In;* phone: 691-6936).

FOOTBALL The BC *Lions,* Vancouver's contenders in the *Canadian Football League,* take on all comers at the city's domed *BC Place Stadium* (see *Special Places*).

GOLF Several private golf courses have exchange privileges with major courses throughout North America. There are over a dozen public links in the Greater Vancouver area, among them two truly outstanding layouts.

TOP TEE-OFF SPOTS

Gleneagles This handsome nine-hole, par 35, 2,600-yard public layout is highly rated among local players. 6190 Marine Dr., West Vancouver (phone: 921-7353).

University Golf Club Situated on the university's *Endowment Lands,* this 18-hole, par 72, 6,584-yard course is one of the best public facilities in all of Canada. 5185 University Blvd. (phone: 224-1818).

The 18-hole *Mayfair Lakes* (5406 No. 7 Rd., Richmond; phone: 276-0505), a par 71 with a 6,641-yard layout, is also highly rated.

HOCKEY The *National Hockey League*'s Vancouver *Canucks* defend the ice at the new *GM Arena* (phone at press time: 681-2280) on Griffith's Way, across from the *BC Place Stadium.*

HORSE RACING Racing at *Hastings Park* at the *Pacific National Exhibition Grounds* (phone: 254-1631) takes place from mid-April to mid-October.

JOGGING *Stanley Park*'s seawall circles the beautiful park. Jogging along the 1-mile-long West Vancouver seawall also is popular.

SAILING Vancouver's several yacht clubs include the venerable *Royal Vancouver Yacht Club* (3811 Point Grey Rd.; phone: 224-1344). Among boat charter outfits is *Island Boat Charters* (Granville Island; phone: 688-6625). Also see *Sailing Canada's Many Waters* in DIVERSIONS.

SKATING From November through late February, a small ice skating rink is set up in the big bubble-covered sunken plaza at *Robson Square.* Office workers twirl and whirl on their lunch hours and after work; the rink is open until 11 PM. No admission charge (no phone).

SKIING The three Coast Range ski areas situated just a half-hour's drive from the city offer urban skiing at its best, especially for those who don't mind their snow hard-packed.

SUPERB SLOPES

Cypress Bowl More recently developed than the other local skiing spots, this area has 23 runs (with vertical drops of up to 1,700 feet) and night skiing on its expert and intermediate runs. Five miles (8 km) from the Upper Levels Hwy. in West Vancouver (phone: 926-5612; 926-6007 for ski conditions).

Grouse Mountain The best-developed of the regional resorts, it has a 1,000-foot vertical drop, four chair lifts, and some satisfyingly steep expert skiing. There also are fine runs for beginners and intermediates. Snowmaking ensures top conditions throughout the mid-December-through-February season, and the hours of operation are from early morning until 11 PM. There's also a restaurant and lounge, and a ski rental shop. At the top of Capilano Rd. in North Vancouver (phone: 984-0661; 986-6262 for ski conditions).

Mt. Seymour In an area known for its sunshine and winter warm spells, this place specializes in family skiing. It features one of the largest ski schools in the Pacific Northwest, the highest base elevation of the three areas, night skiing, and four double chair lifts. About 10 miles (16 km) from the Upper Levels Hwy. in North Vancouver (phone: 986-2261; 879-3999 for ski conditions).

In addition, some of the finest skiing in North America is at Whistler and Blackcomb Mountains, about a one-and-a-half-hour drive from Vancouver. For details on these areas, see *Downhill Skiing* in DIVERSIONS.

SOCCER The Vancouver *86ers,* who hold the North American professional sports record for consecutive victories, are now part of the *American Professional Soccer League.* The season runs from May through September at *Swangard Stadium* (Boundary Rd. at Kingsway, Burnaby; phone: 435-7121).

TENNIS The city maintains a number of municipal courts; the most popular ones are in *Stanley Park* (phone: 257-8489).

THEATER

With a number of professional, semiprofessional, and amateur theater companies, Vancouver is an important source of acting and technical talent for the film and television industries (in North America, Vancouver is third only to Los Angeles and New York in the number of TV shows and movies filmed each year).

CENTER STAGE

Orpheum Theatre Once targeted for demolition, then restored at immense expense in 1975 to its original haute kitsch decor (a theater spokesperson describes the 1927 building as "Spanish Art Deco"), the *Orpheum* is now a National Historic Site and home to the *Vancouver Symphony Orchestra;* it's also the venue for a variety of touring theatrical and musical events. Its soaring dome, ornamental arches, crystal chandeliers, and the *BC Entertainment Hall of Fame*—with tributes to local performers, many of whom have gone on to win international acclaim—can be seen up close on a pre-booked, guided tour. Outside the theater, along *Theatre Row* (Granville St. between Robson and Nelson Sts.), a stars' *Walk of Fame* also pays tribute to local entertainers. 844 Granville St.; entrance on Seymour and Smithe Sts. (phone: 665-3050; 665-3072 to arrange tours).

The *Arts Club* (Granville Island; phone: 687-1644) presents Broadway shows as well as homegrown productions that often go on tour. The evening view from the main stage lounge over False Creek is in itself worth the price of admission. The 2,800-seat *Queen Elizabeth Theatre* (Hamilton and Georgia Sts.; phone: 665-3050) is the stage of choice for touring Broadway shows and Canadian companies; it also features an active program of dance performances, featuring the province's own troupe, *Ballet BC* (phone: 669-5954), as well as regular visits by the *Royal Winnipeg Ballet.* The *Playhouse Theatre Company* (1081 Cambie St.; phone: 873-3311) offers a diverse six-play season, featuring drama, comedy, and satire in classics, new Canadian plays, and Broadway and West End hits. The 1,824-seat, state-of-the-art *Ford Centre for the Performing Arts* (788 Richards St.; phone: 280-2222) was scheduled to open at press time and will feature a roster of mega-musicals, such as its inaugural production, a revival of *Show Boat* created by the same team as the current Broadway hit.

Vancouver also harbors several smaller, but no less entertaining, venues. The *Firehall Arts Centre* (280 E. Cordova St.; phone: 689-0926), once home to the first motorized fire department in North America, now produces three plays a year, as well as hosting several other companies. It is also the venue for a contemporary dance series and the annual *Dancing on the Edge Festival,* held in April. The *Metro Theatre* (1370 SW Marine Dr.; phone: 266-7191), an amateur company that has found its niche in British farce, Agatha Christie–type mysteries, and full-scale musicals, plays to enthusiastic crowds. Sharing the boards at the *Waterfront Theatre* (Granville Island; phone: 685-6217) are the *New Play Centre,* which showcases works by local playwrights, and the *Carousel Theatre,* for the young and young at heart.

In summer, the two most popular theaters are outdoors: *Stanley Park* has the *Theatre under the Stars* (phone: 687-0174), featuring revivals of big Broadway musicals at *Malkin Bowl,* and *Vanier Park* is the venue for *Bard on the Beach* (phone: 875-1533), a Shakespearean program. In September, the Mt. Pleasant area hosts the *Fringe Festival,* a cornucopia of theater (see *Special Events*). Small companies with loyal followings mount productions throughout the season on a variety of stages. For comprehensive listings and reviews, consult newspapers and the weekly *Georgia Straight* (see *Local Coverage*), or call the *Arts Hotline* (phone: 684-2787).

MUSIC

The *Vancouver Opera* (845 Cambie St.; phone: 682-2871) presents five productions from its standard 20-work repertoire (with some occasional surprises) during its October-through-April season at the *Queen Elizabeth*

Theatre (see *Theater,* above). Renowned for his innovative programming, the *Vancouver Symphony Orchestra*'s music director Sergiu Comissiona commands the podium for several weeks a year (guest conductors appear the rest of the season) at the acoustically acclaimed *Orpheum Theatre* (see *Theater*). The symphony orchestra (phone: 684-9100) also takes to the great outdoors each summer with performances in parks, on barges, and, from time to time, atop mountains. Fondly known as the *"Cultch,"* the *Vancouver East Cultural Centre* (1895 Venables St.; phone: 254-9578), a converted church in the East End, is the venue for a wide variety of musical events, from chamber music to jazz. For those who like to start the day with a song, *Music in the Morning* (phone: 736-5650) is a popular series that offers a smorgasbord of concerts by local and international artists in an informal setting. In late June the city welcomes top jazz musicians at the *Vancouver International Jazz Festival;* and in mid-July there's the *Vancouver Folk Music Festival* (see *Special Events* for both).

NIGHTCLUBS AND NIGHTLIFE

Vancouver's eclectic after-hours scene offers something for everyone. Try out the world's first electronic bingo parlor at *Starship on Main* (2655 Main St.; phone: 879-8930), where the action takes place on computer screens. Several alcohol-free casinos have gambling tables, with proceeds from blackjack, roulette, and *sic bo* (an Asian version of craps) going to charities. Downtown, try the *Royal Diamond Casino* (Plaza of Nations, 750 Pacific Blvd. S.; phone: 685-2340) or the *Great Canadian Casino* at the *Renaissance Vancouver* hotel (see *Checking In*). Favorite watering holes include lounges at upscale hotels, such as the *Gérard Bar* at the *Sutton Place Vancouver,* the *Bacchus Lounge* at the *Wedgewood,* and the *Garden Lounge* at the *Four Seasons* (see *Checking In* for all). The *Pelican Bay Bar* in the *Granville Island* hotel (see *Checking In*) is a popular schmoozing grounds for yuppies and baby boomers. Vancouver's two comedy clubs—*Yuk Yuks* (Plaza of Nations, 750 Pacific Blvd. S.; phone: 687-5233) and *Punchlines* (15 Water St.; phone: 684-3015)—are among the best in the country. Reservations are advised at both.

Rock concerts frequently take place at *BC Place Stadium* (see *Special Places*), the *Pacific Coliseum* (*Hastings Park,* Hastings St. and Hwy. 1; phone: 253-2311), and the *Orpheum,* and occasionally at the *Queen Elizabeth Theatre* (see *Theater* for the last two). The *Commodore Ballroom* (870 Granville St.; phone: 681-7838) is now more a concert than dance hall—featuring reggae, jazz, blues, and rock—although occasionally the swing-and-sway set still sashays on its 1930s spring-loaded floor. Current hot spots include the *Starfish Room* (1055 Homer St.; phone: 682-4171), which brings in pop, rock, and country-and-western artists from all over, and the *Roxy* (932 Granville St.; phone: 684-7699), which books live rock 'n' roll seven nights a week. The best touring and local rock acts pack patrons into *Richard's on Richards* (1036 Richards St.; phone: 687-6794). The *Yale* (at the north end of the Granville St. Bridge; phone: 681-9253) has the best R&B in town. Jazz lovers can enjoy local and visiting artists at the *Monterey Lounge* at the *Pacific Palisades* hotel (see *Checking In*); and for Dixieland, swing, and big-band music, there's the *Hot Jazz Society* (2120 Main St.; phone: 873-4131). The *Coastal Jazz and Blues Society* (phone: 682-0706) presents programs at various venues, both indoors and out; call for details. *The Town Pump* (66 Water St.; phone: 683-6695), a cabaret/restaurant, is a casual, sprawling, Gastown club that features some of the city's best live music acts.

Bars close at 2 AM, except on Sundays, when they close at midnight.

Best in Town

CHECKING IN

For a double room per night, expect to pay $130 or more at places listed as expensive; from $75 to $130 at hotels in the moderate range; and from $55 to $75 for those we have rated inexpensive. Many hotels offer weekend and off-season packages at lower rates, often with such bonuses as dining vouchers. All hotels feature air conditioning, private baths, TV sets, and telephones unless otherwise indicated.

For bed and breakfast accommodations, contact the *Best Canadian Bed and Breakfast Network* (1090 W. King Edward Ave., Vancouver, BC V6H 1Z4; phone: 738-7207; fax: 732-4998); *Canada-West Accommodations Bed and Breakfast Reservation Service* (PO Box 86607, North Vancouver, BC V7L 4L2; phone: 929-1424; 800-561-3223; fax: 929-6692); *Old English B & B Registry* (1226 Silverwood Crescent, North Vancouver, BC V7P 1J3; phone: 986-5069; fax: 986-8810); *Westway Accommodation Registry* (PO Box 48950, *Bentall Centre,* Vancouver, BC V7X 1A8; phone: 273-8293; fax: 278-6745); or *Shaughnessy Village* (1125 W. 12th Ave., Vancouver, BC V6H 3Z3; phone: 736-5511; fax: 737-1321). For information on Vancouver area hostels, contact the *Canadian Hostelling Association—BC Region* (1515 Discovery St., Vancouver, BC V6R 4K5; phone: 224-3208; fax: 224-4852). All telephone numbers are in the 604 area code unless otherwise indicated.

EXPENSIVE

Coast Plaza This West End property's primary attractions are its proximity to the beach activity at English Bay and to the delights of *Stanley Park.* Some of the 267 rooms have full kitchens. The property is topped by the 35th-floor *Windows on the Bay* restaurant, and there's a lounge, *Shamper's.* There's a garden patio and a shopping complex on the lower level. A complimentary mini-van takes guests downtown. 1733 Comox St. (phone: 688-7711; 800-663-1144; fax: 688-5934).

Delta Place In the financial district, this lovely hostelry has 197 well-appointed rooms and suites, including Business Zone rooms with fax machines, printers, and computer hookups. Also featured are the *Gates* dining room, the

Clipper lounge, a health club, a pool, squash and racquetball courts, and a full business center. 645 Howe St. (phone: 687-1122; 800-667-2300; fax: 643-7267).

Four Seasons Soaring above *Pacific Centre,* this hotel has two restaurants, including the elegant *Chartwell* (see *Eating Out*). The *Garden Lounge,* with a piano bar, is a favorite meeting spot. The 385 rooms and suites have spectacular city and mountain views. There also are indoor and outdoor pools, an exercise room, and a business center. In the center of the city, at 791 W. Georgia St. (phone: 689-9333; 800-268-6282 in Canada; 800-332-3442 in the US; fax: 684-4555).

Georgian Court Many of the 180 rooms here afford magnificent panoramic views. If you intend to go to a sporting event or trade show at *BC Place* across the street, this is your best bet. One of the city's finest dining rooms, the *William Tell* (see *Eating Out*), is here, along with *Rigney's,* a more casual, sports-oriented bar and grill. Of the 12 floors, six are designated for nonsmokers. 773 Beatty St. (phone: 682-5555; 800-663-1155; fax: 682-8830).

Granville Island Situated near the city's popular covered market, this waterfront hostelry has 54 rooms and suites. Also within are a popular nightspot and the *Pelican Bay* restaurant; outside, seawall pathways lead to the island's restaurants, shops, and theaters. 1253 Johnston St. (phone: 683-7373; fax: 683-3061).

Hyatt Regency This 644-room hotel sits atop the *Royal Centre* shopping mall. The Business Plan floor features office equipment in its rooms. There are two lounges and two restaurants, including *Fish and Co.,* a favorite among seafood lovers. There are also an outdoor heated pool, a sauna, and exercise rooms. 655 Burrard St. (phone: 683-1234; 800-233-1234; fax: 689-3707).

Sutton Place Vancouver This luxury hotel is gracious (the service is superb), appealing, and entirely satisfying. The nearly 400 rooms are beautifully decorated, with sumptuous marble bathrooms; there are 10 nonsmoking floors. Guests can enjoy use of a European spa, plus a pool and sun deck located in *La Grande Residence,* the adjacent residential tower. Dining spots include *Café Fleuri* (see *Eating Out*), with its *Chocoholic Bar* and weekly international buffets; the elegant *Le Club;* and *La Boulangerie,* a deli-style takeout place for sandwiches, desserts, and coffees. The *Gérard Bar,* with its separate entrance, is popular with visiting movie stars and crews. There's also a business center and meeting rooms. 845 Burrard St. (phone: 682-5511; 800-810-6888; fax: 682-5513).

Pan Pacific This hotel's spectacular views of the harbor have been likened to those afforded from Hong Kong's hotels. The building blends artfully with its location; its design includes a wing jutting out over the water. There are 506 luxurious rooms and suites (some classed as ultra-deluxe, with extra amenities). The three restaurants include one offering casual dining and a harbor view, another with Japanese food, and the more formal *Five Sails* (see *Eating Out*), which offers Pacific Rim fare and panoramas of both the water and the North Shore mountains. There is a fitness club, with squash and racquetball courts and a sauna, as well as a business center. 999 Canada Pl. (phone: 662-8111; 800-663-1515 in Canada; 800-937-1515 in the US; fax: 685-8690).

Renaissance Vancouver Overlooking the harbor, this 19-story establishment has 412 rooms and 20 suites. Topped by *Vistas,* a revolving restaurant that serves West Coast–style fare, there is a casino on site, as well as an indoor pool and a weight room. 1133 W. Hastings St. (phone: 689-9211; 800-468-3571; fax: 689-4358).

Hotel Vancouver This property, with a French Renaissance–style green copper roof and gargoyles, has been a landmark since its opening in 1939. Stately and comfortable throughout, it has 538 rooms and suites, all with their original Art Deco elegance intact. The 14th-floor Royal Suite has housed members of the House of Windsor and many other heads of state. The Entrée Gold level offers added amenities such as its own check-in services, a lounge, and a concierge. *Griffins* bistro (see *Eating Out*) is a downtown favorite, and *The Roof* is a romantic restaurant offering dancing to live jazz and swing. The health club features an outdoor deck and a glass-enclosed pool. There is also a full-service business center. 900 W. Georgia St. (phone: 684-3131; 800-441-1414; fax: 662-1907).

Wall Centre Garden Vancouver's newest major hotel is located at the highest point of downtown. In an urban garden bordered by maple and chestnut trees, the 35-story property, with its blue-glass exterior that mirrors superb views, has 243 rooms and 149 luxury suites. Dining facilities include the main dining room, *Azure;* a bistro, *Indigo;* and a lounge, *Cracked Ice.* There is a health club with an indoor pool, and business services are available. 1000 Burrard St. (phone: 893-7100; 800-663-9255; fax: 331-1001).

Waterfront Centre Connected to *Canada Place* on the harbor, it affords spectacular views of the ocean and mountains from most of its 489 rooms and from its outdoor pool and deck. There's a well-equipped fitness center, a business center, a shopping complex with a food court on the lower level, and the *Herons* dining room and lounge (see *Eating Out*), whose Sunday brunch—featuring musicians from the *Vancouver Symphony Orchestra*—is popular. Many rooms are set aside for nonsmokers, and the Entrée Gold level offers its own concierge, lounge, check-in services, and buffet breakfast. 900 Canada Pl. Way (phone: 691-1991; 800-441-1414; fax: 691-1999).

Wedgewood There are 94 attractively decorated rooms in this intimate place with European ambience. A fireplace in the piano lounge makes it especially inviting on rainy nights. The lovely dining room is popular for Sunday brunch. There's also a health spa with a sauna. Across from the *Robson*

Square complex, at 845 Hornby St. (phone: 689-7777; 800-663-0666; fax: 688-3074).

Westin Bayshore Inn It's in the heart of the city, but Coal Harbour is at the doorstep; in fact, yacht owners can moor their vessels at the hotel dock. There are 517 bright, well-decorated rooms and suites (the late Howard Hughes once rented the top floors for a lengthy stay); a selection of elegant shops in the lobby; Beefeater-costumed doormen; a health club with an indoor pool; an outdoor pool; *Trader Vic's* restaurant (see *Eating Out*); and the lobby-level *Garden* restaurant. 1601 W. Georgia St. (phone: 682-3377; 800-228-3000; fax: 687-3102).

MODERATE

Delta Pacific Resort Just 30 minutes from downtown, this airport hostelry's facilities include covered tennis and squash courts, three pools, saunas, a water slide, and a conference center. The 458 rooms are modern, spacious, and comfortable. Executive rooms and full business services are available. There's also a creative center and playground for children. A bus will meet guests at the airport. 10251 St. Edward's Dr., Richmond (phone: 278-9611; 800-268-1133 in Canada; 800-877-1133 in the US; fax: 276-1121).

Georgia With 313 rooms, this hotel evokes plenty of Old World charm. There is a dining room, the *Cavalier;* a winsome British pub, *George V;* and the *Night Court* lounge, which stays open into the wee hours. 801 W. Georgia St. (phone: 682-5566; 800-663-1111; fax: 682-8192).

Holiday Inn Downtown This property offers 242 rooms, plus 36 units (including suites) in a newer tower. The accommodations are quiet, comfortable, and attractive. There's an indoor pool, a restaurant and lounge with live entertainment on weekends, and *Panama Jack's* bar and grill. Also available is a full-service business center. Close to *Robson Square,* at 1110 Howe St. (phone: 684-2151; 800-HOLIDAY; fax: 684-4736).

Landmark Formerly a Sheraton property, this hotel has been refurbished as a new link in the Forum International chain. Along with *Cloud Nine,* the city's first revolving rooftop restaurant, the place has 358 rooms, 12 nonsmoking floors, *Le Café,* a lobby café, and *Café Express,* a self-service coffee and juice bar, and the *Sportscaster* bar and grill. There are also a sauna, a Jacuzzi, and an exercise room, as well as a full-service business center. 1400 Robson St. (phone: 687-0511; 800-830-6144; fax: 687-2801).

O'Doul's This link in the Best Western chain has 130 rooms and suites, a popular restaurant and lounge, an indoor pool, a Jacuzzi, and an exercise room. It's an easy walk to *Stanley Park* and close to shopping. 1300 Robson St. (phone: 684-8461; 800-663-5491; fax: 684-8326).

Pacific Palisades Located on Robson Street, where some of the best shopping in Vancouver is found, this is an all-suites hotel (all 233 units have kitchen facilities) with harbor, mountain, and bay views. Amenities include the *Monterey Lounge and Grill,* a casual spot offering West Coast–style fare and live jazz; a business center; and a fitness center with an indoor pool. 1277 Robson St. (phone: 688-0461; 800-663-1815; fax: 688-4374).

Park Royal This quiet, 30-room hostelry is nestled below the mountains on the banks of the Capilano River, across the Lions Gate Bridge, 20 minutes from downtown; the *Park Royal Shopping Centre* is nearby. The dining room's Sunday brunch and the cozy pub are popular among locals. 540 Clyde Ave. at Sixth St., West Vancouver (phone: 926-5511; fax: 926-6082).

INEXPENSIVE

Barclay In the heart of the West End, within strolling distance of most city center attractions, this European-style property has 75 rooms and 10 suites, plus a restaurant. 1348 Robson St. (phone: 688-8850; fax: 688-2534).

Sylvia A stone's throw from the Pacific Ocean, this eight-story West End hostelry offers great value. The ivy-covered building has 120 rooms, including 16 studio and one-bedroom suites with kitchenettes; its restaurant and bistro are popular among locals. Make reservations at this hotel well in advance, particularly in summer. Across the street from *Stanley Park,* at 1154 Gilford St. (phone: 681-9321).

EATING OUT

Vancouver is in the midst of a restaurant boom, and joining its old "meat-and-potatoes" establishments are first-rate seafood and ethnic dining spots. For a dinner for two, expect to pay $60 or more at restaurants listed in the very expensive category; from $45 to $60 at those in the expensive range; from $30 to $45 at places we have rated moderate; and $30 or less (in some cases much less) at those in the inexpensive category. Prices do not include drinks, wine, or tip. Unless otherwise noted, all restaurants are open for lunch and dinner, and all are in the 604 area code.

VERY EXPENSIVE

Five Sails Located beneath the landmark sails in the *Pan Pacific* hotel, it offers spectacular mountain and harbor views and innovative Pacific Rim cuisine, such as grilled rare *ahi* tuna, and spicy wok-fried tiger prawns. The rack of lamb is cooked to pink perfection. Open daily for dinner only. Reservations advised. Major credit cards accepted. 999 Canada Pl. (phone: 662-8111, ext. 4290; fax: 662-3815).

Teahouse Set in the lush surroundings of *Stanley Park,* this English country home–style establishment is filled with greenery and affords views over English Bay. Hearts of palm salad, smoked salmon, and stuffed mushrooms are on the appetizer menu; entrées include duck, venison, and rack of lamb. There are three sizable dining rooms, plus a small outdoor area for dining in warm weather. Open daily; weekends for brunch. Reservations advised. Major credit cards accepted. Ferguson Point, *Stanley Park* (phone: 669-3281; fax: 687-5662).

EXPENSIVE

Alabaster Located in up-and-coming Yaletown, the specialty of this small, intimate restaurant is northern Italian fare prepared by chef Marcus Weiland. The menu is seasonal and might include grilled monkfish with a scallion cream sauce or salmon with a perky grapefruit and yogurt sauce. Penne with homemade duck sausage and mint pesto can be enjoyed as an appetizer or an entrée. The 50 tables are spaced with plenty of elbow room, so it's an ideal place for quiet conversation. Closed Saturday lunch and Sundays. Reservations advised. Major credit cards accepted. 1168 Hamilton St. (phone: 687-1758; fax: 687-1785).

Amorous Oyster A creative little seafood bistro with an ever-changing blackboard menu, it's known for its excellent service. Closed weekends for lunch. Reservations advised. Major credit cards accepted. A 10-minute cab ride from downtown, at 3236 Oak St. (phone: 732-5916).

Bianco Nero A touch of whimsy separates this classy dining spot from the more formal, predictable places around town. The fare includes traditional pasta and meat dishes, and its extensive wine list is a favorite of theatergoers (the *Vancouver Playhouse* and *Queen Elizabeth Theatre* are nearby). The chocolate mousse served in a clay flowerpot, sprinkled with Oreo cookie crumbs and "planted" with a fresh carnation, is particularly fine. For a more intimate evening, come after curtain time. Closed Saturday lunch and Sundays. Reservations advised. Major credit cards accepted. 475 W. Georgia St. (phone: 682-6376).

Bishop's John Bishop is a true perfectionist, and the output of his kitchen wins wide applause for its superior presentation and taste. Grilled squid salad with jalapeño sauce and smoked cod are among the specialties, as are fine lamb and beef dishes. Although the place is small and located in residential Kitsilano, it also is well known—and well worth the 15-minute taxi ride from downtown. Closed weekends for lunch. Reservations advised. Major credit cards accepted. 2183 W. Fourth Ave. (phone: 738-2025; fax: 738-4622).

Café Fleuri This *Sutton Place* hotel dining room is a good place for celebrity spotting, especially Thursdays through Saturdays, when its decadent *Chocoholic Bar* opens, featuring over 20 dessert selections that range from crêpes to fondue. Favorites on the ever-changing main menu include Dungeness crab cakes served with sauces such as warm curried mayonnaise, and excellent fish preparations. There's a seafood buffet on Fridays and Saturdays, and on weekdays a luncheon theme buffet that changes regularly. The lavish Sunday brunch buffet—accompanied by jazz—is especially popular. Open daily. Reservations advised. Major credit cards accepted. 845 Burrard St., near Robson St. (phone: 682-5511; fax: 682-5513).

Chartwell The formal dining room in the *Four Seasons* hotel offers elegant surroundings, superior service, and cuisine that employs the best in fresh, local ingredients. The rack of lamb with fig and star anise confit, and the steamed Pacific salmon with wild grains and mango-and-lemon-balm chutney are special favorites at dinner. Open daily for breakfast, lunch, and dinner. Reservations advised. Major credit cards accepted. 791 Georgia St. (phone: 689-9333; fax: 689-3466).

Le Crocodile Chef/owner Michel Jacob continues to win the hearts and palates of Vancouverites with his world class French culinary talents. The freshest of seafood, lamb, and fowl are complemented by delectable sauces, graceful presentation, and impressive service, with consistent attention to detail. Closed Saturday lunch and Sundays. Reservations necessary. Major credit cards accepted. 909 Burrard St.; entrance on Smithe St. (phone: 669-4298; fax: 669-4207).

Fish Pond In a former noodle factory at the edge of Gastown, this place serves the best lemon chicken in Vancouver. In the center of the room is a pond where brilliantly colored *koi* are fed at the sound of a gong each evening. Closed weekends for lunch and Sundays in winter. Reservations advised for six or more. Major credit cards accepted. 122 Powell St. (phone/fax: 683-9196).

Le Gavroche Set in a charming West End house, it offers an interesting, changing menu. The game dishes are particularly notable, and the seasonal specialties all are good bets. Desserts are geared to send a weight watcher back to the drawing board. Closed weekends for lunch. Reservations advised. Major credit cards accepted. 1616 Alberni St. (phone: 685-3924; fax: 669-1885).

Griffins The renowned three-tier "convict bread," stuffed with pesto, garlic, olives, and more, could be a meal in itself, but it is just one item of a plentiful buffet in this *Hotel Vancouver* dining room, which has been restored to its original 1930s decor, complete with checkerboard tiles and sunny yellow walls. There's also an à la carte menu (the salmon lasagna wins raves). Saturdays there's an all-you-can-eat pizza special, and at the Tex-Mex–style Sunday brunch, there's a special area for youngsters, where they can don chef's hats and make their own pancakes. Open daily for breakfast, lunch, and dinner. Reservations advised. Major credit cards accepted. 900 W. Georgia St. (phone: 662-1900; fax: 662-1907).

Herons Salmon in all its guises is the specialty of the house, but there is also a varied menu with an emphasis on West Coast cuisine. The bountiful Sunday brunch at this *Waterfront Centre* hotel dining room features music by small combos from the *Vancouver Symphony.* Open daily for breakfast, lunch, and dinner. Reservations advised. Major credit cards accepted. 900 Canada Pl. Way (phone: 691-1991; fax: 691-1999).

Imperial This spacious Chinese restaurant commands a harbor view; the opulent decor features crystal chandeliers and jade carvings. Hong Kong–trained chef Yip Tat Hong prepares creative Cantonese seafood specialties. Dim sum is served at lunch. Open daily. Reservations advised. Visa and American Express accepted. 355 Burrard St. (phone: 688-8191; fax: 688-8466).

Mulvaney's The charming decor—bright and airy, with lots of greenery—is enhanced by the view of the busy False Creek waterfront. Specialties include seafood and Cajun cooking; on Fridays and Saturdays, there's a DJ and dancing. Open daily, including Sunday brunch. Reservations advised. Major credit cards accepted. 9 *Creekhouse,* 1535 Johnston St., Granville Island, next to the *Arts Club Theatre* (phone: 685-6571; fax: 685-4460).

Raincity Grill Pacific Northwest cuisine, an extensive wine list, views of spectacular sunsets over English Bay, and superb service have made this place a winner with locals. The menu and servers advise diners on the perfect marrying of food with wine, such as honey-smoked shark with pinot gris or grilled sweetbreads and pumpkin-seed pesto with chardonnay. Chicken breast with a pecan crust and grilled marlin with sun-dried cranberry relish are especially fine. Open daily. Reservations advised. Major credit cards accepted. 1193 Denman St. (phone: 685-7337; fax: 685-7362).

Star Anise Chef Adam Busby is earning accolades at his intimate dining place, where innovative dishes combine "French respect for food with American playfulness." Try the boned quail stuffed with Dungeness crab. Open daily; weekends for brunch. Reservations advised. Major credit cards accepted. 1485 West 12th Ave. at Granville St. (phone: 737-1485).

Trader Vic's This Polynesian place of tropical delights in the *Westin Bayshore Inn* has long been a favorite, thanks in part to the incomparable views of mountains and harbor. Sample the Bongo Bongo soup (puréed spinach and oysters) to start. Closed weekends for lunch. Reservations advised. Major credit cards accepted. 1601 W. Georgia St. (phone: 682-3377; fax: 687-3102).

Umberto's and Il Giardino di Umberto What began as an Italian eatery in the old yellow *Leslye House,* built in 1896, has grown into two adjacent dining spots. Both the original—*Umberto's*—and the newer *Il Giardino di Umberto* serve traditional northern Italian food, featuring delicious wild fowl and game. Umberto Menghi, the affable and energetic proprietor, divides his evenings between these places and *Settebello* and *Umberto al Porto* (see below). *Il Giardino* is closed Saturday lunch and Sundays. *Umberto's* is open for dinner only; closed Mondays. Reservations necessary. Major credit cards accepted. *Umberto's,* 1380 Hornby St. (phone: 687-6316); *Il Giardino di Umberto,* 1382 Hornby St. (phone: 669-2422; fax for both: 669-9723).

Villa del Lupo Located in a renovated house near trendy Yaletown and not far from the *Queen Elizabeth Theatre* and *BC Place,* this elegant Italian dining room has a mouth-watering menu. Try the fresh Dungeness crab cakes—

the best in town—as an appetizer, and follow them up with one of the typical pasta dishes, unique salads, and rich desserts. Open daily for dinner only. Reservations advised. Major credit cards accepted. 869 Hamilton St. (phone: 688-7436; fax: 688-3058).

William Tell Known as a special-occasion place, this dining spot serves haute cuisine in a luxurious atmosphere. The delicious fare draws heavily on local delicacies. Sunday evenings feature a Swiss farmer's buffet, with an array of roasts and smoked sausages. Open daily. Reservations advised. Major credit cards accepted. 765 Beatty St. (phone: 688-3504; fax: 683-8810).

MODERATE

Bistro! Bistro! In a historic building in the heart of Gastown, this continental bistro is noted for its seafood and pasta and interesting appetizers such as grilled garlic-studded mushrooms with Asiago cheese. Open daily. Reservations advised. Major credit cards accepted. 162 Water St. (phone: 682-2162).

Hard Rock Cafe In a converted bank building, this lively new eatery—Canada's biggest version of the international chain of restaurant/nightspots—seats over 300 people. Famous for its extensive collection of rock 'n' roll memorabilia, the chain's motto is "good food at reasonable prices," with hamburgers a specialty. 686 West Hastings St., near Granville St. (phone: 687-ROCK; fax: 669-0780).

Isadora's A children's menu and a small play area, along with a casual, relaxed atmosphere, make this Granville Island nonsmoking restaurant a big hit with families. Nutrition is high on the agenda; fresh seafood and produce from the nearby market appear in the daily specials. For an unusual treat, try the salmon on bannock (a flat bread). Open daily; weekends for brunch. Reservations advised for six or more. MasterCard and Visa accepted. 1540 Old Bridge St., Granville Island, next to the *Waterfront Theatre* (phone: 681-8816; fax: 681-4538).

The Keg What has become an international restaurant chain began here in Vancouver. Several locations offer hearty fare, with an emphasis on steaks plus a few seafood dishes. There's also a salad bar. It's good family value in a convivial atmosphere. Open daily. Reservations advised. Major credit cards accepted. Locations include the *Keg* on Granville Island (1499 Anderson St.; phone: 685-4735; fax: 685-7006) and the *Keg Downunder* (1122 Alberni St.; phone: 685-4388; fax: 685-4417).

Kettle of Fish Fresh fish and seafood top the menu here, although steaks, chicken, and pasta also are offered. A favorite with first timers is the Combo Plate for two, which features Dungeness crab, Prince Edward Island mussels, pan-fried oysters, BC salmon, blackened snapper, and barbecued catfish. Open daily; closed weekends for lunch. Reservations advised. Major credit cards accepted. 900 Pacific St. (phone: 682-6661; fax: 682-4039).

Milestones at the Beach Boasting a fantastic view of English Bay, this casual spot serves huge portions. The four-page menu offers everything from breakfast entrées to gourmet burgers, hot dogs, pasta, and the best curly fries in town. It's almost always packed with locals. Open daily; weekends for brunch. Reservations advised for dinner. Major credit cards accepted. 1210 Denman St. (phone: 662-3431; fax: 662-7273).

El Patio With its sunny Mediterranean atmosphere and a menu to match, this is the ideal escape on a rainy day. It's even better in balmy weather, when *tapas* are served on the outdoor patio. The menu is a mix of Spanish, Greek, and Italian cooking. It's a popular spot for meals before or after events at the nearby *Queen Elizabeth Theatre* and *BC Place.* Closed Saturday lunch and Sundays. Reservations advised. Major credit cards accepted. 891 Cambie St. at Smithe St. (phone: 681-9149).

Prospect Point Café Prospect Point, with one of the best views in *Stanley Park,* is the site of this café. The inventive menu offers typical West Coast fare—salmon, scallops, and salads—and an imaginative decor increases its appeal. There's outdoor dining in good weather. Open daily. Reservations advised. Major credit cards accepted. *Stanley Park* (phone: 669-2737; fax: 669-6971).

Quattro From the day it opened, this homey Italian restaurant began garnering raves from critics and amateurs alike. One favorite is *strozzapreti paesani,* an unusual hand-rolled pasta served with smoked chicken strips, black olives, smoked *caciocavallo* cheese, and fresh tomatoes. Open daily; closed weekends for lunch. Reservations advised. Major credit cards accepted. 2611 W. Fourth Ave. (phone: 734-4444; fax: 734-4321).

Settebello The accomplished restaurateur Umberto Menghi, who owns four fine establishments in Vancouver, two in nearby Whistler, and one in San Francisco, is the guiding light behind this avant-garde pizzeria. Unusual toppings (duck, Cajun chicken, smoked salmon, and calamari) are the drawing card at this second-story spot. Note, however, that this is not a place for quiet conversation. Open daily. Reservations advised. Major credit cards accepted. 1131 Robson St. (phone: 681-7377; fax: 488-0172).

Umberto al Porto Homemade pasta and an array of Italian specialties are served at this establishment. The upper level offers a terrific view of the harbor and the distant mountains. Located in one of Gastown's most attractive buildings, it's close to most of the area's best shops. Closed Saturday lunch and Sundays. Reservations advised. Major credit cards accepted. 321 Water St. (phone: 683-8376; fax: 683-6682).

Vassilis Taverna At this family-run spot, a favorite with Grecophiles, all the usual favorites are offered, along with a few interesting adaptations. The Greek salad and roast chicken are special treats. Closed weekends for lunch and Mondays. Reservations advised. Major credit cards accepted. 2884 W. Broadway (phone: 733-3231).

INEXPENSIVE

Kitto Peasant-style Japanese comfort food is served here. The Japanese barbecue, called *robata,* is a specialty. Open daily. Reservations advised. Major credit cards accepted. Two locations: 1212 Robson St. (phone: 662-3333) and 833 Granville St. at Robson St. (phone: 687-6622).

Naam At this holdover from the era when West Fourth Avenue was this city's Haight-Ashbury, not a lot has changed since opening day in 1968, when the first flower child "dug" the mismatched furniture and crockery, great food, and friendly vibes. Vegetarians and night owls especially enjoy its low prices, large portions, and made-from-scratch house specialties (bee-pollen cookies, dandelion tea), served 24 hours a day. There's even live music. The beer list includes selections from several microbreweries. Open daily. Reservations advised for parties of seven or more. Major credit cards accepted. 2724 W. Fourth Ave. (phone: 738-7151).

Pink Pearl Just about the most authentic Chinese food this side of Taiwan is offered here. The Sunday morning dim sum brunch is crowded, chaotic, noisy, and absolutely irresistible. The fresh local crab in black bean sauce is reason in itself to visit Vancouver. If you have time for only one Asian meal, make this your stop. Open daily. Reservations advised. Major credit cards accepted. 1132 E. Hastings St. (phone: 253-4316; fax: 253-8525).

Winnipeg

No matter how you approach Winnipeg, it is easy to view the city as no more than an island on a vast prairie ocean that, given a good, strong wind, could simply float away in all that space. The impression is certainly unfair to a city of Winnipeg's substance—it's the capital of Manitoba, a cultural and economic center, and home to 652,000 people—but it is unshakable nevertheless.

The nearest sizable urban centers are Toronto, 1,200 miles (1,920 km) to the east; Minneapolis, 430 miles (688 km) to the southeast; and Calgary, 800 miles (1,280 km) to the west. North of Winnipeg stretch the immense reaches of Manitoba; to the west, the equally huge prairie provinces of Saskatchewan and Alberta. Manitoba itself is a vast province of a quarter of a million square miles, stretching from Hudson Bay to the US border, from the pine forests of the east to an upland rise that leads eventually to the foothills of the Rockies in the west. The capital of all this land is just 60 miles (96 km) north of the US border, at the junction of the Red and Assiniboine Rivers.

In 1670 England's King Charles II granted a franchise for all the lands draining into Hudson Bay to the Hudson's Bay Company, then a fur trading syndicate. (Today the North West Company, formerly the chief rival of the Hudson's Bay Company and since 1821 a subsidiary of it, operates a chain of trading posts in northern Canada. The parent company, now called The Bay, lives on as a chain of department stores across Canada.) To sustain its operation, the Hudson's Bay Company developed an agricultural settlement at the confluence of the Red and Assiniboine Rivers during the 19th century. The deeply silted, rich soil of the Red River basin soon became an asset more important than the fur trade, and the agricultural industry of western Canada was born. By 1870, when Manitoba became part of the confederation of provinces making up Canada, there were 12,000 settlers in the Red River colony.

The union of Manitoba with Canada was not without strife. The entire province had been the domain of several native tribes. Over the course of the long years of intermarriage between the natives and the French (and later English and Scots) fur traders, an ethnic group called the Métis—half-native and half-European—was born. By the late 19th century the Métis were relatively isolated from both the natives and the European settlers who were coming to the area in increasing numbers. Louis Riel, a French-speaking Métis, opposed the takeover of the territory by the confederation of Canada, which failed to recognize his people's claims to the land. The 1870 Red River Rebellion, led by Riel, succeeded in gaining the Canadian government's recognition of the Métis (though this turned out to be only temporary), and Riel himself named the province that was then created—

Manitoba means "spirit that speaks." (Fifteen years later, Riel was to meet his doom in neighboring Saskatchewan, once again in an attempt to defend the Métis's rights.)

The bitterness of the struggle was overlooked but never really resolved in the next decade, when the *Canadian Pacific Railway (CPR)* was under construction. The railroad brought immigrant Eastern European and Chinese laborers into western Canada, changing forever the demographics and ethnic politics of the provinces, and it turned small agricultural centers into boomtowns awash in new prosperity. Prostitution and hard drinking followed, and rowdiness became the order of the day in the newly open West. And while the laborers laid track, the *CPR* laid its plans, becoming a colossus of land, mining, and transportation interests. (Sadly, the *CPR* no longer operates transcontinental routes.)

Because of its location as a gateway to the prairies, Winnipeg was affected by the railroad more than many other cities in western Canada. Laborers who came with the railroad stayed on; settlers from the East took the first trains out and did the same. The city that exists today in all its sophistication still carries the mark of that early development, and the center of Winnipeg's business and cultural life remains the settlers' crossroads, Portage Avenue and Main Street, only a few blocks from the junction of the two major rivers.

For a city its size, Winnipeg offers an extraordinary range of cultural activities. Opera, an internationally acclaimed ballet company, a symphony orchestra, several chamber music groups, two universities, professional sports teams, several theaters, and hundreds of restaurants all contribute to its vitality. Winnipeg also retains a great ethnic diversity. The leading population groups are English-Scottish, German, Ukrainian, French, Native American, Jewish, Polish, Dutch, and Italian. People of Icelandic descent are a small but vital force in the city's business and government life. The newest wave of immigrants comes from the Far East; the Filipino community numbers close to 25,000, and more than 2,500 Vietnamese have settled here.

Winnipeg's North End was the traditional stopping place for newly arrived immigrants; today it is slowly becoming a corridor of high-rise developments and senior citizens' housing projects stretching several miles north on both sides of North Main Street. To the southeast the suburb of St. Boniface is the home of Winnipeg's French-speaking citizens; to the northeast the town of Transcona is a bedroom community for employees of the *Canadian National Railway* and other working people.

The city's most prosperous suburbs lie south of the Assiniboine River. Along Wellington Crescent and to the south of it lie the most prestigious addresses–River Heights, with old, stately homes, and Tuxedo, with sprawling mansions and enclosed grounds. Farther west the suburb of Charleswood has attracted young families. North of the Assiniboine lies the pleasant suburb of St. James, with picturesque homes and quaintly named streets.

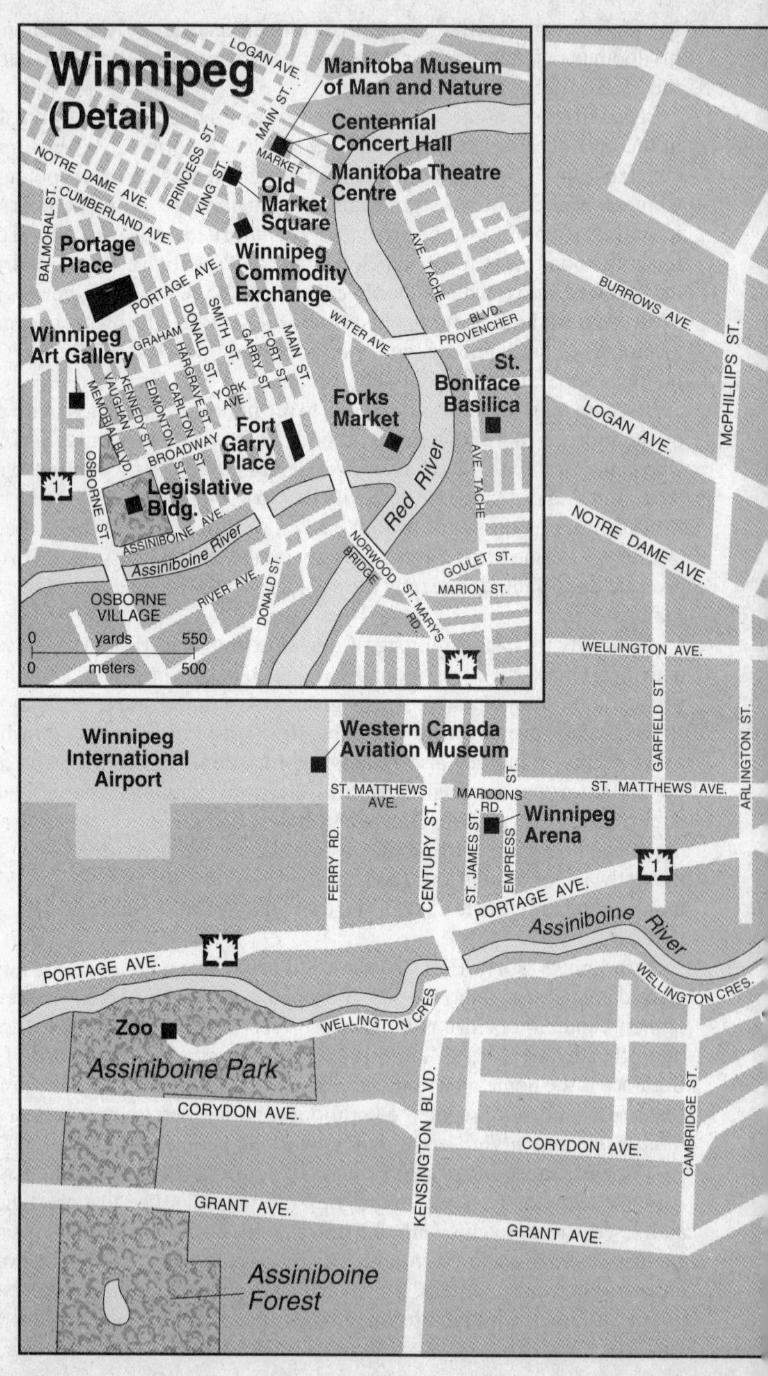

Winnipeg
(Detail)
LOGAN AVE.
MAIN ST.
Manitoba Museum of Man and Nature
Centennial Concert Hall
Manitoba Theatre Centre
MARKET
PRINCESS ST.
KING ST.
Old Market Square
NOTRE DAME AVE.
CUMBERLAND AVE.
BALMORAL ST.
Portage Place
Winnipeg Commodity Exchange
PORTAGE AVE.
AVE. TACHE
BLVD. PROVENCHER
WATER AVE.
Winnipeg Art Gallery
GRAHAM
DONALD ST.
SMITH ST.
GARRY ST.
FORT ST.
MAIN ST.
HARGRAVE ST.
CARLTON ST.
EDMONTON ST.
KENNEDY ST.
VAUGHAN
MEMORIAL BLVD.
YORK AVE.
St. Boniface Basilica
Forks Market
Fort Garry Place
BROADWAY
Red River
OSBORNE ST.
Legislative Bldg.
ASSINIBOINE AVE.
Assiniboine River
NORWOOD BRIDGE
GOULET ST.
MARION ST.
ST. MARY'S RD.
OSBORNE VILLAGE
RIVER AVE.
DONALD ST.
0 yards 550
0 meters 500
1
BURROWS AVE.
McPHILLIPS ST.
LOGAN AVE.
NOTRE DAME AVE.
WELLINGTON AVE.
GARFIELD ST.
ARLINGTON ST.
Winnipeg International Airport
Western Canada Aviation Museum
ST. MATTHEWS AVE.
MAROONS RD.
ST. MATTHEWS AVE.
Winnipeg Arena
FERRY RD.
CENTURY ST.
ST. JAMES ST.
EMPRESS ST.
PORTAGE AVE.
Assiniboine River
PORTAGE AVE.
WELLINGTON CRES.
Zoo
WELLINGTON CRES.
Assiniboine Park
CORYDON AVE.
KENSINGTON BLVD.
CORYDON AVE.
CAMBRIDGE ST.
GRANT AVE.
GRANT AVE.
Assiniboine Forest

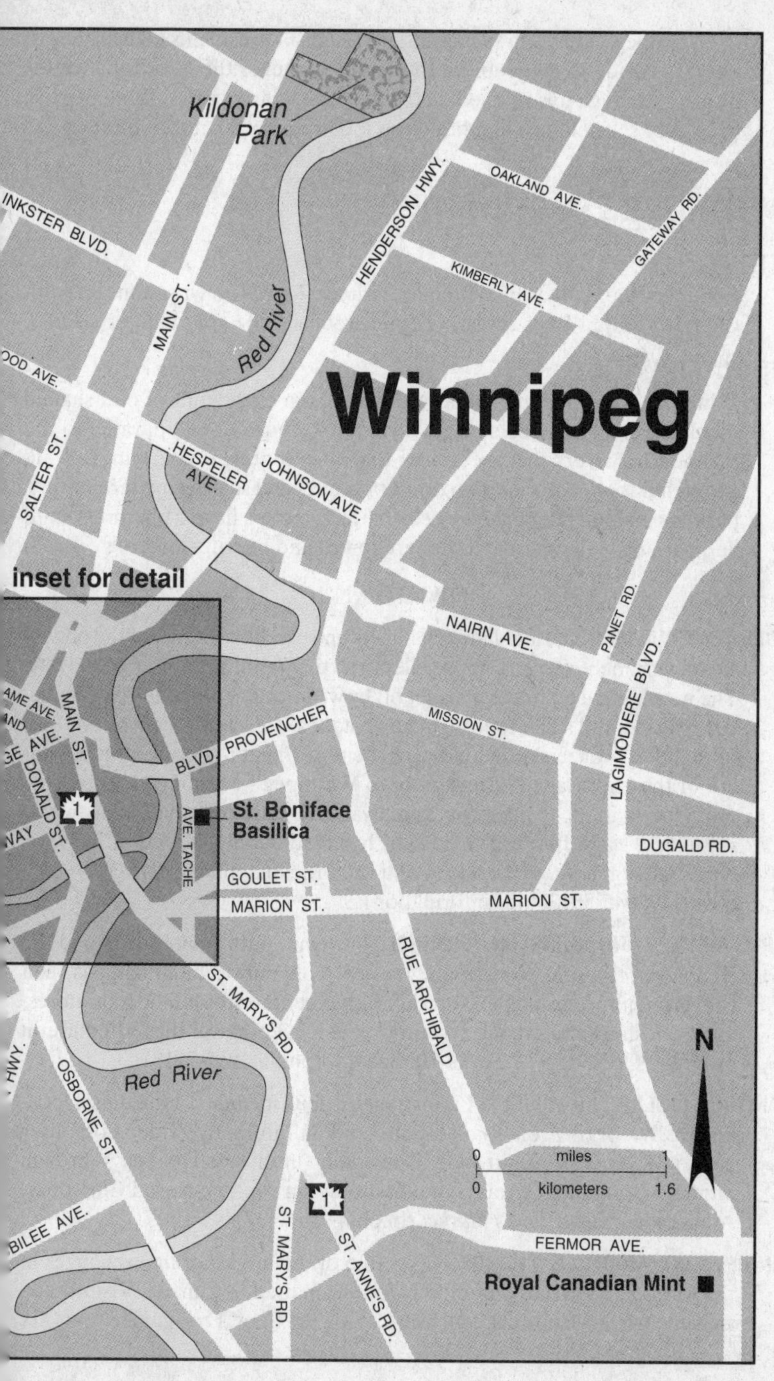
Winnipeg
Kildonan Park
INKSTER BLVD.
MAIN ST.
Red River
HENDERSON HWY.
OAKLAND AVE.
GATEWAY RD.
KIMBERLY AVE.
SALTER ST.
HESPELER AVE.
JOHNSON AVE.
inset for detail
NAIRN AVE.
PANET RD.
LAGIMODIERE BLVD.
MISSION ST.
BLVD. PROVENCHER
DONALD ST.
AVE. TACHE
St. Boniface Basilica
DUGALD RD.
GOULET ST.
MARION ST.
MARION ST.
ST. MARY'S RD.
RUE ARCHIBALD
Red River
OSBORNE ST.
N
miles
kilometers
1.6
ST. MARY'S RD.
ST. ANNE'S RD.
FERMOR AVE.
Royal Canadian Mint

Winnipeg's long, snowy months are tough, but residents take an almost perverse pride in their ability to handle whatever the Manitoba winter brings. Although it is isolated on the vast Canadian prairies, Winnipeg has a sense of self-reliance that has given it both financial and cultural vigor.

Winnipeg At-a-Glance

SEEING THE CITY

For a panoramic view of Winnipeg, visit the *Royal Crown* restaurant, with Canada's only bi-level, revolving dining rooms (see *Eating Out* for details).

SPECIAL PLACES

Winnipeg's downtown commercial center is a crazy quilt of odd-shaped blocks defined by streets originally laid out more or less parallel to the meandering rivers that meet near the city's center. If you want to walk through this area of Victorian office buildings and soaring modern towers, park in a commercial lot: Most city parking meters have a one-hour limit, and parking violators sometimes are towed and heavily fined.

DOWNTOWN

LEGISLATIVE BUILDING The legislative chambers and executive offices of the provincial government serve as an excellent starting point for a tour of the city. The neoclassical architecture is set off by well-groomed, statue-filled lawns. Atop the capitol's 255-foot-high dome stands *Golden Boy,* a five-ton, 13½-foot gilded bronze statue holding a sheaf of wheat under his arm, a symbol of the importance of this grain to Winnipeg's economy. Closed government holidays. Guided tours are available daily every half hour from 9 AM to 6:30 PM in July and August; by reservation only the rest of the year. No admission charge. Broadway and Osborne Sts. (phone: 945-3777; 800-665-0040; 945-5813, tour information).

FORKS MARKET AND JOHNSTON TERMINAL Between South Main Street and the Red River, this site, with elegantly restored old railway buildings, has been converted into a fashionable market with greengrocers, ethnic food stores, antiques shops, and many restaurants. Archaeological digs often are in progress. Open daily. 1 Forks Market Rd. (phone: 957-7618).

MANITOBA CHILDREN'S MUSEUM Permanent exhibits include a 1952 diesel locomotive, a working television studio, and an interactive video computer gallery. There's also a gift shop. Open daily (until 8 PM Thursdays through Sundays in summer; Fridays and Saturdays in winter); closed Christmas. Admission charge. *Forks Market* (phone: 956-5437).

WINNIPEG COMMODITY EXCHANGE This is one of the largest grain exchanges in the world and the only commodity futures market in Canada. Visitors can view the trading from a gallery overlooking the floor. Free guided tours are available by reservation. Closed afternoons and weekends. No admission charge. *Trizec Building* at Portage Ave. and Main St. (phone: 949-0495).

WINNIPEG ART GALLERY From modest beginnings at the turn of the century, this museum has emerged as one of Canada's finest art showplaces. The present triangular building, constructed in 1971 of local Tyndall stone, houses the work of Canadian and European artists, as well as the largest collection of contemporary Inuit sculpture and prints in Canada. The gallery also hosts frequent traveling exhibitions. There's a restaurant on the fifth floor and a gift shop on the main floor. Open daily in July and August; closed Mondays the rest of the year. No admission charge on Wednesdays. 300 Memorial Blvd., just south of Portage Ave. (phone: 786-6641).

PORTAGE PLACE This swanky center is joined by skywalks to such major downtown stores as *The Bay.* On the third level the spectacular *IMAX Theatre,* with a five-and-a-half-story-high, 71-foot-wide screen, shows stunning wildlife and other films custom-made for its huge 70mm format. For program times, call 956-4629. Portage Ave., from Vaughan to Carlton Sts.

OLD MARKET SQUARE During the day on summer weekends, this area teems with produce vendors and antiques peddlers. At night the action shifts to the discos, nightclubs, and restaurants bordering the square; this is also one of the city's red-light districts, so prostitutes congregate here as well. King St. and Bannatyne Ave.

SUBURBS

WESTERN CANADA AVIATION MUSEUM Here is a fascinating collection of aircraft from World War I to the jet age, with a gift shop on the premises. Closed *Christmas* and *New Year's Day.* Admission charge. Near *Winnipeg International Airport,* in Hangar T2, 958 Ferry Rd. (phone: 786-5503).

OSBORNE VILLAGE This is one of Winnipeg's best shopping districts. On each side of the street are small shops selling wicker furniture, books, Tiffany-style lamps, imported Pakistani carvings, handmade gold jewelry, tapes and CDs, fine clothing for women and children, and a variety of exotica. The area boasts several excellent tearooms and restaurants, including the *Tea Cozy* and *Pèppoli* (see *Eating Out* for both). Osborne St., just across the Osborne St. Bridge from the *Legislative Building.*

ASSINIBOINE PARK AND ZOO A 376-acre complex of recreational grounds, botanical gardens, a zoo, a miniature passenger train, and ornate pavilions, this excellent park is just minutes from downtown. In the summer bicycles, including tandems, can be rented for a few dollars a day. But beware: The park's food concessions are limited to snack bars at the botanical gardens, the zoo, and a mid-park pavilion, and the fare—mediocre at best—should be sampled only as a last resort. Open daily. There's a gift shop. Admission charge. Four miles (6 km) west of the city center off Wellington Crescent on Corydon Ave. (phone: 986-6921).

KILDONAN PARK One of Winnipeg's most interesting entertainment complexes, *Kildonan Park* has summertime pools, Canada's only outdoor theater (the *Rainbow Stage,* open July and August), a dining pavilion serving adequate luncheons, and the *Hansel and Gretel Witch's Hut,* a whimsical rendition of the fairy-tale gingerbread house. In summer, walk or cycle along the Red River through the park's dense trees; in winter, skate on the river or toboggan. Open daily. No admission charge. Five miles (8 km) north of the city center on Main St. (phone: 986-3753).

ST. BONIFACE BASILICA The huge church that originally stood on this site was built in 1818; it was followed by a succession of churches that were destroyed by fire and rebuilt. After the fifth church, finished in 1908, burned down in 1968, its old white stone façade was left standing, while yet another church, this one of handsome contemporary design with an attractive wooden interior and remarkably beautiful stained glass windows, was built behind it. In the courtyard separating the old structure from the new is the grave of Louis Riel, the Métis leader hanged for his role in the North-West Rebellion in 1885. The site overlooks the Red River, and the portals of the old church afford a view of the Winnipeg skyline. Near the basilica is the *St. Boniface Museum,* once a convent for the Grey Nuns. Built in 1848, it is the oldest structure in Winnipeg and contains relics of the early settlement of the area by French explorers and fur traders. Open daily (from June 18 through August until 8 PM except Fridays and Saturdays); closed weekends October 2 through June 17. Admission charge. 190 Ave. de la Cathédrale, on the east side of the Red River (phone: 233-7304, for basilica; 237-4500, for museum).

MANITOBA MUSEUM OF MAN AND NATURE Winnipeg's largest museum re-creates life on the prairies and in the North; it also includes a replica of a 17th-century fur-trading ship. Adjacent to the museum is a planetarium with science shows, dioramas, and animal and plant specimens. There's also a gift shop. Open daily May through August; closed Mondays the rest of the year. Admission charge. 190 Rupert Ave. at the *Manitoba Centennial Centre* (phone: 956-2830).

LOWER FORT GARRY Built in the early 1830s by the Hudson's Bay Company, this is the only stone fur-trading fort still intact in North America; it has been designated a national historic site. Costumed employees re-enact the days of the fort's glory. Open daily from late May through August; closed weekdays in September; closed the rest of the year. Admission charge. Twenty miles (32 km) north of Winnipeg on Rte. 9 in Selkirk; from downtown drive north on Main St. until you cross Rte. 101; Main St. then becomes Rte. 9 (phone: 983-3600).

ROYAL CANADIAN MINT One of the most modern facilities of its kind in the world, the mint produces coins for Canada and a number of other countries as well. Closed weekends May 2 though September 2; closed the rest of the year. Admission charge. Lagimodière Blvd. and the Trans-Canada Hwy., 10 miles (16 km) from downtown (phone: 257-3359).

DUGALD COSTUME MUSEUM This is Canada's only display of clothing from 1765 to modern times. Open daily June through August; closed Mondays and Tuesdays April and May, and September through November 5; closed November through March. Admission charge. On Rte. 15, 30 minutes east of downtown (phone: 853-2166).

EXTRA SPECIAL

***Oak Hammock Marsh* is an 8,650-acre wildlife management area where some 250 species of birds rest during their migratory flights. The area is also home to a plethora of mammals, including minks, weasels, deer, and coyotes. Spring and fall are the best bird watching times. Guided tours are available year-round by reservation only. Admission charge. Rte. 67 between Stonewall and Selkirk, about 32 miles (51 km) from downtown (phone: 467-3000).**

Sources and Resources

TOURIST INFORMATION

For general information, brochures, and maps, contact *Travel Manitoba* (155 Carlton St., Seventh Floor, Winnipeg, MAN R3C 3H8; phone: 945-3777; 800-665-0040, ext. 45) or *Tourism Winnipeg* (320-25 Forks Market Rd., Winnipeg, MAN R3C 4L9; phone: 943-1970; 800-665-0204).

LOCAL COVERAGE The *Free Press* and the *Sun* are both dailies. The best city map is the *City of Winnipeg Tourist and Street Guide,* available free from *Travel Manitoba* or *Tourism Winnipeg* (above). *The Manitoba Vacation Planner,* a good guide to the city, is distributed at no charge by *Travel Manitoba.*

TELEPHONE The area code for Winnipeg is 204.

SALES TAX Manitoba has a provincial sales tax of 7% in addition to the 7% federal Goods and Services Tax (GST) levied on most purchases. In many cases visitors can receive refunds of both the provincial and federal taxes. For details on Manitoba tax rebates, contact *Revenue Canada* (phone: 983-3933; 800-282-8076 in Canada); for more information on obtaining rebates on the federal tax, see GETTING READY TO GO.

CLIMATE November through March is a challenge here. With average temperatures hovering around -11F (-24C) during December, January, and February, and with readings of -20F (-29C) not uncommon, precautions against the cold are absolutely necessary. However, summers are warm, with temperatures averaging 68F (20C).

Winnipeg averages a substantial 50 inches of snow each winter. Drivers should carry a shovel, battery booster cables, and a tow rope at all times, and anyone driving in outlying areas or on the rural roads, including the Trans-Canada Highway, should carry some emergency rations, extra gasoline, and flares (for when the snowplows approach with their roar and blinding lights). Despite all this, from about 10 AM to 2 PM during the remarkably sunny days of midwinter, it is possible to walk outside with only light winterwear.

GETTING AROUND

AIRPORT *Winnipeg International Airport* (phone: 983-8410) is accessible by taxi, bus, and limousine, all available 24 hours a day.

BUS *Winnipeg Transit* (phone: 284-7190) operates bus lines throughout the city and suburbs. At press time, the fare was CN$1.35 (about $1 US at press time) for adults; CN 75¢ (55¢ US) for children over four years old. Maps of the system are available at gas stations.

CAR RENTAL All major international companies are represented, most with offices at the airport and downtown.

RIVERBOATS Two companies operate cruises on the Red and Assiniboine Rivers in spring, summer, and early fall. The MS *Paddlewheel Queen,* a replica of an old stern-wheeler, brings an air of the Old South to Winnipeg; evening cruises feature dining and dancing. The MS *Paddlewheel Princess* offers dinners and sightseeing cruises down the Red River to *Lower Fort Garry,* a scenic 20-mile trip. Contact *River Rouge Tours Ltd.* (312 Nairn Ave.; phone: 947-6843) or *Paddlewheel–Gray Line Tours* (PO Box 3930, Station B, Winnipeg, MAN R2W 5H9, or dock at Water Ave. and Gilroy St.; phone: 942-4500).

TAXI Cabs can be hailed in the street; taxi stands are located at the larger hotels and at the airport.

SPECIAL EVENTS

For children and the young at heart, Winnipeg offers the annual *Red River Exhibition* from late June through early July. The *"Ex"* sprawls around the *Winnipeg Arena* (1430 Maroons Rd.) with roller coasters, other rides, and numerous games of chance. For more information, call 772-9464. Another annual event is the *Winnipeg Folk Festival,* a four-day July affair held at *Birds Hill Park,* about 20 miles (32 km) northeast of the city. The festival attracts top names in folk music.

Every August, Winnipeg hosts the two-week *Folkorama* international festival. More than 40 ethnic groups—including Chinese, Greek, Filipino, Ukrainian, and indigenous peoples—celebrate their diverse heritages in colorful pavilions throughout the city with dances, songs, displays, and food.

A *Folkorama* passport provides access to all the pavilions, which are connected by frequent shuttle-bus service operated by the city. Other seasonal festivals with an ethnic accent are *Oktoberfest,* a German party for beer and sausage fans, and the *Festival du Voyageur,* a late-winter event held in the French suburb of St. Boniface, featuring dogsled races, ice sculpture competitions, and hearty food.

MUSEUMS

In addition to those described in *Special Places,* these two museums may be of interest:

PRAIRIE DOG CENTRAL This itinerant museum in a restored 1882 locomotive with passenger cars takes sightseers on a two-hour ride on Sundays from late May through late September. Departures are at 11 AM and 3 PM. Reservations unnecessary. Admission charge. *Portage Avenue Station,* St. James St. (phone: 832-5259).

PROVINCIAL ARCHIVES OF MANITOBA Historical records of the Hudson's Bay Company and photos and letters related to Manitoba's past are featured here. In the lobby are frequently changing historical exhibits of art, maps, and other memorabilia. Closed weekends. No admission charge. 200 Vaughan St. (phone: 945-3971).

SHOPPING

Winnipeg's two largest department stores, *Eaton's* and *The Bay,* are located downtown on Portage Avenue, with branches in many outlying malls. Both are connected to most major buildings and to each other by enclosed skywalks.

Interesting shopping areas include *Osborne Village* and *Old Market Square* (see *Special Places* for both), the *St. Vital Shopping Center* (a 10-minute drive southeast along Main St. from the Portage Ave. intersection), and upscale *Polo Park* (10 minutes west of the city center on Portage Ave.). Most stores are open from 10 AM to 6 PM Mondays through Wednesdays and Saturdays; to 9 PM Thursdays and Fridays; and from noon to 5 PM Sundays. Some shops to explore:

Crafts Guild of Manitoba It carries the work of Manitoban carvers, weavers, and jewelers and specializes in the leather work and carving of local natives and Inuits. 183 Kennedy St. (phone: 943-1190).

David Rice An imaginative selection of locally made jewelry. 100 Osborne St. (phone: 453-6105).

Hangers Fashionable clothing for men and women at low prices. 1761 Wellington Ave. (phone: 788-4805).

Harden & Huyse Belgian Chocolatiers The chocolates sold here are made in Saskatoon by Belgian-trained masters. 843 Corydon Ave. (phone: 287-8241).

Holt Renfrew Canada's preeminent fur retailer. *Portage Place* (phone: 942-7321).

Produce Plus A combination greengrocer, deli, and cheese shop that also sells magnificent tortes and bombes. 520 Academy Ave. (phone: 489-7480).

Ralph Lauren Overruns of the designer's ready-to-wear labels for men, women, and children at prices that may be as much as 90% (!) less than in the States. 2090 Corydon Ave. (phone: 837-7656).

Reiss Furs Fine furs. 275 McDermot St. (phone: 942-7376).

Sydney Gitterman Furs More fine furs. 46 Princess St. (phone: 943-9526).

SPORTS

BASEBALL The *Winnipeg Goldeyes* (phone: 982-2273) compete in the Northern League from early June to early September at *Winnipeg Stadium,* adjacent to the *Polo Park* shopping center, just south of Portage Avenue (1465 Maroons Rd.).

BICYCLING A popular summer diversion here. City parks have marked paths, and bicycles may be rented in *Assiniboine Park* (see *Special Places,* above).

BOXING Matches are held in the *Winnipeg Arena* (1430 Maroons Rd.; phone: 780-8080, for information; 780-SEAT or 800-465-SEAT, for tickets).

CROSS-COUNTRY SKIING Most city parks support some cross-country skiing and snowshoeing, but the best for both activities are *Assiniboine* and *Kildonan Parks* (see *Special Places,* above).

CURLING Originating in Scotland, this game is somewhat related to shuffleboard. In teams of four, the players, or curlers, slide squat, circular stones, each weighing 40 pounds, across an ice rink at goals 46 yards apart. Two assistants run ahead of the curlers, vigorously sweeping the ice with brooms along the path of the stones. Curling takes place at all city ice rinks from September through May.

FISHING Good fishing is possible at Lockport, 20 miles (32 km) north of Winnipeg.

FOOTBALL The *Canadian Football League*'s *Blue Bombers* (phone: 784-2583) make their home at the *Winnipeg Stadium* (see *Baseball*).

GOLF Municipal courses dot the city; perhaps the best of the five public courses is *John Blumberg* (4540 Portage Ave.; phone: 888-8860).

HORSE RACING Thoroughbred and harness racing are held year-round at *Assiniboia Downs* (3975 Portage Ave.; phone: 885-3330).

ICE SKATING For information on Winnipeg's many public ice rinks, call *Winnipeg Parks and Recreation* (phone: 986-3700) or *Travel Manitoba* (phone: 945-3777).

JOGGING Residents do it anywhere and anytime (some hardy souls even brave it in midwinter). Many city parks feature jogging paths.

LACROSSE A sport more common to eastern Canada, lacrosse is played here in *Assiniboine Park* on summer Sundays (see *Special Places,* above).

SNOWMOBILING Restricted to the frozen rivers in Winnipeg proper, it also can be enjoyed at *Birds Hill Park,* 20 miles (32 km) northeast of town. *Joe Rent All* (540 Archibald St.; phone: 233-7000) rents snowmobiles, as well as trailers and hitches to get them where you're going.

SQUASH A number of clubs around town have courts, including the *YMCA* (290 Vaughan St.; phone: 989-4100) and *Court Sports Fitness Club* (1400 Taylor Ave.; phone: 488-3025).

SWIMMING Public pools, mostly indoor, are located at Sinclair and Dufferin Sts. (phone: 986-6530); Dalhousie and Baylor Drs. (phone: 269-7416); 25 Poseidon Bay (phone: 986-5894); 999 Sargent Ave. (phone: 986-3921); 381 Sherbrook St. (phone: 986-5926); and 644 Parkdale St. (phone: 986-6705).

TENNIS There are both public and private courts around the city; for information on public courts, call the *Parks and Recreation Dept.* (phone: 986-3700). In summer championship matches are held at the *Winnipeg Canoe Club* (50 Dunkirk Pl.; phone: 233-5888), where visitors may reserve court time for a fee.

THEATER

Most of Winnipeg's live performances take place during the fall and winter; obtain tickets directly from the performing organizations or, for a service charge, through *Ticketmaster* (phone: 780-3333).

CENTER STAGE

Manitoba Centennial Centre Built in the 1960s, this monumental performing arts complex is home to the internationally acclaimed *Royal Winnipeg Ballet.* The corps, which spends much of the year touring, has four major annual series in Winnipeg (one per season) at the *Centre*'s *Concert Hall* and offers a free summer performance at *Assiniboine Park.* The *Manitoba Opera Association* and the *Winnipeg Symphony Orchestra* make their home here as well. Also on the premises are the *Manitoba Museum of Man and Nature* and the adjacent planetarium (see *Special Places*). 555 Main St. (phone: 956-1360).

The *Manitoba Theatre Centre* (174 Market St.; phone: 942-6537) presents a season of comic and dramatic performances. A companion theater, *The Warehouse* (140 Rupert St.; phone: 943-4849), offers experimental drama with modest ticket prices. The *Prairie Theatre Exchange* (*Portage*

Place at Portage Ave. and Memorial Blvd.; phone: 942-7291) features drama for both children and adults. The *Manitoba Theatre for Young People* (89 Princess St.; phone: 947-0394) stages plays for children. *Le Cercle Molière* (340 Provencher, in the French-speaking suburb of St. Boniface; phone: 233-8053) presents plays and revues in French.

MUSIC

Major performances by the *Winnipeg Symphony Orchestra* (phone: 949-3999) and the *Manitoba Opera Association* (phone: 780-3333) take place in the *Concert Hall* at *Manitoba Centennial Centre* (see *Theater,* above). During July and August musicals are performed at the *Rainbow Stage* (*Kildonan Park;* phone: 784-1280, for information; 780-SEAT or 800-465-SEAT, for tickets).

NIGHTCLUBS AND NIGHTLIFE

Winnipeg's night scene is surprisingly vibrant, considering that it still throbs when temperatures dive well below zero. The greatest concentration of nightclubs is in the downtown warehouse district. *Wise Guys Bar & Grill* (65 Rorie St.; phone: 956-2333) is a popular spot for light rock music, both recorded and live. The *Rollin' Stone Cabaret* (Rorie and McDermot Sts.; phone: 989-2323) and the cavernous *Market Avenue Cabaret* (Market Ave. at the Red River embankment; phone: 942-2222) are both good bets for live rock 'n' roll. Dance music and professional dancers entertain a thirtysomething crowd at the *Bank* (Main St. and Bannatyne Ave.; phone: 943-2582), a nightclub housed in a 1906 bank. *Pockets Bar & Grill* (171 McDermot St.; phone: 957-7665) is an upscale pool hall with good food and a sleek clientele. For a western motif and line dancing, try the *Palomino Club* (1133 Portage Ave.; phone: 772-0454), popular with urban cowpersons. For just plain humor in a dinner-theater setting, try *Rumours* (2025 Corydon Ave.; phone: 488-4520). Most bars are open daily and close at 2 AM.

Best in Town

CHECKING IN

Winnipeg's accommodations range from turn-of-the-century establishments to ultramodern complexes. Many are located in the city center, within easy walking distance of the finer shopping, dining, and entertainment facilities. Expect to pay $90 or more per night for a double room in those hotels classed as expensive, between $50 and $90 at places in the moderate category, and less than $50 at inexpensive places. Most hotels offer significant discounts on weekend and corporate rates. Unless otherwise noted, all hotels feature telephones, TV sets, private baths, and air conditioning. Bed and breakfast accommodations—from modest homes to mansions—also are available in the Winnipeg area. For information, contact *Bed & Breakfast of Manitoba* (533 Sprague St., Winnipeg, MAN R3G 2R9; phone: 783-9797). All hotels are in the 204 area code unless otherwise indicated.

We begin with our favorite haven, which falls in the "expensive" range, followed by recommended hotels listed by price category.

A GRAND HOTEL

Fort Garry Built by the *Canadian National Railway* in 1913 to resemble a Loire Valley château, this downtown establishment has a good restaurant and a strong European flavor. The public rooms boast gilded, coffered ceilings, tapestries, and antiques. The 246 guestrooms are elegantly tranquil; suites leave visitors in awe (the Oriental and Viceregal Suites are unforgettable). On the seventh floor is a European-style casino with roulette, poker, blackjack, and slot machines; jackets and ties are required for men. 222 Broadway Ave. (phone: 942-8251; 800-665-8088; fax: 956-2351).

EXPENSIVE

Delta Winnipeg With 272 rooms atop a high-rise garage, this place has a good location near downtown and shopping, an indoor pool, and, of course, excellent parking facilities. The 12th-floor restaurant offers a broad view of the city. A business center provides extensive services. 288 Portage Ave. (phone: 956-0410; 800-268-1133; fax: 947-1129).

Holiday Inn Airport West One of the area's major hostelries, it is in the rapidly expanding western suburb of St. James. The 228-room hotel has several restaurants and bars and a business center, and the *Unicity Shopping Centre* is nearby. 2520 Portage Ave. (phone: 885-4478; 800-HOLIDAY; fax: 831-5734).

Holiday Inn Crowne Plaza This 406-room hotel is part of a complex of office buildings and apartments, with an indoor pool ringed by pinball machines. There are several restaurants within, but savvy diners will visit either *Between Friends* (French) or *Elephant & Castle* (an English-style pub). Downtown, at St. Mary's Ave. and Carlton St. (phone: 942-0551; 800-HOLIDAY; fax: 943-8702).

Sheraton Winnipeg Near the *Eaton Place Shopping Centre* and the *Winnipeg Convention Centre,* this renovated apartment building features 272 spacious rooms with balconies, a business center, a pool, a sauna, a whirlpool bath, and an outdoor sun deck. The restaurant has an extensive continental menu, and the lounge features live entertainment. 161 Donald St. (phone: 942-5300; 800-325-3535; fax: 943-7975).

Viscount Gort Conveniently located a short drive west of downtown, this 140-room hotel has a coffee shop, an indoor pool, an exercise room, and a sauna. The *Polo Park* shopping center is a five-minute walk away, and the *Winnipeg Stadium* and *Arena*—sites of many competitive sporting events—are only a two-minute drive. Limousine service to the airport and bus station is available. 1670 Portage Ave. (phone: 775-0451; 800-665-1122 in Canada; fax: 772-2161).

Westin In the middle of the financial district and near major department stores, this hotel has 350 guestrooms, a business center, and a good restaurant, the *Velvet Glove* (see *Eating Out*). It's attached to an elaborate shopping and office complex, with ample parking nearby. 2 Lombard Pl. (phone: 957-1350; 800-228-3000; fax: 956-1791).

MODERATE

Comfort Inn by Journey's End South Just within the city's southern boundaries, this dependable, no-frills (except for a restaurant) 79-room motel is close to the *University of Manitoba.* Pembina Hwy. at Perimeter Hwy. (phone: 269-7390; 800-228-5150; fax: 261-7565).

Norwood This turn-of-the-century institution in St. Boniface has 52 rooms, including four suites with oversize color TV sets, plus extensive bar and restaurant facilities and a business center. 112 Marion St. (phone: 233-4475; fax: 231-1910).

Relax Plaza Centrally located, this 156-room property has a pool and a restaurant. 360 Colony St. at Portage Ave. (phone: 786-7011; 800-578-7879; fax: 772-1443).

Travelodge Near the point where the Trans-Canada Highway enters Winnipeg from the east, this 74-room motel is adjacent to a small shopping center. Amenities include an indoor pool with a hot tub, a bowling alley, room service, cable television and VCRs, a restaurant, and a lounge. 20 Alpine, in St. Vital (phone: 255-6000; 800-667-3529 in Canada; 800-578-7878 in the US; fax: 253-1563).

INEXPENSIVE

Grant Motor Inn Modern and well managed, it has 63 rooms and a passable dining room. 635 Pembina Hwy. (phone: 453-8247; fax: 287-2365).

Norlander Also near the *University of Manitoba,* with an attractive Scandinavian-style decor, this place has 36 rooms, a restaurant, and a lounge. 1792 Pembina Hwy. (phone: 269-6955; fax: 261-4543).

EATING OUT

For a seemingly isolated prairie town, Winnipeg can claim a large variety of restaurants that reflect its cultural diversity. Among the offerings are French, Italian, Danish, and Vietnamese fare, in addition to native Canadian dishes. Expensive restaurants charge $40 or more for a meal for two; moderate ones, $25 to $40; and inexpensive places, $15 to $25. Prices include tax but not drinks or tips. Unless otherwise noted, all restaurants are open for lunch and dinner, and all are in the 204 area code.

EXPENSIVE

Amici A northern Italian *ristorante* in downtown Winnipeg, it has a luxuriously formal dining room upstairs and a café downstairs. Imaginative antipasti, chicken stuffed with goat cheese, and lamb roasted with rosemary and fennel are featured. The atmosphere is relaxed and fashionable; the service, superb. Closed Sundays. Reservations advised. Major credit cards accepted. 326 Broadway (phone: 943-4997; fax: 943-0369).

Le Beaujolais In the French-speaking suburb of St. Boniface, this graceful eatery offers imaginative preparations of nouvelle cuisine, such as Atlantic salmon with fresh herbs, and beef tenderloin with shiitake mushrooms. Elegant pastries and deft service enhance the dining experience. Open daily. Reservations necessary. Major credit cards accepted. 131 Provencher (phone: 237-6276; fax: 237-5623).

Café La Scala One of the trendiest spots on Manitoba's trendiest street, this café serves imaginative salads and pasta and desserts such as *tarte aux fruits* for dessert. Closed Sundays in winter. Reservations necessary. Major credit cards accepted. 725 Corydon Ave. (phone: 474-2750).

De Luca's Above a vast Italian grocery, a lavish six-course banquet including a sampling of five wines is offered Saturday nights only. Otherwise, this spot serves inexpensive and abundant Italian lunches daily except Sundays. Reservations well in advance are necessary for the banquet. No credit cards accepted. 950 Portage Ave. (phone: 774-7617; fax: 774-5068).

Earls This casual, "happening" spot has an open grill, an oyster bar, and a wood-burning oven; the eclectic menu offerings—ranging from hamburgers to Thai noodles—make use of excellent fresh ingredients. Open daily. No reservations (except for parties of six or more); expect a wait on weekends. Major credit cards accepted. Downtown, at 191 S. Main St. (phone: 989-0103; fax: 989-2003).

Ichi Ban Japanese Steak House Beautifully decorated, this place incorporates a small artificial meandering river. Besides Japanese-style steaks, it offers sukiyaki, tempura, and a small selection of more exotic dishes. Open daily. Reservations necessary. Major credit cards accepted. 189 Carlton St. (phone: 942-7493; fax: 957-1697).

Pèppoli Here is the architecturally postmodern reincarnation of a legendary restaurant formerly on this site *(Victor's)*. Under the ownership of Heinz Kattenfeld, it has helped turn *Osborne Village* from a slum into a trendy area. The creative menu includes grilled shrimp with sweet potato chips, linguine with goat cheese, and elaborate French desserts. Closed Saturday lunch, Sundays, and holidays. Reservations advised. Major credit cards accepted. 454 River Ave. (phone: 284-3996; fax: 452-3749).

Rae and Jerry's West of downtown, it has good steaks, chicken, fish, and roast beef—the same fare it has been serving since opening in the 1950s. The atmosphere hasn't changed either—it's pure steakhouse retro. Open daily. Reservations necessary. Major credit cards accepted. 1405 Portage Ave. (phone: 783-6155; fax: 783-5797).

Royal Crown Located on top of *Fort Garry Place,* a lavish Baroque apartment complex, this remarkable restaurant has two levels revolving in opposite directions. Dine on continental specialties while enjoying the superb view. Open daily. Reservations necessary. Major credit cards accepted. 83 Garry St. (phone: 947-1990; fax: 943-5595).

Sandpiper and Prairie Oyster Simple decor, avant-garde Southwestern American food, interesting wines, and exquisite desserts (try the sinfully rich chocolate pâté) characterize this elegant, prize winning restaurant and grill (the two are connected by a bar). Note that the grill section is less expensive than the restaurant. Open daily. Reservations necessary. Major credit cards accepted. *Forks Market,* Second Floor (phone: 942-0918; fax: 942-2691).

Tre Visi This trendy, Milan-inspired dining room serves light Italian food; the menu includes elegant pastas, scampi with artichokes, and a variety of desserts. Closed Sundays. Reservations advised. Major credit cards accepted. 173 McDermot Ave. (phone: 949-9032).

Velvet Glove This formal dining room serves elaborate fare, accompanied by harp music Friday and Saturday evenings. Paper-thin smoked salmon and chateaubriand are just two of the menu options. Open daily. Reservations advised. Major credit cards accepted. In the *Westin Hotel,* 2 Lombard Pl. (phone: 985-6255 or 957-1350; fax: 956-1791).

MODERATE

Bistro Bohemia Bright by day, intimate by night, this small establishment serves superb Czech food, as well as a varied menu of other authentic Eastern European dishes. The desserts are magnificent. Closed Sundays. Reservations advised on weekends. Major credit cards accepted. 159 Osborne St. (phone: 453-1944).

Bistro Dansk A frequently changing Danish menu and fine service have made this bistro one of Winnipeg's favorite eateries. Everything is made from scratch—including the rich soups, desserts, and bread. The goulash and roast pork are standouts. Closed Sundays. Reservations advised. Visa accepted. 63 Sherbrook St. (phone: 775-5662).

Civita Designer pizza, fashionable patrons, and avant-garde decor are the hallmarks of this restaurant. During the summer patrons can dine at outdoor tables while listening to strolling street musicians. Open daily. Reservations advised for dinner. Major credit cards accepted. 691-B Corydon Ave. (phone: 453-4616).

Le Croissant A bakery-cum-café, it offers authentic regional French cuisine as well as the light fare and pastries of a tearoom. Closed Mondays. Reservations necessary on weekends. Visa accepted. 268 Taché Ave., St. Boniface (phone: 237-3536; fax: 237-3550).

Edohei Sushi Here, diners sit on traditional tatami mats. In addition to sushi, the menu offers other Japanese specialties, including excellent tempura. Closed Tuesdays, and weekends for lunch. Reservations advised. Major credit cards accepted. 355 Ellice Ave. (phone/fax: 943-0427).

Fork & Cork Swiss fondue and Indonesian fare are the staples of this intimate place. Open daily. Reservations unnecessary. Major credit cards accepted. 218 Sherbrook St. (phone: 783-5754).

Mamma Mia The Italian menu ranges from simple pepperoni pizza to such Neapolitan specialties as homemade sausages and chicken baked with herbs. In summer it's a popular sidewalk café. Open daily. Reservations necessary in summer. Major credit cards accepted. 631 Corydon Ave. (phone: 453-9210).

Settebello Café Already becoming a fixture on chic Corydon, this restaurant/coffee bar has been an instant success. Sandwiches are artistically prepared, and the tortes and cheesecakes are extraordinary. The look is postmodern; the attitude, laid-back. Closed Sunday lunch. Reservations unnecessary. Major credit cards accepted. 788 Corydon Ave. (phone: 477-9105).

Sofia's Caffè Corydon Avenue's most intimate restaurant serves Italian specialties made with fresh ingredients such as homemade sausage. The salads are light and delicately seasoned. Operatic arias play in the background. In summer diners can sit on an outdoor terrace. Open daily. Reservations advised. Major credit cards accepted. 635 Corydon Ave. (phone: 452-3037).

Sugar Reef Caribbean, American Gulf Coast, and Mexican fare are served in a casual atmosphere. In summer the rooftop deck is a good spot to watch the street action below. Open daily. Reservations advised. Major credit cards accepted. 645 Corydon Ave. (phone: 452-7333).

Tea Cozy In *Osborne Village,* this shop serves tea (featuring scones and cucumber sandwiches), coffee, late breakfast, lunch, and (on weekends) dinner in a very British manner. The gingerbread cake with whipped cream is a favorite. Closed weekdays for dinner. Reservations unnecessary. Major credit cards accepted. 99 Osborne St. (phone: 475-1027).

Yamato This friendly Japanese eatery serves everything from sushi and sashimi to teriyaki and tempura. Open daily. Reservations advised. Visa and American Express accepted. 667B Stafford St. (phone: 452-1166; fax: 452-8488).

INEXPENSIVE

Braemar Bakery More than just a place to buy bread, this is a Jamaican restaurant with live Caribbean music on weekends and superb curries and jerk chicken all the time. Open daily. Reservations advised on weekends. Visa accepted. 349 Wardlaw Ave. (phone: 949-7211; fax: 475-0127).

Carlos and Murphy's Built to resemble a Wild West saloon, this Mexican restaurant and bar has good food, a devoted clientele, and an atmosphere conducive to mingling. Closed Sundays for lunch. Reservations unnecessary. Major credit cards accepted. 129 Osborne St. (phone: 284-3510).

D'8 Schtove The weighty Mennonite peasant fare here features stuffed cabbage rolls, beef Stroganoff, and steaks. The sausages are homemade, and the desserts are rich. Open daily. Reservations unnecessary. Major credit cards accepted. 1842 Pembina Hwy. (phone: 275-2294).

Huong Nha Vietnamese and Chinese fare served in a modest but pleasant dining room. Open daily. Reservations unnecessary. Visa accepted. 7-510 Sargent Ave. (phone: 786-1182).

Old Spaghetti Factory In a restored downtown warehouse decorated with turn-of-the-century antiques, including a genuine cable car, it's a favorite with small children. Open daily. Reservations advised. Major credit cards accepted. 291 Bannatyne Ave. (phone: 957-1391; fax: 957-5803).

Pembina Village An informal, friendly, Greek-style steakhouse, it also offers pizza, salads, and souvlaki. Open daily to midnight. Reservations unnecessary. Major credit cards accepted. 333 Pembina Hwy. (phone: 477-5439).

Santa Fe Cafe Mexican food that departs from roadhouse clichés, served in large portions in a room that evokes a pueblo on the prairies. Closed Sunday lunch. Reservations advised. Major credit cards accepted. 121 Osborne St. (phone: 475-7557; fax: 452-9188).

Tap & Grill This modern Greek taverna serves salads, spit-roasted meat, other Aegean fare, and light desserts. Popular choices are souvlaki, chicken stuffed with cheese, and pasta with shrimp. Closed Sundays. Reservations advised on Fridays and Saturdays. Major credit cards accepted. 137 Osborne St. (284-7455; fax: 284-7273).

Zine's Infocafé This new coffeehouse elbows its way to the technological forefront with several computer terminals for patrons to try out new CD-ROM titles, check their E-mail, browse the Internet, or play games. There are also a variety of magazines and newspapers for sale and a standard delicatessen menu, with a few spicy Thai noodle dishes thrown in for good measure. Open daily. No reservations. Major credit cards accepted. 875 Corydon Ave. (phone: 475-5515; E-mail: infocafe@magic.mb.ca).

Diversions

Exceptional Pleasures and Treasures

For the Experience

Quintessential Canada

There is no single Canada; its very identity is linked to its diversity. This is a country of sweeping distances, of sprawling cities and vast wildernesses from maritime Canada in the east, across the Laurentian Mountains, the prairies, and the Rockies, to the lushly vegetated cliffs of the west coast. Beyond the 200-mile-wide layer of settlement and development in southern Canada, the great mass of the country is undeveloped, unchanged from what it was when the great glaciers retreated 10,000 years ago. Drive away from the large, modern, multiethnic cities, and within an hour or two you are in the vast, raw, and beautiful land that explorers and trappers found half a millennium ago.

The country grew up under the protection of two mother nations, France and England, and their influences remain. The touch of the Bourbon monarchs can still be seen in Quebec, right down to the Bourbon fleur-de-lis adorning the provincial flag. In Old Quebec City, the windows of the little *boulangeries* are full of very Parisian-looking (and -tasting) baguettes and croissants. Meanwhile, in English Canada, the knot that still binds the land to the British monarch is visible through the little embossed crown on every Ontario license plate. British tradition is also recalled in the ceremonies of the Royal Canadian Mounted Police and in the west coast city of Victoria, with its horse-drawn carriages, English gardens, ivy-covered buildings, and quaint shops.

British and French, modern and untamed, Canada cannot be captured in a single place or moment, but each of the following crystallizes at least one aspect of this many-faceted land.

CANADA'S ORPHAN ANNIE In 1908, Prince Edward Island native Lucy Maud Montgomery published her first novel, *Anne of Green Gables,* the tale of a spirited young girl who is rescued from an orphanage and brought to live in the PEI town of Cavendish. There, with spirit and wit, she wins the hearts of her adopted family and her small rural community. Anne still charms Prince Edward Island each summer during Charlottetown's annual festival performances of *Anne of Green Gables.* Through most of July and August, the *Confederation Centre of the Arts* presents both evening and matinee performances of a musical version of the beloved tale, which has been translated into 17 languages. True *Anne* aficionados head to Cavendish, an area by the sea 24 miles (38 km) northwest of Charlottetown, and see some of the sites that Anne explored, including "Green Gables" itself, the country farmhouse that was once the home of Anne's creator. The house is now a museum with a large collection of *Anne* memorabilia. In nearby New

London, Lucy Maud Montgomery's birthplace also is open to the public. If you like Little Orphan Annie and Cinderella, you'll love their Canadian cousin.

A FISHING VILLAGE FROM ANOTHER ERA Colorful wooden houses set against a rocky landscape, small boats chugging in and out of a tiny natural harbor, and a magnificent lighthouse define Peggy's Cove. Perched on the eastern shore of Nova Scotia 27 miles (43 km) southwest of Halifax, Peggy's Cove is one of the best-preserved rustic fishing villages in North America. The provincial government has protected the village's maritime character even as the number of townspeople actually engaged in fishing dwindles. Incredibly picturesque, it has attracted a colony of artists and a steady stream of visitors who snap photos at every turn. Immerse yourself in the town's scenery and 19th-century ambience with a walk along the rocks near the water (don't get too near the edge and the sometimes dangerous surf). View the spectacular murals in *St. John's Anglican Church,* painted by a resident artist. For dinner, stop in at one of the local church's regular lobster suppers, or order the local crustacean at the *Sou'wester,* Peggy's Cove's only restaurant. Touristy? Perhaps. But also irresistibly quaint and undeniably appealing.

BATTLES ON ICE Hockey is *the* Canadian game, and Montreal's *Canadiens* provide the best of it on their home ice at the *Forum.* Since the *National Hockey League* was established in 1917, the *Canadiens* have won the *Stanley Cup* trophy more times than any other team and practically owned the championship title for years. This is the arena where Jean Béliveau, Ken Dryden, Jacques Plante, Maurice ("The Rocket") and Henri Richard, and Guy Lafleur, among others, have created legends. During intermissions, follow the rambunctious, hockey-wise crowd as it spills out to the concession stands—the Montreal hot dogs, served with small, spicy pickles called *cornichons,* should not be missed. You'll have to hurry if you want to see the *Canadiens* at the old *Forum,* though: A new arena opens early this year on the site of *Windsor Station.*

THE STAMPEDE The first two weeks of July each year, the residents of Calgary slough everyday work clothes to put on spurs, Stetsons, and broad, Western grins. The *Calgary Exhibition and Stampede,* a flapjacks and rodeo, dancin'-in-the-streets frolic, celebrates the oil and cattle traditions of this city in the foothills of the Rockies. This "Greatest Outdoor Show on Earth" features *World Championship Chuckwagon Races,* lots of live entertainment, a casino, agricultural exhibits, a midway, a parade, and probably the biggest rodeo in the world. The *Half Million Dollar Rodeo,* which takes place daily, ranks as one of the top events on the circuit. Contestants compete for big prizes in such events as bareback bronco riding, steer wrestling, calf roping, wild horse racing, and wild cow milking. It's hard not to get caught up in the spirit of things as this thoroughly modern city turns its back on the banks and the oil companies that are now its main business and revives the myths of the Old West. If you have jeans and cowboy boots, wear 'em. If you have a pickup truck, bring 'er. Quiche is out, beef is in, and everyone—urban and genuine cowboy alike—has a great time.

TEA AT THE EMPRESS The British Empire may be dead, but you'd never know it at the *Empress* hotel in temperate Victoria, British Columbia. The hotel looks like an English country home, but on a vast scale. Built in 1908, the *Empress* is decorated with columns and coffered ceilings, polished floors, and soaring windows that frame elegant salons. The very British tradition of afternoon tea is carried on here to perfection. Served in fragile bone china cups, steaming tea is accompanied by dainty sandwiches, buttery scones, sweet Devonshire cream, and an array of tempting cakes. There are four sittings daily in summer; reserve ahead if you want to be sure to get seated.

THE FALLS Ninety miles (144 km) south of Toronto is a natural wonder of the world, surrounded by a town that gives fresh meaning to the term "honky-tonk." Niagara Falls, formed 10,000 years ago as retreating glaciers left what is called the Niagara Escarpment, were first described in Europe by the Belgian missionary Louis Hennepin in 1678, three years after his arrival in Canada with French explorer René Robert Cavelier de La Salle. At the border of the US and Canada, the ever-popular falls have a mist of romance about them and have long been a favorite of newlyweds—owing, say local historians, to a visit by Napoleon's brother and his new bride on *their* honeymoon. (Today, those wishing to tie the knot here may choose from a number of chapels and hotels catering to honeymooners.) The superhyped falls have been painted by artists, tightroped by lunatics, and shot down in barrels by people never to be seen again. Charles Dickens praised the falls in the mid-19th century, writing, "I seemed to be lifted from the earth."

In 1885, Ontario established a provincial park here to control the madness, but today there are helicopter trips and cable cars over the falls, tram rides and boat rides, exhibits of daredevil barrels, numerous mini-museums, and all manner of tacky sideshows and tourist shops. Despite all that, Niagara Falls remains the world's largest waterfall by volume and a sight that continues to inspire (3.6 million gallons of water flow over the 167-foot-high American Falls every 60 seconds, while more than 37 million gallons a minute crash down the Horseshoe Falls, 158 feet high). The two best viewing towers—the 524-foot *Skylon Tower* and the 416-foot *Minolta Tower*—are on the Canadian side, on a 250-foot escarpment across from the falls. Or take a trip on one of the four boats named *Maid of the Mist* to witness the bottom of the cascade from within the dry security of a raincoat provided with the price of a ticket. Finally, don't miss the show at night, when Horseshoe Falls is lighted by four billion candlepower in rainbow colors. The energy for this Technicolor extravaganza is provided by the falls itself.

ENCOUNTERS WITH THE WILDEST AND THE WOOLIEST Think mountains with sheep clinging to crevices, evergreen forests, and winding rivers where moose drink, and you've pictured the Canada of *Banff National Park,* in Alberta (about 75 miles/120 km west of Calgary). For the best sightings of Canada's wildlife (deer, bighorn sheep, and elk), set out on foot from Banff, a village 10 miles (16 km) inside the eastern gate of the park and the starting point for many of the park's 680 miles of hiking trails. A challenging, two-hour hike up Sulphur Mountain just beyond the town limits could reveal marmots and mountain goats. At the top is a restaurant, at the same altitude where eagles soar in the updrafts. You can ride the gondola back down for free; there is, however, a charge for the ride up.

For a glimpse of Canadian creatures that live farther north, some of which cannot be seen anywhere else, visit Churchill, Manitoba. No road leads from the south to this tiny arctic seaport on the edge of Hudson Bay. From Winnipeg, it's a two-and-a-half-hour flight or two-day train trip. Along the way, the scenery turns from prairie, to forest, to peat bog, to tundra, and, finally, to the bleak shore of the bay. Winter lasts from September to June here, with long nights lit by the aurora borealis. As the subarctic twilight ends, days grow to 21 hours and the marshy muskeg bursts into a riot of life. Tiny arctic flowers grow thick and lush on beds of lichens. Dense clouds of birds (as many as 200 species) migrating north to arctic breeding grounds descend to feed. Four species of fur seals visit the harbor. In July and August, beluga whales give birth to calves in the great rivers that empty into Hudson Bay. You can see, hear, and sometimes even touch the mothers and calves from the whale watching boats that cruise the bay. The whales squeal phrases of greeting, eye their audience, then plunge below to safety. In the fall, polar bears gather in Churchill before they go out onto the ice of Hudson Bay for their winter of fishing. Tundra buggies—huge vehicles with immense tires—offer tours of the bears' haunts, but you may very well run into one of the fantastic white beasts wandering the town's streets. This is the only place in the world where police direct traffic around strolling members of the *Ursus maritimus* family as they search for snacks of kitchen garbage. On *Halloween,* the children of Churchill trick-or-treat under the protection of Mounties toting tranquilizer guns. With its barren but strangely beautiful scenery and its amazing wildlife, Churchill is a weird and wondrous place.

THE MOUNTIES While they are not always treated with the utmost respect in popular culture (dim-witted Dudley Do-Right; the moony, croony Nelson Eddy), they remain a formidable part of Canadian law and order. The Royal Canadian Mounted Police force was established under the name "The North West Mounted Police" in 1873 by the British government as a rural constabulary to guard settlers and keep the peace on the frontier of western Canada. In the late 1890s, they guarded the Klondike gold rush miners, and in 1904—in recognition of their service in the Boer War in South

Africa—King Edward VII granted the Mounties the royal patent. Today close to 16,000 strong, the force still guards the frontiers of the arctic, north and west of Canada, as well as many rural areas in the eastern and western provinces, airports, and major buildings of the federal government. Although today's Mounties ride around in police cars, wear blue uniforms, and investigate modern-day crimes, their mounted tradition and crimson tunics live on in a spectacular horseback show called the *Musical Ride,* which is performed on special occasions across the country. A kind of equine ballet, the spectacle features 32 traditionally clad Mounties on horseback carrying lances and brilliant banners. The horses are trained for three years for the performance. Simpler shows, such as the *Sergeant Major's Parade* and the *Sunset/Retreat Ceremony,* take place at the *Royal Canadian Mounted Police Training Centre and Museum* in Regina, Saskatchewan (Dewdney Ave. W.; phone: 306-780-5838). Visit the center to see modern Mounties in training, then stop in at the museum, whose collection of kits, guns, saddles, logbooks, red tunics, and beaver coats recalls the romantic myths of the Mounties of yore. There is no admission charge for tours or the museum.

HELICOPTER SKIING This is a skier's dream—no lift lines, no crowds, gorgeous mountain vistas, and miles and miles of untouched snow in the wild mountains of western Canada. Lifted by helicopter far above the tree line, you descend a mountain face from near the peak through glacier bowls and beyond to valley bottoms. Runs of 6,600 vertical feet or more are possible. Exhilarating, it's a feeling like no other—and it's long since shed its reputation as a dangerous sport for only the strongest, gutsiest, and most advanced skier. Special powder-snow skis, available from heli-ski operators, make the going easy for intermediate skiers. And ski operators use state-of-the-art technology to monitor snow conditions and guide clients to safe terrain.

The concept of heli-skiing was introduced to Canada in the 1960s, and a vast new world was opened up; comparable terrain simply is unavailable anywhere else in the world. The Bugaboos, in the southeastern section of the Canadian Rockies, alone have some 600 square miles of skiable terrain, and then there are the Cariboos, the Monashees, Valemont, Revelstoke, and the Bobbie Burns. Conditions are good from December through April: Snows are heaviest from December through February, when the mountains are in deep fresh powder; from late February to mid-March, the snow tapers off and the crevasses fill; and, as the days get longer, corn snow appears.

CARNAVAL DE QUÉBEC For a week and a half in early February, icebound Quebec City erupts into an exhilarating northern version of *Mardi Gras* in New Orleans or *Carnaval* in Rio. Some merrymakers don 18th-century costumes (or at least put *tuques* on their heads and tie traditional sashes, *ceintures fléchées,* around their waists); menus feature such Quebec delicacies as maple-sugar pie, *tourtière* (a spicy meat pie), and caribou (a potent mixture of wine and pure alcohol); and there is a dizzying array of activities everywhere you turn.

The fun begins with an opening ceremony in which the mascot Bonhomme Carnaval (a seven-foot snowman with red cap and *ceinture fléchée*) crowns the Carnival Queen at his immense, carved ice palace before thousands of cheering spectators. During the next 10 days, there's an international ice sculpture competition on Place Carnaval, skiing, skating, hockey, tobogganing, luge rides, dogsled races, auto races on ice, and the *International Canoe Race* across the icy, treacherous St. Lawrence. Then there is the annual roll in the snow by bathing-suit-clad participants. At night are fireworks displays, lavish theme parties, the *Queen's Ball,* a parade with brightly lit floats, and a torch-lit ski run. It's an exciting, invigorating experience in a dazzling wonderland of ice and snow.

THE BARD OF THE YUKON English-born poet Robert W. Service went to the Yukon in 1897, just as the region was being flooded with thousands of men in feverish search of gold. There's no better way to evoke the raucous spirit of this era than to read Service's most famous ballad, "The Shooting of Dan McGrew," which tells of a rowdy saloon, a crowd of questionable characters, gold, betrayal, and, finally, two corpses. Service's "The Spell of the Yukon" also captures the spirit of the gold rush. It opens with these lines:

I wanted the gold and I sought it
I scrambled and mucked like a slave.
Was it famine or scurvy I fought it;
I hurled my youth into a grave.

and ends with the poignant

There's gold and it's haunting and haunting;
It's luring me on as of old;
Yet it isn't the gold that I'm wanting
So much as just finding the gold.
It's the great, big, broad land 'way up yonder,
It's the forests where silence has lease;
It's the beauty that fills me with wonder,
It's the stillness that fills me with peace.

Relive the gold rush with a visit to the Yukon's Dawson City, one of the era's biggest boomtowns, where, during the summer, there are daily readings of Service's poems in his log cabin on Eighth Avenue. Spend a day in Dawson living like the prospectors of old. Begin with a few hours at the creek panning for gold, then head to town for an evening of entertainment. First see the *Gaslight Follies,* an authentic 1898 vaudeville production, which is performed nightly (except Tuesdays) in summer at the *Palace Grand Theatre* (one of the few buildings surviving from the 1890s). After the show, try your luck at *Diamond Tooth Gertie's Gambling Hall,* then quench your thirst at one of the town's many saloons, where successful prospectors can still pay for their drinks with gold dust.

Festivals, Fairs, and Fancy Acts

Celebrations abound in Canada, and the motivations behind them are many. Some honor an area's ethnic heritage, or were simply invented to indulge celebrants' fondness for music or dance. Others—like the rodeos, the lobster festivals, and even the mining festivals—fete the local industry. And there are plenty of winter festivals, too, many of them in February.

Provincial tourist authorities can provide lists of the various fairs, exhibitions, and festivals. Below is a compendium of special celebrations off the beaten track (for details on festivals in Canada's major metropolises, see the *Special Events* sections of the individual reports in THE CITIES). Entries are arranged geographically, starting with the eastern provinces and then the western ones; within that framework, entries are arranged alphabetically by province and, within province, by town.

EAST

ACADIAN FESTIVAL, Caraquet, New Brunswick This festival, held during the first two weeks in August (including August 15, the *Acadian National Holiday*), centers around Acadian culture, with music, theater, and visual arts highlighted. Especially noteworthy is the *Blessing of the Fleet,* with fishing boats gaily decorated with garlands and flags. There are also dance performances and folksinging, much of it in French. Information: *Acadian Festival,* Caraquet, PO Box 420, Caraquet, NB E0B 1K0 (phone: 506-727-3423).

MIRAMICHI FOLK SONG FESTIVAL, Newcastle, New Brunswick The oldest festival of its kind in North America, this five-day cultural and historic celebration features musicians from all across Canada performing songs of lumber camps and days at sea. The pieces are sung in French, English, and occasionally other languages as well. Sometimes there's some clickety-clackety spoon playing and tap dancing. Each night a noted entertainer from the province appears. Held annually the first week in August, the festival offers a good opportunity to gather some knowledge of New Brunswick folkways and soak up the atmosphere of this unusual province at the same time. Information: *Susan Butler,* PO Box 13, Newcastle, NB E1V 3M2 (phone: 506-627-1495, days; 506-622-1780, nights).

FESTIVAL BY THE SEA, Saint John, New Brunswick Some 125 entertainers, many representing other Canadian provinces, perform 80 to a hundred stage shows, featuring singing, dancing, and theater productions. Lasting two weeks in August, this festival pays tribute to New Brunswick's marine heritage. Information: *Festival by the Sea,* PO Box 6848, Station A, Saint John, NB E2L 4S3 (phone: 506-632-0086).

SHEDIAC LOBSTER FESTIVAL, Shediac, New Brunswick One of the hot spots of coastal sailing, with miles of sandy beaches, this community, long famous for the lobsters brought ashore by its fishermen, is called the "Lobster Capital of the World." What could be more appropriate, then, than an annual six-day, mid-July bash celebrating those delectable crustaceans? Events typical of such small-town festivities take place, plus lobster-trapping and -boiling exhibitions, lobster-eating contests, and (worth the trip in itself) plenty of lobsters for all. Information: *Shediac Lobster Festival,* PO Box 1923, Shediac, NB E0A 3G0 (phone: 506-532-8932).

ANTIGONISH HIGHLAND GAMES, Antigonish, Nova Scotia The Scottish yearning to link arms with kith and kin, near and far, under the shield of the family clan is expressed at this colorful gathering that takes place for a few days annually in mid-July. The oldest Scottish games in North America are held here, but you don't have to be a Scot to enjoy the fun: There are usually competitions in caber tossing, weight throwing, and Highland dancing and piping, and plenty of tea and oatcakes. Information: *Nova Scotia Tourism Division,* PO Box 549, 1800 Argyle St., Halifax, NS B3J 2R7 (phone: 902-424-4247).

MUSKOKA WINTER CARNIVAL, Gravenhurst, Ontario This popular festival, a four-day weekend held at the end of February in the Muskoka Lakes district 100 miles (160 km) north of Toronto, is known for the assortment of wild and wacky contests on the agenda—motorcycle races, bed races, a *Wreck-um Derby,* snow sculptures, and a talent contest, just to name a few. Information: *Muskoka Winter Carnival* (phone: 705-687-8432) or *Muskoka Tourism Centre,* 9-1 Ontario St., Bracebridge, ONT P1L 2A7 (phone: 800-267-9700).

KITCHENER-WATERLOO OKTOBERFEST, Kitchener, Ontario The German and Pennsylvania Dutch settlers who founded this town around 1800 and named it Berlin never would have imagined that the settlement would give rise to anything like this event, which attracts some 600,000 people and ranks among the biggest celebrations of its kind in North America. German clubs and area service groups sponsor nearly 25 festhalls with tables groaning beneath sausage, sauerkraut, and beer, and, while diners and guzzlers partake, oompah bands merrily entertain. There are concerts, folk-dance shows, performances by brass bands and drum corps, sports tourneys, Canada's largest *Thanksgiving Day* parade, *Thanksgiving* church services, and more. The nine-day event starts during the weekend closest to Canada's *Thanksgiving,* in early October. Information: *Kitchener-Waterloo Oktoberfest, Inc.,* 17 Benton St., PO Box 1053, Kitchener, ONT N2G 4G1 (phone: 519-570-4267).

SHAW FESTIVAL, Niagara-on-the-Lake, Ontario With some help from an energetic citizenry, George Bernard Shaw has done for Niagara-on-the-Lake what Shakespeare did for Stratford. Every year, from May through mid-November, three separate theaters—the *Royal George,* the *Festival,* and the *Court House*—are given over to productions of 10 plays by the celebrated playwright (author of *Pygmalion, Major Barbara,* and *Arms and the Man,* among others) and his contemporaries. Anything written in Shaw's lifetime (1856–1950) may be performed. What began as a small community of devoted actors has become one of the most successful professional theaters in North America. Information: *Shaw Festival,* PO Box 774, Niagara-on-the-Lake, ONT L0S 1J0 (phone: 905-468-2172).

NIAGARA GRAPE AND WINE FESTIVAL, St. Catharines, Ontario Here in the heart of Ontario wine country, the last 10 days of September are dedicated to celebrating the grape harvest. Over 200 events include a charity pancake breakfast, the crowning of the Grape King, a *Pied Piper Parade,* arts and crafts shows, concerts, a royal ball, an amateur wine making contest, and a teddy bear's picnic (where members of the Victorian Order of Nurses patch up damaged teddy bears). Topping it all off is one of the largest parades in North America. Information: *Niagara Grape and Wine Festival,* 145 King St. (Carlisle St. entrance), St. Catharines, ONT L2R 3J2 (phone: 905-688-0212).

STRATFORD FESTIVAL, Stratford, Ontario The festival has put this pleasant little city on the international map. Traditionally known for its star-studded presentations of Shakespeare, the festival has been expanded in recent years to include other classics (Lewis Carroll's *Alice Through the Looking Glass,* for example) and musicals such as Gilbert and Sullivan's *Pirates of Penzance.* The program runs May through November at three playhouses, all within walking distance of the town center. The *Festival Theatre* is in a beautiful park overlooking the Avon River. None of the 2,262 seats is more than 66 feet from the thrust stage. (The famous *Chichester Festival Theatre* in England is a copy of its Canadian cousin.) Backstage tours are available, as are picnic baskets to take into the park (June through September, except Mondays; reservations required). Nearby is the smaller *Tom Patterson Theatre* (also with a thrust stage), named after the journalist who helped found the festival in the early 1950s. The *Avon Theatre,* in central Stratford, has a traditional proscenium arch stage and impressive decor. There are two-for-one ticket days at the *Avon* and reduced rates for students and seniors. An infrared transmitting system is available for the hearing impaired at all theaters. The box office offers one-stop shopping for shows and accommodations. Information: *Stratford Festival,* PO Box 520, Stratford, ONT N5A 6V2 (phone: 519-273-1600; 800-567-1600; fax: 519-273-6173).

CHARLOTTETOWN FESTIVAL, Charlottetown, Prince Edward Island Devoted primarily to showcasing large-scale musical productions, this festival also presents the long-running *Anne of Green Gables* (also see *Quintessential Canada* in this section), children's entertainment, arts and crafts exhibits, and art classes. The June-through-September program was initiated by the *Confederation Centre of the Arts* in 1964. Information: *Public Relations, Confederation Centre of the Arts,* PO Box 848, Charlottetown, PEI C1A 7L9 (phone: 902-628-1864 or 902-566-1267; fax: 902-566-4648).

LOBSTER CARNIVAL AND LIVESTOCK EXHIBITION, Summerside, Prince Edward Island Every July the population of this town (pop. 13,600) swells eightfold, as former residents come home and tourists throng here to watch daily harness races (the highlight is the *Governor's Plate*), a mammoth parade, a talent contest, daily stage entertainment, and delicious lobster suppers. Information: *PEI Tourism, Visitors Services Division,* PO Box 940, Charlottetown, PEI C1A 7M5 (phone: 902-368-4444; fax: 902-368-5737).

WEST

VERNON WINTER CARNIVAL, Vernon, British Columbia This Okanagan Valley community, 110 miles (176 km) from the international border near Penticton, hosts one of Canada's most action-packed events annually in February—10 days of old-fashioned skating parties for kids, wine tastings, performances by the *Vernon Figure Skating Club,* and competitions in snow sculpture, long-distance running, and racquetball. Evenings bring all sorts of theme dances—from Graffiti Night to Western Night. A popular event is hot-air ballooning, with two days of flying competitions. Some 130 events are staged, but despite the scope, there's a friendliness and a homespun feeling here that you won't find at similar events in larger cities. While here, skiers might want to check out the slopes at lovely Silver Star Mountain, which also offers fine dining and on-hill accommodations for 600 (phone: 604-542-0224; also see *Downhill Skiing*). Information: *Vernon Winter Carnival,* 3401 35th Ave., Vernon, BC V1T 2T5 (phone: 604-545-2236), or the *Vernon Tourist Information Centre,* PO Box 520, Vernon, BC V1T 6M4 (phone: 604-542-1415).

NATIONAL UKRAINIAN FESTIVAL, Dauphin, Manitoba Cabbage rolls and pierogi, painted *Easter* eggs and intricate hand-carvings: The culinary and artistic traditions brought by this group of immigrants is extraordinarily rich, as is evident at this four-day event that takes place the first weekend in August. This region of Canada has a large Ukrainian population that has been celebrating its cultural heritage with an annual festival since 1966. The events include music, dance, workshops, Ukrainian foods, displays, four grandstand shows, and a colorful parade. Information: *National Ukrainian Festival,* 119 Main St. S., Dauphin, MAN R7N 1K4 (phone: 204-638-5645), or *Dauphin Chamber of Commerce,* 105 Main St. N., Dauphin, MAN R7N 1C1 (phone: 204-638-4838).

NORTHERN MANITOBA TRAPPERS' FESTIVAL, The Pas, Manitoba One of the oldest festivals in western Canada—originated in 1916—this is a celebration of the heritage and traditions of the northern pioneer. The five-day event, which takes place the second week of February, includes the *World Championship Dog Race,* a 105-mile, three-day-long dogsled race that carries over $30,000 in prize money. Events in the King Trapper category include contests in bannock baking, flour packing, log climbing, moose calling, and a marathon snowshoe race. Other goings-on include craft shows, beerfests, ice fishing, and more. Information: *Trappers' Festival, Inc.,* PO

Box 3327, The Pas, MAN 1R9 0N2 (phone: 204-623-2912), or *Travel Manitoba,* 155 Carlton St., Seventh Floor, Winnipeg, MAN R3C 3H8 (phone: 800-665-0040).

FESTIVAL DU VOYAGEUR, St. Boniface, Manitoba Every year during the third week in February, this district of Winnipeg stages 10 days of parades, concerts of French Canadian music, and all manner of contests (in snow sculpture, jigging, fiddling, hockey, and dogsled racing) in an effort to beat the midwinter blahs. And it seems to work. Information: *Festival du Voyageur,* 768 Taché Ave., St. Boniface, MAN R2H 2C4 (phone: 204-237-7692).

National Parks

A visit to a Canadian national park offers visitors a glimpse into a world of natural beauty that exists scarcely anywhere else on earth: From the rainy coast of the Pacific Rim, with its dense vegetation, to the imposing Canadian Rockies, from rolling prairies to storm-pounded Atlantic shores, the Canadian park system preserves the precious and sometimes fragile ecology of some of the nation's most distinctive regions. Its 70,000 square miles are a vast playground for nature lovers and a rich example of Canada's diverse natural and cultural heritage.

But the system also is designed to please anglers, boaters, golfers, hikers, skiers, campers, swimmers, and photographers. All but the most remote have campgrounds, hiking trails, scenic driving routes, and lively interpretive programs that everyone can enjoy. Details are available from *Department of Canadian Heritage* offices in many cities, or from the individual park offices. A checklist of all the best parks follows. For more detailed information about each region, consult the appropriate section in DIRECTIONS. Entries are arranged geographically, starting with the eastern provinces and then the western ones; within that framework, entries are arranged alphabetically by province and, within each province, by name of park.

EAST

FUNDY NATIONAL PARK, near Alma, New Brunswick Some of the world's highest tides rise here and, in retreating, leave behind vast tidal flats full of periwinkles, limpets, and other sea creatures that make a stroll in the area a delight. Elsewhere in the park, the surf pounds the cave-pocked, 200-foot cliffs, and the rolling inland terrain is cut by deep valleys whose steep rocky walls are ribboned with waterfalls. Visitors can see it all, thanks to some 80 miles of hiking trails, which range from a 30-minute loop trail to a four-day backpacking adventure. Write ahead for tide schedules to help plan your visit. Park facilities are closed mid-October to late May; admission charge. Information: *Fundy National Park,* PO Box 40, Alma, NB E0A 1B0 (phone: 506-887-6000).

KOUCHIBOUGUAC NATIONAL PARK, Kent County, New Brunswick The name means "River of the Long Tides," and the water—often the warmest north of the Carolinas—is shallow and gentle. There also are a multitude of environments: rivers, beaches, bogs, salt marshes, lagoons, fields, forests, and sand dunes. The area, which hosts a profusion of migrating waterfowl in spring and fall, also is home to trout, flounder, and striped bass (anglers need a park fishing license). The reception center screens an award-winning slide presentation about the park. Most park facilities are closed November through April, though trails are open year-round; admission charge. Information: *Kouchibouguac National Park,* Kouchibouguac, Kent County, NB E0A 2A0 (phone: 506-876-2443).

GROS MORNE NATIONAL PARK, near Rocky Harbour, Newfoundland This park, variously described as "North America's least-known national park" and "a *Yosemite Park* with fjords," represents major stages of the earth's evolutionary history. Situated on the province's west coast at the base of the Great Northern Peninsula, this 700-square-mile preserve dominated by the 2,644-foot Gros Morne Mountain is home to some of the nation's most spectacular scenery. There are fjord-like ponds, barren expanses of volcanic rock, heavily wooded forests and alpine meadows, bogs and beaches, tide pools and surf-washed headlands, and waterfalls cascading from such heights that the stream turns to spray before it hits bottom. The flora and fauna are equally diverse, and the fishing is good. Several miles of hiking trails offer the chance to see it all. Note that there are no electrical hookups in the park. The park is open year-round; admission charge. Information: *Gros Morne National Park,* PO Box 130, Rocky Harbour, NFLD A0K 4N0 (phone: 709-458-2066, 709-458-2060, or 709-458-2417; fax: 709-458-2059).

TERRA NOVA NATIONAL PARK, near Glovertown, Newfoundland Canada's easternmost national park, this 153-square-mile expanse of ponds, peat lands, spruce, and fir rolls west from the rugged, rocky coastline adjoining Bonavista Bay and the Labrador Sea. It's punctuated by natural arches, notched by inlets, and fronted by steep cliffs, from which visitors often spot bluish-white icebergs, carried south by the Labrador Current in spring and early summer, or spy some of *Terra Nova*'s inhabitants, such as moose, lynx, and bald eagles. Besides the usual outdoor pursuits—bird watching, hiking, camping, swimming, sailing, snorkeling, scuba diving, cross-country skiing, snowshoeing, golfing, fishing, and canoeing—*Terra Nova* offers free winter camping at Newman Sound, with heated washrooms and showers, and an enclosed kitchen. The park is open year-round; admission charge. Information: *Terra Nova National Park,* Glovertown, NFLD A0G 2L0 (phone: 709-533-2801; fax: 709-533-2706).

CAPE BRETON HIGHLANDS NATIONAL PARK, near Ingonish Beach, Nova Scotia One of the most scenic of Canada's national parks, it occupies a stretch of tundra-, bog-, and forest-covered highlands between the Gulf of St. Lawrence and the Atlantic Ocean. The 180-mile-long Cabot Trail winds along a famous stretch of coastline, where the mountains meet the sea in awe-inspiring cliffs dotted by bizarrely twisted spruce trees. Equally lovely sights greet those who wander down the park's hiking trails. The park is open year-round; admission charge late June through mid-September. Information: *Cape Breton Highlands National Park,* Ingonish Beach, NS B0C 1L0 (phone: 902-285-2691 or 902-285-2270; fax: 902-285-2866).

KEJIMKUJIK NATIONAL PARK, near Maitland Bridge, Nova Scotia These rolling, forested 147 square miles are a paradise for backcountry campers and canoeists, thanks to a good system of canoe routes and hiking trails. A variety of activities is available year-round. The hospitable climate and abundance of wetlands make survival possible here for many species not found elsewhere in Atlantic Canada. Park naturalists give lectures and, in summer, lead guided tours both on foot and by boat. Canoe rentals are available. Admission charge. Information: *Kejimkujik National Park,* PO Box 36, Maitland Bridge, Annapolis County, NS B0T 1N0 (phone: 902-682-2772).

GEORGIAN BAY ISLANDS NATIONAL PARK, near Honey Harbour, Ontario Lake Huron's immense Georgian Bay, sparkling clear and island-dotted, is about two hours north of Toronto. Fifty-nine islands in the southeastern part of the bay belong to this preserve, a favorite of swimmers, anglers, boaters, hikers, and campers. If you don't have your own boat, hire a water taxi or join a tour boat in nearby mainland towns. Open year-round. Information: *Georgian Bay Islands National Park,* PO Box 28, Honey Harbour, ONT P0E 1E0 (phone: 705-756-2415).

POINT PELEE NATIONAL PARK, near Leamington, Ontario The most southern point on Canada's mainland is a huge sand spit jutting into Lake Erie, which is internationally known for its concentrations of migrating birds in spring and autumn and stunning monarch butterfly migration each fall. There are miles of sandy beaches, an interpretive center, a mile-long boardwalk through the marshlands, an observation tower, and bike and canoe rentals. Open year-round. Information: *Point Pelee National Park,* RR1, Leamington, ONT N8H 3V4 (phone: 519-322-2365).

PUKASKWA NATIONAL PARK, near Marathon, Ontario Located 15 miles (24 km) east of Marathon, Ontario, and accessible by Route 627, Pukaskwa encompasses a boreal wilderness of 725 square miles on the rocky landscape of the Canadian Shield. The main reception area at Hattie Cove offers 67 semiserviced campgrounds (with showers), a visitors' center with audiovisual presentations, and walking trails on the nearby headlands and beaches of Lake Superior. The 40-mile coastal hiking trail provides opportunities for day and overnight hikes. The bays, harbors, and coves of the park coastline afford limited protection to sea kayakers, canoeists, and boaters. In winter, the park has a 4-mile (6-km) cross-country ski trail suitable for novices. Open year-round. Information: *Pukaskwa National Park,* Rte. 627, Hattie Cove, Heron Bay, ONT P0T IR0 (phone: 807-229-0801).

ST. LAWRENCE ISLANDS NATIONAL PARK, between Brockville and Kingston, Ontario Canada's smallest national park is scattered over 21 of the famous Thousand Islands in the region between Brockville and Kingston, Ontario. Major activities include boating, hiking, camping, fishing, and just plain old relaxing. Wide-ranging facilities include individual and group campsites, beaches, and interpretive trails. The mainland base at Mallorytown Landing has parking, campsites, a playground, and general day-use facilities. The mainland base is located on the St. Lawrence Bikeway, a 22-mile paved bicycle trail that parallels the St. Lawrence River. Access to the islands is by private boat, boat rental, or water taxi, and facilities are available at most of the many local marinas along the river. Open year-round. Information: *St. Lawrence Islands National Park,* PO Box 469, RR3, Mallorytown, ONT K0E 1R0 (phone: 613-923-5261).

PRINCE EDWARD ISLAND NATIONAL PARK, near Charlottetown, Prince Edward Island A prime example of the kind of sandy Atlantic shoreline that Americans prize on Cape Cod, this stretch of northern PEI is all scalloped bays and inlets, sand dunes, sandy beaches, and salt marshes. More than 200 species of birds have been recorded along the park's 25 miles of coast. There also are seven supervised beaches, three campgrounds, lots of recreational activities, a few fine hotels, and the farmhouse immortalized in Lucy Maud Montgomery's *Anne of Green Gables.* The park is open year-round, though most facilities are closed *Labour Day* to mid-June. Information: *Prince Edward Island National Park,* PO Box 487, Charlottetown, PEI C1A 7L1 (phone: 902-672-6350).

FORILLON NATIONAL PARK, Gaspé Peninsula, Quebec The foghorns moan, and the gulls wheel and cry as Quebec meets the sea at this splendid preserve set on a needle-headed, 92-square-mile triangle of land poking roughly southeastward into the Atlantic. In the easternmost section, 600-foot-high limestone cliffs slice into the sea. The wildlife here is abundant and varied: some 200 species of birds live in the park, and thousands of sea birds visit annually in summer. Whales can usually be spotted off the coast from mid-May to around October, and grey and harbor seals are year-round residents. Inland are forests, peat bogs, dunes, lakes, and dozens of streams. Camping, hiking, biking, scuba diving, and sightseeing cruises keep summer visitors busy, and snowshoeing, winter camping, and cross-country skiing are winter diversions. An interpretation center and interpretive program help visitors discover the park's treasures and beauties. Open year-round. Information: *Forillon National Park,* PO Box 1220, Gaspé, QUE G0C 1R0 (phone: 418-368-5505).

LA MAURICIE NATIONAL PARK, near Shawinigan, Quebec The scenic St. Maurice River flows along the eastern border of this 210-square-mile expanse of glacier-scoured, forest-covered wilderness, and the interconnected lakes and streams that form the river's watershed make for some very good canoeing. Thirteen-mile-long Lake Wapizagonke, contained between two high rocky escarpments, is one of the park's most beautiful spots. Hiking, camping, canoeing, fishing, and cross-country skiing are popular. Two winter shelters provide 44 beds for cross-country skiers. It's open year-round; admission charge. Information: *La Mauricie National Park,* PO Box 758, 146 Blvd. Gaspé, Shawinigan, QUE G9N 6V9 (phone: 819-536-2638 or 819-537-4555).

WEST

BANFF NATIONAL PARK, Banff, Alberta Established in 1885 on the site of hot sulfur springs, this is the country's oldest national park, taking in 2,500 square miles of Canada's most spectacular mountains, alpine meadows, glaciers, forested slopes, rivers, and lakes. The park's network of hiking trails is well developed; visitors can canoe, horseback ride, ski, fish, boat, sail, scuba dive, river raft, bicycle, skate, and climb. The park is open year-round, though some facilities close in winter. Admission charge varies, depending on your length of stay. Information: *Banff National Park,* Box 900, Banff, AB T0L 0C0 (phone: 403-762-1500).

ELK ISLAND NATIONAL PARK, near Edmonton, Alberta In the early 1900s, when the elk in the Beaver Hills were in danger of extinction, a few conservationists banded together to lobby for the government to establish a fenced-in preserve to save the animals from hunters. Now, some 1,500 elk, as well as 500 plains bison and 300 rare wood bison, 350 moose, and 3,000 beavers, make the park their home. Not surprisingly, wildlife viewing is a popular pursuit here, along with picnicking, hiking, and, in winter, snowshoeing and cross-country skiing. The park is open year-round, though some facilities close in winter. Admission charge mid-May through early September. Information: *Elk Island National Park, Visitor Services,* Site 4, RR1, Fort Saskatchewan, AB T8L 2N7 (phone: 403-992-2950).

JASPER NATIONAL PARK, Jasper, Alberta Named for Jasper Hawes, a fur trader of the early 1800s, these 4,200 square miles of lofty peaks and alpine valleys, clear lakes and thundering falls are a backpacker's paradise, thanks to an extensive trail system. This is Canada's largest national park, home to mountain goats, bighorn sheep, moose, elk, and bear. All-weather parkways provide access to such scenic highlights as Maligne Lake, Athabasca Falls, and the renowned Columbia Icefield area. The park is open year-round, though some facilities close in winter. Admission charge varies. Information: *Jasper National Park,* Box 10, Jasper, AB T0E 1E0 (phone: 403-852-6161).

WATERTON LAKES NATIONAL PARK, near Cardston, Alberta It's been said that a maximum of scenery is crammed into a minimum of space in this Canadian section of the *Waterton-Glacier International Peace Park.* For while the park's area is only 204 square miles, its scenery varies greatly as a result of its location in a transitional zone between the prairie and the peaks. There's good hiking on 108 miles of prairie and mountain trails, plus riding, biking, fishing, tennis, golf, swimming, and boating (rentals are available at Cameron Lake). *Waterton* has three campgrounds. In addition, interpretation programs are offered at the *Townsite* and *Crandell* campgrounds. The park is open year-round, though some facilities close from mid-October to mid-May. Admission charge from mid-May through mid-October. Information: *Waterton Lakes National Park,* AB T0K 2M0 (phone: 403-859-2224; fax: 403-859-2650).

GLACIER NATIONAL PARK, near Rogers Pass, British Columbia A trip to this 521-square-mile preserve in the rugged Selkirk and Purcell Ranges is a fascinating geography lesson that teaches visitors that glaciers are dynamic, ever-moving forces, able to slice off whole sections of mountains and carve out their peaks, dig valleys, and polish rock faces as smooth as glass. Evidence of eons of this slicing, carving, and polishing is what makes this park so special. There are wonderful wildflowers as well. Visit the information center at Rogers Pass. The park is open year-round. Information: *Glacier National Park,* PO Box 350, Revelstoke, BC V0E 2S0 (phone: 604-837-7500 or 604-837-6274).

KOOTENAY NATIONAL PARK, Radium Hot Springs, British Columbia The Banff-Windermere Highway, the focal point of this long, skinny preserve, makes its beauties remarkably accessible. Right in front of you are towering peaks by the score, the 128-foot depths of Marble Canyon, rusty-colored paint pots whose iron-rich mud the Native Americans used as body paint, and all manner of wildlife. In May and October, as many as 300 elk may congregate along the road at any given time. There's also a complex of swimming and soaking pools. The park is open year-round; picnic areas, campgrounds, pools, and some trails are wheelchair accessible. Information: *Kootenay National Park,* Box 220, Radium Hot Springs, BC V0A 1M0 (phone: 604-347-9615).

MT. REVELSTOKE NATIONAL PARK, near Revelstoke, British Columbia The views in this 99-square-mile park—particularly from the lookout atop Mt. Revelstoke itself—are astounding; the mountains surrounding the area are exceptionally rugged; and the forests are unusually dense. Alpine meadows bloom bright in late summer and can be seen from the park's hiking trails, which cover over 39 miles. The park is open year-round. Information: *Mt. Revelstoke National Park,* PO Box 350, Revelstoke, BC V0E 2S0 (phone: 604-837-7500).

PACIFIC RIM NATIONAL PARK, near Ucluelet, Vancouver Island, British Columbia This is a wet world. Heavy rains and salt spray produce dense vegetation on the mountains rising abruptly from the sea on the western edge of this 150-square-mile park. Tidal pools trap clusters of hermit crabs, starfish, limpets, and mussels. But not far inland, the peaks are often snow-capped.

Chopped out of the storm-pounded sea cliffs, the West Coast Trail is one of the nation's great hiking adventures, and 6-mile (10-km) Long Beach is among its finest strands. Offshore, visitors can fish, canoe, and camp—in utter solitude—at the Broken Group Islands. The park is open year-round, though some facilities close in the winter. Reservations required for camping. Admission charge. Information: *Pacific Rim National Park,* PO Box 280, Ucluelet, BC V0R 3A0 (phone: 604-726-7721).

YOHO NATIONAL PARK, Field, British Columbia Named by the Cree tribe (*yoho* is an expression meaning "inspiring awe"), this 507-square-mile preserve near the top of the Rockies takes in about 25 peaks over 10,000 feet, countless cascading streams and spectacular falls, and lush forests. The 250-odd miles of trails take hikers through areas inhabited by the park's abundant wildlife. Or visitors can view the park's glories from their cars as they drive along the Trans-Canada Highway. The park is open year-round. Information: *Superintendent, Yoho National Park,* PO Box 99, Field, BC V0A 1G0 (phone: 604-343-6324).

RIDING MOUNTAIN NATIONAL PARK, near Dauphin, Manitoba Riding Mountain is part of a huge 2,000-foot-high plateau. Covered with the kind of thick forest more commonly found in the east, as well as the evergreens and grasslands that are typical of the surrounding prairies, the park's 1,150 square miles are laced with hiking and cross-country ski trails, and a spectrum of wildlife can be spotted. Many visitors come to battle the feisty, voracious northern pike, which is the main game fish, but pickerel, trout, perch, and whitefish can be landed as well. The park is closed mid-October to late May. Information: *Riding Mountain National Park,* Wasagaming, MAN R0J 2H0 (phone: 204-848-2811).

AUYUITTUQ NATIONAL PARK, Baffin Island, Northwest Territories This national park was included in the parcel of land that the Canadian government allocated to the Inuit people in 1991; when "Nunavut," as the area is known, becomes a territory in 1999, the park will no longer be part of the Northwest Territories. The name "Auyuittuq" means "The Land That Does Not Melt," and its 8,290 square miles are dominated by the spiky, 7,000-foot-high Penny Ice Cap, which covers a 2,200-square-mile area. Plants have a tenuous hold on existence in such terrain, but the bright blossoms that dot the meadows in June and July, when the May-through-July midnight sun has worked its magic, are among the park's real beauties. Though there are 40 species of birds, and other wildlife abounds, rocks and mountains are what people come here to enjoy. The celebrated Pangnirtung Pass trek is a must for experienced hikers. April, May, and early June are perfect for winter activities such as snowmobiling and cross-country skiing; in July and August, there's excellent fishing for the prized arctic char in the tidewater of Cumberland Sound. The park is open year-round; no admission charge.

Information: *Superintendent, Auyuittuq National Park,* PO Box 353, Pangnirtung, NWT X0A 0R0 (phone: 819-473-8829; fax: 819-473-8612).

NAHANNI NATIONAL PARK, near Fort Simpson, Northwest Territories The first area to be named to UNESCO's World Heritage List of natural sites, this 1,840-square-mile wilderness surrounding the South Nahanni River is spectacularly beautiful. Unusual plants, high mountains, and incredible canyons are as dazzling as Virginia Falls—an immense cataract that plunges about 300 feet to the river, revealing a four-acre face of whiteness in the process. Access is by chartered aircraft from Fort Simpson, Fort Liard, Fort Nelson, or Watson Lake; very experienced canoeists and rafters can run the river and its tributaries on their own, whereas others can join group expeditions. Visitors also can explore the mountains and valleys on foot. Since this area is very remote, book ahead if you plan to use the services of an outfitter. The park is open year-round; no admission charge. Information: *Nahanni National Park,* Bag 300, Fort Simpson, NWT X0E 0N0 (phone: 403-695-3151).

WOOD BUFFALO NATIONAL PARK, near Fort Smith, Northwest Territories Straddling the Alberta border, this is one of the world's largest national parks, with some 17,300 square miles of wilderness preserve that is home to the largest extant herds of free-roaming bison in the world. It also is the only natural nesting ground of the whooping crane. A UNESCO World Heritage Site, it contains most of the spectacular Peace-Athabasca Delta, one of the planet's biggest freshwater deltas, a habitat for millions of waterfowl. Salt flats with beautiful and unusual vegetation extend throughout the northeastern part of the park. Regularly scheduled flights land at Fort Smith, Northwest Territories, and Fort Chipewyan, Alberta; from those two spots, access is by car or boat. The park is open year-round; no admission charge. Information: *Wood Buffalo National Park,* PO Box 750, Fort Smith, NWT X0E 0P0 (phone: 403-872-2349 or 403-872-2878).

PRINCE ALBERT NATIONAL PARK, near Prince Albert, Saskatchewan Wildlife—moose, deer, elk, caribou, black bears, bison, and beavers—is abundant here, and over 200 species of birds have been recorded (one of Canada's largest white pelican colonies is located at Lavallee Lake, in the park's secluded northwest corner). Thirty miles (48 km) north of Prince Albert (the *Waskesiu Lake Visitor Services Center* is 30 miles/48 km farther north) this nearly-million-acre wilderness park is near the geographical center of the province. Here, a rolling glacial terrain dotted with spruce bogs, large, cold lakes, and aspen uplands is preserved. Interpretive programs explain the fascinating ecosystems seen by hikers and canoeists. The park is open year-round. Information: *Prince Albert National Park,* PO Box 100, Waskesiu Lake, SASK S0J 2Y0 (phone: 306-663-5322; fax: 306-663-5424).

KLUANE NATIONAL PARK RESERVE, near Haines Junction, Yukon Territory A good deal of this park's 8,500 square miles is given over to glaciers and mountains, including 19,520-foot Mt. Logan, Canada's highest peak. The world's largest ice fields outside the polar regions are here. Consequently, *Kluane* is a mountaineer's dream—even though climbing in the Icefield Range always means an expedition. But the park's eastern section is unglaciated, and, by using the old mining roads and some newer trails, visitors can get a feel for a less forbidding *Kluane,* a preserve that boasts an amazing variety of flora, fauna, and terrain. The park is open year-round; no admission charge. Information: *Kluane National Park,* Haines Junction, YT Y0B 1L0 (phone: 403-634-2251).

IF YOU'RE NEARBY

If time and distance are on your side, the following sites are well worth including in your Canadian itinerary. Entries are arranged alphabetically by province and, within province, by name of site.

FORT PRINCE OF WALES, Churchill, Manitoba Accessible only by boat, this smallish ruin is the site of the first Hudson's Bay Company fortified fur trading post at the estuary of the Churchill River. Constructed between 1739 and 1771, the post fell in the next year to three French ships that easily overpowered the undermanned fort. Restored in the mid-1930s, the small structure still conveys the isolation and horrendous conditions that the early armed traders accepted (by winter's end, visitors are told, the walls of the living quarters were lined with sheets of ice, reducing the rooms to frozen closets). Because of the isolation of Churchill itself, the fort is not heavily visited, and old musket balls can still be found coming out of the ground in spring. Visitors should be prepared for the cold, mosquitoes, and the possibility of polar bear attacks (park guides carry weapons just in case). It's open year-round; no admission charge. Information: *Sea North Tours,* Box 222, Churchill, MAN R0B 0E0 (phone: 204-675-2195; fax: 204-675-2198).

FORTRESS LOUISBOURG NATIONAL HISTORICAL SITE, Louisbourg, Nova Scotia A few miles outside of Louisbourg on the Atlantic Coast is a reconstruction of the greatest French fort and trading post on the Atlantic in the mid-18th century; the site covers 55 acres, with most of the reconstructed buildings clustered together. It was built on Cape Breton Island, called Ile Royale by the French, between 1720 and 1745. French policy encouraged Native Americans to raid fishing parties from the English colonies, and as a result New England colonists attacked the fort in 1745. France recovered Louisbourg by treaty, but British troops got it back in 1758, gutting the fortifications. The loss of the fort, together with the capture of Quebec City in 1759, ended New France, and Britain became dominant east of the Mississippi and north to the Arctic. In 1961 reconstruction began here on what became the largest restoration project of its kind in Canada. Today, Louisbourg is a functioning 18th-century town of French culture, where, with obvious theatricality, guards ask visitors if they are English spies, the inn serves French food, and "local residents" dress and act as if New France were still in business. Everything here has been re-created as authentically as possible—there are houses, a bakery, an inn, and military quarters, ranging from the elegant governor's apartment to the spartan soldiers' barracks. The imposing château, a 365-foot-long building with walls two feet thick, is topped by a 250-pound wrought-iron fleur-de-lis. The object was made in the fortress's present forge from early French designs. Inside the walls, four periods of furniture—Louis XIII, Louis XIV, Regency, and Louis XV—are displayed in the governor's sumptuous apartments. It's engaging, provided you like participation. Closed October through May; outside walking tours are offered in May and October. Admission charge. Information: *Fortress Louisbourg National Historic Site,* PO Box 160, Louisbourg, NS B0A 1M0 (phone: 902-733-2280).

GRAND PRÉ NATIONAL HISTORIC SITE, Grand Pré, Nova Scotia Between 1755 and 1763, nearly 14,000 Acadians were expelled from this region by the British, who feared that the peaceful Acadians would challenge their military authority. On September 5, 1755, Lieutenant Colonel John Winslow announced their deportation from the steps of the original *Grand Pré Acadian Church,* an expulsion that was memorialized in Longfellow's poem "Evangeline." Built in the 1920s on what is believed to be the original Acadian church site, the *St. Charles Church,* with its statue of Evangeline out front, is a memorial to the exiled Acadians, many of whom resettled in New Orleans. Nearby, a museum commemorates what the Acadians had and lost. Although the park is open year-round, its buildings are closed to the public from mid-October to mid-May; admission charge. Information: *Grand Pré National Historic Site,* Grand Pré, NS B0P 1M0 (phone: 902-542-3631).

BATOCHE NATIONAL HISTORIC PARK, Rosthern, Saskatchewan In the course of the long years of trade between the Native Americans and the French voyageurs, a culture of people of mixed white and Native American ancestry, called the Métis, developed. These people settled in Manitoba and in an area of Saskatchewan northeast of what is now Saskatoon in the late 1800s. In 1885, Louis Riel, a charismatic French-speaking Métis leader with religious visions who opposed Manitoba's entry into the Confederation of Canada, seized a parish church in Batoche, formed a provisional government, and defied the North West Mounted Police in a shoot-out. The Mounties won. Though of questionable sanity, Riel was hanged for treason, an act that effectively squelched any future danger of Métis rebellions. The ruins of the rebellion sites—located about 7 miles (11 km) north of Route 312 on Route 225 along the South Saskatchewan River—have been memorialized. The site is closed from mid-October to mid-May; admission charge to audiovisual presentation only. Information: *Batoche National Historic Park,* PO Box 999, Rosthern, SASK S0K 3R0 (phone: 306-423-6227/8; fax: 306-423-5400).

Special Havens

Since standardization has begun to overtake the Canadian hotel industry, finding acceptable accommodations is usually not a problem. But where are the hostelries with unique atmosphere, distinctive personality, style, and histories all their own? Not to worry: They're still around, though scattered, from the Maritimes to the Pacific Coast, and sometimes hard to find. A few resorts in this class are well advertised, but locating one with the facilities and activities that suit you can be a taxing chore.

The havens described here—our favorites—are places you'll want to visit when the locale is as important as the activities feasible there. Among them are both resorts and inns. Most resorts feature stables, championship golf courses, biking and hiking paths, pools, beaches, and often nightclubs and similar after-dark diversions. The inns, usually tucked away in some beautiful part of the country for which the innkeeper has a special affinity, are quieter and smaller. In either case, accommodations will cost more than at a less interesting establishment. If money is a consideration, ask about off-season rates, normally offered in spring or fall; summers are always busy, and many properties fill to the rafters with skiers just after the first snowfall. Some hostelries also offer lower rates during the week. It's also wise to inquire whether activities will cost extra at resorts, and don't forget to budget for tips. Entries are arranged geographically, starting with the eastern provinces and then the western ones; within that framework, entries are arranged alphabetically by province and, within province, by name of town or general location.

EAST

MARATHON INN, Grand Manan Island, New Brunswick The bird life that Audubon admired when he visited here in the early part of the 19th century is as rich as ever. In summer, some 300 species feed on the wild strawberries, blueberries, and blackberries that blanket the island—the largest of the trio of Bay of Fundy isles. You'll certainly want to watch the birds, but you'll also want to gather the berries to eat with cream at the inn, admire the lupine and other wildflowers that dot the meadows, and join one of the whale watching tours conducted from August to mid-September. Other activities include playing tennis, swimming, beachcombing, hiking, and bicycling. The hotel itself was built in 1871 atop a hill, so there's almost always a breeze. It's a delight, from the wide hallways leading to the 28 gleaming, lofty-ceilinged guestrooms to the widow's walk that tops the three-story structure. All but six of the rooms overlook the harbor, and most rooms share a bath. The experience is well worth the extra effort it takes to get to the island, which is accessible only by ferry from Black's Harbour, east of Calais, Maine, on the Canadian side of the border. Open year-round. Information:

Marathon Inn, North Head, Grand Manan Island, NB E0G 2M0 (phone: 506-662-8144).

MARSHLANDS INN, Sackville, New Brunswick Built around 1850, the house has been a hostelry for nearly six decades. Before you're packed off to bed at night, innkeepers John and Mary Blakely will ply you with hot chocolate and gingersnaps. In the morning, you're stuffed like a Périgord goose with goodies like baked apples, porridge, country sausage patties, and buckwheat pancakes. For lunch and dinner, choices include such dishes as steak-and-kidney pie, boiled salt cod and pork scraps, and fiddleheads (the top portion of the ostrich fern, a New Brunswick specialty). The Blakelys grow many of the foods that are served in the dining room, which is set in the large gardens behind the inn. The 20 rooms vary; one of the nicer ones has a high four-poster and Oriental rugs. The Tantramar marshes, the summering site for thousands of Canada geese whose honks fill the air during spring and fall migrations, are on the nearby isthmus connecting New Brunswick and Nova Scotia. No wonder Queen Elizabeth took tea here when she toured New Brunswick. Open February through November. Information: *Marshlands Inn,* 59 Bridge St., PO Box 1440, Sackville, NB E0A 3C0 (phone: 506-536-0170).

ALGONQUIN, St. Andrews-by-the-Sea, New Brunswick One of the loveliest of the Canadian Pacific hotels, this restored, rambling, 200-room English country manor of a hostelry, ringed by immaculately manicured lawns and well-tended flower gardens, sits on the edge of Passamaquoddy Bay on a hill overlooking the town, a short walk from the main street. Golfers make pilgrimages to the *Algonquin*'s nine- and 18-hole courses (see *Golf in Canada: A Land of Links* in this section). Guests can swim in Katy's Cove or in the hotel's heated outdoor pool, play tennis or croquet, or go cycling. After such physical exertion, there are several restaurants and evening entertainments from which to choose. Another way to relax is to visit the town for some of Canada's most interesting shopping or for a walking tour of the many late-18th- and early-19th-century houses built by the Loyalists who first settled the area. Open from late May to early October. Reservations are a must in the summer. Information: *Algonquin Hotel,* St. Andrews, NB E0G 2X0 (phone: 506-529-8823; 800-268-9411 in Canada; 800-828-7447 in the US).

ROSSMOUNT INN, St. Andrews, New Brunswick Victorian England must have been a lovely place, or so you would judge from the antiques and portraits of British royalty at this more-than-century-old inn, nestled in the woods at the foot of Chamcook Mountain. There's even a dartboard in the taproom. The 16 bedrooms, all with private baths, are comfortable but plainer than the public rooms. The dining room menu features fresh fish, fruits and berries from the inn's gardens, and bread and desserts baked with whole grains, raw sugar, and honey. (Vegetarian meals are offered.) Walking, hiking, and jogging on trails on the private 87-acre wildlife sanctuary, shopping in town, and playing golf on the nearby course are the favored pastimes. There's also a pool. Smoking is confined to certain areas and is not permitted in the dining room. Information: *Rossmount Inn,* RR2, St. Andrews, NB E0G 2X0 (phone: 506-529-3351).

KELTIC LODGE, Cape Breton Island, Nova Scotia The lonely site of this provincial government resort on a rocky peninsula in magnificent *Cape Breton Highlands National Park* assures each room a marvelous view over a landscape of rugged, heavily wooded highlands reminiscent of the Scottish Hebrides. That alone, or the hotel's proximity to the Cabot Trail, the scenic highway that rings the island, would make it worth a visit. But it also is a relaxing place for longer stays. You can swim in the large pool or in a freshwater lake, or soak up the salt air on a mile-long beach not far away. The surrounding woods are full of trails, ideal for peaceful rambles. There's also the epic Stanley Thompson–designed *Highland Links* golf course (see *Golf in Canada: A Land of Links* in this section) and tennis courts. And when you've worked your appetite up to monstrous proportions, you can satisfy it in a big way: The fresh seafood caught by local fishermen and prepared by French chefs can't be beat. The *Purple Thistle Room* offers fine dining with an accent on nouvelle cuisine and seafood, and there's also the more casual *Atlantic* restaurant. Accommodations are offered in the sedate *Main Lodge,* with 32 rooms; the modern 40-room *White Birch Inn;* or in one of the nine well-appointed cottages (two or four bedrooms, plus a sitting room with a fireplace, in each). Baby-sitting is available on request. Open January through March and June through October. Information: *Keltic Lodge,* PO Box 70, Ingonish Beach, NS B0C 1L0 (phone: 902-285-2880; fax: 902-285-2859).

MILFORD HOUSE, South Milford, Nova Scotia Located in the province's lake district, just 15 miles (24 km) from *Kejimkujik National Park,* this 600-acre country resort was founded in the 1860s as a stopping-off place for travelers. The comfortable main lodge, site of the dining room, a library, and a parlor, features polished wood floors and old-fashioned fireplaces. Guests stay in 27 scattered waterside two- to five-bedroom, fireplace-equipped cottages, each with its own dock. Hearty country fare is the specialty of the house. Though you'll find fresh flowers on your table every day, this very informal establishment is a favorite with families. Canoeing, swimming, and fishing have always been popular activities here, but tennis and golf are possible, too. Confirm your reservations by season's opening in mid-June. Open mid-June through mid-September. Information: *Milford House,* South Milford, RR4, Annapolis Royal, NS B0S 1A0 (phone: 902-532-2617).

AROWHON PINES, Algonquin Provincial Park, Ontario A single highway runs east to west through *Algonquin Provincial Park,* a magnificent 3,000-square-mile stretch of wilderness. Midway, at the end of 5 miles of private road, is this peaceful resort, on the shore of a lake. Moose, deer, red foxes, wolves, bears, and over a hundred species of birds call this region home, and wildlife watching is one of the principal attractions. Another is the food—the dining room here is highly acclaimed. Each of the two- to 12-bedroom cabins has a communal lounge with a fireplace; or reserve one of three suites in a private cabin, also with fireplaces. All meals, plus use of tennis courts, canoes, and windsurfers, are included in the rate. Open mid-May to early October. Information: in summer, *Arowhon Pines, Algonquin Provincial Park,* ONT P0A 1B0 (phone: 705-633-5661; fax: 705-633-5795); in winter, 297 Balliol St., Toronto, ONT M4S 1C7 (phone: 416-483-4393; fax: 416-483-4429).

MILLCROFT INN, Alton, Ontario This 1881 stone knitting mill is one of North America's best examples of an old building adapted to a new use. A glass-walled "dining pod" gives guests a heart-stopping view of the churning falls, and the furnishings are a delightful blend of the contemporary and the antique. Lodgings are in 22 mill rooms or 20 modern condo-type lofts that accommodate four. The restored old manor house, a Victorian building that used to be the miller's home, has 10 deluxe rooms with whirlpool baths. The inn bears the Relais & Châteaux group's stamp of approval. The dining room serves food that the owners describe as "Canadian and natural with a European flair"; its specialties include Atlantic salmon with clover honey and saffron glaze, or tandoori spices and a jasmine tea sauce; salad ragout; and tropical champagne sorbet. The hundred-acre property has a heated outdoor pool, a sauna, a whirlpool bath, and tennis courts. Information: *Millcroft Inn,* Alton, ONT L0N 1A0 (phone: 519-941-8111 or 905-791-4422; fax: 519-857-6130).

LANGDON HALL, Cambridge, Ontario Set on 41 acres in the deep woods about 50 miles (80 km) west of Toronto, this red-brick, white-columned manor was built at the turn of the century as a summer home by Eugene Langdon Wilkes, a wealthy gentleman farmer and distant relation of the Astor family. The place still retains the ambience of its origins—the tranquillity, graceful surroundings, and impeccable service all have guests believing they are nobles spending a fortnight at a country estate. The hotel is a member of the Relais & Châteaux group. The 39 guestrooms and two suites are located in the main house and in a newer Georgian-style house called the *Cloisters.* The rooms and suites set in the romantic nooks and crannies of the main house have comfortable armchairs, Oriental rugs, working fireplaces, and large and comfortable beds; the suites have balconies. Chintz-covered sofas and chairs, working fireplaces, and beds so high that you almost need a ladder to reach them are among the comforts in the *Cloisters*' rooms. After afternoon tea, stroll through the lovely grounds. The candlelit, formal, yet friendly, dining room offers excellent French fare. The tasting menu, offered most Fridays and Saturdays and other times on request, features seven or eight dishes. For those who want to inject activity into their newfound life of leisure, there's a fitness center with a workout room, a sauna, and a whirlpool bath; an outdoor heated pool; a billiards room; a cross-country ski trail; a croquet lawn; mountain bikes; and tennis and volleyball courts. Open year-round. Information: *Langdon Hall,* Cambridge, ONT N3H 4R8 (phone: 519-740-2100; fax: 519-740-8161).

BENMILLER INN, Goderich, Ontario Like so many inns, this one was the result of the original owners' love affair with the locale. In this case, a brother and sister from London, Ontario, fell in love with an area on the banks of the Maitland River near Lake Huron, where they used to come as children. They acquired the area's woolen mill and then a flour mill. When both mills had been restored and furnished with antiques, the mill owners' homes were bought, refurbished, and expanded to include 48 rooms on 70 acres of rolling woodlands. There's great fishing in the surrounding stream and on the river in spring and fall, when the salmon run. Guests also can fish for trout in the pond on the premises, swim in an indoor pool, play tennis (there are two outdoor courts), or relax in the whirlpool bath or sauna. Stratford is only 45 miles (72 km) away. Information: *Benmiller Inn,* RR4, Goderich, ONT N7A 3Y1 (phone: 519-524-2191; 800-265-1711; fax: 519-524-5150).

PINESTONE RESORT, Haliburton, Ontario The fact that you never have to travel very far in Canada to get away from the urban rat race is proved once more at this resort, with a total of 124 rooms in the hotel, villas, chalets, and five-bedroom executive house. Although it is modern and almost citified—with tennis courts, indoor and outdoor pools, an 18-hole golf course, a sauna, a whirlpool bath, a sports bar with a large-screen TV set, a lounge with entertainment six nights a week, and formal and informal dining rooms—the atmosphere is decidedly low-key. Flanking either side of the hotel are a pond and a lake (great for swimming, fishing, and boating); surrounding it all are more woods than anyone could possibly explore on foot even in a whole summer. In winter, guests have access to 56 miles of cross-country skiing trails. There's also snowmobiling, sleigh rides, and ice skating. Downhill skiing is within a half-hour drive. Open year-round. Information: *Pinestone Resort,* PO Box 809, Haliburton, ONT K0M 1S0 (phone: 705-457-1800; 800-461-0357 in Canada).

DEERHURST RESORT, Huntsville, Ontario On Peninsula Lake in the heart of the lovely Muskoka tourist region, this CP Hotels resort has been a landmark since the turn of the century. Its superb recreation facilities include two 18-hole golf courses; heated indoor and outdoor pools; eight outdoor and four indoor tennis courts; three squash courts; a racquetball court; fitness rooms; boat rentals; horseback riding; snowmobiling; skating; and 17 miles of track-set cross-country ski trails. In addition to the standard hotel rooms, there are one-, two-, and three-bedroom condo-style suites, many with fireplaces and whirlpool baths. Pampering services include facials and pedicures.

There are numerous dining rooms and regular nightly stage shows year-round. Information: *Deerhurst Resort*, RR4, Huntsville, ONT P0A 1K0 (phone: 705-789-6411; 800-441-1414; fax: 705-789-2431).

INN AT MANITOU, McKellar, Ontario Small and ultraluxurious, this resort with Relais & Châteaux status is located on a semi-wilderness shore of a north central Ontario lake, not far from the beautiful Georgian Bay area. Some 160 miles (256 km) north of Toronto, it offers a perfect spot for active tennis enthusiasts and nature lovers alike. Guests are accommodated in 22 rooms and 11 suites; the suites have wood-burning fireplaces, and some have whirlpools and saunas. The inn offers three-, four-, and seven-day tennis programs, with a staff of 16 pros to instruct guests on the one indoor and 13 outdoor courts (also see *The Best Tennis Vacations* in this section). Facilities include a heated pool, a sauna and spa with aerobics classes, and boats for sailing on the lake. The delicious food is nouvelle cuisine and "spa cuisine" for the health conscious. The inn offers special rates late May to late June and from *Labour Day* to mid-October. Open May through October. Information: *Inn at Manitou,* McKellar Centre Rd., McKellar, ONT P0G 1C0 (phone: 705-389-2171; fax: 705-389-3818); off-season, 251 Davenport Rd., Toronto, ONT M5R 1J9 (phone: 416-967-3466).

SHERWOOD INN, Muskoka, Ontario Nestled amid 12 acres of 19th-century pines on the shore of Lake Joseph, near Port Carling (two hours north of Toronto), this independently-owned year-round resort offers weekend cooking workshops and, not surprisingly, serves first-rate fare. The elegant main lodge has 17 rooms; and 11 rustic cottages with fireplaces are located on the lake shore. A health club has all the standard exercise equipment, as well as a hot tub. Outdoor activities in summer include tennis, badminton, volleyball, croquet, and shuffleboard; in winter, there is cross-country skiing. Information: Sherwood Inn, Port Carling, ONT P0B 1J0 (phone: 705-765-3131; 800-461-4233).

WINDERMERE HOUSE, Muskoka, Ontario This stately 78-room resort, with all the charm of a country inn, has been a fixture on Lake Rosseau since it was built in the 1870s. The verandah of the main house, many of its rooms, and the Settlers Bay units afford fine views of the beach and the water; other rooms overlook charming gardens. The wealth of diversions include fine dining, dancing, and theater and lounge entertainment. The social director organizes games, movie showings, and children's programs. Sports enthusiasts can enjoy tennis, canoeing, windsurfing, and the 18-hole championship golf course. Open mid-May to mid-October. Information: *Windermere House,* Windermere, ONT P0B 1P0 (phone: 705-769-3611; 800-461-4283; fax: 705-769-2168).

SHAW'S, Brackley Beach, Prince Edward Island A onetime farm, it's been run as a hotel by the Shaw family since the mid-19th century. The proximity of Brackley Beach is among its prime attractions, and for good reason: The beach is 5 miles long, pinkish-tawny, hard-packed, dune-backed—and, more to the point, lapped by waters warm enough for swimming. Guests who tire of the sand and sea can golf, play tennis, take in horse races or a play, or fish, swim, and sail nearby. From June through September, the *Charlottetown Festival* is in full swing not far away. Accommodations are in 18 rooms (some with private baths), 11 cottages, and seven chalets, and there's a dining room, but no TV sets or air conditioning in the rooms. Reserve well in advance. Information: *Shaw's Hotel,* Brackley Beach, PEI C0A 2H0 (phone: 902-672-2022).

DALVAY-BY-THE-SEA, Dalvay Beach, Prince Edward Island This small resort hotel, with a pine-paneled, fireplace-warmed, two-story foyer, has a lot to offer in the way of Victorian charm—which will probably come as a surprise. It was designed around a lovely mansion constructed in 1895 by a partner in the Standard Oil Company, so most visitors expect a more formal and elegant interior decor. But it's not a bit stuffy. There are two cottages, though two dozen of the resort's 26 rooms, most paneled in island pine, are in the mansion proper. Those on the second floor are the loveliest, and some have views over Dalvay Beach, 200 yards away on the least-crowded part of *Prince Edward Island National Park,* and Dalvay Lake, which is at the hotel's doorstep. Guests can swim or splash in the Gulf of St. Lawrence, canoe or row on the lake, play tennis on the hotel's two courts, or try lawn bowling on its green. There are no TV sets or air conditioning in the rooms. Open mid-June through September. Information: *Dalvay-by-the-Sea Hotel,* PO Box 8, Little York, PEI C0A 1P0 (phone: 902-672-2546, winter; 902-672-2048, summer).

LA PINSONNIÈRE, Cap-à-l'Aigle, Quebec This lovely inn enjoys a lovely setting in the heart of Charlevoix, a mere stretch from Pointe-au-Pic, between the St. Lawrence River and the mountains. A pristine, white mansion that was once a private home, it has 28 rooms and suites, some with fireplaces and canopied beds and most with river views. Whale safaris, cruises on the Saguenay Fjord, swimming in the indoor pool, riding, sailing, tennis, sleigh rides, and downhill and cross-country skiing fill the days; theater, concerts, and dining fill the nights. The property is a member of the Relais & Châteaux group, and the owners rely on fresh produce and foodstuffs to produce their fine fare. Closed November. Information: *La Pinsonnière,* 124 Rue St-Raphaël, Cap-à-l'Aigle, Charlevoix, QUE G0T 1B0 (phone: 418-665-4431).

LE CLUB TREMBLANT, Mont Tremblant, Quebec Facing Mont Tremblant, the highest peak in the Laurentians, this resort on the shores of Lac Tremblant has access to some of Canada's best cross-country ski terrain, snowshoeing trails, and downhill skiing. Its live-in ski instructors accompany students to the slopes every morning. The various incarnations of the main inn as private home, boardinghouse, and drinking establishment have given an intriguing patina to an already lovely structure—a typically Canadian mix of big stones and massive beams surrounding a gigantic fireplace. The 122 luxurious one- or two-bedroom condominium apartments are privately owned, but 111 of them, all with fireplaces, are available for rent. It's small enough to be cozy but large enough to offer visitors plenty of things to do: In winter there's skiing; in summer there's swimming, sailing, windsurfing, and fishing on the lake; and there are four tennis courts and a beautifully situated pool. Golf and riding are nearby, and the forest around the lake is great for walks and hikes. For the kids, the club has a playground and hosts a social program. The award-winning dining room serves up dishes with a pronounced French accent. Information: *Le Club Tremblant,* 121 Rue Cuttle, Mont Tremblant, QUE J0T 1Z0 (phone: 819-425-2731; 800-363-2413 in the US; 800-567-8341 in Canada; fax: 819-425-9903).

STATION MONT TREMBLANT LODGE, Mont Tremblant, Quebec This old, well-established resort is the only one actually on Mont Tremblant. A major project is under way that includes the renovation of the inn, and the addition of convention facilities and a new alpine village. So far, the major visible improvements have been a quadruple chair lift on the north side of the mountain and two new ski trails. With 248 rooms in the main lodge and a scattering of small chalets and condominiums, there's plenty of privacy, and the hotel sets a good table. You can ski to the slopes. Information: *Station Mont Tremblant Lodge,* Mont Tremblant, QUE J0T 1Z0 (phone: 819-681-2000; 800-461-8711; fax: 819-681-5999).

LE CHÂTEAU MONTEBELLO, Montebello, Quebec The brochures describing this Canadian Pacific–owned hotel 40 miles (64 km) east of Ottawa in the Ottawa River valley as a magnificent playground aren't stretching the point. The baronial 210-room log palace was once a private club, and when you step across the threshold, you feel just a little bit grander for being there. The scenes are impressive indeed: Fires burning in the massive six-sided, three-story stone fireplace cast flickering light over rafters that look as if they're from the 15th century. Outside are 65,000 acres of dense woodlands dotted by over 70 lakes. There's golf, tennis, hiking, fishing, horseback riding, croquet, indoor and outdoor swimming, cross-country skiing, skating, snowshoeing, sleigh riding, and curling—and on and on. Inside is a fitness area, complete with squash courts, an exercise room, saunas, and whirlpool baths. There are executive suites as well. This is a *seigneurie,* as the French Canadians say, on a very grand scale. Information: *Le Château Montebello,* 329 Rue Notre-Dame, Montebello, QUE J0V 1L0 (phone: 819-423-6341; 800-441-1414; fax: 819-423-5283).

MANOIR DES ERABLES, Montmagny, Quebec This Victorian manor house, less than an hour away from Quebec City across the St. Lawrence, was finished in 1814, when George III was in power and the battle at Waterloo had yet to happen. With only 24 rooms and suites, this inn has an intimate atmosphere. The real charm of the place, however, lies in its maple forest setting. Twice a year, snow geese converge at the Montmagny marshes in vast numbers. Locals—joined by visitors who drop in on these seasonal rites—make an event of the migration. The inn's kitchen is renowned for maple-smoked trout and local sturgeon, goose, venison, and maple sugar cake. There's a pool, and nearby are tennis, golf, downhill and cross-country skiing, hunting, and fishing. Information: *Manoir des Erables,* Blvd. Taché E., Montmagny, QUE G5V 1G5 (phone: 418-248-0100; 800-563-0200; fax: 418-248-9507).

AUBERGE HATLEY, North Hatley, Quebec A romantic country inn overlooking Lac Massawippi, this 1903 hostelry is a charming reminder of the vacation colony created by 19th-century Confederates who, following their defeat by the Yankees, summered in the area with their entourages. Each of its 25 rooms is individually appointed in period antiques, floral wallpaper, and quilted bedspreads; some rooms have fireplaces. Original artwork, leather sofas, beamed ceilings, and an old brick fireplace furnish the spacious living room. Guests can work up an appetite swimming in the pool, or canoeing, sailing, or windsurfing; fishing on the beautiful lake, horseback riding, and nearby tennis and golf facilities, complete the outdoor scene. Chef Alain Labrie oversees the excellent dining room. A member of the prestigious Relais & Châteaux group, the inn is open December to mid-November. Information: *Auberge Hatley,* PO Box 330, North Hatley, QUE JOB 2CO (phone: 819-842-2451; fax: 819-842-2907).

HOVEY MANOR, North Hatley, Quebec The story is told often enough that it's probably true: After the US Civil War, the small groups of Southerners who had summered up north in antebellum days continued to head for Yankeeland—but when the trains arrived there, the travelers pulled the blinds, kept going, and didn't stop until they had crossed the international border. Summer homes were eventually built by a couple of these Southerners, including one Henry Atkinson of Atlanta, who always showed up in North Hatley with two private railway cars, 10 horses and several carriages, and 18 servants. The turn-of-the-century home he built for himself—broad of verandah and white of pillar, inspired by George Washington's *Mount Vernon*—now lends its considerable charm to *Hovey Manor.* All 40 rooms—installed not only in the main house but also ingeniously fitted into the former servants' quarters, icehouse, and pump house—are furnished with Canadian antiques. All rooms have private baths, most face the lake, and suites have fireplaces, whirlpool baths, and private balconies. Each room has its own special decor, and eight are in a new, nonsmoking wing. Sitting atop an 18th-century pine armoire in the reception lobby is the inn's celebrated "haunted" clock, a Gothic-style 80-day chimer that rings only when someone mentions Plumley LeBaron, an early North Hatleyite. The site itself is lovely—a garden slopes down to a private beach facing 10-mile-long Lake Massawippi, surrounded by maples, birches, beeches, and evergreens. In summer, canoeing, sailing, windsurfing, water skiing, fishing, swimming, and tennis (on the inn's single court) are possible, as is golf, on any of the five courses within a 20-minute drive. In winter, skiers schuss the substantial Eastern Townships slopes or take on the manor's 22 miles of cross-country trails. There's also a fully-equipped exercise room, and massages are available. Year-round, diners enjoy the creations of the inn's Belgian chef. Information: *Hovey Manor,* PO Box 60, 595 Hovey Rd., North Hatley, QUE J0B 2C0 (phone: 819-842-2421; 800-661-2421; fax: 819-842-2248).

L'EAU À LA BOUCHE, Ste-Adèle, Quebec This 25-room inn—a member of the Relais & Châteaux group—is about 50 miles (80 km) north of Montreal and the perfect lodging place for a weekend in the Laurentian Mountains. In the winter, the Laurentians are prized for skiing; in the summer, for hiking. Outside, the hotel looks like a roadside *relais;* inside it radiates country warmth, with planked floors and a roaring fire. Food critics give the dining room high ratings for its salmon *au beurre blanc,* baked guinea hen stuffed with cabbage, breast of Barbary duck with coriander, rack of suckling pig, and intelligently chosen wines. The award-winning prix fixe, five-course dinner is expensive but memorable. There's a heated pool, and the inn is also close to golf, skiing, and tennis. Information: *Hôtel l'Eau à la Bouche,* 3003 Blvd. Ste-Adèle, Ste-Adèle, QUE J0R 1L0 (phone: 514-229-2991; fax: 514-229-7573).

AUBERGE GRAY ROCKS, St-Jovite, Quebec Opened in 1906, when the surrounding Laurentians were still virgin forestlands, this massive 150-room inn (at press time, new condos and deluxe suites were in the process of being added) occupies 2,600 acres on the shores of Lac Ouimet, with a commanding view of Mont Tremblant and its own ski hill. It is almost as lively as it is large: There are facilities for swimming and diving on the lake; a complete marina that rents sailboats, windsurfers, and canoes; a 5,000-foot airstrip; 22 Har-Tru tennis courts; a fine 18-hole golf course (see *Golf in Canada: A Land of Links* in this section); a complete fitness center; all manner of other sporting facilities; and lively nightlife. Tennis clinics by Dennis Van der Meer are a big draw in summer, and the program is among Canada's best (see *The Best Tennis Vacations* in this section). In winter, the acclaimed *Snow Eagle Ski School,* based on the hotel's own Sugar Peak, a hundred yards from the main inn, attracts guests from all over the US (see *Downhill Skiing* in this section). Big-mountain skiing at Mont Tremblant is only a short drive away. In the capacious dining room, international cuisine is the order of the day. Information: *Auberge Gray Rocks,* PO Box 1000, St-Jovite, QUE J0T 2H0 (phone: 819-425-2771; 800-567-6767; fax: 819-425-3474).

AUBERGE HANDFIELD, St-Marc-sur-Richelieu, Quebec Accommodations at this charming hostelry in the heart of the peaceful Richelieu River Valley not far from Montreal are in nine old Canadian farmhouses rescued from destruction at the hands of local farmers who were modernizing, then transported to the *Auberge Handfield*'s woods-rimmed property and fitted out with Canadian antiques. There are 55 rooms in the establishment. The main lodge—site of the dining room—is charming, with a big stone fireplace in the lobby. The inn is small enough so you won't get lost but large enough to offer some privacy and to support a good number of facilities, including a kidney-shape pool, a marina, and an activities program that includes corn-on-the-cob parties in fall and sugaring-off parties (at the inn's sugar shack) from the beginning of March through April. The restaurant, with its own fireplace, is noted for its nouvelle cuisine and French Canadian dishes. In winter, there's cross-country skiing; in summer, theater (mainly comedies, performed in French, on a steamboat moored nearby). Information: *Auberge Handfield,* 555 Chemin du Prince, St-Marc-sur-Richelieu, QUE J0L 2E0 (phone: 514-584-2226; 800-667-1087 in Canada).

DES TROIS TILLEULS, St-Marc-sur-Richelieu, Quebec Overlooking the Richelieu River, a 20-minute drive from Montreal, this property was originally a 19th-century mansion. Along with a 24-room rustic inn, the entire property is a member of Relais & Châteaux, the exclusive association of hostelries. In each air conditioned room, guests find a color TV set, radio, and balcony from which they can plot the day's activities in the marina or the pool, on the links or the courts. The inn's highlight is its French cuisine; both owners are French, and the menu is authentic and outstanding. Information: *Hostellerie des Trois Tilleuls,* 290 Rue Richelieu, St-Marc-sur-Richelieu, QUE J0L 2E0 (phone: 514-584-2231; 800-263-2230).

LA SAPINIÈRE, Val David, Quebec In this Laurentians hotel and restaurant, the primary distinction is the kitchen. Between meals, there's canoeing and rowing on a private lake, swimming in an outdoor heated pool, tennis, badminton, shuffleboard, a putting green and driving range, and, in winter, cross-country skiing in the maple, pine, and fir woods that surround the hotel, and downhill skiing at myriad nearby areas. The 70 rooms and suites are large and comfortably appointed. There also are several private salons with fireplaces, five air conditioned meeting rooms, and audiovisual and sound equipment. Information: *Hôtel la Sapinière,* 1244 Chemin de la Sapinière, Val David, QUE J0T 2N0 (phone: 819-322-2020; 800-567-6635; fax: 819-322-6510).

WEST

BANFF SPRINGS, Banff, Alberta Imagine a snow queen's castle rising at the base of an evergreen-covered mountain slope with ice-capped peaks in the distance. This establishment, with 828 rooms and suites, fits the description. Renovations in the early and mid-1990s have ensured that the interior accommodations and amenities reflect the exterior's old-world glamor, while remaining appealingly modern and comfortable. And the site—right in *Banff National Park*—is remarkable: It's surrounded by hundreds of square miles of lofty mountains, deep valleys, stunning glaciers, and crystal lakes. In addition to the hotel's 17 restaurants (including several bar-lounges), there is an extensive spa featuring an indoor pool, an outdoor heated pool, a cascade waterfall, a massage pool, 14 different body treatment rooms, steamrooms, and whirlpools. There is also a spectacularly scenic championship 27-hole golf course (see *Golf in Canada: A Land of Links* in this section), and five tennis courts (see *The Best Tennis Vacations* in this section). Rafting trips are available in warmer weather. In winter, it's a skier's delight; ice skating, ski touring, dogsledding, sleigh rides, and snowshoeing are all possible on the property. Information: *Banff Springs Hotel,* PO Box 960, Banff, AB T0L 0C0 (phone: 403-762-2211; 800-441-1414 in Canada; fax: 403-762-5755).

JASPER PARK LODGE, Jasper, Alberta Towering snow-capped peaks surround this alpine-style village that graces the shores of Lac Beauvert, 3 miles (5 km) from the town of Jasper in *Jasper National Park.* Guests stay in what amounts to a small village of modern cedar chalets and original log cabins—there are 442 units in all, some with adjoining sitting rooms, many with patios and fireplaces. Recreational choices include an aerobics studio, golf, tennis, horseback riding, cycling, whitewater rafting, boating, fishing, and use of the outdoor heated swimming pool and health spa facilities. Ski packages are available as well. Excellent food is served in five dining rooms—including a café and a French restaurant—or in the comfort of one's own cabin, and there's a variety of evening entertainment. Children's recreational programs are offered as well. Open year-round. Rates soar during peak season (mid-May to mid-October). Information: *Jasper Park Lodge,* PO Box 40, Jasper, AB T0E 1E0 (phone: 403-852-3301; 800-441-1414; fax: 403-852-5107).

CHÂTEAU LAKE LOUISE, Lake Louise, Alberta This large (515 bedrooms and suites), French-style château, a Canadian Pacific hotel, has a breathtaking setting on the shores of world-famous Lake Louise—blue-green, beautifully clear, rimmed by mountains, and backed by the blue-white Victoria Glacier. The setting alone would recommend the hotel, but this Gallic beauty is no garden-variety establishment. The resplendence of the interiors almost matches the beauty of the scene outside. Witness the regal pillars in the palatial lobby and the soaring arches of the Victoria Room. Though there is no golf course, the excellent layout at the *Banff Springs* hotel is only 39 miles (63 km) away. On-site facilities include an indoor pool, an exercise room, and a Jacuzzi, as well as dinner dancing, three formal dining rooms, and one informal restaurant. Ice skating, sleigh rides across the frozen lake, pony trekking in the mountains, canoeing and hiking, and downhill and cross-country skiing all are possible diversions here. Note that rooms with a view of the lake are slightly more expensive than those with mountain vistas. Information: *Château Lake Louise,* Lake Louise, AB T0L 1E0 (phone: 403-522-3511; 800-441-1414; fax: 403-522-3834).

POST HOTEL, Lake Louise, Alberta This charming, Bavarian-style jewel in the majestic Canadian Rockies is a member of the prestigious Relais & Châteaux group. The log-constructed building near the pristine Pipestone River is luxurious and cozy. There are 100 rooms, 27 suites, and two one-bedroom cabins; some accommodations feature lofts, fireplaces, and whirlpools. There's also an indoor pool, steamroom, and sauna. The warm, rustic dining room—which retains its 1940s decor—features continental fare prepared by a Swiss-trained chef; there's a cocktail lounge, too. Specialties include Alberta lamb and beef, game birds, and ducks and chickens raised especially for the restaurant. Closed late October to mid-December. Information: *Post Hotel,* PO Box 69, Lake Louise, AB T0L 1E0 (phone: 403-522-3989; 800-661-1586 ; fax: 403-522-3966).

FAIRMONT HOT SPRINGS, Fairmont Hot Springs, British Columbia This hostelry—a long-established resort housed in a handful of newish buildings—is a delight for families. Kids in particular love the 10,000 square feet of steaming natural mineral pools. And then there's the setting—on the side of a mountain in the lovely Kootenay district of the Rockies, surrounded by woods, lawns, and gardens, with nice views over the valley below. There's skiing in winter on the resort's own slopes, which have a thousand-foot vertical, or nearby at big *Kimberley* and *Panorama.* In summer, you can play tennis (there are four courts), golf on two 18-hole courses, or go horseback riding. Additional accommodations are provided at the property's 265-site campground (30 spaces are open in winter). Information: *Fairmont Hot Springs Resort,* Box 10, Fairmont Hot Springs, BC V0B 1L0 (phone: 604-345-6311; 800-663-4979; fax: 604-345-6616).

HASTINGS HOUSE, Ganges, British Columbia Once a seaside estate, today this Relais & Châteaux member on Salt Spring Island (between Vancouver and Victoria, in the Strait of Georgia) has two suites and one guestroom in the vine-covered Tudor-style manor house; six suites and three rooms are available in other buildings on the estate. Accessible by ferry from Vancouver (a three-hour trip) or Victoria (a 35-minute trip), the hotel recalls the mood of a peaceful country manor. The ambience combines rural simplicity with numerous creature comforts: Most units include parlors, fireplaces (the wood is stacked outside the door), and wet bars. After a day of hiking through the pristine forest or along the scenic shore, enjoy one of the dining room's renowned five-course dinners, which may include a salad made with greens grown in the lush gardens, and a superb soufflé for dessert. If you wish to be coddled in the woods, you can do no better than here. (From *Easter* to mid-October, it is essential to reserve a spot on the ferry from Vancouver at least a week in advance by calling *BC Ferries;* phone: 604-669-1211. For travel on long holiday weekends, reserve ferry berths a month in advance.) Open mid-March through November. Information: *Hastings House,* 160 Upper Ganges Rd., Salt Spring Island, BC V8K 2S2 (phone: 604-537-2362; 800-661-9255; fax: 604-537-5333).

HARRISON HOT SPRINGS, Harrison Hot Springs, British Columbia Nestled in the Coast Range, in the upper Fraser River Valley some 90 miles (144 km) east of Vancouver, this impressive old 303-unit resort on the shores of Harrison Lake has recently been renovated and redecorated. The rural landscape around it is dotted with farmhouses and speckled with lakes. Tea is served every afternoon in the upper lobby, and there is nightly dining and dancing. The hot springs are a prime attraction. There's a circular sulfur indoor pool heated naturally to 100F, a curved indoor pool, and an outdoor pool surrounded by a large sun deck. There also are Roman and whirlpool baths, an exercise room, and registered masseurs and masseuses on duty at the health pavilion. There is a sauna; two of the pools are open around the clock. Sports facilities include tennis, shuffleboard, and a nine-hole golf course; also possible are bicycling, water skiing, fishing, boating, and boardsailing nearby. Off the property are scenic boat cruises and helicopter trips. Information: *Harrison Hot Springs Hotel,* 100 Esplanade, Harrison Hot Springs, BC V0M 1K0 (phone: 604-796-2244; 800-663-2266; fax: 604-796-9374).

EMPRESS, Victoria, British Columbia The Edwardian myth of imperial majesty is embodied in this grand hotel at the western edge of the Empire. Designed by Francis Rattenbury, who also created the nearby *Parliament Buildings,* it was ingeniously built on pilings as the land around it was reclaimed from James Bay. When it opened in 1908, it set standards for excellent service that this charming anachronism has stubbornly maintained for nearly a century. The effect of being somewhere in the United Kingdom is inescapable: Double-deck London buses unload at the front door, and the "Upstairs/Downstairs" mood continues through high-ceilinged public rooms with the hushed echo of greatness. Many of the 482 guestrooms afford priceless views of Victoria and the harbor. Also on the premises are three bars, a dining room, a pool, and an exercise room. Several lovely shops offering china and jewelry lend themselves to browsing. Don't miss afternoon tea (also see *Quintessential Canada,* above). Information: *The Empress,* 721 Government St., Victoria, BC V8W 1W5 (phone: 604-384-8111; 800-441-1414; fax: 604-381-4334).

Farm and Ranch Vacations

Holidays at a Canadian farm or ranch can take you back quickly to a childhood you wish you had had—if not to your own youth. They can help introduce youngsters to a way of life that city and suburban kids simply don't encounter elsewhere. They'll milk a cow, talk to the small animals that many farmers keep, prowl through the woods with a dog at their heels, learn to ride, swim in a creek, and explore to their hearts' content. The days fill up quickly with berry picking, horseback riding, haying and combining, visits to auctions in tiny towns you'd otherwise have no reason to visit, or just hanging out in the kitchen while the bread is being baked or the red raspberries, harvested by the gallon from the garden, are being turned into jam. (A farm visit can be a regular cooking school.) The food that shows up on the table—usually simple fare—is meant to satisfy the hearty appetite so easily worked up wherever the air is fresh. The hosts are generally friendly folks with almost infinite tolerance for the ignorance of city slickers. Among them, you'll find more than a few who speak English with an accent—not just French Canadians, but also Canadians from Germany, Ukraine, and other parts of the world.

The nature of the farms changes with the landscape. In the east, you'll find smaller, old-fashioned places of around 200 acres that specialize in dairy or mixed farming, some owned by French Canadian families who can teach you a little of their language. In the Maritimes, you'll find farms of 200 to 2,000 acres specializing in apples, potatoes, or beef and dairy cattle. The larger spreads out west fall into two basic categories: guest (or dude) ranches, where the guest business contributes substantially to the property's income; and working ranches and farms, where guests are a sideline. Guest ranches may offer more luxurious surroundings, a more extensive roster of planned activities, and a wider variety of facilities. Working ranches are make-your-own-fun places, although since they're generally smaller as well, your hosts will always give you plenty of personal attention and many suggestions to keep you busy. Prices can run anywhere from $30 to $85 per night, depending on whether meals are included and on the size and facilities of the farm or ranch; there is usually a discount for children.

Provincial tourism departments can give you information about dude ranches in their province. Farms are represented by associations, all of whose members are inspected regularly and thoroughly and then listed in province-wide directories that are updated annually. When you're picking a farm or ranch, first determine the province you want to visit and exactly what kind of atmosphere you'd like, then write for the listings, and phone the farms that interest you most. For a complete listing of approved farms in Canada, contact these provincial offices:

Alberta: *Alberta Economic Development and Tourism,* PO Box 2500, Edmonton, AB T5J 4L6 (phone: 403-427-4321 in Edmonton; 800-661-8888).

British Columbia: *Tourism British Columbia,* 1117 Wharf St., Victoria, BC V8W 2Z2 (phone: 800-663-6000).

Manitoba: *Manitoba Farm Vacations Association,* RR1, Elm Creek, MAN R0G 0N0 (phone: 204-436-2599).

New Brunswick: *Tourism New Brunswick* (PO Box 12345, Fredericton, NB E3B 5C3; phone: 800-561-0123) and *New Brunswick Farm Vacations* (RR1, Knoxford Rd., Centreville, NB E0J 1H0; phone: 506-276-4787).

Newfoundland/Labrador: *Newfoundland Department of Development, Tourism and Promotions Branch,* PO Box 8730, St. John's, NFLD A1B 4K2 (phone: 709-729-2830; 800-563-6353; fax: 709-576-2830).

Nova Scotia: *Ellen Eisses, Nova Scotia Farm & Country Vacations Association,* RR1 Masstown, NS B0M 1G0 (phone: 902-662-3565).

Ontario: *Sharon Salm-Grose, Ontario Farm and Country Accommodations* (PO Box 8989, Alma, ONT N0B 1A0; phone: 519-846-9788). For a list of farms that specialize in *Christmas* stays, send a legal-size, self-addressed envelope and $1 (CN or US) or an International Postal Coupon.

Prince Edward Island: *Prince Edward Island Department of Tourism and Parks, Visitor Services,* PO Box 940E, Charlottetown, PEI C1A 7M5 (phone: 902-368-4444; fax: 902-368-5737).

Quebec: *Fédération des Agricotours du Québec* (4545 Av. Pierre-de-Coubertin, CP 1000, Succ. M, Montreal, QUE H1V 3R2; phone: 514-252-3138). This organization also runs a rural bed and breakfast program.

Saskatchewan: *Beatrice Magee, Saskatchewan Country Vacations Association* (PO Box 654, Gull Lake, SASK S0N 1A0; phone: 306-672-3970).

FAMILY FARMS

GWYNALTA FARM, Gwynne, Alberta Occupying 400 acres, this central Alberta dairy farm about 40 miles (64 km) from the provincial capital is not tiny, but it's not particularly big and wealthy either. The place is so secluded that neither car nor house can be seen from the edge of the farm's lake. Every morning, deer graze in the yard; quiet nights are spent sitting out on the big deck of Mable Glaser's comfortable old house, watching northern lights dance across the sky. The fishing here is fine, and the water, hills, and forests are too lovely to ignore—look for the bare trace of an old buffalo trail cutting into the trees. Hiking and bird watching are popular in summer, and there's cross-country skiing, snowmobiling, and ice fishing in winter. Be sure to sample the milk collected from the herd of contented black-and-white cows. The farmhouse accommodates up to four people. Information: *Mable Glaser, Gwynalta Farm,* Gwynne, AB T0C 1L0 (phone: 403-352-3587).

CRAZEE AKERZ FARM, Rimbey, Alberta Nestled in lush, rolling countryside, this small farm raises everything from grain to donkeys. Joan and Darrell Carrigan encourage visitors to milk cows, pet sheep, gather eggs, churn butter, and make ice cream. In winter, guests can cross-country ski and skate; in summer, they can boat, swim, or fish on nearby Gull Lake, or go on hayrides. There are three rooms in the main house, plus two rooms in a cottage. Information: *Joan and Darrell Carrigan, Crazee Akerz Farm,* PO Box 1473, Rimbey, AB T0C 2J0 (phone: 403-843-6444).

ASPEN RIDGE, Clear Lake, Manitoba The house where owner Robert Sopuck lives with his guests is what a visitor once dubbed a "log palace," complete with beamed ceilings and a big stone fireplace. That each of the dozen beds has its own down comforter begins to explain the "palace's" appeal to cross-country skiers, though you can't ignore the attraction of heavy snow accumulations and the vastness of the available terrain. Sopuck's 320 rolling acres adjoin government and private land that also is available to skiers, and *Riding Mountain National Park* is just 2 miles (3 km) away. From mid-May through late June and from late August to early October, the area is equally fine for bird watching, since the farm lies right on the Central and Mississippi flyways. And there's always horseback riding at nearby stables. Meals are prepared with indigenous ingredients—geese, ducks, garden vegetables—and include such specialties as kielbasa and cabbage rolls, typical fare of the area's large Ukrainian population. Sopuck also is knowledgeable about edible native plants and is willing to teach interested guests. Information: *Robert Sopuck, Aspen Ridge,* Lake Audy, MAN R0J 0Z0 (phone: 204-848-2964).

LA FERME DES ERABLES I AND II, Aroostook, New Brunswick This 1,200-acre grain-and-potato farm and cattle ranch not far from the Maine border, a couple of miles off the Trans-Canada Highway in the province's northwest corner, belongs to a family that numbers more than 40 when you figure in all the sons, daughters, wives, husbands, and grandchildren. Although they don't all live in the farmhouse, there are always a few of them around, making the place very lively. The whole family is bilingual, and the kids will baby-sit or take you around to see the various neighborhood sights—among them the photogenic 225-foot-high Grand Falls and, in Hartland, to the south, a 1,282-foot-long covered bridge, the world's longest. There is a heated indoor pool. Each farm has only two rooms. Catered bus tours, which place guests in different well-organized homes in the neighborhood, also can be arranged. Open year-round. Information: *Aurèle and Fernande St. Amand, La Ferme des Erables I and II,* Aroostook, NB E0J 1B0 (phone: 506-273-3112 or 506-273-2510).

BROADLEAF FARM, Hopewell Hill, New Brunswick This 1,400-acre cattle farm—big by New Brunswick standards—is a lively, spic-and-span place. The main attractions are the 80 horses. Western riding lessons, hayrides, and trails that take riders out by the water and through the woods are all available. But because the farm's marshy sections attract migrating geese and ducks, the place also is good for bird watching. And it's a good base for trips to nearby *Fundy National Park* and Moncton, for tours of the coastline, and for antiques-hunting trips. The old-fashioned, two-room country house is comfortable, and the food is good and simple, though occasionally you'll be treated to harvests from the marshes—cranberries and mushrooms, as well as exotica like samphire and goosetongue greens. Relax at *Broadleaf Too,* the home of Vernon and Joyce Hudson, right next door and also featuring guestrooms (three). A small area for tents and eight trailer hookups is available; reservations for these sites are necessary. There's also a week-long summer camp for kids. Information: *Darrell and Kathy Weir, Broadleaf Farm,* Hopewell Hill, Albert Co., NB E0A 1Z0 (phone: 506-882-2722), or *Joyce and Vernon Hudson, Broadleaf Too,* Hopewell Hill, Albert Co., NB E0A 1Z0 (phone: 506-882-2803).

ALLEN'S HOLIDAY FARM, Port Elgin, New Brunswick The three TV sets in the big, early-19th-century white frame farmhouse aren't turned on much in summer, because there are so many other things to do: helping out in the garden or on the farm, day-tripping to a nearby beach or to PEI via ferry (20 minutes away), chowing down on big meals of roast meat or fish fresh from the not-too-distant sea, or even putting up raspberry jam, using the fruit from the garden. Information: *Christopher and Dorothy Kean, Allen's Holiday Farm,* RR3, Port Elgin, NB E0A 2K0 (phone: 506-538-2692).

ANDERSON'S HOLIDAY FARM, Sussex, New Brunswick There are sheep, cattle, and a variety of fowl on this 200-acre farm in the heart of dairy country, about an hour's drive from *Fundy National Park.* Kids love the farm's menagerie of ducks, Canada geese, rabbits, ornamental pheasants, and even peacocks. Nearby golf and curling, as well as swimming, tennis, and sightseeing, keep visitors so busy that they need a rest when they get home. Bed and breakfast arrangements can be made. There are three rooms. Open year-round. Information: *Tom and Laura Anderson, Anderson's Holiday Farm,* RR2, Sussex, NB E0E 1P0 (phone: 506-433-3786).

WASHA FARM, Alma, Ontario The grandma's country kitchen of your dreams becomes reality at the 1877 farm of Walter and Sharon Salm-Grose, located in the rich, gently rolling hills of southern Ontario, an hour's drive west of Toronto. Not only is the food all home-cooked, but it's also all homegrown—if not at *Washa,* then at a relative's spread. Feast on fresh sweet corn, beets, spinach, Swiss chard, and peas and potatoes. The grilled veal steaks come from calves raised by Walter's brother, and the pure maple syrup drenching the French toast and blueberry pancakes is supplied by an aunt and uncle in Quebec. Strawberries, blueberries, raspberries, and currants grow wild, and many find their way into Sharon's locally renowned pies. Her coffee cake, muffin, and cookie recipes are the legacy of her mother and grandmother. On weekends, Walter takes over the cooking on the outdoor barbecue grill. It all adds up to a rural gastronomic delight. Information: *Sharon Salm-Grose, Washa Farm,* RR2, Alma, ONT N0B 1A0 (phone: 519-846-9788).

SPRING VALLEY FARM, Hastings, Ontario Sam and Jacqueline Beamish's place is so hospitable that even the wild geese stop off here on their travels, joining the Beamishes' own white geese on their beautiful pond. A sunroom has been added to the century-old farmhouse, and in winter meals are cooked on a magnificent Findlay Oval cookstove. In the family room is a fieldstone fireplace, and the backwoods are ideal for walking or picnicking. The pond is a great spot for tenting, and there's a playhouse for children. Farm tours are available. Located 30 minutes southeast of Peterborough on Route 45, near conservation areas, boating, fishing, golf, and *Lang Pioneer Village.* Information: *Sam and Jacqueline Beamish, Spring Valley Farm,* RR1, Hastings, ONT K0L 1Y0 (phone: 705-696-2878).

FERME CHAMPÊTRE, St-Denis, Saskatchewan Only 25 miles (40 km) east of Saskatoon, this farm has working agricultural lands but keeps the emphasis on fun for its guests. You can help with such tasks as milking, or you can head off to pitch a baseball or horseshoes; there's also volleyball, trail rides in buggies, hayrides, a miniature enchanted forest, and staff dressed in cowboy gear. Visitors stay in cabins or in trailer and tent camping areas. All three meals are served in an Old West–style saloon. French and English are spoken. No credit cards accepted. Information: *Thérèse Denis, Ferme Champêtre,* PO Box 12, St-Denis, SASK S0K 3W0 (phone: 306-258-4635; fax: 305-258-2215).

WORKING RANCHES

HIGHLAND VIEW GUEST RANCH, High River, Alberta Enjoy the fieldstone fireplaces, Victorian antiques, and delicious, home-cooked meals at this 5,760-acre ranch and horse, cattle, and grain operation in Alberta's beautiful foothills country. The McLean family, who have lived and ranched in the area for generations, will be happy to share their knowledge of local history and invite you to try your hand at rounding up cattle, branding, and fencing. Other pursuits include nature walks, trail rides, hayrides, and barbecues, as well as swimming and fishing in the creek. Three bedrooms in the main house and one in the bunkhouse accommodate a total of 10 guests; bathrooms are shared. Open May through September, and throughout December. Information: *Julie and Tim McLean, Highland View Guest Ranch,* RR 2, High River AB T1V 1N2 (phone: 403-395-2246).

TL BAR RANCH, Trochu, Alberta This central Alberta horse and cattle ranch, located between the towns of Red Deer (pop. 60,000) and Drumheller (pop. 6,300) along the Red Deer River in the "Valley of the Dinosaurs," accommodates 10 to 12 guests in a log ranch home and a private cottage. Fishing and swimming are at least as popular here as helping out with the ranch chores, but the surrounding Drumheller Valley, carved over the ages by the Red Deer River, is such a fascinating place that exploring—in canoes, on foot, or on horseback—can be the most interesting activity of all. Dinosaur bones, fossils, and petrified wood have all been found nearby, uncovered by the river. Open weekends from November through April, when off-season rates apply; daily the rest of the year. Information: *Tom and Willie Lynch, TL Bar Ranch,* PO Box 217, Trochu, AB T0M 2C0 (phone: 403-442-2207).

GUEST RANCHES

BLACK CAT GUEST RANCH, Hinton, Alberta This wonderful place is just big enough to provide some privacy—but not too big. It's also beautifully situated, so that each of the 16 guestrooms faces the first range of the Rockies. The large, central living room also affords a view, plus a fireplace, a library, many comfortable chairs, and a pine floor for dancing; the coffeepot is always percolating. In summer, guests ride, hike, and fish at Solomon Creek and the Wild Hay River, canoe on the Athabasca River, and sightsee in nearby areas like the Columbia Icefield. On returning, unwind in the outdoor hot tub with a view of the mountains. Winter's main attraction is cross-country skiing on the 25 miles (40 km) of poplar- and spruce-lined trails that surround the lodge, sometimes along old logging roads. The ranch is better suited for singles and couples than for families. Information: *Amber Hayward, Black Cat Guest Ranch,* PO Box 6267, Hinton, AB T7V 1X6 (phone: 403-865-3084; fax: 403-865-1924).

RAFTER SIX RANCH RESORT, Seebe, Alberta A good-size operation in the mountainous Kananaskis country, about 25 miles (40 km) from Banff, it can accommodate about 60 guests in its solid-log lodge and cabins. The staff numbers around 40 in the summer, so when a few guests decide to go out on a trail ride or take a nature walk, there's always someone from the ranch available to make sure they can do it—and have the best time ever. Breakfast rides, hayrides, whitewater rafting, helicopter sightseeing, and barbecues are regular activities, and occasionally a group from the local Stoney native tribe (the owner is a blood brother) drops by just to visit or, by request, to dance, in full-dress regalia, for guests. On the grounds are a dining room, a coffee shop, a cocktail lounge, an outdoor pool, and an indoor whirlpool bath; the surrounding mountains are so appealing they have been chosen several times as movie locations. Information: *Rafter Six Ranch Resort,* General Delivery, Seebe, AB T0L 1X0 (phone: 403-673-3622; 403-264-1251 direct from Calgary; fax: 403-673-3961).

SUNDANCE GUEST RANCH, Ashcroft, British Columbia This 28-room ranch in the Thompson River Valley is living proof that the Old West still lives. There's sagebrush for miles around, and the friendliest cowhands anywhere will teach even a greenhorn to sit tall in the saddle. Although everything is air conditioned, and there's a tennis court and heated pool, the emphasis is on rustic, whether it's a Saturday night dance attended by cowpokes, or kicking up the trail dust and hearing the howls of coyotes at night. Horseback riding is the raison d'être here, and there are twice-daily trail rides (the ranch usually runs about a hundred horses). The nightlife centers around the giant stone fireplace and bar and Saturday-night dances, and the food—including barbecues—is another attraction. *Sundance Guest Ranch,* PO Box 489, Ashcroft, BC V0K 1A0 (phone: 604-453-2554 or 604-453-2422; fax: 604-453-9356).

TYAX MOUNTAIN LAKE RESORT, Gold Bridge, British Columbia This ranch and outdoor adventure resort is located 90 minutes west of Lilloet in the Cariboo Chilcotin region. The scenic, ice-covered Coast Mountains overlook the gently rolling terrain, intercut with onetime gold-bearing rivers. The resort has a main lodge and seven chalets, together capable of accommodating up to a hundred guests. The lodge's restaurant serves home-style meals. During the summer, spend the days horseback riding, fishing, heli-hiking, canoeing, or panning for gold. There's also a tennis court, Jacuzzi, sauna, and exercise room. Heli-skiing, cross-country skiing, and snowmobiling are available in the winter. Information: *Gus Abel, Tyax Mountain Lake Resort,* Tyaughton Lake Rd., Gold Bridge, BC V0K 1P0 (phone: 604-238-2221; fax: 604-238-2528).

A Shopper's Guide to Canada

The choice of things to buy in Canada is as vast as the country itself. Shoppers in search of items genuinely Canadian will find goods ranging from Inuit-produced crafts to designer fashions from such names as Alfred Sung, Linda Lundstrom, and, for rugged sportswear, Northern Reflections.

The key to satisfying shopping in Canada is timing: There are often pre-*Christmas* sales worth attending, and beginning on *Boxing Day* (December 26) most retail stores drastically reduce prices. Winterwear bargains abound in late winter and early spring, and prices for summer clothing drop by as much as 50% in the fall. Summertime bargains also can be had when city stores reduce prices to attract customers while most urbanites are away on vacation. In small shops and antiques emporiums, you may be able to bargain on individual items of interest.

Sunday shopping rules vary in Canada from one province to another—sometimes even from one town to another. Most provinces allow smaller shops to open Sundays, especially in tourist areas. In 1993, Ontario began to allow unrestricted Sunday shopping, but not all stores remain open; Alberta and British Columbia also have relatively liberal Sunday laws.

Every province except Alberta levies a Provincial Sales Tax (PST)—usually between 7% and 10% (in Newfoundland it's 12%). In addition, the federal government imposes a 7% Goods and Services Tax (GST) on all purchases except prescription drugs, medical services, and basic foods. Non-residents of Canada can get a GST refund of up to CN$500 in goods that will be taken out of Canada. Car rentals and restaurant meals are not eligible for rebates, but hotel and motel accommodations are. Cigarettes and alcohol are not eligible unless purchased at a duty-free shop. Goods bought in Canada and delivered to the purchaser's home country are not subject to a GST. In some provinces, visitors may receive refunds for the PST as well. On entering Canada, ask customs for rebate forms (which sometimes are available at retail stores in the most popular tourist destinations as well), and save your receipts. For further information, contact *Revenue Canada*'s

GST telephone line (phone: 800-668-4748 in Canada; 613-991-3346 in the US).

The following is an item-by-item guide to what to buy in Canada. For listings of recommended shops in Canada's major metropolises, see the *Shopping* sections of the individual reports in THE CITIES.

ANTIQUES AND ART Canadian antiques and works of art can be good buys: pre-Confederation furniture (made before 1867) sells for far less than European or American furniture of the same period. Fine paintings and sculpture by Canadian artists also can be comparatively reasonable in price. Acadian antiques, however, have a certain cachet thanks to Longfellow's poem "Evangeline." They're very rare and expensive—beware of imitations.

CLOTHING Look to Halifax for nautical themes, Quebec and Montreal for the radical and the chic, Winnipeg for bargains, and Calgary and Edmonton for cowboy/cowgirl duds.

CRAFTS AND ARTIFACTS Canadian artisans produce beautiful lace, jewelry, furniture, glassware, and toys; the prices are comparable to (or sometimes higher than) contemporary European and American crafts. A number of places throughout the country specialize in Inuit and native Indian crafts and artifacts. Inuit carvings are abundant, although really fine carvings are rare. Expect to pay $100 for a soapstone seal that will fit in the palm of your hand, $1,000 for something big enough to display on a mantel.

DELICACIES To discover the best of Canadian cuisine, be sure to sample food raised in the region you happen to be visiting. On the Eastern Seaboard, try Atlantic salmon, scallops, mussels, and lobster. On Prince Edward Island, opt for dishes made with the province's famous potatoes ("hodge podge" is a simple but delicious concoction of mashed spuds, fresh vegetables, and plenty of butter). Quebec is known for its maple syrup dishes, its cheeses, and its recipes featuring pork. The fresh whitefish and smoked goldeye fish from Lake Winnipeg are wonderful samples of fresh Ontario and Manitoba fare. The prairies (in Manitoba, Saskatchewan, and Alberta) produce excellent beef and bison (very lean meat with a rich flavor) and a wide variety of grains, including millet, quinoa, amaranth, and Canada's famous, extra-hard wheat. There is also the Saskatoon berry, a red purple delicacy that grows on sheltered prairie hillsides and along riverbanks and makes exquisite pies and puddings. Some of the world's finest lamb is raised in Alberta and British Columbia. From British Columbia's Okanagan Valley come peaches, apricots, and a steadily increasing variety of cherries and apples, many of them old varieties brought back by small-scale, dedicated fruit-growers. While in Vancouver, sample Dungeness crab and salmon, and search out native Indian delicacies such as rabbit, fowl, and other game presented in contemporary dishes. Northern Canada's specialties include muskie, halibut, and arctic char. Major cities boast a profusion of specialty food shops and ethnic food stores and restaurants. And the country is enjoying a resurgence of farmers' markets featuring fresh bread, cheese, meat, seafood, and produce.

FURS Canada came into existence, and the English and French fought a century of wars, largely because of the business of fur trapping. Today, following a decline due to the controversy surrounding the issue of killing animals for their pelts (the Hudson's Bay Company, once the greatest fur enterprise in North America, even closed its fur salons), the fur industry is making a comeback.

Visitors planning to buy a Canadian fur coat for export to another country should be sure that the animal is not listed as an endangered species—such furs are subject to seizure at US (and other) ports of entry. In general, trapped animals are likely to be on the endangered species list, while animals raised on ranches are unlikely to be. So before buying, check with the customs service of the country or countries you plan to enter with your new furs.

The preeminent retailer of furs in Canada is the relatively expensive *Holt Renfrew & Co.,* a fine fashion chain with stores in major cities. The furs here are designer items of uniformly high quality, but you pay for the name. Those willing to invest time as well as money can visit fur districts in Windsor, Toronto, Montreal, Winnipeg, and Vancouver; examine the pelts, sewing, and construction details; and have a coat made to their exact specifications. Bargains are available beginning in January.

For the Body

Downhill Skiing

Skiers in Canada enjoy an invigorating variety of skiing opportunities and a season that—with the help of snowmaking machinery—often expands from early November into April or May. It's possible to ski in the Maritimes, Ontario, Manitoba, and Saskatchewan, but the country's truly world class ski holiday destinations are in Alberta; British Columbia; Quebec, where Parc du Mont Ste-Anne and Mont-Tremblant are superlative ski areas (dress warmly; mountain temperatures here tend to be colder than in BC and Alberta); and, for the adventurous, Newfoundland. Newfoundland's mountains have a raw, refreshing beauty, and the province's handful of resorts are unlike those found in the rest of North America, with their imported, "Alpine" atmosphere. Skiers from around the world are drawn to the phenomenonally scenic Rocky Mountains, with a wide variety of pistes through powder-drenched bowls and trail-cut forests. They also have extensive ski lift facilities and bounteous après-ski opportunities. Helicopter skiing in the ranges of the Rockies known as the Cariboos and Bugaboos, among others, has soared in popularity (see *Wilderness Skiing* in this section). Skiing of the sort found here is quite simply unavailable anywhere else in the world.

For descriptions of major Canadian resorts and more information on helicopter skiing, contact individual provincial tourist offices. Or check newsstands for *Ski Canada* magazine, which reviews resorts and publishes a directory of Canadian ski resorts once a year (19 Albany Ave., Toronto, ON M5R 3C2; phone: 416-595-1252; fax: 416-595-7255). Another great source is the annually updated *White Book of Ski Areas, US & Canada,* available for $16.95 in ski shops and bookstores, or for $19.95 from *Inter-Ski Services, Inc.* (PO Box 9595, Friendship Station, Washington, DC 20016; phone: 202-342-0886; fax: 202-338-1940).

The following is a list of Canada's best slopes beyond the major metropolises. For information on urban slopes, consult the individual reports in *Sports* in THE CITIES. Entries are arranged geographically, starting with the eastern provinces and then the western ones; within that framework, entries are arranged alphabetically by province and, within province, by name of ski area.

EAST

EASTERN TOWNSHIPS (ESTRIE), near Montreal, Quebec Unlike the Laurentians (see below), which were initially built up to serve as summer resorts, the mountains in this northern extension of the Appalachians, less than an hour's drive southeast of Montreal and just north of the Vermont border, were developed primarily for skiing. Each ski area here is the peer of *Mont Tremblant* or any comparable Vermont resort. Mont Sutton, near Sutton, has 54 trails, nine chair lifts, a 1,509-foot vertical, and glade skiing. Owl's Head, near Mansonville, has 27 runs and a 1,770-foot vertical. Mont Orford, near Magog, has a 1,772-foot vertical and 39 trails. Bromont, with a 1,328-foot vertical and 23 trails, is the fourth member of the quartet of major mountains in the area. Headquarter at any one of the four mountains, ski there, and then use your interchangeable lift ticket to sample the other three. All four areas have runs to suit everyone in the family, as well as varied terrain and good lift service.

There also is a wide range of accommodations in the Eastern Townships. Owl's Head has a small lodge right at its base, plus apartment-hotels and condominiums with ski-in/ski-out access to lifts and trails. An expansion at Owl's Head added more snowmaking, two more trails, and a detachable quad chair lift. Owl's Head attracts an almost fanatically loyal crowd that returns year after year. The *Auberge Bromont* (phone: 514-534-2200) at Bromont is a cozy place with views of the illuminated runs. Livelier than Owl's Head and Bromont, Mont Sutton and Mont Orford are both close to a couple of small towns with restaurants and other nighttime activity. Among the more interesting hostelries in this area are *Village Archimède-Viva Sutton* (phone: 514-538-3440; 800-363-1226) at Sutton; the acclaimed *Hovey Manor* (phone: 819-842-2421; 800-661-2421; see *Special Havens*) at North Hatley; and Magog's *Cheribourg* resort (phone: 819-843-3308). Although this is still very much the farming area it was before the lifts went in back in the 1970s, Estrie appeals first and foremost to those who come to ski, with the quality of the skiing among the best in the East. Information: *Mont Orford Resort Centre,* Box 248, Magog, QUE J1X 3W8 (phone: 819-843-6548); *Owl's Head,* Mansonville, QUE J0E 1X0 (phone: 514-292-3342; 800-363-3342); *Sutton Tourist Association* (for lodging) CP 418, Sutton, QUE J0E 2K0 (phone: 514-538-2646 or 514-538-2537) or (for skiing) CP 280, Sutton, QUE J0E 2K0 (phone: 514-538-2545); and *Bromont Ski Area,* CP 29, Bromont, QUE J0E 1L0 (phone: 514-534-2200; 800-363-8920 in Canada); *Sutton Resort,* PO Box 280, Sutton, QUE J0E 2K0 (phone: 514-538-2545). There's also an *All-Resort Line* (phone: 800-355-5755).

LAC BEAUPORT, near Quebec City, Quebec This resort center consists of *Le Relais* and *Mont St-Castin,* whose verticals measure 750 and 550 feet respectively. They do not offer the quality of skiing available at *Mont-Ste-Anne* (see below), but due to their proximity to the city (13 miles/21 km from downtown), each is busy during the week and busier still on weekends. In addition, the nearby food, lodging, and lively après-ski activity are as exceptional as Aspen's. Information: *Le Relais,* 1084 Blvd. du Lac-Beauport, QUE G0A 2C0 (phone: 418-849-1851); and *Mont St-Castin,* 82 Chemin le Tour-du-Lac, Lac Beauport, QUE G0A 2C0 (phone: 418-849-1893).

LAURENTIANS (LES LAURENTIDES), near Montreal, Quebec Beginning about 35 miles (56 km) from Montreal, along the high-speed Laurentian autoroute leading into the hills to the northwest, is a succession of ski communities—more than 20 major ones in all. If only for the extremely high density of runs in the area—some 300 in 40 square miles—the Laurentians would be unique. But the frills of a skiing vacation here also stand out. Some of the region's older Quebecois-style villages have delightful inns, and there are all manner of resorts and small hotels so close to the skiing that you can schuss right to your doorstep. Many of the resorts' dining rooms serve enticing local specialties like *tourtière,* a meat pie, and the sweet, maple sugar–flavored pie known as *tarte au sucre.*

Each ski area here has its own appeal. At the northern end of this string of resorts is *Mont Tremblant,* the dowager queen of Canada's winter resorts. With a vertical drop of 2,100 feet and runs that extend up to 2 miles in length, *Mont Tremblant* offers plenty of good skiing for skiers of all levels of expertise. A detachable quad chair lift and jet T-bar are among its more high-tech features; amenities include restaurants at the top and base of the mountain; a nursery; and snowmaking facilities extending to the very top of the mountain's southern side. The area's many first-rate hotels include the big *Station Mont Tremblant Lodge* (phone: 819-681-2000; 800-461-8711) and the smaller *Le Club Tremblant* (phone: 819-425-2731; 800-363-2413 in the US). Some 3 miles (5 km) away in St-Jovite is the *Auberge Gray Rocks* (phone: 819-425-2771; 800-567-6767 in eastern Canada and the US), a friendly sprawl of a hostelry on 2,600 acres with its own ski hill, Sugar Peak, a hundred yards from the inn. The vertical here is a mere 620 feet, but the proprietors never wasted time deluding themselves that they had the Matterhorn on their hands. Instead, they touted the mountain as ideal for learning and, in 1938, developed the *Snow Eagle Ski School,* with a teaching program so thorough that there are even a couple of instructors whose sole job is keeping the others on their toes. Consequently, hundreds of graduates will testify that the school is North America's best. Other ski areas offer similar delights. *Belle Neige* (phone: 818-322-3311) in Val-Morin, a small hill with a vertical of only about 520 feet, two T-bars, and two chair lifts, is distinguished by the proximity of the *Hôtel la Sapinière* (phone: 819-322-2020; 800-567-6635), the proud possessor of one of Canada's finest kitchens. For all lodgings noted above, see *Special Havens.*

The Laurentians are far from being Canada's biggest mountains, but the atmosphere and amenities go a long way toward making skiing in the east a worthwhile experience. Information: *Association Touristique des Laurentides,* 14142 Rue de La Chapelle, RR1, St-Jérôme, QUE J7Z 5T4 (phone: 514-436-8532).

LE MASSIF, near Quebec City, Quebec Fifty miles (80 km) from town, this is the most unusual ski center east of the Rockies. A 2,614-foot-high escarpment that plunges toward the St. Lawrence River, it has 15 2½-mile intermediate and expert trails that boast some of the best powder snow in eastern Canada. Because the center can accommodate a limited number of skiers per day—despite the addition of new lifts—reservations are a must. Information: *Le Massif,* Rte. 138, CP 68, Petite-Rivière-St-François, QUE G0A 2L0 (phone: 418-632-5876).

MONT-STE-ANNE, near Quebec City, Quebec A regular stop on the *World Cup* circuit, this is the biggest of the local areas. Located in Beaupré, 25 miles (40 km) northeast of the city, it boasts 50 slopes and 12 lifts of varying types that together can transport over 17,000 people an hour. The top three-quarters of the southern slopes are as challenging as any of Vermont's steepest and hairiest runs; there are plenty of varied intermediate and novice runs as well. The snowmaking system covers well over 85% of the skiable terrain, and Mont-Ste-Anne claims to have the highest vertical night skiing in Canada. A "ski à la carte" and three-hour ticket allow skiers flexibility. On clear days, year-round, a gondola climbs 2,640 feet to the summit, commanding a breathtaking view of the St. Lawrence River, Quebec City, and the Ile d'Orléans. The most direct way to get there is to follow Route 138, but for a more scenic tour leave 138 at Beaupré and continue along Route 360; Route 440 is another alternative. Information: *Office du Tourisme et des Congrès de la Communauté Urbaine de Québec,* 60 Rue d'Auteuil, Quebec City, QUE G1R 4C4 (phone: 418-692-2471), and *Parc du Mont Ste-Anne,* CP 400, Beaupré, QUE G0A 1E0 (phone: 418-827-4561; 800-463-1568).

MONT-STE-MARIE RESORT, Lac Ste-Marie, Quebec This ski center has the most extensive facilities and offers the best skiing in west Quebec. It has a vertical drop of 1,250 feet, and its longest run is just over 2 miles. Its two high-speed detachable quad chairs and snowmaking equipment covering all 17 runs have made this ski center number one in the region. The ski chalet has been expanded, and there's an attractive resort complex of condominiums and chalets known for good ski packages. Near Kazabazua, about 50 miles (80 km) from Ottawa. Information: *Mont-Ste-Marie,* Rte. 105, Lac Ste-Marie, QUE J0X 1Z0 (phone: 819-467-5200; 800-567-1256 in Canada).

STONEHAM, near Quebec City, Quebec After *Mont-Ste-Anne* (see above), this is the region's next most extensive ski area, with a 1,380-foot vertical (it also has hosted *World Cup* races). Nestled in a valley, Stoneham is protected from strong winds. Twenty-three of the 25 runs have snowmaking equipment, and 16 of them are lighted; lift capacity is over 14,000 an hour. The resort's condos and hotels are open for summer vacationing. And it's only 13 miles (21 km) from downtown. Information: *Stoneham,* 1420 Av. du Hibou, Stoneham, QUE G0A 4P0 (phone: 418-848-2411; 800-463-6888 in Canada).

WEST

So special and inclusive are the opportunities for winter recreation in the Canadian Rockies that the province of Alberta was chosen to host the

Winter Olympics back in 1988. But much fine skiing can be found in other parts of western Canada as well.

BANFF LAKE LOUISE, Alberta The heart of the Canadian Rockies offers just about everything a skier could want—great slopes, deep powder, some of the continent's most glorious scenery, and a season that consistently extends into May. An alpine resort in a bowl above the tree line, *Sunshine Village* boasts tons of powder, the longest season in the area, on-hill accommodations, and slope-side resort life. The network of forest runs and above-timberline snowfields has a 3,420-foot vertical that is served by eight lifts and a gondola. All of *Sunshine Village*'s resort facilities are in a complex of buildings at the lift base (at 7,200 feet), accessible by gondola from the parking lot at the end of an access road branching off the Trans-Canada. There's also plenty of après-ski activity.

Mystic Ridge and Norquay is Banff's challenge to advanced skiers, but it offers some easy skiing for beginners as well. Site of the celebrated mile-long chute known as the "North American," as well as a couple of other hair-raisers that are nearly as steep, *Mystic Ridge and Norquay* also boasts some of the finest novice terrain anywhere—acres of broad fields covered with ultralight, carefully groomed powder.

The area's most extensive terrain, however—indeed, the nation's largest lift-serviced downhill ski area, the North's answer to Aspen and Squaw Valley—is at *Skiing Louise,* 35 miles (56 km) and 45 minutes down the Trans-Canada from Banff. Here, skiers find 4,000 acres of mogul fields, steep chutes, vast glacial bowls, gentle trails through the glades—and just about any other kind of ski terrain imaginable—on four mountain faces. Some 50 designated runs, reaching up to 5 miles in length, drape down 3,250 vertical feet of hillside and are served by a panoply of lifts. All lodgings are about 2 miles (3 km) from the lift base. The most charming properties are the *Post* hotel (phone: 403-522-3989), known for its kitchen, and the winterized *Château Lake Louise* (phone: 403-522-3511), the grandest of all the Canadian Pacific hotels (see *Special Havens* for both properties).

With shuttle buses linking the three big complexes and the availability of interchangeable lift tickets, mountain-hopping is a common practice here. Many people set up a base in the town of Banff and travel to each of the three ski areas. Accommodations are available in more than 30 hotels in town, including the modern and very comfortable *Banff Park Lodge* (phone: 403-762-4433) and the spired-and-turreted *Banff Springs* hotel (phone: 403-762-2211; see *Special Havens*). Information: *Banff/Lake Louise Tourism Bureau,* PO Box 1298, Banff, AB T0L 0C0 (phone: 403-762-8421) or *Ski Banff/Lake Louise,* PO Box 1085, Banff, AB T0L 0C0 (phone: 403-762-4561; 800-661-1431).

MARMOT BASIN, Jasper, Alberta The Canadian Rockies' third-largest downhill center provides some of the West's finest open slope and bowl skiing off its 7,930-foot summit. Thirty-five of the trails are gentle enough that even the most shaky-kneed novice can sneak a look at the scenery, and there are sunny bowls that make intermediates feel like hotshots. Thirty percent of the trails are rated expert, including an extraordinary deep-powder run accessible via the Knob Chair. The area offers seven varied lifts. *Marmot Basin* offers a nursery for children from 19 months to five years of age, a skier-improvement center with ski week vacation packages, and a rental and retail ski shop. But for all that, *Marmot Basin* would be just another wonderful ski resort, were it not for its location inside spectacular *Jasper National Park.* When you've had enough of the vast downhill slopes, join a cross-country ski tour, a snowshoe tour, a "canyon crawl," or a walking tour guided by park naturalists—or take the 60-mile (96-km) drive down to the Columbia Icefield. *Marmot Basin* is 12 miles (19 km) from Jasper, a family-oriented community of about 4,000, offering a satisfying lineup of après-ski activities and accommodations (no lodging at the hill). For those who want to sample the skiing and activities at Banff (see above), a weekly bus service offers a chance to take in the scenery on the 172-mile (275-km) round trip. Information: *Ski Marmot Basin Ski-Lifts Ltd.,* PO Box 1300, Jasper, AB T0E 1E0 (phone: 403-852-3816); *Jasper Tourism and Commerce,* PO Box 98, Jasper, AB T0E 1E0 (phone: 403-852-3858).

NAKISKA AT MOUNT ALLAN, Kananaskis Village, Alberta The Kananaskis-Nakiska area, site of the *1988 Olympic* alpine competition, is one of Canada's newest ski destinations. It boasts tremendous fall-line skiing, first class facilities, state-of-the-art snowmaking, and western Canada's first two detachable quad chair lifts. Kids have their own ski area, with a handle tow and a day-care center. *Kananaskis Village* includes a general store, a ski rental shop, a post office, and a complex of restaurants, shops, and three hotels. The *Hotel Kananaskis* (phone: 403-591-7711; 403-271-0489 from Calgary; 800-441-1414; fax: 403-591-7770) offers 22 luxury suites and 46 rooms. The *Lodge at Kananaskis* (same phone numbers as the *Hotel Kananaskis*) has 251 rooms and 58 suites. There's a health club, and guests can swim from the pool area to the hot tub located outside under the stars. There's a sauna outside too, and plenty of snow in which to roll. The hotel and lodge, which are connected, are owned by Canadian Pacific (of *Banff Springs* fame); of the two, the lodge is more family-oriented. For more moderately priced accommodations, try Best Western's *Kananaskis Inn* (phone: 403-591-7500; 800-528-1234; fax: 403-591-7633), which has 94 units. Other winter activities include taking horse-drawn sleigh rides, tobogganing, ice skating, and cross-country skiing. Information: *Nakiska Ski Area,* PO Box 1988, Kananaskis Village, AB T0L 2H0 (phone: 403-591-7777; fax: 403-591-7780).

KIMBERLEY, Kimberley, British Columbia The community 2 miles (3 km) from this ski resort in the British Columbia Rockies—50 miles (81 km) north of the international border—has a Bavarian theme complete with a pedestrian mall known as the *Platzl.* Condominiums at the base of the lifts continue this theme. There is extensive summer grooming of the 44 major runs (which are served by two triple chair lifts, one double chair lift, a trio of drag lifts, two handle tows, and a T-bar) and plenty of snowmaking early in the season. Novices and intermediates can ski after dark on one of North America's longest illuminated downhill ski runs (vertical, 2,300 feet). Other facilities include lodges at the top of the hill and winterized campsites, two racquetball courts, and five tennis courts (two indoor, three outdoor) at the base. Information: *Kimberley Ski & Summer Resort,* PO Box 40, Kimberley, BC V1A 2Y5 (phone: 604-427-4881; 800-667-0811; fax: 604-427-3927).

OKANAGAN SIMILKAMEEN (BIG WHITE SKI RESORT, APEX RESORT, AND SILVER STAR), Kelowna, British Columbia This region of pine-clad, lake-dotted mountains whose valleys yield the prodigious harvests of fruit for which the province is so famous is blessed in winter with what some people call Canada's best snow—the famed fast-and-fluffy Okanagan Powder. A good deal of it falls at night, especially during February, so days seem almost predictably sunny, and the valleys stay green almost all winter long. Kelowna (pop. 80,000) is at the midpoint of a trio of good-size ski resorts stretching up and down the valley: *Big White Ski Resort, Apex Resort,* and *Silver Star. Big White,* a resort not unlike Colorado's fine *Keystone,* is a favorite with families. Less than an hour's drive from Kelowna, *Big White*—with a 2,050-foot vertical drop, over 700 acres of groomed trails, and 57 runs—offers high-speed, four-passenger express lifts, doubling the time on the slopes for all skiers at all levels of ability. *Apex Resort,* about 20 miles (32 km) west of Penticton, offers 56 runs (something for every level of skier, with more advanced terrain than at many areas) meandering down 2,000 vertical feet; on-mountain lodgings accommodate up to 320. An area 11 miles (18 km) from Vernon, *Silver Star* has a total of 68 runs—some narrow and tree-lined, some wide-open alpine slopes—with a vertical drop of 2,500 feet; each lift offers access to skiing of all degrees of difficulty. On-mountain accommodations include three hotels (with Swiss, railway, and saloon themes) and three apartment-style condominiums. Information: *Okanagan Similkameen Tourism Association,* 1332 Water St., Kelowna, BC V1Y 9P4 (phone: 604-860-5999; fax: 604-861-7493); *Silver Star,* PO Box 2, Silver Star Mountain, BC V0E 1G0 (phone: 604-542-0224; 800-663-4431; 604-542-1236); *Big White Ski Resort,* PO Box 2039, Station R, Kelowna, BC V1X 4K5 (phone: 604-765-3101; 800-663-2772; fax: 604-765-8200); and *Apex Resort,* Box 1060, Penticton, BC V2A 7N7 (phone: 604-292-8222; 800-387-2739; fax: 604-292-8622).

PANORAMA, near Invermere, British Columbia Nestled in a high mountain valley 12 miles (19 km) from Invermere, this self-contained village provides condominium and hotel accommodations right on the mountain. There are 50 runs and the highest vertical rise (4,300 feet) in the Canadian Rockies. *R. K. Heliskiing* (phone: 604-342-3889) offers heli-ski day packages. Information: *Panorama,* General Delivery, Panorama, BC V0A 1T0 (phone: 604-342-6941; 800-663-2929 in Canada; fax: 604-342-3995).

RED MOUNTAIN, Rossland, British Columbia Named for the color of the tailings of the old Rossland gold mines, this relatively uncrowded mountain a few miles beyond the Washington State border in the southern Monashees is where several Canadian *Olympic* gold medalists have gone from snowplow to slalom. As a result, it's been pegged as a hotshot's mountain. Ski weekers who have grappled with the terrain, a good many of them from Spokane, Washington, 120 miles (192 km) away, still go back home to confirm the truth of the locally popular saying that if you can master Red, you can handle any slope in the world. Nearby Granite provides another 75 runs ranged down 2,800 vertical feet for beginners and intermediates. The mountain's main run is one of Canada's *World Cup* downhill race courses. All trails from both Granite and Red converge at the lift base, where there's a day lodge. Nearby are overnight accommodations in chalets, cabins, and one of the most charming ski hotels anywhere, the nine-room *Ram's Head Inn* (PO Box 636, Rossland, BC V0G 1Y0; phone: 604-362-9577; fax: 604-362-9577). Another great lodging place is the fancy 67-room *Uplander* hotel (PO Box 1510, Rossland, BC V0G 1Y0; phone: 604-362-7375; 800-667-8741; fax: 604-362-7375). The season runs from late November through mid-April. Every year in late January there's a lively winter carnival. Information: *Red Mountain,* PO Box 670, Rossland, BC V0G 1Y0 (phone: 604-362-7384; 604-362-7700, central reservations; 800-663-0105; fax: 604-362-5883).

SUN PEAKS RESORT AT TOD MOUNTAIN, near Kamloops, British Columbia One of a number of Canadian Rockies ski areas in the interior, with 2,850-foot-plus verticals and slopes, Tod Mountain is 33 miles (53 km) from Kamloops, British Columbia, and less than four hours from Vancouver. The deep, dry powder snow, a specialty of the BC interior, the extra-long beginner and intermediate runs (5 and 7 miles, respectively), the steep mogul fields that shoot toward the base, and the "Challenger," which ranks among North America's steepest slopes, all make for first class skiing experiences. Tod has a superb distribution of terrain for skiers at all ability levels, and it can comfortably handle nearly 13,000 skiers a day. With six lifts (two quads, one triple, one double, one T-bar, and one T-bar platter lift), Tod Mountain hasn't yet come close to maximizing its potential. There is also a snowboard park. On-mountain accommodations include bed and breakfast options, condo rentals, and RV hookups. A South Tirolean–style resort village, with a 40-room European-style hotel and restaurant plus shops and dining, is expected to open this year. An 18-hole golf course also is set to open, as the mountain vies for top-resort status. Downtown Kamloops, the nearest rail or air connection to the mountain, is a 45-minute bus or car ride away; on weekends and holidays, shuttle buses run between the mountain and the city. The ski season runs from mid-November to mid-April or early May. Information: *Tod Mountain Development, Ltd.,* PO Box 869, Kamloops, BC V2C 5M8 (phone: 604-578-7222; fax: 604-578-7223).

WHISTLER RESORT, Whistler, British Columbia Nestled in the mountains 75 miles (120 km) north of Vancouver along the spectacular Sea-to-Sky Highway, this resort has long been one of the giants of North American skiing. *Whistler Village* abounds with shops, restaurants, nightspots, galleries, and hotels. One of the best properties in the area where you can ski-in and ski-out is the stately *Château Whistler* (phone: 604-938-8000; fax: 604-938-2020), right at the base of Blackcomb, with its lift and trails, heated indoor and outdoor pools, saunas and Jacuzzis, and several restaurants. Other choices include the *Delta Mountain Inn* (phone: 604-932-1982) at the base of Whistler and the Tirolean-style *Durlacher Hof* (phone: 604-932-1924) and the family-style *Crystal Lodge* (phone: 604-932-2221). The skiing remains unparalleled. The resort's two mountains boast North America's longest lift-served vertical drops—5,280 feet at Blackcomb and 5,020 feet at Whistler Mountain. Side by side, this pair offers close to 7,000 acres of world class ski terrain, with over 200 trails up to 7 miles long (served by more than two dozen lifts) and every type of skiing, from forest-edged trails and paths through the glades to broad groomed slopes and breathtaking high alpine powder bowls. Whistler's snowfall often tops 450 inches a year. The resort frequently hosts the *World Cup* slalom and giant slalom competitions. Open year-round, with a special ski camp on Blackcomb in summer. Information: *Whistler Mountain Ski Corporation,* PO Box 67, Whistler, BC V0N 1B0 (phone: 604-932-3434; fax: 604 932-6374);*Whistler Resort Association,* 4010 Whistler Way, Whistler BC V0N 1B4 (phone: 604-932-4222; 800-944-7853; fax: 604-932-7231); or *Blackcomb Skiing Enterprises*, 4545 Blackcomb Way, Whistler, BC V0N 1B4 (phone: 604-932-3141; fax: 604: 938-7527).

WILDERNESS SKIING

Austrian-born skier and mountain guide Hans Gmoser fell in love with the wild, untamed mountains of western Canada when he came here in 1951 and almost immediately began to explore on skis some of the peaks and slopes that no one before him had ever seen in winter. Before long he was leading tours on a commercial basis. But getting uphill involved such arduous climbs that, for a dozen years, one run a day was the norm—two at the most. Gmoser was continually frustrated by being unable to take full advantage of the immense concentrations of skiable terrain in the area, until he began using helicopters to get his skiers uphill. Heli-skiing was born, and it boomed. Costs are high—from about $2,000 to $3,400 or more for a week-long, all-inclusive package—but intermediate and advanced skiers find the thrill of cascading down 6,600 vertical feet of pristine snow worth the price.

Heli-skiing outfits go to great lengths to keep their guests happy and safe. Guides seek out the best snow and lead skiers around glacier crevasses and away from potentially hazardous areas. They also lend their experienced help to first-time deep-snow skiers. *Canadian Mountain Holidays* (see below) even offers a week-long program for first-time heli-skiers who would like to build up their confidence in skiing this type of terrain. Guests always ski with others of similar ability, and helicopter operators can supply special powder skis that will make the going easier.

Incidents involving avalanches or other dangers are rare. Mike Wiegele, operator of *Mike Wiegele Helicopter Skiing* (see below), says his brand of operation is as safe as any well-established, efficiently operated, lift-serviced ski resort. His company and *Canadian Mountain Holidays,* and others, are involved in a *University of Calgary* avalanche research program that uses the latest technology to study mountain snow conditions and keeps all heli-ski operators informed of problem areas. For additional safety, every member of a heli-skiing party carries an avalanche-rescue transceiver, and radios linking the skiing groups to the helicopters, the base, and the outside world are standard equipment for the guides.

The mountains offer absolutely extraordinary ski terrain. For instance, along the section of the Columbia Mountains' Purcell Range known as the Bugaboos, in the southeasternmost segment of the Canadian Rockies, the skiable area encompasses some 1,000 square miles. And if you have your fill of skiing there, there are always the Cariboos, the Monashees, Valemount, Revelstoke, the Gothics, Galena, Adamant, and the Bobbie Burns to tackle. Each of Hans Gmoser's nine operations is bigger than 40 conventional resorts combined, and optimum snow conditions prevail from December until May. The snow is generally lighter and drier than that found on the West Coast. Nor are there the dry, cold, and fierce winds of the Rockies' eastern slopes. The flakes come in generous quantities—some 1,200 centimeters, or about 39 feet, every year—but there's rarely too much at any one time, and for the most part it is the lightest, driest powder imaginable.

Advanced intermediates experienced with a variety of terrains should find heli-skiing slopes within their abilities—even if they've never before skied powder. For anyone with an adventurous spirit and a little loose cash, heli-skiing is certainly an option. Here are some good operations offering wilderness skiing excursions.

CANADIAN MOUNTAIN HOLIDAYS, Banff, Alberta Hans Gmoser's operation, staffed by certified guides, runs seven-day helicopter ski tours to nine areas in British Columbia. Sometimes skiers headquarter at an isolated mountain lodge; sometimes in a facility in a nearby town. Information: *Canadian Mountain Holidays,* PO Box 1660, Banff, AB T0L 0C0 (phone: 403-762-7100; 800-661-0252).

MIKE WIEGELE HELICOPTER SKIING, Banff, Alberta Mike Wiegele's operation, begun in 1970, offers three-, five-, and seven-day packages in the Cariboos and the Monashees, covering an area of 3,000 square miles of wilderness. Accommodations are in chalets in Blue River, 133 miles (214 km) from Kamloops. Ski weeks can also be arranged for private parties. Information: *Mike Wiegele Helicopter Skiing,* PO Box 249, Banff, AB T0L 0C0 (phone: 403-762-5548; 800-661-9170).

P.K. HELI-SKI, Panorama, British Columbia This British Columbia outfit offers day trips as well as week-long trips for intermediate to advanced skiers, with transportation available from Banff. It's one of the only operators to offer one-day trips. Information: *P.K. Heli-Ski,* PO Box 695, Invermere, BC, V0A 1K0 (phone: 604-342-3889; 403-762-3770).

PURCELL HELICOPTER SKIING LTD., Golden, British Columbia This company has three-, five- and seven-day heli-skiing packages, as well as day trips into the Purcell Mountains. Skiers lodge at the *Prestige Inn.* Information: *Purcell Helicopter Skiing Ltd.,* PO Box 1530, Golden, BC V0A 1H0 (phone: 604-344-5410; fax: 604-344-6076).

SELKIRK WILDERNESS SKIING, Meadow Creek, British Columbia Heated snowcat rather than helicopter is the mode of transport used by this company to bring you to where the deep powder is. A limited number of guests per week are accepted, and they share 20 square miles of varied terrain. Information: *Selkirk Wilderness Skiing Ltd.,* General Delivery, Meadow Creek, BC V0G 1N0 (phone: 604-366-4424; fax: 604-366-4419).

Cross-Country Skiing

It's not necessary to be an Olympic-caliber athlete to enjoy ski touring or cross-country skiing. Nor is it necessary to go anywhere special in Canada to practice the sport. You can ski in city ravines, suburban vest-pocket parks, farmers' fields, and on frozen lakes. But with a long weekend or a week to spare, you'll want to head for the more attractive trails on Canada's hundreds of square miles of public lands. There, given some wisdom in the ways of the winter wilderness, it's a great adventure to break your own trails through the powder. Or tackle one of the many areas where special cross-country ski trails are marked, groomed, and patrolled. The latter can be found at a variety of hostelries: downhill ski resorts, luxury resorts (where après-ski means swimming in a big pool and relaxing in a sauna), dude ranches and guest farms, simple housekeeping cottages in the woods, cozy country inns, and rustic mountain lodges heated by wood stoves and lit by kerosene lanterns. Or you might want to try a lodge-to-lodge or hut-to-hut (tents, actually) tour with accommodations that are a day of skiing apart, on an interconnecting trail (luggage is transported separately by road). For the truly adventurous, there's even helicopter cross-country skiing in Alberta and British Columbia. Interesting articles about the various cross-country skiing areas are published in the magazine *Ski Canada,* found at local newsstands.

In addition to the areas described below, most of the inns and resorts recommended in *Special Havens* and many of the guest farms sketched in *Farm and Ranch Vacations* either maintain their own cross-country ski trail networks or have access to terrain in nearby provincial and national parks. For information on cross-country skiing spots in the major metropolises, see *Sports* in the individual chapters in THE CITIES. Entries are arranged geographically, starting with the eastern provinces and then the western ones; within that framework, entries are arranged alphabetically by province.

EAST

Because of Canada's continuing cross-country skiing boom, most provincial and municipal parks have developed at least one trail and try to keep campgrounds open for die-hard winter lovers. Even the Atlantic provinces have gone in for the sport—*Mactaquac Provincial Park,* 15 miles (24 km) from Fredericton, New Brunswick, keeps locals happy on its small network of trails. There are 40 miles more at Poley Mountain, north of Saint John, not far from Sussex. In Nova Scotia, the *Old Orchard Inn Ski Touring Centre* (PO Box 1090, Wolfville, NS B0P 1X0; phone: 902-542-5751) at Annapolis Valley caters exclusively to cross-country skiers. Wentworth Valley, the wooded area surrounding the *Canadian Hostelling Association*'s handsome, century-old *Wentworth* hostel (RR1, Wentworth, Cumberland Co., NS B0M 1Z0; phone: 902-548-2379), is a delight. The hostel accommodates 45 people (bring your own sleeping bag) and has a cross-country ski rental shop. Reservations are necessary.

In Quebec, *Gaspé Provincial Park* and *Forillon National Park* attract a trickle of experienced skiers looking for a superior wilderness experience. There's an extensive trail network at *Parc du Mont Ste-Anne,* with 134 miles (214 km) of trails of varying degrees of difficulty in the heart of the Laurentian Forest. Located in the picturesque village of St-Férreol-les-Neiges, the cross-country terrain is 5 miles (8 km) east of the *Mont-Ste-Anne* alpine ski center (see *Downhill Skiing* in this section) and 25 miles (40 km) from Quebec City. The trails at the *Duchesnay Forestry Station,* located 25 miles (40 km) northwest of the city (phone: 418-875-2147), are better suited to beginners; they roam through mixed hardwood and fir forests. Finally, within 36 miles (58 km) of Quebec City is *Camp Mercier* (phone: 418-848-2422; 800-665-6527), a trail area just inside the handsome *Laurentides Park,* with both grueling and easier terrain and, usually, better snow.

Quebec's Eastern Townships, also usually thought of in terms of fine alpine skiing, are sprinkled with lodges catering to kick-and-gliders. The *Canadian Ski Marathon*—a mammoth, two-day cross-country ski event that anyone can enter—takes place in the Outaouais region, in the southern section of Quebec, in mid-February. The marathon ranks among the biggest events of its kind in the world. The starting point and finish line alternate each year between *Lac Beauchamp Lodge,* in the Quebec zone of the Ottawa-Hull suburbs, and Lachute, 105 miles (168 km) to the east. For more information, contact *Canadian Ski Marathon* (PO Box 98, Montebello, QUE J0V 1L0; phone: 819-669-7383) or the *Association Touristique de l'Outaouais* (CP 2000, Hull, QUE J8Z 3Z2; phone: 819-778-2222).

Meanwhile, in Ontario, there are myriad resorts in the Huronia district, around Barrie. There's wilderness skiing in the glorious *Algonquin Provincial Park,* while the *Deerhurst Resort* in Huntsville (see *Special Havens*) and the *Bear Trail Inn* (PO Box 158, Whitney, ONT K0J 2M0; phone: 613-637-2662) both have good touring trail systems. The national capital region has numerous conservation areas offering trails of varying lengths; with the exception of *Gatineau Park,* they are all free. For information and maps, call 613-239-5000.

CHADWICK'S KWAGAMA LAKE LODGE, Hawk Junction, Ontario This is a winter wilderness experience for the rugged. Take *Algoma Central Railway*'s *Snow Train* at Sault Ste-Marie and get off at Mile 118.5, amid magnificent backcountry bordering *Lake Superior National Park.* Guides lead you on cross-country skis to the lodge 9 miles (14 km) away (snowmobiles carry the bags) where you can enjoy limitless skiing, great home-cooked meals, and relaxation in a cedar sauna or by the great stone fireplace. Guests sleep in cottages heated by wood stoves. Open *Christmas* through March. Information: *Chadwick's Kwagama Lake Lodge,* Hawk Junction, ONT P05 1G0 (phone: 705-856-1104).

ALGOMA COUNTRY, north of Sault Ste-Marie, Ontario North of this city at the junction of Lakes Superior and Huron is a vast wilderness full of cross-country skiing opportunities, many of them in four provincial parks and one national park. The forests are deep, silent, and unspoiled. Establish a base at a hotel in Sault Ste-Marie and then head out for day trips into these preserves or to the big *Hiawatha Lodge II* (RR5, Landslide Rd., Sault Ste-Marie, ONT P6A 6J8; phone: 705-949-9757). There are no overnight accommodations at the lodge, which is the headquarters of the famous *Sault Finnish Ski Club,* but cross-country skiers can stop here to enjoy the cocktail lounge and other day facilities. In addition to about 21 miles of immaculately groomed trails, there is a 2-mile loop lighted for night skiing (ski and skate rentals available). Alternately, it's possible to headquarter at any one of a number of small, secluded cabins and lodges north and east of Sault Ste-Marie and north of Thessalon in the Mississagi River Valley. The trail networks are not extensive, but the lodges themselves are long on charm. Information: *Algoma-Kinniwabi Travel Association,* 616 Queen St. E., Ste. 203, Sault Ste-Marie, ONT P6A 2A4 (phone: 705-254-4293).

LAURENTIANS, Quebec Three decades ago, cross-country skiing here had the reputation of being for kamikaze types only. Trails were severe, with frequent cliff-like descents. Today, most of the trails have been redesigned, upgraded, and mechanically tracked. This vast sweep of mountains may well be the ultimate cross-country ski resort area, the Aspen of cross-country skiing. The main attraction, besides the skiing, is the abundance of wonderful restaurants and lodging places. But when you consider their diversity and the variety of the skiing terrain, putting together a Laurentians ski vacation can become terribly confusing. A few basic facts about the area may be helpful. To wit: The northern Laurentians' trails are not quite so well marked as those in the south, and the farther east or west you travel from the Laurentians *autoroute,* which bisects the region from north to south, the wilder and less well marked are the ski routes. The trails at the better-known hostelries of the more northerly St-Jovite–Mont Tremblant area are enjoyable; they include *Le Club Tremblant* (phone: 819-425-2731; 800-363-2413 in the US); the *Station Mont Tremblant Lodge* (phone: 819-681-2000; 800-461-8711); *Hôtel la Sapinière* (phone: 819-322-2020; 800-567-6635); and the *Auberge Gray Rocks* (phone: 819-425-2771; 800-567-6767). (All are described in *Special Havens.*)

Most people make their headquarters at one establishment, then spend their vacations exploring its trails and those of its neighbors, accessible via interregional trails. But the very concentration of inns and the proliferation of long-distance trails also suggest the possibility of inn-to-inn touring, and in the south, where the hostelries are situated practically on top of each other, innkeepers are generally obliging about transporting your luggage via hotel bus or taxi to your next overnight stop. Regional trail maps are available from local hotels and ski shops, as is the interregional trail map published by the Laurentian Ski Zone. Information: *Association Touristique des Laurentides,* 14142 Rue de Lachapelle, RR1, St-Jérôme, QUE J7Z 5T4 (phone: 514-436-8532).

WEST

In Manitoba, Saskatchewan, and Alberta, the cross-country skiing mania means that scarcely a snowy weekend passes without swarms of skiers taking to the trails in both urban and wilderness parks. Lodges and guest farms in the area get some of the traffic, including skiers from as far away as Europe. The woodland trails in *Prince Albert National Park* in central Saskatchewan are popular. In Manitoba, the main magnets are *Duck Mountain Provincial Park,* a major wintering ground for elk; *Riding Mountain National Park,* near Wasagaming; and *Whiteshell Provincial Park,* where ski trails lead through black spruce woods and aspen groves. In Alberta, cross-country skiers have access to miles and miles of well-marked trails in *Banff* and *Jasper National Parks,* in the *Kananaskis* area, and at Canmore's *Nordic Centre* (site of the 1988 *Winter Olympics* cross-country skiing events). Some people base themselves at luxury resorts and others at backcountry lodges or huts in order to be able to ski tour the West. Depending on the terrain and the length of your trip, you may want to take a guide. For high-country trips, some skiers rent wider skis and special boots designed especially for telemarking; others tackle the long downhills with their own skinny skis—and they keep up just fine.

ROCKIES, Western Alberta These high and rocky glaciated mountains are well known for the wealth of downhill skiing opportunities they offer—but some of the continent's most dazzling cross-country skiing can be done here as well, in *Banff* and *Jasper National Parks* and in outlying regions. Relatively inexperienced skiers also can find marked trails suited to their abilities. Consult local ski shops and park personnel for help in planning day trips on the extensive trail network here. The dramatic *Banff Springs* hotel (phone: 403-762-2211; 800-441-1414) and the equally imposing *Château Lake Louise* (phone: 403-522-3511; 800-441-1414) offer good access to all levels of trails (see *Special Havens* for both). *Skoki Lodge* (phone: 403-522-3555; fax: 403-522-2095) makes a wonderful base and retreat. It consists of a group of half-century-old log structures, lit by lanterns and candles and heated by fireplaces, and situated in a mountain-rimmed valley 8 miles (13 km) from the nearest road. Delicious meals are prepared on wood stoves, and evenings bring a chance to meet other trekkers around the lodge fireplace. The ski routes traverse woods and meadows, as well as valleys above the timberline. The *Banff Sundance Lodge,* operated by *Warner Guiding and Outfitting* (PO Box 2280, Banff, AB T0L 0C0; phone: 403-762-4551; fax: 403-762-8130), is a solar-powered log cabin on Brewster Creek about 10 miles (16 km) southwest of Banff. It's accessible by an intermediate-level ski trail. The *Shadow Lake Lodge*, operated by *Brewster Rocky Mountain Adventures* (PO Box 964, Dept. S, Banff, AB T0L 0C0; phone: 403-762-5454; fax: 403-762-3953), offers year-round accommodations in six luxurious cabins, with full meals and afternoon tea in the main lodge. The ski trail begins 12 miles (19 km) west of Banff; the lodge lies 9 miles (13 km) from the trailhead.

In *Jasper National Park,* the spectacular Tonquin Valley—edged and overlooked by the renowned "Rampart," rock cliffs that soar up to 10,000 feet in height—is home to *Tonquin Valley Pack and Ski Tours* (PO Box 550, Jasper, AB T0E 1E0; phone: 403-852-3909; fax: 403-852-3763), which offers a 14-mile (22-km) backcountry trip from Jasper to the lodge. The *Alpine Club of Canada* (PO Box 2040, Canmore, AB T0L 0M0; phone: 403-678-3200) operates 18 backcountry huts in western Canada, including the *Wates-Gibson* hut in *Jasper Park*'s Eremite Valley. They also offer accommodations for 54 people in their clubhouse at Canmore. The *Sunshine Village Resort* (PO Box 1510, Banff, AB T0L 0C0; phone: 403-762-6500; 800-762-1676), perched at the top of the gondola, is the single source for on-slope accommodations at one of Banff's big-time ski resorts. There are a number of marked loop trails in the area.

Information: For details about skiing, contact *Banff National Park,* PO Box 900, Banff, AB T0L 0C0 (phone: 403-762-1550), or *Jasper National Park,* PO Box 10, Jasper, AB T0E 1E0 (phone: 403-852-6161); for lists of tour operators, contact the *Banff/Lake Louise Tourism Bureau,* PO Box 1298, Banff, AB T0L 0C0 (phone: 403-762-8421), or *Jasper Tourism,* PO Box 98, Jasper, AB T0E 1E0 (phone: 403-852-3858).

CARIBOOS, British Columbia This province's Interior Ranges—the Cariboos, Purcells, Selkirks, and Monashees—are known for heli-skiing, but there is a lot of excellent cross-country terrain here, too. The region called 100-

Mile House, for instance, has 125 miles of trails and is considered the cross-country skiing capital of British Columbia. The Cariboos, the most westerly of these four groups of peaks, are most like the Rockies in their relatively smooth contours, but snowfall—though it varies considerably from valley to valley—is generally higher. Of the region's resorts and lodges offering prime cross-country skiing, the finest include the *Hills Health and Guest Ranch* (C26, 108 Ranch, 100 Mile House, BC V0K 2Z0; phone: 604-791-5225; fax: 604-791-6384), which has an indoor pool, Jacuzzis, a sauna, and conference facilities; and, across the road, the *Best Western 108 Resort* (C2, RR1, 108 Ranch, 100 Mile House, BC V0K 2E0; phone: 604-791-5211; 800-667-5233; fax: 604-791-6537), a modern, full-service motor lodge with 62 rooms and a wide range of amenities and activities. Surrounding the resort are some 87 miles (140 km) of marked trails through some of the finest cross-country ski terrain in the world; sleigh rides, tobogganing, skating, and ice fishing are also possible. For more details see the "Fraser River" route in *British Columbia,* DIRECTIONS. The *Red Coach Inn* (PO Box 760, 100 Mile House, BC V0K 2E0; phone: 604-395-2266; 800-663-8422 in British Columbia; fax: 604-395-2446) also is a favorite. These establishments are packed the first weekend in February, when the town hosts its 50-kilometer *Cariboo Ski Marathon.* There also are a number of smaller, more rustic places here. The *Circle H Mountain Lodge* (PO Box 7, Jesmond Rd., Clinton, BC V0K 1K0; phone: 604-459-2565), situated at the base of Mt. Bowman, 25 miles (40 km) outside of a blink-and-you-miss-it town called Clinton, is among them. Installed in an old log-and-frame lodge and a number of outlying log cabins, it has about 46 miles of trails with a good mix of terrain for every level of skier. Information: *Cariboo Tourism Association,* PO Box 4900, Williams Lake, BC V2G 2V8 (phone: 604-392-2226; 800-663-5885; fax: 604-392-2838).

ROCKIES, Eastern British Columbia Near the Banff/Lake Louise, Alberta, resorts but on the BC side of the Rockies, there are two lodges you must ski into (so pack light). The first is *Lake O'Hara Lodge* (PO Box 1677, Banff, AB T0L 0C0; phone: 403-678-4110 or 604-343-6418), a timbered lodge about 7 miles (11 km) west of Lake Louise. It was built by the *Canadian Pacific Railway* in 1925. There are 11 rustic rooms in the lodge and shared bathrooms (one men's, one women's). All three meals are served. Then there's the beautifully situated *Mt. Assiniboine Lodge* (PO Box 1527, Canmore, AB T0L 0M0; phone: 403-678-2883; fax: 403-678-4877), a Norwegian-style log cabin built in 1928. The main lodge has six rooms, with a capacity for 12 guests. There are shared showers and flush toilets in summer; guests must use outhouses in winter. Wood, coal, and propane heat are supplied to the fully winterized main lodge. The six private cabins (each accommodating two to four people) are propane-heated and insulated, and guests use outhouses and have access to showers and a wood-heated sauna. Meals are served in the dining room, and lunch is buffet-style. Guided trips (summer hikes, winter cross-country skiing) and equipment rentals are available. At both *Lake O'Hara* and *Mt. Assiniboine*, the cross-country skiing is excellent. Helicopter access to *Mt. Assiniboine* is available certain times of the year; contact the lodge for schedules and cost. Additional information: *Banff/Lake Louise Tourism Bureau* (see *Rockies, Western Alberta*, above).

WILDERNESS MOUNTAIN SKIING IN THE PURCELLS AND THE SELKIRKS, British Columbia The Purcells, just west of the Rockies, and the Selkirks, just west of the Purcells, are some of British Columbia's most rugged mountains. Compared with the Rockies, the slopes are steeper, the tops more pointed, the rocks more jagged, the snow much deeper. This is not the sort of terrain easterners envision when they think of cross-country skiing. Yet once you've mastered the turns, your skis can take you all sorts of places. Most of the activity in this area centers on a handful of tiny mountain lodges of varying degrees of rusticity and remoteness, from which guests go on guided day trips. *Purcell Helicopter Skiing Ltd.* offers both guided ski tours and heli–cross-country ski tours of the one-day variety, as well as longer packages that include heli–cross-country skiing, accommodations, and meals. Information: *Purcell Helicopter Skiing Ltd.*, PO Box 1530, Golden, BC V0A 1H0 (phone: 604-344-5410; fax: 604-344-6076).

The Best Tennis Vacations

Tennis courts are now found in nearly all resort hotels and many big-city hotels in Canada, as well as in just about all the country's townships and municipalities. (Write to the local chamber of commerce or tourist authority of the area you intend to visit for a list.) Bit by bit, the number of resorts devoted exclusively to tennis also has been increasing. Far more common in Canada than the tennis-only resort, however, is the multi-sport resort with a few courts and a pro. Most are located in marvelously scenic country, and offer private lessons or clinics for players of all levels of expertise, as well as other facilities that you can enjoy even if you've never held a racket. For descriptions of tennis facilities in major urban areas, see the *Sports* listings in the individual chapters of THE CITIES. The entries below are arranged alphabetically by province.

BANFF SPRINGS HOTEL, Banff, Alberta Tennis begins here in May, when the weather clears, and continues until October, when temperatures begin to drop. This turreted 828-room château in the heart of the Canadian Rockies offers its guests five Plexipave hard-surface courts and a tennis club. A ball machine and pro are available to help perfect your strokes, and, though the courts aren't lit, you can play until 10 almost every night, when the sun sets in these parts. This establishment is a good bet for a tennis vacation combined with stream fishing, canoeing and rafting, climbing, and golf, as well as swimming in either of two pools. Afterwards, enjoy the hotel's extensive spa facilities, including steam rooms, whirlpools, and a choice (or combination) of about two dozen different body treatments. Information: *Banff Springs Hotel,* PO Box 960, Banff, AB T0L 0C0 (phone: 403-762-2211; 800-441-1414; fax: 403-762-5755). Also see *Special Havens.*

JASPER PARK LODGE, Jasper, Alberta Here is a great hotel (really a lodge surrounded by old-fashioned log cabins and modern cedar chalets), a fine golf course, good fishing, hiking, canoeing and rafting, and all the other Rocky Mountain highs as off-the-court entertainment—plus wonderful tennis. There are four hard-surface courts at your disposal. No clinics are offered, but guests can take lessons from the pro. Information: *Jasper Park Lodge,* PO Box 40, Jasper, AB T0E 1E0 (phone: 403-852-3301; 800-441-1414; fax: 403-852-5107). Also see *Special Havens.*

LAKE OKANAGAN RESORT, Kelowna, British Columbia This 300-acre condominium resort hotel occupies the shores of 90-mile-long Lake Okanagan. There are seven courts (three lighted) and a teaching pro. Accommodations for up to 250 are in guestrooms, suites, studios, and three-bedroom condos, plus Bavarian-style chalets scattered around the wooded grounds and at the edge of the nine-hole, par 3 golf course. Access to local championship courses is available through the pro shop. The area offers access to many other activities, including orchard-country sightseeing—this is Canada's fruit-growing center. Information: *Lake Okanagan Resorts,* 2751 Westside Rd., Kelowna, BC V1Y 8B2 (phone: 604-769-3511; 800-663-3273 in western Canada; fax: 604-769-6665).

DEERHURST RESORT, Huntsville, Ontario Almost a century old, this Muskoka Lakes resort keeps growing to meet demand. It now has eight hard courts outdoors and four indoor courts in an entertainment complex that also features a pool, three squash courts, a racquetball court, a fitness room, men's and women's spas, a beauty salon, a dinner-theater, and pro shops to go with the club's two PGA-level golf courses. Tennis lessons are available from a pro. Information: *Deerhurst Resort,* RR4, Huntsville, ONT P0A 1K0 (phone: 705-789-6411; 800-441-1414; fax: 705-789-2431). Also see *Special Havens.*

HIDDEN VALLEY RESORT, Huntsville, Ontario Set by itself on the shores of what is affectionately known as Pen—for Peninsula—Lake, this establishment boasts three lighted tennis courts, indoor and outdoor pools, racquetball, squash, a universal gym, a whirlpool bath, and a sauna. Sailboats and windsurfers also are available. In winter, the ski slopes of *Hidden Valley Highlands* land you almost at the hotel door. Information: *Hidden Valley Resort,* RR4, Huntsville, ONT P0A 1K0 (phone: 705-789-2301; fax: 705-789-6586).

INN AT MANITOU, McKellar, Ontario This small, ultraluxurious Relais & Châteaux resort located on a semi-wilderness shore of a north-central Ontario lake offers a solid program of three-, four-, and seven-day clinics that stand out because of their high teacher-pupil ratio: A staff of 16 pros is always on hand to provide instruction for the 65 guests who can be accommodated at any given time. Facilities include 13 outdoor courts, an indoor court, ball machines, and video equipment; there's also a pool, a fitness center, a sauna and spa, and boats for sailing on the lake. This is one of North America's best-established tennis resorts, well worth traveling a long distance to experience—and a lot of first-rate tennis players do just that. Reduced rates are offered from late May to late June and from *Labour Day* to mid-October. Information: *Inn at Manitou,* McKellar Centre Rd., McKellar, ONT P0G 1C0 (phone: 705-389-2171; fax: 705-389-3818); off-season: 251 Davenport Rd., Toronto, ONT M5R 1J9 (phone: 416-967-3466). Also see *Special Havens.*

CLEVELANDS HOUSE, Minett, Ontario Tennis is the major attraction at this handsome older lodge—a 165-room families' delight on a hundred lakeside acres in the Muskoka Lakes district, about 140 miles (225 km) north of Toronto. There are 16 courts, and the structured programs—for rank beginners, novices, intermediates, advanced and team players, and children under 14—offer court time and time for viewing indoor films, learning the rules of the game, and discussing tactics and strategies. Ball machines and video equipment are employed when appropriate. Other activities include golf on the challenging nine-hole course, boating, fishing, and swimming. Rooms are located in five lodge buildings and a scattering of bungalows; a wading pool and playground keep kids happy. Open mid-May to mid-October. Information: *Clevelands House,* Box 60, Muskoka Rd. 7, Minett, Muskoka, ONT P0B 1G0 (phone: 705-765-3171; fax: 705-765-6296).

LAURENTIANS, Quebec St-Jovite's *Auberge Gray Rocks,* a complete tennis resort destination, is the grand dame of the Laurentians. Well known for its fine ski instructors, it offers tennis clinics on a par with those of the *Inn at Manitou* (see above). However, there is room here for nearly 500 guests. Tennis clinics follow the methods developed by Billie Jean King's former coach Dennis Van der Meer—that is, plenty of stroke work. Usually, this means 20 hours of instruction (four hours per day for five days) with a pair of instructors for each student on the court at any given time. If you don't want to throw yourself entirely into the game, you don't have to: A small fee entitles guests to a week's unlimited use of the resort's 22 Har-Tru courts. *Le Chantecler,* in Ste-Adèle, and *Villa Bellevue,* on Lake Ouimet, both offer tennis weeks and weekends, private lessons, and clinics. *Villa Bellevue* also has a pro available for lessons, and guests have access to four clay courts and can take full advantage of the resort's lakeshore setting and water sports. The resort also boasts an indoor pool, a spa, an exercise room, and 14 deluxe rooms. *Station Mont Tremblant Lodge* at Mont Tremblant has a half dozen Har-Tru courts; both private and group lessons and seminars for children are available. Guests lodge in a variety of deluxe rooms or in chalets of varying sizes, some with fireplaces. *Le Club Tremblant,* on the edge of Lac Tremblant, has four courts and a tennis pro at its beach club. Information: *Auberge Gray Rocks,* PO Box 1000, St-Jovite, QUE J0T 2H0 (phone: 819-425-2771; 800-567-6767 in eastern Canada and the US); *Station Mont Tremblant Lodge,* Mont Tremblant, QUE J0T 1Z0 (phone: 819-681-2000; 800-461-8711); *Le Club Tremblant,* 121 Rue Cuttle, Mont Tremblant, QUE J0T 1Z0 (phone: 819-425-2731; 800-363-2413 in the US); *Villa Bellevue,* Mont Tremblant, QUE J0T 1Z0 (phone: 819-425-2734; 800-567-6763); and *Le Chantecler,* PO Box 1048, Ste-Adèle, QUE J0R 1L0 (phone: 514-229-3555; 800-363-2420 in the US). See *Special Havens* for additional information on the first three hostelries.

MONT-STE-MARIE RESORT AND CONFERENCE CENTRE, Lac Ste-Marie, Quebec This ski-and-summer resort in the Gatineau Hills some 55 miles (88 km) north of Ottawa offers tennis on four courts that are available daily from 8 AM to 10 PM. When you've had enough on the courts, there are plenty of other sports to enjoy on the resort's 4,500 acres, such as a round of golf on the 18-hole course. Lac à la Truite here is reserved for fishing. You can windsurf, swim, canoe, and kayak on Lake Fournier (canoe and windsurfing equipment can be rented). There's a health club with a sauna and gym equipment, and a full complement of after-dark activities—a must for any complete destination resort as far from the bright lights as this one. Information: *Mont-Ste-Marie,* Lac Ste-Marie, QUE J0X 1Z0 (phone: 819-467-5200; 800-567-1256).

Golf in Canada: A Land of Links

Canada's British heritage is nowhere more obvious than in its abundance of first class golf courses. The season extends year-round on the West Coast, and from March through October in most other regions. You can obtain information on the best courses in British Columbia, Alberta, Saskatchewan, Manitoba, and Ontario from *The Golf Guide,* 16410 137th Ave., Edmonton, AB T5L 4M8 (phone: 403-447-2128). The *Golfer's Course Guide,* (Maple House Press; phone: 905-822-7322) lists courses across the country.

Canada hosts the *Canadian Open* on the PGA circuit, and the *Canadian PGA Tour.* Top female pros compete in the annual *Du Maurier Classic.* For further information on men's tournaments, call the *Canadian Pro Golf Association* (phone: 519-853-5450) or the *Royal Canadian Golf Association* (phone: 905-849-9700). For information on women's events, call the *Canadian Ladies' Golf Association* (phone: 905-849-2542).

With at least 2,500 courses across the country, there are plenty of places for visitors to play. As in the US, many private golf clubs bar transient players. However, if you show up on a weekday with a letter from your own golf club president or home course professional requesting playing privileges at a Canadian club, plus your own membership card, you may be given access. There's no need to go to such trouble, however, at the courses listed below. Most are located at resorts or in public parklands—and they're some of Canada's finest. For information on those courses located in major urban areas, consult the individual reports in *Sports* in THE CITIES. The entries below are arranged geographically, starting with the eastern provinces and then the western ones; within that framework, entries are arranged alphabetically by province and, within province, by name of town.

EAST

EDMUNDSTON GOLF CLUB, Edmundston, New Brunswick The main 18-hole championship layout stretches 6,666 yards and plays to par 73, with one long par 3 over a railway spur. There's also a five-hole, par 3 junior course for youngsters or adult practice. This semiprivate course features a clubhouse and pool overlooking the river and the city. Information: *Edmundston Golf Club,* PO Box 263, Edmundston, NB E3V 3K9 (phone: 506-735-7266 or 506-735-3086).

ALGONQUIN GOLF COURSE, St. Andrews, New Brunswick Part of one of Canada's traditional summer resort hotels, the course borders on Passamaquoddy Bay, east of Calais on the Maine border. One par 71 course has 18 holes, 13 of which are played beside or in sight of the Bay of Fundy; the other is a nine-hole woodland stretch with challenging, narrow fairways. The name of the town in which the course is situated is not gratuitous—it's actually reminiscent of its famous namesake on the east coast of Scotland. Information: *Algonquin Golf Club,* St. Andrews, NB E0G 2X0 (phone: 506-529-8823).

BALLY HALY GOLF AND COUNTRY CLUB, St. John's, Newfoundland Its narrow fairways, side-hill lies, and well-contoured greens would make this 5,800-yard, par 71 course tough enough; because of its coastline location, however, rigorous winds add to its difficulty. Many of the 18 scenic holes, tees, and fairways afford views of the North Atlantic. Information: *Bally Haly Golf and Curling Club,* PO Box 9185, St. John's, NFLD A1A 2X9 (phone: 709-753-6090).

PINES GOLF CLUB, Digby, Nova Scotia This 18-hole, par 71 course and club are owned by the provincial government and operated by the *Tourism Division* of the *Nova Scotia Economic Renewal Agency,* which also runs the fine adjacent hotel. At least as appealing as the course's 6,200 rolling yards are the famous scallops caught hereabouts: In fact, this is one of the best places in Canada to combine good golf and gastronomy. Information: *Pines Golf Club,* c/o *Pines Resort Hotel,* PO Box 70, Digby, NS B0V 1A0 (phone: 902-245-2511; fax: 902-245-6133).

HIGHLAND LINKS, Ingonish Beach, Nova Scotia One of the great adventures in golf, this par 71 course is one you must play many times to savor its true challenge. The superb setting combines seaside, valley, and mountainous terrain in perfect proportion. Tees and greens are placed in only the most perfect positions, and architect Stanley Thompson included walks as long as a half mile between holes to assure maximum enjoyment of this unique layout. The 18-hole layout is 6,588 yards. Anyone considering a round on this course should enjoy walking; motorized golf carts are prohibited to maintain the physical challenge and spirit of the old Scottish links. Closed November through April. Information: *Cape Breton Highlands National Park,* Ingonish Beach, Victoria County, NS B0C 1L0 (phone: 902-285-2600).

LINGAN COUNTRY CLUB, Sydney, Nova Scotia Golf pros who really know Nova Scotia consider this par 72 one of the hardest tracks in all of the Maritimes. You play every foot of the course's 6,664 yards: The distances on the scorecard are deadly accurate, and your short-iron game had better be, too. Definitely not for the timid. Information: *Lingan Country Club,* PO Box 1252, Grand Lake Rd., Sydney, NS B1P 6S9 (phone: 902-562-1112).

GLEN LAWRENCE GOLF AND COUNTRY CLUB, Kingston, Ontario Don't let the rather flat front nine here lull you into a false sense of security. The back nine are considerably more rolling, and this par 71 course represents a fine test. (There's water to conquer on seven holes.) Information: *Glen Lawrence Golf and Country Club,* RR1, Kingston, ONT K7L 4V1 (phone: 613-545-1021).

UPPER CANADA GOLF COURSE, near Morrisburg, Ontario Operated by the *St. Lawrence Parks Commission,* the course boasts unusually large greens and rather rolling fairways. The setting is especially picturesque. A driving range, dining facilities, and a pro shop are on the premises. The par is 72. Information: *Upper Canada Golf Course, St. Lawrence Parks Commission,* PO Box 740, Morrisburg, ONT K0C 1X0 (phone: 613-543-2003).

WHIRLPOOL GOLF COURSE, Niagara Falls, Ontario This par 72 course gets its name from the famous Niagara Whirlpool, and the scenery includes a view of the Niagara Gorge. There are many trees, many traps, and very challenging green positions. Rental clubs are available. Information: *Whirlpool Golf Course, Niagara Parks Commission,* PO Box 150, Niagara Falls, ONT L2E 6T2 (phone: 905-356-1140).

METCALFE GOLF CLUB, near Ottawa, Ontario Among public courses in the area (30 minutes south of Ottawa), this par 72 course is considered one of the most challenging and attractive. The 15th hole, at more than 400 yards, is a very difficult par 5, and there are several daunting dogleg fairways that require precision chips over or through trees. There's a pro shop and pleasant 19th-hole patio bar. Information: *Metcalfe Golf Club,* Metcalfe, ONT K4M 1B3 (phone: 613-821-2701).

GREEN GABLES GOLF COURSE, Cavendish, Prince Edward Island One of the oldest courses on the island (opened in 1939), it owes its name to PEI's leading literary light, Lucy Maud Montgomery. Early in this century, her story of a young orphan girl, *Anne of Green Gables,* entranced the world, and the house in which her fictional heroine lived is adjacent to the golf course. The course itself, a par 72, is a rare blend of rolling terrain with seaside dunes and ponds. Closed November to mid-May. Information: *Green Gables Golf Course, Island Coastal Services Ltd.,* PO Box 151, Charlottetown, PEI C1A 7K4 (phone: 902-892-1062), or *Environment Canada, Parks-PEI,* PO Box 487, Charlottetown, PEI C1A 7L1 (phone: 902-963-2488 or 902-672-2211).

THE LINKS AT CROWBUSH COVE, Lakeside, Prince Edward Island The newest of the province's golf layouts is its first links course (par 72), with a spectacular seaside setting 20 minutes from Charlottetown. There are nine water holes and nine holes surrounded by sand dunes. The clubhouse has a pro shop and a lounge (phone: 902-961-3100). Information: *PEI Visitor Services,* PO Box 940, Charlottetown, PEI C1A 7N5 (phone: 902-368-4444).

BRUDENELL RIVER PROVINCIAL GOLF COURSE, Roseneath, Prince Edward Island Part of *Brudenell River Provincial Park,* this par 72 course has been the site of five *Canadian National Championships.* The riverside setting is well used, with fully half of the 18 holes requiring some passage over a section of the watery landscape. This major recreation complex also includes a marina, tennis, swimming, canoeing and boardsailing, horseback riding, camping, and 50 chalets. Information: *Brudenell River Provincial Golf Course,* c/o *Department of Development and Tourism,* PO Box 2000, Charlottetown, PEI C1A 7N8 (phone: 902-652-2356, October through June; 902-652-2342, the rest of the year).

MILL RIVER PROVINCIAL PARK GOLF COURSE, Woodstock, Prince Edward Island Here's another course (par 72) that's part of a larger provincial park-and-recreation complex. It's worth the trip just to play this superb course's eighth hole, where a bubbling brook boils down the middle of the fairway all the way from tee to green. Information: *Mill River Provincial Golf Course, Department of Development and Tourism,* Woodstock RR3, O'Leary, PEI C0B 1V0 (phone: 902-859-8873).

CARLING LAKE GOLF CLUB, Lachute, Quebec Designed by Harold Watson, this challenging par 72 course occupies a rolling site in the foothills of the Laurentian Mountains. Though at 6,650 yards it's not the longest course in Canada, it boasts many difficult holes that will challenge the talents of even the lowest-handicap player. Information: *Carling Lake Golf Club,* PO Box 670, Route 327 Nord, Pinehill, QUE J0V 1A0 (phone: 514-476-1212).

LE CHÂTEAU MONTEBELLO, Montebello, Quebec The resort courses of the Outaouais area have one thing in common—challenging, rolling terrain. Naturally sculpted ravines and valleys make the most forbidding hazards here, and the entire 6,235-yard course (par 70) is surrounded by dense pine and spruce woods. Information: *Le Château Montebello,* 109 Rue Notre-Dame, Montebello, QUE J0V 1L0 (phone: 819-423-6341).

MANOIR RICHELIEU GOLF CLUB, Pointe-au-Pic, Quebec The precipitous high and low points of this site overlooking the Laurentians make the 6,110-yard, par 70 course both scenic and challenging. Information: *Manoir Richelieu Golf Club,* 19 Rang Terrebonne, Pointe-au-Pic, Charlevoix, QUE G0T 1M0 (phone: 418-665-3703; 800-463-2613); in the off-season, write to 181 Rue Richelieu, Pointe-au-Pic, QUE G0T 1M0.

LE CHANTECLER GOLF CLUB, Ste-Adèle, Quebec It's part of a sizable Laurentian resort with abundant mountain scenery that provides a spectacular golfing backdrop. The 18-hole, par 70 course is next door to the *Chantecler* hotel. The total yardage is 6,200. Information: *Le Chantecler Golf Club,* 2520 Chemin du Golf, PO Box 165, Ste-Adèle, QUE J0R 1L0 (phone: 514-229-3742; 800-363-2420 in the US).

GRAY ROCKS GOLF CLUB, St-Jovite, Quebec Part of the large *Auberge Gray Rocks* complex, the club now boasts two 18-hole, par 72 courses not far from Mont Tremblant that cover gently rolling, wooded terrain. Information: *Gray Rocks Golf Club,* PO Box 1000, St-Jovite, QUE J0T 2H0 (phone: 819-425-2771; 800-567-6767 in the US).

WEST

BANFF SPRINGS GOLF CLUB, Banff, Alberta Set in a valley more than a mile high, this course is surrounded by snow-capped mountains, and you often aim shots at one of the cloud-shrouded peaks. The baronial *Banff Springs* hotel provides a striking background, and every fairway is framed in tall, deep green pine and spruce. The Bow River winds its way down the length of the valley, occasionally tossing up some whitewater. This is perhaps one of the most beautiful (and one of the most difficult) golfing sites in all of Canada. At 6,643 yards, the 18-hole course is par 71. The 9-hole course is 3,482 yards, par 36. Information: *Banff Springs Golf Club,* c/o *Banff Springs Hotel,* PO Box 960, Banff, AB T0L 0C0 (phone: 403-762-6801).

HERITAGE POINTE GOLF CLUB, De Winton, Alberta This challenging site south of Calgary showcases a wide variety of Alberta scenery. Depending on where you are on any of the three nine-hole courses, you'll glimpse the city's downtown core, the Rocky Mountains, the surrounding farmland, or the foothills. The *Pointe* and the *Heritage*, which are nestled in the Pine Creek Valley, are traditional courses; the higher *Desert* course is California links style. The par is 72 for any two courses; 7,044 yards for all three. Information: *Heritage Pointe Golf Club,* 1 Heritage Pointe Drive, De Winton, AB T0L 0X0 (phone: 403-256-2002).

JASPER PARK LODGE GOLF COURSE, Jasper, Alberta This par 71, 6,323-yard course, like the one at *Banff Springs,* was designed in the 1920s by Stanley Thompson. The fairways are carved between the slopes of the Rockies, and the greens are surprisingly lush. Information: *Jasper Park Lodge Golf Course,* c/o *Jasper Park Lodge,* PO Box 40, Jasper, AB T0E 1E0 (phone: 403-852-6090).

KANANASKIS COUNTRY CLUB, Kananaskis, Alberta Alberta's only double set of 18-hole courses features some of the most spectacular scenery in the Canadian Rockies. These finely sculptured greens, bunkers, and fairways, designed by Robert Trent Jones, are a real challenge. Each course is par 72 and 7,100 yards. Information: *Kananaskis Country Club,* PO Box 1710, Kananaskis Village, AB T0L 2H0 (phone: 403-591-7070).

WOLF CREEK GOLF RESORT, Ponoka, Alberta Described as a little piece of Scotland dropped into central Alberta, this highly praised resort annually hosts the Canadian Tour Alberta Open. It has an international, fully staffed golf school and a 20,000-square-foot clubhouse made from hand-peeled spruce logs; the 27-hole course is 6,500 to 6,800 yards, with par 70 on each 18-hole rotation. Information: *Wolf Creek Golf Resort,* RR 3, Site 10, Box 5, Ponoka, AB T4J 1R3 (phone: 403-783-6050).

FAIRMONT HOT SPRINGS GOLF CLUB, Fairmont Hot Springs, British Columbia This resort's two 18-hole, par 72 courses—*Mountainside* and *Riverside*—are surrounded by mountains, giving them compelling vistas. There are two pro shops and golf pros on hand to help you improve your swing. For a change of pace, try the resort's outdoor hot mineral pools, tennis courts, and recreation center. Some sleeping units have lofts and kitchens; camping also is possible. Information: *Fairmont Hot Springs Resort,* Rtes. 93 and 95, PO Box 10, Fairmont Hot Springs, BC V0B 1L0 (phone: 604-345-6311; 800-663-4979; fax: 604-345-6616).

BEST WESTERN 108 GOLF COURSE, 100 Mile House, British Columbia This spread in central British Columbia's Cariboo country, transformed in the 1970s into a 1,500-home development with one of the most luxurious of all Canadian guest ranches, offers magnificent golfing, among many other activities. Its 18-hole, 6,800-yard, par 71, CPGA-approved golf course has been the site of one of western Canada's largest tournaments, and a pro course, a putting green, a chipping green, and an outdoor driving range also are on the grounds. Take some time away from your golf game to play tennis, volleyball, or horseshoes; go horseback riding; swim in a heated pool; or relax in a sauna or whirlpool bath. Information: *Best Western 108 Resort,* PO Box 2, 108 Mile Ranch, BC V0K 2Z0 (phone: 604-791-5211; 800-667-5233; fax: 604-791-6537).

RADIUM GOLF COURSE, Radium Hot Springs, British Columbia The Canadian Rockies provide an impressive backdrop for this 18-hole, 5,271-yard, par 69 course, at the southern edge of *Kootenay National Park,* just minutes from the mineral waters of Radium Hot Springs. (The 118-room *Radium Hot Springs Resort* is between the 16th and 18th fairways.) After a challenging round, guests can enjoy the resort's well-equipped sports complex, which offers tennis, racquetball, squash, an indoor pool, a hot tub, a gym, a sauna, and a massage therapist for those who overdo it. Information: *Radium Hot Springs Resort,* Rtes. 93 and 95, PO Box 310, Radium Hot Springs, BC V0A

1M0 (phone: 604-347-9311; 800-665-3585; fax: 604-347-9588), or *Rocky Mountain Visitors Association of British Columbia,* PO Box 10, 495 Wallinger Ave., Kimberley, BC V1A 2Y5 (phone: 604-427-4838).

UPLANDS GOLF CLUB, Victoria, British Columbia The wind that's always blowing off the surrounding Pacific around here probably makes for the most difficult resident hazard. The private 18-hole, 6,350-yard, par 70 course has been the site of several *Canadian Senior Championships.* Information: *Uplands Golf Club,* 3300 Cadboro Bay Rd., Victoria, BC V8R 5K5 (phone: 604-592-7313, lounge; 604-592-1818, pro shop).

VICTORIA GOLF CLUB, Victoria, British Columbia This 18-hole course is the oldest in the province, founded in 1893, and has about 75 bunkers set beside the Pacific Ocean, where winds make play more challenging. The 6,015-yard layout is a par 70. Information: *Victoria Golf Club,* 1110 Beach Dr., Victoria, BC V8S 2M9 (phone: 604-598-4321; 604-598-4322, pro shop).

CHÂTEAU WHISTLER RESORT GOLF COURSE, Whistler, British Columbia Adjacent to the *Château Whistler* hotel is this 18-hole, par 72 course. It plays 6,635 yards long, and elevation changes of up to 300 feet make for challenging play. The vistas surrounding this course, designed by Robert Trent Jones Jr., lend a spectacular backdrop. Information: *Château Whistler Resort*, PO Box 100, 4612 Blackcomb Way, Whistler, BC V0N 1B4 (phone: 604-938-2092; 604-938-2095, pro shop).

WHISTLER GOLF CLUB, Whistler, British Columbia This beautiful 18-hole, par 72, 6,400-yard championship course was designed by Arnold Palmer. It is surrounded by breathtaking views of snow-capped mountains. Reservations necessary well in advance. Closed mid-October to early May. Information: *Whistler Golf Club,* 401 Whistler Way, Whistler, BC V0N 1B4 (phone: 604-932-4544).

WASAGAMING GOLF COURSE, Wasagaming, Manitoba This province is best known for the rather flat land of the south, but this 6,070-yard, par 72 course overlooking the 9.5 square miles of central Canada's beautiful Clear Lake is unusually demanding because of the rolling terrain, not to mention the difficult lies, the blind approaches to the greens, and the fairway-crossing ravines and creeks. It's about 175 miles (280 km) northwest of Winnipeg, in *Riding Mountain National Park*. Information: *Wasagaming Golf Course,* c/o Jim Dudman, PO Box 52, Wasagaming, MAN R0J 2H0 (phone: 204-848-2597).

FALCON BEACH GOLF COURSE, Whiteshell Provincial Park, Manitoba A creek running through this fine 7,020-yard championship course provides a severe hazard on four of the holes. The fairways are tree-lined and bunkered, the greens are large, undulating, and well-trapped, and the eighth hole was voted the best par 3 in the province (the total par is 72). Information: *Falcon*

Beach Golf Course, c/o *Department of Natural Resources,* Falcon Lake, MAN R0E 0N0 (phone: 204-349-2297 or 204-349-2554).

MURRAY MUNICIPAL GOLF CLUB, Regina, Saskatchewan This gently rolling, 18-hole, par 72, 6,653-yard public course is kept in top shape through an extensive watering system. It's 7 miles (11 km) northeast of downtown Regina. Information: *Murray Municipal Golf Club,* c/o *City of Regina Community Services and Parks Department,* PO Box 1790, Regina, SASK S4P 3C8 (phone: 306-777-7739).

WASKESIU LAKE GOLF CLUB, Waskesiu Lake, Saskatchewan Well trapped and irrigated, and famed for its rolling, wooded terrain, this par 70, Stanley Thompson–designed course is a jewel of the north. Extending for 6,647 yards, it is in the 1,496-square-mile *Prince Albert National Park,* some 143 miles (229 km) north of Saskatoon. Information: *Waskesiu Lake Golf Club,* PO Box 234, Waskesiu Lake, SASK S0J 2Y0 (phone: 306-663-5300, May through September; 306-922-1134, the rest of the year).

Where They Bite: Fishing in Canada

This immense land of bays, lakes, streams, and rivers has the most prolific fishing grounds in the world. There are lakes in the northern wilderness that have scarcely felt the touch of a fishing line. With a little patience, more than a little cash, and some generous help from the outfitters listed below (or any of the hundreds of others whose names are on file with provincial tourist authorities), you can arrange a fly-in wilderness fishing expedition to virtually pristine fishing grounds.

But superior fishing can be found without flying anywhere. Within driving access of most major Canadian cities are splendid fishing grounds; a two-day drive will take you into wilderness country, where you will find guides, fishing lodges of every degree of comfort and luxury, all the back-up facilities you need, and, best of all, hundreds of thousands of fish. Every area of the country has its own specialties: Atlantic salmon in the rivers of the Maritimes (with bluefin tuna in the ocean), muskie and pike in Ontario, arctic char in the far north, steelhead trout and salmon on the Pacific Coast, and lake trout everywhere.

Each province has its own licensing requirements, bag limits, and fishing seasons. Regional tourist offices and the fishing bureaus of the provinces provide this information. For a list of tour operators that offer fishing and other packages to Canada, see GETTING READY TO GO. The entries below are arranged geographically, starting with the eastern provinces and then the western ones; within that framework, entries are arranged alphabetically by province and, within province, by name of town.

EAST

The classic game fish of the East, Atlantic salmon are called the king of fish in this part of the country. They are most abundant in the rivers of New Brunswick and in many areas along the St. Lawrence River, especially around the Gaspé Peninsula. Salmon also can be caught in Nova Scotia, Newfoundland, and Labrador. Prince Edward Island has them as well, although in smaller numbers. Catches are strictly controlled almost everywhere.

Fishing in eastern Canada is hardly limited to the king; plenty of less regal but equally exciting inland river and lake fish run. New Brunswick's rivers and lakes are one of North America's best resources for smallmouth bass. Brook trout and lake trout are common on the seaboard and inland; speckled trout are found in the eastern part of Quebec; *oaunaniche* (pronounced wah-*nah*-nish, a breed of landlocked salmon) in Labrador; and walleye and the hard-fighting pike in Ontario and Quebec. Because of the chill of its fresh water, Prince Edward Island has great brook trout fishing. Brook trout are also popular in Nova Scotia, but the waters most accessible by car are fished pretty heavily, so you'll do better scouting out the wilds. Early in the season (in spring), try bait and lures or streamers; later on, wet and dry flies are more effective.

The Maritimes used to be known for huge bluefin tuna; however, their numbers have diminished in recent years. Throughout the Maritimes, charter boats are not readily available until the end of the lobster season, usually around mid-July, and the fishing gets richer as the summer progresses. Other saltwater fish available in numbers are halibut, hake (off Prince Edward Island), cod, and haddock.

MIRAMICHI RIVER, near Fredericton, New Brunswick The Miramichi is one of the very best salmon rivers on the continent. The season for spring salmon—black salmon—lasts from mid-April to mid-May, while the Miramichi is still high, and fishing is done from a boat. Freshly run from the sea, bright salmon can be taken from mid-June to early October, when the waters recede and much of the river can be waded. Needless to say, the only way a salmon can be taken on any New Brunswick river is with a fly rod. (Be sure to check the latest regulations on catching large salmon. Immediate release is required for any salmon of more than two feet from the tip of the snout to the fork in the tail, measured along the side of the fish.) A number of excellent fishing lodges on the Miramichi have their own "beat" on the river. To name a few: *Wilson's Sporting Camp Ltd.* (McNamee, NB E0C 1P0; phone: 506-365-7962); *Pond's Chalet Resort* (PO Box 8, Ludlow, NB E0C 1N0; phone: 506-369-2612); and *Wade's Fishing Lodge* (PO Box K472, Ammon Rd., Moncton, NB E1C 9V9; phone: 506-843-7311, April through mid-October; 143 Main St., Fredericton, NB E3A 1C6; phone: 506-472-6454, the rest of the year). Information: *Tourism New Brunswick,* PO Box 12345, Fredericton, NB E3B 5C3 (phone: 800-561-0123), and the *Department* *of Natural Resources and Energy, Fish and Wildlife Branch,* PO Box 6000, Fredericton, NB E3B 5H1 (phone: 506-453-2440).

HUMBER RIVER, near Corner Brook, Newfoundland The most productive salmon river on the island, this stream full of vast pools yields some 4,000 salmon averaging around five or six pounds, with 20-pounders not uncommon, between early July and late August. The river, which empties into the Bay of Islands, can be fished upstream by boat or from the shore for about 20 miles from its mouth. Information: *Department of Development, Tourism and Promotions Branch,* PO Box 8730, St. John's, NFLD A1B 4K2 (phone: 709-729-2830; 800-563-6353; fax: 709-576-2830).

GANDER RIVER, near Gander, Newfoundland This is one of Newfoundland's top salmon rivers. More than 3,000 salmon, averaging six pounds, are landed annually; fish up to 18 pounds have been netted. Best from early July to September, the fishing is mostly done out of riverboats with outboard motors, but some of the pools on the Gander can be fished from shore. Information: *Department of Development, Tourism and Promotions Branch* (see above).

EAGLE RIVER, near Goose Bay, Labrador, Newfoundland This river—a hundred miles of foaming rapids, spectacular waterfalls, placid riffles, and beautiful still pools—sees its peak salmon run beginning about mid-July. It's accessible only by float plane. The nearby White Bear River, which also empties into Sandwich Bay, gets a good run of salmon as well, though somewhat later in the summer. The tidal waters at the mouths of both rivers are noted for their abundance of big sea-run brook trout. Information: *Department of Development, Tourism and Promotions Branch* (see above).

EXPLOITS RIVER, near Grand Falls, Newfoundland Here is another of Newfoundland's biggest salmon rivers, emptying into Exploits Bay of Notre Dame Bay. There are about 30 miles of fishable water on the Exploits, and about 1,800 salmon are taken annually, their sizes running up to 18 pounds. Projects in the works may eventually produce annual returns of 100,000 salmon. The best fishing is from early July through August. Information: *Department of Development, Tourism and Promotions Branch* (see above).

RIVER OF PONDS, near River of Ponds, Newfoundland Here is yet another lure for salmon fishers. About 2,500 salmon are landed annually between about July 10, when the first run of fish enters the river, and August 10. A good run of sea trout enters the river in early August. Of the many excellent pools in the River of Ponds, wide and island-dotted Hayward's Pool and Highway Pool are standouts, but good fishing can also be had in the Steady, between River of Ponds Lake and Barrister's Pool, and in Island, Rock, Flat, Dashwood, Cran's, and Mid-Dam Pools. Information: *Department of Development, Tourism and Promotions Branch* (see above).

ALBANY WATERSHED, north of Geraldton, Ontario The wilderness streams and lakes that are part of the Albany River watershed offer a combination of brook trout, walleye, and northern pike fishing. Walleye and brook trout average two to four pounds—and the hard-fighting northern pike from these cold, clean waters occasionally weigh in at 25 pounds. The guides here are Ojibwa, from the native villages of Fort Hope, Webequie, and Lansdowne House. They still live largely off the land by trapping and hunting and are master woodsmen. Limits on the size and number of fish continue to change, so check first with the *Ministry of Natural Resources.* Information: *Ministry of Natural Resources, Geraldton District Office,* PO Box 640, Geraldton, ONT P0T 1M0 (phone: 807-854-1030).

NORTH CHANNEL, near Little Current, Ontario When Franklin D. Roosevelt wanted to go on a Canadian fishing trip after the historic Quebec Conference in 1943, Canadian government officials took him to the North Channel, a rock-studded passage of water between Lake Huron's Manitoulin Island and Ontario's mainland, where FDR reportedly caught as many as 36 bass a day. (Check for current creel limit.) North Channel also has good pike and muskie as well as excellent jumbo perch fishing in spring and summer, plus magnificent scenery. Information: *Ministry of Natural Resources, Espanola District Office,* PO Box 1340, Espanola, ONT P0P 1C0 (phone: 705-869-1330); for a list of fishing lodges, *Northern Ontario Tourist Outfitters Association,* PO Box 1140, North Bay, ONT P1B 8K4 (phone: 705-472-5552).

GEORGIAN BAY, north of Midland, Ontario Part of Lake Huron, this large bay stretches some 200 miles (320 km) from Wasaga to Great Cloche Island off Little Current, and offers some of the province's best fishing—not so much because of its size as its irregular shoreline and the profusion of rocky reefs, bars, and deep channels that create an excellent habitat for smallmouth bass, northern pike, walleyes, muskies, and trout. The eastern shoreline, where the water is especially shallow, offers the most productive smallmouth and pike fishing on the bay. On the eastern shore, Parry Sound provides good fishing for lake trout and lake trout backcross (a hybrid that is 80% lake trout and 20% brook trout); the daily limit for Parry Sound is two. The Honey Harbour, Moon River–Woods Bay, Twelve Mile Bay, Sturgeon Bay, and Magnetawan River areas offer good to excellent muskie action. Largemouth bass are plentiful in select areas along the eastern shore. Severn Sound, to the south, is good for smallmouth, northern pike, and black crappie throughout the summer, and walleye in the spring and late fall. Farther west, the southwestern section from Wasaga Beach to Wiarton offers good rainbow and lake trout backcross angling during the spring, late summer, and fall; in winter, you can fish for them through the ice from Lion's Head to Collingwood. The northeastern area, where the French River enters the bay—accessible only by boat—provides the best walleye action. In winter, there's good ice fishing for black crappie in the Honey Harbour and Twelve Mile Bay areas, and for walleye (in February and March) in the Port Severn–Waubaushene area. Information: *Ministry of*

Natural Resources, Midhurst District Office, Midhurst, ONT L0L 1X0 (phone: 705-725-7500); *Owen Sound District Office,* 611 Ninth Ave. E., Owen Sound, ONT N4K 3E4 (phone: 519-376-3860); *Sudbury District Office,* PO Box 3500, Station A, Sudbury, ONT P3A 4S2 (phone: 705-522-7823); and *Parry Sound District Office,* Lloyd Thurston, District Biologist, 7 Bay St., Parry Sound, ONT P2A 1S4 (phone: 705-746-4201).

EAGLE LAKE, near Vermilion Bay, Ontario Until fairly recently, the angler seeking big muskellunge considered Eagle Lake a must. Although its rocky reefs and bars with sudden drop-offs are a perfect habitat for these fish, the lake has been so heavily fished for muskies, lake trout, and walleye, that the fish are no longer as plentiful as they once were. Outfitters, anglers, and the *Ontario Ministry of Natural Resources* are working to implement regulatory changes and undertake habitat improvements that should help return Eagle to its former status as an ideal fish habitat. Information: *Ministry of Natural Resources, Dryden District Office,* PO Box 730, Dryden, ONT P8N 2Z4 (phone: 807-223-3341); for a list of lodges on the lake, *Patricia Regional Tourist Council,* PO Box 66, Dryden, ONT P8N 2Y7 (phone: 807-223-6792).

QURLUTUK RIVER, near Kuujjuaq, formerly Fort Chimo, Quebec The battling arctic char is king of this stream running through the subarctic tundra country of northern Quebec, and fishing can sometimes be so good that anglers get tired of reeling them in. The average catch runs up to 10 to 15 pounds, and in August, when the spawning season is on, the males are a spectacular bright red. Qurlutuk also has lake and brook trout. The Inuit guides here know the river like a Montrealer knows restaurants. Information: *Ministère du Tourisme du Québec,* PO Box 20000, Quebec City, QUE G1K 7X2 (phone: 514-873-2015; 800-363-7777).

CEDAR LAKES, near Messines, Quebec For a mixed creel, it's hard to beat the easily accessible Cedar Lakes, in the Gatineau River Valley—4-mile-long, 2-mile-wide Big Cedar and 3-mile-long, mile-wide Little Cedar. Smallmouth bass, which pound for pound fight harder than just about any other species, are abundant here; in fact, they are the mainstay of summer fishing. Most catches weigh in at around three pounds, but bigger ones, ranging up to five-and-three-quarter pounds, are not unknown. The Cedars also offer good lake trout fishing (best in May and June) and fairly lively northern pike action (especially in May and June and again from July through September). Lake trout fishing in Cedar Lakes can be combined with a spring black bear hunt in the surrounding wilderness. *Moosehead Lodge* is the only establishment on the lakes (the lodge and eight cabins accommodate a total of 65 people). Information: *Moosehead Lodge,* PO Box 61, Messines, QUE J0X 2J0 (phone: 819-465-2050), or *Ministère du Tourisme du Québec* (see above).

GEORGE RIVER, northeast of Schefferville, Quebec One of the world's great, barely fished salmon rivers, this spectacular stream flows from Michikamau Lake north through the subarctic wilderness, finally draining into Ungava Bay. The season's first angling, right after ice-out, when the streams are swollen with melt water, is for "black" salmon; silvers appear, fresh from the sea, from late July through August or September. Resident brook trout and lake trout can be taken all summer. In September, salmon fishers can combine an angling trip with a hunt for caribou, which migrate through the George River Valley by the thousands at that time of year. During July and August, only fly fishing is allowed on Quebec's designated salmon rivers (the George is among them). Information: *Ministry of Tourism/Northern Quebec*, 4 Pl. Quebec, Quebec City, QUE G1R 4X3 (phone: 418-643-9131; fax: 418-643-6149).

WEST

Western Canada can fulfill an angler's greatest expectations. Great Bear and Great Slave Lakes in the Northwest Territories are legendary for trout fishing. British Columbia's superabundance of trout and salmon have made bass seem run-of-the-mill to local anglers. Lake trout thrive in the Yukon, while the prairie provinces are rich with walleye, northern pike, big lake trout, and, in Manitoba, even trophy brook trout.

KNIGHT INLET, near Campbell River, British Columbia From April to October, spring salmon is the rule rather than the exception here, but there's a limit to the number of large spring you can catch. Big chinook salmon are regularly caught from May through August, while coho are taken from July through September. April and May are the best months to go after trout and steelhead. Given the plentiful population of Dungeness crab, anglers and their families also can go crabbing in the bays. Accommodations, and fishing guides who know the best spots intimately, are available at the *Knight Inlet Fishing Resort* (accessible only by float planes from Vancouver or Campbell River) and at *Stuart Island.* Information for both: *Blair McLean,* PO Box 818, Campbell River, BC V9W 6Y4 (604-286-6016).

DISCOVERY PASSAGE, Quadra Island, near Campbell River, British Columbia The Inside Passage, from the Queen Charlotte Islands to Vancouver, is salmon country, and there are concentrations around Rivers Inlet to the north and the Vancouver-Victoria area to the south. But if big chinook salmon is your game, the Discovery Passage—the 15-mile-long, mile-wide stretch of water running from the bottom of Quadra Island to Seymour Narrows—is where you should fish. Chinooks over 30 pounds—which the area natives call *tyee,* or big salmon—have been taken. Bucktailing—trolling a bucktail fly with fly-fishing tackle—is generally the method to use from April through June, and fly casting is the sport September through October. Some locals say that the best time for *tyee* is during August and the first week in September. Most anglers, however, go for the ferocious coho, which hit hard and then run, leaping like acrobats as the end approaches; it's not uncommon to see schools of them slashing through herring and shrimp from April through

October. The best time for casting to them, both from the shore and from boats, is September and October.

In addition, there are miles of rivers and streams full of steelhead and cutthroat. Almost as outstanding as the fishing is the scenery—miles and miles of fir-clad mountains that rise majestically from the ocean, hundreds of islands tucked away in inlets and bays, and tiny beaches where you can dig for clams and oysters and cook your catch. The area is well known for its killer whales, seals, and sea lions, and its population of bald eagles is one of the world's largest. The celebrated *April Point Fly Fishing Club* makes its headquarters at *April Point Lodge and Fishing Resort* (Quadra Island, about 12 minutes by ferry from the town of Campbell River), a first class operation owned and operated by the Peterson family for decades. The fresh seafood in the dining room is one of the great après-fishing bonuses of an excursion here. Information: *April Point Lodge and Fishing Resort*, PO Box 1, Campbell River, BC V9W 4Z9 (phone: 604-285-2222; fax: 604-285-2411).

UPPER SUSTUT AND FINLAY WATERSHEDS, northwest of Fort St. James, British Columbia For wilderness fishing with both fly tackle and spinning gear, nothing can beat the mountain streams, rivers, and lakes of the rugged Cassiar Mountains. Dolly Varden and rainbow trout run big here. The best time for trout is from May to mid-September; Dolly Varden are plentiful from spring through summer. The feeling of remoteness is seldom found farther south. The striking scenery and abundant wildlife—including moose, caribou, mountain goats, stone sheep, and grizzly bears—are an added bonus. Information: *Ministry of Environment, Lands and Parks, Fish and Wildlife Branch,* 3726 Alfred Ave., Bag 5000, Smithers, BC V0J 2N0 (phone: 604-847-7260; fax: 604-847-7728).

NUELTIN LAKE, north of Thompson, Manitoba On this 120-mile-long lake astride the Manitoba–Northwest Territories border, there's superb angling for arctic grayling averaging a good three pounds, and, in the many secluded, underfished bays, fine northern pike action. But the lake trout are what really put this place on the angler's map. There are strains of lakers here that have learned to use river currents so that they fight like fish twice their size—and when you have a fish on the line as big as the ones in Nueltin, often up to 40 inches long, you have a real battle on your hands. Nueltin often outclasses every other Manitoba lake in the lake trout *Master Angler Award.* The place to stay is *Nueltin Fly-In Lodge,* Manitoba's most northerly lodge. Located on the fringe of the province's northernmost stand of black spruce, only 20 miles (32 km) from the Northwest Territories border, it can be reached only by air. Information: *Nueltin Fly-In Lodge,* in winter, PO Box 1561, Morden, MAN R0G 1J0 (phone: 204-822-4143); in summer, PO Box 1229, Thompson, MAN R8N 1P1 (phone: 204-822-4143); or *Travel Manitoba,* Dept. 9043, 155 Carlton St., Seventh Floor, Winnipeg, MAN R3C 3H8 (phone: 800-665-0040, ext. 49).

BRABANT ISLAND, Mackenzie River, near Hay River, Northwest Territories Not far from Great Slave Lake, this section of the Mackenzie River is outstanding for northern pike and walleye fishing, with superb arctic grayling angling in both the river and local feeder streams. For pike fishing, bring a good selection of big Red Devil and Pixie spoons; for walleyes, an assortment of jigs and spinners. Arctic grayling, a fly fisher's delight, are best attracted with black ant or black gnat fly patterns and small Mepps lures. The area's *Brabant Lodge* has modern, fully equipped cabins. Information: *Brabant Lodge,* PO Box 1095, Hay River, NWT X0E 0R0 (phone: 403-874-2600), and *NWT Tourism Information,* The North Group, PO Box 2107, Yellowknife, NWT X1A 2P6 (phone: 403-873-7200; 800-661-0788).

GREAT BEAR LAKE, north of Yellowknife, Northwest Territories For many North American anglers, the mere mention of this small ocean, 150 miles long and 250 miles wide, conjures up visions of giant lake trout—as well it should. Great Bear Lake has produced more trophy lakers on rod and reel than any other lake on the continent, and the world records for lake trout (65 pounds), as well as those for grayling and lake whitefish, were set in this area. Most lake trout taken here—expect to catch hundreds in a week—weigh in at eight to 12 pounds, while grayling run in the one-to-two-pound class, with three-and-a-half- and four-pounders not uncommon. Arctic char is found a short hop away in the Tree River, accessible through *Plummers Great Bear Lodge* (phone: 204-774-5775), an outpost camp. Reaching any of these fishing grounds is not difficult, and most lodge owners offer transportation from Alberta as part of their package price. Information: *NWT Tourism Information,* The North Group, PO Box 2107, Yellowknife, NWT X1A 2P6 (phone: 403-873-7200; 800-661-0788).

GREAT SLAVE LAKE, near Yellowknife, Northwest Territories Great Slave was the first of the great far northern lakes to be discovered by fishermen. Today, it's famous for excellent lake trout and northern pike. Arctic grayling abound in many feeder streams. Fly fishers can test their skill trying to land whitefish, which can be as challenging as trout. Information: *NWT Tourism Information,* The North Group, PO Box 2107, Yellowknife, NWT X1A 2P6 (phone: 403-873-7200; 800-661-0788).

HANSON LAKE ROAD AREA, northeastern Saskatchewan Winding some 150 miles through magnificent Canadian Shield country, this route takes anglers to some of the best fishing in the north. Such lakes as Little Bear, Deschambault, Jan, and Big Sandy offer some of the most diverse fishing in the province. The route also provides access to the Churchill River system. Many parks, campsites, resorts, and outfitters offer excellent services and access to remote fly-in camps. Information: *Tourism Saskatchewan,* 500-1900 Albert St., Regina, SASK S4P 4L9 (phone: 306-787-2300; 800-667-7191).

LAC LA RONGE, in Lac la Ronge Provincial Park, north-central Saskatchewan This massive lake and the surrounding waters, including the Churchill River system, are home to northern pike, walleye, lake trout, whitefish, and grayling. *Lac la Ronge Provincial Park,* Saskatchewan's largest (851,000 acres), encompasses a hundred lakes. Drive in to this center of northern aviation on an excellent paved highway. Fly-ins are available to more than 100 outfitting camps in the province. Information: *Tourism Saskatchewan* (see above).

Sailing Canada's Many Waters

With its thousands of miles of coastline, Canada offers more good sailing than almost any other country in the world. There are not only the fjord-like shores of British Columbia and the salt-scented Maritimes, but also hundreds of lakes, holding close to half of the world's fresh water. Ontario alone has half a million lakes, many of them navigable and used regularly from May through October. Canadians are enthusiastic sailors, particularly around the Great Lakes (including Toronto), Halifax, and Vancouver. Two hundred private clubs and several hundred marinas across Canada welcome sailors.

For a list of provincial yachting associations, contact the *Canadian Yachting Association* (1600 James Naismith Dr., Suite 504, Gloucester, ONT K1B 5N4; phone: 613-748-5687; fax: 613-748-5688); for lists of marinas, contact provincial tourist authorities. *Transport Canada* (Public Affairs, *Tower C,* Place de Ville, Ottawa, ONT K1A 0N5; phone: 613-990-2309; fax: 613-995-0351) will provide a copy of the *Canadian Coast Guard Safe Boating Guide,* the *Directory of Nautical Information,* and other useful brochures. To order chart catalogs showing chart coverage, related nautical publications, and an international dealership list, contact the *Nautical Mind Bookstore* (249 Queen's Quay W., Toronto ONT M5J 2N5; phone: 416-203-1163; 800-463-9951 in Canada; fax: 416-203-0729). *Canadian Yachting* magazine (395 Matheson Blvd. E., Mississauga, ONT L4Z 2H2; phone: 905-890-1846) and *Pacific Yachting* (1132 Hamilton St., Ste. 202, Vancouver, BC V6B 2S2; phone: 604-687-1581) publish cruising and charter information in every issue, and a comprehensive annual directory of West Coast marinas.

GREAT CRUISING, EAST TO WEST

NOVA SCOTIA'S COAST The shipbuilders of this ocean-washed province were once famous for making square-riggers; today, they build smaller boats—both fishing and pleasure craft—and rent many of them by the day or the week, with or without crew, for cruises along the province's over 4,500 miles of coastline. There's good cruising all along the rocky bay- and inlet-notched headlands and among the scattered off-lying islands from Halifax to Shelburne, particularly around St. Margaret's and Mahone Bay, west of

Halifax. But during the summer, fog rolls in almost every day, and because of the numerous rocks and shoals, you have to know what you're doing. The Northumberland Strait between Pugwash and Canso Strait is another good bet. There's no fog to speak of and very little tide; the water is warm—warmer, in fact, than anywhere else on the Atlantic Coast north of the Carolinas—so you can take a dip after you drop anchor. The Bras d'Or Lakes offer the area's most sheltered saltwater cruising and lovely scenic shoreline without the problems of fog or tide. Throughout Nova Scotia's cruising area, anchorages are generally just a few hours' sail apart, and a dozen or more yacht clubs welcome visitors. Information: *Nova Scotia Economic Renewal Agency, Tourism Division,* 1800 Argyle St., Halifax, NS B3J 2R7 (phone: 902-424-5000).

COASTAL NEW BRUNSWICK The coasts of PEI, Nova Scotia, and New Brunswick—which shelter each other from the blustery Atlantic—together offer some of Canada's finest cruising waters. The prime cruising area is up and down the Northumberland Strait between Pointe-du-Chêne, New Brunswick, and PEI, where you can tie up in tiny fishing villages or little coves, or just cruise along and enjoy the view—mainly of flat-to-rolling countryside occasionally punctuated by a marina or a wharf and a spiky cluster of fishing boats. Information: *Tourism New Brunswick,* PO Box 12345, Fredericton, NB E3B 5C3 (phone: 800-561-0123).

SAINT JOHN RIVER SYSTEM, New Brunswick This is unusual boating for the Maritimes—ideal for families, for dinghy sailors who want to cruise, and for just about anybody else who wants to see what it's like to charter before getting into really big craft. Twenty- and 30-foot boats are fine on these inland waters. They're tree-lined for the most part—pastoral on the upper reaches, fjord-like lower down. Charters can be arranged. Information: *Tourism New Brunswick* (see above; ask for the *Outdoor Adventure Guide*).

SHORES OF PRINCE EDWARD ISLAND The most fantastic thing about this 140-mile-long, 25-mile-wide island as seen from the water is the patchwork-quilt effect of the fields, bright red when they're freshly plowed, and the forests and grasslands, whose greens, especially in early June, are dazzling. The land is relatively flat to low and rolling; here and there is a cluster of farm buildings or a little fishing village. The north shore, sparsely settled and relatively barren, is characterized by longer stretches of beach and more heavily breaking seas. There are fishing harbors in the north, but navigation is tricky, because shifting sands often fill them up. Thanks to the protection afforded by New Brunswick and Nova Scotia, such difficulties are less common on the south shore, where you'll probably do most of your sailing. The Magdalen Islands, some 80 miles (129 km) to the north, are another favored destination. Information: *PEI Sailing Excursions,* Victoria-by-the-Sea, PEI C0A 2G0 (phone: 902-658-2227); the *Charlottetown Yacht Club,* PO Box 1024, Charlottetown, PEI C1A 7M4 (phone: 902-892-9065);

and the *Silver Fox Curling and Yacht Club,* 110 Water St., Summerside, PEI C1N 1A9 (phone: 902-436-2153).

THOUSAND ISLANDS AND THE BAY OF QUINTE, Ontario This province has a good share of lakes and waterways, from the Great Lakes north to Hudson Bay. Around Toronto, the harbor gets so full on weekends that some locals assert they'd rather contend with a highway. For vacation cruising, however, a prime destination is the area at the eastern end of Lake Ontario, where the lake flows into the St. Lawrence River. The Thousand Islands—over 1,700 pink granite or limestone outcroppings ranged between Kingston and Brockville—offer good fishing, fine swimming, and delightful scenery. *St. Lawrence Islands National Park* provides mooring, camping, picnic facilities, and interpretive programs throughout the islands. Long, narrow, and irregular, the Bay of Quinte ranks among the province's prettiest backwaters, and some people prefer it to the Thousand Islands nearby because of the near absence of commercial and power-cruising traffic. The bay, in the heart of historic Prince Edward County, is flanked by prosperous farmlands, wooded slopes, limestone escarpments, sandy beaches, and several of Ontario's oldest towns. To get to the Bay of Quinte from the west, you can either travel around the Isthmus of Murray or, like most boaters, traverse the straight-as-an arrow, 7-mile (11-km) Murray Canal, near Trenton—a lovely trip. The bay also is the southern terminus of the Trent-Severn Waterway, a 240-mile (384-km) inland artery connecting Lake Ontario to Georgian Bay through the heart of central Ontario. Most services can be found in Kingston. Information: *Eastern Ontario Travel Association,* 209 Ontario St., Kingston, ONT K7L 2Z1 (phone: 613-549-3682); *Ontario Travel* (phone: 800-ONTARIO, except from the Yukon and Hawaii); *St. Lawrence Islands National Park,* PO Box 469, RR3, Mallorytown, ONT K0E 1R0 (phone: 613-923-5261); *Venture Yacht Charters,* Portsmouth Olympic Harbour, 53 Yonge St., Kingston, ONT K7M 1E4 (phone: 613-549-1007); and the *Murray Canal,* c/o the Trent-Severn Waterway, PO Box 567, Peterborough, ONT K9J 6Z6 (phone: 705-742-9267).

ONTARIO'S GEORGIAN BAY AND NORTH CHANNEL For fine vacation cruising, a Toronto sailor is apt to travel to Lake Huron's spectacular Georgian Bay, about 60 miles (96 km) northwest of Toronto across the neck of land separating the city from the lake. The vast, bay- and cove-notched, island-dotted expanse of water known as the North Channel—contained to the south by hundred-mile-long Manitoulin Island and to the north by the Ontario mainland—ranks among the world's prime cruising areas. Sun yourself on a lonely rock, pick blueberries, fish, swim, explore long fjord-like bays, and spend nights anchored in the lee of an island or tied up in a deserted cove. Or dock at one of the many resorts and marinas concentrated around Killarney, on the mainland, and Little Current, on Manitoulin Island, for a good meal and some friendly conversation. Powerboating always has been popular here, but sailing is taking over, due to the cost of gas; a few 25- to

35-foot sailboats are available for charter. Information: *Ontario Travel, Queen's Park,* Toronto, ONT M7A 2E5 (phone: 416-965-4008; 800-ONTARIO), and *Ontario Sailing Association,* Ste. 301, 1220 Sheppard Ave. E., Willowdale, ONT M2K 2X1 (phone: 416-426-7221).

LAKE OF THE WOODS, Ontario–Manitoba "Discovered" by Jacques de Noyon in 1688, this historic 70-mile-long, 50-mile-wide section of the fur traders' canoe route between Montreal and the prairies is the largest link in an intricately interconnected chain of lakes. When the multitudinous zigs and zags in the ragged shoreline of the mainland and the over 14,000 scattered islands are taken into account, the coastline measures 65,000 miles. So complex is the layout that you could sail for an entire season and still be a stranger to the many winding bays, cinched channels, and unexplored landfalls. With its clear water and spruce forests scattered with boulders, this is classic Canadian Shield country. Sailing is extremely popular, and there are wide-ranging facilities for boaters along the north shore of Lake of the Woods and in Kenora, Ontario. The latter, a handsomely sited town of about 10,000 once known as Rat Portage because of the muskrats that lived in the area, is home to a museum devoted to local history. The summer brings a lively schedule of fairs, festivals, and regattas, including the *Lake of the Woods International Sailing Association,* one of North America's biggest regattas (probably the biggest staged on an inland lake). There are also cruises on the MS *Kenora* four times a day, covering about 18 miles in and around the islands of the north end of the lake. Fishing—for muskies, lake trout, pickerel, and bass—is plentiful. If Lake of the Woods isn't enough for you, travel farther down the Winnipeg River to the west, where the *Keewatin Boatlift* will put you into the Winnipeg River system in a matter of minutes. Information: *Lake of the Woods Community Development Inc.,* 1500 Rte. 17 E., Kenora, ONT P9N 1M3 (phone: 807-468-8233), and *Ontario Ministry of Natural Resources,* PO Box 5080, Kenora, ONT P9N 3X9 (phone: 807-468-2500/1).

LAKE WINNIPEG, Manitoba This 9,421-square-mile lake is 260 miles long and cinched at the center like a Gibson girl's corseted waist. You won't spot all that many sails in the northern basin even on a sunny day, mostly owing to the relatively small size of the province's population—just over a million. The lake's potential for cruising is practically unlimited. Its "waistline" is the site of a cluster of islands, a number of beautiful natural harbors, the handsome *Hecla Provincial Park,* and the modern *Gull Harbour Resort and Conference Centre.* South of these, the lake's western shore is flat and prairie-like enough that it calls to mind Big Sky country; east of the lake, and north of Hecla Island, you're in Canadian Shield country again, with long sails between anchorages. The paucity of settlements in the north creates a sense of isolation and really brings home what life must have been like for the trappers who settled here during the founding days of the Hudson's Bay Company. The few communities in the northern area are for the most part connected with the Native American reserves that border the lake. However, there are marinas and yacht clubs at Winnipeg Beach, Selkirk, Victoria Beach, Silver Harbour, and Gimli, site of North America's largest Icelandic settlement and, in early August, of a boisterous celebration of this heritage. Information: *Manitoba Sailing Association,* 200 Main St., Winnipeg, MAN R3C 4M2 (phone: 204-925-5650), and *Travel Manitoba,* Dept. 9043, 155 Carlton St., Seventh Floor, Winnipeg, MAN R3C 3H8 (phone: 800-665-0040, ext. 45).

KOOTENAY LAKE, British Columbia Snow-capped mountains plunge right to the water's edge, and sandy beaches line the shore here. Kootenay never freezes—wintertime temperatures are often as high as 50F (10C), with southerly winds. The cold, clear waters are full of lingcod, Rocky Mountain whitefish, kokanee (landlocked sockeye salmon), Dolly Varden, and world-famous trophy rainbow trout. The best trophy fishing (Gerrard rainbow trout up to 35 pounds) is November through March. Because of the cross valleys cutting through the mountains, the prevailing northwest-southeast breezes are occasionally interrupted by squallish winds, sometimes doing a complete reversal in a matter of minutes. Most facilities are in Kaslo, Balfour, and Nelson. Information: *Kootenay Country Tourist Association,* 610 Railway St., Nelson, BC V1L 1H4 (phone: 604-352-6033; fax: 604-352-1656), and *Split Shot Charters,* PO Box 21, Balfour, BC V0G 1C0 (phone: 604-229-5262). For houseboat rentals, contact *Kaslo Shipyard Co.,* PO Box 449, Kaslo, BC V0G 1M0 (phone: 604-353-2686; fax: 604-353-7393).

COASTAL BRITISH COLUMBIA Here, along some of the province's 4,390 miles of coastline, is scenery on a grand scale. Some 2,000 square miles of water stretch from Tsawwassen, in the south, past Vancouver and the Queen Charlotte Islands on to Prince Rupert, which faces the islands across Hecate Strait, just south of the Alaska border. The mountains drop straight into the sea, and the islands are often upholstered with primeval forests of evergreens. Stop to sun yourself on pebbled beaches, take a dip, fish for salmon or other finny creatures in the channels, or dig for clams. You can travel long stretches without seeing a soul; then there will be a yacht club, a government marina, a fishing village, or any one of a couple of dozen provincial marine parks. Because of the moderating influence of the Pacific Ocean, you can enjoy all of this year-round; sometimes views take in white-blanketed ski slopes. Some favorite areas of the 100,000 pleasure-craft owners in British Columbia are the Gulf Islands in the Strait of Georgia around Vancouver; the hundred miles or so beyond that; the Juan de Fuca Strait around Victoria; and the isolated Queen Charlotte Islands, 400 miles (640 km) to the north, a superb cruising ground. Information: *Ministry of Parks,* Mt. Seymour Rd., North Vancouver, BC V7G 1L3 (phone: 604-924-2200), for a list of marine parks, and the *British Columbia Sailing Association,* 304-1367 W. Broadway, Vancouver, BC V6H 4A9 (phone: 604-737-3113; fax: 604-737-0677).

CRUISING SCHOOLS

Almost every charter outfit offers lessons in basic and advanced cruising. A complete list of companies can be obtained from the *Canadian Yachting Association (CYA),* (see introduction to sailing section for details). For other information on sailing schools in the Maritimes, contact the *Nova Scotia Sailing Association,* c/o *Sport Nova Scotia* (5516 Spring Garden Rd., Suite 401, or PO Box 3010, South, Halifax, NS B3J 3G6; phone: 902-425-5450). Here are two of the best.

ATLANTIC YACHTING ACADEMY, headquartered in Dartmouth, Nova Scotia At the school's various locations, good sailors (with experience on the Great Lakes and other fresh waters) can learn to deal with ocean currents and tides; beginners can get acquainted with the difference between port and starboard; and Pacific Coast dwellers and Midwesterners alike can experience the waters of Atlantic Canada. The wonders of these waters include small, secluded coves, where you can anchor and never see another boat; pretty fishing villages; and the wonderful Bras d'Or Lakes, where it's possible to tie up in a cove within arm's reach of a stand of spruce trees whose scent fills the air with an aroma you won't soon forget. Ken Isles, the school's founder, has been active in the movement to standardize sailing instruction in the US and Canada, and he uses these national guidelines in his day- and week-long courses as well as in his navigation and seamanship programs. Registered by the *Canadian Yachting Association,* the academy's instructors also are certified by both the *CYA* and the *Department of Transport.* The academy is affiliated with the *International Sailing Schools Association* and awards national and international certification. Information: *Atlantic Sailing Academy,* PO Box 8232, Station A, Halifax, NS B3K 5L9 (phone: 902-423-7245).

NEW BRUNSWICK SAILING ASSOCIATION, St. John, New Brunswick This group can provide information on sailing instruction on the Bay of Fundy and St. John River. Information: *New Brusnwick Sailing Association,* Station B, St. John, NB E2M 5E6 (phone: 506-738-8677).

Canoeing and Rafting

Eons ago, glaciers scraped Canada's bedrock bare of soil, gouged out great gaping holes and filled them with water, and polished giant boulders and scattered them willy-nilly across the land. This action created the Canadian Shield, a 1.6-million-square-mile horseshoe-shaped expanse of rock whose vast network of river- and stream-linked lakes has been shaping history here since the days before the Europeans arrived. The rivers, streams, and lakes were the highways along which the French and the English explored the land. Later, to facilitate shipping in strategic areas where rapids or waterfalls made navigation difficult, canals and lock systems were added, making Canada's network of waterways among the most extensive in the world. The Northwest Territories alone feature so many streams that 100,000 people could canoe through 100,000 lifetimes and still not cover them all. The Mackenzie River—the trunk of the nation's longest river system—flows some 1,200 miles from its source into the Arctic Ocean. The Quetico area of southern Ontario seems immense to those paddling through, but it's hardly more than a freckle on the map compared with moderate-sized systems like the *Algonquin Provincial Park* in southeastern Ontario or Quebec's *La Vérendrye Provincial Park.* Of Ontario's 250,000 lakes and 20,000 miles of streams, the *Ministry of Natural Resources* has documented some 14,000 miles of the most practical water routes.

The canoeing waters described below chart only a small portion of the possibilities; publications may help you choose others to explore. The *Canadian Recreation Canoeing Association,* 1029 Hyde Park Rd., Suite 5, Hyde Park, ON N0M 1Z0 (phone: 519-473-2109; fax: 519-473-6560), stocks Ken Madsen's excellent regional book, *Rivers of the Yukon,* along with many other books and maps. The association, which publishes Canada's only canoeing and kayaking magazine (*Kanawa*), can suggest local canoe outfitters as well. Lists of outfitters and rental agencies are also available from provincial tourist offices.

Most outfitters can provide maps, but in some areas it may be necessary to order Canadian National Topographic Survey Maps—cartographic reproductions of aerial photographs that pinpoint lakes, rivers, roads, buildings, bridges, and some 90 other manmade and natural features. Those scaled at 1:250,000 give general parameters, while the 1:50,000 series, each map covering approximately one day's paddle, is good for details. To order these or the map indexes that can help you determine which maps you need, contact the *Canada Map Office* (130 Bentley Ave., Nepean, ONT K1A 0E9; phone: 613-952-7000). Also ask for their two useful brochures, *How to Use a Map* and *Maps and Wilderness Canoeing,* free of charge. (Remember, maps are only general guides; seasonal and other conditions must be taken into account.) For a list of tour operators offering outdoor adventure packages along Canada's inland waterways, see GETTING READY TO GO.

ONTARIO'S VAST PROVINCIAL PARKS The hardwood forest–covered ridges that make up this part of the Canadian Shield characterize *Algonquin, Killarney,* and *Quetico Provincial Parks.* Although these areas, just across the US border, are very popular, there is little danger of crowding even in the busy summer months. *Algonquin Provincial Park,* which occupies some 2,925 square miles of highlands between the Ottawa River and Lake Huron's Georgian Bay, boasts over a thousand miles of canoe routes and good fishing for lake and brook trout. Notable destinations here include ultradeep, cliff-ringed Lake Eustache; the breathtaking Natch Rapids on the Petawawa River (towered over by 300-foot-high cliffs); and Hailstorm Creek, where an occasional moose can be spied. To the northwest is *Quetico Provincial*

Park, with 900 miles of water routes that are essentially as the Ojibwa and the voyageurs found them; some of the portages (most shorter than those in *Algonquin*) are the same ones trod by the famous fur trade governor Sir George Simpson, the explorer La Vérendrye, and the itinerant artist Paul Kane. Additional routes are found in 118,600-acre *Killarney Provincial Park,* near Georgian Bay. Day trips are possible here, but the area is better for outings of about three days or longer, and the scenery is stunning. Outfitting services are in Atikokan and Thunder Bay for trips into *Quetico* and the lakes to the west and north outside the park; in Dwight, South River, and Whitney for *Algonquin Park* trips (advance information and reservations from *The Portage Store*, *Algonquin Park,* ONT P0A 1K0; phone: 705-633-5622, summer only); and in Killarney Village for trips into *Killarney Park.* Due to *Killarney*'s popularity, however, visitors should make reservations; contact *Killarney Outfitters* (Rte. 637, Killarney, ONT P0M 2A0; phone: 705-287-2828; 800-461-1117 in Ontario and the US) or *White Squall* (RR1, Nobel, ONT P0G 1G0; phone: 705-342-5324).

Information: For overviews of canoe routes in the three parks, write to *Ministry of Natural Resources, Algonquin Park District Office,* PO Box 219, Whitney, ONT K0J 2M0 (phone: 705-633-5572); for *Quetico* information, the *Atikokan District Office,* 108 Saturn Ave., Atikokan, ONT P0T 1C0 (phone: 807-597-6971); and, for Killarney information, the *Sudbury District Office,* PO Box 3500, Station A, Sudbury, ONT P3A 4S2 (phone: 705-522-7823). For listings of outfitters, contact *Ontario Travel, Queen's Park,* Toronto, ONT M7A 2E5 (phone: 416-965-4008; 800-ONTARIO).

NORTHERN ONTARIO Here in the heart of Canadian Shield country south of James and Hudson Bays are hundreds of thousands of lakes and as many more streams. The huge expanses of cool silent forests, patched here and there with outcroppings of polished rock and scattered with huge glacial boulders, are often penetrable only by canoe. Many of the waterways are virtually unexplored. Some 53,000 square miles are drained by the swift-flowing Albany River and its tributaries. Among the province's great wilderness waterways, the Albany was once a major fur trade route between *York Factory* on Hudson Bay, Lake of the Woods, and Winnipeg. On the upper reaches of the river, which flows through the middle of northern Ontario from its headwaters at Lake St. Joseph, you can still portage the many rapids and falls on wide pathways used by the oversized canoes known as York boats. The pools at the base of the rapids and falls make for some of the river's best fishing. Tributaries include the Kabinakagami, Kenogami, Little Current, Nagagami, and Ogoki Rivers. But there are hundreds of routes to follow. Most canoe trips here are fly-in propositions. Outfitters are located in the areas around Geraldton, Hearst, Longlac, Nakina, Armstrong, and Sioux Lookout. Information: for a list of outfitters, contact *Ontario Travel* (see above). The *Ministry of Natural Resources Public Information Centre,* MI-73, Macdonald Block, 900 Bay St., Toronto, ONT M7A 2C1 (phone:

416-314-2000), publishes guidebooks to the provincial parks. Some bookstores sell the helpful *Canoe Routes of Ontario,* which offers an overview of principal watersheds and canoeing possibilities. For information about guided and unguided trips, contact the *Wildwaters Wilderness Fishing Shop,* 119 N. Cumberland St., PO Box 2777, Thunder Bay, ONT P7A 4M3 (phone: 807-345-1765; fax: 807-345-1394).

RIDEAU CANAL, Ottawa to Kingston This 123-mile-long waterway between Lake Ontario and the Ottawa River was built in the early 19th century as a part of Canada's defense against the US. It's now used as a recreational waterway, as gradually increasing numbers of boats cruise its waters every summer. The trip is pleasant. Boats pass through 45 locks, masterpieces made of hand-hewn stone blocks, all but three of which are still operated by hand. Everyone stops at Jones Falls for the awe-inspiring view of the massive horseshoe dam built more than 150 years ago by the British army. The lockkeepers are happy to describe the odd-shaped buildings at some of the lock stations, originally designed as fortified structures, and to fill visitors in on other points of interest in the area. Newboro Lock brings you to the full height of the canal, where you begin a gradual descent through the Rideau Lakes. One of Ontario's fine cruising and fishing grounds, with a wealth of tree-tufted islands, it is surrounded by forests, fields, weedy shallows, sleepy little villages and towns, cottages, and marinas. At the canal's northern extremity, the Ottawa Locks, you begin a fascinating 79-foot descent through eight flight locks to the Ottawa River. Information: *Superintendent, Rideau Canal,* 12 Maple Ave. N., Smiths Falls, ONT K7A 1Z5 (phone: 613-283-5170); for tour and boat rental information, *Ontario Travel* (see above).

OTTAWA RIVER, near Pembroke, Ontario Canada has bigger rivers than this tributary of the St. Lawrence, which was once used by the voyageurs on their journeys between Montreal and Lake Huron, and many of the paddle-snapping rapids that challenged the early Canadians have been tamed by hydro dams. But the island-sprinkled Rocher-Fendu area, one-and-a-half hours west of the nation's capital and just east of *Algonquin Park,* is a stretch of water so rough that it's safe to run it only in a large rubber raft—even when it's at summer levels. When the river is at flood stage during May and June, the towering explosion waves are the equal of wild water anywhere in the world. However, there are less turbulent spots where guides can teach you to body surf. If you can't sample Canada's whitewater in the West, don't miss the one- and two-day trips on the Ottawa. There's also lots of off-water activity, including bungee jumping. Information: *Wilderness Tours,* PO Box 89, Beachburg, ONT K0J 1C0 (phone: 613-646-2291); *OWL Rafting,* Box 29, Forrester's Falls, ONT K0J 1V0 (phone: 613-238-7238); and *River Run,* PO Box 179, Beachburg, ONT K0J 1C0 (phone: 613-646-2815; 800-267-8504 in Canada).

THOMPSON, FRASER, AND CHILCOTIN RIVERS BY RAFT, British Columbia Raft tour operators on these three dynamic streams have been turning city slickers into river rats for years. The big, swift-flowing Fraser, the granddaddy of Canadian streams and one of the largest and deepest in all of North America, flows at an average of 150,000 cubic feet per second, as compared with the mighty Colorado, whose maximum flow is regulated at 25,000 cubic feet per second. In some areas, the Fraser dips and dives past the ruins of gold rush towns, and sometimes it roars through deep canyons over roller-coaster rapids. Those at Hell's Gate, below Boston Bar, are the most famous, but the Moran and Bridge River rapids are even wilder.

Alone, the Fraser would make an exciting trip. But most operators in the area offer floats that combine a number of miles on the big streams with sections on one or more of their tributaries and interconnected lakes. One such trip, on the upper reaches of the Fraser system, begins at the turquoise, 54-mile-long Chilko Lake, ringed on all sides with hanging glaciers and mountains, to its outlet and the crystal-clear Chilko River, then heads down the Chilko and into the Chilcotin, which flows into the Fraser. Scenery ranges from arid benchlands to cool evergreen forests, and in canyons you'll see rare California bighorn sheep, moose, bears, deer, and more. Shorter versions of this trip, which begin on the Chilcotin about 20 miles upstream from its confluence with the Fraser, just above the lower of the Chilcotin's two best stretches of whitewater, also are available. Still shorter trips are offered on the powerful Thompson, a more southerly Fraser tributary that flows roughly southward from Savona via Ashcroft to Lytton through an arid sagebrush-and-bunchgrass land dotted with abandoned mines and cabins. The weather here is scorching, but the whitewater spray will keep you cool. Information: *Kumsheen Raft Adventures,* Box 30, Lytton, BC V0K 1Z0 (phone: 604-455-2296; fax: 604-455-2297), and *Canadian River Expeditions,* PO Box 1023, Whistler, BC V0N 1B0 (phone: 604-938-6651; fax: 604-938-6621).

BOWRON LAKES PROVINCIAL PARK, near Barkerville, British Columbia Located in the northernmost Cariboos near the Fraser River some 70 miles (112 km) east of Quesnel, this 304,000-acre preserve offers one of Canada's classic wilderness canoe trips. In 73 miles you'll cover a chain of mountain lakes and portions of the Bowron and Cariboo Rivers and float past meadows and thick forests of spruce, lodgepole pine, western hemlock, western red cedar, and some deciduous trees, providing striking contrast in the fall. Your chances of seeing moose grazing in the marshes, beavers building dams in the flats, and bears feeding on abundant salmon in the streams are quite good. The clear waters, which flow roughly in a clockwise direction, offer good fishing for Dolly Varden, kokanee, rainbow trout, whitefish, and lake trout. Involving only about 5 miles of portaging, with no single portage longer than 1.5 miles, this trip is best from early June through October; insects are less prevalent beginning in September. Information: for canoe rentals, *Becker's Canoe Outfitters,* PO Box 129, Wells, BC V0K 2R0 (phone: 604-992-8864; fax: 604-992-3886), and *Bowron Lake Lodge and Resorts Ltd.,* 672 Walkem St., Quesnel, BC V2J 2J7 (phone: 604-992-2733; fax: 604-992-1551); for other information, *D. J. Park Contractors,* 358 Vaughan St., Quesnel, BC V2J 2T2 (phone: 604-992-3111; fax: 604-992-6624).

SOUTH NAHANNI RIVER, southwestern Northwest Territories One of the continent's finest wild streams takes in incredible vertical-walled canyons 4,000 feet high, karst landforms and caves, and high mountains sprinkled with hot springs. Then there are the tremendous Virginia Falls, showing a four-acre face of white spray and foam where they plunge—about 300 feet, or over twice the distance of Niagara. Unusual plants, luxuriant grasses, balsams, poplar, spruce, and all manner of wildlife—including grizzlies, Dall sheep, golden eagles, and trumpeter swans—can be seen here. The ridge walking that some canoe-trippers undertake for a break from their paddling is some of Canada's finest. The 1,840-square-mile *Nahanni National Park,* through which the river flows, publishes a booklet detailing a 183-mile-long section of the South Nahanni, which takes in waters ranging in difficulty from Grade I to Grade IV, and a 78-mile-long section of the Flat River—mostly Grades I and II, except for the Cascade of the Thirteen Steps, which must be portaged. Outside the park, the South Nahanni flows into the Liard, which joins the Mackenzie at Fort Simpson; both of these former fur-trade arteries can be canoed. The tributaries of the Liard—particularly the Beaver, Grayling, Rabbit, Red, and Toad Rivers—offer fine Dolly Varden and arctic grayling fishing. For nonexperts, group raft and canoe trips on shorter sections of the stream are available. Information: *Nahanni River Adventures,* 182 Valleyview Dr., Box 4869, Whitehorse, YT Y1A 4N6 (phone: 403-668-3180; fax: 403-668-3056); *Black Feather Wilderness Adventures,* 40 Wellington St. E., Toronto, ONT M5E 1C7 (phone: 416-861-1555; fax: 416-862-2314); Yellowknife, NWT X1A 2L9 (phone: 403-873-7200; 800-661-0788); and *Nahanni National Park,* Postal Bag 300, Fort Simpson, NWT X0E 0N0 (phone: 403-695-3151).

GREAT BARREN GROUND RIVERS, Northwest Territories Canada's northernmost region—the more than one million square miles of tundra between the forest-clad Mackenzie Valley and Hudson Bay, plus the Northern Yukon and the Ungava Plateau of northern Quebec and Labrador—are so finely veined with rivers and so liberally dotted with lakes that the area is as much water as it is land. During the brief summer, this is a canoeing ground without equal. Much of the land is rolling tundra, upholstered with dwarf shrubs, mosses that are sometimes emerald in hue, plus lichens, grasses, and sedges. Here and there, this palette of greens is spattered with the brilliant blues, reds, and yellows of tiny arctic flowers. Stunted spruce trees huddle together along the shores of some of the rivers. But occasionally, too, trees stand tall along the eskers (gravel ridges deposited by rivers that flowed under the glaciers). In the hundred or so miles south of the tree line are forests of widely spaced spruce, pine, and birch, and exotic and abundant wildlife. Herds of caribou file across the tundra every spring and fall on their way to and from the tree line in a mysterious migration that no one understands thoroughly. The tens, or even hundreds, of thousands of caribou often seen traveling together constitute the largest herds of wild animals left on earth. Ducks, geese, and wading birds breed in the kettle ponds and lakes. Canada geese, grizzlies, white tundra wolves, loons, musk oxen, falcons, and tundra swans are commonly seen. Because humans are unknown to many of the wild creatures here, they are more readily approached than elsewhere. The fishing can be spectacular. In midsummer, you can paddle through the wee hours of the morning by the eerie half-light of the midnight sun. In late summer the northern lights play magically across the sky. A trip in the Barren Grounds will be one you won't ever forget—whether you take it on the well-known Coppermine; the Thelon, which flows through a wooded game sanctuary; the Thelon's tributary, the short, swift Hanbury; the furious 615-mile-long Back River, which flows into the Arctic; or the Anderson, Burnside, Dubawnt, Horton, or Kazan. Guides are recommended for non-experts. Information: *Canoe Arctic Inc.*, Alex Hall, PO Box 130, Fort Smith, NWT X0E 0P0 (phone: 403-872-2308).

Mountain Climbing

Vast expanses of glaciers, whitish-blue icefalls, and breath-stopping peak-behind-peak views are all part of Canada's mountainous lure. Stunning as they are when seen from afar, they are still more bewitching when explored up close.

Novice climbers always should go out with a more experienced person or a registered guide; joining a group climb offered by one of the schools listed below is another option. More advanced mountaineers can discuss routes with climbers from a local club. For a list of tour operators offering outdoor packages that include vertical adventures, see GETTING READY TO GO.

CANADA'S CLASSIC CLIMBING

For an idea of the incredible scope and variety of the climbing in Canada, simply flip through the pages of the climbing guides available through the *Alpine Club of Canada.* The books are thick, the details multitudinous, the descriptions concise, and the possibilities—mind-boggling.

Canada's loftiest peak, 19,850-foot Mt. Logan, and the surrounding St. Elias Mountains—within *Kluane National Park* in the Yukon—generally fall into the category of expedition climbs. But the sheer number of mountains in Canada also guarantees the mountaineer an abundance of peaks to assail, usually with several routes to the top. While extremely difficult north face routes abound, the summits of most of these giants are also accessible by easier routes.

COLUMBIA ICEFIELD, near Jasper, Alberta Shaped somewhat like a saucer and rimmed with some of the highest peaks in the Rockies, this tremendous, 120-square-mile accumulation of ice lying astride the Continental Divide in *Jasper* and *Banff National Parks* sends its melt water to three oceans—the Arctic, 765 miles away via the Athabasca, the Slave, and the Mackenzie rivers; the Atlantic, by way of the Saskatchewan River, Lake Winnipeg, and Hudson Bay; and the Pacific, via the Columbia River through British Columbia and Washington State. The 11,340-foot Snow Dome, a bland-looking peak where all these river systems originate, is, in specialists' terms, the hydrographical apex of the continent. But in popular mountaineering imagination, the Snow Dome takes a back seat to a number of other peaks in the area, among them 12,294-foot Mt. Columbia, the highest in Alberta, and Mt. Athabasca. Mt. Athabasca is popular because, though only 11,452 feet high, it is very accessible from the Icefields Parkway, and because the North Glacier route, the standard route to the summit, is fairly straightforward for experienced glacier travelers and snow climbers. The Silverhorn Route is also particularly pleasant and only moderately difficult. A score of other popular peaks also offer fine challenges. Information: *Jasper National Park,* PO Box 10, Jasper, AB T0E 1E0 (phone: 403-852-6161).

MT. EDITH CAVELL, near Jasper, Alberta The summit, named after a British nurse, has been famous since the early days of exploration. Its views of the Tonquin Valley are especially fine because, at 11,033 feet, the peak is by far the highest in the vicinity of Jasper townsite. Getting there is within the skills of most competent mountaineers in good shape, weather permitting. The western slopes, for instance, are technically easy, requiring little more than scrambling with an ice axe, and perhaps crampons. The East Ridge, known for the exposed position it often puts climbers in, with sheer drop-offs on either side, is a mixed snow-and-ice route, not technically difficult but requiring rock, snow, and ice work in quickly changing sequences, so it can take 16 to 18 hours round trip. Expert mountaineers can tackle several routes on the north face. Information: *Jasper National Park,* PO Box 10, Jasper, AB T0E 1E0 (phone: 403-852-6161).

MT. ROBSON, near Jasper, Alberta Located in eastern British Columbia alongside the Alberta border in *Mt. Robson Provincial Park,* this 12,972-foot giant, the highest in the Canadian Rockies, is so big that it creates its own weather. Clouds often hang over Robson when the skies around it are clear for miles. The base is at 2,800 feet, so most climbs to the summit last three to 10 days. The standard route, up the south face, is heavily glaciated and leads over a series of ledges; here the climber will encounter many seracs and crevasses in unstable icefalls, unique frosted cornice formations called the Gargoyles, and ice and snow that can be very dangerous. Most of the mountain is raked by avalanches. To climb Robson by any route is a major mountaineering challenge—even experienced climbers frequently turn back. There is no easy way to the top, but certified guides can be found in Jasper and Banff.

Hans Schwarz of Jasper is a recognized authority on the mountain's idiosyncrasies. Information: *Jasper Climbing School and Guide Service,* Hans Schwarz, PO Box 452, Jasper, AB T0E 1E0 (phone: 403-852-3964), and *Mt. Robson Provincial Park,* PO Box 579, Valemount, BC V0E 2Z0 (phone: 604-566-4325).

MT. TEMPLE, MT. VICTORIA, AND MT. LEFROY, next to Lake Louise, Alberta Ascents of these three 11,000-foot-plus peaks—the ones featured on standard postcards of Lake Louise—mean long climbs that most mountaineers prefer to make in two days. First climbed in 1897, Lefroy's summit is accessible via several routes. The Mouse Trap Route to Abbot's Pass (where climbers camp overnight in a stone structure that accommodates 24), a snow route known for its changing glaciers, is moderately difficult but fairly straightforward. Behind the hut, there is a 2½-mile (4-km) traverse to the north peak of Mt. Victoria. The three peaks (southern, center, and northern) of Mt. Victoria make a spectacular ridge, popular for climbing and photographing. Temple, one of the bigger of the Rockies' 11,000-foot peaks, is most frequently climbed by the moderately demanding route up its southwest face from Sentinal Pass. Its particular challenges arise from the frequent and deceptively dangerous snow patches. At the top, if the weather holds, there's an unforgettable view of Paradise Valley below and the scattering of tiny lakes surrounded by wave after wave of mountains. Consult *Alpine Club of Canada* publications for detailed information. Information: *Banff National Park,* PO Box 900, Banff, AB T0L 0C0 (phone: 403-762-1550).

AUYUITTUQ NATIONAL PARK, Baffin Island, Northwest Territories Baffin Island, above Hudson Bay, is home to some of the most unusual and demanding of Canada's climbs, and big-wall climbers from Yosemite, Europe, and Japan come here to test the extremely difficult rock walls. In most cases, it's not that the peaks are technically tough; rather, climbing here poses problems simply because of the isolation. The park's outstanding features are Mt. Aasgard, with its beautiful peak, and the spiky 7,000-foot Penny Icecap, which covers 2,200 square miles. Information: *Superintendent, Auyuittuq National Park,* Pangnirtung, NWT X0A 0R0 (phone: 819-473-8962).

MOUNTAIN CLIMBING SCHOOLS

Good training at the hands of a competent guide develops solid skills and instills the good judgment and "mountain sense" that keep most climbers from heading into danger, and helps them get out of scrapes when they do occur unexpectedly. For a good introduction to mountain climbing, enroll in one of the one- or two-day beginner rock climbing courses offered by several Canadian mountaineering schools. These will teach you the basics For your next step, consider a climbing week in which lecture-practice sessions are combined with several peak ascents in the area of the base camp

The cost is $500 or more, and usually includes equipment rental, but not accommodations or meals. Alternatives include one-day intermediate programs, or one- or two-day snow-and-ice courses aimed at intermediates and beginners with some experience. The organizations listed below offer a good variety of programs.

BANFF ALPINE GUIDES, Banff, Alberta From May through September, certified mountain guides offer custom-designed rock and ice climbing courses and private guided climbs. Custom ski touring is offered in April and May. Information: *Banff Alpine Guides,* PO Box 1025, Banff, AB T0L 0C0 (phone: 403-678-6091).

HOSTELLING INTERNATIONAL CANADA–SOUTHERN ALBERTA, Calgary, Alberta Among the varied outdoor programs presented in collaboration with area outdoor-activity operators, the association promotes mountaineering, hiking, downhill ski packages, and trekking. Information: *Hostelling International Canada–Southern Alberta Region,* Suite 203, 1414 Kensington Rd. NW, Calgary, AB T2N 3P9 (phone: 403-283-5551; fax: 403-283-6503).

ALPINE CLUB OF CANADA, Canmore, Alberta Canada's only national mountaineering club, established in 1906, annually sponsors a variety of week-long mountain lovers' get-togethers. Training weeks teach snow, rock, and ice climbing skills to beginners and leadership skills to the experienced. Mountaineering camps, set up in areas with a variety of exceptional hiking and climbing opportunities, provide trainees with a chance to go out on daily climbs or to form climbing parties with kindred spirits. The club operates 18 backcountry huts and can accommodate 54 in its Canmore clubhouse. Venues for all *Alpine Club of Canada* programs change from year to year. Information: *Alpine Club of Canada,* PO Box 2040, Canmore, AB T0L 0M0 (phone: 403-678-3200; fax: 403-678-3224).

CANADIAN SCHOOL OF MOUNTAINEERING, Canmore, Alberta Chief guide Ottmar Setzer is also part-time proprietor of the *Haus Alpenrose Lodge,* where most of the school's students are housed. Summer programs include eco-hikes (for nature study), four- or five-day backpacking courses, classic-summit climbs (for intermediate climbers), rock climbing weeks or weekends, snow and ice climbing, mountain scrambles (advanced hiking), and rock-and-snow combination courses. Winter offerings include telemark skiing, ski mountaineering courses, and waterfall ice climbing courses, among others. Information: *Canadian School of Mountaineering,* 629 Ninth St., PO Box 723, Canmore, AB T0L 0M0 (phone: 403-678-4134).

JASPER CLIMBING SCHOOL AND GUIDE SERVICE, Jasper, Alberta Hans Schwarz, the local authority on Mt. Robson, shares his knowledge and experience at his climbing school, which offers summer and winter courses. Information: *Jasper Climbing School,* PO Box 452, Jasper, AB T0E 1E0 (phone: 403-852-3964).

FEDERATION OF MOUNTAIN CLUBS, Vancouver, British Columbia This year-round school offers weekend to six-day courses for beginning, intermediate, and advanced climbers in hiking, climbing, and backcountry travel. Information: *Federation of Mountain Clubs of BC,* 1367 W. Broadway, Vancouver, BC V6H 4A9 (phone: 604-737-3053; fax: 604-738-7175).

Hiking and Backpacking

One of the best ways to explore Canada's great mountains and forests is on foot. Even on short nature trails you'll see many small, hidden wonders—tiny flowers nestling under broken tree trunks, or the intricate lace patterns of the ferns, for example—while longer trips can take you deep into Canada's vast wilderness areas. Most national and provincial parks offer good opportunities for hiking; some have really extensive trail systems. In addition, Canada offers countless scenic long-distance trails.

A growing number of nature enthusiasts are experiencing the thrill of heli-hiking. *Canadian Mountain Holidays* specializes in this area—depositing clients in unspoiled alpine settings, then later whisking them away to remote lodges offering all the comforts of big-city hotels. Information: *Canadian Mountain Holidays,* PO Box 1660, Banff, AB T0L 0C0 (phone: 403-762-7100; 800-661-0252; fax: 403-762-5879.)

For further information on hiking in Alberta and British Columbia, consult Brian Patton's *The Canadian Rockies Trail Guide* or Will Harmon's *Hiker's Guide to Alberta;* both can be ordered from the *Banff Book and Art Den* (PO Box 1420, Banff, AB T0L 0C0; phone: 403-762-3919; fax: 403-762-4126) for about $13, plus postage and handling. *Explore* magazine, available at newsstands, contains articles on backpacking opportunities throughout Canada. For a list of tour operators offering outdoor adventure packages that include forays afoot, see GETTING READY TO GO.

Here's a sampling of some of the nation's hiking hot spots. Entries are arranged alphabetically by province and, within province, by name of town.

BANFF NATIONAL PARK, Banff, Alberta Some 950 miles of trails cut through this 2,500-square-mile preserve, winding through forests of spruce and pine, over high alpine meadows filled with delicately colored flowers, and under high peaks ribboned with waterfalls. Some lead to areas of scenic beauty known around the world—Lake Louise, Skoki Valley, Sunshine Meadows, Egypt Lake, and Moraine Lake and the Valley of the Ten Peaks. Information: *Banff National Park,* PO Box 900, Banff, AB T0L 0C0 (phone: 403-762-1550).

WATERTON LAKES NATIONAL PARK, near Cardston, Alberta The 108 miles of trails in this 204-square-mile preserve explore the prairies-to-mountains transitional country that gives the area its distinctive character. Most of the trails can be hiked in a day, but backcountry camps are available. There are three main trail systems, one radiating from the town of Waterton Park, one from the Akamina Parkway and Cameron Lake, and one from the Red Rock Canyon area. Information: *Waterton Lakes National Park,* Waterton Park, AB T0K 2M0 (phone: 403-859-2224).

JASPER NATIONAL PARK, Jasper, Alberta With some 4,200 square miles of land, and a network of over 600 miles of trails, the hiking possibilities here are mind-boggling. Some of the more famous take in Brazeau Lake, Jonas Pass, and Amethyst Lake in the Tonquin Valley, with its towering ramparts. The three national parks nearby—*Banff, Kootenay,* and *Yoho*—double the amount of available hiking terrain in the area. In Jasper, *Happy Trails* offers customized backpacking and horse-assisted (horses carrying heavy gear) trips for hikers and runners lasting anywhere from an afternoon to a week. Information: *Jasper National Park,* PO Box 10, Jasper, AB T0E 1E0 (phone: 403-852-6161), and *Happy Trails,* PO Box 1446, Jasper, AB T0E 1E0 (phone: 403-852-5493).

TWEEDSMUIR PROVINCIAL PARK, near Bella Coola, British Columbia This 2.4-million-acre wilderness is British Columbia's largest provincial park. The south part of the park lies some 229 miles (369 km) by partially paved road from the nearest town of any size. Consequently, much of the park's southern section has changed little since the area's first explorations by European scouts, over a century and a half ago. For the hiker, this means that self-sufficiency is paramount. There is a trail network, but still plenty of space for wilderness travel. Nearly every North American landform can be found somewhere within the park boundaries—glaciers and snowfields, lakes and rivers, plains and forest-clad hills. With its large lake system, the northern area is a marine park, accessible only by boat, helicopter, or floating plane. The brightly tinted peaks of the Rainbow Mountains, in the east-central part of the park, are especially striking. Licensed guides are available. Information: *Park Supervisors, BC Parks, South Tweedsmuir Provincial Park,* 640 Borland St., Williams Lake, BC V2G 4P1 (phone: 604-398-4414), and *Visitor Services Coordinator, Skeena District,* Bag 5000, Smithers, BC V0J 2N0 (phone: 604-847-7565).

CHILKOOT TRAIL, from Dyea, Alaska, to Bennett, British Columbia From the winter of 1897 until the fall of 1898, some 30,000 persons trekked the 33 often steep and usually rocky miles between these two towns, lured on by the promise of gold. Today you'll see the same sweeping views of rocky peaks and tranquil lakes, and the trail occasionally still turns up traces of the gold rush days—old boots, rusted tin cans, stoves, and other artifacts. The hike is demanding, so come well prepared. The *White Pass & Yukon Railway* (phone: 907-983-2217; 800-343-7373) has service between Skagway and Bennett, BC. From May through August, bus service also is available between Whitehorse and Skagway. Information: *Klondike Gold Rush National*

Historical Park, PO Box 517, Skagway, AK 99840 (phone: 907-983-2921), and *Parks Canada,* 205-300 Main St., Whitehorse, YT Y1A 2B5 (phone: 403-667-3910).

YOHO NATIONAL PARK, Field, British Columbia In the heart of the Rockies, this park is famous for its towering peaks, alpine valleys, thundering waterfalls, and turbulent streams. Some 250 miles of trails lead into the high country, where the views go on forever, and through the valleys, threaded with glacial streams. Backcountry lodges within the park's boundaries can be incorporated into hiking and walking tours; some facilities and trails are wheelchair accessible. Information: *Superintendent, Yoho National Park,* PO Box 99, Field, BC V0A 1G0 (phone: 604-343-6324), and *Yoho Visitors Centre* (phone: 604-343-6783).

MT. ASSINIBOINE PROVINCIAL PARK, near Invermere, British Columbia Matterhorn-like, 11,870-foot Mt. Assiniboine dominates the scenery in this fine 96,350-acre expanse of jagged peaks and shining lakes, blue-white glaciers, and wildflower-dotted meadows. Although the preserve is one of the Rockies' loveliest, it's also among the wildest. Transportation here is on foot only or, with permission, on horseback or by helicopter from Canmore, Alberta. Although supplies and equipment are not available, there is a concessionaire-operated resort and four alpine shelters known as the *Naiset Cabins.* Reservations are necessary at the lodge. The wilderness experience here ranks among Canada's finest. *Banff* and *Kootenay National Parks* adjoin *Assiniboine.* Information: *BC Parks–East Kootenay District,* PO Box 118, Wasa, BC V0B 2K0 (phone: 604-422-3212; fax: 604-422-3326), and *Mt. Assiniboine Lodge,* PO Box 1527, Canmore, AB T0L 0M0 (phone: 403-678-2883; fax: 604-929-2425).

MANNING PROVINCIAL PARK, Manning Park, British Columbia This 176,000-acre preserve, situated some 140 miles (225 km) east of Vancouver just north of the international border, is somewhat more developed than many BC parks. Several self-guiding nature trails, many guided walks, and a variety of day hikes are available in the area. The park itself is the southern terminus of the Canadian leg of the Pacific Crest Trail, which ends in Mexico. Information: *Ministry of Parks,* 1610 Mt. Seymour Rd., North Vancouver, BC V7G 1L3 (phone: 604-924-2200).

KOKANEE GLACIER PROVINCIAL PARK, near Nelson, British Columbia Preserving some 158,000 acres of rugged Selkirk Mountains country and accessible only by gravel road and by trail, this park's craggy peaks, canyons, glaciers, and jewel-like tarns are well worth the effort it takes to reach them. The main trail, from Gibson Lake to Joker Mill, winds through some of the most spectacular countryside and past five crystal-clear lakes. Another trail, beginning at the *Slocan Chief Hut,* takes hikers up to the 8,500-foot level and to the Kokanee Glacier. This is not the wildest of BC's parks, but some degree of expertise is required to handle the terrain, even in summer.

Information: *BC Parks–West Kootenay District,* Site 8, Comp. 5, RR3, Nelson, BC V1L 5P6 (phone: 604-825-4421; 604-825-9509).

GLACIER NATIONAL PARK, near Rogers Pass, British Columbia Most trails here begin at or near the Trans-Canada Highway, which bisects the park, and then climb steeply into jagged mountains covered with lovely forests of conifers below and spectacular glaciers and snowfields above. Trails lead hikers near the 10-square-mile Illecillewaet Icefield, one of the park's most awe-inspiring, and to Mt. Abbott, Mt. Sir Donald, and the Asulkan Glacier. Most of the trails are short enough for a day's hike, but overnight trips are also possible. A visit to the *Rogers Pass Information Centre* is well worth a break in the day's hiking. Here, exhibits and movies provide information about the park's avalanche-control program, the world's largest, as well as other aspects of the park. Park staff members will help plan hikes and answer questions. Information: *Glacier National Park,* PO Box 350, Revelstoke, BC V0E 2S0 (phone: 604-837-7500).

WEST COAST TRAIL, PACIFIC RIM NATIONAL PARK, Vancouver Island, British Columbia The western shore of this island is rocky and cliff-bound. In days gone by, storms drove ships onto the rocks, and the sailors who survived the shipwrecks perished because they couldn't get up the cliffs. Such tragedies earned the area the name "Graveyard of the Pacific." The 48-mile-long West Coast Trail, carved out as an escape hatch, has become one of the nation's most popular hiking trails. This is demanding backpacking. Now a part of *Pacific Rim National Park,* it is also one of the most spectacular, offering fine views of foamy surf and sky. The northern terminus is at Bamfield, on Pachena Bay; the southern trailhead is in Port Renfrew. Reservations required. Park admission fee. Information: *West Coast Trail Information Centres* (phone: 604-728-3234, mid-May through September only; 800-663-6000 for reservations), and *Pacific Rim National Park,* PO Box 280, Ucluelet, BC V0R 3A0 (phone: 604-726-7721).

RIDING MOUNTAIN NATIONAL PARK, Wasagaming, Manitoba Part of the Manitoba Escarpment, Riding Mountain is actually a plateau rising up from the surrounding prairie, with undulating hills, meadows, lakes, and streams accessible via over 30 hiking trails in summer and over 20 cross-country ski trails in winter. Information: *Superintendent, Riding Mountain National Park,* Wasagaming, MAN R0J 2H0 (phone: 204-848-2811).

DOBSON TRAIL, near Moncton, New Brunswick Meandering for 37 miles from Riverview into *Fundy National Park,* this is one of the more beautiful of Canada's long trails because of the primitive Albert County woods-and-valleys landscape it covers. In the park, the trail becomes the Cross Fundy Hiking Trail, providing access to other trails along quick-flowing streams that lead to the bold, irregular coastline. The Dobson Trail, marked with blue blazes, is recommended only for experienced hikers. *A Hiking Guide to New Brunswick,* by Marianne and H. A. Eiselt (Goose Lane Editions), is a collection of maps detailing more than a hundred trails; order it directly from the publisher (469 King St., Fredericton, NB E3B 1E5; phone: 506-450-4251; fax: 506-459-4991). Information: *Tourism New Brunswick,* PO Box 12345, Fredericton, NB E3B 5C3 (phone: 800-561-0123).

BRUCE TRAIL, near Hamilton, Ontario This 430-mile hiking trail winds over the scenic Niagara Escarpment from Queenston on the Niagara River to the village of Tobermory on the tip of the Bruce Peninsula, between Lake Huron and Georgian Bay. A complete guide and maps are available. Information: *Bruce Trail Association,* PO Box 857, Hamilton, ONT L8N 3N9 (phone: 905-529-6821 or 905-529-6823).

ALGONQUIN PROVINCIAL PARK, near Huntsville, Ontario This immense preserve has long been known for its extensive canoeing. But the *Ministry of Natural Resources,* responsible for the area's administration, is cutting trails into the dense forests of hardwoods and conifers that cover the Canadian Shield in the area. Two of these are the Western Uplands Backpacking Trail, made up of three loops of 19, 33, and 42 miles; and the Highland Backpacking Trail, whose two loops are 11 and 22 miles long. Some trails skirt the edges of the lakes, some meander around boggy areas, and some climb ridges. The scenery is always lovely, and a permit system preserves the isolated feeling. Information: *Algonquin Park District Office, Ministry of Natural Resources,* PO Box 219, Whitney, ONT K0J 2M0 (phone: 705-633-5572).

RIDEAU TRAIL, Kingston, Ontario A 235-mile-long system, it follows trails and secondary roads on its meandering way from the shores of Lake Ontario through marshes, forests, and fields to Chaudière Falls in Ottawa, and then to the north. The scenery varies from serene to spectacular, and historic sites and wildlife are frequently in evidence. Come prepared for mosquitoes, which you may find in the swampy areas in late spring and early summer. The *Rideau Trail Guidebook* is a good investment; order it from the *Rideau Trail Association.* Information: *Rideau Trail Association,* PO Box 15, Kingston, ONT K7L 4V6 (phone: 613-545-0823 or 613-239-5000).

GATINEAU PARK, near Hull, Quebec This preserve's 88,000 acres are flanked by the Gatineau and Ottawa Rivers, not far from Ottawa, a region well known for its hills. They rise as high as 1,367 feet from the valleys, which are at about 600 feet, and most are crisscrossed with more than 120 miles of hiking trails. Winding to waterfalls and beaver ponds, to historic ruined buildings and overlooks of the valleys to the south, some trails loop back to Lac Philippe, site of beaches, picnic grounds, a campground, and semi-wilderness campsites. Zero environmental-impact canoe-camping is possible at Lac la Pêche. Information: *Gatineau Park Division, National Capital Commission,* 161 Laurier Ave. W., Ottawa, ONT K1P 6J6 (phone: 819-827-2020; 800-465-1867).

Hunting

Canada's untracked wilderness is just about any hunter's dream. Modern-day hunters can return to a more primitive age to stalk big game, such as elk, moose, caribou, and bears, or smaller prey, like grouse, partridge, geese, and ducks. Canadians view their wildlife as a precious natural resource. Game species are professionally managed to ensure their future well-being, and government regulations strictly control hunting seasons. Each province has its own licensing requirements, and the federal government restricts the hunting of migratory birds. Each province has its own permit regulations and costs, too; therefore, it is absolutely essential that the hunter contact the province to keep abreast of regulations for specific areas.

In general, hunting is an activity best pursued in autumn, when game populations are at their peak. (Sunday hunting is prohibited in many areas.) Bag limits for small game and birds are generous across the country, but the numbers of larger game are strictly limited. Non-resident hunters should check with *Customs Canada* before bringing rifles, shotguns, and hunting dogs (which must have rabies shots) into Canada. Handguns are strictly prohibited.

The following entries are arranged geographically, starting with the eastern provinces and then the western ones; within that framework, entries are arranged alphabetically by province.

EAST

Hunting in eastern Canada centers around upland game birds, such as partridge, grouse, and woodcocks, but some areas are also outstanding for moose, caribou, white-tailed deer, and black bears. Hunters from all over the world are drawn to the picturesque province of New Brunswick in pursuit of woodcocks. These long-billed game birds are especially common in Kent, Charlotte, Albert, Westmorland, Kings, Queens, York, Victoria, Carleton, and Northumberland Counties; guides with good dogs are available.

NEW BRUNSWICK Charlotte County (which includes Grand Manan Island), as well as Victoria, Kings, York, Carleton, and Queens Counties, is one of the best spots in eastern Canada to hunt white-tailed deer. While the length of the deer season varies from area to area (from three to four weeks), it generally opens in late October or early November. Non-resident hunters must be accompanied by a guide. Information: *Fish and Wildlife Branch,* PO Box 6000, Fredericton, NB E3B 5H1 (phone: 506-453-2440).

NEWFOUNDLAND Newfoundland's western coast is one of Canada's prime moose, black bear, and caribou hunting areas. The big-game populations have been well managed by the government, so hunters with local guides stand a good chance of success. The hunting season for moose and caribou opens in mid-

September. Obtain licenses well in advance from outfitters listed in the *Newfoundland and Labrador Hunting and Fishing Guide.* Information: *Newfoundland Department of Development, Tourism and Promotions Branch,* PO Box 8730, St. John's, NFLD A1B 4K2; phone: 709-729-2830; 800-563-6353; fax: 709-576-2830.

CHAPLEAU AREA, Chapleau, Ontario This expanse of rugged, lake-dotted, boreal forest is one of the top hunting spots in eastern Canada. Black bear hunting is excellent in both the spring and fall; hunting for moose and small game is best in fall. Several lodges and outfitters in the area handle fly-in trips, accommodations, and equipment rentals. There are also six Ontario provincial parks, four with developed campsites, and two waterway parks. The town of Chapleau is the gateway to the *Chapleau Crown Game Preserve,* the largest wildlife preserve in the world. Information: *Ministry of Natural Resources,* 190 Cherry St., Chapleau, ONT P0M 1K0 (phone: 705-864-1710).

PELEE ISLAND, in Lake Erie, Ontario Among hunters who prize pheasants above all other game birds, this island is justly famous. The pheasant season is split into two periods of two days each during the fall; an additional season is scheduled during winter. Pelee Island takes on a holiday-like atmosphere as all the islanders welcome visiting hunters. There are some guides with hunting dogs on the island, but hunters are advised to bring their own if possible. Information: *Township Clerk-Treasurer,* Township of Pelee, Pelee Island, ONT N0R 1M0 (phone: 519-724-2931), and *Ministry of Natural Resources, Chatham District Office,* PO Box 1168, Chatham, ONT N7M 5L8 (phone: 519-354-7340).

JAMES AND HUDSON BAY, Moosonee, Ontario Snow, blue, and Canada geese all breed and rest in huge numbers along the rugged, unspoiled western shores of James and Hudson Bays. In September and early October during migration, when geese and ducks mass along the coastal flats to feed, the hunting is superb. Cree goose-hunting camps operate during this peak season and have cabins and canoes. Based in these comfortable spots, hunters go out with native Cree guides. Information: *Ministry of Natural Resources, Moosonee District Office,* PO Box 190, Moosonee, ONT P0L 1Y0 (phone: 705-336-2987).

ILE AUX GRUES (Crane Island), near Quebec City, Quebec This spit of grass and mud in the St. Lawrence River is one of the best hunting grounds for water fowl in eastern Canada. When greater snow geese stop over by the thousands on the tidal flats during their southward migration in October, hunting conditions are ideal. The area is also rich in black ducks, teal, and snipe Several government publications provide information on registration and services offered throughout the province. Information: *Ministère du Tourisme du Québec,* PO Box 20000, Quebec City, QUE G1K 7X2 (phone: 514-873-2015; 800-363-7777), and *Recreation, Hunting, and Fishing Department*

(*Ministère du Loisir de la Chasse et de la Pêche*), 150 Blvd. René-Lévesque E., Quebec City, QUE G1R 4Y3 (phone: 418-643-3127).

UNGAVA, near Kuujjuaq (formerly Fort Chimo), Quebec The rolling, tundra-covered hill country south of Ungava Bay is the best caribou area in Canada, thanks to careful management that has allowed the herds to grow to some 700,000 strong. As a result, the number of available hunting licenses has been increased (but there's a two-caribou-per-license limit), and several Inuit from Kuujjuaq have started outfitting hunters. Hunting season is August through October, but most lodges close by the end of September. Information: *Ministère du Tourisme du Québec* (see above) and *Quebec Inuit and Indian Outfitters,* M. Claud Fournier, Marketing Director, PO Box 163, Duhamel, QUE J0V 1G0 (phone: 819-428-4228).

WEST

Western Canada is stocked with an unparalleled variety of game. The mountains of Alberta, British Columbia, and the Yukon are internationally famous for their big-game hunting, while the prairies of Manitoba and Saskatchewan have abundant waterfowl and upland game, such as grouse, pheasant, Hungarian partridge, and snipe.

WILLMORE WILDERNESS, north of Jasper National Park, Alberta This vast Rocky Mountain wilderness is one of the largest strongholds of trophy bighorn sheep on the continent. No motorized transport is allowed in the area, so hunters must either hike or trek in on horseback, with a string of pack horses in tow, much like the country's earliest explorers. The park is home to an abundance of elk, mountain goats, deer, and moose. Information: *Alberta Department of Environmental Protection, Edmonton Information Centre,* 9920 108th St., Edmonton, AB T5K 2M4 (phone: 403-944-0313).

SPATSIZI PLATEAU, near Dease Lake, British Columbia Together with the Level Mountain Range, located west of Dease Lake, this provincial park just east of the Stewart Cassiar Highway offers some of the province's best hunting for mountain goat and caribou. Hunting is allowed within park boundaries by special permit only. The season runs from early to mid-August through mid-October, but the best time to hunt is after mid-September, after the animals have acquired their thick winter coats. *Spatsizi,* a native term meaning red goats, refers to the color the normally white goats' fur takes on when they roll around in the area's red volcanic dust to protect themselves from insects. Information: *BC Parks,* 800 Johnson St., Victoria, BC V8V1X4 (phone: 604-387-5002)

QUEEN CHARLOTTE ISLANDS, off the coast of British Columbia Black-tailed deer are abundant on these islands, because their only natural predator here is an occasional black bear. To control the population, the *British Columbia Fish and Wildlife Branch* allows hunters to bag 10 deer per year, with a possession limit of three. Information: *BC Environment—Wildlife Branch,* 780 Blanshard St., Victoria, BC V8V 1X4 (phone: 604-387-9717).

INTERLAKE REGION, between Lakes Manitoba and Winnipeg, Manitoba Sharp-tailed and ruffed grouse have always been a primary hunting attraction in this area, and they are still. In good years, the sharp-tailed grouse are unbelievably abundant, especially during peak season in late September, and through October. (The town of Ashern, so enamored of the sharp-tailed grouse that it has erected a 17-foot, 3,800-pound statue of the creature alongside Provincial Highway 6, annually stages a celebrated *One-Box Sharp-tail Hunt,* in which teams of selected VIP guests race to bag the largest number of birds with one box of shells.) In 1989, the population of ruffed grouse peaked. Lately, however, because of a resoundingly successful habitat management program, the Interlake Region also has become one of the nation's best spots for goose hunting. An estimated one million snow geese and 1.4 million Canada geese migrate through Manitoba, and the two lakes act as a funnel, so that most of the birds stop to feed and rest in the area. Around Grant's Lake and Oak Hammock Marsh, within sight of the Winnipeg skyline, several hundred thousand birds can be seen at any given time. As a result of the healthy population, bag limits are liberal. Information: *Department of Natural Resources,* 1495 St. James St., PO Box 22, Winnipeg, MAN R3H 0W9 (phone: 204-945-7812).

POTHOLE COUNTRY, from Minnedosa to the Assiniboine River, Manitoba Thanks to an abundance of sloughs, potholes, and other wetlands, this area is a prime place for duck hunting; however, the number of mallards and pintails has declined annually, and hunting is good only in isolated spots. A habitat management program has been introduced, so with luck the birds' population will increase soon. Goose hunting is excellent throughout much of southern Manitoba. The province's snow goose and Canada goose populations are healthy and expanding. Roughly one million snow geese and one million Canada geese wing their way through southern Manitoba each fall. Information: *Department of Natural Resources* (see above).

MACKENZIE MOUNTAINS, near Norman Wells, Northwest Territories Sheep still die of old age without ever having seen a human being in the rugged Mackenzies—probably among the best Dall sheep ranges on the continent. Here rams with full-curl horns measuring 35 to 38 inches are common, while trophies-size specimens with 40- to 42-inch horns are bagged in season (July 15 through October). Information: *NWT Tourism Information, The North Group,* Yellowknife, NWT X1A 2P6 (phone: 403-873-7200; 800-661-0788).

Ice Skating and Hockey

Canadian winters and ice go together. From December until spring, ponds, lakes, rivers, and streams turn into natural rinks. The tradition of bundled-up businessmen skating to their offices originated with the French traders who skated over the frozen waterways from one trading post to another with their goods. Then, inspired by the ingenuity of the French, the Iroquois strapped bones to their feet and joined the sport, and English soldiers in turn began holding competitions for the most creative and intricate patterns cut into ice. Indoor rinks first appeared in Quebec City and Montreal in the 1880s.

Today, skating is enormously popular all over the country. Hockey dominates the scene, although figure skating also is booming. The *Canadian Figure Skating Association* (phone: 613-748-5635) has 176,000 members, and some 1,400 clubs nationwide stage seminars for skaters and interclub competitions, sending the winners on to sectional, divisional, national, and international contests. For information on skating and hockey in major urban areas, see the *Sports* sections in the individual chapters in THE CITIES.

CANADA'S UNIQUE OPEN-AIR SKATING

BANFF SPRINGS HOTEL, Banff, Alberta Like many big, mountain resort hotels, this one provides its guests with an ice skating facility. Although the rink isn't *Olympic* caliber, it's worth taking a few spins around just to enjoy the grand scenery: jagged, snow-capped peaks rising steeply at the edge of the mile-wide Bow River valley, where the hotel sits. Afterward, warm up over a hot buttered rum or a bowl of soup at the hotel's winterized golf clubhouse. Information: *Banff Springs Hotel,* PO Box 960, Banff, AB T0L 0C0 (phone: 403-762-2211; 800-441-1414 in Canada; fax: 403-762-5755). See also *Special Havens* in this section.

LAURENTIANS, Quebec The trick here is to arrive after a spell of weather long enough and cold enough to ice over the myriad ponds, lakes, and streams of this lovely area—but before the snow. Then you can skate for miles, play hockey to your heart's content, or trace figures so large that giants might have made them. The great outdoors is one vast skating rink. But even after the snowfall, there's no dearth of places to skate in this skate-happy region. Almost every village has its rink—if not an oval set up in the schoolyard, then a section of a nearby lake kept plowed for the season. Rinks at several of the area's best resorts (among them *Auberge Gray Rocks* at St-Jovite and the *Hôtel la Sapinière* at Val David; see *Special Havens* for both) are usually kept clear, as are the lakes at Ste-Adèle and Ste-Agathe. The former has a half-mile oval to speed around as well as the regular rink-sized area. And there are indoor rinks as well. The delight of skating here also derives from what goes après. The unique European flavor of après-ski in the Laurentians applies to "après-skate" as well, with long sessions at the hearths of cozy inns, the satiation of ravenous appetites in one of the many fine restaurants in the quaint villages, and a lively Québécois nightlife. Information: *Association Touristique des*

Laurentides, 14142 Rue de Lachapelle, RR1, St-Jérôme, QUE J7Z 5T4 (phone: 514-436-8532).

HOCKEY MUSEUMS

The *Hockey Hall of Fame and Museum* is described in *Toronto* in THE CITIES. Fans may also want to make a pilgrimage to the sport's other shrine, in Kingston, Ontario.

INTERNATIONAL HOCKEY HALL OF FAME AND MUSEUM, Kingston, Ontario People have been playing hockey in Kingston ever since it was called shinny, back in the 1880s, and the collections here record the history of the game through the present. There's the stick used in the big game between *Queen's* and *Royal Military College* on Kingston harbor ice around 1886, the first colored hockey cards (1906–09), an early *NHA* player contract signed by Alf Smith of Ottawa for $500 a year, the famous No. 9 sweaters of Rocket Richard and Gordie Howe, and Dit Clapper's No. 5, retired by the Boston *Bruins* in 1947—not to mention the battered skates of Scotty Davidson and referee Mike Rodden, Gordie Howe's gloves, and much more. Open daily from June through September; by appointment the rest of the year; admission charge. Information: *International Hockey Hall of Fame and Museum,* York and Alfred Sts., PO Box 82, Kingston, ONT K7L 4VS (phone: 613-544-2355).

Directions

Introduction

On the following pages are 35 driving tours through the very different areas of Canada's 10 provinces and two territories. From Prince Edward Island to British Columbia's Vancouver Island, they traverse Canada's most spectacular routes, roads, and natural wonders: surf-washed coasts, glaciers and cobalt-blue lakes, dramatic mountain peaks, dense forests, and barren tundra. These are journeys, too, into the past, along paths first traveled by Canada's Inuit and other native peoples and French fur traders. You also can follow routes that take in tiny fishing villages, vast colonial fortifications, or the trail to fortune followed by prospectors during the Klondike gold rush. The remote and northerly regions of Canada offer the exploration-minded some of the most magnificent unspoiled landscapes left on this planet; in such areas, however, although roads are generally good and closely monitored, it is crucial to be prepared for fewer services and for extremes of weather.

In this section are 12 chapters, one for each province or territory. The chapters introduce the region, then describe two to four suggested driving tours, each lasting about three to five days, although all can be expanded by the individual traveler. Visitors with more time may want to string several of these routes together or spend two or three weeks on just one.

If you have just a little time, you will find that any single itinerary provides a healthy sampling of sights and atmosphere, as well as mentioning the essentials, like where to find a nearby restaurant or snack bar. The *Best en Route* section at the end of each tour is a qualitative guide to accommodations along the way: small inns, clean and comfortable motels, country hotels, campgrounds, and off-the-main-road havens. Prices mentioned in the beginning of each *Best en Route* section are quoted in US dollars.

The tours are not exhaustive. No book could cover every inch of Canada, but these chapters can help you reach its essence and make your trip a most memorable one.

Alberta

Perhaps the most beautiful drive in western Canada starts at Calgary, Alberta's largest city, and follows the spine of the Rocky Mountains north through *Banff National Park* to Lake Louise and *Jasper National Park.* Shared with the Pacific province of British Columbia, these mountains are part of the diverse geography that distinguishes Alberta from its sister prairie provinces, Saskatchewan and Manitoba. Covering 255,285 square miles, Alberta is the largest and most westerly of the prairie and plains provinces, but it is the least prairie-like. In the west, on the Alberta–British Columbia border, are the Rocky Mountains; in the southeast corner of the province are badlands and desert; and along the border with the Northwest Territories (of which the province was a part until 1905) is a wilderness of forests, lakes, and rivers.

The economy here also diverges from the traditional prairie concerns of farming and ranching. Oil discoveries in central and southern Alberta, especially the Leduc Fields find in 1947, propelled the province into a period of growth. In those boom times, Alberta's oil business grew to such proportions that the provincial government set up a trust fund to assure future development as oil reserves waned. Edmonton and Calgary are the centers of the province's oil industry. Some 80% of Alberta's 2.5 million people live in its cities, and the two major oil centers are home to most of them. (For complete reports on Calgary and Edmonton, see THE CITIES.) Alberta is the only province with no provincial sales tax, affording its residents one of the lowest tax rates in the country.

Where there is oil there are generally fossil remains, and, true to the rule, paleontological excavations in Alberta's badlands earlier in this century turned up more than a hundred dinosaur skeletons. Paleontologists continue to unearth new species of dinosaurs in *Dinosaur Provincial Park,* near the southeastern town of Brooks. In the same part of the country is the Siksika nation, one of Canada's largest communities of Native Americans.

Visitors with a yen to enjoy Alberta's natural beauty up close can take advantage of the province's numerous opportunities for trail riding, river rafting, cycling, mountain climbing, and even dogsledding. Farm and ranch vacations offer families a chance to milk cows, ride horses, gather farm-fresh eggs, and breathe the country air. Note that hunting is forbidden in all of Alberta's provincial parks.

In the following pages, we outline three driving routes, each lasting three or four days, that take in the most compelling sights and dramatic scenery of this varied province. Southern Alberta is thoroughly explored in the Lethbridge-Calgary drive, which includes beautiful *Waterton Lakes National Park.* The high points of any Alberta trip are *Banff* and *Jasper National Parks,* and a drive through them from Calgary is described in the second

Alberta route. Edmonton is the ultimate destination of the third route, from *Cypress Hills Provincial Park* through the dinosaur-rich badlands and the Siksika Reserve—formerly known as the Blackfoot Reserve (the Siksika are one of three Blackfoot tribes).

For more information about the province, including maps of Alberta and extensive accommodation and campground guides, contact the *Alberta Economic Development and Tourism Department* (PO Box 2500, Edmonton, AB T5J 2ZA; phone: 403-427-4321; 800-661-8888).

NOTE

When making calls in Alberta outside the local calling area from which you are dialing, you must use the area code, which is 403.

Lethbridge to Calgary via Waterton Lakes National Park

This 250-mile (400-km) route begins at the prairie city of Lethbridge, swings through southwestern Alberta, then heads north to Calgary. It crosses *Waterton Lakes National Park* in the Rocky Mountains at Alberta's southwestern corner and passes several places of interest along the route. On the way to *Waterton Lakes,* Cardston is the site of the *Alberta Temple,* Canada's first Mormon temple. North of *Waterton Lakes,* fishing is good around Pincher Creek, and at Fort Macleod stands a re-creation of a North West Mounted Police (NWMP) fort. The route is easily traveled, and you can take it at your own pace. The whole area enjoys bright blue sky and clean air. The best time for traveling this route is from spring to fall, since many attractions close down for the winter. For detailed information about and maps of *Waterton Lakes National Park,* Lethbridge, and other parts of this area, contact the *Chinook Country Tourist Association* (2805 Scenic Dr., Lethbridge, AB T1K 5B7; phone: 403-320-1222; 800-661-1222 in western Canada and the northwestern US; fax: 403-380-3209).

LETHBRIDGE The commercial center for the surrounding farm and ranch country sits on the banks of the Oldman River. A pleasant, orderly place, Lethbridge (pop. 63,400) has blossomed over the last 20 years into a far cry from its first days in the 1860s, when *Fort Whoop-Up* was built by whiskey traders from the US to sell liquor to both white settlers and natives, often with tragic results. A reconstruction of the fort stands in *Indian Battle Park,* in town on the riverbank. Although it's not located on the same spot as the original *Fort Whoop-Up,* the re-created fort is authentic—all that's missing is the rotgut. The park was the site of an 1870 battle between the Cree and Blackfoot nations that lasted for days. Details of the epic battle are explained at an interpretive center, with exhibits inside the fort. An old coal train carries visitors on a guided tour through the park. The park and interpretive center are open daily; closed early September through late May. There's an admission charge (phone: 403-329-0444).

Cross the Oldman River just south of *Indian Battle Park* and continue south on the bypass road for an excellent view of the *University of Lethbridge* campus. The university's unusual buildings were designed to complement the coulees (deep, sharp trench erosions in rock) in the surrounding terrain. From the western end of the bypass road, the university looks like a large ship nestled in the folds of the surrounding hills.

On the east side of town, on Mayor Magrath Drive, *Henderson Park* offers a variety of diversions, including a golf course and Henderson Lake, where there's swimming, boating, and fishing. On the shore of the lake is Lethbridge's premier attraction—*Nikka Yuko Garden,* a beautiful Japanese garden designed and constructed in Japan under expert supervision, then shipped in pieces and assembled without nails in Lethbridge. The *Nikka Yuko* guides, Japanese women in traditional dress, explain the philosophy of the intricate pebble designs, the manicured trees and shrubs, and the miniature pools and waterfalls. The centerpiece is a replica of a Japanese tea house, but, alas, it does not serve refreshments. The garden is open daily; closed October to mid-May. There's an admission charge (phone: 403-328-3511).

Hungry travelers can head for *Billy MacIntyre's Cattle Company* (1621 Third Ave. S; phone: 403-327-2727) for its award-winning home-style cooking; or relax amid antiques and two wood-burning fireplaces at *Carole's Café and Bar* (314 Eighth St. S; phone: 403-328-6575).

For a fascinating day trip or overnight camping expedition, travel southeast of Lethbridge to the *Writing-on-Stone Provincial Park.* Drive about 50 miles (80 km) south on Route 4 to Milk River, then 20 miles (32 km) east on Route 501 to the park turnoff, and 6 miles (10 km) south to the park. This archaeological preserve is rich in ancient tribes' rock paintings and carvings, and it features a reconstructed NWMP outpost once used to control whiskey smuggling. The park's parched sandstone hills have been a sacred spot for native tribes for at least 700 years. Surrounded by rare cottonwood trees and the wind-carved rock pillars known as hoodoos, the campground offers opportunities for swimming, canoeing, and fishing. This is rattlesnake country, but don't be alarmed: The rangers keep the campground clear and assure visitors that the local rattlers are timid creatures, unlike their aggressive relatives farther south. Be on the safe side, though, and wear boots when hiking in wilderness terrain. The park is open daily; no admission charge. For information, stop by the *Alberta Economic Development and Tourism Information Centre,* on the southern edge of Milk River on Route 4 (297 Milk River, AB T0K 1M0; phone: 403-647-2364), which is open daily.

En Route from Lethbridge Mayor Magrath Drive becomes Route 5, the direct road to *Waterton Lakes National Park,* 81 miles (130 km) southwest of Lethbridge. The route crosses rolling prairie and coulees beneath an incredibly blue, seemingly infinite sky on the way to the next stop, Cardston, 48 miles (77 km) south of Lethbridge.

CARDSTON This small town is the home of the *Alberta Temple,* the country's first Mormon temple, dedicated in 1923. Information on the Mormon church and its history is available at the visitors' center, but the temple itself is open only to preapproved church members. On Main Street, the *C. O. Card Home and Museum* preserves the house of the leader who first brought the Mormons from Utah to Alberta in the 1880s. The interior accurately reflects the decor and furnishings of early Alberta pioneer homes, providing a fine sense of the atmosphere of a Mormon household. The museum is closed Sundays and September through March; no admission charge (phone: 403-653-4322). If the temple and the museum don't sufficiently make the point that the town is Mormon, note also that Cardston is "dry"; look elsewhere for a cold beer.

On the southern outskirts of town, look for the *Remington-Alberta Carriage Center* (623 Main St.; phone: 403-653-5139), where you can try your hand at harnessing a horse and see the factory where horse-drawn vehicles are built. It's open daily; admission charge.

Cardston also marks the southern border of the Blood tribe's reserve, with 7,000 residents, the largest in Canada. Every June, the Blood perform the *Sun Dance* religious ritual; it is one of the few Plains tribes maintaining this tradition. The dance, however, is not a public event.

If you need gas, fill up in Cardston: Gas stations are few and far between on the next stretch of highway.

En Route from Cardston Except for a couple of small towns, Leavitt and Mountain View, this is mostly open country, the approach to the foothills of the Rockies. Thirty-one miles (50 km) west of Cardston on Route 5 is *Waterton Lakes National Park.*

WATERTON LAKES NATIONAL PARK This park joins the United States' *Glacier National Park* at the US border in Montana to form the *International Peace Park.* Set in a part of the Rockies more ancient than the Banff-Jasper area, the park has its own stunning beauty: jagged mountains with contrasting purple, red, and green rock; chains of connected valleys; and innumerable mountain streams, waterfalls, and lakes. The *Waterton Park* townsite is on the northern shore of Upper Waterton Lake, several miles in from the park gate on Route 5. It is an active park center of motels, restaurants, stores, and campgrounds. *Shoreline Cruise* boats (phone: 403-859-2362) offer leisurely two-hour cruises of Upper Waterton Lake, crossing the international border and stopping briefly at Goat Haunt, Montana. *Shoreline Cruise* also rents boats and provides a water shuttle service to the starting point of the 5.4-mile (8.6-km) *Crypt Lake Hike,* which winds through a natural mountain tunnel offering trekkers views of spectacular waterfalls. The town has docking facilities and a boat launch. (Motorboats are restricted to the main lakes.) Just north of town is the starting point of the Red Rock Canyon hiking trail network. Before heading into the wilds, visit the *Bayshore Inn* in town (see *Best en Route*); its views are beautiful, augmented by an old-fashioned dining room that serves fresh mountain trout and Alberta beef. The *Prince of Wales* hotel, a château-like hostelry up the hill from town (see *Best en Route*), has a magnificent view and dining room as well. Also see *National Parks* in DIVERSIONS.

During the winter, snowdrifts often block the roads to *Waterton Lakes National Park,* and most facilities are closed. However, if the roads are open, a drive through the snow-covered mountains affords superb scenery and splendid views of wildlife. If you do visit in winter, be sure there's plenty of gas in the car. Winter visitors can stay at the *Kilmorey* motor lodge or *Crandell Mountain Lodge*—both offer cross-country skiing (see *Best en Route* for both).

En Route from Waterton Lakes Take Route 6 north from the northern exit of the park. After 30 miles (50 km), you will reach the town of Pincher Creek, reputed to be the windiest spot in Alberta. The chinook (the prevailing strong westerly wind from the Rockies) hits Pincher Creek full force as it whistles off the mountains. In town, the *Pincher Creek Museum and Kootenai Brown Historical Park* (James Ave. and Grove St.; phone: 403-627-3684) has several restored pioneer log cabins, one of which was built in 1889 by Kootenai Brown, the area's most illustrious pioneer. Call ahead for hours; admission charge. Trout fishing is good in the rivers around Pincher Creek and in *Beauvais Lake Provincial Park,* just west of town. The park is open daily.

A detour west at Pincher Creek on Route 3 will provide a peek into an interesting chapter of Alberta's past. About 20 miles (32 km) west of the Pincher Creek junction lies Crowsnest Pass, a community comprising five small villages along Route 3: Bellevue, Hillcrest Mines, Frank, Blairmore, and Coleman. This area was the birthplace of the province's earliest coal mining and the scene of one of its greatest tragedies, the Frank Slide. The *Frank Slide Interpretive Centre* (Rte. 3; phone: 403-562-7388) tells the story of the night in 1903 when 90 million tons of rock broke off Turtle Mountain and buried part of the mining town of Frank and an estimated 75 people. The center is open daily year-round; admission charge. The nearby *Leitch Collieries* stone ruins (Rte. 3, on the outskirts of Crowsnest Pass; phone: 403-562-7388) are now an interpretive center depicting the history of the coal mining industry. It's open daily; no admission charge. The *Crowsnest Pass Eco-Museum* (phone: 403-562-8831), a nonprofit organization dedicated to preserving historic sites in the Crowsnest Pass area, operates two projects that are worth a look. The *Bellevue Mine* was the site of an explosion in 1910 that killed 30 people. Tours of the mine itself are given daily mid-May through August; by appointment the rest of the year. There's an admission charge. In the neighboring community of Coleman is the *Coleman Journal Building* (7702 18th Ave.), which houses several printing presses used by the Pulitzer Prize–winning newspaper when it existed early in the century. Tours of the facility are given Wednesdays through Sundays from 10 AM to 4 PM in summer; by appointment the rest of the year. There's no admission charge.

Returning east on Route 3, the road heads northeast of Pincher Creek toward Fort Macleod, 29 miles (46 km) away. On the way, the road passes through part of the Peigan Reserve and its main town, Brocket. From here, Fort Macleod is a half-hour drive.

FORT MACLEOD The *Fort Macleod Museum* (219 25th St.; phone: 403-553-4703) features eight 19th-century buildings within a stockade. Although it is not a reconstruction of the original fort, it does display numerous artifacts from that era and offers a thought-provoking glimpse into early frontier life. The original fort was built in 1874 by the North West Mounted Police (NWMP). The Mounties were the umpires of the territories, refereeing among the settlers, natives, whiskey traders, ranchers, and immigrants. They were hardly impartial, being essentially forces of eastern expansionism, but they represented what law did exist. Exhibits in the fort museum detail the history of the NWMP and local native cultures, and Mounties in the uniform of the period perform original horseback drills. The museum is open daily May through mid-October; closed weekends the rest of the year. There's an admission charge.

Take a stroll through downtown Fort Macleod, whose streets are lined with historic buildings dating back to the turn of the century. The downtown core has been declared a provincial historic site—the first such designation in Canada–and its more than 30 protected buildings include an old sandstone hotel, a Roman Catholic church, the *Town Hall,* a post office, and the *Empress Theatre* (phone: 403-553-4403), a former vaudeville roadhouse and silent movie theater that now stages professional live theater in July and August. Guided tours of the downtown area are offered by Fort Macleod's historical preservation society (phone: 403-553-2500). The *Fort Macleod Rodeo,* one of the better small-town competitions of its kind, usually takes place the first 10 days of July.

About 9 miles (14 km) northwest of Fort Macleod on Route 516, nestled in the Porcupine Hills, is *Head-Smashed-In Buffalo Jump.* Named a World Heritage Site by UNESCO, the 5,700-year-old jump was used by the Blackfoot tribe, who would stampede buffalo herds over the cliffs and then slaughter them for food. The interpretive center here has five display galleries, an audiovisual presentation, and a gift shop. It's open daily; admission charge (phone: 403-553-2731; 403-265-0048 toll-free from Calgary).

En Route from Fort Macleod Follow Route 2 north toward Calgary, 103 miles (165 km) away, passing through several interesting small towns en route. About 23 miles (37 km) north of Fort Macleod, you may choose to rest up at *Anola's Bed and Breakfast,* a highly rated farm establishment east of Claresholm (see *Best en Route*) or simply to continue north on Route 2 for 24 miles (38 km) to Nanton. You also can take Route 520 west of Claresholm for a winding, 80-mile (128-km) tour of the foothills. This route is unpaved and passes through remote territory, but it does offer a glimpse of real ranching country and some fantastic scenery. In fact, Clint Eastwood filmed much of his Oscar-winning western *Unforgiven* in the area. Take Route 520 until it meets Route 22. Follow Route 22 south for 13 miles (20 km), then turn west onto Route 517, which will join the Forestry Trunk Road (Rte. 940) in the *Rocky Mountains Forest Reserve.* Traveling north on the Trunk Road, you will pass the spectacular Livingstone Falls. Shortly beyond Livingstone Falls, turn east on Route 532, which leads out of the forest reserve. At the junction with Route 22, head south for about 7 miles (11 km) to *Chain Lakes Provincial Park,* which has 140 picnic sites (including six that are wheelchair accessible), camping facilities, cooking shelters, fishing, and a boat launch in an isolated, relaxing environment. The park is open daily; no admission charge (phone: 403-646-5887; fax: 403-646-3141). From Chain Lakes, Route 533 goes directly to Nanton in about 45 minutes. Nanton is famous for its sparkling, ice-cold water, available from taps beside the highway. In a lovely old brick building on the road out of town is *Emporium Antiques* (1901 20th Ave.; phone: 403-646-2437), with a large selection of furniture, china, tableware, and other pieces that reflect the ranching community that occupied the area at the turn of the century. Though these items aren't yet old enough to be genuine antiques, they're still worth a look. Fifteen miles (24 km) north on Route 2 is High River.

HIGH RIVER Many Albertans believe this little town typifies western life. Always a center for ranchers, it also has become home for many people who work in Calgary but want to live in a small town. Many of its shops carry arts and crafts made in the area, so if you're looking for a souvenir, High River might be able to supply it. The unique Western articles produced by such stores as *Eamor's Saddlery* (504 Centre St.; phone: 403-652-2614) and *Olson's Silver and Leather Co.* (610 Centre St.; phone: 403-652-2744) are prized around the world. Each June, the town hosts the *North American Chuckwagon Championships and Guy Weadick Memorial Rodeo.* The chuckwagon races attract the same drivers and rigs that appear in the famous *Calgary Exhibition and Stampede,* but here you get a much closer view of the action. For the dates of the championships, contact the *High River Chamber of Commerce* (PO Box 5244, High River, AB T1V 1M4; phone: 403-652-3336). The *Little Britches Rodeo,* in mid-May, features junior cowboys and cowgirls, as young as seven years, "mutton" busting (yes, we do mean riding sheep), steer wrestling, and calf roping. The *Museum of the*

Highwood (First St.; phone: 403-652-7156) has a good geological collection and exhibits on local history. It's open daily mid-May through September; closed weekends the rest of the year; admission charge. Look for the vivid murals on downtown buildings depicting High River's early days. The quaint house at 153 Macleod Trail is home to the *Gooseberries Tea Room and Gift Shop* (phone: 403-652-3226), where you can enjoy lunch or afternoon tea in pleasant, pastel surroundings.

En Route from High River It is a direct 24-mile (38-km) drive on Route 2 to Calgary. For a bit of homey sustenance, head southwest on Route 2A (off Rte. 2) for about 5 miles (8 km) to the small town of Okotoks. The community is considered one of the most livable in the country, owing to its lovely setting and the down-home friendliness of its residents. The Victorian-style *Ginger Tea Room and Gift Shop* (43 Riverside Dr.; phone: 403-938-2907) serves Saskatoon berry pie (in season) and its own blend of Okotokian tea. The aptly named Big Rock southwest of town on Route 7 is North America's largest glacial erratic (rock deposited far from its original source by the movement of glaciers).

BEST EN ROUTE

There are plenty of motels and campgrounds along this route, but except for those in Waterton Park and Lethbridge, high-quality places are difficult to find. Most motels are simple, functional, and little else. Similarly, overnight campsites meet only basic needs. The area abounds in charming bed and breakfast establishments like the *Robin's Nest* (see below); for information about similar accommodations in the area, contact the *High Country Bed and Breakfast Association* (PO Box 61, Millarville, AB T0L 1K0; phone: 403-931-3514). Expect to pay $60 or more per night for a double room in a hotel listed as expensive; $45 to $60 at a hotel rated moderate; $15 to $45 at one in the inexpensive range; and less than $15 for most campground sites, which fall into the very inexpensive category. Most campsites operate on a first-come, first-served basis; be sure to arrive by midafternoon at the latest, especially on weekends. All hotels have private baths, a restaurant, TV sets, and telephones unless otherwise indicated. For each location, lodgings are listed alphabetically by price category.

LETHBRIDGE

Lethbridge Lodge This modern, 191-room hotel has a spectacular view of the Oldman River Valley. It features a plant-filled atrium, a dining room, a country-western tavern, a pool, business services, and a Jacuzzi. 320 Scenic Dr. (phone: 403-328-1123; 800-661-1232; fax: 403-328-0002). Expensive.

Motel Magic Located on Scenic Drive near the *Lethbridge Lodge,* this 87-room motel includes one unit with a kitchenette. There also are nonsmoking rooms, business services, a whirlpool, an exercise room, and free continental breakfast. No restaurant. 100 Third Ave. S (phone: 403-327-6000; 800-661-8085; fax: 403-320-2070). Moderate.

Sandman Inn Features of this 139-room establishment include a 24-hour restaurant, a cocktail lounge, an indoor pool and sauna, a fitness center, business services, and a tavern. 421 Mayor Magrath Dr. (phone: 403-328-1111; 800-726-3626; fax: 403-329-9488). Moderate.

Parkside Inn A few blocks from the Japanese gardens and *Henderson Lake Park,* this hotel has 65 rooms; there's also a dining room, a cocktail lounge, business services, and a coffee shop. 1009 Mayor Magrath Dr. (phone: 403-328-2366; fax: 403-328-5933). Inexpensive.

Super 8 Lodge This 92-room motel features a dining room, an outdoor pool, a hot tub, a sauna, laundry facilities, and business services. Pets welcome. Mayor Magrath Dr. and Seventh Ave. (phone: 403-329-0100; 800-661-8091 in Canada; fax: 403-327-3600). Inexpensive.

Henderson Lake Campground Just across the road from the park and the east end of the lake are a hundred camping sites, many with sewer, electric, and water hookups. There also are stoves, fireplaces, tables, showers, and flush toilets. Closed November through March (phone: 403-328-5452). Very inexpensive.

CARDSTON

Flamingo Eight of the 38 units in this motel have kitchenettes. There's also an outdoor pool and coin laundry. At the south end of town, at 848 Main St. S. (phone: 403-653-3952; fax: 403-653-3863). Inexpensive.

Lee Creek Campground Here are 63 camping sites, plus hookups, cooking facilities, tap water, showers, and flush toilets. Closed October through April. In Cardston (phone: 403-663-3667). Very inexpensive.

Police Outpost Provincial Park Operated by the provincial department of recreation and parks, these 46 camping sites offer cooking facilities, a fish-cleaning stand, a boat launch, pump water, and pit toilets. There are no hookups. Six miles (10 km) south of Cardston on Rte. 2, then follow signs west 14 miles (23 km) to the park (phone: 403-653-2522). Very inexpensive.

WATERTON PARK

Bayshore Inn In this motel overlooking the lake are 70 units, including 19 nonsmoking rooms. There's also a dining room, a cocktail lounge, and business services. Try the outdoor, lakefront hot tub. Closed October 15 through March. 111 Waterton Ave. (phone: 403-859-2211; fax: 403-857-2291). Expensive.

Crandell Mountain Lodge This lodge has 13 units, some with kitchenettes and views from a deck, and four three-room suites with full kitchens; there's no dining room. 102 Mount View Rd. (phone: 403-859-2288; fax: 403-859-2288). Expensive.

Kilmorey Right on the lake at the entrance to Waterton Park townsite, this motor lodge has 25 rooms, an award-winning dining room, a cocktail lounge with fireplaces, and a rustic atmosphere. Near the *Bayshore Inn,* at 117 Evergreen Ave. (phone: 403-859-2334; fax: 403-859-2342). Expensive.

Prince of Wales The best in the area. A château on a hill with a splendid view of the mountains and the lake, this is a perfect headquarters for a park visit. There are 81 rooms, a dining room, a cocktail lounge, and a tearoom. Closed mid-September through May. Rte. 5 (phone: 406-226-5551 for reservations in season; fax: 403-859-2630). Off-season, write to Mail Station 0928, Phoenix, AZ 85077 (phone: 602-248-6000). Expensive.

Townsite Campground Conveniently located in the town of Waterton Park along the lake, with 238 sites; showers; flush toilets; and power, water, and sewer hookups. Closed mid-October to mid-May (phone: 403-859-2224). Very inexpensive.

Waterton Homestead Campground Here are 260 camping sites, including 70 trailer spots with electric, sewer, and water hookups, showers, flush toilets, and laundry facilities. Closed September 15 through April. Two miles (3 km) north of the *Waterton Lakes National Park* gate on Rte. 6 (phone: 403-859-2247). Very inexpensive.

PINCHER CREEK

Heritage Inn This modern hotel has 42 rooms, including executive and honeymoon suites, and features business services, restaurants, a pub, and a lounge (phone: 403-627-5000; fax: 403-627-3936). Moderate.

CLARESHOLM

Anola's Bed and Breakfast Snuggle under "Grandma's quilts" in the cozy, one-bedroom guest cottage filled with antiques or settle into the private, two-bedroom suite in Anola and Gordon Laing's country home. There's also a hot tub. Nine miles (15 km) east of Claresholm, off Rte. 520 (phone: 403-625-4389; fax: 403-625-2277). Inexpensive.

Sportsman An inn with 41 units (some have queen-size waterbeds, and all have cable TV), it also has a dining room and plug-ins (for warming up car engines in cold weather). On Rte. 2, at the south end of town (phone: 403-625-3347; fax: 403-625-4042). Inexpensive.

HIGH RIVER

Highlandview Guest Ranch A working horse, cattle, and grain ranch in the foothills, with room for 10 in the main ranch house and bunkhouse; accommodations share bathrooms. Attractions include Victorian antiques, flower gardens, and ranch-style cooking. Guests can swim and fish in the creek that runs through the property, take buggy rides or trail rides, enjoy nature walks, and help with ranch chores. Rates include breakfast or all meals. Six miles (10 km) south of High River via Rte. 2A, then 16 miles (25 km) west on Rte. 540 (phone: 403-395-2246 or 403-395-2154). Moderate.

OKOTOKS

Robin's Nest This bed and breakfast establishment on a historic family farm offers spectacular mountain scenery, abundant wildlife, and proprietress Dorothy Jackson's excellent cooking—including fresh trout for breakfast. Each of the two modern cabins has a private bath; the two guestrooms in the main house share a bath. Plummer's Rd., off Rte. 22 (phone: 403-931-3514). Moderate.

Calgary to Banff and Jasper National Parks

Immense as they are, stretching from the Yukon Territory to New Mexico, the Rocky Mountains are only part of a much larger chain that reaches deep into Mexico. This huge mountain range tells the story of creation, and one of the beautiful chapters of that story is revealed on the drive between *Banff* and *Jasper National Parks,* the showpieces of the Canadian West.

These two vast, adjoining parks cover hundreds of square miles of the Rocky Mountains on the Alberta–British Columbia border, some of the finest mountain scenery in the world. The 259-mile (414-km) road from Calgary to *Banff,* past beautiful Lake Louise, the Columbia Icefields, and on to *Jasper,* follows the spine of the Continent. Whether for summer or winter sport or because it is simply one of the most wonderful drives in North America, this is the most popular destination in the West.

Banff is a nature sanctuary as well as a major resort. Around the town itself are luxurious hotels, elegant restaurants, art galleries, crafts shops, ski resorts, and entertainment centers. Since it is one of Canada's most popular vacation areas, be prepared for crowds at the major attractions and considerable traffic on the park's winding roads.

Jasper is somewhat less commercially developed, although the town of Jasper has creature comforts aplenty. And for those who want to commune with nature in peace and quiet, both parks have miles of uncrowded hiking trails, secluded riverside picnic sites, and wilderness paths into the raw, undeveloped Rockies. Note that in both parks it is illegal to feed, touch, or tease the wild animals. Watch out for animals on the highway both during the day and at night.

For maps of Banff and Jasper, contact the *Banff Lake Louise Tourism Bureau* (PO Box 1298, 93 Banff Ave., Banff, AB T0L 0C0; phone: 403-762-8421; fax: 403-762-8545) or *Jasper Tourism and Commerce* (PO Box 98, 632

Connaught Dr., Jasper, AB T0E 1E0; phone: 403-852-3858; fax: 403-852-4932). A list of tourism operators in the areas of *Banff* and *Jasper Parks* may be obtained from the *Alberta Economic Development and Tourism Department* (see chapter introduction).

En Route from Calgary The entrance to *Banff National Park* lies about 70 miles (112 km) west of Calgary. Both the four-lane, divided Route 1 (the Trans-Canada Hwy.) and the parallel Route 1A lead directly to the park entrance. If you take the Trans-Canada Highway, stop at *Canada Olympic Park,* on the western edge of the city, site of the *1988 Winter Olympic* games and the world's only *Olympic Hall of Fame.* It's open daily; admission charge (phone: 247-5452). Route 1A passes through several small towns and the Stoney tribe's reserve. If you have time, it's a more relaxing way to go. Our route follows Route 1A.

The Crowchild Trail in Calgary becomes Route 1A as you head west. You may recognize some of the rolling foothills and forested areas in this part of the province from films and television. The region's beauty has attracted the makers of *Lonesome Dove: The Series, The Black Fox Trilogy* (a miniseries starring Christopher Reeve), *North of 60* (a popular Canadian series), *Legends of the Fall* (with Anthony Hopkins, Brad Pitt, and Aidan Quinn), and *Last of the Dog Men* (with Tom Berenger and Barbara Hershey)—to name but a few. Just outside Calgary, the small town of Cochrane is worth a stop for those who'd like to ramble over the grassy site of the first large ranch in Alberta, established in 1881. Climb to the rocky perch of the *Cochrane Ranch*'s famous horse and rider statue, and investigate the nearby *Western Heritage Centre* (at press time set to open later this year) to learn about historical and contemporary agricultural practices, rodeos, and ranching. Contact the *Town of Cochrane Administration Office* (phone: 403-932-2075) for more information. Cochrane has several new housing developments, built mainly for people who work in Calgary but who prefer to live in Cochrane's small-town atmosphere. The town is also home to a growing community of artists and craftspeople. Look for unique antiques and gifts at *Old and Crafty* (420 First St. W.; phone: 403-932-5332), and watch the owners of *Studio West* (205 Second Ave. SE; phone: 403-932-2611) create sculptures of horses and riders from molten bronze. The town's downtown area boasts an eclectic mix of boutiques, tea shops, gift stores, and the famous *MacKay's Homemade Ice Cream Shop* (220 First St. W.; phone: 403-932-2455). About 10 miles (16 km) from Cochrane on Route 1A is the Stoney Reserve, where the Stoney tribe still lives.

STONEY RESERVE Located on the highway, the main village on the reserve is Morley, settled in the 1800s by Methodist missionary George McDougall. It is the site of the tribe's schools, administrative office, and recreation center. Tiny *McDougall Memorial United Church,* built in 1875, is the second-oldest building on its original site in Alberta. While there are no restaurants or major retail stores here, it is possible to purchase leather goods, feather- and beadwork, and jewelry made by the residents of the reserve at the *Chief Chiniki Restaurant and Handicraft Centre* (just south of Rte. 1 at the Morley overpass; phone: 403-881-3960) and at *Nakoda Lodge* (phone: 403-881-3949; fax: 403-881-3901; gift shop open Sundays only), a large cedar-log facility built by the Stoney on the shore of Hector Lake, 10 miles (16 km) west of Morley. The lodge, which also includes 50 motel units, is the site of workshops and educational retreats. Sunday brunches are offered year-round. Note that the Stoney value their privacy. While you are welcome to visit the town and other places open to visitors, don't wander off the main highway. The residents have the right to ask you to leave; the reserve is their property.

A few miles west of Morley, near the banks of the Bow River, the Stoney have set aside land for a public campground, called *Stoney Park.* The facilities include some beautifully wooded camping spots. Camping permits are available from *Nakoda Lodge* (see above), and the scenery is spectacular. Some of the sites overlook a fenced buffalo paddock; to the west, the mountains seem close enough to touch. *Stoney Park* and Morley also can be reached from the Trans-Canada Highway.

En Route from the Stoney Reserve Route 1 and Route 1A draw closer together as they approach *Banff National Park.* Just past the town of Exshaw—its large Canada Cement factory visible from both highways—the two roads join and continue a few miles to Canmore. Within a mile or two of this intersection are two guest ranches, *Brewster's Kananaskis* and the *Rafter Six Ranch Resort* (see *Best en Route* for both). The latter's Sunday brunches and dinners are legendary feasts of western fare. Originally a coal mining town, Canmore has become a thriving center, with many grocery stores, shops, art galleries, motels, and fast-food outlets serving Banff's overflow tourist industry. For a leisurely meal, try *Sinclair's* (Eighth St.; phone: 403-678-5370). Like the early mountain explorer it's named after, this place has a taste for adventure, offering such dishes as spicy Bombay chicken served in Rocky Mountain clay pots made by a local potter, innovative pasta dishes, and haute pizza. It's open daily July and August; closed Mondays the rest of the year.

From Canmore, it's easy to explore *Kananaskis Country,* a year-round recreational area developed by the provincial government. This 2,400-square-mile mountain wilderness has facilities for hiking, biking, horseback riding, cross-country skiing, fishing, and snowmobiling. On the town's outskirts, the *Canmore Nordic Centre* has 42 miles (70 km) of skiing and hiking trails open to the public daily (phone: 403-678-2400).

Follow Route 1 east of Canmore to Route 40 and travel 13 miles (22 km) south to Mt. Allan, site of the *1988 Winter Olympic* alpine events. Call *Ski Nakiska* (phone: 403-591-7777) for public skiing information. Two miles (3 km) farther south on Route 40 are the two challenging and beautiful 18-

hole golf courses at the *Kananaskis Country Club* (phone: 403-591-7070); for details, see *Golf in Canada* in DIVERSIONS. The gates to *Banff National Park* are just beyond Canmore.

BANFF NATIONAL PARK In 1841 Sir George Simpson, governor of the Hudson's Bay Company, was the first white man to explore this area. It remained untouched until the 1880s, when the *Canadian Pacific Railway* prepared to lay track nearby and businessmen decided to exploit the hot springs at the base of Sulphur Mountain by building a hotel and spa. As the resort gained popularity, the town of Banff grew.

Although it's possible to drive nonstop through *Banff National Park* or a portion of it, don't. It's far more enjoyable to view the sights at leisure and participate in some of the activities offered along the way. Plan at least an overnight stay; two days are even more desirable. The admission charge to the park varies, depending on your length of stay (phone: 403-762-1550). Campers will find sites throughout the park. (And remember, all national park campsites are first-come, first-served.) For those who prefer motels or hotels, there are adequate accommodations in the town of Banff (about 10 miles/16 km beyond the park entrance), at Lake Louise, 35 miles (56 km) beyond, and along the longer stretch of road between Lake Louise and the boundary of *Jasper National Park* (see *Best en Route*). Reserve rooms well in advance; this is a popular area. It also is one of Canada's foremost ski destinations: The resorts of *Skiing Louise* (phone: 403-522-3555; fax: 403-522-2095) and *Mystic Ridge and Norquay* (phone: 403-762-4421; fax: 403-762-8133) have excellent downhill slopes, and *Sunshine Village* (phone: 403-762-6500; fax: 403-762-6513), 14 miles (22 km) west of town, has full ski facilities and overnight accommodations. (For more information, see *Downhill Skiing* and *Cross-Country Skiing* in DIVERSIONS.)

The town of Banff is the center of the park's attractions and the home base for exploring the southern part of the park. It's a major tourist center, and its stores, bookshops, art galleries, and restaurants are often crowded but endlessly intriguing. At the *Cave and Basin,* you can view the subterranean cave where Banff's famous hot springs were discovered in 1883 and follow a boardwalk through the warm-water marsh where unexpected varieties of plants, animals, and fish thrive. It's open daily; and there's an admission charge (phone: 403-762-1557). The *Banff Park Museum,* western Canada's oldest natural history museum, has been declared a national historic site. It looks exactly as it did when it was built in 1903 and exhibits taxidermy specimens of all indigenous species of *Banff* and *Jasper National Parks* (Banff Ave. and Buffalo St., next to the Bow River Bridge; phone: 403-762-1558). It's open daily; admission charge. The *Whyte Museum of the Canadian Rockies* (111 Bear St.; phone: 403-762-2291) exhibits the work of both local and national Canadian artists. The museum also houses the *Archives of the Canadian Rockies,* a collection of rare books and photographs. The museum is open daily mid-May through mid-October; closed Mondays the rest of the year; admission charge.

Built in 1888, Canadian Pacific's *Banff Springs* hotel (see *Best en Route*) is the descendant of the original resort that first established *Banff* as a vacation spot. Three architects worked on the hotel's design, creating a style that can only be described as 16th-century French château with touches of Scottish manse. Fossilized stone used throughout the structure reinforces its castle-like appearance. Nearby is the *Upper Hot Springs Pool* (Mountain Ave.; phone: 403-762-1515). The pool is not intended for swimming but for soaking in the soothing natural sulfur waters. The water—not just warm, but hot—is especially relaxing after a day of hiking or skiing. The pool is open daily until 11 PM (until 10 PM late September through mid-June, except Fridays and Saturdays); closed one week around *Easter* and a week in mid-October. There's an admission charge.

A number of stores here sell clothing, ceramics, weavings, paintings, and sculptures. *Quest* (105 Banff Ave.; phone: 403-762-2722) has a good collection of Inuit prints and soapstone carvings, jewelry, and wood, clay, and leather crafts.

The town of Banff also is the home of the *Banff Centre,* Canada's premier arts institution and one of the best of its kind in the world. Annually, more than 1,000 world class artists are enrolled at this education complex. Two modern theaters offer drama, dance, and music performances throughout the year. The center's annual *Banff Festival of the Arts,* held June through August, features a variety of concerts, exhibitions, dance, drama, and other productions. For information on events, call 403-762-6300 (800-413-8368 in Alberta and British Columbia).

Despite Banff townsite's many attractions, the real interest lies in the mountains, lakes, and forests surrounding it. A good way to begin exploring the countryside is to head for the two mountains near town. To the northwest, a winding road up Mt. Norquay offers commanding views from many stopping points. To the southeast, the *Sulphur Mountain Gondola* takes riders up to a tea house and hiking trails at the summit of the mountain. It's closed from late November through December; open daily the rest of the year. There's an admission charge (phone: 403-762-2523 or 403-762-5438).

Several short hiking trails lead out from the town of Banff. A fascinating 1½-mile loop in Sundance Canyon crosses streams and climbs rocks. Behind the parking lot at Upper Hot Springs, a 2½-mile climb takes about an hour and loops back to the hot springs. Guided horseback trail rides are available from *Warner Guiding and Outfitting* (132 Banff Ave.; phone: 403-762-4551).

Rocky Mountain Raft Tours (phone: 403-762-3632) offers a three-hour excursion on the Bow River on a large rubber raft; hour-long scenic float trips leave four times daily. Obtain tickets at the bus station, located at 100 Gopher Street, or at the *Banff Springs* hotel. A few miles west of town, at

Lake Minnewanka, operators offer two-hour motorboat tours of the lake as well as canoe rentals.

Several companies offer assistance to travelers who want to tour the Rockies by bicycle. *Rocky Mountain Cycle Tours* (phone: 403-678-6770; 800-661-2453; fax: 403-678-4451) offers bike rentals for self-guided tours, as well as a full cycling package, including meals, instruction, support van, accommodations, and guide service. *Backroad Bicycle Tours* (phone: 800-533-2573; fax: 510-527-1444) offers six-day trips starting at *Banff National Park,* traveling up the Columbia Icefields Parkway, and ending at *Jasper National Park.* To rent bikes by the hour or day, call *Park 'n' Pedal* (226 Bear St.; phone: 403-762-3191).

Helicopter operators offer a broad range of skiing, hiking, and sightseeing packages and tours in the area. Try *Canadian Mountain Holidays* (phone: 403-762-7100; 800-661-0252), which offers both winter and summer alpine holidays.

An easy way to enjoy the park's splendid scenery is simply to drive through it. A number of major peaks, like Cascade Mountain, Castle Mountain, and Mt. Brett, are short distances away from the town of Banff, and there are plenty of seldom-traveled trails throughout the area for easy hikes. Park personnel will help you to find them. A word of caution that can't be repeated too often: The constant presence of human beings has made the animals unafraid of people. Nevertheless, they are still wild; they can be dangerous and unpredictable. Also, in feeding or attempting to play with wild animals, you risk harming them. It is cruel and stupid—not to mention illegal—to feed park animals: Don't do it.

LAKE LOUISE Thirty-five miles (56 km) northwest of Banff townsite, this spot must not be missed. You can make it a separate overnight stop, a day's round-trip journey from Banff, or the first stop in a full day of driving north. Early in the morning, Lake Louise is a special treat. Beautifully clear and blue-green, it is surrounded by mountains and backed by the Victoria Glacier. As the sun rises, the mountains and the glacier are mirrored on the lake's surface. Since sunrise can be as early as 4 AM, it helps to stay overnight. The only hotel right on the lake is the *Château Lake Louise* (see *Best en Route*). Guests can request a wake-up call to see the sunrise spectacle.

For years the lake was an undisturbed preserve of the rich and the powerful, but over the years democracy (and economics) caught up with it. Lake Louise is now accessible to all, and remains beautiful at any time, sunrise or midday. There is ample privacy and serenity for everyone; a great way to get away from other people here is to rent a canoe or a horse. Lake Louise also has Canada's largest ski area (phone: 403-522-3555; 800-258-7669 in western Canada; fax: 403-244-3774).

En Route from Lake Louise Route 93 heads north toward *Jasper National Park* through the large remaining section of *Banff Park* and some of the most striking scenery you may ever see. This section of Route 93 is called the Icefields Parkway. From the road you can see 12 of the 25 highest peaks in the Rockies, and glaciers up to a thousand feet thick. Take your time, because the highway winds and climbs. About 22 miles (35 km) past Lake Louise, you can stop for coffee and a meal at *Num-Ti-Jah Lodge* on Bow Lake (phone: 403-522-2167). Also be sure to stop and absorb the views at Hector Lake, Peyto Lake, and Bow Summit. Forty-six miles (74 km) north of Lake Louise is the boundary of *Jasper National Park.*

JASPER NATIONAL PARK *Jasper*'s natural wonders complement rather than repeat those of *Banff.* The 92-mile (147-km) drive provides amazing views of rugged peaks, pristine wilderness, and up-close wildlife. Like *Banff, Jasper* has many hiking and cross-country skiing trails and lots of pristine nature. There's an admission charge (phone: 403-852-6161).

Immediately after crossing into *Jasper* you are still in glacier country. Directly inside the park's boundary is the Columbia Icefield, from which the Saskatchewan, Columbia, and Athabasca Rivers rise. Covering 160 square miles, the ice field lies across the Continental Divide. One toe of the Athabasca Glacier, which is 600 to 1,000 feet thick, spills down the mountain; visitors can ride across the ice in specially equipped "sno-coaches" (May to mid-October; phone: 403-762-6735), or park and follow the foot trail leading to an excellent view of the mountain's cliffs and the abutting Angel Glacier. Back on Route 93A, it is a short drive to the town of Jasper.

Although Jasper has been growing rapidly in recent years, the town still has a more relaxed, less formal atmosphere than that of Banff. One of the first things visitors will notice as they drive into town is the large totem pole in the center of the open square near the railway station. From the Queen Charlotte Islands of British Columbia, it is one of the finest examples of a nearly extinct art. Jasper's many other attractions include the *Jasper Tramway* (Whistlers Mt. Rd., off Rte. 93A; phone: 403-852-3093), which ascends 7,400-foot-high Whistlers Mountain, offering a spectacular view of the Athabasca Valley and *Jasper National Park.* There is a café at the top station and hiking trails leading even higher. Since this is the tree line, there are lovely specimens of rock flowers and moss. Numerous marmots—a type of groundhog—scurry from burrow to burrow. The *Tramway* is open daily; closed mid-October to mid-April. There's an admission charge. *Jasper Raft Tours* (phone: 403-852-3613); *Maligne River Adventures* (phone: 403-852-3370); and *Whitewater Rafting* (phone: 403-852-7238) offer whitewater excursions on the Athabasca River in large rubber rafts. *Rocky Mountain Voyager,* with colorfully costumed guides, provides rides in 32-foot canoes on Lac Beauvert (phone: 403-852-5595). *Pyramid Riding Stables* (Pyramid Lake Rd.; phone: 403-852-3562) and *Skyline Trail Rides* at the *Jasper Park Lodge* (see *Best en Route,* below, and *Special Havens* in DIVERSIONS) provide guided trail rides. *Jasper Park Lodge* also boasts a renowned 18-hole golf course (phone: 403-852-6090). To find a scenic spot for a quiet picnic, cross the footbridge to the tiny island in Pyramid Lake. For an elegant meal, try *Becker's Gourmet Restaurant* at *Becker's Chalets* (Jasper-Banff Hwy.; phone: 403-852-3535; fax: 403-852-7202), whose reputation has spread far beyond Jasper.

Take the side road from Jasper south to Maligne Lake for the popular one-and-a-half-hour motor cruise—it's worth the detour. Fishing guides and boat rentals are available. Nearby Maligne Canyon offers breathtaking scenery. Trails lead down to the end of the deep, narrow gorge. The Miette Hot Springs, 25 miles (40 km) from Jasper near the park's eastern boundary, has three naturally hot pools, including the hottest one in the mountains. There's also *Marmot Basin,* one of the finest ski areas in the Rockies, 12 miles (19 km) south of town via Route 93A (phone: 403-852-3816).

BEST EN ROUTE

Although motels, hotels, and campgrounds are plentiful along this route, reservations are recommended far in advance during the summer, when rates soar (especially within the two national parks). The *Banff Lake Louise Tourism Bureau* and *Jasper Tourism and Commerce* (see introduction to route for both) can recommend a reservations service. Although room rates here are higher than elsewhere in Alberta, this is also the only area in the province that has a real choice of accommodations. Expect to pay more than $200 per night for a double room in a place we list as very expensive; $95 to $200 at a hotel in the expensive range; $55 to $95 at one in the moderate category; and less than $55 at a place rated inexpensive. All hotels feature private baths, TV sets, and telephones unless otherwise indicated. Campgrounds provide very inexpensive accommodations, usually less than $15 per night. Most campsites operate on a first-come, first-served basis; be sure to get to your chosen place by mid-afternoon at the latest, especially on weekends. Consult the campground guide available from the *Alberta Economic Development and Tourism Department* (see chapter introduction) for a list of campgrounds that do accept reservations. *Hostelling International Canada* operates numerous inexpensive properties in this area. For more information, contact *Hostelling International Canada–Southern Alberta Region* (1414 Kensington Rd. NW, Calgary, AB T2N 3P9; phone: 403-283-5551; fax: 403-283-6503). For each location, lodgings are listed alphabetically by price category.

CANMORE

Green Gables Inn Many of the 61 units in this attractive Best Western hotel have fireplaces and whirlpool baths. An exercise room, conference facilities, private patios, and the highly praised *Chez François* dining room add to the inn's appeal. On Rte. 1A (phone: 403-678-5488; 800-661-2133; fax: 403-678-2670). Moderate.

Greenwood Inn Completed just last year, this 150-room hotel has tastefully decorated rooms, full bathrooms with double sinks, hair dryers, a spa, a restaurant, a lounge, a gift shop, and business facilities. Rte. 1A (phone: 403-678-3625; 800-263-3625; fax: 403-678-3765). Moderate.

Rocky Mountain Ski Lodge This alpine abode houses 82 units, including one- and two-bedroom accommodations with fireplaces and kitchens; some of the standard rooms also have kitchen facilities. The lodge also has a steamroom, conference room, and outdoor playground and picnic area. There's no restaurant. Rte. 1A (phone: 403-678-5445; 800-665-6111 in Canada; fax: 403-768-6484). Moderate.

Spray Lakes West Shore Campground Ten miles (16 km) south of Canmore along Smith Dorrien/Spray Trail, this property has 50 tent and trailer sites with stoves, tables, a boat launch, and outdoor toilets. It's run by the provincial parks department. Closed late November through early May (phone: 403-591-7222). Very inexpensive.

KANANASKIS COUNTRY

Lodge at Kananaskis This luxurious facility in a pristine wilderness setting has 253 rooms, some suites with fireplaces, an indoor pool, a whirlpool, a sauna, and a good dining room. Located near Mt. Allan's *Nakiska* ski resort and the *Kananaskis Country Club*'s two 18-hole golf courses, 13 miles (21 km) south of Rte. 1 on Rte. 40 (phone: 403-591-7711; 800-441-1414; 403-271-0459 in Calgary; fax: 403-591-7770). Expensive.

Rafter Six Ranch Resort The solid-log lodge and cabins at this guest ranch accommodate about 60 guests. For additional details see *Farm and Ranch Vacations* in DIVERSIONS. About 25 miles (40 km) east of Banff, near Seebe (phone: 403-673-3622; 403-264-1251 direct from Calgary—no long-distance charges apply; fax: 403-673-3961). Expensive.

Brewster's Kananaskis Guest Ranch Established in 1923, the Brewster family homestead offers 33 comfortable cabins and chalets with antiques and a lovely view of the Bow River and the mountains. There also is a dining room and a cocktail lounge, as well as horseback riding and river rafting. Located 1 mile (1.6 km) north of Seebe on Rte. 1X (phone: 403-673-3737; fax: 403-673-2100). Moderate.

Mount Engadine Lodge An alpine lodge, it sits alone in primal forest and mountain country. Amenities include a dining room, living room, lounge, sauna, outdoor Jacuzzi, and fireplace. There's a choice of dormitory or private accommodations (the lodge sleeps a total of 24 guests, and baths are shared), plus wholesome meals and opportunities for alpine hiking, cross-country skiing, mountain biking, and fishing. Rates include meals and guided hikes. Closed April through June 20 and October through *Christmas.* Take Smith

Dorrien Rd. south of Canmore to the Mount Shark turnoff (phone: 403-678-4080; fax: 403-678-2109). Moderate.

BANFF

Banff Springs This castle of a hotel has 828 rooms (including 36 suites). For additional details see *Special Havens* in DIVERSIONS. Spray Ave. (phone: 403-762-2211; 800-441-1414; 800-268-9411 in Canada; fax: 403-762-5755). Very expensive.

Rimrock Resort The view from this luxurious hotel is matched only by that commanded from the venerable *Banff Springs.* There are 345 rooms (including 41 suites), two restaurants, two lounges, exercise facilities, a Jacuzzi, an indoor pool, and business services. 100 Mountain Ave. (phone: 403-762-3356; 800-372-9270; fax: 403-762-4132). Very expensive.

Banff Park Lodge The downtown area is two blocks from this modern, quiet, 210-room hostelry, with dining rooms, a cocktail lounge with live entertainment, business facilities, a heated indoor pool, a steamroom, and a whirlpool. 222 Lynx St. (phone: 403-762-4433; 800-661-9266; fax: 403-762-3553). Expensive.

Mount Royal A pleasant hostelry in the center of town, it has 138 rooms and offers a dining room, a pub, and a cocktail lounge; a Jacuzzi, sauna, and exercise area; and business services. 138 Banff Ave. (phone: 403-762-3331; 800-267-3035 in western Canada; fax: 403-762-8938). Moderate.

Swiss Village On the eastern outskirts of Banff townsite, this lodge has 49 motel units, some with kitchenettes and fireplaces, plus 22 bungalows. There's a restaurant in the adjacent *Inns of Banff Park* hotel. 600 Banff Ave. (phone: 403-762-4581; 800-661-1272; fax: 403-762-2434). Moderate.

Tunnel Mountain Campgrounds The national parks service operates two trailer campgrounds (open mid-May through mid- or late-September) and one tent and trailer campground (open year-round), about 1.5 miles (2.5 km) northeast of the town of Banff on Tunnel Mountain Road. There are a total of 1,144 sites; full hookups, showers, and flush toilets are provided. No reservations (phone: 403-762-1550). Very inexpensive.

LAKE LOUISE

Château Lake Louise In addition to its spectacular Lake Louise setting, this property has 515 luxurious roms. For additional details see *Special Havens* in DIVERSIONS. Off Rte. 1, on Lake Louise (phone: 403-522-3511; 800-441-1414; fax: 403-522-3834). Very expensive.

Lake Louise Inn This motel has 222 units, including 53 rooms with kitchenettes and 40 with fireplaces. There also are a restaurant, laundry facilities, a tennis court, a pool, a Jacuzzi, a sauna, and an exercise room. 210 Village Rd.

(phone: 403-522-3791; 800-661-9237 in western Canada and the US; fax: 403-522-2018). Expensive.

Post Hotel A member of the Relais & Châteaux group, this charming log-constructed building houses 73 rooms, 27 suites, and an excellent dining room; there also are two one-bedroom cabins. Many of the accommodations have fireplaces. For additional details see *Special Havens* in DIVERSIONS. Closed late October to mid-December. 200 Pipestone (phone: 403-522-3989; 800-661-1586; fax: 403-522-3966). Expensive.

JASPER

Charlton's Chateau Jasper Here are 120 luxurious rooms and suites, a dining room offering nightly entertainment, business services, and an indoor pool and whirlpool. 96 Geikie St. (phone: 403-852-5644; 800-661-9323 in Canada; fax: 403-852-4860). Very expensive.

Jasper Park Lodge This highly acclaimed, sprawling alpine resort on Lac Beauvert has 442 guestrooms in cedar chalets and log cabins, plus four dining rooms and an 18-hole championship golf course. For additional details see *Special Havens* in DIVERSIONS. Lodge Rd. (phone: 403-852-3301; 800-441-1414; fax: 403-852-5107). Very expensive.

Lobstick Lodge Five blocks from the center of Jasper, this motel has kitchenettes in all 138 units, plus a sauna, steamroom, outdoor and indoor hot tubs, executive suites, and gamerooms. Geikie St. (phone: 403-852-4431; 800-661-9317 in western Canada; fax: 403-852-4142). Expensive.

Pyramid Lake Resort This terraced lakeside property features 64 units, many with kitchenettes, whirlpool baths, and gas fireplaces, as well as a dining room and fishing and boating facilities; there are no telephones in the units. Motor boats, canoes, paddleboats, and windsurfing and cross-country ski equipment can be rented. Three-and-a-half miles (5 km) northwest of Jasper, on Pyramid Lake Rd. (phone: 403-852-4900; fax: 403-852-7007). Moderate.

Cypress Hills Provincial Park to Edmonton via the Dinosaur Country

Modern technology has taken the bad out of badlands. These marginal desert areas were places where, years ago, a traveler on foot or horseback could easily die without due precaution, native intelligence, and desert savvy. Today there is nothing bad about them. In the distances a car can cover, they need hardly be dangerous, and chances are, unless you've done desert driving, the image you carry in your mind of "badlands" doesn't begin to account for their color, striking rock formations, or severe beauty.

All the better reason to make this drive from *Cypress Hills Provincial Park* in southeastern Alberta across the province's badlands and plains to Edmonton, in the center of the province. In its course, the 400-mile (640-km) drive encompasses all the area's grave beauty and harsh splendor.

Alberta's badlands contain many surprises. *Cypress Hills Provincial Park,* in the middle of a desert, is a teeming, green forest with a crazy-quilt ecology. Northwest of *Cypress Hills,* the city of Medicine Hat offers a variety of urban attractions. West through the badlands, at the towns of Brooks and Drumheller, are the skeletons and fossils of dinosaurs and other extinct creatures discovered in this area. There are excellent opportunities for visitors to see these remains and to explore the fossil beds themselves.

The Siksika (formerly Blackfoot) Reserve, between Brooks and Drumheller, provides a look back into native history and an insight into the tribe's present culture. In Alberta's midlands, the desert gives way to rich farm country. Near Red Deer, several lake resorts well equipped for recreation provide a welcome contrast to the arid terrain. North of Red Deer, an easy trip through Alberta's farm communities leads to the major city of Edmonton. While there is much driving on this route—and in the summer the weather is apt to be hot—there are excellent facilities all along the way, including many farms offering bed and breakfast services, and the sights make the driving worth it. If necessary, the whole route could be covered in two crowded days of just glimpsing the scenery. But since the best attractions lie slightly off the main roads, a more leisurely pace makes sense. A three- or four-day drive allows you to see each sight thoroughly and to stay overnight at spots you find particularly attractive.

For detailed maps and information on accommodations and more in the *Cypress Hills*–Medicine Hat–Brooks area, contact the *Southeast Alberta Travel and Convention Association* (PO Box 605, Medicine Hat, AB T1A 7G5; phone: 403-527-6422; fax: 403-528-2682); for the Drumheller area, contact the *Big Country Tourist Association* (PO Box 2308, Drumheller, AB T0J 0Y0; phone: 403-823-5885; fax: 403-823-7942); and for the Red Deer area, contact the *David Thompson Country Tourist Council* (4836 Ross St., Red Deer, AB T4N 5E8; phone: 403-342-2032; fax: 403-346-1290).

CYPRESS HILLS PROVINCIAL PARK *Cypress Hills Park* lies just west of Saskatchewan and north of Montana. From the US, take Montana's Route 232, which becomes Canada's Route 41; *Cypress Hills* is 50 miles (80 km) beyond the border. West of Saskatchewan on the Trans-Canada Highway (Rte. 1) is a turnoff south onto Route 41, shortly after you enter Alberta. Another 21 miles (34 km) brings you to *Cypress Hills.*

This park is one of nature's startling oddities. Surrounded by the prairie's rolling hills, *Cypress Hills* is a wide plateau, 2,000 feet higher than the surrounding countryside and nearly 5,000 feet above sea level. It is covered by a heavy pine forest, supports a wide variety of wildlife, and contains three lakes, the largest of which is Elkwater. This landscape should by all reason exist hundreds of miles farther south. Here in abundance are mountain and woodland orchids, hawthorns, violets, and crocuses. Coyotes, moose, deer, elk, and all manner of birds are found in the forest.

Near the park's northern boundary are the town of Elkwater and Elkwater Lake, where you can swim, boat, windsurf, and rent bicycles and canoes. The town has a service station and one motel, the *Green Tree* (phone: 403-893-3811), with 19 units. The park's 13 campgrounds have more than 530 sites for both trailers and tents (for campground reservations, call 403-893-3782). During the winter, there are facilities for cross-country skiing and downhill skiing at *Hidden Valley* (phone: 403-893-3961), with a lodge and quad-chair lift.

En Route from Cypress Hills Provincial Park Take Route 41 north to Route 1 (Trans-Canada Hwy.). Head west on Route 1 for about 45 minutes to Medicine Hat.

MEDICINE HAT Medicine Hat is a tree-filled city (population 45,900) whose prosperity is based on the 780 billion cubic feet of natural gas that lie beneath it. This gas reserve, Canada's largest, is 99% pure and pumped directly into the turn-of-the-century lamps that light the revitalized downtown area. Legends concerning the origin of the city's name abound. According to one story, a Cree medicine man lost his headdress during a battle with the Blackfoot, and the Cree consequently lost the battle. Medicine Hat contains more than 70 parks connected by 40 miles (65 km) of trails for hiking, biking, and cross-country skiing. The *Medicine Hat Museum and Art Gallery* (1302 Bomford Crescent SW; phone: 403-527-6266) reveals the history of the Canadian West through exhibits, reconstructions, and photographic displays. Open daily; no admission charge. Near the *Tourist Information Centre* (Trans-Canada Hwy. at Southridge Dr.; phone: 403-527-6422) stands the steel, 20-story-tall *Saamis Teepee,* which was constructed for the opening ceremony of the 1988 *Olympic Winter Games* in Calgary and now overlooks an archaeological dig. Guided tours are offered by the *Saamis Teepee Association.* There's no admission charge (phone: 403-527-6773). Native arts and crafts are on sale at the *Dream Catcher* store next to the teepee. The site is open May through September; closed the rest of the year. Medicine Hat also boasts four excellent golf courses.

En Route from Medicine Hat Continue west on Route 1. For the most part, it is open country until the town of Brooks, 70 miles (112 km) out of Medicine Hat. This stretch of highway provides a good overview of Alberta's badlands. Prominent here and throughout much of southern Alberta are coulees, sharp trenches worn by wind and water into masses of rock. You will see a few of the formations of curiously columned rock called hoodoos. Those interested in horticulture may want to stop in Brooks at the *Crop*

Diversification Centre–South, which conducts tours of its landscaped gardens. It's closed mid-September through May; open daily the rest of the year. There's no admission charge (phone: 403-362-3391). The *Brooks and District Museum* (568 Sutherland Dr.; phone: 403-362-5073) takes visitors back in time, as they walk through an old church and schoolhouse with maps, schoolbooks, and inkwells intact. Open daily; closed September through April. There's an admission charge.

The main attraction, however, is *Dinosaur Provincial Park,* northeast of Brooks, which contains the largest dinosaur fossil bed in the world. The park lies about 15 miles (24 km) north of Brooks; take Route 873 north and follow the signs.

DINOSAUR PROVINCIAL PARK Located on the banks of the Red Deer River, the park—a World Heritage Site—was once lush seaside swampland, the home of 11 species of duck-billed dinosaurs. Today its valleys and hills are covered with juniper, sagebrush, and prickly pear cactus, and it is one of the world's richest fossil grounds. The action of the river has gradually eroded the rock bed, creating spectacular hoodoos and revealing layer upon layer of colored minerals. In the process, the river uncovered the remains of the dinosaurs.

Scientists, including world-renowned paleontologist H. C. Sternberg, unearthed 120 dinosaur skeletons in the area in the late 1800s, duly distributing them to museums around the world. Discoveries of additional skeletons and species of dinosaur continue to be made during digs every summer.

The park has been kept as natural as possible, with some skeletons on display in the badlands, housed in protective buildings. Visitors are welcome to take self-guided tours of the parkland and to join bus tours (for a small fee) that venture several times a day into restricted areas of this fragile landscape. Note that all fossils and bones are protected by law; you are not allowed to keep any you may find.

Also in the park is a well-equipped campground that's open May through mid-October (phone: 403-378-4342; fax: 403-378-4247), and *John Ware's Cabin,* a museum depicting life on an early Alberta ranch. A former slave from South Carolina, Ware settled here in the late 1800s, when little was known of this valley. He eventually ran a thousand head of cattle on the Red Deer River. The park also is the site of the *Royal Tyrrell Museum of Palaeontology Field Station,* an interpretive center where visitors can watch paleontologists at work. The park is open daily (for day use only), but the cabin and the interpretive center are closed September through April; no admission charge (phone: 403-378-4342).

En Route from Dinosaur Provincial Park The next major destination is Drumheller, to the northwest, where there are more dinosaurs. Pick up the Trans-Canada Highway (Rte. 1) again at Brooks and continue west. After about 38 miles (64 km), you'll come to Route 56, which you can follow north 39 miles (65 km) to Drumheller. Or, you can continue on Route 1 for another 10 miles (16 km) until you find the turnoff for Cluny. The towns of Cluny and Gleichen border the Siksika nation's reserve. Here, in 1877, Crowfoot, chief of the Blackfoot nation, signed Treaty No. 7, which mandated peace between the natives and white settlers. South of Cluny on Route 842, you will pass a sign pointing the way to Crowfoot's grave. Up the ridge is a burial ground containing the graves of many natives who died of starvation and poverty after the treaty was signed. At the edge of the graveyard, surrounded by a black fence, is Crowfoot's grave. At the east end of Cluny alongside Route 842, look for the *Bow River Trading Post,* which sells everything from Siksika-made moccasins, clothing, jewelry, and other crafts to audiotapes of actual powwows (phone: 403-734-3255). Eight miles (13 km) west of Cluny on Route 1 is the turnoff for Gleichen. On the south side of town are the buildings of *Old Sun College.* Here the Siksika operate a museum of local ethnographic history. (Their ongoing efforts continue to bring back artifacts dispersed throughout Canada over the past century.) To view the museum, contact the *Siksika Cultural Department* (PO Box 1100, Siksika, AB T0J 3W0; phone: 403-734-3070 or 403-294-1435). Information on the museum and crafts stores is also available from the Siksika nation's administrative office in the mall at the Route 1–Gleichen turnoff.

Return to the Trans-Canada Highway and continue to the turnoff to Route 21, 18 miles (29 km) farther west. Head north on Route 21 for 23 miles (37 km) and turn east on Route 9. Another 29 miles (46 km) will bring you to Drumheller. Over the course of this route, you will have reentered the badlands.

Along Route 9, 16 miles (26 km) southwest of Drumheller, stop for a refreshing cup of tea and home-baked desserts at *That's Crafty* (phone: 403-677-2207; closed Sundays and January through March). The store, housed in a converted barn, carries the work of local artisans.

You may want to turn off Route 9 at Route 840 and head south about 6 miles (10 km) to the historical hamlet of Rosebud, where you can enjoy a country-style dinner, followed by family or variety theater at *Rosebud School of the Arts* (phone: 403-677-2001; 800-267-7553), as well as browse through an art gallery, a crafts shop, an antiques store (in an old railway caboose), and a museum of pioneer history. Contact *Rosebud School of the Arts* for information on all Rosebud attractions.

Six miles (10 km) southwest of Drumheller, off Route 9, Horse Shoe Canyon is an excellent example of badlands landscape. From the canyon floor, the rock piles rise in strange shapes, and the canyon's walls are layers of contrasting green, red, brown, and gold. There are fine vantage points along the canyon's rim, and trails lead down into the canyon itself.

DRUMHELLER This city (pop. 6,300) boasts an excellent museum—the *Royal Tyrrell Museum of Palaeontology* (see below)—and a spectacular landscape. Here over the ages, the Red Deer River has carved the Drumheller Valley deep into the plains. The region is filled with hoodoos and exposed layers of stone, gullies, and canyons. And, as at Brooks, the river has uncovered the remains of prehistoric animals.

Many of Drumheller's attractions are found along the Dinosaur Trail, a 30-mile (48-km) tourist road that begins at the outskirts of town, travels through the badlands north and west of the city, and returns to town. Despite its name, the Dinosaur Trail contains a variety of attractions relating to local life and history and is more commercial than *Dinosaur Provincial Park.* Entering the trail at the north end of Drumheller, follow Route 838 (North Dinosaur Trail) through spectacular badlands scenery to the *Homestead Antique Museum,* a unique collection of just about anything that relates to life in the Drumheller area since the turn of the century. The museum is closed mid-October through April; open daily the rest of the year. There's an admission charge (phone: 403-823-2600).

Continue west to the *Royal Tyrrell Museum of Palaeontology* (Dinosaur Trail; phone: 403-823-7707). Between 60 and 120 million years ago, this area was a tropical swamp inhabited by dinosaurs. Today, remnants of that era can be seen at this $30-million museum and research center, named for geologist Joseph Tyrrell, who found the first dinosaur bones in the area in 1884. The collection and its illustration of the epochs of history are stunning. One of the museum's prize pieces is the albertosaurus skull that Tyrrell discovered in the area. There are more than 40 dinosaur skeletons and 45,000 dinosaur specimens, and the exhibits on the development of life in the area feature films, videos, and interactive computer terminals. (One computer program lets you "build your own dinosaur," then explains whether or not such a creature could survive in the prehistoric era you've selected.) Visitors also can watch the museum's scientists at work preserving and mounting dinosaur fossils. Step into the *Palaeoconservatory,* a greenhouse filled with tropical plants similar to those that thrived in Alberta between 70 and 300 million years ago. The museum is open daily mid-May through early September; closed Mondays the rest of the year; admission charge.

The next site on the trail is the *Little Church,* an aptly named universal house of worship that accommodates six. Beyond the church is Horsethief Canyon. The road commands an excellent view of the canyon's fine desert landscape. After Horsethief Canyon, the *Bleriot Ferry* (one of the few remaining cable ferries in Alberta) takes you and your car across the Red Deer River, passing thousands of fossilized oysters on the opposite bank. The ferry operates free of charge daily; closed early November through mid-April.

The route now turns south onto South Dinosaur Trail (Rte. 837) and descends again into the river valley, passing the community of Nacmine and entering Drumheller from the west. This badlands section of the route passes the family-oriented *Drumheller Prehistoric Park,* which contains life-size replicas of dinosaurs plus a rock and fossil shop. The park is closed mid-October through March; open daily the rest of the year. There's an admission charge (phone: 403-823-6144).

You also can take an hour's drive east from Drumheller, on Route 10, to East Coulee. This route, along Hoodoo Drive, goes deeper into the river valley, passes some abandoned coal mine shafts, and reveals more hoodoos and some mushroom-shaped rock formations. Four miles (6 km) east of Drumheller, near Rosedale, a swinging bridge spans a deep section of the valley. At East Coulee is the *Atlas Coal Mine Museum.* Once the region's major working coal mine, the site now has an interpretive center and walking trail. Surface tours of the mine are available. The museum is closed early September through mid-May; open daily the rest of the year. There's an admission charge (phone: 403-822-2220). The restored *East Coulee School Museum* (Second Ave.; phone: 403-822-3970), built circa 1930, features a restored classroom, a crafts shop, a tearoom, an old-fashioned candy store, and an art gallery. It's closed weekends September to late May; open daily the rest of the year; admission charge.

En Route from Drumheller The quickest way to reach the city of Red Deer and, from there, the highway to Edmonton, is on Route 9 west from Drumheller, which becomes Route 72 and, 72 miles (115 km) west of Drumheller, intersects Route 2. To go directly to Red Deer, go north on Route 2, a four-lane highway, for 43½ miles (70 km), or take a brief detour west on Route 580 to the *Pasu Farm Gallery,* a working sheep farm with a gallery, tearoom, and shop selling handwoven wool, moccasins, leather goods, unique jewelry, and mohair tapestries. It's 5 miles (9 km) west of Carstairs, which is on Route 2A, just west of Route 2; call ahead for hours (phone: 403-337-2800).

It also is possible to make the trip to Red Deer by way of secondary roads through countryside that lacks any major tourist attractions but does have interesting scenery. Follow Route 56 north from Drumheller for about 25 miles (40 km), then cut west on Route 585. After 22 miles (35 km), Route 585 intersects Route 21 at Trochu, where you'll find the *St-Ann Ranch Bed and Breakfast,* an antiques-furnished ranch house (see *Best en Route*). Head north on Route 21 for 19 miles (31 km) until it intersects Route 42. Take Route 42 west for 24 miles (38 km) to Route 2 just south of Red Deer.

RED DEER This city (pop. 60,000) is the convention capital of the province and a fast-growing industrial center. Although Red Deer is not a major tourist attraction, it does feature one worthwhile museum: the *Red Deer and District Museum* (47th Ave. and 45th St.; phone: 403-343-6844), which is devoted to pioneer history. It's open daily; no admission charge. If hunger strikes, try *Killian's Restaurant* at the city's north end (*Parkland Mall,* Gaetz Ave.; phone: 403-346-8555) or *Smitty's,* an attractive alternative to the standard truck stop diner (Rte. 2 south of town; phone: 403-340-8484). In addition, the *Red Deer Lodge* and the *Black Knight Inn* both have dining rooms (see *Best en Route*).

Of greater interest to a vacationer is the area just west of the city on Route 11. Here in wooded countryside is the town of Sylvan Lake, a resort popular with Albertans, with several commercial campgrounds and a public beach on the south shore of the lake. This popular area may be crowded, so those in need of some serious solitude should drive around to the north shore of the lake, site of *Jarvis Bay Provincial Park.* The park offers trailer sites, showers, picnic facilities, swimming, and fishing. It charges a fee for camping but not picnicking. For camping reservations call 403-887-5522.

En Route from Red Deer It's an easy 93 miles (149 km) north to Edmonton on either Route 2, the major highway, or Route 2A, which passes through towns along the way. The countryside is pleasant and at times spectacular. Sights include two more lake resorts west of the highways. Red Deer also can be the starting point for a trip west on Route 11, the David Thompson Highway. Along this 154-mile (246-km) road lies the *Rocky Mountain House National Historic Park,* which was built on the site of several former trading posts. The road continues, crossing unspoiled country, through the *Rocky Mountains Forest Reserve* and terminates at the boundary of *Banff* and *Jasper National Parks.*

Fifteen miles (24 km) north of Red Deer is the town of Lacombe, home of the *Canadian Agriculture Department*'s research station (58th St. and C&E Trail; phone: 403-782-3316), where scientists develop new varieties of wheat and grain. The station is closed to visitors on weekends, and tours must be booked ahead; no admission charge. Seven miles (11 km) west of Lacombe on Route 12, at Gull Lake, is *Aspen Beach Provincial Park,* the best of the area's lake resorts, with more than 680 campsites in three campgrounds, power hookups, showers, swimming, fishing, boat launches, and boat rentals (phone: 403-748-4066 for camping reservations). Continue north for another 19 miles (30 km) on Route 2 or 2A to Route 13. Follow Route 13 west to reach *Pigeon Lake Provincial Park,* with 292 campsites, as well as showers, swimming, fishing, boat launches, hiking trails, concession stands, and boat rentals (phone: 403-586-2644 for camping reservations). Route 13 east from Route 2 leads for 12 miles (19 km) to the town of Wetaskiwin, at the junction of Route 2A. Here, the *Reynolds Museum* (4118 57th St.; phone: 403-352-5855), devoted to agriculture and transportation, has one of North America's largest collections of antique and classic cars, fire engines, and airplanes. It's open year-round; admission charge. The final 42 miles (67 km) north travel through farmland past the town of Leduc to Edmonton.

BEST EN ROUTE

Medicine Hat, Brooks, Drumheller, and Red Deer have good motels; there also are several good campgrounds and bed and breakfast establishments. The area boasts no truly luxurious or major resort motels, but most are pleasant and comfortable, with the fanciest at Red Deer. It's advisable to reserve your room far in advance in the summer, especially in the Drumheller area. Per night, expect to pay from $55 to $75 for a double room at hotels in the expensive range; from $40 to $55 in those we list as moderate; from $20 to $40 at inexpensive places; and less than $20 at most campgrounds, which we have classed as very inexpensive. All hotels feature private baths and TV sets, unless otherwise indicated. For each location, lodgings are listed alphabetically by price category.

MEDICINE HAT

Medicine Hat Lodge Giant indoor water slides, a hair salon, a casino, a whirlpool and steamroom, and business services are some of the features of this 189-room lodge just off Route 1 at the city's eastern entrance. The lodge also has its own pub, cocktail lounge, and restaurant. 1051 Ross Glenn Dr. SE (phone: 403-529-2222; 800-661-8095 in Canada; fax: 403-529-1538). Expensive.

Imperial This motel has 102 units with telephones, a restaurant, an exercise room, laundry facilities, an indoor pool, a sauna, and a whirlpool. At the eastern entrance to the city, at 3282 13th Ave. SE (phone: 403-527-8811; 800-661-5322; fax: 403-526-7039). Inexpensive.

Gas City Campground Considered one of the best in the province, this 97-site property is open May to early September. One mile (1.6 km) west of Rte. 1 on Seventh St. SW (phone: 403-526-0644). Very inexpensive.

BROOKS

Douglas Country Inn This nonsmoking establishment offers seven rooms, a full country breakfast included in the rate, a TV room, and heated kennels for pets. The dining room serves dinner nightly except Sundays. Four miles (7 km) north of Brooks on Route 873 (phone: 403-362-2873; fax: 403-362-2100). Moderate.

Heritage Inn A link in the Heritage chain, this property features 82 rooms, a restaurant and cocktail lounge, a tavern, an exercise room, and a sauna, as well as business services. On Main St., just off the Trans-Canada Hwy. (phone: 403-362-6666; fax: 403-362-7319). Moderate.

Tillebrook Provincial Park On 344 acres, its 120 tent and trailer sites have laundry facilities, electrical hookups, showers, and flush toilets. Open May to mid-October for camping; for day use only the rest of the year. Four miles (7 km) southeast of Brooks on Rte. 1 (phone: 403-362-4525). Very inexpensive.

DRUMHELLER

Drumheller Inn This 100-room inn features an indoor pool, a whirlpool, meeting facilities, a dining room, and a lounge. 100 S. Railway Ave. (Rte. 9) SE (phone: 403-823-8400; fax: 403-823-5020). Expensive.

Dinosaur Trail RV Resort This tent and trailer camp has more than 200 sites, canoe rentals, laundry facilities, an outdoor pool, mini-golf, and a recreation hall. Closed October through April. About six miles (11 km) west of Drumheller on Route 838/North Dinosaur Trail (phone: 403-823-9333). Very inexpensive.

TROCHU

St-Ann Ranch Bed and Breakfast This four-story ranch house, which dates from 1905, has five antiques-filled rooms (three with private baths). There's also a restored pioneer cottage featuring two rooms with fireplaces and a shared kitchen. Reservations necessary far in advance. The tea house on the premises is open afternoons May through August; the entire establishment is closed Mondays. Rte. 585, at the east end of town (phone: 403-442-3924). Moderate.

TL Bar Ranch A horse and cattle ranch between Drumheller and Red Deer, this place accommodates 10 to 12 people in a log ranch house and a cottage (some private baths are available). Closed weekdays from November through April. Also see *Farm and Ranch Vacations* in DIVERSIONS. PO Box 217, Trochu, AB T0M 2C0 (phone: 403-442-2207). Moderate.

RED DEER

Red Deer Lodge Considered the best in town, this motel has 233 rooms with color TV sets and telephones, including six lovely one-bedroom suites with kitchenettes. The motel also offers meeting facilities; a hot tub; an excellent dining room and lounge; a poolside coffee shop; and two pubs—a sports bar and a country-and-western bar. The property is built around a landscaped indoor courtyard with a pool. 4311 49th Ave. (phone: 403-346-8841; 800-661-1657; fax: 403-341-3220). Expensive.

Black Knight Inn This 98-room hostelry has telephones and color TV sets, an indoor pool, a sauna, a dining room, a cocktail lounge, and banquet/meeting facilities. There's a discount for seniors. 2929 Gaetz Ave. (phone: 403-343-6666; 800-661-8793 in Alberta; fax: 403-340-8970). Moderate.

British Columbia

Canada's third-largest province, British Columbia (BC) also is its wettest. BC is bordered on the west by the Pacific Ocean; on the south by the states of Washington, Montana, and Idaho; on the east by Alberta; and on the north by the Northwest and Yukon Territories and Alaska. The Alaskan panhandle also runs a long way down the province's northwest flank. BC covers 366,255 square miles, enough land to make 73 Connecticuts or 300 Rhode Islands. Despite the fruit lands of the Okanagan Valley, the trim pastures of Vancouver Island's east coast, and the vegetable farms of the Fraser River delta east of Vancouver, less than 10% of the land is now or ever will be cultivated or used as pasture. The rest is covered by pristine forests, towering mountains, and vast expanses of semiarid sagebrush land.

Three quarters of the province's population lives at the southwestern tip, in the provincial capital of Victoria (pop. over 283,000) and in the Pacific port city of Vancouver, Canada's third largest (pop. 1.6 million). For a detailed report on Vancouver, see THE CITIES; for more on the province's superb skiing, see *Downhill Skiing* and *Cross Country Skiing* in DIVERSIONS.

The four routes outlined below include a trip up Vancouver Island to Port Hardy, where ferries depart for Prince Rupert, gateway to the Yukon and Alaska; a journey up the Fraser River road; a drive from Kamloops east to the stunningly beautiful mountain parks on the Alberta border; and a wilderness itinerary that starts mid-province at Prince George and leads to the Yukon. For information about ferry routes in BC, contact *British Columbia Ferries* (1112 Fort St., Victoria, BC V8V 4V2; phone: 604-386-3431; 604-685-1021 in Vancouver). The *Victoria Line* (US office: 101 Alaskan Way S., Seattle, WA 98104; phone: 206-625-1880 in Seattle; 604-480-5555 in Victoria; 800-668-1167 for recorded information; fax: 206-625-1881; 604-480-5222) offers a deluxe car/passenger ferry link between Seattle and Victoria that runs daily from mid-May to late September; reservations are necessary for cars, but not for foot passengers. For further information on the province, contact *Tourism British Columbia* (1117 Wharf St., Victoria, BC V8W 2Z2; phone: 604-387-1428; 800-663-6000; or 802-865 Hornby St., Vancouver, BC V6Z 2G3; phone: 604-663-6000) or *Tourism Victoria* (812 Wharf St., Victoria, BC V8W 1T3; phone: 604-382-2127; 800-663-3883 for hotel reservations only).

Vancouver Island

Some US citizens still grumble about the Oregon Treaty, ratified by Britain and the US in 1846, which established the 49th Parallel as the line of demarcation for most of the US-Canada border. The focus of the complaints is the little patch in the far west where Vancouver Island drops just below the

49th, putting the beautiful town of Victoria firmly into what should be—but is not—US territory.

This island has snow-capped mountains, long white beaches, waters teeming with salmon, and fine, deep harbors. This 310-mile (496-km) trip from Victoria to Port Hardy takes in the coastal resort towns of Qualicum Beach and Parksville and the salmon runs in the renowned Campbell River. It also reveals some of Vancouver Island's history, which stretches back to the times when the native Haida, Kwakiutl, Sooke, and Cowichan were its only inhabitants. Although their populations were nearly wiped out by disease and war, the Cowichan still fish for salmon in the Cowichan River in much the same way their ancestors did thousands of years ago. Their legacy also can be seen in the giant totem poles in Victoria's *Thunderbird Park;* in petroglyphs at the edges of evaporating pools; and in the legends surrounding such geographical landmarks as Forbidden Plateau in Courtenay.

In contrast is the influence of Canadians of British heritage living in the provincial capital. Although you won't see a bobby on every corner, afternoon tea at the *Empress* hotel is a decidedly Anglo tradition (see *Quintessential Canada* in DIVERSIONS). It's easy to spend days visiting Victoria's museums, shops, and English-style pubs. Considered the most British city in Canada, it may seem a bit stuffy and formal, yet it lends a distinctive air to a journey largely characterized by wilderness scenery.

VICTORIA Jutting into the Strait of Juan de Fuca, the provincial capital is named after Queen Victoria, and it reflects the Britain of her reign. Its Victorian architecture, spacious parks, manicured gardens, and people (many of British descent) all add to this harbor city's Empire appeal.

Established as a Hudson's Bay Company post in 1843, the city went through a rowdy boomtown period almost two decades later, when fortune seekers stopped on their way to pan for gold in the Fraser River. Downtown's Bastion Square—with its renovated criminal courthouses, supply center for miners, maritime museum, restaurants, and shops with modern goods but mid-19th-century architecture–recaptures that time.

But thousands of years before any European set foot on the North American continent, the island's natives used deer antlers to chop down cedars for building homes and canoes. Visitors to *Thunderbird Park* (adjacent to the *Royal British Columbia Museum;* see below) not only will see a Kwakiutl dance house but will feel the power of the mythical thunderbird, thought to be a representation of the huge California condor. The bird was believed to have created thunder by fluttering its wings, and lightning by flashing its eyes. Carvings of this creature crest totem poles (some original, some copies) throughout the park, which is open daily. There's no admission charge.

Visitors to the *Royal British Columbia Museum* (675 Belleville St.; phone: 604-387-3014) will see one of the world's best collections of Northwest

Coast tribal art and view re-created street scenes and turn-of-the-century storefronts. It's open daily; admission charge. On a visit to the museum, you may hear the 62-bell *Carillon* that stands in front of the building. It was a gift from the people of the Netherlands for the *1967 Canadian Centennial.* Down the street is the *Royal London Wax Museum* (470 Belleville St.; phone: 604-388-4461), which contains surprisingly realistic likenesses of some prominent figures in history and fantasy, ranging from Queen Victoria to Pinocchio. It's open daily; there's an admission charge.

Nestled on the east side of the *Royal BC Museum* is the historic *Helmcken House* (10 Elliott Sq.; phone: 604-387-3011). Original furnishings and medical instruments belonging to Victoria's first doctor, John Helmcken, are on display. In early December, actors in 1860s garb portray a Victorian family engaged in traditional *Christmas* pastimes. *Helmcken House* is closed mid-December to mid-May; open daily the rest of the year. Admission is by donation.

Considered one of Canada's finest art museums, the *Art Gallery of Greater Victoria* (1040 Moss St.; phone: 604-384-4101) is home to North America's only Shinto shrine. It also features a large Japanese and Chinese collection plus European works from the 15th to the 20th centuries. The gallery is closed Sunday mornings; there's an admission charge.

The provincial *Parliament Buildings* (Government and Belleville Sts.), ornate Victorian structures built of andesite and native granite, are open to the public on weekdays. They are outlined at night by 3,000 lights.

Much Anglo influence is evident in the city's Victorian residences, past and present. *Craigdarroch Castle* (1050 Joan Crescent Dr.; phone: 604-592-5323) was once the home of a wealthy matron lured to Victoria by her husband's promise of a palatial abode. Robert Dunsmuir, a coal baron, built the castle for his Scottish wife but died before its completion. The castle is open daily; admission charge.

On the grounds of the *Olde England Inn* (see *Best en Route*) is a replica of the thatch cottage where Shakespeare's wife, Anne Hathaway, once lived; it's furnished with 16th-century antiques. Also part of the complex are a replica of the house where Shakespeare was born and of a 17th-century Plymouth tavern. Guided tours are available. The complex is open daily; admission charge.

Gardening enthusiasts will find the living, growing museum at the *Horticulture Centre of the Pacific* (505 Quayle St.; phone: 604-479-6162), with its rhododendron vale, kiwi arbor, and dozens of flowering shrubs and ornamental grasses, to be of particular interest. Open daily, except *Christmas;* admission charge.

To add to its atmosphere of bygone decorum, *Point Ellice House* (2616 Pleasant St.; phone: 604-387-4697) serves English high tea in its garden. Built in 1861 in mid-Victorian Italianate style by Victoria pioneer John Work for his daughter, the house contains many of its original furnishings and artifacts. Call to confirm tea times. The house is closed early

October to mid-May; open daily the rest of the year. Admission is by donation.

The *Crystal Gardens* (713 Douglas St.; phone: 604-381-1277), for decades the town's main swimming pool, is today a unique, multilevel tropical paradise filled with lush plantings, flamingos, and other tropical birds and animals housed in a great old-fashioned glass hall. It's open daily; admission charge. Another tropical indoor garden, with hundreds of colorful, exotic free-flying butterflies, is the *Victoria Butterfly Gardens* (1461 Benvenuto Ave.; phone: 604-652-3822). It's closed January and February; open daily the rest of the year. There's an admission charge.

Victoria's shops offer good values in woolens, china, crystal, jade, antiques, and handicrafts, many with a British influence. Walk down Government Street for antiques stores, clothiers, and afternoon tea spots, all with a traditional feel. One interesting place is *Sydney Reynolds* (801 Government St.; phone: 604-383-3931), Victoria's oldest china shop, which carries on the trade in a quaint old building.

For British fare more substantial than tea and crumpets, head for the *Sticky Wicket* (919 Douglas St.; phone: 604-383-7137) or *Barb's Place* (310 St. Lawrence St., by *Fisherman's Wharf;* phone: 604-384-6515). Other restaurants cater to more international whims: The *Taj Mahal* (679 Herald St.; phone: 604-383-4662) serves Indian food; the *Japanese Village* (734 Broughton St.; phone: 604-382-5165) has genuine Japanese cuisine; *La Petite Colombe* (604 Broughton St.; phone: 604-383-3234) features French fare; and *Met Bistro* (1715 Government St.; phone: 604-381-1512) offers California-style cooking. Or order a box lunch from *Sam's Deli* (805 Government St.; phone: 604-382-8424) and picnic under the oaks in *Beacon Hill Park* (Quadra St. and Superior St.). Although any place in the city is good for bird watching (sparrows and purple finches perch on apartment windowsills downtown), in the 154-acre oasis of *Beacon Hill Park,* native wild ducks and black (English) swans sail serenely across the ponds, and majestic eagles soar.

For a worthwhile side trip, take Route 17 or 17A north for a few miles and follow the signs to *Butchart Gardens.*

BUTCHART GARDENS About 90 years ago the estate of Jennie Butchart was a limestone quarry. Over the years she transformed this dismal scene into a horticulturist's dream: an English garden with thousands of rose beds, arches, and arbors; a Japanese garden with maple trees, hydrangeas, bamboo, and the rare Tibetan blue poppy; and a formal Italian garden with a cross-shaped lily pond and sculptured trees and hedges. Two restaurants among the 50 acres of manicured lawns, ponds, lakes, and exotic and native flowers offer breakfast, lunch, and afternoon tea, and the *Seed and Gift Store* sells the seeds of many of the flowers on the site. The gardens are illuminated by thousands of hidden lights evenings June through September, when occasionally musical performances are held. The gardens are open daily, with late evening hours in summer; there's an admission charge (phone: 604-652-4422).

En Route from Victoria Follow signs to Route 1, marked Nanaimo. Duncan is 38 miles (61 km) north.

DUNCAN On the banks of the Cowichan River, this small, bucolic town survives on lumbering (its traditional industry), farming, and fishing. The river is known for European brown trout and Pacific salmon. The lifestyle of the area's first residents, the Northwest Coast natives, is examined at the *Native Heritage Centre* (at the entrance to town, 200 Cowichan Way; phone: 604-746-8119). Native carvers display their skills in a carving house, and knitters create prized Cowichan sweaters in the gift gallery. At the *Longhouse,* you can see *Great Deeds,* a captivating film about the Cowichan culture. The on-site restaurant features abundant native fare. The complex is open daily; admission charge. Also visit the *British Columbia Forest Museum* (Hwy. 1, 1 mile/1.6 km north of town; phone: 604-746-1251). Organized around the theme "Man in the Forest: Yesterday, Today, and Tomorrow," the museum explores all aspects of the lumber industry, from the raw beauty and power of forests of 250- to 350-year-old Douglas firs to the reseeding and replanting operations under way today. The museum also has a wonderful collection of early lumbering equipment, including donkey engines, handcarts, and various saws. It's closed late September through April; open daily the rest of the year. There's an admission charge.

Anglers may want to take a side trip to Cowichan Bay, 4 miles (6 km) west on Route 18. Once a prime (and still reasonably good) area for sport fishing, the bay is now covered with log booms to feed nearby mills. You can rent a boat and fish for salmon here in late summer and early fall, but the best fishing has been declared off limits to visitors by local natives, within whose reserve most of the Cowichan River runs.

En Route from Duncan Head north on Route 1 to the turnoff to Chemainus, renowned as "The Little Town That Could." In a project that involved many of the residents of the town, which once was sustained by a lumber mill, artists took over the sides of stores and buildings to turn the main street into a festival of murals. Each painting depicts an aspect of the area's history, from steam locomotives and general stores to loggers and seamen, and more are added every year.

Northwest of Chemainus, the mountains and sea close together again, funneling travelers through Ladysmith, which lies on the 49th Parallel, the Canada-US border for mainland British Columbia. Continue on Route 1 to Nanaimo, 32 miles (51 km) from Duncan.

NANAIMO More than a century ago, seven native tribes lived in harmony along the shores of the Strait of Georgia. The discovery of coal in 1852—and the concomitant arrival of British miners—destroyed that peace. Less than a decade after a native showed the coal and its whereabouts to a Hudson's

Bay Company employee trading in a fort here, the company added a turreted bastion, complete with cannon, to protect the workers from native attacks. Modern-day visitors can follow a narrow cow path–like road uphill to view the bastion, now a museum.

Forest products have since replaced coal mining as Nanaimo's main industry. Recently, tourism has become important, and the city's waterfront facilities have been redeveloped. An interesting addition is the Swy-a-Lana Lagoon, the world's only manmade tidal lagoon. In mid-July, Nanaimo's harbor is the site of one of Canada's wackiest contests. Participants race 35 miles over the often-stormy Strait of Georgia to the mainland in motorized bathtub-like contraptions. This popular event, the *World Champion Bathtub Race,* attracts entrants from around the world (also see "Special Events" in *Vancouver,* THE CITIES). The more traditional sport of fishing also is popular in the strait, where salmon, trout, and steelhead proliferate all year.

En Route from Nanaimo Just north along the waterfront on Route 19 is Departure Bay, with marina facilities for boats and yachts. At Parksville, follow Route 4 west to the charming village of Coombs, where goats stand atop the roof of the general store. Coombs also is home to *Butterfly World,* where more than a thousand free-flying butterflies of about 80 different species can be observed in a 5,000-square-foot greenhouse. It's closed November through March; open daily the rest of the year. There's an admission charge (phone: 604-248-7026). From here, a small mountain pass descends into the Alberni Valley and runs west for 30 miles (48 km) to Port Alberni. Along the way, the pass cuts through *MacMillan Park,* one of the best examples anywhere of untouched forest. It's also the home of *Cathedral Grove,* a cluster of tall West Coast cedars and Douglas firs rising high above the forest floor.

PORT ALBERNI Visitors to this mill city are usually more interested in the area's sport fishing than the downtown attractions. Near here, anglers can find sockeye salmon and cohos in the harbor or follow a narrow paved road 6 miles (10 km) northwest to Sproat Lake, noted for its trout. From Sproat Lake, Route 4 leads west and then south to *Pacific Rim National Park* for some of the best beachcombing in North America. Here, seals, sea lions, and shore birds inhabit 250 square miles of craggy headlands, curving, white sandy beaches, interior lakes, and estuaries. For information on the park, contact *Pacific Rim National Park* (PO Box 280, Ucluelet, BC V0R 3A0; phone: 604-726-7721). The park is open daily, though some facilities close in the winter; there's a charge for overnight stays.

At the northwest edge of *Pacific Rim National Park* is Tofino, a pretty little fishing village and the site of an annual whale watching festival around late March.

En Route from Port Alberni Retrace Route 4 to Parksville, a resort town with long sandy shores splashed by shallow warm water. Just south of town, *Rathtrevor Beach Park* has camping and picnic facilities. North of Parksville on Route 19 is Qualicum, with more beaches. South of Qualicum on Route 4A, *Little Qualicum Falls Provincial Park* offers a day's hiking or overnight camping. The park is open daily; there's a charge for overnight stays from April through October. From Qualicum, head north on Route 19 for 39 miles (62 km) to Courtenay, located in the southeastern section of the Comox River Valley. Bounded by high mountains and carved out by clear lakes and the river, this area is home to grouse, ducks, geese, and pheasant.

COURTENAY The British established this town in the late 1880s as a major farming community. It's now a popular recreational area, with golf courses, lodges, and restaurants. A native tribe had formerly lived here, atop a mountain known as the Forbidden Plateau. Its name derives from the legend of an enormous monster that was believed to have slain women and children there while their men were away. Those not frightened by the legend may make the trip up the plateau on foot for world class wilderness climbing. Both Forbidden Plateau (phone: 604-334-4744; 604-338-1919 for snow report) and Mt. Washington (phone: 604-338-1386; 604-338-1515 for snow report) offer challenging ski runs during the winter.

En Route from Courtenay Head 14 miles (22 km) north along the coast to *Miracle Beach Park,* a public campsite with spaces for 193 tents and a great beach to comb for driftwood. Continue north on Route 19 to Campbell River, 28 miles (45 km) from Courtenay.

CAMPBELL RIVER Although this town is a mining and lumbering port, its fame comes from its excellent salmon fishing. In fact, the most sought-after honor among the fishing fraternity here is membership in the *Tyee Club.* Only those who have caught a *tyee* salmon weighing more than 30 pounds from a rowboat, on light tackle, in one of two local ponds can join.

The town enjoys the advantage of the largest river on the island. If you want to rent a boat, tackle, or other fishing equipment, head to the shores of the river, which flows through *Strathcona Provincial Park* (west on Route 28). Mountain climbers will be challenged by Mt. Albert Edward and Mt. McBride, both over 6,000 feet. The park is open daily; there's a charge for overnight stays from May through September.

About 81 miles (130 km) north on Route 19 is Port McNeill, known for its Vanishing River, which disappears into the earth, indicating the existence of a vast subterranean maze of caves and tunnels. This leg of Route 19 continues for about 25 miles (40 km) to Port Hardy, where visitors can board the *Queen of the North* ferry for a 274-mile (438-km) voyage through the Inside Passage to Prince Rupert on the mainland (for information, contact *British Columbia Ferries;* see introduction to this chapter).

BEST EN ROUTE

One of the most popular vacation spots in Canada, Vancouver Island offers a wide variety of accommodations, from basic modern motels and clean campsites to elaborate hotels. During the peak season (May through September), it is wise to book ahead. For a double room for one night, expect to pay from $110 to $265 in an expensive hotel; from $60 to $110 in a moderate hotel, bungalow, or cottage; and from $30 to $60 in an inexpensive inn or bed and breakfast establishment. Campsites in the area run $10 or less. All hotels have private baths unless otherwise indicated. For a complete listing of accommodations, contact *Tourism British Columbia* (see chapter introduction). For each location places are listed alphabetically by price category.

VICTORIA AREA

Aerie A short drive north of downtown Victoria is this secluded, European-style resort. From its picturesque setting atop the Malahat Summit to its 23-karat-gold-plated dining room ceiling, original oil paintings, and lovely hand-crafted furniture, the surroundings are exquisite. The 12 individually decorated rooms and suites feature Jacuzzis, fireplaces, and balconies affording breathtaking views of the Pacific Ocean and Gulf Islands. The dining room serves first-rate continental fare. Located 19 miles (30 km) from Victoria on the Trans-Canada Hwy. (Rte. 1) at Malahat (phone: 604-743-7115; fax: 604-743-4766). Expensive.

Beaconsfield Inn Set in a handsome Edwardian mansion, this elegant and serene bed and breakfast establishment is on a quiet residential street three blocks from Victoria's Inner Harbor. The nine lovely rooms and suites are furnished with antiques and have private baths; most also feature fireplaces and Jacuzzis. A full breakfast, afternoon tea and sherry, and champagne and chocolates are included in the rate (there's no restaurant). This is the perfect place for a romantic getaway. 998 Humbolt St., Victoria (phone: 604-384-4044). Expensive.

Coast Victoria Harbourside A 132-room waterfront resort hotel, it boasts an indoor-outdoor pool, exercise facilities, and the popular *Blue Crab* restaurant. 146 Kingston St., Victoria (phone: 604-360-1211; 800-663-1144; fax: 604-360-1418). Expensive.

Empress This elegant giant, which opened in 1908, still reigns as the island's largest and best-known hotel. The 482-room bulwark of British custom has, with the help of a $45-million restoration in the late 1980s, added up-to-the-minute innovations while retaining its charm. Facilities include three bars, the *Empress Room* restaurant, the *Bengal Lounge,* the *Garden Café,* a pool, and an exercise room. Afternoon tea is a not-to-be-missed experience for guests and non-guests alike. For additional details see *Quintessential Canada* and *Special Havens* in DIVERSIONS. 721 Government St., Victoria (phone: 604-384-8111; 800-441-1414; fax: 604-381-4334). Expensive.

Hastings House A Relais & Châteaux member, this country hotel is situated on an island 12 miles (19 km) north of Victoria. The casual elegance of its four rooms and eight suites is complemented by its seaside location and proximity to golf, tennis, and sailing. There is a dining room; breakfast is included in the rate. For additional details see *Special Havens* in DIVERSIONS. Closed late November to mid-March. Accessible by ferry from Swartz Bay. 160 Upper Ganges Rd., Salt Spring Island (phone: 604-537-2362; 800-661-9255; fax: 604-537-5333). Expensive.

Laurel Point Inn Situated on Victoria's inner harbor, it offers plush, modern facilities, including an indoor/outdoor pool, tennis, a dining room and bar, balconies with views, banquet facilities, and 201 guestrooms. 680 Montreal St. (phone: 604-386-8721; 800-663-7667; fax: 604-386-9547). Expensive.

Oak Bay Beach This 50-room Tudor-style seaside resort hotel showcases priceless antiques throughout. There is a fine dining room, the *Tudor Room by the Sea,* and an English-style pub called the *Snug;* afternoon high tea with scones and Devonshire cream is served daily. The hotel's own yachts offer breakfast, luncheon, or sunset dinner cruises and are available for salmon fishing charters. A short drive from downtown, at 1175 Beach Dr., Victoria (phone: 604-598-4556; 800-668-7758; fax: 604-598-4556). Expensive.

Ocean Pointe Overlooking the Inner Harbour, this 250-room hotel features a pool, a sauna and spa facilities, the *Victorian* dining room, the casual *Boardwalk* restaurant-deli, and access to a waterside walkway. 45 Songhees Rd., Victoria (phone: 604-360-2999; 800-667-4677; fax: 604-360-1041). Expensive.

Olde England Inn This gabled Tudor-style hotel offers 63 rooms with antiques galore, including Victorian furniture, canopy beds, and suits of armor–the bed in one room is purported to be the one King Edward VII of England used in *Warwick Castle.* Set on acres of lawns, the hotel and the adjacent replica of Anne Hathaway's thatch cottage and other 17th-century buildings are popular tourist attractions. The restaurant specializes in hearty dishes like roast beef and Yorkshire pudding. Located in the suburb of Esquimalt, at 429 Lampson St. (phone: 604-388-4353). Expensive.

Ramada Huntingdon Manor Inn Sporting an English manor-house theme, this 116-room hotel is located in the historic James Bay area close to the *Parliament Buildings.* On the premises are a library, a sauna, a Jacuzzi, the *Hunters' Club* lounge, and the *Royal Stables* dining room. The inn is within easy walking distance of many attractions. 330 Quebec St., Victoria (phone: 604-381-3456; 800-663-7557; fax: 604-382-7666). Expensive.

LADYSMITH

Inn of the Sea A great place to get away from it all while enjoying the benefits of a luxury hotel, it boasts 60 well-appointed rooms and suites with ocean views. Guests can relax in a Jacuzzi, swim in the heated pool, play tennis, or charter a cruise through the Gulf Islands before indulging in a fine meal in the dining room. A floating dock provides mooring for guests' boats. 3600 Yellow Point Rd. (phone: 604-245-2211; 800-663-7327 in western Canada; fax: 604-245-3442). Expensive.

Yellow Point Lodge One of the island's top getaways occupies 180 acres overlooking the sea. The establishment can accommodate a hundred guests in rustic log-and-sandstone cottages and in the main lodge. Walking trails, tennis, a pool, a dining area, and cozy gamerooms with fireplaces for a quiet round of chess or backgammon are all here. 3700 Yellow Point Rd. (phone: 604-245-7422; fax: 604-245-7411). Expensive.

NANAIMO

Coast Bastion Inn An attraction on the town's revitalized waterfront, this 15-story, 179-room hotel features a well-equipped health club with a gym, whirlpool, sauna, and an outdoor deck. There's also a restaurant and popular pub/nightclub. 11 Bastion St. (phone: 604-753-6601; 800-663-1144; fax: 604-753-4155). Moderate.

PARKSVILLE

Bayside Inn Minutes off the highway on sandy Parksville Bay, this full-service, 60-room inn offers ocean and mountain views. There's also a dining room, a lounge, an indoor pool and whirlpool, a fitness center, a putting green, and tennis, racquetball, and squash courts. 240 Dogwood St. (phone: 604-248-8333; 800-663-4232 in western Canada; fax: 604-248-4689). Expensive.

CAMPBELL RIVER

Painter's Lodge At the oldest and best-known fishing property in town, the guest list includes celebrities and plain folk drawn to the great salmon fishing. The 94 rooms are distributed among the main lodge, five other buildings, and four cottages with fireplaces. Amenities include a dining room, a pub, a lounge, a heated pool, boats, guides, access to float planes, a full-service spa, a running track, tennis courts, and a children's entertainment center. 1625 MacDonald Rd. (phone: 604-286-1102; 800-663-7090; fax: 604-286-0158). Expensive.

Strathcona Park Lodge This family-oriented resort, on the northeast edge of *Strathcona Provincial Park,* offers 46 rooms in four chalets, plus 12 cabins. The main dining hall serves buffet-style meals, and there is fine dining in the *Hi-Bracer* room. Visitors can enjoy boats, kayaks, canoes, fishing, and swimming on the park's 50-mile lake system. Rock climbing and hiking are nearby. Special packages and fishing guide services are available. Rte. 28 (phone: 604-286-3122; fax: 604-286-6010). Moderate.

QUADRA ISLAND

April Point Commanding a view of the island's fjords and snow-fringed mountains, this salmon fishing resort offers boats, guides, helicopter trips to fishing and hiking destinations, swimming, waterskiing, and sailing nearby. It can accommodate 115 guests in lodgings that range from double rooms to units for 10 people. There also is a dining room. The large yacht marina features full facilities, including engine repair service. Closed November through March. From Campbell River, take the 10-minute car ferry ride to Quadra Island (phone: 604-285-2222; fax: 604-285-2411). Expensive.

Tsa-Kwa-Luten Lodge A creation of the Cape Mudge native tribe, the lodge (its name means "gathering place") is located on the bluffs overlooking Discovery Passage. There are 28 large guestrooms with lofts, patios, or decks in the main house, in addition to four handsome two-bedroom cabins and a guesthouse that sleeps up to 12. Many of the rooms have fireplaces. Built of the wood of massive Douglas firs, the lobby is a contemporary interpretation of a Native American longhouse; there's also a dining room. Veteran guides take guests fishing in sturdy Boston whalers for a variety of salmon. The fascinating *Kwagiulth Museum and Cultural Centre,* with displays of local artifacts, is nearby. Closed November through March. Take the 10-minute car ferry from Campbell River; the lodge is a 10-minute drive from the ferry landing. Quathiaski Cove (phone: 604-285-2042; 800-665-7745 in the western US and Canada; fax: 604-285-2532). Expensive.

Fraser River

From the time Native Americans were the sole inhabitants of this continent until the 19th century, when prospectors were struck with gold fever, the Fraser River—with its deadly whirlpools, jagged shoals, and white rapids—blocked the road to the deer and elk hunting grounds, fur trading routes, and gold mines of the Cariboo Mountains. Roads and bridges have made the river less of an obstacle, though it is still just as wild. This 850-mile (1,360-km) journey follows the river, from the Fraser Valley delta around Hope, rich in fur trading history and alive with farm fairs and festivals, through the scenic but perilous Fraser Canyon, carved out by the raging river, to the cattle-ranching country north of Cache Creek, where the spirit of the Wild West still lives.

In the farmlands to the south, the Fraser is calm, but farther north, at Hell's Gate and Devil's Cauldron, the river churns through narrow cliff walls. Although most people watch these white waters from an aerial tramway at Yale, some brave souls don life jackets, cling tightly to a rubberized raft, and hurtle over and through the boiling cauldron. In July, millions of salmon streak the water red as they force their way upstream through rapids and over rocks to spawn and die. The river's course also leads into cowboy country. Visitors can live on a ranch, pitch hay in the stables, round up cattle, or ride horseback through the bush. And it's also a trip through gold rush country, where the reconstructed village of Barkerville evokes the era of lucky strikes.

En Route from Vancouver Travel east on Route 1 to Langley, a dairy- and truck-farming community overlooking the Fraser River. Nearby is *Fort Langley,* a restored Hudson's Bay Company fort (now a national historic park), located on the last point on the Fraser River that seagoing vessels can navigate. For details on the fort, see "Special Places" in *Vancouver,* THE CITIES. A visit to the fort recalls this site's boom period in 1859, when fierce competition meant gold seekers often spent as much as $1,500 daily outfitting themselves for expeditions. The camp was dominated by the Hudson's Bay Company, which even organized dances for the prospectors. But this was more than a company town; it was the site of the founding of British Columbia. Each November 19, Langley sponsors a banquet and historical program in tribute to the day in 1858 when Governor James Douglas signed the decree making BC a British colony.

Head southeast on Route 1, passing Abbotsford, noted for its *International Air Show* (one of the biggest on the continent) held in early August (see "Special Events" in *Vancouver,* THE CITIES). Continue on Route 1, skirting the Vedder River, where anglers fish for salmon in May and June, coho in the fall, and steelhead trout from December through June. A few miles east, the road cuts through Chilliwack, a small farming town on the Fraser delta abutting the cliffs at the foot of the Coastal Range. From the snow-capped peaks of Mt. Slesse and Mt. Clemme, melting snow cascades over the dark green pines, veiling the rocks and trees underneath and inspiring the name Bridal Falls. Near the town runs the 35-mile Chilliwack River, swimming with Dolly Varden trout. The town is noted for its horses, and in May it hosts the *Chilliwack Horse Show.*

South of Chilliwack (follow the signs) is Sardis, where Salish sell handwoven articles in old native designs. Four miles (7 km) south of Route 1 on Vedder Road is Cultus Lake, within a provincial park with camping sites and picnic areas. Each June, crews race war canoes across the 3-mile-wide lake as part of the *Indian Festival.* The park is closed *Labour Day* through April; open daily the rest of the year. There's a charge for overnight stays. Continue east on Route 1 to Hope, 96 miles (154 km) from Vancouver.

HOPE Surrounded by mountains, this small town (pop. 4,000) is best known as the entrance to the Fraser River Valley. In 1848 the Hudson's Bay Company established Fort Hope—a fitting name, considering the dangers of the Fraser River just upstream. The name stuck until 1965, when the town was incorporated as Hope. In 1858 prospectors stopped here before paddle-wheeling up the river to the gold fields; today, visitors still stock up on camping supplies here before striking out for the wilderness.

Interesting aspects of the town include the *Hope Museum* (Water St. off Rte. 1; phone: 604-869-7322 or 604-869-2021), which has pioneer relics. It's closed *Labour Day* to mid-May, and Tuesdays and Wednesdays mid-May through June; open daily the rest of the year. Admission is by donation. The *Rainbow Junction Community Arts Centre,* in a restored railway station (Rte. 1 and Old Hope–Princeton Way), sells local arts and crafts. Sculptures of local wildlife carved with chain saws from huge logs are situated throughout the downtown area. *Hope Brigade Days,* held the first weekend after *Labour Day,* features a demolition derby and logging sports. For more information, contact the *Hope Travel Info Centre* (919 Water Ave.; phone: 604-869-2021). It's open weekdays, except in July and August, when office hours are daily until 8 PM.

The area around Hope offers first-rate hiking, climbing, and, thanks to the updrafts caused by the mountainous terrain, hang gliding. The town basks in the shadow of 6,000-foot Mt. Hope. Goats scamper on its ledges, and black bears, deer, and raccoons live within its forests.

Ten minutes from downtown (follow the signs) is the *Coquihalla Canyon Recreation Area,* where a walk along abandoned rail lines, through four tunnels, and over two railway bridges right through the otherwise inaccessible canyon affords spectacular vistas. The setting has been used for several movies, including *Rambo: First Blood* with Sylvester Stallone and *Shoot to Kill* with Sidney Poitier.

En Route from Hope Fill your tank in Hope, as there are few gas stations along the next leg of the route. From here, travelers may choose from two routes. The faint of heart can head northeast on the Coquihalla Highway (Rte. 5) for a short, relatively unadventurous trip north for 114 miles (182 km) to the junction with Route 97, which heads west for 46 miles (74 km) to rejoin the route outlined below at Cache Creek. More intrepid travelers can head north from Hope on Route 1 to Yale, the gateway to Fraser Canyon, where the river becomes a twisting, treacherous run of water due to snow runoff from the Rocky, Selkirk, and Cariboo Mountains. At Yale, squeezed between the reddish bluffs of the Cascade Mountains and the Coastal Range, the river rages.

Prospectors once used rope ladders to hoist themselves and their horses, mules, and even camels over the sheer cliff walls here that at some points rise 7,000 feet. (One enterprising outfitter introduced camels to lug heavy loads of mining gear, but their stench so repelled the mules, horses, and prospectors that the unfortunate creatures were abandoned along the way.) The prospectors also built a makeshift route (Cariboo Rd.) along the bedrock of the canyon. Although still precipitous in parts, today's road is made infinitely easier by highways and tunnels. Yale's *Pioneer Cemetery* dates back to gold rush days; one of BC's oldest churches, *St. John the Divine,* is a historic site. A slide show at the *Yale Museum* illustrates Fraser Canyon history and current attractions. It's closed *Labour Day* through April; open daily the rest of the year. There's an admission charge (phone: 604-863-2324).

A few miles north of Yale, the canyon constricts to form Hell's Gate, where visitors can board an aerial tramway and peer down at fierce rapids. Each July, salmon make the tortuous 24-day journey up the federal fishway steps to spawn and then die at the mouth of the Adams River. The tramway is closed October through March; open daily the rest of the year. There's an admission charge (phone: 604-867-9277).

North of Hell's Gate on Route 1 is Boston Bar, where you can tour the *J. S. Jones Lumber Mill.* The mill is closed weekends; there's no admission charge (phone: 604-867-9214). A good stopping place in the area is the unpretentious *Blue Lake Resort* (phone: 604-867-9246), just north of Boston Bar, with a log main building, rustic cedar cabins, and camping facilities. Nineteen miles (30 km) farther north is Jack Ass Mountain, a precipitous ridge on the canyon cliffs. A few miles farther north is Lytton, where the Fraser Canyon ends and the Thompson River Valley begins.

The Thompson and Fraser Rivers converge here, and at their banks fortune seekers still pan for gold and search for jade. A more reliable quest is for the steelhead trout swimming in these fast-flowing waters from late October to spring. The Thompson River knifes through mountains, revealing 10,000-year-old rocks and nurturing a semiarid terrain of sagebrush, bunchgrass, and prickly pear cacti. An exciting way to experience both the tranquillity and the turbulence of the river is to board a motorized rubber raft in Lytton.

Either rafting the Thompson or traveling Route 1 will take you to *Gold Pan Campsite Provincial Park,* on the banks of the Thompson. From here, mountain sheep can be seen scampering along the cliffs' stratified edges. The park is closed January through March; open daily the rest of the year. There's a charge for overnight stays May through September.

From Lytton, travel north to Spences Bridge. During the summer, roadside vendors along the way sell honey, fruit, and apple juice. The town is a native reserve where remains of the *wikiups* (houses used by nomadic tribes) still stand. Although chukars, other partridge, deer, and grouse still inhabit this region, avid hunting has reduced their numbers greatly.

From Spences Bridge, Route 1 rises to ranching country. Some 27 miles (43 km) north is Ashcroft. A mile (1.6 km) out of town is *Ashcroft Manor,* a pioneer ranch settled by the first Lieutenant Governor of British Columbia, Clement Cornwall. Although Cornwall was the very personification of the pioneer spirit, he was English to the core. When he led guests on "modified" fox hunts, everyone wore traditional garb. (Hunts were modified because the quarry was coyote, not fox, of which few exist in BC.) The riding habits and hunting gear are on display in the restored manor, which also has a tearoom and a crafts shop. It's closed mid-October to mid-March;

open daily the rest of the year. There's no admission charge (phone: 604-453-9983). A few miles north is Cache Creek, at the junction of Routes 1 and 97.

CACHE CREEK A stopover in the last century for prospectors seeking gold in the Cariboos, this city today serves as a halfway point between the lower Fraser and Cariboo region. Surrounded by the semi-arid ranching country of the Thompson Flats, Cache Creek is a center for cattle ranching and copper mining and a base for freshwater sport fishing. Although no gold is found here today, the legends of the boomtown era live in the town's name. An ignominious (and perhaps fictional) bandit stole 80 pounds of gold from a successful miner and hid it here before disappearing, but the alleged cache has never been found.

En Route from Cache Creek Follow Route 97 north through the dry hills surrounding Cache Creek. On the way, you can take a side trip east to Loon Lake for small rainbow trout, or follow a dirt road farther northeast to Lake Bonaparte for the bigger trout. Although named after a British duke, the town of Clinton, 25 miles (40 km) north of Cache Creek, has the spunky Old West character that comes from its history as a roadside stop on the trail to the Cariboo gold fields: It was 47 Mile House on the Gold Rush Trail.

Take Route 97 about 10 miles (16 km) north of Clinton; here, 2½ miles (4 km) off the main road, amid heavily forested areas and grassy meadows, is *Chasm Provincial Park.* The park is the site of the Painted Chasm, a box canyon cut into multicolored layers of volcanic bedrock by melting glacial waters. The park is open for day use only; there's no admission charge. Farther north on Route 97 is 100 Mile House, 47 miles (75 km) from Clinton.

100 MILE HOUSE The men who blazed the Cariboo wagon road from Lillooet to the gold fields of Cariboo were paid by the mile, which may explain why 100 Mile House is a good deal short of 100 miles from the start of the trail. The town is known for its annual 50-kilometer *Cariboo Ski Marathon,* which draws more than 2,000 cross-country skiers every February (also see *Cross-Country Skiing* in DIVERSIONS).

En Route from 100 Mile House Back on Route 97, the road runs through rolling, wooded country dotted with lakes, where waterfowl live on the marshy borders. One of these lakes, Lac La Hache, beside the highway, has some of the best kokanee (landlocked salmon) fishing in the province. Continue north on 97 (watch out for chipmunks and squirrels crossing the highway) to Williams Lake, 56 miles (90 km) from 100 Mile House.

WILLIAMS LAKE During the Chilcotin Indian War of 1864, Willy'um, chief of the Shuswap (now the Sugar Cane tribe), saved the white settlers here from being massacred. To show their thanks, the settlers named the town after him. Although a stone marks the spot where the natives held their tribal meetings (called *Colunetze*, "gathering place of lordly ones"), the spirit of the place was later violated by the rowdier culture of the gold panners. Typical of the town's Wild West heritage is the *Williams Lake Stampede* each July, in which top riders, many of them native ranch hands, compete in such traditional rodeo events as bronco riding and cattle wrestling. Parallel to this hillside town is 6-mile-long Williams Lake.

For an interesting detour, head east on a series of dirt roads to the forested rolling terrain around Horsefly and Quesnel Lakes, which are surrounded by the mountains of Big Timothy and Mt. Stevenson, both over 7,000 feet. The lakes are full of trout and kokanees, and a hiker may sight a moose, deer, or black bear among the cottonwoods.

En Route from Williams Lake Follow Route 97 north along the edges of the Fraser River through 75 miles (120 km) of ranching, logging, and mining country to Quesnel, a former Cariboo gold rush town and now a lumbering center. During the summer, the main streets are lined with colorful petunias. Salmon fishing is good where the Quesnel River enters the Fraser. From here, head east on Route 26 to Barkerville, a restored gold-mining boomtown near 1,300-acre *Bowron Lake Provincial Park.*

BARKERVILLE In 1862, a Cornish fortune seeker named Billy Barker arrived here and staked a claim on a small parcel of land. After digging 40 feet down and finding nothing but dirt, Barker was almost ready to give up and head north. But he and his mates persisted, and two feet deeper they found a pocket of gold nuggets worth $600,000 ($9 million by today's standards). Attracted by Barker's find, thousands of prospectors swarmed here, making this town the biggest city north of San Francisco and west of Chicago. Like the city named for him (now a ghost town restored for tourists), Billy Barker's success was short-lived. Barker married a more successful gold digger than himself: His wife cleaned him out, leaving him to die penniless in a Victoria nursing home.

Today, at *Barkerville Historic Town,* visitors can pan for gold nearby, ride a stagecoach, and watch a period melodrama at the *Theatre Royal.* There are no performances at the *Theatre Royal* Saturdays in May; during the summer there are no shows on Fridays. The town's attractions are closed *Labour Day* through April, though the historic streets remain open year-round. There's an admission charge mid-June to *Labour Day* (phone: 604-994-3332). In winter, cross-country skiing and snowmobiling are popular area activities.

A few miles east is *Bowron Lake Provincial Park,* a sanctuary for moose, beavers, caribou, mountain goats, grizzly bears, and wolves. In the lakes and streams swim Kamloops, Dolly Varden, and lake trout. You can canoe on Lakes Bowron, Indianpoint, and Isaac, portaging between them. The park is closed November through May; open daily the rest of the year. There's a charge for overnight stays and for canoeing on the park's lake system.

BEST EN ROUTE

Sagebrush ranges and wooded plateaus are the backdrop for ranch holidays, some of the best vacation bets in the region. On working cattle ranches, where hundreds of branded cattle graze on the short grasses, you can help the hands round them up. Or stay in up-to-date accommodations on a ranch, and ride sleek, Arabian horses over blazed trails. Wherever you stay, the food is sure to be fresh and plentiful. The nightly entertainment is usually a gathering of cowpokes—both urban and authentic—sitting around the fireplace listening to cowboy music. The range of prices is wide, from expensive accommodations for two costing about $1,300 a week to more moderate ones for about $400 a week. Although most ranches are open year-round, the horseback riding is supplemented with cross-country skiing during the bitterly cold winters.

ASHCROFT

Sundance Guest Ranch This dude ranch caters to people who like to ride everything from Arabian to quarter horses. Guests, divided into groups according to their riding abilities, are accompanied on twice-daily trail rides. All 28 rooms have private baths. For additional details, see *Farm and Ranch Vacations* in DIVERSIONS. Five miles (8 km) south of Ashcroft off Highland Valley Rd. (phone: 604-453-2554 or 604-453-2422; fax: 604-453-9356). Expensive.

100 MILE HOUSE

Best Western 108 Resort Fans of cross-country skiing, horseback riding, swimming, golfing, or tennis should know about this motor lodge, where fishing and canoeing are possible right on the property, and bird watching locales are nearby. All 62 rooms have balconies, color TV sets, and private baths; there also is a whirlpool bath, sauna, and heated outdoor pool. In summer, a big draw is the resort's championship 18-hole golf course (see *Golf in Canada* in DIVERSIONS), while winter visitors can take advantage of some 87 miles (140 km) of marked trails through some of the greatest cross-country ski terrain in the world; also available are sleigh rides, tobogganing, skating, and ice fishing. In the dining room, European cuisine often takes a back seat to West Coast favorites like smoked salmon. The resort is also accessible via a 5,000-foot paved airstrip. Telqua Dr. (phone: 604-791-5211; 800-667-5233; fax: 604-791-6537). Moderate.

CHILKO LAKE

Chilko Lake Resort/Hotel Although situated in utter wilderness, this modern, 36-room resort—which also includes individual cabins—has all the urban amenities. There's a dining room in the rustic main lodge, an indoor pool, gamerooms, and nearby tennis and volleyball courts and a riding stable.

Boats are available for excellent lake and river fishing, and snowmobiles are for rent in winter. The resort is a three-and-a-half hour drive west of Williams Lake on Route 20; at Tatla Lake, turn south and follow signs to the property. PO Box 6016, Williams Lake, BC V2G 3W2 (phone: 604-481-1107; 800-667-8773; fax: 604-481-1135). Expensive.

The Pacific National Parks

One hardly thinks of national parks coming in groups, but they do in eastern British Columbia, where several mountain chains—the Purcells, Selkirks, and Rockies—tumble together to form a jagged tangle of glaciers, chasms, peaks, and snowfields unparalleled in the Western Hemisphere. The Trans-Canada Highway cuts like a blade through this wondrous knot, connecting Kamloops in the west with *Banff National Park* across the Alberta border. To preserve these mountain wildernesses, huge areas have been designated national parks (with access through Revelstoke on the Trans-Canada Highway). Preservation, however, does not preclude human presence. There are luxurious baths near the hot springs of Kootenay, and numerous well-maintained hiking trails link the most interesting spots in the parks.

Mounts Revelstoke, Glacier, Yoho, Kootenay, and the Bugaboos make up parts of the long chain separating BC from the rest of Canada, creating its unique weather systems and the feeling of a separate Pacific Coast culture. The 280-mile (448-km) trip from Kamloops on Route 1 (the Trans-Canada Hwy.) skirts Mt. Revelstoke, bisects *Glacier* and *Yoho National Parks,* and passes near the entrance to *Kootenay Park.*

For thousands of years, the mountains of the Continental Divide stood in splendid isolation. Awed by the size of their glacier-torn peaks and chasms, few natives ventured into them. Below, however, certain lakes were fished, and ocher beds in the Kootenay Mountains were used for their natural paint. Early fur traders approached the mountains with circumspection, too; it wasn't until the railroad came through that the mountains were even partially explored by Europeans. The arrival of trains, which engineers threaded over precarious mountain passes, made the Canadian West vastly more accessible and established a section of a rail route often said to be one of the most spectacular in the world.

KAMLOOPS Sprawled across the sagebrush hills and dry brown mountains, this city is a major junction for Routes 1 and 5. More significant to the visitor is the name the natives gave this site—Cumcloups, "the meeting of the waters"—for this is where the north and south branches of the Thompson River converge, creating Kamloops Lake. (Kamloops trout, which jump a few feet into the air after being hooked, live in the lake.) The nearby mountains are rife with deer, moose, grizzly bears, caribou, and elks. For hunting, fishing, and other tourist information, contact the *Kamloops Travel*

Information Centre (1290 W. Trans-Canada Hwy., Kamloops, BC V2C 6R3; phone: 604-374-3377; fax: 604-828-9500). The center is open daily mid-May through *Labour Day;* closed weekends the rest of the year.

The pioneering spirit of the early European settlers is commemorated in some of the city's festivals and celebrations. The spring-summer season brings an indoor rodeo, a bluegrass music festival, and an international air show.

En Route from Kamloops Head east along Route 1 to "the world's richest 300 acres," according to the road sign. Here are the Adams River spawning beds, where in late October millions of salmon spawn and die after fighting their way up the Fraser and Thompson Rivers. Continuing east, the road follows the Columbia River through the mountains of the Monashee Range to Revelstoke, 131 miles (210 km) from Kamloops, near the western entrance to *Mt. Revelstoke National Park.*

MT. REVELSTOKE NATIONAL PARK So enchanted were the residents of Revelstoke with the variety of natural rock formations, trees, and animals in the nearby Clachacudainn Mountains that in 1914 they persuaded the government to designate a hundred square miles of it a national park. Thanks to their efforts, modern-day visitors can walk 40 miles of trails, including one that meanders 16 miles through valleys cloaked in trembling aspen, black cottonwood, and Rocky Mountain maple. Hillsides are covered with rain forests of western white pine, western red cedar, western hemlock, Douglas fir, and spruce below the timberline, and paths wind through mountain meadows of blazing Indian paintbrush, arnica, and valerian to Eva Lake, and to masses of colorful rock, thought to be 500 million years old. Although the heavy snowfalls (between 30 and 40 feet annually) scare off most big animals, a variety of birds—including the wren, finch, Canada jay, and even the golden eagle—soar above it all.

Before you climb the peaks, including Mt. La Forme (8,400 ft.) and Mt. Cyr (8,520 ft.), or camp in the wild, contact the Superintendent of Parks in Revelstoke (PO Box 350, Revelstoke, BC V0E 2S0; phone: 604-837-7500 or 604-837-6274). The park is open daily; there's an admission charge.

En Route from Revelstoke Follow Route 1 toward Golden, 93 miles (149 km) northeast. On the way is *Glacier National Park.*

GLACIER NATIONAL PARK High up in the Selkirk and Purcell Ranges is this 521-square-mile park, where huge snowfalls occur each year; much of the snow never disappears. Earlier snows compact, harden, and through their sheer weight create glaciers that crawl down the mountainside. Ragged summits, including 10,818-foot Mt. Sir Donald, and steep canyon walls have been carved out and polished by the slow-motion flow of countless rivers of ice forming and descending to the plains over thousands of years.

For anyone who's always wanted to see a glacier up close, this is the place. There are more than 400 here, with trails leading to two of them

Illecillewaet and Asulkan. Another trail leads to the Nakimu Caves of Cougar Valley, a seemingly endless maze of underground limestone passages. (Only experienced speleologists may enter after obtaining written permission from the Parks Superintendent.) Although the snowfall limits the growth period below the timberline to two months, look for the glacial lily, alpine anemone, and heather, all of which bloom in the summer. Note: Avalanches sometimes menace the paths and highways, and the underbrush can be too thick to pass in places (always check conditions with park rangers; see below).

For a place to stay, check out the remote *Purcell Lodge* (PO Box 1829, Golden, BC V0A 1H0; phone: 604-344-2639; fax: 604-344-5520), a rustic inn on an alpine meadow east of the park with full facilities, a breathtaking view of the timberline meadows and the ice-capped Purcell and Selkirk Ranges, downhill and cross-country skiing in winter, and hiking in summer. It's accessible by helicopter from Golden. For a map of trails, lakes, glaciers, and campgrounds, contact *Parks Canada Administration Offices, Glacier National Park* (PO Box 350, Revelstoke, BC V0E 2S0; phone: 604-837-7500 or 604-837-6274). The park is open daily; there's an admission charge.

En Route from Glacier National Park Continue to Golden, the gateway to *Yoho National Park, Kootenay National Park,* and the beginning of the Rocky Mountains, looming high above to the east. Because it served as a storage area during the construction of the railroad, the city was originally called The Cache. When a nearby community was named Silver City, The Cache's leaders—not to be outdone—changed the name of their city to Golden.

YOHO NATIONAL PARK The Rockies here include 28 peaks that soar over 10,000 feet. These astounding heights were given the name Yoho ("inspiring awe") by the Cree, who traveled through here long before the 1858 Palliser expedition penetrated Kicking Horse Pass (the treacherous eastern passage through the Rocky Mountains into *Yoho National Park*). More than 250 miles of hiking trails crisscross this 507-square-mile reserve. The Yoho Valley Trail extends from the highway to Takakkaw Falls; from here there are trails such as Laughing Falls and Yoho Glacier. Look for mountain goats, hoary marmots, and pikas. For more information on the park, contact the Superintendent, *Yoho National Park* (PO Box 99, Field, BC V0A 1G0; phone: 604-343-6324). The park is open daily; admission charge.

KOOTENAY NATIONAL PARK This 543-square-mile park runs parallel to the Continental Divide on the western slopes of the Rockies. Trails lead to Marble Canyon, created by the waterfall at Tokumm Creek. There also are glaciers, alpine meadows, and ocher beds that Kootenay, Stoney, and Blackfoot natives used as natural paint pots.

A fault at the base of Redstreak Mountain is the source that gives rise to Radium Hot Springs pools. Water seeps through faults deep in the earth where the rock masses are hot. When it meets this hot mass, it turns to steam and quickly rises through fissures to meet the cool air. The steam condenses to water at a temperature of 113F (45C) and is channeled to thermal soaking and swimming pools. For more information on the park, contact *Kootenay National Park* (PO Box 220, Radium Hot Springs, BC V0A 1M0; phone: 604-347-9615). The park and hot springs are open daily; there's an admission charge. Also see *National Parks* and *Golf in Canada* in DIVERSIONS.

BEST EN ROUTE

Almost all of the following establishments are near the national parks. For an expensive double room or cottage for one night, expect to pay $110 or more; in a moderate place, from $60 to $110; and in an inexpensive one, $60 or less. All establishments have private baths. *Glacier, Yoho,* and *Kootenay National Parks* offer developed campsites on a first-come, first-served basis. For wilderness camping in *Mt. Revelstoke,* check with the Superintendent of Parks (see above).

KAMLOOPS

Coast Canadian Inn This 94-room place has the most modern facilities in town, including a heated outdoor pool (seasonal), a pub, and a dining room. 339 St. Paul St. (phone: 604-372-5201; 800-663-1144; fax: 604-372-9363). Expensive.

REVELSTOKE

Three Valley Gap Motor Inn This sprawling, 167-room lakefront resort is a reconstructed boomtown as well as a place to spend the night. Owner Gordon Bell transported from old BC towns bits and pieces of gambling halls, gin mills, and cabins—20 historic structures in all—and reassembled them here. The structures are filled with authentic period furnishings such as a long bar, roulette wheels, and spittoons. Dining is available in a cafeteria and two restaurants. Closed mid-October through April. Twelve miles (19 km) west of Revelstoke on Rte. 1 in Three Valley Gap (phone: 604-837-2109; fax: 604-837-5220). Moderate.

YOHO NATIONAL PARK

Emerald Lake Lodge A rustic, 85-room place overlooking the lake, it is 5 miles (8 km) north of Route 1. There's a dining room, a lounge, gamerooms, outdoor hot tubs, and a sauna. Field (phone: 604-343-6321; 800-663-6336; fax 604-343-6724). Expensive.

KOOTENAY NATIONAL PARK

Blakley's Bungalows Each of these 23 secluded cottages has its own kitchen; some have fireplaces. Rte. 93, Radium Hot Springs (phone: 604-347-9918) Inexpensive.

Prince George to the Yukon

For thousands of years, the northern part of British Columbia has been wilderness—snow-capped mountains; forests of spruce and pine alive with caribou, moose, and grizzlies; deep lakes teeming with arctic grayling and Dolly Varden trout; and churning rivers carving out mountain passes. It's a great place for hunters, anglers, and hikers.

But civilization is following the gravel and the blacktop of the Alaska Highway into the wilderness. Explorers already have dug for oil successfully; mining companies are busily extracting minerals; and lumber companies have cut forests. However, most of this 860-mile (1,376-km) trip from Prince George up Route 97 to Dawson Creek and north along the Alaska Highway takes you through pristine territory.

This is a region of extremes, from the farming valleys of the Peace River region to the 7,536-foot peak of Mt. St. George in *Stone Mountain Park;* from the cold waters of Muncho Lake to the 120F (49C) waters of Liard Hot Springs; from dense evergreen forests to oceans of wheat near Dawson Creek; from 20 hours of darkness in cruel, frigid winters to 20 hours of sunlight in pleasant, mild summers.

Do not wander too far from the road in these northerly parts unless you have a guide or extensive wilderness training; the area beyond has few trails and few facilities for the trekker. Caution also is advised for anyone who wants to explore the rapids of the Peace River. As for driving conditions, be aware that the Alaska Highway, although now mostly paved, can be hazardous when icy in winter or muddy in summer. This trip may not be for everybody, but if you want to experience the kaleidoscope of colors produced by the northern lights as they streak across an unpolluted black sky, this is one of the places to do it.

For complete hunting, fishing, and touring information, contact the *Peace River Alaska Highway Tourist Association* (PO Box 6850, Fort St. John, BC V1J 4J3; phone: 604-785-2544). To fly into the wilderness, contact *Air BC* (*Dawson Creek Airport;* phone: 604-782-1720). Guides, licenses, and tourist information are available year-round from the chambers of commerce in towns along the Alaska Highway. For road reports, call 800-663-4997 in Canada.

PRINCE GEORGE Before railway and road workers extended the *Canadian Pacific Railway* and paved Routes 97 and 16 through the heart of town, this was a slumbering Hudson's Bay Company trading post. Today, however, it is the crossroads of the north (to Whitehorse and Yellowknife), south (to Vancouver and the Okanagan Valley), east (to Jasper and Edmonton), and west (to Prince Rupert). Truckloads of timber, farm produce, and minerals cross through this city daily. To the visitor, all this activity means modern hotels, restaurants, and museums. Stop by the *Prince George Art Gallery*

(2820 15th Ave.; phone: 604-563-6447); it's closed Sunday mornings year-round and Mondays early September to June. There's an admission charge. Other sites of interest include the *Prince George Regional Railway and Forest Industry Museum* (850 River Rd.; phone: 604-563-7351; closed Tuesdays, Wednesdays, and *Labour Day* through mid-May; admission charge) and the *Fort George Regional Museum* (20th Ave. entrance to *Fort George Park;* phone: 604-562-1612). The latter is open daily June to early September; closed mornings and Mondays the rest of the year; admission charge. There is a par 71 golf course at the *Prince George Golf Club* (2515 Recreation Plaza; phone: 604-563-0357). Festivals are big entertainment here year-round, even during the chilly winters. February's highlight is *Snow Daze,* with its variety of unorthodox sporting events, such as the *World Championship Snow Golf Tournament,* in which wildly costumed contestants with homemade golf clubs designed to fit their theme play nine rounds in the snow. Other popular events include the *Prince George Airshow* and the *Salmon Valley Country Music Festival,* both held in July. Prince George has over 120 parks, including *Connaught Hill,* with elaborate gardens and panoramic views.

But it is the city's location near the confluence of the Nechako and Fraser Rivers that lends it special appeal. From here, anglers travel to nearby lakes swimming with rainbow trout, and hunters hike to the backwoods to bag black bears, deer, and moose. For tourist information, including a list of hunting guides, visit the *Prince George Travel Information Centre* (1198 Victoria St.; phone: 604-562-3700; 800-668-7646; fax: 604-563-3584); it's closed weekends. From mid-May to *Labour Day,* a satellite office is open daily (to 8 PM beginning in July) at the junction of Routes 97 and 16 (phone: 604-563-5493).

En Route from Prince George Follow Route 97 (the John Hart Highway) north for 32 miles (51 km) to Summit Lake, on the Continental Divide. From this Rocky Mountain ridge, water flows either north to the Arctic Ocean or south to the Pacific or Atlantic. Continue north on Route 97 and take Route 39 to MacKenzie, established in 1966 to process the dense forests nearby. Those interested in the lumber industry may tour the two pulp mills here. The town's prime attraction is the 5,960-foot lookout on Morfee Mountain; from here, Williston Lake (the largest artificial lake in the province) and the miles of surrounding wilderness can be seen. The lake is rich in lake trout, while black bears and moose roam within the jack pine forest.

Return to Route 97. After cutting through the lowest pass in the Rockies, the road reaches Chetwynd, on the slopes of the Rockies. Look for the chain-saw sculptures of wildlife dispersed throughout the downtown area. Beyond the local coal mines are good moose and deer territory and fine grayling and jackfish lakes. For hunting and fishing information contact the *Chetwynd Chamber of Commerce* (PO Box 1000, Chetwynd, BC V0C

1J0; phone: 604-788-3345; fax: 604-788-7843). It's open daily to 8 PM July to *Labour Day;* closed weekends the rest of the year.

From Chetwynd, Route 97 stretches from the foothills of the mountains to the vastness of the prairies. Dawson Creek is the center of the province's most vital grain-producing region and also on the edge of fine moose-grazing terrain. Its lakes are stocked with northern pike, arctic grayling, whitefish, and Dolly Varden and rainbow trout. All wilderness information is available from the *South Peace Historical Society Travel Information Centre* (900 Alaska Ave., Dawson Creek, BC V1G 4T6; phone: 604-782-9595; fax: 604-782-9538). It's open daily mid-May to mid-September; closed Sundays and Mondays the rest of the year.

Dawson Creek also is the start (Mile 0/Km 0) of the Alaska Highway, a paved road built during World War II by the US Army Corps of Engineers as a defense measure. All distances along the highway are indicated by Mile/Km figures. Follow the highway to Fort St. John (Mile 49/Km 79).

FORT ST. JOHN Although this is a busy lumbering, oil-exploration, and cattle-ranching center, tourists are drawn here by the area's fine hunting, fishing, hiking, and canoeing amid rugged, forested mountain terrain. Before venturing out, stop at the *Chamber of Commerce* (9323 100th St., Fort St. John, BC V1J 4N4; phone: 604-785-6037) to hire a guide or get a map; it's closed weekends. At the same address is the *Fort St. John and District Travel Information Centre,* where information is available on hunting, fishing, and other tourist attractions (phone: 604-785-3033). The center is open daily until 8 PM from May 24 through September; closed weekends the rest of the year.

For many years after this site was settled as a fur-trading center (*Rocky Mountain House,* now a native reserve, was the fort), these northern residents depended upon fishing and hunting for their livelihood. When oil was discovered nearby back in the 1950s, the community went through a building boom. Although the discovery brought a modicum of sophistication to the wilderness, the town still stages traditional events such as a rodeo in June and the *World Gold Panning Championship* in August.

En Route from Fort St. John About 8 miles (13 km) north of town is Charlie Lake, teeming with arctic grayling and gray trout. As the road winds through forested hills and valleys to Pink Mountain (during autumn, the multicolored leaves take on a pinkish hue from a distance), you may see a moose, black bear, or grizzly parade across the gravel road. Stargazers rave about the view of the northern lights from here in the late fall and early winter.

Head northwest to the last fairly large city on the highway, Fort Nelson (Mile 300/Km 483). Beyond this gas-processing and shipbuilding center on the river of the same name is the wilderness, inhabited by grizzlies and wolverines. For travel information on the area, contact *Bag Service 399* (Fort Nelson, BC V0C 1R0; phone: 604-774-2541).

Continue west over Summit Pass, the highest elevation on the highway, through *Stone Mountain Provincial Park.* From the highway, hikers can follow a 4-mile trail (one of the few improved ones) alongside the North Testa River to Flower Spring Lake, where caribou graze in meadows around the banks. The towering peaks of Mt. St. George and Mt. St. Paul make for very challenging climbs, but there are smaller neighboring mountains. By the side of the road, Summit Lake is the park's biggest lake, home of lake trout and arctic grayling; there are boating facilities. The park is closed November through April; open daily the rest of the year. There's a charge for overnight stays. At Mile 456/Km 734 is *Muncho Lake Provincial Park.*

MUNCHO LAKE PROVINCIAL PARK Here, 218,476 acres of white spruce and lodgepole pine forests thin to scrub alpine spruce, lichen, and moss above the timberline. Dominating the park is Muncho Lake (*muncho* means "big water" in the native language), ringed by moose-inhabited forests. Along an 8-mile trail following Nonda Creek (near the northeastern boundary of the park), hikers will see goats, beavers, black bears, and Stone sheep. The park is closed November through April; open daily the rest of the year. There's a charge for overnight stays.

A few miles north of the park is the Liard River, at Mile 496/Km 798. Named Liard (French for "poplar") after the trees lining its banks, the river was once a prime artery for fur traders. Today, visitors can rent equipment and hire a guide to canoe the river; try the *Highland Glen Lodge* (below). Here, too, are the Liard Hot Springs, soothingly hot no matter how cold the air. Even during the winter, visitors don bathing suits and slip into the thermal waters, while, in summer, bathers soak within view of the miniature orchids that grow wild on the nearby hills. Near the springs is a free 80-unit campsite. Lodging and guide service are available May through October only from the *Highland Glen Lodge* (PO Box 3190, Fort Nelson, BC V0C 1R0; phone: 604-776-3481 May through October; 604-774-2909 the rest of the year; fax: 604-774-2908).

BEST EN ROUTE

What most establishments along this route lack in luxury (and character since most are boxy concrete structures) they make up for in cleanliness and efficiency. For a double room for one night, establishments listed in the expensive category charge $55 or more; a moderate room costs $40 to $55. Unless otherwise noted, all establishments have private baths. There also are numerous campsites in and around the towns along the route check with the town chambers of commerce for locations. Sites are rented on a first-come, first-served basis. For each location, hotels are listed alphabetically by price category.

PRINCE GEORGE

Coast Inn of the North This 152-room establishment offers everything a traveler could possibly want, from a restaurant and lounge to a pool and sauna. 77

Brunswick St. (phone: 604-563-0121; 800-663-1144; fax: 604-563-1948). Expensive.

Holiday Inn Downtown, this full-service member of the international chain has 139 rooms, a restaurant, a lounge, a pub, a casino, and free covered parking. Other facilities include an indoor pool, a sauna, and a whirlpool. 444 George St. (phone: 604-563-0055; 800-HOLIDAY; fax: 604-563-6042). Moderate.

Sandman Inn In a modern building, this 71-room property provides a restaurant, a pool, and a sauna. 1650 Central St. (phone: 604-563-8131; 800-726-3626; fax: 604-563-8613). Moderate.

MACKENZIE

Alexander MacKenzie This 99-room hotel has just about everything: a shopping center, laundry facilities, a beer parlor, a dining room, a hot tub, and a sauna. 403 MacKenzie Blvd. (phone: 604-997-3266; 800-663-2964 in BC). Moderate.

Powder King Ski Village Within walking distance of the slopes, this 55-room hotel has a dining room, a cafeteria, a bar, day-care facilities, and triple-chair and T-bar lifts. Closed Tuesdays and Wednesdays. Rte. 97 (phone: 604-997-6323; fax: 604-997-5421). Moderate.

DAWSON CREEK

Peace Villa At Mile Zero, this motel offers 46 carpeted rooms, a sauna, cable TV, and complimentary coffee. Restaurants are within walking distance. 1641 Alaska Ave. (phone: 604-782-8175; fax: 604-782-3040). Moderate.

FORT ST. JOHN

Mackenzie Inn This modern, seven-story, 67-room motel has an indoor pool, a coffee shop, a restaurant, a bar and lounge, and nightly entertainment. 9223 100th St. (phone: 604-785-8364; 800-663-8313 in Canada; fax: 604-785-7547). Moderate.

Pioneer Inn Here are 125 rooms, with amenities such as an indoor pool, a sauna, a weight room, and a Jacuzzi. Also on the premises are a dining room, lounge, and coffee shop. 9830 100th Ave. (phone: 604-787-0521; 800-663-8312; fax: 604-787-2648). Moderate.

FORT NELSON

Fort Nelson Motor Hotel This 135-room complex has color TV sets, an indoor pool, a shopping arcade, and a Hawaiian-style dining room. Mile 300 on Rte. 97 (phone: 604-774-6971; 800-663-5225 in western Canada; fax: 604-774-6711). Moderate.

Manitoba

Manitoba got its name from its original inhabitants, members of the Cree tribe. They believed in the spirit Manitou, whose drum was the voice of rushing water. European explorers first traversed the territory in the early 17th century in search of the Northwest Passage. The first actually to settle here were French, but in the 19th century communities of Mennonites, Icelanders, and Ukrainians built settlements throughout the plains as well.

Rugged, sparsely settled, and vast, Manitoba covers 251,000 square miles of diverse terrain, including gigantic Lake Winnipeg and the myriad lakes and rivers surrounding it. Bordered by North Dakota and Minnesota to the south, Saskatchewan to the west, Ontario to the east, and the Northwest Territories to the north, the province is home to just over a million people, many of whom make their living by farming or mining. About two thirds live in Winnipeg, the capital (for details, see *Winnipeg* in THE CITIES).

There is plenty of wilderness for sportspeople and other visitors to explore. Keep in mind, though, that Manitoba's climate covers Canada's extremes. Bone-chilling winters can drop the mercury to below -40F (-40C). In the southern part of the province, however, temperatures can reach the 90s F (30s C) in summer, when most people explore the lakes, marshes, waterfalls, and granite ledges of this enormous province.

The first driving route in this chapter covers the Whiteshell region, from Winnipeg east on the Trans-Canada Highway and south to the Mennonite town of Steinbach, Falcon Lake, *Whiteshell Provincial Park,* the Winnipeg River, and Pinawa. The second takes in the northern part of the province, proceeding west from Winnipeg on the Trans-Canada Highway to Portage la Prairie, northwest to Neepawa, a former fur trading post, then north through picturesque river valleys to *Riding Mountain National Park,* The Pas, and Flin Flon, home of the *Flin Flon Trout Festival* in early July. The third destination—the fascinating subarctic seaport of Churchill—can be reached only by air or rail.

For further information on the province, contact *Travel Manitoba* (155 Carlton St., Seventh Floor, Winnipeg, MAN R3C 3H8; phone: 204-945-3777; 800-665-0040, ext. 45).

Whiteshell

Millions of years ago, glaciers covered the high mountains and plains of eastern Manitoba. The movement of the huge ice sheets eroded deep craters and gullies that eventually filled with crystal-clear water. Sliding through the mountains, the ice exposed quartz and granite layers, grinding them down to gentle hills. Later, the exposed Precambrian-era rock was covered with a thin layer of soil supporting thick forests of barely rooted evergreens

This is topography typical of the geological area known as the Canadian Shield.

The Whiteshell tour begins in Winnipeg, running 209 miles (334 km) east on the Trans-Canada Highway to Falcon Lake. The hills, valleys, forests, lakes, and streams of this region offer some of the best fishing, hunting, hiking, and recreation in the province. There's also a replica of a Mennonite village near the town of Steinbach, where villagers still grind grain in a wind-powered gristmill. The resort communities of Falcon Lake and West Hawk Lake have fine beaches, sailing, and waterskiing. In *Whiteshell Provincial Park,* the wilderness is traversed by the fast-flowing Winnipeg River. In fact, most of this tour winds through the park, which offers hiking trails alongside moose, deer, and black bear territories and deep lakes where trophy-size northern pike, walleye, and smallmouth bass can be caught. To the north are granite bluffs topped with precariously balanced evergreen and spruce trees. Also in the park are vestiges of the glacier days—shallow marshy lakes, now speckled with nesting geese and ducks. In the winter, tobogganers and downhill skiers careen down the park's snow-covered hills; cross-country skiers glide along the forest trails; and anglers drill holes in the lakes' frozen surfaces to ice fish.

En Route from Winnipeg Heading southeast on Highway 1, the rich, expansive farmlands of the southwest gradually give way to the jagged granite outcroppings of the Canadian Shield. At the junction of Routes 1 and 12, travel south on Route 12 for a glimpse of two towns—Ste-Anne and Steinbach—as different from each other in lifestyle as this century is from the last.

Ste-Anne is one of Canada's few predominantly French-speaking communities outside of Quebec. The *Musée Pointe des Chênes* (Arena Rd.; phone: 204-422-5505) exhibits the cultural artifacts of the ancestors of its people. It's open by reservation only; no admission charge.

Ten miles (16 km) farther south is Steinbach, the center of thriving grain farms where Mennonites have lived and farmed since escaping religious persecution in Russia in 1873.

STEINBACH Strictures based on religious teachings are the rule of the town. But religion does not ban an annual festival—*Steinbach Pioneer Days*—when locals demonstrate for visitors old-time farming methods such as reaping, flailing, and plowing and such homemaking chores as spinning, weaving, and churning butter. It's held during *August Long Weekend,* the weekend preceding the first Monday in August, in the *Mennonite Heritage Village,* 1½ miles (2 km) north of Steinbach on Route 12.

Regardless of when you visit this village, you can watch and talk to the Mennonites—most speak both English and a Low German dialect—as they grind whole-wheat grains in one of Canada's few wind-powered gristmills. Flour is sold here for those who'd like to bake their own bread, but others prefer to eat the bread and other Mennonite food (try the *varenyky,* a cheese- or potato-filled dumpling) offered here at the livery barn, which, along with the blacksmith shop and houses, makes up the village complex. The complex is open daily; there's an admission charge (phone: 204-326-9661).

En Route from Steinbach Return to Route 1. Traveling east, you soon reach *Sandilands Provincial Forest,* filled with acres of pine, spruce, and other evergreens. Its nursery raises trees to landscape the province's parks. The park's *Interpretative Centre* offers guided tours in July and August (except Tuesdays and Wednesdays); by arrangement only for groups mid-May through June and September through mid-October. There's a charge for tours (phone: 204-453-3182).

Beyond the forest, a bit north of Route 1 on Route 11 and 51 miles (82 km) from Winnipeg, is Hadashville, an excellent spot to reel in northern pike while canoeing on the Whitemouth River. Continue east on Route 1 to Falcon Lake, the southern entrance to *Whiteshell Provincial Park.*

FALCON LAKE In Falcon Lake's less wild sections are sailing, horseback riding, and waterskiing facilities, a guarded swimming beach, a major shopping center, an 18-hole golf course (see *Golf in Canada* in DIVERSIONS), and tennis courts. The Beaver Creek circular hiking trail (at the entrance to Falcon Beach) penetrates the more pristine wilderness of the Canadian Shield, where beavers construct dams and an occasional deer whizzes through the spruce. Despite the popularity of this resort, an angler can still find an isolated inlet in which to reel in smallmouth bass, northern pike, and walleye.

During the winter, you can travel east on Route 301 for a few miles to the *Falcon Lake Ski Resort* (see *Best en Route*), which has 14 slopes of beginner and intermediate trails.

WHITESHELL PROVINCIAL PARK Here are 1,065 square miles of one of Canada's best wilderness, canoeing, fishing, hunting, and vacation lands. The park stretches from Falcon Lake in the south to the swiftly flowing Winnipeg River in the north, and east to the Ontario border. Dramatic waterfalls—such as Rainbow Falls on the northeastern tip of White Lake—crash over granite and snowy quartz before tumbling into rivers, lakes, and streams edged by forests of jack pine, spruce, and elm. Ruffed grouse feed in the vast wild-rice beds encircling small lakes, and Canada geese and ducks make the marshes around Hart, Betula, White, and Jessica Lakes their home. Traversing land topped with a layer of caribou moss and spots of muskeg (decayed vegetation), hunters search in spring and fall for the black bear, in recent years the only big game allowed to be taken in the park. For those who prefer driving a golf ball, smashing a tennis ball, or catching the rays on a beach, the resorts of Falcon Lake (see above) and West Hawk Lake (see below) are the places to stay. For a rundown on everything the park offers, read *The Manitoba Explorer's Guide,* available free from *Travel Manitoba* (see introduction to this chapter); or call the *Parks Department*

Offices at Falcon Lake (phone: 204-349-2201) or West Hawk Lake (phone: 204-349-2245).

WEST HAWK LAKE Thousands of years ago, a meteor fell to earth and formed this lake (also known as Crater Lake), at 365 feet the deepest in Manitoba. No matter how hot the summer day, this water is spine-tingling cold. Swimmers may mind, but it certainly doesn't bother the smallmouth bass. Those who'd rather not try to land one of these fighting fish (and then fry it up at one of the area's 150 campsites) can still savor the local specialty at one of the resort's restaurants.

En Route from West Hawk Lake Leave the Trans-Canada Highway, heading northwest on Route 44. Just west of Caddy Lake, where you can rent canoes and boats to fish for smallmouth bass, is Lily Pond. A small, shallow lake lined with hard rock visible on all shores, it gets its name from the yellow and white flowers floating on the surface. The cliff across the road has light-colored "lenses" of granite formed about two and a half million years ago, when molten rock forced its way in between layers of the harder, older rock.

At the junction of Route 307 near the town of Rennie (the site of hunting and drive-in fishing lodges) is the *Alf Hole Goose Sanctuary* (Rte. 44; phone: 204-369-5470 or 204-369-5232). In 1937 a railroad worker named Alf Hole raised four abandoned Canada goslings in his home. These four returned the next year, bringing more of their flock. Now, 200 geese return here each spring. At the sanctuary's center are exhibits on the life cycle of the Canada goose. It's open daily May through September; closed the rest of the year. There's no admission charge.

Head north on Route 307, driving in between Jessica and White Lakes, with Rainbow Falls cascading over a granite ledge. Continue north for about 2 miles (3 km) past Betula Lake to the Bannock Point petroforms. Archaeologists believe these petroforms of people, turtles, snakes, fish, and birds were arranged by the native Ojibwa in configurations to track the movement of the sun and the moon. The Cree, Saulteaux, and Ojibwa once rode through these hills and valleys, but all that remains of them in the area are their weapons and stuffed replicas of the bison and elk they once pursued.

From here, the highway cuts through Precambrian country at its best—sparkling lakes, verdant evergreen forests, and towering granite cliffs. At the end of Natalie Lake is Seven Sisters Falls, on the Winnipeg River. The river is not the same as it was in the days when trappers, adventurers, and natives canoed its stormy surface. That Winnipeg was filled with rapids, sudden swirling pools of water, and dangerous obstacles like decaying evergreen trees felled by lightning storms. Today the river is calmer, its rapids tamed by several power dams, the largest of which is at Seven Sisters Falls. Canoeing on these waters is nothing like paddling the uncharted wilderness waters in the northern bush, but it does have its moments: You glide on cool, fresh water teeming with sturgeon and smallmouth bass, through sheltering forests of birch, bur oaks, and evergreens. Along the rugged cliffs are granite and rock formations that geologists believe to be among the oldest in the world—two and a half *billion* years old. When you've had enough canoeing for the day, camp at one of the many sites dotting the Winnipeg River and, if you've been lucky, dine on your catch of the day.

Take Route 11 north to Route 211. Eight miles (13 km) east on Route 211, on the Winnipeg River, is Pinawa, Atomic Energy of Canada's research site.

PINAWA During the summer, general tours of the research site (including a portion of the reactor building and laboratories) are conducted at 10 AM and 1:30 PM. The plant is off limits to pregnant women and children below the sixth grade. It's closed Sundays in July and August; closed weekends the rest of the year; no admission charge (phone to reserve tours: 204-753-2311; 800-665-0436 in Canada).

En Route from Pinawa Head south on Route 11 to Route 44, which meanders west through tall cliffs of dolomite limestone. (Blocks of it were used to build Winnipeg's *Legislative Building.*) If you're making this trip in late February, stop at Beausejour for the *Canadian Power Toboggan Championship,* a commercial event in which major snowmobile manufacturers from the US and Canada demonstrate their sophisticated equipment in heart-stopping races.

At the junction with Route 59 at Lockport, turn south toward Winnipeg. The last leg of this journey passes *Birds Hill Provincial Park*—8,300 acres of aspen, poplar, and cedar groves and thickets of strawberries and blueberries. The park offers opportunities for camping, hiking, and horseback riding only half an hour from the big-city bustle of Winnipeg. It's open daily; there's an admission charge per vehicle (phone: 204-222-9151).

BEST EN ROUTE

Most of the hotels, inns, and campsites along this route take advantage of the beautiful natural settings of pine and spruce forests and clear lakes. In the expensive resorts, expect to pay between $50 and $75 per night for a room for two; the places listed as moderate charge $25 to $50. All hotels feature air conditioning and private baths unless otherwise indicated. Camping is inexpensive, costing from $10 to $20 per night. On summer weekends, some of the more popular campsites fill up fast. For reservations at campsites, contact *Travel Manitoba* (see introduction to this chapter). For each location, places are listed alphabetically by price category.

STEINBACH

Dutch Connection A 25-unit motor inn, it features European touches and color TV sets. Its restaurant serves authentic Low Countries food in a dining room that's right out of a Rembrandt painting. 88 Brandt Rd. at Rte. 12 (phone: 204-326-2018; fax: 204-326-4666). Moderate.

Frantz This 20-unit modern motel with color TV sets was built outside the town limits to avoid the ban on alcoholic beverages. Facilities include a cocktail lounge and bar plus a coffee shop. South of Rte. 52 (phone: 204-326-9831). Moderate.

WHITESHELL PROVINCIAL PARK

Falcon Lake Close to its namesake, this resort has 35 units, each with a color TV set. There's also a cocktail lounge, a restaurant, and an indoor pool. Falcon Lake (phone: 204-349-8400; fax: 204-349-8401). Expensive.

Tallpine Lodge All 15 of these homey housekeeping units have Jacuzzis and fireplaces, and some have private saunas. There's no restaurant, but a quaint souvenir shop is nearby. West Hawk Lake (phone: 204-349-2209). Expensive.

Caddy Lake Campground If you crave peace and quiet, camp here in one of the 26 sites near Caddy Lake, with a playground, store, and boat ramp. Six miles (10 km) west of West Hawk Lake on Rte. 44 (no phone). Inexpensive.

Falcon Beach Campground On summer weekends this is one of the most popular spots in the park. There are 300 tent sites and 117 trailer sites. From here you can rent equipment and boats for fishing on the lake. Falcon Lake (phone: 204-349-2231). Inexpensive.

West Hawk Campground The 83 campsites and 71 trailer sites here are close together, but tall pines give each a degree of privacy. Often noisy on summer weekends, this provincial government facility offers picnic shelters and boat rentals. West Hawk Lake (phone: 204-349-2245). Inexpensive.

RENNIE

Inverness Falls Resort Ten deluxe cottages and two spartan cabins are set in a spacious, wooded setting. The complex has a coffee shop and a store, a tackle and bait shop with fishing and hunting licenses for sale, a fly-out fishing service, and canoe and boat rentals. Brereton Lake (phone/fax: 204-369-5336). Moderate.

The North

In the northern wilderness the dark, dense forest meets clear, blue lakes; rabbits, deer, and foxes peep from the bush; fish leap from the water; and campfires crackle under pans of just-caught walleye.

And then there's that other world of the north—the shouts and whoops at the *Flin Flon Trout Festival;* the crack of the mushers' whips over the heads of lead dogs during the *World Championship Dog Race* at The Pas, during February's *Northern Manitoba Trappers' Festival;* the buzz of chain saws in the pulp and paper operations; the brightly colored *Easter* eggs in the Ukrainian town of Dauphin; and the camaraderie of a people more than willing to share their good times with visitors.

The tour route outlined below travels from the wheat farming communities of the interior to the flatlands of Hudson Bay. En route are the extensive wilderness preserves of *Riding Mountain National Park* and the lumber and mining towns of The Pas and Flin Flon.

En Route from Winnipeg Head west on the Trans-Canada Highway (Rte. 1) for 44 miles (70 km) to Portage la Prairie, where a fair is held each summer in celebration of the strawberry, an important local crop.

PORTAGE LA PRAIRIE Many of the early French explorers carried canoes through this area on their way to Lake Manitoba in unsuccessful searches for northwest trade routes to the Far East and its riches. More than a century later, a different type of explorer settled here, after discovering that the rich black soil of the prairies nourished wheat. The transient life of explorers—such as Pierre Gaultier de La Vérendrye, who built *Fort la Reine* here in 1738—and the more settled ways of farmers—such as John Sutherland Sanderson, who established the first homestead in western Canada here—are dramatically described at the *Fort la Reine Museum and Tourist Bureau* (Rte. 1A E.; phone: 204-857-3259). A trading post, blacksmith shop, and stable make up the museum, which also includes an early log homestead and a trapper's cabin. It's open daily; closed mid-September to mid-May. There's an admission charge.

There is much more to Portage la Prairie than its past. In July the town puts on the strawberry festival and, in the same month, the lively *Portage Fair.* A permanent attraction is *Island Park* on Crescent Lake (Saskatchewan Ave. at Royal Rd.; no phone), a preserve with a horseshoe-shaped lake, sanctuaries for deer, a large resident flock of Canada geese, hiking trails, tennis courts, and a golf course. The park is open daily; no admission charge.

En Route from Portage la Prairie Follow the Yellowhead Highway (Rte. 16) northwest for 63 miles (101 km) to Neepawa, where a plaque commemorates the 900-mile (1,440-km) road that fur traders traveled from the Red River settlement to Fort Edmonton, Alberta.

Neepawa is noted for its salt mines. The Canadian Salt Company once pumped brine out of an underground salt lake which still exists near the center of town. During July, Neepawa culture buffs paint, sing, and play instruments under the tutelage of topnotch teachers in the week-long *Holiday Festival of Arts.* Students and teachers (some from the *Winnipeg Symphony Orchestra*) perform concerts and plays.

Continuing west on Route 16, in the Minnedosa River Valley—an area of rolling hills decked with oak trees—lies the town of Minnedosa (pop. 2,500). Hunters flock here each autumn for the fine goose and duck hunting. For non-hunters, there's Minnedosa Lake, northeast of town, offering delightful swimming, picnicking, and camping. Each July Minnedosa puts on the *Country Fun Festival,* a family fair at which local musicians stage everything from square dances to rock concerts.

North of Minnedosa, Route 10 climbs into sandy, hilly country, then traverses grassy plains to the plateau of *Riding Mountain National Park.*

RIDING MOUNTAIN NATIONAL PARK Surrounded by the Canadian plains, this is a recreational park and nature preserve of prairies and rolling hills, hardwood and evergreen forests, and crystal-clear lakes and streams.

Northern pike and rainbow trout swim in the park's deep, cold lakes—Clear Lake, Lake Katherine, and Deep Lake, to name a few—while beavers build dams in marshy, shallow creeks. On the meadow to the west bloom the bright yellow blossoms of shrubby cinquefoil and purplish gaillardia. On the prairies around Lake Audy, herds of buffalo roam through the scrubby grasses. An exhibit nearby relates the history of the bison—almost extinct except for one species. Throughout the park are wolves, elk, white-tailed deer, and moose. A walk along one of the numerous hiking paths will bring you to the log cabin of Archibald Belaney—more commonly known by his native name of Grey Owl—a British naturalist who, in the early 20th century, drew and wrote about the creatures living in the forest around him.

During the winter, cross-country skiers can follow several trails through the park. If the prospect of schussing down the steepest downhill slope in the province attracts you, take a trip to Mt. Agassiz on the east side of the park near McCreary.

The southeastern entrance to the park is at the resort community of Wasagaming (meaning "clear water"), on the shores of Clear Lake. Regularly stocked with trout, the lake has facilities for fishing, boating, and sailing. Wasagaming also boasts an 18-hole, par 72 golf course (so near Clear Lake that a misguided drive may cost you a ball; see *Golf in Canada* in DIVERSIONS), tennis and badminton courts, a roller-skating rink, a dance pavilion, and a cinema. Also in Wasagaming is the *Elkhorn Resort* (see *Best en Route*), where horses may be rented for trail rides through the park.

For information about overnight and day hikes and trails, visit the park's information center (Wasagaming Dr.; phone: 204-848-7275 or 204-848-7272) in Wasagaming, which is open daily; there's an admission charge to the park.

En Route from Riding Mountain National Park Follow Route 10 north to Dauphin, 43 miles (69 km) from Wasagaming.

DAUPHIN After the transcontinental railroad was finished in 1896, Ukrainian immigrants moved north with visions of fertile farmland and homesteading grants, and they were not disappointed. Over the years the rich soil of the Dauphin

Valley nurtured their crops of wheat, barley, and potatoes. Today, the town is noted for its flour and lumber mills as well as its farming.

On the first weekend in August, the town holds the *National Ukrainian Festival* as a tribute to its ancestry. The celebration offers much to see and do: Riders in traditional Ukrainian cossack garb travel through the valley; artisans demonstrate *pysanka* (*Easter*-egg decorating); and people gather for dancing, singing, and eating delicious home-cooked foods. These last include piroshki (boiled or fried pastry stuffed with potatoes and/or cheese), borscht (beet soup), and kielbasa (sausage). The food is quite heavy—dieters beware. (Also see *Festivals, Fairs, and Fancy Acts* in DIVERSIONS.)

En Route from Dauphin Follow Route 10 as it veers west and then north. At the junction with Route 367 in Garland, head west for about 10 miles (16 km) to *Duck Mountain Provincial Park* for wilderness camping and excellent fishing. The park's thickly wooded, rolling terrain is dotted with dozens of deep, clear lakes that brim with trout, splake, muskellunge, walleye, northern pike, and perch. The forests and meadows support birds and game animals. There are campgrounds throughout the park, but the whole area has a remote, otherworldly feel. The highest point in Manitoba is Baldy Mountain (2,727 feet), where in August and September you can hear the bugling of elks. The *Nicholas Copernicus Observance Committee* has mounted a sundial on this mountain to help those hiking the Copernicus Hill Trail keep track of the hour.

Back on Route 10, head north and west to the town of Swan River, where between 1787 and 1821 the Hudson's Bay Company competed with the Northwest Company's franchise to trade with the native Plains groups. The *Swan River Valley Museum* (1 mile/1.6 km north of town on the banks of the river; phone: 204-734-3585) depicts the history of that era through its collection of old photographs and indigenous artifacts. It's closed mid-September through April; open daily the rest of the year (until 8 PM in July and August). There's an admission charge. At the end of July, the town hosts the *Northwest Roundup,* when farmers exhibit beef cattle, cowboys rope steer, and everybody eats pancake breakfasts at sidewalk buffets.

From Swan River, Route 10 runs north through miles of evergreen forests and skirts clear lakes, including the second largest in the province, Lake Winnipegosis. Those who stop to fish may catch great northern pike or glimpse a black bear, moose, or deer in the trees along the lake.

On Route 10 north of Lake Winnipegosis, you'll pass a stretch of floating muskeg known as "the bog." It's 144 miles (230 km) from Swan River to The Pas.

THE PAS The Pas (pronounced *Pah*) boasts not only fine fishing and hunting but also some of the country's liveliest festivals. In mid-February the town stages the four-day *Northern Manitoba Trappers' Festival,* with several dogsledding races. The largest and most prestigious is the *World Championship Dog Race,* during which professional mushers from all over Canada and the US race teams of huskies and other breeds along a 105-mile course. Townspeople compete in log-wrestling and log-felling events as well as the less rugged contests of moose and goose calling. Both spectators and participants can enjoy buffet dinners with continuous entertainment, beer fests, and pancake breakfasts. Lumberjacks, miners, anglers, trappers, and The Pas's other residents get into the spirit by wearing beads and buckskin while hunting the mythical "ice worm" and by crowning one woman Miss Fur Queen of the North. (Also see *Festivals, Fairs, and Fancy Acts* in DIVERSIONS.)

In mid-August, the native Opasquiak host the *Opasquiak Indian Days* festival. One of the most popular events is a race in which contestants carry heavy bags of flour and canoes on their backs. Visitors are welcome to compete. (Less energetic souls may prefer simply to buy beaded moccasins and jackets in the reserve's shopping mall.)

En Route from The Pas Continue north on Route 10. The road skirts *Clearwater Lake Provincial Park,* known for its unpolluted crystalline blue water (bush pilots flying 1,500 feet above have reported spotting rocks lying 35 feet below the surface). The trout here are so healthy that experts use the lake as an index by which to measure pollution in other waters. The lake's shores are home to ducks and geese; moose and other big game roam in the nearby woods. Flin Flon is 87 miles (139 km) north.

FLIN FLON In 1915, gold miners here named this town after an old, tattered novel about Josiah Flintabbatey Flonatin, the discoverer of a city of gold. The name was soon shortened to Flin Flon. A statue of Flonatin, designed by cartoonist Al Capp, welcomes visitors. Although little gold is found here now, the industry of the town is dominated by the *Flin Flon Mine,* where visitors can see the surface operations of the nonferrous metal mines; lumbering is Flin Flon's other major industry.

The town also is a great place for fishing. The first weekend of July, the town hosts the *Flin Flon Trout Festival,* with cash prizes for the biggest lake trout and northern pike. A festival queen presides over the event, which includes pancake breakfasts and a canoe race.

En Route from Flin Flon Return south on Route 10 to the junction with Route 39, then follow Route 39 as it enters *Grass River Provincial Park.* The truly untouched wilderness here is awe-inspiring: The terrain is composed of layers of limestone bedrock, Precambrian granite, and permafrost, and is covered with somewhat stunted, dense evergreen forests. You may even see caribou with their young. The park is open daily; for day use only October to mid-May. There's a charge for overnight stays (phone: 204-472-3331).

BEST EN ROUTE

Lodging for two for one night ranges from expensive ($35 or more) hotels and inns to moderately priced ($15 to $35) bungalows and hunting/fishing lodges. Unless otherwise indicated, all hotels have private baths and air conditioning. Camping in provincial or federal sites averages $5 to $10 for two people per night and is on a first-come, first-served basis. If you want a truly rustic experience, grab your sleeping bag and camp out under the stars near Lake Audy, home of the bison. It's free, and it might be the most memorable night of your trip. For each location, places are listed alphabetically by price category.

RIDING MOUNTAIN NATIONAL PARK

Elkhorn Resort and Conference Centre This is an ideal spot for those who want to combine ranch living with all the accoutrements of a resort. Besides horseback riding, hayrides, and horseshoe courts, this ranch, with 62 rooms in a main lodge and 16 chalets, has a dining room, cocktail lounge, indoor pool, and sauna. Near Clear Lake and the Clear Lake golf course (phone: 204-848-2802; fax: 204-848-2109). Expensive.

Thunderbird Bungalows These 22 log cabins surround a spacious lawn and are separated from one another by thick clumps of pine trees. Within walking distance of Clear Lake, the complex also has a heated outdoor pool but no dining room. Closed November through April (phone: 204-848-2521). Expensive.

Aspen Ridge This farm is very popular with cross-country skiers. The attraction is not only the 320 rolling acres but also the accommodations: six rooms (with shared baths) in a lovely log home, complete with beamed ceilings and a huge stone fireplace. Also see *Farm and Ranch Vacations* in DIVERSIONS. Near *Riding Mountain National Park* (phone: 204-848-2964). Moderate.

Wasagaming Campground Not far from the bustling resort community of Wasagaming is this federal government campground with space for 343 tents and 72 trailers. Amenities include barbecue pits, wood stoves, a playground, a store, laundry facilities, and boat rentals. Closed mid-September through April. Near Clear Lake (phone: 204-848-7275; 800-707-8480). Inexpensive.

DUCK MOUNTAIN PROVINCIAL PARK

Blue Lakes Campground Thick forests of pine and spruce shelter and create privacy for the 99 tent sites here. At night, the dark, dense forests, unlit by electricity or trailer lights, make the campgrounds pitch black. On the property are a boat ramp and store. Closed November through April. Near Blue Lake (phone: 204-546-2701). Inexpensive.

THE PAS

Wescana Inn This property has 77 comfortable units (with amenities such as coffeemakers), a restaurant, and a sauna. 425 Fischer Ave. (phone: 204-623-5446; 800-665-9468; fax: 204-623-3383). Expensive.

CLEARWATER LAKE PROVINCIAL PARK

New Vickery Lodge With 10 modest units (accommodating 40) for serious anglers, the lodge has a guide service, canoes, boats, a fly-out fishing service, and a coffee shop. Closed November through April. On the southern edge of the park, 23½ miles (38 km) northeast of The Pas (phone: 204-624-5429). Expensive.

Carpenter's Clearwater Lodge This simple property caters to hunters and fisherfolk, who get their licenses here. There are 11 cabins but no restaurant. Weekly rates are available. On the southern edge of the park, 23 miles (37 km) northeast of The Pas (phone: 204-624-5467). Moderate.

FLIN FLON

Victoria Inn This modern, 76-unit motel is near the park in which stands the Flonatin statue. It offers an indoor pool, a sauna, a dining room, a cocktail lounge, and airport limousine service. Off Rte. 10 (phone: 204-687-7555; fax: 204-687-5233). Expensive.

Churchill

For diehard adventurers, Manitoba's *real* pioneer country begins at the subarctic seaport of Churchill. The northern terrain features muskeg bogs with a few spindly dwarfed spruce clinging to gray rocks and tundra. This region's frigid winter extends from mid-October to mid-June, but the cold climate and short summer are no reason to skip this journey.

To get to Churchill by air, take *Canadian Airlines International* (phone: 204-632-1250 in Winnipeg; 800-665-1177 in Canada; 800-426-7000 in the US) from Winnipeg, The Pas, or Thompson. Three days a week, *VIA Rail* (123 Main St., Winnipeg, MAN R3C 2P8; phone: 800-561-8630 in Canada; 800-561-3949 in the US) offers a two-night, one-day train journey that leaves from Winnipeg. Accommodations range from coach to sleeping cars, and a dining car offers spirits and sustenance. Organized tours of the area are operated by the *Great Canadian Travel Company* (54 Donald St., Winnipeg, MAN R3C 1L6; phone: 204-949-0199; fax: 204-949-0188).

CHURCHILL This subarctic seaport lies on the southwestern shore of Hudson Bay, a vast arm of the Atlantic Ocean extending deep into Canada's north. A town of 800 winter-hardened people, Churchill has no road connection to the south. Along the bleak shore of the bay, trees grow to be little more than wind-worn stumps, yet a thriving world of wildlife, some of which cannot be seen anywhere else in the world, dwells near—and even in—the town. During the long subarctic nights, the vivid aurora borealis (northern lights) illuminates the town with the brightness of street lamps. In spring, which comes in mid-June, flowers create a riot of color.

Inuit, or native, peoples lived in the Churchill region as early as 1700 BC; European settlement began in the winter of 1619–20, when the Danish seafarer Jens Munck wintered near the present townsite during his fruitless search for the Northwest Passage. Of the original crew of 65, only Munck and two other sailors survived to return to Denmark. In 1717 the Hudson's Bay Company established a trading post at Churchill. Later in the 18th century, *Fort Prince of Wales,* a national historical site (phone: 204-675-8863; fax: 204-675-2026), was built to defend British colonial fur-trading interests. It's open daily year-round; admission charge. The fort can be reached by tour boats; contact *Sea North Tours* (phone: 204-675-2195; fax: 204-675-2198). (For more details on the fort, also see *National Parks* in DIVERSIONS.)

Today, vast numbers of snow geese, Canada geese, sandhill cranes, and 200 other bird species migrate through Churchill on their way to and from summer breeding grounds. Four species of fur seals visit Churchill harbor, fishing for abundant char, grayling pike, and cisco. Beluga whales, now protected against commercial hunting, frolic in the bay's waters near town from June to early September. And polar bears, which migrate to the frozen ice of the bay from surrounding land in the fall, often roam Churchill's streets from September through November, making it the only town in the world with an itinerant population of *Ursus maritimus.* At the peak of the bear migration, which occurs around *Halloween,* the beasts, drawn by smells of food and garbage, are kept under control by Royal Canadian Mounted Police and environmental officials armed with tranquilizer dart guns. Tundra buggies, huge vehicles with immense tires and tracks, offer tours to the polar bears' haunts. Souvenirs, including eight-foot-long narwhal tusks, polar bear rugs, mukluk boots, Inuit-carved soapstone, fur-trimmed parkas, and moose-hair earrings, can be bought at the *Arctic Trading Company* (Kelsey Blvd. and Bernier St.; phone: 204-675-8804).

BEST EN ROUTE

In Churchill a double room per night ranges from expensive ($35 or more) hotels and inns to more moderately priced ($15 to $35) lodgings. All hotels below have private baths and TV sets and are listed alphabetically by price category.

Churchill Motel This well-equipped, 26-room facility with a restaurant is in the heart of town, at Kelsey Blvd. and Franklin St. (phone: 204-675-8853; fax: 204-675-8228). Expensive.

Seaport This full-service hostelry has 21 rooms and a restaurant; it can be noisy. Munck St. and Kelsey Blvd. (phone: 204-675-8807; fax: 204-675-2795). Expensive.

Tundra Inn Comfortable accommodations are found in this 31-room establishment with a dining room. 34 Franklin St. (phone: 204-675-8831; fax: 204-675-2764). Expensive.

New Brunswick

Tucked under the Gaspé Peninsula, New Brunswick shares a long border with Maine. Its maritime status is firmly established with its extensive seacoast on the Gulf of St. Lawrence and reiterated in the Bay of Fundy, where waves that sometimes crest nearly as high as 50 feet crash against the southeastern shore. This land of forested hills is crossed by rivers that enrich the earth and foster agriculture. After lumbering and mineral production, potato farming is the major industry.

Conservation is vital to a province so dependent for survival on its natural resources, and a strict program protects New Brunswick's forests from depletion. The province's real natural wonder, the Fundy tide, however, is in no danger of depletion. Tides in the Bay of Fundy—the world's highest—are the primal force behind another of the province's water-linked phenomena, the reversing falls at Saint John and Hopewell Rocks, a striking formation carved by water out of indigenous limestone.

This land of woods and water was settled by French-speaking Acadians in the early 18th century. The French built forts to protect these settlers, but in 1755, when the British captured the forts, the Acadians were expelled. Some returned 30 years later and were given land. (More than 35% of the province's population of about 725,000 is French-speaking.) The other early settlers were New Englanders, British immigrants, and Loyalists who came from the US during and after the American Revolution.

Much of New Brunswick is rural. Its major urban areas are Moncton (pop. 107,000), a distribution center; Saint John (pop. 125,000), a manufacturing center; and Fredericton (pop. 46,500), the provincial capital and gathering place of artists and craftspeople who produce and sell their wares.

New Brunswick is a paradise for hikers and bird watchers—some 250 species of birds can be found in the province. The *New Brunswick Actlvity Guide* describes hundreds of miles of hiking trails and provides trail lengths, and the *Package Catalogue* details a variety of package trips, accommodations, and activities. The guide and catalogue are available from *Tourism New Brunswick* (see below).

The Fundy coast route links the cities along New Brunswick's southern coast, where the Loyalist heritage is still devoutly maintained. At Saint John, Canada's oldest incorporated city, you can watch the river run upstream, forced by the strength of the Fundy tide. *The Saint John River Valley* itinerary includes Fredericton and the beautiful rolling hills of the region's low-tide farming area. *The Acadian Coastal Drive* follows the eastern coast through fishing, farming, and lumbering villages. In the summer, begin this trip with a bang at the mid-July *Shediac Lobster Festival,* which celebrates the homely crustacean.

For further information, contact *Tourism New Brunswick* (PO Box 12345, Fredericton, NB E3B 5C3; phone: 800-561-0123). Any New Brunswick tourist information center can make reservations for your stay in the province during the high season, from June to mid-September. Many tourist attractions close from early September through May, and the phones may be disconnected during that time.

The Fundy Coast

When open warfare broke out between Great Britain and the American colonies in April 1775, not all of George III's American subjects grabbed a musket to fight for independence. Some salvaged what they could of their estates and dashed across the border into New Brunswick. This route follows the path of the Loyalists—those who remained loyal to the British crown—after they fled the rebellious colonies.

The drive runs beside the Bay of Fundy, whose waves (which have been measured as high as 48.5 feet) dash the coast with awesome power. At Hopewell Cape and St. Martins, the tides have sculpted giant "flowerpots" out of sandstone. The tide plays such an important role in this area that those planning to visit should request a timetable in advance from the provincial tourism office to learn the best time to see the magnificent tidal action. A word of caution about swimming in the Bay of Fundy: High tides mix the water so that the temperature never gets much above 65F (16C). Swimming in New Brunswick is tamer on the eastern coast, along the Northumberland Strait, where the water is shallow and warm (see *The Acadian Coastal Drive*).

The small coastal communities developed a strong shipbuilding industry in the early 1800s. The famous *Marco Polo,* the fastest sailing ship of the mid-19th century, was built in Saint John. When wooden sailing ships became obsolete, deep-sea fishing became the main industry of the smaller coastal centers.

Even though commercial fishing is the fourth-largest industry in the province (behind forestry, mining, and agriculture), the Bay of Fundy still yields cod, halibut, flounder, herring, crab, scallops, lobster, and sardines in abundance. If you come to this region to fish, you'll also have the chance to catch speckled trout or landlocked Atlantic salmon. Deep-sea fishing enthusiasts can hire boats in St. Andrews. For a real taste of the sea, try the Fundy Isles, all of which are accessible by sea: Grand Manan and Deer Island from the mainland by ferry; Campobello by ferry from Deer Island and by bridge from Lubec, Maine. Whale watching is an opportunity not to be missed; check with the *St. Andrews Chamber of Commerce* (phone: 506-529-3555) for an environmentally conscientious charter.

The Fundy coast also is a farming and dairy area, and a land of covered bridges. Then there's *Fundy National Park,* which offers opportunities to canoe and to hike its 50 miles of trails. This route begins at St. Stephen, on the US-Canada border, and winds for 210 miles (336 km) to Moncton, near the Nova Scotia border. The route does not have four-lane highways, although the roads are excellent. Nor does it have a boisterous nightlife, though Saint John is fairly sophisticated.

ST. STEPHEN Your introduction to colonial history begins here. Residents of the two border communities—St. Stephen and Calais, Maine—ignored the War of 1812, which Canadian historians regard as an attempt by the United States to annex Canada. The atmosphere was so doggedly nonviolent that gunpowder sent by the British to defend St. Stephen was loaned to Calais for their *Fourth of July* festivities. Visit a landmark named after the war's local peacekeeper, the *Kirk McColl United Church* (King St.; phone: 506-466-1380). The friendship is renewed each August at the *International Festival.*

British Loyalist memorabilia are on display at the *Charlotte County Historical Society Museum* (*James Muerchie Building,* 443 Milltown Blvd.; phone: 506-466-3295), which is open daily June through August (by appointment in September); closed the rest of the year; donations welcome. A popular British Loyalist settlement in the 1780s, St. Stephen is now known for its chocolate, lumber, and canning industries. Arthur Ganong invented the chocolate bar here in 1910, and Ganong Brothers Ltd. is still turning out candy; stop in at *Ganong's Chocolatier* (Water St.; phone: 506-465-5611) for some delicious bites. A chocolate festival is held here in early August. The *Crocker Hill Herb Garden* (on the St. Croix River; phone: 506-466-4251) is a pleasant stop for a cup of herbal tea.

Those who can't wait to sink their hooks into some of the famous landlocked salmon in the Chiputneticook Lakes region to the north of St. Stephen should plan ahead with outfitters in that area. For a copy of the booklet *New Brunswick Accommodations and Campground Guide,* contact *Tourism New Brunswick* (see chapter introduction).

You may want to follow Route 1 east for 5 miles (8 km) to *Oak Bay Provincial Park,* 8 miles (13 km) from the US-Canada border. The park has 112 campsites, with services for trailers, plus an excellent saltwater beach on the bay. It's closed mid-September to mid-May; admission charge (phone: 506-466-2661).

En Route from St. Stephen Take Route 127 south for 10 miles (16 km) to St. Andrews. Along the way, stop for the exceptional view of Dochet's Island, where, in the winter of 1604, Champlain lost half his temporary settlement to scurvy.

ST. ANDREWS At the close of the Revolutionary War in 1783, British Loyalists in Castine, Maine, were horrified to learn that the US-Canada border had been moved to the other side of the St. Croix River. Almost the entire community moved across the Bay of Fundy to the havens of British protection. Those who could afford it moved their homes, along with their possessions, and some of these houses still stand in the center of town. Fourteen of the buildings date back to the 1700s.

The local *Canadian Club* organizes walking tours of the historic homes one afternoon in late July in odd-numbered years. The *Historical Society* arranges limited tours for conventions at the *Algonquin* hotel (see *Best en Route*). Information on walking tours and arrangements for local boat cruises, whale watching, bird watching, and diving is available from the *St. Andrews Chamber of Commerce* (PO Box 89, St. Andrews; phone: 506-529-3555). The *Sunbury Shores Arts and Nature Centre* (139 Water St.; phone: 506-529-3386) sponsors shore walks and gives presentations on marine ecology. Additionally, St. Andrews is a great place to tour by bicycle; rentals are available at the *Algonquin* hotel (see *Best en Route*), among several other places.

Historic sites in town include the *Blockhouse* (Joe's Point Rd.; phone: 506-529-4270), the last of 12 built to defend St. Andrews during the War of 1812, and the *Greenock Church* (1822) on Montague Street, whose pulpit was built without using a single nail, copied from one in Greenock, Scotland.

Since St. Andrews is a popular resort area, reservations are advisable in summer at most hotels and restaurants. Two excellent seafood spots are *Conley's Lighthouse* (*Conley's Wharf;* phone: 506-529-3082) and *The Gables* (143 Water St.; phone: 506-529-3440). Another choice for fine dining is *L'Europe Dining Room* (48 King St.; phone: 506-529-3818). Just outside town is the *Rossmount Inn* (see *Best en Route*), noted for its Victorian decor and pleasant dining.

The town boasts some of the best shopping in New Brunswick. The *Sea Captain's Loft* (211 Water St.; phone: 506-529-3300) features hand-blown glass and woolens; *Cottage Craft* (in the town square; phone: 506-529-3190) offers locally made and imported woolens; and *Tom Smith's Studio* (136 Water St.; phone: 506-529-4234) has fine-quality pottery.

Antiques lovers shouldn't miss the *Ross Memorial Museum* (188 Montague St.; phone: 506-529-3906). The restored home of the Reverend and Mrs. Henry Phipps Ross, it features the couple's extensive collection of furniture from the mid-18th to the early 20th century. It's closed mid-October to late May; donations welcome.

The *Huntsman Marine Science Centre* (Brandy Cove Rd.; phone: 506-529-8895) is a 15-minute walk from town. In its aquarium are tanks with sturgeon, salmon, sea cucumbers, and other local marine life. There is also an excellent film on the area's sea life and a playful group of seals in residence. (Its laboratory, a large oceanographic institute, is closed to the public.) The *Centre* is closed from early October to late May; admission charge.

The *Algonquin* hotel (see *Best en Route*) has two golf courses open to the public: a nine-hole woodland course and an 18-hole, par 71 course, with 13 fairways near Passamaquoddy Bay (for details, see *Golf in Canada* in DIVERSIONS).

En Route from St. Andrews Ask local residents for directions to join Route 1 east toward St. George. Along the way are five of New Brunswick's approximately 70 covered bridges. Letete and Black's Harbour, reached by way of St. George, are the departure points for a side trip from the Fundy Coast to a chain of beautiful islands nestled between the US and Canadian shores.

FUNDY ISLES A trip to these little-known islands in the Bay of Fundy takes time and planning (which explains why they remain little known and unspoiled). The Canadian coast offers access by sea to each island, including Campobello, which is also reachable via the International Bridge in Lubec, Maine. During late summer, it's very common to see whales in this area. Many right whales (also called Greenland whales) migrate to the Bay of Fundy in August and September; other varieties here include the humpback and finback. This also is a popular bird watching area.

Grand Manan The largest of the Fundy Isles can be reached by ferry from Black's Harbour, 6 miles (10 km) south of St. George on Route 778. Reasonably priced ferries leave five times daily (three times on Sundays) from July through September and less often the rest of the year. Often dolphins ride the bow waves, acting as escorts.

Grand Manan is the place for those who want to see whales cavorting offshore and who also appreciate the beauty of a delicate wildflower. Hiking enthusiasts should pick up a copy of the *Hiking Guide to Grand Manan,* available in gift shops, to enjoy some of the island's 19 trails, many of which wind near spectacular seascapes.

The island's 2,000 residents live off and with the sea. Its fisherfolk catch tons of herring, scallops, clams, and lobsters daily. A paved road runs the 15-mile length of the island. The village of North Head boasts the *Shorecrest Lodge,* run by two naturalists, and the *Compass Rose,* a smaller inn with highly regarded food (see *Best en Route*). Additional accommodations can be found at Grand Harbour and Seal Cove. The island's only beer and liquor store is in Castalia, 5 miles (8 km) south of Grand Harbour.

On the west coast, Dark Harbour is the "dulse capital of the world." Known for its high iodine content, dulse is edible seaweed sold in health-food stores all over the continent. Pick your own and dry it on the beach—just ask a local resident how to do it. Dulse production is the island's second most lucrative industry. It's an acquired taste, so don't expect love at first bite, but certainly give it a try. The *Manan Island Inn and Spa* (see *Best en Route*) uses dulse in its pricey health treatments.

People come here from all over to photograph the tall, spiky wildflowers called lupens. Other wildflowers, strawberries, blueberries, and blackberries can be found in the meadows and near the picturesque lighthouses at either end of the island.

A free government ferry runs from Ingall's Head Village to White Head Island. Residents claim that a 33-foot great white shark, the largest catch ever recorded, was landed just off White Head. Boats can also be chartered at Ingall's Head for trips to the Three Islands, home of the *Bowdoin Scientific Station,* a sanctuary for many of the 250 species of birds found on Grand Manan. Charters also are available for two-hour trips to Machias Seal Island, where you can see seals, puffins, and an occasional whale. Inquire at the *Shorecrest Lodge* (see *Best en Route*) about whale watching expeditions; sightings are practically guaranteed in the mating season.

Deer Island From St. George, take Route 772 south to Letete; from there, hop on the free government-run ferry to Deer Island. On the island is a quiet campground and the world's three largest lobster pounds. From July to *Labour Day,* a private ferry makes the journey from here to Campobello Island. From the ferry you can see the Old Sow, the second-largest whirlpool in the world. The *West Isles World Bed and Breakfast* (phone: 506-747-2946) offers rooms, cottages, and whale watching cruises.

Campobello Island You can get to Campobello either by the ferry mentioned above or from US Route 1 over the International Bridge at Lubec, Maine. The island features good hiking and walking trails, a lighthouse, and a great nine-hole golf course.

Like most of the Fundy Coast, the island was originally settled by the French and later by British Loyalists from New England. Campobello was given to Captain William Owen in 1767 in exchange for an arm he lost in battle. Benedict Arnold and his wife lived at Snug Cove for a while, but the island draws its fame from Franklin Delano Roosevelt, the American president who spent many summers here. The *Roosevelt-Campobello International Park* on the southern end of the island encompasses the former 11-acre Roosevelt estate. Many Roosevelt artifacts are on display, including the leather chair he used for Washington cabinet meetings and a childhood letter to Santa Claus. Guided tours are available from May through September. The park is closed October through April; donations are welcome (phone: 506-752-2922).

En Route from the Fundy Isles Rejoin Route 1 at St. George heading toward Saint John, 50 miles (80 km) away. Along the way is *New River Beach.* This attractive 835-acre provincial park facing the Bay of Fundy affords spectacular ocean views, and the park has 115 campsites, as well as services for trailers. Lepreau Falls is 3 miles (5 km) beyond *New River Beach* on Route 1. The falls are 80 feet high but can be significantly shorter at high tide. Not one of the seven wonders of New Brunswick, they are nonetheless a good place to stop and relax for a few minutes. Another peaceful spot is Dipper Harbour, just off Route 1 on the way to Saint John, where you'll find *Fundy Haven* (phone: 506-659-2231), an excellent little restaurant.

As you approach Saint John (not to be confused with St. John's, the capital of neighboring Newfoundland) from the west, note that Route 1 merges with Route 7 and becomes the Saint John Throughway.

SAINT JOHN This is New Brunswick's largest city, one of its most historic, and the heart of Loyalist country. Thousands of Loyalists arrived in this port in 1783 after the US was officially recognized by the Treaty of Paris. The city celebrates *Loyalist Day* each July. Saint John's harbor is open year-round, so much of the activity in its commercial port occurs after the St. Lawrence Seaway freezes in winter. It has been a shipping center since the early 19th century, when Loyalists began a shipbuilding industry here. Although similar maritime cities failed with the obsolescence of wooden sailing ships, Saint John thrived. From the observation booth at the *Saint John Drydock*—the largest facility of its kind in North America—visitors can see tankers under construction. The Irving Oil refineries also are located here.

When you arrive at Saint John, check at the *Tourism and Visitor Centre* (*City Hall,* 11th Floor; phone: 506-658-2990), open daily year-round, to find out the times for high and low tides at the Reversing Falls. For optimum viewing, observe the tidal action twice—at or near both high and low tide. During low tide in the Bay of Fundy, the water drops 15 feet below river levels, forcing the river to crash through a narrow gorge in the harbor. At high tide, the rush reverses, and bay waters flow upriver. A 13-minute interpretive film explaining the phenomenon is shown regularly at the *Reversing Falls Tourist Centre* (Rte. 100 at the Reversing Falls Bridge; phone: 506-658-2937), which is closed mid-October to mid-May.

Market Slip, the site of the first Loyalist landing—on May 18, 1783—is a good point of orientation to downtown Saint John and the city's historical beginnings. A fine way to see New Brunswick's oldest city is to take a walking tour. Brochures that give excellent directions and historical information for three tours of Victorian homes, local merchant heritage, and Saint John's Loyalist history are available at the *Tourism and Visitor Centre* (see above).

Most Loyalist sites are within easy walking distance of the harbor. *Barbour's General Store* (phone: 506-658-2939), with staff in period costume, is just a few feet from the "tourist tug." Tours of the circa-1810 *Loyalist House* (120 Union St.; phone: 506-652-3590) provide an excellent introduction to the family life, culture, and skills of early Saint John craftspeople. Another historic site is the *Old Loyalist Burying Ground* (1783). The *Aitken Bicentennial Exhibit Centre* (20 Hazen Ave.; phone: 506-633-4870) features rotating exhibits on science, art, and culture in New Brunswick. It's closed weekends; no admission charge.

Adjacent to *Market Slip,* with its sidewalk cafés, is *Market Square,* a colorful restoration, featuring the public library, shops, and restaurants, including *Grannan's* (phone: 506-634-1555), as well as an agglomeration of fast-food bars serving international fare. *La Belle Vie* (Lancaster Ave.; phone: 506-635-1155) serves French and international fare, and *Incredible Edibles* (Princess St.; phone: 506-633-7554), a short walk from *Market Square,* features pasta, salad, and seafood.

From either Charlotte or Germain Street, enter the block-long *Old City Market,* which has been open since 1876. Vegetables, meat, fresh lobster, and fish, as well as hand-knitted items and various crafts for both infants and adults, are sold here.

Relics of the shipbuilding era can be seen at the *New Brunswick Museum* (277 Douglas Ave.; phone: 506-658-1842). In the 1880s, before the actual construction of a ship, detailed models were built, and these replicas are displayed here. Don't miss the miniature of the 1,625-ton *Marco Polo,* the fastest sailing ship of its time. The museum is open year-round; admission charge. In August, the city's *Festival by the Sea* draws more than a thousand song-and-dance performers from all over Canada. (See *Festivals, Fairs, and Fancy Acts* in DIVERSIONS.)

Direct ferry service to Nova Scotia from Saint John—a three-hour trip—begins at the foot of Lancaster Street. The *Princess of Acadia* (phone: 506-636-4048) plies the bay three times daily in summer (twice on Sundays).

About 40 miles (64 km) east along Route 111 (detour on to Rte. 825 to see more of the Bay of Fundy) is St. Martin's, a quiet, undeveloped village and home of the *Quaco Inn* (see *Best en Route*).

En Route from Saint John The most direct road to Sussex, 49 miles (79 km) northeast, is Route 1. However, a drive through the farming district of the Kingston Peninsula and the Kennebecasis River Valley is recommended. Many of New Brunswick's remaining covered bridges are located here, and the area features some of the province's most scenic countryside. A complete list of covered bridges is available from *Tourism New Brunswick* (see chapter introduction).

Take Route 100 through Rothesay to Gondola Point, and cross the Kennebecasis River by free car ferry (the ferry operates year-round from 6 AM to 10 PM; other times on demand) to Reeds Point. Follow Route 850 north to Route 124 east, and rejoin Route 1 at Norton. Continue along Route 1 for 12 miles (19 km) through the heart of the dairy district to Sussex. There, stay at *Anderson's Holiday Farm* to experience dairy life (see *Best en Route*). The *Broadway Café* (phone: 506-433-5414) is directly across from the train station in the middle of town.

From Sussex, pick up the Trans-Canada Highway (Rte. 2) northeast toward Moncton for 10 miles (16 km) to Route 114, also known as the Fundy Coastal Drive, and follow that road south to *Fundy National Park.*

FUNDY NATIONAL PARK Most of this 80-square-mile park sits on a plateau a thousand feet above sea level. Its thick forests are laced with 50 miles of hiking trails used by the resident moose, black bears, foxes, deer, bobcats, and beavers as well as by visitors. Its interior streams are excellent for trout and salmon fishing. Guides are available for the nature trails, but you can explore for yourself with relative ease.

The entrance on Route 114 is through dense forests, but 2½ miles (4 km) before Alma, a small city at the southeastern corner and home of the park headquarters. Stop at Hastings Hill for the view where the road opens suddenly for a vista of Chignecto Bay. Campers can stock up on supplies at Alma (lobster is plentiful), and visitors to *Fundy National Park* can eat at the *Fundy Park Chalets and Coffee Shop* (in the park; phone: 506-887-2808).

A heated saltwater pool is close to the chalets. Visit the beach, however, even if you don't plan to swim. The coastline is dotted with caves cut into the side of the 200-foot cliffs by the pounding surf. This exploration can be dangerous: Park officials warn that, should you lose track of the time, the tide will rise faster than you can climb to safety. Check at park headquarters for a timetable.

A nine-hole golf course, tennis courts, and a lawn-bowling green are available for use through the provincial government. For more information, contact *Fundy National Park* (PO Box 40, Alma, NB E0A 1B0; phone: 506-887-2000). Park facilities are closed mid-October to late May; admission charge.

En Route from Fundy National Park From Alma, follow inland Route 114 or Route 915—which follows the coast and offers great bird watching—east for about 28 miles (45 km) to Hopewell Cape, where the mighty tides have created sculptures from sandstone known locally as "flowerpot rocks." From Hopewell Cape, proceed north on Route 114 for 50 miles (80 km) to Moncton, "the hub city of the Maritimes."

MONCTON The second-largest city in New Brunswick, Moncton is an important distribution center for the other Maritime Provinces. Rail connections to Montreal, Nova Scotia, the Prince Edward Island ferry, and the Northumberland coast pass through the city. It has been an important rail center since 1872, when it was designated maritime headquarters of the *Intercolonial Railway*.

The *Free Meeting House* (Steadman St. and Mountain Rd.) was built in 1821 as an interdenominational place of worship until churches could be built. Just across the street, the *Moncton Museum* has displays on the city's history as a rail center. It's open year-round; donations welcome (phone: 506-853-3003). From the museum, walk down King Street toward the Petitcodiac River to *Boreview Park.* The action of the Fundy tide creates a phenomenon similar to the Reversing Falls in Saint John: Twice daily, a wave—known as the Tidal Bore—rushes upstream as the tide rises in the Bay of Fundy 25 miles away. But for all this activity, the wave is usually only one foot high. At Magnetic Hill, cars seem to be pulled uphill. For the most part, though, Moncton's synthetic attractions prevail—its large shopping malls and huge water theme park, *Magic Mountain* (Exit 388 off Rte. 2; phone: 506-857-9283), which has boats, wave pools, and slides.

For a taste of the sea, try *Cy's Seafood* restaurant (170 Main St.; phone: 506-382-0032; closed Sundays). For sophisticated but expensive French cuisine, splurge at *Chez Jean Pierre* (21 Toombes St.; phone: 506-382-0332).

BEST EN ROUTE

Most of the accommodations listed here are older establishments, with friendly staffs and homey atmospheres. In heavily traveled areas, we also note some standard places where you have a better chance of getting a room without reservations. In the popular resort areas, you must have a reservation for July and August—for the *Algonquin* in St. Andrews, reservations are advisable during the entire summer season. The government publication *New Brunswick Accommodations and Campground Guide* lists hundreds of smaller hotels, cabins, guesthouses, and bed and breakfast establishments. For a copy, contact *Tourism New Brunswick* (see chapter introduction).

For a double room for one night, expect to pay more than $75 in an expensive hotel; from $40 to $75 in a moderate one; and $40 or less at an inexpensive place. All hotels feature such amenities as air conditioning, private baths, TV sets, and telephones unless otherwise indicated. For each location, places are listed alphabetically by price category.

ST. STEPHEN

Auberge Wandlyn This motel has 50 modern rooms and a restaurant specializing in seafood and steaks. 99 King St. (phone: 506-466-1814; 800-561-0000 in eastern Canada; 800-561-0006 in the US). Moderate.

ST. ANDREWS

Algonquin One of the best hotels in the Canadian Pacific chain, it has 200 rooms, a restaurant, a coffee shop, two lounges, and a clubhouse adjoining the two golf courses—a nine-hole and an 18-hole (guests pay no greens fees). There also are tennis courts and bicycles for touring the city. Open late May to early October. Also see *Special Havens* in DIVERSIONS. 184 Adophus St. (phone: 506-529-8823; 800-268-9411 in Canada; 800-828-7447 in the US; fax: 506-529-4194). Expensive.

Rossmount Inn The decor in this 16-room establishment is eclectic in the fashion of a well-traveled Victorian gentleman's home: Persian rugs, French art, and colorful English wallpaper adorn the parlor. The dining room concentrates on a healthy menu. The guestrooms are not air conditioned. Also see *Special Havens* in DIVERSIONS. RR2, St. Andrews, NB E0G 2X0 (phone: 506-529-3351; fax: 506-529-1920). Expensive to moderate.

GRAND MANAN

Manan Island Inn and Spa This renovated, Victorian-style bed and breakfast establishment features eight large guestrooms furnished with antiques. The charming sitting room has a fireplace and large bay windows with lace curtains. There also is a spa with hydrotherapy, facials, manicures, and mas sage services. North Head (phone: 506-662-8624 or 506-662-3407). Expensive to moderate.

Marathon Inn Sitting on a hill, this lovely historic inn has 28 guestrooms, none air conditioned but many with harbor views and original furnishings. There are tennis courts, an outdoor pool, a dining room, and a lounge that can get noisy on weekends and in the summer. Most rooms share a bath. Whale watching trips can be arranged in summer. Open year-round. Also see *Special Havens* in DIVERSIONS. North Head (phone: 506-662-8144). Expensive to moderate.

Compass Rose Nine guestrooms in two charming old houses look out to the sea. The excellent dining room faces a deck overlooking the harbor. North Head (phone: 506-662-8570). Moderate.

Shorecrest Lodge An old-fashioned country inn with 15 guestrooms, a lounge, and dining room, it is run by two naturalists who give direction and information on exploring Grand Manan. North Head (phone: 506-662-3216). Moderate.

SAINT JOHN

Delta Brunswick This modern motel with 255 rooms is centrally located and has a pool, a sauna, a whirlpool bath, a gameroom, a lounge with live entertainment, bars, and a good, moderately priced dining room. 39 King St. (phone: 506-648-1981; fax: 506-658-0914). Expensive.

Saint John Hilton Here is a luxury hotel nicely situated in the renovated historic harbor-front area—the best of the 197 rooms overlook the bay. The *Turn-of-Tide* dining room is first class. *Market Sq.* (phone: 506-693-8484; 800-HILTONS; fax: 506-657-6610). Expensive.

Parkerhouse Inn Located just off King's Square, this Victorian property has stained glass windows, a curving staircase, fireplaces, a solarium, 14 guestrooms, and a dining room. 71 Sydney St. (phone: 506-652-5054; fax: 506-636-8076). Expensive to moderate.

ST. MARTIN'S

Quaco Inn In this old, lovingly restored sea captain's home are nine guestrooms with great beds. The dining room serves excellent local foods for breakfast and dinner. In the village, on St. Martin's Rd. (phone: 506-833-4772). Moderate.

ROTHESAY

Shadow Lawn Country Inn Built in 1871, this inn has eight rooms furnished with a mixture of antiques and castoffs. The dining room, which serves breakfast, and dinner by reservation, is elegant, but the owner makes the gratuity a mandatory part of the bill instead of an offering. Rte. 100 (phone: 506-847-7539). Expensive to moderate.

SUSSEX

Rory's Mountain Motel This property includes a lounge, a restaurant, a log-constructed convention center, and 22 rooms and housekeeping units. 1019 Main St. (phone: 506-433-1558). Moderate.

Anderson's Holiday Farm Set on 200 acres of rolling farmland, this charming place has three guestrooms and as broad a spectrum of animals as you can imagine—sheep, ducks, Canada geese, rabbits, and even peacocks. There's golf, curling, tennis, and swimming, too. Open year-round. Also see *Farm and Ranch Vacations* in DIVERSIONS. RR2 (phone: 506-433-3786). Moderate to inexpensive.

FUNDY NATIONAL PARK

Caledonia Highlands Inn and Chalets These 44 modern units afford spectacular views. There's no dining room. In *Fundy National Park,* on the main park road at the summit of the hill overlooking the Bay of Fundy (phone: 506-887-2930). Moderate.

HOPEWELL HILL

Broadleaf Farm A good stopping-off place between *Fundy National Park* and Moncton, this 1,400-acre cattle farm with two guestrooms is lively and fun. Besides the 80 horses (which you can learn to ride Western-style), there are hayrides, hiking trails, and prime bird watching. The food is usually simple, although local exotica—such as goosetongue greens—sometimes appears on the menu. Next door, *Broadleaf Too* also has accommodations (three rooms), and there is a small area for tents and trailer hookups. Also see *Farm and Ranch Vacations* in DIVERSIONS. Hopewell Hill (phone: 506-882-2722, *Broadleaf Farm;* 506-882-2803, *Broadleaf Too*). Moderate to inexpensive.

MONCTON AREA

Beausejour Reservations are a must at one of New Brunswick's finest establishments. The 316 rooms are decorated in early Acadian style; also featured are a lounge, two restaurants, and an outdoor pool. The *Windjammer Room* specializes in steaks and seafood, and *L'Auberge* serves Acadian dishes. Special rates are available with vouchers from the tourist information centers. In town, at 750 Main St. (phone: 506-854-4344). Expensive.

Marshlands Inn In the neck of land connecting New Brunswick and Nova Scotia are the Tantramar Marshes, the launching pad for thousands of Canada geese each year. On the edge of the marshes, this inn, built around 1850 is the launching pad for people traveling between the two provinces and for bird watchers and naturalists exploring the marshes. There are 20 rooms in this lovely old home, and even if you can't stay overnight, come for a delicious meal. Open February through November. Also see *Special Havens* in DIVERSIONS. Twenty-five miles (40 km) southeast of Moncton, in Sackville. Write to PO Box 1440, 59 Bridge St., Sackville NB E0A 3C0 (phone: 506-536-0170). Expensive to moderate.

Canadiana This century-old house has 20 rooms, a restaurant, and cable television. In Moncton, at 46 Archibald St. (phone: 506-382-1054). Moderate.

Different Drummer This bed and breakfast establishment has eight rooms and loads of charm. In Sackville, at 82 W. Main St. (phone: 506-536-1291). Moderate.

The Saint John River Valley

The Saint John River once served as a major transport route between the St. Lawrence River and the Bay of Fundy. This was the territory of the powerful Maliseet, the nomadic tribe that wandered throughout the northernmost Allegheny Mountains. Their swift canoes carried them all the way to Nova Scotia in the warm months. In fact, most canoes in use today are based upon the Maliseet design. There are six Native American reserves along the route.

The Saint John River Valley route, from the busy commercial port of Saint John to the pulp and paper center at Edmundston, is 264 miles (422 km) long. It starts in the rolling hills and agricultural region of the Kingston Peninsula, passing New Brunswick's largest freshwater lake and the provincial capital of Fredericton.

The river turns north at Meductic toward Hartland—with the world's longest covered bridge—and continues through New Brunswick's potato district to Perth-Andover. A pleasant side trip to undeveloped, 43,000-acre *Mt. Carleton Provincial Park* returns to Route 2 at Grand Falls.

One of the two best Atlantic salmon and canoeing rivers in North America is the Restigouche—accessible from St-Léonard—which leads to Chaleur Bay on New Brunswick's northern border. Other spots for canoeing and fishing are marked along the way. *Tourism New Brunswick* (see chapter introduction) offers a free fishing guide and an *Outfitters* brochure that will you help plan a fishing or canoeing expedition, plus topographical maps of any section of the province at modest prices.

AINT JOHN For details on Saint John, consult the entry in *The Fundy Coast* route, above.

En Route from Saint John If you came from the east through the dairy district surrounding Sussex, take Route 7 directly to Fredericton, 64 miles (102 km) north (see below).

If you came from the west along the Fundy Coast, a trip through the Lower Saint John River Valley on the Kingston Peninsula is recommended. Many of the province's more than 70 covered bridges can be found on the peninsula. The rolling countryside has not yet been tainted by industrialization. Take Route 100 north for 12 miles (19 km) to Quispamsis. From there, the road is well marked to Gondola Point, where you (and you car) can take the free ferry (year-round, on demand 24 hours) to Reeds Point, only five minutes away. From there, take Route 850 north for 18 miles (29 km) to a second ferry across the Belleisle Bay (again free, year-round, on demand 24 hours). Route 124 west will take you to the ferry at Evandale. (Don't be afraid to ask residents for directions to the covered bridges or to the best place to stop for a leisurely picnic.) From Evandale, take Route 102 north for 17½ miles (28 km) to Gagetown.

GAGETOWN This is the home of the *Queens County Museum* (Front St.; phone: 506-488-2966; closed mid-September to mid-June; no admission charge) and a handful of crafts shops, as well as the Loomcrofters, weavers of tartans and other fabrics whose workshop is in a blockhouse, the oldest building on the Saint John River, dating from the late 18th century. Also in Gagetown is *Colpitt's* (Main St.; phone: 506-488-2979), a marina and old-fashioned general store; and the *Loaves and Calico Country Inn and Café* (Tilley and Mill Sts.; phone: 506-488-3018), which features tasty homemade treats.

Look for cattle grazing on the islands in the middle of the Saint John River. If you pass at the right time of day, you can see cattle being transported back and forth on wooden flatboats, as they have been for over a hundred years. Apple orchards dot the meadowlands.

En Route from Gagetown Route 102 skirts the southern bank of the river as it bends to the west toward Fredericton. At Oromocto, 24 miles (38 km) northwest of Gagetown, the *Canadian Forces Base Gagetown* (phone: 506-422-2630; open year-round; no admission charge) has an army museum. There are some crafts, gift, and antiques shops in the area. Route 102 joins Route 7 into Fredericton.

FREDERICTON The French were the original settlers here until 1759, when they were ousted by British troops. British Loyalists sailed up the Saint John River in 1783, promptly establishing a British city on the spot. The first major settlement in the "interior," Fredericton still is a prosperous city with many small industries in addition to the major employers, the *University of New Brunswick* and the provincial government offices. *Officer's Square*, part of the original British military compound, has been restored, complete with soldiers in red coats and an hourly changing of the guard, accompanied by a piper, in summer.

This "city of the stately elms" was designated the provincial capital in 1785 by Governor Thomas Carleton, to the chagrin of Saint John. The *Ol*

Government House (1828) on Woodstock Road, until 1893 the official residence of provincial governors, was the headquarters of the district's Royal Canadian Mounted Police.

Other sites of note are centrally located on Queen Street. The Anglican *Christ Church Cathedral* (1853) is considered one of the best examples of Gothic architecture in North America. The cathedral's east stained glass window was donated by *Trinity Church* in New York City.

The silver dome of the *Legislative Building* (Queen St.; phone: 506-453-2338) dominates the skyline. Its *Assembly Chamber* has two giant Reynolds portraits of King George III and Queen Charlotte (the provincial capital was named after their second son, Frederick). A 1783 edition of the *Domesday Book* and a complete set of folio-size Audubon bird books are displayed in the *Legislative Library,* annexed to the rear of the main building. The building is closed late August through May; no admission charge.

One can't visit Fredericton without being aware of the city's admiration for Lord Beaverbrook (1879–1964). Born William Maxwell Aitken in Maple, Ontario, and raised in Newcastle, New Brunswick, Lord Beaverbrook became a self-made millionaire before the age of 30, making his fortune in the formation of Canada Cement from the merger of 13 smaller companies. Beaverbrook owned London's *Daily Express,* was a member of the British Parliament from 1910 to 1916, and served in Winston Churchill's cabinet during World War II. Lord Beaverbrook's legacy is evident in Fredericton's buildings, including several on the *University of New Brunswick* campus, such as the *University Library;* the *Playhouse,* home of *Theatre New Brunswick* (Queen St.; phone: 506-458-8344); and the *Beaverbrook Art Gallery* (703 Queen St.; phone: 506-458-8545). The gallery was built in 1958 as a gift to the people of New Brunswick by its namesake. With a number of works by Botticelli, Reynolds, Gainsborough, Constable, Turner, and Hogarth, its standout piece is the 10-by-13½-foot *Santiago El Grande* by Spanish surrealist Salvador Dalí. Other holdings include the paintings and prints of Cornelius Krieghoff, one of the first European artists to choose Canadian landscapes and frontier subjects, and 20th-century daubings by Lord Beaverbrook's friend Winston Churchill. The gallery is closed *Christmas;* admission charge. Just behind the art gallery is the *Green,* a massive landscaped park between Queen Street and the Saint John River with benches, walking paths, and a pleasant view of the water.

The Fredericton area has become a crafts center. Area shops feature batik, pewterware, stained glass, hooked rugs, handwoven clothing, sterling silver jewelry, enamelware (such as miniature paintings on copper buttons), wooden toys, candles, and fine pottery. A list of handicraft studios throughout the province is available from *Tourism New Brunswick* (see chapter introduction). Visit *Aitken's Pewter* (81 Regent St.; phone: 506-450-8188) for tableware, jewelry, and collectibles, and *Shades of Light* (228 Regent St.; phone: 506-455-1318) for a panoply of local crafts.

A few of the best places to eat are the trendy *Bar-B-Q Barn* (540 Queen St.; phone: 506-455-2742), which features chicken, ribs, escargots, and crêpes, and *Mei's* (Regent St.; phone: 506-454-2177), a good, small Chinese restaurant. There's also a good restaurant at the *Sheraton Inn Fredericton* (see *Best en Route*), with a lovely view of the Saint John River. Fredericton's farmers' market on Saturday mornings (George St. between Regent and Saint John Sts.) is a must for crafts, produce, and local color.

A worthwhile side trip, especially interesting for anglers, is to Doaktown, about two hours northeast of Fredericton. Follow Route 8 north along the Miramichi River, world-famous for its abundance of Atlantic salmon, to Doaktown. Like many New Brunswick towns, it is small, but it is a headquarters for hunting, fishing, and canoeing outfitters. For the *Outfitters* brochure, contact *Tourism New Brunswick* (see chapter introduction). Even if you don't fish, you'll be intrigued by Doaktown's *Miramichi Atlantic Salmon Museum* (Main St.; phone: 506-365-7787), which attractively chronicles the history of Atlantic salmon, displays myriad colorful flies used to lure the fish, and explains the conservation policies necessary to protect them. The museum is closed October through May; admission charge. At the other end of Main Street is the *Doak Historic Park,* where costumed guides provide interpretive tours of a house and farm. It's closed October through June; no admission charge (phone: 506-365-4363). The Doak family came from Ayershire, Scotland; they planned to sail south and settle in Kentucky, but storms forced their ship off course to a port on the Miramichi. The area they settled later was named Doaktown.

En Route from Fredericton The Trans-Canada Highway (Rte. 2) runs west along the Saint John River almost to the Quebec border. Follow it for 15 miles (24 km) to *Mactaquac Provincial Park.*

MACTAQUAC PROVINCIAL PARK This "super park" is one of the newest and largest provincial parks. Because of its wide range of facilities and close proximity to Fredericton, it also is crowded most of the summer. In the late 1960s, the New Brunswick Electric Power Commission built the hydroelectric dam from which the park takes its name. The dam flooded the Saint John River Valley for 60 miles (96 km), all the way to Woodstock.

Boating, water skiing, swimming, and fishing are among the popular pastimes at this mammoth, 1,400-acre park. Pickerel, smallmouth bass, and trout are among the fish in the dam's 34-square-mile head pond. Sailboat and powerboat marinas serve the lake, which has two long beaches. There are guided nature trails, programs for children, playgrounds supervised by qualified counselors skilled in arts and crafts instruction, and nearly 300 campsites with kitchen shelters, heated washrooms, and showers. The park is closed mid-May to mid-October; admission charge (phone: 506-363-3011).

The *Park Lodge* (phone: 506-363-4145), with a bar and restaurant, rents clubs for use on its championship 18-hole golf course, one of the best in the province. A good choice for lodging is the *Chickadee Lodge* (see *Best en Route*).

En Route from Mactaquac Provincial Park The Trans-Canada Highway (Rte. 2) leads south and then west to Kings Landing, 5 miles (8 km) away.

KINGS LANDING This is the last bastion of Loyalist tradition along the Saint John River route. The *Kings Landing Historical Settlement* (3 miles/5 km west of the Rte. 3 intersection on the Trans-Canada Hwy.; phone: 506-363-5805) was constructed when the rising waters of Mactaquac Dam threatened to wash away several sites of historic importance along the river. Over 50 buildings—including a school, church, carpenter's shop, and forge—were moved to higher ground. In the shops, the costumed staff of the settlement make horseshoes, plane lumber, and demonstrate other early crafts. Children will enjoy an hour-long behind-the-scenes tour, during which they can don period costumes, see how buildings were constructed, and eat cookies made on the premises. In the settlement, the *Kings Head Inn* (phone: 506-363-5613) offers wholesome meals from 1800s-vintage recipes. The entire settlement is closed mid-October through May; admission charge.

En Route from Kings Landing Route 2 runs west along the south bank of the river for 29 miles (46 km), passing Prince William and turning north at Meductic (see below). Just before Meductic, Route 122 leads south to the Chiputneticook Lakes region, with landlocked salmon and trout. When you get to Canterbury on Route 122, ask outfitter Albert Conklin of the *Skiff Lake Inn Sporting Camps* (phone: 506-279-2119) about canoeing on the Eel River. Depending on the season, the Eel can be the ultimate white-water destination in New Brunswick.

MEDUCTIC This is the site of a fort built by the Maliseet for protection against the raiding Mohawks. Until the 1960s, excavations of the ancient Maliseet burial grounds were under way. Living Maliseet petitioned the *Department of Indian Affairs* to cease the digging, and the excavations were brought to a halt. Crafts are available at some reserves along the way.

En Route from Meductic Follow Route 2 northwest for about 13 miles (21 km) to Woodstock.

WOODSTOCK Featuring elm-lined streets, this quiet town depends primarily on agriculture for its economy. Visit the restored *Old Courthouse* (1833) in Upper Woodstock, which doubles as the *Carleton County Historical Society Museum* (phone: 506-328-9706). Closed September through June (except by appointment); donations welcome. Note that if you return to the US at the Woodstock-Houlton, Maine, border, duty-free shops here stock English woolens, china, and crafts from Canada and all over.

En Route from Woodstock Route 2 leads north to Hartland, site of the world's longest covered bridge (1,282 feet). The origin of many of New

Brunswick's potatoes, Hartland also is a popular resort for salmon and trout fishing. From Hartland, Route 2 crosses to the east bank of the Saint John River, then returns to the west bank at Florenceville. The *Tobique Reserve,* near Perth-Andover, is a good place to buy native handicrafts. It also is home to *York's* (phone: 506-273-2847), one of Canada's best-known dining spots. Immense meals—including lobster, duck, crab, turkey, steaks, clams, scallops, chicken, and pork chops, with five kinds of bread, soup, salad, and strawberry shortcake or pie—are served at a moderate price. Second helpings are free; there's no menu; no liquor is served; and no reservations are accepted. It's closed early October through April.

From Perth-Andover, follow Route 109 northeast to Plaster Rock, home of several outfitters for canoeing, hunting, and fishing on the Tobique River, and the gateway to New Brunswick's largest park, *Mt. Carleton Provincial Park.* The drive northeast into the park from Plaster Rock takes about an hour. There is a 30-mile (48-km) stretch of gravel road, but speeds of 50 to 60 miles (80 to 96 km) per hour are safe except in the early spring, when roads get bumpy from frost heaves. Interior roads are plentiful—although not marked on most maps—thanks to extensive logging in the area. The logging trucks also travel 50 miles (80 km) per hour on the narrow road, so be careful.

MT. CARLETON PROVINCIAL PARK This 43,000-acre park is reserved for wilderness campers. Be forewarned: There are no accommodations, aside from nearly 285 campsites. There are, on the other hand, moose, deer, otters, muskrats, brook trout, and Atlantic salmon. Mt. Carleton is the highest peak (2,690 feet) in New Brunswick. A canoe set down on one of the Nepisiguit Lakes will take you all the way to the Bathurst Power Dam by way of the Nepisiguit ("Angry River").

To plan your trip through this wilderness, contact the Park Superintendent (PO Box 180, St. Jacques, NB E0L 1K0; phone: 506-235-2025, Park Superintendent; 506-506-735-2525, regional operations) or a local outfitter in Plaster Rock (see above).

En Route from Mt. Carleton Provincial Park Return southwest to Plaster Rock, and follow Route 108 north toward Grand Falls. En route is scenic New Denmark, the largest settlement of Danish people in Canada. Spectacular scenery surrounds the town, and the *Valhalla* restaurant (Foley Brook Rd.; phone: 506-553-6614) serves good Danish food.

GRAND FALLS The 75-foot Grand Falls are among Canada's highest cataracts The best view is from the walkway along the gorge, higher than Niagara's. Tours are available of the hydroelectric powerhouse.

The best canoeing and fishing on this route are to be found along the Restigouche River, which winds northeast for almost 100 miles (160 km) to Chaleur Bay on the Quebec border, accessible via Route 17 to

Campbellton. After the Miramichi River on the east coast, this is the best salmon river in the province.

En Route from Grand Falls Route 2 runs north to St-Léonard, about 11 miles (18 km) away. This hamlet between Grand Falls and Edmundston is home to *Madawaska Weavers* (Main St.; phone: 506-423-6341), producers of fine handwoven products, which boasts Britain's Princess Anne among its customers. Edmundston is 23 miles (37 km) farther northwest.

EDMUNDSTON The inhabitants of the northern part of the province are predominantly of French origin, since British soldiers drove them out of southern New Brunswick in 1784. Although logs are no longer floated to the pulp and paper mills, the Saint John River is polluted for many miles below Edmundston (from mills on the US side, according to locals). If you visit in August, don't miss the *Foire Brayon Festival*—the largest French Canadian festival outside of Quebec.

The spires of the Roman Catholic *Cathedral of the Immaculate Conception* (145 Rice St.) can be seen from all over the city. *Lac-Baker* and *Les-Jardins Provincial Parks* are nearby. Also worth exploring is the *Madawaska Museum* (195 Hebert Ave.; phone: 506-735-7254), which has exhibits on the art and culture of northwestern New Brunswick, reflecting the many cultural groups—English, Acadian, and Scottish—that have made their home here. It's closed late September to mid-June; admission charge.

Worth special mention in the gastronomic department are Edmundston's *Bel Air* (174 Victoria St.; phone: 506-735-3329), with an eclectic menu of Chinese and Italian dishes, and *Seafood Paradise* (at the same address; phone: 506-739-7822), which serves French Canadian fare and a variety of seafood dishes.

For golfers, the superb *Edmunston Golf Club* (PO Box 263, Edmundston, NB E3V 3K9; phone: 506-735-7266 or 506-735-3086) is a par 73 (for details, see *Golf in Canada* in DIVERSIONS). Whitewater canoeing on the Saint John River above Edmundston is the best in the province. Mont Farlagne offers excellent skiing, along with good restaurants and motels.

BEST EN ROUTE

Many small lodges and tourist homes can be found along this route. Reservations are necessary during July and August; if the motels are full, consult the *New Brunswick Activity Guide,* available from *Tourism New Brunswick* (see chapter introduction). For accommodations in Saint John, consult the "Best en Route" section in *The Fundy Coast* route, above. At expensive hotels, expect to pay more than $75 per night for a double room; at moderate ones, from $40 to $75; and at an inexpensive place, $40 or less. All hotels feature such amenities as air conditioning, private baths, TV sets, and telephones unless otherwise indicated. For each location, places are listed alphabetically by price category.

GAGETOWN

Steamers Stop Inn This friendly hostelry with a spacious verandah overlooks the Saint John River. All seven guestrooms are furnished with antiques. There is a good dining room. Front St. (phone: 506-488-2903). Moderate.

FREDERICTON

Best Western Mactaquac Inn Year-round sporting activities, from golf, hiking, swimming, and salmon fishing to skiing, are available here. In addition to 75 luxurious guestrooms, visitors can enjoy a first-rate restaurant and an exercise room. Ten minutes west of Fredericton on the Trans-Canada Highway, in the hills overlooking the Saint John River, at RR6 (phone: 506-363-5111; 800-561-5111; fax: 506-363-3000). Expensive.

Lord Beaverbrook With 165 rooms, this is part of the Keddy's Motor Inn chain. An indoor pool, a bar, a hot tub, a sauna, and the popular *Maverick Room* restaurant (open to midnight) are attractions here. 659 Queen St. (phone: 506-455-3371; 800-561-7666; fax: 506-455-1441). Expensive.

Sheraton Inn Fredericton The largest hotel in town, it features 223 guestrooms and 15 luxury suites, along with a fine restaurant, an exercise room, and indoor and outdoor pools. The location on the banks of the Saint John affords lovely views. 225 Woodstock Rd. (phone: 506-457-7000; 800-325-3535; fax: 506-457-4000). Expensive.

Auberge Wandlyn This 116-room family motel features a dining room, a lounge, a pool, a sauna, and conference rooms. 58 Prospect St. (phone: 506-452-8937; 800-561-0000 in eastern Canada; 800-561-0006 in the US). Expensive to moderate.

Carriage House Bed and Breakfast Built in 1875 for the former mayor, this two-story mansion includes two balconies, a ballroom, a coffee bar, and seven guestrooms. There's no restaurant, but full breakfast, coffee, and other meals are served on request. 230 University Ave. (phone: 506-452-9924). Moderate.

PRINCE WILLIAM

Chickadee Lodge Fine bed and breakfast accommodations are found in this five-room facility. There are two lounge areas with fireplaces and a dining room. It also boasts a spectacular view of Mactaquac Headpond. The proprietor acts as a guide during hunting season. Open May to late November. Rte. 2 (phone: 506-363-2759). Moderate.

WOODSTOCK

Auberge Wandlyn Located on Route 95 near the US-Canada border, this motel has 50 rooms and a restaurant. It's usually crowded in July and August (phone: 506-328-8876; 800-561-0000 in eastern Canada; 800-561-0006 in the US; fax: 506-328-4828). Expensive to moderate.

Queen Victoria Bed and Breakfast This quaint, cozy two-room inn features Victorian decor with antiques, and a gazebo. 133 Chapel St. (phone: 506-328-8382). Moderate.

AROOSTOOK

La Ferme des Erables I and II Watch a real potato farm in action, fish for trout, hike, swim in a heated indoor pool, or golf nearby. The photogenic Grand Falls and the world's longest covered bridge are worth exploring while you're here. Just two rooms at each farm. Also see *Farm and Ranch Vacations* in DIVERSIONS. Open year-round. In Aroostook, a few miles north of Perth-Andover, on Rte. 1 (phone: 506-273-3112 or 506-273-2510). Inexpensive.

GRAND FALLS

Lakeside Lodge and Resort Eight rooms are in the lodge and seven chalets on 65-acre Pirie Lake, where many outdoor activities are possible. The dining room serves three meals daily plus Sunday brunch. Pirie Lake (phone: 506-473-6252). Expensive to moderate.

Près du Lac Noted for its hospitality, this motel has a hundred attractive rooms (some nonsmoking), an indoor pool, whirlpool baths, a sauna, a gym, miniature golf, and a restaurant. Trans-Canada Hwy. (phone: 506-473-1300; 800-528-1234; fax: 506-473-5501). Expensive to moderate.

EDMUNDSTON

Howard Johnson's In the heart of town, this motel features 103 rooms, a pool, a sauna, whirlpool baths, a family restaurant, and a dining room. 100 Rice St. (phone: 506-739-7321; 800-654-2000; fax: 506-725-9101). Expensive to moderate.

Le Brayon Hospitable and attractive, this motel has 32 rooms, seven chalets, and a dining room serving breakfast and dinner. St. Basile, Rte. 2E (phone: 506-263-5514). Moderate.

The Acadian Coastal Drive

Acadia, the name France gave its holdings on the Atlantic Seaboard in the 17th century, suffered bitterly in the 18th century at the hands of the British. Acadian residents of Nova Scotia and southern New Brunswick who refused to pledge allegiance to the British Crown fled to northeast New Brunswick in 1755, when British soldiers burned their settlements under orders from colonial Governor William Shirley in Massachusetts. Thousands of French settlers were thus driven out of Nova Scotia and New Brunswick, and their saga is immortalized in Henry Wadsworth Longfellow's "Evangeline, a Tale of Acadia." Some of the tenacious French slowly drifted back to their northeast corner, establishing settlements in the forest, out of sight of marauding British soldiers. Without help from members of the native Micmac, many could not have survived the harsh winters.

The people on the eastern coast of New Brunswick still rely largely on fishing, farming, lumbering, and mining, despite the growth of new industry nearby. Eastern New Brunswick's climate, tempered by the Gulf Stream, is radically different from that of the Bay of Fundy. Long sandbars at several points along the coast create some of the best and warmest beaches north of the Carolinas.

The 270-mile (432-km) drive outlined below starts at Shediac, host of an annual lobster festival, and then follows Route 11 to Bathurst on the northern coast. Cocagne, a tiny village on the other side of the Caissie Cape, comes alive every summer, when hydroplanes speed down the Cocagne River estuary at 200 miles per hour in a regatta.

Farther north, the two small communities of Rexton and Richibucto once were the home of a flourishing shipbuilding company. At *Big Cove Reserve,* 5 miles (8 km) inland from there, some remaining Micmac still make canoes. Nearby *Kouchibouguac National Park,* one of the world's richest ecosystems, harbors moose, black bears, and a variety of waterfowl. The park features a 16-mile-long beach.

The people of Miramichi are proud of their Anglo past, especially of Lord Beaverbrook, the British newspaper magnate who grew up in the area. The city sits on the Miramichi River, famous for its Atlantic salmon and trout.

The northeastern coast of New Brunswick offers some of the province's best deep-sea fishing. A world-record bluefin tuna weighing in at 1,200 pounds was caught off Miscou Island in Chaleur Bay in 1976.

The Acadian Coastal Drive ends at Bathurst, a wood-pulp and paper-industry center on Chaleur Bay. From there, Route 11 continues northwest to the Quebec border at Matapédia.

SHEDIAC One of the province's most hospitable communities, this town (pop. 5,000) claims to be the "lobster capital of the world," hosting the annual six-day *Shediac Lobster Festival* in mid-July. A lobster-eating contest, bicycle and 10-km foot races, and a big parade, with the requisite fireworks, all make up the festivities. (Also see *Festivals, Fairs, and Fancy Acts* in DIVERSIONS.)

Nearby is *Parlee Beach Provincial Park,* with a 142-site tent and trailer campground, close to the province's largest beach. If you've tested the icy waters of the Bay of Fundy on the south shore, these waters will seem downright tepid in comparison. The long sandbars and shallow water make it perfect for children.

Shediac also has some of the best seafood restaurants in the province. *Fisherman's Paradise* (Main St.; phone: 506-532-6811) serves up exceptional lobster rolls, which can make a complete dinner. The chowder is considered the best in the region, portions are gigantic, and prices are moderate. Another excellent seafood restaurant, *Chez Françoise* (93 Main St.; phone: 506-532-4233), is located in an old mansion. For a snack, try the sticky buns at the aptly named *Sticky Bun Shop* (470 E. Main St.; phone: 506-532-3137).

En Route from Shediac Follow Route 11 north for 13 miles (21 km) to Cocagne.

COCAGNE This picturesque fishing village (pronounced Ko-*kann*) was settled in 1767 by Acadians expelled from Nova Scotia by the British. Even today, most residents speak French as well as English.

The annual *International Hydroplane Regatta* is held here in early August in the wide Cocagne River estuary. It draws entries from all over the US and Canada and over 40,000 spectators.

For a side trip, drive north for about 7 miles (11 km) on Route 530 to Caissie Cape, site of several lighthouses and a good beach that is less crowded than Parlee in Shediac.

En Route from Cocagne About 11 miles (18 km) north on Route 11 is Bouctouche.

BOUCTOUCHE If you haven't sampled oysters yet, try some in Bouctouche (pronounced Book-*tush*), "the oyster bed of New Brunswick," as this small fishing village and busy port is known. Some of the best can be had at the *Bouctouche Bay Inn* (see *Best en Route*).

Antonine Maillet, an author whose works about the Acadians and their heritage are well known throughout Canada, was born here in 1929 and now lives in Montreal. An interpretive center, *Le Pays de la Sagouine* (on the south bank of the river on Acadie St.; phone: 506-743-8519), reproduces the setting of her most famous novel, *La Sagouine,* which depicts the life of an Acadian washerwoman in the 1930s. Exhibits show the village and lifestyle described in the text, and scenes from a play based on the story are performed. Tours of the site are given daily; call ahead for an appointment. The center is closed October to mid-June; admission charge.

There are several good beaches on the coastline north of Bouctouche. Also nearby is the *Bouctouche Reserve,* with a small Native American handicrafts shop, *Creations Corinne Baker Jaillet* (phone: 506-743-5920), open daily.

En Route from Bouctouche Route 11 goes directly to Rexton, about 16 miles (26 km) north, but Route 134 is the prettier drive, winding close to the coast and through small communities along the way.

REXTON This charming coastal village was settled by a group of Scots early in the 19th century. Among its earliest residents were the Jardine brothers—

Robert and John—from Dumfriesshire, Scotland, who established one of the first shipbuilding companies in the town and built Kent County's first square-rigger in 1820. Since then, Rexton's relationship to the sea has never faltered. John Jardine, incidentally, returned to Great Britain in 1844 to settle in Liverpool, where his son David became chairman of the *Cunard Line* some years later. Rexton also is the birthplace of Andrew Bonar-Law, who became Prime Minister of Britain in 1922. His home is now a museum (*Bonar-Law Historic Park;* phone: 506-523-7615). It's closed from late September to late July; donations are welcome.

Habitant (Rte. 138; phone: 506-523-4421), in nearby Richibucto, is one of the best places to eat between Shediac and Bathurst. The cooking is plain but reliable; fish is the best bet.

En Route from Rexton Head northwest for 30 miles (48 km) on Route 11 to Kouchibouguac, a gateway to *Kouchibouguac National Park*.

KOUCHIBOUGUAC NATIONAL PARK New Brunswick's "other national park" offers a mixture of forest, open fields, and beach. An offshore sandbar, the primary swimming area, runs the entire length of the shoreline. With sand dunes dotted with tufts of sea grass, the area resembles some of the quieter, less developed parts of Cape Cod. Three rivers flow through the park into Kouchibouguac Bay, forming tidal estuaries and quiet lagoons on the coast.

The park is a flat coastal plain with no stunning vistas, except along the shore at low tide, but the spruce, pine, and birch forests are home to a varied wildlife population, including black bears, moose, and deer. Some of the smaller streams have beaver dams. And if you run short of provisions during your stay, try your hand at clam digging. The Northumberland Strait is free of the poisonous red tides that occasionally plague the Bay of Fundy. Try the lobster suppers at *Bon Accueil* (phone: 506-876-4310), a restaurant in the park. It's closed October through May. *Kouchibouguac National Park* also features an outdoor theater, self-guided trails through fragile habitats, and awareness programs on acid rain and other subjects. An award-winning audiovisual presentation is shown at the information center.

Kouchibouguac has 218 campsites (tent and trailer) and four wilderness campgrounds for backpackers and canoeists (free). Canoes, boats, sailboards, and bicycles can be rented; sailboarding lessons also are available. At 93 square miles, this park is slightly larger than *Fundy National Park*, and, because it is off the heavily traveled route to Nova Scotia, it's not as crowded. For more information, contact *Kouchibouguac National Park* (Kouchibouguac, NB E0A 2A0; phone: 506-876-2443). The park is closed November through April (trails are open year-round); admission charge.

En Route from Kouchibouguac National Park The trip to Miramichi via Route 117 through seaside Acadian villages—Point Sapin; Escuminac, where there is a monument to lost fishermen; and Baie Ste-Anne, home of former world champion boxer Yvon Durelle—is twice as long as the more direct Route 11, but more enjoyable. The coastal road has lighthouses, several good beaches, and occasional stops for home-cooked Acadian food; the 22-mile (35-km) drive on Route 11 passes through wilderness forest.

MIRAMICHI In January 1995, the adjacent towns of Chatham and Newcastle were incorporated into the municipality of Miramichi. The Miramichi River runs into the Miramichi Bay at the former townsite of Chatham. Jacques Cartier landed here in 1534, when the native Micmac ruled the area. This region provided timber for Samuel Cunard's shipbuilding industry in the early 19th century, before the invention of the steamship led to the demise of wooden ships in the late 1800s.

According to legend, the Middle Island was lifted from the forest (forming a lake there) and dropped into the Miramichi River. Sure enough, just a mile away is a lake the exact size and shape of Middle Island. In 1847, Irish immigrants fleeing the potato famine were quarantined on Middle Island after an outbreak of cholera on their ship. The island became first a hospital and then a burial ground for most of the ship's passengers and crew. It is now a park with a beach for swimming.

Miramichi's Newcastle side features a number of lovely old homes reflecting the booming shipbuilding days under the Cunards. Max Aitken (later Lord Beaverbrook) was raised here in the *Old Manse* (225 Mary St.), the parsonage of his Presbyterian minister father. Aitken became a British newspaper magnate and New Brunswick's great benefactor. In 1917, when he was made a peer, he took his new name from the Beaver Brook stream north of town. In 1950, he restored the *Old Manse* as a library, then donated it—along with a copious book collection—to the town. He also donated the *Town Hall,* theater, and town square, where his ashes rest.

In August, the *Miramichi Folk Song Festival* takes place here, with musicians from all across the country performing songs in French and English. (See *Festivals, Fairs, and Fancy Acts* in DIVERSIONS.) From Miramichi, avid anglers can follow Route 8 southwest to Doaktown, site of fabulous fishing (see the Fredericton entry in *The Saint John River Valley* route, above).

En Route from Miramichi Head north on Route 8, which intersects Route 11 at Ferry Road. Continue north on Route 11 on the shore of Miramichi Bay. About eight miles (13 km) northeast of Miramichi at Bartibog Bridge is the *MacDonald Farm Historical Park*, a restoration of an early-19th-century farm. Costumed guides provide interpretive tours of the farm site and the sandstone farmhouse, built around 1820 by Alexander MacDonald. There also are self-guided nature trails on the property. The park is closed late September to late June; admission charge (phone: 506-773-5761).

Burnt Church, 22 miles (35 km) north on a tiny side road off Route 11, is now a native reserve. It was the site of a French church burned in 1759 by British troops on their way to Quebec. All along the shore are excellent sandy beaches. Continue north for 60 miles (96 km) to Tracadie.

TRACADIE Although the name sounds French, Tracadie is a Micmac name meaning "a good place to camp." Many French settlers, divested of all of their possessions during the infamous expulsion, moved back to this area in the 1780s. This corner of New Brunswick is almost entirely French-speaking, but communication is rarely a problem.

Fish are plentiful here. There are salmon in the Tracadie River, and deep-sea fishing charters are available. Or just head down to the beach and dig up some clams. If you come up empty-handed, try one of the local take-outs, which often are very good. A leper colony once existed here, a fact recalled at the *Tracadie Historical Museum* (Main St.; phone: 506-395-2212). Closed mid-August through May. The small *Val-Comeau Provincial Park,* 5 miles (8 km) south of Tracadie, has 55 campsites, a beach, and a picnic area.

En Route from Tracadie Follow Route 11 north away from the coast to Pokemouche; from there, take Route 113 east to Shippagan.

SHIPPAGAN The fishing industry in the northeast corner of New Brunswick employs many people, but there is another industry as well: Peat moss is harvested out of the earth and piled to dry in the sun to reduce its weight. The government is experimenting with a peat-burning electrical plant in the area. The *Marine Centre,* a tribute to the fishing industry, illustrates sea life in the Gulf of St. Lawrence and the Northumberland Strait. It features a replica of a lighthouse, a "touch tank," and displays of live fish and seals. It's closed October through mid-May (phone: 506-336-4771).

On Lamèque Island, accessible by bridge from Shippagan, the village of Lamèque hosts the *International Baroque Music Festival* in early July and the *Peat Moss Festival* in late July. From Little Shippagan, on the northern tip of Lamèque Island, take the free ferry to Miscou Island, site of endless white sand beaches and a fish restaurant. Deep-sea fishing boats can be chartered in the quest for giant bluefin tuna, averaging 800 pounds. *Miscou Island Camping* (phone: 506-344-8638) has 56 campsites and a few cabins.

En Route from Shippagan Return south to Route 11 at Pokemouche, picking up Route 11 north for 10 miles (16 km) to Caraquet.

CARAQUET On Chaleur Bay, this small fishing community is rich with Acadian tradition. Settled in 1757, Caraquet is home to one of the largest commercial fleets in New Brunswick. You can buy reasonably priced fresh seafood at the wharf. Small wooden fishing boats bob in the water as their owners prepare lobster traps. Just east of Caraquet is a wooden shipbuilding company, one of the last of its kind.

In August, Caraquet hosts the *Acadian Festival,* with a traditional *Blessing of the Fleet* (to protect the fisherfolk) conducted by Catholic priests. (See *Festivals, Fairs, and Fancy Acts* in DIVERSIONS.) Residents will tell you of a fiery ghost ship often seen in Chaleur Bay on stormy nights. Sightings of the ship with sails ablaze also have been reported across the bay in Quebec.

The town's small *Acadian Museum* will introduce you to the Acadian way of life. It's closed from early October to mid-June (phone: 506-727-3269).

The dining rooms of the unpretentious *Paulin* hotel (see *Best en Route*) serve some of the best scallops on the north coast. By calling ahead, visitors can arrange to have an authentic Acadian meal, such as chicken *fricôt,* a thick, savory stew, or, in season, a fresh-from-the-sea lobster feast.

En Route from Caraquet Follow Route 11 west for about 8 miles (13 km) to *Acadian Village.*

ACADIAN VILLAGE This 500-acre village was built in the 1970s to commemorate the hardships endured by French settlers expelled by the British. Early Acadian homes, a working tavern, a school, and a blacksmith's shop were dismantled piece by piece from other parts of the province and reassembled here. Craftspeople demonstrate how to make cedar shingles, soap, and candles. All clothing worn by staff is produced on site.

Since there was little arable land in the Caraquet area, the tenacious French exiles built a system of dikes to recover swampy marshland from the sea, a skill they imported from their homeland on the Brittany coast. The site for the re-creation was chosen in part because it has a number of these 18th-century engineering marvels. Other features of the village include a restaurant serving Acadian fare, such as *poutine râpe,* grated potatoes wrapped around pork and then steamed or fried. *Acadian Village* is closed from early September to early June; admission charge (phone: 506-727-3467). In nearby Grande-Anse, the unique *Pope's Museum* features portraits of all the popes, a scaled-down replica of *St. Peter's,* and historic nuns' and priests' habits. It's closed early September to early June; admission charge (phone: 506-732-3003).

En Route from Acadian Village Follow Route 11 west to Bathurst.

BATHURST Until the early 1950s, Bathurst's economy was shackled to pulp and paper production. When zinc and copper deposits were discovered in 1953, Bathurst's faltering economy boomed. Because of this heavy industry, much of Bathurst is not particularly attractive, though the city has lively discos and taverns. A free tour of the world's largest zinc mine can be arranged by calling 506-546-6671. There are several good beaches nearby on Nepisiguit Bay at Youghall, Caron Point, and Chaleur. For more information on Bathurst, contact *Tourism Visitors Services* (PO Drawer D, Bathurst, NB E2A 3Z1; phone: 506-548-0410).

One of New Brunswick's top eating places is in Nigadoo, 9 miles (14 km) north on Route 134. By the Nigadoo River Bridge, *La Fine Grobe* (phone: 506-783-3138) affords a pretty view of Nepisiguit Bay. The fine, expensive menu is mainly French, with some Acadian dishes. The restaurant usually closes in September, and then the owners begin their "real" jobs: Georges and Hilda Frachon are potters, painters, and silk screeners, and fine examples of their work are on display in the restaurant. The restaurant opens again in May. During the summer, a reasonably priced luncheon menu is served on the terrace. Make reservations for dinner at least a day in advance.

En Route from Bathurst Routes 11 and 134 go to the Quebec border at Matapédia, 81 miles (130 km) to the west. Route 134, which follows the coast, is more scenic. At Petit Rocher, northwest of Bathurst on Route 134, the *Mining and Mineral Museum* gives visitors "hands-on" experience with geologic resources of the area. It's closed early September through May; admission charge (phone: 506-783-8714).

Continuing west on Route 11 or 134, the Eel River bar is one of the longest natural sandbars in the world, with salt water on one side and fresh water on the other. A few miles farther on Route 134 is Dalhousie, an attractive town known for processing wood products; its shoreline boasts interesting rock formations that attract rock hounds. Its *Restigouche Regional Museum* (437 George St.; phone: 506-684-4685) depicts the area's pioneering days, as well as the development of fishing and farming. It's closed early September through May; admission charge. The *Chaleur Phantom* departs daily for tours of the beautiful Bay of Chaleur, and a ferry runs from Dalhousie to Misquasha, Quebec. *Chaleur Provincial Park* and *Inch Arran Municipal Park* are popular for swimming and camping. For more information, contact Dalhousie's tourism office (phone: 506-684-5352), which is closed from *Labour Day* through mid-June.

Campbellton, at the western end of the Bay of Chaleur, is an important outfitting and service center for sport fishers. The last naval engagement of the Seven Years' War was fought offshore at Campbellton in 1760. Founded 13 years later, the city was named after Sir Archibald Campbell, the lieutenant-governor of the province. The city's waterfront park has a lighthouse and a 28-foot-long model of an Atlantic salmon. The *Restigouche Gallery* (39 Andrew St.; phone: 506-753-5750) is a national exhibition center for regional artists. It's open year-round; donations are welcome.

BEST EN ROUTE

For accommodations in Moncton, consult the "Best en Route" section of *The Fundy Coast* route, above. Be aware of festivals and other special events before deciding where to make reservations. For example, Cocagne's *International Hydroplane Regatta* draws 40,000 spectators, but the town is so tiny that residents take in guests during the festival—a good way to meet Acadians. For details, write to the *Festival Committee* (*Hôtel de Ville,* Cocagne, NB E0A 1K0; no phone). In French-speaking northeastern New Brunswick, most hotel and motel staff members are bilingual.

For a double room for one night, expect to pay $75 or more for expensive accommodations; from $40 to $75 for moderate ones; and $40 or less in an inexpensive hotel. All hotels feature such amenities as air conditioning, private baths, TV sets, and telephones unless otherwise indicated.

The Northwest Territories

The Northwest Territories (known as the NWT) comprise the largest parcel of land in Canada: More than 1.3 million square miles stretch from Ellesmere Island, just off Greenland's northern coast, to the Mackenzie Mountain range at the Yukon border. Alternately barren and pine forested, there are mountains and plateaus, as well as vast lakes and foaming white-water rivers. The territories' wilderness offers endless variations for hikers, other nature lovers, hunters, and anglers.

This huge area is home to only 64,000 people, many of them Inuit and members of other Native American tribes. (Inuit—pronounced *In*-oo-it—means "the people" in the Inuktitut language and is the proper term for Native Americans of the far north. The term "Eskimo," picked up by early settlers, is considered derogatory.) Nearly 25% of the total territorial population resides in Yellowknife, the capital; another 20%, more or less, lives elsewhere in the Great Slave Lake area. The lives of many of the native inhabitants are characterized by life-and-death struggles with nature, including hunting and fishing for survival, and encounters with caribou and bears, moose, walrus, and whales. The conflict between the desire to preserve nature and the demands of human beings for resources continues, with wildernesses being explored for mineral deposits—especially oil—by mining companies. So far, much of the business and enterprise center around the Yellowknife environs near the Alberta border (by far the most accessible spot for entering the territories).

The Northwest Territories have undergone considerable political evolution. In 1991, the Canadian government allocated more than half of the territories for self-government by the 18,000 Inuit who live here. Called Nunavut (an Inuit term meaning "our land"), the area stretches from the northern tip of Hudson Bay nearly to the North Pole. In 1992, the accord was approved by a majority of Northwest Territories voters and ratified by resident Inuit; at press time, the Canadian Parliament was scheduled to hold a final vote on the region's special status. The expected ratification will mean improved political and economic control for the Inuit, including land and limited resource development rights in the area, which some experts think may yield valuable oil, gas, and precious metals. (Further devolution will make Nunavut an official territory by 1999.)

This agreement does not, however, signal the end of petitions for self-government by Canada's native peoples. The Dene (pronounced De-*nay,* meaning "people" in Slavey, the language spoken by the Slavey peoples, members of the Dene nation) and the Métis (Canadians of mixed European and Native American ancestry) who live in the western part of the Northwest Territories also have claims to be dealt with, some conflicting; negotiations with Ottawa are in progress.

In exploring this vast region, we have concentrated on Great Slave Lake, circled by smaller and larger towns and providing a wonderful introduction to the human and natural environment of the territories; a trip to *Nahanni National Park* in the southwestern corner, north of British Columbia (accessible via the Liard Highway and then by charter aircraft); and the Dempster Highway, the 450-mile (720-km) route between Dawson City in the Yukon and Inuvik in the Northwest Territories, a road that crosses the wandering grounds of one of the world's largest herds of wild caribou. For further information, contact *NWT Tourism Information, The North Group* (PO Box 2107, Yellowknife, NWT XIA 2P6; phone: 403-873-7200; 800-661-0788).

Hay River to Yellowknife

To journey in the Northwest Territories is to travel between two cultures—one driven by the needs and technologies of contemporary society, the other a traditional, native way of life that's disappearing fast. The northern frontier's more bustling towns are not very different from those farther south, with most of the amenities and some of the worries of any remotely urban environment. The northern homelands, however, are scattered in the far north and elsewhere, where native people still practice traditional crafts and rely on hunting, fishing, and trapping to live, even while incongruous aspects of modern life impinge on their society.

Nowhere are these forces more evident than around the Northwest Territories' mighty Great Slave Lake, home of the Dogrib and Slavey people, members of the Dene nation. Here, too, is thriving Yellowknife, the capital of the territories. The drive around the lake from Hay River to the capital crosses the Mackenzie River, offering in the process a glimpse of the area's majesty. Through it all blow the winds of change, as gas and oil discoveries in the wake of the Alaska Pipeline project have brought to the relations between government and people—especially native people—a new edge and urgency.

HAY RIVER This junction community (pop. 3,200) on Great Slave Lake provides access to all the settlements on the Mackenzie Highway system. The Hudson's Bay Company built the first trading post here in 1868, but the population didn't grow until the highway system was completed and oil and gas exploration begun. A railway finished in 1964 to carry lead-zinc ore from Pine Point to smelters established the town as a transportation center; Pine Point has since closed. Freight bound for High Arctic settlements is loaded onto barges here for the 1,200-mile voyage down the Mackenzie River to the Arctic Ocean, a precarious lifeline depending heavily on the weather: The survival of the Mackenzie River and High Arctic communities relies on these once-a-year supply drops of food, fuel, and construction material.

Drive past the airport into Hay River's Old Town, where the wharves of barging companies are piled high with supplies bound for exotic places like Holman Island, Fort Good Hope, and Tuktoyaktuk. Old Town also is the home of the commercial fishermen who ply the waters of Great Slave Lake, winter and summer, bringing in trout, whitefish, northern pike, and inconnu. Some of the pike is shipped to France, where it's made into pâté.

Old Town is an area of small, old frame houses built on the flood plain of the Hay River delta. After two disastrous floods, it was moved to higher ground upriver. New Town is dominated by a 17-story high-rise, completed in 1973 in anticipation of the Mackenzie Valley pipeline, a project for which Hay River was a staging area. The *Diamond Jenness School* (named after the anthropologist who first studied northern native culture around 1910) is across the street. The school is a striking example of northern-flavored architecture. Its shocking purple color was the choice of the students; disconcerted by the color at first, everyone is now proud of it, and the building has become a landmark.

Although relatively small, Hay River provides most amenities. Several motels and hotels here offer good service, and some have restaurants and bars. The *Back Eddy* restaurant (Capital Crescent; phone: 403-874-6680), a block from downtown, has the best steaks around. Unleaded gas is available in the gas stations and garages, and tourists can find just about any camping supplies.

If you have time, take a 167-mile (269-km) drive southeast on Route 5 to *Wood Buffalo National Park,* home to hundreds of bird species, including the rare whooping crane, as well as the world's last free-roaming herd of bison. The park is open daily year-round; no admission charge (phone: 403-872-2349). For more information, see *National Parks* in DIVERSIONS.

En Route from Hay River Drive 22 miles (35 km) south on Route 2 to Enterprise; along the way are two gas stations and two restaurants. Turn west onto Route 1 to start the 276-mile (445-km) drive that skirts Great Slave Lake, the second-largest lake in Canada, after Great Bear Lake, to Yellowknife. Gas up either in Hay River or Enterprise—it's a 67-mile (107-km) drive from Enterprise to the next gas station, in Spruce Grove. Also check to see if the ferry is running across the Mackenzie River to Fort Providence (see below).

The highway is paved almost entirely, and driving conditions are generally good. Here the road follows a ridge overlooking a wide, wooded plain covered with the familiar jack pine. In the distance is the wide expanse of Great Slave Lake. For a spectacular view—and a look at one of the far north's many paradoxes—turn off onto the Hart Lake fire tower access road, 29 miles (46 km) out of Enterprise. The well-marked road leads to a picnic site, 500 yards beyond which, along the marked path, is a 250-foot escarpment, the remains of a coral reef.

Another 23 miles (37 km) leads to the well-marked turnoff to Kakisa and the *Lady Evelyn Falls Campsite,* with 10 tent sites and five RV pads. Drinking water and firewood are available. Below the 48-foot falls, fishing is good, and grayling are common. A 10-minute drive past the campsite is the village of Kakisa (pop. 30), where the Slavey still live off the land, hunting moose, fishing for pike and whitefish, and trapping muskrat and beavers. Their small but well-kept log cabins are nestled in groves of pine and birch. There are no tourist services here. If you want to launch a boat, inquire first, because fishing nets are strung out around the lake. When boating, watch for the net floats, so as to avoid tangling your outboard in the nets and damaging both.

Eleven miles (18 km) from the Kakisa turnoff on Route 1 is the junction of Routes 1 and 3. Turn north on Route 3 for 15 miles (24 km) to the Mackenzie River ferry crossing to Fort Providence. The *Merv Hardie* (phone: 403-873-7799; 800-661-0751 in Canada) takes vehicles (for free) across the mile-wide river after the ice breakup and before the freeze-up. In winter, travelers drive right across the river on the four-foot-thick ice, which supports up to 55 tons. There are delays each spring and fall, during breakup and freeze-up, when these rivers cannot be crossed at all. At that time, when highway communications are interrupted, perishable goods must be flown into Yellowknife. (Before the road to Yellowknife was built, goods were freighted all the way across the ice of Great Slave Lake.)

FORT PROVIDENCE Across the river, a 5-mile (8-km) drive leads to the Fort Providence access road. A motel, restaurant, bar, gas station, and store are located between the junction and the settlement (pop. 660), 3 miles (5 km) up the road.

Father Henri Grollier, a Catholic priest, built a mission on nearby Big Island in 1858, but he moved it here three years later, and the settlement gradually grew around it. At the west end of the village is a monument to Sir Alexander Mackenzie, who passed through here in 1789 in his search for the Pacific Ocean. He didn't find the Pacific, but he was the first European to get his baggage wet in the Arctic Ocean: He camped on a beach in the Mackenzie delta, just out of sight of the ocean. Everyone was sleeping when the tide came in, flooding the camp. Mackenzie called the river that now bears his name the River of Disappointment. The Dene along the river call it *Deh Cho,* or the Mighty River.

Two excellent craft shops in the village produce some of the best Dene handiwork in the valley: made-to-measure parkas, moose-hair tufting, porcupine quills, and beadwork designs. Each settlement in the valley has its own style of artwork. One crafts shop is in the *Snowshoe Inn* (phone: 403-699-3511; fax: 403-699-4300), across the street from the motel; the other is in a cabin operated by the Fort Providence Dene Band; it is near the *Big River Service Centre* (phone: 403-699-3401; fax: 403-699-3210).

Anglers can rent boats at either of the service stations for some excellent grayling and pike fishing, but watch out for the blackflies. These pesky bugs bite anywhere, so bring a good insect repellent or head net. A mile from the junction of the access road, a beautiful campsite on the top of the river bluffs has secluded tenting and RV pads and a dumping station for RVs. Tugs can often be seen pushing laden barges downriver, heading for the High Arctic.

En Route from Fort Providence Head north on Route 3 for 131 miles (211 km) to Edzo or 142 miles (228 km) to Rae. On the east side of the highway is the *Mackenzie Bison Sanctuary.* The government transplanted 19 wood buffalo here from the Fort Smith area in the early 1960s; now the herd numbers well over 500. The only pure herd of wood buffalo left in North America, the animals generally can't be seen from the highway, since they range close to the shores of the lake. But an occasional moose does come browsing in the numerous lakes and sloughs along the highway, and if you're lucky, you'll see a sandhill crane.

The North Arm picnic site, 112 miles (179 km) north of Fort Providence, affords a picturesque view of Great Slave Lake's North Arm, dotted with numerous islands.

RAE and EDZO These towns (total pop. 1,520) make up the largest Dene community in the NWT. The Dogrib tribe was mostly nomadic, following the migratory caribou in winter and fishing the plentiful lakes in summer. At the turn of the century, this area produced tons of dried meat for Hudson Bay traders. Dr. John Rae established a post on the lake's North Arm, several miles from the present settlement, in 1852. It was moved in 1906 to its present site, where some log cabins still remain from old *Fort Rae.*

In 1965—while the Mackenzie Highway was being extended to Yellowknife—the government established Edzo as a replacement model community. However, the residents refused to move to the new place, even though it occupied a higher, drier, and more sanitary location with a modern school, a nursing station, and housing. They were loath to abandon their homes built on the rocks and muskeg, where they could launch canoes into Marian Lake from their backyards. Some finally did move, but the old community of Rae survives, strong as ever. There are no services in Edzo, but Rae has two gas stations. Walking around the village, you'll see numerous snowmobiles, sled dogs tied up waiting for winter snows, and fish hung up on drying racks.

Edzo was named after a Dogrib chief who brought peace to the area in the mid-1800s. His antagonist was Chief Akaitcho of the Yellowknife Dene, who lived from Yellowknife Bay north almost to Coppermine. The Yellowknife preyed on the Dogrib, chasing them out of hunting and fishing grounds. According to legend, in a confrontation between the two, Edzo spoke so long and eloquently that Akaitcho was afraid to wage war again. Akaitcho helped Captain John Back in his trek to the Arctic Ocean up the

Back River in 1832. The Yellowknife disappeared as a distinct tribal unit after 1928, when their ranks were decimated by a flu epidemic. The survivors gradually moved into other tribal settlements, assimilating as they went.

Frank's Channel, which separates Rae and Edzo, marks the geological divide between the sedimentary basin, an extension of the Canadian prairies, and the Precambrian Shield. The highway to Yellowknife takes on a few more curves as it skirts lakes and sloughs nestled among hard rock outcrops. The familiar spruce and pine grow shorter here as they struggle for footholds in any dip and crevice that can hold a few inches of soil. This is also the area of permafrost, where only a few top feet of ground thaw in summertime. Gas up in Rae for the drive to Yellowknife.

En Route from Rae and Edzo Proceed southeast on Route 3 for 62 miles (99 km) to Yellowknife. Driving into town, you'll probably notice the *Bristol Monument,* a *Bristol* freighter set atop a prominent rock outcrop. This plane made aviation history in 1967 when, flown by *Wardair* pilot Don Braun, it touched down at the North Pole, the first wheeled aircraft to do so. A relic of World War II, the *Bristol* helped open many an isolated camp and mine in the NWT by freighting in construction materials, even bulldozers.

YELLOWKNIFE The capital of the Northwest Territories, this city (pop. 17,000) owes its existence to two gold mines and its growth to the government offices that administer this huge region. Home to about a quarter of the territories' population, Yellowknife has a profile marked by high-rises and office buildings sprouting out of the surrounding taiga (evergreen forest). It's come a long way since 1789, when Laurent Leroux, a Northwest Company trader, built his trading post on Yellowknife Bay. Alexander Mackenzie passed through here in his roundabout search for the river that now bears his name, and explorer John Franklin traveled up the Yellowknife River to the Arctic Coast via the Coppermine River in 1819.

The Hudson's Bay Company closed down the Yellowknife trading post in 1823, after its 1821 amalgamation with its longtime fur-trading rival, the Northwest Company. Little attention was paid the area for the next 75 years. Prospectors on their way to the Klondike via the Mackenzie River found traces of gold in the hard rock in 1896, but it wasn't until 1930 that a major gold discovery precipitated a boom in the area. Con Mines, on the southern edge of Yellowknife, became the first to operate in the area, in 1938. The second, Giant Yellowknife Mines, began production in 1945.

Take a walk around Old Town Yellowknife on the peninsula where, in the 1930s and 1940s, shacks fought for space on the bare rocks. They are long gone, but today the *Bush Pilot's Monument* perches on one of the rocks overlooking the waters of Great Slave Lake. The cairn commemorates the legendary bush pilots who opened the far north with their daring exploits in rickety planes. From the vantage point offered by the monument, visitors can watch floatplanes take off, flying tourists to remote fishing lakes and prospectors to other potential bonanzas. Below the monument on the Back Bay side is the restored *Wild Cat Café* (phone: 403-873-8850; closed September through May), one of the few surviving landmarks in Old Town where you still can have a meal.

The *Prince of Wales Northern Heritage Centre* (off Hwy. 4, the Ingraham Trail; phone: 403-873-7551) is on the shore of Frame Lake, a three-block walk from downtown. It houses extensive displays of northern artifacts, ranging from Inuit carvings to dioramas of wildlife. Also in this well-rounded collection is a piece of *Cosmos 954,* the Soviet satellite that crashed into the Barrenlands 300 miles (480 km) east of Yellowknife in 1978. It's closed *New Year's Day, Christmas,* and Mondays during the winter; open daily 10:30 AM to 5:30 PM from June 1 through September 1; no admission charge.

Yellowknife's hotels and motels offer a wide range of services and prices. The town also boasts more than 25 dining establishments, some with liquor licenses. Stores can fill just about every need, but remember that prices in far-off Yellowknife are about 30% higher than in southern Canada, due to transport costs. Many sell soapstone carvings and handicrafts. The largest collections can be found in *Northern Images* (in the *YK Mall* at Franklin and 48th Sts.; phone: 403-873-5944) and the *Aurora Art Gallery* (*Scotia Centre* at Franklin and 51st Sts.; phone: 403-873-4256). Both stock the internationally famous Holman Island and Cape Dorset prints and etchings.

Golf buffs arriving in town around the longest day of the year, June 21, can participate in the *Canadian North Yellowknife Midnight Classic* at the *Yellowknife Golf Club* (phone: 403-873-4326). This annual event draws participants and celebrities for a tee-off under the sunlit midnight sky. The course is unique—the turf is sand, the greens are oiled sand, and ravens are the biggest hazards. The large, plucky birds have been known to steal a ball from under the nose of a golfer. Contestants are armed with raven repellent, liquid refreshment, and extra balls, among other things. The *Folk on the Rocks* music festival is held in mid-July.

Many campsites are within easy reach of Yellowknife. The closest to town, the *Fred Henne Park* (across from the airport; phone: 403-920-2472), has drinking water, tenting sites, and pads for RVs, with dumping facilities. At the park, consider taking the interesting Prospector's Trail, a self-guided, two-hour interpretive hike around Long Lake that explains the area's unique geology, flora, and fauna. *Fred Henne Park* can get crowded on weekends because it has the only sandy swimming beach close to town, attracting residents in the short but sunny summers. The park is closed mid-September to mid-May; admission charge to campgrounds and a day charge to use picnic sites.

En Route from Yellowknife Those wishing to get away from the crowds can drive along the 50-mile (80-km) Ingraham Trail, named for Yellowknife hotelier Vic Ingraham. The trail was to be the start of the ambitious Roads to Resources, skirting Great Slave Lake and linking many potential mine sites, but the project was abandoned in the late 1960s.

Along the trail are hiking paths, boat launches, picnic sites, and camping (with drinking water and firewood) at *Prelude Lake* and *Reid Lake Territorial Parks.* Fishing is a popular area pastime, with lake trout, northern pike, walleye, whitefish, and arctic grayling the primary catches in the waterways off the trail. It's also a very good place for canoeing. Those who venture out here in winter might see the Bathurst caribou herd, which migrates as far south as this road. Other winter activities include ice fishing, cross-country skiing, and snowshoeing. Fishing licenses are necessary. They are available at Northwest Territories border information booths, most sport fishing lodges, sporting goods and hardware stores, the *Royal Canadian Mounted Police (RCMP) Renewable Resources* offices, and the *Department of Fisheries and Oceans* offices.

Drive 2 miles (3 km) past the Giant Mines property on Route 4; *Yellowknife River Park* is right across the bridge. Here, a boat launch provides access to the northern pike–rich river. Or you can fish for grayling and whitefish at Tartan Rapids, 7 miles (11 km) upstream, where Prosperous Lake empties into the river. There are plenty of pike in the shallows and weed beds that will rise to a homemade lure, but red devils are a favorite.

There are three other picnic sites over the next 12 miles (19 km), each providing hiking trails and fishing. *Prelude Lake Territorial Park,* at the end of a 1-mile (1.6-km), well-marked turnoff, has a boat launch, a beach, and good trout fishing. The *Prelude Lake Lodge* (phone: 403-920-4654) offers accommodations, boat and motor rentals, and a café. Watch for sudden shifting winds when boating on the larger lakes. If you get into difficulty, make for the nearest land and wait out the weather; even the smaller lakes kick up sizable waves, and the water here is extremely cold.

At Km 48 is a parking area at the beginning of the well-marked scenic trail to Cameron River Falls. The three-quarter-mile trail opens on a 45-foot waterfall, and side trails lead to another, smaller waterfall downstream. Eight miles (13 km) farther is *Reid Lake Territorial Park,* the best along the Ingraham Trail. Water, wood, and a boat launch are available, plus plenty of good fishing. This 27-site camping area is only 7 miles (11 km) from the end of the road, at Tibbit Lake.

BEST EN ROUTE

Due to the scarcity of accommodations here, make reservations as far in advance as possible. Expect to pay $75 or more per night for a double room in the places listed in Hay River, and $90 or more in Yellowknife. All feature private baths. Lodgings are listed alphabetically by location.

HAY RIVER

Caribou In the new section of Hay River (built up since a big flood in 1967), this motel features 29 rooms with kitchenettes, phones, and TV sets; steambaths; whirlpool baths; car plug-ins; a dining room; and a lounge. PO Box 1114, Hay River, NWT X0E 0R0 (phone: 403-874-6706).

Cedar Rest Right on the highway, this motel has 29 suites and 12 rooms with kitchenettes, all with waterbeds and satellite TV. There's no restaurant. PO Box 540, Hay River, NWT X0E 0R0 (phone: 403-874-3732).

Harbour House A bed and breakfast establishment with six rooms, it also has a crafts center. Boats, canoes, and surfboards are available, as is take-out food. PO Box 54, Hay River, NWT X0E 0R0 (phone: 403-874-2233).

Hay River In Old Town, this cedar-log place has 16 renovated rooms available in winter, 38 in summer, all with TV sets and phones. A dining room, a café, a lounge, country-and-western entertainment, and a convenience store are other amenities. PO Box 1659, Hay River, NWT X0E 0R0 (phone: 403-874-6022).

Migrator This motel has 24 rooms; six have kitchenettes (there's no dining room on the premises). On the main highway between Old and New Towns. PO Box 1847, Hay River, NWT X0E 0R0 (phone: 403-874-6792; fax: 403-874-2938).

Ptarmigan Inn A 41-room hotel, it is part of a complex which also houses a restaurant, dining lounge, downstairs bar, barbershop, and bank. PO Box 1000, Hay River, NWT X0E 0R0 (phone: 403-874-6781; fax: 403-874-3392).

YELLOWKNIFE

Discovery Inn This establishment has 41 rooms, a family-style restaurant, a lounge, and conference facilities. Downtown (phone: 403-873-4151; fax: 403-920-7948).

Explorer A modern place, it has 124 guestrooms, all with color TV sets and air conditioning. Other facilities include the *Bedrock Café,* fine dining in the *Factors Club,* a cocktail lounge, and a gift shop. 48th St. and 49th Ave. (phone: 403-873-3531; fax: 403-873-2789).

gloo Inn Halfway between Old Town and New Town, this motel has 44 rooms, some with kitchen facilities. The diner serves simple sandwiches. Franklin Ave. (phone: 403-873-8511; fax: 403-873-5547).

Northernlites Located one block from downtown, Yellowknife's newest motel has 20 guestrooms (six with kitchenettes), all with color TVs and cable. No dining room. 49th St. (phone: 403-873-6023).

ellowknife Inn Conveniently located downtown, it has 150 rooms, a café, a bar, a lounge, a newsstand, and one of the best dining places in town, the *Mackenzie*

Dining Room. The menu includes such northern Canadian dishes as arctic char, caribou steaks, and musk ox. The café is frequented by businessfolk, travelers, and the mining and aviation fraternity. 49th St. and 50th Ave. (phone: 403-873-2601; fax: 403-873-2602).

YWCA Here are 32 rooms (for men and women), many with kitchenettes. No restaurant. Weekly and monthly rates are available. 5004 54th St. (phone: 403-920-2777; fax: 403-873-9406).

The Nahanni

In the southwestern corner of the Northwest Territories is *Nahanni National Park*, a destination that appeals primarily to hard-core wilderness trekkers and canoeists: The main purpose of a visit to *Nahanni,* besides the lure of burying oneself in its 1,840 square miles of mountains, lakes, and wilderness, is the South Nahanni River, one of the purest, wildest, roughest stretches of whitewater left in the world, where motorized craft are forbidden. Because it is a wilderness destination, the park and river are most accessible by charter aircraft (see below); the two jumping-off places for flight access are Fort Liard and Fort Simpson. Usually, visitors fly into the north end of the park and paddle canoes or rafts downstream. To reach Fort Liard or Fort Simpson, take the Liard Highway, which starts at Fort Nelson, British Columbia, and runs through the Liard Valley. You also can reach Fort Simpson from Fort Providence, a 201-mile (324-km) drive west on Route 1, a well-graveled, all-weather highway. The trip will take four to five hours if you drive straight through. Ten miles from Fort Simpson, a free ferry provides transportation across the Liard River.

Two air services depart from Fort Liard and Fort Simpson: *Deh Cho Air Ltd.* (*Liard Valley Band Development Corp.*, Fort Liard, NWT X0E 0A0; phone: 403-770-4103; fax: 403-770-3555) and *Simpson Air* (PO Box 260, Fort Simpson, NWT X0E 0N0; phone: 403-695-2505; fax: 403-695-2925). They will transport both you and your canoe into *Nahanni National Park.* *Simpson Air* also has a canoe rental service.

FORT SIMPSON The Northwest Company established the Fort of the Forks here in 1803, to trade for the rich beaver and marten furs that fashion-hungry Europe demanded. This town (pop. 1,150) at the confluence of the Liard and Mackenzie Rivers is named for Sir George Simpson, governor of the Hudson's Bay Company in 1821, when it amalgamated with its rival, the Northwest Company. If you walk around town, you'll see an occasional small, steam engine river tug lying on the shores, a vestige of the time when Fort Simpson was an important stopping point for river barges that loaded up with food, fuel, and furs for their voyages up and down the Mackenzie. The town has great potential for agriculture, and for many years church missions grew their own potatoes and grains and raised cattle here. Th federal government established an experimental farm in Fort Simpson but closed it in 1969; once the highway was built, it cost less to import all the food needed from outside.

NAHANNI NATIONAL PARK This reserve is a long, skinny piece of land designed to protect the ecology of the Nahanni River. The river flows past natural hot springs, hills of soft calcium, canyons twice as deep as the Grand Canyon, and other features so unusual that the *UN* has designated the park a World Heritage Site. At 300 feet, the river's Virginia Falls is twice the height of Niagara.

Legends about the area tell of a lost tribe of native people (Nahanni means "the people over there"), tropical valleys, and sightings of Sasquatch, the legendary Bigfoot. The tales arose from prospectors traveling up the Liard River on their way to the Klondike gold rush in the Yukon. In 1904, three McLeod brothers entered the Nahanni Valley looking for gold. Rumor has it that they found gold nuggets the size of grapes. The following year, two of the brothers returned to the valley and disappeared. Three years later, their headless bodies were found, giving the name to Headless Valley, where they had their cabin. Their fate remains a mystery, but legends—of cabins mysteriously burning and of murders—persist. Others have gone in search of the McLeod brothers' mother lode, but no one has found it. One man, Albert Faille, spent his life looking, making more than 30 trips into the valley. The portage route around Virginia Falls is the one he cut on his travels.

In *Nahanni National Park,* visitors can look for orchids growing around the falls, take a dip in sulfur hot springs, hike the trails into the mountains, or stalk wildlife with a camera. Dall sheep can be seen on the mountain-sides, moose and bears in the valley, and woodland caribou in the upper valleys.

Those planning to canoe the river must be experienced in whitewater. Register your travel plans with the national parks warden at the Fort Simpson headquarters (see below) or the Nahanni Butte warden station at the entrance to the park (no phone). The RCMP also handle a wilderness travel registration service throughout the far north. If you're heading into the bush, tell them where you're going and when you expect to return. If something happens, help will be on the way once you're reported overdue. For information on outfitters offering canoeing and rafting trips on the Nahanni River, see *Canoeing and Rafting* in DIVERSIONS.

The park is open daily year-round; no admission charge. For further information, contact *Nahanni National Park* (Bag 300, Fort Simpson, NWT X0E 0N0; phone: 403-695-3151).

BEST EN ROUTE

Due to the scarcity of accommodations in the Northwest Territories, reservations should be made as far in advance as possible. In Fort Simpson, whose hostelries follow, expect to pay $75 or more per night for a double with private bath; accommodations at campgrounds are considerably less expensive (from $10 to $20 for two persons per night). For information on accommodations, campsites, and outfitters in *Nahanni National Park,* contact the park via the address or phone above.

Lindberg Landing This two-bedroom log house and rustic cabin will accommodate 14. On the main street (phone: mobile operator JR3-6644).

Maroda A 15-room motel with TV sets and kitchenettes, it also has a gift shop. On the main street (phone: 403-695-2602; fax: 403-695-2273).

Nahanni Inn In this hotel are 70 rooms with cable TV and telephones; four suites have kitchens. A restaurant and cocktail lounge are on the premises. Overlooking the Mackenzie and Liard Rivers, the property is on the main street (phone: 403-695-2201/2/3/4; fax: 403-695-3000).

Dawson City to Inuvik

The Dempster, one of the newest NWT highways, snakes 475 miles (760 km) from the rolling hills around historic Dawson City, Yukon, to above the Arctic Circle. The road ends at Inuvik, NWT, on the eastern edge of the majestic Mackenzie River delta, so it is necessary to drive on the same route to return. Named after a Royal Canadian Mounted Police corporal who found the ill-fated Dawson patrol (see *Fort McPherson,* below), the highway is the only public access road reaching this far north in North America.

Since the Dempster Highway is in such a remote area, facilities are scarce. Only two places between Dawson and Inuvik offer accommodations, but there are plenty of campsites.

The drive takes you to the top of the world, from the forested slopes of the Yukon, across the Eagle Plain wintering grounds of the porcupine caribou herd, to the alpine tundra of the Richardson Mountains. There will be plenty of opportunities to observe and photograph wildlife along the route, so have your camera ready. The migration of the 150,000 head of porcupine caribou across the highway may temporarily close the road, but since this massive movement coincides with freeze-up and breakup periods, when the ferry is not in service, the highway will probably be closed anyway. The Dempster Highway is open year-round, but travelers should be well prepared for adverse driving conditions in winter. Make sure your tires are good, and always carry extra gas in the trunk. In case of breakdowns, there are garages in Dawson, Inuvik, and Fort McPherson. It's wise to have a down-filled jacket as well. During the summer, nighttime temperatures can be chilly in high altitudes and near lakes and rivers. A wide variety of food and supplies is available in both Dawson and Inuvik, and you can get the basics in Fort McPherson and Tsiigehtchic.

BEFORE YOU GO

Make sure to inquire in advance about the condition of the highway; whether the ferry is operating across the Peel and Mackenzie Rivers; and whether the gas and lodge facilities at Eagle Plains are open (phone: 403-979-2678; 800-661-0752 in Canada).

En Route from Dawson City Drive east on Route 3 to its intersection with Route 11, then turn north. There is a gas station at this junction; the next gas available beyond the Ogilvie River is at Eagle Plains, 256 miles (412 km) from Dawson.

The *Tombstone Campgrounds* (no phone), a government-run operation on a ridge above the Klondike River 45 miles (72 km) north of the junction of Routes 3 and 11, offers minimal conveniences. Another 78 miles (125 km) through rolling, forested hills takes you to yet another government campsite on the Ogilvie River (named for the Yukon commissioner at the time of the gold rush). Farther along the way is the *Eagle Plains* hotel (phone: 403-979-4187). Caribou stragglers are sometimes visible on the Eagle Plains; the porcupine caribou herd migrates from the North Slope of Alaska into the Yukon interior. As you near the NWT border and the Richardson Mountains, you might see Dall sheep. In June, snowbanks will still line the sides of the road. Once you hit the NWT-Yukon border, the cable-operated ferry across the Peel River to Fort McPherson is only 47 miles (75 km) away.

FORT MCPHERSON This is a settlement of about 700 Gwich'in people, a tribe of the Dene, on the Peel River. The Gwich'in rely on hunting, trapping, and government work for survival. The area is rich in mink, muskrat, lynx, and beaver. The present site, established in 1840 by Alex Isbister and John Bell, Northwest Company fur traders, was originally named Fort Bell. Later its name was changed to honor Murdoch McPherson, chief trader for the Hudson's Bay Company. The RCMP established this as one of their main patrol posts in the early 1900s.

In the winter of 1910–11, Inspector F. J. Fitzgerald of the RCMP attempted a patrol from McPherson to Dawson with three companions. Lacking competent guides, the patrol lost its way in heavy snows, missing a crucial turn that would have led to a pass. Hopelessly lost, they turned back; two members made it as far as 20 miles from home before they perished. The bodies were found by Corporal W. D. Dempster. Fort Fitzgerald, formerly Smith's Landing (south of Fort Smith), was renamed to honor the inspector. For provisions, stop at the *Tetlit Co-op* in town (phone: 403-952-2417; fax: 403-952-2602).

En Route from Fort McPherson Tsiigehtchic lies just east of Fort McPherson, and between the two communities are two picnic areas that afford excellent views of the river rapids. Both are great spots for whitefish and grayling.

As you approach the ferry crossing at Tsiigehtchic, you'll come to a ridge with a splendid view of the Arctic Red River pouring into the MacKenzie River. Unbelievably, swans nest in this area.

TSIIGEHTCHIC This is a traditional fishing camp for the Gwich'in, who catch their winter supply of northern pike and whitefish for themselves and their dogs here; you can see fish drying on racks around the town. The settlement gained some permanence when Father Jean Seguin, of the Oblate of Mary Immaculate (OMI), established a Roman Catholic mission here in 1868. Eventually, Hudson's Bay set up a trading post here. Only three families lived at the camp 40 years ago; now the population numbers about a hundred.

En Route from Tsiigehtchic A government-run ferry takes passengers (and their cars) across the mile-wide Mackenzie River. The highway then continues parallel to the mighty river. Along the 84-mile (134-km) stretch to the next territorial campground, *Chuk Park,* which has all the basic conveniences, are four sites for picnics, fishing, shutterbugging, and relaxing. To view the scenery along the highway, most travelers just pull off on the shoulder of the road. Inuvik is 80 miles (128 km) from Tsiigehtchic.

INUVIK This Inuvialuit word means "place of man" (the Inuvialuit are the Delta and Western Arctic Inuit). Located in the Mackenzie delta, this is a modern town by far north standards. It officially opened in 1958 as a replacement community for Aklavik, 36 miles (58 km) away on the western side of the delta. Government engineers thought Aklavik would be swept into the Mackenzie because of the constant erosion of the riverbanks. However, Aklavik's motto is "The Town That Wouldn't Die," so few moved to the new center, despite promises of better services and housing. Aklavik is still alive and well, but all government offices relocated to the new site. Still mainly a government town (pop. 3,200), Inuvik enjoyed a boom period when companies were drilling into the delta to find oil and gas reserves. Most of the petroleum exploration now is in the Beaufort Sea, centered out of Tuktoyaktuk (more commonly known as Tuk), 70 miles (112 km) north, a modern town with most conveniences.

Inuvik offers a good example of how people adapt to a frigid environment. Until the late 1970s, when the main street was paved, wooden boardwalks protected one's boots from the thick, springtime mud. Vestiges of these sidewalks can still be found in some areas of town. Buildings are built on piles driven into the permafrost—ground permanently frozen to depths of 300 feet. If they were built aboveground, heat from the building would melt the permafrost, causing the ground to settle and the building to sink. It's impossible to bury sewer and water lines for the same reason. Digging through permafrost is like digging through rock, and if the lines were buried, they would have to be heated to prevent them from freezing. Instead, service lines are laid on top of the ground in utilidors, insulated corridors connecting buildings.

Permafrost has some advantages. The town's hunters and trappers association, for example, tunneled into a ridge to make a community freezer. Thirty feet underground, meat stays frozen no matter how hot the summer. Summer temperatures may reach the high 80s F (30s C); the summer mean is in the 50s F (10C to 20C).

The Inuvik branch of *Northern Images* (115 Mackenzie Rd.; phone: 403-979-2786; fax: 403-979-4430) is housed in an octagonal building, where you can purchase soapstone carvings by internationally recognized Inuit carvers; silk screens and soapstone lithographs from Holman Island and Sachs Harbour, 400 air miles to the northeast; and wolf, muskrat, coyote, and Inuvik duffel parkas and coats made in the shops of Tuk and Aklavik. Inquire at *Northern Images* about seeing native craftspeople at work.

Boats and guides are available for fishing the twisting channels of the resource-rich Mackenzie delta. The fishing is splendid in nearby lakes, accessible by chartering a small plane. Inuvik's *Happy Valley Campground* is a good choice if you'd like to pitch your tent where there are views of the lakes and channels.

Inuvik is the transportation center for the delta and western Arctic region, providing regularly scheduled flights to such centers as Sachs Harbour, Holman Island, Tuktoyaktuk, Aklavik, and Fort McPherson. Each of these has accommodations for those who'd like to spend a day or two watching how the Inuvialuit live off the land, sealing, whaling, and hunting.

BEST EN ROUTE

Due to the scarcity of accommodations in the Northwest Territories, it is necessary to make reservations as far in advance as possible. In Inuvik, expect to pay $100 or more per night for a double room with bath in the places listed below.

Eskimo Inn A downtown establishment, it has 78 rooms and a wide range of services, including a café, lounge, and dining room. Mackenzie Rd. (phone: 403-979-2801; fax: 403-979-3234).

Finto This 51-room motel with a restaurant is on the edge of town. Mackenzie Rd. (phone: 403-979-2647; fax: 403-979-3442).

Mackenzie This hostelry has 33 rooms, two lounges, a coffee shop, a large dining room with a fireplace, and a 150-seat nightclub. Mackenzie Rd. (phone: 403-979-2861; fax 403-979-3317).

Nova Scotia

Nova Scotia is a province of two parts: The peninsula of Nova Scotia is connected to the mainland by a narrow isthmus over the Bay of Fundy; Cape Breton Island, the northern extreme of the province, is linked to the rest of the peninsula by a mile-long causeway. The Atlantic Ocean pounds the long eastern shore of this Maritime Province, while the Bay of Fundy and Gulf of St. Lawrence lie to the west. From its southern tip in the Bay of Fundy to the northern St. Lawrence Gulf coast, the province encompasses 21,425 square miles of fishing villages, farms, ferry towns, and cities with excellent harbors.

Nova Scotia is a mosaic of half a dozen cultural influences, beginning with its pre-European forbears, the Micmac. The French and the English struggled for decades to control the land that some 18th-century wags called "Nova Scarcity." During the 1600s, settlement by both countries was sporadic; but in 1720, when the French built their strategic *Fortress Louisbourg* on Cape Breton Island, the tussle over Nova Scotia began in earnest. Twenty-five years later, a band of New Englanders captured the fort. Rather than rejoice, Britain handed it back to France in return for France's aid in opposing the claim to the British throne of Scotland's Bonnie Prince Charlie. Enraged, the New Englanders demanded an English base in Nova Scotia, and the result was Halifax. As Britain's control over the peninsula tightened, they expelled the French-speaking Acadians and destroyed *Fortress Louisbourg.* These moves helped to steer the rest of Canada into the arms of the British Empire.

Other groups soon arrived in Nova Scotia: Germans settled on the Atlantic shore, southwest of Halifax, turning Lunenburg into a thriving port; waves of Loyalists rushed in after the American Revolution; shiploads of Irish came, seeking relief from the potato famines of the 1840s; Scots, displaced by the Highland Clearances, landed at Pictou County on the northwestern shore and at Cape Breton with its Highland-like glens; and blacks settled near Halifax after the War of 1812.

Halifax is the capital of Nova Scotia and the commercial, administrative, and military center of the four Maritime Provinces. (For a complete report on *Halifax,* see THE CITIES.) Halifax and Dartmouth, soon to be incorporated—along with the town of Bedford and surrounding Halifax County—as one sprawling municipality, face one another across Halifax Harbour midway along Nova Scotia's long Atlantic Coast. Although these are the province's largest urban centers, many people start their tours of the area from Yarmouth, on the southwestern coast where the Atlantic and the Bay of Fundy meet. This is the docking point of ferries from both Portland and Bar Harbor, Maine. We have divided the province into three routes: from Yarmouth along the Bay of Fundy to Amherst, through Acadian country;

from Yarmouth south and east along the Atlantic shore to the Strait of Canso, through the Atlantic Coast uplands and a series of fascinating fishing villages; and from Amherst east across the Strait of Canso through Cape Breton Island, including a stop at the restored *Fortress Louisbourg* and a drive along the beautiful Cabot Trail. This last route goes through an area settled by Scots and so filled with lochs and glens that it is almost a miniature Scotland.

Nova Scotia Check-In (1800 Argyle St., Suite 515, Halifax, NS B3J 3N8; phone: 902-425-5781; 800-565-0000 in Canada; 800-565-6096 in the US; fax: 902-420-1286), a government agency, provides information on more than 700 properties throughout the province, including hotels, inns, resorts, campgrounds, and bed and breakfast establishments; it also has details on car rentals. In addition, the agency will make guaranteed reservations and supply weather forecasts and other useful information.

If the idea of touring the province by bicycle appeals to you, *Freewheeling Bicycle Adventures* (RR 1, Boutiliers Point, NS B0J 1G0; phone: 902-857-3600; fax: 902-857-3612) can help arrange a trip. The company organizes treks through Nova Scotia and arranges accommodations in local hostelries. The booklet *Bicycle Tours in Nova Scotia* includes 20 popular routes and other useful information; write to the Touring Chairman, *Bicycle Nova Scotia* (PO Box 3010 South, Halifax, NS B3J 3G6).

For more information, contact *Nova Scotia Tourism* (136 Commercial St., Portland, ME 04101; phone: 207-772-6131) or the *Tourism Division, Nova Scotia Economic Renewal Agency* (PO Box 549, 1800 Argyle St., Halifax, NS B3J 2RT; phone: 902-424-5000; fax: 902-424-2668).

Yarmouth to Amherst

The 324-mile (518-km) drive from Yarmouth to Amherst is a ramble through French Nova Scotia along the stunning coastline forged by the powerful tide of the Bay of Fundy. It passes through Acadian villages where the locals still speak the dialect imported by the region's first French settlers. Crossing Annapolis Valley, it skirts the province's most prosperous farmlands. Near the end of the route is tragic Springhill, where a 1958 mining disaster claimed over 70 lives.

The route virtually traces the province's history. Here, visitors can walk through the first settlements established in the early 1600s; view the battlegrounds where the French and the English vied for new lands; and remember Longfellow's star-crossed lovers, Evangeline and Gabriel, whose story commemorates the fate of the Acadians.

Along the route, rocky, wind-blown fishing villages give way to thriving agricultural communities. The 170-mile (272-km) Bay of Fundy, always nearby on the left, gradually narrows and becomes shallower. This results in the world's highest tides at the bay's eastern end, the Minas Basin. Generations of Nova Scotians have watched these tides with fascination, some dreaming of the day when that enormous power might be harnessed to provide inexpensive energy for industry.

Although the roads along the Bay of Fundy are sometimes narrow and winding, they are generally good. This trip most often follows Routes 1 and 2, the Evangeline Trail and the Glooscap Trail, signposted routes set up by the *Tourism Division.* The journey's numerous gastronomic attractions include fish and other Acadian dishes in French Nova Scotia and, a bit farther on, abundant seasonal produce from roadside stands in the Annapolis Valley. There also are countless opportunities to pull over and watch the fishing boats in the weirs, see the gulls diving, or simply enjoy the cool bay breeze.

To get to Yarmouth, take a ferry from either Portland or Bar Harbor, Maine; some transport cars and have overnight berth accommodations. For reservations on the MV *Bluenose,* which departs from Bar Harbor, contact *Marine Atlantic* (PO Box 250, North Sydney, NS B2A 3M3; phone: 902-794-5700; 800-341-7981 in the US). The ferry runs daily from mid-June to mid-September, two or three times weekly the rest of the year. The ferry from Portland, the MS *Scotia Prince* (phone: 800-482-0955 in Maine; 800-341-7540 in Canada and elsewhere in the US), includes such cruise features as duty-free shopping, a casino, a formal dining room, and a nightclub with live entertainment. Reservations on both ferries are subject to cancellation if tickets are not picked up one hour before sailing. Additionally, *Air Canada* offers direct flights to Yarmouth from Boston.

At Yarmouth, arrange for membership in the *Order of the Good Cheer,* North America's oldest social club. Samuel de Champlain, the great explorer and historian, formed the group more than 375 years ago in an attempt to cheer up his men in the face of the loneliness, disease, and harsh weather of the New World. Today, it is open to all those who visit Nova Scotia for at least three days. There are no initiation fees or dues, and members of the order never meet formally. They are, however, required to have a good time, remember Nova Scotia pleasantly, speak kindly of the province, and come back again. Visitors, most of whom have no trouble fulfilling these requirements, can join the club at the *Nova Scotia Government Tourist Bureau* at the ferry dock.

YARMOUTH This attractive town's narrow, lighthouse-guarded harbor serves as a haven for ferries and herring seiners. (The latter are boats named for seines, the large, weighted nets used by fishermen.) These craft can be seen coming and going in the harbor or docked below Main Street. Yarmouth (pop. 7,780) is the largest seaport in the province west of Halifax and a transportation and commercial center for much of western Nova Scotia. Its downtown features much original 19th-century architecture. Also noteworthy is the *Fire Fighters Museum of Nova Scotia* (451 Main St.; phone: 902-742-5525), with some fire-fighting equipment over a hundred years old.

Open daily July and August; closed Sundays June and September; closed weekends the rest of the year; admission charge. At the *Yarmouth County Historical Society Museum* (22 Collins St.; phone: 902-742-5539), a runic stone linked to the Norse explorations of AD 1000 is on display. This relic is cited as evidence that Europeans came to North America long before Columbus. Closed Sunday mornings from June to mid-October; closed mornings, Mondays, and some Sundays the rest of the year; admission charge.

Yarmouth has some fine seafood restaurants. *Harris' Quick 'n' Tasty* (Rte. 1 in Dayton, 3 miles/5 km north of Yarmouth; phone: 902-742-3467) also serves chicken and beef dishes. It's closed December 15 through February.

En Route from Yarmouth Travel along Route 1 through the Hebron area's "lupine trail." In June, a blanket of white, pink, and blue flowers is spread along the road. You might see oxen as you pass by Port Maitland. Here, just over 4 miles (6 km) east of Route 1, the Lake George fish hatchery annually releases millions of trout and salmon into the lakes and streams of western Nova Scotia. Thousands of black-backed gulls nest on the islands in Lake George. Crossing into the municipality of Clare (actually a collection of 27 small villages), you enter the district settled by Acadians, the early French settlers who named Nova Scotia "Acadie." They were expelled from the province in 1755 by the British, though later many returned. In fact, 335 Acadian families are said to have walked from Boston to Digby in 1768. In Clare the residents still speak French, but expect neither a Parisian nor a Quebecois accent. Just as the language has been preserved, so have the culture and traditions. Even the smallest community along the "French shore" is dominated by a large Catholic church.

Following Route 1, consider a side trip to North and South Bear Coves, where cliffs meet the ocean. After returning to Route 1, you soon reach *Clare Park* at Smuggler's Cove. During Prohibition, when liquor was shipped illegally to the US, the maze of coves here provided rumrunners with hideaways. Their lair can be found at the bottom of the footpath leading down to the picnic area. Continue to Meteghan, 35 miles (56 km) north of Yarmouth.

METEGHAN This small town (pop. 900) is typical of the area's coastal communities. It was settled in 1785 by the Acadians; the *Vieille Maison,* one of its oldest homes, has been preserved as a museum. Acadian guides in traditional costume give tours in English daily in July and August; closed the rest of the year; admission charge (phone: 902-645-2599). Meteghan's skilled shipbuilders gained international recognition in 1966, when they built a three-quarter-size replica of Donald McKay's famous American clipper ship *Flying Cloud.*

En Route from Meteghan Continue north on Route 1 to Church Point.

CHURCH POINT In this tiny village is the tallest wooden church in North America. Adjacent to the campus of *Université Ste-Anne,* it and its small museum are open daily with bilingual guides July to mid-October; by appointment only the rest of the year; no admission charge (phone: 902-769-2832). The province's only French degree-granting institution, the university was founded in 1891 by Eudist (the Congregation of Jesus and Mary) priests from France and has traditionally attracted local students and those of Acadian descent. The *Acadian Festival of Clare,* usually held here in the second week of July, features local crafts, music, and French Canadian specialties such as *rappie* pie (grated potatoes and chicken or rabbit baked in a crust). The celebration is the oldest Acadian festival in the Maritime Provinces.

En Route from Church Point Less than a mile from Church Point is Grosses Coques, meaning "large clams." It's said that the clams in this district are the largest on the North American coast. Reportedly, they were so plentiful that the first settlers lived on them throughout their first winter. A stone memorial commemorates the site of their first chapel, built in 1769, and a tablet marks the site of the first frame house in the multiple village township of Clare. A 1½-mile drive to the left of Grosses Coques Bridge is Major's Point and a long, blue slate beach. The site of the first Acadian cemetery, this driftwood-studded expanse is thick with clams; it also is a great spot for bird watching. St. Bernard is a few miles north on Route 1.

ST. BERNARD Even though its population is only about 320, St. Bernard supports a large stone cathedral with a seating capacity of a thousand. Construction of the church, built with all local materials and labor, was started in 1910 and finished in 1942.

En Route from St. Bernard Leaving St. Bernard, look for the road to the left leading to New Edinburgh, about 2 miles (3 km) away. A loop will return you to Route 1, but along the way are beautiful views of the seashore and countryside. Traces of the first town site in New Edinburgh, settled by three Scottish Loyalists in 1783, still remain. Continue along Route 1 (which becomes Route 101 in several miles) to Weymouth.

WEYMOUTH Settled by Loyalists in 1783, this town (pop. 380) was named after Weymouth, Massachusetts. Colonel Moodie of North Carolina, a famous Loyalist, settled in this district and wrote an interesting diary of his experiences in the American Revolution. Weymouth is situated on St. Mary's Bay at the mouth of the Sissiboo River (a native name meaning "big river"), where trading schooners once loaded. The town's stores are built on logs to allow the river's tides to pass underneath, and periodically the first floors of the stores flood.

En Route from Weymouth Five miles (8 km) northeast of Weymouth is Plympton, with an interesting variety of antiques and crafts shops. Just past

Plympton is *Savary Park,* a picnic site with a fine tide-pool beach and large groves of white birch and evergreen trees.

Five miles (8 km) farther east is Marshalltown, the former home of the late Maud Lewis, a painter of primitives that won her international acclaim. Her work may be seen at the *Folk Art Building* in *Upper Clements Family Vacation Park* (4 miles/6 km west of Annapolis Royal on Rte. 1; phone: 800-565-PARK in Canada) as well as at the *Art Gallery of Nova Scotia* in Halifax (see *Halifax* in THE CITIES). To the right off Route 101 is Acaciaville (pop. 141), whose hills command fine views of Digby on the east and the Bay of Fundy on the west. Continue on Route 101 for a few miles to Digby.

DIGBY Like Yarmouth, Digby is a ferry town, served by *Marine Atlantic*'s MV *Princess of Acadia* (phone: 902-245-2116), which carries cars and passengers to and from Saint John, New Brunswick, three times a day. Digby was named for Robert Digby, a British admiral who commanded the HMS *Atlanta,* the ship that brought 1,500 Loyalists from New England in 1783. One of Nova Scotia's more popular summer resorts, it offers horseback riding, canoeing, and swimming, and it's a good base for deep-sea fishing and whale watching excursions. Climb to the top of the hill by the high school for a beautiful view of Annapolis Basin, then perhaps stop in for a meal at the *Pines* resort (see *Best en Route*). Digby also is the center of a highly profitable scallop fishery, and in August the town celebrates *Digby Scallop Days.* For details, check with the *Municipal Visitor and Information Centre* (95 Montague Row; phone: 902-245-5714); it's closed mid-October through May; open daily the rest of the year (to 8 PM mid-June to mid-October). Also try the *Nova Scotia Visitor Information Centre* (at the ferry terminal on Shore Rd.; phone: 902-245-2201); it's closed mid-October through April; open daily the rest of the year (until 8:30 PM mid-June to mid-October).

For a scenic side trip from Digby, follow the spit of land known as Digby Neck south to its end at Brier Island. The trip, on Route 217, includes two short ferry rides and covers a distance of about 86 miles (138 km). Depending on how often the ferries run, it could take as long as seven hours.

Heading out on Digby Neck, you'll pass a number of sheep farms. Make a right turn downhill toward the Bay of Fundy into Centreville, one of the province's prettiest fishing villages. Several beautiful old churches dot the road. Just past Centreville is a picnic area at Lake Medway, also a good spot for a swim. The lake, which is stocked with trout, is usually 15 to 20 degrees warmer than the numbingly cold Bay of Fundy. Sandy Cove, 4 miles (6 km) farther down the road, is at the bottom of a big hill.

SANDY COVE Leaving Route 217, take the road to the right and follow its meandering path to the long sandy beach on the Bay of Fundy side, which affords visitors a good view of weir fishing, common only in the Bay of Fundy area. The weirs are long, thin trees driven into the seabed and lined with fishnets. Stretching out from the shore in a straight line, they form a semicircle at the end, where fish are trapped after following the straight section. If you are lucky, you might see fishermen entering a weir with their boats to scoop up the fish. For good seafood and homemade bread in a dignified setting, try the *Olde Village Inn* (Old Post Rd.; phone: 902-834-2202), a restored 1890s inn. Picnic baskets are available, and all types of outdoor activities—including whale watching—can be arranged.

Continue on Route 217 past Mink Cove and Little River, two prosperous fishing villages. Mink Cove is well known for its amethyst and quartz, often sought by rock hounds. The next village is East Ferry, where travelers (and their cars) can board the *Joshua Slocum* ferry for the 10-minute trip to Tiverton on Long Island, the island separating the mainland from Brier Island. From Tiverton, it's 10 miles (16 km) across the island to Freeport, whence a second ferry goes to Brier Island.

BRIER ISLAND This was the home of Joshua Slocum, who in July 1895 bade goodbye to his mother and set off to become the first person to circumnavigate the earth single-handedly. He accomplished the feat in his 37-foot sloop, *Spray,* which he had built himself. Slocum completed his journey in three years, finally arriving at Gloucester, Massachusetts. A plaque on the southern end of Brier Island memorializes the solitary navigator. From here, follow the short walking trail along the cliffs, with the waves crashing below. The island is a popular spot for bird and whale watchers.

Most visitors also take some time to wander about Westport, the small community where the ferry docks. Bird watchers will be impressed with the many species of both land birds and seabirds that visit the area during migration periods. For advice on the province's best birding spots, contact the *Nova Scotia Bird Society* through the *Nova Scotia Museum of Natural History* in Halifax (phone: 902-424-7353).

Before heading back to Digby on the ferry, you may want a snack from the take-out counter by the ferry wharf, which features fish and chips—the fish, naturally, are fresh out of the water.

En Route from Digby Heading east on Route 101, consider stopping at Smith's Cove for a visit to *St. Anne's Birchbark Chapel* on the grounds of the *Harbourview Country Inn* (phone: 902-245-5686), off Route 101. Over 60 years old, the chapel was built by a local craftsman in honor of an Anglican bishop who was a longtime summer visitor.

The better restaurants on this leg of the journey are all located off Route 101 (Exits 24 and 25) at Smith's Cove. *The Harbourview Country Inn* (see above) offers fresh seafood and homemade bread in a casual, turn-of-the-century setting; it's closed October through May, and reservations are advised. *Hedley House* (phone: 902-245-2585), on the grounds of the *Hedley House* motel, serves fresh fish and vegetables; the atmosphere is on the formal side. The restaurant is closed October 20 through April. The *Mountain Gap* resort (phone: 902-245-5841; 800-565-5020; fax: 902-245-2277) also prepares good meals (especially seafood); it's closed October 15 to May 11, and reservations are advised. A few miles past Smith's Cove, take Exit 24 off Route 101 south to the town of Bear River.

BEAR RIVER Known as the Switzerland of Nova Scotia, Bear River is especially beautiful during the annual *Cherry Carnival* in July. The river itself fronts a charming street lined with century-old shops, each built on stilts as a precaution against floods. A few miles outside of town, a full-scale Dutch windmill affords a pleasant view of the river and a tearoom from which to enjoy it.

En Route from Bear River Head back north to Deep Brook, where Route 1 continues east to Clementsport, a community settled by Loyalists in 1784. Many of its homes were once occupied by sea captains. The old Loyalist *Church of St. Edward,* consecrated in 1788, is now an interesting museum. Its hours vary; check with the *Anglican Parish of Clements* (phone: 902-638-8147). There's no admission charge to the museum. A few miles down the road is Annapolis Royal, site of the *Fort Anne National Historic Park.*

FORT ANNE NATIONAL HISTORIC PARK This 28-acre site was Canada's first national historic park. Charles de Menou d'Aulnay established a settlement here in 1635, calling it Port Royal after an earlier French colony in the area that was destroyed by the English (see below). A section of the settlement's first fortress is still maintained. Since its construction, the fort has been the object of attacks by the English, the French, New Englanders, native people, and even pirates.

In 1690, brigands burned the church here and destroyed 28 homes, immolating a mother and her children in one building. During the winter of 1709, after three attacks by New Englanders had been repulsed in the previous five years, three privateers sheltered at Port Royal. They had with them 55 Boston ships that they had seized during the summer. Stung by this latest outrage, the New Englanders launched another expedition in 1710, and in eight days the fort was taken from the French and the settlement was renamed Annapolis Royal after Queen Anne. The key to the fort was carried to Boston (it was returned in 1922 and placed in the *Fort Anne Museum*). After its capture in 1710, the fort was attacked many more times, and England maintained a garrison of soldiers here until 1854.

The complex has been preserved pretty much as it was then. The British officers' quarters, erected by the Duke of Kent, father of Queen Victoria, originally comprised 30 rooms, each with a fireplace and a view of the fort and Annapolis Basin. Now the officers' quarters are a museum, featuring an Acadian room with its original wall beams and ceiling, a complete collection of Acadian kitchen utensils and clothing, and a historic library. *Fort Anne* is open daily mid-May to mid-October; closed weekends the rest of the year; no admission charge (phone: 902-532-2898).

En Route from Fort Anne National Historic Park Two miles (3 km) from Annapolis Royal, turn left for the 7-mile (11-km) drive to *Port Royal National Historic Park.*

PORT ROYAL NATIONAL HISTORIC PARK The tiny village of Port Royal is the oldest permanent white settlement north of Florida in North America. An exact replica of the original *Port Royal Habitation* that Samuel de Champlain and Pierre du Gua de Monts built in 1605 is on the original site. The building's timber framing was mortised, tenoned, and pinned together in the old manner, with no spikes or nails. It was here that Champlain founded the *Order of the Good Cheer.* The park is open daily, but the buildings are closed Sunday mornings and October 15 to May 15; admission charge (phone: 902-532-2898).

En Route from Port Royal Back on Route 1, continue 30 miles (48 km) east to Bridgetown, traveling into the Annapolis Valley, framed by the North and South Mountains. Proceeding farther into the valley, you'll probably feel an increase in the temperature, since the mountains protect the area from the winds and fog off the Bay of Fundy. Thanks to this clement weather, the valley is famous for its produce, particularly apples. The region is probably most beautiful at apple blossom time, in late May or early June. A pleasant dairy and fruit farming community, Bridgetown (pop. 1,037) is at the head of the Annapolis River. Paradise, at the junction of the Paradise and Annapolis Rivers, marked the eastern limit of French settlements in the Port Royal region. Near Paradise is the *Eden Golf and Country Club* (phone: 902-665-4257); non-members are welcome at its nine-hole course. As you explore the area, keep an eye open for signs of fairs and church suppers, known for their terrific home-cooked food. Continue a few miles east on Route 1 to Lawrencetown.

LAWRENCETOWN This is the regional headquarters for sport fishing and hunting. Signs in town direct visitors to spots where guides with canoes can be hired. The town also has a land surveying and photogrammetry (surveying using aerial photography) school, the only such institution in the country. A five-day *Annapolis County Agricultural Exhibition* is held here in August.

En Route from Lawrencetown The next main community along the way is Middleton, so named because it is about halfway between Annapolis Royal and Kentville (61 miles/98 km east of Annapolis Royal). Five miles (8 km) off the road from Middleton, at Mt. Hanly, is a scenic view of the Annapolis Valley. From here the road passes into Kings County, the province's best farmland. In addition to apples, plums, pears, and cherries, the area supports a substantial dairy industry. Along the rivers flowing into the Minas Basin, great stretches of diked marshes yield root crops, grain, and hay. Kingston, a key agricultural service area, hosts the province's largest steer barbecue on the second Saturday in July. The 18-hole *Paragon* golf course (phone: 902-765-2554) also is in Kingston. Canada's largest antisubmarine air base is located at Greenwood, just off Route 1; the military community (pop. 9,000) has its own schools, churches, and recreational facilities. Kentville is about 25 miles (40 km) from Kingston.

KENTVILLE This village of Kings County is the home of the *Apple Blossom Festival,* held in late May or early June. The *Old Kings Courthouse Heritage Museum* (37 Cornwallis St.; phone: 902-678-6237) houses materials related to the county's social and natural history, as well as the genealogical records of the *Kings Historical Society.* It's closed weekends (Sundays only in July and August); no admission charge. *Memorial Park* has tennis courts, baseball diamonds, and a public pool.

En Route from Kentville On the way to Wolfville, 9 miles (14 km) east of Kentville, photographers and hikers can take a lovely side trip. Route 358 winds through several attractive communities before coming to The Lookoff, a spot that offers a spectacular view of Minas Basin, the valleys of six rivers, and parts of five counties. Explore Scots Bay farther down the road, with low cliffs and a broad rocky beach where agates and other stones continually come ashore, particularly in spring and early summer. From the end of the road, a hiking trail leads to Cape Split, one of the best walks in the province. Much of the trail is inland, but it emerges at the tip of the cape and ends with a breathtaking panorama from 150-foot cliffs.

WOLFVILLE At the center of the Acadian land Henry Wadsworth Longfellow immortalized in "Evangeline," this town also is the home of *Acadia University,* founded by the *Nova Scotia Baptist Education Society* in 1838. The closest town to Grand Pré, Wolfville is a convenient base for explorations in this historic area. Nearby Evangeline Beach offers saltwater bathing that is almost warm.

GRAND PRÉ The name Grand Pré means "great meadow," but the community is better known as the site of one of the oldest French settlements in the province and the setting for Longfellow's poem "Evangeline." Between 1755 and 1763, nearly 14,000 Acadians were forced from their homes by the British, who believed that the Acadians would challenge their military authority. Following the subsequent peace, many of the exiled Acadians returned to Nova Scotia, but most of the current residents of Grand Pré are descendants of New Englanders. *Grand Pré National Historic Site,* a memorial to the deported Acadians, features a statue of Evangeline and a reconstructed Acadian church that now serves as both a museum and an interpretative center. Although the park is open daily, its buildings are closed to the public mid-October to mid-May; no admission charge (phone: 902-542-3631).

Worth a visit, too, is the *Church of the Covenanters* (off Rte. 1, at the intersection for Grand Pré, on a hill across from the *Irving* gas station), constructed by New England planters in 1790, with quaint box pews and a pulpit halfway to the ceiling. In addition, visitors can tour the estate vineyards of *Grand Pré Wines* (Exit 10 off Rte. 101; phone: 902-542-1753) by appointment daily except Sundays; no admission charge.

Continuing on, the road soon reaches Hants County, where agricultural land gives way to an area of lumbering and light industry.

HANTSPORT Located along the Avon River, Hantsport served a large number of oceangoing clipper ships in the middle of the last century. Today it is a major shipping port for the gypsum quarried near Windsor. *Observation Lookoff* provides an excellent view of the river tides and the loading of the boats. William Hall, the first black to win the Victoria Cross for heroism, died in Hantsport. The son of an escaped Virginia slave, he was recognized for assisting in the relief of the city of Lucknow in India during the Indian Mutiny.

En Route from Hantsport Continue south for 6 miles (10 km) to Windsor.

WINDSOR Off King and Fort Edward Streets stands the oldest blockhouse in Canada, the only remaining building of *Fort Edward,* built here by the British in 1750. The fort is closed *Labour Day* to June 15; open daily the rest of the year. There's an admission charge (phone: 902-542-3631). The *Haliburton Memorial Museum* (Clifton Ave.; phone: 902-798-2915) is the former residence of Judge Thomas Charles Haliburton (1796–1865), the author and humorist who created the fictional character Sam Slick. It's closed Sunday mornings and October 15 through May; no admission charge. The *Hants County Exhibition* is held here annually in September. Started in 1765, it's believed to be the oldest fair in Canada. *King's College School,* the oldest educational institution in the British Commonwealth outside the United Kingdom, also is located here.

En Route from Windsor Take Route 1 to Three Mile Plains before turning left onto Route 14 toward Brooklyn. At Brooklyn, take Route 215 toward Summerville along the Glooscap Trail. This route parallels the drive from Grand Pré to Hantsport and Windsor on the other side of the Avon River. Like Hantsport, this area has active gypsum and barite mines and an anhydrite quarry. As you pass Tennycape, look to your left to Economy Point, on the other side of Minas Basin. The tides here have been measured at 54 feet—the highest in the world. Plans for a dam between Economy Point and Burntcoat Head to harness the power of the Bay of Fundy high tides have long been debated, but as yet nothing definite has materialized. The small town of Noel, settled by families from Northern Ireland in 1762, is farther along the shore. Local lore has it that the legendary Captain Kidd brought his pirate ship to Noel to be remasted. It's said that although he threw bars of silver to those who supplied timbers, the locals would not touch the pirate's ill-gotten gains.

The road now follows the path of the Shubenacadie River to South Maitland, where a pronounced tidal bore appears twice each day. This wall of whitewater advances over the muddy bottom, signaling the advent of another high tide. From Shubenacadie, pick up Route 2 north. Head for

Stewiacke's Provincial Wildlife Park, with a large variety of native animals and birds. It's closed October 15 to May 15; open daily the rest of the year. There's an admission charge (phone: 902-758-2040). Continue north on Route 2 for 17 miles (27 km) to Truro.

TRURO This town (pop. 11,700) is a major service community for the surrounding area. *Victoria Park,* a thousand-acre natural playground, has two picturesque waterfalls. At the *Nova Scotia Agricultural College* (Bible Hill; phone: 902-839-6671) is a demonstration farm open to visitors. It's closed weekends; visits by appointment only. There's no admission charge. In August, Truro hosts the *Nova Scotia Provincial Exhibition,* the largest attraction of its kind in the province. From June through October, visitors also can take in harness racing at Truro. The *Best Western Glengarry* has daily buffets featuring beef and seafood dishes. Equally good is the food at the *Palliser* hotel, whose dining room offers a view of the tidal bore. (For details on both hotels, see *Best en Route.*) To check on the arrival of this natural phenomenon, which rolls into the Salmon River at the rate of a foot a minute, call *Dial-a-Tide* (phone: 902-426-5494).

En Route from Truro Take Route 2 west following the Glooscap Trail through Masstown, where a number of dikes built by the Acadians still function. Farther along, there's good striped bass fishing near the mouth of the Bass River. Continuing west, Route 2 climbs Economy Mountain, whose peak commands a spectacular vista of Minas Basin, then enters the community of Five Islands (pop. 199). According to Native American tradition, the god Glooscap, in a fit of anger, hurled five pieces of land at a beaver, creating the town. Moose Island, one of the five, is supposed to be the hiding place of pirate treasure; the others are called Egg, Diamond, Pinnacle, and Long. From here Route 2 passes through a narrow gorge between two wood-covered hills, then travels to Parrsboro, 55 miles (88 km) northwest of Truro.

PARRSBORO A port town, Parrsboro is across the Minas Basin from Cape Blomidon. Weir fishing, like that done in the Bay of Fundy near Digby, is carried on here. In August, amateur geologists from across the continent gather for the annual *Rockhound Roundup.* Amethysts, agates, and other attractive minerals may be found along the shores. Follow the main street through Parrsboro; about 1 mile (1.6 km) from town, on the left, you'll see *Ottawa House,* once the summer home of Sir Charles Tupper, a native of Amherst who became Prime Minister of Canada in 1896.

At the three-way intersection near the center of Parrsboro is the *Fundy Geological Museum,* with an interesting collection of minerals, gems, and fossils. It is open daily; admission charge (phone: 902-254-3814). Outside the museum, a cairn commemorates the plane that left Parrsboro in 1919 to fly the first airmail service between Nova Scotia and the US. A giant statue of Glooscap stands nearby; by pushing a button, visitors can hear the legend of the Native American god. Check at the visitor information center (Eastern Ave.; phone: 902-254-3266) for tide times and information on a beach tour and rockhounding; it's open daily from late May through September.

From Parrsboro, take a short side trip west on Route 209 to Advocate Harbour and Spencer's Island. The winding road, rising from sea level to 750 feet, unveils a series of extraordinary vistas. At Fox River you can see the picturesque rock formation of Cape Split across Minas Channel. The high hill on the right is known as Woods Mountain. Farther along is Port Greville, which was at one time a great shipbuilding center; yachts and motorboats are still built here. Pollack, haddock, and halibut are caught along this shore, and charter boats are readily available.

SPENCER'S ISLAND This tiny community is, in fact, not an island. A ship called the *Mary Celeste* was built here in 1861. Eleven years later, on October 27, Captain Ben Briggs and 10 others, including his wife and their 10-year-old daughter, left New York for Genoa in the hundred-foot brigantine. Twenty-seven days later, the Nova Scotian brigantine *Del Gratia,* commanded by Captain Morehouse of Bear River, Digby County, came upon the *Mary Celeste,* sailing erratically. No one was found on board, and the one lifeboat was gone. Although there were no signs of violence, the compass was knocked out and ruined, and the navigation instruments had been removed. There had not been any storms, and the last entry in the log was marked for 8 AM, two days earlier. No trace of the passengers or the lifeboat was ever found. At nearby Advocate Harbour is a rock formation known as the Three Sisters; legend claims it is the spot where Glooscap's three sisters were all turned into stone. Head back to Parrsboro.

En Route from Parrsboro Rejoin Route 2 and head toward Springhill, 29 miles (46 km) east. On the way is Mapleton, the center of the local maple-sugar industry. It's said that natives of the area, while cooking potatoes in maple sap, discovered that the sticky substance becomes sweet and thick when boiled. Maple sugar and superior maple cream are sold in candy stores in the area.

SPRINGHILL This town (pop. 5,000) has a tragic history. Coal mining began here in 1872, and the town was known for having the deepest mine in the country. In 1891, however, 125 miners lost their lives, and in 1956, an explosion in the No. 4 mine killed 39. Just after *Christmas* the following year, fire destroyed half of the downtown business district, and in 1958 over 70 miners died on the job. In the two years following this disaster, 2,400 people left the town to seek employment elsewhere. And the town's run of bad fortune wasn't over: In 1975, another fire destroyed 75% of the business district. The mines have closed, but their story is detailed at the *Miner's Museum* (Black River Rd., off Rte. 2; phone: 902-597-3449), where mine tours are conducted daily from May 21 to early October; closed the rest of the year; admission charge. For a side trip on a much lighter note, stop at the *Anne Murray Centre* (Main St.; phone: 902-579-8614), exhibiting memorabilia related to the well-known singer who is Springhill's favorite daughter. It's open daily late May through October 10; by appointment only the rest of the year; admission charge.

En Route from Springhill The next town is Amherst, 22 miles (35 km) north, the inland gateway to Nova Scotia and the geographical center of the Maritime Provinces. It is built on rising ground above the famous Tantramar marshes. The *Drury Lane Steak House* (phone: 506-536-1252), in a building dating from 1780 with period decor, is 3 miles (5 km) from Amherst just across the border in New Brunswick, at the junction of Routes 2 and 16. Some claim it's one of the best restaurants in Canada.

BEST EN ROUTE

The road from Yarmouth to Amherst includes a variety of interesting accommodations, including a grand old hotel that used to be run by a railroad, an old sea captain's home, and a country lodge. We've rated places charging over $65 for a double room per night as expensive, and those from $40 to $65 as moderate. For each location, hotels are listed alphabetically by price category.

YARMOUTH

Rodd's Grand One of the most modern hostelries in town, it has 138 rooms, *The Ship's Bell* restaurant, a lounge, a pool, and a whirlpool. Some rooms offer lovely views of the harbor. 417 Main St. (phone: 902-742-2446; 800-565-RODD; fax: 902-742-4645). Expensive.

Rodd Colony Harbour Inn This place has a lovely view of Yarmouth Harbour. Its facilities include the *Colony* restaurant, with a varied menu featuring seafood dishes, plus a lounge and meeting rooms. Some of the 65 units have minibars. At the ferry terminal (phone: 902-742-9194; 800-565-RODD; fax: 902-742-6291). Moderate.

Victorian Vogue This bed and breakfast establishment has six guestrooms in a historic house built in 1896. There are two shared baths, and one room has a private bath. 109 Brunswick St. (phone: 902-742-6398). Moderate.

DIGBY

Pines By far the best-equipped establishment in the area, this is a grand old place. Originally operated by the *Canadian Pacific Railway,* it's now run by the provincial government. There are 83 rooms, 30 cottages, an excellent 18-hole golf course (see *Golf in Canada* in DIVERSIONS), tennis courts, a pool, and hiking trails. Also on the premises are a lounge with entertainment and the *Annapolis Room,* known for its fine cuisine (especially its seafood and tenderloin steaks). Box lunches and package deals are available. Closed mid-October to late May. 103 Shore Rd. (phone: 902-245-2511; 800-667-4637; fax: 902-245-6133). Expensive.

Admiral's Landing At this bed and breakfast establishment, guests have a choice of 10 rooms, three with private baths. A sun porch overlooks the harbor. No pets. 11 Montague Rd. (phone: 902-245-2247). Moderate.

SOUTH MILFORD

Milford House Close to *Kejimkujik National Park*, south of Annapolis Royal in the center of the province, this country lodge is devoted primarily to the joys of canoeing, fishing, and swimming. The main lodge has a dining room, library, and sitting room; the 27 lakeside cabins—ranging from two to five bedrooms—have fireplaces and individual docks. Tennis and golf are nearby. Closed mid-September to mid-June; two cabins with kitchen facilities are open year-round. Also see *Special Havens* in DIVERSIONS. Fourteen miles (23 km) south of Annapolis Royal via Rte. 8 (phone: 902-532-2617). Expensive.

WOLFVILLE

Blomidon Inn Formerly a sea captain's home, this is a restored 1877 property with 26 guestrooms (five of which are suites), a parlor with a fireplace and a baby grand piano, a library, two dining rooms, an outside terrace, and a tennis court. Packages are available for honeymooners, eagle watching, and wine tasting. No pets. 127 Main St. (phone: 902-562-2291; 800-565-2291; fax: 902-542-7461). Expensive.

Tattingstone Inn The 10 rooms here are distributed among a main house, cottage, and carriage house. Built in the late 1800s, the inn is a registered historic property. The pleasant features include a dining room where the rack of lamb and salmon are recommended, plus a pool, tennis court, steamroom, and music room. No smoking or pets allowed. 434 Main St. (phone: 902-542-7696; fax: 902-542-4427). Expensive.

Victoria's Historic Inn and Motel Built in 1893 by a local apple merchant, the inn has 10 guestrooms, five motel units, and three honeymoon suites, as well as a good dining room, Jacuzzi, and whirlpool bath. 416 Main St. (phone: 902-542-5744; fax: 902-542-7794). Expensive.

Old Orchard Inn Overlooking the university town of Wolfville, this inn has 110 rooms and 30 rustic chalets. There also is a restaurant, the *Acadian Room* (try the chateaubriand and seafood dishes), plus nightly entertainment, cross-country skiing, an indoor pool, saunas, tennis courts, bicycle rentals, and a children's playground. Take Exit 11 off Rte. 101, or Rte. 358 off Rte. 1 (phone: 902-542-5751; fax: 902-542-2276). Moderate.

TRURO

Palliser This resort's floodlit view of the tidal bore is its chief attraction. Facilities include 41 units and one cottage, as well as a restaurant. Breakfast is included in the rate. Closed November through April. Rte. 102 (phone: 902-893-8951; fax: 902-895-4585). Expensive.

Best Western Glengarry Spacious grounds, a restaurant with a daily lunch buffet, a coffee shop, and a heated outdoor pool are all draws at this 90-unit motel. 150 Willow St. (phone: 902-893-4311; 800-528-1234; fax: 902-893-1759). Moderate.

PARRSBORO

Sunshine Inn An 11-unit motel, it boasts a playground, fishing, boating, swimming, and a picnic area. Box lunches are available. No restaurant. Closed November through April. Rte. 2, a mile (1.6 km) north of Parrsboro (phone: 902-254-3135). Moderate.

Yarmouth to the Strait of Canso

Along the southern and eastern shores of Nova Scotia are dozens of quaint, hospitable fishing villages that have been crucial to the local economy since the province was first settled. The route also offers some very impressive scenery, but don't be surprised when the view suddenly disappears behind a bank of fog, though morning coastal fog often burns off before noon. Wraiths of mist might even create the right mood for exploring Oak Island, where the infamous Captain Kidd is thought to have hidden his treasure. (Look for the treasure if you want, but be warned that you won't be the first. Lives have been lost and fortunes spent in fruitless search.) The fog might also help you appreciate the dangers faced daily by the local fishermen.

Starting at Yarmouth, the 477-mile (763-km) route weaves along Atlantic coastal highways, then proceeds via the forested eastern shore to Cape Auld on the Strait of Canso. The area's economy is profoundly affected by its proximity to the Grand Banks fishing grounds off Canso in the Atlantic Ocean. The first part of the journey, the "lighthouse route," includes several stretches of good white-sand beach. The second part—or "marine drive"—on the other side of the Halifax-Dartmouth metropolitan area offers brooks, streams, sheltered coves, and forests. Throughout the trip, you'll notice a New England influence in the architecture, a reminder of the thousands who came here after the American Revolution because of their loyalty to England. You'll also see the cultural imprint of the province's Scottish, French, and German settlers.

YARMOUTH For details on Yarmouth, see the *Yarmouth to Amherst* route, above.

En Route from Yarmouth Take Route 3 east to Tusket, a community settled in 1785 by Dutch United Empire Loyalists from New York and New Jersey. Beyond Tusket the road through Argyle and Central Argyle passes by rugged coast and largely uninhabited countryside. Located at the head and on both sides of Pubnico Harbour are the Pubnico communities. Crossing into Shelburne County, you soon come to Shag Harbour. Here, at the top of Chapel Hill near the *United Baptist Church,* there's a splendid view of the water and Cape Sable Island. At night, five lighthouses are visible from this point. Continue on to Barrington.

BARRINGTON A number of buildings here are preserved as museums. The *Old Meeting House,* built in 1765 and used by settlers for public meetings and later as a place of worship, is now the oldest Nonconformist church in the country. Located on Route 3 just west of the bridge in Barrington, it serves today as a museum. Open daily except Sunday mornings mid-June through September; closed October through mid-May. There's no admission charge (phone: 902-637-2185). The *Old Woolen Mill* is just east of the bridge. Built in the early 1880s, it dyed and spun its own yarns from the wool of sheep raised on the neighboring headlands and islands. After the yarn was prepared, clattering looms produced bolts of twills and flannels to be used for blankets and suits. The last waterpowered woolen mill to operate in eastern Canada, it was in private use until 1962. The mill museum is closed Sundays and October through May; no admission charge (phone: 902-637-2185). Also in town you'll find the only tourist bureau in the province with a Cape Island fishing boat tied alongside (Barrington Bay; phone: 902-637-2625). It's closed mid-September through late May; open daily the rest of the year.

En Route from Barrington Take Route 330 toward Clark's Harbour, crossing over the 4,000-foot Cape Sable Island Causeway. Continue along Route 220 through Newellton to West Head, turning right to the governmen wharf. On the right, just before the wharf, the *Cape Sable Island Fisherman's Cooperative* has a salt fish processing operation and a lobster pound capable of storing 50,000 crustaceans. Visitors are invited to tour the plant; cal ahead for hours (phone: 902-745-3444).

Continue on Route 330 to Clark's Harbour, a total of 57 miles (91 km south of Yarmouth. It was in Clark's Harbour that the Cape Island boat a particularly seaworthy craft, was designed in 1907. The broad-beame wooden vessel is quite popular with fishermen because it's difficult to capsize. Continue on Route 330 past Lower Clark's Harbour and South Side On the way back to Barrington and Route 3, you'll see countless lobste traps stacked on the shore (it's open season here from November to May) Heading north on Route 3, you will see the Clyde River, which passe through the villages of Upper and Middle Clyde, hamlets that once consisted of homesteads for lumbermen. Today the homesteads are used a summer residences or hunting and fishing lodges. Just before Shelburn (about 23 miles/37 km east of Barrington) is Birchtown, first settled by a thousand blacks who came here during the Loyalist migration in 1783. At that time Birchtown was the largest free black settlement in North America.

SHELBURNE This town was founded in 1784 by a contingent of United Empire Loyalists, many of whom were members of the New York aristocracy. To a great extent it retains its original atmosphere, especially in the *Ross-Thomson House* (Charlotte La.; phone: 902-875-3141), a museum of the only extant shop from the 18th century in the province. At one time it sold such items as yard goods, rum, and china; today it displays a variety of artifacts from the Loyalist period. The rest of the house is filled with period furniture and the delicious odor of pungent spices from around the world, exactly what an enterprising and wide-ranging sea captain might have brought home to his wife. The house is closed October 15 through May; open daily the rest of the year. There's no admission charge.

Shelburne always has been associated with the sea. It was here that many of the world's great yachts were built, and here that Donald McKay, one of the greatest yacht builders, learned his trade. Appropriately, one of the oldest lighthouses in Nova Scotia, *Cape Roseway Light,* is here, on McNutt Island at the entrance to Shelburne's harbor. The island is a lovely place for summer picnics, but only sailors need apply—it's accessible only by boat.

En Route from Shelburne Continue on Route 3, also called Route 103 in this area. You'll pass through Jordan Falls, a tiny community where the novelist Zane Grey once caught a record tuna. From Jordan Falls, follow Route 3 to Lockeport, 18 miles (29 km) from Shelburne.

LOCKEPORT Founded in 1755 by settlers from Plymouth, Massachusetts, Lockeport is known for its crescent beach, more than a mile of hard sand. Near it is the *Little School Museum,* the town's first schoolhouse, built in 1845. Refurbished by the *Lockeport Garden Club,* it contains many artifacts of the time. Closed Sunday mornings and *Labour Day* through June; no admission charge (no phone).

En Route from Lockeport Proceeding east on Route 103, you soon enter Queens County and travel past Port Joli. In the winter and spring this area, with its plentiful supply of eel grass, lures large numbers of beautiful Canada geese. Shooting—in season—is allowed only when the birds fly over the hills that separate the Port Joli and Port Hebert harbors. A few miles farther is White Point Beach, a popular resort area. There's an attractive beach near the *White Point Beach Lodge* resort (see *Best en Route*), but the water is usually cold. Nearby is the nine-hole seaside course of the *Liverpool Golf and Country Club* (phone: 902-683-2485), at which non-members who pay the greens fee are welcome.

IVERPOOL Once the site of a native village, Liverpool was founded in 1760 by New Englanders of Pilgrim stock. The town has an exciting history. It was visited by Samuel de Champlain and Pierre du Gua de Monts in 1604 and was the home of the privateer Joseph Barss Jr. In the War of 1812, Barss captured more than a hundred American vessels; his home, built in 1798, is now *Lane's Privateer Inn* (27 Bristol Ave.; phone: 902-354-3456). On the grounds of *Old Fort Point,* a park located at the east end of Main Street, are monuments to the exploits of Barss and others. The *Simeon Perkins House* (Main St.; phone: 902-354-4058) was built in 1766 by this famous Nova Scotia colonel, merchant, and diarist. The Cape Cod–style home contains rare artifacts of trading, Yankee privateering, and the American Revolution. Closed Sunday mornings and October 15 through May. Perkins's diary, on display at the adjacent *Queens County Museum,* gives an account of the town between 1766 and the War of 1812; the museum is closed Sunday mornings. Admission to both the *Simeon Perkins House* and the museum is by donation.

En Route from Liverpool Follow Route 331 past Mill Village and through the delightful fishing villages of Vogler's Cove and West Dublin. Farther along the road, in a major park, you'll find Risser's Beach, one of the many excellent beaches in this area. The water's warm enough for a summer swim. The many summer homes in the region can be seen from the road as it begins to follow the LaHave River toward Bridgewater, 28 miles (45 km) from Liverpool. This river, which is noted for its good salmon fishing, is called the Rhine of Nova Scotia, both for its beauty and because the surrounding area was settled by people of German descent. The area is of particular historic interest as the scene of numerous attempts by the French to establish settlements in the 1600s.

BRIDGEWATER The *DesBrisay Museum* (Jubilee Rd.; phone: 902-543-4033) has a collection of old coins, possessions of early settlers, native artifacts, and curios from the sea. Closed Sunday mornings May 15 through September; from October through May 14, closed mornings and Mondays (open Wednesdays until 9 PM). There's no admission charge. Also worth seeing is the *Dean Wile Carding Mill* (Victoria Rd.; phone: 902-543-4033), a water-powered wool operation dating to about 1860 that cleans and untangles fibers before spinning. Closed Sunday mornings and October through May; no admission charge. The *South Shore Exhibition and International Ox Pull,* featuring oxen from the US competing against local champions, is held here annually in early July.

En Route from Bridgewater Follow Route 332 south along the LaHave River (toward the ocean) to Riverport.

RIVERPORT The *Ovens Natural Park* (Feltzen South Rd.; phone: 902-766-4621) boasts a series of caverns worn into the rocky cliffs by the pounding surf. It once was the site of a brief but furious gold rush: For six months in 1861 it yielded $120,000 worth of gold. A boomtown sprang up and quickly disappeared. There is a good lookout point, and from late June through mid

September visitors can pan for gold on the gravel beach (except on Mondays), visit the restaurant and crafts shop, and take guided tours of the caves, both on foot (daily except Mondays) and in Zodiac inflatable boats (daily). The park is open daily; facilities are closed October 16 to May 14. There's an admission charge.

En Route from Riverport Follow Route 332 north for a few miles to Lunenburg.

LUNENBURG Probably the most important fishing port in North America, Lunenburg is the headquarters of the Highliner Division of National Sea Products, a Nova Scotia company with plants from Florida to Newfoundland. Here visitors are certain to get an indication of the enormous role fishing plays in the life of the province. According to estimates, national sea-related companies employ 10,000 people, with twice that number indirectly dependent on the firms.

Lunenburg is also the home of the fishing schooner *Bluenose,* undefeated in international races between 1921 and 1946; it's depicted on the back of the Canadian dime. An exact replica (except for some modern conveniences), *Bluenose II,* was constructed at Lunenburg's Smith and Rhuland yard and launched in 1963. Built by a brewery for promotional purposes and now owned by the provincial government, it tours around the province and goes to US coastal cities, but spends most of the summer in Halifax, from where it makes daily cruises. The Smith and Rhuland yard also built the *Bounty,* which was used in the film *Mutiny on the Bounty,* starring Marlon Brando.

The *Lunenburg Fisheries Museum* is at the water end of Duke Street. Housed in two ships—the *Theresa E. Connor,* the last Lunenburg schooner to fish the Grand Banks with dories, and the *Cape Sable,* a steel-hulled trawler—the museum also has an aquarium. It's closed October 15 through May; open daily the rest of the year. There's an admission charge (phone: 902-634-4794). The *Nova Scotia Fisheries Exhibition and Fishermen's Reunion* is held in Lunenburg in early September and features competitive events such as dory races and scallop-shucking contests. Have dinner at the *Boscawen Inn* (150 Cumberland St.; phone: 902-634-3325), a restored Victorian mansion overlooking the harbor. It specializes in fresh local seafood and home-cooked meals; it also offers 17 guestrooms furnished with antiques. It's closed January through *Easter.*

En Route from Lunenburg Head north for about 5 miles (8 km) to Mahone Bay.

MAHONE BAY Founded in 1754, Mahone Bay is a scenic town at the head of a bay sprinkled with 365 islands. During the War of 1812 an American ship, the *Young Teazer,* was chased into Mahone Bay by a British man-of-war. On board the American vessel was a British deserter. Realizing that the *Young Teazer* couldn't escape and that he would be hanged if captured, the Briton threw a torch into the powder magazine and blew the ship apart. Legend has it that on the anniversary of the explosion, June 27, a ghost ship, engulfed in flames, can be seen in the bay.

Three pretty churches standing side by side at the head of the bay make an attractive photograph. Take tea at the *Tingle Bridge Tea House* (Main St.; phone: 902-624-9770), which features more than 50 different blends, daily lunch specials, and enticing desserts.

For an interesting side trip, make arrangements to visit Oak Island. Privately owned, it can be visited only with permission; call the owner, Don Blankenship (phone: 902-627-2376), in advance. To get to Oak Island, continue on Route 3, and take the turnoff to the *Oak Island Inn* (see *Best en Route*).

OAK ISLAND According to legend, an enormous treasure is buried here. Some say it's the plunder of Captain Kidd; other stories link it to British military engineers attempting to hide valuables during the American Revolution or to pirates who used the island as a communal bank. In any event, millions of dollars have been spent, and six people killed, trying to unearth the cache, but nothing of consequence has been found. The search for the treasure began in 1796, when three hunters from nearby Chester noticed a depression in the land and thought someone had been digging there. The next day they began their own excavation. At 10 feet they discovered a layer of planks; at 20 feet they found a second layer; and at 90 feet they discovered still more layers. Using more sophisticated methods, the diggers went to 96 feet, at which point water rushed in, flooding the pit. Subsequent drillings met the same fate, although oak casks and loose metal were encountered.

En Route from Mahone Bay Follow Route 103 to Chester.

CHESTER A scenic town popular with many American families who have summered here for generations, Chester was settled in 1759 by New Englanders. Graced with two harbors, Chester also has municipal tennis courts (next to the village ice rink) and an 18-hole golf course that's open to visitors, the *Chester Golf and Country Club* (phone: 902-275-4543). A yacht club hosts some of the province's most spirited regattas. *Race Week* in late August features dozens of craft, many flying beautiful spinnakers. From Chester a ferry travels to Big and Little Tancook Islands, famed for cabbages and sauerkraut; pick up the ferry at Water Street (check locally for schedules). The *Captain's House* restaurant (129 Central St.; phone: 902-275-3501) offers good meals and a splendid view of the Back Harbour. Other eateries of note are *The Rope Loft* (Water St.; phone: 902-275-3430), in an old fishermen's shack, and *Windjammer* (attached to the motel on Rte. 3 at the southern turnoff to the town; phone: 902-275-3567). Both have good seafood at reasonable prices. For fresh take-out seafood, try *Hilchie's* (Water St.; phone: 902-275-4846), which is open daily in the summer only.

En Route from Chester Continue east on Route 3 to Hubbards.

HUBBARDS This pleasant community has a small fish plant and is the home of many summer residents. A nice private beach is open to visitors for a small charge; it has a snack bar and picnic facilities.

En Route from Hubbards Heading toward Halifax, Route 3 passes many clean, supervised beaches and attractive sea views. Queensland Beach is particularly popular, because the water usually reaches 70F (21C) by late summer. At Upper Tantallon, turn off to the right on Route 333 toward Glen Haven and Peggy's Cove. At one time, many of the houses here were occupied by lone fishermen—a species now all but extinct. Today commuters travel from their homes here to jobs in Halifax, and summer homes dot the roadside. Even so, old fishing villages like Indian Harbour and Paddy's Head still thrive.

PEGGY'S COVE This rustic fishing village is probably the most photographed spot in the province. A barren landscape of granite projections and piled boulders stands in stark contrast to the brightly painted homes of the village, perched at the edge of the crashing sea. For details, see *Quintessential Canada* in DIVERSIONS. The *Sou' Wester* (phone: 902-823-2561) nearby features hearty chowder and delicious gingerbread; it closes at 6 PM.

En Route from Peggy's Cove It seems as if giants have dropped the huge boulders you'll see as you head toward Halifax through the bare countryside on Route 333. They are the result of glacial movements; the boulders lie where they were when the ice melted. Weeping Widow's Island in Shad Bay has been the scene of several unsuccessful treasure hunts. At Shad Bay, take a short drive out to Prospect, a robust fishing village facing out to sea from a spit of land. Each July the village has a chowder chow-down, with lots of hearty soup and baked goods. At the end of Route 333, signs to Route 102 lead via the Bayers Road Exit into Halifax.

HALIFAX The largest city on Canada's east coast, Halifax merits a tour of its own. For complete details, see *Halifax* in THE CITIES.

En Route from Halifax Just after the *Halifax Shopping Centre* on the right side of Bayers Road, make a left turn onto Connaught Avenue. Continue on Connaught until you see signs to the A. Murray MacKay Bridge. Cross the toll bridge and follow Route 111 past the Micmac Rotary, with lakes on both sides. This is the beginning of the marine drive, which is marked with distinctive signs. At Woodlawn, near the *Penhorn Mall Shopping Centre,* take Route 207 toward Cole Harbour and Lawrencetown. The Cole Harbour Dike area is a good spot for bird watching for Canada geese and other waterbirds. Lawrencetown has a fine sandy beach, which is supervised in season but has a sometimes strong and dangerous undertow. Its waves can be adequate for surfing, though hardly challenging to an expert. Beyond Lawrencetown, Three Fathom Harbour, Seaforth, and West Chezzetcook are all picturesque villages. Early in the morning, the villagers go to sea in small boats; in the afternoon they can be seen cleaning their catch on the wharves. At Musquodoboit Harbour you enter a lumbering area, the center of which is Head of Jeddore. Nearby Lake Charlotte is one of the province's best hunting and fishing districts. Continue east on Route 7 to Tangier.

TANGIER This was one of the province's first gold mining areas. Nearby, at the *Moose River Gold Mines,* one of the most famous dramas in Nova Scotia history was acted out. On April 12, 1936, the day before *Easter,* three Toronto men were trapped in the 141-foot shaft they were inspecting. Six days later, signals indicating that the three were alive came through a hole drilled by rescue crews. Five days later, the men were finally reached, but one of them had died. The story received worldwide attention.

At Tangier look for signs to *J. Willy Krauch and Sons Smoke Shop* (phone: 902-772-2188). Krauch was internationally known for the quality of his smoked fish—he even supplied smoked salmon to Queen Elizabeth. His sons now carry on the business in traditional style.

En Route from Tangier On the way to Sherbrooke, about 62 miles (99 km) northeast of Tangier, you'll pass through Sheet Harbour, a thickly wooded area known for deer. Inland from Sheet Harbour is the 200-square-mile *Liscomb Park Game Sanctuary,* where moose, mink, muskrat, and other animals roam the forests; it's an ideal spot for photography buffs. Trout fishing also is excellent here, but anglers must be accompanied by registered guides. Port Dufferin, named after the Marquis of Dufferin, is another area where gold has been found. Farther along the route is Necum Teuch, a Native American term for "beach of fine sand." Before reaching Ecum Secum ("red bank"), you'll cross into Guysborough, mainland Nova Scotia's easternmost county. At Liscomb Mills, look for the *Liscombe Lodge* (see *Best en Route*), whose restaurant is attractive yet informal. The lodge also outfits trout and salmon fishing trips.

SHERBROOKE Visit *Sherbrooke Village,* an area of town in which 17 buildings, including a post office, drugstore, jail, school, church, blacksmith's shop, and sawmill, have been restored to their appearance of 1860 to 1880, when Sherbrooke boomed with gold mining, shipbuilding, and lumbering activity. Costumed guides provide tours. Closed mid-October through May; open daily the rest of the year. There's an admission charge (phone: 902-522-2400).

En Route from Sherbrooke Beyond Sherbrooke, at the junction of Routes 7 and 276, take Route 276 right to Goshen, then proceed on Route 316 15 miles (24 km) south toward Country Harbour, with Harbour Island at its mouth. Although its magnificent waters are virtually unspoiled by commerce, the harbor has been mentioned as a possible site for marine industrial development. From Country Harbour, the route passes through numerous other small fishing towns of rugged beauty. At the junction of Routes

316 and 16, take a swing east to Canso, the mainland point closest to the rich Atlantic fishing grounds. First inhabited by the French in the 1500s, Canso always has been heavily dependent on fishing for its prosperity. Return on Route 16 to Guysborough, an important lumber and pulpwood center. Then take Route 344 to Mulgrave on the Strait of Canso. Mulgrave faces Port Hawkesbury across the strait; the two towns have benefited from the ice-free, deepwater harbor resulting from the construction of the Canso Causeway, the world's largest, which was built in the 1950s. Auld Cove, the mainland end of the causeway, is the last stop on this route.

BEST EN ROUTE

The hotels and motels on this route provide generous facilities for canoeing, camping, fishing, and swimming. Expect to pay $65 or more per night for a double room in an expensive hotel; $40 to $65 for accommodations listed as moderate; and less than $40 for accommodations in the inexpensive category. All places feature private baths, TV sets, and telephones unless otherwise indicated. For each location, hotels are listed alphabetically by price category.

SHELBURNE

Ox Bow Motel This place has 47 spacious rooms, an outdoor heated pool, a gameroom, an enclosed playground, bird watching trails, meeting facilities, and a restaurant and coffee shop. On the shores of Lake George (phone: 902-875-3000; fax: 902-872-2000). Moderate.

LIVERPOOL

White Point Beach Lodge With 47 rooms and 40 cottages, this resort offers daily beach parties and barbecues on a white sandy beach. Also available to guests are a freshwater lake, boats, tennis courts, a nine-hole golf course, nature trails, fishing, and horseback riding. The resort has a restaurant which offers daily specials. Packages are available. Off Rte. 103, Exit 20A or 21 on Rte. 3 (phone: 902-354-2711; 800-565-5068 in Canada; fax: 902-354-7278). Expensive.

Lanes Privateer At the east end of the Liverpool Bridge spanning the Mersey River, this 27-room motel comes with all the conveniences, including a lounge and dining room, called *1798,* that specializes in seafood. There are also meeting and banquet rooms and a boat launch (phone: 902-354-3456: fax: 902-354-7220). Moderate.

Hopkins House This bed and breakfast establishment in a pre–War of 1812 Loyalist home has three guestrooms and two shared baths. There's a TV set in a main lounge, but no telephones in the rooms. Full breakfast is included. 120 Main St. (phone: 902-354-5484). Inexpensive.

BRIDGEWATER

Auberge Wandlyn Inn Part of an eastern Canadian motel chain, it has 74 rooms, a coffee bar, a dining room, a sports bar, an indoor pool, and a sauna. 50 North St. (phone: 902-543-7131; 800-561-0006 in the US; 800-561-0000 in eastern and central Canada; fax: 902-543-7170). Moderate.

WESTERN SHORE

Oak Island Inn With a view of Oak Island and Mahone Bay, this 74-unit inn has a sauna, a whirlpool, tennis, tanning and exercise rooms, a volleyball court, and hiking trails. The full-service marina offers boat and sailboat rentals and deep-sea fishing charters. The *Atlantic* dining room, which features seafood, is closed weekdays during the off-season. Take Exit 9 or 10 from Rte. 103 to the "Lighthouse Route" and look for *Oak Island Inn* signs (phone: 902-627-2600; 800-565-5075; fax: 902-627-2020). Expensive.

CHESTER

Mecklenburgh Inn In this bed and breakfast establishment are four guestrooms (none with telephones) and two shared baths. There's a TV set in the lounge. Full breakfast is included, and picnic lunches, bicycles, and rowboats are available. Closed November through May. 78 Queen St. (phone: 902-275-4638). Moderate.

Windjammer This 18-unit motel has landscaped grounds set back from the highway. There's a pool, mini-golf, the *Windjammer* restaurant, and a picnic area with barbecues. West of town on Rte. 3 (phone: 902-275-3567). Moderate.

HUBBARDS

Anchorage House and Cabins Gordon and Judy Morrison are the friendly proprietors of this lovely old house, whose four cozy guestrooms are decorated with homemade quilts and antique furnishings. There also are three cabins and five housekeeping cottages. Accommodations have TV sets, but no telephones. A restaurant, the *Trellis Café,* is nearby on the main street. Trout ponds, fishing charters, and small-boat and bicycle rentals are available. 6612 Shore Club Rd. (phone: 902-857-9402; fax: 902-857-1419). Moderate.

LISCOMB MILLS

Liscombe Lodge The best accommodations on the eastern shore are found at this government-owned facility on the Liscomb River. The attractive property has 65 units, including cottages, chalets, and rooms in the main lodge; there's also a pleasant restaurant. Tennis, boat and canoe rentals, a playground, lawn games, freshwater fishing, guides and equipment, yacht mooring, and hiking trails are on the premises. Pets are allowed in the chalets only. Babysitting is available on request. Usually closed mid-October through May; call for exact dates. On Rte. 7; look for *Liscombe Lodge* signs (phone: 902-779-2307; fax: 902-779-2700). Expensive.

Amherst around Cape Breton Island

Beginning in Amherst, this 530-mile (848-km) route passes through farmlands bordering the warmest salt water north of the Carolinas, crosses the Strait of Canso, and then swings around Cape Breton Island to its terminus in Port Hawkesbury. Alexander Graham Bell, who spent his summers on the island, thought this was the most beautiful scenery in North America. Rolling hills plunge into verdant valleys, stony cliffs overlook the ocean, and inland lochs and glens are reminiscent of Scotland. The trip culminates at *Fortress Louisbourg,* Canada's largest historical restoration.

The first part of the route leads through lands settled mostly by Scots. It was at Pictou that the *Hector* landed in 1773 with 33 families and 25 unmarried men, all refugees from the Highlands. On the 11-week journey across the Atlantic, 18 passengers died, but the *Hector*'s voyage was just the start of a migration that gave the area its decisively Scottish character.

Throughout the drive, keep an eye out for good meals in out-of-the-way places. Along Route 6, bordering the Northumberland Strait, look for signs advertising lobster suppers, often sponsored by church and community groups. The waters around the island contain some of the world's richest lobster grounds. Of particular note is the *Pictou Lobster Carnival* (usually held in early July).

AMHERST This town is named after Lord Jeffrey Amherst (1717–97), the English baron and Governor General of British North America from 1760 to 1763 who also gave his name to the Massachusetts town and college, to Amherstburg, and to Amherst Island in Ontario. Amherst is the first community directly east of the Nova Scotia–New Brunswick border. The main provincial tourist bureau (phone: 902-667-8429) is on Route 104 west of town. It's closed late October through mid-May; open daily the rest of the year.

En Route from Amherst Take Route 6 on the Sunrise Trail, a stretch of highway following the shore of the Northumberland Strait to the Canso Causeway. Stop by Heather Beach, typical of many along this road, and then head for Pugwash, 42 miles (67 km) from Amherst.

PUGWASH In Pugwash—which has street signs in English and Gaelic—you'll feel the first tangible evidence of the Scottish influence in the area. The site of a major salt mine, it produces a thousand tons of the mineral a day. The small town was made famous earlier this century as the site of the annual

Thinkers Conference, instituted by the late industrialist Cyrus Eaton, who was born here.

En Route from Pugwash Continue southeast on Route 6 to Wallace, known for over a hundred years for sandstone quarries that have provided material for such famous buildings as the *Houses of Parliament* in Ottawa and *Province House* in Halifax. From Wallace, the road passes the Malagash Peninsula, known for its lobsters and oysters and for a salt mine discovered in 1916. The finding was a key one for Nova Scotia, since the fishing industry required thousands of tons of salt yearly. Today, most of the province's salt comes from the Pugwash mine (see above). Continue south to Tatamagouche.

TATAMAGOUCHE Eight-foot-tall Anna Swan was born near this village (pop. 550) in 1846. She went on to star in P. T. Barnum's circus and to marry Captain Martin Van Buren Bates, also eight feet tall. Her skirt and other mementos are on display at the *Fraser Cultural Center* (Main St.; phone: 902-657-3285). It's closed November through April; open daily until 8 PM the rest of the year. There's no admission charge.

From Tatamagouche, take a side trip south on Route 311 to Balmoral Mills, where the *Nova Scotia Museum* (Main St.; phone: 902-424-7353) operates a gristmill dating from 1874. Privately owned until 1966, the restored mill still grinds grain into flour with old-fashioned waterwheels providing the power; its products are for sale. The museum and mill are closed Sunday mornings and October 15 through May; no admission charge (phone: 902-657-3016, mill). The *Balmoral Motel and Mill Room* (Main St.; phone: 902-657-2000) serves Canadian and German dishes; it's closed November to May 25. Drysdale Falls, 23 feet high with a marvelous swimming area below, are nearby.

En Route from Tatamagouche Head east on Route 6 to Brule, known for its warm water, sandy beaches, golf course, and campgrounds. Crossing into Pictou County, you enter an increasingly industrialized area, whose residents rely more on factories than on the sea or farmlands for their livelihood. At Toney River you might see Irish moss being baled and dried. Pictou is 38 miles (61 km) from Tatamagouche.

PICTOU This small city, along with four surrounding towns, forms the province's third-largest industrial area, ranking behind Halifax-Dartmouth and Sydney. It is home to a shipbuilding yard, a lobster cannery, and a knife manufacturer. In 1773, the *Hector* brought the first settlers here from Scotland. Pictou is the site of an annual three-day *Lobster Carnival,* usually held in early July, and the *Pictou County–North Colchester Exhibition* early in September. Thomas McCulloch's house (Old Haliburton Rd.; phone: 902-485-4563) overlooking the mouth of West River at Pictou Harbour, was built in the early 19th century. Today, it's a museum devoted to tracing the lives of prominent Pictonians of Scottish ancestry. Closed Sunday mornings and

October 15 through May; no admission charge. Check with the *De Coste Centre for the Performing Arts* (phone: 902-485-8848) for evening events.

En Route from Pictou Travel south to Route 104 and Stellarton, where coal was discovered in 1798. At 48 feet, the Foord Seam here is believed to be the thickest seam of coal in the world. Also in Stellarton is the *Nova Scotia Museum of Industry* (Exit 24 off Rte. 104; phone: 902-755-5425), which has impressive exhibits of railroad artifacts, including two antique steam locomotives. Open daily until 8 PM; admission charge. New Glasgow is near Stellarton, north of Route 104.

NEW GLASGOW Named after Glasgow, Scotland, this town was originally the center of Pictou County coal mining. Today it's known for its steel foundries, clay works, and machine shops. The first settlers along the banks of the East River were mostly bachelors. It's reported that once, when a ship bearing new settlers docked in Halifax, three of the single men trekked all the way there on foot to find brides. After the Halifax weddings, the new couples hiked the entire distance back. Along nearby Abercrombie Road is the *Abercrombie Country Club* (phone: 902-752-6249), featuring an 18-hole golf course and a curling rink.

En Route from New Glasgow At Sutherland River, take Route 245 north toward Merigomish. At Malignant Cove (named for a British man-of-war wrecked here), follow Route 337 east to Cape George. Beautiful sea views grace the road at this point, and there's a lighthouse at the tip of the cape. Continue on Route 337 around the cape to Antigonish.

ANTIGONISH Halfway between Halifax and Sydney, Antigonish was founded by Loyalist soldiers and their families after the American Revolution. Each year, around the middle of July, this pretty town hosts the *Highland Games,* a traditional celebration that's a kind of *Olympics* of the clans (for details, see *Festivals, Fairs, and Fancy Acts* in DIVERSIONS).

Antigonish also is the home of *St. Francis-Xavier University* and its sister institution, the *Coady Institute.* The university won recognition in 1920 for the Antigonish Movement, a self-help program for community development that stressed the use of cooperatives and credit unions. Today, students from more than 80 countries study community development at the *Coady Institute* on the campus. One of the best restaurants in town is the *Lobster Treat* (241 Post Rd.; phone: 902-863-5465), a converted schoolhouse that serves fresh, well-prepared food.

En Route from Antigonish Follow Route 104 west to the Strait of Canso and the Canso Causeway. Completed in 1955, the nearly mile-long causeway took three years to build and required over 10 million tons of fill, mostly from Cape Porcupine on the mainland side of the strait. The 13-mile-long Strait of Canso is an ice-free "superport" that permits the world's largest ships to enter and dock with ease.

Take Route 19 north along the western shore of Cape Breton Island through Inverness County. At the start of this route at Creignish, the road rises to 850 feet, a good point from which to see the whole Strait of Canso and St. George's Bay; then it's down again past the farms that support most of the residents, who farm and fish for a living. The villages around Judique were once known for the size and violence of their male residents—huge Highlanders who challenged each other at dances and other social events.

Farther on, Port Hood (pop. 500) was much larger during its coal mining days, but the pits have been closed for some time since the mines flooded. From Port Hood, you pass through the farming and sheep-raising area of Mabou and Strathlorne, then through Inverness, a coal mining center since 1865. At Margaree Forks, the *Margaree Lodge* offers good fresh fish and vegetables in an attractive setting (see *Best en Route*).

Before joining the Cabot Trail, a highway named after explorer John Cabot, who's said to have landed here just after Columbus reached America, detour east to the *Salmon Museum* at Northeast Margaree. A stone's throw from the Margaree River, this small museum has marvelous displays of old fishing equipment, both legal and illegal. Closed October 15 to June 15; open daily the rest of the year. There's an admission charge (phone: 902-248-2848). The Margaree River, by the way, yielded the largest salmon ever caught in the province: a 45-pounder nabbed in 1933.

As you leave Margaree Forks, you enter an area of the province where French is the first language. Belle Côte might be called the Acadia of Inverness County, for the inhabitants retain the language and traditions of their Norman ancestors. At St-Joseph du Moine are large, undeveloped deposits of limestone and extensive cranberry bogs. At Grand Etang is a cooperative lobster-canning plant run by local fishermen. Chéticamp is a few miles beyond Grand Etang.

CHÉTICAMP Opposite *St. Peter's Church* at the south end of the village is the *Acadian Museum* (744 Main St.; phone: 902-224-2170), with frequent demonstrations of spinning and weaving (in season). Crafts, including hooked rugs, are for sale, and Acadian meals are served. It's closed mid-October through April and weekends in May; open daily the rest of the year (until 9 PM late June through mid-September). Guided tours are available in season. There's no admission charge. *Laurie's* motel (Main St.; phone: 902-224-2400; fax: 902-224-2069) serves homemade mincemeat and fresh fish.

En Route from Chéticamp Three miles (5 km) beyond Chéticamp is *Cape Breton Highlands National Park.*

CAPE BRETON HIGHLANDS NATIONAL PARK Forming part of a vast tableland, this 370-square-mile area contains the island's most spectacular scenery. The landscape is reminiscent of the coast of Scotland: Steep cliffs, often hundreds of feet high, loom over a stony shore. Barrens give way to deep, green valleys crisscrossed by rivers and streams. Foxes, lynx, and bears roam the park's forests, and over a hundred bird species nest here. Facilities include many hiking trails and a number of campgrounds and picnic spots. Golfers can test their skills on a challenging 18-hole course (see *Golf in Canada* in DIVERSIONS). For more information contact the park (phone: 902-285-2691 or 902-285-2270; fax: 902-285-2866).

Although it often climbs mountains only to drop suddenly back to sea level, the road through the park is good, and an alert driver will have no difficulty. The curves are sharp and the grades steep, however. French Mountain, at an elevation of 1,492 feet, is the highest point on any highway in the province. The road also climbs MacKenzie Mountain (1,222 feet), descending, by a series of switchbacks, to Pleasant Bay. Three rivers—the MacKenzie, the Pond, and the Red—converge here. From the bay, the road swings to the east up the side of North Mountain, climbing 1,460 feet. You'll have good views of the park's spectacular gorges as you descend into Sunrise Valley. As you come around the park toward the east coast of the island, turn left to Neil Harbour.

Named after an early settler, Neil Harbour is an English-speaking fishing village and one of the best spots on the island to plunge into a way of life as dependent on the sea as it was a century ago. Steep grades and more dramatic sights characterize the Cabot Trail before Ingonish.

Local legend says that the name "Ingonish" is Portuguese, and that the Portuguese had a fishing base here as early as 1521. Early in the 17th century the French established an active settlement here, and by 1740, 54 fishing vessels were sailing out of Ingonish. From here continue to Ingonish Beach, the site of the administrative quarters for the park. The community also is a major provincial resort area, with the impressive *Keltic Lodge* (see *Best en Route*) as its centerpiece.

En Route from Cape Breton Highlands National Park From Ingonish, the road passes *Cape Smokey* (phone: 902-285-2778), a winter ski area. A chair lift is available in the summer for those who want to take in the view from the mountaintop. From this peak, you can clearly see the results of a disastrous forest fire that occurred back in 1968.

The villages of Wreck Cove, Skir Dhu, Breton Cove, and North Shore are next along the trail. Just south of Indian Brook, take Route 312 toward Jersey Cove. From here, a short ferry trip (it operates 24 hours a day) takes you (and your car) to Englishtown. Just to your right as you disembark is the grave of Angus MacAskill, the fabled Cape Breton giant who died in 1863 at the age of 38. MacAskill grew to a well-proportioned height of seven feet, nine inches and weighed 425 pounds. His boot, on display at the *Nova Scotia Museum* in Halifax, is 14½ inches long. From Englishtown, you can pick up Route 105 south to Sydney, Nova Scotia's steel center. Instead of going directly to Sydney, however, make a side trip to Baddeck, heading west on Route 105 for 33 miles (53 km).

BADDECK This is where Alexander Graham Bell summered the last 35 years of his life, during which time he worked on a host of projects. His descendants still live here, occupying the home at Beinn Bhreagh (Gaelic for "beautiful mountain") where Bell and his wife lived. The Bells' graves are nearby. Although visible from the government wharf in Baddeck, the house is not open to visitors. The fascinating *Alexander Graham Bell Museum* (at the east end of town on Rte. 205; phone: 902-295-2069), however, is. The building is in the shape of a trahedra, a form of four triangular faces used by Bell in his huge person-carrying kites. Inside are photos and artifacts that indicate the extraordinary range of Bell's interests, including sheep breeding, medicine, aeronautics, and naturally, the telephone. Open daily (until 9 PM in July and August); admission charge. Aided by Bell, J. A. D. McCurdy flew an early airplane, the *Silver Dart,* across icy Bras d'Or Lake near here on February 23, 1909—the first flight made in the British Empire. Baddeck, a fishing and sailing center, is extraordinarily picturesque, especially in summer, when the harbor is filled with sailboats. *Gisele's Country Inn* (387 Shore Rd.; phone: 902-295-2849) provides bike rentals.

En Route from Baddeck Take Route 105 back to Englishtown, and from there south to Sydney. Passing over Kelly's Mountain (again), you'll have excellent views of St. Ann's Bay and Bras d'Or Lake. Cross the Bras d'Or Bridge, and proceed to North Sydney, where ferries travel to Newfoundland. Route 125 leads to Sydney.

SYDNEY On a deep natural harbor facing Newfoundland across the Cabot Strait, Sydney is a center of shipping and industry. Its first settlers were Loyalists from New York led by Abraham Cuyler, a former Mayor of Albany. Scottish Highlanders were the next group to put down roots. The third-largest city in Nova Scotia, Sydney has a population of 29,400; the *University College of Cape Breton* here has over a thousand students. Steel production, the main industry, is synonymous with the Sydney Steel Corporation (SYSCO).

En Route from Sydney Head south on Route 22 for 20 miles (32 km) to the *Fortress Louisbourg.*

FORTRESS LOUISBOURG Built by the French between 1720 and 1745, *Fortress Louisbourg* was once the headquarters of the French fleet. Today the fort has been reconstructed to resemble its 18th-century incarnation as much as possible. It's on the Atlantic Coast, just outside the town of Louisbourg. The fort is closed October through May, although outside walking tours are offered in May and October (in English at 10 AM and 2 PM); open daily the rest of the year. There's an admission charge (phone: 902-733-2280). After touring the fort, drive to Lighthouse Point, Careening Point, and Royal Battery—other areas of scenic beauty and historical importance in the 20-square-mile *Fortress Louisbourg Park.* A trip to Kennington Cove, constructed by American volunteers during the siege of 1745, also is a worthwhile stop.

En Route from Fortress Louisbourg A loop diversion from Route 22 proceeds through Main à Dieu. This small, quaint fishing village was almost completely wiped out by a huge forest fire in 1976. As you approach the town, you'll see the charred trunks of trees in the surrounding forest.

On the road back to Sydney, look for the exit to Route 125 that quickly connects with Route 4 heading south. Route 4 passes along the shore of saltwater Bras d'Or Lake, a favorite yachting site on the Atlantic Coast. At Chapel Island, near Soldiers Cove, is a shrine where the Micmac hold an annual three-day religious festival in July. Next, the road passes through St. Peter's across St. Peter's Canal, which was built in 1869 to connect 400-square-mile Bras d'Or Lake and St. Peter's Bay on the Atlantic.

ST. PETER'S The first Europeans to occupy this area were the Portuguese, who called the community San Pedro; they used it as a fishing base between 1521 and 1527. In the next century the French explorer Nicholas Denys exploited the fishing grounds and exported lumber to France. Located on the west side of St. Peter's Canal, the *Nicholas Denys Museum* contains Micmac artifacts and mementos of the early French and British settlers. Closed October through May; open daily the rest of the year. There's an admission charge (phone: 902-535-2379). Until 1745 the port, known first as St. Pierre and later renamed Port Toulouse, was a stronghold of French power and a major supply channel for *Fortress Louisbourg,* but in that year New Englanders attacked and captured *Louisbourg* for the English. Later returned to France by treaty, *Louisbourg* fell for the second time in 1758. At that time British settlers ousted the French and changed the port's name to St. Peter's. Visit the 90-acre picnic and camping park on the east side of St. Peter's Canal. Here you can hike to the top of Mt. Granville, the original site of *Fort Granville,* built in 1793. The remains of its ramparts are still visible.

En Route from St. Peter's Before reaching Port Hawkesbury, take a short side trip to Isle Madame, linked to the mainland by a bridge. The paved loop passes through several scenic Acadian villages. One of these, Arichat, features an 1838 cathedral, the century-old *Bishop's Palace* (now a hospital), and *Le Noir Forge Museum.* The museum is closed October through April; hours vary (call ahead to confirm). There's no admission charge (phone: 902-226-2800). Returning to the mainland, take Route 4 through Cleveland, a tiny lumbering community named after the US president, to Port Hawkesbury.

BEST EN ROUTE

An interesting alternative to hotels and motels is one of Cape Breton Island's bed and breakfast houses. To make a reservation, call the *Cape Breton Tourist Information Bureau* (phone: 800-565-9464). Some of the accommodations listed below offer an American Plan (meals included) and/or a Modified American Plan (dinner and breakfast) in addition to the conventional European Plan (no meals). Per night, expect to pay more than $65 for a double room at those hotels listed as expensive, and from $40 to $65 in the moderate category. All establishments have private baths unless otherwise indicated. For each location, hotels are listed alphabetically by price category.

ANTIGONISH

Best Western Claymore To be in the center of the action—especially during the midsummer *Highland Games*—try this comfortable motel with 76 rooms and 10 suites, located near the town's shopping center. St. George's Bay can be chilly, making the motel's heated indoor and outdoor pools all the more attractive. On site is a steak-and-seafood restaurant, the *Lochinvar.* Church St. (phone: 902-863-1050; 800-528-1234; fax: 902-863-1050). Expensive.

INVERNESS

Inverness Beach Village Here are 40 fully equipped cottages with kitchens; there's also a dining room. Closed October 15 to June 15. A quarter-mile north of Inverness on Rte. 19 (phone: 902-258-2653). Moderate.

MARGAREE FORKS

Margaree Lodge Overlooking the Margaree Valley, this 46-unit establishment can arrange deep-sea fishing trips, salmon and trout fishing excursions, and guides. Facilities include a dining room and a pool. Closed October 15 to June 15. Junction of Rte. 19 and Cabot Trail (phone: 902-248-2193; fax: 902-248-2170). Moderate.

MARGAREE VALLEY

Normaway Inn In addition to the charming nine-room country inn on this lovely estate are 14 comfortable cabins. Good food and hospitality are here in ample supply. The owner often shows films about the area or arranges traditional entertainment—one or two Cape Breton fiddlers, step dancers, or storytellers sometimes perform for guests in the living room. In the lobby are listings of local concerts and square dances. Amenities include badminton, tennis courts, bicycle rentals, and equipment for salmon fishing. There are also walking trails and horseback riding. The dining room features hearty but elegantly served dishes. Closed October 15 to June 17. Two miles (3 km) off the Cabot Trail on Egypt Rd. (phone: 902-248-2987; 800-565-9463; fax: 902-248-2600). Expensive.

CHÉTICAMP

Park View Looking over the Gulf of St. Lawrence and the Cape Breton Highlands are 17 rooms and a restaurant that serves steaks, seafood and homemade bread and pastries; deep-sea and freshwater fishing with guides can be arranged. Closed October 20 to May 24. At the entrance to *Cape Breton Highlands National Park* (phone: 902-224-3232; fax: 902-224-2596). Moderate.

INGONISH AND INGONISH BEACH

Keltic Lodge Surrounded by terrain that looks astoundingly like the Scottish Hebrides, this resort offers a variety of accommodations—32 rooms in the *Main Lodge,* 40 rooms in the modern *White Birch Inn,* and nine two- to four-bedroom cottages with fireplaces. Complementing the spectacular setting are an 18-hole golf course (see *Golf in Canada* in DIVERSIONS), nature trails, and tennis courts. The beach is nearby, and guests can enjoy swimming in a pool or a freshwater lake. Closed April, May, November, and December; exact winter dates depend on snow conditions, since alpine and cross-country skiing are offered. Also see *Special Havens* in DIVERSIONS. Near the east gate of *Cape Breton Highlands National Park,* at Herman Falls (phone: 902-285-2880; fax: 902-285-2859). Expensive.

Glenghorm This resort has 21 acres of landscaped property, including beach frontage, with 68 motel units, five efficiencies, 11 cottages, a pool, and a dining room. Closed November through April. Cabot Trail (phone: 902-285-2049; fax: 902-285-2395). Moderate.

BADDECK

Inverary Inn This charming inn has 24 rooms, 14 cottages, 50 motel units, and lots of room for children to play, including a playground. Indoor and outdoor pools, a sauna, a hot tub, an exercise room, complimentary boat tours, tennis courts, meeting rooms, and banquet facilities round out the amenities. The *Lake View* dining room overlooks the ocean, and there's the more informal *Lakeside Café.* Complimentary bicycles and boats are available for guests' use. On Shore Rd., Rte. 205 (phone: 902-295-3500; 800-565-5660 in Canada; fax: 902-295-3527). Expensive.

Silver Dart Overlooking Bras d'Or Lake on a hill above the road, this motel has 88 modern units, a restaurant, a waterfront area, walking trails, and bicycle rentals. Closed November through April. On Shore Rd., Rte. 205 (phone: 902-295-2340; fax: 902-295-2484). Moderate.

PORT HAWKESBURY

Auberge Wandlyn Inn Near a small shopping center, this inn has 74 units, a restaurant, a heated pool, a sauna, a whirlpool bath, a tanning bed, badminton and volleyball courts, and other exercise facilities. Five miles (8 km) south of the Canso Causeway, at 689 Reeves St. (phone: 902-625-0320; 800-561-0000 in eastern and central Canada; 800-561-0006 in the US; fax: 902-625-3876). Moderate.

Ontario

This centrally located province offers a cross section of Canada's past and present, its multiethnic heritage, and its diverse terrain. Ontario's southern border includes Niagara Falls, and its waterways always have been essential to Canada's national livelihood. Four of the five Great Lakes are wholly or partly within Ontario, and the early fur-trapping and trading posts established on their shores have grown to become essential arteries in Canada's industrial heart. Today, Ontario's more than 10 million inhabitants also make it the country's most populous province.

The peninsula surrounded by Lakes Ontario, Erie, and Huron dominates the economic life of the province and is itself dominated by Toronto, the provincial capital, on Lake Ontario. With more than three million people, Toronto is the country's most populous metropolitan area (for a detailed report, see *Toronto* in THE CITIES). Above Toronto, in a small nubbin of Ontario jutting into neighboring Quebec, is Ottawa, the national capital (for a complete report, see *Ottawa* in THE CITIES). This corner of the province is exceedingly fertile, its gardens and farms yielding most of Ontario's vegetables.

With 412,000 square miles, Ontario is Canada's second-largest province, after Quebec. The Great Lakes peninsula is just a small part of Ontario: The province reaches above the lakes to Hudson Bay, including in its domain rich lake districts, mining and lumber country, and endless miles of wilderness accessible only by foot, canoe, or plane.

Culturally, geographically, and historically, Ontario divides rather neatly into three driving routes. The first is a tour of the peninsula's "little England": from Windsor, on the Canadian side of the Detroit River, to Stratford, through the heart of Canada's English culture, where architecture, historic sites, and even the green gardens conspire to be as much like an English shire as possible. The Lake Ontario route includes the traditional Heritage Highways of the early voyageurs and settlers. It begins at Niagara and follows the western shore of Lake Ontario north to Hamilton and Toronto. Following the shape of Lake Superior in a broad inland arc is the third route, Yonge Street—reputed to be the longest street in the world. Yonge (pronounced *Young*) starts in downtown Toronto and wanders over 1,000 miles (1,600 km) north and then west, one of the major links between civilization and Ontario's vast wilds.

Camping is offered in 220 provincial parks, four of the six national parks and in some of the 304 conservation areas, as well as in hundreds of private sites. Hunting and fishing licenses for nonresidents are available at *Ontario Ministry of Natural Resources (MNR)* offices and most sporting goods stores. The same sources issue permits required for nonresidents of Canada to camp on government land north of the French and Mattawa

Rivers. The region is becoming very popular, and regulations controlling the number of campers are intended to preserve the wilderness. (Higher camping fees may be charged by parks in need of extra ecological protection.) Note that in wintertime, parks are unstaffed but can still be visited in daylight hours.

For further information, contact *Ontario Travel* (*Queen's Park,* Toronto, ONT M7A 2E1; phone: 800-ONTARIO). A 24-hour campsite-vacancy report can be obtained by calling 416-314-0998. The toll-free information number (phone: 800-ONTARIO) also can be used to make hotel, motel, and campground reservations. This *Central Reservation and Information Service (CRIS)* serves primarily small operations that are not part of another central toll-free reservation system. Tourists can call *CRIS* daily between 9 AM and 9 PM. Places that accept a reservation via *CRIS* and cannot honor it are responsible for finding alternative accommodations for the visitor.

Windsor to Stratford: Ontario's England

Just as Quebec is the guardian of Canada's French culture, the southern tip of Ontario is the citadel of Canada's British culture and tradition. On the route from Windsor, across the river from Detroit, the place-names tell the story: Chatham, London, Stratford, Waterloo, and Kitchener, to name a few. The cities and sites on this route are close to one another; its entire length is only 160 miles (256 km). The drive ends at Stratford on the River Avon, home of the summerlong *Stratford Festival,* a world class presentation of the works of William Shakespeare and other renowned playwrights.

This temperate, southerly spur of Canada yields substantial crops of corn, sugar beets, and tobacco. The native people who lived here grew pumpkins, beans, and maize in what was once the southernmost portion of the Huron nation. Once the local Huron left the more violent Iroquois Confederacy to concentrate on farming as a way of life, the area became a contested war zone; after that, only members of what was called the Neutral tribe, who supplied flint tools and weapons to all combatants, were able to dwell here.

European settlers began occupying the area shortly after 1763, when the British took control. It wasn't until the 1820s, however, when the Canada Company was formed to promote development of the Huron Tract, that the "land between the lakes" really began to thrive.

The route described below is designed to take a couple of days and to include the most interesting places on the peninsula. From Windsor, it travels through Amherstburg and around the point of the peninsula to the north shore of Lake Erie, lined with small fishing villages and farming communities, like Leamington and Port Stanley, before turning north. Farther inland are the towns of London and Stratford. Each began as an agricultural center and retains the aura of a giant farmers' market. Acres of farmland are punctuated by inns, taverns, and hostelries, all remarkably British in appearance and atmosphere.

WINDSOR Windsor is situated on a small peninsula surrounded by Lakes Erie and St. Clair, and the sheer beauty of its position belies the city's status as a hub of Canada's automotive industry, one of the country's busiest points of entry from the US, and the southernmost city in all of Canada, across the Detroit River from the automotive capital of America. This busy city is actually *south* of Detroit, connected by one of the only two international underwater tunnels in the world (the other being the English Channel tunnel), as well as by conventional bridges. Like Detroit, the city has been affected by economic recession and flagging automobile sales.

Windsor has been economically important ever since European explorers first used the St. Lawrence River to penetrate deeper into the new continent, portaging across the Niagara Peninsula and continuing by water past Windsor and Amherstburg on the Detroit River.

The city is filled with spacious, colorful parks such as *Dieppe Gardens,* which overlooks the river at Oullette Avenue and Riverside Drive. Here, in 1749, French settlers began the first agriculturally based European community in Ontario. Nearby plaques commemorate Windsor's involvement in the Mackenzie Rebellion (1838) and in the growth of the *Great Western Railway,* which connected it with Niagara Falls in 1854.

The *Jackson Park Sunken Garden* (Tecumseh Rd. and Rte. 3B), while lovely at all times, is especially bewitching in the evening, when 400 custom-designed lights illuminate the most exquisite blooms and underwater lights turn fountains into rainbow machines. The focal point is the unique sculpture *Coordination,* donated by Windsor artist Hans Hennecke. The garden contains 12,000 rosebushes of 450 different varieties. This certainly explains why Windsor, called the "City of Roses," attracts rose lovers from all over North America. A battle-scarred *Lancaster* bomber in the center of the garden pays tribute to the 398 Royal Canadian Air Force flyers who died during World War II. The garden is open year-round.

The *Art Gallery of Windsor* (3100 Howard Ave.; phone: 519-969-4494) has a permanent collection of Canadian paintings and sculptures, including superb Inuit soapstone carvings; some works date back to the early 18th century. Closed Sunday mornings and Mondays; no admission charge. During the second and third weekends of June, the *Carousel of Nations* (at locations throughout the city) features ethnic food, entertainment, and dress. It's a warm-up for the big *International Freedom Festival*, which runs from late June to early July, celebrating the *Fourth of July* as well as Canada's independence day (*Canada Day*) on July 1.

A magnet for visitors is the *Oullette Avenue Mall,* which in summer is lined with leafy trees and musicians in addition to its array of interesting stores. Look for Erie and Ottawa Streets if you like shopping in an Asian or European atmosphere. The largest shopping center in the city is *Devonshire Mall* (3100 Howard Ave.; phone: 519-966-3100), with 175 stores, including *Sears* and *The Bay. Windsor Market* (over several blocks in the downtown area) is a great place to go for fresh fruits, vegetables, meat, and bread. There is a wide variety of good restaurants, including outdoor cafés, and an abundance of ethnic foods—from schnitzel to curried goat.

There's harness racing at *Windsor Raceway* (6 miles/10 km south on Rte. 18; phone: 519-969-8311). The seating areas are completely enclosed and heated, since the season runs from late October through April. Races take place Wednesdays through Sundays at 7:30 PM.

"Sight sipping" tours of wineries in the area are very popular. *Colio Wines* (Harrow; phone: 519-738-2241) offers afternoon tours daily except Sundays (reservations are needed for groups of 10 or more). The *D'Angelo Estate Winery* (Anderdon Township; phone: 519-736-7959) is open daily from 11 AM to 6 PM May through December; Saturdays (by appointment) January through April. *Hiram Walker* (phone: 519-254-5171, ext. 499; 313-965-6611, ext. 499 in the US) provides one-hour tours of its Windsor distillery daily at 2 PM year-round, except for three weeks starting in mid-July and on national holidays. Tours begin in the lobby at the corner of Walker Road and Riverside Drive.

The *Windsor Casino* (445 Riverside Dr. W.; phone: 519-258-8100; fax: 519-258-3146), which opened in 1994, drew about 16,000 visitors daily in its first year. Open round-the-clock, the casino has some 1,700 slot machines and 68 table games (some of the 48 blackjack tables are wheelchair-accessible). The gaming currency is Canadian, and winnings are tax-free in Canada. You have to be 19 or older to get in. The three-story building includes a VIP lounge, a nonsmoking floor, and a food court. Valet parking is available in the lots adjoining the casino; a third, larger parking lot nearby has a free shuttle service. The casino is temporarily housed next door to the city tourist bureau and close to several major hotels. At press time, it was expected that the casino eventually will be moved a short distance away to a $375-million structure built especially for it.

En Route from Windsor Amherstburg is 15 miles (24 km) south of Windsor via Route 18, through a section of Essex County that was deeply involved in the War of 1812 between British Canada and the US. A plaque about 5 miles (8 km) north of the town marks the site of the first major battle.

AMHERSTBURG *Fort Amherstburg* was erected in 1796 by the British after *Fort Detroit* was ceded to the Americans following the Jay Treaty of 1794 (which defined the boundaries between the US and Canada). The fort, which gradually became known as *Fort Malden,* was a strategic point in the defense of Canada in both the War of 1812 and Mackenzie's 1838 Rebellion. It was here that General Isaac Brock met with Shawnee Chief Tecumseh to plan the capture of Detroit, which was accomplished by a joint expedition. However, their loss of control over Lake Erie forced the British to abandon and burn the fortifications at both Detroit and Amherstburg. The fort was partially rebuilt following the war, then converted in 1857 into a government asylum for mental patients. The property was used by a private company after the asylum was moved some 13 years later, and in 1939 *Fort Malden,* some of its original earthworks intact, was declared a National Historic Park. The *Fort Malden National Historic Museum* (100 Laird Ave.; phone: 519-736-5416), an 11-acre riverfront park, includes a restored barracks, a military pensioner's cottage, and two buildings with exhibits and artifacts. There are also picnic facilities. Closed on national holidays November through April; no admission charge.

Another military museum in town is the *Colonel François Baby Museum* (254 Pitt St. W.; phone: 519-253-1812), originally the home of the commander of the area's armed forces. During the early 1800s, François Baby was a key figure in military, political, and social circles, but his fierce loyalty to the British created some tension within the French Canadian community. His stone mansion was occupied by American troops during the War of 1812. Damaged by fire, it was rebuilt and altered many times over the years; in 1958, it became a museum, displaying many items about the area's history, such as changing fashion trends and the evolution of the press and news coverage. Closed Mondays; no admission charge.

The *Park House Museum* (214 Dalhousie St.; phone: 519-736-2511) is doubly interesting because of its pre-1800 construction and because it was moved here from Detroit in 1799. The interior is done in 1850s style. It's closed Mondays and Saturdays, September through May; open daily the rest of the year. Black heritage, from its origins in Africa through slavery to emancipation and settlement in Essex County, is traced in the *North American Black Historical Museum* (277 King St.; phone: 519-736-5433). It's closed October through January; Mondays and Tuesdays the rest of the year.

The *Waterfront* ice-cream parlor (*Navy Yard Park;* phone: 519-736-5553) is worth a visit. The dining room at *Duffy's* motel (see *Best en Route)* is highly regarded, as is *Rosa's* Italian restaurant (phone: 519-736-2177), across from *Duffy's.*

En Route from Amherstburg Take Route 18A south to Holiday Beach (phone: 519-662-1475). Here you can camp overnight, enjoy the sandy beach, picnic area, and stocked fishpond, or simply sit and watch the boats go by. During the migration seasons, this is one of the best places in Ontario for viewing hawks and waterfowl.

Returning to Route 18, you will soon pass through the small agricultural town of Harrow, site of a research station that specializes in crop studies. There are dozens of fruit and vegetable stands along the way. Continue east to Kingsville, 35 miles (56 km) southeast of Windsor.

KINGSVILLE This is Canada's most southerly town, 35 miles (56 km) south of Detroit. Its dominant attraction, founded in 1904 by naturalist Jack Miner, is the *Jack Miner Bird Sanctuary,* which continues under the guidance of his son, Jasper, and grandson, Kirk. Most of what is known about migration routes comes from the Miner family. When Jack began banding birds with his name and address, hunters returned the bands to him, giving the location of their kill. Miner was then able to follow the birds' flight patterns. The sanctuary is located on the great central flyway; this protected region of 300 acres is used by waterfowl, including an estimated 30,000 geese, during their seasonal migrations to and from breeding grounds in the Hudson Bay area. The last two weeks in March, the first week in April, and late October through November are the best times to visit. An "air show," when the birds are flushed into the air, takes place daily October through November at 4 PM. The sanctuary and its museum are closed Sundays; no admission charge (phone: 519-733-4034).

Partners, a family restaurant that serves simple, satisfying fare such as sandwiches and burgers, is located 1 mile (1.6 km) from the sanctuary at the intersection of Division and Road 3 West (phone: 519-733-5955).

Immediately south of Kingsville and west on Route 18A are two beautiful sandy beaches on Lake Erie. Linden Beach has about 2,600 feet of shoreline; Cedar Beach has about 400. They are excellent for swimming and sunning; both are free, but neither has a lifeguard. Kingsville also is the jumping-off point for ferries to Pelee Island (phone: 519-733-4474; 519-326-2154 in summer only from Leamington).

PELEE ISLAND Between Ontario and Ohio, Pelee is Lake Erie's largest island, with 10,000 acres of farmland. It is a popular summer resort, with sandy beaches, cottage rentals, and the *International Pheasant Hunt.* Only a limited number of hunters—US and Canadian—are allowed a crack at the 20,000 pheasants released from late October to early November; call the township clerk for information (phone: 519-724-2931; also see *Hunting* in DIVERSIONS). The *Pelee Island Winery* (phone: 519-733-6551) has a self-guided tourist pavilion and a do-it-yourself barbecue area (you can buy a steak on-site to go with your wine). Guided tours also are available. The winery is closed Sundays January through April. There is a small fee for the tram ride from the ferry to the winery.

En Route from Kingsville Follow Route 18 east from the bird sanctuary for 3 miles (5 km) to the turnoff going north on Route 3 to the tiny village of Ruthven. In Ruthven, the *Colasanti Tropical Gardens* are a major attraction for plant lovers. Three acres of greenhouses feature one of North America's largest displays of tropical houseplants, including a great variety of cacti, plus parrots and other tropical birds. There is also a petting zoo and crafts shop. (If plant shopping, remember that only "indoor variety" plants may be taken into the US.) Meals are available in a large banquet hall. Closed *New Year's Day* and *Christmas* (phone: 519-326-3287). From Ruthven, continue east on Route 3 to Leamington, at the junction of Routes 18 and 77.

LEAMINGTON Billed locally as the "tomato capital of Canada," this canning center almost floats in a sea of surrounding vegetable fields. The keystone of Leamington's economy is the H. J. Heinz Company of Canada, which has been processing foods here for worldwide markets since 1914. The *Thirteen Russell Street Steak House* (13 Russell St.; phone: 519-326-8401) is a charming restaurant, built at the turn of the century. The *Dock* restaurant (at the end of Erie St. S.; phone: 519-326-2697), on the edge of the wharf, offers a great view of the lake.

From Leamington, *Point Pelee National Park* is accessible via Route 33 south. This 4,000-acre sand spit (there are no camping facilities) has 14 miles of beaches and is crisscrossed with trails and boardwalks; some services are closed in winter (phone: 519-322-2365). Also see *National Parks* in DIVERSIONS.

En Route from Leamington It's about 85 miles (136 km) on Route 3 to St. Thomas (see below), following Lake Erie's north shore past several seaside communities and provincial parks. Eight miles (13 km) along the way is Wheatley, where you can stop to photograph the picturesque harbor. There's also a mile of sandy beach, picnic grounds, a nine-hole golf course, and nearby *Wheatley Provincial Park,* with 210 wooded campsites.

From Wheatley, follow Route 3 past pleasant port towns and numerous orchards and farms selling pears, peaches, plums, and apples from roadside stands. Take the turnoff for County Road 12 southeast to Erieau.

ERIEAU This tiny village, which fronts Lake Erie and Rondeau Bay with a fabulous 1,900-foot beach, is a renowned center of commercial and recreational fishing for muskie, pike, coho salmon, bass, perch, and smelt during the runs in April. Check with the *Rondeau Bay Marina* (phone: 519-674-5931) for information on boat rentals and fishing charters.

En Route from Erieau Return to Route 3; accessible from the junction of Routes 3 and 51 is *Rondeau Provincial Park.*

RONDEAU PROVINCIAL PARK Another of Lake Erie's famous sandy spits, this is the second-oldest park in Ontario (1894). Enclosing sheltered, 9-mile Rondeau Bay, it's a major preserve for birds, reptiles, white-tailed deer, and Carolinean forest. There are beaches, a swimming area, nature and hiking trails, picnic grounds, tennis courts, a riding stable, bicycling, miniature golf, a fishing dock, a store, and interpretive programs. During the fall, hunting of waterfowl is allowed; winter activities include skating, ice fishing, and iceboat racing. The park is open year-round.

En Route from Rondeau Provincial Park For about 30 miles (48 km), Route 3 parallels the north shore of Lake Erie. A detour north on Routes 40/78 takes you to Dresden and *Uncle Tom's Cabin Historic Site.* Harriet Beecher Stowe's novel of the same name was partly based on the life of the Reverend Josiah Henson, a fugitive black slave who built a cabin and founded a vocational school for other fugitives in Dresden. His descendants, who now run the site, are quick to challenge the pejorative meaning now linked to the name "Uncle Tom"; it is engraved on Henson's headstone as a tribute. Closed Sunday mornings and October through mid-May; admission charge (phone: 519-683-2978).

Back on Route 3, you will come to *John E. Pearce Provincial Park,* with secluded picnic sites, a woodland hiking trail, and a superb view over Lake Erie from its cliffs (no swimming access). During migration season, you can see (and photograph) a variety of hawks. The park is for day use only.

The name Talbot is common in this region. In the early 1800s, Colonel Thomas Talbot, a member of Lieutenant Governor John G. Simcoe's staff, received land in return for recruiting settlers. Eventually he controlled 60,000 acres, organizing 27 townships from Long Point to the Detroit River. At Talbotville Royal, take Route 4 south to St. Thomas and Port Stanley for a delightful diversion.

ST. THOMAS Set in the gently rolling landscape of Elgin County's tobacco belt, St. Thomas is one of the loveliest cities in southwestern Ontario. It is well known for its fine architecture, dating back some 130 years.

The *Elgin County Pioneer Museum* (32 Talbot St.; phone: 519-631-6537) was built in 1848–49 for pioneer physician Elijah Duncombe. Its displays relate to the early development of the community, with exhibits of numerous pioneer tools and crafts as well as regional birds. Closed Mondays; admission charge.

St. Thomas's hundred-acre *Pinafore Park* (Elgin and Elm Sts.) features a wildlife sanctuary, a picnic area, tennis courts, a baseball diamond, and, on weekends, a genuine steam locomotive that occasionally travels the narrow-gauge railway. The *St. Thomas Memorial Arena* (80 Wilson Ave.; phone: 519-631-4015) hosts a major two-day antiques show every November.

PORT STANLEY On the north shore of Lake Erie, about a 15-minute drive south on Route 4, is this picturesque fishing village (pop. 1,700).

Port Stanley holds a festival called *Calipso* (an acronym for *C*ome *a*nd *L*ive *i*n *P*ort *S*tanley, *O*ntario), in early August, with bonfires, an outdoor market, a boat parade, and dancing to a steel band. The *Kettle Creek Queen* (phone: 519-782-3566), a paddle wheeler, offers hour-long cruises May through September at 1:30 and 3 PM. The town also boasts Canada's only privately owned passenger train service. Run by volunteers, the 45-minute round trip links Port Stanley, Union, and St. Thomas. It operates daily in July and August; weekends in spring and fall; and Sundays only in winter (phone: 519-782-3730).

En Route from Port Stanley Follow Route 24 along the north shore of Lake Erie to Port Bruce, where the road connects with Route 73. Another 15 minutes of driving will bring you to the tobacco town of Aylmer.

AYLMER Located in the heart of a thriving agricultural area, these heavily fertilized and irrigated fields of sandy soil are prime for the production of flue-cured tobacco. Aylmer also plays host to some 60,000 whistling swans that stop here on their yearly migration to the Arctic during April and May.

En Route from Aylmer Take Route 3 west back to its junction with Route 4 at St. Thomas, and follow Route 4 (joined by Route 2) until it becomes Wharncliffe Road, inside London.

LONDON This city sits at the fork of the north and south branches of the Thames River. The river, called Aspenessippi by the natives, reminded Governor Simcoe of the English Thames, and with his usual disregard for the established, he promptly changed its name. Capable of sudden floods, the Thames meanders through the heart of London, passing commercial enterprises and gracious old homes on quiet, tree-lined streets.

London is known as the "Forest City," the product of a farsighted and extensive tree-planting program undertaken more than a century ago and continued today. The city still plants a thousand trees in its civic squares, 1,500 acres of parkland, and along busy thoroughfares every year. Strolling along these shady streets, you'll discover museums, art galleries, antiques shops, specialty stores, excellent restaurants and hotels, and, as in the original London, a surprising variety of parks.

On the banks of the Thames, *Springbank Park* is a source of justifiable pride to Londoners. Its 350 acres include broad expanses of lawn, colorful flower beds, a careful selection of trees, picnicking facilities, and *Storybook Gardens,* a theme park designed for children. *Storybook Gardens* is closed October through April. From the dock, you can take a cruise along the Thames on the paddle wheeler *Storybook Queen* or a 20-minute ride on the *Tinkerbell* (boat schedules vary).

Reservoir Park, on the highest point of land in London, offers a beautiful vista of the Thames Valley and the downtown area.

Fanshawe Park, operated by the *Upper Thames Conservation Authority,* was established to combat the traditional problem of flooding in the Thames watershed. The dam and reservoir, built in 1953, remain the largest flood-control structures in Ontario. Normally used at its low level for recreational activities, the lake is capable of holding 38,880 acre-feet of water in emergencies. While functioning as protection for downstream communities, the 4-mile lake and park area provide beaches, swimming, sailing, fishing, hiking, picnicking, campgrounds (open May through September), an 18-hole golf course, and *Fanshawe Pioneer Village* (entrance off Fanshawe Park Rd.; phone: 519-457-1296). The last is a museum complex that authentically reproduces a typical crossroads Canadian community of the pre-railway 19th century. Buildings include log cabins, a barn, blacksmith's and weaver's shops, carriage makers, a general store, a Presbyterian church, a brewery, and a replica of the original Free Press Building. Closed November through April; admission charge.

Sifton Bog (Oxford St., east of Sanitorium Rd.) is a 15,000-year-old black spruce floating bog that contains rare specimens of orchids and certain medicinal plants; the round leaves of the sundew, for instance, can be dried and powdered for use as a cold medication. Huge masses of bright green sphagnum moss—60 feet deep in places—float in the bog; the moss has been used by Native Americans as a disposable diaper, by medicine men as an antiseptic, and by World War I medics as a field dressing. The center of the bog can be reached on a boardwalk, from which the bottom is visible through crystal-clear water. Carnivorous plants seem to do well around the edges of the area, and attentive bog watchers may spot lemmings.

The *Royal Canadian Regiment Museum* (*Wolseley Hall;* phone: 519-660-5102) has a spectacular collection of weapons, uniforms, and memorabilia from Canada's oldest regular infantry regiment. It is closed Mondays and holidays; no admission charge. At the *London Regional Children's Museum* (21 Wharncliffe Rd. S.; phone: 519-434-5726), kids can climb down a manhole and see underground telephone cables; study the stars; and rummage through a huge box of props and come up dressed as a Roman soldier or Native American. Open daily; admission charge.

The *London Museum of Archaeology* (1600 Attarwandaron Rd.; phone: 519-473-1360), on a bluff overlooking Snake Creek and the Medway River, shows life as it was for the natives before Europeans arrived. It is open daily; admission charge. Also worth seeing is the *Banting Museum* (442 Adelaide St. N.; phone: 519-673-1752), which originally was the laboratory where Sir Frederick Banting did much of his research on using insulin as a treatment for diabetes. (In nearby Banting Square, the Flame of Hope burns to symbolize the continuing search for a cure for this disease.) At the museum, visitors can view exhibits related to this work, which earned the scientist a Nobel Prize. The museum is closed Sundays, Mondays, and the last two weeks of December; admission charge.

The *London Regional Art and Historical Museum* (421 Ridout St.; phone: 519-672-4580) is an architectural gem in a superb natural setting. It features the works of leading national and international artists, plus a permanent collection of more than 2,000 historical and current works. It's closed mornings and Mondays; no admission charge. The *Guy Lombardo Music Centre* (205 Wonderland Rd. S.; phone: 519-473-9003) traces the story of "Mr. New Year's Eve" and his *Royal Canadians.* Born in London, Guy and his siblings formed a band that played for presidents at the *White House* and became synonymous with "Auld Lang Syne" and ringing in the *New Year* in New York. It's open daily May through September; by appointment the rest of the year.

London's pride and joy is its *Grand Theatre* (471 Richmond St.; phone: 519-672-8800; 800-265-1593 in Canada), whose professional productions range from serious drama to comedy and musicals.

A great way to see the city is to take a walking tour prepared by the historians of London's public library. Check with the visitors' bureau at *City Hall* (Wellington St. and Dufferin Ave.; phone: 519-661-5000) or the library (305 Queens Ave.; phone: 519-661-5100). Less active folks can catch a double-decker tour bus from *City Hall,* which runs daily.

London is reputed to have a larger shopping area per capita than any other Canadian metropolis. Stop into the *Antiquarian* (Richmond and Horton Sts.; phone: 519-432-4422), famous for its antiques and wide variety of figurines unavailable elsewhere; then go over to *Covent Garden Market* (off Market La., in the center of London) for some fresh fruit, a wedge of cheese, some warm, crusty bread, and homemade cookies to round off your picnic. This same part of downtown London teems with good restaurants of all kinds. The *Great West Steak House* (240 Waterloo St.; phone: 519-438-4149) enjoys a reputation for generous portions and reasonable prices.

In the *Longwoods Road Conservation Area* is the *Ska-Nah-Doht Native American Village* (Oneida for "a village stands again"). Reconstructed with longhouses of cedar and elm bark, the village is perched on a sandy bluff overlooking the forks of a stream. The Attawandaron occupied this area 400 years ago. An agricultural tribe, they were as rooted to this place as their carefully tended fields and refused to become involved in the Iroquois-Huron conflict. They became known as the Neutrals, and like neutrals in so many wars, they traded their skillfully made flint tools and weapons to combatants throughout the area. *Ska-Nah-Doht* strives to re-create faithfully the activities of the entire village. Corn and squash are planted and harvested on plots cleared by felling trees and burning out the stumps. A stockade encircles the central village, complete with a sweat lodge (similar to a sauna, but used for religious ceremonies), a council chamber, fish-drying racks, and a special dwelling belonging to the shaman, the group's spiritual leader. The village is closed weekends *Labour Day* to *Victoria Day;* the park area (12 miles/19 km west of London, off Rte. 2; phone: 519-264-2420) is open year-round. Admission charge weekends from *Victoria Day* to late June; daily from late June to *Labour Day.*

En Route from London If you're staying on the west side of town, take Route 4 north to its junction with Route 7 at Elgenfield, and follow Route 7 into Stratford. From downtown London, follow Route 90 or Route 2 east to Ingersoll, where Route 19 leads north into the Stratford area. Routes 7 and 19 intersect outside of Stratford and enter the festival city as one road

STRATFORD Stratford is in the heart of what were once the prized farmlands of the Huron nation. The Upper Canada (as Ontario was then called) government gave about a million acres to the Canada Company to sell to settlers, and in 1932 a community sprang up around a mill on a small tributary of the Thames River. The proprietor of the only inn in the area, William Sargint, hung a likeness of William Shakespeare over the door, and the place became known as the *Shakespeare Inn*; it was the focal point of community activities. Before long the community adopted the name Stratford, and the tributary was renamed the Avon. It has since been widened where it passes through *Upper Queen's Park* (in front of the *Festival Theatre*) and is a favorite boating and picnicking spot for theatergoers. In the summer, a jazz group plays on a barge.

Until a generation ago Stratford was best known for its train-repair facilities and furniture manufacturing, but Shakespeare changed all that. The *Stratford Festival* (PO Box 520, Stratford, ONT N5A 6V2; phone: 519-273-1600; 800-567-1600; fax: 519-273-6173) takes place May through mid-November and no longer limits itself to performances of plays by Shakespeare. Other classics—from Lewis Carroll to Molière—plus musicals and even gritty dramas like the boxing story *In The Ring* have been added in recent years. The box office now offers one-stop shopping for tickets and for accommodations approved by the *Stratford Chamber of Commerce.* (Also see *Festivals, Fairs, and Fancy Acts* in DIVERSIONS) Hotels and motels are generally good, and bed and breakfast establishments are a way of life here. The *Visitor Information Centre* (York St., two blocks from the *Tom Patterson Theatre*; phone: 519-273-3352) displays pictures of bed and breakfast properties in the area.

Restaurants are the natural companions of theaters, and Stratford has achieved an excellent balance in variety and cost. Built more than a century ago as a church, the *Church Restaurant and Belfry* (70 Brunswick St.; phone: 519-273-3424) is a gastronomic landmark, with prices to match. The same goes for *Rundle's* (9 Cobourg St.; phone: 519-271-6442) and the *Old Prune* (151 Albert St.; phone: 519-271-4157), both of which specialize in French fare on a fixed-price basis. (Here's a sample from the *Old Prune* menu: salmon strudel in an aromatic carrot-ginger broth, with a tumeric-cucumber chutney.)

At the *Queens' Inn* in Stratford (see *Best en Route*), the *Boar's Head* pub offers hearty, inexpensive meals—the pub pie and locally brewed ale will sustain you through the longest Shakespearean epic. Most other restaurants are in the moderate price range. For something unusual, try the honey-mustard shrimp or shrimp Thai noodles at the *Sun Room* (55 George St.; phone: 519-273-0331).

En Route from Stratford Toronto is 95 miles (152 km) away. Those who can extend their trip should stop along the way in the town of Cambridge, where the *Langdon Hall* hotel pampers its guests in a country manor setting (see *Best en Route*).

BEST EN ROUTE

If you're traveling during the summer, make reservations as early as possible; good places are booked far in advance. Fortunately, there is no shortage of good motels and campgrounds in this area, and you can expect all creature comforts to be available—this isn't the North Woods. For a double room for one night, expect to pay $75 or more at an expensive hotel;

from $55 to $75 at one in the moderate category; and from $40 to $55 at a place we rate inexpensive. All hotels feature such amenities as air conditioning, private baths, TV sets, and telephones unless otherwise indicated. Campgrounds provide very inexpensive lodgings, costing $20 or less. For each location, places are listed alphabetically by price category.

WINDSOR

Compri Windsor If you enjoy socializing and a "club" atmosphere, this hotel is for you. A large room overlooking the river is devoted to table games and has an area for children. There's no dining room, but snacks are available. There are 207 guestrooms, an exercise room, an indoor pool, a whirlpool, and a sauna. 333 Riverside Dr. W. (phone: 519-977-9777; 800-267-9777; fax: 519-977-1411). Expensive.

Travel Lodge This hotel offers 160 pleasant rooms, a dining room, an indoor pool, and a whirlpool bath. Downtown, at 33 Riverside Dr. E. (phone: 519-258-7774; 800-525-9055; fax: 519-258-0020). Expensive to moderate.

Ivy Rose Even the highest rates at this motel—which buy whirlpool baths and a private movie channel—are reasonable by Ontario standards. Some of the 91 pleasant, spacious rooms have water beds. There's a dining room, playground, and heated outdoor pool. 2888 Howard Ave., across from the *Devonshire Shopping Mall* (phone: 519-966-1700; 800-265-7366; fax: 519-966-1700). Moderate to inexpensive.

Windsor South KOA In this popular 50-acre campground are 178 sites and three cabins, water/electric hookups, a dumping station, a laundry room, and a store. Recreational facilities include a gameroom, bingo, hayrides, an outdoor pool, and a stocked fishing pond. Open year-round. 4855 Ninth Concession, 7 miles (11 km) south on Howard Ave., west of Rte. 401 (phone: 519-735-3660). Very inexpensive.

AMHERSTBURG

Duffy's This attractive and well-equipped motel overlooking the Detroit River has been renovated and expanded from 17 to 35 rooms. There are three Jacuzzi suites, a dining room popular with the locals, a pool, and a marina with 70 boats. 306 Dalhousie St. (phone: 519-736-2101; fax: 519-736-2103). Moderate.

Holiday Beach Conservation Area Formerly owned by the province, this campground on a beautiful 2,000-foot sandy beach on Lake Erie offers 32 sites for seasonal rent, 59 tent sites, and 10 overnight sites with water and power hookups. Central facilities include a dump tank, flush toilets, fireplaces, a store, and a shelter. Trail motorcycles and all-terrain vehicles are not permitted. In addition to a bird sanctuary and bird-observation platform, a pond is stocke with rainbow trout for fishing derbies. Nine miles (14 km) south of Amherstburg off Rte. 18 (phone: 519-736-3772). Very inexpensive.

KINGSVILLE

Lakeshore Terrace On the shores of Lake Erie, this place has 40 rooms, a restaurant, and a beach. There's a golf course nearby. 85 Park St. E. (phone: 519-733-4651). Moderate.

Adams Golden Acres The 27 rooms and efficiency units here are on grounds set back from the road. About half the units have kitchenettes; there is no restaurant. A playground and a golf course are located nearby. One mile (1.6 km) west on Rte. 18 (phone: 519-733-6531). Inexpensive.

Pleasant Valley Trailer Park This campground 1 mile (1.6 km) from Lake Erie has 135 sites with electrical and water hookups (all but 20 have sewer hookups), fireplaces, a dump station, flush toilets, showers, a shelter, laundry facilities, a video gameroom, and a pool. Nearby are restaurants, riding, hiking trails, and golf. One mile (1.6 km) west on Rte. 18 (phone: 519-733-5961). Very inexpensive.

PELEE ISLAND

Pelee Island This two-story, 14-room lakefront establishment has many good features. Breakfast, lunch, and dinner are served in the pleasant dining room. There's a rocky beach in front of the hotel; a sandy beach is a short drive away. At the West Dock (phone: 519-724-2912). Moderate.

LEAMINGTON

Pelee Amenities at this 94-room motel include a sauna, a whirlpool bath, an indoor pool, a coffee shop, a dining room, a beach, and, nearby, a golf course. A few minutes' south of town on Rte. 33 (phone: 519-326-8646). Moderate.

Sun Parlor A quiet motel, it has 18 units, some with water beds and six with kitchens. There's also a dining room. Close to tennis courts and a sports complex, at 135 Talbot St. W. (phone: 519-326-6131). Moderate to inexpensive.

Wigle's Set on spacious, landscaped grounds, this attractive motel has 24 units, a playground, a coffee shop, and a dining room. 135 Talbot St. E. (phone: 519-326-3265). Inexpensive.

RONDEAU PROVINCIAL PARK AREA

Queen's Here are 17 units; a restaurant, playground, and golf course are nearby. On Rte. 3, a mile (1.6 km) west of Blendheim and about 11 miles (18 km) west of the park (phone: 519-676-5477). Inexpensive.

Rondeau Provincial Park Here are 258 campsites, 106 with electrical hookups. Other facilities include flush toilets, laundry facilities, showers, fireplaces, a store, a shelter, a sanitary dump, a launching ramp, and a natural beach. Restaurants, boat rentals, a marina, hiking trails, and horseback riding are nearby. Four miles (6 km) south on Rte. 51 (phone: 519-674-1750). Inexpensive.

PORT STANLEY

Kettle Creek Inn Built in 1849, this delightful European-style inn has won several awards for its food. In summer, dinner is served in the gazebo on the lawn. There are 10 rooms and five suites with private balconies, whirlpool baths, and gas fireplaces. Maine St. (phone: 519-782-3388; fax: 519-782-4747). Expensive.

LONDON

Golden Pheasant All 41 rooms here come with extra-long beds and radios. Other pluses include a heated outdoor pool, a playground, a restaurant, and a coffee shop. Rte. 22, 1 mile (1.6 km) west of Rte. 4 (phone: 519-473-4551; fax: 519-471-2265). Moderate.

Motor Court The 26 rooms here are noted for their variety; among the choices are water beds, air beds, honeymoon suites, housekeeping units, a sauna, and a whirlpool bath. There's no restaurant, but plenty of fast-food establishments are nearby. 1883 Dundas St. E., near the airport (phone: 519-451-2610). Moderate to inexpensive.

Fanshawe Park Conservation Area This 3,000-acre park has more than 639 campsites, 400 with electrical hookups and 239 with water. There also are flush toilets, showers, ice, fireplaces, a store, a shelter, launching ramps, a pool, and a beach. Nearby are boat rentals and hiking; pets are allowed. Open early May to early October. 691 Ontario St. (phone: 519-451-2800). Very inexpensive.

Happy Hills On 175 acres are 350 sites, all with electrical and water hookups; a dumping station; flush toilets; showers; ice; fireplaces; a shelter; and a heated pool. Motorbikes not allowed. Miniature golf, a horseshoe pitch, and hayrides provide the diversions. From Rte. 7, take Embro Rd. 11 miles (18 km) southwest (phone: 519-475-4471). Very inexpensive.

STRATFORD

As You Like It This motel has 18 comfortable rooms equipped with refrigerators air conditioning, telephones, and TV sets; also on the premises are a sunny breakfast room and outdoor heated pool. It has a quiet country atmosphere and has won solid ratings in recent years. 379 Romeo St. (phone: 519-271-2951). Expensive.

Queen's Inn First built in 1850 and rebuilt in 1905 after a fire, this landmark hotel in the city center was owned by the same family from 1914 to 1970. After a period of decline, it was renovated in the early 1990s. The 30 guestrooms are delightfully decorated in period furniture. The *Queen Victoria Room* offers formal dining; good pub fare is available in the *Boar's Head.* Room rates are usually much lower on Mondays (non-theater night). 161 Ontario St. (phone: 519-271-1400). Expensive.

Shakespeare Inn More Bavarian than Bard, this crisp, clean inn on the main street of the tiny village of Shakespeare, a seven-minute drive from Stratford, has 50 units and suites, as well as a café. Hwys. 7 and 8 (phone: 519-625-8050). Expensive to moderate.

St. Vincent Guest House Stratford abounds in bed and breakfast establishments, and in general they enjoy a reputation for high standards. Typical is this one, a cozy home with a patio, a garden, and a gazebo overlooking the Avon River. It has a self-contained unit with a kitchen that's stocked with coffee and teas. 50 St. Vincent St. S. (phone: 519-271-9866). Moderate.

CAMBRIDGE

Langdon Hall A member of the prestigious Relais & Châteaux group, this hotel is set in the deep woods. Once a turn-of-the-century summer home, the manor offers 39 guestrooms (most with fireplaces) and two suites, a candlelit dining room specializing in French and regional fare, a billiards room, a sauna, and a whirlpool. Also see *Special Havens* in DIVERSIONS. Exit 275 off Rte. 401 on Homer Watson Rd., south to Langdon Rd. (phone: 519-740-2100; fax: 519-740-8161). Expensive.

The Heritage Highways

The Heritage Highways are a network of roadways originating at the popular border crossing of Niagara Falls, skirting Lake Ontario and extending along the banks of the St. Lawrence River to the tip of the Gaspé Peninsula in Quebec. They follow the byways developed from trails first blazed by the natives and later by European explorers and settlers. This drive, from Niagara Falls to Toronto, constitutes 74 miles (118 km) of the 377 miles (603 km) of these historical highways in Ontario, comprising both high-speed express routes and meandering roadways.

From Niagara Falls, the route leads quickly to Ontario's past, into the 1800s village of Niagara-on-the-Lake, home of the *George Bernard Shaw Festival.* It then traverses the extensive wine- and fruit-producing district spanning the Niagara peninsula. After rounding the western end of Lake Ontario, the route goes on to the metropolitan areas of Hamilton and Toronto.

NIAGARA FALLS Canada's most famous border city has been a major magnet for travelers for centuries. The thundering falls are formed as the waters of the Niagara River are forced through a narrows before plunging almost 200 feet over limestone cliffs. A small island in the river splits the whitewater juggernaut into two falls: the straight-crested American Falls—167 feet high and 1,060 feet wide; and the Horseshoe (Canadian) Falls—158 feet high and 2,600 feet wide. Another, smaller waterfall, Bridal Veil, lies on the American side, but the Canadian side commands grander views (from two observation towers). The towns on both sides cater to the tourist trade, with the Canadian side perhaps slightly less commercial. Abuses by humans do not, however, constitute the threat to the falls' beauty that natural phenomena do. The shale and limestone foundations of the riverbed are slowly being washed away by the sheer force of the plunging water. As this erosion continues, the falls will be forced backward until they flatten out entirely, becoming just a series of rapids in the river.

Meanwhile, if you can dream up an offbeat angle from which you'd like to view the falls, chances are someone has already thought of it and has turned it into a prosperous business. The *Falls Incline Railway* (phone: 905-356-0943) provides transportation up and down the escarpment in twin cable rail cars from *Easter* weekend to mid-October. For an aerial view, you can take the *Niagara Spanish Aerocar* (phone: 905-354-5711), a cable car that makes a dizzying 1,800-foot trip over the Whirlpool Rapids from March through late October; go on a helicopter ride; or gaze from one of the several observation towers. The two best viewing towers are on the Canadian side on a 250-foot bank across from the falls. The taller one is the 524-foot *Skylon Tower* (phone: 905-356-2651), with a viewing height about 770 feet above the base of the falls, complete with a revolving dining room, a lounge, and an indoor/outdoor observation deck, all on three levels atop its structural base. A variety of shops and an amusement area are located below. The shorter, 416-foot *Minolta Tower* (viewing height of about 665 feet) features the *Pinnacle Restaurant* (phone: 905-356-1501), offering international cuisine and five theme gift shops. Both towers are open daily to midnight.

At ground level are a number of ways to approach the falls. *People Movers* are ultramodern buses that run between the falls and the *Aerocar* (see above), allowing passengers to get on and off at any of several stops. Of the various boat trips, the *Maid of the Mist* is the most famous. (Actually, there are four sightseeing boats named *Maid of the Mist,* so the wait for a ride is never too long.) Wearing hooded raincoats (supplied), you can enter the Table Rock Scenic Tunnels to view points behind the falls. There's also a spray-doused viewing station at the foot of the falls. The tunnels are open daily year-round; admission charge.

On the hillside opposite the falls, near the end of Rainbow Bridge, is the *Niagara Falls Museum* (5651 River Rd.; phone: 905-356-2151), including the *Daredevil Hall of Fame,* honoring those who challenged the falls in barrels and on rafts (some made it; others perished). The museum is open daily year-round. There's also *Ripley's Believe It or Not Museum* (4960 Clifton Hill; phone: 905-356-2238); *Tussaud's Waxworks Museum* (4915 Clifton Hill; phone: 905-374-6601), with life-size statues of kings, presidents, and other notables and nasties; and the *Houdini Museum* (4983 Clifton Hill; phone: 905-356-4869). All museums are open daily year-round and charge admission. *Marineland* (7657 Portage Rd.; phone: 905-356-9565) offers popular daily shows featuring whales, dolphins, and sea lions. Open daily year-round; admission charge includes access to an adjacent game farm and a summer midway boasting the world's largest roller coaster.

One feature at Niagara Falls is *Tivoli Miniature World* (5930 Victoria Ave.; phone: 905-357-4100), formerly located in nearby Vineland. It has marvelous 1:50-scale replicas of such world landmarks as *St. Peter's Basilica,* the *Eiffel Tower,* and the *Kremlin.* Closed November through March.

Note that souvenirs of the falls are available at many of the smaller towns along the route, where they may be cheaper than they are here. Non-falls-related items (such as traditional woolen clothing and Inuit carvings) also are likely to be cheaper elsewhere. For more details on the falls' history and facilities, see *Quintessential Canada* in DIVERSIONS.

For a change of pace, you can sample the wares of a local vintner. Although once the subject of much derision, Canadian wine has improved greatly; taste it for yourself during a tour of *Bright's Wines* (4887 Dorchester St.; phone: 905-357-2400), one of Ontario's largest and most prestigious wineries. Tours are given daily; groups of 10 or more should make reservations.

En Route from Niagara Falls The Niagara Parkway parallels the river northward toward Lake Ontario, running through a delightful system of parks and historic sites on its 18-mile (29-km) route to Niagara-on-thc-Lake.

About 5 miles (8 km) north of Niagara Falls is the *Niagara Parks Commission*'s *Botanical Gardens,* with acres of magnificent flowers and gardens. Just beyond is the *Floral Clock,* a working timepiece some 40 feet across comprising thousands of brilliantly colored plants that bloom from early spring to the first frost. The indoor gardens are open daily year-round; closed November to mid-April outdoors; no admission charge.

Queenston Heights Park at Queenston, just a few miles north of Niagara Falls, marks the slopes where the British eventually defeated American troops attempting to overtake Queenston in October 1812. British General Sir Isaac Brock, one of Upper Canada's most prominent war heroes, died here while leading the first counterattack against American soldiers.

Nearby, in Queenston Village, is the *Laura Secord Homestead* (Partition St.; phone: 905-262-4851), a restored 1800s dwelling. Laura Secord became a heroine during the War of 1812 by walking 19 miles to reveal the plans of an American attack to a British officer. Although he already knew of the attack from other sources, her courage in defying the soldiers who had occupied her home eventually was rewarded by the Prince of Wales (later Edward VII). Closed mid-October to mid-May.

NIAGARA-ON-THE-LAKE On the west bank of the Niagara River at its mouth on Lake Ontario, this historic village (1781) was one of the earlier settlements in southern Ontario. Originally Butlersburg, its name was changed to Newark in 1792 when it became the first capital of Upper Canada. During this period, *Fort George,* the principal British outpost on the Niagara frontier, was erected nearby. The town was occupied by American soldiers during the War of 1812, and both the town and *Fort George* were destroyed in 1813, when the troops abandoned the area.

Eventually rebuilt, this town has some excellent examples of 19th-century architecture. Stately homes with wide doorways adorned with decorative transoms line avenues shaded by ancient trees. The revived community, the point of entry to Canada for many Mennonite and Amish settlers, was dubbed Niagara-on-the-Lake in 1906. Today the main street, Queen Street, houses several crafts shops selling quilts, hand-crafted furniture, and other period items. *Greaves Jam* (phone: 905-468-7831), staffed by its fourth generation of cooks, still produces jam in the small kitchen behind the store. The *Niagara Apothecary Museum* (phone: 905-468-3845) no longer dispenses the medicaments of the 1860s on its shelves but merely displays them. It's closed early September to early May; no admission charge.

The town's biggest attraction, which draws theater lovers from all over and presents top-name talent in several productions, is the annual *George Bernard Shaw Festival* (phone: 800-724-2934 in the US; 800-267-4759 in Canada), held late May through mid-November at the *Royal George Theatre,* the *Court House Theatre,* and the ultramodern *Festival Theatre.* For details, see *Festivals, Fairs, and Fancy Acts* in DIVERSIONS.

The *Inniskillin Wine Boutique,* located amid vineyards on Service Road 66 off the parkway, showcases what are widely regarded as some of the best wines produced in Canada. The cellar contains limited-edition vintages, and the *Champagne Loft* shows how champagne is made, down to the all-important art of turning the bottles by hand during fermentation. Tours are offered daily (phone: 905-468-3554).

Fort George, on the outskirts of town (Picton St.; phone: 905-468-3938), was rebuilt in 1815, and it was reconstructed as a tourist attraction in the 1930s after a period of disuse. Now it is staffed by colorfully dressed troops who regularly display their expertise. The fort is open daily mid-May through October; weekdays only November through March; and weekends only April through mid-May.

En Route from Niagara-on-the-Lake The Queen Elizabeth Way (QEW) a high-speed auto route, is easily accessible via the Stone Road (Rte. 55) about 7 miles (11 km) southwest of town. It leads into St. Catharines (about 16 miles/26 km from Niagara-on-the-Lake) and then follows the shore of Lake Ontario toward Hamilton. The Scenic Blossom Route (Rte. 87) to St. Catharines follows the lakeshore west from Niagara-on-the-Lake through a broad fruit-growing area where roadside stands sell the season's fresh produce. Many small towns here were founded by German settlers.

ST. CATHARINES Located among the vines and orchards of Ontario's prime fruit and wine-producing district, St. Catharines has been nicknamed the "Garden

City." A visit to the *Farmer's Market* (outdoors near *City Hall* and the federal buildings), which is held Tuesdays, Thursdays, and Saturdays, demonstrates how well the town and region have earned their claim to unusually abundant harvests and gardens.

Settled by English Loyalists before the American Civil War, the city was an important Underground Railroad terminus. Today it is a major stop for travelers to the area's many festivals. Late September's *Niagara Grape and Wine Festival* celebrates the ripening of the grapes in true bacchanalian style, with 10 days of eating, drinking, parades, and contests of strength and skill (for more information, see *Festivals, Fairs, and Fancy Acts* in DIVERSIONS). Second in size only to the famous one in England, the *Royal Canadian Henley Regatta* in August attracts champion rowers here from all over the world. Local newspapers provide details on the best vantage points.

The Welland Canal facilitates passage between Lakes Ontario and Erie for ships unable to negotiate the Niagara River (and Falls). A series of locks compensate for the 326-foot variation in water level between the two lakes. At the northern end of the canal (which divides Niagara-on-the-Lake and St. Catharines), an observation platform near Lock 3 offers a close look at the lock as seagoing freighters rise and fall with the water level (take the Glendale Ave. exit from the QEW eastbound or the Niagara St. exit westbound, and follow signs).

Peter D's (Fourth St.; phone: 905-687-8888) is a pleasant and reasonably priced family eatery. Ontario Street boasts a wide variety of restaurants; *Archie's at the Parkway* (phone: 905-688-2324) is a good bet.

En Route from St. Catharines Use Canal Road to get back onto Route 87, the Scenic Blossom Route, and continue west along Lake Ontario, passing by several boat-launching areas and beaches. Near Henley Island, Route 87 becomes Route 34 and turns south to intersect Route 818. Follow Route 818 for a side trip to Jordan, a few miles inland.

JORDAN Before the construction of the canal, Jordan was an important shipping center, providing access to Lake Ontario through Twenty Mile Creek. The area's economy is now based on its prominence as a wine-producing center. A group of early structures is part of the *Jordan Historical Museum of the Twenty* (3802 Main St.; phone: 905-562-5242), named after the creek responsible for the settlement's growth. The *Vintage House* (ca. 1840) and the *Jacob Fry House* (ca. 1815) display many items used by the early Mennonite settlers, including a wedding dress and several of the patterns and equipment used by Samuel Fry, a weaver. The buildings are closed November through March.

The *Balls Falls Conservation Area,* just off Route 8, features two medium-size waterfalls, the larger about 90 feet high, and an 1809 gristmill. The Bruce Trail, one of the original routes through the peninsula, cuts across the Balls Falls area on its 430-mile (688-km) stretch from Niagara Falls to Lake Huron.

En Route from Jordan Return to Route 818 and continue along the lakeshore toward Hamilton. Between Grimsby and Hamilton, a short detour on Route 6 leads to *Hamilton Airport,* home of the *Canadian Warplane Heritage Museum* and a superb collection of World War II aircraft. Open daily year-round; admission charge (phone: 905-679-4183).

HAMILTON History credits United Empire Loyalists with selecting this site in 1778, but not until 1813, when businessman George Hamilton laid out a pattern of lots and roadways, did the city really sprout. Shortly after a canal was cut through the sandbar (which had landlocked the city's most usable port area), Hamilton rose to prominence as a Great Lakes shipping port and Canada's largest steel-producing city.

Dundurn Castle—built in 1832 by Sir Allan MacNab (later Prime Minister of pre-confederated Canada) and named for his ancestral homeland in Scotland—is a 36-room Regency villa overlooking Hamilton Harbour. Restored in 1967, it is the site of concerts and other outdoor events. It's open daily year-round, but with shorter hours October through mid-June; guided tours are available. There's an admission charge (phone: 905-546-2872).

A short distance northwest are the *Royal Botanical Gardens* (Rte. 2; phone: 905-527-1158), with over 2,000 acres of gardens and a 1,200-acre wildlife sanctuary. Open daily year-round; admission charge. The gardens host the *Sugaring-off Festival,* a two-week celebration of maple syrup making and pancake eating, held annually in March at the *Rock Chapel Sugar Shanty* (a 15-minute drive north on Rte. 6).

En Route from Hamilton Take the QEW east across Hamilton Harbour on the Burlington Skyway Bridge, heading toward Toronto, 44 miles (70 km) northeast. You are now entering the heart of Ontario's economy, the Golden Triangle, which stretches from Hamilton to Oshawa (on the far side of Toronto). Avoid driving through this congested area during afternoon rush hour. Take time out in Burlington, if possible, to visit the *Joseph Brant Museum* (1240 North Shore Blvd. E.; phone: 905-634-3556), a tribute to one of the most powerful native chiefs. It is housed in a replica of the cedar home built for him in about 1800. Open daily; admission charge. In mid-July, check out the *Highland Games,* a week-long festival including bagpipe contests, dancing, and the traditional throwing of the caber (the Scottish sport of throwing a log or tree trunk as a test of strength).

Halfway between Hamilton and Toronto is the community of Oakville filled with beautiful parklands and homes of the wealthy. The *Glen Abbey* golf course (1306 Lakeshore Rd. E.; phone: 905-844-1800), designed by Jack Nicklaus for championship play, is the permanent site of the *Canadian Open,* held every June. Its clubhouse is a former monastery.

Nearby *Bronte Creek Provincial Park* (Exit 109 off the QEW; phone 905-827-6911) has a children's farm, a play loft, a 1.6-acre pool, and win ter ice skating outdoors; the rink becomes a basketball court in the warmer months. It's open daily.

Back on the QEW, continue to the Gardiner Expressway and take the Yonge Street turnoff into downtown Toronto.

TORONTO For details on the provincial capital, see *Toronto* in THE CITIES.

BEST EN ROUTE

Due to the high volume of tourist traffic flowing through the province, most hotel accommodations fall in the expensive and moderate price categories. Those charging $75 or more per night for a double are considered expensive; those costing from $55 to $75 are moderate; and those charging $50 or less are inexpensive. All hotels feature such amenities as air conditioning, private baths, TV sets, and telephones unless otherwise indicated. Campgrounds provide very inexpensive accommodations, usually costing no more than $20. Reservations are advised at all places, at all times, and should be made weeks in advance during the summer and fall. For each location, places are listed alphabetically by price category.

NIAGARA FALLS

Ameri-Cana About 4 miles (6 km) outside the hustle and bustle of downtown, amid spacious grounds with a play area, this motor inn has 120 rooms, including honeymoon and Jacuzzi suites, as well as several efficiencies and kitchen units. There are indoor and outdoor sports facilities and a restaurant. A good base of operations if you've got a small mob with you. 8444 Lundy's La. (phone: 905-356-8444; 800-263-3508; fax: 905-356-8576). Expensive.

Brock The best-known hostelry in town offers a good view of both sets of falls from many of its 233 rooms. The *Rainbow Room* is a popular dining spot. 5685 Falls Ave. (phone: 905-374-4445; 800-263-7135; fax: 905-357-4804). Expensive.

Foxhead Inn The inn has about 400 modern rooms, many of which overlook the falls, and a full range of features—including a pool, an excellent dining room, and a sports complex. 5875 Falls Ave. (phone: 905-374-4444; 800-263-7135; fax: 905-357-9550). Expensive.

Michael's Inn A comfortable motor inn overlooking the river and gorge, it has a pool and dining facilities. Many of the 130 rooms offer good falls views from their balconies. 5599 River Rd. (phone: 905-354-2727; 800-263-9390; fax: 905-374-7706). Expensive.

Parkwood Some of the 32 rooms here have refrigerators. There is an outdoor pool and a picnic area nearby, but no dining room. 8054 Lundy's La. (phone: 905-354-3162). Moderate.

Niagara Falls KOA This appealing 350-site campground has many wooded areas and grassy tent sites as well as RV facilities. If you like tent camping, this is the place. Most sites have power and water hookups; there also are fireplaces, flush toilets, showers, two heated outdoor pools, an indoor pool, hot tubs, shuffleboard, a gameroom, a trampoline, and miniature golf. One mile (1.6 km) west of the QEW on Rte. 20 (phone: 905-354-6472 or 905-356-2267). Very inexpensive.

NIAGARA-ON-THE-LAKE

Angel Inn Originally built in 1779 as a three-room log cabin, the inn always has been a center of local history and politics. Let one of the staff members fill you in on the events that took place here. A hotel since 1823, it is full of authentic colonial pieces and collector's items. The beds in the nine rooms and suites are canopied and embellished with petit point. There is a dining room, a wine bar, and an English pub. Queen St. at Regent St. (phone: 905-468-3411). Expensive.

Pillar and Post There are fireplaces in half of the 90 rooms in this interesting place. Amenities include a sauna, whirlpool bath, outdoor pool, dining room, and crafts and antiques shop. Complimentary morning coffee and a newspaper are provided. King and John Sts. (phone: 905-468-2123). Expensive.

Prince of Wales A truly magnificent, restored, 105-room inn, it is highlighted by the royal suite (and bed) occupied by the Prince of Wales in the 1920s. Meals are served in a fine dining room and a casual cafeteria. Theater and winter packages are available. 6 Picton St. (phone: 905-468-3246). Expensive.

Queen's Landing This elegant Georgian inn overlooks the Niagara River and is directly across the street from the *Shaw Festival.* Many of the 137 guestrooms have canopy beds, fireplaces, and whirlpool baths. There's also a fully equipped exercise room, indoor swimming and lap pools, a sauna, and bicycle rentals. The dining room serves distinctive Canadian dishes, including Brome Lake duckling. Byron St. (phone: 905-468-2195). Expensive.

Moffat Part of this delightful inn dates to 1835. It's on the main street, close to shops and theaters, with 22 individually decorated rooms (some with fireplaces), a solarium lounge and bar, and a restaurant. 60 Picton St. (phone: 905-468-4116). Expensive to moderate.

ST. CATHARINES

Parkway Inn An attractive and convenient downtown spot, it features 125 rooms and enough amenities to satisfy anyone: a sauna, a whirlpool bath, bowling, an indoor pool, and good dining facilities. 327 Ontario St. at the QEW (phone: 905-688-2324). Expensive to moderate.

Crossroads Minutes from Niagara Falls and the famous Seaway twin locks, this motor inn has 20 pleasant rooms, a dining room, and a sports bar serving food until midnight. Exit 406 at Glendale Ave. W. to Merritt St. (phone: 905-227-1183). Moderate.

Highwayman Noted for its cozy atmosphere, this inn has 50 rooms, a restaurant, and an outdoor pool. Winery tours can be arranged. 420 Ontario St. (phone: 905-688-1646). Moderate.

Yonge Street: Toronto to Thunder Bay

Listed in the *Guinness Book of World Records* as the longest street in the world, Yonge Street runs 1,142 miles (1,827 km) from downtown Toronto on Lake Ontario to the province's far southwestern border with Minnesota and Manitoba. It is a trip from urban sophistication to frontier-like austerity, through the rich farmland of southern Ontario's "English counties," across the harsh, mineral-rich mining districts of the Canadian Shield, and through the trapping and fur country north of the Great Lakes. Called Route 11 once it leaves Toronto, Yonge Street knifes across the width of southern Ontario, touching all the features that have forged the province's culture.

Lieutenant Governor John Simcoe began planning the route in 1793, and construction of the roadway began the following year. Its original purpose was to provide a rapid military and commercial route to northern Ontario and the Upper Great Lakes; it became a major force in the settlement of Ontario and a prime factor in knitting this diverse province into a political entity.

The road grew as Ontario grew. At first it served the fur-trading routes, but the discovery of rich mineral deposits in the Canadian Shield, north and west of the lakelands, pulled the road northward, past Lake Nipissing, across the central crest of the Canadian Shield, and on to towns like Kirkland Lake, whose main street is filled with raw gold ore. At its western end, Route 11 cuts south, skirting the shores of Lake Nipigon, past Ouimet Canyon to Thunder Bay, a gateway to the west. This section of Ontario is pure heaven for hunters, anglers, and rock hounds.

TORONTO For a detailed report on the city, see *Toronto* in THE CITIES.

En Route from Toronto The 60-mile (96-km) journey to Barrie, on the shore of Lake Simcoe, begins on Yonge Street (Rte. 11) going north. About 13 miles (21 km) from downtown Toronto is suburban Richmond Hill, known as Mt. Pleasant until the Duke of Richmond renamed it in 1819.

Newmarket, 11 miles (18 km) beyond Richmond Hill, is the site of a Quaker meetinghouse, the first church erected in the lands north of Toronto; it has stood on the west side of Yonge Street since 1810. Another early 1800s structure, also built by Quakers, has been incorporated into the *Pine Orchard Union Church.* The history of Newmarket's settlement is illustrated by the exhibits at the *Whitchurch-Stouffville Museum* (14732 Woodbine Ave., Vandorf; phone: 905-727-8954), set in an 1880s house slightly southeast of the town. One of the few craftsmen in North America still making wooden barrels by hand gives demonstrations here Sunday afternoons in June and on an irregular basis the rest of the summer. The museum sells videotapes of the demonstrations. Closed Mondays mid-May through August; closed weekends the rest of the year; no admission charge.

From here, Yonge Street leads toward the Holland River, with thousands of acres of rich, black farmland reclaimed by patient Dutch farmers during the early 1930s. The broad swath of bottomland opening to view as the road approaches is Holland Marsh. Careful management of this once unproductive swamp and floodplain by residents of this still very Dutch district resulted in one of Ontario's prettiest and most productive vegetable-growing areas. Take the turnoff to Holland Landing (about 25 miles/40 km from Toronto) at the foot of the hill.

HOLLAND LANDING This was the original terminus of Simcoe's Yonge Street. From the settlement of Holland Landing, soldiers and settlers would follow the route of the early trappers to Georgian Bay by taking the Holland River to Lake Simcoe and connecting with the Severn River to the north. This water route comprises the upper section of the Trent-Severn Waterway, which begins on Lake Ontario at Trenton.

Before leaving Holland Landing, visit the hamlet of Sharon, about 1 mile (1.6 km) east. This settlement was established by a Quaker splinter group known as the Children of Peace, or Davidites, so named because they were led by one David Willson. Central to the community was the *Temple of Peace,* erected in the first half of the 19th century and designed to reflect aspects of the sect's beliefs through its architecture. Now partially restored, it is a museum of local history owned by the *Sharon Temple Museum Society* (18974 Leslie St.; phone: 905-478-2389). It's closed Mondays and Tuesdays May through June and September through October; closed Mondays July through August; closed the rest of the year. There's an admission charge.

En Route from Holland Landing The commercial hub of Holland Marsh, Bradford is 6 miles (10 km) beyond the Holland Landing turnoff. Yonge Street goes through the town, then crosses a series of river valleys that carry just a hint of the northern highlands to come; occasional glimpses of distant Lake Simcoe, Ontario's sixth-largest lake, are visible as the road nears Barrie.

BARRIE This gateway to Ontario's pleasant lake district, a year-round tourist center, is on Kempenfeldt Bay, an inlet of Lake Simcoe. Summers here are devoted to sailing, swimming, water skiing, and just about every other water sport, while winters are given over to snowmobiling, alpine and cross-coun try skiing, as well as ice fishing. Simcoe's smallmouth bass and lake trout bite year-round.

Barrie returns to the 19th century at the *Simcoe County Museum and Archives* (5 miles/8 km north of town on Rte. 26; phone: 705-726-9300). In it is a replica of an 1840s street, with carefully reconstructed shops and other buildings; several traveling exhibits and restored pioneer buildings detail changes in the area since 2000 BC. The museum also holds several special events throughout the year: On *Pioneer Day* (the second Sunday in June), steam engines and demonstrations of blacksmithing are displayed; the first Sunday in July sees the annual *Rose Festival;* and there is a quilt, rug, and craft fair during the third weekend in September. To celebrate the *Christmas* season, a choral group performs carols accompanied by a bell choir on the second Sunday in December. The museum is open daily; admission charge.

Springwater Provincial Park (6 miles/10 km west of town on Rte. 26) aims to preserve the environment that created this resort area a century ago. Some of the park's animals roam free, but for visitors' safety others are caged. Its busy beaver dam is one of the most interesting sights. The park is open daily.

On the waterfront, the *Crazy Fox* restaurant (268 Bradford; phone: 705-737-5000) makes wonderful pasta and seafood. For exotic desserts, try *Michael and Marion's* (89 Bayfield; phone: 705-721-1188). Barrie's favorite nightspot is the *Raceway* (Essa Rd.; phone: 705-726-9400), rebuilt in 1985 after being flattened by a tornado. The track facilities, including a dining room, are all topnotch, and the grandstand is glass-enclosed for year-round viewing. There usually are 10 harness races per program on Wednesdays and Saturdays; post time is 7:30 PM.

En Route from Barrie Follow Route 27 northwest for 24 miles (38 km) to Midland.

MIDLAND In the early years of Canada's development, in the 1630s, French Jesuit missionaries established one of the first inland European settlements here in the heart of the Huron nation. They made it their headquarters for spreading Christianity in Canada. During the Iroquois Wars against the Huron and their French allies in the 1640s, half a dozen Jesuits were killed: Fathers Jean de Brebeuf and Gabriel Lalament, subjected to torture fires at St. Ignace in March 1649, are buried here at the *Martyrs' Shrine,* which commands a spectacular view of Georgian Bay and the Wye River and overlooks the mission of *Ste-Marie-among-the-Hurons.* Completely rebuilt with a museum, the mission illustrates the lives of the Native Americans and the Jesuits. Both are on Route 12, about 3 miles (5 km) east of Midland, on opposite sides of the highway. Closed early October to late May; the shrine holds mass daily (phone: 705-526-7838).

Across from the shrine is the *Wye Marsh Wildlife Centre,* 2,500 acres of forests, fields, and marsh run by a nonprofit conservation organization.

Open year-round, it offers daily conservation programs July through August, guided canoe tours by appointment, and 14 miles (22 km) of cross-country ski trails in winter (phone: 705-526-7809). A wildlife festival at the center in September features woodcarving championships, an art show and sale, folk music, and conservation displays.

To explain and describe something of life before and after the coming of the French, Midland has reconstructed a 1615 Huron village in *Little Lake Park* (King St. S.; phone: 705-526-2844) and an accompanying *Huronia Museum;* together, they provide an excellent picture of early Native American and fur-trader life. Open daily; admission charge.

From Midland, Yonge Street (Rte. 11) traces the shore of Lake Simcoe for 19 miles (30 km) to the narrows separating it from Lake Couchiching to the north. In his notes, Samuel de Champlain tells of this place, called Michekum by the local native tribe, meaning "fence." The fence consisted of a series of stakes driven into the lake bottom, almost closing the passage, much like a vertical dam. The natives set fishnets in the breaks, capturing Lake Simcoe's bounty. This particular weir, recorded by Champlain, resulted in the lake's being called Lac aux Claies (Lake of Sticks), or simply Le Clie, until Governor Simcoe renamed it in honor of his father.

En Route from Midland Follow Route 12 to Orillia.

ORILLIA A plaque at *Couchiching Park* relates the story of Chief William Yellowhead's Mississauga tribe of Ojibwa (called Chippewa in the US), who fought with the British during the War of 1812 and in 1830 settled in the Orillia area, traditional fishing grounds. European settlers came to Orillia less than a decade later, forcing the natives to abandon their lands at the juncture of Lakes Simcoe and Couchiching (now called Atherley Narrows) and to relocate to the Rama Reserve.

Painter Frank Carmichael (the youngest artist of the original Group of Seven) was born and raised in Orillia, and Stephen Leacock (a well-known humorist and writer, who has more books in print than any other Canadian author) lived in the Lake Simcoe area from the age of six and built a 19-room mansion on Old Brewery Bay in 1908. He spent some of the most productive years of his life here. On display at the *Leacock Home,* a National Historic Site, are the author's letters, notes, manuscripts, desk, and other memorabilia. In all likelihood, Leacock's *Sunshine Sketches of a Little Town* is based on life in Orillia. Open daily late June to *Labour Day;* by appointment the rest of the year (phone: 705-326-9357).

The old *Orillia Opera House* (West and Mississauga Sts.), built in 1895, is a local landmark that has come alive again as home to the *Sunshine Festival Theatre Company* (phone: 705-326-8011), a professional group that presents a summer season of comedies and light musicals. Orillia's *Ossawippi Express* (210 Mississauga St. E.; phone: 705-329-0001) is a restaurant housed in antique and turn-of-the-century railway cars (complete with brass fittings and Tiffany-style lamps); affording a marvelous view of Lake Couchiching, it serves continental dishes. The restaurant is closed Mondays.

A good way to view the entire Lake Simcoe area is to take a sightseeing flight available from *Orillia Aviation* (phone: 705-325-6153); the company also runs two fishing camps on nearby lakes and will fly passengers in for one-, two-, or five-day stays. Additionally, two-hour Lake Couchiching cruises aboard the *Island Princess* are available daily from July through August (May through October for groups). The dock is at the east end of Mississauga Street (phone: 705-538-1563 or 705-325-2628). Other area waterway cruises can be arranged via the same phone numbers.

En Route from Orillia The scenery changes north of Orillia, as farms grow smaller, fewer, and farther apart; rocky outcroppings become more frequent; and wooded hills, rivers, and streams tumble after one another in surprising profusion. It's an easy 23 miles (37 km) along Route 11 to Gravenhurst, at the southern tip of Lake Muskoka.

GRAVENHURST This town began as a hardworking, rambunctious lumber town but became a favorite summer resort in the early 1900s. Rumors persist that its name originated in Washington Irving's *Bracebridge Hall* (which indulges in some mischievous and fictitious geography). It is also the doorway to the fall foliage route, when the changing season paints the maples and birches blazing reds and oranges. The autumnal change, which begins early here, is heralded by dances, country fairs, parades, and fireworks displays that match the bright colors of the leaves. The RMS *Segwun,* the oldest steamship still operating in Canada (it dates from 1886), has daily one-hour cruises June through October from *Sagamo Park* (phone: 705-687-6667).

Gravenhurst's favorite son is Norman Bethune, a doctor who became famous as a medical officer with the Chinese communists. Mao dedicated an essay to Bethune after the revolution, and his home is a destination for Chinese diplomats to this day. *Bethune Memorial House* (235 John St.; phone: 705-687-4261), a former church manse where Bethune was born, has been restored to its original 1890 appearance and contains exhibits depicting Bethune's life and accomplishments. It's closed weekends late October to late May; admission charge.

The *Muskoka Winter Carnival,* held over four days covering the last full weekend in February, is a lively, popular event, with everything from motorcycle races on ice to a jazz festival. (For details, see *Festivals, Fairs, and Fancy Acts* in DIVERSIONS.) Just north of Gravenhurst at the *Reay Road KOA* campsite, thousands take part in a cross-country ski race the first week in March (phone: 705-687-2333).

A highway sign claims Gravenhurst is "halfway to the North Pole," a theme developed at *Santa's Village* theme park (west of town, on Santa's Village Rd.; phone: 705-645-2512). Here, children can ride a paddle wheel boat or miniature train; see Santa and his helpers; play with a farm full of animals; and enjoy go-carts, a Rollerblade track, and batting cages. It's open daily, mid-June through early October; there's an admission charge.

Sloan's Restaurant (155 Muskoka St. S.; phone: 705-687-4611) is as much a historic landmark as it is a fine place to eat; try the fresh blueberry pie.

En Route from Gravenhurst Ten miles (16 km) north of Gravenhurst, on the east side of Lake Muskoka, lies Bracebridge, which also may (or may not) have derived its name from Washington Irving's work. A *Kite Festival* is held here in *Jubilee Park* the first week in May.

Instead of heading straight to Huntsville, you can take Route 169 to Parry Sound to enjoy a sightseeing cruise aboard the *Island Queen* (phone: 705-746-2311). The navigational skills of the crew in some tight and spectacular rocky channels are almost as breathtaking as the scenery. The 550-passenger ship makes three-hour trips from June to mid-October. From Parry Sound, take Route 141 to Rosseau and then Route 3 to Huntsville, 22 miles (35 km) from Bracebridge.

HUNTSVILLE Located between the Lake of Bays and Lake Vernon, Huntsville serves as the western entrance to *Algonquin Provincial Park* and as a resort center for this watershed area. Anglers can try their skill on lake, rainbow, and brook trout, which are plentiful in these waters. Hunters will find moose and deer in the woods but may have better luck going after waterfowl. An international triathlon takes place the second week in May.

ALGONQUIN PROVINCIAL PARK Created in 1893 as a wildlife sanctuary to protect the headwaters of five major rivers, this is a natural environment park; as such, it is one of the province's most varied recreational areas. Only one road, Route 60 (which intersects Route 11 at Huntsville), runs through the park, though other access roads lead to the grounds. The southern third of the park, closest to the highway, is fairly heavily developed, with a logging museum, visitors' center, tent and trailer sites, and basic sanitation facilities. The remainder of this 2,910-square-mile park is crossed by two major hiking trails and a thousand miles of canoe routes over calm lakes, rushing rivers, and an occasional portage over rough ground. No motor vehicles are allowed in the backcountry. The park is open daily year-round. Information on outfitters associated with the park, the lodges and campgrounds along Route 60, and seasonal activities is available from the Park Superintendent, *Algonquin Provincial Park, Ministry of Natural Resources* (PO Box 219, Whitney, ONT K0J 2M0; phone: 705-633-5572).

En Route from Huntsville Yonge Street (Rte. 11) continues north for about 74 miles (118 km) into the hills of the Canadian Shield toward North Bay, on Lake Nipissing. Burk's Falls, on the Magnetawan River, is about 24 miles (38 km) from Huntsville; Sand Lake, a few miles east of town, is within canoeing distance of the backwaters of *Algonquin Provincial Park.* Sundridge, 12 miles (19 km) farther north, also provides a water route (from Bernard Lake) into the park area. The lakes surrounding South River, 6 miles (10 km) past Sundridge, are sheer joy for fishing enthusiasts and are excellent testing grounds for more rigorous expeditions into the great north.

NORTH BAY Popular with hunters, trappers, and anglers as a staging area for expeditions into the northern and western reaches of Ontario, North Bay began as a camp along the portage used by natives, explorers, and fur traders between the Ottawa River and Georgian Bay. Nearby Mattawa, 40 miles (64 km) east of North Bay at the junction of the Mattawa and Ottawa Rivers, began as a Hudson's Bay Company trading post. This marked the turnoff point of the canoe trade routes leading west rather than due north. Today you can trace some of these routes aboard an excursion boat. The *Chief Commanda II* offers a variety of cruises from May through mid-September, departing from the *Main Street Dock* (phone: 705-472-4500).

North Bay became internationally known in 1934, when the Dionne quintuplets were born here. The Dionne log home, near the tourist center on the Seymour Street bypass, is furnished with family memorabilia. Closed early October to mid-May; admission charge (phone: 705-472-8480).

En Route from North Bay About 36 miles (58 km) up the road is *Marten River Provincial Park.*

MARTEN RIVER PROVINCIAL PARK Ontario's wilderness country begins past here, in a transitional zone where the yellow birch of the southern forests (used in Native American canoe building) merges with northern black spruce, balsam fir, and pines. It's open year-round.

En Route from Marten River Provincial Park Route 11 enters the *Temagami Forest Reserve,* traveling through its 4.2 million acres of protected forests, lakes, and rivers. This is the entrance to northeastern Ontario's mining and timber regions and the towns that grew up around them.

TEMAGAMI The town of Temagami appears out of the wilderness about 60 miles (96 km) past North Bay on Lake Temagami ("Deep Lake"), where the water in places reaches depths of 1,500 feet and the trout weigh up to 30 pounds. This oddly shaped lake, which extends long fjords and bays in every direction, encompasses some 1,600 islands and 370 miles of shoreline and has 5,000 square miles of interconnecting canoe routes and hiking and mountain bike trails (phone: 705-569-3344; 800-661-7609). The *Lady Evelyn–Smoothwater Wilderness Park* contains the Ishpatina Ridge—at 2,275 feet, the so-called rooftop of Ontario.

En Route from Temagami From iron ore country at Temagami to the silver ore area at Cobalt is a drive of 18 miles (29 km) on Route 11 to the 11B Bypass, then a few miles farther on Route 11B. Slightly south of the 11B cutoff is the *Highway Bookshop* (phone: 705-679-8375). Besides carrying a variety of area maps, excellent canoe-route guides, and works by Canadian and Native American authors, the shop stands squarely on the portage between the Montreal River, heading west, and Lake Timiskaming, on the route down the Ottawa River toward Montreal.

COBALT One night in September 1903, blacksmith Fred LaRose threw his hammer at what he thought was a glittering-eyed fox—and struck the world's richest silver vein. Traces of cobalt were found mixed into the silver, and miners flocked to the site. The mining boom died out in the 1930s but revived in the late 1940s, when new methods made additional silver extraction feasible, and the cobalt ore, once discarded as waste, became important for medical, military, and manufacturing uses.

Cobalt's history is reflected in the treasure trove of silver and cobalt displayed in the *Northern Ontario Mining Museum* (24 Silver St.; phone: 705-679-8301), across from the post office. The museum, which sells jewelry made from Cobalt silver, will arrange tours of local mines. Open daily June through September; closed mornings and weekends the rest of the year; admission charge.

The frontier lifestyle that characterized Cobalt's origins is commemorated in the *Miner's Festival* (first week of August) with rock-breaking, canoeing, and fiddling contests; flea markets; French Canadian step dancing; a parade; and a beauty contest.

En Route from Cobalt Continuing north on the Route 11B Bypass to its reunion with Route 11 just past New Liskeard, the road passes the beaches of Lake Timiskaming at Haileybury and the dairy farms of New Liskeard, which are a bit unusual in these chilly northern woods. It's about 70 miles (112 km) from Cobalt to Kirkland Lake, a short distance east of Route 11 on Route 66.

KIRKLAND LAKE This place is as close as you may ever come to a street "paved with gold," since a road construction crew accidentally used rock with gold ore rather than waste rock when filling in the roadbed of Kirkland Lake's Government Road (otherwise known as the Golden Mile). By the time they realized what had happened, it would have cost more than the value of the ore to recover the gold. Since the discovery of gold in 1912, the Kirkland Lake district has yielded over a billion dollars' worth of the prized metal. For more information, contact the *Kirkland Lake Chamber of Commerce* (20 Duncan St. N., Kirkland Lake, ONT P2N 3L1; phone: 705-567-5444; 705-634-2707 for summer tourist information).

The mansion built by Sir Harry Oakes, owner and manager of the Kirkland Lake gold mine, has been converted into a museum (Château Dr.; phone: 705-568-8800); it has a variety of Inuit and native artifacts plus some interesting pieces of old mining gear. Open daily; admission charge.

En Route from Kirkland Lake Double back westbound on Route 66 to Route 11, then travel about 9 miles (14 km) north to the signpost marking the crest of the Arctic watershed. You'll recognize the spot easily: From here on, all the lakes and rivers flow north toward James and Hudson Bays.

A little fancy footwork on the nearby slopes puts photographers in position for some great shots of the incredible expanses of countryside and streams. The area is rugged and rocky, another rich mineral stockpile of the Canadian Shield, producing silver, zinc, nickel, copper, lead, tin, cadmium, and more gold than any other source in North America. This region, known as the Porcupine Camp district, also is popular for big-game hunting, fishing, swimming, golf, and other outdoor activities. It is a little over 27 miles (43 km) on Yonge Street from the Route 66 intersection to the Route 101 access into Timmins.

TIMMINS Europeans explored and traded in this area during the 1700s, but it was the discovery of gold in 1909 that created the Porcupine gold rush that drew settlers to the site. A forest fire in 1969, which took over 70 lives and destroyed more than 500,000 acres of timberland, dampened the miners' enthusiasm only slightly, and today over 40,000 people live and work in the area. The town is proud of its importance as a major mineral-producing center, and the *Timmins Chamber of Commerce* (PO Box 985, Rte. 101, Timmins, ONT P4N 7H6; phone: 705-360-1900) can arrange tours of various locations.

Kettle Lakes Provincial Park, on the Route 101 access east of town, is a beautiful area for camping, hiking, canoeing, fishing, and blueberry picking. To protect the park's environment, no motorboats are allowed. Open year-round.

En Route from Timmins Take Route 610 east to Route 67 to return to Yonge Street and Iroquois Falls (see below). Stop at the plaque marking the site of a 1700s Hudson's Bay trading post on Barber's Bay. The fur trade started its growth here, and modern mining operations continually explore the area, but timber has remained the economy's constant. Canada's forests cover about 1.25 million square miles (half the country's surface area), and Ontario's timber industries employ some 75,000 people. Many of the area mills welcome visitors, and the pulp- and paper-making process is really something to see.

IROQUOIS FALLS It's startling to find a planned community, with parklands and broad avenues, in the midst of these forests and hills. This mill town and model community is interesting to visit, especially because of its contrast to the surrounding wilds. One of Ontario's newsprint producers, Abitibi-Price, was founded here in 1912 and offers tours of its mill, explaining how logs are made into paper; the town *Chamber of Commerce* (phone: 705-232-4656) arranges them.

En Route from Iroquois Falls Yonge Street continues north to Cochrane, some 30 miles (48 km) from the Iroquois Falls access road. Route 11 has begun to arch slightly west ever since New Liskeard, but here it takes a definite turn and begins its journey across the frontiers of western Ontario.

COCHRANE A major industrial, mining, lumbering, and rail center, Cochrane was established at the turn of the century, in the opening days of the area's mineral discoveries. It was the railroad that made, and still makes, Cochrane an important jumping-off point for mineral exploration and for hunting and fishing expeditions into the far north and the Hudson Bay region.

The *Polar Bear Express* train still crosses the wide Arctic watershed from Cochrane to the remote community of Moosonee, near the mouth of the Moose River on James Bay. Here, on a river island called Moose Factory, a lone fortress was erected in the early 1670s, the second such "trading post" under the auspices of the Hudson's Bay Company. A plaque near the site of the original post commemorates English explorer Henry Hudson, who first sailed into Hudson Bay—and was set adrift here with his sons. Several early buildings, including a smithy and a gunpowder magazine, are grouped together with a museum describing the post area's growth over the centuries. Cree prayer books are among the artifacts. Another aspect of the area's history is explained on the riverbank in Moosonee at the *Révillon Frères Museum* (no phone). The British-French conflict for control of the New World focused on the choice territory around this extensive inlet more than once; the museum describes much of that conflict. It is open afternoons daily from mid-June through early September. Only the tracks of the *Ontario Northland Railway* share the immense territory around Moosonee with the moose, bears, caribou, deer—and an occasional human being.

The 372-mile (596-km) journey to Moosonee and back takes about four hours each way and can be made in one day, with time for sightseeing in Moosonee. The *Polar Bear* train runs daily, June 26 to September 6, departing at 8 AM and arriving back in Cochrane about 9:30 PM (phone: 705-272-4228, Cochrane station; 705-336-2210, Moosonee station). Canoes and bulky hunting equipment are not allowed on this train, but they are permitted on a companion service, the *Little Bear,* which stops anywhere on request; the journey takes about a day each way. The *Little Bear* departs from Cochrane Tuesdays and Thursdays in summer, and Mondays, Wednesdays, and Fridays in winter, returning the next day. Book your passage well in advance, as both trains are popular. Group fares for families are available. For more information on the trains, as well as accommodations in Moosonee, contact the *Ontario Northland Railway* (*Passenger Service Department,* North Bay, ONT P1B 8L3; phone: 705-495-4200).

In keeping with Cochrane's background as a rail center, a locomotive and several cars dating back to the days of the railway construction are filled with memorabilia of the era. In forthright frontier style, the *Railway Museum* is on a spur track at Cochrane's *Union Station.* Closed early October to mid-June (phone: 705-272-5378).

En Route from Cochrane Yonge Street wheels westward from here, tracing 285 miles (456 km) of thinly settled frontier outlining the Hudson Bay lowlands to the north and the fringes of population centers around the westernmost Great Lake, Superior, to the south. The small towns along Route 11 (Smooth Rock Falls, Kapuskasing, Mattice, Hearst, Longlac, and Geraldton) all cater to the camper, sport fisher, hunter, and canoeist. Thousands of miles of unspoiled rivers and untrampled forest and a truly memorable experience await the daring vacationer. Those who prefer less strenuous adventure will find innumerable fly-in hunting and fishing camps operated by experienced outfitters. Some of the best of these are operated by the Cree in the James Bay and Hudson Bay areas, where the fall goose and duck hunting is superb. Take advantage of the half-dozen provincial parks along the way; they encompass a wide variety of terrain and geographical oddities. (For more information, call the *Ontario Tourism Authority* at 800-668-2746.)

Twenty miles (32 km) west of Cochrane is *Greenwater Park,* centered on a 200-foot esker ridge (glacial gravel deposit) formed over 15,000 years ago. Its 26 small lakes are filled with trout. About 45 miles (72 km) from *Greenwater Park* is *René Brunelle Park.* In the midst of a belt of clay earth, this is an oasis of fertile land in the rocky Canadian Shield. About 23 miles (37 km) northwest of Route 11 on the Fushimi Forest Access Road is *Fushimi Lake Park.*

The clay belt extends here from Remi Lake, but the cooler climate keeps the growing season too short for farming. The fish, however, seem to thrive. About 25 miles (40 km) beyond *Fushimi Lake Park,* south of Yonge Street via Route 631, is *Nagagamisis Park* on Nagagamisis Lake. It offers boating, fishing, swimming, and a bit of history, as the area once was the site of a native camp. And on the eastern outskirts of Geraldton is *Macleod Park,* on the shores of Kenogamisis Lake. It is extremely popular for swimming and boating; the numerous islands and inlets around the lake are full of pike, pickerel, whitefish, and yellow perch.

GERALDTON This small timber and mining community was founded in the wake of gold discoveries in the 1930s; today, Geraldton is the western starting point for expeditions into the James Bay area. Here, Yonge Street begins to curve toward the western extremity of Lake Superior and its coastal towns and cities.

En Route from Geraldton Jellicoe, about 30 miles (48 km) west of Geraldton, was originally a divisional point for rail lines leading north from the Thunder Bay tributary into the James Bay–Hudson Bay region; it later became a mining town for a short time. Between here and Beardmore, some 16 miles (26 km) west and south on Route 11, sharp-eyed rock hounds can often pick up semiprecious gemstones like agate and jasper beside the highway. The timber and gold resources of Beardmore, on the southeast shore of Lake Nipigon (the largest inland lake in Ontario), preceded the town's current industries—hunting and fishing outfitting and tourism.

Yonge Street continues south from here, along the shore of Lake Nipigon through Macdiarmid, Orient Bay, Reflection Lake, and Gorge Creek. It's about 50 miles (80 km) to Route 11's juncture with Route 17 at Nipigon (see below), on the northwest shore of Lake Superior. Between Beardmore and the fisheries at Macdiarmid, Lake Nipigon becomes visible to the west, and the tall palisades of the Pijitawabik region peer down over the highway from the eastern side.

BLACKSAND PARK Overlooking Pijitawabik Bay on Lake Nipigon, the beach of black sand that gives this park its name lies across from the legendary nesting place of the Thunderbird. Ojibwa stories tell of the wrath of the Thunderbird, who abandoned his home and destroyed his secluded mountaintop retreat as Europeans began invading the remote territory. Occasionally he still vents his rage through summer thunderstorms.

En Route from Blacksand Park The area around the lakeshore of Nipigon and farther south to Lake Superior and the Minnesota border has yielded native artifacts (mostly pre-Ojibwa, or pre-Chippewa) and enough archaeological evidence to substantiate the early presence of Norsemen—Vikings—in the Minnesota–Thunder Bay lands around Lake Superior.

NIPIGON Spread across three terraces created by glacier-wrought changes in the water level, the city lies at the mouth of the Nipigon River on Nipigon Bay. The river always has been a major route inland, and this sheltered area near its mouth was inhabited by the Ojibwa for ages before European fur traders turned Nipigon into the first year-round white settlement on Superior's north shore. The fur trade no longer draws explorers, but the opportunity to hook a champion trout beckons many. The world's largest brook trout, a 14½-pound monster, was taken here.

En Route from Nipigon The 64 miles (102 km) on Routes 11 and 17 between Nipigon and Thunder Bay (see below) are filled with fantastic rock formations. Red Rock Cuesta, a wall of red cliffs south of the roadway, is 2 miles long and about 700 feet high. The red hue is caused by horizontal layers of limestone tinted by hematite.

Ouimet Canyon is an amazing earth carving 500 feet wide, almost 2 miles long, and 300 to 500 feet deep into volcanic rock and red mudstone. Several tall, freestanding columns have broken away from the sheer cliff walls. One of these is called Indian Head because of its classic profile; other columns have tumbled, breaking into huge boulders hundreds of feet below. There are few guard rails, and if you happen to venture to the edge and peer straight down, you'll see large cracks in the canyon floor. No one knows which section will break free next, so be extremely cautious.

The canyon floor is a unique environment. Little sunlight warms these depths, and the cold holds back the flowering and greening of spring until late summer. In deeper areas, where even the summer sun brings no warmth, snow and ice cover the ground most of the year, and arctic plants like firs, arctic moss, and a type of liverwort thrive miles south of their usual southernmost growing areas.

This is not a place to allow children to run around unsupervised, and many adults find some of the canyon trails a little hair-raising, especially when it comes to stepping over crevices that seem to extend to the canyon floor. From the trail along the canyon's south rim, Lake Superior is visible in the distance, its surface dotted with tiny islands. At this point, Superior's Black Bay lies opposite, formed between Nipigon Bay's sheltering southern peninsula and Thunder Bay's northern Sibley Peninsula.

The *Dorian Fish Hatchery,* just off Route 17/11 near Ouimet, breeds speckled and lake trout to keep area population levels high. A few miles farther is the *Thunder Bay Amethyst Mine* (30 miles/48 km south of Nipigon, 5 miles/8 km off Rte. 17/11 on E. Loon Rd.), uncovered by a crew cutting a logging road into the woods. Visitors can climb into the pits and collect their own stones or purchase inexpensive samples. The mine is closed early October through April. From the mine, Route 587 travels the length of Sibley Peninsula from the village of Pass Lake, on Route 17/11, to *Sleeping Giant Provincial Park.*

SLEEPING GIANT PROVINCIAL PARK Although the park lies outside the town's boundaries, the port of Thunder Bay (see below) claims its most visible and memorable landmark as its own—the Sleeping Giant. The natural sculpture is as perfect as anything created by humans, carved into exposed surfaces of the Canadian Shield over a span of centuries. Ojibwa legend tells of Nanibijou (or Nanabozho), a giant demigod who discovered a rich vein of silver. He warned the tribe not to reveal the metal's presence to anyone, saying that if a white man were to learn of it, the tribe would perish and he would turn to stone. The silver was buried on a tiny island at the far end of the peninsula, and the tribe was sworn to secrecy; nevertheless, one warrior made himself silver weapons that fell into the hands of the Sioux. Spotting the Sioux bringing European traders as they approached Sibley Peninsula across Lake Superior, Nanibijou caused a windstorm to sink their canoes. Fulfilling his own destiny, Nanibijou was turned to stone by the Great Spirit, and the next morning the Ojibwa looked out upon him, transformed into the thousand-foot-tall, 7-mile-long mountain peninsula called the Sleeping Giant.

It wasn't until 1868 that someone stumbled onto the native silver cache on Silver Islet, an island barely large enough to be worthy of notice. A haphazard pick stroke exposed $10,000 worth of the metal, and a 14-year boom began. During that time, many lives were lost as miners were trapped in frequently flooded shafts. Today, a causeway built in the 1930s makes access a lot safer, and the island's century-old houses, general store, and rare photographs of the desperate miners and their families are an interesting adjunct to the park and its legend. The park is open year-round.

En Route from Sleeping Giant Provincial Park Back on Yonge Street (Rte. 17/11), it's about 24 miles (38 km) to Thunder Bay, traveling along the bay's shoreline under the watchful eyes of the Sleeping Giant.

THUNDER BAY Created when two communities sheltered by Sibley Peninsula merged in 1969, Thunder Bay is one of Canada's largest and busiest ports and one of the best harbors on the Great Lakes. Route 17/11 approaches from the northeast, through the gentle hills above the city. Lake Superior and the massive grain elevators that characterize the lakehead dominate the city's south; Mt. McKay stands, taller than its fellow mountains, toward Thunder Bay's southwest corner. The Kaministikwa River, which runs past Mt. McKay, empties into the harbor through a broad delta divided into three navigable channels.

This sheltered river mouth was the meeting place of natives and fur trappers bringing skins to barter with the fur buyers carting European goods up the St. Lawrence. *Fort Kaministquia,* a French outpost, was erected here in the 1670s; in 1801 the British (who had assumed control of the area) built *Fort William,* the main supply post for the Northwest Company after the settlement of the US-Canadian boundaries revealed the company's earlier headquarters to be in US territory. Until it merged with the Hudson's Bay Company 20 years later, all of the Northwest Company's goods moved through this point. Each summer, more than 2,000 voyageurs gathered here.

Fort William was extensively rebuilt on the bank of the Kaministikwa River, 9 miles (14 km) upstream from the original site, together with an entire village of about 50 buildings and an Ojibwa camp. The active trading center is staffed with a full complement of trappers, voyageurs, traders, and natives, all going about as if it were still the early 1800s. There are demonstrations of barrel making. Closed November through April (phone: 807-577-8461). Cruises to *Fort William* and of the harbor can be arranged through *Welcomeship Ltd.* (phone: 807-344-2512 or 807-577-7875).

A 140-acre section of Thunder Bay North is devoted to *Centennial Park,* a wooded area with trails along the Current River and a working 1910 logging camp. The camp and some other facilities are open in summer only. There are five ski areas in the mountains of this compact region, a short drive southwest of downtown Thunder Bay: *Big Thunder* (phone: 807-475-4402; 800-667-8386 in Canada); *Candy Mountain* (phone: 807-475-5633); *Loch Lomond* (phone: 807-475-7787); *Mount Baldy* (phone: 807-683-8441); and *Norwester Resort* (phone: 807-473-9123).

Thunder Bay boasts its own waterfall, Kakabeka Falls (18 miles/29 km northwest of town on Route 17/11), which is spectacular—but only on weekends. A hydroelectric dam on the Kaministikwa River controls the water flow, so during the week the falls are usually no more impressive than a drainpipe in a drought. Locally, the falls are called "Only on a Sunday Falls," because that's when the water is let loose in full force (or almost), tumbling over the 128-foot-high, 225-foot-wide ledge into the gorge below. According to legend, in the days before the dam an Ojibwa princess captured by a band of Sioux was forced to lead her captors to her tribe. Instead, she guided the Sioux warriors over the falls, and all were killed. Her spirit is said to be visible in the spray, although the dam has probably cut down the frequency of her appearances.

There's no lack of variety in the restaurants in the Lakehead area. *Hoito's* (314 Bay St.; phone: 807-345-6323) has excellent Finnish food, and *Duck Chan's* (130 May St. N.; phone: 807-622-2601) is the place to go for Chinese fare. Both are inexpensive. The moderately priced *Circle Inn* (686 Memorial Ave.; phone: 807-344-5744) offers good fare, including Sunday brunch, in pleasant surroundings. All three restaurants are open daily.

One of Thunder Bay's most popular camping-activity areas is *Chippewa Park,* 300 wooded acres with a beach, a small zoo, several children's rides, and a wide variety of facilities for travelers. It's south of town, off Route 61, on access road 61B. Closed early September to mid-May. Just east of the city on the Trans-Canada Highway (Rte. 17) is an impressive bronze statue of Terry Fox, the Canadian teenager who in 1980 set out to run across Canada, east to west, after losing a leg to cancer. He wanted to draw attention to the disease and raise money for research. Fox's incredible journey of nearly 2,000 miles ended here, when the cancer spread and a short time later took his life. His run brought in millions of dollars for cancer research. In early July, the *Great Canadian Rendezvous* is celebrated here with a week-long festival.

BEST EN ROUTE

Along this route, there's a wide range of hotel prices. In the northern areas, rates may include guide services, fishing permits, and equipment, in addition to rooms. Accommodations farther north tend to be more rustic than those in southern Ontario, as most visitors are seeking outdoors-oriented vacations and/or good hunting and fishing. Between Hearst and Geraldton, for example, virtually the only places to stay are park campgrounds.

Be sure of what you're buying when you make reservations. Don't plan on finding vacancies easily in summer; hotel and camping space can be scarce. An establishment charging $70 or more for a double per night is considered expensive; one costing from $50 to $70, moderate; and a place charging $50 or less, inexpensive. All hotels feature such amenities as air conditioning, private baths, TV sets, and telephones unless otherwise indicated. Campgrounds are considered very inexpensive, costing $20 or less.

From mid-June to the first week of September, call 416-314-0998 for information on campsite availability in southern Ontario. To prevent overcrowding, some provincial parks impose daily quotas on canoe routes and backpack trails. For information on reserving a canoeing permit or campsite in these parks, call 416-314-2000, collect. For each location, places are listed alphabetically by price category.

BARRIE

Journey's End Its 60 rooms offer all the comforts you'd expect from Canada's largest motel chain, but there's no restaurant. Exit Rte. 400 at Dunlop St. to Hart Dr. (phone: 705-722-3600). Moderate.

Willow Creek Trailer Park In addition to 175 campsites, most with water and electrical hookups, there are showers, flush toilets, fireplaces, a pool, and a store. *Spring Water Christian Campground* (phone: 705-725-8020). Very inexpensive.

ORILLIA

Fern Occupying a mile of Lake Couchiching shore, this 102-room, family-oriented resort has a three-room dining area, five tennis courts, free golf, two heated terrace pools, an indoor pool with a fitness/recreation center and hot tubs, water skiing, windsurfing, *bocci,* and supervised children's activities. In the rooms, suites, and cottages are more than 80 fireplaces. Nightly entertainment takes place in *Bertyl's Bar* and *The Club.* Take Rte. 12 to Rama Rd. (phone: 705-325-2256; 800-567-3376; fax: 705-327-5647). Expensive.

Sundial This popular motor inn with 92 rooms and a view of Lake Simcoe has a restaurant, an indoor pool, a sauna, and a whirlpool bath. 600 Sundial Dr. (phone: 705-325-2233; 800-461-0288 in Canada). Moderate.

Knight's Inn "Friendliness and cleanliness" is the motto here. There are 40 rooms, a gameroom, and a lounge; plenty of restaurants are within walking distance. 265 Memorial Ave. (phone: 705-326-3554). Moderate to inexpensive.

GRAVENHURST

Pine Dale A pleasant resort comprising 21 efficiency units and one cabin, it's on the shore of Gull Lake, surrounded by pine groves, with a recreation hall, a beach, and a dock; fishing and boat rentals can be arranged. Pinedale Rd. (phone: 705-687-2822). Moderate.

BRACEBRIDGE

Aston Resort This is a comfortable, 67-room resort with a dock and a beach on Lake Muskoka for fishing, free windsurfing and water skiing, or just sunning and swimming. It also has an outdoor pool, a sauna, a whirlpool bath, golf, tennis (with instruction), and a restaurant. Open June through September. Off Rte. 118 (phone: 705-764-1177). Expensive.

Bangor Lodge Six tennis courts, a semiprivate nine-hole golf course, a dining room, and an outdoor pool complement 98 rooms and five cottages at this family-run operation. Open June through September. Golden Beach Rd. (phone: 705-645-4791). Expensive.

HUNTSVILLE

Deerhurst Resort A 365-room, multi-facility sports resort that has been catering to guests for about a century, the inn has standard hotel rooms as well as one-, two-, and three-bedroom suites, plus three dining areas. Also see *Special Havens* in DIVERSIONS. Muskoka Rd. (phone: 705-789-6411; 800-441-1414; fax: 705-789-2431). Expensive.

Hidden Valley More like a family inn than part of a hotel chain, this 93-room establishment offers racquet sports, a sauna, an indoor pool, a whirlpool bath, an outdoor pool, a beach, a dock, and boats for water skiing or fishing. In the center of the skiing area, surrounded by a lake and golf course, on Hidden Valley Rd. (phone: 705-789-2301). Expensive.

Highland Court Motel At the west end of town, it offers spotless, well-furnished accommodations, including four suites and 11 rooms, each equipped with a small refrigerator, a kettle, and coffee. 208 Main St. W. (phone: 705-789-4424). Moderate to inexpensive.

ALGONQUIN PROVINCIAL PARK

Arowhon Pines This tranquil resort occupies the shore of its own lake. There are two- to 12-bedroom cabins plus one private cabin. The restaurant is superb. Open mid-May to early October. Also see *Special Havens* in DIVERSIONS. *Algonquin Provincial Park* (phone: 705-633-5661 in summer; 416-483-4393 in winter; fax: 705-633-5795 in summer; 416-483-4429 in winter). Expensive.

Lake of Two Rivers Campground Of the park's eight campgrounds, this one (with 241 sites) has the most facilities, including showers, a store, a laundry area, fireplaces, and nearby boat rentals (phone: 705-633-5538; fax: 705-633-5581). Very inexpensive.

NORTH BAY

Best Western Lakeshore One of many reliable hostelries located on this part of the lake shore, it has 130 rooms, an indoor pool, a sauna, a good restaurant, and a coffee shop. Guests can arrange to play on a nearby golf course. 700 Lakeshore Dr. (phone: 705-474-5800; 800-461-6199). Expensive to moderate.

Ascot In this high-quality inn are 31 rooms and a sauna; continental breakfast is available. Centrally located, near buses, rail, beaches, sports, shopping, and other entertainment. 255 McIntyre St. W. (phone: 705-474-4770; fax: 705-497-1437). Moderate.

Champlain Tents and Trailer Park A full range of services is available here, including electrical hookups at many of the 55 sites, showers, flush toilets, fireplaces, a playground, and a store, all set on Lake Nipissing. 1202 Premier Rd. N. (phone: 705-474-4669). Very inexpensive.

MARTEN RIVER

Land O'Lakes A base for guided wilderness canoe trips, this picturesque and well-equipped spot offers 11 comfortable housekeeping cottages, a cluster of campsites, showers, toilets, a store, and a beach. Open May to late October. Rte. 11 (phone: 705-892-2322; fax: 705-892-2126). Moderate to inexpensive.

Rock Pine Motel It has only eight rooms, but it's in a picturesque setting, and there's a restaurant, a gift shop, and boat rentals. Pets are allowed. Located 31 miles (50 km) north of North Bay on Rte. 11 (phone: 705-892-2211). Inexpensive.

COBALT

Marsh Bay On beautiful Marsh Bay on the Montreal River, this establishment has five housekeeping cottages, campsites, boat rentals, and guide services. Marsh Bay Rd., off Rte. 11 (phone: 705-679-8810). Moderate.

KIRKLAND LAKE

Esker Lakes Park About a half-hour from town, the park lies just within the Arctic watershed on Panagapka Lake. Thirty-two of the 135 campsites have electric hookups. There are showers, flush toilets, and a store, and boat rentals are available in the park, but there's a restriction on motorboats. Access from Rte. 66 (phone: 705-567-4849). Inexpensive.

TIMMINS

Riverside Inn Attractions at this 116-room property include an indoor pool, nearby golf, free local phone calls, rooms with king-size beds and refrigerators, a good dining room, and a bar with a six-foot TV screen. Within walking distance of the *Timmins Square Shopping Centre,* at 1800 Riverside Dr. (phone: 705-267-6241; 800-461-3795). Moderate.

Best Western Colonial Inn Set on the Mattagami River, near cross-country and downhill skiing, it has 25 clean, well-equipped rooms. 1212 Riverside Dr. (phone: 705-268-5200). Moderate to inexpensive.

COCHRANE

Westway Here are 42 units but no restaurant. 21 First St., on Rte. 11 (phone: 705-272-4285; fax: 705-272-4429). Moderate to inexpensive.

Greenwater Provincial Park You should have no trouble getting one of the park's 90 sites (35 with electricity), as this fairly remote area is not one of Ontario's busiest. All the basic facilities are here, including showers, laundry, and a beach. Access from Rte. 668, off Rte. 11 (phone: 705-272-6335). Very inexpensive.

KAPUSKASING

Apollo A popular place, it has 44 large rooms and an indoor pool. Several restaurants are located nearby. Rte. 11 (phone: 705-335-6084). Moderate to inexpensive.

Two Bridges En route to the spectacular *Polar Bear Express* train ride, this motel has 23 rooms, some of which are housekeeping units; all have refrigerators. Complimentary morning coffee and a newspaper plus use of the minigolf course are offered. Rte. 11 (phone: 705-335-2281). Inexpensive.

GERALDTON

Park Bay View Twenty rooms are equipped with all the necessities, and the dining room serves good home cooking. A beach picnic area and golf are nearby. Rte. 11 (phone: 807-854-1716). Moderate.

THUNDER BAY

Airlane South of town and close to the airport, this hostelry features 170 rooms and a full array of creature comforts, including an indoor pool, a sauna, a whirlpool bath, three restaurants, and a nightclub. Complimentary limo service to the airport. 698 Arthur St. W. (phone: 807-577-1181; 800-465-5003 in Canada; fax: 807-475-4852). Expensive.

Landmark Renovated in 1993, this is another of Thunder Bay's best accommodations. Its 106 rooms have all the usual amenities, and the pool has a 161-foot water slide. There's also a restaurant. It's close to major shopping areas, and airport limo shuttle service is available around the clock. Dawson Rd. and Thunder Bay Expy. (phone: 807-767-1681; 800-465-3950 in Minnesota, Michigan, and Wisconsin; fax: 807-767-1439). Expensive to moderate.

Prince Edward Island

This crescent-shaped island in the gulf of the St. Lawrence River attracts over half a million visitors every summer. Unspoiled by modern freeways and heavy industry, Prince Edward Island (PEI) is known for its farmlands, which roll to the edge of cliffs. Rich red soil, evergreen forests, and red sand beaches with long-legged blue herons add bold dashes of color, as do the cheerily painted fishing villages perched at the sea's edge. For visitors seeking an enchanting, uncrowded, and unhurried land, PEI is a small utopia.

Once described humorously as two long beaches with potato fields in between, PEI is the tiniest of Canada's 10 provinces. Some 130,000 people live in the province, which is 140 miles long and from 4 to 40 miles wide, encompassing 2,184 square miles. In 1864, Charlottetown, the provincial capital, was the site of the first discussions on the Canadian Confederation; Canada became a confederation in 1867, and PEI joined in 1873.

Accessible to motorists by two ferry routes across the Northumberland Strait, the island is served almost entirely by one-lane roads (which make for wonderful car or bicycle expeditions). Most touring on the island starts at Charlottetown, in the southern corner of the center section. From there, travelers can go north and west along the Blue Heron Drive or east along the Kings Byway, or explore the westernmost section of the island on a route known as Lady Slipper Drive.

For further information, contact the *Prince Edward Island Department of Tourism, Visitor Services* (PO Box 940, Charlottetown, PEI C1A 7M5; phone: 902-368-4444; 800-565-7421 in Nova Scotia and New Brunswick; 800-565-0267 elsewhere in Canada and the US; fax: 902-368-5737).

Blue Heron Drive

This route leads north and west from Charlottetown to the island's northern shore, a stretch of 25 miles (40 km) of national park beaches and red sandstone capes that ends at the tourist town of Cavendish. Just beyond is New London Bay, the home of the beautiful blue herons for which the route is named. From here the drive turns south toward the southern shore of the island to return to Charlottetown.

CHARLOTTETOWN The provincial capital is 38 miles (61 km) from the Wood Islands ferry landing and 34 miles (54 km) from Borden. Its downtown area features beautiful tree-lined streets and rows of wood-frame houses. The only incorporated city in the province, Charlottetown still retains the air of a colonial seaport, but with 20th-century conveniences.

The French originally settled Port la Joie across the harbor from Charlottetown in 1720. In 1758, the British took over Port la Joie's fort, renaming the island St. John's. Charlottetown, which became its capital in 1768, grew slowly, even with an influx of British Loyalists at the close of the American Revolution. Today, Charlottetown's population stands at 31,000, about one-quarter of PEI's entire population.

The *Confederation Centre of the Arts* (Queen and Grafton Sts.; phone: 902-628-1864) is the city's focal point. Built in the mid-1960s on the site of the original city market, this national museum, art gallery, and theater makes up for its stark concrete lines with impressive exhibits and acclaimed performances. It's open year-round; admission charge to the art gallery. Behind *Confederation Centre* is *Province House* (phone: 902-566-7362), the site of the original Canadian Confederation talks. On display in its second-floor *Confederation Chamber* are the original chairs and table around which the founders of the country sat in the mid-19th century, along with other mementos of island history. *Province House* is now the home of the provincial legislative assembly. It's open daily year-round; no admission charge.

Theatergoers should attend the *Confederation Centre*'s annual summer festival performance of *Anne of Green Gables,* based on the beloved novel about a young orphan by Lucy Maud Montgomery (for details, see *Quintessential Canada* in DIVERSIONS). Bordering the *Confederation Centre* is the downtown shopping district. Some of Charlottetown's oldest retail stores, including *Henderson & Cudmore* (phone: 902-892-4215), an exclusive men's clothing shop, now form part of the *Confederation Court Mall.* Nearby is the 19th-century red brick *City Hall,* with a mansard roof and 66-foot tower; on the ground floor is a visitors' information center (phone: 902-566-5548), which is open daily in summer. On weekdays in July and August, guided walking tours of Charlottetown depart from here hourly.

Those who wish to explore the city on their own should begin with a walk down Richmond Street. This block-long row of Victorian buildings across from the *Confederation Centre* contains cafés, bars, and arts and crafts shops. The tiny *Black Forest Café and Bakery* (146 Richmond St.; phone: 902-628-2123) specializes in homemade breads, soups, and pastries. To purchase a variety of crafts and artifacts made on the island, visit the *Island Crafts Shop* (156 Richmond St.; phone: 902-892-5152), which is operated by the PEI *Craftsmen's Council.* It's open daily.

Along Great George Street is *St. Dunstan's Basilica,* the seat of the province's Roman Catholic diocese. Built in 1919, the present-day *St. Dunstan's* is the fourth Roman Catholic church on this site; its two Gothic spires, rising to a height of 200 feet, dominate the city's skyline. At the bottom of Great George Street is *Peake's Wharf,* a redeveloped harborfront area with a marina, boutiques, and a boardwalk. *Peake's Quay* (36 Lower Water St.; phone: 902-368-1330) has a restaurant, a bar, and a deck with umbrella-shaded tables. The moderately priced menu includes sandwiches, salad, and seafood. The *Root Cellar* (34 Queen St.; phone: 902-892-6227) is one of the best natural foods stores in eastern Canada; it's closed October through April. The *Merchant Man Pub* (23 Lower Queen St.; phone: 902-892-9150) has local and imported draft beer. The menu concentrates on Thai food, plus seafood, sandwiches, and crêpes. It's open to midnight daily in summer; closed for lunch Sundays year-round.

No stay in Charlottetown would be complete without a stroll through the 40-acre *Victoria Park,* on the harbor. Along the southern shore, you'll pass the old cannon guarding the harbor and see the city's striking silhouette. Bordering the grounds of *Victoria Park* is *Government House* (1835), the official residence of the province's governor. Nearby, at the corner of West and Kent Streets, is *Beaconsfield.* This stately old wood-frame house is the home of the *PEI Museum and Heritage Foundation*, filled with colonial and Victorian furniture. Free tours are available in the summer. It's closed weekends; no admission charge (phone: 902-368-6600).

Every August, Charlottetown sponsors *Old Home Week,* a week of livestock and handicraft exhibitions, country music, and a midway. The highlight is a huge, two-hour parade through the city's streets and the *Gold Cup and Saucer Race* at the racetrack, featuring some of the best trotters in eastern Canada.

Charlottetown has six movie theaters, an 18-hole golf course, and a selection of good restaurants and lounges. Most of the city's larger restaurants accept major credit cards, and many close Sundays for lunch. The *Lord Selkirk Room* at the *Prince Edward* hotel (see *Best en Route*) is the city's most formal and expensive dining room, serving salmon, lobster, chateaubriand, veal, and such seasonal dishes as venison and braised breast of duck. It's closed Sundays and for lunch. Also in the hotel is *Obsessions,* an inexpensive café that stays open daily until about 5:30 PM. *Sirinella Ristorante* (83 Water St.; phone: 902-628-2271), across the street from the hotel, is the city's best Italian restaurant. Its menu includes meat, seafood, and pasta dishes prepared by an Italian-born chef. It's closed for lunch on weekends, and closed Sundays October through April. The *Griffon* dining room at the *Dundee Arms* (see *Best en Route*) is expensive, but the menu justifies the prices: Lobster, scallops, and pepper steaks are the most popular entrées. The *Claddagh Room* (129 Sydney St.; phone: 902-892-9661) has the city's widest selection of seafood, and the *Olde Dublin Pub* upstairs boasts imported draft beer from Ireland and Scotland. The inexpensive *Off Broadway Café* (125 Sydney St.; phone: 902-566-4620) features crêpes, Acadian meat pies, and rich desserts. In the wee hours, *Cedar's* (81 University Ave.; phone: 902-892-7377) has low-priced, hefty sandwiches and Lebanese food. It's open until midnight Mondays through Thursdays (1 AM on Fridays and Saturdays); closed Sunday lunch.

En Route from Charlottetown Take Route 2 (St. Peter's Rd.) north about two miles, and then take Route 15 (Brackley Point Rd.) for 7½ miles (1[illegible] km) to Brackley Beach. The *Dunes Studio Gallery* (Rte. 15, phone: 902

672-2586) has an art gallery, gift shop, and café, operated by potter Peter Jansons. It's closed November through April. Continue on Route 15 to *Prince Edward Island National Park*.

PRINCE EDWARD ISLAND NATIONAL PARK Its miles of dunes are fronted by the sea and backed by salt marshes, cliffs and sea-torn rock formations. Of the more than 200 species of birds here, the most compelling is the great blue heron, gangling lord of the wetlands. This 25-mile stretch of shoreline is at once delicate and durable, a wonder of ecology and balance. The park begins at Tracadie Bay and Dalvay Beach and ends at Cavendish Bay. The herons are easiest to find at Rustico Island and New London Bay. The park is open year-round, though most facilities are closed *Labour Day* to mid-June; admission charge from late June through August (phone: 902-672-6350).

BRACKLEY BEACH The area has a wide range of cabins, tourist farmhouses, campgrounds, and hotels, including *Shaw's* hotel and cottages (see *Best en Route*). The national park campground at Rustico Island is just west of the beach on Gulf Shore Road. Overlooking beautiful Rustico Bay are 148 campsites set in 113 acres of evergreen forest.

STANHOPE BEACH Over three dozen cottage operations—many of them along the Gulf Shore Road—provide ample accommodations for the thousands of visitors who summer here. Weekly housekeeping rates range from $350 to $750. For those on more modest budgets, the 25-acre national park campground, cut out of a spruce forest, has 104 campsites and 14 sites for trailers. Roadside shopping, laundry facilities, and bicycle rentals are available in the area.

DALVAY BEACH This is the least crowded area of the national park. It has only one bathhouse and a sheltered cooking facility. Nearby, on the shores of Dalvay Lake, is the stately *Dalvay-by-the-Sea* hotel (see *Best en Route*). Along the Gulf Shore Road, watch for the nature trail, which features a bubbling spring, a pioneer cemetery, and a log bridge. (Don't try the nature trail in the summer without a liberal application of insect repellent.) From Dalvay Beach, walk 2 miles (3 km) east along the shoreline to the Tracadie Harbour area, where waterskiers abound.

En Route from Prince Edward Island National Park Follow Route 6 west to Oyster Bed Bridge. For a pleasant, short side trip, take Route 251 to the picturesque community of Wheatley River. A hundred yards before the crossroads at Wheatley River is *The Weathervane* antiques store (phone: 902-621-0070). Lynn and Cynthia Foley, among the island's most knowledgeable dealers, are always willing to give tips to visiting antiques hunters. The *PEI Preserve Company* (Rte. 224 in New Glasgow; phone: 902-964-2524) makes its own preserves and mustards, and its pleasant tearoom serves imported teas and coffees and home-baked desserts.

On the drive on Route 6 between Oyster Bed Bridge and North Rustico, blue herons wade along the inlets formed by the Wheatley and Hunter Rivers in search of small fish. From North Rustico, continue to Cavendish.

CAVENDISH Local author Lucy Maud Montgomery set her novel *Anne of Green Gables* in this area. Some of the rustic paths that the fictional Anne explored have been turned into a golf course (see *Green Gables Golf Course* in *Golf in Canada* in DIVERSIONS), but visitors can still see the Lover's Lane, the Babbling Brook, the Haunted Woods, and the Lake of Shining Waters. *Green Gables,* the country farmhouse immortalized in the children's classic, is open daily; admission charge (phone: 902-963-2675).

En Route from Cavendish Cavendish Beach is the busiest of all Canada's national park beaches, and Route 6 between Cavendish and Stanley Bridge is an almost continuous strip of motels, lodges, summer cottages, roadside shops, and attractions for children.

The Stanley Bridge area is famous for its beautiful inlets. This part of Prince Edward Island has a tradition of community lobster suppers held nightly during the summer, which has become a cherished part of island life. The tradition began in the community and parish halls of New Glasgow, St. Ann's, and New London, and is still going strong today. For about $20, lucky guests have a choice of hot or cold lobster, New York sirloin, or pork chops, accompanied by seafood chowder, potatoes, corn, coleslaw, and rolls, finished off with pie and ice cream. For information, call 902-964-2351, or follow signs pointing the way.

Farther along Route 6 in New London is Lucy Maud Montgomery's birthplace (6 Kensington Cove; phone: 902-886-2596). The house in which the author was born contains her wedding dress, veil, shoes, and scrapbook. Open daily; admission charge.

From New London, take Route 20 northwest for 6 miles (10 km) to the town of Park Corner and the *Anne of Green Gables Museum*. Located in a house in which the author lived at various times during her life, the museum contains the island's largest collection of Montgomery memorabilia, including autographed copies of the first edition of her world-famous novel. The museum has a tearoom, a gift shop, and, outside, a playground. It's open daily; admission charge (phone: 902-886-2884).

From Park Corner, proceed directly south on Route 101 to Kensington, and follow Route 2 southwest to the junction with Route 1A at Travellers Rest. From here, take Route 1A southeast 5 miles (8 km) to Ross Corner and from there to Borden Point, site of the ferry landing from New Brunswick. From there, follow Routes 10 and 1 east to Victoria.

VICTORIA In this quaint seaside village is the *Orient* hotel (see *Best en Route*) and nearby, the *Victoria Playhouse* (phone: 902-658-2025). The *Island Chocolate Company* (Main St.; phone: 902-658-2320) sells chocolates and gift items

The *Landmark Café* (Main St.; phone: 902-658-2286), located in an old country store, is the village's most popular eating spot. It stays open late for theatergoers.

En Route from Victoria Turn off Route 1 onto Route 19 at DeSable for a picturesque drive east along the south shore. At Rocky Point, *Fort Amherst National Historic Park* is the site of the first French settlement on the island (1720), but only the earthworks built by the British after they captured it in 1758 remain today. The site features a museum and a picnic area. It's open daily; no admission charge (phone: 902-675-2220).

To return to Charlottetown, continue along Route 19 to New Dominion; cross the causeway to Cornwall, where Route 1 leads directly into the capital.

BEST EN ROUTE

Prince Edward Island has an ample supply of accommodations of every sort: hotels, motels, bed and breakfast establishments, farms that take visitors, cottages, and lodges. Because of the national park, the Blue Heron Drive is dotted with small cottages and tourist homes available for rental; book well in advance for July and August. These places are listed in the comprehensive *Visitors Guide,* available free from the *PEI Department of Tourism* (see introduction to this chapter).

For a double room per night, expect to pay $80 or more at a place in the expensive category; from $50 to $80 at one in the moderate range; and $50 or less at an inexpensive place. All hotels feature private baths and air conditioning, TV sets, and telephones in rooms, and accept major credit cards, unless otherwise indicated. Most campgrounds are very inexpensive, costing $20 or less per night. For each location, places are listed alphabetically by price category.

CHARLOTTETOWN

Dundee Arms This establishment includes a refurbished 90-year-old house, plus a modern 10-room hotel. Of the eight rooms in the older building, some are furnished with antiques and brass beds; they're slightly less expensive than the modern rooms. The *Griffon* dining room serves excellent food. 200 Pownal St. (phone: 902-892-2496; fax: 902-368-8532). Expensive.

Elmwood At the end of a tree-lined drive, this Victorian inn is a short walk from *Victoria Park.* The three well-appointed suites have antique furniture and private baths; two have fireplaces. Breakfast is included in the rate, but there is no restaurant. 121 N. River Rd. (phone: 902-368-3310). Expensive.

Prince Edward Overlooking the waterfront, this 10-story, 213-room Canadian Pacific establishment is Charlottetown's finest, with two restaurants, a lounge, a heated indoor pool, saunas, and a fully equipped exercise room.

It is joined to a convention center and a small indoor shopping plaza. 18 Queen St. (phone: 902-566-2222; fax: 902-566-2282). Expensive.

Duchess of Kent Inn The seven spacious rooms in this antique, clapboard-and-shingled bed and breakfast establishment have period furnishings, hardwood floors, and shared baths. No TV sets, telephones, or air conditioning. Kitchen facilities are available, and continental breakfast is provided on request. No credit cards accepted. A block and a half from the center of the city, at 218 Kent St. (phone: 902-566-5826). Inexpensive.

DALVAY BEACH

Dalvay-by-the-Sea A lovely 26-room resort on Dalvay Lake, it features tennis courts, lawn bowling, and rowboats. The dining room serves French and English dishes. No TV sets, telephones, or air conditioning in the rooms. Open mid-June through September. Also see *Special Havens* in DIVERSIONS. Rte. 6, in *Prince Edward Island National Park* (phone: 902-672-2048 in summer, 902-672-2546 in winter; or write to PO Box 8, Little York, PEI C0A 1P0 in winter). Expensive.

BRACKLEY BEACH

Shaw's The Shaw family has been welcoming guests here for over 130 years. Adjacent to the national park, this hostelry has 18 rooms, 11 cottages, and seven chalets, one with a sauna and two with whirlpool baths. The rate includes two meals a day in the dining room. A lounge is on the premises; sailboats and windsurfing are available. No TV sets or air conditioning in the rooms. Also see *Special Havens* in DIVERSIONS. Rte. 15 (phone: 902-672-2022). Expensive.

SOUTH RUSTICO

Barachois Inn This handsome Victorian home has been turned into a bed and breakfast establishment with two suites and two rooms, all furnished with artwork and antiques, some with four-poster beds. No TV sets, telephones, or air conditioning in the rooms. No credit cards accepted. Rte. 243 (phone: 902-963-2194). Moderate.

CAVENDISH

Kindred Spirits Country Inn and Cottages For warm hospitality, this 10-room inn with 16 housekeeping units is a great place to stay, especially if you enjoy buffet breakfasts. Closed mid-October to mid-May. Rte. 6 in the center of town (phone: 902-963-2434). Moderate.

VICTORIA

Orient This heritage inn, built around the turn of the century, has four rooms and two suites, all with private baths (but no TV sets or telephones). There's a tearoom and dining room on the premises. Closed November through April. Main St. (phone: 902-658-2503). Moderate.

The Kings Byway

The Kings Byway starts at the strawberry fields across the river from Charlottetown, then cuts across the island's hilly interior tobacco-growing region to the eastern shore. The many provincial parks along the route have facilities for camping and swimming; the largest is the 1,700-acre *Brudenell River Provincial Park,* with 90 campsites. Within the park is the *Brudenell Resort* (see *Best en Route*), home of the best golf course on Prince Edward Island (see *Golf in Canada* in DIVERSIONS).

En Route from Charlottetown For a detailed report on Charlottetown, see the *Blue Heron Drive* route, above. Follow Grafton Street east over the Hillsborough Bridge to the village of Southport. Nearby Tea Hill and Alexandra are noted for their neatly kept country houses and thriving berry farms. During July, self-pick farms in this area sell strawberries and raspberries at low prices.

Continue along Route 1A for 8 miles (13 km) beside Pownal Bay, and take the Trans-Canada Highway (Rte. 1) east at Mount Mellick. Proceed 6 miles (10 km) to Orwell.

ORWELL Located at the main crossroads of the tiny hamlet of Orwell is *Orwell Corner Historic Village,* a restored farm community that depicts the life of PEI's early settlers. The pioneer mood and setting of the mid-19th-century village are re-created by the historic site's store, post office, keeper's house, church, and barn, all of which have been restored. The museum is closed Mondays late June through *Labour Day;* closed weekends mid-May through late June and *Labour Day* through late October; closed the rest of the year. There's an admission charge (phone: 902-651-2013). Just up the road is the *Sir Andrew MacPhail Homestead*. Set in the woods, the 19th-century house has been restored and turned into a tearoom. It's closed October through May (phone: 902-651-2789). A 24-site campground is nearby.

En Route from Orwell Return to Route 1 and drive west about 6 miles (10 km) to Cherry Valley, and pick up Route 3. At Poole's Corner 14 miles (23 km) east on Route 3, stop at the *King's Byway Visitor Information Centre,* which features a multimedia exhibition of King's County history and culture. It's closed September through May. No admission charge (phone: 902-838-2972). Turn right on Route 3 to the *Brudenell River Provincial Park* and the *Brudenell Resort*.

BRUDENELL RESORT This 1,700-acre retreat (see *Best en Route*) is the perfect spot to spend a few days relaxing. On its grounds are an 18-hole golf course, two tennis courts, open playing fields, and a small-craft marina on the river. The resort is family-oriented, with scheduled activities for children.

Nearby is the *Brudenell River Provincial Park*, with 90 campsites (some with services for trailers). Guests staying in the park are entitled to use the resort's facilities. The park is closed October through May; no admission charge (phone: 902-652 2756).

En Route from Brudenell For a picturesque drive northeast through rural Prince Edward Island, follow Route 311 through Cardigan along the shore of the Boughton Peninsula. At Dundas, scene of the province's annual summer plowing match, follow Route 310 to Spry Point. In Spry Point, *The Ark* (phone: 902-583-2400), a unique building that once was a government-sponsored energy-efficient living demonstration project, has been turned into a charming, eight-room inn. Set in a greenhouse, its restaurant serves local fish and vegetables. From Spry Point, follow Route 310 north toward Souris.

SOURIS This town got its name from the French word for "mice" after an invasion of these rodents early in the province's history. Some of the island's finest white-sand beaches are found on the 9-mile (14-km) stretch between Souris and Bothwell.

Souris is the departure point for a side trip to the French-speaking Magdalen Islands, located 84 miles (134 km) north of Prince Edward Island in the Gulf of St. Lawrence. Part of Quebec, the Magdalens can be reached by ferry from a pier just beyond the outskirts of Souris.

En Route from Souris Nearby *Red Point Provincial Park* has 26 campsites nestled behind a small woods close to the shore. The park has a picnic area, a large children's playground, and an excellent beach. It is closed *Labour Day* to mid-June; no admission charge (phone: 902-357-2463).

The *Basin Head Fisheries Museum* (S. Lake Souris; phone: 902-357-2966) also is nearby, with exhibits on the history of fishing in the province—and in many respects the history of fishing *is* the history of the province. The museum is closed *Labour Day* to mid-June; admission charge.

BEST EN ROUTE

While there are few large hostelries along this route, there are many lodges and cottages with no more than five rooms all along the drive. Many of these are listed in the *Visitors Guide,* available free from the *PEI Department of Tourism* (see introduction to this chapter). For a double room for one night, expect to pay $80 or more in an expensive hotel; from $50 to $80 in a moderate place; and $50 or less in an inexpensive one. All hotels feature private baths unless otherwise indicated. Campgrounds are very inexpensive, costing $20 or less per night. For each location, places are listed alphabetically by price category.

BRUDENELL

Brudenell Resort Just west of Georgetown, this 1,700-acre park and resort area has 50 one-room chalets and 50 hotel rooms, each with a phone and TV set. The property has the island's best golf course; two tennis courts;, a small-craft marina on the Brudenell River, which meanders through the park and resort; a pool—really preferable to swimming in the river—and a restaurant. Open May to mid-October. For information, write to the *Brudenell Resort, c/o Rodd Inns,* PO Box 22, Cardigan, PEI C0A 1G0 (phone: 902-652-2332); in winter, *Rodd Inns,* PO Box 432, Charlottetown, PEI C1A 7K7 (phone: 902-892-7448). Expensive.

BAY FORTUNE

Inn at Bay Fortune Once the summer home of playwrights, actors, and actresses, this place has 11 cozy rooms, some with fireplaces, and a dining room. Closed mid-October through May. Between Spry Point and Souris, on Rte. 310 (phone: 902-687-3745). Expensive.

SOURIS

Matthew House Inn This restored and immaculately kept Victorian house overlooks the water. Each of the eight guestrooms has a full or half bath. The inn has four fireplaces, a dining room, a library, a parlor, a sun deck, and a shaded porch. A block from the center of town, on Breakwater St. (phone: 902-687-3461). Moderate.

Red Point Provincial Park A small, seven-acre site situated about 8 miles (13 km) east of Souris, it features 24 campsites, 14 trailer hookups, a supervised beach, a playground, and kitchen facilities. Rte. 16 (phone: 902-357-2463). Very inexpensive.

Lady Slipper Drive

The western third of Prince Edward Island should not be missed. This is Acadian country, home of the island's French-speaking population, the descendants of the early French settlers who established villages here before the British took over in 1758. Two Acadian museums along the 171-mile (274-km) route—the *Acadian Museum* and the *Acadian Pioneer Village*—re-create the way of life of the French settlers.

UMMERSIDE This town of well-kept residential streets and wood-frame houses (pop. 13,600) is sometimes referred to as PEI's western capital. With its fine old clock tower, *Town Hall* (1886) makes the perfect starting point for a walking tour of the neighborhood, some of whose houses resemble stately châteaux. *The Eptek Centre* (phone: 902-436-4737) in the *Waterfront Mall* features art and other exhibits open to the public. Nearby, the yacht club offers a view of Bedeque Bay and Holman Island, the site of a hotel destroyed by fire in 1904. A short stroll from the yacht club is *Spinnaker's Landing,* a boardwalk with boutiques, snack bars, and an outdoor lounge where local musicians perform most nights during the summer. The *Lobster Carnival and Livestock Exhibition* in mid-July is a popular annual festival (see *Festivals, Fairs, and Fancy Acts* in DIVERSIONS).

En Route from Summerside Follow Central Street to Route 2; a left turn takes you through suburban St. Eleanors. At Miscouche, the *Acadian Museum* (23 Main Dr. E.; phone: 902-436-6237) displays antiques from the early 19th century, including farm implements, trade tools, and portraits. It's open daily year-round; admission charge.

For 6 miles (10 km) beyond Miscouche, Route 2 cuts through a barren stretch of swamp and scrub. Turn left (south) on Route 124 to get to Mont-Carmel.

MONT-CARMEL Overlooking Egmont Bay and dominated by the two black spires of *Notre Dame Church,* this city serves nicely as the gateway to Acadian Prince Edward Island: Mont-Carmel and its surrounding villages are staunchly French Canadian (and French-speaking). Photographers should note the cemetery adjacent to *Notre Dame,* with several ornate statues atop stone pillars.

Cap-Egmont, 3 miles (5 km) west of Mont-Carmel on Route 11, is the site of the *Acadian Pioneer Village*, a re-creation of an early-19th-century log cabin settlement, with a church, a common house, a blacksmith shop, a school, and a water well. It's closed mid-September to mid-June; admission charge (phone: 902-854-2227). *Etoile de Mer* (Mont-Carmel St.; phone: 902-854-2227), in a spacious log building, is the island's most authentic Acadian restaurant. Its dishes include meat pies and *rapure,* a dish of grated potatoes wrapped around pork, then steamed or fried.

En Route from Mont-Carmel Follow Route 11 north for 14 miles (22 km) to Mt. Pleasant; from there, take Route 2 to Route 14 at Carleton, and proceed southwest to West Point. This drive around Egmont Bay leads to PEI's westernmost shore. At West Point, *Cedar Dunes Provincial Park* has camp- and trailer sites (see *Best en Route*) and a beach on the bay. Also inside the park is the *West Point Lighthouse* (see *Best en Route*), a hotel with a chowder house and a crafts shop. Route 14 follows the shoreline north to Cape Wolfe, named after General James Wolfe, who stopped here in 1759 on his way to lay siege to Quebec.

The island's western shore from Cape Wolfe all the way north to Christopher Cross is dotted with small fishing villages and provincial parks. If you want to "get away from it all," the campgrounds and beaches here are uncrowded even at the height of summer. From Cape Wolfe, follow the Lady Slipper Drive north to Campbelltown; then take Route 145 inland to *Mill River Provincial Park*.

MILL RIVER PROVINCIAL PARK This 500-acre park and camping area (phone: 902-859-8786) near the town of O'Leary has a heated indoor pool, tennis courts, and an 18-hole golf course (see *Golf in Canada* in DIVERSIONS).

MILL RIVER FUN PARK On Route 2 in nearby Woodstock, this place is worth visiting if you're traveling with children. Its highlights are an outdoor pool and water slides, miniature golf, paddle and bumper boats, a petting zoo, and a 650-seat amphitheater for daytime entertainment. Closed *Labour Day* to mid-June; admission charge (phone: 902-859-2071). The *Rodd Mill River* resort (see *Best en Route*) also is in Woodstock.

En Route from Mill River Provincial Park East of the park, Malpeque Bay's oyster beds have made Prince Edward Island famous for bivalves. Near the bay, *Green Park Provincial Park* (see *Best en Route*) is perhaps the island's most beautiful camping spot. On the way into the park, the road winds through spruce and white birch forests and open fields. From here, the route returns to Summerside.

BEST EN ROUTE

Except for Summerside, the western section of Prince Edward Island is sparsely populated. Small accommodations are listed in the *Visitors Guide,* available free from the *PEI Department of Tourism* (see introduction to this chapter). For a double room per night at expensive places, expect to pay $80 or more; at moderate establishments, from $50 to $80; and at inexpensive places, $50 or less. All hotels feature private baths unless otherwise indicated. Campgrounds, including those in provincial parks along the shore, provide very inexpensive accommodations for $15 or less. For each location, places are listed alphabetically by price category.

SUMMERSIDE

Loyalist Country Inn The town's newest accommodations are on the waterfront across from *Spinnaker's Landing.* There are 42 well-appointed, comfortable rooms and eight housekeeping units, as well as a restaurant and lounge. 195 Harbour Dr. (phone: 902-436-4330). Expensive.

Silver Fox On a residential street, this restored house decorated with antiques is one of PEI's nicest inns. There are six rooms; rates include a continental breakfast. There's a restaurant. 61 Granville St. (phone: 902-436-4033). Moderate.

WEST POINT

West Point Lighthouse Located in *Cedar Dunes Provincial Park* (see below), this restored, more-than-century-old lighthouse has nine antiques-furnished guestrooms. A chowder house and crafts shop are on the premises. Closed October to mid-May. Off Rte. 14 (phone: 902-859-3605). Moderate.

Cedar Dunes Provincial Park Next to a stretch of beach with lifeguards are 20 campsites, 22 trailer sites, two-way electrical hookups, and laundry facilities. Just off Rte. 14 (signposted) in the lighthouse area (phone: 902-859-8785). Very inexpensive.

WOODSTOCK

Rodd Mill River This 80-room resort is considered one of the most scenic in Atlantic Canada. Among its amenities are tennis and squash courts, an 18-hole championship golf course, a heated indoor pool, a dining room, and a lounge. Closed December through April. Off Rte. 2 (phone: 902-859-3555). Expensive.

CASCUMPEC

Cold Comfort Farm Don't let the name throw you—it's a family joke. This handsome bed and breakfast establishment in an old home has three guestrooms, two with double beds (there's a shared bath). There are no TV sets, telephones, or air conditioning in the rooms. Closed mid-September through mid-June. Rte. 12, a few miles east of *Mill River Provincial Park* (phone: 902-853-2803). Inexpensive.

GREEN PARK PROVINCIAL PARK AREA

Doctor's Inn This fine example of a traditional PEI country home is a mile or so southwest of the park, in Tyne Valley. Owners Paul and Jean Offer have just two rooms available on a bed and breakfast basis, with a shared bath. Operators of a seven-acre market garden, they are excellent cooks and will serve guests and others (with reservations) a delicious dinner in the dining room. Rte. 167 off Rte. 12 (phone: 902-831-2164). Inexpensive.

Green Park Provincial Park Overlooking oyster-rich Malpeque Bay is one of the island's most scenic campgrounds. On its 219 acres are 18 campsites and 19 trailer hookups, with running water and flush toilets. A shipbuilding museum is located in the 19th-century *Yeo House,* also on the grounds. Rte. 12 (phone: 902-831-2370). Very inexpensive.

Quebec

Quebec, known as "the Distinct Society" and the center of French language and culture in North America, is a province unlike any other. Forever fearful of being swallowed up by the surrounding sea of English speakers, French Quebeckers (or Québécois) place great importance on protecting and promoting their linguistic and cultural identity. The result has been recurring political disputes between Quebec and the federal government, with Quebec trying to achieve more autonomy—either as a province with greater legislative powers or as an independent country. But these debates, which at times can reach passionate levels, have had no negative effect on day-to-day living. Most Quebeckers—Anglophone or Francophone—would like the issue resolved once and for all. It could even be said that this debate, propelled by nationalist pride, has helped maintain the vitality and richness of Quebec's cultural and social life. And for visitors, that adds spice to a province that combines a North American lifestyle with Old World charm.

In the early years of European settlement, Quebec was part of New France, an area that nominally extended from Hudson Bay to the Gulf of Mexico. In 1642, a permanent settlement called Ville-Marie was established and later renamed Montreal. Louis XIV declared Quebec a French colony in 1663, but a century later it fell to the British in the famous Battle of the Plains of Abraham—now a historic park site in Quebec City.

Canada itself came into being in 1867 as a country of four provinces, including Quebec, whose language and institutions were accorded protection under the founding British North America Act. French is still the official language of Quebec, and both English and French are recognized as official languages for Canada as a whole. About 83 percent of Quebec's 7.2 million residents speak French as their mother tongue. Although in rural areas, you will hear English being spoken very rarely, most people who work in the service and tourism industries can speak English. Montrealers are bilingual for the most part, and in Quebec City, communicating in English does not pose any problem. The population of Native Americans (including Cree, Mohawk, Huron, and Micmac) totals about 53,000, while there are about 6,800 Inuit people in northern Quebec.

Quebec is Canada's largest province, covering 594,860 square miles. Its capital, Quebec City (regional pop. 630,000), is its third-largest city, after Greater Montreal (pop. 3.1 million) and Laval (pop. 325,000). (For individual reports on Quebec City and Montreal, see THE CITIES.)

In the vast areas beyond the urban centers, the terrain of this province is varied, with fertile farmland both in the south and along the St. Lawrence River, rolling hills to the east, and the striking Laurentian mountains to the north. Summers in central and southern Quebec can be hot and humid, while winters are cold and snowy. Both spring and fall are pleasantly temperate.

We have divided Quebec into four driving routes: the Eastern Townships, near the US border, dotted with ski resorts and lakes; the Laurentian Mountains, rich in parks, lakes, and vacation resorts; the Gaspé Peninsula, with windswept fishing villages and fabulous ocean wildlife (whales, seals, and seabirds); and a remote archipelago of a dozen islands called Iles-de-la-Madeleine (Magdalen Islands), rich sources of fish and lobster.

For further information, contact *Tourisme Québec* (1001 Square Dorchester, PO Box 979, Montreal, QUE H3C 2W3; phone: 514-873-2015; 800-363-7777 in Canada and the US, except Alaska; fax: 514-864-3838). In addition, the *Fédération des Agricotours du Québec* (4545 Av. Pierre-de-Coubertin, PO Box 1000, Station M, Montreal, QUE H1V 3R2; phone: 514-252-3138) publishes a helpful guide, *Best Bed and Breakfasts in Quebec,* which covers bed and breakfast establishments, farm holidays, and small country inns. It's available in many US travel bookstores or by writing to the *Fédération;* at press time it cost about $10 US (including postage). For camping information, call *Camping Québec* (phone: 514-651-7396; 800-363-0457 in Quebec and Ontario). To reserve chalet, lodge, and camping accommodations in provincial parks and wildlife preserves, contact the *Ministère de l'Environnement et de la Faune* (Department of Environment and Wildlife; Blvd. René-Lévesque E., Quebec City, QUE G1R 4Y1; phone 418-890-6527; 800-665-6527 in Quebec). Information on hunting and fishing can be obtained from the same department (phone: 418-643-3127; 800-561-1616 in Quebec).

The Eastern Townships

Sometimes called Quebec's best-kept secret, this scenic area of woods and glacial lakes in the upper reaches of the Appalachians is just an hour's drive from Montreal. Long popular with vacationing Montrealers, the Eastern Townships region has been attracting people from farther afield in recent years as its reputation as a resort area grows. Opportunities to enjoy horseback riding, swimming, sailing, and festivals abound in summer; brilliant foliage and apple country attract autumn vacationers; and downhill and cross-country skiing, snowmobiling, and snowshoeing are the winter draws. The area boasts numerous alpine (downhill) ski centers, more than 800 miles of cross-country ski trails, and close to 100 miles of snowshoeing tracks. (For more details, see *Downhill Skiing* and *Cross-Country Skiing* in DIVERSIONS.) Every February, in the village of Valcourt, an international festival celebrates the snowmobile, which was invented in this area. The region's proximity to the American border states of Maine, New Hampshire, and Vermont, just across the road in some cases, makes it a favorite stopping-off place for New Englanders on their way to Montreal and for Montrealers traveling to the States.

The Eastern Townships area was originally settled mostly by former New Englanders who poured over the nearby border between 1774 and 1840 to escape first the American Revolution and later the government of the independent United States of America. Known in Canada as United Empire Loyalists (loyal to the King of England), these immigrants set up farms similar to their former homes south of the border. Before this influx, the earliest inhabitants were the Abenaki and other, smaller native groups. Today, about 85% of the area's residents are Francophone; they refer to the townships as "les Cantons de L'Est," while the government officially calls the region "L'Estrie," a combination of the word "est," meaning east, and "patrie," for homeland. For more information on the Eastern Townships region, contact the *Maison Régionale du Tourisme de l'Estrie* (L'Estrie Regional Tourism Office; Rte. 10, St-Alphonse de Granby, QUE JOE 2AO; phone: 514-375-8774; 819-820-2020; 800-263-1068).

En Route from Montreal Head east on either the high-speed Eastern Townships Autoroute (Rte. 10) or the older, winding (and far more scenic) Route 112. The latter passes through Rougemont, a small town known for its apple orchards and cider mills. In the fall, it's a great place to pick, buy, and eat apples and to watch them being pressed into cider. In fact, throughout the region there are orchards where visitors can pick their own apples. Watch for roadside signs. Granby is 53 miles (85 km) from Montreal.

GRANBY The townships truly begin here, on Route 112, just off the autoroute. The *Granby Zoo*—in addition to having some 1,000 animals, a children's petting section, plenty of rides, and a picnic area—claims to have the only reptile farm in Canada. The *Granby Zoo* (347 Bourget St.; phone: 514-372-9113) is closed early September to mid-May; it's open daily the rest of the year. There's an admission charge. The *Lac Boivin Nature Preserve* (700 Drummond St.; phone: 514-375-3861), in the heart of Granby, is a marsh habitat traversed by walking trails. It's open daily; no admission charge.

En Route from Granby A few miles south, just off the autoroute, is Bromont, one of a quartet of major mountains developed for skiing in the area.

BROMONT This area is most popular during the winter, thanks to the *Station Touristique Bromont* (150 Rue Champlain; phone: 514-534-2200), which has some of the longest illuminated night ski runs in Canada. During the summer, test the mountainside water slides or enjoy the lake's fine swimming and sailing. Bromont also is known for horseback riding at the *Centre Equestre Bromont* (100 Chemin Laprairie; phone: 514-534-3255). In June, there's an international equestrian competition, attracting Olympic caliber riders. In addition, the town is a prime destination for shoppers: A huge flea market takes place on Sundays throughout the summer, just off Route 10, and there are a large number of factory outlet stores (Route 10, Exit 78).

En Route from Bromont Head south on Route 241 to Route 104, which leads east to the Lac Brome and Sutton area, near the Vermont border. Take Route 139 south to reach some of eastern Canada's best skiing at Mont Sutton (phone: 514-538-2545), which has a 1,500-foot vertical drop, more than 50 downhill trails, and excellent cross-country trails. Every weekend between mid-September and early October, walking and hiking foliage tours are available. For a more unusual way to see the terrain, take a ride on one of the park's llamas; llama rides are offered year-round. For more information, contact *Sutton Natural Environment Park* at Mont Sutton (phone: 514-538-4085) or the *Sutton Tourism Bureau* (phone: 800-565-8455). During warmer months (generally June through October), a Saturday-morning farmer's market takes place here. From Sutton, head north on Route 215, then east on Route 104 to Lac-Brome, formerly Knowlton (and still called that by many locals).

LAC-BROME A choice vacation spot, this country dotted with cottages sprawls along the shore of Lac-Brome, made famous by its delicious ducklings. Summer activities center around the lake and the town of Lac-Brome; during the winter skiing is possible at nearby Mont Glen (phone: 514-243-6142). The *Brome County Historical Museum* (130 Lakeside Rd.; phone: 514-243-6782) is housed in buildings dating back to the turn of the century. Its exhibits of furnishings and tools re-create the life of the Loyalist settlers. It's closed September through May; open daily the rest of the year. There's an admission charge. A number of quaint boutiques in the area offer good browsing grounds.

En Route from Lac-Brome Return to Route 215 north and continue past the junction with Route 10 to Waterloo, a little valley village set against the rolling Eastern Townships mountains. Founded by Loyalists during the 1790s, Waterloo has a fine architectural heritage. The old right-of-way where the railway once passed through town is now a 13-mile (21-km) bicycle path, called *L'Estriade*, that leads to Granby. Another 29-mile (47-km) path begins at *Safari Tour* (475 Blvd. Horizon, or Exit 89 off Route 10; phone: 514-539-0501), an unusual and imaginative nature park and museum, with butterfly, beetle, and insect displays in one area and an adventure theme park featuring Indiana Jones–type characters and "adventure expeditions" in another. Reservations are recommended for the expeditions, which change regularly but might be a treasure hunt, a search for a "lost city," or a mission to rescue the occupants of a downed airplane. The park is open daily year-round; there's an admission charge. From Waterloo, hop on the autoroute and head east about 15 miles (24 km) to the Magog-Orford area.

MAGOG This town (pronounced *May*-gog) lies at the northernmost tip of Lac Memphrémagog. Tourists and seasonal residents often picnic and swim at the public beach on Merry Point. The motor launch *Adventure II* (phone:

819-843-8068) makes three daily 1¾-hour tours of the lake from June through September; a day-long cruise to Newport, Vermont, is also available. While touring the lake, keep an eye out for "Memphré," the legendary lake monster, who, like the Loch Ness monster, has so far avoided positive identification. Many locals are convinced he exists in the depths of this large, long lake, though the only evidence is a handful of grainy photographs. The *Traversée International du Lac Memphrémagog* (International Swim Marathon) attracts thousands of spectators in mid-July for the grueling swim across the lake—27 miles (42 km) from Newport, Vermont, to Magog. Top world swimming marathoners are part of the field. To celebrate the turning of the leaves at the end of September, the town hosts the *Flambée des Couleurs* (Blaze of Colors). The *Auberge l'Etoile sur-le-Lac,* right in the heart of town (1150 Rue Principale W.; phone: 819-843-6521; 800-567-2727), is an excellent spot to sample the area's Lac-Brome duckling.

MONT ORFORD Both exits 115 and 118 off the autoroute lead to Mont Orford, known for its ski center (phone: 819-843-6548; 800-567-7315), its scenic Lac Stukely, and a provincial campground. *Mont Orford Provincial Park* also has a 500-seat concert hall, part of the *Orford Arts Centre* (Exit 118 on Rte. 141 N.; phone: 819-843-3981; 800-567-6155 in Quebec and Ontario) and scene of the *Festival Orford.* One of Canada's best-known annual music festivals, this event runs from late June to mid-August. The summer home of the country's national youth orchestra, *Les Jeunesses Musicales,* the Orford hills come alive with the sound of classical, jazz, and popular music indoors and out. (Sunday brunch and supper concerts are extremely popular.) Students from all over the world attend the center's summer music school, and the public is invited to some of the master classes.

The area also features the *Mont Orford* 18-hole public golf course, closed mid-October through April (Chemin du Parc; phone: 819-843-5688); summer chair-lift rides at the ski center (see above); and a number of resorts.

En Route from Mont Orford The autoroute goes directly to Sherbrooke (see below), but a more scenic route involves a quick backtrack to Magog along Route 141 to Ayer's Cliff. On the lake's southern banks, Ayer's Cliff offers a wide range of summer and winter facilities and equipment, including cottages, pedal boats, kayaks, rowboats, and fishing tackle. It is home to the *Ripplecove Inn,* an old-fashioned resort complex (see *Best en Route*); a public beach; and a number of antiques stores. Just past Ayer's Cliff, take Route 143 north around the jagged shoreline of Lac Massawippi and its resort community and on to North Hatley.

NORTH HATLEY One of the area's most popular destinations, the village is spread out along the northern banks of Lac Massawippi. This is the site of two of the Eastern Townships' better-known inns and a summer theater. The *Piggery Theatre* (on Rte. 108, just a few minutes west of town; phone: 819-842-2431), one of only two English-language theaters in the area (the other is in Lac-Brome), has a wide-ranging repertoire, from Broadway hits to Canadian productions. The theater's restaurant serves tasty country suppers before curtain time. Both *Hovey Manor,* with its art gallery, and the *Auberge Hatley,* a member of the Relais & Châteaux group, are in North Hatley (see *Best en Route* as well as *Special Havens* in DIVERSIONS for both), as are a number of craft studios and galleries. For a light meal and locally made beer, check out the outdoor deck at the *Pilsen* restaurant (55 Rue Principal; phone: 819-842-2971). The *Lake Massawippi Festival,* held from late April to late June, is highlighted by organ recitals at *Ste-Elisabeth Church* and Sunday brunch "Sons et Brioches" concerts at the *United Church.*

En Route from North Hatley Continue north for about 16 miles (26 km) to Sherbrooke. On the way is the small town of Lennoxville, site of one of Canada's leading learning institutions, *Bishop's University,* established in 1843. The buildings that spread over the peaceful little campus were inspired by the architecture at *Oxford University* in England. Lennoxville's main street harbors a number of well-stocked antiques shops, and the *Musée Uplands* (50 Park St.; phone: 819-564-0409 in summer; 819-569-1179 the rest of the year) features displays relating to the area's history. It's closed Mondays; admission charge.

SHERBROOKE Sherbrooke is the area's industrial and cultural center. With about 80,000 inhabitants, this city, dating back to 1791, is home to the large *University of Sherbrooke.* It also is the home of a number of art galleries and museums, including the *Sherbrooke Museum of Fine Arts* (174 Palais St.; phone: 819-821-2115), which features a collection of 19th-century art inspired by local scenery. It's closed Mondays; admission charge. The town also has several imposing churches, including the *Sherbrooke Cathedral* (downtown at 130 Rue Cathédral) and an old seminary that now houses the *Musée du Seminaire de Sherbrooke* (222 Rue Frontenac; phone: 819-564-3200), a natural science museum. The museum is closed Mondays; there's an admission charge. During the winter Sherbrooke is served by alpine and cross-country skiing facilities in several scenic municipal parks and at Mont Bellevue (phone: 819-821-5872), a mountain just blocks from the downtown core.

BEST EN ROUTE

This area is known for its excellent inns, but there also is a variety of accommodations in resort hotels, motels, and bed and breakfast establishments. Expect to pay $125 or more for a double room per night in the expensive range; from $65 to $125 in the establishments listed as moderate; and $65 or less in the inexpensive category. All hotels feature private baths unless otherwise indicated. For each location, establishments are listed alphabetically by price category.

GRANBY

Bon Soir This 43-unit motel has a pool. There's no dining room, but the motel is within walking distance of most Granby restaurants. 1587 Rue Principale (phone: 514-378-7947; fax: 514-378-5564). Moderate.

Le Castel de l'Estrie In this comfortable, 136-unit hotel are four rooms with fireplaces and a good dining room. It also is one of the four hostelries in the area that offers bargain ski packages in winter, and golf and *Granby Zoo* packages in summer. 901 Rue Principale (phone: 514-378-9071; 800-363-8953; fax: 514-378-9930). Moderate.

BROMONT

Auberge Bromont With 50 motel units close to ski slopes, cross-country ski trails, and a public 18-hole golf course, it also has an outdoor pool, tennis, and a fairly good restaurant. 95 Montmorency St. (phone: 514-534-2200; fax: 514-534-1700). Expensive.

Le Château Bromont Based on the full service European-style spa concept, this 154-room resort offers a restaurant, squash and racquetball courts, saunas, hot tubs, and indoor and outdoor pools. Golf, skiing, and nature trails are at its doorstep. 90 Stanstead St. (phone: 514-534-3433; 800-304-3433; fax: 514-534-0514). Expensive.

La Petite Auberge One of the attractions of this rustic six-room inn is its very good dining. Other pluses include an outdoor pool, saunas, and a pleasant terrace. Ski slopes are nearby. 360 Blvd. Pierre-Laporte (phone: 514-534-2707; fax: 514-534-1067). Inexpensive.

SUTTON

La Paimpolaise This 28-room property is close to ski slopes. It also has good guest services, a fair dining room, and a large outdoor Jacuzzi; in summer, tennis is available. 615 Maple St. (phone: 514-538-3213; 800-263-3213; fax: 514-538-3970). Moderate.

Horizon A modern place, it offers 48 rooms, an indoor pool and sauna, tennis, and a dining room that features old-fashioned roast pig on Thursday nights. Cross-country ski trails ribbon the property. 297 Chemin Mont-Sutton (phone: 514-538-3212; fax: 514-538-6669). Inexpensive.

MONT ORFORD

Auberge Chéribourg and Villas This 97-room hostelry has two outdoor pools, an indoor pool and spa, tennis, and a first-rate dining room. Rte. 141 N. (phone: 819-843-3308; 800-567-6132 in Quebec; fax: 819-843-2639). Expensive.

Auberge Estrimont The best place to stay in the area, this 82-unit resort features rooms in a main house as well as 19 chalets with fireplaces and kitchens.

The main house has a good dining room. Squash and racquetball courts, a sauna, and a pool round out the facilities; golf packages that take advantage of four of the area's layouts are available as well. Exit 118 off Rte. 10, at 44 Av. de l'Auberge (phone: 819-843-1616; 800-567-7320; fax: 819-843-4909). Expensive.

Auberge du Parc Orford Right in the park, it boasts 42 units equipped with kitchenettes, plus a restaurant, café, pool, and grocery store. 1259 Chemin de la Montagne (phone: 819-843-8887; fax: 819-843-1280). Moderate.

Auberge la Grande Fugue Located in *Mont Orford Provincial Park,* this new hostelry is part of the international youth hostel network but it's open to everyone. There are 180 beds in dormitory-style rooms (only 60 are available in July and August because many music students lodge here). In addition there are six family suites and eight double rooms. Open May through October. In *Mont Orford Provincial Park* (phone: 819-843-8595). Inexpensive.

NORTH HATLEY

Auberge Hatley A member of the Relais & Châteaux group, this country inn was built in 1903 as a summerhouse on a beautiful piece of property overlooking Lac Massawippi. The 25 colonial-style rooms are comfortably furnished with antique pieces; some have fireplaces. Alain Labrie oversees the excellent dining room. For more details see *Special Havens* in DIVERSIONS. 325 Chemin Virgin (phone: 819-842-2451; fax: 819-842-2907). Expensive.

Hovey Manor Formerly a private estate, this highly regarded manor house inn is furnished with antiques. Most of the 40 rooms have views of Lac Massawippi; suites feature wood-burning fireplaces, whirlpool baths, and private balconies. There's also a fine dining room. For more details see *Special Havens* in DIVERSIONS. 595 Hovey Rd. (phone: 819-842-2421; 800-661-2421; fax: 819-842-2248). Expensive.

AYER'S CLIFF

Ripplecove Inn On Lake Massawippi, this intimate, country inn is minutes away from five alpine ski centers. It has 25 units, including a log cabin that accommodates up to seven people, plus one of the best restaurants in the entire region—Montrealers often drive an hour or so just to enjoy this hostelry's award-winning food. Guests also make good use of the two private beaches, the pool, badminton and volleyball courts, and the inn's canoes, kayaks, and pedal boats. 700 Ripplecove Rd. (phone: 819-838-4296; 800-668-4296; fax: 819-838-5541). Expensive.

The Laurentians

One of the oldest mountain ranges in the world, the Laurentians skirt the southern boundary of the Canadian Shield, providing a splendid wilderness backyard for the large population living in the St. Lawrence River Valley. Cutting a broad swath across southern Quebec, these ancient, glacier-shaped mountains are dotted with lakes and rivers, and the slopes close to Quebec City and Montreal are world-famous ski resorts. Twenty alpine ski areas offering 350 trails (accommodating up to 50,000 skiers at one time) are located within 40 miles of Montreal. The mountains are not towering; Mont Tremblant, the best known, is 3,000 feet high. But the Laurentians are easily accessible, making this huge recreation area a popular year-round destination. In addition to excellent downhill skiing, the region offers some 500 lakes and rivers, about 250 miles of walking and cycling trails, and 745 miles of marked cross-country ski trails in the Maple Leaf network (also see *Cross-Country Skiing* in DIVERSIONS).

Carefully controlled hunting is permitted, though in certain areas it's restricted to Quebec residents. There are also numerous areas for fishing and winter ice-fishing. All wildlife is carefully monitored, and hunting and fishing guidelines ensure that no species is threatened. To hunt or fish, everyone must have a permit. Non-residents must also respect bag and catch limits, as well as firearms regulations. For those planning to hunt or fish outside provincial wildlife reserves, the assistance of an outfitter is recommended. Because of the close interaction between hunter (or angler) and outfitter, much of the enjoyment of the trip depends upon personalities; talk to one or two outfitters before making arrangements. Companies recommended by the *Quebec Outfitters Association* (phone: 418-527-5191; 800-567-9009 in Canada) are listed in the *Laurentides Tourist Guide,* published by *Tourisme Québec* (see the introduction to this chapter).

CENTRAL QUEBEC: THE ST-MAURICE VALLEY

One of Quebec's major industrial cities, Trois-Rivières, halfway between Montreal and Quebec City, straddles the mouth of the St-Maurice River. The city's French name is based upon the three channels formed by the islands in the river delta where it meets the St. Lawrence. The area's rich timberlands, providing lumber, and the river, providing transportation and power, were vital in the creation of this hectic industrial and shipping center. It is fitting that this busy city, with a past as old as Canada itself—Cartier toured the St-Maurice River Valley in 1535, and Champlain erected a trading post here in 1615—should guard the entrance to one of the most beautiful sections of Quebec. Although many of the valley's communities are industrial centers drawing upon neighboring resources, they are dedicated to preserving the forests and rivers that surround them.

Trois-Rivières can be reached from Montreal via the high-speed Route 40 or Route 138, Canada's first highway, which opened in 1737. At that time it was known as "le chemin du Roy" or King's Road. Part of it follows the St. Lawrence River before turning inland and passing through several small villages. For additional information contact the regional tourism office, *Tourisme Mauricie-Bois Francs* (1180 Rue Royale, Second Floor, Trois Rivières, Quebec G9A 4J1; phone: 819-375-1222; 800-567-7603; fax: 819-375-0301).

TROIS-RIVIÈRES This prosperous industrial city warrants at least an afternoon's stop to tour its much-improved historic district; here are many cafés, such as *Café Morgane* (Rue des Forges; phone: 819-694-1116), which serves excellent desserts; there are also reasonably priced restaurants here, such as *Café Mozart* (324 Rue Bonaventure; phone: 819-371-9483). In addition, in this area is the beautifully restored *Manoir Boucher-de-Niverville* (168 Rue Bonaventure; phone: 819-375-9628), a 1730 house that displays antique furniture and artifacts belonging to the town's first seigneurs. The house is closed weekends; there's no admission charge. There's also an interpretation center with displays related to the first iron-making forge in Canada at *Les Forges du St-Maurice National Historic Site* (10,000 Blvd. des Forges; phone: 819-378-5116). It's closed *Labour Day* to mid-May; open daily the rest of the year. There's an admission charge. The town hosts several festivals, including the *International Festival of Vocal Art* in late June, a blues festival in early July, a festival of street performers in August, and a three-day Grand Prix auto race in early August.

En Route from Trois-Rivières Take Route 55 north about 25 miles (40 km) to Grand-Mère, where the road becomes Route 155. The southeast entrance to *La Mauricie National Park* is a secondary road from St-Jean-des-Piles, about 8 miles (13 km) from Grand-Mère.

LA MAURICIE NATIONAL PARK Encompassing some 200 square miles of glacier-torn mountains, the park comprises 60 lakes and an untold number of rivers. Near the park entrance at Lac la Pêche are 208 campsites; there are 219 more at Lac Wapizagonke and another 91 at Mistagance. All campsites have running water, flush toilets, and showers, but no electricity. There are two welcome centers *(centres d'accueil):* one at St-Jean-les-Piles (phone: 819-538-3232), and the other in St-Mathieu, off Route 55 at exit 217, before Grand-Mère (phone: 819-532-2414). Both are open daily mid-May through mid-October, and closed the rest of the year. Sites for *camping primitif*—wilderness camping in areas accessible only by canoe—surround these lakes. Beyond the areas nearest the welcome centers, a canoe is the only means of transportation to the many wilderness campsites in the backcountry. It is necessary to portage about 1¼ miles to reach the next lake; frequent portages are required to explore the rest of the area. The park provides canoe rentals and detailed maps indicating three- to five-day canoe-camping trips through the area. A license is necessary if you plan to catch trout dinners while you camp—and remember, a four-day food supply can be heavy. Hunting is not permitted. Even if you don't choose to rough it for a few days, do take a day trip (by canoe) on Lac

Pêche. Along the lake are several sandy shores where you can beach your canoe and walk in unspoiled forests. At the north end of the lake is half a mountain, sheared away by a passing glacier long ago so that the mountain's solid rock interior is exposed. Lac Wapizagonke lies between two such rocky walls 13 miles long. Exploration has revealed native pictographs on these cliffs, but their origins are unknown. The park is open daily year-round; admission charge (phone: 819-536-2638). Also see *National Parks* in DIVERSIONS.

If this area is too tame or confining for your taste, bear in mind that it borders on the even wilder reserves of *St-Maurice* (to the north; see below) and *Mastigouche* (to the west).

ST-MAURICE RESERVE If it's really untamed woodland you're looking for, this is a fine place to start. For 150 years, hunters and anglers from all over North America have come here to engage in their favorite outdoor pursuits. The reserve covers 617 square miles of wild mountains, rivers, and woods. There is now access to the reserve by car over a new bridge (with a toll) at Rivière-Mattawin—about 42 miles (67 km) from Grand-Mère. A few hunting chalets are available, but getting one in July or August is not easy. In all provincial parks you have to apply for hunting accommodations in advance, and names are chosen randomly. In the off-season, it's easier. For details on all accommodations in Quebec reserves, call the *Ministère de l'Environnement et de la Faune* (Department of Environment and Wildlife; see the introduction to this chapter). Camping is the alternative, and no reservations are required. Bear and small-game hunting is permitted; moose hunting permits are restricted and again depend on the luck of the draw. Fishing is abundant, and visitors can canoe to their hearts' content; however, only a few canoe rentals are available in the park. There's a park reception center at Rivière-Matawin (phone: 819-646-5687; fax: 819-646-5680). The park is open daily year-round; there's no admission charge.

LA TUQUE Venture farther along Route 155 (about 75 miles/120 km from Grand-Mère) to this town that developed around the forest industry. It offers the *Domaine Touristique de La Tuque* (La Tuque Recreation Area; phone: 819-523-6151; 819-523-4424 in summer) which encompasses 20 lakes, a ski center, and an 18-hole golf course. Hunting and fishing are major activities here. More than a dozen outfitters can find a place for you at one of over 130 camps and lodges in the broader region. Area game includes moose, deer, rabbits, and various fowl. A municipal campground (phone: 819-523-5533), off Route 155 north, has 344 sites, a pool, a recreation hall, and boat access to the Bostonnais River. A couple of miles west of the city on Route 155 is *Bostonnais Falls Park,* where there are hiking trails and picnic areas and cross-country skiing in winter. It's open year-round; no admission charge. From here, Lac St-Jean is 82 miles (131 km) north.

NORTH OF QUEBEC CITY: RÉSERVE FAUNIQUE DES LAURENTIDES

En Route from Quebec City Take Route 175 from downtown for 30-mile (48-km) drive to the wildlife reserve's southern entrance. The 5,637 square miles of the reserve offer beautiful scenery and a variety of activities, and it's only minutes away from the city. Hiking, canoeing, camping, cross-country skiing, and hunting and fishing are all possible here. Black bear hunting is permitted in June, and moose and small game can be taken in the fall; the fishing season runs from mid-May to early September. Year-round, visitors can rent cabins with bathrooms and kitchens at some 20 locations, and there are three campgrounds—the largest at La Loutre on Lac Jacques-Cartier, with 104 sites for tents and trailers, and offering canoeing, sailing, and fishing. There are another 30 sites at the northern edge of the park off Route 169 on Lac de la Belle Rivière. In the middle of the reserve is the area called "les Portes-de-l'Enfer"—the gates of hell—so named because in the early days, it was hellish trying to travel through this sector during spring flooding. Here, there are nine fully-equipped chalets, a dining room, and guide services. The wildest sector of the park is around Lac Brûlé, accessible by hydroplane only. It has four chalets, but no running water. For general park information call 418-686-1717; for reservations call 800-665-6527. The reserve is open daily year-round; there's no admission charge.

SAGUENAY–LAC ST-JEAN

En Route from the Réserve Faunique des Laurentides Continuing out of the park, Route 169 takes you into the land of "les Bleuets" (Blueberries), the nickname that residents of the region have given themselves. Besides an enormous array of outdoor activities, the beauty of Lac St-Jean itself (22 miles in diameter), and summer and winter festivals, the area is known for its blueberries. Try some of the local blueberry wine. Follow Route 169 west 40 miles (65 km) from the northern edge of the park to Lac St-Jean and along the lake to the town of Roberval. The *Traversée Internationale* (International Swim) across the lake is held here in late July, with accompanying music and street celebrations in and around town. In St-Felicien, a few miles farther along Route 169 at the western end of the lake, is the *Zoo de St Félicien* (phone: 418-679-0543; 800-667-5687 in Canada) where the people are in cages (cars, actually) and the animals roam freely (or mostly). It's open daily from mid-May through September; there's an admission charge. For information, contact the regional tourist office, *Tourisme Saguenay–Lac St-Jean* (198 Rue Racine E., Chicoutimi, Quebec G7H 1R9; phone: 418-543-9778; 800-463-9651 in Quebec; fax: 418-543-1805).

Follow the Saguenay River down to where it empties into the St. Lawrence; take Route 169 east from Roberval to the intersection with Route 170 at Métabetchouan, and follow Route 170 past the town of Chicoutimi to St-Siméon. Along the way, the route passes the *Parc du Saguenay* (418-272-2267 or 418-544-7388), which offers breathtaking views of the magnificent, cliff-lined fjord formed by the river here. Such landscapes are a rarity outside the Arctic Circle, and Greenland sharks and other northerly sea creatures can be found in the Saguenay Fjord's waters as far as 60 miles (90 km) upstream from the St. Lawrence. There's an interpretation center along Route 170 near Rivière-Eternité that offers guided excursions, and 84 camping and trailer sites (phone: 418-272-3008). Walking trails through the park provide some panoramic views; there's even a 50-mile (80-km) walking trail that stretches all the way from Baie Eternité to Tadoussac. Boat shuttles (passengers only, no cars) link the two sides of the river at several points within the park. Since a road goes through it, the park is technically open daily year-round, but the information and interpretation centers are closed November through April and open daily the rest of the year. There's no admission charge.

From St-Siméon, on the banks of the St. Lawrence, drive north on Route 138 for 52 miles (86 km) to Tadoussac, on the far bank of the Saguenay.

TADOUSSAC This small town is perched at the mouth of the Saguenay. From here, excursions—in either rubber dinghies or slightly larger cruising vessels—leave in search of a glimpse of the beluga whale, a protected species whose numbers have been decimated by pollution and collisions with ships in the St. Lawrence. Whale-watching cruises sail several times daily from the *Hôtel Tadoussac* (165 Rue Bord de l'Eau; phone: 418-235-4421; 800-561-0718 or 800-463-5250; fax: 418-235-4607; also see *Best en Route*). The company that owns the hotel also runs a four-hour excursion ferry service between the hotel and Quebec City. The *Saguenay Marine Park,* whose mandate is to protect the valuable underwater environment of the area, has set up interpretation centers on the marine environment of the Saguenay and St. Lawrence Rivers in various locations along the Saguenay. There is a center in Tadoussac at 182 Rue de l'Eglise (phone: 418-235-4703 or 418-237-4383; 800-463-6769 in Canada).

En Route from Tadoussac Heading back toward Quebec City, take a short ferry ride back across the Saguenay to Baie-Ste-Catherine. Then, from St-Siméon, you can take a car ferry (phone: 418-638-2856 or 418-862-5094; no reservations) across the St. Lawrence to Rivière-du-Loup. Or you can simply continue along Route 138 to La Malbaie.

LA MALBAIE About 27 miles (44 km) beyond La Malbaie on Route 138 is the *Parc des Hautes-Gorges-de-la-Rivière-Malbaie,* a jewel of the Charlevoix region. The river valley is awe inspiring, cut into a deep gorge, with steep rock faces and several waterfalls. There's excellent hiking and climbing as well as canoeing and camping (phone: 418-439-4402). The park is open daily year-round; there's no admission charge.

Or turn left at La Malbaie onto Route 362 to Pointe-au-Pic, formerly known as Murray Bay, where luxurious steamships carrying well-heeled city travelers once docked. Their destination was the *Manoir Richelieu,* a grand, stately hotel that has recently been given a massive facelift (see *Best en Route*). For those seeking cozier quarters, there is no shortage of bed and breakfast establishments and small, charming inns in the area. For information contact *Tourisme Charlevoix* (630 Blvd. de Comporté, La Malbaie, Quebec G5A 1T8; phone: 418-665-4454; 800-667-2276; fax: 418-665-3811).

Just south of here is St-Irénée, the site of a magnificent historic estate called *Le Domaine Forget,* where a summerlong series of classical and jazz concerts is held in an idyllic setting overlooking the St. Lawrence. Call well in advance to make reservations for these popular events (phone: 418-452-3535 or 418-452-8111). Farther along is Baie-St-Paul, an artists' paradise. This tiny town shelters numerous art galleries and exhibition areas and sponsors many art-related special events. Check with the local tourist office in the *Centre d'Art de Baie-St-Paul* (phone: 418-435-3681) for details; it's open daily year-round. From Baie-St-Paul, Quebec City is a 90-mile (150-km) drive.

NORTH OF MONTREAL: SKI COUNTRY

En Route from Montreal When English-speaking Montrealers refer to "the Laurentians" (or sometimes simply "Up North"), they're talking about this area less than an hour from the city. From Montreal, two routes—the high-speed Route 15 and the winding Route 117—lead north into the heart of resort country. The city of St-Jérôme, the gateway to the Laurentians, is only 15 miles (24 km) away (see below). *Tourisme Laurentides* (14142 Rue de la Chapelle, RR #1, St-Jérome, Quebec J72 5T4; phone: 514-436-8532; fax: 514-436-5309) can provide details on the region. Or stop at the tourist center at exit 39 off Route 15 (phone: 514-436-8532); it's open daily year-round.

Before stopping in St-Jérôme, some may want to take a short tour of the Lanaudière region just east of the Laurentians; take Route 25 from Montreal, followed by Route 125. In the town of Ville des Laurentides (turn onto Route 337) is the *Wilfred Laurier National Historic Park,* the former home of Canada's seventh prime minister and now a museum chronicling his life and times. It's open daily mid-April to mid-October; no admission charge (phone: 514-439-3702). Returning west along Route 158, cross Routes 25 and 125 and head for the town of Joliette, the heart of the region. Here, the annual *Lanaudière International Festival* takes over local parks, theaters, churches, and a 10,000-seat outdoor amphitheater with a series of superb classical and jazz concerts performed by internationally-known artists. The festival runs from late June to mid-August. Some concerts are free, but most charge admission (phone: 514-759-7636). A few miles farther north off Route 125, just outside Rawdon, is *Earle Moore's Canadiana Village,* a reconstructed 19th-century community of 42 buildings that contains the largest private collection of Canadiana in the country. It's closed Mondays and from *Labour Day* to mid-May; admission charge (phone: 514-834-4135). *Tourisme Lanaudière* (3642 Rue Queen, CP 1210, Rawdon,

Quebec J0K 150; phone: 514-834-2535; 800-363-2788 in Quebec; fax: 514-834-8100) can provide more details on the area's attractions.

ST-JÉRÔME This town was established in 1834 and was largely developed by Curé Antoine Labelle who was concerned about the exodus of large numbers of young people to New England in the latter 1800s. His fervent efforts to open the wild lands of Canada's north and west and his explorations to establish new communities made him a well-loved folk hero throughout the country. A bronze statue of him dominates the park opposite the downtown cathedral. St-Jérôme marks the beginning of a new 125-mile-long *Linear Park,* which not long ago was the railway line for the "Petit Train du Nord." Not all of the park is open yet, but you can walk, cycle, or cross-country ski along parts of it from here, Ste-Agathe-des-Monts (below), or Mont Laurier, about 120 miles (192 km) north of St-Jérôme. It's open daily; no admission charge (no phone).

PRÉVOST This municipality now encompasses a town formerly known as Shawbridge, and it was here in 1928 that Jackrabbit Johanssen, considered the father of Laurentian skiing, laid out the slalom run that started it all. The famed *Maple Leaf Trail,* covering 745 miles (1,192 km) of cross-country trails from here to Mont Tremblant, was established by Johanssen during the early 1930s. The *Jackrabbit Laurentian Ski Museum* is in Piedmont, five miles (8 km) away (Rte. 15, Exit 60, 220 Rue Beaulne; phone: 514-227-2886). It's closed Mondays and Tuesdays; admission charge.

This area also marks the beginning of the alpine ski region—some 20 centers are located within a 38-mile (60-km) radius. Near Piedmont, Mont Avila and Mont Olympia (Rte. 15, Exit 58 for both) both offer nighttime skiing, and there are more than two dozen cross-country trails. At *Ski Morin Heights* (Rte. 15, Exit 60) there are 22 runs, and 21 at Mont Gabriel (Rte. 15, Exit 64). At St-Sauveur (Rte. 15, Exit 60), Mont St-Sauveur offers 28 slopes and a vertical drop of 700 feet. St-Sauveur is also a prime area for nightlife, with many fine restaurants, cafés, and bars. All five of these centers (Avila, Olympia, Morin Heights, Gabriel, and St-Sauveur) can be reached through a central phone number (phone: 514-227-4671; 800-363-2426). Two other ski centers in this area are Mont Christie (Côte St-Gabriel E., St-Sauveur; phone: 514-226-2412), with 12 slopes, and Mont Habitant (12 Blvd. des Skieurs, St-Sauveur; phone: 514-227-2637), with nine. In nearby Ste-Adèle, there are two centers, *Le Chantecler* (see *Best en Route*) offering night skiing, and *Côtes 40-80* (phone: 514-229-2921).

This spacious resort area, called St-Sauveur-des-Monts, is also popular during the summer. There are three 18-hole golf courses at Ste-Adèle, and one each at Piedmont and Mont Gabriel. There are also dozens of private campgrounds. In Bellefeuille, just south of Prévost, is the *Lac Lafontaine* campground (phone: 514-431-7373), with 294 sites. The 173-site *Pin d'Erable* campground (phone: 514-436-8319) is located in St-Hippolyte, east of Prévost. Mont St-Sauveur has a water slide park, the *Parc Aquatique* (phone:

514-227-4671 or 514-871-0101; 800-363-2426 in Quebec and Ontario), which includes a pool that generates four-foot waves and has six slides, including two that are built into the mountainside. The area also offers canoeing, a sailing school, horseback riding, and numerous public beaches. Several summer theaters stage productions, most often in French but some also in English. Last but not least, this region's popularity is increased by several excellent dining establishments; *L'Estérel* rates among the finest (see *Best en Route*).

STE-AGATHE-DES-MONTS This city on Lac-des-Sables is the hub of a resort area only 60 miles (96 km) from Montreal that dates back to the 1850s. The Val-Morin and Val-David sport centers are less than 20 miles (32 km) away. There are 22 slopes at Alta (2114 Rte. 117; phone: 819-322-3206) and another 16 at Vallée Bleue (1418 Chemin Vallé Bleue; phone: 819-322-3427), all in Val-David; Belle Neige (Rte. 117; phone: 819-322-3311) also has 14 slopes, and Mont Sauvage (Av. 2; phone: 819-322-2337) has nine, bringing the village of Val-Morin's total to 23. Nearby, in St-Adolphe d'Howard (southwest of Ste-Agathe via Route 329), L'Avalanche—not exactly a well-chosen name—has eight slopes (1657 Chemin de L'Avalanche; phone: 819-327-3232). As popular for its restaurants as for its slopes is Val-David, which takes the culinary awards for this area. Leading the way is the restaurant of *La Sapinière* hotel (see *Best en Route,* below, and *Special Havens* in DIVERSIONS).

For summer activities, there are campgrounds at Val-David—*La Belle Etoile* has 117 sites (phone: 819-322-3207), and *Laurentian* has 71 (phone: 819-322-2281)—as well as a 556-site municipal campground, the *Parc des Campeurs,* in Ste-Agathe-des-Monts (phone: 819-324-0482; 800-561-7360 in Quebec). *Alouette Boat Tours* (phone: 819-326-3656) sponsors excursions on Lac-des-Sables that leave from the dock in the center of town daily during the summer.

En Route from Ste-Agathe-des-Monts The village of St-Faustin, 14 miles (22 km) north on Route 117, marks the location of one access road to giant *Mont Tremblant Park.* This small resort area is popular with hunters; Mont Blanc, with 35 ski slopes, is equally attractive to skiers (phone: 819-688-2444; 800-567-6715). St-Faustin also boasts two 18-hole golf courses, including the *Royal Laurentien* (phone: 819-326-2347). Campers will find 93 sites in the *Domaine Desjardins* (phone: 819-688-2179). St-Jovite, a major resort area, is 6 miles (10 km) farther on Route 117.

ST-JOVITE Two ski centers provide a total of 83 slopes in the St-Jovite/Mont Tremblant area: *Station Mont Tremblant Lodge,* the biggest, has 61 slopes and a maximum vertical drop of over 2,100 feet; *Auberge Gray Rocks* offers 22 slopes (see *Best en Route,* below, and *Special Havens* in DIVERSIONS). For additional information, see *Downhill Skiing* and *Cross-Country Skiing* in DIVERSIONS.

Camping in the area is plentiful, with a 239-site provincial campground at Mont-Tremblant, north of St-Jovite along Rte 327 near Lac Monroe. Serious diners can sample the fare at the *Auberge Gray Rocks* and *Le Club Tremblant* (see *Best en Route* for both).

For those who've been exploring the Lanaudière area to the east, an alternate approach from Montreal to *Mont Tremblant Park* is via Routes 25 and 125, a total of 83 miles (133 km) from Montreal. This route passes through the villages of Chertsey and St-Donat. Although there is skiing in the St-Donat area—the two major hills, Mont Garçeau and Val St-Côme, have 34 trails—the region is definitely better outfitted for hunting and fishing. *L'Auberge Gaudet* (Rte. 329 in St-Donat; phone: 819-424-2714) takes top culinary honors in the area, but there's special satisfaction in a meal prepared over an open fire in the woods, especially if you caught (or shot) dinner yourself. Make arrangements with one of the many outfitters in the area to start hunting or fishing expeditions from here.

MONT TREMBLANT PARK Created in 1895 by the Quebec government, this park is used almost all year. Skiing, snowmobiling, and snowshoeing are the principal winter activities, with camping, canoeing, and moose hunting in season. (The park harbors some 30 animal species, including bears, deer, marten, mink, and porcupines, all easily visible from some of the more remote trails.) Only eight cottages are available for rent, but there are plenty of campgrounds throughout the park. The park is open daily year-round; there's no admission charge (phone: 819-688-2281).

NORTH OF HULL: THE GATINEAU VALLEY AND LA VÉRENDRYE

This region, called the Outaouais (or Ottawa in English), owes its settlement to both French explorers and American industrialists. Fur trader Nicholas Gatineau, who gave his name to a river, a city, and a valley, explored this area in 1650. The city of Hull, which lies across the Ottawa River from Canada's capital city of Ottawa, was founded by Philemon Wright from Massachusetts, who helped build the first lumber mill in 1801. Another American, E. B. Eddy, started the match factory that put Hull on the map about 50 years later. As a result of Hull's American roots, there is a large population of Anglophones as well as Francophones in the area, which has grown into an administrative center as part of the National Capital Region. For more information about this area contact *Tourisme Outaouais* (103 Rue Laurier, Hull, QUE J8X 3V8; phone: 819-778-2222; fax: 819-778-7758) or *National Capital Region Tourism* (40 Elgin St., Suite 202, Ottawa, ONT K1P 1C7; phone: 800-465-1867).

HULL While many people flock to Ottawa to see the Canadian *Parliament Buildings* and all the other attractions of a capital city, Hull also offers interesting sights, including the new riverfront *Canadian Museum of Civilization* (100 Rue Laurier; phone: 819-776-7000). It offers a wide variety of ever-changing exhibits, though it focuses on Indian and Inuit art; its *Grand Hall* is devoted to 900 years of native and Canadian history. The museum is closed Mondays from October through April. There's an admission charge, except on Sundays before noon. A new provincially regulated casino is scheduled to open this year near Lac Leamy, about two miles (3 km) from downtown.

En Route from Hull An unusual way to see the Gatineau River Valley is on the Hull-Chelsea-Wakefield *Steam Train,* built in 1907 and one of the last steam-powered trains still in operation in Canada. The train makes a half-day, 36-mile (64-km) round trip from Hull to Wakefield and back daily from May through October. Reservations are necessary (phone 819-778-7246; 800-871-7246).

Follow Route 105 toward *La Vérendrye Reserve,* 120 miles (192 km) north. *Gatineau Park,* just outside of Hull, has four principal lakes and 10 times that number of smaller ones. Although hunting is prohibited, fishing is allowed in all lakes and rivers, and canoe rentals are available. In winter, the park offers downhill and cross-country skiing. Lac Philippe has an attractive campground with 258 sites (phone: 819-456-3016) as well as a large public beach, picnic tables, and boat rentals.

Also in the park is *Moorside,* the 575-acre summer estate of former Canadian Prime Minister William Lyon Mackenzie King, which he willed to the public. On the grounds is an English garden with a curious collection of ruins. Located just off the Gatineau Parkway, the estate is closed mid-October through April; open daily the rest of the year. There's an admission charge (phone: 819-827-2020 or 613-239-5000).

In towns all along Route 105—Gracefield, Bouchette, Messines, and Maniwaki—there are outdoor adventure companies and outfitters (*pourvoiries* in French) which can arrange anything from canoeing and snowshoeing to hunting and fishing expeditions. In all, there are about 30 outfitters to choose from, any of whom can help find the best hunting spots for moose, deer, rabbit, or duck, and the best fishing holes for speckled trout, lake sturgeon, and walleye. In addition, there's no shortage of campsites, chalets, and lodges in the area, ranging from primitive to luxurious. In Maniwaki there's an interesting interpretation center on the history of forest fire prevention, called *Château Logue* (8 Rue Comeau; phone: 819-449-7999). It's open daily May through October; there's an admission charge

Continue on Route 105 to Grand-Remous, 20 miles (32 km) north of Maniwaki, where Route 117 intersects it and heads west to *La Vérendrye Reserve.* This area, too, offers many outfitters for the sporting-minded Consult the list in the *Outaouais Tourist Guide,* available from *Tourisme Outaouais* (see above).

LA VÉRENDRYE Established in 1939 to protect wildlife from the onslaught of hunters invading this area, the park preserves the natural habitat of moose, bears wolves, mink, beavers, marten, rabbits, loons, and many other species. Route 117 travels through the heart of the 5,174-square-mile expanse located a the western end of the Laurentian Mountain Range. Hunting is limited to moose and small game, and black bears in spring, but the fishing—for pike, walleye, smallmouth bass, and lake and speckled trout—is unlimited. Contact *Auberge le Domaine* (see *Best En Route*), the only inn in the park, for details on access rights. Limited numbers of canoe rentals and cottages are available in the park, which is open daily. There's no admission charge (phone: 819-438-2017).

BEST EN ROUTE

The Laurentians offer some of the most pleasant and also some of the most rustic accommodations in Canada. In the ski resort areas north of Montreal—around Val-David, for instance—are several of the best in the country. The selection below singles out the best in any given area, though not necessarily the least expensive. If your budget is tight, avail yourself of one of the many inexpensive roadside motels, but be prepared for less than perfection. For the hotels that follow, expensive places cost $75 or more per night for a double room; moderate lodges and bed and breakfast places charge from $50 to $75; and inexpensive places cost $50 or less. In the prime ski resort areas, seasonal prices are regularly $200 per day or higher for two, not including extras like ski rentals and lift tickets. Check to see what is included before making reservations. All hotels feature private baths unless otherwise indicated. Note that Mont Tremblant has a central reservation service (phone: 819-425-8681; 800-567-6760) for booking accommodations at any of its chalets and condominiums, or lodgings at a select number of area hotels. For each location, places are listed alphabetically by price category.

SHAWINIGAN

Auberge L'Escapade Near the town of Grand-Mère, this is an excellent, comfortable place to stay, offering 40 well-equipped rooms, a dining room, an 18-hole golf course, cross-country skiing, and snowmobiling. Conveniently located at 3383 Rue Garnier (phone: 819-539-6911; 800-461-6911 in Quebec; fax: 819-539-7669). Moderate.

TADOUSSAC

Hôtel Tadoussac Set on a swath of land leading down to a beach, this 149-room property offers a good view of the St. Lawrence River. Other features include a lovely dining room that has both a view and a good gastronomic reputation. Also offered are tennis, golf, and horseback riding. 165 Rue Bord de l'Eau (phone: 418-235-4421; 800-561-0718 or 800-463-5250; fax: 418-235-4607). Expensive.

LA MALBAIE

Manoir Richelieu Just south of La Malbaie, this dowager hotel offers 314 rooms and suites, an excellent dining room, and a full range of services. There is a swimming pool, golf, tennis, cross-country skiing, and now the new *Casino de Charlevoix.* 181 Avenue Richelieu, Pointe-au-Pic (phone: 418-665-3703; fax: 418-665-3093). Expensive.

STE-ADÈLE

Le Chantecler Located in the vicinity of Ste-Agathe-des-Monts and its wealth of outdoor activities, this resort has 302 well-appointed rooms; a restaurant; tennis, squash, and racquetball courts; saunas; a whirlpool bath; an indoor pool; and a beach. It provides a full range of summer and winter sports. Lac Rond, Chemin du Chantecler (phone: 514-229-3555; 800-363-2420; fax: 514-229-5593). Expensive.

L'Eau à la Bouche A member of the distinguished Relais & Châteaux group, it is nestled against a hillside with a lovely view of the Laurentians. There are 25 comfortable rooms with terraces, a pool, and a first-rate restaurant. For more details see *Special Havens* in DIVERSIONS. 3003 Blvd. Ste-Adèle (phone: 514-229-2991; fax: 514-229-7573). Expensive.

Château Neuville This red brick hotel offers 57 stylishly decorated rooms, plus both an indoor and outdoor pool and proximity to all the area's outdoor activities. 3080 Blvd. Ste-Adèle (phone: 514-229-6641; fax: 514-229-9016). Moderate.

VILLE D'ESTÉREL

L'Estérel Set on a lake not far from the Val-David and Val-Morin ski areas, this place offers 135 rooms, a restaurant and cafeteria, an indoor sports complex, and convention facilities. A pool, a sauna, an 18-hole golf course, and tennis courts are on the premises and fishing and boating are available. Blvd. Fridolin Simard (phone: 514-228-2571; 800-363-3623; fax: 514-228-4977). Expensive.

VAL-MORIN

Far Hills Inn This cozy 72-room inn is set up in the hills overlooking a lake, with excellent cross-country skiing and close to downhill skiing. It also offers an indoor and an outdoor pool, tennis, mountain biking, and horseback riding. Rue Far Hills (phone: 819-322-2014; 800-567-6636; fax: 819-322-1995). Expensive.

VAL-DAVID

La Sapinière An hour's drive from Montreal, this is one of the exceptional inns of eastern Canada, with 70 well-appointed rooms and suites. Its primary distinction is its kitchen (and pastry chef Jean-Pierre Monjon). Restaurant open daily for lunch and dinner. Reservations necessary (a few weeks in advance) for weekend dining. Major credit cards accepted. Also see *Special Havens* in DIVERSIONS. 1244 Chemin de la Sapinière (phone: 819-322-2020; 800-567-6635; fax: 819-322-6510). Expensive.

MONT TREMBLANT

Auberge Villa Bellevue The Dubois family has owned this 99-room lodge—which includes a condominium complex—for three generations. Luc Dubois, former head coach of the Canadian ski team, is the director of the hotel's ski school, while the rest of the family concentrates on keeping the accommodations comfortable and maintaining the restaurant's high standards. On Lac Ouimet (phone: 819-425-2734; 800-567-6763 in Canada; fax: 819-425-2734). Expensive.

Le Club Tremblant This luxury condominium complex is not to be confused with the other resort bearing a similar name (see below). On Lac Tremblant, less than a mile (1.6 km) from Mont Tremblant's lift station, the resort is independently owned and has been recognized by the province's tourism association for its quality. Recently renovated, it offers 122 one- and two-bedroom condominium suites with fireplaces. It has four tennis courts, a private beach and marina, an outdoor heated pool, an indoor sports complex, and access to nearby skiing and other recreational activities. Also see *Special Havens* in DIVERSIONS. 121 Rue Cuttle (phone: 819-425-2731; 800-363-2413 in the US; 800-567-8341 in eastern Canada; fax: 819-425-9903). Expensive.

Station Mont Tremblant Lodge Skiing is serious business in this former jet setters' playground, founded by Philadelphia native Joe Ryan in 1938 and recently purchased by Intrawest. There are 248 units in the lodge and an ever-expanding community of chalets and condominiums on the slopes and in the base village. In addition there are seven restaurants. Ski facilities are constantly being upgraded; the center now has 61 trails and boasts the longest bubble-covered, high-speed quad lift in North America. Other facilities include a new 18-hole golf course and a beach on Lac Tremblant. Also see *Special Havens* in DIVERSIONS. 3005 Chemin Mont Tremblant (phone: 819-681-2000; 800-461-8711; fax: 819-681-5999). Expensive.

ST-JOVITE

Auberge Gray Rocks Just down the road from Mont Tremblant, this 91-year-old resort has actually reduced its rooms to 150, in order to add an arts and crafts center and other facilities. But there are plans to add 40 new condominiums and deluxe suites in the main lodge. The resort offers 22 ski slopes and a well-known ski school; in summer there's a tennis camp, as well as canoeing, swimming, sailing, and horseback riding. A second 18-hole golf course will open this year. In the main lodge there is a dining room, bar, and complete fitness center with a heated pool. Also see *Special*

Havens in DIVERSIONS. Rte. 327, 3 miles (5 km) north of St-Jovite (phone: 819-425-2771; 800-567-6767; fax: 819-425-3474). Expensive.

Le St-Jovite An excellent service staff and a good dining room make this 71-room establishment a pleasurable place to stay. 614 Rue Ouimet (phone: 819-425-2761). Moderate.

GATINEAU–LA VÉRENDRYE

Auberge le Domaine Being right inside this vast park adds a special air to your stay. The resort offers 35 rustic but very comfortable chalets (some accommodating up to 12 people) in three different areas of the park, as well as a four-unit motel. There's also a cafeteria, a grocery store, a service station, and laundry facilities. The staff will provide everything you need for hunting, fishing, and other outdoor adventures. Family packages are available. Rte. 117 (phone: 819-435-2541 May through October; 819-623-6759 the rest of the year). Moderate.

The Gaspé Peninsula

The southern shore of the St. Lawrence River ends at a 175-mile-long peninsula of land that looks like the crest of a curling wave rolling in from the Gulf of St. Lawrence. This is the Gaspé Peninsula. To the west is the ever-widening St. Lawrence River as it enters the gulf; to the north and east, the gulf itself and Anticosti Island; to the southeast, the Baie des Chaleurs (Bay of Warmth), which separates Gaspé from New Brunswick.

Considered one of the oldest landmasses on the planet, the Gaspé supports life forms that have long since disappeared from other areas. The Chic-Choc Mountains, called Sigsoon ("rocky mountains") by the native Micmac, create a high-altitude sanctuary for centuries-old alpine fir and for the rangifer (wood caribou), which are virtually extinct elsewhere. The heavily wooded valleys and highland regions rate among the world's best for moose, deer, and upland game-bird hunting, and the Chic-Chocs' rivers are among the finest sources of Atlantic salmon.

When Cartier first sailed through the Strait of Belle Isle and entered the Gulf of St. Lawrence, the lands of Labrador and Newfoundland were thought to be cold, barren, and forbidding—fit for fisheries and little else. After cruising the western shore of Newfoundland and discovering the Iles-de-la-Madeleine, he entered the Baie des Chaleurs. The more tolerable climate and fertile lands prompted him to explore the peninsula, called Gespeg ("land's end" or "extremity") by the resident Micmac. Before returning to France, Cartier sailed in the summer of 1534 from the Baie des Chaleurs around the rugged shoreline of the Gespeg and across the mouth of the St. Lawrence River to Ile d'Anticosti. During his next voyage he explored the river, hoping it would provide the route to the spice lands of the East—the Northwest Passage. His reports of the beautiful and fertil lands of the Gaspé (as the peninsula rapidly came to be called by the Europeans) and visions of the wealth of resources yet undiscovered attracted settlers to New France.

The massive scale of this primitive area is illustrated by the unique Percé Rock, which stands silent and alone just off the Gaspé coast. It is 1,420 feet long and nearly 300 feet tall, and its weight is estimated at 400 million tons. During his voyage Cartier anchored his three ships in its protective shadow.

The coastal fishing settlements established by the French and other Europeans began as isolated, independent villages relatively oblivious to one another. In some sense this isolation is an abiding characteristic of Gaspé life. Few of the original inland villages have grown much, since most settlers arriving in successive waves followed the St. Lawrence farther inland. Commercial growth has been limited largely to tourist services. The principal highway, Route 132, was completed in 1928 and runs through the Matapédia River Valley, following the rocky coastline and the shoreline of the St. Lawrence.

But there is more to the Gaspé than the small fishing villages with their century-old dwellings, the handmade sails mounted on wooden fishing boats, and the stories of shipwrecks and ghosts. There is the unspoiled beauty of forests that are home to moose, bears, and caribou; trout leaping from mountain streams; and the seemingly indomitable mountains. All this makes an appealing package for hunters, anglers, naturalists, artists, and latter-day explorers.

This route originates across the river from Quebec City and jumps quickly to Rivière-du-Loup, proceeding along the south bank of the St. Lawrence on Route 132. Route 20, the Trans-Canada Highway, can help cut down on your travel time between the two cities, or you can take one of the many ferries between the south and north shores; these are mentioned in the descriptions below. From Rivière-du-Loup, the route follows the St. Lawrence on Route 132 and circles the peninsula. The entire journey covers some 220 miles (352 km), beginning at Quebec City and ending at the Ste-Flavie–Mont Joli area.

For additional information about this region contact *Tourisme Chaudières-Appalaches* (800 Autoroute Jean-Lesage, Bernières, QUE G7A 1C9; phone: 418-831-4411; fax: 418-831-8442); *Tourisme Bas St-Laurent* (189 Rue Hôtel de Ville, Rivière-du-Loup, QUE G5R 5C4; phone: 418-867-3015; 800-563-5268; fax: 418-867-3245); or *Tourisme Gaspésie* (357 Rte. de la Mer, Sainte-Flavie, QUE G0J 2L0; phone: 418-775-2223; fax: 418-775-2234).

QUEBEC CITY This beautiful bit of history is more than a provincial capital: It embodies the soul of French Canada. Unless you have visited the city before, it is a necessary introduction to this unique province. For a detailed report, see *Quebec City* in THE CITIES.

En Route from Quebec City The Pont du Québec (Quebec Bridge) and the Pont Pierre-Laporte lead to both Routes 20 and 132. Via Route 20, the 123-mile (197-km) trip to Rivière-du-Loup takes about two-and-a-half hours; on the more scenic Route 132, the trip takes about an hour longer. Although Route 20 does have rest areas, it is necessary to exit onto Route 132 for food and gas. Six miles (10 km) out of Quebec City, Route 132 passes through Lévis-Lauzon.

LÉVIS-LAUZON It was here, in 1648, that Father Pierre Bailloquet celebrated the south shore's first mass. From terraces overlooking the river, the city of Quebec unfolds in a magnificent panorama. Pointe Lévis, directly opposite Quebec City, was used for a variety of purposes over the years, including the defense of the walled city. On April 18, 1793, Marie-Josèphe Corriveau was hanged near the Plains of Abraham (outside Quebec) after being convicted of murdering her second husband with an ax. After she was hanged, the body of La Corriveau, as she was nicknamed, was then displayed in an iron cage on Pointe Lévis—in view of Quebec City. Today, La Corriveau lives on in the region's memory as a local Lizzie Borden.

The *Alphonse-Desjardins House,* built in 1882–84 (8 Rue Mont-Marie; phone: 418-835-2090), is now a museum commemorating the founder of North America's first savings and loan institution, Les Caisses Populaires Desjardins, which opened in 1901 in this building's kitchen. The museum is open daily; no admission charge. The unimaginatively named *Fort Number 1* (41 Chemin du Gouvernement; phone: 418-835-5182; 800-463-6769 in Canada), one of three defense sites still standing in Quebec City's original fortification system, was built by the British army between 1865 and 1872 to protect the railway linking Maine to Lévis; it is now a national historic site. It's closed *Labour Day* to mid-May; open daily the rest of the year. There's an admission charge.

En Route from Lévis-Lauzon A little farther northeast is the city of Montmagny and the Ile-aux-Grues archipelago—a group of 21 small islands that are prime viewing and hunting grounds for waterfowl. Each spring and fall, thousands of Canada geese and other migrating birds invade the shoreline flats, and hunters (only in the fall) gather in droves for the occasion. One of these islands, Grosse-Ile, played a major role in Canadian history. During the 19th and early 20th centuries, millions of European immigrants came to Canada, many carrying infectious disease such as cholera and typhus. Normal hospital quarantine measures were not enough, so the isolated Grosse-Ile was designated a major quarantine station from 1832 to 1937. It is now a national historic site, and visitors can step back in time and feel the hopes and fears of the thousands of people who passed through or died, here. There are about 100 remaining buildings, including two chapels. Guided tours are available from Montmagny; contact *Parks Canada* (phone: 418-563-4009; 800-463-6769) or *La Corporation pour la mise en* *valeur de Grosse-Ile* (phone: 418-248-4832) for details. The site is open daily June through September; there's an admission charge.

In mid-October, the massive migration southward of hundreds of thousands of snow geese is marked in Montmagny with the *Festival de l'Oie Blanche.* During this time, there are tours to a bird sanctuary on an island in the St. Lawrence, where visitors can view the nesting site of the white geese at close range. To obtain festival information, or to make tour reservations, contact *Le Bureau de Festival de l'Oie* (phone: 418-248-3954). More information about the migratory habits of the geese and other area fowl and wildlife is available at *Le Centre Educatif des Migrations* in Montagny (53 du Bassen Nord; phone: 418-248-0466 or 248-4565), which is open daily from April 15 to November 15. There's an admission charge.

Montmagny celebrates its 350th anniversary in 1996. Festivities are scheduled for June 21–24 and June 28–July 1; for details call *Tourism Montmagny* (phone: 418-248-9196).

St-Jean-Port-Joli is 50 miles (80 km) from Lévis.

ST-JEAN-PORT-JOLI Known as the handicrafts capital of the region, this village is well worth visiting. Just before entering town, Route 132 passes a large group of shops selling wood sculptures, antiques, and crafts. The well-known Bourgault family provided the impetus for this loose association in 1936 by bringing their own shop and personal artistry in woodcarving to the area. Soon they were joined by craftspeople working in a variety of materials. An unrestored church, built in 1776 and classified as a historic landmark, stands alongside the road at the edge of the village; its sculptured wooden detail is exquisite. The *Musée des Anciens Canadiens* (332 Av. de Gaspé W.; phone: 418-598-3392) contains works of well-known woodcarvers. It's closed November through April except for private tours (book in advance); open daily the rest of the year. There's an admission charge. In town, try *Auberge du Faubourg* (280 Av. de Gaspé W.; phone: 418-598-6455) for lunch.

En Route from St-Jean-Port-Joli Continue along Route 132 through a series of charming little villages—St-Roch-des-Aulnaies, Kamouraska, Notre-Dame-du-Portage. For good camping along the river and spectacular sunsets, try *Camping des Aulnaies* (St-Roch-des-Aulnaies; phone: 418-354-2225) or *Camping Rivière-Ouelle* (Rivière-Ouelle; phone: 418-856-1484). Rivière-du-Loup is 58 miles (93 km) from St-Jean-Port-Joli.

RIVIÈRE-DU-LOUP The town's name is derived from the *loups-marins* seals that at one time made frequent appearances in the St. Lawrence at its junction with the du Loup River. Although the seals are rarely seen nowadays, the town has kept the name—except from 1850 to 1919, when it was called Fraserville for the Scots seigneurial family that bought the settlement in the 1780s. With its back to the hills, this terraced town affords excellent views of the St. Lawrence River and three small islands. Each spring, a number of eider ducks nest on the easternmost isle of the group, Ile Blanche.

The town is a popular gathering spot for hunters and anglers preparing to enter the Gaspé. Guides point out the best nearby places to start. A good place for dinner is the *Saint-Patrice* (169 Rue Fraser; phone: 418-862-9895).

En Route from Rivière-du-Loup It is possible to ferry across the St. Lawrence River from here to St-Siméon on the north shore. The ferry runs April through December (and sometimes later), usually making several trips daily, depending upon demand (phone: 418-862-9545 or 418-862-5094). The Gaspé region lies ahead on Route 132, 83 miles (133 km) away, at the town of Ste-Flavie. Twenty-nine miles (46 km) northeast of Rivière-du-Loup is the fishing village of Trois-Pistoles.

TROIS-PISTOLES The town's name has been traced back to a legendary incident in 1621, when oarsmen crossing one of the many rivers in the area dropped a silver cup worth three "pistoles," the currency of the day, into the water. Their cry of *"Voilà trois pistoles perdues!"* ("Three pistoles lost!") gave rise to the town's name. Today, the town is known for its fishing. One of the offshore islands bears the name Ile aux Basques, and three Basque whale-oil furnaces, used for heating, cooking, and boiling down whale blubber, have been reconstructed on the island. Check with the visitors' center (468 Rue Vézina, Trois-Pistoles; phone: 418-851-4949) for permission to visit the furnaces. *Le Marmiton* (70 Rue Notre-Dame W.; phone: 418-851-3202) is a good place to eat.

En Route from Trois-Pistoles Twenty-five miles (40 km) from Trois-Pistoles is the small town of Bic, a beautiful place to stop.

BIC The story told around here is that during the creation of the earth, an overworked angel in charge of mountains and islands decided to end the day right here—leaving Bic surrounded by heavenly hills and a mosaic of islands and reefs. Not that early inhabitants always acted in an angelic way—the names of sites in the *Parc du Bic* reveal unpleasant stories from the past: Ile du Massacre and Cap Enragée. In 1533 a band of about 200 Micmac were driven from shelter in a cave and murdered by a party of Iroquois raiders. But there is also an Ile d'Amours (Isle of Loves). A marine delight, the park is home to a rich diversity of sea mammals, mollusks, and birds. There is an interpretation center, bicycle and foot paths, a beach, and a campsite, *Camping du Bic* (directly off Rte. 132; phone: 418-736-4711). The park is closed October through May; open daily the rest of the year. There's no admission charge (phone: 418-736-5035; 418-727-3779 in winter).

En Route from Bic Continue northeast for 7 miles (11 km) to Rimouski.

RIMOUSKI This city (pop. 30,000) rates as one of the urban centers of the region. In 1950 almost 25% of the city was destroyed by fire, an event that provided space for the growth of many modern facilities and subsequently attracted people and industry.

As the route enters the Gaspé, hunting and fishing improve, and the city of Rimouski is no exception. For river fishing information, contact the provincial *Ministère de l'Environnement et de la Faune* (Department of Environment and Wildlife; see the introduction to this chapter); make hunting arrangements at the government-run *Rimouski Reserve* (phone: 418-722-3516), which allows deer and small-game hunting. The name Rimouski means "land of moose," and these prize animals can be hunted (one per person) during late October. The season lasts only one or two weeks; call the *Ministère de l'Environnement et de la Faune* for the exact dates.

The city has a regional art museum, the *Musée Régional de Rimouski* (35 Rue St-Germain W.; phone: 418-724-2272); it's closed Mondays and Tuesdays in winter; admission charge. Six miles (10 km) east of town there's an intriguing sea museum, the *Musée de la Mer et Lieu Historique National de Pointe-au-Père* (1034 Rue du Phare; phone: 418-724-6214). The museum has displays on the area's maritime history; it recounts the tragic story of the 1914 sinking of the *Empress of Ireland,* in which more than 1,000 passengers died. It's open daily mid-June through mid-October; admission charge. In August the city hosts a jazz festival, and in September an *International Film Festival* is held here.

En Route from Rimouski Continue east to the sandy beaches of Ste-Luce, an old whaling village that has grown into a popular water sports resort. Visitors can charter boats for deep-sea fishing right from the village wharf. In the village of Ste-Luce-sur-Mer (a separate but indistinguishable entity) is a French restaurant in the *Auberge Sainte-Luce* (see *Best en Route*). About 12 miles (19 km) from Rimouski, Route 132 splits and circles the peninsula in two directions. Since most traffic goes clockwise around the Gaspé, we've mapped a counterclockwise route to avoid crowds and aggravation.

The drive from Ste-Flavie to Matapédia (see below), at the Restigouche estuary on the Baie des Chaleurs, is just under 100 miles (160 km) and can be negotiated in about two-and-a-half hours, but don't rush. The route follows an old Native American trail through the valley of the Matapédia River, aptly nicknamed "River of the 222 Rapids," which boasts some of the most beautiful scenery in the world.

Head inland through the farming and hunting villages of Ste-Angèle-de-Mérici and St-Moïse to Sayabec, at the head of Lac Matapédia. In the nearby forestry museum, the *Centre Naturanimo* (St-Cléophas; phone: 418-536-3078), is the trunk of a 700-year-old cedar tree and a fir tree growing *within* a cedar. The center also includes a zoo, a small farm, an amusement park, and kiosks selling handicrafts. It's closed mid-September to mid-May; open daily the rest of the year. There's an admission charge.

A bit farther along, Val-Brillant has the good fortune to front a really fine beach that sprawls along the western side of Lac Matapédia. Take a few minutes to stop and relax. Down the road at Amqui, a secondary road leads to the *Matapédia Wildlife Reserve* encompassing 66 square miles of rivers, small lakes, and mountains. It's open daily; no admission charge (phone: 418-865-2080 or 418-756-6174).

Lac-au-Saumon, dominating a small lake formed by a widening of the Matapédia River, was originally settled by a group of Acadians from the Iles-de-la-Madeleine. The area around the village, a favorite of many freshwater anglers, is filled with trout streams and small waterfalls. In general, this stretch of the route offers six fishing zones, four of which do not require reservations, so it's possible just to stop off and fish for a spell. Try your luck and skill with the Atlantic salmon that run in the river. Those who prefer to watch can visit the *Domaine Matamajaw* in Causapscal, a few miles farther down the road (48 Rue St-Jacques; phone: 418-756-5999), an interpretive center that recounts the history of salmon fishing. It's open daily June through September; admission charge. Observant visitors also may view the sport along the Les Fourches Trail, at the junction of the Matapédia and Causapscal Rivers. Visiting anglers can hire local fishing guides by calling *ZEC Casault* (phone: 418-756-3670); for general information about permits and salmon fishing in the area, call *SEPAQ* (phone: 418-643-3127), or the *Corporation for the Management of the Matapédia and Patapédia Rivers* (phone: 418-756-3304 or 418-756-6174).

After you've taken your limit (check local regulations), continue through the small farming village of Ste-Florence. From here, the road to the village of Routhierville winds around the river, giving panoramic views of the rushing water below. There are a number of scenic rest areas en route. The only access to the village is across an old 259-foot covered bridge. From Routhierville to Matapédia, 24 miles (38 km) south, there's little but farmland and river . . . and good fishing.

MATAPÉDIA This small village is at the juncture of the Restigouche and Matapédia Rivers. First settled by a group of Loyalists in 1808, the village was bolstered by the arrival of Irish immigrants in 1832 and Acadians in 1860. The Restigouche flows on from here into the Baie des Chaleurs. The delta itself, today a major salmon fishing area, played a role in the area's history as well. On July 9, 1760, in a sea battle between the French and British, the ships *Machault* and *Bienfaisant* were scuttled in the north channel of the river delta, and a third French ship, the *Marquis de Malauze,* burned to its waterline. The hull of the *Marquis de Malauze* was refloated in 1939, and divers have recovered many artifacts from all three ships, including complete sets of dishes, kitchen utensils, and pieces of equipment.

En Route from Matapédia Stay on Route 132 as it bears east and begins to follow Cartier's route along the south coast of the peninsula. Restigouche built on the site of a 17th-century Capuchin mission, is just a few mile away. The *Bataille-de-la-Restigouche National Historic Park* (Pointe-à-la Croix; phone: 418-788-5676), which commemorates the last naval battl between France and England in 1760, is the resting place of the hull of the *Machault* and many of its recovered artifacts. A monument in front of the *Church of St. Anne* commemorates the conversion of a Micmac tribe to Christianity in 1610. The park is closed early September to mid-June; open daily the rest of the year. There's an admission charge.

Farther along Route 132, beyond Escuminac, a secondary road leads south onto a point occupied by the town of Miguasha, site of a superb natural science park of the same name. Its cliffs hold specimens of plant and fish fossils—some dating back 365 million years—that attract researchers from all over the world. It's closed mid-October through May; admission charge (phone: 418-794-2475). The point, and the city of Dalhousie on the opposite shore in New Brunswick, mark the beginning of the Baie des Chaleurs and the end of the Restigouche estuary. Carleton is 14 miles (22 km) farther.

CARLETON This city is an excellent example of the bicultural heritage of the Gaspé. Originally established in 1756, it was named Petite-Tracadie by Acadian refugees who had been expelled from British-controlled areas of the Maritime region. Later it was renamed Carleton in honor of the British governor-general of the province by Loyalists who relocated here after the American Revolution. The city remains French-speaking, however, and the *Notre Dame Oratory* on Mont St-Joseph still dominates the town. From this point, almost 2,000 feet above the bay, the mountains of the Gaspé can be seen to the east, north, and west, and the shore of New Brunswick is visible across the bay to the south. A minibus makes scheduled trips up the mountainside from the *Baie Bleue* hotel (see *Best en Route*).

When you come down from the mountain, check into the provincial campground, *Camping Carleton* (phone: 418-364-3992), if possible. It's on a ridge overlooking the bay, and the sunrise makes it worth getting up early to watch and perhaps take an early-morning swim. Cartier named this the Bay of Warmth for good reason; the water is warm enough for swimming even when it's chilly in surrounding areas. Early risers also can look for pieces of agate reflecting in the water; the beach is loaded with them. Of course, the water here is loaded with other things, too, like mackerel, smelts, and flatfish that can be caught right from the wharf; charter boats are available for deep-sea fishing for sea trout, cod, and halibut. If you'd rather watch the animal life than mount it on your wall, just wander along the beaches and observe the sea terns, herons, and gannets that congregate here.

En Route from Carleton About 15 miles (24 km) east on Route 132 is Maria.

MARIA This town is the site of one of the two Micmac reservations on the Baie des Chaleurs. A roadside cooperative operated by the Micmac sells snowshoes and handwoven baskets produced by the tribe. The natives' village (phone: 418-759-3441), open to visitors, features a church in the shape of a tepee. Access is via a secondary road to the right of the crafts stand.

En Route from Maria Stay on Route 132 across the Cascapédia River. Just before the the town of New Richmond, there's an opportunity to make a shortcut north across the peninsula on Route 299 directly to *Gaspé Park* (Parc de la Gaspésie; see below). If you follow the peninsula, you'll reach New Richmond, a small town founded by Loyalists and one of several Gaspé communities where many English-speaking people live. Visit the *British Heritage Center* (351 Blvd. Perron Ouest; phone: 418-392-4487), which features a re-created village portraying more than a century of early local history. It's open daily from mid-June to early September; admission charge. Bonaventure, the next town on the route, is 25 miles (40 km) from Maria.

BONAVENTURE A popular resort on the south shore of the Gaspé, Bonaventure was named after one of the many ships that carried French nobles on tours of the region during the late 1500s. A fishing port, the village was burned by the British after the battle of the Restigouche estuary. A group of Acadians rebuilt the village in the same year, following their forced exile from Britain's Nova Scotia colony. The *Acadian Museum* (97 Av. du Port-Royal; phone: 418-534-4000), in an original wooden structure, contains many period pieces, including kitchen utensils, looms, furniture, and a fossil collection. It's closed mid-September to mid-June; open daily the rest of the year. There's an admission charge.

From the church in Bonaventure, you can take a short side trip inland to see *La Grotte* (the caves) in St-Elzéar (198 Rue de l'Eglise; phone: 418-534-4335; 418-534-3655). The caves have intriguing stalactite and stalagmite formations; there's also a museum on-site. Reservations are required for cave tours; suitable clothing and boots are provided. The caves are closed October through May; open daily the rest of the year. There is an admission charge. Children under 10 are not permitted.

En Route from Bonaventure Many of the villages on this part of the coast were settled by British Loyalists around the time of the American Revolution; others were established by Acadians fleeing the British in Nova Scotia. The fact that such radically different, polarized groups were able to settle within a few miles of each other and not fight is amazing—especially considering the frequency of conflicts between Britain and France. One example of British influence in the area is the town of New Carlisle. And yet it's the birthplace of René Lévesque, an immensely popular political figure of French ancestry who was elected Quebec's premier from 1976 to 1985 as head of the independence party, the Parti Québécois. Continue along Route 132 to Port-Daniel.

PORT-DANIEL AND PORT-DANIEL PARK Port-Daniel is at the end of the beach-lined deep-water bay where Cartier anchored his ships for a week during his explorations. He called it Conche St-Martin (St. Martin Cove), but it was renamed for one of the many sea captains who later visited the area. Whether Cartier explored the Port-Daniel River and the mountains from which it flows i unknown, but the river and surrounding peaks offer some of the most splendid scenery in Gaspé. The park, 8 miles (13 km) north of town on a small secondary road, encompasses 18 separate trout lakes as well as the Port-Daniel River, known for Atlantic salmon fishing. The mountains in the north end of the park average 900 feet and support an interesting variety of foliage. There's no admission charge to the park, which is open daily June through *Labour Day* (phone: 418-396-2789). A lovely place to stay is *Motel Chaleur et Chalets* (see *Best en Route*), situated on 80 acres of parkland.

En Route from Port-Daniel It is about 52 miles (83 km) from here to Percé, the entrance to beautiful *L'Ile Bonaventure Park.* Facing east into the Gulf of St. Lawrence, the stretch of coast between has seen many shipwrecks, and its coastal villages are filled with tales of ghosts, phantom ships, and treasure. L'Anse-aux-Gascons, a few miles east of Port-Daniel, was the scene of the wreck of an English ship during the 19th century. The villagers rescued a few survivors and took the cargo of 40,000 gold louis for their pains. True to storybook fantasy, one of the sailors later married the daughter of the fisherman who saved him. Although it is unlikely that a search of the coastal rocks will turn up any of the treasure, the shore is filled with pieces of agate.

The villagers in Grande-Rivière and Ste-Thérèse-de-Gaspé still hold pretty much to the ways of their ancestors, using open-air cod-drying racks to prepare their daily catches. According to legend, Cap-d'Espoir, 42 miles (67 km) from Port-Daniel, is haunted by the ghost of a stray ship from Admiral Walker's fleet, which crashed into the rocks in 1711. It's said that the ship can sometimes be seen on summer nights, crashing onto the rocky cape; try to arrive here around dusk to watch for it to reappear. In the morning continue to Percé to watch the sun rise behind the immense rock that seems to guard the town.

PERCÉ With a population of over 4,600, this qualifies as a major town in the Gaspé, but it's just a small fishing village with many attractions for visitors. Percé Rock is a natural wonder that defies accurate description. The rock, which juts nearly 300 feet out of the sea, is 1,420 feet long, and 300 feet wide, with a natural, 50-foot-high arch at its eastern end. A few feet from this monolith stands a natural stone tower, all that remains of a second arch in the rock that collapsed in 1845. At dawn, when the sun rises *through* the remaining arch, the entire stone changes from something inorganic to a luminescent presence. The road to Petite Irlande commands a particularly good view of the rock. During low tide, you can walk out to the rock on a convenient sandbar at the foot of Mont Joli (first find out when the tide will come *in*) to inspect the fossils (from the Devonian period, the fourth phase of the Paleozoic Era, just before trees began to appear on the east coast of North America) on the sides of the monolith.

The village is laid out in a semicircle surrounding two bays, with capes between and within a larger semicircle created by the slopes of the mountains that isolate it from the rest of the peninsula. The peak of Mont Ste-Anne, used by the Micmac in their sun-worshiping ceremonies, can be reached by walking up the dirt road near the *Eglise St-Michel.* The road is navigable by car, but driving is not recommended; mini-bus tours are offered at the site. If you proceed on foot, count on a round-trip hike of about two-and-a-half to three hours. The 1,230-foot summit makes an ideal vantage point from which to plan further explorations. From here, Percé Rock, Bonaventure Island, and the entire village can be seen at a glance. Another trail behind the *St-Michel* church leads to a small cave and waterfall.

In the town itself, the *Percé Wildlife Interpretive Centre* (79 Rang de l'Irlande; phone: 418-782-2721) uses dioramas and a filmstrip to illustrate the stages of development that produced Percé Rock and the irregular coastline of the peninsula. The center is closed mid-October to early June; open daily the rest of the year. There's an admission charge.

Aside from its geography, Percé's other attraction is food. More than two dozen establishments serve excellent seafood and French dishes; one to try is *La Normandie* hotel-motel (Rte. 132, at 221 Rte. des Failles; phone: 418-782-2112; 800-463-0820 in Quebec, summer only; expensive). But don't limit yourself to one or two places—the food here is half the fun of the trip.

From Percé's wharf, many boat tours depart to Bonaventure Island. Once the home of a community of fishermen-farmers, it now belongs exclusively to the birds. The dominant species—gannets—number about 50,000, although there also are kittiwakes, gulls, razor-billed auks, murres, and occasional sea pigeons and sea parrots. Most of the island's new residents have established nests along the cliffs that line the shore and can easily be photographed. The island is a sanctuary under the control of the *Tourism, Fish, and Game Commission.*

En Route from Percé From Percé to Gaspé is a comfortable morning's drive—just under 50 miles (80 km)—through countryside that varies from cliffs to sandy beaches. The tiny village of Coin-du-Banc lies in a small pass that marks the exit from the guardian mountains of Percé and the entrance to the northern sectors of the peninsula. Its beach attracts avid windsurfers.

About 25 miles (40 km) from Percé is the resort center of *Auberge Fort Prével* (see *Best en Route*), whose restaurant, one of the best in the province attracts diners from all over the world. From spring to early autumn th resort is a government training school catering to the hotel-restaurant trade The settlement here began after a British sailor, George Prevel, floate onto a nearby shore—either swept overboard or shipwrecked—married local girl, and set up housekeeping. During World War II, coastal gun were installed and barracks erected. Extensively redecorated, these build ings make up the heart of the resort.

GASPÉ This industrial hub of the peninsula is a deep-water port and the railhea of the region, linking the city with Montreal, Quebec City, and Matapédi The town fronts the Baie de Gaspé, where three of the region's maj

Atlantic salmon rivers—the Dartmouth, York, and St-Jean—converge. *Pisciculture de Gaspé* (686 Blvd. York, 5 miles/8 km inland on Rte. 198; phone: 418-368-3395), a fish hatchery near the mouth of the York River, stocks lakes and rivers all over the province with almost one million salmon and trout per year. It's open daily, with guided tours offered during the summer; no admission charge. Anglers can go after the grown ones in all three rivers (within the limits set by law) as long as arrangements are made in advance with the lower Saint-Laurent and Gaspé government office (phone: 418-643-1616); or check limits in the current *Fishing, Hunting, and Trapping Guide,* available at tourist offices. Make reservations 48 hours ahead of time, since the number of anglers is controlled. It's sometimes possible to get a space on only 24 hours' notice, but don't count on it.

In town, the *Gaspé Museum* (80 Blvd. de Gaspé; phone: 418-368-5710) has a permanent display on Gaspé history and mounts temporary exhibitions during the summer on regional art, ethnology, and culture. It's open daily; admission charge.

En Route from Gaspé About 10 miles (16 km) outside Gaspé, Route 132 takes a sharp turn eastward, outlining the peninsula containing *Forillon National Park,* while Route 197 cuts across the western end of the park, joining Route 132 on the other side. Encompassing some 92 square miles of widely varying landscape and vegetation, the park occupies almost all of the small peninsula. Its low areas are almost marine (saltwater plants, sand dunes, grottoes, and occasional seals), while the mountains in the center nurture a variety of alpine vegetation, including species of plants that have survived since the Ice Age. Altogether, there are nine distinct levels of climatic variation and a spectacular array of wildlife—moose, black bears, white-tailed deer, foxes, lynx, mink, otters, muskrat, and others. Scuba diving and nature walks are among the park's varied activities. Three private campgrounds in the park area provide most facilities (phone: 418-892-5100). The park's reception centers in the village of Penouille, on the south coast of the peninsula along Route 132, are closed *Labour Day* to early June; they are open daily the rest of the year. There's an admission charge to the park (phone: 418-368-5505). Also see *National Parks* in DIVERSIONS.

It is believed a Viking outpost may have been established on the site of the village of Penouille during the 11th century, and that Freydis (Eric the Red's illegitimate sister) may have visited the site—which would make her the first European female to set foot in Canada. The difficulty in proving this has been compounded by the destruction of the early French settlements here by English troops on three separate occasions (in 1690, 1711, and 1759). A few miles farther, the village of Cap-aux-Os was named for the large collection of whale bones found here by the earliest settlers. While this does not prove that Vikings actually landed on this shore, it lends credence to the theory.

Forillon Park draws its name from *pharillon,* or "little lighthouse," the designation given to one of the tall towers of rock at the eastern tip of the peninsula, the site of signal fires that warned sailors off the rocky cape. On the north side of the peninsula, Cap-des-Rosiers is said to be the site of more shipwrecks than any other point on the Canadian coast. Its lighthouse, *Phare du Cap-des-Rosiers* (Rte. 132; phone: 418-892-5613 or 418-368-5710), was built in 1858 and is a historic monument. It's closed early September to late June; open daily the rest of the year. There's an admission charge.

The *Manoir Le Boutillier* in L'Anse-au-Griffon has an exhibit that chronicles the Gaspé's cod fishing heritage. The center also has an auditorium, a crafts shop, a playground, and a café. It's closed October to late June; open daily the rest of the year. There's no admission charge (phone: 418-892-5150).

Routes 132 and 197 reunite near Rivière-au-Renard, where descendants of a group of Irish sailors shipwrecked at Cap-des-Rosiers make up a large part of the population. The *Centre et Circuit d'Interprétation des Pêches Contemporaines* (Rtes. 197 and 132; phone: 418-269-5292) is an interpretation center that houses exhibits reflecting the traditional way of life in this region. Bus tours of fish-processing plants on the peninsula, included in the admission charge to the center, leave from here several times a day. Route 132 continues along the coast to L'Anse-Pleureuse, 68 miles (110 km) north. Between L'Anse-Pleureuse and Ste-Anne-des-Monts are 42 miles (67 km) of irregular roadway, running so close to the water in places that spray splashes the cars, then climbing 1,200 feet over a rocky cape. Stop at the village of Mont-St-Pierre, and take an hour to climb the mountain on foot or drive up the jeep trail. From the peak, you can look out over the vast Gulf of St. Lawrence or face slightly westward and strain to see Pointe-des-Monts, at the base of the gulf on the north shore. Mont-St-Pierre, with its glider launching pads, is considered the glider capital of eastern Canada. The *Mont-St-Pierre* hotel-motel, which serves good food at low prices, makes a timely stopping place (see *Best en Route*).

Approaching the village of Tourelle, 37 miles (59 km) from L'Anse-Pleureuse, keep an eye out for falling rocks; the highway runs between the beach and the mountains, and in 1963 part of the village was wiped out by a landslide.

STE-ANNE-DES-MONTS On arrival in Ste-Anne-des-Monts, get off Route 132 and take the old road along the shore. Most of the older buildings were destroyed by fire in 1925, but the *Théodore Lamontagne Residence,* now known as the *Auberge Château Lamontagne* (170 Av. 1; phone: 418-763-2589), still watches over the bay. It's worth the 5-mile (8-km) drive off Route 132 to see the house and grounds and to try out its restaurant. The road crosses the Ste-Anne River, where salmon fishing is allowed under government guidelines (see the current *Fishing, Hunting, and Trappin*

Guide, available from tourist offices). Between the hatchery upstream and the fish coming from the St. Lawrence, it is a good spot to land a salmon. Route 299 leads inland 25 miles (40 km) to *Gaspé Park.* A fine place in the area for dinner is the *Auberge Gîte du Mont-Albert* (see *Best en Route*), right off Route 299 in the middle of the park. The inn specializes in classic French cooking as well as regional dishes of the Gaspé and Quebec Province, and it's known for its high caliber of service. During the academic year, students from the *Quebec Institute of Tourism and Hostelry* show off their skills for guests.

GASPÉ PARK (PARC DE LA GASPÉSIE) This park covers almost 500 square miles of magnificent mountainous land, preserving a portion of the natural beauty that prompted Cartier's praise of the area. This is one of the few places in the province where herds of caribou, moose, and deer still roam in the same area. The highest peaks of the Chic-Choc Mountains preserve alpine vegetation that exists nowhere else at such a southerly latitude.

An arm of the Appalachian chain, the Chic-Choc Mountains run the length of the park and most of the peninsula, from the Matapédia River Valley to the eastern capes. They average 3,500 feet, and the highest peaks—such as the McGerrigle—scrape the skies at 4,100 feet. It was the height of these slopes that kept the alpine flora from dying out during the last (Wisconsin) ice age, which lasted from about 15,000 to 5,000 BC. The alpine fir, representative of the period, rarely grows more than eight feet tall. Mont Jacques-Cartier has the largest concentration of these plants. Both Mont Jacques-Cartier and the McGerrigle are frequented by herds of caribou most of the year. They remain in the cool of these peaks in the summer, venturing down to the lower region only during winter.

The park's vegetation changes with the altitude: Peat bogs on the valley floor give way to forested slopes, then to lichen, moss, and low shrubs on the windblown crests. Mont Albert is a naturalist's dream. Its base is lined with conifers such as firs and spruces, which gradually mix with subalpine forests of stubby alpine firs. Toward the peak, the trees are replaced by alpine tundra and arctic vegetation—shrubs and moss—and in the barren areas, the intense cold and frost have shattered massive chunks of exposed rock into gigantic boulders.

The park is crisscrossed by a network of hiking trails and drivable roads. Most conveniences are available in the park area. Trail guides and trained naturalists are on duty on an irregular basis, and many activities can be arranged with the help of the staff. Although hunting is strictly prohibited, the park's lakes and rivers yield speckled, sea, and Quebec red trout as well as hard-fighting Atlantic salmon. During the winter, these slopes attract cross-country skiers from all over the world. This is still very much an untamed forest; the animals (including black bears) have rights to the area. It gets dark quickly in the mountain forests, so always keep track of time, and return to your campsite or car before dark, or you may get lost. The parks use a check-in, checkout system designed to keep track of all those wandering in the forest, but it could take time to find you. Call ahead for information before heading into the park. Its reception center is closed early September to early June; open daily the rest of the year. There's no admission charge to the park (phone: 418-763-3301).

Two bordering parks, *Les Réserves Fauniques Matane* and *Dunière,* are extensions of *Gaspé Park* in geography and content but are administered separately. The principal access to these areas is via Route 195 from Matane.

En Route from Gaspé Park Return to Route 132 and continue west along the south bank of the St. Lawrence River for 55 miles (88 km) to Matane.

MATANE This industrial town was settled in 1795, but it remained basically a Micmac village until 1845. During the mid-19th century, it evolved into a river pilot station and grew with the lumber trade. Its name is based on the native word for "beaver pond." Ferries (phone: 418-562-2500; 800-463-2420 in Quebec) connect Matane with Godbout and Baie-Comeau on the north shore of the St. Lawrence River. Juicy Matane shrimp is a Quebec seafood favorite. The last week of June, the *Shrimp Festival* pays tribute to this delicacy with various activities, including shrimp tastings and sports events (phone: 418-562-0404). Atlantic salmon fishing in the Matane River also is excellent. A stopover at *Le Barrage Mathieu-D'Amours Fish Ladder,* a short walk from the *Hôtel des Gouverneurs* (250 Av. du Phare E.; phone: 418-566-2651; 800-463-2820 in Quebec), allows visitors to observe the salmon as they struggle upstream in *Des Iles Park.* The park lighthouse is a museum and tourist information center for the area (968 Av. du Phare W.; phone: 418-562-1065). It's open daily year-round; no admission charge.

En Route from Matane About 32 miles (51 km) from Matane is *Jardins de Métis Park.*

JARDINS DE MÉTIS PARK This park began as a private estate, one of the many English-style manors established in the area during the Victorian era. Its formal gardens have been adapted to include approximately 4,000 plants of many different climates. There are 500 species of alpine shrubs, annuals, and perennials, as well as experimental plantings of a group of aquatic plants. The success of these plantings is a tribute to Elsie Reford, who began the gardens in 1922. *Villa Reford*—her former home and the centerpiece of the park—houses a museum, restaurant, and crafts shop. It's closed mid-September to early June; open daily the rest of the year. There's an admission charge (phone: 418-775-2221).

BEST EN ROUTE

The range of lodgings on the Gaspé Peninsula is wide, with inns that boast renowned dining rooms in several parks and rustic, simple motel or even campground accommodations elsewhere. Expect to pay $65 or more per night for a double room in the places listed as expensive; between $45 and $65 in those categorized as moderate; and $45 or less in inexpensive places. These prices are valid for the summer season; off-season rates may be half as much. All hotels feature private baths unless otherwise indicated. For each location, hotels are listed alphabetically by price category.

NOTRE-DAME-DU-PORTAGE

Les Pèlerins sur Mer A four-room bed and breakfast that provides what such a place should—pleasant accommodations, a good breakfast, and a relaxing atmosphere. Sit on the front balcony and watch the sun set across the river behind the mountains. 756 Rte. du Fleuve (phone: 418-867-2806). Inexpensive.

RIVIÈRE-DU-LOUP

Auberge de la Pointe Occupying a good spot on the river's edge, this inn boasts fine dining and 125 comfortable rooms distributed among nine buildings. Facilities include an indoor pool and health center, indoor and outdoor games areas, bicycle paths, and a trolley that runs around the property. Autoroute Jean Lesage, exit 507 (phone: 418-862-3514; 800-463-1222). Expensive.

Lévesque Not plush but comfortable, it offers 96 rooms, a fitness center, an outdoor pool, and an excellent dining room that serves French Canadian food. 171 Rue Fraser (phone: 418-862-6927; 800-463-1236 in Canada; fax: 418-867-5827). Expensive.

Universel A 119-room motel in the center of town, it has all the facilities of most large hotels. The rooms are comfortable; the service, excellent. There's a restaurant and a piano bar. 311 Blvd. Hôtel-de-Ville (phone: 418-862-9520; 800-463-4495; fax: 418-653-4486). Moderate.

Journey's End A link in the economical hotel chain, it has 69 clean, comfortable accommodations. There is no restaurant. 85 Blvd. Cartier (phone: 418-867-4162; 800-668-4200; fax: 418-867-1687). Inexpensive.

TROIS-PISTOLES

Le Bocage A bed and breakfast with warmth and atmosphere, this old ancestral home's six rooms are furnished with antiques. The breakfast is very good, and the river view is lovely. 124 Rte. 132 E. (phone: 418-851-3602). Inexpensive.

RIMOUSKI AREA

Auberge Universel A small-scale version of a full-service establishment, it features 63 rooms and a restaurant. 130 Av. Belzile (phone: 418-724-6944; 800-463-4495; fax: 418-653-4486). Expensive.

Auberge Sainte-Luce This 30-room motel is best known for its good restaurant. Closed October through April. Six miles (10 km) from Rimouski, at 46 Rte. du Fleuve W., in Ste-Luce (phone: 418-739-4955; fax: 418-739-4923). Inexpensive.

MATAPÉDIA

Restigouche On the banks of the Restigouche and Matapédia Rivers, this comfortable, 40-room motel is popular among salmon fisherfolk. Most rooms overlook the estuary; there's also a good dining room, a pool, tennis courts, and a horseshoe pitching area. 3 Rue du Saumon (phone: 418-865-2155; fax: 418-865-2848). Moderate.

CARLETON

Baie Bleue This hotel-motel features 95 rooms. Guests have access to a heated pool, a beach, and tennis courts. The hotel's *La Seigneurie* restaurant is the best in the area, with fine French and Canadian dishes and seafood. 482 Blvd. Perron (phone: 418-364-3355; 800-463-9099 in Canada; fax: 418-367-6165). Expensive.

Shick Shock Thirty-four comfortable rooms, a restaurant, a bar, and a view are the draws at this motel. 1746 Blvd. Perron (phone: 418-364-3288). Inexpensive.

PORT-DANIEL

Motel Chaleur et Chalets This 80-acre site offers 10 rooms, some in the motel and some in cottages. These excellent accommodations are surrounded by lovely parkland for walking or cross-country skiing. 160 Rte. de la Pointe (phone: 418-396-5667). Moderate.

CHANDLER

Fraser French and Canadian specialties and seafood are served in the restaurant at this 40-unit motel, which also has a heated outdoor pool. 325 Rte. 132, in Chandler, about halfway between Bonaventure and Percé (phone: 418-689-2281; 800-463-1404 in Canada, except Manitoba and British Columbia; fax: 418-689-6628). Expensive.

St. Laurent This is an older place with 44 comfortable rooms, good service, a heated outdoor pool, and a restaurant. 499 Av. Réhel (phone: 418-689-3355; fax: 418-689-5752). Moderate.

PERCÉ

Le Bonaventure sur Mer This 90-room hotel-motel overlooks Percé Rock and offers comfortable accommodations, a bar, and a good restaurant. Closed November through April. 367 Rte. 132 (phone: 418-782-2166; 800-463-4212 in Canada; fax: 418-782-5323). Expensive.

Mirage du Rocher Percé In this 60-room motel complex, the second-floor rooms have balconies overlooking the beach and Percé Rock. Recreational facilities include tennis courts and a heated pool. The coffee shop serves breakfast only. Closed November to mid-May. 288 Rte. 132 (phone: 418-782-5151; 800-463-9011 in Canada and the northeastern US in season only; fax: 418-782-5536). Expensive.

Pic de l'Aurore Overlooking Percé Rock, this 18-unit motel has a fair dining room. There are also accommodations in 17 log cabins on the woodsy grounds. Closed mid-October through May. 1 Rte. 132 (phone: 418-782-2151). Expensive.

Manoir Percé A 38-unit establishment, it boasts a nice dining room and a lovely location with an ocean view. 212 Rte. 132 (phone: 418-782-2022; 800-463-0858 in Quebec; fax: 418-782-5195). Moderate.

FORT PRÉVEL

Auberge Fort Prével This is a comfortable, 78-unit motel-chalet and resort area built from World War II army barracks. It features a nine-hole golf course, tennis courts, a health center, and an excellent restaurant with a terrace serving French dishes that capitalize on the area's fresh seafood. Closed late September to mid-May. There are activities for kids, and a variety of excursions can be arranged. Rte. 132, St-Georges-de-Malbaie (phone: 418-368-2281; fax: 418-368-1364). Moderate.

GASPÉ

Auberge des Commandants Certainly the best lodging spot on the Gaspé Peninsula, it has 56 rooms and overlooks the bay. Amenities include a dining room and a cocktail lounge. 178 Rue de la Reine (phone: 418-368-3355; 800-462-3355 in Quebec; fax: 418-368-1702). Expensive.

Adams A motel near the gulf, it has 98 nice rooms, good service, and a dining room offering seafood and French dishes. 2 Rue Adams, Rte. 132 (phone: 418-368-2244; 800-463-4242 in Quebec; fax: 418-368-6963). Moderate.

MONT-ST-PIERRE

Mont-St-Pierre This 12-room motel on the ocean includes a good restaurant. 60 Rue Prudent-Cloutier (phone: 418-797-2202). Moderate.

STE-ANNE-DES-MONTS

Monaco des Monts Here are 46 rooms and good dining facilities. The guest services are average. 90 Blvd. Ste-Anne W. (phone: 418-763-3321; 800-361-6162; fax: 514-861-4016 in Montreal). Moderate.

Auberge Gîte du Mont-Albert Besides 48 newly renovated rustic rooms and 15 chalets that look out at the surrounding forest, this hotel-motel has a famous restaurant. There are also three campgrounds and an outdoor pool. Closed December through April (except for the chalets). About 25 miles (40 km) south of Ste-Anne-des-Monts on Rte. 299 (phone: 418-763-2288; fax: 418-763-7803). Expensive.

Iles-de-la-Madeleine

The Iles-de-la-Madeleine (Magdalen Islands)—anchored in the Gulf of St. Lawrence about 130 miles east by southeast of the Gaspé Peninsula, about 55 miles northeast of the tip of Nova Scotia's Cape Breton Island, and 60 miles east of Prince Edward Island—are an unusual and satisfyingly remote getaway spot. However, increasing tourism has made residents worry about preserving their way of life and the fragile ecology of these beautiful isles.

Only seven of the dozen or so islands, islets, and reefs in this archipelago are inhabited, so that even as travelers discover them, it is easy to find a dune-lined beach where you can be alone with the sea. The major islands of the Magdalens cluster together and are connected by causeways. They are Ile-du-Cap-aux-Meules, the largest of the islands and the starting point of most tours (at its community Cap-aux-Meules); Ile-du-Havre-aux-Maisons; Ile-aux-Loups; La Grosse-Ile; Ile-de-la-Grande-Entrée to the northeast; and Ile-du-Havre-Aubert to the southeast. Accessible only by ferry is Ile-d'Entrée. Most of the coastal rocks are a soft grayish red, laced with sandstone and gypsum (betraying hints of volcanic ancestry), stained ocher by the seawater and salt air, and carved over centuries into weird formations. Tall pillars overlook chasms and the crashing ocean. Atop overhanging ledges, picnic sites command panoramic views of neighboring islands and the gulf; below are enchanting caves. These natural formations and the fine sandy beaches with their dunes and warm waters make this quiet archipelago a summer destination of romance and mystery.

The lifestyle of the Madelinot villagers reflects the quietude of the islands, affected most by the surrounding sea. Lobster, herring, mackerel, scallops, and halibut are the mainstays of the economy, and most of the people belong to island-based cooperatives that freeze, can, smoke, ship, and market their catch. Until recently, the annual seal hunt was the second component of the economy. But because of an internationally organized anti-sealing campaign, attempts are under way to develop other resources to replace seal hides in the marketplace. However, many other sectors of the fishery also are suffering, because of depletion of fish stocks.

Of the 15,000 inhabitants occupying this 55,000-acre haven, most are of Acadian origin; about a thousand of the islanders are of Scottish ancestry; while many others descend from shipwrecked sailors of all nationalities.

The relative isolation of the islands, even from each other, has allowed communities established by early settlers to retain their individuality. For example, Scottish communities are concentrated on Grosse-Ile and Ile-d'Entrée. "Magdalen Islands" or "Grindstone" appears on many local fishing vessels, and even French maps of the islands are strewn with such names as Old Harry, Leslie, and Cap (Cape) Alright.

During the spring and fall migrations, the Iles-de-la-Madeleine become a bird watcher's haven. More than 50 species of waders, ducks, alcids (a family of diving birds), and other waterfowl, plus many varieties of land birds, take sanctuary here. In summer, the surrounding seas are like fields ripe for harvest. The deep-sea fishing for bluefin tuna is as good here as anywhere in the world. The early summer is reserved for lobsters taken fresh from the gulf (you can buy them at wharves) and cooked on the beach; the later summer is perfect for swimming and long afternoons of basking on the dunes. Winters here are beautiful in their solitude, but few (except the seals) appreciate them.

Since the summer days are apt to attract many travelers, and since there are only about 350 hotel rooms—and about 200 campsites—available, it is advisable to make arrangements far in advance. The best approach to Iles-de-la-Madeleine is by air: *Inter-Canadian* (phone: 418-969-2771 or 418-692-1031; 800-361-0200 in Quebec) flies from Montreal and Quebec City to Havre-aux-Maisons, with stops at Mont-Joli and Gaspé; *Air Alliance/Air Canada* (phone: 418-969-2888; 800-361-8620 in Quebec) also offers daily flights. Many travelers prefer to drive to Cap Tormentine, New Brunswick, and take a ferry to Prince Edward Island. From the wharf at Borden, PEI, they drive across the island to Souris for the NM *Lucy Maud Montgomery* ferry to Cap-aux-Meules. Between Cap Tormentine and Borden, PEI, there is continuous service and little waiting time. The trip from Souris to the Madeleines takes five hours, with only one departure daily (at 2 PM, except Tuesdays, when it leaves at 2 AM; in high season, a daily 2 AM ferry is added); schedules can change on short notice. Beginning in mid-March, reservations are taken for the round trip. For reservations and information about the ferry, call the *Cooperative de Transport Maritime Aérien* (*CTMA;* phone: 902-687-2181 in Souris; 418-986-6600 or 418-986-3278 in Cap-aux-Meules). Visitors also can travel by ship on the *CTMA Voyageur,* which transports cargo and up to 15 passengers from Montreal to the Iles-de-la-Madeleine. The ship departs Montreal on Fridays and arrives on Sunday afternoons; return trips depart Iles-de-la-Madeleine on Tuesdays and arrive in Montreal on Fridays.

A new summer ferry service between the Iles-de-la-Madeleine and Carleton on the Gaspé Peninsula was inaugurated in 1995. The ferry transports cars and has a dining room, a bar, a movie theater, and entertainment, as well as a few cabins (reservations required) for those who want to sleep during the 14½-hour trip. The ferry runs from July through August with departures every other day; for schedule information and reservations, contact *Croisiéres Carleton-les-Iles* (phone: 418-364-6207).

To get to Cap Tormentine from Montreal or Quebec City, take Route 20 east along the south shore of the St. Lawrence River to Rivière-du-Loup, then pick up Route 185 across the Gaspé and into New Brunswick, where it becomes Route 2 to Moncton. Cap Tormentine is just a short distance away from here via local roadways. From New England, pick up US 1 from US 95 in Portland, Maine. It leads into Canadian Route 1, which goes through Saint John, New Brunswick, where it intersects Route 2 heading toward Moncton.

Whether you arrive at 8 in the morning or the evening, the first view of Ile-d'Entrée—a large grassy hillock protruding from the sea—is astounding. As you pass Cap Rouge and Pointe-du-Sud-Ouest, look for the hiking trails leading along the cliffs, and pick a spot among the red rock formations to visit later. The ferry docks at Cap-aux-Meules in a sheltered bay full of small fishing vessels and visiting sailing sloops. Local ferry service on the SP *Bonaventure* (phone: 418-985-5705) to Ile-d'Entrée originates here. A tourist information booth is located at the exit from the ferry dock. To the left of the wharf is the formation known as Gros-Cap. Ile-du-Cap-aux-Meules, the largest island in the archipelago, is the most heavily populated. Three municipalities are centered here: Cap-aux-Meules (a small district on the eastern shore of the island); Fatima (encompassing the north end of the island and a long beach and reef extending north from the perimeter); and L'Etang-du-Nord (occupying the southern end of the island).

Items made by the islanders are sold at reasonable rates on the islands. Cold, lonely winters provide many hours for exacting, detailed work. Carved pieces of whalebone and seal fur items are among the popular choices. The fish wells, where freshly caught fish and lobsters are kept ready for shipment, may be visited to see how the locals pursue their arduous living from the sea. There is an excellent marina on the Gulf of St. Lawrence, with some interesting fish and sea mammals on display. Nine-meter sailboats with a captain can be rented, and fishing trips are scheduled daily, weather permitting. Check with the *Association Touristique des Iles* (128 Débarcadère Cap-aux-Meules; phone: 418-986-2245) for information on sailing and fishing excursions, boat rentals, and sailing schools.

Chemin du Gros-Cap leads to the Gros-Cap Scenic Area, which lies in the Etang-du-Nord district. A provincial campground with 75 sites is located just past Cap Rouge, about 4 miles (6 km) from the wharf. This point, like most of these exposed hills and cliffs, is subject to the 20-mph winds that created the rock carvings, so dress appropriately—wear a sweater and/or windbreaker on windier days. The same road, Chemin du Gros-Cap, curves inland toward La Vernière, with a beautiful old wooden church near Butte du Vent, the highest point on the islands. The entire archipelago may be seen from this summit, and on a clear day you can see Cape Breton Island, almost 60 miles (96 km) away.

Route 199, the highway that links most of the islands into a cohesive landmass, leads south from La Vernière through the Plage de la Martinique (Martinique Beach) and across a causeway to Ile-du-Havre-Aubert. A similar connecting beach links the western sides of these two islands, creating a lagoon called Havre-aux-Basques (Basque Harbor). Along this western leg of Ile-du-Cap-aux-Meules, in the Etang du Nord district, the remains of several wooden ships—among the many wrecked here—can be seen in the shallow offshore waters. The roadway bears east and follows the beach of Ile-du-Havre-Aubert to the village of Havre-Aubert. This busy harbor looks much like the bay at Cap-aux-Meules, populated by Madelinot fishers and fisheries. The *Musée de la Mer* (Marine Museum) portrays the history not only of the archipelago but also of sailing and fishing in the area. It is open daily; admission charge (phone: 418-937-5711). There is a reconstructed Madelinot village nearby. Two of the five campgrounds in the islands are located on the southern coast, near the village of Bassin. *Belle Plage* (phone: 418-937-5408) has 46 sites, and *Plage du Golfe* (phone: 418-937-5224 or 418-937-5115) has 72 sites. Check the *Iles-de-la-Madeleine Tourist Guide* (available at the tourist office near the ferry terminal) for facilities available at each.

If you drove from Ile-du-Cap-aux-Meules on Route 199, then you should certainly return along the Plage-de-l'Ouest (West Beach). Try to keep an eye out for the shipwrecks in the gulf on the left, and be sure to glance over at the waters of the lagoon to your right.

When you arrive at Ile-du-Cap-aux-Meules, take the road leading north through the village of Etang-du-Nord and toward Fatima. A private, 115-site campground, *Le Barachois* (phone: 418-986-6065 or 418-986-5678), overlooks the northwest shore. This district on the northern end of the island extends along the Dune-du-Nord, a long, wide, sandy arm of dune-filled beach that connects with the outstretched southerly arm of Grosse-Ile. At various points this elongated beach is called Plage-de-l'Hôpital and Plage-de-la-Pointe-au-Loup. Here, too, a second arm paralleling the first (the northern extension of Ile-du-Havre-aux-Maisons) forms a lagoon between these two beaches.

Route 199 crosses this lagoon and runs along the west side on the Dune-du-Nord beach. The Grosse-Ile district occupies two islands that form a severe V shape, pointing north. The western side is Grosse-Ile; the other, obviously, is Ile-de-l'Est. Not so obvious is exactly where one island ends and the other begins. Traveling north, Route 199 passes through the village of Leslie, which was settled by Scots. To a large extent, their language has been lost in the French, but some customs of the families date back to early Scotland. Spend a little time in the village to get a taste of the Scottish-Madelinot atmosphere. The highway turns sharply south across the mouth of the bay (Baie Clarke) that forms the northern tip of the lagoon and continues in the direction of Old Harry on Ile-de-l'Est. The entire northern section comprises two beach shorelines, the Plage-de-la-Pointe-de-l'Est (from Grosse-Ile along the western side of the V) and the Plage-de-la-Grande-Echouerie—perhaps one of the most beautiful beaches in the world (along the eastern side of the island). The panorama of Ile-de-Brion to the north, over the dunes and the gulf, is magnificent, and the southern view of the lagoon is equally so, especially at sunset.

Route 199 goes into the village of Old Harry, where the Anglican chapel and a mini-museum in the *Old English Schoolhouse* are located. The museum has exhibits tracing the development and history of education in the town. Closed *Labour Day* through June; open daily the rest of the year. There's an admission charge (phone: 418-985-2116).

Continue through the village to Ile-de-la-Grande-Entrée, a peninsula extending south from Ile-de-l'Est that helps to form the Lagune-de-la-Grande-Entrée, to a large bay, known as Havre-de-la-Grande-Entrée. Camping space on the island is limited to the 38-site *Grande-Entrée Campground* (phone: 418-985-2833); *Club Vacances "Les-Iles"* (phone: 418-985-2833) also is near Bassin aux Huîtres and offers a campground, a 24-room motel, a restaurant, and a lounge.

Since the highway does not cross the mouth of the lagoon (Chenal-de-la-Grande-Entrée) to the northern extension of Ile-du-Havre-aux-Maisons (Plage-de-la-Dune-du-Sud), the return trip means retracing your path through Leslie and the Dune-du-Nord.

Halfway south on the Dune-du-Nord, take Route 199 across a causeway to Ile-du-Havre-aux-Maisons. This island comprises most of the eastern shoreline of the archipelago, so it's not so odd that most of the shipwrecks occurred on its shores as boats sailed west to the New World. The northern section of the island is relatively barren, but the southern end is well settled. Be sure to visit the lighthouse at Cap Alright and the shipwreck at nearby Pointe Basse.

From here to Cap-aux-Meules is a quick ride west and south—across a short causeway and down the west coast of the island.

A short, one-day visit to Ile-d'Entrée makes for a pleasant excursion, featuring rock formations, birds, and its own fishing port.

BEST EN ROUTE

Although the islands are not exactly overflowing with hotel space, a few places handle guests very nicely. Fluctuating exchange rates, inflation, and seasonal demand make prices difficult to predict, but most establishments are moderately priced. In the places listed as expensive, plan on spending about $100 a night for a double room; at moderate places, from $60 to $100; and inexpensive places will cost $60 or less. All hotels feature private baths. The *Association Touristique des Iles* (see above) also publishes the *Iles-de-la-Madeleine Tourist Guide* and operates a reservation service from March through mid-September. In addition to the campgrounds mentioned in the text, camping is allowed almost anywhere. Just follow basic rules of courtesy, and ask permission before setting up; don't camp on anyone's front lawn. For each location, hotels are listed alphabetically by price category.

ILE-DU-HAVRE-AUX-MAISONS

Auberge de l'Islet An excellent motel, it has 20 units (all with TV sets and telephones) plus a restaurant. Closed mid-September to mid-May. Dune-du-Sud (phone: 418-969-2955; fax: 418-969-4736). Moderate.

Au Vieux Couvent In a restored convent, the nine rooms here are spartan, but the bar gets a crowd almost every night. The restaurant specializes in island mussel dishes. Closed mid-September through May. Rte. 199 (phone: 418-969-2233; fax: 418-969-4693). Inexpensive.

CAP-AUX-MEULES

Château Madelinot Four of the 72 units in this motel have kitchenettes; all have TV sets and telephones. There's a dining room, an indoor pool and whirlpool, and a fitness center. Rte. 199 (phone: 418-986-3695; 800-661-4537; fax: 418-986-6437). Expensive.

Bellevue In the main village, atop a hill overlooking the sea, this establishment offers 33 comfortable rooms and a restaurant. 40 Rue Principale (phone: 418-986-4477; fax: 418-986-4414). Moderate.

HAVRE-AUBERT

La Marée Haute A small, rustic four-room inn facing the Sandy Hook dunes. It has a fireplace and a restaurant serving local dishes. 25 Chemin des Fumoirs (phone: 418-937-2492). Moderate.

Saskatchewan

Its southern grasslands and vast farmlands may give the impression that Saskatchewan is completely a prairie province, but, in fact, trees cover much of its 251,700 square miles. The change in terrain is most noticeable at *Prince Albert National Park,* the forested entrance to Saskatchewan's northerly wilds. Past the town of La Ronge, traveling by air is a virtual necessity. Many roads have only gravel surfaces, and service stations are rare. This inconvenience does not stop the great number of campers, hikers, and anglers who make their way by plane to the region's remote camps and lodges.

Another interesting aspect of Saskatchewan is its history of political innovation. In 1944, it elected North America's first socialist government, which introduced electricity to 99% of its farms, established government-owned businesses, and instituted broad-reaching school-modernization programs. For more historical perspectives, visit the branches of the *Western Development Museum* dotting the province. The long-standing presence of the Royal Canadian Mounted Police (RCMP) can be seen in the capital, Regina, which is the site of the force's training academy and museum.

Today, with about a million people fairly evenly divided between city and country, the province is still sparsely populated. Farming and wheat production, supplemented by oil production, are the leading industries.

In the following pages we offer two itineraries across Saskatchewan: east to west on the Trans-Canada Highway, slicing through the heart of the rich prairie farmland and Regina in the province's southerly quarter; and south to north, from the US North Dakota border at Estevan through Saskatoon—the province's other major urban center—to splendid *Prince Albert National Park,* poised on the edge of the vast wilderness stretching to the Northwest Territories. These routes can be combined for even longer tours.

Those who wish to experience the rural life of Saskatchewan can arrange farm vacations through the *Saskatchewan Country Vacation Association* (PO Box 654, Gull Lake, SASK S0N 1A0; phone: 306-672-3970). For further information, including maps, contact *Tourism Saskatchewan* (500-1900 Albert St., Regina, SASK S4P 4L9; phone: 306-787-2300 in Regina; 800-667-7191 elsewhere in Canada and the US).

The Trans-Canada Highway across Saskatchewan

The Trans-Canada Highway (Rte. 1), running 370 miles (592 km) through Saskatchewan's southern prairies and wheat fields, provides a good way to see much of the province. Passing through the cities of Regina, Moose Jaw, and Swift Current, it is best used as a principal east-west path from which to detour north and south to the many interesting sights located on secondary roads.

En Route from Manitoba Route 1 enters Saskatchewan from Manitoba in the east, passing through a series of small communities. At Whitewood, 41 miles (66 km) from the provincial border, stop at *Chopping's Museum* (Rte. 1; phone: 306-735-2255) for prairie Victoriana. Then turn south on Route 9 to *Moose Mountain Provincial Park,* one of the most popular of Saskatchewan's parks, 38 miles (61 km) from Whitewood.

MOOSE MOUNTAIN PROVINCIAL PARK With Kenosee Lake at its center, the park comprises rolling terrain covered with aspen, white birch, and spruce. Its origins go back to 1906, when R. B. Clark established a resort beach along the lake. The present park's chief building is a chalet-like, stonework field house. Built in 1930, it was damaged by fire and reconstructed as a relief project during the Depression. Today, besides functioning as a visitors' reception area and park headquarters, it contains meeting rooms and a small museum. Park accommodations range from a modern motel to cabins to about 330 campsites.

The park's recreational facilities include an 18-hole golf course, beaches for swimming, privately operated riding stables, biking and hiking trails, tennis courts, a water slide, and supervised children's activities. In addition, there is good lake fishing for pike, pickerel, and perch. A 15-mile (24-km) gravel road stretches into the forest area, where one may see moose or elk grazing in the early morning or early evening. The park, which houses some 450 beaver lodges, also is a nesting place for geese and a wide variety of other birds, including wood ducks, blue herons, and vultures. The park is open year-round; no admission charge (phone: 306-577-2131 or 306-577-4503).

Nearby is *Cannington Manor Provincial Historic Park,* site of a 19th-century venture in community building. In 1882, Captain Edward Mitchell Pierce and his son came here to establish a traditional English manor system in the New World. The middle class Pierce, hoping to lead the life of an aristocratic Victorian squire on this land, established five tenant homestead farms, a wagon shop, a paint business, and sawmills. The inherent impracticality of the scheme, coupled with Pierce's costly indulgence in horse racing, caught up with the community, and the effort was abandoned after 15 years. Today, visitors can see the original church and reconstructions of the blacksmith and carpenter shops. The original schoolhouse has been turned into a museum of memorabilia from the colony. *Cannington Manor* is closed September 5 to May 19; no admission charge (phone: 306-787-9573).

En Route from Moose Mountain Provincial Park Return to Whitewood and rejoin Route 1, heading west through prairies and farming communities. On the way is the town of Wolseley, where you can have a meal at *Le Parisien* restaurant (on Rte. 1; phone: 306-698-2801). Sixty-eight miles (109 km) from Whitewood is the town of Indian Head, site of the *Canada Agricultural Experimental Farm* (Rte. 1; phone: 306-695-2274; fax: 306-695-3445). Here, you can examine its landscaping and demonstration gardens of grain, vegetables, flowers, and trees. The farm is closed October through April; no admission charge. Turn north on Route 56 to Fort Qu'Appelle and the Qu'Appelle Valley area.

QU'APPELLE VALLEY On the shores of a chain of lakes, this valley is a region of bush and light forest. Its ready supply of wood for fuel and building made it attractive to pioneers, and it thus became an early stop on the fur trade route and a haven for the area's first European settlers. It is significant in Native American history because a faction of the Sioux nation, fleeing north after the Battle of Little Big Horn, sought refuge here. Pauline Johnson, a popular Native American poet of the turn of the century, commemorated the valley in several works. The valley now is known for its parks and its arts and crafts.

The town of Fort Qu'Appelle is at the junction of Routes 56, 10, and 35. In town, *Qu'Appelle Crafts* (310 Broadway St. W.; phone: 306-332-6025) and the *Hansen Ross Pottery Studio* (298 Bay St.; phone: 306-332-5252) feature local handicrafts and pottery. A short ride south on Route 56 leads to *Katepwa Point Provincial Park,* whose name in Cree means "Who calls?" *Katepwa* is a lakeside area designed primarily for day use and family activity. A short distance west of Fort Qu'Appelle is *Echo Valley Provincial Park,* another lakeside retreat, which offers swimming and fishing.

En Route from the Qu'Appelle Valley Follow Route 10 southwest for 46 miles (74 km) to Regina.

REGINA Saskatchewan's capital (pop. 184,000) began in 1882 as a small frontier settlement near a spot named Pile o' Bones for its large number of buffalo skeletons. Feeling the need for another name, the residents christened the new town Regina, in honor of Queen Victoria. Today, the modern city offers a full range of urban facilities. One interesting place is the *Royal Canadian Mounted Police Museum and Training Academy* (off Dewdney Ave. on the west side of the city; phone: 306-780-5777), which provides an excellent opportunity to view the past and present of the RCMP. The nation's major display of Mountie history, its exhibits focus on the history of the North West Mounted Police (now the RCMP) in the Old West, including uniforms and weapons, models of forts, photographs, and pictorial representations of historic moments. There are more unusual attractions as well: the crow's nest of the *St. Roch,* a ship instrumental in the establishment of a Northwest Passage; the tobacco pouch that Sitting Bull brought with him when he fled to Canada; and, since Saskatchewan was the center of the Riel Rebellion of the 1880s, the crucifix Louis Riel carried to his execution. The museum also devotes considerable space to the culture of the native Plains group; there's even a corner dedicated to the singing duo Jeanette MacDonald and Nelson Eddy, who made the Mounties famous with the film *Rose Marie.*

Visitors may observe recruits exercising and drilling at the *Training Academy,* the RCMP's national center for basic training. You may also want to catch the ceremonial drills, in which the Mounties march in their smart uniforms; the *Sergeant Majors' Parade* takes place Mondays and Thursdays at 1 PM. Guided tours are available weekdays. It's open year-round, call for hours; no admission charge.

Many other places to visit are located in *Wascana Centre,* a 2,300-acre park built around artificial Wascana Lake in the central part of town. Here is the *Legislative Building,* the provincial seat of government, and the main campus of the *University of Regina.* On the complex's north side, on the corner of College Avenue and Albert Street, is the *Royal Saskatchewan Museum* (2445 Albert St.; phone: 306-787-2815), which concentrates on the province's flora and fauna largely through exhibits and paintings. Other sections are devoted to Native American life. The museum further sponsors conservation and archaeological projects, whose results are on exhibit. Open daily year-round; no admission charge.

Nearby, at the corner of Albert Street and 23rd Avenue, is the *MacKenzie Art Gallery* (3475 Albert St.; phone: 306-522-4242), with European art from the Renaissance onward and contemporary Canadian and US works. It's closed weekends; no admission charge. Also on the grounds of *Wascana Centre* is the *Diefenbaker Homestead.* Relocated here from Borden, Saskatchewan, this was the family home of John Diefenbaker, a former Prime Minister of Canada (1957–63). Even if you're not interested in Canadian politics, you may find a visit to the homestead interesting, since it is furnished in an authentic pioneer manner. It's closed early September to mid-May; no admission charge (phone: 306-522-3661).

Also in *Wascana Centre,* the *Saskatchewan Centre of the Arts* (200 Lakeshore Dr.; phone: 306-565-4500) houses a theater that accommodates touring productions. Near the arts center, on the lakeshore, is a waterfowl sanctuary; the observation point on the opposite bank is an excellent spot to view Canada geese, ducks, swans, and other shorebirds. The *Saskatchewan Science Centre* (Winnipeg St. and Wascana Dr.; phone: 306-791-7914) has hands-on science exhibits and live stage demonstrations in the *Powerhouse of Discovery,* and shows films on a five-story screen several times a day in the *Kramer IMAX Theatre.* It's open daily in summer and closed most Mondays in winter; admission charge.

The *City Centre* features many cultural attractions. In the public library (12th Ave. and Lorne St.), the *Prairie History Room* (phone: 306-777-6011) exhibits documents on local history, and the *Dunlop Art Gallery* (phone:

306-777-6040) shows the work of local artists. The library is closed weekend mornings; no admission charge. Located in the old *City Hall* is the *Globe Theatre* (1801 Scarth St.; phone: 306-525-9553), Regina's professional company. (The historical drama *The Trial of Louis Riel* is staged each summer at the *MacKenzie Art Gallery*—see above.) Nearby, at 11th Avenue and Scarth Street, is the stylish *Cornwall Centre* shopping mall. Also nearby on Hamilton Street is the *Galleria,* an architecturally trendy collection of boutiques.

Definitely worth a visit is the *Agridome* (in *Exhibition Park,* a few blocks west of *City Centre;* phone: 306-781-9200), a multipurpose complex for concerts, conventions, expositions, and sporting events, among other attractions. There's horse racing at the *Queensbury Downs* track, located in the complex, and the *Buffalo Days* fair is held here each August. There are nine golf courses encircling the city, and the Saskatchewan *Roughriders* play football at *Taylor Field* (Albert St. and Dewdney Ave.; phone: 306-525-2181 or 306-569-2323; 800-667-8179 in Saskatchewan).

Regina boasts several interesting dining spots. *Bartleby's* (1920 Broad St.; phone: 306-565-0040) features an Old West atmosphere, with a stand-up bar, a player piano, and antique decorations. The fare is reasonably good, too. *Elephant & Castle* (11th Ave. and Scarth St.; phone: 306-757-4405) is an English-style pub serving beer and good food. Excellent continental cuisine and legendary desserts can be had at *Memories* (1711 Victoria Ave.; phone: 306-522-1999). When the *Saskatchewan Science Centre* (see above) is open, its *Edgewater Café* serves basic burgers and sandwiches; in the evenings, the restaurant offers good French fare. *Applause Feast and Folly,* in the *Regina Inn* (see *Best en Route*), is a dinner-theater.

En Route from Regina It is 44 miles (70 km) west to Moose Jaw via Route 1. On the way, take an interesting side trip by turning north just before Moose Jaw on Route 301 to *Buffalo Pound Provincial Park*, a 13-mile (21-km) drive.

BUFFALO POUND PROVINCIAL PARK Here, 260 acres of fenced-in land provide a grazing area for a herd of buffalo. The park is an excellent place to observe these animals in something close to a natural state. Outside the buffalo pound, the park offers hiking along old paths through some interesting scenery. Fishing is permitted in Buffalo Pound Lake, and there are tennis courts and a pool. The park has a cafeteria, a grocery store, and more than 200 campsites. During the winter, it operates the *White Track Ski Resort,* with tobogganing, downhill and cross-country skiing, and ice fishing. The park is open year-round; admission charge (phone: 306-693-2678 or 306-694-3659).

En Route from Buffalo Pound Provincial Park Return south on Route 301 to rejoin Route 1 to Moose Jaw.

MOOSE JAW This industrial city (pop. 35,000) is set in the heart of wheat country. Of greatest interest here is the *Moose Jaw Zoo,* home to animals from all over the world—perhaps a welcome change of pace from moose and buffalo. The children's section emphasizes Saskatchewan wildlife. The zoo is open daily May 1 through September 15, weekends only the rest of the year; admission charge (phone: 306-693-8112). At the junction of Routes 1 and 2, one of Saskatchewan's four *Western Development Museums* provides a visual record of the area's growth in culture and technology, from pioneer days onward. The Moose Jaw branch specializes in the history of transportation, with exhibits ranging from wagons and dogsleds to trains and airplanes. The museum is open year-round; admission charge (phone: 306-693-5989).

Most of Moose Jaw's other attractions are annual events. The *International Band Festival* is a mid-May competition that draws marching bands from all over North America. Early July brings a summer fair and the *Saskatchewan Air Show,* which features demonstrations of antique and modern planes. The *Parke Lodge Motor Inn* (Rtes. 1 and 2; phone: 306-692-0647) and the *Best Western Heritage Inn* (see *Best en Route*) have dining rooms.

En Route from Moose Jaw Swift Current is a straight, 109-mile (174-km) drive west on Route 1, but travelers interested in history should follow the more circuitous route described below, which takes in *St. Victor Petroglyphs Historic Park* and the reconstructed fort at *Wood Mountain Historic Park.* Take Route 2 south for 88 miles (141 km); a side road leads you a few miles farther into the first park.

ST. VICTOR PETROGLYPHS HISTORIC PARK The petroglyphs here are carvings made in a sandstone rock face by native people in prehistoric times. Pictured are animal and human figures and totemic renderings of human faces. Getting to the carvings is a somewhat strenuous venture: You have to follow a path to the foot of a cliff, then climb a series of stairs to get to the ledge. Since the figures have faded through erosion, they are best seen when the sunlight is not directly on them. The park is open year-round; no admission charge (phone: 306-694-3664).

En Route from St. Victor Petroglyphs Historic Park Return to Route 2, heading south for a short distance to an unpaved road leading to Route 358, about 10 miles (16 km) west. Follow Route 358 south to its junction with Route 18 to the entrance road to *Wood Mountain Historic Park.*

WOOD MOUNTAIN HISTORIC PARK The two reconstructed buildings from the North West Mounted Police post that existed here from 1874 to 1918 feature photographs and artifacts relating to the history of the fort and its most memorable episode. After the Battle of Little Bighorn, Sitting Bull brought the Sioux nation north from Montana to settle for several years in this vicinity.

En Route from Wood Mountain Historic Park Follow Route 18 west to Val Marie in *Grasslands National Park.* Then take Route 4 north to the town of Swift Current, 122 miles (195 km) from *Wood Mountain Historic Park*.

SWIFT CURRENT This town (pop. 16,000) preserves an Old West spirit while still providing all the amenities of modern times. Its pioneer tradition is expressed in the *Frontier Days* celebration and rodeo, held annually around July 1, and an amateur fiddling contest that takes place in late September. Swift Current also has the *Canadian Country Music Hall of Fame* (1100 Fifth Ave. NE; phone: 306-773-7854), featuring memorabilia and portraits of famous Canadian country music stars. With several hotels, the town makes a good overnight stop (see *Best en Route*). Major attractions are not plentiful here, but interesting exhibits on pioneer history can be seen at the *Swift Current Museum* (105 Chaplin St. E.; phone: 306-778-2775). It's open year-round; no admission charge. Artwork is on exhibit at the *Swift Current Library and Art Gallery* (411 Herbert St. E.; phone: 306-778-2752). The library is closed Sunday mornings, and the gallery's closed all mornings; no admission charge.

For an interesting side trip, drive north on Route 4 for 24 miles (38 km) to *Saskatchewan Landing Provincial Park*. A marker pinpoints the spot where generations of pioneers had to ford or ferry across the South Saskatchewan River to reach the Battlefords Trail, the route into northern Saskatchewan. Native grave sites and tepee rings are in the hills throughout the park. Another interesting site here is the *Victorian Goodwin Mansion*, built of fieldstone in 1900. The park is open year-round; admission charge (phone: 306-375-2434 or 306-375-2912).

En Route from Swift Current Heading west, Route 1 soon penetrates ranching country. North of the highway are the Great Sand Hills, an open area of dune-like hills harboring an abundance of wildlife. For a closer look, turn north on Route 37 at Gull Lake, 34 miles (54 km) west of Swift Current.

Continuing west, Route 1 intersects with Route 21 after another 46 miles (74 km). Turn south on Route 21, which soon leads into Maple Creek. Here the *Old Timer's Museum* (105 Chaplin St.; phone: 306-662-2474) concentrates on local history. It's open year-round; no admission charge. About 22 miles (35 km) farther south on Route 21 is *Cypress Hills Interprovincial Park*.

CYPRESS HILLS INTERPROVINCIAL PARK The Cypress Hills are a twist of nature—hilly, high-level plateaus covered with rich forests set in the midst of flat dry, low-scrub prairie. Scientists believe that 30 million years ago, a river flowing eastward left a deposit of cobblestone in the area that was gradually lifted into prominence by the erosion of the surrounding strata. Later when the Wisconsin Glacier moved across Canada, it bypassed the 80 square miles that today form the summits of the hills.

Cypress Hills offers a respite from the flatness of the prairies. It is filled with buttes, ridges, and plateaus surrounded by huge areas of rolling ranch land. On the shoreline of an artificial lake are a chalet, condominiums, an cabins. This main area has a nine-hole golf course, tennis courts, a pool, and a beach. Hiking trails lead around the park; the trail to Bald Butte promontory is especially scenic. You can drive through cattle country and see curiously shaped rock formations and the impressive Conglomerate Cliffs. The woodland is a good place to observe deer, moose, and other wildlife. During the winter, the park offers downhill and cross-country skiing, snowmobiling, skating, and tobogganing. In addition to cabins, the park has 400 camping spaces. Most of the park's facilities are closed *Labour Day* to mid-May; admission charge (phone: 306-662-4411).

En Route from Cypress Hills Interprovincial Park Directly west of *Cypress Hills, Fort Walsh* can be reached if you don't mind some rougher-than-usual driving. From Maple Creek (see above), Route 271 leads directly to *Fort Walsh*.

FORT WALSH NATIONAL HISTORIC PARK *Fort Walsh* was the original headquarters of the North West Mounted Police. In the Cypress Hills area, a battle took place in 1873 between US and Canadian traders and the Assiniboin tribe. The traders lost badly, and the hue and cry that followed resulted in the establishment of the Mounties. Built in 1874, *Fort Walsh* served as the main patrol center until 1882. The old fort has been duplicated at its original site, with original artifacts lending authenticity, but there are no historical reenactments or Mounties in period uniforms. What distinguishes *Fort Walsh* from other Mountie reconstructions is the isolated setting evocative of a bygone age. Nearby is *Farwell's Trading Post,* restored to 1872 conditions and staffed with costumed guides. The park is closed early October to mid-May; admission charge (phone: 306-662-3590 or 306-662-2645).

BEST EN ROUTE

Since the Trans-Canada is a principal highway, there's no lack of adequate accommodations along this route. Some of Regina's hotels and inns are elaborate, with entertainment and recreational facilities. Elsewhere, the motels tend to be functional and modern. Expect to pay $60 or more per night for a double room in an expensive hotel; from $35 to $60 at one in the moderate range; from $20 to $35 at a place we list as inexpensive; and $20 or less at campgrounds, considered very inexpensive. All hotels feature such amenities as air conditioning, private baths, and TV sets unless otherwise indicated. For each location, places are listed alphabetically by price category.

MOOSE MOUNTAIN PROVINCIAL PARK

enosee Inn Here are 53 deluxe, modern, and semi-modern hotel rooms and cabins plus a restaurant. Open year-round (phone: 306-577-2099, Park Superintendent). Inexpensive.

Fish Creek and Lynwood Campground This government-operated property has 333 campsites, 186 with electricity. Showers, flush toilets, firewood, laundry, and a grocery store are on the premises. Open mid-May to early September. Just 1.5 miles (2.5 km) west of the park entrance (phone: 306-577-2144). Very inexpensive.

WOLSELEY

Banbury House Inn A small Edwardian mansion-turned-hotel, it has nine guestrooms, a cozy bar, and a dining room. Front St. (phone: 306-698-2239). Moderate.

REGINA

Ramada This hotel has 255 rooms, an indoor pool, a water slide, and extensive dining facilities. In the *Saskatchewan Trade and Convention Centre,* at 1919 Saskatchewan Dr. (phone: 306-525-5255; 800-854-7854; fax: 306-781-7188). Expensive.

Regina Inn This good business hotel in the center of town has 239 rooms and convention facilities. An outdoor whirlpool bath, an exercise room, two restaurants, and a cocktail lounge round out the amenities. 1975 Broad St. (phone: 306-525-6767; 800-667-8162 in Canada; fax: 306-352-1858). Expensive.

Hotel Saskatchewan Radisson Plaza A lavishly restored Beaux Arts–style hotel, i has 215 rooms and two restaurants, one elegant and the other casual 2125 Victoria Ave. (phone: 306-522-7691; 800-667-5828 in Canada; 800-333-3333 in Canada and the US; fax: 306-757-5521). Expensive.

Landmark With 188 distinctively furnished units, this inn also boasts a restaurant bar, heated indoor pool, sauna, whirlpool bath, and water slide. 4150 Alber St. (phone: 306-586-5363; 800-667-8191 in Canada; fax: 306-586-0901) Expensive to moderate.

Delta Regina This 251-unit property has an indoor heated pool and several restau rants. Victoria Ave. and Broad St. (phone: 306-569-1666; 800-268-1133 i Canada; 800-877-1133 in the US; fax: 306-525-3550). Moderate.

Imperial 400 A 200-room motel with dining, convention, and entertainment faci ities, it also has a sauna, whirlpool bath, indoor pool, and water slide. 425 Albert St. (phone: 306-584-8800; fax: 306-584-0204). Moderate.

Regina Travelodge This motel has 200 rooms, a three-story water slide, a restau rant, and an Irish pub. 4177 Albert St. (phone: 306-586-3443; 800-255-305 fax: 306-586-9311). Moderate.

Seven Oaks A motel, this place has 156 guestrooms, a heated indoor pool, wat slides, a dining room, and a coffee shop. 777 Albert St. (phone: 306-75 0121; 800-667-8063 in Canada; fax: 306-565-2577). Moderate.

MOOSE JAW

Best Western Downtown Here are 28 units with an adjacent restaurant. 45 Athabasca St. E. (phone: 306-692-1884; 800-528-1234; fax: 306-692-4442). Moderate.

Best Western Heritage Inn In addition to 88 rooms, facilities here include an indoor pool, whirlpool bath, dining room, and cocktail lounge. 1590 Main St. N. (phone: 306-693-7550; 800-528-1234; fax: 306-692-5660). Moderate.

SWIFT CURRENT

Imperial 400 This motel has 142 units, an indoor pool, a sauna, a dining room, and a lounge. 1150 Begg St. E. (phone: 306-773-2033; fax: 306-773-4911). Expensive to moderate.

Horseshoe Lodge The 45 units here afford a good view of the countryside. There is a dining room, cocktail lounge, and heated outdoor pool. Rte. 1E on N. Service Rd. (phone: 306-773-4643; fax: 306-773-0309). Moderate.

MAPLE CREEK

Maple Grove Motel This establishment has 14 rooms and six serviced trailer sites, so one may be a guest or park a recreational vehicle. Rte. 21 and First Ave. W. (phone: 306-662-2658; fax: 306-662-4118). Moderate to inexpensive.

Estevan to the Northern Lakes

From south to north, Saskatchewan stretches for a long distance. From Estevan, near the North Dakota border, to Prince Albert, the northernmost city, it's 363 miles (581 km), and travelers who choose to head farther north or make side trips in the southern part of the province can easily double the mileage. You can arrange the southern part of the journey to include Regina and Saskatoon, Saskatchewan's two major cities, and to take in many of the province's most interesting attractions. The route can be exciting, since it reaches partway into Saskatchewan's great northern wilderness. This region's fine fishing lures some travelers here; others are attracted by the chance to observe open, undisturbed nature. While many sites are accessible only by plane, roads do lead a fair distance into the wilderness. If you choose, you may end your northward trek at *Prince Albert National Park,* which offers a taste of the wilderness while staying close to civilization.

TEVAN A small city (pop. 10,500), Estevan is a major center for oil and coal resources. *Boundary Dam,* just south of town on Route 47, is the largest lignite-burning power station in Canada. It's open year-round (call in advance for tours, June through *Labour Day*); no admission charge (phone: 306-634-1300). Southeast, *Woodlawn Regional Park* houses a reconstruction of a North West Mounted Police barracks from the 1870s. It's open year-round, and there's an admission charge (phone: 306-634-2324). The *Estevan Brick Wildlife Display* features a collection of area animals. Open year-round; donations are accepted (phone: 306-634-2531).

En Route from Estevan The most direct route to Regina, northwest on Route 39, covers miles of semiarid terrain. Fifty-three miles (85 km) away is Weyburn, the next major town. Here, the *Soo Line Historical Museum* (411 Industrial La.; phone: 306-842-2922) is devoted to exhibits on local history. It's open daily July through August and closed weekends the rest of the year; admission charge. The town library has a small art gallery. Forty-four miles (70 km) farther, at the village of Corinne, Route 39 joins Route 6, which leads north for 28 miles (45 km) to Regina. A few miles past Corinne, however, Route 39 leads to Wilcox, site of *Notre Dame College,* founded by Father Athol Murray. The *Tower of God,* a place of worship on campus, is open 24 hours a day (phone: 306-732-2080).

The southern edge of Saskatchewan contains much badlands territory. For a look at really spectacular terrain, head west from Estevan on Route 18 for 73 miles (117 km) to the edge of the Big Muddy Badlands. Then head north on Route 6 for 66 miles (106 km) to Regina.

REGINA For a full account of Regina and its attractions, see *The Trans-Canada across Saskatchewan* route, above.

En Route from Regina Route 11, a divided highway, continues northwest for 154 miles (246 km) to Saskatoon (see below). A side trip to *Gardiner Dam* at Lake Diefenbaker is worthwhile, however. To reach the dam, turn west on Route 44 at Davidson, about halfway between Regina and Saskatoon on Route 11. After 31 miles (50 km), Route 44 crosses Route 19. Turn north on Route 19 and take the turnoff heading west to the dam, 10 miles (16 km) away.

GARDINER DAM Canada's largest rolled-earth dam, *Gardiner* is an impressive sight Over 3 miles long and a mile wide at its base, the dam rises to a height o 210 feet. It lies across the South Saskatchewan River, its backwater turnin a 140-mile section of the river into Lake Diefenbaker. *Danielson Provincia Park,* established around the dam, provides facilities for camping, swim ming, fishing, and boating. A visitors' pavilion (phone: 306-857-2027) explain the workings of the dam, and self-guided tours are available. Farther sout along the lakeshore on Route 19 is *Douglas Provincial Park,* which also offer a full range of lake activities, adjacent to the smaller *Qu'Appelle Dam.* Jus north of *Douglas* on Route 19, the *Elbow Museum and History Society* in th community of Elbow (Saskatchewan St.; phone: 306-854-2125 or 306-85 2285) contains a pioneer sod house. The Plains tribes used the original 40 ton glacial boulder in their offerings to the spirit Manitou. The museum closed September through June; admission charge.

En Route from Gardiner Dam Return to Route 19, and travel north for 14 miles (22 km) to the intersection with Route 15. Turn east on Route 15; another 14 miles (22 km) will return you to Route 11 at Kenaston. Continue north on Route 11 for another 25 miles (40 km) to the turnoff for *Blackstrap Provincial Park,* which boasts an artificial mountain. In addition to this somewhat treacherous hill, *Blackstrap* has fishing, swimming, and a campground. From here, it is 20 more miles (32 km) north to Saskatoon.

SASKATOON On the banks of the South Saskatchewan River, Saskatoon (pop. 185,600) is known as the City of Bridges. The riverfront and its many parks reveal a skillful blending of urban design with the work of nature. Downtown, the *Delta Bessborough* hotel is a landmark (see *Best en Route*).

Saskatoon's *Western Development Museum* (Lorne Ave. in the southern part of the city; phone: 306-931-1910) includes *Boomtown 1910,* an indoor reconstruction of a frontier main street and stores a city block long. There are no false fronts; all the buildings—a barbershop, hotel, print shop, firehouse, town hall, dry goods store, drugstore, bank, school, and church—were brought to the museum from a small village and are fully furnished with material from the early 1900s. Cars and buggies are parked on the street, and a railway station is at one end of town. Also in the *Western Development Museum* is the old-fashioned *Palace Theatre*, which shows silent movies and historical films, and the *Saskatchewan* hotel, whose balcony is a good place from which to observe *Boomtown 1910.* Other exhibits in the museum include vintage cars and farm machinery. Some of the old farm machinery is used in threshing competitions during the fair that is held at the nearby exhibition grounds during the third week of July. The museum is open year-round; admission charge.

The *University of Saskatchewan Museum of Natural Sciences and Geology* (in the *Arts Building;* phone: 306-966-5683) devotes much space to dinosaur skeletons and to local flora, fauna, and geology. It's closed weekend mornings and holidays; no admission charge. The small, privately operated *Ukrainian Museum of Canada* (910 Spadina Crescent E.; phone: 306-244-3800) houses exhibits of traditional clothing and handicrafts. It's closed Sunday mornings and holidays; admission charge.

The *Mendel Art Gallery and Conservatory* (Spadina Crescent, on the riverfront; phone: 306-975-7610) hosts visiting exhibitions; its permanent collection includes Canadian, European, and Inuit art. The *Saskatchewan Craft Gallery* (813 Broadway Ave.; phone: 306-653-3616) also emphasizes local work. Old timekeeping devices are available at *Wilkie's Antique Clocks* (1202 22nd St. W.; phone: 306-665-2888). Other interesting shops include *Past and Present Antiques* (327 21st St. W.; phone: 306-242-9379); *Prairie Pottery* (150B Second Ave. N.; phone: 306-242-8050); and the *Trading Post* (226 Second Ave. S.; phone: 306-653-1769). On the east side of town, off 115th Street, the *Forestry Farm Park and Zoo* exhibits 300 live animals native to North America; on its grounds are picnic areas and a stocked fish pond. It's open year-round; admission charge (phone: 306-975-3382).

Saskatoon's top restaurants include the *St. Tropez Bistro* (243 Third Ave. S.; phone: 306-652-1250), which serves French fare; *Cousin Nik's* (1110 Grosvenor; phone: 306-374-2020) for Greek food; and *Taunte Maria's* (51 First St. E.; phone: 306-931-3212), which offers hearty Mennonite food.

The city's annual events include a Ukrainian festival in mid-May, a jazz festival in June, *Louis Riel Day* and the annual fair in July, Shakespearean plays in July and August, and a multicultural festival in August.

En Route from Saskatoon Route 11 leads north to an area of considerable historical interest. *Batoche National Historic Park* may be reached by turning east on Route 312 at Rosthern (36 miles/58 km north of Saskatoon), traveling 10 miles (16 km), and then turning north on Route 225 for 6 miles (10 km). At Batoche, a decisive battle took place in 1885 between Louis Riel and his Métis forces and General Middleton and his troops. The Métis were Canadians of French–Native North American heritage who were largely neglected by the Canadian government, and their sense of injustice spilled into armed revolt. But the defeat of their leader, Riel, at Batoche marked the end of their uprising. Although one more battle took place at Steele Narrows, the Riel Rebellion was over. Most of the signs of the battle have disappeared, but bullet scars remain on the walls of the *St-Antoine de Padoue Church* rectory. Inside the building, photographs and displays commemorate the battle, and the graves of slain Métis are nearby. The site is closed from mid-October to mid-May; admission charge to audiovisual presentation only (phone: 306-423-6227/8; fax: 306-423-5400). By returning to Route 312 and heading east a few miles, then traveling south on an unpaved road for 11 miles (18 km), you can see the *Fish Creek Battlefield*, where the rebellion began.

Follow Route 312 back to Route 11 and continue north for a short distance to the *Duck Lake Regional Interpretive Centre.* The museum includes exhibits on the Riel Rebellion, a jail that once housed the native rebe Almighty Voice, and material relating to the native community at Duc Lake. It's open daily mid-May to early September, and by appointment th rest of the year; admission charge (phone: 306-467-2057). From *Duck Lake* a trip of 18 miles (29 km) west on Route 212 leads to *Fort Carlton Histori Park.* Partially reconstructed, *Fort Carlton* was an early Hudson's Ba Company outpost. Inside the fort is a replica of an early *Hudson's Bay* store and several other buildings have been furnished in period decor. The for is closed from early September to mid-May; admission charge (phone: 306 787-2854 or 306-953-2322). Returning to Route 11, head north 35 mile (56 km) to the city of Prince Albert.

PRINCE ALBERT Considered the gateway to the north, Prince Albert is the poin where the rolling prairies give way to heavily treed, lake-dotted parkland The *Prince Albert Historical Museum* is housed in an old fire hall built i

1866. Its exhibits, which relate to area history, include ubiquitous NWMP artifacts. The museum is closed from early September to mid-May; admission charge (phone: 306-764-2992). Adjacent to it is a blockhouse dating from the Riel Rebellion. The *Lund Wildlife Exhibit,* downtown on the shore of the North Saskatchewan River, contains an excellent taxidermy collection of North American animals. It's closed October to mid-May; admission charge (phone: 306-764-4471 or 306-764-2860).

Prince Albert also offers a chance to sample artwork. *The Little Gallery* (Central Ave.; phone: 306-763-7080) presents shows in a building that was once an opera house. The *Prince Albert Arts Centre* (Central Ave.; phone: 306-953-4811) exhibits the work of local, national, and international artists. In addition, the public library on 12th Street houses a small art and crafts gallery.

The most interesting local event here is an annual festival held in February, with dogsled races and king trapper competitions, in which contestants try to duplicate legendary pioneer acts of strength by lifting 600-pound loads onto their backs and cutting wood at great speed; visitors can sample traditional Native American dishes. A more conventional summer fair is usually held the first week in August.

As a departure point for expeditions north, either by road or by air, Prince Albert offers a bewildering number of routes from which to choose. For example, a 155-mile (248-km) drive via Routes 3, 55, and 924 leads northwest to Dore Lake for fishing.

En Route from Prince Albert One trip not to be missed is the relatively short journey to *Prince Albert National Park.* Head north on Route 2; after 21 miles (34 km), a turnoff west onto Route 263 will take you right into the park. Travel 26 miles (42 km) north through the park to the main townsite at Waskesiu Lake.

PRINCE ALBERT NATIONAL PARK Here is an excellent introduction to Saskatchewan's northern wilderness. Characteristic of the north country, the 960,000-acre park is filled with lakes, ponds, and streams formed thousands of years ago by receding glaciers. The terrain is hilly and forested, with white and black spruce, poplar, and birch prominent. Animals, including elk, moose, deer, and bears, are abundant. Waskesiu Lake, with the park's townsite on its shores, is the main center of water activity, but Crean and Kingsmere, two other large, neighboring lakes, also are popular, as are the smaller Namekus, Hanging Heart, and Sandy. There also are many less crowded lakes and streams and hiking trails.

The Waskesiu townsite has several hotels, motels, and cabins, and grounds in and around the park provide about 500 camping sites. Waskesiu is also the base for most recreational facilities, such as tennis courts; an 18-hole golf course (see *Golf in Canada* in DIVERSIONS); riding stables; lawn bowling greens; rentals of houseboats, motorboats, rowboats, and canoes; a boat launch, if you've brought a craft; and a paddle wheeler (phone: 306-663-

5322; fax: 306-663-5424) that makes touring excursions on the lake. Most other lakes are accessible by road, but Crean and Kingsmere can be reached only by boat from Waskesiu. Fishing for lake trout is particularly good at Crean and Kingsmere. From the boat dock on the northwest shore of Kingsmere, a long hike leads to the home of Grey Owl, an Englishman adopted by the Ojibwa who became one of Canada's greatest naturalists.

Though the park is open year-round, many motels, campgrounds, and park facilities close in early October and reopen in April or May. The *Lakeview* hotel (phone: 306-663-5311), with 44 modern rooms, is one place where you can enjoy the summer season; in addition, *Château Park Chalets* have 10 two-bedroom units open year-round (phone: 306-663-5566). Cross-country skiing, ice fishing, and skating are available, with more winter activities planned. For information on the park, call 306-663-5322; also see *National Parks* in DIVERSIONS.

En Route from Prince Albert National Park You might decide to end your northward journey here. For a stronger taste of the wilderness or some serious fishing, head north on Route 2 to La Ronge, 92 miles (147 km) from the Waskesiu park gate through unpopulated countryside.

LA RONGE The town sits on the southwest shore of Lac La Ronge, a large lake surrounded by many smaller lakes and streams. A good fishing spot in its own right, it serves as a launching point for trips to resorts deeper into the wilderness, either by car on the Route 102 continuation of Route 2 or by plane from La Ronge's small airport. In town are a few motels, some resorts and a small campground; on the north shore of the lake, another 13 miles (21 km) on Route 2, is *Lac La Ronge Provincial Park,* where camping, more or less in the rough, is permitted.

Lac La Ronge is a good place to catch lake trout, and the Churchill River, just to the north, has plenty of walleye and pike. While it is certainly possible to fish entirely on your own here, especially if you've brought your own boat, resorts in the area provide guides. The *Kikinahk Friendship Centre* (phone: 306-425-2051); *Red's Camps* (phone: 306-425-2163; or mobile operator Saskatoon JW3-2067 on the La Ronge channel); and *Camp Kinisoo* (phone: 306-425-2024) are all licensed fishing outfitters accessible by road. If you want to stay at or use the facilities of one of these resorts, make reservations several months in advance. Even if you wish simply to rent a boat, you will do well to inquire ahead. The fishing season is short, and places fill up fast.

Lac La Ronge and the Churchill River are excellent for canoeing as well. *Tourism Saskatchewan* has mapped out 56 routes in northern Saskatchewan, several of them in the La Ronge area. A brochure detailing these routes is available on request from *Tourism Saskatchewan* (see introduction to this chapter).

En Route from La Ronge Anglers can continue the search for perch, pike, walleye, and lake trout farther north by road; wilderness buffs can use the same route to satisfy their sense of adventure. Note that north of La Ronge, roadside facilities are being developed, and an occasional gas station can be found, but it is nonetheless wise to leave with a full tank and to keep your eye on the fuel gauge.

Just beyond the *Lac La Ronge Provincial Park,* Route 2, which became a gravel road several miles back, changes its designation to Route 102 and continues northeastward. For about 58 miles (93 km), it passes a series of smaller lakes, such as McLennan and Brabant, with a number of small, primitive campgrounds along the lakeshores. Shortly past Brabant Lake, the road forks. Route 102 continues on for 27 miles (43 km) to the southern shore of large Reindeer Lake, where there is a small campground; Route 905 heads north to Wollaston Lake. The Wollaston Lake camps all offer fly-in packages; the most prominent, *Wollaston Lake Lodge* (phone: 800-328-0628 in Saskatchewan), is almost exclusively a fly-in operation. Come with a full tank of gas and a good spare tire, and drive very carefully on the gravel surface.

An alternate fishing route from La Ronge is to backtrack south for 12 miles (19 km) on Route 2 to the intersection with Route 165. Route 165 runs east through open country for 60 miles (96 km) to Route 106, which heads east for 18 miles (29 km) to the shores of Deschambault Lake, a good spot for pike. Before Deschambault, the *Northern Lights Lodge* (phone: mobile operator JP3-2028) and *Deschambault Lake Resort* (phone: 306-632-2166 or mobile operator JP5-8233) are both accessible from the highway. After Deschambault, Route 106 continues northeast for 25 miles (40 km) to the junction with Route 135. Route 135 leads north for a few miles to Jan Lake, famous for its pike fishing. Of the five licensed outfitter lodges there, the *Great North Lodge* (phone: 306-632-4516) and *Miniquay Lodge* (phone: 306-632-4515) are among the most developed. Pelican Narrows, another excellent fishing spot, is 25 miles (40 km) farther north on Route 135.

The *Saskatchewan Outfitters Association* (PO Box 2016, Prince Albert, SASK S6V 6K1; phone: 306-763-5434; fax: 306-922-6044) offers a list of resorts and outfitters that should be consulted by anyone seriously planning a fishing trip. For more details on angling, also see *Where They Bite: Fishing in Canada* in DIVERSIONS. Again, make reservations at fishing camps months in advance.

EST EN ROUTE

The most—and most comfortable—hotels are in Regina and Saskatoon; Regina's hotels are discussed in the previous *Best en Route* section. For accommodations in this area, expect to pay $60 or more per night for a double at a place in the expensive category; from $40 to $60 at one listed as moderate; from $20 to $35 at a hotel rated inexpensive; and $20 or less at the campground listed as very inexpensive. Although only a few motels and one campground are listed here, you'll find a steady supply along this route. Unless otherwise noted, all rooms in hotels feature air conditioning, TVs, and private baths. For each location, places are listed alphabetically by price category.

WEYBURN

Weyburn Inn In addition to 70 rooms, there is a coffee shop, dining room, and cocktail lounge. 5 Government Rd. (phone: 306-842-6543; fax: 306-842-2210). Moderate.

SASKATOON AREA

Delta Bessborough This French Revival château is named for a British Governor General of Canada of the 1930s. On a scenic riverbank site, it has 227 rooms and two restaurants. 601 Spadina Crescent (phone: 306-244-5521; 800-268-1133 in Canada; 800-877-1133 in the US; fax: 306-665-7262). Expensive.

Holiday Inn Adjacent to a shopping mall and the *Centennial Auditorium,* this 187-unit motel has a heated indoor pool, restaurant, and cocktail lounge with entertainment. First Ave. and 22nd St. E. (phone: 306-244-2311; 800-HOLIDAY; fax: 306-664-2234). Expensive.

Ramada This hotel has 291 rooms in an 18-story tower. There also are 14 luxury suites with wet bars, and two restaurants. The recreation complex includes two water slides, a sauna, a whirlpool bath, and an indoor pool. Satellite TV and nightly entertainment are available. Downtown, at 405 20th St. E (phone: 306-665-3322; 800-228-9898 in Canada; 800-854-7854 in Canada and the US; fax: 306-665-5531). Expensive.

Saskatoon Inn Two minutes from the airport, this establishment features a central courtyard with tropical plants. Each of its 249 rooms has a queen-size bed, and there is a sauna, a whirlpool bath, an indoor pool, nightly entertainment, a lounge, a coffee shop, and a restaurant. 2002 Airport Dr. (phone: 306-242-1440; 800-667-8789 in Canada; fax: 306-244-2779). Expensive.

Sheraton-Cavalier The hotel has 250 units, a pool, a sauna, and a whirlpool bath. The restaurant-nightclub overlooks the river. 612 Spadina Crescent E (phone: 306-652-6770; 800-325-3535; fax: 306-244-1739). Expensive.

Sands Centrally located, it features 148 modern rooms, a restaurant, convention facilities, an indoor pool, a sauna, nightly entertainment, and free parking. There's also an indoor golf dome with a driving range and putting green. 806 Idylwyld Dr. N., on Yellowhead Rte. 16 (phone: 306-665-6500; 800-667-6500 in Canada; fax: 306-665-1973). Expensive to moderate.

Travelodge Near the airport are 220 units, an indoor pool with a water slide, a sauna, a whirlpool bath, an exercise room, and a restaurant. 106 Circle Dr. W. (phone: 306-242-8881; 800-255-3050; fax: 306-665-7378). Expensive to moderate.

Parktown In this place are 109 units, a heated indoor pool, a sauna, a whirlpool bath, a restaurant, and a disco. 924 Spadina Crescent E. (phone: 306-244-5564; 800-667-3999 in Canada; fax: 306-665-8698). Moderate.

Circle Drive Suites Close to the airport, this motel has 192 rooms, a restaurant, a pool, and satellite TV. Airport and Circle Drs. (phone: 306-665-8121; 800-667-3529 in Canada; fax: 306-665-0064). Moderate to inexpensive.

Ferme Champêtre At this working farm, guests can engage in both agricultural chores (such as milking) and sports-oriented activities (like horseshoes and volleyball). Accommodations are in cabins as well as trailer and tent camping areas. There's no restaurant. Open May through September. No credit cards accepted. Also see *Farm and Ranch Vacations* in DIVERSIONS. In St-Denis, 25 miles (40 km) east of Saskatoon on Rte. 5 (phone: 306-258-4635; fax: 306-258-2215). Moderate to inexpensive.

King George Centrally located, it has 104 rooms, a restaurant, and extensive shopping in an underground arcade. 157 Second Ave. N. (phone: 306-244-6133; 800-667-1234 in Canada; fax: 306-652-4672). Moderate to inexpensive.

Brighton House Bed and Breakfast With four guest bedrooms (one with private bath), this is a congenial home near the center of town. Visa accepted. 1308 Fifth Ave. N. (phone: 306-664-3278). Inexpensive.

PRINCE ALBERT

Coronet Here are a hundred units, an indoor pool, a whirlpool bath, a sauna, a dining room, and a cocktail lounge with entertainment. 3551 Second Ave. W. (phone: 306-764-6441; fax: 306-763-8250). Moderate.

Imperial 400 In addition to its 137 units, this motel has a heated indoor pool and coffee shop. 3580 Second Ave. W. (phone: 306-764-6881; fax: 306-763-6533). Moderate.

Marlboro Inn In this 112-unit hostelry are an indoor pool, a dining room specializing in smorgasbord, and a cocktail lounge. 67 13th St. E. (phone: 306-763-2643; fax: 306-763-6336). Moderate.

PRINCE ALBERT NATIONAL PARK

Skyline A 21-unit motel, it has no restaurant. Reservation deposit required. Open April through October. Waskesiu (phone: 306-663-5461, summer; 306-763-1112, winter). Moderate.

Beaver Glen Campground Here are 213 sites, showers, flush toilets, a dump station, and firewood. Operated by *Parks Canada.* Open mid-May to late September. Near the Waskesiu townsite (phone: 306-663-5322; fax: 306-663-5424). Very inexpensive.

The Yukon Territory

For thousands of years, only Native Americans lived in the Yukon. Then, in the 19th century, the Hudson's Bay Company pushed northwest in its search for fur. Under the auspices of the company, Robert Campbell and John Bell explored the upper watercourse of the Yukon River and the northern sections of the territory in the 1840s. Trappers and traders followed the trail of Hudson's Bay trading posts, and in 1869 the Alaska Commercial Company moved in, extending the system of trading posts. Prospectors began drifting into the area as early as 1863, encouraged by finds of gold traces along the course of the Yukon River.

Acquired from the Hudson's Bay Company in 1870, the land became a provisional district in 1895, when there were just a thousand settlers of European descent in the territory. After 1898, as news spread of the first major gold strike, approximately 100,000 gold seekers, mostly Americans, rushed in—and encountered hardships for which they were ill prepared. They crept over treacherous mountain passes like a stream of ants, hauling the ton or more of supplies required for self-sufficiency. Less than half ever reached the fabulous gold fields, and of these, perhaps 20,000 actually panned for gold. Only 4,000 found anything of value, since the richest claims had been staked long before the hordes reached the fabled creek beds.

The Klondike gold rush of 1898 lasted less than five years, but the epic human drama changed the face of Canada's pristine Yukon Territory forever. The incident that started the gold rush created several millionaires but ruined most of those involved, among them one of the original discoverers. A miner named Robert Henderson told fellow prospector George Washington Carmack of a location he either knew or suspected had gold. Carmack, an educated white man who was married to a native Stick woman, began to work the juncture of the Klondike and Yukon Rivers with his two Stick brothers-in-law. He found a huge nugget on August 16, 1896, registered it the next day, and he, Skookum Jim, and Tagish Charlie (his brothers-in-law) laid claim to the area where Rabbit Creek (later Bonanza Creek) met the Eldorado Creek. Henderson, who was never told of the find, lost the chance to stake a claim to one of the biggest strikes in the Klondike. Henderson established a claim on another rich section, but failing health prevented him from working it himself. He sold it for $3,000 to another miner, who took an estimated half million in gold from the claim. In his later years, Henderson was awarded a government pension as codiscoverer of the Klondike gold fields, but he died a poor man in Vancouver.

The best place to learn about this intriguing era is not in murky museum hallways but on the "Trail of '98" itself. By following the path of the gold-crazed "stampeders," as they were called, travelers can retrace this piece of history, adding substance and a sense of adventure to a Yukon trip.

Most miners sailed from West Coast ports into Lynn Canal and past Juneau to a point of land formed by the juncture of the Skagway and Taiya Rivers. Here, the stampeders prepared for the overland trek to the headwaters of the Yukon River; from there, it was another 500 miles (800 km) to the gold fields at Dawson.

Pressed to cross the mountains in time to reach the Yukon River before freeze-up, the stampeders used two passes, the Chilkoot and the White. The Chilkoot, paralleling the Taiya River into the mountains, is 32 miles (51 km) long; the White, which follows the Skagway River for a distance, is 41 miles (66 km) long. The two passes meet on the shores of Lake Bennett, at the headwaters of the Yukon River, where the stampeders could load their goods on boats and float to the fields. The camps they established and the trading posts they patronized grew into towns, forming a thin lifeline into the wilderness.

The Yukon Territory is shaped like a right-angle triangle—wide at the bottom and tapered at the top. Its base rests on the 60th Parallel, which also marks the northern boundary of British Columbia; the upright, western edge leans against Alaska. The northern end, lying within the Arctic Circle, opens on Beaufort Sea. The jagged eastern border of the Yukon is shared with the Northwest Territories.

Although the 1898 gold rush, the building of the Alaska Highway in 1942, and other encroachments of civilization have taken their toll on Canada's last frontier, the Yukon remains largely untamed wilderness. Just over 30,000 people live in this 187,000-square-mile area, and three-quarters of them are concentrated in Whitehorse (pop. 22,250), the capital. Dawson City and Watson Lake are the next largest communities, each with fewer than 2,000 inhabitants. The remaining population lives in tiny, isolated communities. An excellent transportation system, however, gives an estimated 300,000 annual visitors access to the Yukon wilds.

For air travel to the Yukon, contact *Air North* (phone: 403-668-2228); *Alkan Air* (phone: 403-668-2107; 800-661-0432 in western Canada); or *Canadian Airlines International* (phone: 403-294-2000; 800-363-7530 in Canada; 800-426-7000 in the US). Smaller carriers provide charter service from the outside and between distant points within the territory.

For bus travel throughout the Yukon, contact *Alaskon Express* (300 Elliott Ave. W., Seattle, WA 98119; phone: 206-281-0576; 800-544-2206); *Atlas Tours Ltd.* (609 W. Hastings St., Fifth Floor, Vancouver, BC V6B 4W4; phone: 604-682-5820); *Atlin Express* (PO Box 291, Atlin, BC V0W 1A0; phone: 604-651-7617); *Gold City Tours* (PO Box 960, Dawson City, YT Y0B 1G0; phone: 403-993-5175); *Greyhound of Canada* (2191 Second Ave., Whitehorse, YT Y1A 3T8; phone: 403-667-2223); *Norline Coaches* (PO Box 5237, Whitehorse, YT Y1A 4Z1; phone: 403-668-3355); *North West Stage Lines* (2191 Second Ave., PO Box 4932, Whitehorse, YT Y1A 4S2; phone: 403-668-7240); *Rainbow Tours* (212 Lambert St., Whitehorse,

YT Y1A 1Z4; phone: 403-668-5598); or *Watson Lake Bus Lines* (PO Box 469, Watson Lake, YT Y0A 1C0; phone: 403-536-7381).

Package tours can be arranged through *Atlas Tours Ltd., Gold City Tours, Rainbow Tours* (see above), and *Gray Line Yukon/Westours* (300 Elliott Ave. W., Seattle, WA 98119; phone: 800-544-2206).

For backcountry expeditions in the Yukon, more than a hundred outfitters arrange hunting and fishing trips and other wilderness encounters. *Access Yukon* (same address and phone as *Rainbow Tours,* above) offers river trips, heli-hiking, trail riding, and sightseeing tours, both with and without guides. Three other operators to try are *Arctic Edge Ltd.* (PO Box 4850, Whitehorse, YT Y1A 4N6; phone: 403-633-5470; 800-661-0469 in the US), which provides 10- to 21-day wildlife and natural history expeditions by canoe, raft, backpack, dog team, and skis; the *Inconnu Lodge* (PO Box 4730, Whitehorse, YT Y1A 4N6; phone: 403-667-4070), a fishing and recreational resort on the east side of the Yukon; and *Kluane Adventures* (PO Box 5396, Haines Junction, YT Y0B 1L0; phone: 403-634-2282), which offers hiking, horseback riding, bicycling, and canoeing trips in *Kluane National Park Reserve.*

Contact *Tourism Yukon* (see below) for a complete list of services, an up-to-date copy of the hunting and fishing regulations, and a list of outfitters. Careful wildlife management is needed to prevent depletion of herds, so the territory is divided into 20 active registered guiding areas; one outfitter has sole rights to guiding and outfitting in each. Any hunter from beyond the Yukon's borders must be accompanied by a licensed guide. Grizzly, black, and brown bears, Dall and stone sheep, woodland and barren-ground caribou, moose, and mountain goats are abundant, as are white-tailed and rock ptarmigan, four types of grouse, and various ducks and geese. Bag limits are more than generous.

Like the mountains, the fish here are big and plentiful. The largest lake trout taken in recent years was 87 pounds; catches of 20 to 30 pounds are common. With a daily limit of five each for northern pike (averaging three to four feet), arctic grayling, Dolly Varden, rainbow trout, and salmon; two arctic char; and three lake trout (with a two-day limit in your possession at any one time), you know the fish are striking, and there is no closed season. Guides, while not required for fishing trips, are nonetheless recommended.

Hunting season starts in early spring and extends into late fall, but the principal tourist season runs from mid-May to mid-September. Summer daytime temperatures often soar to the high 80s F (30s C), but average July temperatures are in the high 60s F (20s C). Yukon winters, with readings as low as −50F (−45C), are no time to tour. Some roads, like the Taylor/Top of the World Highway (in Alaska, it's the Taylor Highway; in Canada, the Top of the World Highway) are closed in winter. Make travel arrangements, especially hotel reservations, as far in advance as possible, at least 90 days. Even reservations at popular restaurants should be made in advance.

A few quick notes about traveling in the Yukon: Most of the highways are asphalt, but some roads are still gravel. Although these are generally well maintained, it's a good idea to put protective covers over headlights and screens on windshields to protect them from flying rocks and stones. Also note that unleaded gasoline is not available in the Yukon, and gas is quite a bit more expensive here than in the US. The roads are patrolled thoroughly, and services are spread along most highways, but spare tires and changing equipment are a must. First-aid kits and some dehydrated foods aren't a bad idea either; if you are traveling during winter, they're a necessity. The same is true of a camp stove, to provide heat in case of emergency.

When camping or just cooking on the side of the road, avoid foods that are highly aromatic, since most animals are sensitive to smells. Caribou, moose, and grizzly, black, and brown bears abound. Do not be alarmed by them, but remember they are wild, and lives have been lost through unnecessary and (usually) foolish acts. *Do not try to corner a bear* or in any way force it to move against its will. If confronted, back away slowly and quietly. Don't feed bears or any other animals, and burn all waste and foodstuffs when you're through.

In this chapter, two routes run through the territory. The Dawson Circle Route, which explores the contemporary Yukon, begins and ends in the capital, Whitehorse, traveling through mining areas and crossing into nearby Alaska. The Trail of '98 follows the path used by most prospectors as they crossed the Chilkoot Pass through the St. Elias Mountains and then rafted 500 miles north on the Yukon River to the gold fields at Dawson. The trip is still ruggedly unforgettable, though far easier now with cars and roads.

For further information, contact *Tourism Yukon* (PO Box 2703, Whitehorse, YT Y1A 2C6; phone: 403-667-5340).

The Dawson Circle Route

For a broad view of the Yukon Territory, follow this route, which travels 333 miles (533 km) northwest from Whitehorse to Dawson via the Klondike Highway (Rte. 2). From Dawson, the Top of the World Highway joins with the Alaska Highway at Tetlin Junction, a distance of 170 miles (272 km). Returning to Whitehorse, the entire route—about 1,125 miles (1,800 km)—offers an excellent overview of the area. Cameras and binoculars are a must.

Allow at least six days and five nights to travel the complete circle. Those who want to fish or hike can easily extend the trip.

WHITEHORSE Between a 200-foot clay escarpment and the banks of the Yukon River lies Whitehorse. The Yukon's capital since 1953, this city had its origins in the Klondike gold rush. In the spring of 1898, thousands of stampeders drifted down the Yukon River through Miles Canyon, only to encounter the treacherous Squaw and White Horse Rapids. After the first few boats were wrecked and their passengers drowned, the stampeders constructed a wooden tramway system around the canyon and the rapids. A small settlement developed at the northern end of the tramway, where the stampeders stopped before continuing downriver. This settlement, on the opposite side of the river from the present city, was called White Horse. The White Horse Rapids were eventually tamed by the construction of a power dam.

From June through August, you can take a two-and-a-half-hour cruise through Miles Canyon aboard the MV *Schwatka.* A running commentary details the history of the canyon and the rapids. Transportation to the dock on Schwatka Lake is available from major hotels. For tickets and additional information, contact the *MV Schwatka Yukon River Cruise* (PO Box 4690, Whitehorse, YT Y1A 2R8; phone: 403-668-2042). Those who'd rather drive can take the south access road from Whitehorse to Miles Canyon. Turn left just before the railroad tracks, and follow the road around the west side of Schwatka Lake. The canyon also can be reached via an access road from Km 1470 on the Alaska Highway. A suspension footbridge spans the canyon, leading from the parking area to a trail on the opposite side. The site of Canyon City, where the stampeders built the initial stage of a tram line above the rapids, is off to the right about 7 miles (11 km). Although little remains of Canyon City, the walk is a pleasant one, and the path is easy. Even if you're not up to walking the full distance, the area is excellent for picnics.

Construction of the *White Pass and Yukon Railway* was carried out south from Whitehorse and north from Skagway, Alaska, from 1898 to 1900, when the two lines met at Carcross, at the Yukon border. The northern terminus of the railroad was on the west bank of the Yukon River. The original town of White Horse moved across the river, too, where the new settlement was called Closeleigh, after English stockholders in the railway. However, people soon started calling the settlement Whitehorse again, and the name stuck.

During the gold rush years, Whitehorse was a busy place. As the trains rolled into the station, stern-wheelers docked along the riverbank, filling with people and cargo destined for Dawson. The old wooden pilings still protrude from the river behind the *White Pass Station* on First Avenue.

Ironically, the rail link from Skagway was completed about a year after the gold rush ceased. Subsequently, Whitehorse's population decreased drastically. Copper mining sustained the town for a while, but by the 1920s this proved unprofitable, and the population dwindled to less than 400.

By the river, at the end of Second Avenue, rests the SS *Klondike,* a restored stern-wheeler. Magnificent boats such as this were once a common sight as they made their way downstream toward Dawson. Long after the gold rush, they retained their position as a major means of transportation. The *Klondike,* built in 1936, carried ore concentrates from the silver mine at Mayo to freight cars at Whitehorse until 1955. Daily tours of the ship (phone: 403-667-4511) are offered in summer; admission charge.

Most visitors like to spend a day or two browsing around and shopping in Whitehorse. Since the downtown area is compact, it's easy to walk to most of the stores. Typically northern items, such as gold nugget jewelry and Inuit carvings and prints, are available. *Northern Images* (Fourth Ave. and Jarvis St.; phone: 403-668-5739) has a beautiful, if expensive, collection of soapstone carvings. *Murdoch's Gem Shop* (Main St.; phone: 403-667-7403) is another good but fairly expensive place. Yukon items such as mukluks, parkas, and beaded jewelry can be purchased at *Yukon Native Products* (4230 Fourth Ave.; phone: 403-668-5935); the *Yukon Gallery* (2093 Second Ave.; phone: 403-667-2391); and *Mac's Fireweed Books & Gifts* (203 Main St.; phone: 403-668-2434).

Relics from the gold rush period can be seen at the *MacBride Museum* (First Ave. and Wood St.; phone: 403-667-2709). As well as housing the first telegraph key used in the Yukon during the gold rush and one of the original engines used on the *White Pass and Yukon Railway,* the museum has a collection of mounted local wildlife, such as wolves, Dall sheep, and grizzly bears. It's open daily May through September; admission charge.

You'll feel as though you're in the southwestern US at *Arizona Charlie's* restaurant in the *Westmark Klondike Inn* (see *Best en Route*). Other good bets for dinner include *Angelo's* (202 Strickland St.; phone: 403-668-6266), which serves Italian dishes; *Panda's* (212 Main St.; phone: 403-667-2632), for good European fare in a Klondike setting; and the *Parthenon* (204 Main St.; phone: 403-668-4243), specializing in Greek and other European cuisines. The dining room in the *Westmark Whitehorse* hotel (see *Best en Route*) features prime ribs, trout, salmon, and steaks. At *Porter's Place* (*Porter Creek Mall;* phone: 403-663-3299), steaks, seafood, and Italian and Greek food are the bill of fare. *The Cellar* (101 Main St.; phone: 403-667-2572) is popular for its prime ribs, steaks, and seafood.

The big evening show in town is the *Frantic Follies* at the *Westmark Whitehorse* hotel, a gold rush vaudeville production with whooping cancan dancers and honky-tonk piano music. There are one or two performances nightly, from May to mid-September; get tickets during the day, since they may run out by evening.

En Route from Whitehorse Head northwest to Carmacks, just over 100 miles (160 km) away. Take the Alaska Highway (Rte. 1) for about 7 miles (11 km) to the Klondike Highway (Rte. 2) turnoff, and follow that road toward Carmacks. A secondary roadway, the Takhini Hot Springs cutoff, is 3½ miles (5.6 km) north and leads to a hot springs area 6½ miles (10 km) off the main highway. A cement pool holding the naturally hot waters is open from 8 AM to 10 PM; swimwear can be rented at the springs. On-site dining facilities feature German food. The springs are open year-round (phone: 403-633-2706).

Back on the Klondike Highway, continue north for 55 miles (88 km) to *Braeburn Lodge* (phone: radio operator 2M-3987, Fox channel). Here, you'll get the largest servings of food anywhere in the Yukon, and at good prices. On opposite sides of the highway, the Twin Lakes are 16 miles (26 km) north of Braeburn. These two small lakes and the surrounding picnic sites are great places to stop. If the pike and grayling cooperate, you can catch lunch or dinner.

CARMACKS Named after George Carmack, whose discovery of gold sparked the Klondike gold rush, Carmacks is a small, predominantly native settlement. About 450 people live at this onetime stern-wheeler port. Stop for a cold beer or coffee at the *Carmacks* hotel (Klondike Hwy., PO Box 160, Carmacks, YT Y0B 1C0; phone: 403-863-5221), and gas up your vehicle.

En Route from Carmacks Dawson is 224 miles (358 km) north of Carmacks on the Klondike Highway, and unless you want to camp along the way, there's not much to detain you en route. But that's not to say the drive is uneventful. The road to Dawson passes over dome-shaped mountains and wends its way along forested lakeshores. As on any Yukon highway, you'll find yourself absorbed in the beauty surrounding you.

Fourteen miles (22 km) north of Carmacks are the Five Fingers Rapids. Although not comparable to the dangerous White Horse Rapids, they posed some problems for the old stern-wheelers. Ringbolts, through which heavy cables were threaded to pull the riverboats upstream, are still embedded in the rocks of Five Fingers. This is a good spot to pull over and gaze upon the Yukon River flowing steadily 500 feet below.

Another 30 miles (48 km) north is the *Minto Resorts* campground (phone: 403-633-5251). Yukon River trips to historic Ft. Selkirk, an abandoned town, leave from the campground. Twenty-two miles (35 km) farther north is Pelly Crossing, a Native American community (pop. 275). Facilities here include the *Fort Selkirk Trading Post,* a gas station, and a store with groceries and native handicrafts. Continue 45 miles (72 km) north to Stewart Crossing.

STEWART CROSSING This town features a lodge with a café and tavern, a campground, and a service station. From here, we recommend a spectacular side trip northeast on the historic Silver Trail, which takes in the ghost towns of Elsa and Keno City. While off the beaten path, the detour is worth the time, offering stunning scenery and friendly residents along the way. Obtain more information on the region through the *Silver Trail Tourism Association* (PO Box 268, Mayo, YT Y0B 1M0; no phone).

Mayo is 33 miles (53 km) from Stewart Crossing on Route 11. On the way, you may want to stop at the *Hungry Mountain Farm* (Mile 14/Km 22, PO Box 112, Mayo, YT Y0B 1M0; phone: 403-667-1054). Situated on a terrace above the Stewart River, the farm was homesteaded back in the 1930s and features a hydroponic greenhouse, a market garden, guest facilities, and a variety of alternative energy sources, including a water turbine and solar panels. At press time, renovation of the farm was under way.

MAYO This town (pop. 450) developed as a supply center and shipping depot for the silver-lead concentrate mined in the area. Steamships carried supplies up the Stewart River to Mayo, floating back downstream loaded with ore. After the 1950s, when roads were built, the ore was trucked from here to Whitehorse. Besides a grocery store, a variety store, a deli, a service station, and two motels, the town offers handmade crafts, available through individual artisans. In town, visit the *Binet House Interpretive Centre* (PO Box 160, Mayo, YT Y0B 1M0; phone: 403-996-2317), which features a geologic and environmental history of the area and information about local activities. No admission charge. *Duncan Creek Golddusters* (Duncan Creek/Mayo Lake Road, PO Box 174, Mayo, YT Y0B 1M0; mobile phone: JJ3-6558, Elsa channel) conducts gold panning and guided tours of a family mining operation and has gold jewelry for sale.

En Route from Mayo The Mt. Haldane Trail, at the Haldane Access Road, is 18 miles (29 km) east of Mayo. The 4-mile (6-km) trail rises to 6,023 feet, and views from the top include the towns of Elsa and Mayo and an expanse of mountains, forests, and lakes. Elsa, 28 miles (45 km) from Mayo, was home to the United Keno Hill Mines, which closed in 1989 due to depressed silver prices. They were among Canada's oldest and most productive.

From Elsa, continue for 9 miles (14 km) to Keno City, once a bustling mining town but now home to only about 25 people, a few log buildings, and a small hotel with a bar. At 6,200 feet, it offers spectacular views of the surrounding mountains. The *Keno City Mining Museum* (General Delivery, Keno City, YT Y0B 1J0; phone: 403-998-2792) exhibits blacksmithing and mining tools, old photographs, written history of the region, and other memorabilia.

Five hiking trails from Keno City meander to patches of berries, wildflowers, and "sorting circles," sunken areas containing stones and grass-green moss. If you continue up Keno Hill beyond the city, you pass by historic silver mining sites and, after 3 miles (5 km), reach the top of the hill (known locally as the "Top of the World"). The spot commands a spectacular view. Return to Stewart Crossing.

En Route from Stewart Crossing On the Klondike Highway, 15 miles (24 km) northwest is the *Moose Creek Lodge* (mobile phone: JL3-9570, Stewart channel), with five rustic cabins and a café serving hearty, homemade food such as sourdough pancakes and pastries. The lodge is open May through September. From this point, it's 98 miles (157 km) more to Dawson.

Eighty-seven miles (139 km) from Stewart Crossing is the *Klondike River Lodge* (phone: 403-993-6892) and the Dempster Highway turnoff north. This is a good place to stop, gas up, and get a bite to eat. Those who want to see pristine wilderness can detour north on the Dempster Highway for

45 miles (72 km) to *Tombstone Mountain* (no phone), a government campground near the north fork of the Klondike River. There are very few services along this road, built to connect Yukon communities with Ft. McPherson and Inuvik in the Northwest Territories. The distance from the Dempster Highway turnoff to Dawson is 28 miles (45 km).

DAWSON For one brief year, this former moose pasture at the confluence of the Klondike and Yukon Rivers was hailed as the San Francisco of the north. The first eager stampeders arrived in Dawson during the late fall of 1897. There were already 3,500 people in town at that time, many of them old-time prospectors who had been panning the creeks of the north for years. But there was no food to be bought in Dawson that autumn, as the supply ships didn't make it through before the water froze. Warnings were given—and fortunately heeded by some—to evacuate and head for the nearest outpost, 350 miles away, preventing a full-fledged disaster. Among those who remained, food was so scarce that one man traded a mountain sheep for a single sack of flour. Later, Canada insisted that each person bring a year's supply of food and clothing.

More stampeders—and all their goods—arrived in the spring, and the law of supply and demand began to operate in textbook fashion. One man lugged 200 dozen eggs over the trail, selling them for $18 a dozen. Within an hour he'd sold them all for a total of $3,600. By the week's end, with supplies arriving daily, the market was so saturated with eggs that the price had dropped to a mere $3 a dozen.

In the early summer of 1898, the many thousands who had been waiting impatiently on the shores of Lindeman and Bennett Lakes started arriving in Dawson, only to discover that the richest claims they had sought so fanatically had been staked even before anybody outside had heard of the Klondike. The supplies these men had so laboriously transported over the mountains were sold at any price to raise the fare home, and Dawson's muddy streets took on the appearance of a huge marketplace.

An air of decadent extravagance permeated the city of 30,000. "Dance hall queens" bathed in champagne, and butlers were installed in a few of the gloomy, one-room cabins of prospectors living along the hillsides and creeks. Posh hotels complete with chandeliers, Persian carpets, and Turkish baths sprang up along Front Street. In their dining rooms, such delicacies as lobster Newburg, cold tongue, and Bengal Club chutney were prepared by San Francisco chefs. The luxuries were brought to Dawson because the Klondike kings—the men who first staked the creekbeds in 1896 and 1897—had invested their fortunes in hotels, dance halls, and shipping companies. Thus, ships laden with Paris fashions and fresh oysters docked continuously at Dawson's shore during the summer of 1898.

One of the wealthiest original prospectors was "Big Alex" McDonald, also known as the "King of the Klondike." He owned many claims, one of the richest yielding $5,000 a day. His fame was such that, while in Rome, he was granted an audience with the pope. Curiously, Big Alex exhibited a distinct contempt for gold. He left bowls full of nuggets on his sideboard and urged guests to help themselves, explaining he had no use for the things. Big Alex's attitude was shared to some extent by the stampeders of 1898. Few hoarded the precious metal they had sought. After the trial of their trek, many men simply collected a small supply of nuggets and dust, then rushed down to Dawson's dance halls and frantically disposed of their riches.

The dance halls lining Front Street housed drinking and gambling rooms; upstairs were numerous rooms where the dance hall queens entertained in private. There also was a theater for vaudeville and plays. When the shows were over, it became a large dance floor that shook until dawn with the stomping of feet. In the gaming rooms, where fortunes quickly were won or lost, the stakes were high, ranging up to $150,000 in a poker game. So pervasive was gambling, in fact, that two men are reported to have wagered $10,000 in a spitting duel. The city's brief life was a carnival gone mad, with people who lived and played hard; by the summer of 1899, it was over, ended by rumors of a new gold find near the mouth of the Yukon River.

So the fever set in once again. In one week alone, 8,000 people left Dawson for Nome, Alaska. Some remained, but the Dawson they created was a changed one: An air of respectability prevailed, and the city served as the territory's capital until 1953. The digging for gold continued, but the individual prospector was quickly replaced by companies of men using massive dredges. The damage these huge machines did to the creekbeds and hillsides is still apparent.

Today, about 1,700 people live in Dawson through the long, cold, dark winters. Most residents are either employed by the government or involved in the summer tourism industry; others still live along the creeks, mining for gold. The city has been designated a historical complex, and restoration projects are ongoing.

Numerous fires during 1898 destroyed all but a few of the gold rush–era structures, so the derelict buildings visible today date back only to the early 1900s. One 19th-century survivor is Arizona Charlie Meadows's *Palace Grand Theatre* (King St. and Third Ave.), dating from 1899. After the gold rush ended, the building sat in ruins until 1962, when it was rebuilt by the Canadian government. During the day, tours of the theater are given, and on summer nights except Tuesdays, from the end of May through early September, an 1898-style vaudeville production, the *Gaslight Follies,* is staged.

A pleasant way to spend a few hours in the afternoon is to take a Yukon River cruise aboard the *Yukon Lou* (phone: 403-993-5482). The boat departs at 1 PM daily, and coffee and muffins are served. Along the way, you may catch a glimpse of the stern-wheeler graveyard ashore. The *Yukon Queen* (phone: 403-668-5225) makes day trips from Dawson to Eagle, Alaska.

Visitors to Dawson should try their luck at *Diamond Tooth Gertie's Gambling Hall* (Fourth Ave. near Queen St.; no phone), named for one of the dance hall queens of 1898. The stakes may not be as high as before, but people have been known to walk out richer than when they arrived—and also poorer. There's a bar, and floor shows each evening feature colorful cancan dancers and a singer-hostess you'd swear was Gertie herself. *Gertie's* is open nightly to 2 AM, mid-May through September.

Another attraction in Dawson is a poetry reading by the "ghost" of Robert Service, the Yukon's gold rush bard. The free readings are held daily on the lawn of Service's log cabin (Eighth Ave. near Church St.) at 10 AM and 3 PM, June through September 15. (For additional details, see *Quintessential Canada* in DIVERSIONS.)

After a day in Dawson, most people feel the urge to try their hand at gold panning. This can be done at *Guggie Ville* (phone: 403-993-5008), at the Bonanza Creek turnoff, which also has a campground with showers, hookups, and a gift shop. George Carmack's original claim and the largest wooden-hulled gold dredge in the world are nearby, and transportation to the gold fields is available. For more information, contact the *Visitor Information Centre* (Front and King Sts.; phone: 403-993-5566 or 403-993-5575), which is closed weekends mid-September through mid-May.

Dawson's *Discovery Days* celebration is held the weekend before the third Monday in August. Raft races, handicrafts displays, and a parade are among the many activities. The city also is the site of its own *Labour Day* weekend craziness, with an annual *Outhouse Race:* Contestants pull and push brightly colored shacks (with one person sitting inside) through the city streets.

En Route from Dawson It's a long and circuitous drive from Dawson to Beaver Creek, 603 miles (963 km) south. Along the way, you'll be traveling on one of the most impressive roads in the world—the Top of the World Highway. You'll wind a way up to mountaintops from which you can gaze at the surrounding splendor, then descend to lush valleys.

Head west from Dawson to the US-Canadian border crossing, which is only open from 9 AM to 9 PM (Yukon time). There are no services along this stretch, so plan accordingly. The village of Boundary, Alaska, is 4 miles (6 km) into US territory, and services are available there. From Boundary, head south to Tetlin Junction; from there, follow the road southeast to Beaver Creek, back in the Yukon, where the border crossing is open 24 hours a day.

BEAVER CREEK This town has the distinction of being the most westerly community in Canada. With a population of about a hundred, it is a by-product of the Alaska Highway construction, created to provide highway services. Its three motels with lounges and cafés do an admirable job. There's a campground at the *Westmark Inn Beaver Creek* (see *Best en Route*) and a government campground with 20 sites (and great fishing) at Snag Junction, 13 miles (21 km) beyond Beaver Creek.

En Route from Beaver Creek Head southeast on the Alaska Highway toward Haines Junction, 186 miles (298 km) away and an important entry to *Kluane National Park Reserve.* Some 109 miles (174 km) from Beaver Creek is Burwash Landing, a lakeside community of about a hundred people. Virtually all of its homes and cabins are heated by wood fires, and most look out over Kluane Lake. Forty-six miles long, the lake is filled with trout, grayling, steelfish, and pike. The trout can weigh up to 40 pounds, so be prepared. The *Talbot Arms* motel (phone: 403-841-4461) and *Sehja Services RV Park* (phone: 403-841-4807) are located on the lakeshore, as is the *Burwash Landing* resort, one of the nicest spots in the Yukon (see *Best en Route*). While in Burwash, explore the *Kluane Museum of Natural History* (Alaska Hwy., Mile 1093, Burwash Landing; phone: 403-841-5561). The museum and its crafts shop are closed early September to mid-May; admission charge. Destruction Bay, another small community created by highway construction, is 10 miles (16 km) farther.

Another 23 miles (37 km) from Destruction Bay is the Slim's River Bridge, which crosses an ancient glacier moraine at the head of Kluane Lake and offers amazing views. Sheep Mountain borders the highway near this spot; with an alert eye, you may see Dall sheep on the hillside. As you explore the area, remember that walking over spring vegetation could damage the animals' winter supply of food. Sheep Mountain also is the site of a *Kluane National Park Reserve* interpretive center (phone: 403-634-2251), which is closed mid-May to early September.

KLUANE NATIONAL PARK RESERVE This magnificent 8,500-square-mile area is characterized by soaring snow-capped peaks that rise through the clouds. Within the park are the world's largest ice fields outside of the polar regions and Canada's highest peak, 19,550-foot Mt. Logan, which rises majestically from these fields.

The 8,000-foot mountains that border the highway are draped in white spruce, aspen, and balsam poplar until the tree line is reached at about 4,000 feet. Above, colorful arctic and alpine flowers dot the mountainsides, as do stunted species of shrubs. The jagged mountaintops are crowned in wreaths of snow. Check in with park authorities at their headquarters in Haines Junction (see below) to find out about hiking and canoe routes. The center also shows an award-winning audiovisual presentation on the park. Many of *Kluane*'s trails are marked, and maps are available. Experienced climbers who want to attempt the mountains and glaciers must first report to the park warden at headquarters. The park is open year round; no admission charge.

HAINES JUNCTION In the shadow of the park, this community (pop. 700) came into being with the construction of the Alaska Highway in 1942. The park headquarters and a visitors' information center share the same building (11[illegible] Logan St.; phone: 403-634-2251); both are open year-round. Most visitors stay in one of the town's handful of hotels and visit the park by day. If you prefer to camp, there is a government campground at Pine Lake, 3 miles (5 km) east of Haines Junction.

En Route from Haines Junction A 98-mile (157-km) drive completes the circle back to Whitehorse. Forty-one miles (66 km) from Haines Junction, you'll pass through the nearly deserted trading post of Champagne. At one time, it serviced the Dalton Trail, which ran from Pyramid Harbor on the Lynn Canal to the Yukon's interior. Frontiersman Jack Dalton cut the trail, and 2,000 head of beef cattle were successfully driven across it in 1898. From the trading post, it's 57 miles (91 km) east to the lights of Whitehorse.

BEST EN ROUTE

So many travelers are attracted to the Yukon each year that it's necessary to reserve hotel rooms as far in advance as possible. To get first crack at top accommodations, book a June vacation in January. Plan on spending $110 or more per night a for double room at places in the expensive category; between $65 and $110 in a hotel listed as moderate; and from $40 to $65 at a place classified as inexpensive. All hotels feature such amenities as private baths, TV sets, and telephones unless otherwise indicated. Reservations must be accompanied by a guaranteed deposit, usually the equivalent of one night's stay. Also contact the *Northern Network of Bed and Breakfasts* (PO Box 954, Dawson City, YT Y0B 1G0; phone: 403-993-5644) for accommodations in several communities. Campgrounds are very inexpensive: Per night, per site, private campgrounds charge from $8 to $25; government campsites are given out on a first-come, first-served basis for about $8. For each location, places are listed alphabetically by price category.

WHITEHORSE

Best Western Gold Rush Inn Behind its Klondike-style façade are 80 units, a gift shop, laundry facilities, a lounge, and a dining room. 411 Main St. (phone: 403-668-4500; 800-528-1234). Expensive.

Westmark Klondike Inn Here are 98 rooms, a coffee shop, a good restaurant, a lounge, a gift shop, and a sauna. The hotel is closed from September 15 through May 15. 2288 Second Ave. (phone: 403-668-4747; 800-999-2570 in Canada; 800-544-0970 in the US; fax: 403-667-7639). Expensive.

Westmark Whitehorse This popular spot for businesspeople and tourists has 181 rooms, a café, a dining room, a lounge, a gift shop, a barbershop, an art gallery, and even a travel agency *(Atlas Travel Tours)* and a tour operator *(Grayline Tours).* The hotel offers an airport shuttle service and is home of the *Frantic Follies Vaudeville* revue. 201 Wood St. (phone: 403-668-4700; 800-999-2570 in Canada; 800-544-0970 in the US; fax: 403-668-2789). Expensive.

Regina The lobby of this 53-room establishment is stocked with Yukon memorabilia. Amenities include a dining room. 102 Wood St. (phone: 403-667-7801). Moderate.

MacKenzie's RV Park Here are 54 serviced and 22 unserviced sites, free gold panning, a general store, video games, showers, and laundry facilities. Km 1484 on the Alaska Hwy., 6 miles (10 km) north of downtown Whitehorse (phone: 403-633-2337). Inexpensive.

Pioneer Trailer Park There are 129 camping spaces, 73 full and 16 partial hookups, 40 wooded campsites, laundry facilities, showers, restrooms, a store, a recreation hall, and an RV wash. Open mid-May through September. Km 1465 on the Alaska Hwy., 5 miles (8 km) south of Whitehorse (phone: 403-668-5944). Very inexpensive.

Robert Service Campground A popular campground on the banks of the Yukon River, it has 40 tents-only campsites as well as restrooms, picnic tables, and a nature trail. Open late May to early September. On the South Access Rd., 1 mile (1.6 km) from downtown. Contact the *City of Whitehorse Parks & Recreation Department,* 2121 Second Ave. (phone: 403-668-8325). Very inexpensive.

Wolf Creek Government Campground If you don't want to pay for all the amenities, this is a good spot. It has 29 RV/tent sites, 11 tent-only sites, and free wood. Open mid-May to mid-October. Twelve miles (19 km) south of Whitehorse on the Alaska Hwy., at Km 1459 (no phone). Very inexpensive.

MAYO

Bedrock This motel features 12 air conditioned units, a lounge, and meal and RV services. Continental breakfast is included in the rate. Box 69, Mayo, YT Y0B 1M0 (phone: 403-996-2290). Moderate.

Country Charm Quiet and comfortable, this bed and breakfast establishment is near Five Mile Lake. No smoking is allowed on the premises. The owners offer sightseeing and fishing tours May through August. PO Box 34, Mayo, YT Y0B 1M0 (phone: 403-996-2918, summer; 403-633-4225, winter). Moderate.

North Star There are kitchenettes and showers in each of the nine units at this motel; no restaurant. PO Box 151, Mayo, YT Y0B 1M0 (phone: 403-996-2231). Moderate.

DAWSON

Downtown This hotel features four VIP suites, 56 rooms, a Jacuzzi, a conference room, and the *Jack London Grill.* Second Ave. and Queen St. (phone: 403-993-5346). Expensive.

Eldorado Here are 52 rooms, two VIP suites, and the *Bonanza* dining room. Third Ave. and Princess St. (phone: 403-993-5451; fax: 403-993-5256). Expensive.

Westmark Inn Dawson City A modern motel, it has 131 rooms, a gift shop, a lounge, and a dining room. The hotel is closed mid-September through mid-May. Fifth Ave. and Harper St. (phone: 403-993-5542, mid-May through mid-September; 800-999-2570 in Canada; 800-544-0970 in the US; fax: 403-993-5623). Expensive.

GuggieVille About a mile (1.6 km) south of downtown at the Bonanza Creek turnoff, this campground has showers and hookups, along with a gift shop and a gold panning operation. Klondike Hwy. (phone: 403-993-5008). Very inexpensive.

Yukon River Campground A good government campground immediately across the Yukon River from Dawson, it offers 74 RV/tent sites and 20 sites for tents only. A ferry service operates daily, 24 hours a day from mid-May to mid-September; from 7 AM to 11 PM from mid-September to mid-October. Contact *Parks and Outdoor Recreation, Government of the Yukon* (phone: 403-667-5648). Very inexpensive.

BEAVER CREEK

Westmark Inn Beaver Creek This good facility has 174 rooms (with no phones or TV sets), a dining room with a dinner show, a gift shop, a recreation area with miniature golf, and a lounge with a TV set. Make reservations before leaving Whitehorse. Open May 15 to September 15. Km 1934, Alaska Hwy. (phone: 403-862-7501; 800-999-2570 in Canada; 800-544-0970 in the US; fax: 403-862-7902). Expensive.

Westmark Inn Campground Here are 67 serviced campsites, showers, a laundromat, a small store, and a dump station, with a lounge and restaurant nearby. Open June through mid-October. Km 1934, Alaska Hwy. (phone: 403-862-7501; 800-999-2570 in Canada; 800-544-0970 in the US). Very inexpensive.

BURWASH LANDING

Burwash Landing Resort This lodge on Kluane Lake has 28 units (none with phones), a restaurant, a lounge, and, nearby, a wildlife museum. There also are 184 campsites. Staff can arrange glacier flights and fishing and boating trips. Km 1759, Alaska Hwy. (phone: 403-841-4441). Moderate.

Kluane Wilderness Village This place has 25 log cabins and six deluxe motel units plus 77 campsites and a restaurant. Neither the cabins nor the motel units have phones; there are no TV sets in the cabins. Km 1798, Alaska Hwy. (phone: 403-841-4141). Moderate.

Kluane Park Inn On the Alaska Highway a hundred yards before it meets the Haines Highway at the entrance to *Kluane National Park Reserve*'s visitor reception center, this popular spot has 20 rooms without phones, a cocktail lounge, and a recreation room. The inn is closed December 23 through January 1. Make reservations before leaving Whitehorse (phone: 403-634-2261; fax: 403-634-2273). Moderate.

The Trail of '98

Once the 100,000 or so stampeders landed at Skagway and Dyea, Alaska (8½ miles/13½ km west of Skagway), between 1896 and 1900, the 32-mile (51-km) Chilkoot Pass was the primary route inland. It had been established by the Chilkat tribe, who held a monopoly on trade between the seacoast and the Stick tribe on the far side of the mountains. The native inhabitants guarded their trade link violently, exacting a heavy toll from those who wished to cross the pass and occasionally killing a disagreeable traveler. A show of arms by a US gunboat convinced the tribe to make other arrangements. Thereafter, prospectors and explorers paid the natives as guides and packers for use of the trail.

During the pre–gold rush years, about a thousand people took this route into the newly opened area, and interest in the unexplored lands grew. As more people flocked to the Yukon, the Chilkat lost control of the pass; soon only those affluent travelers who could afford their assistance paid the Chilkat as packers. Most stampeders carried their own goods along the well-worn trail. (During the early stages of the rush, Canadian authorities required each stampeder to bring with him a year's supply of food, clothing, and equipment in an effort to stem deaths due to starvation and exposure.) In 1886 a Canadian surveying expedition discovered the White Pass, just a few miles east.

It's possible to cruise into Skagway aboard the *Alaska Marine Highway System* (PO Box 25535, Juneau, AK 99802-5535; phone: 907-465-3941; 800-642-0066) from Bellingham, Washington. Its ferries carry passengers and vehicles. Many travelers enjoy cruising one way and driving back the other. Additionally, the Skagway-Carcross road makes it possible to drive down from Whitehorse throughout the year, and airports in both Skagway and Whitehorse make travel into the Yukon easier than any trail hand could have dreamed possible.

SKAGWAY In 1887, a gold-seeking retired sea captain named William Moore erected a cabin and a wharf on a point of land at the mouth of the Skagway River on the eastern side of the head of the Lynn Canal. Moore believed a trail of gold he had traced up from South America would lead to a massive strike here in the north. On the west side of the Lynn stood the set tlement of Dyea, at the mouth of the Taiya River, in a direct line with the Chilkoot Pass. Moore foresaw that, with a railroad through the White Pass, more facilities would be needed, and he fully expected to be the founder of the town of Skagway as it grew around his homestead.

When news of the gold strike at Bonanza Creek reached the outside world, the flow of travelers Moore had expected turned into a flood, forcing him to abandon his plans. The gold-crazed mob tore him from his cabin and took over his wharf. A city of tents and temporary buildings sprang up, obscuring Moore's claim. (His cabin still stands, just off Skagway's main thoroughfare, Broadway Street, behind *Kirme's* jewelry store.) Several years later, Moore took the matter to court and received some compensation for his losses. Eventually, his dream of a railroad through the White Pass was realized, but by that time the Chilkoot Pass had become symbolic of the courage and determination of the stampeders.

An attempt to cross the White Pass during the late fall of 1897 was disastrous. Five thousand people embarked on a 41-mile trek that would become a continuous frozen hell. Early rains and rocky trails created a morass that swallowed men and horses whole, slowing the pace to a crawl and holding them captive until the winter snows caught them exposed in the mountains. Men and horses died by the dozens in a battle against time, the elements, and often other men. Only the hardiest few made it through to the Yukon River before the winter freeze-up.

Some returned to Skagway to await the spring thaw; many died on the path named Dead Horse Trail. Bits and pieces of their goods and equipment still line the trail in mute testimony. Those who survived the journey to Skagway were weary and frustrated. As tensions grew, the sound of gunfire became commonplace. With no laws to constrain them, mobs ruled the small town of tents and impromptu buildings. By midwinter, Skagway's population hovered around 5,000. Not all were bound for the Klondike: Their fortunes lay in providing entertainment for those en route to the gold fields. Saloons and gambling and dance halls crowded the already congested streets.

The chaos of those early days was made to order for a particular type of businessman: the con artist. Soapy Smith was an expert at his trade. With a band of felons, thugs, and prostitutes backing him, Smith set out to dominate the town of Skagway. Posing as a civic-minded member of the business community, he persuaded the chamber of commerce of the righteousness of his activities, and the false-fronted buildings lining Skagway's streets camouflaged his bogus business dealings.

By February 1898, Skagway's residents, realizing that Smith had gotten out of hand, requested US troops to take charge of the town. Legend has it that, in July of that year, Smith robbed a prospector of over $2,000 in gold dust. Word soon spread among the community that if the money wasn't returned, other prospectors would avoid the town. Faced with that loss of income, the residents formed a vigilante committee to force Smith to return the money. He refused and, after getting drunk (remember, this is a legend), went out to face the mob. Smith had already fought with another townsman, Frank Reid, earlier that day, challenging him to return with a gun. The first man Smith encountered that night was Reid. Shots were fired, and both men fell. Reid lasted two weeks before expiring; Smith was left dying in the street. Rumors persist that Reid couldn't have fired the fatal shot, but no one ever took credit for the deed. Today, the two men lie buried side by side in the *Gold Rush Cemetery.* Smith's former mistress was the only mourner at his funeral, as his gang members had already been shipped out of town. Reid's funeral, on the other hand, was reportedly the largest in Skagway's history.

En Route from Skagway The most natural way to explore the Yukon is to follow the route taken by the first travelers into the region: Hike the Chilkoot Pass (see below) to Bennett, British Columbia, then raft down the Yukon to Dawson. For the less actively inclined, the *White Pass and Yukon Railway* (PO Box 435, Skagway, AK 99840; phone: 907-983-2217; 800-343-7373 elsewhere in the US) operates narrow-gauge passenger trains daily between Skagway and Bennett. Through-service rail/bus excursions from Skagway to Whitehorse and vice versa are available. The railway was completed in 1900, just after the gold rush, and the train is a fascinating way to tour this area, since the tracks closely follow the route of those stampeders who fought their way from Skagway to Bennett in the fall of 1897; they then parallel the watercourse north to Whitehorse.

CHILKOOT PASS The most dramatic event in the history of the gold rush was the assault by 22,000 stampeders upon the 3,739-foot summit of the Chilkoot Pass during the winter of 1897–98. Bent under the weight of their packs, these men trudged up a 40° slope for more than six hours as temperatures fell to -60F (-51C), only to find themselves a mere thousand feet from where they had begun. Only a fanatical devotion to the gold they believed lay beyond enabled them to persevere. Finally reaching the summit and depositing their goods, often losing them in the 70 feet of snow that fell that winter, the weary men slid back down to strap on another pack and make the climb again. For the average stampeder, who could pack only 50 pounds at a time, it took 40 trips to bring his required ton of supplies to the peak. Other trials lay ahead, but having conquered the pass, they were no longer *cheechakos* (naive newcomers to the north).

The first tramway was constructed from the base to the summit in December 1897; four more were in operation by the spring of 1898. The most effective tramway transported goods from Canyon City, 8 miles north of Dyea, to the summit at a rate of nine tons per hour. But the cost of the tramways exceeded the budgets of some of the stampeders, who trudged along as goods whisked by overhead. It took the average stampeder three months to lug his supplies the 32 miles across the pass from Dyea to Lake Bennett.

Modern-day hikers traveling the Chilkoot Pass allow four days for the trip from Dyea to Bennett. The trail is well marked and patrolled daily by park rangers. They are stationed at Sheep Camp (Mile 13) on the Alaskan side and at Lindeman (Mile 25.5) on the Canadian side. Cabins at three points along the trail are open to hikers, but don't bet on finding a vacancy; plan to sleep in a tent. While the trail is not too difficult, it is no mere stroll through the park. Those not in good physical condition should take the bus instead.

Maps and information are available from the *National Park Service, Klondike Gold Rush National Historic Park* (phone: 907-983-2921) and the *Skagway, Alaska, Visitor Information Bureau* on the Chilkoot Pass (phone: 907-983-2854). Archie Satterfield's *Klondike Park from Seattle to Dawson City* (available from Fulcrum Publishing, 350 Indiana St., Golden, CO 80401-5093; phone: 303-277-1623; 800-992-2908 in the US; fax: 800-726-7112) is an entertaining guide.

The hike up the Chilkoot Pass begins near Dyea. Those who'd rather not walk to the starting point can drive or take a taxi from Skagway right to the trail head at the south end of the Taiya River Bridge. A row of old pilings and a few rotten timbers about a mile away mark the old Dyea townsite. The nearby *Slide Cemetery* contains the graves of about 60 people killed in the *Palm Sunday* avalanche of April 3, 1898. Modern-day hikers should remember that snowstorms can occur at any time, even in the middle of summer, and winter snow often remains through June. Exercise extreme care in crossing any unbroken area of snow; you never know what's underneath.

Except for the initial one-quarter mile, which is very steep, the first 7 miles (11 km) of the trek are fairly easy, at times offering glimpses of the 5,000-foot (and higher) St. Elias and Coastal Mountain Ranges ahead. Farther on, the trail drops to the bank of the river. Across its banks are magnificent blue-green glaciers whose icy streams tumble noisily into the Taiya. Eventually, the path rises over a trail of boulders and scrambles down to cross an old moss- and lichen-covered glacial moraine. Stunted conifer trees and wildflowers decorate the area. At Mile 7.75, the *Canyon City Shelter* startles with its sudden appearance. The one-room cabin has a wood-burning stove, a table, and benches. Forget about using the stove; in fact, unless a storm is brewing, you'll probably be more comfortable outside the cabin than in.

About a half-mile up the trail, an old suspension bridge across the Taiya River leads to the original Canyon City site, now reduced to some half-rotten cabins and a garbage dump. At one time, hotels, saloons, and stores stood here. Along the one steep climb about a mile beyond the bridge is a handrail. *Pleasant Camp,* at Mile 10, is a beautiful place. Since the *Sheep Camp Shelter* is only 3 miles (5 km) farther, not as many people stop here as at either Canyon City or Sheep Camp, which once had a population of about 1,500. The dilapidated remains of Sheep Camp are on the opposite bank of the Taiya.

From here, the trail rises about a thousand feet in 2 miles (3 km). Once you break the tree line, at about 1,900 feet, it's loose rock from here on. Rangers place markers daily along the safest path, but if they're down for any reason, just keep heading carefully up.

Mile 16, where goods to be hauled up by tram were weighed, is known as the Scales. The half-mile from the Scales to the summit is virtually straight up, roughly a thousand feet, to the notch that marks the Chilkoot Pass. As you climb toward the top, Chilkoot bears off slightly to the left. A second trail, which tends to be dangerous, leads to the right until it crosses the peak, then cuts back to the left. Avoid this route, since the rocks may break loose. Climbers should allow extra space ahead and behind them, since a lot of rock gets kicked up. Keep an eye on the hiker ahead of you, and unless you are the leader, don't turn your back on the slope. If you're in doubt about which trail to take, look for tramway cables on the ground—that's the Chilkoot.

The snow blanketing the peaks extends almost a mile down the reverse slope, right to the shores of Crater Lake, at Mile 17.5. The trail from Crater Lake to Long Lake winds through mountain flowers, heather, and colorful moss and lichen. Near the entrance to a canyon that opens on Long Lake is a waterfall, formed by Coltsfoot Creek, which waters the first trees you see since breaking the tree line on the American side of the pass. This area, at Mile 21.5, is called Happy Camp. From here, a rocky trail leads down to the lake. The land near Long Lake is a masterwork of natural gardening. The trail gently crosses back and forth to and from the bank of the lake, winding among tarns and water holes carved into the ground by glaciers and filled with freshly melted snow. Alpine firs and hemlocks, their growth stunted by the harsh weather, give this wild expanse the look of a Japanese bonsai garden.

Atop the cliffs overlooking Deep Lake, at Mile 23, are several beautiful campsites surrounded by waterfalls. There are many islands in Deep Lake; its north end, which feeds into Lake Lindeman, is a hazardous stretch of rapids. The trail emerges from the forest at the head of Lake Lindeman, at Mile 25.5, site of a Canadian ranger station and a cabin for hikers. The lake is a good resting spot; the stampeders who arrived too late to float down the river that winter set up a town here, whose remains can be seen easily. There's a second cabin at Mile 26, along the side of the lake. The Chilkoot Trail ends at the head of Lake Bennett, at Mile 32.

BENNETT Since the stream that connects Lindeman and Bennett Lakes is large enough to be navigated and rocky enough to be dangerous, many of the stampeders built boats at Lindeman during the winter and tried to sail down to Lake Bennett after breakup. Some of them made it; others foundered on the rocks. They established a larger camp at Bennett, and, following breakup in May 1898, more than 7,000 small craft left for the gold fields at Dawson. The camp was vacated within a matter of days.

En Route from Bennett If you really wanted to duplicate the Trail of '98 experience, you'd build a boat before continuing. It's more feasible, however, to arrange canoe rentals for the remainder of the journey. Experienced canoeists realize the importance of having the correct gear and accurate maps; a novice shouldn't attempt the trip without a guide.

The Klondike Highway provides car and bus access to Log Cabin or Fraser. The *White Pass and Yukon Railway* (see above) offers hikers service back to Skagway and Fraser, where bus service to Whitehorse or Skagway is available.

You can canoe 26 miles (42 km) to Carcross, at the north end of Lake Bennett.

CARCROSS This quiet community (pop. 350) lies in a mountain-rimmed valley with a sandy shore opening on the lake. For those staying in Whitehorse who choose not to take the Trail of '98, Carcross is easily reached by car via Route 2 south, a distance of about 45 miles (72 km). On the left is the Carcross Desert, reputed to be the smallest in the world. Emerald Lake, named for its shimmering green waters, also is along this roadway.

Before the gold rush, Carcross was known as Caribou Crossing; when migrating herds of caribou came here to cross the narrows between Bennett and Nares Lakes, the Tagish natives camped in the area to hunt. It was here, in 1900, that the two sections of the railroad, one coming south from Whitehorse and the other north from Skagway, were linked with the traditional golden spike.

Stop at the *Carcross Visitor Centre* (Klondike Hwy., Km 106; phone: 403-821-4431), closed *Labour Day* through May, where you can hear the history of the SS *Tutshi,* a 1917 stern-wheeler that until 1955 plied the headwaters of the Yukon River. The boat was destroyed in 1990 in a fire. Nearby sits the *Duchess,* an old *White Pass and Yukon Railway* engine; next to it is a mail wagon dating from the early 1900s. *Watson's* general store (Main St.; phone: 403-821-3803), built in 1911, also is intriguing. It still is heated by a wood-burning Yukon barrel stove, as is the *Caribou* hotel's tavern (Main St.; phone: 403-821-4501).

En Route from Carcross Continue the journey to Whitehorse by car, or canoe down the Yukon River to Whitehorse or all the way to the gold fields at Dawson, 500 miles (800 km) northwest.

YUKON RIVER There's no better way to tour the Yukon Territory than on the river that gives this wild land its name. Greatly feared by the Klondikers, the rapids have been tamed by the construction of a power dam necessitating the only portage on the entire route. Once past Whitehorse and Miles Canyon, utter wilderness takes over. There may be a cabin or two along the riverbank, but more likely the only signs of life you'll encounter will be an occasional moose or bear. Eventually you'll turn a bend in the river; there, on the right bank, is the tarnished ghost of Dawson, the city of gold.

BEST EN ROUTE

To stay in hotels in the Yukon, make arrangements far in advance; six months is a good rule of thumb. For a moderately priced double room for one night, expect to pay from $55 to $95; for an inexpensive room, from $40 to $55. Reservations must be accompanied by a guaranteed deposit, usually the equivalent of one night's stay. Privately owned campgrounds charge about $8 per day, per site; government-operated sites also cost about $8 per night and are given out on a first-come, first-served basis. Since this is an outdoor route, you'll spend much of your trip sleeping in a tent or in cabins operated by an outfitter/guide. Detailed maps of the Yukon watercourse are available from the Alaska Northwest Publishing Company (PO Box 4-EEE, Anchorage, AK 99509).

For information on accommodations in Whitehorse and Dawson, see *The Dawson Circle Route*, above. The following places, all in Skagway, are listed alphabetically by price category.

Golden North All 32 rooms in this lovely place are furnished with period antiques. All but four have private baths; none have TV sets. There's an 1898 bar, a beauty shop, and a restaurant, and sightseeing services can be arranged. Third St. and Broadway (phone: 907-983-2451). Moderate.

Sgt. Preston's Bordering on Skagway's historic district, each of the 23 rooms here (some with private baths) has access to the street. There's no restaurant, but fresh coffee and donuts are served every morning. Sixth St., between Broadway and State (phone: 907-983-2521). Moderate.

Skagway Bed & Breakfast Inn The atmosphere at this intriguing and friendly guesthouse is pure 1897. In fact, the core of the building dates back to the gold rush. With only 12 rooms, it is small but very popular. There are no phones or TVs in the rooms, and not all have private baths. Breakfast and dinner are available. Next to the post office on Broadway, between Sixth and Seventh Sts. (phone: 907-983-2289). Moderate.

Portland House This nine-bedroom inn in the historic district was built in 1897. Baths are shared, and a restaurant is on the premises. Fifth St., near Broadway (phone: 907-983-2493). Inexpensive.

Glossary

Climate Chart

Average temperatures (in °F)

	January	***April***	***July***	***October***
Calgary	2–23	27–49	49–74	30–54
Edmonton	-3–15	29–49	53–74	32–52
Halifax	20–33	33–48	57–73	44–58
Montreal	9–23	36–52	63–79	43–57
Ottawa	4–20	33–51	58–80	39–57
Quebec City	6–20	32–47	58–78	39–53
Toronto	18–30	38–53	62–80	45–60
Vancouver	33–42	41–54	55–70	45–56
Winnipeg	-10–8	29–48	56–79	34–54

Weights and Measures

APPROXIMATE EQUIVALENTS

	Metric Unit	Abbreviation	US Equivalent
Length	1 millimeter	mm	.04 inch
	1 meter	m	39.37 inches
	1 kilometer	km	.62 mile
Capacity	1 liter	l	1.057 quarts
Weight	1 gram	g	.035 ounce
	1 kilogram	kg	2.2 pounds
	1 metric ton	MT	1.1 tons
Temperature	0° Celsius	C	32° Fahrenheit

CONVERSION TABLES

METRIC TO US MEASUREMENTS

	Multiply:	by:	to convert to:
Length	millimeters	.04	inches
	meters	3.3	feet
	meters	1.1	yards
	kilometers	.6	miles
Capacity (liquid)	liters	2.11	pints
	liters	1.06	quarts
	liters	.26	gallons
Weight	grams	.04	ounces
	kilograms	2.2	pounds

US TO METRIC MEASUREMENTS

	Multiply:	by:	to convert to:
Length	inches	25.0	millimeters
	feet	.3	meters
	yards	.9	meters
	miles	1.6	kilometers
Capacity	pints	.47	liters
	quarts	.95	liters
	gallons	3.8	liters
Weight	ounces	28.0	grams
	pounds	.45	kilograms

TEMPERATURE

Celsius to Fahrenheit	(°C x 9/5) + 32 = °F
Fahrenheit to Celsius	(°F - 32) x 5/9 = °C

Index